More information about this subseries at https://link.springer.com/bookseries/7410

Avishek Adhikari · Ralf Küsters ·
Bart Preneel (Eds.)

Progress in Cryptology – INDOCRYPT 2021

22nd International Conference on Cryptology in India
Jaipur, India, December 12–15, 2021
Proceedings

 Springer

Editors
Avishek Adhikari 🆔
Presidency University
Kolkata, India

Ralf Küsters 🆔
University of Stuttgart
Stuttgart, Germany

Bart Preneel 🆔
University of Leuven and imec
Leuven, Belgium

ISSN 0302-9743   ISSN 1611-3349 (electronic)
Lecture Notes in Computer Science
ISBN 978-3-030-92517-8   ISBN 978-3-030-92518-5 (eBook)
https://doi.org/10.1007/978-3-030-92518-5

LNCS Sublibrary: SL4 – Security and Cryptology

This Springer imprint is published by the registered company Springer Nature Switzerland AG
The registered company address is: Gewerbestrasse 11, 6330 Cham, Switzerland

Preface

It is with great pleasure that we present the proceedings of the 22nd International Conference on Cryptology (INDOCRYPT 2021) held in Jaipur, India, during December 12–15, 2021, as a hybrid conference.

INDOCRYPT is an international cryptography conference held every year in December, under the aegis of the Cryptology Research Society of India (CRSI). In the two decades since the inaugural edition in 2000, INDOCRYPT has established itself as a reputable international venue for publishing cryptology research, as well as a valuable resource for promoting research in India. It is currently organized in cooperation with the International Association for Cryptologic Research (IACR).

This year's conference was organized by a team centered at the LNM Institute of Information Technology (LNMIIT), Jaipur, India, in association with R C Bose Center for Cryptology and Security and The Chatterjee Group Centres for Research and Education in Science and Technology (TCG CREST), Kolkata, India. Due to the ongoing COVID-19 pandemic, the conference was organized as a hybrid event to facilitate global participation. Past editions of INDOCRYPT were held in various cities in India: Kolkata (2000, 2006, 2012, 2016), Chennai (2001, 2004, 2007, 2011, 2017), Hyderabad (2002, 2010, 2019), New Delhi (2003, 2009, 2014, 2018), Bangalore (2005, 2015), Kharagpur (2008), and Mumbai (2013). INDOCRYPT 2020 was organized virtually.

The Program Committee (PC) for INDOCRYPT 2021 consisted of 71 experts from around the world. About 56% of the PC (including two of the chairs) was based in Europe, 24% in India (including one chair), and the rest from other countries, including Australia, Canada, China, Singapore, and the USA.

The conference attracted 66 submissions. Of these, one paper was rejected by the PC chairs for not meeting the submission guidelines. The remaining 65 papers were reviewed by the PC, with the help of 29 external reviewers and using the HotCRP conference management system. All papers received between three and five independent reviews in a double-blind reviewing process. We take this opportunity to thank all the PC members and the external reviewers for an outstanding job! Despite the short review period, on the whole, the reviews were rigorous and detailed. In a handful of submissions, the reviews uncovered subtle errors; at the discretion of the PC, the authors were given a chance to respond. At the end of the review phase, 27 papers were selected for publication in these proceedings, seven of which went through a shepherding process to ensure that various concerns raised by the reviewers were addressed before publication. As usual, the final uploaded versions were not reviewed by the PC, and the authors bear the full responsibility for their contents.

The 66 submissions received involved 199 authors from 25 countries. Among the accepted papers, European authors had a share of about 30%, North American authors about 13%, Indian authors about 32%, and authors from the rest of Asia about 25%; the top five countries contributing to this list were India (32%), USA (12%), Germany, Japan, and China (9% each).

The program also included three invited talks by Karthik Bhargavan (Inria Paris, France), María Naya-Plasencia (Inria Paris, France), and Adi Shamir (Weizmann Institute of Science, Israel), a tutorial by Daniel J Bernstein (University of Illinois at Chicago, United States and Ruhr University Bochum, Germany), and a rump session to announce new results and works in progress.

We would like to thank CRSI for entrusting us with putting together the program for INDOCRYPT 2021. Thanks to the authors of all the submissions, and the contribution of the entire PC and the external reviewers, we have ended up with a rich and exciting program. We would also like to acknowledge the major contribution of the organizers, headed by the General Chair Ravi Prakash Gorthi of LNMIIT Jaipur, India. In particular, we thank the Organizing Chair, Jayaprakash Kar of LNMIIT Jaipur, India, and his efficient team for helping us in a range of tasks, including putting together the conference webpage with all the relevant information and instructions for the authors. We are thankful to Microsoft, Google, DRDO, the R C Bose Center for Cryptology and Security, TCG CREST and NTRO for providing us the financial support. We also thank Springer for continuing to support INDOCRYPT by publishing the proceedings as part of the LNCS series. Finally, we thank all the participants in the conference, including the authors of all the submissions, the attendees, and the presenters, for their enthusiastic participation. We hope you enjoyed INDOCRYPT 2021 and find these proceedings to be valuable and enjoyable!

December 2021

Avishek Adhikari
Ralf Küsters
Bart Preneel

Organization

Chief Patron

Rahul Banerjee   LNMIIT Jaipur, India

General Chair

Ravi Prakash Gorthi   LNMIIT Jaipur, India

Organizing Chair

Jayaprakash Kar   LNMIIT Jaipur, India

Organizing Committee

Shweta Bhandari   LNMIIT Jaipur, India
Nilotpal Chakraborty   LNMIIT Jaipur, India
Poulami Dalapati   LNMIIT Jaipur, India
Mohit Gupta   LNMIIT Jaipur, India
Saurabh Kumar   LNMIIT Jaipur, India
Preety Singh   LNMIIT Jaipur, India

Program Committee Chairs

Avishek Adhikari   Presidency University Kolkata, India
Ralf Küsters   University of Stuttgart, Germany
Bart Preneel   University of Leuven and imec, Belgium

Program Committee

Manuel Barbosa   University of Porto, Portugal
Paulo Barreto   University of Washington, USA
Lejla Batina   Radboud University, The Netherlands
Sebastian Berndt   University of Lubeck, Germany
Ward Beullens   University of Leuven, Belgium
Karthikeyan Bhargavan   Inria, France
Raghav Bhaskar   Data61, CSIRO, Australia
Joppe Bos   NXP Semiconductors, Belgium

Yann Rotella	Université Paris-Saclay, France
Adeline Roux-Langlois	Université de Rennes and IRISA, CNRS, France
Bimal Roy	Indian Statistcal Institute, Kolkata, India
Sushmita Ruj	Indian Statistical Institute, Kolkata, India
Kouichi Sakurai	Kyushu University, Japan
Somitra Sanadhya	Indian Institute of Technology, Jodhpur, India
Vishal Saraswat	Bosch Engineering and Business Solutions, India
Santanu Sarkar	Indian Institute of Technology, Madras, India
Dominique Schröder	Friedrich-Alexander-University Erlangen-Nürnberg, Germany
Peter Schwabe	Radboud University, The Netherlands, and Max Planck Institute, Germany
Sourav Sen Gupta	Nanyang Technological University, Singapore
François-Xavier Standaert	Université de Louvain, Belgium
Pierre-Yves Strub	École Polytechnique, France
S. P. Suresh	Chennai Mathematical Institute, India
Willy Susilo	University of Wollongong, Australia
Meiqin Wang	Shandong University, China
Qingju Wang	University of Luxembourg, Luxembourg
Michael Zohner	Hochschule Fulda, Germany

Additional Reviewers

Cyril Bouvier	Sikhar Patranabis
Avik Chakraborti	Bernardo Portela
Debasmita Chakraborty	Lucas Prabel
Amit Kumar Chauhan	Ivan Pryvalov
Jayashree Dey	Joost Renes
Christoph Dobraunig	Laltu Sardar
Subhranil Dutta	Aein Rezaei Shahmirzadi
Maria Eichlseder	Yu Shen
Adela Georgescu	Kr Amit Singh Bhati
Brian Goncalvez	Najmeh Soroush
Satrajit Ghosh	Ida Tucker
Senyang Huang	Nils Wisiol
Mario Larangeira	Harry W. H. Wong
Jack P. K. Ma	Yongjun Zhao
Tapas Pal	

Invited Talks

High-Assurance High-Performance Cryptographic Software

Karthikeyan Bhargavan

Inria Paris, France
karthikeyan.bhargavan@inria.fr

Every year, many new cryptographic algorithms, constructions, and protocols are proposed, standardized, and deployed across a variety of platforms. However, implementing these cryptographic mechanisms remains a challenging and error-prone task, typically entrusted to a few specialists who understand both the subtleties of cryptographic design and the intricacies of the target hardware architectures. The resulting code is comprehensively tested, fuzzed, and subject to manual reviews and audits by experts both before and after deployment. Despite all these measures, however, bugs in cryptographic software are regularly uncovered, often resulting in embarassing attacks.

In this talk, we will show how formal verification can be used to bring higher assurance to cryptographic software development [1]. In particular, we will examine the HACL* verified cryptographic library, which implements a full suite of modern crypto algorithms and is used by mainstream software like the Mozilla Firefox web browser, the WireGuard VPN, the Tezos blockchain, and the ElectionGuard voting software.

We will discuss the verification and compilation methodology used by HACL* to generate portable C code for each cryptographic algorithm [5]. We will see how this methodology can be extended to generate verified C code optimized for single-instruction-multiple-data (SIMD) architectures [3]. We will also show how verified C code from HACL* can be safely composed with verified assembly code for improved performance [4]. By combining these techniques, the verified code in HACL* is as fast as (and sometimes faster than) the unverified hand-optimized C and assembly code in mainstream cryptographic libraries.

Despite its critical importance, the cryptographic library is only one component in a cryptographic software stack that typically also includes communication protocols, key management, and application code. We will conclude by discussing how the formal verification guarantees of the HACL* cryptographic library can be combined with symbolic protocol analysis to build provably secure implementations of modern real-world cryptographic protocols like TLS 1.3, Signal, and ACME [2].

References

1. Barbosa, M., et al.: SoK: computer-aided cryptography. In: IEEE Symposium on Security and Privacy (S&P), pp. 777–795 (2021)
2. Bhargavan, K., et al.: DY*: a modular symbolic verification framework for executable cryptographic protocol code. In: IEEE European Symposium on Security and Privacy (EuroS&P) (2021)

3. Polubelova, M., et al.: HACLxN: verified generic SIMD crypto (for all your favourite platforms). In: ACM SIGSAC Conference on Computer and Communications Security (CCS), pp. 899–918 (2020)
4. Protzenko, J., et al.: EverCrypt: a fast, verified, cross-platform cryptographic provider. In: IEEE Symposium on Security and Privacy (S&P), pp. 983–1002 (2020)
5. Zinzindohoué, J., Bhargavan, K., Protzenko, J., Beurdouche, B.: HACL*: a verified modern cryptographic library. In: ACM SIGSAC Conference on Computer and Communications Security (CCS), pp. 1789–1806 (2017)

Quantum Safe Symmetric Cryptography

María Naya-Plasencia

Inria Paris, France
maria.naya_plasencia@inria.fr

During this talk we will introduce the context and summarize the state-of-the-art of the main quantum symmetric cryptanalysis results, providing the details of some particularly interesting cases. We will also present the scenario of some related open problems that are yet to be solved or improved.

A New Theory of Adversarial Examples in Machine Learning

Adi Shamir

Department of Computer Science, Weizmann Institute of Science, Rehovot, Israel

The extreme fragility of deep neural networks when presented with tiny perturbations in their inputs was independently discovered by several research groups in 2013. Due to their mysterious properties and major security implications, these adversarial examples had been studied extensively over the last eight years, but in spite of enormous effort they remained a baffling phenomenon with no clear explanation. In particular, it was not clear why a tiny distance away from almost any cat image there are images which are recognized with a very high level of confidence as cars, planes, frogs, horses, or any other desired class, why the adversarial modification which turns a cat into a car does not look like a car at all, and why a network which was adversarially trained with randomly permuted labels (so that it never saw any image which looks like a cat being called a cat) still recognizes most cat images as cats. The goal of this talk is to introduce a new theory of adversarial examples, which we call the Dimpled Manifold Model. It can easily explain in a simple and intuitive way why they exist and why they have all the bizarre properties mentioned above. In addition, it sheds new light on broader issues in machine learning such as what happens to deep neural networks during regular and during adversarial training. Experimental support for this theory, obtained jointly with Odelia Melamed and Oriel BenShmuel, will be presented and discussed in the last part of the talk.

Contents

Side-Channel Attacks

Fault Attacks

Post-Quantum Cryptography

Public Key Encryption and Protocols

Cryptographic Constructions

Blockchains

Authenticated Encryption

Revisiting the Security of **COMET** Authenticated Encryption Scheme

Shay Gueron[1,2], Ashwin Jha[3], and Mridul Nandi[4(✉)]

[1] University of Haifa, Haifa, Israel
[2] Amazon Web Services, Seattle, USA
[3] CISPA Helmholtz Center for Information Security, Saarbrücken, Germany
ashwin.jha@cispa.de
[4] Indian Statistical Institute, Kolkata, India

Abstract. COMETv1, by Gueron, Jha and Nandi, is a mode of operation for nonce-based authenticated encryption with associated data functionality. It was one of the second round candidates in the ongoing NIST Lightweight Cryptography Standardization Process. In this paper, we study a generalized version of COMETv1, that we call gCOMET, from provable security perspective. First, we present a comprehensive and complete security proof for gCOMET in the ideal cipher model. Second, we view COMET, the underlying mode of operation in COMETv1, as an instantiation of gCOMET, and derive its concrete security bounds. Finally, we propose another instantiation of gCOMET, dubbed COMETv2, and show that this version achieves better security guarantees as well as memory-efficient implementations as compared to COMETv1.

Keywords: COMET · ICM · Provable security · Rekeying · Lightweight · AEAD

1 Introduction

Lightweight cryptography has seen a sudden surge in demand due to the recent advancements in the field of Internet of things (IoT). The NIST lightweight cryptography standardization project [1], henceforth referred as the NIST LwC project, intends to address this demand by standardizing lightweight authenticated encryption (AE) and cryptographic hash schemes.

The first round of NIST LwC project had 56 candidates, of which 32 were selected to continue to second round. Among these 32 candidates around 15 schemes were based on (tweakable) block ciphers. In this paper we focus on one particular block cipher based candidate, called COMET [2] by Gueron et al., that uses nonce and position based re-keying and a COFB [3] or Beetle [4] like feedback operation.

COMET can be viewed as an ideal cipher based alternative for Beetle [4] and COFB [3]. Indeed, the designers state that the mode of operation can be viewed

© Springer Nature Switzerland AG 2021
A. Adhikari et al. (Eds.): INDOCRYPT 2021, LNCS 13143, pp. 3–25, 2021.
https://doi.org/10.1007/978-3-030-92518-5_1

as a mixture of CTR [5] and Beetle. COMET is parameterized by the block size of the underlying block cipher. Accordingly, COMET-n means COMET with block size n. It has two versions, one with $n = \kappa$, and the other with $n = \kappa/2$, where κ denotes the key size of the block cipher. The concrete submissions using COMET mode are based on AES-128/128 [6], Speck-64/128 [7,8], CHAM-128/128 [9], and CHAM-64/128 [9]. Some of the standout features of COMET are as follows:

1. DESIGN SIMPLICITY: The design of COMET is extremely simple. Apart from the block cipher evaluations, it only requires simple shift and XOR operations.
2. SMALL STATE SIZE: Theoretically, COMET requires only $(n + \kappa)$-bit internal state, which makes it one of the smallest AEAD candidate in the ongoing NIST LwC project.
3. EFFICIENCY: COMET is single-pass, which makes it quite efficient in both hardware and software. Apart from the block cipher call, only 1 shift and at most 2 XOR operations are required per block of input. This places COMET among the fastest candidates in the ongoing NIST LwC project. In fact, according to the publicly available software implementation and benchmarking by Weatherley [10], COMET outperforms all other candidates by a significant margin.

1.1   Motivations and Related Works

In this paper, we concentrate on the provable security of the COMET mode of operation. The designers made the following claims with respect to the security of COMET:

- COMET-128 is secure while the data complexity, denoted D, is at most 2^{64} bytes, and the time complexity, denoted T, is at most 2^{119}.
- COMET-64 is secure while $D < 2^{45}$ bytes, and $T < 2^{112}$.

Note that, the designers make a better claim with respect to the privacy of COMET-64. However, for the sake of uniformity, we mention the more conservative bound claimed for the integrity of COMET-64. In [11], Khairallah presented the first cryptanalytic work on COMET. Later, as noted by the designers [12], Bernstein, Henri and Turan [13] shared two observations on the security of COMET-64. While these works do not invalidate the security claims due to a breach in the data complexity limit, they do demonstrate a possible tightness of the security claims. Shortly after Khairallah's work, at NIST Lightweight Cryptography Workshop 2019, the designers presented a brief sketch of the security proof [12] for COMET-128. However, their proof approach was not applicable to COMET-64. In this paper, we aim to give a comprehensive proof of security for the COMET mode of operation.

1.2   Our Contributions

Our contributions are twofold:

1. We propose a generalization of COMET, dubbed as gCOMET (see Sect. 3). We intend to employ the recently introduced proof strategy of Chakraborty

Table 1. Summary of security bounds for COMET and COMETv2 as per the results in this paper.

Submissions	Data (D)	Time (T)	Data-Time (DT) Trade-off
COMET-128	2^{63} bytes	$2^{125.19}$	$2^{184.24}$
COMET-64	2^{42} bytes	2^{112}	$2^{152.24}$
COMETv2-128	2^{64} bytes	$2^{125.19}$	$2^{184.24}$
COMETv2-64	2^{63} bytes	$2^{121.58}$	$2^{152.24}$

et al. [14] to prove the security of gCOMET. Consequently, in Sect. 4 and 5, we extend the tools and results used in [14]. We give a detailed security proof for gCOMET in Sect. 6.

2. We view COMET as an instance of gCOMET and obtain concrete security bounds for both versions of COMET. Specifically, we show that
   - COMET-128 is secure while: $D < 2^{63}$ bytes and $T < 2^{125.19}$ and $DT < 2^{184.24}$.
   - COMET-64 is secure while: $D < 2^{42}$ bytes and $T < 2^{112}$ and $DT < 2^{152.24}$.

Further, we observe that two simple changes in the design of COMET, improves the performance and increases the security (by avoiding the attacks in [11,13]). We call this new version, COMETv2. In terms of security, we show that
   - COMETv2-128 is secure while: $D < 2^{64}$ bytes and $T < 2^{125.19}$ and $DT < 2^{184.24}$.
   - COMETv2-64 is secure while: $D < 2^{63}$ bytes and $T < 2^{121.58}$ and $DT < 2^{152.24}$.

We summarize the concrete security bounds for different variants of COMET and COMETv2 in Table 1. Our security bounds validate the security claims for COMET-128, as given in [2]. For COMET-64, our bounds are slightly lower than the ones claimed by the designers. However, we note that we could not find any matching attacks. So, the exact security of COMET-64 is still an open problem.

2 Preliminaries

NOTATIONAL SETUP: Let $\mathbb{N}$ denote the set of all natural numbers and $\mathbb{N}_0 := \mathbb{N} \cup \{0\}$. Fix some $n \in \mathbb{N}$. We write $(n]$ to denote the set $\{0, \ldots, n-1\}$. For $m, k \in \mathbb{N}_0$, such that $m \geq k$, we define the falling factorial $(m)_k := m!/(m-k)!$. Note that, $(m)_k \leq m^k$. For $m, n \in \mathbb{N}$, $A_{m \times n}$ denotes an $m \times n$ binary matrix (or simply A_n, when $m = n$). The identity matrix of dimension n is denoted I_n and the null matrix of dimension $m \times n$ is denoted $0_{m \times n}$. We write $\operatorname{rank}(A_n)$ to denote the rank of A_n. For any square matrix A_n, we define the period of A_n, denoted $\operatorname{cycle}(A_n)$, as the smallest integer k such that $A_n^k = I_n$. We drop the dimensions of the matrix, whenever they are understood from the context.

We use $\{0,1\}^n$ and $\{0,1\}^+$ to denote the set of all n-bit strings, and non-empty binary strings, respectively. ε denotes the empty string and $\{0,1\}^* :=$ $\{0,1\}^+ \cup \{\varepsilon\}$. For any string $B \in \{0,1\}^+$, $|B|$ denotes the number of bits in B, also referred as the length or size of B. We use little-endian format of indexing, i.e., for any $B \in \{0,1\}^+$, we write and view B as a $|B|$-bit binary string $b_{|B|-1} \cdots b_0$, i.e., the most significant bit $b_{|B|-1}$ lies on the left. For $B \in \{0,1\}^+$, $(B_{\ell-1}, \ldots, B_0) \xleftarrow{n} B$, denotes the n-bit block parsing of B into $(B_{\ell-1}, \ldots, B_0)$, where $|B_i| = n$ for $0 \le i \le \ell - 2$, and $1 \le |B_{\ell-1}| \le n$. For $A, B \in \{0,1\}^+$, and $|A| = |B|$, $A \oplus B$ denotes the "bitwise XOR" operation on A and B. For $A, B \in \{0,1\}^*$, $A\|B$ denotes the "string concatenation" operation on A and B. For $A, B \in \{0,1\}^*$ and $X = A\|B$, A and B are called the prefix and suffix of X, respectively.

For $q \in \mathbb{N}$, X^q denotes the q-tuple $(X_0, \ldots, X_{q-1})$. For $q \in \mathbb{N}$ and any set $\mathcal{X}$ such that $|\mathcal{X}| \ge q$, we write $(\mathcal{X})_q$ to denote the set of all q-tuples with pairwise distinct elements from $\mathcal{X}$, i.e., $|(\mathcal{X})_q| = (|\mathcal{X}|)_q$. For a finite set $\mathcal{X}$, $X^q \xleftarrow{\$} \mathcal{X}$ denotes the uniform at random sampling of q variables $X_0, \ldots, X_{q-1}$ from $\mathcal{X}$ in with replacement fashion.

2.1   Authenticated Encryption: Definition and Security Model

AUTHENTICATION ENCRYPTION WITH ASSOCIATED DATA: An authenticated encryption scheme with associated data functionality, or AEAD in short, is a tuple of algorithms $\mathsf{AE} = (\mathsf{E}, \mathsf{D})$, defined over the key space $\mathcal{K}$, nonce space $\mathcal{N}$, associated data space $\mathcal{A}$, plaintext space $\mathcal{P}$, ciphertext space $\mathcal{C}$, and tag space $\mathcal{T}$, where:

$$\mathsf{E} : \mathcal{K} \times \mathcal{N} \times \mathcal{A} \times \mathcal{P} \to \mathcal{C} \times \mathcal{T} \quad \text{and} \quad \mathsf{D} : \mathcal{K} \times \mathcal{N} \times \mathcal{A} \times \mathcal{C} \times \mathcal{T} \to \mathcal{P} \cup \{\bot\}.$$

Here, E and D are called the encryption and decryption algorithms, respectively, of AE. Further, it is required that $\mathsf{D}(K, N, A, \mathsf{E}(K, N, A, M)) = M$ for any $(K, N, A, M) \in \mathcal{K} \times \mathcal{N} \times \mathcal{A} \times \mathcal{P}$. For all key $K \in \mathcal{K}$, we write $\mathsf{E}_K(\cdot)$ and $\mathsf{D}_K(\cdot)$ to denote $\mathsf{E}(K, \cdot)$ and $\mathsf{D}(K, \cdot)$, respectively.

IDEAL BLOCK CIPHER: For $n \in \mathbb{N}$, let $\mathsf{Perm}(n)$ denote the set of all permutations of $\{0,1\}^n$. For $n, \kappa \in \mathbb{N}$, $\mathsf{ICPerm}(\kappa, n)$ denotes the set of all families of permutations $\pi_K := \pi(K, \cdot) \in \mathsf{Perm}(n)$ over $\{0,1\}^n$, indexed by $K \in \{0,1\}^\kappa$. A block cipher with key size κ and block size n is a family of permutations $\mathsf{IC} \in \mathsf{ICPerm}(\kappa, n)$. For $K \in \{0,1\}^\kappa$, we denote $\mathsf{IC}_K(\cdot) = \mathsf{IC}_K^+(\cdot) := \mathsf{IC}(K, \cdot)$, and $\mathsf{IC}_K^-(\cdot) := \mathsf{IC}^{-1}(K, \cdot)$. Throughout this paper, we denote the key size and block size of the block cipher by κ and n, respectively. In this context, a binary string X, with $|X| \le n$, is called a full block if $|X| = n$, and partial block otherwise. A block cipher is said to be an ideal cipher if for all $K \in \{0,1\}^\kappa$, $\mathsf{IC}_K \xleftarrow{\$} \mathsf{Perm}(n)$.

AEAD SECURITY IN THE IDEAL CIPHER MODEL (ICM): Let $\mathsf{AE}_{\mathsf{IC}}$ be an AEAD scheme, based on the ideal cipher IC, defined over $(\mathcal{K}, \mathcal{N}, \mathcal{A}, \mathcal{P}, \mathcal{C}, \mathcal{T})$. In this paper, we fix $\mathcal{K} = \{0,1\}^\kappa$, $\mathcal{N} = \{0,1\}^n$, $\mathcal{T} = \{0,1\}^\tau$, and $\mathcal{C} = \mathcal{P} = \mathcal{A} = \{0,1\}^*$, for some fixed $\kappa, \eta, \tau \in \mathbb{N}$. Accordingly, we denote the *key size, nonce size,* and *tag size* by κ, η, and τ, respectively. Let

$$\mathsf{Func} := \{f : \mathcal{N} \times \mathcal{A} \times \mathcal{P} \to \mathcal{C} \times \mathcal{T} \; : \; \forall (N, A, M) \in \mathcal{N} \times \mathcal{A} \times \mathcal{P}, \; |f(N, A, M)| = |M| + \tau\},$$

and $\Gamma \leftarrow_{\$} \mathsf{Func}$. Let $\perp$ denote the degenerate function from $(\mathcal{N}, \mathcal{A}, \mathcal{P}, \mathcal{T})$ to $\{\perp\}$. For brevity, we denote the oracle corresponding to a function by the function itself, and bidirectional access to IC is denoted by the superscript $\pm$.

Definition 2.1. *The AEAD advantage of any adversary $\mathscr{A}$ against $\mathsf{AE_{IC}}$ is defined as,*

$$\mathbf{Adv}^{\mathrm{aead}}_{\mathsf{AE_{IC}}}(\mathscr{A}) := \left| \Pr_{\substack{K \leftarrow_{\$} \mathcal{K} \\ \mathsf{IC}^{\pm}}} \left[\mathscr{A}^{\mathsf{E_K, D_K, IC}^{\pm}} = 1 \right] - \Pr_{\Gamma, \mathsf{IC}^{\pm}} \left[\mathscr{A}^{\Gamma, \perp, \mathsf{IC}^{\pm}} = 1 \right] \right|, \qquad (1)$$

where $\mathscr{A}^{\mathsf{E_K, D_K, IC}^{\pm}}$ and $\mathscr{A}^{\Gamma, \perp, \mathsf{IC}^{\pm}}$ denote $\mathscr{A}$'s response after its interaction with $(\mathsf{E_K, D_K, IC}^{\pm})$ and $(\Gamma, \perp, \mathsf{IC}^{\pm})$, respectively.

In this paper, we assume that the adversary is *non-trivial* and *nonce respecting,* i.e., it never makes a duplicate query, it never makes a query for which the response is already known due to some previous query, and it does not repeat nonce values in encryption queries. Throughout, we use the following notations to parametrize adversary's resources:

- q_e and q_d denote the number of queries to $\mathsf{E_K}$ and $\mathsf{D_K}$, respectively. σ_e and σ_d denote the sum of input (associated data and plaintext/ciphertext) lengths across all encryption and decryption queries, respectively. We also write $q_c = q_e + q_d$ and $\sigma_c = \sigma_e + \sigma_d$ to denote the combined construction query resources.
- q_p denotes the number of primitive queries.

An adversary $\mathscr{A}$ that abides by the above resources is referred as a $(q_e, q_d, \sigma_e, \sigma_d, q_p)$-adversary. We remark here that q_c and σ_c correspond to the *online complexity* (grouped under data complexity $D = q_c + \sigma_c$), and q_p corresponds to the *offline complexity* (grouped under time complexity $T = q_p$) of the adversary.

2.2 Expectation Method

We discuss the expectation method by Hoang and Tessaro [15] in context of AEAD security in the ideal cipher model. Consider a computationally unbounded and deterministic adversary $\mathscr{A}$ that tries to distinguish the real oracle $\mathcal{R} := (\mathsf{E_K, D_K, IC}^{\pm})$ from the ideal oracle $\mathcal{I} := (\Gamma, \perp, \mathsf{IC}^{\pm})$. We denote the query-response tuple of $\mathscr{A}$'s interaction with its oracle by a transcript ω. Sometime this may also include any additional information the oracle chooses to reveal to the adversary at the end of the query-response phase of the game. We will consider this extended definition of transcript.

Let R (res. I) denote the random transcript variable when $\mathscr{A}$ interacts with $\mathcal{R}$ (res. $\mathcal{I}$). The probability of realizing a given transcript ω in the security game with an oracle $\mathcal{O}$ is known as the *interpolation probability* of ω with respect to $\mathcal{O}$. Since $\mathscr{A}$ is deterministic, this probability depends only on the oracle $\mathcal{O}$ and the transcript ω. A transcript ω is said to be *attainable* if $\Pr[\text{I} = \omega] > 0$.

Theorem 2.1 (Expectation method [15]**).** *Let Ω be the set of all transcripts. For some $\epsilon_{\text{bad}} \geq 0$ and a non-negative function $\epsilon_{\text{ratio}} : \Omega \to [0, \infty)$, suppose there is a set $\Omega_{\text{bad}} \subseteq \Omega$ satisfying the following:*

- $\Pr[\text{I} \in \Omega_{\text{bad}}] \leq \epsilon_{\text{bad}}$;
- *For any $\omega \notin \Omega_{\text{bad}}$, ω is attainable, and*

$$\frac{\Pr[\text{R} = \omega]}{\Pr[\text{I} = \omega]} \geq 1 - \epsilon_{\text{ratio}}(\omega).$$

Then, for any adversary $\mathscr{A}$, we have

$$\mathbf{Adv}_{\text{AE}_{\text{IC}}}^{\text{aead}}(\mathscr{A}) \leq \epsilon_{\text{bad}} + \text{Ex}\left[\epsilon_{\text{ratio}}(\text{I})\right].$$

A proof of this theorem is available in multiple papers including [15,16]. The H-coefficient technique due to Patarin [17,18] is a simple corollary of this result, where ϵ_{ratio} is a constant function.

3   Generalized **COMET** Mode of Operation

COunter Mode Encryption with authentication Tag, or COMET in abbreviation, is a block cipher mode of operation by Gueron, Jha and Nandi [2] that provides authenticated encryption with associated data functionality. At a very high level, it can be viewed as a mixture of CTR [5], Beetle [4], and COFB [3] modes of operation. In this section, we provide a slightly generalized description of the COMET mode of operation, that we call gCOMET.

3.1   Parameters and Building Blocks

The gCOMET mode of operation is based on a block cipher IC with n-bit block and κ-bit key size.

PARAMETERS: In the following, we describe various parameters used in gCOMET along with their limits:

1. *Block size:* The block size n of IC also denotes the block size of gCOMET. It is analogous to the *rate* parameter used in Sponge-based schemes [4,19].
2. *Key size:* The key size κ is simply the key size of the underlying block cipher IC, that follows $\kappa \geq n$.
3. *State size:* The $(n+\kappa)$-bit input size of the underlying block cipher IC denotes the state size $\mathfrak{s}$ of gCOMET.

4. *Control and Invariant-prefix size:* gCOMET uses a small number of bits, called *control bits* (or, control) for separating the various phases of execution, such as associated data (AD) processing and plaintext processing, and identifying full and partial block data. We denote the control size by c and it follows $c \ll \kappa$. In fact, the control bits can be described in very few bits. For instance, COMET [2] uses $c = 5$.

   On a related note, we also use an auxiliary parameter c', called the *invariant-prefix size*, following the relation $c' \geq c$. For example, COMET uses $c' = \kappa/2$.

5. *Nonce size:* The nonce size η follows the relation:

$$\begin{aligned} \eta \leq n & \qquad \text{if } n = \kappa, \\ \eta \leq \kappa - c & \qquad \text{if } n < \kappa. \end{aligned} \tag{2}$$

6. *Tag size:* The tag size τ follows the relation $\tau \leq n$.

From the above discussion, one can see that gCOMET is primarily parameterized by the block size n and the key size κ, and all other parameters are bounded in terms of these two. Accordingly, we write fatCOMET and tinyCOMET to denote gCOMET with $n = \kappa$ and $n < \kappa$, respectively. In each case, the nonce size η is a fixed number that follows the condition given in Eq. (2). For the sake of simplicity, we assume $\eta = n$ for fatCOMET and $\eta = \kappa - c$ for tinyCOMET.

BUILDING BLOCKS: Apart from the block cipher IC, gCOMET has three more components that are described below:

Control Sequence Generator: We define the control sequence generator as the function $\Delta : \mathbb{N}_0 \times \mathbb{N}_0 \to (\{0,1\}^c)^+$ such that $|\Delta(a,m)| = (a + m + 2)c$ for all $a, m \in \mathbb{N}_0$.

Feedback Functions: Let Φ be an invertible linear map over $\{0,1\}^n$ and $\Phi' := \Phi \oplus I$, the pointwise sum of Φ and I, where I denotes the identity map over $\{0,1\}^n$. We define the feedback functions as follows:

- $L_{ad} : \{0,1\}^n \times \{0,1\}^n \to \{0,1\}^n$ is defined by the mapping

$$(X, A) \longmapsto X \oplus A.$$

- $L_{pt} : \{0,1\}^n \times \{0,1\}^n \to \{0,1\}^n \times \{0,1\}^n$ is defined by the mapping

$$(X, M) \longmapsto (X \oplus M, \Phi(X) \oplus M).$$

- $L_{ct} : \{0,1\}^n \times \{0,1\}^n \to \{0,1\}^n \times \{0,1\}^n$ is defined by the mapping

$$(X, C) \longmapsto (\Phi'(X) \oplus C, \Phi(X) \oplus C).$$

Key-Update Function: Let Ψ be an invertible linear map over $\{0,1\}^{\kappa-c'}$. We define the update function $U : \{0,1\}^\kappa \to \{0,1\}^\kappa$ by the binary matrix

$$U := \begin{bmatrix} I_{c'} & 0_{c' \times \kappa-c'} \\ 0_{\kappa-c' \times c'} & \Psi \end{bmatrix},$$

where Ψ is viewed as a $(\kappa - c')$ square matrix with elements from $\{0,1\}$. The above definition implies that c' controls the prefix size of the key that remains unchanged in the key updation. This motivates our nomenclature for c' as the invariant-prefix size parameter.

3.2 Description of gCOMET

In the following, we describe the main phase of gCOMET's encryption/decryption algorithm for a tuple of input (K, N, A, I) where K, N, A, and I denote the key, nonce, associated data and plaintext (ciphertext in case of decryption), respectively:

Initialization Phase: This phase computes the initial state for the algorithm. This is the only phase where the two gCOMET versions, namely fatCOMET and tinyCOMET differ. Specifically,

In fatCOMET, we have

$\text{init}_{n,\kappa}(K, N, A, I)$:

1: $a \leftarrow \left\lceil \frac{|A|}{n} \right\rceil$, $m \leftarrow \left\lceil \frac{|I|}{n} \right\rceil$, $\ell = a + m$
2: $\delta^{\ell+2} \leftarrow \Delta(a, m)$
3: $Y_0 \leftarrow K$
4: $Z'_0 \leftarrow \text{IC}_K^+(N) \oplus \delta_0 \| 0^{\kappa-c}$
5: **return** $(Y_0, Z'_0, \delta^{\ell+2}, a, m, \ell)$

In tinyCOMET, we have

$\text{init}_{n,\kappa}(K, N, A, I)$:

1: $a \leftarrow \left\lceil \frac{|A|}{n} \right\rceil$, $m \leftarrow \left\lceil \frac{|M|}{n} \right\rceil$, $\ell = a + m$
2: $\delta^{\ell+2} \leftarrow \Delta(a, m)$
3: $Y_0 \leftarrow \text{IC}_K^+(0^n)$
4: $Z'_0 \leftarrow K \oplus \delta_0 \| N$
5: **return** $(Y_0, Z'_0, \delta^{\ell+2}, a, m, \ell)$

Data Processing Phase: This phase consists of two modules corresponding to associate data processing, denoted proc_ad, and plaintext/ciphertext processing, denoted proc_pt/proc_ct. Each of these modules only execute for non-empty data. The modules are identical except for the feedback functions. For non-empty data the processing is as follows:

$\text{proc\_ad}(Y_0, Z'_0, A, \delta^{\ell+2})$:

1: $(A_{a-1}, \ldots, A_0) \xleftarrow{n} A$
2: **for** $i = 0$ to $a - 1$ **do**
3: $\quad Z_i \leftarrow \text{U}(Z'_i)$
4: $\quad X_i \leftarrow \text{IC}_{Z'_i}^+(Y_i)$
5: $\quad Y_{i+1} \leftarrow \text{L}_{ad}(X_i, A_i)$
6: $\quad Z'_{i+1} \leftarrow Z_i \oplus \delta_{i+1} \| 0^{\kappa-c}$
7: $\quad$ **return** (Y_a, Z'_a)

$\text{proc\_pt}(Y_a, Z'_a, I, \delta^{\ell+2})$:

1: $(I_{m-1}, \ldots, I_0) \xleftarrow{n} I$
2: **for** $j = 0$ to $m - 1$ **do**
3: $\quad k \leftarrow a + j$
4: $\quad Z_k \leftarrow \text{U}(Z'_k)$
5: $\quad X_k \leftarrow \text{IC}_{Z_k}^+(Y_k)$
6: $\quad (Y_{k+1}, O_j) \leftarrow \text{L}_{pt}(X_k, I_j)$
7: $\quad Z'_{k+1} \leftarrow Z_k \oplus \delta_{k+1} \| 0^{\kappa-c}$
8: $\quad O \leftarrow (O_{m-1}, \ldots, O_0)$
9: $\quad$ **return** (Y_ℓ, Z'_ℓ, O)

$\text{proc\_ct}(Y_a, Z'_a, I, \delta^{\ell+2})$:

1: $(I_{m-1}, \ldots, I_0) \xleftarrow{n} I$
2: **for** $j = 0$ to $m - 1$ **do**
3: $\quad k \leftarrow a + j$
4: $\quad Z_k \leftarrow \text{U}(Z'_k)$
5: $\quad X_k \leftarrow \text{IC}_{Z_k}^+(Y_k)$
6: $\quad (Y_{k+1}, O_j) \leftarrow \text{L}_{ct}(X_k, I_j)$
7: $\quad Z'_{k+1} \leftarrow Z_k \oplus \delta_{k+1} \| 0^{\kappa-c}$
8: $\quad O \leftarrow (O_{m-1}, \ldots, O_0)$
9: $\quad$ **return** (Y_ℓ, Z'_ℓ, O)

Tag Generation Phase: This is the final step and generates the tag.

$\text{proc\_tg}(Y_\ell, Z'_\ell, \delta_{\ell+1})$:

1: $Z'_\ell \leftarrow Z'_\ell \oplus \delta_{\ell+1} \| 0^{\kappa-c}$
2: $Z_\ell \leftarrow \text{U}(Z'_\ell)$
3: $T := X_\ell \leftarrow \text{IC}_{Z_\ell}^+(Y_\ell)$
4: **return** T

Algorithm 3.1 gives the complete algorithmic description of gCOMET, and Fig. 1 illustrates the major components of the encryption/decryption process.

Algorithm 3.1. Encryption/Decryption algorithm in gCOMET.

1: **function** gCOMET$_{[IC]}$.E(K, N, A, M)
2:    $C \leftarrow \perp$
3:    $(Y_0, Z_0', \delta^{\ell+2}, a, m, \ell) \leftarrow \text{init}_{n,\kappa}(K, N, A, M)$
4:    **if** $a \neq 0$ **then**
5:       $(Y_a, Z_a') \leftarrow \text{proc\_ad}(Y_0, Z_0', A, \delta^{\ell+2})$
6:    **if** $m \neq 0$ **then**
7:       $(Y_\ell, Z_\ell', C) \leftarrow \text{proc\_pt}(Y_a, Z_a', M, \delta^{\ell+2})$
8:    $T \leftarrow \text{proc\_tg}(Y_\ell, Z_\ell', \delta_{\ell+1})$
9:    **return** (C, T)

1: **function** gCOMET$_{[IC]}$.D(K, N, A, C, T)
2:    $(Y_0, Z_0', \delta^{\ell+2}, a, m, \ell) \leftarrow \text{init}_{n,\kappa}(K, N, A, C)$
3:    **if** $a \neq 0$ **then**
4:       $(Y_a, Z_a') \leftarrow \text{proc\_ad}(Y_0, Z_0', A, \delta^{\ell+2})$
5:    **if** $m \neq 0$ **then**
6:       $(Y_\ell, Z_\ell', M) \leftarrow \text{proc\_ct}(Y_a, Z_a', C, \delta^{\ell+2})$
7:    $T' \leftarrow \text{proc\_tg}(Y_\ell, Z_\ell', \delta_{\ell+1})$
8:    **if** $T' = T$ **then**
9:       is_auth $\leftarrow 1$
10:   **else**
11:      is_auth $\leftarrow 0$, $M \leftarrow \perp$
12:   **return** (is_auth, M)

---

4 Expected Maximum Multicollision Sizes

We briefly revisit some results on the expectation of maximum multicollision size in a random sample. These results are largely based on the extensive analysis already given in [14]. We mostly reuse the strategy from [14] to derive some new results required in case of COMET. For space limitation, we postpone the proofs of all the propositions in this section to the full version of this paper [20].

Before delving into the results we state a simple observation (also given in [14]) that will be useful in bounding the expectation of any non-negative random variable. For any non-negative random variable Y bounded above by q, and $\rho \in \mathbb{N}$, we have

$$\text{Ex}[Y] \leq \rho - 1 + q \times \Pr[Y \geq \rho]. \tag{3}$$

4.1 For Uniform Random Sample

For $n \geq 1$, let $X^q \leftarrow_\$ \{0,1\}^n$. We define the maximum multicollision size random variable, denoted $\Theta_{q,n}$, for the sample X^q as follows

$$\Theta_{q,n} := \max_{a \in \{0,1\}^n} |\{i \in (q) : X_i = a\}|,$$

and write $\mu(q, n)$ to denote $\text{Ex}[\Theta_{q,n}]$.

Proposition 4.1. *For $n \geq 2$,*

$$\mu(q, n) \leq \begin{cases} 3 & \text{if } q \leq 2^{\frac{n}{2}}, \\ \frac{4n}{\log_2 n} & \text{if } 2^{\frac{n}{2}} < q \leq 2^n, \\ 5n \left\lceil \frac{q}{n2^n} \right\rceil & \text{if } q > 2^n. \end{cases}$$

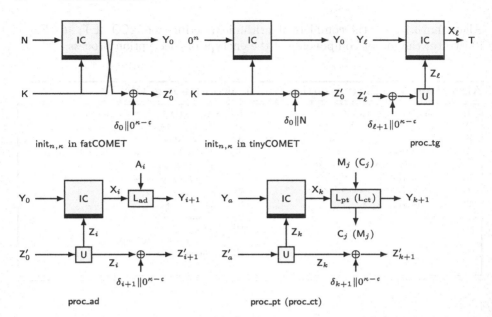

Fig. 1. Various phases in the encryption/decryption algorithm of gCOMET. Here, $i \in (a]$, $j \in (m]$ and $k = a + j$.

For Ideal Cipher Samples. Let $(z_0, y_0), \ldots, (z_{q-1}, y_{q-1})$ be a q-tuple of distinct pairs of key and input to an ideal cipher IC with n-bit input block, such that $z_i \neq z_j$ for all $i \neq j$. For $i \in (q]$, let $X_i = IC_{z_i}(y_i)$. We define

$$\widehat{\Theta}_{q,n} := \max_{a \in \{0,1\}^n} |\{i \in (q] : X_i = a\}|,$$

and write $\widehat{\mu}(q, n)$ to denote $\mathsf{Ex}\left[\widehat{\Theta}_{q,n}\right]$. Since all the keys are pairwise distinct, the sample X^q is statistically indistinguishable from a sample following uniform distribution. Thus, using Proposition 4.1, we get the following proposition for ideal cipher generated samples.

Proposition 4.2. *For $n \geq 2$,*

$$\widehat{\mu}(q, n) \leq \begin{cases} \frac{4n}{\log_2 n} & \text{if } q \leq 2^n \\ 5n \left\lceil \frac{q}{n2^n} \right\rceil & \text{if } q > 2^n. \end{cases}$$

Note that, identical result holds for samples generated through inverse calls to the ideal cipher as well.

For Linear Post-processing: Consider a variant of the above given problem, where we are interested in multicollisions on $(L(X_i))_{i \in (q]}$ for some linear map L over $\{0,1\}^n$ with $\mathsf{rank}(L) = r$. Obviously, $r \leq n$. We define

$$\widehat{\Theta}'_{q,n,r} := \max_{a \in \{0,1\}^n} |\{i \in (q] : L(X_i) = a\}|,$$

and write $\widehat{\mu}'(q, n, r)$ to denote $\mathsf{Ex}\left[\widehat{\Theta}'_{q,n,r}\right]$.

Proposition 4.3. *For $n \geq 2$,*

$$\widehat{\mu}'(q, n, r) \leq \begin{cases} \frac{4n}{\log_2 n} & \text{if } q \leq 2^r \\ 5n \left\lceil \frac{q}{n 2^r} \right\rceil & \text{if } q > 2^r. \end{cases}$$

4.2 Sum of Ideal Cipher Sample

Let $(z_0, y_0, x_0'), \ldots, (z_{q-1}, y_{q-1}, x_{q-1}')$ be a q-tuple such that (z_i, y_i) are pairwise distinct and (z_i, x_i') are pairwise distinct, where $z_i \in \{0,1\}^\kappa$ and $y_i, x_i' \in \{0,1\}^n$. Let L be a linear map over $\{0,1\}^n$ with $\mathsf{rank}(\mathsf{L}) = r$. For $i \in (q)$, let $z_i' = \mathsf{U}(z_i)$ and $\mathsf{C}_i = \mathsf{L}(\mathsf{IC}_{z_i}^+(y_i)) \oplus \mathsf{IC}_{z_i'}^-(x_i')$. We define

$$\Theta'_{q,n,r} := \max_{a \in \{0,1\}^n} |\{i \in (q) : \mathsf{C}_i = a\}|,$$

and write $\mu'(q, n, r)$ to denote $\mathsf{Ex}\left[\Theta'_{q,n,r}\right]$. We want to bound $\mu'(q, n, r)$.

Proposition 4.4. *For $n \geq 4$, we have*

$$\mu'(q, n, r) \leq 2n \left\lceil \frac{22nq}{2^r} \right\rceil.$$

5 Super-Chain Structure

In [14], Chakraborty et al. proposed the *multi-chain* structure. They use this tool to give a tight security bound for Sponge-type AEAD constructions like Beetle [4] and SpoC [21]. In this section, we give an extension of the multi-chain structure in our notations. This extended tool will be used later in the security analysis of gCOMET.

LABELED DIRECTED GRAPH: Let $\mathcal{L} = \{(z_i, y_i, x_i) : i \in (q)\}$ be a list of triples such that $(z_i, y_i) \neq (z_j, y_j)$ and $(z_i, x_i) \neq (z_j, x_j)$ for all $i \neq j \in (q)$, where $z_i \in \{0,1\}^\kappa$ and $x_i, y_i \in \{0,1\}^n$ for all $i \in (q)$. We write $\mathsf{range}(\mathcal{L}) = \{(z_i, x_i) : i \in (q)\}$. Let L be a linear map over $\{0,1\}^n$. To $\mathcal{L}$ and L, we associate a labeled directed graph $\mathcal{G}_{\mathcal{L}}^{\mathsf{L}} = (\mathsf{range}(\mathcal{L}), \mathcal{E})$ over the set of vertices $\mathsf{range}(\mathcal{L})$ with edge set $\mathcal{E}$. For all edge $((z, x), (z', x')) \in \mathcal{E}$ with label $c \in \{0,1\}^n$, denoted $(z, x) \xrightarrow{c} (z', x')$, we have $\mathsf{L}(x) \oplus c = y'$ and $\mathsf{U}(z) = z'$. By extending the notation, a labeled walk $\mathcal{W} = (w_0, \ldots, w_k)$ with label c^k is defined as $\mathcal{W} : w_0 \xrightarrow{c_0} w_1 \xrightarrow{c_1} w_2 \cdots w_{k-1} \xrightarrow{c_{k-1}} w_k$. We usually write it as $w_0 \xrightarrow{c^k} w_k$, where k is referred as the length of the walk. We simply write $\mathcal{G}$, dropping the list $\mathcal{L}$ and linear function L, whenever they are understood from the context.

Definition 5.1 (Chain). *A chain, denoted $\mathcal{C}(c^{k+1})$, with label c^{k+1} in $\mathcal{G}_{\mathcal{L}}^{\mathsf{L}}$ is simply a labeled walk $(z_{i_0}, x_{i_0}) \xrightarrow{c^k} (z_{i_k}, x_{i_k})$ with an additional parameter called sink, denoted $\mathsf{sink}[\mathcal{C}(c^{k+1})]$, and defined as follows*

$$\mathsf{sink}[\mathcal{C}(c^{k+1})] := \begin{cases} x_{i_k} & \text{if } c_k = \varepsilon \\ \mathsf{L}(x_{i_k}) \oplus c_k & \text{if } c_k \neq \varepsilon. \end{cases}$$

We call $\mathcal{C}(c^{k+1})$ a complete (resp. partial) chain if $c_k = \varepsilon$ (resp. $c_k \neq \varepsilon$). We define the source and key of the chain as $\mathsf{src}[\mathcal{C}(c^{k+1})] := x_{i_0}$ and $\mathsf{key}[\mathcal{C}(c^{k+1})] := z_{i_0}$, respectively. Length of $\mathcal{C}(c^{k+1})$, denoted $\#\mathcal{C}(c^{k+1})$, is simply the length of the walk, i.e., k.

In context of this work, a chain is a graphical representation of (a part of) an execution of gCOMET encryption/decryption process, where the label of the chain plays the role of the input string, the key and source of the chain denote the starting point in the execution and the sink denotes the end point. Looking ahead momentarily, in our analysis we will need a special collection of chains starting from a common source and ending in (possibly) distinct sinks.

Definition 5.2 (Super-chain). *A t-sink super-chain, denoted $\mathcal{S}(c^{k+1})$, with label c^{k+1} in $\mathcal{G}_{\mathcal{L}}^{\mathsf{L}}$ is a set of chains $\{\mathcal{C}_0(d_0), \ldots, \mathcal{C}_{l-1}(d_{l-1})\}$ such that*

- *for $i \in (k]$, $c_i \in \{0,1\}^n$ and $c_k = \epsilon$.*
- *for $i \in (l]$, $d_i = c^{j+1}$ for some $j \in (k+1]$.*
- *for distinct $i, j \in (l]$, $\mathsf{src}[\mathcal{C}_i(d_i)] = \mathsf{src}[\mathcal{C}_j(d_j)]$ and $\mathsf{key}[\mathcal{C}_i(d_i)] \neq \mathsf{key}[\mathcal{C}_j(d_j)]$.*
- *$|\{(\mathsf{sink}[\mathcal{C}_i(d_i)], \#\mathcal{C}_i(d_i)) : i \in (l]\}| = t$.*

Size of $\mathcal{S}(c^{k+1})$, denoted $|\mathcal{S}(c^{k+1})|$, is simply the cardinality of $\mathcal{S}(c^{k+1})$, i.e., l.

A super-chain can be viewed as a collection of parallel chains starting at a common decryption query block (source of the super-chain), albeit with different keys, and ending at any one of the possible encryption query blocks or the committed tag value. If an adversary succeeds in generating a super-chain of significant size for a sequence of ciphertext blocks, then it can herd the corresponding decryption query to a desired tag value (or intermediate encryption query block) with significantly high probability. Simply put, a non-trivial[1] forgery would imply that the adversary succeeds in herding a decryption query to one of the chains in the super-chain. As a consequence, we aim to upper bound the size of the super-chain. Note that the multi-chain structure of [14,22] is a special case of super-chain structure, where $t = 1$ and for all $i \in (l]$, $d_i = c^{k+1}$. These extra conditions imply that all the chains are of length k, and they end in a common sink.

5.1 Maximum Size of t-Sink Super-Chain of Length k

Consider a non-trivial adversary $\mathscr{A}$ interacting with an ideal cipher oracle $\mathsf{IC}^{\pm}$. Suppose, $\mathscr{A}$ makes q queries to $\mathsf{IC}^{\pm}$. For $i \in (q]$, let $(\widehat{\mathsf{Z}}_i, \widehat{\mathsf{Y}}_i, \widehat{\mathsf{X}}_i, \widehat{\mathsf{d}}_i)$ denote the i-th query-response tuple, where $\widehat{\mathsf{Z}}_i \in \{0,1\}^\kappa$, $\widehat{\mathsf{Y}}_i, \widehat{\mathsf{X}}_i \in \{0,1\}^n$, and $\widehat{\mathsf{d}}_i \in \{0,1\}$. If $\widehat{\mathsf{d}}_i = 0$, $\mathscr{A}$ queries $(\widehat{\mathsf{Z}}_i, \widehat{\mathsf{Y}}_i)$ and gets response $\widehat{\mathsf{X}}_i := \mathsf{IC}^+(\widehat{\mathsf{Z}}_i, \widehat{\mathsf{Y}}_i)$ (forward query), else it queries $(\widehat{\mathsf{Z}}_i, \widehat{\mathsf{X}}_i)$ and gets response $\widehat{\mathsf{Y}}_i := \mathsf{IC}^-(\widehat{\mathsf{Z}}_i, \widehat{\mathsf{X}}_i)$ (backward query). We store the q query-response tuples in a list $\mathcal{L}$. Sometimes, we also write $\mathcal{L}' := ((\widehat{\mathsf{Z}}_0, \widehat{\mathsf{Y}}_0, \widehat{\mathsf{X}}_0), \ldots, (\widehat{\mathsf{Z}}_{q-1}, \widehat{\mathsf{Y}}_{q-1}, \widehat{\mathsf{X}}_{q-1}))$ which drops information about

---

[1] A forgery attack that does not involve exhaustive guessing of internal state or key.

query direction. Fix a linear map L over $\{0,1\}^n$ and consider the graph $\mathcal{G}_{\mathcal{L}'}^L$. Let $W_{t,k}(\mathcal{L}')$ denote the maximum over the size of all t-sink super-chains of length k in $\mathcal{G}_{\mathcal{L}'}^L$. Then, $W_{t,k}(\mathcal{L})$ is a random variable where the randomness is induced by IC.

Lemma 5.1. *Let* $\nu := \max\limits_{i \in (q)} \left| \{j : \widehat{Z}_j = \mathsf{U}(\widehat{Z}_i)\} \right|$. *For any non-trivial adversary* $\mathscr{A}$ *and an ideal cipher* IC, *we have*

$$\mathsf{Ex}\left[W_{t,k}(\mathcal{L})\right] \le 2\widehat{\mu}(q,n) + (t-1) \cdot \widehat{\mu}'(q,n,\mathsf{rank}(\mathsf{L})) + k \cdot \mu'(q\nu, n, \mathsf{rank}(\mathsf{L})).$$

The proof of this lemma is postponed to the full version of this paper [20].

6   Security of gCOMET

In this section, we give a detailed security analysis of gCOMET. Theorem 6.1 gives the combined AEAD security of gCOMET in the ideal cipher model.

Theorem 6.1. *For* $N, r > 0$, *let* $\mathsf{cycle}(\Psi) = N$ *and* $\mathsf{rank}(\Phi') = r$. *Then, for* $n, \nu_{ed} > 0$, $\sigma_c < \min\left\{N, 2^{n-2}\right\}$, $q_p < 2^{\kappa-2}$ *and* $(q_e, q_d, \sigma_e, \sigma_d, q_p)$-*adversary* $\mathscr{A}$, *we have*

$$\mathbf{Adv}^{\mathsf{aead}}_{\mathsf{gCOMET}}(\mathscr{A}) \le \left(\frac{2q_p}{2^\kappa} + \frac{6\sigma_c}{2^{\kappa-c'}} + \frac{4\sigma_d}{2^{\kappa-c'+n}}\right)\mu(\sigma_c, n) + \frac{4q_d}{2^\kappa}\widehat{\mu}(q_p, n) + \frac{q_c}{2^{\kappa-c'}}$$

$$+ \min\left\{\frac{2\sigma_d\sigma_e}{2^\kappa}\widehat{\mu}'(q_p, n, r), \frac{2\sigma_d\sigma_e}{2^{\kappa-c'}} + \frac{2\sigma_d}{2^\kappa}\widehat{\mu}'(q_p, n, r)\right\} + \frac{q_p + \sigma_c}{2^\kappa}$$

$$+ \frac{2\sigma_d}{2^\kappa}\mu'(q_p\nu_{ed}, n, r) + \frac{q_p\sigma_c}{\nu_{ed}2^\kappa} + \frac{2q_d(\sigma_e + q_e)}{2^{\kappa-c'+n}} + \frac{4q_p\sigma_d}{2^{\kappa+n}} + \frac{2q_d}{2^n}. \quad (4)$$

The proof is given in the rest of this section. In relation to the expectation method (high level tool used in the proof), we largely reuse the definitions and notations from Sect. 2.2.

6.1   Initial Setup and Description of Oracles

We denote the query-response tuple of $\mathscr{A}$'s interaction with its oracle by a transcript $\omega = \{\omega_e, \omega_d, \omega_p\}$, where $\omega_e := \{(\mathsf{N}^i, \mathsf{A}^i, \mathsf{M}^i, \mathsf{C}^i, \mathsf{T}^i) : i \in (q_e)\}$, $\omega_d := \{(\bar{\mathsf{N}}^j, \bar{\mathsf{A}}^j, \bar{\mathsf{C}}^j, \bar{\mathsf{T}}^j, \bar{\mathsf{D}}^j) : j \in (q_d)\}$, and $\omega_p := \{(\widehat{\mathsf{Z}}_k, \widehat{\mathsf{Y}}_k, \widehat{\mathsf{X}}_k, \widehat{\mathsf{d}}_k) : k \in (q_p)\}$. Here,

- $(\mathsf{N}^i, \mathsf{A}^i, \mathsf{M}^i, \mathsf{C}^i, \mathsf{T}^i)$ denotes the i-th encryption query-response tuple, where N^i, A^i, M^i, C^i, and T^i, denote the nonce, associated data, message, ciphertext, and tag, respectively. Let $\left\lceil \frac{|\mathsf{A}^i|}{n} \right\rceil = a^i$, $\left\lceil \frac{|\mathsf{C}^i|}{n} \right\rceil = \left\lceil \frac{|\mathsf{M}^i|}{n} \right\rceil = m^i$, and $\ell^i = a^i + m^i$.
- $(\bar{\mathsf{N}}^j, \bar{\mathsf{A}}^j, \bar{\mathsf{C}}^j, \bar{\mathsf{T}}^j, \bar{\mathsf{D}}^j)$ denotes the j-th decryption query-response tuple, where $\bar{\mathsf{N}}^j$, $\bar{\mathsf{A}}^j$, $\bar{\mathsf{C}}^j$, $\bar{\mathsf{T}}^j$, and $\bar{\mathsf{D}}^j$, denote the nonce, associated data, ciphertext, tag, and the authentication result, respectively. $\bar{\mathsf{D}}^j$ equals to a message $\bar{\mathsf{M}}^j$ when authentication succeeds, and $\perp$ otherwise. Let $\left\lceil \frac{|\bar{\mathsf{A}}^i|}{n} \right\rceil = \bar{a}^j$ and $\left\lceil \frac{|\bar{\mathsf{C}}^i|}{n} \right\rceil = \bar{m}^j$, and $\bar{\ell}^j = \bar{a}^j + \bar{m}^j$.

- $(\widehat{Z}_k, \widehat{Y}_k, \widehat{X}_k, \widehat{d}_k)$ denotes the k-th primitive query-response tuple, where $\widehat{Z}_k$, $\widehat{Y}_k$, $\widehat{X}_k$, and $\widehat{d}_k$, denote the key, input, output, and direction of query, respectively. $\widehat{d}_k = 0$ if the k-th query is forward, and $\widehat{d}_k = 1$ if the k-th query is backward.

In addition, for all $(i, j) \in (q_e] \times (\ell^i + 1]$ and $(i', j') \in (q_d] \times (\bar{\ell}^i + 1]$, (Z_j^i, Y_j^i, X_j^i) and $(\bar{Z}_{j'}^{i'}, \bar{Y}_{j'}^{i'}, \bar{X}_{j'}^{i'})$ are defined analogous to Fig. 1 and Algorithm 3.1.

IDEAL ORACLE DESCRIPTION: The ideal oracle works as follows:

- For the i-th primitive query:
     return $\widehat{X}_i = \mathsf{IC}^+(\widehat{Z}_i, \widehat{Y}_i)$ if $\widehat{d}_i = 0$, and return $\widehat{Y}_i = \mathsf{IC}^-(\widehat{Z}_i, \widehat{X}_i)$ otherwise.
- For the i-the encryption query:
  - $(X_0^i, \ldots, X_{\ell^i}^i) \leftarrow_\$ \{0, 1\}^n$.
  - for $j \in (m^i]$ and $k = a^i + j$, set $(Y_{k+1}^i, C_j^i) = \mathsf{L}_{\mathrm{pt}}(X_k^i, M_j^i)$ and $T^i = X_{\ell^i}^i$.
  - for $j \in (a^i]$, set $Y_{j+1}^i = \mathsf{L}_{\mathrm{ad}}(X_j^i, A_j^i)$.
  - return (C^i, T^i).
- For the i-th decryption query: simply return $\perp$.

Note that, the sampling mechanism in the ideal world is slightly indirect in nature. We compute ciphertext and tag outputs by first sampling X values and then using operations identical to gCOMET. However, owing to the invertibility of Φ, the marginal distribution of (C, T) is identical to the case where they are sampled uniform at random.

REAL ORACLE DESCRIPTION: The real oracle faithfully responds to $\mathscr{A}$'s encryption, decryption, and primitive queries using $\mathsf{IC}^\pm$.

Releasing Additional Information: After the query-response phase is over, the oracles additionally release $(X_0^i, \ldots, X_{\ell^i}^i)$ to the adversary. We add $(X_0^i, \ldots, X_{\ell^i}^i)$ to the encryption transcript, i.e. $\mathcal{I}_e$ in case of ideal oracle and R_e in case of real oracle. Note that, A, M, X tuples completely define $(Y_1^i, \ldots, Y_{\ell^i}^i)$.

Decryption Blocks Information from Encryption Blocks: Consider a decryption query $i \in (q_d]$. If $\bar{N}^i \neq N^{i'}$, for all $i' \in (q_e]$, then we define the index of longest common prefix, denoted p_i as -1. If there exists a unique index $i' \in (q_e]$, such that $\bar{N}^i = N^{i'}$, then we have

$$p_i := \begin{cases} \max\{j : (\bar{A}_0^i, \ldots, \bar{A}_{j-1}^i) = (A_0^{i'}, \ldots, A_{j-1}^{i'})\} & \text{if } \bar{A}^i \neq A^{i'}, \\ \max\{\bar{a}^i + j : (\bar{C}_0^i, \ldots, \bar{C}_{j-1}^i) = (\bar{C}_0^{i'}, \ldots, \bar{C}_{j-1}^{i'})\} & \text{otherwise.} \end{cases}$$

It is clear that whenever $p_i \geq 0$, then $(\bar{Z}_0^i, \bar{Y}_0^i) = (Z_0^{i'}, Y_0^{i'})$. Further, $\bar{Y}_j^i$, and $\bar{X}_j^i$ are determined for all $j \in (p_i + 1]$, due to $Y_j^{i'}$, $X_j^{i'}$, and $\bar{C}_j^i$. Note that, this holds in both the real and ideal world due to the way we define the ideal oracle responses.

At this point, the transcript random variables, viz. R and I, are completely defined. For the sake of notational simplicity, we use the same notation to represent the constituent random variables in the transcripts of both the world. However, they can be easily separated via their probability distribution which will be determined from their exact definitions in the two worlds. For any transcript ω, we define

- $\theta_e^b := \max\limits_{c \in \{0,1\}^n} |\{(i,j) \in (q_e] \times (m^i + 1] : Y_j^i = c\}|.$
- $\theta_e^f := \max\limits_{c \in \{0,1\}^n} |\{(i,j) \in (q_e] \times (m^i + 1] : X_j^i = c\}|.$

Definition 6.1 (Useful index and transcript set). *For $\nu > 0$, the ν-useful index set corresponding to some primitive transcript ω_p, is defined as the maximal set $\mathcal{I}$, such that for all $i \in \mathcal{I}$ we have $\left|\{j \in (q_p] : \widehat{Z}^j = \widehat{Z}^i\}\right| \le \nu$, and the ν-useful transcript set is defined as $\mathcal{Q}_\nu := \{(\widehat{Z}^i, \widehat{Y}^i, \widehat{X}^i) : i \in \mathcal{I}\}$.*

A useful set signifies the keys that do not occur often in primitive queries. Specifically, our aim is to bound the number of keys that appear in both primitive and construction queries. Since, the construction key is not released to the adversary one can get good bounds on ν. Looking ahead momentarily, a useful set will represent the subset of primitive queries that the adversary can use to herd some decryption query to the desired tag value.

6.2 Ratio of Interpolation Probabilities

Fix a transcript $\omega := (\omega_e, \omega_d, \omega_p)$. Since the transcript is attainable, we must have $\omega_d = \perp^{q_d}$. Analogous to the transcript $(\omega_e, \omega_d, \omega_p)$, we also view I and R as (I_e, I_d, I_p) and (R_e, R_d, R_p), respectively.

IDEAL WORLD: With respect to the encryption transcript, the ideal oracle samples exactly $\sigma_e + q_e$ mutually independent blocks uniformly at random. The decryption transcript holds with probability 1 as the ideal oracle always responds with $\perp$. Using the independence of construction and primitive transcripts in ideal world, we have

$$\Pr[I = \omega] = \Pr[I_e = \omega_e, I_d = \omega_d, I_p = \omega_p] = \Pr[I_p = \omega_p] \times \frac{1}{2^{n(\sigma_e + q_e)}}. \quad (5)$$

Consider the multiset, $\mathcal{Z}_p := \{\widehat{Z}^i : i \in (q_p]\}$. Let $(L_0, \ldots, L_{s-1})$ denote the tuple of distinct keys in $\mathcal{Z}_p$ and λ_i^p be the multiplicity of L_i in $\mathcal{Z}_p$ for all $i \in (s]$. Then, in Eq. (5) we have

$$\Pr[I = \omega] = \frac{1}{\prod_{i \in (s]}(2^n)_{\lambda_i^p}} \times \frac{1}{2^{n(\sigma_e + q_e)}}. \quad (6)$$

REAL WORLD: The interpolation probability of ω with respect to the real oracle $\mathcal{R}$ is slightly involved. In particular, we bound the interpolation probability for a special class of values for the internal transcript (i.e. K, Y_0, Z and $\bar{Z}$) that are compatible with ω. Loosely, the quadruple $(K, Y_0, Z, \bar{Z})$ is incompatible when it might result in some inconsistent input/output relations for the underlying ideal cipher. Formally, we say that $(K, Y_0, Z, \bar{Z})$ is incompatible with the external transcript ω, if one of the following events hold:

BO : $\exists i \in (q_p]$, such that $K = \widehat{Z}^i$.

B1 : $\exists (i,j) \in (q_e] \times (\ell^i + 1]$, such that $\mathsf{K} = \mathsf{Z}_j^i$.

B2 : $\exists (i,j) \in (q_d] \times (\bar{\ell}^i + 1]$, such that $\mathsf{K} = \bar{\mathsf{Z}}_j^i$.

B3 : $\exists i \in (q_e]$, such that $\mathsf{Z}_0^i = *\|0^{\kappa - c'}$.

B4 : $\exists i \in (q_d]$, such that $\bar{\mathsf{Z}}_0^i = *\|0^{\kappa - c'}$.

B5 : $\exists (i,j) \in (q_e] \times (\ell^i + 1], (i',j') \in (q_e] \times (\ell^{i'} + 1]$, such that $(\mathsf{Z}_j^i, \mathsf{Y}_j^i) = (\mathsf{Z}_{j'}^{i'}, \mathsf{Y}_{j'}^{i'})$.

B6 : $\exists (i,j) \in (q_e] \times (\ell^i + 1], (i',j') \in (q_e] \times (\ell^{i'} + 1]$, such that $(\mathsf{Z}_j^i, \mathsf{X}_j^i) = (\mathsf{Z}_{j'}^{i'}, \mathsf{X}_{j'}^{i'})$.

B7 : $\exists (i,j) \in (q_e] \times (\ell^i + 1], i' \in (q_p]$, such that $(\mathsf{Z}_j^i, \mathsf{Y}_j^i) = (\widehat{\mathsf{Z}}^{i'}, \widehat{\mathsf{Y}}^{i'})$.

B8 : $\exists (i,j) \in (q_e] \times (\ell^i + 1], i' \in (q_p]$, such that $(\mathsf{Z}_j^i, \mathsf{X}_j^i) = (\widehat{\mathsf{Z}}^{i'}, \widehat{\mathsf{X}}^{i'})$.

B9 : $\exists (i,j) \in (q_e] \times (\ell^i + 1]$ such that $|\{j \in (q_p] : \widehat{\mathsf{Z}}^j = \mathsf{Z}^i\}| \geq \nu_{ed}$.

B10 : $\exists (i,j) \in (q_d] \times (\bar{\ell}^i + 1]$ such that $|\{j \in (q_p] : \widehat{\mathsf{Z}}^j = \bar{\mathsf{Z}}^i\}| \geq \nu_{ed}$.

For brevity we accumulate the incompatibility events in certain compound events as follows:

Kcoll : B0 ∪ B1 ∪ B2 ∪ B3 ∪ B4.

EEmatch : B5 ∪ B6.

EPmatch : B7 ∪ B8.

PKcount : B9 ∪ B10.

The Kcoll event handles all the scenarios which might lead to key recovery or internal key collisions. EEmatch handles the event that two encryption query block states collide, and EPmatch handles a similar scenario for an encryption query block and a primitive query. The event PKcount is more of a technical requirement that accounts for the adversarial strategy of exhausting a particular encryption/decryption block key via primitive queries. If this happens, then the adversary can guess the block cipher outputs (or inputs) with higher probability. Let

$$\mathtt{Comp} := \neg\,(\mathtt{Kcoll} \cup \mathtt{EEmatch} \cup \mathtt{EPmatch} \cup \mathtt{PKcount})\,.$$

Then, in the real world we have

$$\Pr\,[\mathsf{R} = \omega] \geq \Pr\,[\mathsf{R} = \omega, \mathtt{Comp}]$$

$$\geq \Big(1 - \Pr\,[\neg\mathtt{Comp}]\Big) \times \Pr\,[\mathsf{R} = \omega \mid \mathtt{Comp}]$$

$$\geq \Big(1 - \Pr\,[\neg\mathtt{Comp}]\Big) \times \Pr\,[\mathsf{R}_p = \omega_p \mid \mathtt{Comp}]$$

$$\times \Pr\,[\mathsf{R}_e = \omega_e \mid \mathtt{Comp} \wedge \mathsf{R}_p = \omega_p]$$

$$\times \Pr\,[\mathsf{R}_d = \omega_d \mid \mathtt{Comp} \wedge (\mathsf{R}_p, \mathsf{R}_e) = (\omega_p, \omega_e)]. \quad (7)$$

For any compatible quadruple $(\mathsf{K}, \mathsf{Y}_0, \mathsf{Z}, \bar{\mathsf{Z}})$, in addition to the multiset $\mathcal{Z}_p$, consider the following two multisets,

$$\mathcal{Z}_e := \{\mathsf{Z}_j^i : i \in (q_e] \times (m^i]\} \qquad \mathcal{Z}_d := \{\bar{\mathsf{Z}}_j^i : i \in (q_d] \times (\bar{m}^i]\}$$

We extend $(L_0, \ldots, L_{s-1})$ to $(L_0, \ldots, L_{s-1}, \ldots, L_{s'-1})$ for some $s' \geq s$ to denote the tuple of distinct keys in $\mathcal{Z}_p \cup \mathcal{Z}_e$ and let λ_i^t be the multiplicity of L_i in $\mathcal{Z}_t$ for all $t \in \{p, e\}$ and $i \in (s']$. Then, by continuing Eq. (7) we have

$$\Pr\left[\mathsf{R} = \omega\right] \geq \left(1 - \Pr\left[\neg\mathsf{Comp}\right]\right) \times \frac{1}{\prod_{i \in (s')}(2^n)\lambda_i^p} \times \frac{1}{\prod_{i \in (s')}(2^n - \lambda_i^p)\lambda_i^e}$$
$$\times \Pr\left[\mathsf{R}_d = \omega_d \mid \mathsf{Comp} \wedge (\mathsf{R}_p, \mathsf{R}_e) = (\omega_p, \omega_e)\right]$$

$$\overset{(*)}{\geq} \left(1 - \Pr\left[\neg\mathsf{Comp}\right]\right) \times \frac{1}{\prod_{i \in (s)}(2^n)\lambda_i^p} \times \frac{1}{2^{n(\sigma_e + q_e)}}$$
$$\times \left(1 - \Pr\left[\mathsf{R}_d \neq \omega_d \mid \mathsf{Comp} \wedge (\mathsf{R}_p, \mathsf{R}_e) = (\omega_p, \omega_e)\right]\right)$$

$$\frac{\Pr\left[\mathsf{R} = \omega\right]}{\Pr\left[\mathsf{I} = \omega\right]} \overset{(**)}{\geq} \left(1 - \Pr\left[\neg\mathsf{Comp}\right] - \Pr\left[\mathsf{R}_d \neq \omega_d \mid \mathsf{Comp} \wedge (\mathsf{R}_p, \mathsf{R}_e) = (\omega_p, \omega_e)\right]\right).$$
$$(8)$$

At inequality $(*)$ we use two facts. First, ω_p contains only s distinct keys, and second, $\sum_{i \in (s')} \lambda_i^e = \sigma_e + q_e$. Inequality $(**)$ follows from Eq. (6). In Lemma 6.1 and 6.2 we bound $\Pr\left[\neg\mathsf{Comp}\right]$ and $\Pr\left[\mathsf{R}_d \neq \omega_d \mid \mathsf{Comp} \wedge (\mathsf{R}_p, \mathsf{R}_e) = (\omega_p, \omega_e)\right]$, respectively.

Lemma 6.1. *For $\sigma_c < \min\left\{N, 2^{n-2}\right\}$ and $q_p \leq 2^{\kappa-2}$, we have*

$$\Pr\left[\neg\mathsf{Comp}\right] \leq \frac{q_p + \sigma_c + q_p(\theta_e^b + \theta_e^f)}{2^\kappa} + \frac{q_c + 2\sigma_e(\theta_e^b + \theta_e^f)}{2^{\kappa - \mathfrak{c}'}} + \frac{q_p \sigma_c}{\nu_{ed} 2^\kappa}.$$

The proof of this lemma is postponed to the full version of this paper [20].

Lemma 6.2. *Let E denote the event $\mathsf{Comp} \wedge (\mathsf{R}_p, \mathsf{R}_e) = (\omega_p, \omega_e)$. For $\sigma_c < \min\left\{N, 2^{n-2}\right\}$ and $q_p \leq 2^{\kappa-2}$, we have*

$$\Pr\left[\mathsf{R}_d \neq \omega_d \mid \mathsf{E}\right] \leq \frac{2q_d(\sigma_e + q_e) + 4\theta_e^b \sigma_d}{2^{\kappa - \mathfrak{c}' + n}} + \frac{2\theta_e^b q_d}{2^{\kappa - \mathfrak{c}'}} + \frac{4q_p \sigma_d}{2^{\kappa + n}} + \frac{2q_d}{2^n}$$
$$+ \sum_{i \in (q_d)} \min\left\{\frac{2\mathsf{W}_{\bar{\ell}^i \sigma_e, \bar{\ell}^i}(\mathcal{Q}_{\nu_{ed}})}{2^\kappa}, \frac{2\bar{\ell}^i \sigma_e}{2^{\kappa - \mathfrak{c}'}} + \frac{2\mathsf{W}_{\bar{\ell}^i, \bar{\ell}^i}(\mathcal{Q}_{\nu_{ed}})}{2^\kappa}\right\}.$$

The proof of this lemma is postponed to the full version of this paper [20]. On substituting these bounds in Eq. (8), and applying Theorem 2.1, we get

$$\mathbf{Adv}_{g\mathsf{COMET}}^{\mathrm{aead}}(\mathscr{A}) \leq \left(\frac{q_p}{2^\kappa} + \frac{4\sigma_c}{2^{\kappa - \mathfrak{c}'}} + \frac{4\sigma_d}{2^{\kappa - \mathfrak{c}' + n}}\right) \mathsf{Ex}\left[\theta_e^b\right] + \left(\frac{q_p}{2^\kappa} + \frac{2\sigma_e}{2^{\kappa - \mathfrak{c}'}}\right) \mathsf{Ex}\left[\theta_e^f\right]$$
$$+ \sum_{i \in (q_d)} \min\left\{\frac{2\mathsf{Ex}\left[\mathsf{W}_{\bar{\ell}^i \sigma_e, \bar{\ell}^i}(\mathcal{Q}_{\nu_{ed}})\right]}{2^\kappa}, \frac{2\bar{\ell}^i \sigma_e}{2^{\kappa - \mathfrak{c}'}} + \frac{2\mathsf{Ex}\left[\mathsf{W}_{\bar{\ell}^i, \bar{\ell}^i}(\mathcal{Q}_{\nu_{ed}})\right]}{2^\kappa}\right\}$$
$$+ \frac{q_p + \sigma_c}{2^\kappa} + \frac{q_c}{2^{\kappa - \mathfrak{c}'}} + \frac{q_p \sigma_c}{\nu_{ed} 2^\kappa} + \frac{2q_d(\sigma_e + q_e)}{2^{\kappa - \mathfrak{c}' + n}} + \frac{4q_p \sigma_d}{2^{\kappa + n}} + \frac{2q_d}{2^n}. \quad (9)$$

Note that, θ_e^b and θ_e^f correspond to $\Theta_{\sigma_e,n}$ and $\Theta_{\sigma_d,n}$ respectively (see Sect. 4.1). Thus, $\mathsf{Ex}\left[\theta_e^b\right], \mathsf{Ex}\left[\theta_e^f\right] \le \mu(\sigma_c, n)$. Further, $|\mathcal{Q}_{\nu_{ed}} \times \mathcal{Q}_{\nu_{ed}}| \le q_p \nu_{ed}$, as $\mathcal{Q}_{\nu_{ed}}$ is a ν_{ed}-useful transcript set. The result follows from these facts and the application of Lemma 5.1.

6.3   Desired Properties from Ψ and Φ' Matrices

Theorem 6.1 sheds some light on the properties required from Ψ and Φ' in order to get a secure gCOMET instance. Specifically, in a secure gCOMET instance we must have:

- *Large period for Ψ matrix*: Let ℓ denote the maximum permissible message length. For any $i > j \in (\ell]$, and some non zero $Z \in \{0,1\}^\kappa$, we want to avoid $\mathsf{U}^i(Z) = \mathsf{U}^j(Z)$. In words, this roughly translates to key repetition within an encryption/decryption query. We can rewrite it as $\mathsf{U}^{i-j} = \mathsf{I}$. Clearly, if $\mathsf{cycle}(\mathsf{U}) \ge \ell$, then we are done. Now, due to the nature of U, we have $\mathsf{cycle}(\mathsf{U}) = \mathsf{cycle}(\Psi)$. Hence, the property $\mathsf{cycle}(\Psi) \ge \ell$ helps in avoiding key repetitions within a query.
- *Small value for $\mathfrak{c}'$*: As evident from Theorem 6.1, the value of $\mathfrak{c}'$ directly affects the security bound, as $\mathsf{rank}(\Psi) = \kappa - \mathfrak{c}'$. In other words, smaller the value of $\mathfrak{c}'$, higher the rank of Ψ, which directly translates to better security guarantee for gCOMET.
- *High rank for Φ' matrix*: In decryption phase, the rank of Φ' function quantifies the effect of the previous block cipher output on the next block cipher input. For example, if $\Phi' = 0$ (possible when $\Phi = \mathsf{I}$), the next input is independent of previous output. In other words, the adversary can fully control the next input. In particular, the adversary can collide the input of a large number of blocks. This can be verified from Theorem 6.1 as well, where some multicollision bounds are inversely proportional to $\mathsf{rank}(\Phi')$.

7   Instantiating gCOMET

For any $S \in \{0,1\}^+$ and $s \in (|S|]$, $S \ggg s$ denotes the "circular right shift by s" operation on S. The set $\{0,1\}^{\kappa-\mathfrak{c}'}$ can be viewed as the Galois field $\mathrm{GF}(2^{\kappa-\mathfrak{c}'})$ consisting of $2^{\kappa-\mathfrak{c}'}$ elements. Let $f(x)$ denote the primitive polynomial used to represent the field $\mathrm{GF}(2^{\kappa-\mathfrak{c}'})$, and α_f denote a fixed primitive element in this representation. The set $\{0,1\}^{\kappa-\mathfrak{c}'}$ can also be viewed as a $(\kappa - \mathfrak{c}')$-dimensional vector space over $\mathrm{GF}(2)$. In this context, α_f can be viewed as an invertible linear map over $\{0,1\}^{\kappa-\mathfrak{c}'}$. By a slight abuse of notation, we denote the binary matrix associated with α_f by α_f itself. It is well-known that $\mathsf{cycle}(\alpha_f) = 2^{\kappa-\mathfrak{c}'} - 1$.

7.1   COMETv1 and Its Security

The NIST LwC candidate COMET, hereafter referred as COMETv1, can be easily obtained from gCOMET in the following manner:

Algorithm 7.1. Control sequence generator for COMETv1 (left) and COMETv2 (right).

1: **function** $\Delta(A, I)$	1: **function** $\Delta(A, I)$
2: $\quad a \leftarrow \left\lceil \frac{|A|}{n} \right\rceil, m \leftarrow \left\lceil \frac{|I|}{n} \right\rceil, \ell := a + m$	2: $\quad a \leftarrow \left\lceil \frac{|A|}{n} \right\rceil, m \leftarrow \left\lceil \frac{|I|}{n} \right\rceil, \ell := a + m$
3: $\quad \delta^{\ell+2} \leftarrow (0^5)^{\ell+2}$	3: $\quad \delta^{\ell+2} \leftarrow (0^5)^{\ell+2}$
4: $\quad$ **if** $a \neq 0$ **then**	4: $\quad$ **if** $a \neq 0$ **then**
5: $\qquad \delta_0 \leftarrow \delta_0 \oplus 00001$	5: $\qquad \delta_1 \leftarrow \delta_1 \oplus 00001$
6: $\qquad$ **if** $n \nmid |A|$ **then** $\delta_{a-1} \leftarrow \delta_{a-1} \oplus 00010$	6: $\qquad$ **if** $n \nmid |A|$ **then** $\delta_a \leftarrow \delta_a \oplus 00010$
7: $\quad$ **if** $m \neq 0$ **then**	7: $\quad$ **if** $m \neq 0$ **then**
8: $\qquad \delta_a \leftarrow \delta_a \oplus 00100$	8: $\qquad \delta_{a+1} \leftarrow \delta_{a+1} \oplus 00100$
9: $\qquad$ **if** $n \nmid |I|$ **then** $\delta_{\ell-1} \leftarrow \delta_{\ell-1} \oplus 01000$	9: $\qquad$ **if** $n \nmid |I|$ **then** $\delta_\ell \leftarrow \delta_\ell \oplus 01000$
10: $\quad \delta_{\ell+1} \leftarrow \delta_{\ell+1} \oplus 10000$	10: $\quad \delta_{\ell+1} \leftarrow \delta_{\ell+1} \oplus 10000$
11: $\quad$ **return** $(a, m, \ell, \delta^{\ell+2})$	11: $\quad$ **return** $(a, m, \ell, \delta^{\ell+2})$

- Key size, κ is set to 128.
- Block size, n is set to 128 and 64 in fatCOMETv1 and tinyCOMETv1, respectively.
- The control size $\mathfrak{c}$ is set to 5 and the invariant-prefix size $\mathfrak{c}'$ is set to $\kappa/2 = 64$.
- Δ is defined in Algorithm 7.1 (left).
- Φ is defined by the mapping $(X_3, X_2, X_1, X_0) \longmapsto X_1 \| X_0 \| (X_2 \ggg 1) \| X_3$, where $(X_3, X_2, X_1, X_0) \xleftarrow{n/4} X$. One can verify that $\mathrm{rank}(\Phi') = n - 1$.
- The Ψ function is defined as the binary matrix α_f, where α_f denotes the primitive element of $\mathrm{GF}(2^{64})$ with respect to $f(x) = x^{64} + x^4 + x^3 + x + 1$.

In Corollary 7.1, we apply Theorem 6.1 and relevant multicollision bounds from Propositions 4.1–4.4, to obtain security bounds for fatCOMETv1 and tinyCOMETv1.

Corollary 7.1. *For $n \geq 4$, $q_p < 2^{126}$, and any $(q_e, q_d, \sigma_e, \sigma_d, q_p)$-adversary $\mathscr{A}$, we have*

1. For $\sigma_c < 2^{64}$, and $\nu_{ed} = \frac{2^{55}}{\sqrt{11}}$:

$$\mathbf{Adv}^{\mathrm{aead}}_{\mathsf{fatCOMETv1}}(\mathscr{A}) \leq \frac{q_p}{2^{125.19}} + \frac{\sigma_c}{2^{59.75}} + \frac{\sigma_d \sigma_e}{2^{120.8}} + \frac{q_p \sigma_c}{2^{180.24}}.$$

2. For $\sigma_c < 2^{39}$, and $\nu_{ed} = \frac{2^{24}}{\sqrt{11}}$:

$$\mathbf{Adv}^{\mathrm{aead}}_{\mathsf{tinyCOMETv1}}(\mathscr{A}) \leq \frac{q_p}{2^{121.58}} + \frac{\sigma_c}{2^{55.98}} + \frac{\sigma_d \sigma_e}{2^{126}} + \frac{q_p \sigma_d}{2^{149.24}} + \frac{q_p \sigma_e \sigma_d}{2^{188.68}}.$$

Corollary 7.1 clearly shows that fatCOMETv1 (or the NIST submission COMET-128) is secure while $\sigma_c < 2^{63.75}$ bytes[2] (data complexity), $q_p < 2^{125.19}$ (time com-

---

[2] Each block of fatCOMETv1 is built of 16 bytes.

plexity), and $q_p \sigma_c < 2^{184.24}$ (data-time trade-off). Similarly, under the assumption that $\sigma_c < 2^{42}$ bytes[3] (data complexity), tinyCOMETv1 (or the NIST submission COMET-64) is secure while $q_p < 2^{112}$ (time complexity) and $q_p \sigma_c < 2^{152.24}$ (data-time trade-off).

In the full version of this paper [20], we summarize the two known cryptanalytic works [11,13] on COMETv1. Although these works are largely inconsequential in relation to the validity of COMETv1's security claims, they show that large value of $\mathfrak{c}'$ can lead to a large class of weak keys. We observe that the value of $\mathfrak{c}'$ can be reduced significantly without much degradation in performance. Particularly, we observe that the Ψ function can be defined over a larger field which avoids the above given strategies. In fact, a similar remedy has been also offered in [11].

7.2 COMETv2 and Its Security

We describe a variant of COMETv1, called COMETv2, that differs in the following components:

- The control size $\mathfrak{c}$ is set to 5 and the invariant-prefix size $\mathfrak{c}'$ is set to 8.
- The Δ function is defined in Algorithm 7.1 (right).
- The Ψ function is defined as the binary matrix α_f, where α_f denotes the primitive element of $GF(2^{120})$ with respect to $f(x) = x^{120} + x^9 + x^6 + x^2 + 1$.

From the above discussion, it is clear that COMETv2 differs from COMETv1 in just two components, namely Δ and Ψ functions. The modified Δ function helps in reducing the hardware footprint as the earlier version required an additional n-bit of memory. Further, the strategies from [11,13] have significantly higher data/time complexity against COMETv2 due to the small value of $\mathfrak{c}'$ and the updated Ψ function.

In Corollary 7.2, we apply Theorem 6.1 and relevant multicollision bounds from Propositions 4.1–4.4, to obtain security bounds for fatCOMETv2 and tinyCOMETv2.

Corollary 7.2. *For $n \geq 4$, $q_p < 2^{126}$, and any $(q_e, q_d, \sigma_e, \sigma_d, q_p)$-adversary $\mathscr{A}$, we have*

1. *For $\sigma_c < 2^{64}$, and $\nu_{ed} = \frac{2^{55}}{\sqrt{11}}$:*

$$\mathbf{Adv}^{\mathrm{aead}}_{\mathsf{fatCOMETv2}}(\mathscr{A}) \leq \frac{q_p}{2^{125.19}} + \frac{\sigma_c}{2^{115.62}} + \frac{\sigma_d \sigma_e}{2^{120}} + \frac{q_p \sigma_c}{2^{180.24}}.$$

2. *For $\sigma_c < 2^{62}$, and $\nu_{ed} = \frac{2^{24}}{\sqrt{11}}$:*

$$\mathbf{Adv}^{\mathrm{aead}}_{\mathsf{tinyCOMETv2}}(\mathscr{A}) \leq \frac{q_p}{2^{121.58}} + \frac{\sigma_c}{2^{63}} + \frac{\sigma_d \sigma_e}{2^{120}} + \frac{q_p \sigma_d}{2^{149.24}}.$$

---

[3] Each block of tinyCOMETv1 is built of 8 bytes.

ON THE BENEFITS OF fatCOMETv2 OVER fatCOMETv1: Note that the advantage expressions for the two versions look similar. However, fatCOMETv2 has subtle advantages over fatCOMETv1. For instance, when we restrict $q_p < 2^{119}$ (NIST prescribed), the dominating terms are

- for v1: $\sigma_d \sigma_e / 2^{120} + \sigma_c / 2^{59}$
- for v2: $\sigma_d \sigma_e / 2^{120}$

In fact, the additional term $\sigma_c / 2^{59}$ for v1, is not just an artifact of the proof. Indeed, the previous works by Khairallah [11] and Bernstein et al. [13] (although violate the designers' prescribed limits) achieve a lower bound which almost matches this term using encryption queries only. On the other hand, our security proofs guarantee that even such strategies do not work against v2. Clearly, when $\sigma_e \approx 2^{60}$, $\sigma_d \ll 2^{60}$ and $q_p \ll 2^{119}$, v2 has much better security than v1. This is an improved security feature of v2, in addition to the fact that it has obvious implementation advantages. Note that, for $q_p > 2^{119}$ or $\sigma_e, \sigma_d \approx 2^{60}$, the two versions enjoy similar security guarantees.

8   Conclusion

In this paper, we proposed a generalization of the COMET mode of operation, called gCOMET, and gave a detailed security proof of gCOMET. We view COMET as an instance of gCOMET and derive its security bounds. Finally, we propose a refinement of COMET, called COMETv2, that seems to have better performance and security as compared to COMET. We note that our security proofs are not complemented with matching attacks, and it is possible that the security bounds can be improved, particularly for the COMET-64 versions.

Acknowledgments. Shay Gueron is supported by The Israel Science Foundation (grants No. 1018/16 and 3380/19); NSF-BSF Grant 2018640; The BIU Center for Research in Applied Cryptography and Cyber Security and the Center for Cyber Law and Policy at the University of Haifa, both in conjunction with the Israel National Cyber Bureau in the Prime Minister's Office. Ashwin Jha's work was carried out in the framework of the French-German-Center for Cybersecurity, a collaboration of CISPA and LORIA. Mridul Nandi is supported by the project "Study and Analysis of IoT Security" under Government of India at R. C. Bose Centre for Cryptology and Security, Indian Statistical Institute, Kolkata.

References

1. NIST: Lightweight cryptography (2018). https://csrc.nist.gov/Projects/Lightweight-Cryptography. Accessed 31 Aug 2020
2. Gueron, S., Jha, A., Nandi, M.: COMET: counter mode encryption with tag. Submission to NIST LwC Standardization Process (Round 1) (2019). https://csrc.nist.gov/CSRC/media/Projects/Lightweight-Cryptography/documents/round-1/spec-doc/comet-spec.pdf. Accessed 26 June 2020

3. Chakraborti, A., Iwata, T., Minematsu, K., Nandi, M.: Blockcipher-based authenticated encryption: how small can we go? In: Fischer, W., Homma, N. (eds.) CHES 2017. LNCS, vol. 10529, pp. 277–298. Springer, Cham (2017). https://doi.org/10.1007/978-3-319-66787-4_14

4. Chakraborti, A., Datta, N., Nandi, M., Yasuda, K.: Beetle family of lightweight and secure authenticated encryption ciphers. IACR Trans. Cryptogr. Hardw. Embed. Syst. **2018**(2), 218–241 (2018)

5. Dworkin, M.: Recommendation for Block Cipher Modes of Operation - Methods and Techniques. NIST Special Publication 800–38A, National Institute of Standards and Technology, U. S. Department of Commerce (2001)

6. NIST: Announcing the Advanced Encryption Standard (AES). Fedral Information Processing Standards Publication FIPS 197, National Institute of Standards and Technology, U. S. Department of Commerce (2001)

7. Beaulieu, R., Shors, D., Smith, J., Treatman-Clark, S., Weeks, B., Wingers, L.: The SIMON and SPECK lightweight block ciphers. In: Proceedings of the 52nd Annual Design Automation Conference, pp. 175:1–175:6 (2015)

8. Beaulieu, R., Shors, D., Smith, J., Treatman-Clark, S., Weeks, B., Wingers, L.: SIMON and SPECK: block ciphers for the Internet of Things. IACR Cryptology ePrint Archive **2015**, 585 (2015)

9. Koo, B., Roh, D., Kim, H., Jung, Y., Lee, D.-G., Kwon, D.: CHAM: a family of lightweight block ciphers for resource-constrained devices. In: Kim, H., Kim, D.-C. (eds.) ICISC 2017. LNCS, vol. 10779, pp. 3–25. Springer, Cham (2018). https://doi.org/10.1007/978-3-319-78556-1_1

10. Weatherley, R.: Performance of AEAD algorithms on AVR (2020). https://rweather.github.io/lightweight-crypto/performance_avr.html#perf_avr_overall. Accessed 14 Sept 2020

11. Khairallah, M.: Weak keys in the rekeying paradigm: application to COMET and mixfeed. IACR Trans. Symmetric Cryptol. **2019**(4), 272–289 (2019)

12. Gueron, S., Jha, A., Nandi, M.: On the security of COMET authenticated encryption scheme. Presented at NIST Lightweight Cryptography Workshop 2019 (2019). https://csrc.nist.gov/CSRC/media/Presentations/on-the-security-of-comet-authenticated-encryption/images-media/session2-gueron-security-of-comet.pdf. Accessed 14 Sept 2020

13. Bernstein, D.J., Gilbert, H., Turan, M.S.: Observations on COMET. Personal Communication (2020)

14. Chakraborty, B., Jha, A., Nandi, M.: On the security of sponge-type authenticated encryption modes. IACR Trans. Symmetric Cryptol. **2020**(2), 93–119 (2020)

15. Hoang, V.T., Tessaro, S.: Key-alternating ciphers and key-length extension: exact bounds and multi-user security. In: Robshaw, M., Katz, J. (eds.) CRYPTO 2016. LNCS, vol. 9814, pp. 3–32. Springer, Heidelberg (2016). https://doi.org/10.1007/978-3-662-53018-4_1

16. Jha, A., Nandi, M.: Applications of h-technique: revisiting symmetric key security analysis. IACR Cryptology ePrint Archive **2018**, 1130 (2018)

17. Patarin, J.: Etude de Générateurs de Permutations Basés sur les Schémas du DES. Ph.D. thesis, Université de Paris (1991)

18. Patarin, J.: The "Coefficients H" technique. In: Avanzi, R.M., Keliher, L., Sica, F. (eds.) SAC 2008. LNCS, vol. 5381, pp. 328–345. Springer, Heidelberg (2009). https://doi.org/10.1007/978-3-642-04159-4_21

19. Bertoni, G., Daemen, J., Peeters, M., Van Assche, G.: Duplexing the sponge: single-pass authenticated encryption and other applications. In: Miri, A., Vaudenay, S. (eds.) SAC 2011. LNCS, vol. 7118, pp. 320–337. Springer, Heidelberg (2012). https://doi.org/10.1007/978-3-642-28496-0_19
20. Gueron, S., Jha, A., Nandi, M.: Revisiting the security of COMET authenticated encryption scheme. IACR Cryptology ePrint Archive **2021** (2021)
21. AlTawy, R., et al.: SpoC: an authenticated cipher submission to the NIST LWC competition. Submission to NIST LwC Standardization Process (Round 2) (2019). https://csrc.nist.gov/CSRC/media/Projects/Lightweight-Cryptography/documents/round-2/spec-doc-rnd2/spoc-spec-round2.pdf. Accessed 09 July 2020
22. Chakraborty, B., Jha, A., Nandi, M.: On the security of sponge-type authenticated encryption modes. IACR Cryptology ePrint Archive **2019**, 1475 (2019)

tHyENA: Making HyENA Even Smaller

Avik Chakraborti[1], Nilanjan Datta[2(✉)], Ashwin Jha[3],
Cuauhtemoc Mancillas-López[4], and Mridul Nandi[5]

[1] University of Exeter, Exeter, UK
a.chakraborti@exeter.ac.uk
[2] Institute for Advancing Intelligence, TCG CREST, Kolkata, India
nilanjan.datta@tcgcrest.org
[3] CISPA Helmholtz Center for Information Security, Saarbrücken, Germany
ashwin.jha@cispa.de
[4] Computer Science Department, CINVESTAV-IPN, Mexico City, Mexico
cuauhtemoc.mancillas@cinvestav.mx
[5] Indian Statistical Institute, Kolkata, India
mridul@isical.ac.in

Abstract. This paper proposes a lightweight short-tweak tweakable
blockcipher (tBC) based authenticated encryption (AE) scheme tHyENA,
a tweakable variant of the high profile NIST LWC competition submission HyENA. tHyENA is structurally similar to HyENA, however, proper
usage of short-tweaks for the purpose of domain separation, makes the
design much simpler compact. We know that HyENA already achieves
a very small hardware footprint, and tHyENA further optimizes it. To
realize our claim, we provide NIST API compliant hardware implementation details and benchmark for tHyENA against HyENA and several
other well-known sequential feedback-based designs. The implementation
results depict that when instantiated with the tBC TweGIFT, tHyENA
achieves an extremely low hardware footprint - consuming only around
680 LUTs and 260 slices while maintaining the full rate and the almost
birthday bound security. To the best of our knowledge, this figure is
significantly better than all the known implementation results of other
lightweight ciphers with sequential structures.

Keywords: Authenticated encryption · Lightweight · tBC · HyENA ·
Feedback based AE · TweGIFT

1 Introduction

In the last few years, lightweight cryptography has seen a growing popularity due
to increasing security demands for lightweight IoT applications such as sensor
networks, healthcare applications, distributed control systems, cyber-physical
systems, etc., where highly resource-constrained devices communicate and need
to be operated with the low hardware area, low power or low energy. Lightweight
cryptography is about developing cryptographic solutions for these resource-
constrained environments and this research direction has been triggered by the
ongoing NIST Lightweight Standardization Competition (LWC) [19] followed by

© Springer Nature Switzerland AG 2021
A. Adhikari et al. (Eds.): INDOCRYPT 2021, LNCS 13143, pp. 26–48, 2021.
https://doi.org/10.1007/978-3-030-92518-5_2

CAESAR [11]. As a result, in recent years, the cryptographic community has witnessed a rise in various lightweight authenticated encryption proposals.

One popular approach to design lightweight AE schemes is to use a sequential structure as it consumes lesser hardware footprint. Blockcipher (BC) based sequential AE schemes typically use a feedback function on the previous blockcipher output, an auxiliary secret state, and the current input (message or associated data) block. It outputs the next blockcipher feedback, updates the auxiliary secret state and the current output block (in case of message blocks). Thus, blockcipher-based sequential AE schemes can be well described by the underlying blockcipher, the auxiliary secret state, and the feedback function. Consequently, the efficiency and the hardware footprint of the AE scheme also largely depend on these three components (the underlying blockcipher, the feedback function, and the auxiliary secret state). In the following context, we assume that we have an ultra-lightweight and efficient primitive to instantiate the AE scheme. The efficiency of a construction is primarily dependent upon the *rate*, the number of data blocks processed per primitive call. It is well known that a trivial upper bound on the rate is 1. In this paper, we concentrate only on rate-1 authenticated encryptions with a small hardware footprint such that we can achieve a lightweight construction along with a high throughput.

1.1   Rate-1 Feedback Based Authenticated Encryption

Zhang et al. in [25], proposed a plaintext feedback-based mode iFEED that has rate 1. However, it requires a large state size of $(3n + k)$ bits, where n is the underlying blockcipher's state size, and k is the key size. CPFB by Montes et al. [18] is a notable scheme that reduces the state size to $(2n + k)$ bits, at the cost of a reduction in the rate to 3/4. In CHES 2017, Chakraborti et al. [7] proposed COFB the first feedback-based AE scheme that achieves rate-1 with an impressive state size of just $1.5n + k$ bits. The main feature of COFB is a novel feedback function, called *combined feedback*.

In [8,9], Chakraborti et al. studied a generalized feedback-based rate-1 AE scheme and showed that it is a necessity for any rate-1 feedback-based AE mode to have an auxiliary state of $n/2$-bit to achieve security up to $2^{n/2}$ queries, depicting the optimality of COFB in the auxiliary state size. However, they have observed that the use of the combined feedback requires $2.5n$-bit XORs, which could be improved further using a *hybrid feedback* HYFB, which results in a hybrid of plaintext feedback and ciphertext feedback. Based on the HYFB feedback function, Chakraborti et al. in [5] proposed a rate-1 AE mode called HyENA, that uses an $n/2$-bit auxiliary secret state, but significantly reduces the XOR count from $2.5n$-bit to $1.5n$-bit. This seems to achieve the smallest footprint for any rate 1 blockcipher based authenticated cipher owing to the fact that it requires the optimal auxiliary state, optimal linear operations. The optimality of the linear operations can be conjectured from the facts that (i) to implement a feedback function that takes $2n$-bit input and produces n-bit output, one needs at least n-bit binary operation, and (ii) XOR is one of the most simple operations, and hence n-bit XORs seem to achieve the trivial lower bound of any feedback function.

1.2 Our Contribution

In this paper, we primarily focus on highly optimizing HyENA, i.e. significantly minimizing the hardware footprint. To achieve the goal, we use a short tweak tweakable blockcipher based on the well-known blockcipher GIFT [1] to propose a tweakable variant of HyENA, dubbed as tHyENA. This new variant is structurally much simpler and removes the redundant operations to reduce the hardware footprint. tHyENA inherits all the desirable properties of HyENA: (i) single-pass (one primitive call per data block), (ii) inverse-free (no need for blockcipher decryption), (iii) extremely low state size and XOR count. Precisely, the use of tweaks for the purpose of domain separation makes the construction simpler and removes all the constant field multiplications making the mode even lighter. We instantiate tHyENA with an ultra-lightweight short-tweak tweakable blockcipher TweGIFT (designed over the blockcipher GIFT [1]). We also provide concrete hardware implementation details of tHyENA. The hardware results depicts that tHyENA with TweGIFT consumes the least hardware area among all the feedback type (tweakable) block cipher based designs.

1.3 tHyENA in DSCI Light-Weight Competition

In 2020, National CoE, the joint initiative of the Data security council of India and the Ministry of Electronics and IT (MeitY), announced a lightweight cryptography competition named "Lightweight Cipher Design Challenge 2020" [20]. One of the primary objectives of the challenge is to design new lightweight authenticated ciphers, and the best designs will be considered for developing the prototype for ready industry implementation. The algorithm tHyENA has been nominated as one of the top three candidates in the challenge and has been selected for the final round. Interestingly, the construction achieves the lowest hardware footprint, making it to be the most light-weight design, in terms of area, in the competition.

2 Preliminaries

For $n \in \mathbb{N}$, we write $\{0,1\}^*$ and $\{0,1\}^n$ to denote the set of all binary strings (including the empty string λ), and the set of all n-bit strings, respectively. Throughout we fix even integer n as the block size in bits, and often refer to n-bit strings as *blocks*. For all $X \in \{0,1\}^*$, $|X|$, referred as the length of X, denotes the number of bits in X. For any $X \in \{0,1\}^n$, X_L and X_R denote the most and least significant $n/2$ bits of X, respectively. For all practical purposes, we use the little endian format for representing binary strings, i.e., the least significant bit is the right most bit. We use the notation $\oplus$ to denote binary addition. For two strings $X, Y \in \{0,1\}^*$, $X\|Y$ denotes the concatenation of X and Y. We use the notation $(X_{\ell-1}, \ldots, X_0) \xleftarrow{n} X$ to denote parsing of the string X into ℓ blocks such that for $0 \leq i \leq \ell - 2$, $|X_i| = n$ and $1 \leq |X_{\ell-1}| \leq n$. For any predicate $\mathcal{E}$, the expression $\mathcal{E}?a : b$ evaluates to a if $\mathcal{E}$ is true, and b otherwise. For any binary string X with $|X| \leq n$, we define the padding function Pad as

$$\mathsf{Pad}(X) = \begin{cases} X & \text{if } |X| \bmod n = 0 \\ 0^{n-|X|-1}\|1\|X & \text{otherwise.} \end{cases}$$

For any binary string X, the truncate function $\mathsf{Trunc}_i(X)$ returns the least significant i bits of X.

The set $\{0,1\}^{n/2}$ can be viewed as the finite field $\mathbb{F}_{2^{n/2}}$ consisting of $2^{n/2}$ elements. We interchangeably think of an element $A \in \mathbb{F}_{2^{n/2}}$ in any of the following ways: (i) as an $n/2$-bit string $a_{\frac{n}{2}-1} \ldots a_1 a_0 \in \{0,1\}^{n/2}$; (ii) as a polynomial $A(x) = a_{\frac{n}{2}-1}x^{n/2-1} + a_{\frac{n}{2}-2}x^{\frac{n}{2}-2} + \cdots + a_1 x + a_0$ over the field $\mathbb{F}_2$; (iii) a nonnegative integer $a < 2^{n/2}$; (iv) an abstract element in the field. Addition in $\mathbb{F}_{2^{n/2}}$ is just bitwise XOR of two $n/2$-bit strings, and hence denoted by $\oplus$. $P(x)$ denotes the primitive polynomial used to represent the field $\mathbb{F}_{2^{n/2}}$, and α denotes the primitive element in this representation. The multiplication of $A, B \in \mathbb{F}_{2^{n/2}}$ is defined as $A \odot B := A(x) \cdot B(x) \pmod{P(x)}$, i.e. polynomial multiplication modulo $P(x)$ in $\mathbb{F}_2$.

For a finite set $\mathcal{X}$, $\mathsf{X} \leftarrow \mathcal{X}$ denotes the uniform at random sampling of X from $\mathcal{X}$. Let $\gamma = (\gamma[1], \ldots, \gamma[s])$ be a tuple of equal-length strings. We define $\mathsf{mColl}(\gamma) = m$ if there exist distinct $i_1, \ldots, i_m \in [1..s]$ such that $\gamma[i_1] = \cdots = \gamma[i_m]$ and m is the maximum of such integer. We say that $\{i_1, \ldots, i_m\}$ is an m-multi-collision set for γ.

Tweakable Blockcipher: For $n, \tau, \kappa \in \mathbb{N}$, $E\text{-}n/\kappa/\tau$ denotes a tweakable blockcipher family E, parameterized by the block length n, key length κ, and tweak length τ. For $K \in \{0,1\}^\kappa$, $T \in \{0,1\}^\tau$, and $M \in \{0,1\}^n$, we use $E_K^T(M) := E(K, T, M)$ to denote invocation of the encryption function of E on key K, tweak T, and input M.

2.1 Authenticated Encryption

An authenticated encryption (AE) is a symmetric-key primitive that provides both data confidentiality (or privacy), and authenticity of the input plaintext. Often, practical scenarios additionally require authenticity for some associated data. In this case, we extend the ambit of AE to AE with associated data functionality or AEAD, which guarantees privacy for the input message and authenticity for the input message and associated data.

Formally, an AEAD scheme AE is a tuple of algorithms (Enc, Dec) defined over the key space $\mathcal{K}$, nonce space $\mathcal{N}$, associated data space $\mathcal{A}$, message and ciphertext space $\mathcal{M}$, and tag space $\mathcal{T}$, where:

$$\mathsf{AE.Enc} : \mathcal{K} \times \mathcal{A} \times \mathcal{N} \times \mathcal{M} \to \mathcal{M} \times \mathcal{T} \qquad \mathsf{AE.Dec} : \mathcal{K} \times \mathcal{N} \times \mathcal{A} \times \mathcal{M} \times \mathcal{T} \to \mathcal{M} \cup \{\bot\},$$

and $\bot$ denotes the error symbol indicating authentication failure.

The encryption function AE.Enc instantiated with key $K \in \mathcal{K}$, takes a nonce $N \in \mathcal{N}$ (which is usually a unique value for each invocation), an associated data $A \in \mathcal{A}$, and a plaintext $M \in \mathcal{M}$ as input, and outputs a tagged-ciphertext (C, T) where $|C| = |M|$. The corresponding decryption function AE.Dec instantiated with key K, takes $(N', A', C', T') \in \mathcal{N} \times \mathcal{A} \times \mathcal{M} \times \mathcal{T}$, and returns a decrypted plaintext M' when (N, A, C, T) authenticates successfully, and it returns the error symbol $\perp$ otherwise. For all key $K \in \mathcal{K}$, we write $\mathsf{AE.Enc}_K(\cdot, \cdot) := \mathsf{AE.Enc}(K, \cdot, \cdot)$ and $\mathsf{AE.Dec}_K(\cdot, \cdot, \cdot) := \mathsf{AE.Enc}(K, \cdot, \cdot, \cdot)$. For correctness in decryption, it is required that $\mathsf{AE.Dec}(K, N, A, \mathsf{AE.Enc}(K, N, A, M)) = M$ for all $(K, N, A, M) \in \mathcal{K} \times \mathcal{N} \times \mathcal{A} \times \mathcal{M}$.

In addition to the block size n, we fix positive even integers κ and η to denote the *key size* and *nonce size*, respectively, in bits. Throughout this document, we fix $n = 128$, $\kappa = 128$, $\eta = 96$, and tag size $= n$.

2.2 Security Definitions

ADVERSARY: A (q, t)-adversary $\mathcal{A}$ is an interactive algorithm with access to an oracle, that runs in time at most t, and makes at most q oracle queries. By convention, $t = \infty$ denotes computationally unbounded (information-theoretic) and deterministic adversaries. Throughout, we make the plausible assumption that the adversary is *non-trivial*, i.e., it never makes a duplicate query. Whenever, the adversarial queries are allowed to be of arbitrary length, we parametrize the adversary with additional parameters. For example, an adversary that makes queries of length at most ℓ blocks, and total length of all queries at most σ blocks is referred as (q, ℓ, σ, t)-adversary. We write $\mathcal{A}^{\mathcal{O}} \Rightarrow x$ to denote the compound operation: "adversary $\mathcal{A}$ outputs x after interacting with oracle $\mathcal{O}$".

TWEAKABLE BLOCKCIPHER SECURITY: The security of any tweakable blockcipher family is formalized in terms of the notion of *tweakable pseudorandom permutation*. Formally, the tweakable pseudorandom permutation or *TPRP advantage* of any adversary $\mathcal{A}$ against tweakable blockcipher E is defined as

$$\mathbf{Adv}_E^{\mathsf{tprp}}(\mathcal{A}) := \left| \Pr[\mathcal{A}^{E_K} \Rightarrow 1] - \Pr[\mathcal{A}^{\Pi} \Rightarrow 1] \right|,$$

where Π is a uniform at random tweakable permutation sampled from the set of all tweakable permutations over $\{0, 1\}^n$ with tweak space $\{0, 1\}^\tau$. For $\epsilon \geq 0$, the blockcipher E is called a (q, t, ϵ)-TPRP if

$$\mathbf{Adv}_E^{\mathsf{tprp}}(q, t) := \max_{\mathcal{A}} \mathbf{Adv}_E^{\mathsf{prp}}(\mathcal{A}) \leq \epsilon,$$

where the maximum is taken over all (q, t)-adversary.

AEAD SECURITY: The security of any nonce-based AEAD scheme can be modeled in terms of the NAEAD notion,. In this model, the adversary is nonce-respecting, i.e., assuming single-key setting, no pair of distinct encryption queries share the same public nonce value. Formally, the NAEAD advantage of any adversary $\mathcal{A}$ against AEAD scheme AE is defined as

$$\mathbf{Adv}_{\mathsf{AE}}^{\mathsf{naead}}(\mathcal{A}) := \left| \Pr[\mathcal{A}^{\mathsf{AE.Enc}_K, \mathsf{AE.Dec}_K} \Rightarrow 1] - \Pr[\mathcal{A}^{\$, \perp} \Rightarrow 1] \right|,$$

where $ returns an independent and uniform at random string of length $\tau + |M|$ for each queried message M. Note that, we overload the $\perp$ notation to denote the *"always fail"* oracle, which returns $\perp$ in all cases, except when $\mathcal{A}$ makes a query (N, A, C, T), such that there exists an earlier query (N, A, M) to $ and (C, T) is the corresponding response, in which case the always fail oracle returns M. For $\epsilon \geq 0$, the AEAD AE is called a $(q_e, q_v, \ell_e, \ell_v, \sigma_e, \sigma_v, t, \epsilon)$-NAEAD if

$$\mathbf{Adv}^{\mathsf{naead}}_{\mathsf{AE}}(q_e, q_v, \ell_e, \ell_v, \sigma_e, \sigma_v, t) := \max_{\mathcal{A}} \mathbf{Adv}^{\mathsf{naead}}_{\mathsf{AE}}(\mathcal{A}) \leq \epsilon,$$

where the maximum is taken over all $(q_e, q_v, \ell_e, \ell_v, \sigma_e, \sigma_v, t)$-adversary, i.e., all adversary $\mathcal{A}$ such that

- the number of encryption queries is bounded by q_e; each encryption query length is at most ℓ_e blocks; and the total length across all encryption queries is at most σ_e blocks.
- the number of decryption queries is bounded by q_v; each decryption query length is at most ℓ_v blocks; and the total length across all decryption queries is at most σ_v blocks.

In addition, we let $q = q_e + q_v$, $\ell = \ell_e + \ell_v$ and $\sigma = \sigma_e + \sigma_v$.

Note on AEAD Security Conventions: It is worth noting here that the NAEAD security notion subsumes [13,23] the conventional security notions such as privacy and integrity, and provides a combined and uniform security argument for the concerned AEAD scheme. Although our security analysis will follow the NAEAD notion, we briefly define the conventional notions as we present our security claims in terms of the conventional notions.

PRIVACY SECURITY: We define the *privacy advantage* of any adversary $\mathcal{A}$ against AEAD scheme AE as

$$\mathbf{Adv}^{\mathsf{priv}}_{\mathsf{AE}}(\mathcal{A}) := \left| \Pr[\mathcal{A}^{\mathsf{AE.Enc}_K} = 1] - \Pr[\mathcal{A}^{\$} = 1] \right|.$$

INTEGRITY SECURITY: We say that any adversary $\mathcal{A}$ *forges* an AEAD scheme AE, if $\mathcal{A}$ is able to compute a tuple (N, A, C, T) satisfying $\mathsf{AE.Dec}_K(N, A, C, T) \neq \perp$, without querying (N, A, M) for some M to $\mathsf{AE.Enc}_K$ and receiving (C, T), i.e., (N, A, C, T) is a non-trivial forgery. The *forging advantage* for $\mathcal{A}$ is defined as

$$\mathbf{Adv}^{\mathsf{int\text{-}ctxt}}_{\mathsf{AE}}(\mathcal{A}) := \Pr[\mathcal{A}^{\mathsf{AE.Enc}_K, \mathsf{AE.Dec}_K} \text{ forges}].$$

3 tHyENA Authenticated Encryption Mode

The tHyENA authenticated encryption mode receives an encryption key $K \in \{0,1\}^\kappa$, a nonce $N \in \{0,1\}^r$, an associated data $A \in \{0,1\}^*$, and a message $M \in \{0,1\}^*$ as inputs, and returns a ciphertext $C \in \{0,1\}^{|M|}$ and a tag $T \in \{0,1\}^n$.

The decryption algorithm receives a key $K \in \{0,1\}^\kappa$, an associated data $A \in \{0,1\}^*$, a nonce $N \in \{0,1\}^r$, a ciphertext $C \in \{0,1\}^*$ and a tag

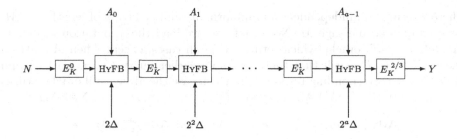

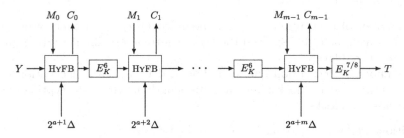

Fig. 1. tHyENA authenticated encryption mode for a block associated data and m block message.

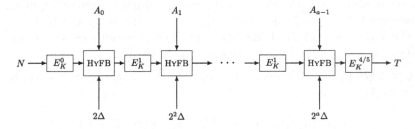

Fig. 2. tHyENA authenticated encryption mode for a block associated data and empty message.

$T \in \{0,1\}^n$ as inputs and return the plaintext $M \in \{0,1\}^{|C|}$, corresponding to the ciphertext C, if the tag T authenticates. Complete specification of tHyENA is presented in Algorithm 5 and the corresponding pictorial description can be found in Fig. 1, 2, 3, 4. We use the same hybrid feedback function as defined in [5]. For completeness, we have given the corresponding pictorial representation in Fig. 6 and 7 (Fig. 5).

3.1   Features and Design Rationale

Here, we summarize the salient features and design rationale of tHyENA:

(i) Inverse-Free: tHyENA is an inverse-free authenticated encryption algorithm. Both encryption and verified decryption of the algorithm do not require

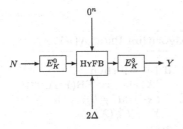

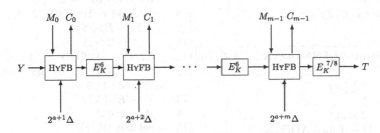

Fig. 3. tHyENA authenticated encryption mode for empty associated data and m block message.

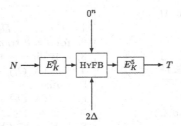

Fig. 4. tHyENA authenticated encryption mode for empty associated data and empty message.

any decryption call to the underlying block cipher. This reduces the overall hardware footprint significantly, especially in the combined encryption-decryption implementations.

(ii) Optimal: tHyENA requires $(a + m + 1)$ many block cipher invocations to process an a block associated-data and m block message. In [6], it has been shown that this is the optimal number of non-linear primitive calls required for any nonce based authenticated encryption. This feature is particularly important for short messages from the perspective of energy consumption, which is directly dependent upon the number of non-linear[1] primitive calls.

---

[1] In general, non-linear primitives consume significantly more energy as compared to linear counterparts.

Algorithm tHyENA-ENC(K, N, A, M)

1. $Y \leftarrow E_K^0(N)$
2. $\Delta \leftarrow Y_R$
3. $\Delta \leftarrow 2 \odot \Delta$
4. $(Y, \Delta) \leftarrow \text{PROC-AD}(Y, A)$
5. if $|M| \neq 0$ then
6. $(Y, C) \leftarrow \text{PROC-TXT}(Y, \Delta, M, +)$
7. $T \leftarrow Y$
8. return (C, T)

Algorithm tHyENA-DEC(K, N, A, C, T)

1. $Y \leftarrow E_K^0(N)$
2. $\Delta \leftarrow Y_R$
3. $\Delta \leftarrow 2 \odot \Delta$
4. $(Y, \Delta) \leftarrow \text{PROC-AD}(Y, A)$
5. if $|C| \neq 0$ then
6. $(Y, M) \leftarrow \text{PROC-TXT}(Y, \Delta, C, -)$
7. $T' \leftarrow Y$
8. if $T' = T$ then return M
9. else return $\perp$

Algorithm HYFB(Y, Δ, M)

1. $C \leftarrow \text{Trunc}_{|M|}(Y) \oplus M$
2. $\overline{M} \leftarrow \text{Pad}(M), \overline{C} \leftarrow \text{Pad}(C)$
3. $B \leftarrow (\overline{M}_L \| (\overline{C}_R \oplus \Delta))$
4. $X \leftarrow B \oplus Y$
5. return (X, C)

Algorithm HYFB$^-$(Y, Δ, C)

1. $M \leftarrow \text{Trunc}_{|C|}(Y) \oplus C$
2. $\overline{M} \leftarrow \text{Pad}(M), \overline{C} \leftarrow \text{Pad}(C)$
3. $B \leftarrow (\overline{M}_L \| (\overline{C}_R \oplus \Delta))$
4. $X \leftarrow B \oplus Y$
5. return (X, M)

Algorithm PROC-AD(Y, A)

1. if $|A| = 0$ then
2. $(X, \star) \leftarrow \text{HYFB}(Y, \Delta, 0^n)$
3. $t \leftarrow (|M| \neq 0)? \ 3 : 5$
4. $Y \leftarrow E_K^t(X)$
5. else
6. $(A_{a-1}, \ldots, A_0) \xleftarrow{n} A$
7.   for $i = 0$ to $a - 2$
8. $(X, \star) \leftarrow \text{HYFB}(Y, \Delta, A_i)$
9. $Y \leftarrow E_K^1(X)$
10. $\Delta \leftarrow 2 \odot \Delta$
11. $(X, \star) \leftarrow \text{HYFB}(Y, \Delta, A_{a-1})$
12. $t \leftarrow ((|M| \neq 0)$ and $(|A_{a-1}| = n))? \ 2 : 3 : 4 : 5$
13. $Y \leftarrow E_K^t(X)$
14. $\Delta \leftarrow 2 \odot \Delta$
15.   return (Y, Δ)

Algorithm PROC-TXT(Y, Δ, D, dir)

1. $(D_{d-1}, \ldots, D_0) \xleftarrow{n} D$
2. for $i = 0$ to $d - 2$
3.   if $\text{dir} = +$ then
4. $(X, O_i) \leftarrow \text{HYFB}(Y, \Delta, D_i)$
5.   else
6. $(X, O_i) \leftarrow \text{HYFB}^-(Y, \Delta, D_i)$
7. $\Delta \leftarrow 2 \odot \Delta$
8. $Y \leftarrow E_K^6(X)$
9. if $\text{dir} = +$ then
10. $(X, O_{d-1}) \leftarrow \text{HYFB}(Y, \Delta, D_{d-1})$
11. else
12. $(X, O_{d-1}) \leftarrow \text{HYFB}^-(Y, \Delta, D_{d-1})$
13. $t \leftarrow (|D_{d-1}| = n)? \ 7 : 8$
14. $Y \leftarrow E_K^t(X)$
15. return $(Y, (O_{d-1} \| \ldots \| O_0))$

Fig. 5. Formal Specification of tHyENA Authenticated Encryption and Decryption algorithm. For any n-bit string S, we define S_L (and S_R) as the most (and least) significant $n/2$ bits of S i.e. $(S_L, S_R) \xleftarrow{n/2} S$. We use the notation $\star$ to denote values that we do not care.

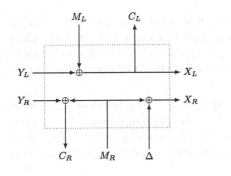

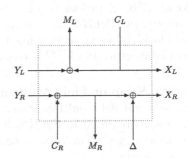

(a) HyFB+ module.   (b) HyFB- module.

Fig. 6. HyFB+ and HyFB- module of tHyENA for full data blocks.

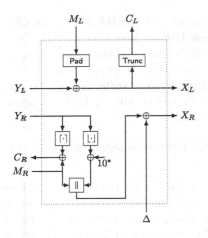

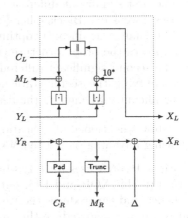

(a) HyFB+ module.   (b) HyFB- module.

Fig. 7. HyFB+ and HyFB- module of tHyENA for partial data blocks.

(iii) Low State-Size: tHyENA requires a state size as low as $3n/2$-bits along with the key state.

(iv) Low XOR Count: To achieve optimal, inverse-free authenticated ciphers with low state, a possible direction is to use the combined feedback approach where (i) the previous block cipher output is XORed with the plaintext to generate the ciphertext, and (ii) the next block cipher input is defined as the XOR of the plaintext with some linear function of the previous block cipher output. This technique was used in the popular authenticated encryption mode COFB [7]. It is easy to see that such combined feedback function require at least $2n$ bits of XOR operations (when operated on n bit data), along with some additional XOR operations required for the linear function mentioned above. On the contrary, in tHyENA, we use the concept of hybrid feedback or HyFB, where the block cipher input is defined partially via ciphertext feedback and partially via plaintext feedback. This reduces the number of the XOR operations to only n bits.

(v) No Swap or Field Multiplication by 3 or 3^2: tHyENA does not require the constant field multiplications by 3 or 3^2, or the swap operation during finalization, as required in HyENA. It uses the short tweaks efficiently to handle all the necessary domain separations. This is extremely helpful in having very low area footprint.

3.2 HyENA vs tHyENA

There are two significant changes in the tHyENA design over HyENA [5].

- The first significant difference between tHyENA and HyENA is that tHyENA uses Tweakable Blockcipher (TBC) whereas HyENA uses Blockcipher (BC). This change significantly optimizes the hardware area and throughput. It also improves the proof structure (the proof is more well structured now).
- The second significant difference is the secret internal state update. We are simplifying the secret state update and can reduce the update overheads significantly by making the design more compact.

The above-mentioned modifications ensure that the new design tHyENA has the following advantages over HyENA:

(i) First, HyENA uses 3 : 1 128-bit Multiplexors and other field multiplications with 3 (68-bit XOR and 1-bit left) or 3^2 (uses field multiplication by 3 twice in sequence and this reduces the throughput) that acquire a significant amount of hardware area and reduce the throughput. The main reason behind this usage of multiplexors and field multiplication is the domain separation of the inputs (that means, differentiating nonce, message, associated data, and the number of data bits in the last input block for each data type). We use a novel technique of using a TBC instead of a BC (and additional operations). Generally, in most of the TBC-based algorithms, the tweak is used as a counter. In this design, we take a completely different approach and we use the tweak to separate the domains. In general, there are few domains in most of the designs and a small 4-bit tweak is sufficient to separate the domains (e.g., the 4-bit tweak can separate $2^4 = 16$ domains) and circuit area for tweak updates can be reduced a lot. In tHyENA, we use a TBC that deals with small 4-bit tweaks and the area for this tweak processing circuit is very small (only a few 4-bit XORs) as compared to 3 : 1 128-bit Multiplexors plus field multiplication by 3 or 3^2. This technique, can significantly reduce the hardware area and increase the throughput a bit.

(ii) Second, using a TBC makes the design simpler and removes several avoidable operations (for example, constant field multiplications with 3 or 3^2, and the swap operation can be avoided in tHyENA). This makes the construction cleaner, more modular (e.g., we can now replace the blockcipher and several avoidable operations with a simple TBC). The security proof is now much simpler, well structured, and easily readable. To be precise, we adopt the Coefficient H technique for the security proof and HyENA has 8 bad cases to consider. However, due to the simpler structure of tHyENA, we need only 3 bad cases for the security proof of tHyENA.

3.3 Instantiation of tHyENA with TweGIFT

We instantiate tHyENA with tBC TweGIFT-128, or simply TweGIFT, the 128-bit tweakable block cipher with 4-bit tweak and 128-bit key. As the name suggests, it is a tweakable variant of the GIFT [1] block cipher. TweGIFT is composed of 40 rounds and each round is composed of five operations: SubCells, PermBits, AddRoundKey, AddRoundConstant, and AddTweak. The first four operations are identical to that of GIFT. In AddTweak, the 4-bit tweak is first expanded to a 32-bit value:

$$(x_1, x_2, x_3, x_4) \rightarrow (X, X, X, X), \ X \leftarrow (x_1, x_2, x_3, x_4, S \oplus x_1, S \oplus x_2, S \oplus x_3, S \oplus x_4),$$

where $S = x_1 \oplus x_2 \oplus x_3 \oplus x_4$. Then the 32-bit value is XORed to the state at an interval of 5 rounds. Technically speaking, it adds the expanded 32-bit tweak to bit positions $4i + 3$, $i = 0 \ldots 31$. A detailed description can be found in [2].

4 On the Security of tHyENA Mode of Operation

In this section, we prove the NAEAD security of tHyENA in shape of the following theorem.

Theorem 1. *Let* $Q = q_e + \sigma_e + q_v + \sigma_v$. *For* $Q \leq 2^{\frac{n}{2}-1}$, *we have*

$$\mathbf{Adv}^{\text{naead}}_{\text{tHyENA}}(q_e, q_v, \ell_e, \ell_v, \sigma_e, \sigma_v, t) \leq \mathbf{Adv}^{\text{tprp}}_E(Q, t') + \frac{2\sigma_e}{2^{n/2}} + \frac{2\sigma_e^2}{2^n} + \frac{q_v}{2^n} + \frac{2n\sigma_v}{2^{n/2}}.$$

where $t' = t + O(Q)$.

Without loss of generality, we can assume that $Q \leq 2^{n/2-1}$, since otherwise the result is vacuously true. First, we replace the block cipher E_K with a uniform random tweakable permutation Π using the standard hybrid argument, and then replace Π with a uniform random tweakable function $\Gamma : \{0,1\}^\tau \times \{0,1\}^n \rightarrow \{0,1\}^n$ using the standard TRP-TRF switching lemma. The cost of these transitions is accounted in the first two terms of our bound. We will employ the Coefficient-H technique for the rest of the proof. Before delving further into the proof we briefly describe this technique in the next subsection.

4.1 Coefficient-H Technique

The coefficient-H technique by Patarin [21,22] is a tool to upper bound the distinguishing advantage of any deterministic and computationally unbounded distinguisher $\mathcal{A}$ in distinguishing the real oracle $\mathcal{R}$ from the ideal oracle $\mathcal{I}$. We describe the technique in context of the NAEAD security game, i.e., we take $\mathcal{R} = (\mathsf{AE.Enc}, \mathsf{AE.Dec})$ and $\mathcal{I} = (\$, \perp)$.

The collection of all queries and responses that $\mathcal{A}$ made and received to and from the oracle is called the transcript of $\mathcal{A}$, denoted as ω. Let Λ_{re} and Λ_{id} denote the transcript random variable induced by $\mathcal{A}$'s interaction with $\mathcal{R}$ and $\mathcal{I}$, respectively. Let Ω be the set of all transcripts. A transcript $\tau \in \Omega$ is said to be *attainable* if $\Pr[\Lambda_{\mathsf{id}} = \omega] > 0$, i.e., it can be realized by $\mathcal{A}$'s interaction with $\mathcal{I}$.

Theorem 2. *For $\epsilon_1, \epsilon_2 \geq 0$, suppose there is a set $\Omega_{\mathsf{bad}} \subseteq \Omega$, that we call the set of bad transcripts, such that the following conditions hold:*

- $\Pr[\Lambda_{\mathsf{id}} \in \Omega_{\mathsf{bad}}] \leq \epsilon_1$; *and*
- *For any $\tau \notin \Omega_{\mathsf{bad}}$, τ is attainable and $\dfrac{\Pr[\Lambda_{\mathsf{re}} = \tau]}{\Pr[\Lambda_{\mathsf{id}} = \tau]} \geq 1 - \epsilon_2$.*

Then, for any computationally unbounded and deterministic distinguisher $\mathcal{A}$, we have

$$\mathbf{Adv}_{\mathsf{AE}}^{\mathsf{naead}}(\mathcal{A}) \leq \epsilon_1 + \epsilon_2.$$

We skip the proof of Theorem 2 as it is readily available in several previous works including [10,17].

4.2   Notations and Initial Setup

Fix a $(q_e, q_v, \ell_e, \ell_v, \sigma_e, \sigma_v, \infty)$-adversary $\mathcal{A}$ that interacts with either the real oracle, i.e.,

$$\mathcal{R} := (\mathsf{tHyENA.Enc}, \mathsf{tHyENA.Dec}),$$

or the ideal oracle, i.e., $\mathcal{I} := (\$, \perp)$, making at most

1. q_e encryption queries $(N_i^+, A_i^+, M_i^+)_{i=1..q_e}$, each of length $l_i^+ \leq \ell_e$, with an aggregate of total σ_e many blocks, and
2. attempts to forge with q_v many queries $(N_i^-, A_i^-, C_i^-, T_i^-)_{i=1..q_v}$, each of length $l_i^- \leq \ell_v$, having a total of σ_v many blocks.

We assume that for $1 \leq i \leq q_e$, M_i^+ and A_i^+ have m_i^+ and a_i^+ blocks respectively, and for $1 \leq j \leq q_v$, C_j^- and A_j^- have m_j^- and a_j^- blocks respectively. So, $l_i^+ = m_i^+ + a_i^+$ and $l_j^- = m_j^- + a_j^-$. We use the notation X, Y to denote the intermediate variables. Let

$$(S_i[0], S_i[1], \cdots, S_i[l_i^+ - 1]) \leftarrow (A_i^+[0], \cdots, A_i^+[a_i^+ - 1], M_i^+[0], \cdots, M_i^+[m_i^+ - 1]).$$

Let $(\lambda_i^+[j] : 1 \leq i \leq q_e, 0 \leq j \leq l_i^+)$ denote the tweak sequence in the encryption queries. Similarly, we have the tweak sequence $(\lambda_i^-[j] : 1 \leq i \leq q_v, 0 \leq j \leq l_i^-)$ in the decryption queries. Note that, one can easily deduce these tweak sequences just by observing the query inputs.

If bitwise representation of n-bit string G is $(G_{n-1} \cdots G_0)$. Then for $u > w$, we denote $(G_u \cdots G_w)$ by G_{u-w} which is a $u - w + 1$-bit substring of G from u^{th} bit to wth bit of G.

4.3 Overview of Attack Transcript

We begin with a description of the ideal oracle which consists of two phases.

- **Online phase:** For the ith encryption query $(N_i^+, A_i^+ = (A_i[0], \ldots, A_i^+[a_i - 1]), M_i^+ = (M_i^+[0], \ldots, M_i^+[m_i - 1]))$, the oracle samples $(Y_i^+[a_i^+], \ldots, Y_i^+[l_i^+]) \leftarrow_\$ \{0,1\}^{n(m_i^+ + 1)}$ independently. It next sets the tag $T_i^+ = Y_i^+[l_i^+]$ and $C_i^+ = (C_i^+[0], \ldots, C_i^+[m_i^+ - 1])$ where $C_i^+[j] = Y_i^+[j + a_i^+] \oplus M_i^+[j]$ for $0 \leq j \leq m_i^+ - 1$ and returns (C_i^+, T_i^+) to $\mathcal{A}$.
- **Offline phase:** After $\mathcal{A}$ makes all the queries the oracle samples other Y^+ values as $Y_i^+[j] \leftarrow_\$ \{0,1\}^n$, for $0 \leq j \leq a_i - 1$.

For convenience, we slightly modify the experiment where we reveal to the adversary $\mathcal{A}$ (after $\mathcal{A}$ made all its queries and obtains corresponding responses but before it outputs its decision) the Y^+-values and now the adversary can set all intermediate values $X_i^+[j]$ using $S_i[j]$ and $Y_i^+[j]$. Note that $\Delta_i^+ = \lfloor Y_i^+[0] \rfloor$ and $\Delta_i^- = \lfloor Y_i^-[0] \rfloor$.

Overall, the transcript of the adversary $\omega := (\omega_e, \omega_v)$ be the list of queries and responses of $\mathcal{A}$ that constitutes the query response transcript of $\mathcal{A}$, where

- $\omega_e = (N_i^+, A_i^+, M_i^+, X_i^+, Y_i^+, T_i^+)_{i=1..q_e}$,
- $\omega_v = (N_j^-, A_j^-, C_j^-, T_j^-, \perp)_{j=1..q_v}$.

A prefix for a decryption query is defined as the common prefix blocks between the decryption query input string and an encryption query (if any) output string prepended with the nonce and the associated data. The length of the longest common prefix for the ith decryption query is denoted as p_i. Note that if the decryption query uses a fresh nonce (not occurred during encryption queries), then it does not share any common prefix with any of the encryption queries then we set $p_i = -1$.

4.4 Identifying and Bounding Bad Events

We say that a transcript is bad if one of the following conditions is satisfied:

B1: $\mathtt{mcoll}(\lceil X^+ \rceil) > n$, where $\lceil X^+ \rceil := (\lceil X_i^+[j] \rceil : 1 \leq i \leq q_e, 1 \leq j \leq l_i^+)$.

B2: there exists $(i, j) \neq (i', j')$, such that, $\lambda_i^+[j] = \lambda_{i'}^+[j'] \wedge X_i^+[j] = X_{i'}^+[j']$.

B3: there exists $i, (i', j')$, such that, $\lambda_i^-[p_i + 1] = \lambda_{i'}^+[j'] \wedge X_i^-[p_i + 1] = X_{i'}^+[j']$.

The following lemma bounds the probability of bad transcripts in ideal oracle.

Lemma 1. *For* $\sigma_e \leq 2^{\frac{n}{2}-1}$, *we have*

$$\Pr[\Lambda_{\mathsf{id}} \in \Omega_{\mathsf{bad}}] \leq \frac{2\sigma_e}{2^{n/2}} + \frac{2\sigma_e^2}{2^n} + \frac{nq_v}{2^{n/2}}.$$

Proof. By definition of bad transcripts, we have

$$\Pr[\Lambda_{\mathsf{id}} \in \Omega_{\mathsf{bad}}] = \Pr[\mathsf{B1} \vee \mathsf{B2} \vee \mathsf{B3}]$$
$$\leq \Pr[\mathsf{B1}] + \Pr[\mathsf{B2}] + \Pr[\mathsf{B3}|\neg\mathsf{B1}]. \tag{1}$$

Now, we bound the probability terms on the right hand side one by one:

Bounding $\Pr[\mathsf{B1}]$: The event $\mathsf{B1}$ is a multicollision event for uniformly chosen n many $n/2$-bit strings out of σ_e many $n/2$-bit strings. As the Y^+-values are sampled uniformly and independently in the ideal game, we have,

$$\Pr[\mathsf{B1}] \leq \frac{\binom{\sigma_e}{n}}{2^{n/2(n-1)}} \leq \left(\frac{2\sigma_e}{2^{n/2}}\right)^n \leq \frac{2\sigma_e}{2^{n/2}}. \tag{2}$$

The last inequality follows from the assumption that $\sigma_e \leq 2^{\frac{n}{2}-1}$.

Bounding $\Pr[\mathsf{B2}]$: For any $(i,j) \neq (i',j')$, $\lambda_i^+[j] = \lambda_{i'}^+[j']$ and $j, j' > 0$, we have the following two possibilities:

(a) $j < l_i^+, j' < l_{i'}^+$: for any $(i,j) \neq (i',j')$, the event $X_i^+[j] = X_{i'}^+[j']$ is nothing but two non-trivial linear equations. One is on $\lceil Y_i^+[j-1] \rceil$ & $\lceil Y_{i'}^+[j'-1] \rceil$ and other is on $\delta_j \odot \Delta_i^+$ & $\delta_{j'} \odot \Delta_{i'}^+$ for some constants δ_j & $\delta_{j'}$. For $i \neq i'$, we have $\lceil Y_i^+[j-1] \rceil, \lceil Y_{i'}^+[j'-1] \rceil, \Delta_i^+$ and $\Delta_{i'}^+$ are independent and uniformly distributed. For $i = i'$, we have $\delta_j \neq \delta_{j'}$ and $\lceil Y_i^+[j-1] \rceil, \lceil Y_{i'}^+[j'-1] \rceil$ are independent and uniformly distributed. Hence this event has probability at most 2^{-n}. Therefore,

$$\Pr[X_i^+[j] = X_{i'}^+[j']] \leq \frac{(\sigma_e - q_e)^2}{2^n}.$$

(b) $j = l_i^+, j' = l_{i'}^+$: This can be handled in a similar manner as case (a). So, we have

$$\Pr[X_i^+[j] = X_{i'}^+[j']] \leq \frac{q_e^2}{2^n}.$$

Therefore,

$$\Pr[\mathsf{B2}] \leq \frac{(\sigma_e - q_e)^2 + q_e^2}{2^n} \leq \frac{2\sigma_e^2}{2^n}. \tag{3}$$

Bounding $\Pr[\mathsf{B3}|\neg\mathsf{B1}]$: The condition $\neg\mathsf{B1}$ implies that there are at most n possible choices for (i',j') for any fixed choice of i'. Once we fix (i',j'), we get an equality relation in the least significant $n/2$ bits. Now, we have the following cases:

(a) $p_i = -1$: This case is actually not possible. As $\lambda_i^-[0] = \lambda_{i'}^+[j]$ if and only if $j = 0$. But $N_i^- \neq N_{i'}^+$ (since $p_i = -1$), whence $X_i^-[0] \neq X_{i'}^+[j']$.

(b) $0 \leq p_i < l_i^- - 1$: Since $p_i \geq 0$, we have $N_i^- = N_k^+$ for some k. Suppose $k \neq i'$. Then we obtain a non-trivial linear equation on $\Delta_{i'}^+$. Therefore, the probability in this case is at most $\frac{nq_v}{2^{n/2}}$. Now, suppose $k = i'$. Then we must have $j' \neq p_i+1$. Otherwise we get $C_i^-[p_i] = C_k^+[p_i]$ which contradicts the definition of p_i. Hence we get the probability at most $\frac{q_v}{2^{n/2}}$.

(c) $p_i = l_i^- - 1$: In this case, j' must equal to $l_{i'}^+$ (as $\lambda_i^-[p_i + 1] = \lambda_{i'}^+[j']$). Following similar line of argument as in case (b), we get a bound of $\frac{nq_v}{2^{n/2}}$.

$$\Pr[X_i^-[l_i^-] = X_{i'}^+[j'] \wedge \neg\text{B1}] \leq \frac{nq_v}{2^{n/2}}.$$

By accumulating all the cases above, we get

$$Pr[\text{B3}|\neg\text{B1}] \leq \frac{nq_v}{2^{n/2}}. \tag{4}$$

The result follows from Eq. (1)–(4). □

4.5   Good Transcript Analysis

We fix $\omega \in \Omega_{\text{good}}$. Let $\omega = (\omega_e, \omega_v)$, where

$$\omega_e = (N_i^+, A_i^+, M_i^+, X_i^+, Y_i^+, T_i^+)_{i=1..q_e},$$

and

$$\omega_v = (N_i^-, A_i^-, C_i^-, T_i^-, \perp)_{i=1..q_v}.$$

First, it is easy to see that

$$\Pr[\Lambda_{\text{id}} = \omega] = 1/2^{n(\sigma_e + q_e)} \tag{5}$$

Next, we consider the real world. As $\neg\text{B2}$ holds, all the inputs of the tweakable random function are distinct and hence all the Y^+-values are independent and uniformly distributed. Therefore, $\Pr[\Lambda_{\text{ree}} = \omega_e] = \frac{1}{2^{n(\sigma_e + q_e)}}$. Now, we have

$$\begin{aligned}
\Pr[\Lambda_{\text{re}} = \omega] &= \Pr[(\Lambda_{\text{ree}}, \Lambda_{\text{rev}}) = (\omega_e, \omega_v)] \\
&= \Pr[\Lambda_{\text{rev}} = \omega_v | \Lambda_{\text{ree}} = \omega_e] \times \Pr[\Lambda_{\text{ree}} = \omega_e] \\
&= \frac{1}{2^{n(\sigma_e + q_e)}} \times \Pr[\Lambda_{\text{rev}} = \omega_v | \Lambda_{\text{ree}} = \omega_e] \\
&= \frac{1}{2^{n(\sigma_e + q_e)}} \times (1 - \Pr[\Lambda_{\text{rev}} \neq \omega_v | \Lambda_{\text{ree}} = \omega_e]) \tag{6}
\end{aligned}$$

Let **E** be the event that $\forall 1 \leq i \leq q_v, p_i + 1 < j \leq l_i^-$, $X_i^-[j] = X_{i'}^+[j']$ and $\lambda_i^-[j] = \lambda_{i'}^+[j']$ for some (i', j'). *Here we remark that, in case of* HyENA *one needs to consider another type of collision, where* $X_i^-[j] = X_i^-[j'']$ *for some* $j' < j''$. *However, this is not required in our case due to dedicated tweak for tag generation.* As the event $\neg\text{B3}$ holds for the good transcript, $Y_i^-[p_i + 1]$ is uniformly random. Due to the property of feedback function, $X_i^-[p_i + 2]$ is also uniformly random.

Now we need to calculate $\Pr[\Lambda_{rev} = \omega_v | \Lambda_{ree} = \omega_e]$.

$$\Pr[\Lambda_{rev} = \omega_v | \Lambda_{ree} = \omega_e] = 1 - \Pr[\Lambda_{rev} \neq \omega_v | \Lambda_{ree} = \omega_e]$$
$$= 1 - (\Pr[\Lambda_{rev} \neq \omega_v, \mathsf{E} | \Lambda_{ree} = \omega_e] + \Pr[\neg\mathsf{E} | \Lambda_{ree} = \omega_e]) \tag{7}$$

Here, $\Pr[\Lambda_{rev} \neq \omega_v, \mathsf{E} | \Lambda_{ree} = \omega_e]$ is the probability that $\exists 1 \leq i \leq q_v$ such that T_i^- is correct. But $T_i^- = Y_i^-[l_i^-]$ and the event E implies that $Y_i^-[l_i^-]$ is uniformly random. Hence $\Pr[\Lambda_{rev} \neq \omega_v, \mathsf{E} | \Lambda_{ree} = \omega_e]$ is the probability of guessing T_i^- correctly. Therefore,

$$\Pr[\Lambda_{rev} \neq \omega_v, \mathsf{E} | \Lambda_{ree} = \omega_e] \leq \frac{q_v}{2^n} \tag{8}$$

Now, consider $\Pr[\neg\mathsf{E} | \Lambda_{ree} = \omega_e]$. The event $\neg\mathsf{E}$ can be described as: for all $1 \leq i \leq q_v$ and $p_i + 1 \leq j \leq l_i^-$, $X_i^-[j] = X_{i_1}^+[j_1]$ for some i_1, j_1. The event $\neg\mathsf{B1}$ holds for good transcripts. Hence (i_1, j_1) can take at most n values. Then for a fixed i, we have

$\Pr[X_i^-[j] = X_{i_1}^+[j_1]] \leq \frac{n.l_i^-}{2^{n/2}}$. Since $\sum_{1 \leq i \leq q_v}(l_i^-) \leq \sigma_v$, summing over all $1 \leq i \leq q_v$, we have

$$\Pr[\Lambda_{rev} \neq \omega_v, \neg\mathsf{E} | \Lambda_{ree} = \omega_e] \leq \frac{n\sigma_v}{2^{n/2}} \tag{9}$$

From Eq. (5)–(9), we get

$$\Pr[\Lambda_{re} = \omega] \geq \frac{1}{2^{n(\sigma_e + q_e)}} \times \left(1 - \frac{q_v}{2^n} - \frac{n\sigma_v}{2^{n/2}}\right)$$
$$\geq \Pr[\Lambda_{id} = \omega] \times \left(1 - \frac{q_v}{2^n} - \frac{n\sigma_v}{2^{n/2}}\right).$$

The result follows from Coefficient-H Theorem 2 in combination with Lemma 1.

A Note on the Security of TweGIFT. In our AEAD algorithm, we utilize the tweakable pseudorandom permutation security of TweGIFT. Since TweGIFT is an extension of GIFT-128 blockcipher – a well-known and studied cipher – it benefits from the extensive analysis [12,16,24,26] already present for GIFT-128. Indeed, for tweak value 0 (the setting for majority of TweGIFT calls made in our algorithm), TweGIFT is exactly similar to GIFT-128 blockcipher, whence all the cryptanalytic results directly translate to this case. In addition, TweGIFT-128 has also been analyzed as a dedicated tweakable blockcipher in [2–4].

Table 1. Clock cycles per message byte for tHyENA

Message length (Bytes)											
16	32	64	128	256	512	1024	2048	4096	16384	32768	262144
cpb	10.3125	6.469	4.547	3.586	3.105	2.865	2.745	2.685	2.655	2.633	2.629	2.625

5   Hardware Implementation Results

tHyENA aims to achieve a lightweight implementation on low resource devices. tHyENA has a simple structure with a blockcipher and a few linear operations. It has a small state size and the complete circuit size is dominated by the underlying blockcipher. In this section we provide hardware implementation details of tHyENA instantiated with the GIFT blockcipher.

5.1   Clock Cycle Analysis

We provide a conventional way for speed estimation, i.e., the number of clock cycles to process input bytes. Since tHyENA processes at least one associated data (AD) block (one dummy block when AD is empty), we calculate the cpb assuming one AD block and m message blocks. We use 40 round GIFT and need 40 cycles for the GIFT module. We use 2 more cycles to compute the feedback and update the Δ value. Overall, tHyENA needs $(42(m+1)+81)$ cycles. Table 1 shows the number of average cycles per input message bytes, which we call cycles per byte (cpb). The cpb is $(42(m+1)+81)/16m$ and it converges to 2.625 for very large m.

5.2   Hardware Architecture

tHyENA is based on E-t-M paradigm and the message blocks are processed along with the associated data blocks to generate the ciphertext blocks and the tag. We use the same circuit for both the associated data and ciphertext processing as they are computed similarly. Only a change in the blockcipher tweak value for the two types of input data is required to distinguish. We provide the hardware architecture and briefly describe the individual components of this architecture. For the sake of simplicity, we remove the control unit from Fig. 8 and present a separate control unit in Fig. 9. The main components in the hardware circuit are briefly described below.

State Registers. The hardware circuit consists of two registers. The primary state register is used to store the internal state, this register is internally used by the TweGIFT module. The Δ register is used to store the Δ value, this register is internally used by the X2 module.

Module TweGIFT. The module TweGIFT is used to compute one round of the underlying tweakable blockcipher. TweGIFT uses an n-bit internal register to hold the blockcipher internal state. This register is updated with a new state

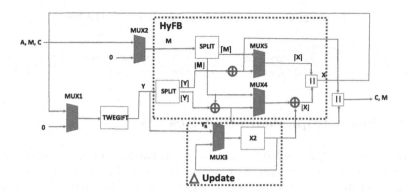

Fig. 8. Hardware architecture diagram

value whenever the state is updated with the round function or other operations. TweGIFT also uses an internal control unit, that we are omitting from the description for simplicity.

Other Modules. Apart from the above two main components, we have a $\|$ module that concatenates two strings into one, a SPLIT module that splits the internal state into two parts, and X2 module that multiplies Δ by 2. The SPLIT module is mainly used in the hybrid feedback function.

Remark 1. (Combined Encryption and Decryption) In this implementation, we mainly focus on a combined encryption-decryption circuit. We observe that we can also implement encryption-only circuits even with a small decrease in hardware area and with the same throughput.

5.3 Control Unit

We also describe the control unit in our implementation. We first list the control signals and next we describe the states in the control unit.

☐ **Data Signals**. The hardware circuit uses several internal data signals controlled by the finite state machine (FSM). The circuit uses the following signals.

- **Start**: This signal signifies the start of the circuit. This signal makes a transition from the **WAIT** to the **COMP_E_K(N)** state.
- **Rdy**: This signal signifies the start of the corresponding module.
- **Empty AD**: This signal signifies whether the associated data is empty or not.
- **Last AD**: This signal signifies whether the current associated data block is the last or not.
- **Last Msg**: This signal signifies whether the current message block is the last or not.

□ **FSM**. This module controls the hardware circuit for tHyENA. **FSM** generates and controls signals to operate the state transitions. It generates and sends signals to different modules and divides the functionalities of the circuit into several states. This is depicted in Fig. 9. Note that, for the sake of simplicity we omit the control unit of the TweGIFT module. This module uses its own architecture and control unit.

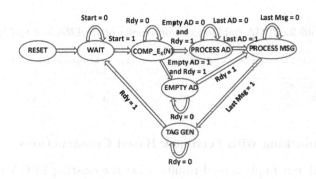

Fig. 9. Finite state machine

- **RESET**: This state resetss all the circuit parameters.
- **WAIT**: This state signifies the start of the circuit. **COMP_E$_K$(N)**. This state corresponds to the first blockcipher call
- **PROCESS AD**: This state corresponds to the processing of the associated data blocks.
- **PROCESS MSG**: This state corresponds to the processing of the message blocks.
- **EMPTY AD**: This state signifies that the associated data is empty and the control goes to the message processing phase.
- **TAG GEN**: This state corresponds to the tag generation phase and the control goes to this state from the **PROCESS MSG** state after the last message is processed.

Note that, for decryption, the process is the same, with just a few changes in some control signals.

5.4   Implementation Results

We implement tHyENA on Virtex 7 (xc7v585tffg1761-3), using VHDL and VIVADO. The implementation follows the NIST LWC API. The result includes all the overheads caused by this API. Table 2 presents the implementation results. We follow the RTL approach and a basic iterative type architecture with 128-bit datapath. The areas are provided in the number of LUTs and slices. Frequency (MHz), Throughput (Gbps), and throughput-area efficiencies are also reported in addition to the hardware areas. Table 2 presents the mapped hardware results of tHyENA.

We have also made our own implementation for the NIST submission HyENA under the same setup and using the NIST LWC API. The results for HyENA is given in Table 2 below. The results reveal that both tHyENA and HyENA achieve the same frequency but tHyENA is significantly better than HyENA in hardware area.

Table 2. FPGA implementation results of tHyENA and HyENA

Design (Platform)	Slice registers	LUTs	Slices	Frequency (MHz)	Throughput (Gbps)	Mbps/LUT	Mbps/Slice
tHyENA (Virtex 7)	472	679	261	555	1.73	2.548	6.628
HyENA (Virtex 7)	470	725	280	555	1.73	2.386	6.179

5.5 Benchmarking with Feedback Based Constructions

We benchmark our implemented results using the existing FPGA results (note that, all the other benchmarking candidates are feedback-based similar as tHyENA) on Virtex 7. We provide comparisons with the implementations from the references cited in Table 3 below.

Table 3. Comparison of lightweight feedback based AE modes on Virtex 7. '-' denotes results not available.

Scheme	Rate	LUT	Slices	T'put (GBps)	Mbps/LUT	Mbps/Slice
tHyENA-TweGIFT128	**1**	**679**	**261**	**1.73**	**2.548**	**6.628**
HyENA-GIFT128	1	725	280	1.73	2.386	6.179
COFB[GIFT] [8,9]	1	771	316	2.230	2.892	6.623
COFB[GIFT]-CAESAR-API [8,9]	1	1041	355	1.164	1.174	2.604
COFB[AES] [8,9]	1	1440	564	2.933	2.031	5.191
COFB[AES]-CAESAR-API [8,9]	1	1496	579	2.747	1.842	4.395
ESTATE-TweGIFT128 [4]	1/2	681	263	0.84	1.23	3.20
SUNDAE-GIFT128 [4]	1/2	931	310	0.84	0.90	2.71
CLOC-AES [14]	1/2	3145	891	2.996	0.488	1.724
CLOC-TWINE [14]	1/2	1689	532	0.343	0.203	0.645
CLOC-AES-Optimized [14,15]	1/2	–	595	0.695	–	1.17
SILC-AES [14]	1/2	3066	921	4.040	1.318	4.387
SILC-LED [14]	1/2	1685	579	0.245	0.145	0.422
SILC-PRESENT [14]	1/2	1514	548	0.407	0.269	0.743

Acknowledgements. The authors would like to thank all the anonymous reviewers of Indocrypt 2021 for their valuable comments. Prof. Mridul Nandi is supported by the project "Study and Analysis of IoT Security" by NTRO under the Government of India at R.C.Bose Centre for Cryptology and Security, Indian Statistical Institute, Kolkata. Dr. Ashwin Jha's work was carried out in the framework of the French-German-Center for Cybersecurity, a collaboration of CISPA and LORIA.

References

1. Banik, S., Pandey, S.K., Peyrin, T., Sasaki, Yu., Sim, S.M., Todo, Y.: GIFT: a small present. In: Fischer, W., Homma, N. (eds.) CHES 2017. LNCS, vol. 10529, pp. 321–345. Springer, Cham (2017). https://doi.org/10.1007/978-3-319-66787-4_16
2. Chakraborti, A., Datta, N., Jha, A., Mancillas-López, C., Nandi, M., Sasaki, Yu.: Elastic-tweak: a framework for short tweak tweakable block cipher. IACR Cryptol. ePrint Arch. **2019**, 440 (2019)
3. Chakraborti, A., Datta, N., Jha, A., Mancillas-López, C., Nandi, M., Sasaki, Yu.: INT-RUP secure lightweight parallel AE modes. IACR Trans. Symmetric Cryptol. **2019**(4), 81–118 (2019)
4. Chakraborti, A., Datta, N., Jha, A., Mancillas-López, C., Nandi, M., Sasaki, Yu.: ESTATE: a lightweight and low energy authenticated encryption mode. IACR Trans. Symmetric Cryptol. **2020**(S1), 350–389 (2020)
5. Chakraborti, A., Datta, N., Jha, A., Mitragotri, S., Nandi, M.: From combined to hybrid: making feedback-based AE even smaller. IACR Trans. Symmetric Cryptol. **2020**(S1), 417–445 (2020)
6. Chakraborti, A., Datta, N., Nandi, M.: On the optimality of non-linear computations for symmetric key primitives. J. Math. Cryptol. **12**(4), 241–259 (2018)
7. Chakraborti, A., Iwata, T., Minematsu, K., Nandi, M.: Blockcipher-based authenticated encryption: how small can we go? In: Fischer, W., Homma, N. (eds.) CHES 2017. LNCS, vol. 10529, pp. 277–298. Springer, Cham (2017). https://doi.org/10.1007/978-3-319-66787-4_14
8. Chakraborti, A., Iwata, T., Minematsu, K., Nandi, M.: Blockcipher-based authenticated encryption: how small can we go? IACR Cryptol. ePrint Arch. **2017**, 649 (2017)
9. Chakraborti, A., Iwata, T., Minematsu, K., Nandi, M.: Blockcipher-based authenticated encryption: how small can we go? J. Cryptol. **33**(3), 703–741 (2020)
10. Chen, S., Steinberger, J.: Tight security bounds for key-alternating ciphers. In: Nguyen, P.Q., Oswald, E. (eds.) EUROCRYPT 2014. LNCS, vol. 8441, pp. 327–350. Springer, Heidelberg (2014). https://doi.org/10.1007/978-3-642-55220-5_19
11. CAESAR Committee: CAESAR: Competition for Authenticated Encryption: Security, Applicability, and Robustness. http://competitions.cr.yp.to/caesar.html/
12. Eskandari, Z., Kidmose, A.B., Kölbl, S., Tiessen, T.: Finding integral distinguishers with ease. In: Cid, C., Jacobson, M.J., Jr. (eds.) Selected Areas in Cryptography - SAC 2018, Revised Selected Papers. LNCS, vol. 11349, pp. 115–138. Springer, Cham (2018). https://doi.org/10.1007/978-3-030-10970-7_6
13. Fleischmann, E., Forler, C., Lucks, S.: McOE: a family of almost foolproof online authenticated encryption schemes. In: Canteaut, A. (ed.) FSE 2012. LNCS, vol. 7549, pp. 196–215. Springer, Heidelberg (2012). https://doi.org/10.1007/978-3-642-34047-5_12
14. Iwata, T., Minematsu, K., Guo, J., Morioka, S., Kobayashi, E.: CLOC and SILC. Submission to CAESAR (2016). https://competitions.cr.yp.to/round3/clocsilcv3.pdf
15. Kumar, S., Haj-Yihia, J., Khairallah, M., Chattopadhyay, A.: A comprehensive performance analysis of hardware implementations of CAESAR candidates. IACR Cryptology ePrint Archive 2017:1261 (2017)
16. Liu, Y., Sasaki, Yu.: Related-key boomerang attacks on GIFT with automated trail search including BCT effect. In: Jang-Jaccard, J., Guo, F. (eds.) ACISP 2019. LNCS, vol. 11547, pp. 555–572. Springer, Cham (2019). https://doi.org/10.1007/978-3-030-21548-4_30

17. Mennink, B., Neves, S.: Encrypted Davies-Meyer and its dual: towards optimal security using mirror theory. In: Katz, J., Shacham, H. (eds.) CRYPTO 2017. LNCS, vol. 10403, pp. 556–583. Springer, Cham (2017). https://doi.org/10.1007/978-3-319-63697-9_19
18. Montes, M., Penazzi, D.: AES-CPFB v1. Submission to CAESAR (2015). https://competitions.cr.yp.to/round1/aescpfbv1.pdf
19. NIST: Lightweight cryptography. https://csrc.nist.gov/Projects/Lightweight-Cryptography
20. National Centre of Excellence. Light-weight Cipher Design Challenge. https://www.dsci.in/ncoe-light-weight-cipher-design-challenge-2020/
21. Patarin, J.: Etude de Géńerateurs de Permutations Basés sur les Schémas du DES. Ph.D thesis. Inria, Domaine de Voluceau, France (1991)
22. Patarin, J.: The "Coefficients H" technique. In: SAC 2008, pp. 328–345 (2008)
23. Rogaway, P., Shrimpton, T.: A provable-security treatment of the key-wrap problem. In: Vaudenay, S. (ed.) EUROCRYPT 2006. LNCS, vol. 4004, pp. 373–390. Springer, Heidelberg (2006). https://doi.org/10.1007/11761679_23
24. Sasaki, Yu.: Integer linear programming for three-subset meet-in-the-middle attacks: application to GIFT. In: Inomata, A., Yasuda, K. (eds.) IWSEC 2018. LNCS, vol. 11049, pp. 227–243. Springer, Cham (2018). https://doi.org/10.1007/978-3-319-97916-8_15
25. Zhang, L., Wu, W., Sui, H., Wang, P.: iFeed[AES] v1. Submission to CAESAR (2014). https://competitions.cr.yp.to/round1/ifeedaesv1.pdf
26. Zhu, B., Dong, X., Yu, H.: MILP-based differential attack on round-reduced GIFT. In: Matsui, M. (ed.) CT-RSA 2019. LNCS, vol. 11405, pp. 372–390. Springer, Cham (2019). https://doi.org/10.1007/978-3-030-12612-4_19

Panther: A Sponge Based Lightweight Authenticated Encryption Scheme

K. V. L. Bhargavi(✉) ⓘ, Chungath Srinivasan(✉) ⓘ, and K. V. Lakshmy ⓘ

TIFAC-CORE in Cyber Security, Amrita School of Engineering,
Amrita Vishwa Vidyapeetham, Coimbatore, India
{c_srinivasan,kv_lakshmy}@cb.amrita.edu

Abstract. In the modern era, lots of resource-constrained devices have exploded, creating security issues that conventional cryptographic primitives cannot solve. These devices are connected to an unsecured network such as internet. These lightweight devices not only have limited resources, but also lead to the demand for new lightweight cryptographic primitives with low cost, high performance, low cost of deployment, and effective security outcomes. After reviewing various encryption schemes, designs, and security details, this paper provides a secure cipher Panther, which performs both encryption and authentication using the best components. The design of the Panther is based on a sponge structure using Topelitz matrix and NLFSR (Non-Linear Feedback Shift Register) as the main linear and non-linear components, respectively. Security analysis shows that it is not affected by advanced cryptographic analysis proposed in recent cryptographic literature.

Keywords: Authenticated Encryption (AE) · Sponge construction · Authenticated Encryption with Associated Data (AEAD) · Lightweight cipher

1 Introduction

The rapid explosion of technological development has created many new devices like RFID, IoT, sensor networks and smart cards which makes everything smarter. In addition, these devices operate in a variety of environments. The device connects to the Internet, disrupting communication with the attacker's target and creating various security loop holes. The data should be encrypted and/or authenticated. There are three challenges with these new devices. 1) Secure encryption, authentication only or encryption and authentication 2) Cost of execution, limitation of space and resources 3) Performance latency, power consumption, available capacity and memory.

Lightweight Cryptography: Lightweight ciphers [18] helps us to achieve proper security goals like confidentiality, integrity and authenticity in lightweight environments. Over the past 50 years, symmetric key encryption has come a long way. During 1970's DES followed by RC4 competitions were held. Then, in 2005,

© Springer Nature Switzerland AG 2021
A. Adhikari et al. (Eds.): INDOCRYPT 2021, LNCS 13143, pp. 49–70, 2021.
https://doi.org/10.1007/978-3-030-92518-5_3

the eSTREAM competition was held. At the end of 2008, the SHA3 hash competition and in 2013, the CAESAR encryption competition were held as shown in Fig. 1. There are many symmetric key cryptographic primitives existing in the literature but they cannot meet the security requirements of resource-constrained devices. Traditional encryption technologies like AES, SHA2, SHA3, and RSA are suitable for server and desktop environments, but require a lot of processing and memory. CAESAR and NIST competitions focused on finding new methods to meet security requirements in lightweight environments like ACORN, ASCON [9], Elephant [10], WAGE [1]. The main constraints to consider are power, gate equivalence and cost. Since, the resource constrained devices are operated by batteries for power and the size of hardware available is less. Lightweight cryptography needs to find a balance of trade-off among them while designing cryptographic primitives for the respective application.

Fig. 1. Development in cryptographic primitives

Authenticated Encryption: Plain encryption differs from Authenticated Encryption (AE). AE provides both confidentiality and authentication, whereas plain encryption just provides confidentiality. The integrity and privacy of confidential messages exchanged across an insecure channel should be guaranteed. The demand for AE arose from the realisation that integrating distinct authentication and confidentiality of the block cipher operating modes in a secure manner will be hard and prone to errors. AE [16] provides confidentiality through encryption, integrity and assurance of message origin will be provided by authentication. This technique can be used to design a lightweight cryptographic algorithm which provides essential security in resource constrained environment. There are few situations where we need to encrypt and authenticate one part of data and the other part of data requires only authentication which is known as associated data, like the header in the packet need not to be encrypted but need to be authenticated and content to be encrypted and authenticated, then we use the technique AEAD. Since, a single approach will provide all the features of security, we are opting for AEAD technique.

The algorithm generates ciphertext and an authentication tag from key, plaintext, and associated data given as input during encryption. When decrypting the ciphertext, the algorithm takes the key, authentication tag and related data, which then returns plaintext or an error, if the tag doesn't match with the ciphertext.

AEAD: Both AE and AEAD are encryption algorithms which provide data confidentiality and also ensures authenticity. The destination address of a network packet is contained in the packet header, which must be publicly accessible in order to send the packet. As a result, the header should be authenticated rather than being encrypted. Associated data must be authenticated before being transmitted. Then we will use authenticated encryption with associated data technique where associated data is not encrypted and the message is encrypted and a tag used to authenticate both associated data and plaintext.

Sponge Based AEAD: The sponge function [15] has a finite internal state that accepts a variable length bit stream as input and outputs a specified length bit stream. It is capable of creating a variety of cryptographic techniques like MAC, masking functions, hash algorithms, pseudo random generator, Authenticated Encryption, password hashes. For generating authenticated tag a sponge function is used as defined in Hash-One [17], but does not provides encryption. Sponge based AEAD can be easily adapted to meet the requirements and do not require key scheduling. In the CAESAR competition on AE, sponge construction is used in 10 of the 57 submissions, and in the NIST LWC competition, sponge construction is utilised in 20 of the 56 submissions. These results indicate that sponge-based constructions will be beneficial in a range of next-generation cryptographic primitives, not just in the proposed SHA-3 hashing standard.

The sponge function employs a permutation or transformation function that works with bits of width b. A finite state with size b bits is partitioned into 2 sections in the sponge construction. The capacity c is the inner part, and the bit rate r is the outer part, where $b = r + c$ bits. Initialization, absorption, and squeezing phases are used to process the given input, which is divided into r bit blocks. The state will be populated in initialization phase using the intial vector (IV) and key as input. During absorption phase, processing of associated data and plaintext will happen. The input data is divided into r bits and then send to the processing. The ciphertext will be obtained while processing the plaintext. In the squeezing phase, the authenticated tag is obtained from the internal state.

1.1 Our Contribution

There is a need for new AE techniques because the conventional techniques are prone to attacks as they are unrealistic in constrained environments. The main constraints in lightweight environments are physical implementation area, power consumption, resources, performance, proper security. An analysis of numerous authenticated encryption schemes, their designs, and security aspects was conducted as part of a literature review. We propose an approach to design a secure cipher using sponge based lightweight AEAD technique named Panther. The inputs for the algorithm are variable length associated data, plaintext and a key. We send these inputs to the sponge and extract the ciphertext of length equal to the plaintext and an authentication tag of given length. We have used panther to transmit real-time traffic in an insecure network like internet. We have also analyzed panther against few cryptographic attacks to prove the strength of the cipher. The results showed that panther is immune to various cryptanalytic attacks which are proposed against other ciphers in the recent cryptographic literature.

Outline of the Paper: We formally present a thorough description of our proposed encryption, Panther, in Sect. 2. In Sect. 3, we describe the benefits of several components used in the proposed cipher. Security analysis of Panther is detailed in Sect. 4 followed by conclusion and future scope in Sect. 5.

2   Proposed Cipher

As indicated in Fig. 2, Sponge is a one-for-all cryptography primitive model created by Bertoni et al. It works in an iterative manner. It comprises of a 328-bit state divided into 82 blocks of four bits each. The sponge's state size splits into two parts r and c. The state's bit rate s_r is 64 bits, collected from the last four blocks (16 bits) in each register P, Q, R, S, while the remaining blocks are used to fill the sponge's capacity s_c.

$$s_r = P15||P16||P17||P18||Q16||Q17||Q18||Q19||R17||R18||R19||R20||S18||S19||S20||S21$$
$$s_c = state - s_r$$

2.1   Notations Used in Panther

All algorithms described in the paper works on the internal state of 328 bits. The 328 bits is splitted into P, Q, R, S registers. The notations mentioned throughout the paper are listed in Table 1.

2.2   Encryption and Decryption Methods in Panther

The sponge-based AEAD technique is one of the most successful way to develop an AEAD algorithm. We utilised sponge construction to create ciphertext and a variable-length authentication tag. The cipher's internal state is made up of four NLFSR's of lengths 19, 20, 21, and 22 over the field F_{2^4} and the field polynomial $x^4 + x^3 + 1$. The sponge's capacity is 264 bits, while the rate is 64 bits. The length of each key and initial vector (IV) is 128 bits.

We use Panther to acquire ciphertext and tag in the encryption algorithm, as illustrated in Fig. 2. The key, IV, plaintext (PT) and associated data (AD) are inputs to the encryption function E, which returns ciphertext (CT) and a tag for authentication, written as $E(key, IV, AD, PT, hashlen) = (CT, tag)$.

The internal state is iterated 92 times during the initialization and finalization phases using state update function, where as the processing of AD, PT, and CT states are updated four times, as illustrated in Algorithm 1.

Figure 3 depicts the decryption and verification process, which is described as $D(key, IV, AD, CT, tag) \in \{PT, Error\}$.

The decryption process in Algorithm 2 is having three phases: The initialization phase is followed by absorption phase, in which we will perform ciphertext processing. The input to this phase is ciphertext blocks which will be xored with rate bits of sponge and produces plaintext as output. The ciphertext block xored with rate bits of sponge will be forwarded as rate part of the state for further state updation function. The last phase is finalization phase, in which the tag is

Table 1. Notations

Notation	Description
Key	Secret key of size 128 bits
IV	Initialization vector of size 128 bits
PT	Plaintext of arbitrary length
CT	Ciphertext of arbitrary length
AD	Associated data of arbitrary length
Error	Error, verification of tag is failed
State	The internal state of sponge of size 328 bits
T_p	Toeplitz matrix
S_b	S-Box
f_i	Feedback polynomial for register i
g_i	Interconnection polynomial for register i
rc	Round constant
F	State update function
$\overline{x}$	Complement of x
s_r, s_c	Bit rate of size 64 bits, capacity of sponge of size 264 bits
P, Q, R, S	Size of internal state is 328 bits which splits into P, Q, R, S
$\oplus$	XOR
$\otimes$	Field multiplication over F_{2^4}
$0^*\|\|1$	Zeros followed by 1
$>>$	Right Shift

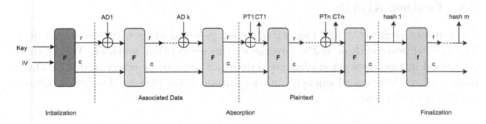

Fig. 2. Sponge based AEAD encryption

Algorithm 1. Encryption

1: **function** ENCRYPTION($key, IV, AD, PT, hashlen$)
2:     $state = 0$
3:     $state = $ Initialize(key, IV)   ▷ Initialization Phase
4:     $state = $ AdProcessing($state, AD$)   ▷ Absorption Phase   ▷ AD Processing
5:     $state, CT = $ PlaintextProcessing($state, PT$)   ▷ Plaintext Processing
6:     $tag = $ Finalization($state, hashlen$)   ▷ Finalization Phase
        return CT, tag

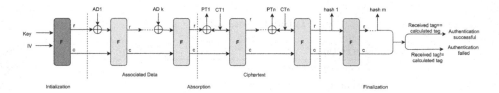

Fig. 3. Sponge based AEAD decryption

verified. If the result of encryption tag is same as the tag obtained during the decryption process, the tag is verified, and the plaintext obtained matches the original message. Otherwise, an error is returned.

Algorithm 2. Decryption

1: **function** DECRYPTION(key, IV, AD, CT, tag)
2:     $state$ = Initialize(key, IV)   ▷ Initialization Phase
3:     $state$ = AdProcessing($state, AD$)   ▷ Absorption Phase   ▷ AD Processing
4:     $state, PT$ = CiphertextProcessing($state, CT$)   ▷ Ciphertext Processing
5:     $decTag$ = Finalization(state, hashlen)   ▷ Finalization Phase
6:     **if** $tag == decTag$ **then**
         return PT
7:     **else**
         return Error

2.3 Panther AEAD

To generate ciphertext and tag, we use sponge-based authenticated encryption. The decryption method is the inverse of the encryption method. The data is processed in the absorption phase and does not need to be encrypted. The three phases of authenticated encryption are initialization phase, absorption phase, and finalization phase.

2.4 Initialization Phase

The inputs are key and IV, both of which are 128-bit long. The key is loaded first, then IV. The remaining bits are made up of 64 bits of key complemented bits, seven 1's, and a 0 at the end. Using state update function F, state is updated for 92 times. The initialization process is explained via the Algorithm 3.

2.5 Absorption Phase

The absorption phase partitions both associated data and plaintext into r bit chunks. The input bits are XORed with state bits and interleaved with state update function F. The associated data is organised into k 64-bit blocks. Each

---

Algorithm 3. Initialization Phase

1: **function** INITIALIZE(key, IV)
2:     **for** $i = 0$ to 127 **do**
3:         $state[i] = key[i]$
4:         $i++$
5:     **for** $i = 0$ to 127 **do**
6:         $state[i + 128] = IV[i]$
7:         $i++$
8:     **for** $i = 0$ to 63 **do**
9:         $state[i + 256] = \overline{key[i]}$
10:         $i++$
11:     **for** $i = 0$ to 7 **do**
12:         $state[i + 320] = 1$
13:         $i++$
14:     $state[327] = 0$
15:     $state = \text{F}(state, 92)$ ▷ State update function
        return state

---

of these k blocks is updated four times with function F. Plaintext is divided into n blocks of 64 bits each after processing k blocks. We will obtain ciphertext while processing the plaintext. Once all of the input blocks have been processed, the state is updated 92 times before switching to the squeezing phase. The absorption mechanism is explained in Algorithm 4.

2.6 Ciphertext Processing

In decryption process we will perform ciphertext processing as shown in the Algorithm 5. The received ciphertext is divided into blocks of 64 bits and given to this phase as input. The state bits are XORed with ciphertext. Here, in this step we will retrieve the PT.

2.7 Finalization Phase

Here, the rate part s_r of the internal state of sponge is given as output blocks which is interlaced with four applications of function F. The user's hash length input determines the number of output blocks. The authentication tag is the result of this phase. The Algorithm 6 describes this phase.

2.8 State Update Function

The cipher's internal state is made up of four NLFSR of length 19, 20, 21, and 22 over F_{2^4}. The state is updated 92 times during the initialization and finalization stages, and four times during the intermediate rounds. The feedback polynomial value, the interconnection polynomial value, and the round constants are all calculated here for each NLFSR feedback. The results of the four NLFSR are

Algorithm 4. Absorption Phase

1: **function** ADPROCESSING($state, AD$)
2:     $adlen = \text{length}(AD)$
3:     **if** $adlen\%64! = 0$ **then**
4:         $pad = 64 - (adlen\%64) - 1$
5:         $AD = AD||1||0^{pad}$
6:     $AD_1, AD_2...., AD_k = AD$ ▷ Dividing into k blocks
7:     **for** $i = 1$ to k **do**
8:         **for** $j = 0$ to 63 **do**
9:             $s_r[j] = s_r[j] \oplus AD[i][j]$ ▷ Array of rate bits
10:            $F(state, 4)$ ▷ State update function
        return state
11: **function** PLAINTEXTPROCESSING($state, PT$)
12:     $ptlen = length(PT)$
13:     **if** $ptlen\%64! = 0$ **then**
14:         $pad = 64 - (ptlen\%r) - 1$
15:         $PT = PT||1||0^{pad}$
16:     $PT_1, PT_2, \cdots, PT_n = PT$ ▷ Dividing into n blocks.
17:     $ct = 0$
18:     **for** $i = 1$ to n **do**
19:         **for** $j = 0$ to 63 **do**
20:             $s_r[j] = s_r[j] \oplus PT[i][j]$
21:             $CT[ct] = s_r[j]$
22:             $ct + +$
23:         **if** $i < n$ **then**
24:             F$(state, 4)$ ▷ State update function
        return $CT, state$

Algorithm 5. Ciphertext processing

1: **function** CIPHERTEXT PROCESSING($state, CT$)
2:     $CT_1, CT_2...., CT_K = CT$ ▷ Dividing into k blocks of each size r
3:     $n = 0$
4:     **for** $i = 1$ to k **do**
5:         **for** $j = 0$ to 63 **do**
6:             $PT[n] = s_r[j] \oplus CT[i][j]$
7:             $s_r[j] = CT[i][j]$
8:         **if** $i < k$ **then**
9:             F$(state, 4)$ ▷ State update function
        return $state, PT$

then sent to a filter function, which performs linear and nonlinear operations. Then the registers will be shifted by one block. The $P18, Q19, R20, S21$ blocks are updated with the new result. The polynomial $x^4 + x^3 + 1$ is used to perform field multiplication (Figs. 4 and 5).

Algorithm 6. Finalization Phase

1: **function** FINALIZATION($state, hashlen$)
2:     F($state, 92$)
3:     $t = 0$
4:     **if** $hashlen\%64 == 0$ **then**
5:         **for** $i = 0$ to $(hashlen/64) - 1$ **do**
6:             **for** $j = 0$ to 63 **do**
7:                 $tag[t] = s_r[j]$
8:                 $t = t + 1$
9:             F($state, 4$)
10:     **else**
11:         **for** $i = 0$ to $(hashlen/64) - 1$ **do**
12:             **for** $j = 0$ to 63 **do**
13:                 $tag[t] = s_r[j]$
14:                 $t = t + 1$
15:             F($state, 4$)
16:         **for** $j = 0$ to $(hashlen\%64) - 1$ **do**
17:             $tag[t] = s_r[j]$
18:             $t = t + 1$
       return tag

Algorithm 7. State update function

1: **function** F($state, n$)
2:     **for** $i = 1$ to n **do**
3:         $f_p = P_0 \oplus P_7 \oplus P_{10} \oplus P_6 \otimes P_{18}$ ▷ Step 1: Calculate Feedback Polynomial
4:         $f_q = Q_0 \oplus Q_4 \oplus Q_6 \oplus Q_7 \oplus Q_{15} \oplus Q_3 \otimes Q_7$
5:         $f_r = R_0 \oplus R_1 \oplus R_{15} \oplus R_{17} \oplus R_{19} \oplus R_{13} \otimes R_{15}$
6:         $f_s = S_0 \oplus S_1 \oplus S_4 \otimes S_{10} \oplus S_{11} \otimes S_{18}$
7:         $g_p = Q_9 \oplus R_{10} \oplus S_{12}$ ▷ Step2: Calculate Interconnection Polynomial
8:         $g_q = P_4 \oplus R_2 \oplus S_5$
9:         $g_r = P_{12} \oplus Q_{11} \oplus S_{16}$
10:         $g_s = P_{16} \oplus Q_{17} \oplus R_2$
11:         $rc_1, rc_2, rc_3, rc_4 = (0111)_2, (1001)_2, (1011)_2, (1101)_2$ ▷ Step3: Round Constant selection
12:         $l_1 = f_p \oplus g_p \oplus rc_1$ ▷ Step4: Creating inputs for filter function
13:         $l_2 = f_q \oplus g_q \oplus rc_2$
14:         $l_3 = f_r \oplus g_r \oplus rc_3$
15:         $l_4 = f_s \oplus g_s \oplus rc_4$
16:         $[d_1, d_2, d_3, d_4]^T = T_p * [l_1, l_2, l_3, l_4]^T$ ▷ Step5: toeplitz multiplication(T_p is toeplitz matrix)
17:         $[t_1, t_2, t_3, t_4]^T = T_p * [S_b[d_1], S_b[d_2], S_b[d_3], S_b[d_4]]^T$ ▷ Step6: S-box(S_b) followed by toeplitz multiplication
18:         $P >> 1, Q >> 1, R >> 1, S >> 1$ ▷ Step7: Shift the Registers
19:         $P18, Q19, R20, S21 = t_1, t_2, t_3, t_4$
20:         $n + +$
       return $state$

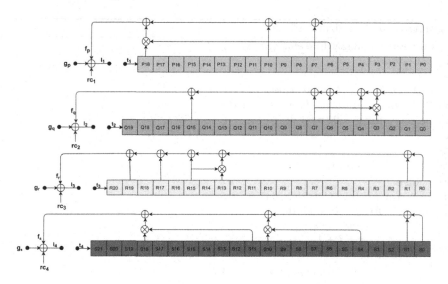

Fig. 4. f_i function

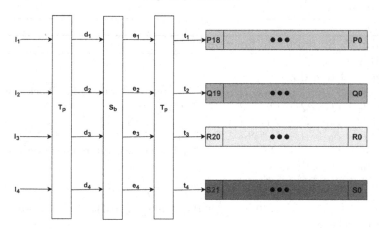

Fig. 5. $l_i \rightarrow t_i$ function

2.9   Toeplitz Matrix

Diffusion layers are constructed using MDS (Maximum Distance Separable) matrices. It is a square matrix with non-singular submatrices. The toeplitz matrices can be used to reduce the complexity of multiplication by using shift and xor operations. The field polynomial should be chosen so that fewer gates are required. As a linear layer, we're utilising the toeplitz matrix. Toeplitz matrices have a constant in descending diagonal from left to right. A typical 4×4 toeplitz matrix looks like

$$T = \begin{bmatrix} t_0 & t_1 & t_2 & t_3 \\ t_{-1} & t_0 & t_1 & t_2 \\ t_{-2} & t_{-1} & t_0 & t_1 \\ t_{-3} & t_{-2} & t_{-1} & t_0 \end{bmatrix}$$

We don't need to keep all of the matrix element, just the first row and first column will suffice. As a result, we can reduce storage complexity. Diffusion and confusion attributes are included in every state change. A matrix is said to be "circulant" if each row is a left circulant shift of the preceeding row. Toeplitz Matrices that circulate are known as circulant matrices. We are using a 4×4 Toeplitz matrix which is both MDS and circulant.

$$T_p = \begin{bmatrix} 1 & 1 & t & t^{-1} \\ t^{-2} & 1 & 1 & t \\ 1 & t^{-2} & 1 & 1 \\ t^{-1} & 1 & t^{-2} & 1 \end{bmatrix}$$

Consider the primitive element t, which is a root of $t^4 + t^3 + 1$, then the matrix $T_p(t)$ has an XOR count $10 + 4 \times 3 \times 4 = 58$.

2.10 Substitution Box

S-boxes are the fundamental building blocks of practically all modern stream ciphers, and they play a critical role in maintaining security. In a cipher, they're one of the most important nonlinear components. To make the cipher resistant to all types of cryptanalytic attacks, they must be carefully developed or chosen. We have selected a 4×4 S-box from well studied and tested Present [8] cipher.

d_i	0	1	2	3	4	5	6	7	8	9	A	B	C	D	E	F
$S_b[d_i]$	C	5	6	B	9	0	A	D	3	E	F	8	4	7	1	2

3 Design Rationale

Our proposed scheme's goal is to achieve the best possible balance of size, speed in terms of software, hardware and security. Because of its well-known hardware efficiency, we used an NLFSR in the state update of sponge. To withstand standard cryptographic attacks and to ensure that every state bit impacts the entire state, the state is updated in a nonlinear fashion using toeplitz followed by S-box followed by toeplitz matrix. The majority of our design is based on well-researched and standard primitives.

Because the message given into the internal state of the sponge, we can get nearly free authentication security. The huge number of iterations in the initialization is primarily intended to ensure that the secret key is better safeguarded when IV is repeated.

The problem is that because we employed nonlinear feedback registers in our sponge construction for state updation, it is difficult to track differential propagation in the state, especially if we wish to provide robust security of 128-bit. Our strategy is to address this issue so that authentication security may be simply assessed by concatenating four different sized linear feedback shift registers. This mechanism used to guarantee, if once exists a difference in the state, the S-box and toeplitz function and tap positions will help to eliminate the differential propagation. We have chosen the suitable tap points for all NLFSR's to guarantee high security.

3.1 Choice of the Mode for Authenticated Encryption

Our authenticated encryption mode design idea is based on the sponge methodology [5]. When compared to other available building approaches, such as various block cipher or stream cipher modes the sponge-based design offers several advantages. The sponge construction has been thoroughly researched, examined, and verified as secure for a variety of applications. Furthermore, the sponge construction is utilised in Keccak, the SHA-3 winner. Other capabilities such as hash, MAC, and cipher can be added as needed. The design is elegant and simple, with a large internal state and no need of key scheduling. We can compute plaintext and ciphertext blocks in parallel without having to wait for the complete message or message length input. Encryption and decryption uses the same permutation which reduces low implementation overhead. We chose the rate bits in a non-sequential manner to make the keystream more unpredictable. Our design includes a 92-round keyed initialization and finalisation phase, which is more robust than prior sponge-based authenticated encryption designs. Though an attacker is able to recover the internal state of sponge while data processing, this does not imply that key will be retrieved completely during trivial forgeries. Bertoni [6] proved that the sponge's security is $O(2^{c/2})$. The security in our cipher is $O(2^{132})$.

3.2 Positioning of the Key and IV

The primary objective of loading the initial values into the state is to keep the different instances separate. In our design, the key is loaded to the first 128 bits of the state, followed by IV for the following 128 bits, and the remaining bits are loaded with the complement of 64 bits from beginning then seven 1's and a zero. Even though both the key and the IV are zeros, the positioning of key, IV prevents the whole state undergoing zero.

3.3 Choice of Rate Positions

The internal state consists of a rate component and a capacity part, with the rate part allowing the attacker to insert messages into the state. The state's rate locations are determined by the security and efficiency of the hardware implementation. From a security standpoint, the chosen rate locations allow the feedback polynomial to disperse the input bits as quickly as feasible after absorbing the message into the state, resulting in quicker confusion and diffusion. Using the shifting property, the length of the process of updating the rate positions is reduced.

3.4 Substitution Layer Selection

A 4×4 S-Box is used in the substitution layer, chosen from the well known PRESENT cipher and was created to enhance diffusion in lightweight environments. The direct outcome for hardware efficiency will be attained by employing a 4×4 S-box which is generally significantly smaller than an 8×8 S-box. Because this S-box has been thoroughly researched and tested, it will be resistant to both differential and linear attacks, as well as well-suited to hardware implementation efficiency. The nonlinear function S-box adds difference noise to the feedback to reduce forgery attempts success rate.

The characteristics of this S-box are as follows: Nonlinearity $= 4$, differential uniformity $= 4$. The S-box has a balanced output, and there are no fixed points in the S-box.

3.5 Choice of Linear Layer

A circulant matrix is a matrix in which each row represents one cyclic shift from the preceding row. Because the entire matrix may be produced from the initial row, these matrices are useful in hardware design. MDS matrices has been utilised as the diffusion layer because of the highest diffusion power. For example, the diffusion layer of AES uses MDS matrix. The toeplitz matrix, which is both an MDS and a circulant matrix was chosen. We picked the Toeplitz matrix because it has a lower XOR count, which means less hardware is needed, and we don't have to store all of the elements in the matrix as it is circulant, which decreases storage complexity. For storing the matrix, we just require a single-dimensional array with $(2n - 1)$ items. The diffusion characteristics of Toeplitz, which is an MDS matrix, are well known. Under the irreducible polynomial $x^4 + x^3 + 1$, the minimal value of the XOR count of a 4×4 MDS matrix over F_{2^4} is $10 + 4 \times 3 \times 4$.

4   Security Analysis

4.1 Linear and Differential Cryptanalysis

Linear Cryptanalysis: It attempts to exploit high possibility of linear expressions with ciphertext bits, plaintext bits, and key bits occurring. This is a known plaintext attack, which implies that attacker will be aware of few pairs of plaintext with their corresponding ciphertexts. On the other side, the attacker has no idea what plaintexts and ciphertexts are exposed. It is plausible to suppose the attacker is aware of some random pairs of plaintexts and ciphertexts in many applications and circumstances. The aim of this attack is to figure out expressions with high or low likelihood of occurrence. When a cipher tends or does not hold a linear equation, it has weak randomisation capabilities.

We need to calculate the linear probability bias that is the deviation of linear expression probability from $1/2$. If a linear expression holds with probability p_L for some randomly picked plaintexts with associated ciphertexts then probability bias is $p_L - 1/2$. If the value of the probability bias is high then more linear cryptanalysis may be used with some known plaintexts. We take into account the features of the single non linear component: the S-box to create linear expressions. It is feasible to construct linear approximations among pairs of input and output bits in the S-box after the non-linearity features of the S-box have been identified.

The Table 2 depicts all linear approximations of the S-box used in the cipher.

Table 2. LAT table

	0	1	2	3	4	5	6	7	8	9	A	B	C	D	E	F
0	+8	0	0	0	0	0	0	0	0	0	0	0	0	0	0	0
1	0	0	-2	-2	0	0	-2	+6	+2	+2	0	0	+2	+2	0	0
2	0	0	-2	-2	0	0	-2	-2	0	0	+2	+2	0	0	-6	+2
3	0	0	0	0	0	0	0	0	+2	-6	-2	-2	+2	+2	-2	-2
4	0	+2	0	-2	-2	-4	-2	0	0	-2	0	+2	+2	-4	+2	0
5	0	-2	-2	0	-2	0	+4	+2	-2	0	-4	+2	0	-2	-2	0
6	0	+2	-2	+4	+2	0	0	+2	0	-2	+2	+4	-2	0	0	-2
7	0	-2	0	+2	+2	-4	+2	0	-2	0	+2	0	+4	+2	0	+2
8	0	0	0	0	0	0	0	0	-2	+2	+2	-2	+2	-2	-2	-6
9	0	0	-2	-2	0	0	-2	-2	-4	0	-2	+2	0	+4	+2	-2
A	0	+4	-2	+2	-4	0	+2	-2	+2	+2	0	0	+2	+2	0	0
B	0	+4	0	-4	+4	0	+4	0	0	0	0	0	0	0	0	0
C	0	-2	+4	-2	-2	0	+2	0	+2	0	+2	+4	0	+2	0	-2
D	0	+2	+2	0	-2	+4	0	+2	-4	-2	+2	0	+2	0	0	+2
E	0	+2	+2	0	-2	-4	0	+2	-2	0	0	-2	-4	+2	-2	0
F	0	-2	-4	-2	-2	0	+2	0	0	-2	+4	-2	-2	0	+2	0

It is now quite straightforward to create a secure round function. An S-box layer plus a diffusion layer built on MDS code gives a high security margin against differential and linear attacks straight away, even when the number of rounds is minimal.

Differential Cryptanalysis: This is a chosen plaintext attack where the attacker selects inputs and outputs to infer key. It exploits high likelihood of few plaintext differences goes into the cipher's final round. Using this highly likely differential characteristic and by utilising information flowing into the last round of the encryption, we may extract bits from the last layer of sub keys.

It makes use of information from XOR of 2 inputs(input difference) and XOR of 2 outputs (output difference). The attacker selects an input difference x, and has several tuples (x_1, x_2, y_1, y_2), with x_1, x_2 as inputs and y_1, y_2 as outputs. Attacker guesses the key value of the previous round for each pair of y_1 and y_2 and decrypts the XOR at the last but one round. Checks whether the result matches the most likely outcome and keeps track of the number of matches in a frequency table for each key. The correct key will have a high frequency.

The distribution table for differences in S-boxes measures how many pairings with a certain difference of input leads to a certain difference of output. It's a crucial step in finding high-probability transitions and building the differential characteristics, which will be employed later in the attack. The difference distribution table (DDT) of the S-box is provided in Table 3. All iterative differences are copied to the diagonal of the DDT. The S-box has a differential uniformity of 4 and a differential branch number of 3.

Table 3. DDT table

	0	1	2	3	4	5	6	7	8	9	A	B	C	D	E	F
0	16	0	0	0	0	0	0	0	0	0	0	0	0	0	0	0
1	0	0	0	4	0	0	0	4	0	4	0	0	0	4	0	0
2	0	0	0	2	0	4	2	0	0	0	2	0	2	2	2	0
3	0	2	0	2	2	0	4	2	0	0	2	2	0	0	0	0
4	0	0	0	0	0	4	2	2	0	2	2	0	2	0	2	0
5	0	2	0	0	2	0	0	0	0	2	2	2	4	2	0	0
6	0	0	2	0	0	0	2	0	2	0	0	4	2	0	0	4
7	0	4	2	0	0	0	2	0	2	0	0	0	2	0	0	4
8	0	0	0	2	0	0	0	2	0	2	0	4	0	2	0	4
9	0	0	2	0	4	0	2	0	2	0	0	0	2	0	4	0
A	0	0	2	2	0	4	0	0	2	0	2	0	0	2	2	0
B	0	2	0	0	2	0	0	0	4	2	2	2	0	2	0	0
C	0	0	2	0	0	4	0	2	2	2	2	0	0	0	2	0
D	0	2	4	2	2	0	0	2	0	0	2	2	0	0	0	0
E	0	0	2	2	0	0	2	2	2	2	0	0	2	2	0	0
F	0	4	0	0	4	0	0	0	0	0	0	0	0	0	4	4

Differential Attack Using ML Technique: Following in the traditions of Gohr's [11] work on deep learning-based round reduction cryptanalysis(DL), Baksi [3] discusses a deep learning-based solution for differential attacks on non-Markov ciphers by simplifying the differentiating problem into a classification strategy, they used a range of models with varied widths and numbers of neurons, such as Convolutional Neural Networks (CNN) and MultiLayer Perceptron

(MLP). We utilized Tensorflow, Keras, and the Adam algorithm as optimizer function. We trained the model offline by introducing a large number of input differences (t) into the cipher and storing all of the output differences as training data. The accuracy of ML model training reports is ($\alpha = 0.6$) $> 1/t$. Hence, we can move on to the next phase. During the online phase, we trained the ML model by treating it like an oracle and putting it to the test with a variety of random input differences. The accuracy ($\alpha = 0.4$) $< 1/t$ is revealed by the results. We can therefore ensure that the proposed cipher acts as an random oracle and has good random characteristics.

4.2 Slide Re-synchronization Attack

The attack objective is to discover the related keys and initial values. With a probability of 2^{-2}, there appears a related (key', IV') pair for each pair (key, IV). The slide attack [7] when applied to the stream ciphers initialization is known as the slide re-synchronization attack. Attacker takes advantage of this fact and then try to find the related pair

$$(key', \ IV') = ((k'_0, k'_1, \cdots, k'_{127}), (IV'_0, IV'_1, \cdots, IV'_{256}, k'_{127}))$$

with a probability of 2^{-2}, this yields the 1-bit shifted keystream sequence. Their attack strategy is based on two observations:

1. States of the key initialization process are similar to each other.
2. Key set up and keystream generation are similar.

The relationship between (key, IV) and (key', IV') is $key = (k_0, k_1, \cdots, k_{127})$ $\implies key' = (k_1, k_2...., k_{127}, b)$, where $b \in \{0, 1\}$, $IV = (IV_0, IV_1, \cdots, IV_{127})$ $\implies$ $IV' = (IV_1, IV_2...., IV_{127}, 1)$. They showed that stream ciphers which have similar states in the initialization process and using similar mechanisms for key setup and keystream generation are vulnerable to slide resynchronization attacks. While it does not yet produce an effective key recovery attack, it indicates an initialization vulnerability that may be overcome with a small amount of work. Our cipher resists this attack as we are using other NLFSR's data while updating the state. Some of the initialization bits are a mix of complement of key, so it won't undergo slide-resynchronization attack.

4.3 Time Memory Trade-Off Attack

This is one of the general attacks on any cipher. It has mainly two phases

1. Preprocessing Phase
2. Realtime Phase

In preprocessing phase, attacker try to understand the structure of the cipher design and then creates a summary of all the findings in some tables. Attacker invests more time in this phase to gather as much information as possible.

In real time phase, attacker uses the pre-computed tables in the earlier phase to obtain keys in a quicker way. Hellman [13] is famous for the well-known time/memory trade-off exploit. It employs any parameter combination that satisfies $TM^2 = N^2$, $P = N, D = 1$. The best T and M options are determined by the relative costs of these computing resources. Hellman obtains the precise trade-off $T = N^{2/3}$ and $M = N^{2/3}$ for block ciphers by selecting $T = M$. Babbage [2] and Golic [12] separately described the simplest time memory trade-off attack which will be referred as BG attack. They reduced preprocessing time to half ($P = M$) and also the attack time to half ($T = D$).

To prevent tradeoff attacks (TMTO attacks) with l bit key and v bit IV, the internal state size must be at least twice as large as the key size. Then the basic TMTO attack would have complexity at least $O(2^l)$, which is equivalent to the exhaustive key search.

Assume pre-computation time to be 2^p. The attacker observes 2^d frames and mounts an online attack with time 2^t and memory 2^m to recover the secret key K of one frame. Then the TMTO attack would satisfy the following constraints.

$$p = l + v - d$$
$$t \geqslant d \tag{1}$$
$$t + m = l + v$$

In the pre-computation phase, we generate keystream sequences, i.e. frames, for 2^m random (Key, IV) pairs and store them in a list in memory. Next in the online phase, we observe 2^d frames using which we are trying to recover the corresponding secret key K. From the birthday paradox, it follows that one of these frames will be broken when

$$m = d = (l + v)/2 \tag{2}$$

From the above Eqs. (1) and (2), it means that the size of IV should be approximately l bits; otherwise the TMTO attack will be faster than the brute-force attack. In our design, $l = v = 128$. Assume $d = 64$, i.e. we could observe 2^{64} frames. Then from (1), we have $p = 192$, $t \geqslant 128$ and $m \leqslant 128$. This implies that the complexity of TMTO attack on our design is at least same as that of brute-force attack.

4.4 Fault Attack

Fault attacks [14] is one of the powerful attacks on any cipher and have shown to be efficient against various stream ciphers. It's uncertain whether or not these attacks are truly possible. Adversary is allowed to flip bits in any of the shift register is one scenario in a fault attack. However, the attacker will not have complete control over the amount of defects or their precise position. A much more powerful assumption is that the opponent can flip precisely one bit, but at a position that he is unable to control. He also has the ability to reset the encryption and introduce a new flaw. If the attacker can repeatedly reset the encryption, each time generating a new defect in a known place that he can estimate from the output difference. Given the more realistic premise that the adversary is unable to control the amount of faults inserted, determining the induced difference from the output differences appears to be more challenging. In the NLFSR, it is feasible to introduce flaws. These flaws will propagate non-linearly in the NLFSR, making their evolution more difficult to forecast. As a result, it appears that inserting faults into the NLFSR is more challenging than LFSR.

4.5   Correlation Attack

The proposed architecture passes all structural tests [19], includes key/keystream correlation test, which evaluates correlation of key and the associated keystream by fixing an IV. The IV/keystream correlation test is the second test, which looks at the correlation of IV and related keystream by fixing a key. The next one is the frame correlation test, which examines the correlation of keystreams with several IV's. The results showed the cipher is resilient against correlation attack.

Correlation attack takes advantage of any correlation between the keystream and the LFSR output in the cipher. The keystream may be thought of as a noisy or distorted version of the LFSR output. The issue of determining the LFSR's internal state is therefore reduced to a decoding problem, with keystream representing the received codeword and LFSR internal state representing the original message. However, unlike LFSR-based ciphers, the recommended state of the ciphers changes in a non-linear form, making it impossible to determine how an attacker should combine these equations to retrieve the condition.

4.6   Cube Attack

We investigated the proposed cipher by selecting 100 cubes and generated 1000 keystream bits corresponding to each cube. For computing the equations we have set the IV vectors to zero at positions other than the cube. Random 128 bit vector is generated and used as key K. Then for each cube and i^{th} keystream bit $F_i(K, IV)$, the polynomial $\sum_{IV \in C} F_i(K, IV)$ is verified for linearity by checking the relation (3) for sufficient number of random key pairs (X, Y).

$$\sum_{IV \in C} F_i(X + Y, IV) = \sum_{IV \in C} F_i(X, IV) + \sum_{IV \in C} F_i(Y, IV) + \sum_{IV \in C} F_i(0, IV) \quad (3)$$

Note that the nonlinearity of the component functions of S-box is 4 and its algebraic immunity is 2. Also for the proposed cipher after 92 rounds of the initialization phase, the degree of the output polynomial is estimated to be very high. As a result, it would be hard for an attacker to gather low-degree relations among the secret key bits.

4.7   Diffusion of Key and IV over the Keystream

This test verifies that every single bit of a key and an IV on the keystream has been diffused. To meet the diffusion condition, every single bit of key and IV must have an equal probability of affecting the keystream. Small differences in key or IV must produce huge change in the keystream. This test begins with the selection of randomly chosen key and IV and produces a length of keystream (L). New keystreams are produced by altering key and IV bits. Create a matrix $(k + v) \times L$ by applying XOR on original keystream and bit changed keystreams. This method is done for N times and resulting matrices are summed up. To evaluate diffusion property for the matrix entries we apply Chi-Square Goodness of Fit test. When N is high, the elements in the matrix follows normal distribution of mean $N/2$, variance $N/4$, resulting in a secure cipher.

We have picked [0–498], [499–507], [508–516], [517–525] and [526–1024] as the category boundaries using these estimated probabilities. To pass the Chi-square goodness of fit test, which has four degrees of freedom and a significance threshold of $\alpha = 0.01$ the resultant chi-square value should be $\chi^2 \leqslant 13.277$. Here, the observed and predicted values are compared, and our design passed with a average chi-square value of $\chi^2 = 4.4$ after analyzing various sample sizes.

4.8   Banik's Key-Recovery Attack

The existence of roughly 2^{30} IV's for each key in Sprout was originally noted out in this work [4], so that the LFSR state becomes entirely 0state following the Key-IV mixing phase. The LFSR does not get feedback from the output bit during the keystream phase, and so remains in the zero state throughout the evolution of cipher weaken the cipher's algebraic structure. Their work was used to report the following: In practical time, key-IV pairings were discovered that produced keystream bits with a period of 80. In the multiple IV mode, a key recovery attack was recorded. The attacker searches keystream for a fixed secret key and several secret IVs, then waits until one of the IVs is queried, causing the LFSR to fall into the all zero state after the key-IV mixing. Because the cipher's algebraic structure was weakened, simple equations on the key bits could be derived, which could be solved to discover the secret key.

To overcome this, we used a constant 1 in the last bits of the state in Panther, so that when the cipher eventually enters keystream generation mode, the NLFSR state is never all zero because the last bits are 1's, and it never falls into the all zero trap.

4.9   Result of NIST Tests

For testing pseudo random sequence generators we can use the Statistical Test Suite SP800-22 of NIST. It consists of 16 tests that check if the bits produced by each encryption method are random. 1000 files are used to perform this test, each of which has a 10^6 bit sequence and corresponds to a distinct key and IV. In the parentheses beside each test, the input parameters used for the test are

Table 4. NIST results

S. No.	Statistical tests	p-value	Proportion
1	Frequency	0 851383	1.0000
2	Block frequency ($m = 100000$)	0.657933	0.9905
3	Forward cumulative sums	0.062821	0.9815
4	Backward cumulative sums	0.678686	0.9900
5	Runs	0.145326	1.0000
6	Longest runs of ones ($M = 1000$)	0.657933	0.9900
7	Non-overlapping template ($m = 9, B = 000000001$)	0.494392	0.9905
8	Universal ($L = 9, Q = 5120$)	0.419021	1.0000
9	Overlapping template ($m = 9$)	0.171867	0.9860
10	Spectral DFT	0.202268	0.9968
11	Approximate entropy ($m = 10$)	0.759756	0.9900
12	Rank	0.699313	0.9853
13	Random excursions ($x = \pm 1$)	0.568055	0.9968
14	Random excursions variant ($x = -1$)	0.534146	0.9880
15	Linear complexity ($M = 500$)	0.319084	0.9853
16	Serial ($m = 16$)	0.514124	1.0000

listed in Table 4. If we take a sample data of 1000 binary sequence size, the minimal passing rate for each statistical test is about equal to 0.980567%. We may conclude from Table 4 that the suggested cipher passed all NIST randomness tests since the p-value uniformity of every test is larger than or equal to 0.01.

4.10   Diffusion of Plaintext over Message Authentication Code

This test verifies that each plaintext bit on the hash has been diffused. Each bit of plaintext should have an equal probability of influencing hash creation to fulfil the diffusion property. Minor changes in the plaintext should cause the hash to alter in an unpredictable way. First, a constant key and IV are chosen in the Diffusion test. We chose the key and IV to be zero, and a 256-bit plaintext is generated. New hashes are then produced by altering each bit of the plaintext. The original plaintext hash values are then XORed with these hash values. A matrix of size $msg \times L$ was created using these vectors. This process is iterated N times and the resultant matrices will be calculated by adding in real numbers. To evaluate the diffusion of matrix entries apply the Chi-Square Goodness of Fit test.

When N is high, the elements in the matrix follows normal distribution with a mean of $N/2$, variance of $N/4$, resulting in a secure cipher. We have taken $N = 1024$, $L = 256$, $msg = 256$ and the limits for each category with these approximate probabilities are chosen as, [0–498], [499–507], [508–16], [517–525] and [526–1024]. To pass the Chi-square goodness of fit test, which has four degrees of freedom and a significance threshold of $\alpha = 0.01$ the resultant chi-square value should be $\chi^2 \leqslant 13.277$. Here, the observed and predicted values are compared, and our design passed with a average chi-square value of $\chi^2 = 3.83$ after analyzing various sample sizes with random key and IV.

5   Conclusion and Future Work

Because of picking the best components with the least hardware load and adequate security, the suggested sponge based approach can be employed in lightweight environments. To update the state, the design employs NLFSR and a toeplitz matrix. The proposed design has good pseudo randomness and diffusion qualities, which is a criterion for a good design according to the literature. The suggested technique can be used in resource-constrained devices to achieve adequate security goals at a cheap cost. Panther was used to send real-time traffic via an unsecured network. We tested the strength of Panther using a variety of cryptography attacks. The future scope is to test the suggested scheme's resilience and strength employing more cryptanalytic attacks in a realistic manner.

References

1. Aagaard, M., AlTawy, R., Gong, G., Mandal, K., Rohit, R., Zidaric, N.: WAGE: an authenticated cipher. Submission to NIST Lightweight Cryptography Standardization Project (announced as round 2 candidate on August 30, 2019) (2019)
2. Babbage, S.: Improved "exhaustive search" attacks on stream ciphers. In: 1995 European Convention on Security and Detection, pp. 161–166. IET (1995)
3. Baksi, A., Breier, J., Chen, Y., Dong, X.: Machine learning assisted differential distinguishers for lightweight ciphers. In: 2021 Design, Automation & Test in Europe Conference & Exhibition (DATE), pp. 176–181. IEEE (2021)
4. Banik, S.: Some results on Sprout. In: Biryukov, A., Goyal, V. (eds.) INDOCRYPT 2015. LNCS, vol. 9462, pp. 124–139. Springer, Cham (2015). https://doi.org/10.1007/978-3-319-26617-6_7
5. Bertoni, G., Daemen, J., Peeters, M., Van Assche, G.: On the indifferentiability of the sponge construction. In: Smart, N. (ed.) EUROCRYPT 2008. LNCS, vol. 4965, pp. 181–197. Springer, Heidelberg (2008). https://doi.org/10.1007/978-3-540-78967-3_11
6. Bertoni, G., Daemen, J., Peeters, M., Van Assche, G.: Duplexing the sponge: single-pass authenticated encryption and other applications. In: Miri, A., Vaudenay, S. (eds.) SAC 2011. LNCS, vol. 7118, pp. 320–337. Springer, Heidelberg (2012). https://doi.org/10.1007/978-3-642-28496-0_19
7. Biryukov, A., Wagner, D.: Slide attacks. In: Knudsen, L. (ed.) FSE 1999. LNCS, vol. 1636, pp. 245–259. Springer, Heidelberg (1999). https://doi.org/10.1007/3-540-48519-8_18
8. Bogdanov, A., et al.: PRESENT: an ultra-lightweight block cipher. In: Paillier, P., Verbauwhede, I. (eds.) CHES 2007. LNCS, vol. 4727, pp. 450–466. Springer, Heidelberg (2007). https://doi.org/10.1007/978-3-540-74735-2_31

9. Dobraunig, C., Eichlseder, M., Mendel, F., Schläffer, M.: ASCON v1.2. Submission to the CAESAR Competition (2016)
10. Dobraunig, C., Mennink, B.: Elephant v1 (2019)
11. Gohr, A.: Improving attacks on round-reduced Speck32/64 using deep learning. In: Boldyreva, A., Micciancio, D. (eds.) CRYPTO 2019. LNCS, vol. 11693, pp. 150–179. Springer, Cham (2019). https://doi.org/10.1007/978-3-030-26951-7_6
12. Golić, J.D.: Cryptanalysis of alleged A5 stream cipher. In: Fumy, W. (ed.) EURO-CRYPT 1997. LNCS, vol. 1233, pp. 239–255. Springer, Heidelberg (1997). https://doi.org/10.1007/3-540-69053-0_17
13. Hellman, M.: A cryptanalytic time-memory trade-off. IEEE Trans. Inf. Theory **26**(4), 401–406 (1980)
14. Hoch, J.J., Shamir, A.: Fault analysis of stream ciphers. In: Joye, M., Quisquater, J.-J. (eds.) CHES 2004. LNCS, vol. 3156, pp. 240–253. Springer, Heidelberg (2004). https://doi.org/10.1007/978-3-540-28632-5_18
15. Krishnan, L.R., Sindhu, M., Srinivasan, C.: Analysis of sponge function based authenticated encryption schemes. In: 2017 4th International Conference on Advanced Computing and Communication Systems (ICACCS), pp. 1–5. IEEE (2017)
16. Maimut, D., Reyhanitabar, R.: Authenticated encryption: toward next-generation algorithms. IEEE Secur. Priv. **12**(2), 70–72 (2014)
17. Mukundan, P.M., Manayankath, S., Srinivasan, C., Sethumadhavan, M.: Hash-one: a lightweight cryptographic hash function. IET Inf. Secur. **10**(5), 225–231 (2016)
18. Rohit, R.: Design and cryptanalysis of lightweight symmetric key primitives. University of Waterloo (2020)
19. Turan, M.S., Doganaksoy, A., Calik, C.: Detailed statistical analysis of synchronous stream ciphers. In: ECRYPT Workshop on the State of the Art of Stream Ciphers (SASC 2006) (2006)

Symmetric Cryptography

Crooked Indifferentiability of Enveloped XOR Revisited

Rishiraj Bhattacharyya[1($\boxtimes$)], Mridul Nandi[2], and Anik Raychaudhuri[2]

[1] NISER, HBNI, Bhubaneswar, India
[2] Indian Statistical Institute, Kolkata, India

Abstract. In CRYPTO 2018, Russell, Tang, Yung and Zhou (RTYZ) introduced the notion of crooked indifferentiability to analyze the security of a hash function when the underlying primitive is subverted. They showed that the n-bit to n-bit function implemented using enveloped XOR construction (EXor) with $3n + 1$ many n-bit functions and $3n^2$-bit random initial vectors can be proven secure asymptotically in the crooked indifferentiability setting. We identify several major issues and gaps in the proof by RTYZ, We argue that their proof can achieve security only in a restricted setting. We present a new proof of crooked indifferentiability where the adversary can evaluate queries related to multiple messages. Our technique can handle function-dependent subversion.

Keywords: Crooked indifferentiability · Subverted random oracle · Simulator · Enveloped XOR Hash

1 Introduction

BLACKBOX REDUCTION AND KLEPTOGRAPHIC ATTACK. Many of the modern cryptographic constructions are analyzed in a modular and inherently blackbox manner. The schemes or protocols are built on underlying primitives only exploiting the functionality of the primitives. While analyzing the security, one shows a reduction saying, a successful attack on the construction will lead to an attack against the underlying primitive. Unfortunately, this approach completely leaves out the implementation aspects. While the underlying primitive may be well studied, a malicious implementation may embed trapdoor or other sensitive information that can be used for the attack. Moreover, such implementation may well be indistinguishable from a faithful implementation [21]. These types of attacks fall in the realm of *Kleptography*, introduced by Young and Yung [21]. While the cryptographic community did not consider kleptography as a real threat, the scenario has changed in the past few years. The kleptographic attack has been a real possibility in the post-Snowden world. A line of work has appeared aiming to formalize and provide security against kleptographic attack [2,10,17,18]. Specifically, in [2], Bellare, Paterson, and Rogaway showed that it is possible to mount algorithm substitution attacks against almost all known

© Springer Nature Switzerland AG 2021
A. Adhikari et al. (Eds.): INDOCRYPT 2021, LNCS 13143, pp. 73–92, 2021.
https://doi.org/10.1007/978-3-030-92518-5_4

symmetric key encryption schemes to the extent that the attacker learns the secret key.

RANDOM ORACLE AND INDIFFERENTIABILITY. The *Random Oracle* methodology is a very popular platform for proving the security of cryptographic constructions in the black-box fashion. In this model, all the parties, including the adversary, are given access to a common truly random function. One proves the security of a protocol assuming the existence of such a random function. During the implementation of the protocol, the random function is replaced by a hash function H. The *Indifferentiability* framework and the composition theorem [13] assert that if the hash function H is based on an ideal primitive f, and Indifferentiable from a random function, then the instantiated protocol is as secure as the protocol in the random oracle model (assuming the security of the ideal primitive f). Indifferentiability from Random Oracle has been one of the mainstream security criteria of cryptographic hash functions. Starting from the work of Coron, Dodis, Malinaud, and Puniya [9], a plethora of results [1,4–7,12,14–16] have been proven, showing indifferentiability of different constructions based on different ideal primitives.

CROOKED INDIFFERENTIABILITY. In CRYPTO 2018, Russel, Tang, Yung and Zhou [19] introduced the notion of crooked indifferentiability as a security notion for hash functions in the kleptographic setting. Like classical indifferentiability, the game of crooked-indifferentiability challenges the adversary to distinguish between two worlds. In the real world, the adversary has access to the underlying ideal primitive f, and the construction C, which has subroutine access to $\tilde{f}$, the subverted implementation of f.[1] The implementation $\tilde{f}$ on input an element x, queries the function (possibly adaptively) at maximum $\tilde{q}$ many points and, based on the transcript, decides the evaluation of x. As the adversary likes the subversion to go undetected, it is assumed that $\tilde{f}$ differs from f only on some negligible fraction (ϵ) of the domain.

In the ideal world, the construction is replaced by a Random Oracle $\mathcal{F}$. The role of f is played by a simulator with oracle access to $\mathcal{F}$ and the subverted implementation $\tilde{f}$. The job of the simulator is to simulate f in such a way that $(C^{\tilde{f}}, f)$ is indistinguishable from $(\mathcal{F}, S^{\mathcal{F}, \tilde{f}})$. To avoid trivial attacks, the framework allows a *public* random string R to be used as the salt in the construction. The string R is fixed after the adversary publishes the implementation but stays the same throughout the interaction. All the parties, including the simulator and the adversary, get R as part of the initialization input. We note that even in the weaker setting of Random Oracles with auxiliary input, a random salt is required to prove security [8,11].

ENVELOPED XOR CONSTRUCTION AND ITS CROOKED-INDIFFERENTIABILITY. We recall the Enveloped XOR construction. We fix two positive integers n and l. Let $\mathcal{D} := \{0, 1, \ldots, l\} \times \{0, 1\}^n$. Let H be the class of all functions $f : \mathcal{D} \rightarrow \{0, 1\}^n$.

---

[1] The domain extension algorithms are simple and the correctness of their implementations are easy to verify.

For every $x \in \{0,1\}^n$ and an initial value $R := (r_1, \ldots, r_l) \in (\{0,1\}^n)^l$, we define

$$g_R(x) = \bigoplus_{i=1}^{l} f(i, x \oplus r_i) \quad \text{and} \quad \mathsf{EXor}(R, x) = f(0, g_R(x)).$$

In [19], Russel *et al.* proved crooked-indifferentiability of the enveloped-xor construction. Their analysis is based on an interesting rejection sampling argument.

1.1 Our Contribution

Another Look at Russel et al.'s Proof. We uncover that the techniques of [19], while novel and interesting, bear significant shortcomings. The consistency of the simulator is not proven. Moreover, their technical treatment requires that the subversion for the final function $f(0, \cdot)$ be independent of g_R. In other words, the proof is applicable against a restricted class of subversion. Finally, the proof does not consider the messages queried to $\mathcal{F}$. We elaborate the issues in Sect. 3.

A New Proof of the Crooked-Indifferentiability of Enveloped XOR. We present a new proof of the crooked-indifferentiability of Enveloped XOR. Interestingly, our techniques do not involve heavy technical machinery. Rather, we identify core domain points related to functions and use simple tools like Markov inequality.

1.2 Overview of Our Technique

We observe the Enveloped XOR (EXoR) construction is in the class of Generalized Domain Extensions considered in [5]. It is known that for a GDE construction with independent functions and preimage awareness, the indifferentiability advantage is bounded by the probability that the final chaining query is not fresh. However, EXoR construction instantiated with the crooked functions (denoted by $\widetilde{\mathsf{EXor}}$) is not part of GDE. The main issue is that the final output of $\widetilde{\mathsf{EXor}}$ need not be the output of $f(0, \cdot)$ evaluation, as required by the condition of GDE.

We consider an intermediate construction $\overline{\mathsf{EXor}}(R, m) = f(0, \tilde{g}_R(m))$. In other words, the intermediate construction restricts that the finalization function $f(0, \cdot)$ is not subverted. $\overline{\mathsf{EXor}}$ is a GDE construction and crooked-indifferentiability of $\overline{\mathsf{EXor}}$ can be proved following the structure of [5]. In particular, the generic simulator of [5], adopted for $\overline{\mathsf{EXor}}$ along with access to $\tilde{f}$ work out here along with the consistency arguments. Our proof is modularized via the following two claims.

- Claim 3 shows distinguishing advantage for $(f, \overline{\mathsf{EXoR}})$ and $(f, \widetilde{\mathsf{EXoR}})$ is bounded by probability of hitting a crooked point or domain point for f_0 (Bad1).
- Claim 4 shows the distinguishing advantage of intermediate world $(f, \overline{\mathsf{EXoR}})$ and the ideal world of crooked indifferentiability is bounded by the probability of Bad2 event. This event is classified into two main categories. In the first

category, while responding to a query to the primitive (or the simulator), input $\tilde{g}_R(m)$ appeared already in the transcript. In the second category, the input $\tilde{g}_R(m)$ appeared in the extended transcript which includes all queries of a subverted computation $\tilde{f}(x)$ of a crooked point x.

The challenge remaining is to bound the probability of the bad events. Our proof works with a counting approach. We say a point $\alpha \in \{0,1\}^n$ is robust with respect to a function f, if all points which queries α is not subverted with all but negligible probability, if the output $f(\alpha)$ is re-sampled. A point is good if it is queried by only a few robust and un-crooked points. By averaging argument, we show that for overwhelming fraction of candidate f, R, for every message m, there will exist an index i such that $m \oplus r_i$ is good for function $f(i, \cdot)$. Now, we can say that even though $f(i, m \oplus r_i)$ was queried by other points, they are robust. If we re-sample at $(i, m \oplus r_i)$ the subverted outputs of those robust points will not change. Thus, we can talk about $\tilde{g}_R(m)$ independently to the outputs of the function $\tilde{f}(0, \cdot)$.

Finally, we shall show that the output distribution of $\tilde{g}_R(m)$ is close to uniform. We could find a rejection resampling lemma on two or more points, and argue the uniformity of $\tilde{g}_R(m)$. However, we simplify things further. We observe that with high probability over the output values of $f(i, m \oplus r_i)$ for every i for which $m \oplus r_i$ is good in f, the transcript of the previous internal queries remains unchanged. Hence, we consider the conditional probabilities by conditioning on all possible transcripts and take union bound to show near uniformity of $\tilde{g}_R(m)$.

Relation of GDE Constructions with Our Results and Further Uses. A majority of this work focuses on $\overline{\text{EXor}}$ construction which is a GDE construction (defined in [5]). GDE constructions cover a wide range of domain extension algorithms. We believe that many ideas developed in this result to deal with the $\overline{\text{EXor}}$ construction can be extended to investigate the crooked-indifferentiability of different GDE constructions. However the bad events and their analysis will depend on the particular construction being investigated.

Revised Proof by Russel et al. After we communicated our findings to the authors of [19], they acknowledged the issues, and uploaded a major revision in eprint [20]. Our proof is done independently and significantly differ from their revised proof in some crucial aspects.

2   Notations and Preliminaries

NOTATIONS. Let $\mathbb{N} = \{0, 1, \ldots\}$ be the set of natural numbers. If $k \in \mathbb{N}$, then $\{0,1\}^k$ denotes the set of all k-bit binary strings. If x and y are two strings xy denote the concatenated string. We write $x \xleftarrow{\$} S$ to denote the process of choosing x uniformly at random from a set S and independently from all other random variables defined so far. For a positive integer l, we use $(l]$ and $[l]$ to denote the set $\{1, \cdots, l\}$ and $\{0, 1, \ldots, l\}$ respectively. The positive integer n is our security parameter and we write $\mathcal{R} := \{0, 1\}^n$.

CLASS OF FUNCTIONS. $\mathsf{H} := \mathsf{H}_{\mathcal{D},n}$ denotes the set of all n-bit functions from $\mathcal{D}$ to $\mathcal{R}$. In this paper we mainly consider $\mathcal{D} :=: [l] \times \{0, 1\}^n$ and let $f : [l] \times \{0, 1\}^n \rightarrow \mathcal{R}$ denotes a family of l many functions from $\{0, 1\}^n$ to itself. *We often use the shorthand f to denote the family $\{f_0 := f(0, \cdot), \cdots, f_l := f(l, \cdot)\}$ when the function family is given as oracles.*

For any tuples of pairs $\tau = ((x_1, y_1), \ldots, (x_s, y_s))$ we write $\mathcal{D}(\tau)$ (called domain of τ) to denote the set $\{x_i : 1 \leq i \leq s\}$. We say a function f agrees with τ if for all $(x, y) \in \tau$, $f(x) = y$. For every $x \in \mathcal{D}$, $\alpha \in \mathcal{R}$, we use $f|_{x \rightarrow \alpha}$(or simply f_α whenever x is understood) to denote the following function:

$$f|_{x \rightarrow \alpha}(y) = \begin{cases} f(y) & \text{if } x \neq y \\ \alpha & \text{if } x = y \end{cases}.$$

Adversaries and Distinguishing Advantage. An *adversary* A is an algorithm possibly with access to oracles $\mathcal{O}_1, \ldots, \mathcal{O}_\ell$ denoted by $\mathsf{A}^{\mathcal{O}_1, \ldots, \mathcal{O}_\ell}$. The adversaries considered in this paper are computationally unbounded. The complexities of these algorithms are measured solely on the number of queries they make. An algorithm $\mathcal{A}$ having access to an oracle is called q-query algorithm if it makes at most q queries to its oracle. Similarly, an oracle algorithm having access to two oracles is called (q_1, q_2)-query algorithm, if it makes at most q_1 and q_2 queries to its first and second oracles respectively. Adversarial queries and the corresponding responses are stored in a transcript τ. So, $\mathcal{D}(\tau)$ denotes the list of inputs (queries) in the transcript.

Definition 1 (Distinguishing Advantage). *Let F^l and G^l be two l-tuples of probabilistic oracle algorithms for some positive integer l. We define* advantage *of an adversary $\mathcal{A}$ at distinguishing F^l from G^l as*

$$\Delta_{\mathcal{A}}(F^l \; ; \; G^l) = \left| \Pr[\mathcal{A}^{F_1, F_2, \cdots, F_l} = 1] - \Pr[\mathcal{A}^{G_1, G_2, \cdots, G_l} = 1] \right|.$$

If $\mathcal{A}$ makes a total of q queries, it is called a q-query distinguisher.

2.1 Modeling Subversion Algorithms and Crooked-Indifferentiability

We recall the related terms and notations introduced in [19] in our terminologies. A $(q, \tilde{q})$ *implementor* is an q-query oracle algorithm $\mathcal{A}^{\mathcal{O}}$. $\mathcal{A}$ outputs the description of another oracle algorithm $\tilde{F}^{\mathcal{O}}$ (called subversion algorithm) which makes at most $\tilde{q}$ many queries to its oracle. For a correct subversion algorithm of a function $f \in \mathsf{H} := \mathsf{H}_{\mathcal{D},n}$, we must have $\tilde{f} := \tilde{F}^f = f$. However, a crooked-implementor may not behave correctly.

Definition 2 (crooked implementer). *A $(q, \tilde{q})$ implementer $\mathcal{A}_1$ is called ϵ-crooked for a function family H, if for every $f \in \mathsf{H}$ and $\tilde{f} \leftarrow \mathcal{A}_1^f$,*

$$\Pr_{\alpha \xleftarrow{\$} \mathcal{D}} [\tilde{f}(\alpha) \neq f(\alpha)] \leq \epsilon.$$

Let τ_0 denote the transcript of oracle queries of $\mathcal{A}_1^f$. We may assume that ϵ is negligible[2] and the transcript τ_0 is hardwired in $\tilde{f}$ and all the $\tilde{q}$ queries made by $\tilde{f}$ are different from $\mathcal{D}(\tau_0)$ (as the response is known from the transcript). The subversion algorithm $\tilde{f}$ on input x queries $\gamma_1(x), \gamma_2(x), \ldots, \gamma_{\tilde{q}}(x)$, and based on the query-responses outputs $\tilde{f}(x)$. Without loss of generality, we assume $\gamma_1(x) = x$. We write $Q(x) := Q_f(x)$ to denote the set of all queries as defined above. We write

$$Q_f^{-1}(y) := \{x : y \in Q_f(x)\},$$

the set of all points x, in which the computation of $\tilde{f}(x)$ queries y. The set does not depend on the value of $f(x)$. Mathematically, let $f_\beta = f|_{y \to \beta}$ then $Q_f^{-1}(y) = Q_{f_\beta}^{-1}(y)$ for all β.

Crooked Indifferentiability. A crooked distinguisher is a two-stage adversary; the first stage is a subverted implementor and the second stage is a distinguisher.

Definition 3 (crooked distinguisher). *We say that a pair $\mathcal{A} := (\mathcal{A}_1, \mathcal{A}_2)$ of probabilistic algorithms $((q_1, \tilde{q}, \epsilon), q_2)$-crooked distinguisher for H if*
(i) $\mathcal{A}_1$ is a ϵ-crooked $(q_1, \tilde{q})$ implementer for H and
(ii) $\mathcal{A}_2(r, \tau_0, \cdot)$ is a q_2-query distinguisher where r is the random coin of $\mathcal{A}_1$, and τ_0 is the advice-string, the transcript of interaction of $\mathcal{A}_1$ with f.

Note that the random coin r of $\mathcal{A}_1$ and the transcript of $\mathcal{A}_1$ are shared with $\mathcal{A}_2$ to emphasis that $\mathcal{A}_1$ and $\mathcal{A}_2$ are joint adversary working in two different stages.

Definition 4 (H-crooked-indifferentiability [19]). *Let $\mathcal{F}$ be an ideal primitive and C be an initial value based $\mathcal{F}$-compatible oracle construction. The construction C is said to be $((q_1, \tilde{q}), (q_2, q_{\mathrm{sim}}), \epsilon, \delta)$-**crooked-indifferentiable** from $\mathcal{F}$ if there is a q_{sim}-query algorithm S (called simulator) such that for all $((q_1, \tilde{q}, \epsilon), q_2)$-crooked distinguisher $(\mathcal{A}_1(r), \mathcal{A}_2(r, \cdot, \cdot))$ for H, we have*

$$\Delta_{\mathcal{A}_2(r, \tau_0, R)}\big((f, C^{\tilde{f}}(R, \cdot)) \; ; \; (S^{\mathcal{F}, \tilde{F}}(\tau_0, R), \mathcal{F})\big) \leq \delta \tag{1}$$

where τ_0 is the advice string of $\mathcal{A}_1^f$ and R is the random initial value of the construction sampled after subverted implementation is set.

TWO-STAGE DISTINGUISHING GAME. Now we explain the distinguishing game. In the first stage, $\mathcal{A}_1^f$ outputs $\tilde{F}$ after interacting with a random oracle f as

---

[2] Given an implementation, one may check the correctness of the algorithm by comparing the outputs of the implementation with a known correct algorithm. More precisely, we sample $\alpha_1, \ldots, \alpha_t \stackrel{\$}{\leftarrow} \{0,1\}^m$ and then for all $0 \leq i \leq l$, we check whether $\tilde{f}(\alpha_i) = f(\alpha_i)$ holds. If it does not hold, the implementation would not be used. It is easy to see that for ϵ-crooked implementation the subversion would not be detected with probability at least $(1 - \epsilon)^t$. So for a negligible ϵ, this probability would be still close to one for all polynomial function t and so the implementation can survive for further use.

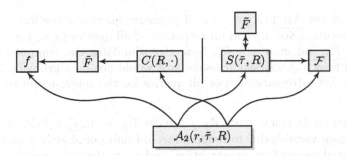

Fig. 1. The crooked-indifferentiability notion. In the first phase of real world, $\mathcal{A}_1$ interacts with f and returns an oracle algorithm $\tilde{F}$ (which would be accessed by the construction C in the second phase). In the second phase the random initial value R will be sampled and given to construction C and also to $\mathcal{A}_2$. In ideal world, simulator $S^{\mathcal{F}}$ gets the transcript of the first phase as advice string, blackbox access to the subverted implementation $\tilde{F}$ and the initial value R.

discussed before. A random initial value R, for the hash construction C is sampled. In the real world, $\mathcal{A}_2$ interacts with the same f of the first stage and the construction $C^{\tilde{f}}(R, \cdot)$. In the ideal world, the simulator S gets the advice-string τ_0, the initial value R and blackbox access to the subverted implementation $\tilde{F}$ and a random oracle $\mathcal{F}$. Simulator is aimed to simulate f so that behavior of $(f, C^{\tilde{f}})$ is as close as $(S, \mathcal{F})$ to the distinguisher $\mathcal{A}_2$ (Fig. 1).

CONVENTION ON CROOKED DISTINGUISHERS: Note that there is no loss to assume that both $\mathcal{A}_1$ and $\mathcal{A}_2$ are deterministic (so we skip the notation r) when we consider computational unbounded adversary[3]. We also assume that $\mathcal{A}_2$ makes all distinct queries and distinct from the queries made by $\mathcal{A}_1$ (as the simulator has the advice string and so it can respond honestly). We skip the notation τ_0 as an input of $\mathcal{A}_2$ as it is fixed throughout the game. As the advice string is fixed, we consider it as part of the transcript. Specifically, the transcript τ_0, view of $\mathcal{A}_2$ at the start of the second stage is set as the advice string τ_0. We fix the advise string τ_0 throughout the paper. We write f to denote the random function agreeing on τ_0. In other words, $f \xleftarrow{\$} \Gamma_{\tau_0} = \{f : f(x) = y, (x, y) \in \tau_0\}$.

Enveloped XOR Construction. Recall that, in the real world, the distinguisher is interacting with the subverted construction $\widetilde{\mathsf{EXor}}$ which is defined as

$$\widetilde{\mathsf{EXor}}(R, M) = \tilde{f}(0, \tilde{g}_R(M)) \quad \text{where} \quad \tilde{g}_R(M) = \bigoplus_{i=1}^{l} \tilde{f}(i, M \oplus r_i).$$

We also define a hybrid construction $\overline{\mathsf{EXor}}[f](R, M) = f(0, \tilde{g}_R(M))$. Now consider an adversary $\mathcal{A}$ interacting with $(f, \overline{\mathsf{EXor}} := \overline{\mathsf{EXor}}[f])$.

---

[3] $\mathcal{A}_1$ can fix the best random coin for which the distinguishing advantage of $\mathcal{A}_2$ is maximum.

ASSUMPTION ON ADVERSARY. For all primitive queries of the form (j, x) with $j > 0$, we return $\overline{\mathsf{EXor}}(m)$ and all responses of all queries $(a, \alpha_a), a \in [l]$ where $\alpha_a = m + R_a$ and $m = x + R_j$. Note that simulator can compute m and so responding $\overline{\mathsf{EXor}}(m)$ honestly for simulator would not be a problem. Moreover, we assume that adversary disclose all queries for the construction to the simulator.

TRANSCRIPT OF INTERACTION. For $j \geq 0$, let $\mathsf{Tr}_j := (R, \tau_j, \pi_j)$ denote the transcript (random variable due to randomness of f only) of $\mathcal{A}$ after j queries where R is the initial value of the construction, and τ_j, π_j denote the query-responses for the primitive and the construction respectively. Note that τ_j contains τ_0 for all j.

3   Revisiting the Crooked Indifferenitability Security of EXoR [19].

A Brief Detour: Classical Indifferentiability Simulator for EXor. Before describing the crooked indifferentiability simulator, we would like to briefly recall the principle behind the indifferentiability simulator and proof principles behind EXor construction in the classical setting.

The goal of the simulator is to simulate each $f(i, \cdot)$ honestly so that for every queried message m, it holds that $\mathsf{EXor}(R, m) = \mathcal{F}(m)$ for all queried m. Without loss of generality, assume that whenever the adversary makes queries $f(i, x)$ for $i > 0$, it also makes queries $f(j, x \oplus r_i \oplus r_j)$ for all $j > 0$ simultaneously. In other words, it makes a batch query of the form $(f(j, m \oplus r_j))_{1 \leq j \leq l}$ for some $m \in \{0, 1\}^n$. We simply say that the adversary $\mathcal{A}$ queries m to g_R and obtains responses $(f(j, m \oplus r_j))_{1 \leq j \leq l}$.

On receiving a batch query $g_R(m)$, the simulator will honestly sample outputs for the corresponding $f(i, m \oplus R_i)$ queries for all $i \in (l]$, and compute $g_R(m)$ by xoring those sampled outputs. Also, the simulator will save the queried m along with the computed $g_R(m)$ in a list L. For a $f(0, x)$ query, the simulator will first search in L, whether for some m, it has given $x = g_R(m)$ as output. If yes, the simulator simply returns $\mathcal{F}(m)$. If no such entry exists, the simulator samples an output z uniformly at random and returns z.

Now, we briefly recall how the indifferentiability is proved for this simulator. There are two bad events.

- for distinct m, m', it holds that $g_R(m) = g_R(m')$. In this case, the simulator, on query $f(0, g_R(m))$ can not be consistent with both $\mathcal{F}(m)$ and $\mathcal{F}(m')$ with any significant probability.
- For a batch query $g_R(m)$ the output is such that it matches with a previous $f(0, .)$ query. In this case, the simulator has already given output to the $f(0, .)$ query which, with all but negligible probability, is not equal to $\mathcal{F}(m)$.

One can indeed summarize these bad events as one; $g_R(m) \in E$, where E is the set of $f(0, .)$ queries made by the adversary.

The Simulator for Crooked Indifferentiability. We now describe the main indea behind the simulator in the crooked indifferentiability setting. The same principle was used in [19]. Note, here the main goal of the simulator is different. It needs to simulate $f \xleftarrow{\$} \mathsf{H}$ as honestly[4] as possible such that $\widetilde{\mathsf{EXor}}(R, m) = \mathcal{F}(m)$ for all queried m. Thus the simulator needs to ensure that the output of the random oracle matches with the *subverted implementation* of EXor.

The simulator maintains a list L of pairs (α, β) to record $f(\alpha) = \beta$ for $\alpha \in \mathcal{D}$ and $\beta \in \{0,1\}^n$. It also maintains a sub-list $L^A \subseteq L$ consisting of all those pairs which are known to the distinguisher. Both lists are initialized to z (the advice-string in the first stage which we fix to any tuple of q_1 pairs). $L_0 = L_0^A = z$. Now we describe how the simulator responds.

1. (Query $f(0, w)$) We call this query a Type-1 Query. Type-1 Queries are returned honestly. If $((0, w), y) \in L$ for some y, the simulator returns the same y. Otherwise, it samples y uniformly from $\{0,1\}^n$, updates the list L and L^A, and returns y.
2. (Query $g_R(m)$) We call this Type-2 Query. For a query $g_R(m)$ (i.e. batch query) the simulator computes $\tilde{f}(\alpha_j)$ for all j, one by one by executing the subverted implementation $\tilde{F}$, where $\alpha_j = (j, m \oplus R_j)$. During this execution, simulator responds honestly to all queries made by the subverted implementation and updates the L-list by incorporating all query responses of h. However, it updates L^A list only with $(\alpha_j, f(\alpha_j))$ for all j. Let $\tilde{g} := \bigoplus_j \tilde{f}(\alpha_j)$. If $(0, \tilde{g}) \in \mathcal{D}(L)$, the simulator **aborts**. If the simulator does not abort, it makes a query $\mathcal{F}(m)$ and adds $((0, \tilde{g}), \mathcal{F}(m))$ into the both lists L and L^A.

For $f(0, w)$ made by $\mathcal{A}_2$ where $w = \tilde{g}_R(m)$ for some previous query m to g_R, the simulator responds as $\mathcal{F}(m)$.

CAUTIONARY NOTE. Even though $\mathcal{F}$ is a random oracle, we cannot say that the probability distribution of the response of $(0, \tilde{g})$ in the ideal world is uniform. Note that, the adversary can choose m after making several consultations with $\mathcal{F}$. In other words, m can be dependent on $\mathcal{F}$. For example, the adversary can choose a message m for which the last bit of $\mathcal{F}(m)$ is zero. Thus, the response for the query $(0, w)$ always has zero as the last bit (which diverts from the uniform distribution). However, the randomness can be considered when we consider joint probability distribution of all query-responses.

Transcript: Now we describe what is the transcript to the distinguisher and for the simulator in more detail. First, we introduce some more relevant notations.

1. Let L^F denote the set of all pairs $(m', \tilde{z})$ of query response of $\mathcal{F}$ by $\mathcal{A}_2$.
2. Let L^g denote the set of all pairs (m, β^l) of query response of g_R oracle (batch query) made by $\mathcal{A}_2$ to the simulator where $\beta^l := (\beta_1, \ldots, \beta_l)$ and $\beta_j = h(j, m \oplus R_j)$ for all j. According to our convention all these m must be queried to $\mathcal{F}$ beforehand.

---

[4] By honestly we mean perfectly simulating a random function. If the responses are already in the list it returns that value, otherwise, it samples a fresh random response and includes the input and output pairs in the list.

3. As we described, we also have two lists, namely L and its sublist L^A, keeping the query responses of h oracle.

Now we define the transcript and partial transcript of the interaction. We recall that q_1 is the number of queries in the first stage and $\mathcal{A}_2$ is a (q_F, q_2)-query algorithm. Let $q = q_2 + q_F$ For any $1 \leq i \leq q$, we define the partial transcript of $\mathcal{A}$ and the simulator as $\tau_i^A := (L_i^F, L_i^A)$ and $\tau_i^S := (L_i, L_i^g)$ respectively, where L_i^F, L_i^A, L_i, L_i^g denote the contents of the corresponding lists just before making ith query of the distinguisher. So when, $i = 1$, $L_1^A = L_1 = z$ and the rest are empty and when $i = q + 1$, these are the final lists of transcripts. Let $\tau_i := (\tau_i^A, \tau_i^S)$ and $\tau := (\tau^A, \tau^S)$ denote the joint transcript on ith query or after completion respectively. As the adversary is deterministic, the simulator is also deterministic for a given h and $\mathcal{F}$, and we have fixed z, a (partial) transcript is completely determined by the choice of R, h and $\mathcal{F}$ (in the ideal world). We write $(R, f, \mathcal{F}) \vdash \tau_i^S$ if the transcript τ_i^S is obtained when the initial value is R, the random oracles are $\mathcal{F}$ and f. We similarly define $(R, f, \mathcal{F}) \vdash \tau_i^A$ and $(R, f, \mathcal{F}) \vdash \tau_i$.

3.1   Techniques of [19]

Overview of the Techniques in [19]. We assume, without any loss of generality that the second stage adversary $\mathcal{A}_2$ queries m to $\mathcal{F}$ before it queries to g_R oracle. In addition, like before, we assume that it makes batch queries.

For every query number i, we define a set $E_i := \mathcal{D}(L_i) \cup \mathsf{subv}_f$ where subv_f is the set of all crooked elements for f. The event BAD_i holds if and only if $(0, \tilde{g}_R(m_i)) \in E_i$ where m_i denotes the ith query of $\mathcal{A}$ (made to g_R oracle of the simulator). So, the crooked indifferentiable advantage is bounded by $\sum_{i=1}^{q_2} \Pr(\tilde{g}_R(m_i) \in E_i)$. The authors wanted to show that the distribution of $\tilde{g}_R(m_i)$ is almost uniform. They proposed the following theorem.

(Theorem 5 from [19]). With overwhelming probability (i.e., one minus a negligible amount) there exists a set $\mathcal{R}_{\tau_0} \subseteq (\{0, 1\}^n)^l$ and for every i, a set of transcripts $\mathcal{T}_i^A$ (before ith query) such that for all $R \in \mathcal{R}_{\tau_0}$, $\tau_i := (L_i^F, L_i^A) \in \mathcal{T}_i^A$, and $m \notin \mathcal{D}(L_i^g)$,

$$\Pr_f[(0, \tilde{g}_R(m)) \in E_i \mid (R, f, \mathcal{F}) \vdash \tau_i] \leq \text{poly}(n)\sqrt{|E_i|} + \text{negl}(n).$$

The authors claimed that crooked indifferentiability of EXor can be derived from the above theorem. To describe the issues we need to dive into the main idea which is to show that $\tilde{g}_R(m)$ behaves close to the uniform distribution over $\{0, 1\}^n$. Thus the above probability would be negligible as $q_1/2^n$ and $|\mathsf{subv}_f|/2^n$ is negligible. By using Markov inequality, authors are able to identify a set of overwhelming amount of pairs (R, f), called *unpredictable* pair, such that for any unpredictable (R, f) all m, there exists an index i such that

1. $\Pr_\beta[\alpha_i \in \mathsf{subv}_f \mid f(\alpha_i) = \beta]$ is negligible and
2. $\alpha_j \notin Q_f^{-1}(\alpha_i)$ for all $j \neq i$, where $\alpha_j = m \oplus R_i$.

Thus, if we resample $\beta = f(\alpha_i)$ then with overwhelming probability $\tilde{f}|_{\alpha_i \to \beta}(\alpha_i) = f|_{\alpha_i \to \beta}(\alpha)$ (i.e. α_i is not crooked and returned a random value) and all corresponding values for indices j different from i will remain same. So, $\tilde{g}_R(m) = \beta + A$ where A does not depend on choice of β. Thus, the modified distribution is close to uniform (as almost all values of β will be good). In particular the authors made the following claim:

Claim 1. *Under the modified distribution (i.e. after resampling),* $\Pr[\tilde{g}_R(m) \in E_1] \leq q_1/2^n + \epsilon + p_n$ *where* p_n *denotes the probability that a random pair* (R, f) *is not unpredictable.*

As the choice of i depends on the function f and so a new rejection resampling lemma is used to bound the probability of the event under the original distribution (i.e. before resampling).

Lemma 1 (Rejection Resampling [19]). *Let* $X := (X_1, \ldots, X_k)$ *be a random variable uniform on* $\Omega = \Omega_1 \times \Omega_2 \times \cdots \times \Omega_k$. *Let* $A : \Omega \to (k)$ *and define* $Z = (Z_1, \ldots, Z_k)$ *where* $Z_i = A_i$ *except at* $j = A(X^k)$ *for which* Z_j *is sampled uniformly and independently of remaining random variables. Then for any event* $S \subseteq \Omega$, *it holds that*

$$|S|/|\Omega| \leq \sqrt{k \Pr(Z \in S)}$$

With this rejection resampling result and the Claim 1, the authors concluded the following under original distribution:

$$\Pr_{h*}(\tilde{g}_R(x) \in E_1) \leq \sqrt{l \cdot \Pr_{\text{resampled } h}(\tilde{g}_R(x) \in E_1)} \leq \sqrt{l \cdot (q_1/2^n + \epsilon + p_n)}.$$

3.2   Issues with the Technique of [19]

Now we are ready to describe the issues and the limitations of the techniques in [19]. To prove the general case (i.e. for any query), the authors provide a proof sketch where they argued that with an overwhelming probability of realizable transcript $\mathcal{T}$ and for all $\tau \in \mathcal{T}$, $\Pr(\tilde{g}_R(m_i) \in E_i \mid \tau)$ is negligible.

The Number of Queries to $\mathcal{F}$ is Essential. An incompleteness of the proof of [19] comes from the fact that the analysis does not consider the $\mathcal{F}$ queries of the distinguisher. The bound is almost vanishing if $q_1 = 0$ and $q_2 = 2$ and there is no crooked point. However, a distinguisher can search for $m \neq m'$ such that $\mathcal{F}(m) = \mathcal{F}(m')$. Conditioned on collision at the final output, the event $g_R(m) = g_R(m')$ holds with probability about $1/2$. On the other hand, for the honest simulation of all f values, g value will collide with very low probability. If the adversary can make $2^{n/2}$ many queries to $\mathcal{F}$, the above inconsistency can be forced. Hence, *the probability upper bound of Theorem 5 of* [19] *can not be independent of the number of queries made to* $\mathcal{F}$.

Inconsistency for Multiple Queries: Controlling Query Dependencies for the Same Index. Authors claimed that for all unpredictable (R, h), for all m, an index i exists on which the resampling can be done *without affecting the transcript*. Recalling the notion of unpredictable (R, h) we see that the resampling is done on an index i, that is honest ($\tilde{f}(i, m \oplus R_i) = f(i, m \oplus R_i)$), and $f(i, m \oplus R_i)$ is not queried by $f(j, m \oplus R_j)$ for any other j. From here, the authors argued that the transcript of the interaction remains same, if we resample at such i. This claim is justified for a single message and not for multiple queries. We note that it is easy to construct a subverted implementation $\tilde{F}$ for which all inputs of f for a batch response are queried during some other previous query. For example, if it queries $f(i, x \oplus 1^n)$ for an input (i, x), and the distinguisher makes two batch queries queries, $\tilde{g}_R(m \oplus 1^n)$, and $\tilde{g}_R(m)$. The simulator, while simulating $\tilde{g}_R(m \oplus 1^n)$ responds to all the queries made by $\tilde{f}(i, m \oplus 1^n \oplus R_i)$, and in particular the value of $f(i, m \oplus R_i)$ is now gets fixed. *So an appropriate analysis was missing in case of multiple queries.*

The Bad Event E_i Depends on the Function f. The main technical claim of [19] that $\Pr_{\text{resampled } f}(\tilde{g}_R(x) \in E)$ is small because $\tilde{g}_R(x)$ is uniformly distributed under resampling distribution of f and size of E is negligibly small. However the crooked set of $f(0, \cdot)$ may depend on the other functions $f(1, \cdot), \ldots, f(\cdot)$. Thus the event E is not independent of $\tilde{g}_R(x)$. In particular, one cannot upper bound the $\Pr(\tilde{g}_R(x) \in E)$ as $|E|/2^n$. This is one of the crucial observation which actually makes the crooked security analysis quite a complex task.

4   Basic Setup: Good Pairs and Critical Set

SUBVERTED INPUTS. For a function $f \colon \mathcal{D} \to \mathcal{R}$ agreeing on τ_0, we define

$$\mathsf{subv}_f = \{x \mid x \in \mathsf{Dom}(\tau_0) \vee \tilde{f}(x) \neq f(x)\},$$

union of the set of all subverted points for the function f and the $\mathsf{Dom}(\tau_0)$. We consider elements of the domain of τ_0 as subverted points as the outputs of those have no entropy and is hard coded into an implementation. Thus, we treat all those inputs as subverted points. Clearly, for all function f,

$$|\mathsf{subv}_f| \leq q_1 + \epsilon|\mathcal{D}|.$$

where q_1 denotes the size of τ_0. Let $\epsilon_1 := \epsilon + q_1/|\mathcal{D}|$.

Definition 5 (robust point). *Let f agree on τ_0. A point y is called* robust *in f (or the pair (y, f) is called robust) if for all $x \in Q_f^{-1}(y)$,*

$$\Pr_{\beta} \left[x \in \mathsf{subv}_{f_\beta} \right] \leq \sqrt{\epsilon_1}$$

where $\beta \xleftarrow{\$} \mathcal{R}$ and $f_\beta := f|_{y \to \beta}$.

Note that robustness of y in f does not depend on the value $f(y)$. In other words, if y is robust in f then so in $f|_{y \to \beta}$ for all β.

Definition 6 (popular point). *A point* $y \notin \mathrm{Dom}(\tau_0)$ *is called* popular *for a function* f *if* $|Q_f^{-1}(y)| > \epsilon_1^{-1/4}$.

Recall that the subversion algorithm $\tilde{f}$ makes at most $\tilde{q}$ many queries for any y. So, $\sum_y |Q_f^{-1}(y)| \leq \tilde{q}|\mathcal{D}|$. Using the simple averaging argument the number of popular points are at most $\tilde{q}\epsilon_1^{\frac{1}{4}}|\mathcal{D}|$.

$$\Pr_{x,f}[x \text{ is popular in } f] \leq \tilde{q}\epsilon_1^{\frac{1}{4}} \tag{2}$$

We call the robust pair (y, f) **good** if (1) y is not popular for f and (2) for all $x \in Q_f^{-1}(y)$, $x \notin \mathrm{subv}_f$. In particular for good (y, f), it holds that $y \notin \mathrm{subv}_f$ and $y \notin \mathrm{subv}_{f_\beta}$ with high probability over randomness of β where $f_\beta := f|_{y \to \beta}$.

Lemma 2. *For a random* $y \xleftarrow{\$} \mathcal{D}$, *we have*

$$\Pr_{y,f}[(y, f) \text{ is not good}] \leq 3\tilde{q}\epsilon_1^{\frac{1}{4}}.$$

Proof. We define two indicator functions:

$$d(x, f) = \begin{cases} 1, & \text{if } x \in \mathrm{subv}_f \\ 0, & \text{otherwise} \end{cases} \qquad d_{j,\beta}(x, f) = \begin{cases} 1, & \text{if } x \in \mathrm{subv}_{f|_{\gamma_j^{(x)} \to \beta}} \\ 0, & \text{otherwise.} \end{cases}$$

In other words, $d(x, f)$ simply indicator function for capturing crooked points and $d_{j,\beta}(x, f)$ is an indicator function capturing whether a point x becomes crooked for f after replacing the jth query output by β. For $1 \leq j \leq \tilde{q}$, let $D^j(x, f) = \mathbb{E}_\beta(d_{j,\beta}(x, f))$. For any function $g \in \Gamma_{\tau_0}$, let $\mathcal{S}_{x,g} := \{(f, \beta) : f|_{\gamma_j^{(x)} \to \beta} = g\}$. It is easy to see that we have $|\mathcal{S}_{x,g}| = 2^n$. Now, for each j,

$$\mathbb{E}_{x,f}(D^j(x, f)) = \mathbb{E}_{x,f} \mathbb{E}_\beta (d_{j,\beta}(x, f))$$

$$= \sum_{x,f,\beta} \Pr(f) \Pr(x) \Pr(\beta) \cdot d_{j,\beta}(x, f)$$

$$= 2^{-n} \sum_{(f,\beta) \in \mathcal{S}_{x,g}} \sum_{x,g} \Pr(g) \Pr(x) \cdot d(x, g)$$

$$= \sum_{x,g} \Pr(g) \Pr(x) \cdot d(x, g)$$

$$= \mathbb{E}_{x,g} d(x, g) \leq \epsilon + \frac{q_1}{|\mathcal{D}|} := \epsilon_1$$

Applying Markov inequality, we get for every $j \in (\tilde{q}]$

$$\Pr_{x,f}\left[D^j(x,f) \geq \epsilon_1^{\frac{1}{2}}\right] \leq \frac{\mathbb{E}_{x,f}\left(D^j(x,f)\right)}{\epsilon^{\frac{1}{2}}} \leq \epsilon_1^{\frac{1}{2}} \qquad (3)$$

We recall there are three ways x can be not good in f.

$$\Pr_{f,x}\left[(x,f) \text{ is not good}\right] \leq \Pr_{f,x}\left[x \text{ is popular for f}\right] +$$

$$\Pr_{f,x}\left[x \text{ is queried by some point in subv}_f\right] +$$

$$\Pr_{f,x}\left[(x,f) \text{ is not robust} \mid x \text{ is not popular for f}\right]$$

As there are at most $\epsilon_1|\mathcal{D}|$ many points in subv_f,

$$\Pr_{f,x}\left[x \text{ is queried by some point in subv}_f\right] \leq \tilde{q}\epsilon_1.$$

From the definition of robust points and Eq. 3

$$\Pr_{x,f}\left[x \text{ is non robust in f} \mid x \text{ is not popular for f}\right] \leq \epsilon_1^{-1/4}\sum_{j=1}^{\tilde{q}}\Pr_{x,f}\left[D^j(x,f) \geq \epsilon_1^{\frac{1}{2}}\right]$$

$$\leq \tilde{q}\epsilon_1^{\frac{1}{4}}$$

Adding above two inequalities and Eq. 2

$$\Pr_{f,x}\left[x \text{ is not good in f}\right] \leq \tilde{q}\left(\epsilon_1 + \epsilon_1^{\frac{1}{4}} + \epsilon_1^{\frac{1}{4}}\right) \leq 3\tilde{q}\epsilon_1^{\frac{1}{4}}$$

$\square$

Critical Set. We consider a set $\mathcal{G}$ of pairs (R, f) of initial values R and functions f satisfying the condition that for every $m \in \{0,1\}^n$ there exists $1 \leq i \leq l$ such that $(\alpha_i := (i, m \oplus R_i), f)$ is good. The following lemma says that for a uniform random string R (initial value) and a randomly chosen function f agreeing on τ_0, with high probability (R,f) is in the critical set.

Lemma 3. *Let* $\tilde{q} \leq 2^{n/2}, \epsilon_1 \leq \frac{1}{2^{16}}$ *and* $\ell > 2n$. *It holds that*

$$\Pr_{R,f}((R,f) \notin \mathcal{G}) \leq 3\tilde{q}\epsilon_1^{1/8} + 2^{-n}.$$

Proof. We know that $\Pr_f\left[\Pr_x[(x,f) \text{ is not good}] > \epsilon_1^{1/8}\right] \leq 3\tilde{q}\epsilon_1^{1/8}$. We say f is convenient if $\Pr_x[(x,f) \text{ is not good}] \leq \epsilon_1^{1/8}$. Fix a convenient f

$$\Pr_R[(R,f) \notin \mathcal{G}]$$

$$\leq \sum_m\prod_{i=1}^{l}\left(\Pr_{R_i}[(i, m \oplus R_i) \text{ is not good in } f]\right)$$

$$\leq 2^n \times \left(\epsilon_1^{1/8}\right)^l \leq 1/2^n.$$

In the first step, the sum is taken over $m \in \{0,1\}^n$. The last inequality follows from $l > n$, and $\epsilon_1 \leq \frac{1}{2^{16}}$. Hence, we have

$$\Pr_{R,f}((R,f) \notin \mathcal{G}) \leq \Pr_f [f \text{ is not convenient}] + \Pr_R [(R,f) \notin \mathcal{G}|f \text{ is convenient}]$$

$$\leq 3\tilde{q}\epsilon_1^{1/8} + 1/2^n. \qquad \qquad \square$$

5   Crooked-Indifferentiability of Enveloped XOR Construction

In this section we analyze the crooked-indifferentiability security of the EXOR construction. Our main result in this section is Theorem 2.

Theorem 2. *Let* $l = 3n + 1, \tilde{q} \leq 2^{n/2}$ *and* $\epsilon_1 = \epsilon + \frac{q_1}{(l+1)2^n} \leq \frac{1}{16}$. *Let* $f : [l] \times \{0,1\}^n \to \{0,1\}^n$ *be a family of random functions and* $\mathsf{EXor} : \{0,1\}^n \to \{0,1\}^n$ *be the enveloped-xor construction. Then there exists a simulator S such that for all all* $((q_1, \tilde{q}), (q_2, q_{sim}), \epsilon, \delta)$ *crooked distinguisher* $\mathcal{A} = (\mathcal{A}_1, \mathcal{A}_2)$

$$\mathbf{Adv}_{\mathcal{A},(\mathsf{EXor},f)}^{\text{crooked-indiff}} \leq (4l^2\tilde{q})q_2^2/2^n + (4\tilde{q} + 2l)q_2\epsilon_1^{1/16}$$

The simulator is described in Fig. 2 which makes at most q_2 query to the random oracle $\mathcal{F}$ and makes $q_2 l \tilde{q}$ many calls to the subverted implementation $\tilde{f}$.

Proof. We recall that, in the real world, the distinguisher is interacting with the subverted construction $\widetilde{\mathsf{EXor}}$ which is defined as

$$\widetilde{\mathsf{EXor}}(R, m) = \tilde{f}(0, \tilde{g}_R(m)) \quad \text{where} \quad \tilde{g}_R(m) = \bigoplus_{i=1}^{l} \tilde{f}(i, m \oplus r_i).$$

We also define a hybrid construction $\overline{\mathsf{EXor}}[f](R, m) = f(0, \tilde{g}_R(m))$. Now consider an adversary $\mathcal{A}$ interacting with $(f, \overline{\mathsf{EXor}} := \overline{\mathsf{EXor}}[f])$ in the second phase.

Bad Events. We consider the bad event happening immediately after ith query of the adversary which is of the form (j, x_i) for $j > 0$. We write $m_i = x_i + R_j$. We define four bad events.

1. BAD1_i holds if $(0, \tilde{g}_R(m_i)) \in \mathsf{subv}_f$
2. $\text{BAD2}a_i$ holds if $(0, \tilde{g}_R(m_i)) \in \mathsf{Dom}(\tau_{i-1})$
3. $\text{BAD2}b_i$ holds if $\tilde{g}_R(m_i) = \tilde{g}(m_j)$ for some $j < i$
4. $\text{BAD2}c_i$ holds if $(0, \tilde{g}_R(m_i)) \in Q(x)$ for some $x \in \mathsf{Dom}(\tau_i)$ and $x \in \mathsf{subv}_f$.

Let $\text{BAD1} = \vee_i \text{BAD1}_i$, $\text{BAD2} = \vee_i(\text{BAD2}a_i \vee \text{BAD2}b_i \vee \text{BAD2}c_i)$, and $\text{BAD} = \text{BAD1} \vee \text{BAD2}$.

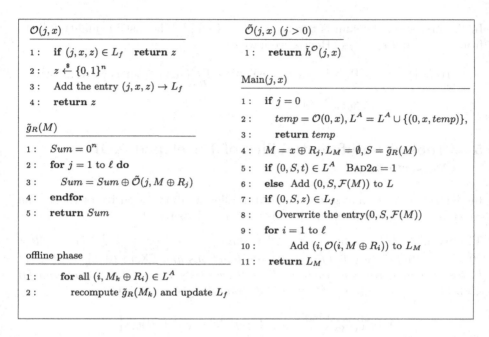

Fig. 2. Simulator for EXor: Offline Phase is executed after all the distinguisher queries.

Claim 3

$$\Delta_{\mathcal{A}_2(r,\tilde{\tau},R)}\big((f, \overline{EXor}(R,\cdot)) \; ; \; (f, \widetilde{EXor}(R,\cdot))\big) \leq \Pr(\text{Bad1})$$

where Bad1 holds while $\mathcal{A}$ interacting with $(f, \overline{EXor})$.

Proof of the above claim is straightforward as both worlds behave identically until Bad1 does not hold.

We have defined our simulator $S^{\mathcal{F}}$ in Fig. 2 where $\mathcal{F} : \{0,1\}^n \to \{0,1\}^n$ is a random function. The simulator has also observed the above bad events in particular, Bad2. Now we claim that the hybrid construction and the ideal world is indistinguishable provided Bad2 does not hold (in the hybrid world) while $\mathcal{A}$ interacting with $(f, \overline{EXor})$.

Claim 4

$$\Delta_{\mathcal{A}_2(r,\tilde{\tau},R)}\big((f, \overline{EXor}(R,\cdot)) \; ; \; (S^{\mathcal{F},\tilde{f}}(\tilde{\tau}, R), \mathcal{F})\big) \leq \Pr(\text{Bad2}).$$

We call a transcript good if Bad2 does not hold. In case of simulator world, whenever Bad2 does not hold, simulator maintains extended transcript which is consistent with the hybrid world. As the simulator set all outputs of the function either randomly or through outputs of $\mathcal{F}$, realizing any such good transcript τ' has probability $2^{-n\sigma}$ where $\sigma = |\tau' \setminus \tau_0|$. We have already seen that the probability of realizing a good transcript in the hybrid world is exactly $2^{-n\sigma}$. In other words, the both worlds behave identically until BAD2 does not hold. Combining Claims 3 and 4, we get

$$\mathbf{Adv}^{\text{crooked-indiff}}_{\mathcal{A},(\text{EXor},f)} \leq \Pr[\text{BAD}].$$

The proof of Theorem 2 follows from the following lemma. □

Lemma 4

$$\Pr[\text{BAD}] \leq (4l^2\tilde{q})q_2^2/2^n + (4\tilde{q} + 2l)q_2\epsilon_1^{1/16}$$

The lemma is proved in Sect. 6.

6 Proof of Lemma 4

We write $f \Rightarrow_j \text{Tr}_j$ to denote the event that after j queries to $(f, \overline{\text{EXor}})$, an adversary obtains the transcript Tr_j. We skip the notation j if it is understood from the context.

Definition 7. *A transcript* Tr_{i-1} *is good if*

$$\Pr((R,\mathsf{f}) \in \mathcal{G} \mid \mathsf{f} \Rightarrow \text{Tr}_{i-1}) \geq 1 - 3\tilde{q}\epsilon_1^{1/16}.$$

Applying Markov inequality on Lemma 3, we have $\Pr(\text{Tr}_{i-1}$ is good) $\geq 1 - \epsilon_1^{1/16}$. Let us fix a good transcript Tr_{i-1} (which also determines m_i for the ith query) and a function f agreeing on Tr_{i-1} such that $(R,f) \in \mathcal{G}$.

Definition 8. *For any fix* k, *we say that* f *is called* Tr_i-*good if (i)* $f \Rightarrow \text{Tr}_{i-1}$ *and (ii)* (α_k, f) *is good.*

Claim 5. *For any* Tr_i-*good* f *there exists a set* S *of size at least* $2^n(1 - \epsilon_1^{1/4})$ *such that for all* $\beta \in S$, $f_\beta := f|_{\alpha \to \beta}$ *is also* Tr_i-*good.*

Proof. We fix a function $f \in \Gamma_{R,\tau_{i-1},\pi_{i-1}}$ such that (α_k, f) is Tr_i-good. Now we identify a set of good values of β such that $f_\beta := f|_{\alpha_k \to \beta} \in \Gamma_{R,\tau_{i-1},\pi_{i-1}}$ such that (α_k, f) is Tr_i-good. In other words, setting the output of f on the point α_k to β keeps the pair (α_k, f_β) good. For every $x \in \text{Dom}(\tau_{i-1}) \cap Q_f^{-1}(\alpha_k)$, let B_x denote the set of all bad β values for which good condition of (α_k, f) gets violated. By definition, $|B_x| \leq \epsilon_1^{1/2}$ and hence $|\cup_x B_x| \leq 2^n\epsilon_1^{1/4}$. We define

$$S = \mathcal{D} \setminus \cup_{x \in Q_f^{-1}(\alpha_k)} B_x.$$

Note that for all $\beta \in S$, (α_k, f_β) is Tr_i-good. □

Due to the above claim, we have

$$\Pr(\mathsf{f}(\alpha_k) = z \mid (\alpha_k, \mathsf{f}) \text{ is } \mathsf{Tr}_i\text{-good},) \leq \frac{1}{|S|} \leq \frac{1}{2^n(1 - \epsilon_1^{1/4})} \leq \frac{2}{2^n}.$$

The last inequality holds because $\epsilon_1 \leq \frac{1}{16}$. Now note that for any event E, we have

$$\Pr_{\mathsf{f}}(E|\mathsf{Tr}_{i-1}) \leq \Pr_{\mathsf{f}}(E \wedge (R, \mathsf{f}) \in \mathcal{G}|\mathsf{Tr}_{i-1}) + 3\tilde{q}\epsilon_1^{1/16}$$

$$\leq \sum_{k=1}^{l} \Pr_{\mathsf{f}}(E \wedge (\alpha_k, \mathsf{f}) \text{ is } \mathsf{Tr}_{i-1}\text{-good} \mid \mathsf{Tr}_{i-1}) + 3\tilde{q}\epsilon_1^{1/16}$$

$$\leq \sum_{k=1}^{l} \Pr_{\mathsf{f}}(E \mid (\alpha_k, \mathsf{f}) \text{ is } \mathsf{Tr}_{i-1}\text{-good}) + 3\tilde{q}\epsilon_1^{1/16}$$

For the last inequality we simply use the fact that

$$\Pr_{\mathsf{f}}((\alpha_k, \mathsf{f}) \text{ is } \mathsf{Tr}_{i-1}\text{-good} \mid \mathsf{Tr}_{i-1}) \leq 1.$$

Now we bound individually each bad events and then we can multiply by l then add all the terms to get the bound.

Bound of $\Pr(\text{BAD}2a_i \cup \text{BAD}2b_i)$. Fix a Tr_i-good f. Let $B2$ denote the set of all elements containing $\tilde{g}_R(m_j)$ (for all $j < i$) and all elements from $\mathcal{D}(\tau_{i-1})$ of the form $(0, *)$. Note that the set $B2$ and $\sum_{j \neq k} \tilde{f}(m_i + R_j)$ does not depend on the value $f(\alpha_k)$ provided $f(\alpha_k) \in S$. Hence,

$$\Pr_{\mathsf{f}}(\text{BAD}2a_i \cup \text{BAD}2b_i \mid (\alpha_k, \mathsf{f}) \text{ is } \mathsf{Tr}_{i-1}\text{-good}) \leq 2i/2^n.$$

Bound of $\Pr(\text{BAD}2c_i)$. We first note that for all $\beta \in S$ and an input x which queries α_k, x is not crooked and a robust point. Let $A = \mathcal{D}(\tau_i)\backslash(\{\alpha_k\}\cup Q_f^{-1}(\alpha_k))$. Let $\tilde{A}$ denote the set of all points queried by the elements of A. Suppose $\tilde{g}_R(m_i) \notin \tilde{A}$. Then, for every x from the domain of τ_i querying $\tilde{g}_R(m_i)$ must query α_k and hence $\text{BAD}2c_i$ does not hold. So, $\text{BAD}2c_i$ can hold only if $\tilde{g}_R(m_i) \in \tilde{A}$. Once again by randomness of $f(\alpha_k)$, we have

$$\Pr(\text{BAD}2c_i \mid (\alpha_k, \mathsf{f}) \text{ is } \mathsf{Tr}_{i-1}\text{-good}) \leq 2\tilde{q}il/2^n.$$

Bound of $\Pr(\text{BAD}1_i)$. Clearly, $\tilde{f}_\beta(x)$ can be different from $\tilde{f}(x)$, only if $x \in Q_f^{-1}(\alpha_k)$. Moreover for every $x \in Q_f^{-1}(\alpha_k)$, as both (α_k, f) and (α_k, f_β) are good, it holds that $x \notin \mathsf{subv}_f$ and $x \notin \mathsf{subv}_{f_b}$. Thus for any such Tr_i-good f, f_β, we have the following conditions: $\mathsf{subv}_f = \mathsf{subv}_{f_\beta}$. Thus,

$$\Pr[\text{BAD}1_i \mid (\alpha_k, f) \text{ good}, \mathsf{Tr}_i \text{ good}] \leq 2\epsilon_1$$

So,

$$\Pr[\text{BAD}_i \mid \text{Tr}_{i-1}] \leq 4l^2 q_2 \tilde{q}/2^n + 2l\epsilon_1 + 3\tilde{q}\epsilon_1^{1/16}$$

Finally, we add the probability that we realize a not good transcript Tr_{i-1} and we obtain bound for $\Pr(\text{BAD}_i)$. By taking union bound over $i \in [q_2]$, we get

$$\Pr[\text{BAD}] \leq 4l^2 q_2^2 \tilde{q}/2^n + 2lq_2\epsilon_1 + 3\tilde{q}q_2\epsilon_1^{1/16} + q_2\epsilon_1^{1/16}$$
$$\leq (4l^2\tilde{q})q_2^2/2^n + (4\tilde{q} + 2l)q_2\epsilon_1^{1/16}$$

This finishes the proof of Lemma 4.   □

References

1. Andreeva, E., Mennink, B., Preneel, B.: On the indifferentiability of the Grøstl hash function. In: Garay, J.A., De Prisco, R. (eds.) SCN 2010. LNCS, vol. 6280, pp. 88–105. Springer, Heidelberg (2010). https://doi.org/10.1007/978-3-642-15317-4_7
2. Bellare, M., Paterson, K.G., Rogaway, P.: Security of symmetric encryption against mass surveillance. In: Garay, J.A., Gennaro, R. (eds.) CRYPTO 2014, Part I. LNCS, vol. 8616, pp. 1–19. Springer, Heidelberg (2014). https://doi.org/10.1007/978-3-662-44371-2_1
3. Bellare, M., Rogaway, P.: The security of triple encryption and a framework for code-based game-playing proofs. In: Vaudenay, S. (ed.) EUROCRYPT 2006. LNCS, vol. 4004, pp. 409–426. Springer, Heidelberg (2006). https://doi.org/10.1007/11761679_25
4. Bertoni, G., Daemen, J., Peeters, M., Van Assche, G.: On the indifferentiability of the sponge construction. In: Smart, N. (ed.) EUROCRYPT 2008. LNCS, vol. 4965, pp. 181–197. Springer, Heidelberg (2008). https://doi.org/10.1007/978-3-540-78967-3_11
5. Bhattacharyya, R., Mandal, A., Nandi, M.: Indifferentiability characterization of hash functions and optimal bounds of popular domain extensions. In: Roy, B., Sendrier, N. (eds.) INDOCRYPT 2009. LNCS, vol. 5922, pp. 199–218. Springer, Heidelberg (2009). https://doi.org/10.1007/978-3-642-10628-6_14
6. Bhattacharyya, R., Mandal, A., Nandi, M.: Security analysis of the mode of JH hash function. In: Hong, S., Iwata, T. (eds.) FSE 2010. LNCS, vol. 6147, pp. 168–191. Springer, Heidelberg (2010). https://doi.org/10.1007/978-3-642-13858-4_10
7. Chang, D., Nandi, M.: Improved indifferentiability security analysis of ChopMD hash function. In: Nyberg, K. (ed.) FSE 2008. LNCS, vol. 5086, pp. 429–443. Springer, Heidelberg (2008). https://doi.org/10.1007/978-3-540-71039-4_27
8. Coretti, S., Dodis, Y., Guo, S., Steinberger, J.: Random oracles and non-uniformity. In: Nielsen, J.B., Rijmen, V. (eds.) EUROCRYPT 2018, Part I. LNCS, vol. 10820, pp. 227–258. Springer, Cham (2018). https://doi.org/10.1007/978-3-319-78381-9_9
9. Coron, J.-S., Dodis, Y., Malinaud, C., Puniya, P.: Merkle-Damgård revisited: how to construct a hash function. In: Shoup, V. (ed.) CRYPTO 2005. LNCS, vol. 3621, pp. 430–448. Springer, Heidelberg (2005). https://doi.org/10.1007/11535218_26
10. Degabriele, J.P., Paterson, K.G., Schuldt, J.C.N., Woodage, J.: Backdoors in pseudorandom number generators: possibility and impossibility results. In: Robshaw, M., Katz, J. (eds.) CRYPTO 2016, Part I. LNCS, vol. 9814, pp. 403–432. Springer, Heidelberg (2016). https://doi.org/10.1007/978-3-662-53018-4_15

11. Dodis, Y., Guo, S., Katz, J.: Fixing cracks in the concrete: random oracles with auxiliary input, revisited. In: Coron, J.-S., Nielsen, J.B. (eds.) EUROCRYPT 2017, Part II. LNCS, vol. 10211, pp. 473–495. Springer, Cham (2017). https://doi.org/10.1007/978-3-319-56614-6_16

12. Dodis, Y., Reyzin, L., Rivest, R.L., Shen, E.: Indifferentiability of permutation-based compression functions and tree-based modes of operation, with applications to MD6. In: Dunkelman, O. (ed.) FSE 2009. LNCS, vol. 5665, pp. 104–121. Springer, Heidelberg (2009). https://doi.org/10.1007/978-3-642-03317-9_7

13. Maurer, U., Renner, R., Holenstein, C.: Indifferentiability, impossibility results on reductions, and applications to the random oracle methodology. In: Naor, M. (ed.) TCC 2004. LNCS, vol. 2951, pp. 21–39. Springer, Heidelberg (2004). https://doi.org/10.1007/978-3-540-24638-1_2

14. Mennink, B.: Indifferentiability of double length compression functions. In: Stam, M. (ed.) IMACC 2013. LNCS, vol. 8308, pp. 232–251. Springer, Heidelberg (2013). https://doi.org/10.1007/978-3-642-45239-0_14

15. Moody, D., Paul, S., Smith-Tone, D.: Improved indifferentiability security bound for the JH mode. Cryptology ePrint Archive, Report 2012/278 (2012). http://eprint.iacr.org/2012/278

16. Naito, Y.: Indifferentiability of double-block-length hash function without feed-forward operations. In: Pieprzyk, J., Suriadi, S. (eds.) ACISP 2017, Part II. LNCS, vol. 10343, pp. 38–57. Springer, Cham (2017). https://doi.org/10.1007/978-3-319-59870-3_3

17. Russell, A., Tang, Q., Yung, M., Zhou, H.-S.: Cliptography: clipping the power of kleptographic attacks. In: Cheon, J.H., Takagi, T. (eds.) ASIACRYPT 2016, Part II. LNCS, vol. 10032, pp. 34–64. Springer, Heidelberg (2016). https://doi.org/10.1007/978-3-662-53890-6_2

18. Russell, A., Tang, Q., Yung, M., Zhou, H.S.: Generic semantic security against a kleptographic adversary. In: Thuraisingham, B.M., Evans, D., Malkin, T., Xu, D. (eds.) ACM CCS 2017, pp. 907–922. ACM Press (2017). https://doi.org/10.1145/3133956.3133993

19. Russell, A., Tang, Q., Yung, M., Zhou, H.-S.: Correcting subverted random oracles. In: Shacham, H., Boldyreva, A. (eds.) CRYPTO 2018, Part II. LNCS, vol. 10992, pp. 241–271. Springer, Cham (2018). https://doi.org/10.1007/978-3-319-96881-0_9

20. Russell, A., Tang, Q., Yung, M., Zhou, H., Zhu, J.: Correcting subverted random oracles. IACR Cryptol. ePrint Arch. 2021, 42 (2021). https://eprint.iacr.org/2021/042

21. Young, A., Yung, M.: The dark side of black-box cryptography or: should we trust capstone? In: Koblitz, N. (ed.) CRYPTO 1996. LNCS, vol. 1109, pp. 89–103. Springer, Heidelberg (1996). https://doi.org/10.1007/3-540-68697-5_8

Sequential Indifferentiability
of Confusion-Diffusion Networks

Qi Da[1,2], Shanjie Xu[1,2], and Chun Guo[1,2,3(✉)]

[1] Key Laboratory of Cryptologic Technology and Information Security of Ministry
of Education, Shandong University, Qingdao 266237, Shandong, China
[2] School of Cyber Science and Technology, Shandong University,
Qingdao, Shandong, China
{daqi,shanjie1997}@mail.sdu.edu.cn, chun.guo@sdu.edu.cn
[3] State Key Laboratory of Information Security, Institute of Information
Engineering, Chinese Academy of Sciences, Beijing 100093, China

Abstract. A large proportion of modern symmetric cryptographic
building blocks are designed using the Substitution-Permutation
Networks (SPNs), or more generally, Shannon's confusion-diffusion
paradigm. To justify its theoretical soundness, Dodis et al. (EURO-
CRYPT 2016) recently introduced the theoretical model of *confusion-
diffusion networks*, which may be viewed as keyless SPNs using *random
permutations* as S-boxes and combinatorial primitives as permutation
layers, and established provable security in the plain indifferentiability
framework of Maurer, Renner, and Holenstein (TCC 2004).

We extend this work and consider Non-Linear Confusion-Diffusion
Networks (NLCDNs), i.e., networks using *non-linear permutation layers*,
in weaker indifferentiability settings. As the main result, we prove that
3-round NLCDNs achieve the notion of sequential indifferentiability of
Mandal et al. (TCC 2012). We also exhibit an attack against 2-round
NLCDNs, which shows the tightness of our positive result on 3 rounds. It
implies correlation intractability of 3-round NLCDNs, a notion strongly
related to known-key security of block ciphers and secure hash functions.
Our results provide additional insights on understanding the complexity
for known-key security, as well as using confusion-diffusion paradigm for
designing cryptographic hash functions.

Keywords: Block ciphers · Substitution-permutation networks ·
Confusion-diffusion · Indifferentiability · Correlation intractability

1 Introduction

Modern block ciphers roughly fall into three classes. The first class consists of
Feistel networks and their generalizations, with DES, LBlock [41], and many
other block cipher standards as popular instances. The second class are the
Lai-Massey structures designed for IDEA [27,28]. This paper focuses on the
last class, namely the *Substitution-Permutation Networks* (SPNs). Concretely,
an SPN yields an wn-bit block cipher via iterating the following three steps:

© Springer Nature Switzerland AG 2021
A. Adhikari et al. (Eds.): INDOCRYPT 2021, LNCS 13143, pp. 93–113, 2021.
https://doi.org/10.1007/978-3-030-92518-5_5

1. *Key-addition*: XOR a round key with the wn-bit state;
2. *Substitution*: break down the wn-bit state into w disjoint chunks of n bits, and evaluate a small n-bit permutation, typically called an S-box, on each chunk;
3. *Permutation*: apply a keyless permutation to the whole wn-bit state.

The S-boxes are usually highly non-linear. On the other hand, while modern block ciphers tend to use linear or affine mappings for the *Permutation*, there is actually no a priori restriction, and the use and advantages of non-linear permutations was recently explored [29].

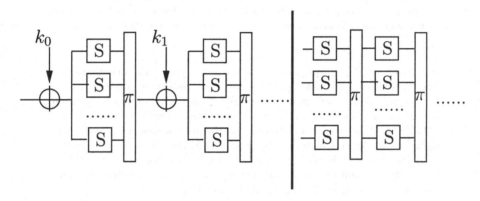

Fig. 1. Comparison of SPN and CDN, with SPN on the left and CDN on the right

The SPNs well fit into the *confusion-diffusion paradigm*: usually, the substitution is viewed as "confusion", while the permutation is viewed as "diffusion". The idea of confusion-diffusion goes back to the seminal paper of Feistel [17] and even back to Shannon [37]. Various popular primitives have been built upon this, including block ciphers such as the AES [13] and RECTANGLE [43] and hash functions such as the KECCAK-f permutations of the SHA [5]. Motivated by this popularity, SPNs have been the topic of various researches [12,35,40]. In particular, modeling the S-boxes as random or pseudorandom functions/permutation, SPNs can be proved as a strong pseudorandom permutation SPRP (i.e., indistinguishability from a truly random permutation), the standard security notion for block ciphers [7,18,25,33].[1] We refer to [18] for a detailed survey of these SPRP results. In these security proofs, the S-boxes act as the only source of cryptographic hardness, while the permutation layers only supply auxiliary *combinatorial* properties. This limits the provable security to the domain-size of

---

[1] We remark that, as proving such security for concrete block ciphers such as AES seems out of the reach of current techniques, it is actually the usual approach to idealize some underlying primitives and prove that the high-level structure meets certain security definitions.

the S-boxes, which is unfortunately as small as 8 bits in, e.g., the AES. Consequently, provable results on SPNs do not relate to any concrete SPN-based block ciphers. Instead, they should be viewed as theoretical support for the SPN approach to constructing block ciphers. Indeed, the above results have confirmed (in a widely recognized theoretical model) that, the use of non-linear permutation layers ensures more security than linear ones. The provable bounds become meaningful when the "S-boxes" enjoy sufficiently large domains, e.g., when the "S-boxes" themselves are block ciphers such as the AES or cryptographic permutations such as the KECCAK-f. Therefore, on the practical side, the above results yield domain extension of block ciphers or permutations.

1.1 Indifferentiability of Confusion-Diffusion Networks

The aforementioned SPRP notion is formalized using the indistinguishability framework. A generalization of indistinguishability, named *indifferentiability*, was introduced by Maurer et al. [32]. Briefly, a construction $C^{\mathcal{F}}$ built upon an ideal primitive $\mathcal{F}$ is indifferentiable from the ideal cryptographic primitive $\mathcal{G}$, if there exists an efficient simulator $\mathcal{S}^{\mathcal{G}}$ such that the two systems $(C^{\mathcal{F}}, \mathcal{F})$ and $(\mathcal{G}, \mathcal{S}^{\mathcal{G}})$ are *indistinguishable*. The role of the simulator is to imitate the behavior of $\mathcal{F}$, such that it appears like the "underlying primitives" of the ideal primitive $\mathcal{G}$. The consistency of the simulation is possible by accessing $\mathcal{G}$.

Indifferentiability comes with a secure composition lemma, meaning that an indifferentiable cryptographic scheme could safely replace its ideal counterpart, even in the settings *with no secret keys*. Unsurprisingly, indifferentiability was soon adopted as a standard for evaluating cryptographic constructions, with applications to hash functions [4,10], block cipher paradigms [1,11,22], and encryption schemes [3]. Due to this success, the authors won the TCC Test-of-Time award at TCC 2016-B [31].

The indifferentiability analysis of SPNs was initiated by Dodis et al. [16]. In detail, they introduced the model of *Confusion-Diffusion Networks* (CDNs), which may be viewed as SPNs *without key-additions*. In other words, CDNs is SPNs without key (see Fig. 1). Their CDN models are purely built upon public random S-boxes and non-cryptographic "D-boxes" (i.e., permutation layers), and indifferentiability measures the distance between such CDNs and wide random permutations. When the "D-boxes" are non-linear (and thus achieve a stronger diffusion), they showed that 5 rounds are sufficient for indifferentiability, and the concrete security bounds increase with the number of rounds. When the "D-boxes" are linear (as in common SPN ciphers), they showed that 9 rounds are sufficient for indifferentiability. This confirmed (in a widely recognized theoretical model) that, the use of non-linear diffusion layers ensures more security than linear ones. Dodis et al. also exhibited an attack against 2-round CDNs with arbitrarily strong (yet non-idealized) D-boxes [16, Section 3]. These justify the soundness of using fixed-key block ciphers as "random looking" permutations for constructing hash functions [36] and other sophisticated cryptosystems [21].

1.2   Weaker Variants of Indifferentiability

By incorporating different restrictions, the definition of indifferentiability has been generalized to various variants. Firstly, Yoneyama et al. [42], Dodis et al. [15], and Naito et al. [34] independently proposed the concept of *public indifferentiability*, in which the simulator $\mathcal{S}^{\mathcal{G}}$ is aware of all queries made by the distinguisher to the target ideal primitive $\mathcal{G}$. This captures the settings in which $\mathcal{G}$ only evaluated on public inputs, which fits into the use of, e.g., digital signatures. At TCC 2012, Mandal et al. [30] proposed another weakened variant named *sequential indifferentiability* (*seq-indifferentiability* for short), which restricts the distinguisher's queries to be "primitive-construction-sequential". Namely, the distinguisher consists of two phases. In the first phase, it queries the (simulated) "underlying primitive" $\mathcal{F}$ or $\mathcal{S}^{\mathcal{G}}$ in arbitrary, without making any query to the "construction" $\mathcal{C}^{\mathcal{F}}$ or $\mathcal{S}^{\mathcal{G}}$. In the second phase, it queries the "construction" $\mathcal{C}^{\mathcal{F}}$ or $\mathcal{G}$ in arbitrary, without making any query to the "primitive" $\mathcal{F}$ or $\mathcal{S}^{\mathcal{G}}$. It finally outputs the decision. Seq-indifferentiability is actually equivalent to the aforementioned public indifferentiability for natural constructions [30], while the former is easier to handle in the security analyses. In addition, seq-indifferentiability implies *correlation intractability* of Canetti et al. [6], i.e., there is no "non-trivial" relation between the inputs and outputs of the construction.

1.3   Our Results

As noted [39], indifferentiability appears imperfect for block cipher paradigms: security proofs are highly involved, and complexities of provably secure schemes appear far beyond necessary. In contrast, the notions of seq-indifferentiability and correlation intractability are directly linked to known-key security of block ciphers [9,26], and are already sufficient for establishing security for block cipher-based hash functions. Due to these, several papers have characterized the seq-indifferentiability and correlation intractability of Feistel networks [30,39] and variants of Even-Mansour ciphers [8,23]. Though, the natural extension of this line of works to CD networks remains open.

With the above discussion, we characterize the sequential indifferentiability of NLCDNs, i.e., CD networks with non-linear D-boxes. [16] investigated full indifferentiability of CD networks (with both non-linear and linear D-boxes), while we study the weaker notion of sequential indifferentiability of CD networks with non-linear D-boxes only. As mentioned before, the motivation is that sequential indifferentiability was believed more suitable for known-key security of block ciphers, to some extent.

In this respect, our first observation is that Dodis et al.'s attack on 2-round NLCDNs [16, Section 3] is not sequential in any sense, and our first contribution is a primitive-construction-sequential distinguisher against 2-round NLCDNs with *any* (non-idealized) D-boxes. Depending on the D-boxes in use, the running time of our distinguisher may be exponential. Though, the *query complexity* is merely

2, indicating that 2-round CD networks are *insecure in the information theoretic setting.*

As positive results, we prove that 3-round NLCDNs are seq-indifferentiable, as long as the D-boxes satisfy some moderate conditions. The number of rounds is 40% less than that required for plain indifferentiability.[2] In addition, as discussed, the round complexity is *tight* in the information theoretic setting. As mentioned before, these imply that 3-round NLCDNs (tightly) achieve correlation intractability, and are thus sufficient for known-key security of CD networks (in the sense of correlation intractability).

Interpretations. Since initiated [26], models or adversarial goals for known-key attacks has incurred intensive discussion. In fact, for the AES, the 7- [26] and 8-round known-key distinguishers [19, Sect. 4.1] attacked correlation intractability of the round-reduced ciphers, while the 10-round distinguishers [19, Sect. 4.2] and beyond [20] are closer to breaking "indifferentiability-like" properties. The meaningfulness and influences of these two sorts of known-key models have incurred intensive discussion or even debt [19, 20].

By our results, for the natural paradigm underlying common block ciphers including the AES, the complexity for correlation intractability is 40% less than the complexity for indifferentiability. This matches the aforementioned cryptanalytic practice. While similar results have been shown with respect to the iterated Even-Mansour ciphers [8, 14], the model of CD network is more fine-grained (despite the inherently weak bounds), and we thus believe it sheds some lights on known-key attack model from the perspective of provable security.

1.4 Other Related Work

Certain models for SPNs could be proved secure against certain cryptanalytic approaches [12, 33, 35, 40]. As a variant of indifferentiability, public indifferentiability is introduced independently by Dodis et al. [15], Naito et al. [34] and Yoneyama et al. [42]. Mandal et al. [30] introduce a new and simpler variant of indifferentiability called seq-indifferentiability. Soni and Tessaro [38] introduced another form of seq-indifferentiability called *CP-sequential indifferentiability*, which restricts the distinguisher's queries to be "construction-primitive-sequential". Some other variants of indifferentiability were introduced in [2, 9] in order to formalize known-key security of block ciphers. Finally, Dodis et al. [16] shows the first positive results for the indifferentiability security of the CDNs. Based on this work, we prove that 3-round NLCDNs achieve seq-indifferentiability.

1.5 Organization

We supply necessary notations and definitions in Sect. 2. Then present our attack on 2-round NLCDNs in Sect. 3. Our main result, the seq-indifferentiability proofs for 3-round NLCDNs, is then given in Sect. 4. Finally, Sect. 5 concludes.

---

[2] Recall that 5 rounds are needed for NLCDNs to achieve plain indifferentiability [16].

2   Preliminaries

2.1   Notations

We write $[w]$ for the set of integers $\{1, \ldots, w\}$. We denote by bold letters, e.g., $\mathbf{x}$, bit strings of length wn, where $|\mathbf{x}|$ stands for its length. Using n-bit S-boxes, such a string $\mathbf{x}$ will be divided into w blocks, each of which is of n bits. For $i \in [w]$, the i-th n-bit block of $\mathbf{x}$ is denoted $\mathbf{x}[i]$ (i.e., $|\mathbf{x}[i]| = n$). We let $N = 2^n$ to simplify notations.

A random (invertible) permutation $\mathcal{Z} : \{+, -\} \times \{0, 1\}^{wn} \rightarrow \{0, 1\}^{wn}$ accepts queries of the form $(+, \mathbf{x})$ (i.e., forward queries) or $(-, \mathbf{y})$ (i.e., backward queries). As our positive result addresses a 3-round CDN with non-linear diffusion layers (NLCDN for short), we use A_j, B_j, C_j to refer to the S-boxes in the 1st, 2nd, and 3rd rounds (as sketched in Fig. 3). The idealized model of such a 3-round NLCDN relies on a tuple of $3w$ independent random permutations $\mathcal{P} = (\mathcal{P}_{A_1}, \ldots, \mathcal{P}_{A_w}, \mathcal{P}_{B_1}, \ldots, \mathcal{P}_{B_w}, \mathcal{P}_{C_1}, \ldots, \mathcal{P}_{C_w})$, where $\mathcal{P}_{\mathcal{T}_j} := \{+, -\} \times \{0, 1\}^n \rightarrow \{0, 1\}^n$ for every $\mathcal{T} \in \{A, B, C\}$ and every $j \in [w]$. To simplify notations, we assume that $\mathcal{P}$ provides a single interface $\mathcal{P}(\mathcal{T}_j, \delta, x)$ for all the $3w$ permutations, where $\mathcal{T}_j \in \{A_1, \ldots, A_w, B_1, \ldots, B_w, C_1, \ldots, C_w\}$ indicates the S-box being queried, $\delta \in \{+, -\}$ indicates the direction of the query, and $x \in \{0, 1\}^n$ indicates the concrete queried value.

2.2   Confusion-Diffusion Networks

The CDN and NLCDN constructions First, we formalize r-round confusion-diffusion networks. Fix integers $w, n, r \in \mathbb{N}$ as parameters. Let

$$\mathcal{P} = \{P_{i,j} : (i, j) \in \{r \times w\}\}$$

be an array of wr permutations from $\{0, 1\}^n$ to $\{0, 1\}^n$, i.e., $P_{i,j}$ is a permutation from $\{0, 1\}^n$ to $\{0, 1\}^n$ for each $i \in [r]$ and each $j \in [w]$ and will serve in the confusion layers. Given $\mathbf{x} \in \{0, 1\}^{wn}$, we denote $\overline{\mathcal{P}}_i(\mathbf{x})$ as

$$\overline{\mathcal{P}}_i(\mathbf{x}) = P_{i,1}(\mathbf{x}[1]) \| P_{i,2}(\mathbf{x}[2]) \| \ldots \| P_{i,w}(\mathbf{x}[w])$$

which means the i-th confusion layer. In other words, $\overline{\mathcal{P}}_i$ is a permutation of $\{0, 1\}^{wn}$ and can also be defined by setting

$$\overline{\mathcal{P}}(\mathbf{x})[j] = P_{i,j}(\mathbf{x}[j]).$$

Let

$$\Pi = (\pi_1, \ldots, \pi_{r-1})$$

be an arbitrary sequence or $r - 1$ permutations and each of them from $\{0, 1\}^{wn}$ to $\{0, 1\}^{wn}$. It will be the diffusion layer, which only has certain (simple) combinatorial properties rather than sophisticated cryptographic properties.

With all the above, the function CDN is written as

$$\mathsf{CDN}_\Pi^\mathcal{P}(\mathbf{x}) = \overline{\mathcal{P}}_r(\pi_{r-1}(\ldots \overline{\mathcal{P}}_2(\pi_1(\overline{\mathcal{P}}_1(\mathbf{x}))) \ldots)) = \mathbf{y} \tag{1}$$

The value w and r will be called *width of confusion layer* and *rounds*. As mentioned, in our primary focus 3-round NLCDNs, we use A, B, C instead of $\overline{\mathcal{P}}_1, \overline{\mathcal{P}}_2, \overline{\mathcal{P}}_3$ for the S-boxes.

Combinatorial Properties of the Diffusion Layers. We now use the definitions in [16] to formalize the properties that the diffusion layers Π have to fulfill in order to result in a secure CD network. Given a vector $\mathbf{x}$ and two indices $j, j' \in [w]$, we let $\pi^{\mathbf{x}}_{j,j'} : \{0,1\}^n \to \{0,1\}^n$ be the function from $\{0,1\}^n$ to $\{0,1\}^n$ obtained by restricting the i-th block of input of π to $\mathbf{x}[i]$ $(i \neq j)$, by replacing $\mathbf{x}[j]$ with the input $x \in \{0,1\}^n$, and by considering only the j'-th block of output. The properties are defined unidirectionally: π might satisfy a property but π^{-1} does not.

Then, the quantity MaxPreEx is defined as

$$\mathsf{MaxPreEx}(\pi) = \max_{\mathbf{x}, j, h, y} \left| \{x \in \{0,1\}^n : \pi^{\mathbf{x}}_{j,h}(x) = y\} \right|.$$

Briefly, it formalizes the maximal number of $x \in \{0,1\}^n$ such that, once "extended" to a wn-bit string $\mathbf{x}$ in a pre-defined manner, the corresponding wn-bit image $\mathbf{y} = \pi(\mathbf{x})$ has at least one n-bit block equal $y \in \{0,1\}^n$. We further define

Then, the quantity MaxColl is defined as

$$\mathsf{MaxColl}(\pi) = \max_{\mathbf{x}, \mathbf{x}', j, h} \left| \{x \in \{0,1\}^n : \pi^{\mathbf{x}}_{j,h}(x) = \pi^{\mathbf{x}'}_{j,h}(x)\} \right|.$$

Briefly, it formalizes the maximal number of $x, x' \in \{0,1\}^n$ such that, once "extended" to a wn-bit strings $\mathbf{x}$ and $\mathbf{x}$', the corresponding wn-bit images $\mathbf{y} = \pi(\mathbf{x})$ and $\mathbf{y}' = \pi(\mathbf{x}')$ collide on at least one n-bit block. A concrete non-linear D-box with $\mathsf{MaxPreEx}(\pi) = \mathsf{MaxColl}(\pi) \approx O(w)$ was given in [16, Appendix D].

2.3 Sequential Indifferentiability and Correlation Intractability

We first informally introduce indifferentiability, and we concentrate on CDNs to ease understanding. In this setting, a distinguisher $\mathcal{D}$ is trying to distinguish an idealized $\mathsf{CDN}^{\mathcal{P}}$ from a random wn-bit permutation $\mathcal{Z}$, with the help of the underlying random S-boxes $\mathcal{P}$. Hence, in the real world, $\mathcal{D}$ is interacting with two oracles, namely $(\mathsf{CDN}^{\mathcal{P}}, \mathcal{P})$. In the ideal world, the "position" of the non-existing oracle $\mathcal{P}$ will be filled by a simulator $\mathcal{S}^{\mathcal{Z}}$. By these, $\mathsf{CDN}^{\mathcal{P}}$ is *indifferentiable from* $\mathcal{Z}$, if there exists an efficient simulator $\mathcal{S}^{\mathcal{Z}}$ making queries to $\mathcal{Z}$, such that the ideal system $(\mathcal{Z}, \mathcal{S}^{\mathcal{Z}})$ and the real system $(\mathsf{CDN}^{\mathcal{P}}, \mathcal{P})$ are *indistinguishable* in the view of any distinguisher $\mathcal{D}$.

The sequential indifferentiability (seq-indifferentiability in short) setting also considers a distinguisher $\mathcal{D}$ trying to distinguish the ideal $(\mathcal{Z}, \mathcal{S}^{\mathcal{Z}})$ and the real $(\mathsf{CDN}^{\mathcal{P}}, \mathcal{P})$. Unlike the above (plain) indifferentiability, seq-indifferentiability focuses on *sequential distinguishers* (*seq-distinguishers* for short), i.e., a certain type of distinguishers that issue queries in a strict order. Concretely, a seq-distinguisher $\mathcal{D}$ is *primitive-construction-sequential*, if it proceeds with three steps: (1) $\mathcal{D}$ queries the (real or ideal) construction $\mathsf{CDN}^{\mathcal{P}}$ or $\mathcal{Z}$, without querying the (real or simulated) primitive $\mathcal{S}$ or $\mathcal{S}^{\mathcal{Z}}$; (2) $\mathcal{D}$ queries the primitive $\mathcal{S}$ or $\mathcal{S}^{\mathcal{Z}}$, without querying the construction $\mathsf{CDN}^{\mathcal{P}}$ or $\mathcal{Z}$; (3) $\mathcal{D}$ outputs its decision. This order is reflected by the numbers in Fig. 2.

Using the notion of seq-distinguishers, the definition of seq-indifferentiability due to [8] is as follows.

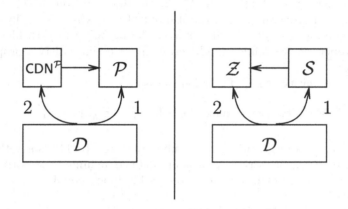

Fig. 2. The definition of sequential indifferentiability. The numbers near the arrows indicate the order of distinguisher's query. If the distinguisher first query "1", it could query "2" next. If it first query "2", it could not query "1" any more

Definition 1 (Seq-indifferentiability). *The idealized network* $\mathsf{CDN}^{\mathcal{P}}$ *with oracle access to random permutations* $\mathcal{P}$ *is statistically and strongly* $(q, \sigma, t, \varepsilon)$-*seq-indifferentiable from a random wn-bit permutation* $\mathcal{Z}$, *if there exists a simulator* $\mathcal{S}^{\mathcal{Z}}$ *such that for any sequential distinguisher* $\mathcal{D}$ *making at most* q *queries,* $\mathcal{S}^{\mathcal{Z}}$ *issues at most* σ *queries to* $\mathcal{Z}$ *and runs in time at most* t, *and it holds*

$$\left| \Pr\left[\mathcal{D}^{\mathsf{CDN}^{\mathcal{P}}, \mathcal{P}} = 1\right] - \Pr\left[\mathcal{D}^{\mathcal{Z}, \mathcal{S}^{\mathcal{Z}}} = 1\right] \right| \leq \varepsilon.$$

As mentioned, seq-indifferentiability already implies correlation intractability in the idealized model [8,30]. The notion *correlation intractability* was introduced by Canetti et al. [6] to capture the feature that there is no exploitable relation between the inputs and outputs of the function ensembles in question. It was transposed to idealized models to guarantee similar feature on idealized constructions. Formally, we first give the definition (from [8]) of evasive relation.

Definition 2 (Evasive Relation). *An* m-*ary relation* $\mathcal{R}$ *over pairs of binary sequences is said* (q, ϵ)-*evasive with respect to the random wn-bit permutation* $\mathcal{Z}$, *if for any PPT oracle Turing machine* $\mathcal{M}$ *issuing at most* q *oracle queries, it holds*

$$\Pr\left[(x_1, \ldots, x_m) \leftarrow \mathcal{M}^{\mathcal{Z}} : ((x_1, \ldots, x_m), (\mathcal{Z}(x_1), \ldots, \mathcal{Z}(x_m))) \in \mathcal{R}\right] \leq \epsilon.$$

Definition 3 (Correlation Intractability). *Let $\mathcal{R}$ be an m-ary relation. The idealized network $\mathsf{CDN}^{\mathcal{S}}$ with oracle access to the random S-boxes $\mathcal{S}$ is (q, ϵ)-correlation intractable with respect to $\mathcal{R}$, if for any oracle Turing machine $\mathcal{M}$ issuing at most q oracle queries, it holds*

$$\Pr\big[(x_1, \ldots, x_m) \leftarrow \mathcal{M}^{\mathcal{P}} : ((x_1, \ldots, x_m), (\mathsf{CDN}^{\mathcal{P}}(x_1), \ldots, \mathsf{CDN}^{\mathcal{P}}(x_m))) \in \mathcal{R}\big] \leq \epsilon.$$

With the above definitions, the implication of seq-indifferentiability is formally stated as follows [8].

Theorem 1. *For an idealized block cipher construction $\mathcal{C}^{\mathcal{F}}$ which has oracle access to ideal primitives $\mathcal{F}$ and makes at most c queries to $\mathcal{F}$ in total, if $\mathcal{C}^{\mathcal{F}}$ is $(q+cm, \sigma, \epsilon)$-seq-indifferentiable from another ideal primitive $\mathcal{G}$ (m is the number of binary sequences), then for any m-ary relation $\mathcal{R}$ which is $(\sigma+m, \epsilon_{\mathcal{R}})$-evasive with respect to $\mathcal{G}$, $\mathcal{C}^{\mathcal{F}}$ is $(q, \epsilon + \epsilon_{\mathcal{R}})$-correlation intractable with respect to $\mathcal{R}$.*

3   Attack 2-Round CD

The attack against 2-round CDN is neither primitive-construction-sequential nor construction-primitive-sequential in [16]. In this section we exhibit a primitive-construction-sequential distinguisher against 2-round CDN making only 2 oracle queries to mitigate the gap. The assumption on the D-boxes is that it is an efficiently computable function rather than an oracle. The running time of our distinguisher may be exponential $O(2^n)$ or even $O(2^{wn})$. Though, it remains valid in the *information theoretic setting*, and confirms the *tightness* of our positive result on 3 rounds.

1. Find $b, d_1, d_2 \in \{0,1\}^n$ such that $D(b\|d_1)[1] = D(b\|d_2)[1]$;
2. Query the right oracles for $A_1^{-1}(b) \to a$, $A_2^{-1}(d_1) \to c_1$, and $A_2^{-1}(d_2) \to c_2$.
3. Query the left oracle P for $P(a\|c_1) \to f_1\|h_1$ and $P(a\|c_2) \to f_2\|h_2$, and outputs 1 if and only if $f_1 = f_2$.

If P is the 2-round CDN oracle, it necessarily holds $f_1 = f_2$ since $D(b\|d_1)[1] = D(b\|d_2)[1]$, which means the distinguisher always outputs 1. On the other hand, to simulate consistently in the ideal world, the simulator has to run ahead to find a pair of inputs/outputs $y_1 = \mathcal{Z}(+, a\|c_1)$ and $y_2 = \mathcal{Z}(+, a\|c_2)$ of the random permutation $\mathcal{Z}$ such that $y_1[1] = y_2[1]$, the probability of which is $O(q^2/2^n)$ within q queries. The distinguishing advantage is thus $1 - O(q^2/2^n) \approx 1$ for any simulator making $q \ll 2^{n/2}$ queries to P.

4   Sequential Indifferentiability of 3-Round NLCDNs

The main result of this work is formally stated as follows.

Theorem 2. *Assuming that $\mathcal{P} = (\mathcal{P}_{A_1} \ldots \mathcal{P}_{A_w}, \mathcal{P}_{B_1} \ldots \mathcal{P}_{B_w}, \mathcal{P}_{C_1} \ldots \mathcal{P}_{C_w})$ is a tuple of 3w independent random n-bit permutations, then the 3-round confusion-diffusion network with oracle access to $\mathsf{CDN}^{\mathcal{P}}$ is strongly and statistically*

$(q, \sigma, t, \varepsilon)$-*seq-indifferentiable from a wn-bit random permutation* $\mathcal{Z}$, *where* $\sigma = q^w, t = O(q^w)$ *and*

$$\varepsilon = \frac{4q^w(q^w + q)}{N - q^w - q} + \frac{4w(q^w + q)^2(\mathsf{MaxPreEx}(\pi) + \mathsf{MaxCoPr}(\pi))}{N - q^w - q} + \frac{1}{N^w}. \quad (2)$$

As mentioned in Sect. 2.2, a non-linear D-box construction with

$$\mathsf{MaxPreEx}(\pi) = \mathsf{MaxCoPr}(\pi) \approx O(w)$$

was given in [16, Appendix D]. It easy to verify that the other terms in Theorem 2 are all of the order $O(q^{2w}/N)$, which further means

$$\varepsilon = O\Big(\frac{q^{2w}}{2^n}\Big).$$

By Theorem 1, we have that for any $(q^w, \epsilon_{\mathcal{R}})$-evasive relation, the 3-round NLCDN is $(q, \epsilon_{\mathcal{R}} + O(q^{2w}/2^n))$-correlation intractable with respect to $\mathcal{R}$. We stress that $\mathsf{MaxPreEx}(\pi) = \mathsf{MaxCoPr}(\pi) \approx O(w)$ and thus the above concrete results are only achievable with *non-linear* D-boxes [16] (which is not surprising in turn).

To prove it, we: (1) build a simulator (Sect. 4.1); (2) bound the complexity of the simulator (Sect. 4.2); (3) introduce the intermediate system for the proof (Sect. 4.3); (4) prove that the simulator simulates well (Sects. 4.4 and 4.5).

4.1   Overview of the Simulator

We follow the approach of explicit randomness technique of [8,11], namely, letting the simulator $\mathcal{S}$ have explicit access to $\mathcal{P}$ and query it to obtain necessary random values. We denote by $\mathcal{S}(\mathcal{P}, \mathcal{Z})$ the simulator for 3 round CDN which access $\mathcal{P}$ (and $\mathcal{Z}$).

To keep track of previously answered queries, $\mathcal{S}$ internally maintains $3w$ tables $(A_1, \ldots, A_w, B_1, \ldots, B_w, C_1, \ldots, C_w)$ that have entries in the form of (x, y) for $x, y \in \{0,1\}^n$. For $\mathcal{T} \in \{A, B, C\}$ and $j \in [w]$, we denote by $\mathcal{T}_j^+(x)$ the n-bit value such that $(x, \mathcal{T}_j^+(x)) \in \mathcal{T}_j$, and write $\mathcal{T}_j^+(x) = \bot$ if there is no pair of the form $(x, \star)$ in $\mathcal{T}_j$. Similarly by symmetry, we denote by $\mathcal{T}_j^-(y)$ the n-bit value such that $(\mathcal{T}_j^-(y), y) \in \mathcal{T}_j$, and write $\mathcal{T}_j^-(y) = \bot$ once no such pair exists. For $\delta \in \{+, -\}$, we denote by $\bar{\delta}$ the opposite of δ. For example, when $\delta = +$, $\mathcal{T}_j^{\bar{\delta}}$ refers to $\mathcal{T}_j^-$.

The basic idea is Coron et al.'s simulation via chain completion technique [11], which has achieved succes in (weaker) indifferentiability proofs of a variety of idealized block ciphers. It requires the simulator $\mathcal{S}$ to *detect* "partial" computation chains formed by the queries of the distinguisher, and *completes* the chains in advance by querying the random permutation $\mathcal{Z}$, so that $\mathcal{S}$ is ready for answering queries in the future. To simulate answers that are consistent with $\mathcal{Z}$, $\mathcal{S}$ has to use the answer from $\mathcal{Z}$ to define some simulated answers: this action is called *adaptation*. Specifically, our simulator views every tuple of w queries to the (2nd round) S-boxes $B_1, ..., B_w$ as a partial chain, and completes it by defining entries in $A_1, ..., A_w$ or $C_1, ..., C_w$ depending on the context, as depicted in Fig. 3.

$\mathcal{S}$ offers an interface Query$(\mathcal{T}_j, \delta, x)$ to the distinguisher (which is the same as the interface of $\mathcal{P}$), where $\mathcal{T} \in \{A, B, C\}$ and $j \in [w]$ indicate the concrete S-box being queried, $\delta \in \{+, -\}$ indicates whether this a direct of inverse query, and $x \in \{0, 1\}^n$ is the actual queried value. Upon a query Query$(\mathcal{T}_j, \delta, x)$, $\mathcal{S}$ checks the table $\mathcal{T}_j$ to see whether the corresponding answer $\mathcal{T}_j^\delta(x)$ is already defined. When this is the case, it returns $\mathcal{T}_j^\delta(x)$ to finish this response. Otherwise, it draws a random response $y \leftarrow \mathcal{P}(\mathcal{T}_j, \delta, x)$ from the random permutation $\mathcal{P}$ and invokes a private procedure SetTable$(\mathcal{T}_j^\delta, x, y)$. The latter procedure adds (x, y) to $\mathcal{T}_j$.

Then, if $= B$, $\mathcal{S}$ invokes another private procedure AdaptC (resp. AdaptA) if $\delta = +$ (resp. $\delta = -$) to complete detected partial chains as mentioned before. In detail, when $\delta = +$, then for every $\mathbf{x}^B[j] = x$, $\mathcal{S}$ calls AdaptC, which further computes $\mathbf{x}^C = \pi_2(\mathbf{y}^B)$, $\mathbf{x}^A = Block(A, -, \pi_1^{-1}(\mathbf{x}^B))$,[1] and queries $\mathcal{Z}(-, \mathbf{x}^A) \rightarrow \mathbf{y}^C$. The procedure AdaptC then adapts: for $j = 1, ..., w$, it defines $(\mathbf{x}^C[j], \mathbf{y}^C[j])$ as a new entry of the table C_j. Entries to-be-adapted may cause inconsistency when an entry of the form $(\mathbf{x}^C[j], \star)$ or $(\star, \mathbf{y}^C[j])$ already exists in C_j. In this case, our simulator *overwrites* the existing entries and breaks the bijectivity of the partially defined maps. This is the major source of inconsistency, and its unlikeness constitutes a main intermediate goal of our remaining proofs. The procedure AdaptA is similar to the above by symmetry. The chain completion strategy is illustrated in Fig. 3. $\mathcal{S}$ eventually returns $\mathcal{T}_j^\delta(x)$ as the response. This means queries of the form (A_j, δ, x) or (C_j, δ, x) won't trigger chain detection, and are simply answered with randomness from $\mathcal{P}$. The formal description in pseudocode is given in Algorithm 1.

4.2   Simulator Efficiency

As the first step, we must prove that the complexity of the simulator $\mathcal{S}$ is polynomial in q.

Lemma 1. *If the simulator receives at most q queries in total, then for every $j \in [w]$, the tables $A_1, ..., A_w, B_1, ..., B_w, C_1, ..., C_w$ of $\mathcal{S}$ has $|B_j| \leq q$, $|A_j| \leq q^w + q$, and $|C_j| \leq q^w + q$. The simulator executes AdaptA and AdaptC for at most q^w times, makes at most q^w queries to $\mathcal{Z}$ and runs in time $O(q^w)$.*

Proof. For $j \in [w]$, it is clear that $|B_j|$ only increases by at most 1 when the distinguisher makes a query to Query(B_j, δ, x), and thus $|B_j| \leq q$. On the other hand, $|A_j|$ may increase in two cases:

(1) The distinguisher makes a query to Query(A_j, δ, x), and
(2) $\mathcal{S}$ executes AdaptA$(\mathbf{x}^B, \mathbf{y}^B)$.

---

[1] The private procedure Block$(\mathcal{T}, \delta, \mathbf{t})$ computes a complete S-box layer on the input $\mathbf{t} \in \{0, 1\}^{wn}$, where $\mathcal{T} \in \{A, B, C\}$ and $\delta \in \{+, -\}$.

Algorithm 1. Simulator $\mathcal{S}(\mathcal{Z}, \mathcal{P})$

1: **procedure** Query($\mathcal{T}_j, \delta, x$)
2:　if $\mathcal{T}_j^\delta(x) = \bot$ **then**
3:　　$y \leftarrow \mathcal{P}(\mathcal{T}_j, \delta, x)$
4:　　SetTable($\mathcal{T}_j, x, y$)
5:　　**if** $\mathcal{T} = B$ and $\delta = +$ **then**
6:　　　**forall** $\mathbf{x}^B, \mathbf{y}^B$ s.t. $\mathbf{x}^B[j] = x$ **do**
7:　　　　AdaptC($\mathbf{x}^B, \mathbf{y}^B$)
8:　　**if** $\mathcal{T} = B$ and $\delta = -$ **then**
9:　　　**forall** $\mathbf{x}^B, \mathbf{y}^B$ s.t. $\mathbf{y}^B[j] = x$ **do**
10:　　　　AdpatA($\mathbf{x}^B, \mathbf{y}^B$)
11:　**return** $\mathcal{T}_j^\delta(x)$
12:
13: **private procedure** AdaptC($\mathbf{x}^B, \mathbf{y}^B$)
14:　$\mathbf{x}^C = \pi_2(\mathbf{y}^B)$
15:　$\mathbf{x}^A = \mathrm{Block}(A, -, \pi_1^{-1}(\mathbf{x}^B))$
16:　$\mathbf{y}^C = \mathcal{Z}(+, \mathbf{x}^A)$
17:　**forall** $j \in \{1, \ldots, w\}$ **do**
18:　　SetTable($C_j, \mathbf{x}^C[j], \mathbf{y}^C[j]$)

19: **private procedure** AdaptA($\mathbf{x}^B, \mathbf{y}^B$)
20:　$\mathbf{y}^A = \pi_1^{-1}(\mathbf{y}^B)$
21:　$\mathbf{y}^C = \mathrm{Block}(C, +, \pi_2(\mathbf{y}^B))$
22:　$\mathbf{x}^A = \mathcal{Z}(-, \mathbf{y}^C)$
23:　**forall** $j \in \{1, \ldots, w\}$ **do**
24:　　SetTable($A_j, \mathbf{x}^A[j], \mathbf{y}^A[j]$)
25:
26: **procedure** SetTable($\mathcal{T}_j^\delta, x, y$)
27:　$\mathcal{T}_j^\delta(x) \leftarrow y$
28:　$\mathcal{T}_j^\delta(y) \leftarrow x$
29:
30: **private procedure** Block($\mathcal{T}, \delta, \mathbf{t}$)
31:　**forall** $j \in \{1, \ldots, w\}$ **do**
32:　　**if** $\mathcal{T}_j^\delta(\mathbf{t}[j]) = \bot$ **then**
33:　　　$\mathbf{u}[j] \leftarrow \mathcal{P}(\mathcal{T}_j, \delta, \mathbf{t}[j])$
34:　　　SetTable($\mathcal{T}_j, \mathbf{t}[j], \mathbf{u}[j]$)
35:　　$\mathbf{u}[j] \leftarrow \mathcal{T}_j^\delta(\mathbf{t}[j])$
36:　**return u**

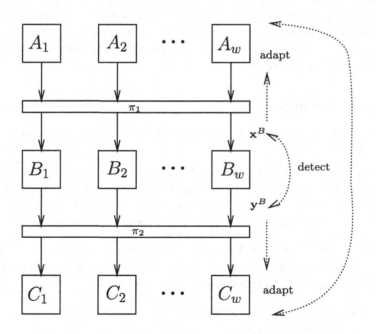

Fig. 3. Our simulation strategy.

The procedure AdaptA is executed once for every wn-bit "combined" string $\mathbf{x}^B \in B_1 \times \cdots \times B_w$ detected by $\mathcal{S}$. Therefore, the number of executions is at most q^w. This plus the increment due to the q adversarial queries yield $|A_j| \leq q^w + q$. The argument for $|C_j| \leq q^w + q$ is similar by symmetry. Then, each execution of AdaptA/AdaptC makes 1 query to $\mathcal{Z}$, which establishes the q^w query complexity. Finally, the simulator computations are clearly dominated by the executions of AdaptA/AdaptC, and this establishes the $O(q^w)$ time complexity.   □

4.3   Intermediate Systems

We follow [8] and use three games to facilitate the proof (see Fig. 4). The game G_1 captures the interaction between the distinguisher and the ideal world $(\mathcal{Z}, \mathcal{S}(\mathcal{Z}, \mathcal{P}))$. $\mathcal{Z}$ is a wn-bit random permutation and $\mathcal{P}$ is a tuple of n-bit independent random permutation $(\mathcal{P}_{A_1} \cdots \mathcal{P}_{A_w}, \mathcal{P}_{B_1} \cdots \mathcal{P}_{B_w}, \mathcal{P}_{C_1} \cdots \mathcal{P}_{C_w})$, plays the role of S-boxes in CDN which is mentioned in Sect. 2.3. The simulator $\mathcal{S}(\mathcal{Z}, \mathcal{P})$ has access to both $\mathcal{Z}$ and $\mathcal{P}$. Our rules for constructing game strictly follow the rules constructed in [1,8], and all use random permutation $\mathcal{P}$ as source of randomness. The game G_3 captures interaction between the distinguisher and the real world $(\mathsf{CDN}^{\mathcal{P}}, \mathcal{P})$. We construct a intermediate system G_2. It lies between G_1 and G_3 and functions as a bridge to simplify the proof. The intermediate game G_2 captures the interaction between the distinguisher and the system $(\mathsf{CDN}^{\mathcal{S}(\mathcal{Z}, \mathcal{P})}, \mathcal{S}(\mathcal{Z}, \mathcal{P}))$, i.e., it is modified from G_1 by replacing $\mathcal{Z}$ with the CDN construction. In other words, the right oracle is the simulator $\mathcal{S}(\mathcal{Z}, \mathcal{P})$ with oracle access to random permutation $\mathcal{Z}$, but now the left oracle is CDN construction with oracle access to $\mathcal{S}(\mathcal{Z}, \mathcal{P})$.

4.4   Probability of Overwriting

As mentioned before, during executing the procedures AdaptA and AdaptC, our simulator may overwrite already defined entries and cause inconsistency. In this section we show this event of overwriting, in fact, happens with a bounded probability.

The event overwriting only occurs during the execution of SetTable. We begin by considering the probability of line 4 and line 34. These lines only cause overwriting when the sampled values collide with the value previously added by AdaptA or AdaptC. Since the size of A_j and C_j is $q^w + q$ by Lemma 1, the obtained $y \leftarrow \mathcal{P}(\mathcal{T}_j, \delta, x)$ is uniform in at least $N - q^w - q$ possibilities. The probability that y already exists is $\frac{2(q^w+q)}{N-q^w-q}$ since there are at most $q^w + q$ random assignment in tables A_j and C_j. The procedure AdaptA, resp. AdaptC, is executed by at most q^w times. By these, we have

$$\Pr\left[line\ 4,\ 34\ overwrite\right] \leq \frac{2q^w(q^w + q)}{N - q^w - q}. \tag{3}$$

Then, we consider the overwriting in AdaptC or AdaptA. During executing the former AdaptC, the occurrence of overwriting is due to $C_j(x) \neq \perp$

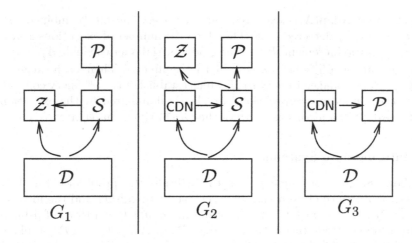

Fig. 4. Games and the involved primitives used in our proof.

or $C_j^{-1}(y) \neq \perp$. Assume that table C_j already have k pairs ($k \leq q^w + q$) $(\mathbf{x}_1^C, \mathbf{y}_1^C), \ldots, (\mathbf{x}_k^C, \mathbf{y}_k^C)$ before this execution. By construction (line 14), we define $\mathbf{x}_i^C = \pi_2(\mathbf{y}_i^B)$ has chance to cause the following two types of overwriting:

- PreEx: $\mathbf{x}_i^C[j] \in C_j, (1 \leq i \leq k, 1 \leq j \leq w)$
- Coll: $\mathbf{x}_i^C[j] = \mathbf{x}_{i'}^C[j], (1 \leq i \leq i' \leq k, 1 \leq j \leq w)$

where C_j is represented as the domain of table C_j. In other words, $C_j = \{x \in \{0,1\}^n : C_j(x) \neq \perp\}$. It is clear that PreEx and Coll includes all the possibilities of bad events in AdaptC. By Lemma 1, the size of C_j is at most $q^2 + q$. We first discuss the probability of occurrence of PreEx. As mentioned before, we denoted $\pi_{j,j'}^{\mathbf{x}}$ be the function from $\{0,1\}^n$ to $\{0,1\}^n$. It represents in the D-boxes, we split the input x and output y into the j-th and j'-th block. We now define:

$$\mathsf{MaxPreEx}(\pi_2) = \max_{\mathbf{x},j,h,y} \left| \{x \in \{0,1\}^n : \pi_{j,h}^{\mathbf{x}}(x) = y\} \right|.$$

Since the size of C_j is at most $q^w + q$, $\mathbf{x}_i^C$ is uniformly random in a set of size at least $N - q^w - q$, So we can find the probability of occurrence of PreEx for $\mathbf{x}_i^C[j] = \pi_2(\mathbf{y}^B)$ at most:

$$\frac{\mathsf{MaxPreEx}(\pi_2)|C_j|}{N - q^w - q}.$$

For all $\mathbf{x}^C$, the probability would be at most:

$$\Pr\left[\prod_{i=1}^{k}\prod_{j=1}^{w} \mathsf{PreEx}\right] \leq \frac{wk(q^w + q)\mathsf{MaxPreEx}(\pi_2)}{N - q^w - q}. \tag{4}$$

Next, we consider the probability of Coll. Coll occurs if and only if $\mathbf{x}_i^C[j] = \mathbf{x}_{i'}^C[j]$. There are two different situations here: if $\mathbf{x}_i^C$, $\mathbf{x}_{i'}^C$ are from distinct calls, the probability of $\mathbf{x}_i^C[j] = \mathbf{x}_{i'}^C[j]$ is at most:

$$\frac{\mathsf{MaxPreEx}(\pi_2)}{N - q^w - q}.$$

In this case, the value range of bad event has only one value. $|\mathcal{C}_j|$ is replaced by 1. If $\mathbf{x}_i^C$, $\mathbf{x}_{i'}^C$ are from the same calls, the probability of $\mathbf{x}_i^C[j] = \mathbf{x}_{i'}^C[j]$ is at most:

$$\frac{\mathsf{MaxColl}(\pi_2)}{N - q^w - q},$$

which we define that:

$$\mathsf{MaxColl}(\pi_2) = \max_{\mathbf{x} \neq \mathbf{x}', j, h} \left| \{ x \in \{0, 1\}^n : \pi_{j,h}^{\mathbf{x}}(x) = \pi_{j,h}^{\mathbf{x}'}(x) \} \right|.$$

We let $\mathsf{MaxCoPr}(\pi) = \max(\mathsf{MaxPreEx}(\pi), \mathsf{MaxColl}(\pi))$, thus:

$$\Pr \left[\prod_{i=1}^{k} \prod_{i'=1}^{k} \prod_{j=1}^{w} \mathsf{Coll} \right] \leq \frac{wk^2 \mathsf{MaxCoPr}(\pi_2)}{N - q^w - q}. \tag{5}$$

Gathering Eqs. (4) and (5), and using $k \leq q^w + q$, the probability to have overwriting due to executing AdaptC is bounded by

$$\Pr[\text{AdaptC } overwrites] \leq \frac{wk(q^w + q)\mathsf{MaxPreEx}(\pi_2)}{N - q^w - q} + \frac{wk^2 \mathsf{MaxCoPr}(\pi_2)}{N - q^w - q}$$
$$= \frac{w(q^w + q)^2 (\mathsf{MaxPreEx}(\pi_2) + \mathsf{MaxCoPr}(\pi_2))}{N - q^w - q}. \tag{6}$$

Similar reasoning holds for AdaptA executions by symmetry, giving rise to the same bound

$$\Pr[\text{AdaptA } overwrites] \leq \frac{wk(q^w + q)\mathsf{MaxPreEx}(\pi_1)}{N - q^w - q} + \frac{wk^2 \mathsf{MaxCoPr}(\pi_1)}{N - q^w - q}$$
$$= \frac{w(q^w + q)^2 (\mathsf{MaxPreEx}(\pi_1) + \mathsf{MaxCoPr}(\pi_1))}{N - q^w - q}. \tag{7}$$

Gathering Eqs. (3) and (7), we evetually have the probability of overwriting.

$$\Pr[Overwriting] \leq \frac{2q^w(q^w + q)}{N - q^w - q} + \frac{2w(q^w + q)^2 (\mathsf{MaxPreEx}(\pi) + \mathsf{MaxCoPr}(\pi))}{N - q^w - q}, \tag{8}$$

where $\mathsf{MaxPreEx}(\pi)$, $\mathsf{MaxColl}(\pi)$, and $\mathsf{MaxCoPr}(\pi)$ stand for the maximal quantity among the two diffusion layers π_1, π_2, i.e.,

$$\mathsf{MaxPreEx}(\pi) = \max \left(\mathsf{MaxPreEx}(\pi_1), \ldots, \mathsf{MaxPreEx}(\pi_2^{-1}) \right)$$
$$\mathsf{MaxColl}(\pi) = \max \left(\mathsf{MaxColl}(\pi_1), \ldots, \mathsf{MaxColl}(\pi_2^{-1}) \right)$$
$$\mathsf{MaxCoPr}(\pi) = \max \left(\mathsf{MaxCoPr}(\pi_1), \ldots, \mathsf{MaxCoPr}(\pi_2^{-1}) \right).$$

4.5   Statistical Distance Between Games

In this section, we will complete the final step of the proof. Recall from Sect. 4.3 that we built three games to imitate real world and ideal world. First, we consider the transition from G_1 to G_2. Note that both G_1 and G_2 has the same pair $(\mathcal{Z}, \mathcal{P})$, $\mathcal{Z}$ is the random wn-bit permutation and $\mathcal{P}$ is a tuple of random permutations $\mathcal{P}_{\mathcal{T}_j}$. The pair is *bad*, if the simulator overwrites an entry of the table $\mathcal{T}_j$, specifically, A_j, C_j during G_2; otherwise, the pair is *good*.

We first address the statistical distance between G_1 and G_2.

Lemma 2. *For any distinguisher $\mathcal{D}$ making at most q queries, the statistical distance between G_1 and G_2 is bounded by*

$$\left| \Pr\left[\mathcal{D}^{G_1(\mathcal{S}(\mathcal{Z},\mathcal{P}),\mathcal{Z})} = 1\right] - \Pr\left[\mathcal{D}^{G_2(\mathcal{S}(\mathcal{Z},\mathcal{P}),\mathrm{CDN}^{\mathcal{S}(\mathcal{Z},\mathcal{P})})}\right]\right| \leq \Pr\left[(\mathcal{Z},\mathcal{P}) \text{ is bad}\right].$$

Proof. Since the distinguisher is sequential in the sense of Definition 1, in G_1 and G_2, it necessarily first queries $\mathcal{S}(\mathcal{Z},\mathcal{P})$ and then $\mathcal{Z}$ (in G_1) or $\mathrm{CDN}^{\mathcal{S}(\mathcal{Z},\mathcal{P})}$ (in G_2) only. If the pair is good, the answers $\mathcal{D}$ received from G_1 and G_2 are the same since they stem from the same randomness source. On the other side, $\mathcal{Z}$ is an ideal primitive and CDN is the structure that exists in the real state, they could not trigger bad event. So, the statistical distance between G_1 and G_2 is determined by pair $(\mathcal{Z},\mathcal{P})$ and will not be greater than the pair $(\mathcal{Z},\mathcal{P})$ is bad. Bad event will not triggered by $\mathcal{S}$ unless the pair $(\mathcal{Z}, \mathcal{P})$ is bad. Hence, the statistical distance between G_1 and G_2 is actually the probability of bad events. □

Next, we consider the transition from G_2 and G_3, i.e. the transition from $(\mathcal{Z},\mathcal{P})$ to $\mathcal{P}$ which is the most important part. Thus, we use the *randomness mapping argument* of Holenstein et al. [24]. In detail, we define a map Γ on tuples of random permutations $(\mathcal{Z},\mathcal{P})$. When the pair $(\mathcal{Z},\mathcal{P})$ is bad, $\Gamma(\mathcal{Z},\mathcal{P}) = \bot$ which is a special symbol. Otherwise, $\Gamma(\mathcal{Z}, \mathcal{P})$ is the tuple of $3w$ tables $\beta = (\beta_1, ..., \beta_{3w})$ standing at the end of the execution $G_2(\mathcal{Z}, \mathcal{P})$. It is easy to see such tables $\beta = (\beta_1, ..., \beta_{3w})$ defines $3w$ partial permutations and a partial permutation is a function $\beta_i : \{+, -\} \times \{0,1\}^n \rightarrow \{0,1\}^n \cup \{*\}$ such that for all $x, y \in \{0,1\}^n, \beta_i(+, x) = y \neq * \Leftrightarrow \beta_i(-, y) = x \neq *$. The map Γ is defined for good pairs $(\mathcal{Z},\mathcal{P})$ as follows: run $\mathcal{D}^{G_2(\mathcal{Z},\mathcal{P})}$, and consider the tables $\mathcal{T}_j$ of the $\mathcal{S}$ at the end of the execution; then fill all undefined entries of the $\mathcal{T}_j$ with the special symbol $*$.

We say that a tuple of permutation $\mathcal{P}$ extends a tuple of partial permutation $\beta = (\beta_1, ..., \beta_{3w})$, denoted $\mathcal{P} \vdash \beta$, if for each β_i and $\mathcal{P}$ agree on all entries such that $\beta_i(\delta, x) \neq *$. By the definition of the randomness mapping, for any good tuple of partial permutation β, the output of $\mathcal{D}^{G_2(\mathcal{Z},\mathcal{P})}$ and $\mathcal{D}^{G_3(\mathcal{P})}$ are equal for any pair $(\mathcal{Z},\mathcal{P})$ such that $\Gamma(\mathcal{Z}, \mathcal{P}) = \beta$ and any tuple of permutations $\mathcal{P}$ such that $\mathcal{P} \vdash \beta$. We can conclude that for all β, the distance $\Delta(G_2, G_3)$ between G_2 and G_3 is bounded by

$$\Delta(G_2, G_3) = \left| \Pr\left[\mathcal{D}^{G_2(\mathcal{Z}, \mathcal{P})} = 1\right] - |\Pr\left[\mathcal{D}^{G_3(\mathcal{P})} = 1\right]\right|$$

$$\leq \Pr[(\mathcal{Z}, \mathcal{P}) \text{ is bad}] + \sum \Pr[\Gamma(\mathcal{Z}, \mathcal{P}) = \beta] - \sum \Pr[\mathcal{P} \vdash \beta]. \quad (9)$$

For $\mathcal{D}^{G_3(\mathcal{P})}$, let $\bar{q}_{T_j}$ be the good execution of $\mathcal{P} \vdash \beta$, then:

$$\Pr[\mathcal{P} \vdash \beta] = \prod_T \prod_{j=0}^{w} \prod_{l=0}^{|\bar{q}_{T_j}|-1} \frac{1}{N-l}. \quad (10)$$

For $\mathcal{D}^{G_2(\mathcal{Z}, \mathcal{P})}$, let $\bar{p}_{T_j}$ be the good pair of $\Gamma(\mathcal{Z}, \mathcal{P}) = \beta$, then:

$$\Pr[\Gamma(\mathcal{Z}, \mathcal{P}) = \beta] = \left(\prod_{l=0}^{|\mathcal{Z}|-1} \frac{1}{N^w - l} \right) \cdot \left(\prod_T \prod_{j=1}^{w} \prod_{l=0}^{|\bar{p}_{T_j}|-1} \frac{1}{N-l} \right). \quad (11)$$

Lemma 3. *Under the conditions of (10) and (11), for $T \in \{B\}$, $|\bar{p}_{T_j}| = |\bar{q}_{T_j}|$, and for $T \in \{A, C\}$, if there exist two non-negative integers a, c such that $a + c = |\mathcal{Z}|$, then $|\bar{q}_{A_j}| = |\bar{p}_{A_j}| + a$, $|\bar{q}_{C_j}| = |\bar{p}_{C_j}| + c$*

Proof. Recall that G_3 is the real world, $|\bar{q}_{T_j}| = |T_j|$ since there is no adapt mechanism in it. In G_2, $|B_j|$ will never be adapted, so $|\bar{p}_{T_j}| = |T_j| = |\bar{q}_{T_j}|$ if $T \in \{B\}$. $|A_j|$ and $|C_j|$ is adapted when the simulator call procedures AdaptA or AdaptC. Noted that $\mathcal{Z}$ is only called by AdaptA or AdaptC, so the times AdaptA or AdaptC called is equal to the size of table $\mathcal{Z}$. Assume that AdaptA is called a times and AdaptC is called c times, so clearly $|\mathcal{Z}| = a + c$. Due to the adapt mechanism of G_2, $|\bar{q}_{A_j}| = |\bar{p}_{A_j}| + a$, $|\bar{q}_{C_j}| = |\bar{p}_{C_j}| + c$. $\square$

We divide (10) by (11), and apply Lemma 3:

$$\frac{\Pr[\mathcal{P} \vdash \beta]}{\Pr[\Gamma(\mathcal{Z}, \mathcal{P}) = \beta]} = \frac{\prod_T \prod_{j=0}^{w} \prod_{h=0}^{|\bar{q}_{T_j}|-1} \frac{1}{N-h}}{\left(\prod_{h=0}^{|\mathcal{Z}|-1} \frac{1}{N^w - h} \right) \cdot \left(\prod_T \prod_{j=1}^{w} \prod_{h=0}^{|\bar{p}_{T_j}|-1} \frac{1}{N-h} \right)}$$

$$\geq \prod_{h=0}^{a-1} \frac{1}{(N-h)^w} \cdot \prod_{h=0}^{c-1} \frac{1}{(N-h)^w} \cdot \prod_{h=0}^{a+c-1} (N^w - h)$$

$$= \frac{N^w - 1}{N^w} \cdot \prod_{h=1}^{a-1} \frac{1}{(N-h)^w} \cdot \prod_{h=1}^{c-1} \frac{1}{(N-h)^w} \cdot \prod_{h=2}^{a+c-1} (N^w - h)$$

$$= \frac{N^w - 1}{N^w} \cdot \frac{\prod_{h=a}^{a+c-1}(N^w - h)}{\prod_{h=1}^{c-1}(N-h)^w}$$

$$\geq \frac{N^w - 1}{N^w} = 1 - \frac{1}{N^w}.$$

$$(12)$$

Gathering Eqs. (12) and (9), we have

$$\Delta(G_2, G_3) \leq \Pr[(\mathcal{Z}, \mathcal{P}) \text{ is bad}] + \sum \Pr[\Gamma(\mathcal{Z}, \mathcal{P}) = \beta] - \sum \Pr[\mathcal{P} \vdash \beta]$$

$$= \Pr[(\mathcal{Z}, \mathcal{P}) \text{ is bad}] + \sum \Pr[\Gamma(\mathcal{Z}, \mathcal{P}) = \beta]\left(1 - \frac{\Pr[\Gamma(\mathcal{Z}, \mathcal{P}) = \beta]}{\Pr[\mathcal{P} \vdash \beta]}\right)$$

$$\leq \Pr[(\mathcal{Z}, \mathcal{P}) \text{ is bad}] + \sum \Pr[\Gamma(\mathcal{Z}, \mathcal{P}) = \beta] \cdot \frac{1}{N^w}$$

$$\leq \Pr[(\mathcal{Z}, \mathcal{P}) \text{ is bad}] + \frac{1}{N^w}. \tag{13}$$

Using Lemma 3 again, we eventually have Eq. (2).

$$\left| \Pr\left[\mathcal{D}^{G_1(\mathcal{Z}, \mathcal{P})} = 1\right] - \left| \Pr\left[\mathcal{D}^{G_3(\mathcal{P})} = 1\right] \right| \right.$$

$$\leq \Delta(G_2, G_3) + \Pr[(\mathcal{Z}, \mathcal{P}) \text{ is bad}]$$

$$= 2\Pr[(\mathcal{Z}, \mathcal{P}) \text{ is bad}] + \frac{1}{N^w} \tag{14}$$

$$= \frac{4q^w(q^w + q)}{N - q^w - q} + \frac{4w(q^w + q)^2\left(\mathsf{MaxPreEx}(\pi) + \mathsf{MaxCoPr}(\pi)\right)}{N - q^w - q} + \frac{1}{N^w}.$$

5   Conclusion

We characterize the sequential indifferentiability of Confusion-Diffusion Networks (CDNs). Assuming using random permutations as S-boxes and non-linear permutations as the diffusion layer, we exhibit a sequential distinguisher against 2-round CDNs (strengthening Dodis et al.'s negative result [16]) and prove sequential indifferentiability for 3-round CDN. Non-linear D-boxes satisfy certain combinatorial requirements, and this is crucial for the proof of Sect. 4.4. This was also central for the full indifferentiability results of [16]: as mentioned in our Introduction, using non-linear D-boxes 5 rounds are proved indifferentiable, while 9 rounds are needed for linear D-boxes. Hence, to achieve sequential indifferentiability, the exact number of rounds required by non-linear CDNs is 3, which is better than that (5 rounds) needed for full indifferentiability. These complement Dodis et al.'s results in the full indifferentiability setting [16] and deepen the theory of known-key security of block ciphers.

Acknowledgments. We sincerely appreciate the anonymous reviewers for their insightful feedback that helps us improving our presentations greatly. Chun Guo was partly supported by the Program of Taishan Young Scholars of the Shandong Province, the Program of Qilu Young Scholars (Grant No. 61580089963177) of Shandong University, the National Natural Science Foundation of China (Grant No. 62002202), and the Shandong Nature Science Foundation of China (Grant No. ZR2020MF053).

References

1. Andreeva, E., Bogdanov, A., Dodis, Y., Mennink, B., Steinberger, J.P.: On the indifferentiability of key-alternating ciphers. In: Canetti, R., Garay, J.A. (eds.) CRYPTO 2013. LNCS, vol. 8042, pp. 531–550. Springer, Heidelberg (2013). https://doi.org/10.1007/978-3-642-40041-4_29

2. Andreeva, E., Bogdanov, A., Mennink, B.: Towards understanding the known-key security of block ciphers. In: Moriai, S. (ed.) FSE 2013. LNCS, vol. 8424, pp. 348–366. Springer, Heidelberg (2014). https://doi.org/10.1007/978-3-662-43933-3_18

3. Barbosa, M., Farshim, P.: Indifferentiable authenticated encryption. In: Shacham, H., Boldyreva, A. (eds.) CRYPTO 2018, Part I. LNCS, vol. 10991, pp. 187–220. Springer, Cham (2018). https://doi.org/10.1007/978-3-319-96884-1_7

4. Bertoni, G., Daemen, J., Peeters, M., Van Assche, G.: On the indifferentiability of the sponge construction. In: Smart, N. (ed.) EUROCRYPT 2008. LNCS, vol. 4965, pp. 181–197. Springer, Heidelberg (2008). https://doi.org/10.1007/978-3-540-78967-3_11

5. Bertoni, G., Peeters, M., Van Assche, G., et al.: The Keccak Reference (2011)

6. Canetti, R., Goldreich, O., Halevi, S.: The random oracle methodology, revisited (preliminary version). In: 30th Annual ACM Symposium on Theory of Computing (STOC), pp. 209–218. ACM Press, May 1998. https://doi.org/10.1145/276698.276741

7. Cogliati, B., et al.: Provable security of (tweakable) block ciphers based on substitution-permutation networks. In: Shacham, H., Boldyreva, A. (eds.) CRYPTO 2018, Part I. LNCS, vol. 10991, pp. 722–753. Springer, Cham (2018). https://doi.org/10.1007/978-3-319-96884-1_24

8. Cogliati, B., Seurin, Y.: On the provable security of the iterated Even-Mansour cipher against related-key and chosen-key attacks. In: Oswald, E., Fischlin, M. (eds.) EUROCRYPT 2015, Part I. LNCS, vol. 9056, pp. 584–613. Springer, Heidelberg (2015). https://doi.org/10.1007/978-3-662-46800-5_23

9. Cogliati, B., Seurin, Y.: Strengthening the known-key security notion for block ciphers. In: Peyrin, T. (ed.) FSE 2016. LNCS, vol. 9783, pp. 494–513. Springer, Heidelberg (2016). https://doi.org/10.1007/978-3-662-52993-5_25

10. Coron, J.-S., Dodis, Y., Malinaud, C., Puniya, P.: Merkle-Damgård revisited: how to construct a hash function. In: Shoup, V. (ed.) CRYPTO 2005. LNCS, vol. 3621, pp. 430–448. Springer, Heidelberg (2005). https://doi.org/10.1007/11535218_26

11. Coron, J.-S., Holenstein, T., Künzler, R., Patarin, J., Seurin, Y., Tessaro, S.: How to build an ideal cipher: the indifferentiability of the Feistel construction. J. Cryptol. 29(1), 61–114 (2014). https://doi.org/10.1007/s00145-014-9189-6

12. Daemen, J., Rijmen, V.: The wide trail design strategy. In: Honary, B. (ed.) Cryptography and Coding 2001. LNCS, vol. 2260, pp. 222–238. Springer, Heidelberg (2001). https://doi.org/10.1007/3-540-45325-3_20

13. Daemen, J., Rijmen, V.: The Design of Rijndael, vol. 2. Springer, Heidelberg (2002)

14. Dai, Y., Seurin, Y., Steinberger, J., Thiruvengadam, A.: Indifferentiability of iterated Even-Mansour ciphers with non-idealized key-schedules: five rounds are necessary and sufficient. In: Katz, J., Shacham, H. (eds.) CRYPTO 2017, Part III. LNCS, vol. 10403, pp. 524–555. Springer, Cham (2017). https://doi.org/10.1007/978-3-319-63697-9_18

15. Dodis, Y., Ristenpart, T., Shrimpton, T.: Salvaging Merkle-Damgård for practical applications. In: Joux, A. (ed.) EUROCRYPT 2009. LNCS, vol. 5479, pp. 371–388. Springer, Heidelberg (2009). https://doi.org/10.1007/978-3-642-01001-9_22

16. Dodis, Y., Stam, M., Steinberger, J., Liu, T.: Indifferentiability of Confusion-Diffusion networks. In: Fischlin, M., Coron, J.-S. (eds.) EUROCRYPT 2016. LNCS, vol. 9666, pp. 679–704. Springer, Heidelberg (2016). https://doi.org/10.1007/978-3-662-49896-5_24

17. Feistel, H., Notz, W.A., Smith, J.L.: Cryptographic techniques for machine to machine data communications. IBM Thomas J. Watson Research Center (1971)

18. Gao, Y., Guo, C., Wang, M., Wang, W., Wen, J.: Beyond-birthday-bound security for 4-round linear substitution-permutation networks. IACR Transactions on Symmetric Cryptology, pp. 305–326 (2020). https://doi.org/10.13154/tosc.v2020.i3.305-326

19. Gilbert, H.: A simplified representation of AES. In: Sarkar, P., Iwata, T. (eds.) ASIACRYPT 2014. LNCS, vol. 8873, pp. 200–222. Springer, Heidelberg (2014). https://doi.org/10.1007/978-3-662-45611-8_11

20. Grassi, L., Rechberger, C.: Revisiting Gilbert's known-key distinguisher. Des. Codes Cryptogr. 88(7), 1401–1445 (2020). https://doi.org/10.1007/s10623-020-00756-5

21. Guo, C., Katz, J., Wang, X., Yu, Y.: Efficient and secure multiparty computation from fixed-key block ciphers. In: 2020 IEEE Symposium on Security and Privacy, San Francisco, CA, USA, 18–21 May 2020, pp. 825–841. IEEE Computer Society Press (2020). https://doi.org/10.1109/SP40000.2020.00016

22. Guo, C., Lin, D.: A synthetic indifferentiability analysis of interleaved double-key Even-Mansour ciphers. In: Iwata, T., Cheon, J.H. (eds.) ASIACRYPT 2015. LNCS, vol. 9453, pp. 389–410. Springer, Heidelberg (2015). https://doi.org/10.1007/978-3-662-48800-3_16

23. Guo, C., Lin, D.: Separating invertible key derivations from non-invertible ones: sequential indifferentiability of 3-round Even–Mansour. Des. Codes Crypt. 81(1), 109–129 (2015). https://doi.org/10.1007/s10623-015-0132-0

24. Holenstein, T., Künzler, R., Tessaro, S.: The equivalence of the random oracle model and the ideal cipher model, revisited. In: Fortnow, L., Vadhan, S.P. (eds.) 43rd ACM STOC, pp. 89–98. ACM Press, June 2011. https://doi.org/10.1145/1993636.1993650

25. Iwata, T., Kurosawa, K.: On the pseudorandomness of the AES finalists - RC6 and serpent. In: Goos, G., Hartmanis, J., van Leeuwen, J., Schneier, B. (eds.) FSE 2000. LNCS, vol. 1978, pp. 231–243. Springer, Heidelberg (2001). https://doi.org/10.1007/3-540-44706-7_16

26. Knudsen, L.R., Rijmen, V.: Known-key distinguishers for some block ciphers. In: Kurosawa, K. (ed.) ASIACRYPT 2007. LNCS, vol. 4833, pp. 315–324. Springer, Heidelberg (2007). https://doi.org/10.1007/978-3-540-76900-2_19

27. Lai, X.: On the design and security of block ciphers. Ph.D. thesis, ETH Zurich (1992)

28. Lai, X., Massey, J.L.: A proposal for a new block encryption standard. In: Damgård, I.B. (ed.) EUROCRYPT 1990. LNCS, vol. 473, pp. 389–404. Springer, Heidelberg (1991). https://doi.org/10.1007/3-540-46877-3_35

29. Liu, Y., Rijmen, V., Leander, G.: Nonlinear diffusion layers. Des. Codes Crypt. 86(11), 2469–2484 (2018). https://doi.org/10.1007/s10623-018-0458-5

30. Mandal, A., Patarin, J., Seurin, Y.: On the public indifferentiability and correlation intractability of the 6-round Feistel construction. In: Cramer, R. (ed.) TCC 2012. LNCS, vol. 7194, pp. 285–302. Springer, Heidelberg (2012). https://doi.org/10.1007/978-3-642-28914-9_16

31. Maurer, U., Renner, R.: From indifferentiability to constructive cryptography (and back). In: Hirt, M., Smith, A. (eds.) TCC 2016, Part I. LNCS, vol. 9985, pp. 3–24. Springer, Heidelberg (2016). https://doi.org/10.1007/978-3-662-53641-4_1

32. Maurer, U., Renner, R., Holenstein, C.: Indifferentiability, impossibility results on reductions, and applications to the random oracle methodology. In: Naor, M. (ed.) TCC 2004. LNCS, vol. 2951, pp. 21–39. Springer, Heidelberg (2004). https://doi.org/10.1007/978-3-540-24638-1_2

33. Miles, E., Viola, E.: Substitution-permutation networks, pseudorandom functions, and natural proofs. In: Safavi-Naini, R., Canetti, R. (eds.) CRYPTO 2012. LNCS, vol. 7417, pp. 68–85. Springer, Heidelberg (2012). https://doi.org/10.1007/978-3-642-32009-5_5

34. Naito, Y., Yoneyama, K., Wang, L., Ohta, K.: How to confirm cryptosystems security: the original Merkle-Damgård is still alive! In: Matsui, M. (ed.) ASIACRYPT 2009. LNCS, vol. 5912, pp. 382–398. Springer, Heidelberg (2009). https://doi.org/10.1007/978-3-642-10366-7_23

35. Park, S., Sung, S.H., Lee, S., Lim, J.: Improving the upper bound on the maximum differential and the maximum linear hull probability for SPN structures and AES. In: Johansson, T. (ed.) FSE 2003. LNCS, vol. 2887, pp. 247–260. Springer, Heidelberg (2003). https://doi.org/10.1007/978-3-540-39887-5_19

36. Rogaway, P., Steinberger, J.: Constructing cryptographic hash functions from fixed-key blockciphers. In: Wagner, D. (ed.) CRYPTO 2008. LNCS, vol. 5157, pp. 433–450. Springer, Heidelberg (2008). https://doi.org/10.1007/978-3-540-85174-5_24

37. Shannon, C.E.: Communication theory of secrecy systems. Bell Syst. Tech. J. **28**(4), 656–715 (1949)

38. Soni, P., Tessaro, S.: Public-seed pseudorandom permutations. In: Coron, J.-S., Nielsen, J.B. (eds.) EUROCRYPT 2017, Part II. LNCS, vol. 10211, pp. 412–441. Springer, Cham (2017). https://doi.org/10.1007/978-3-319-56614-6_14

39. Soni, P., Tessaro, S.: Naor-Reingold goes public: the complexity of known-key security. In: Nielsen, J.B., Rijmen, V. (eds.) EUROCRYPT 2018, Part III. LNCS, vol. 10822, pp. 653–684. Springer, Cham (2018). https://doi.org/10.1007/978-3-319-78372-7_21

40. Sun, B., Liu, M., Guo, J., Rijmen, V., Li, R.: Provable security evaluation of structures against impossible differential and zero correlation linear cryptanalysis. In: Fischlin, M., Coron, J.-S. (eds.) EUROCRYPT 2016. LNCS, vol. 9665, pp. 196–213. Springer, Heidelberg (2016). https://doi.org/10.1007/978-3-662-49890-3_8

41. Wu, W., Zhang, L.: LBlock: a lightweight block cipher. In: Lopez, J., Tsudik, G. (eds.) ACNS 2011. LNCS, vol. 6715, pp. 327–344. Springer, Heidelberg (2011). https://doi.org/10.1007/978-3-642-21554-4_19

42. Yoneyama, K., Miyagawa, S., Ohta, K.: Leaky random oracle (extended abstract). In: Baek, J., Bao, F., Chen, K., Lai, X. (eds.) ProvSec 2008. LNCS, vol. 5324, pp. 226–240. Springer, Heidelberg (2008). https://doi.org/10.1007/978-3-540-88733-1_16

43. Zhang, W., Bao, Z., Lin, D., Rijmen, V., Yang, B., Verbauwhede, I.: Rectangle: a bit-slice lightweight block cipher suitable for multiple platforms. Sci. China Inf. Sci. **58**(12), 1–15 (2015)

Elastic-Tweak: A Framework for Short Tweak Tweakable Block Cipher

Avik Chakraborti[1], Nilanjan Datta[2(✉)], Ashwin Jha[3],
Cuauhtemoc Mancillas-López[4], Mridul Nandi[5], and Yu Sasaki[6]

[1] University of Exeter, Exeter, UK
a.chakraborti@exeter.ac.uk
[2] Institute for Advancing Intelligence, TCG CREST, Kolkata, India
nilanjan.datta@tcgcrest.org
[3] CISPA Helmholtz Center for Information Security, Saarbrücken, Germany
ashwin.jha@cispa.de
[4] Computer Science Department, CINVESTAV-IPN, Mexico City, Mexico
cuauhtemoc.mancillas@cinvestav.mx
[5] Indian Statistical Institute, Kolkata, India
mridul@isical.ac.in
[6] NTT Secure Platform Laboratories, Tokyo, Japan
sasaki.yu@lab.ntt.co.jp

Abstract. Tweakable block cipher (TBC), a stronger notion than
standard block ciphers, has wide-scale applications in symmetric-key
schemes. At a high level, it provides flexibility in design and (possibly)
better security bounds. In multi-keyed applications, a TBC with short
tweak values can be used to replace multiple keys. However, the existing TBC construction frameworks, including TWEAKEY and XEX, are
designed for general purpose tweak sizes. Specifically, they are not optimized for short tweaks, which might render them inefficient for certain
resource constrained applications. So a dedicated paradigm to construct
short-tweak TBCs (tBC) is highly desirable. In this paper, as a first contribution, we present a dedicated framework, called the Elastic-Tweak
framework (ET in short), to convert any reasonably secure SPN block
cipher into a secure tBC. We apply the ET framework on GIFT and AES
to construct efficient tBCs, named TweGIFT and TweAES. These short-
tweak TBCs have already been employed in recent NIST lightweight competition candidates, LOTUS-LOCUS and ESTATE. As our second contribution, we show some concrete applications of ET-based tBCs, which
are better than their block cipher counterparts in terms of key size, state
size, number of block cipher calls, and short message processing. Some
notable applications include, Twe-FCBC (reduces the key size of FCBC
and gives better security than CMAC), Twe-LightMAC_Plus (better rate
than LightMAC_Plus), Twe-CLOC, and Twe-SILC (reduces the number of
block cipher calls and simplifies the design of CLOC and SILC).

Keywords: TBC · GIFT · AES · TWEAKEY · XEX · ESTATE,
LOTUS-LOCUS

© Springer Nature Switzerland AG 2021
A. Adhikari et al. (Eds.): INDOCRYPT 2021, LNCS 13143, pp. 114–137, 2021.
https://doi.org/10.1007/978-3-030-92518-5_6

1 Introduction

Since their advent in late 1970's, block ciphers [1,2] have become the ubiquitous building blocks in various symmetric-key cryptographic algorithms, including encryption schemes [3], message authentication codes (MACs) [4], and authenticated encryption [5]. Due to their wide-scale applicability, block ciphers are also the most well-analyzed symmetric-key primitives. As a result, the cryptographic community bestows a high degree of confidence in block cipher based designs. Block cipher structures are more or less well formalized and there are formal ways to prove the security of a block cipher against the classical linear [6] and differential [7] attacks. The literature is filled with a plethora of block cipher candidates, AES [2] being the most notable among them. AES is currently the NIST standard block cipher [2], and it is the recommended choice for several standardized encryption, MAC and AE schemes such as CTR [3], CMAC [4], AES-GCM [8] etc. A recent block cipher proposal, named GIFT [9] has generated a lot of interest due to its ultra-lightweight nature.

1.1 Some Issues in Block Cipher Based Designs

KEY SIZE OF DESIGNS: Several designs use more than one independent block cipher keys, which could be an issue for storage constrained applications. Some notable examples of such designs are sum of permutations [10,11], EDM [12], EWCDM [12], CLRW2 [13], GCM-SIV-2 [14], Benes construction [15]. While some of these designs have been reduced to single key variants, reducing a multi-keyed design to single-key design is, in general, a challenging problem.

AUXILIARY SECRET STATE: FCBC, a three-key MAC by Black and Rogaway [16], is a CBC-MAC type construction. CMAC [4], the NIST recommended MAC design, reduces number of keys from three to one by using an auxiliary secret state (which is nothing but the encryption of zero block). Though CMAC is NIST recommended MAC design, it costs an extra block cipher call (compared to FCBC) and holds an additional state. This may be an issue in hardware applications, where area and energy consumption are very crucial parameters. Further FCBC [17,18] allows more number of queries per key, as compared to CMAC [19].

SIMPLICITY OF DESIGNS: Design simplification, is a closely related topic to the single-keyed vs. multi-keyed debate. A simple design could be beneficial for real life applications, and better understanding of designs themselves. Often, the single-keyed variant of a block cipher based design is much more complex than the multi-keyed version, both in implementation and security analysis. This is due to the several auxiliary functions used chiefly for domain separation. For instance CLOC and SILC [20] use several functions depending upon the associated data and message length. In contrast, the multi-keyed variants of CLOC and SILC would be much simpler.

SHORT MESSAGE PROCESSING: An essential requirement in lightweight applications is efficient short input data processing, while minimizing the memory consumption and precomputation. In use cases with tight requirements on delay and latency, the typical packet sizes are small (way less than 1 Kilobytes) as large packets occupy a link for longer duration, causing more delays to subsequent packets and increasing latency. For example, Zigbee, Bluetooth low energy and TinySec [21] limit the maximum packet lengths to 127 bytes, 47 bytes and 128 bytes, respectively. Similarly, CAN FD [22], a well-known transmission protocol in automotive networks, allows message length up to 64 bytes. The packet sizes in EPC tag [23], which is an alternate to the bar code using RFID, is typically 12 bytes.

Cryptographic designs with low latency for shorter messages could be highly beneficial for such applications. As it turns out, for many designs short message performance is not that good due to some constant overhead. For instance CMAC uses one block cipher call to generate a secret state, and SUNDAE [24] uses the first call of block cipher to distinguish different possibilities of associated data and message lengths. So, to process a single block message, SUNDAE requires two block cipher calls. CLOC and SILC [20] have similar drawbacks. They cost 2 and 4 calls to process a single block message. LightMAC_Plus [25], feeds a counter-based encoded input to the block cipher, which reduces the rate.[1]

1.2   Motivation of Short-Tweak TBC

TWEAKABLE BLOCK CIPHERS: The Hasty Pudding cipher [26], an unsuccessful candidate for AES competition, was one of the first tweakable block ciphers.[2] Later, Liskov et al. in formalized this in their foundational work on tweakable block ciphers [27]. Tweakable block ciphers (TBCs) are more versatile and find a broad range of applications, most notably in authenticated encryption schemes, such as OCB [28], COPA [29], and Deoxys [30]; and message authentication codes, such as ZMAC [31], NaT [32], and ZMAC+ [33]. TBCs can be designed from scratch [26,34,35], or they can be built using existing primitives like block ciphers, and public permutations. LRW1, LRW2 [27], CLRW2 [13], XEX [36] and XHX[37] are some examples of the former category, whereas Tweakable Even-Mansour [32] is an example of the latter.

Tweakable block cipher can actually solve most of the aforementioned issues in block ciphers quite easily. A secure TBC with distinct tweaks is actually equivalent to independently keyed instantiations of a secure block cipher. This naturally gives a TBC based single-keyed design for any block cipher based multi-keyed design. For example, one can use this equivalence to define a single-keyed version of FCBC which is as secure as FCBC. This resolves the issues with CMAC. In some cases, TBCs can also avoid the extra block cipher calls. It also helps to simplify designs like CLOC and SILC.

In all these cases, we observe that a short tweak space (in most of the cases 2-bit or 4-bit tweaks) is sufficient. In other words, a short-tweak tweakable block cipher (in short we call tBC) would suffice for resolving these issues. An tBC is

---

[1] No. of message blocks processed per block cipher call.
[2] It used the term "spice" for tweaks.

better than large tweak TBCs in two respects: (i) state size for holding tweak is small, and most importantly (ii) tBC would potentially be more efficient than large tweak TBCs.

THE TWEAKEY FRAMEWORK: At Asiacrypt'14, Jean et al. presented a generic framework for TBC construction, called TWEAKEY [38], that considers the tweak and key inputs in a unified manner. Basically, the framework formalized the concept of tweak-dependent keys. The TWEAKEY framework gave a much needed impetus to the design of TBCs, with several designs like Kiasu [39], Deoxys [30], SKINNY and Mantis [40] etc. As TWEAKEY is conceptualized with general purpose tweak sizes in mind, it is bit difficult to optimize TWEAKEY for tBC. For instance, take the example of SKINNY-128. To process only 4-bit tweak, the additional register is limited but their computation modes must move from TK1 to TK2, which increases the number of rounds by 8. This in turn affects the throughput of the cipher. Although, some TWEAKEY-based designs, especially Kiasu-BC [39] do not need additional rounds, yet this is true in most of the existing TWEAKEY-based designs. We also note here that Kiasu-BC, which is based on AES, is weaker than AES by one round, as observed in several previous cryptanalytic works [41–43].

So, there is a need for a generic design framework for tBC, which (i) can be applied on top of a block cipher, (ii) adds minimal overheads, and (iii) is as secure as the underlying block cipher.

XE AND XEX: Rogaway [36], proposed two efficient ways of converting a block cipher into a tweakable block cipher, denoted by XE and XEX. These methods are widely used in various modes such as PMAC [44], OCB [45], COPA [29], ELmD [46] etc. However, XE and XEX have several limitations with respect to a short tweak space, notably (i) security is limited to birthday bound, and (ii) precomputation and storage overhead to generate the secret state. In addition, it also requires to update the secret state for each invocation, which might add some overhead.

1.3   Our Contributions

Our main contributions can be divided into two parts:

1. ELASTIC-TWEAK FRAMEWORK: In this work, we address the above issues and propose a generic framework, called the Elastic-Tweak framework (ET in short), to transform a block cipher into a short tweak TBC. We consider "short tweaks" of size less than equal to 16 bits and greater than equal to 4 bits. This small size ensures that the tweak storage overhead is negligible. In this framework, given the block cipher, we first expand the short tweak using linear code, and then inject the expanded tweak at intervals of some fixed number of rounds, say r. Designs under this framework can be flexibly built over a secure block cipher, and are as secure as the underlying block cipher.

The ET framework distributes the effect of the tweak into the block cipher state that can generate several active bytes. In particular we choose a linear code with high branch number to expand the input tweak. This design is particularly suitable for short tweaks to ensure the security against differential cryptanalysis because the small weight of the short input always results in a large weight of the output.

Another advantage of the framework is the easiness of the security evaluation. First, for zero tweak value, the plaintext-ciphertext transformation is exactly the same as the original cipher (i.e. it has backward compatibility feature). Therefore, to evaluate the security of the new construction, we only need to consider the attacks that exploit at least one non-zero tweak. Second, the large weight of the expanded tweak ensures relatively high security only with a small number of rounds around the tweak injection. This allows a designer to focus on the security of the r-round transformation followed by the tweak injection and further followed by the r-round transformation, which is called "$2r$-round core".

We instantiate this framework with several designs over two well known block ciphers AES [2] and GIFT [9] with different tweak sizes varying from 4 to 16. Several of these candidates have already been extensively analyzed in [47,48] in terms of security and performance due to their use in NIST lightweight competition candidates, LOTUS-LOCUS [49] and ESTATE [50]. However, we refer the full version [51] for the thorough security analysis (Sect 4, [51]) and performance evaluation (Sect 3.4 and Appendix C, [51]).

2. APPLICATIONS OF tBC: Here we demonstrate the applicability of tBC in various constructions:

1. **Reducing the Key Size in Multi-Keyed Modes:** The primary application of tBC is to reduce the key space of several block cipher based modes that use multiple independently sampled keys. We depict the applicability of tBC on FCBC MAC, Double Block Hash-then-Sum (DbHtS) paradigm, Sum of permutations, EDM, EWCDM, CLRW2, GCM-SIV-2 and the Benes construction.

2. **Efficient Processing of Short Messages:** tBC can be used to reduce the number of block cipher calls, which in turn reduces the energy consumption for short messages. We take the instance of Twe-LightMAC_Plus to demonstrate this application of tBC. Twe-LightMAC_Plus achieves a higher rate as compared to it's original counterpart LightMAC_Plus. In addition, the number of keys is reduced from 3 to 1. However, this is also applicable to Twe-CLOC and Twe-SILC (tBC based counterparts of CLOC and SILC [20] respectively).

3. **Replacement for XE and XEX.** tBC can be viewed as an efficient replacement of XE and XEX especially when we target short messages (say of size up to 1 MB). In such cases, instead of using a secret state (that we need to precompute, store and update), one can simply use tBC with the block-counters as the tweak. The applicability of this paradigm can be depicted on several MAC modes such as PMAC; encryption mode such as COPE and AEAD modes such as ELmD, COLM.

In addition to the above applications, we show that tBCs can also simplify the internal structures of various block cipher based authenticated encryption modes. For example, CLOC, SILC use several auxiliary functions mainly for domain separation. We propose tBC-based variants for these, named Twe-CLOC and Twe-SILC, which simplify the original designs (by cleaning up the auxiliary functions) and reduces the number of block cipher calls. These in turn help in reducing the area of hardware implementation, and significantly increasing the throughput for short messages.

2 Preliminaries

NOTATIONS: For $n \in \mathbb{N}$, $[n]$ denotes the set $\{1, \ldots, n\}$, and $\{0,1\}^n$ denotes the set of all n-bit binary strings. We use $\{0,1\}^+$ to denote the set of all non-empty binary strings. $\perp$ denotes the empty string and $\{0,1\}^* = \{0,1\}^+ \cup \{\perp\}$. For any string $X \in \{0,1\}^n$, $|X|$ denotes the number of bits in X, and for $i \in [|X|]$, x_i denotes the i-th significant bit ($x_{|X|}$ being the most significant bit). For $X \in \{0,1\}^+$ and $n \in \mathbb{N}$, $(X)_{[\ell]} := (X_1, \ldots, X_\ell) \xleftarrow{n} X$, denotes the n-bit block parsing of X into $(X)_{[\ell]}$, where $|X_i| = n$ for $[\ell - 1]$, and $X_\ell \in [n]$. For $k \le n \in \mathbb{N}$, and $X \in \{0,1\}^n$, $\lfloor X \rfloor_k := X_1 \ldots X_k$. The expression $a\ ?\ b\ :\ c$ evaluates to b if a is true and c otherwise.

For $n, m \in \mathbb{N}$, $\mathsf{Perm}(n)$ denotes the set of all permutations over $\{0,1\}^n$, and $\mathsf{Func}(m, n)$ denotes the set of all functions from $\{0,1\}^m$ to $\{0,1\}^n$. For $n, \kappa \in \mathbb{N}$, $\mathsf{TPerm}(\kappa, n)$ denotes the set of all families of permutations $P_k := P(k, \cdot) \in \mathsf{Perm}(n)$ indexed by $k \in \{0,1\}^\kappa$. By extending notation, we use $\mathsf{TPerm}(\kappa, \tau, n)$ to denote the set of all families of permutations $P_{k,t} \in \mathsf{Perm}(n)$, indexed by $(k, \tau) \in \{0,1\}^\kappa \times \{0,1\}^\tau$.

(TWEAKABLE) BLOCK CIPHER: A block cipher with key size κ and block size n is a family of permutations $\mathsf{E} \in \mathsf{TPerm}(\kappa, n)$. For a fixed key $k \in \{0,1\}^\kappa$, we write $\mathsf{E}_k(\cdot) = \mathsf{E}(k, \cdot)$, and its inverse is written as $\mathsf{E}_k^{-1}(\cdot)$. A tweakable block cipher with key size κ, tweak size τ, and block size n is a family of permutations $\mathsf{E} \in \mathsf{TPerm}(\kappa, \tau, n)$. For a fixed key $k \in \{0,1\}^\kappa$ and tweak $t \in \{0,1\}^\tau$, we write $\mathsf{E}_k^t(\cdot) = \mathsf{E}(k, t, \cdot)$, and its inverse is written as $\mathsf{E}_k^{-t}(\cdot)$. Throughout this paper we fix $\kappa, \tau, n \in \mathbb{N}$ as the key size, tweak size, and block size, respectively, of the given (tweakable) block cipher.

2.1 Security Definitions

(TWEAKABLE) RANDOM PERMUTATION AND RANDOM FUNCTION: For any finite set $\mathcal{X}$, $\mathsf{X} \leftarrow_\$ \mathcal{X}$ denotes uniform and random sampling of X from $\mathcal{X}$. We call $\Pi \leftarrow_\$ \mathsf{Perm}(n)$ a (uniform) random permutation, and $\widetilde{\Pi} \leftarrow_\$ \mathsf{TPerm}(\tau, n)$ a tweakable (uniform) random permutation on tweak space $\{0,1\}^\tau$ and block space $\{0,1\}^n$. Note that, $\widetilde{\Pi}^i$ is independent of $\widetilde{\Pi}^j$ for all $i \ne j \in \{0,1\}^\tau$. We call $\Gamma \leftarrow_\$ \mathsf{Func}(m, n)$ a (uniform) random function from $\{0,1\}^m$ to $\{0,1\}^n$.

We say that a distinguisher is "sane" if it does not make duplicate queries, or queries whose answer is derivable from previous query responses. Let $\mathbb{A}(q, t)$ denote the class of all sane distinguishers, limited to at most q queries and t computations.

TWEAKABLE STRONG PSEUDORANDOM PERMUTATION (TSPRP): The TSPRP advantage of any distinguisher $\mathcal{A}$ against $\widetilde{\mathsf{E}}$ instantiated with key $\mathsf{K} \leftarrow_\$ \{0, 1\}^\kappa$, is defined as

$$\mathbf{Adv}_{\widetilde{\mathsf{E}}}^{\mathsf{tsprp}}(\mathcal{A}) := \left| \Pr[\mathcal{A}^{\widetilde{\mathsf{E}}_\mathsf{K}^\pm} = 1] - \Pr[\mathcal{A}^{\widetilde{\Pi}^\pm} = 1] \right|.$$

The TSPRP security of $\widetilde{\mathsf{E}}$, is defined as

$$\mathbf{Adv}_{\widetilde{\mathsf{E}}}^{\mathsf{tsprp}}(q, t) := \max_{\mathcal{A}} \mathbf{Adv}_{\widetilde{\mathsf{E}}}^{\mathsf{tsprp}}(\mathcal{A}). \tag{1}$$

TPRP or tweakable pseudorandom permutation and its advantage $\mathbf{Adv}_{\widetilde{\mathsf{E}}}^{\mathsf{tprp}}(q, t)$ is defined similarly when adversary has no access of the inverse oracle.

PSEUDORANDOM FUNCTION (PRF): The PRF advantage of distinguisher $\mathcal{A}$ against a keyed family of functions $\mathsf{F} := \{\mathsf{F}_K : \{0, 1\}^m \to \{0, 1\}^n\}_{K \in \{0,1\}^\kappa}$ is defined as

$$\mathbf{Adv}_{\mathsf{F}}^{\mathsf{prf}}(\mathcal{A}) := \left| \Pr_{\mathsf{K} \leftarrow_\$ \{0,1\}^\kappa} [\mathcal{A}^{\mathsf{F}_\mathsf{K}} = 1] - \Pr[\mathcal{A}^{\Gamma} = 1] \right|.$$

The PRF security of F against $\mathbb{A}(q, t)$ is defined as

$$\mathbf{Adv}_{\mathsf{F}}^{\mathsf{prf}}(q, t) := \max_{\mathcal{A}} \mathbf{Adv}_{\mathsf{F}}^{\mathsf{prf}}(\mathcal{A}). \tag{2}$$

The keyed family of functions F is called weak PRF family, if the PRF security holds when the adversary only gets to see the output of the oracle on uniform random inputs. This is clearly a weaker notion than PRF. We denote the weak prf advantage as $\mathbf{Adv}_{\mathsf{F}}^{\mathsf{wprf}}(q, t)$.

IV-BASED ENCRYPTION: An IV-Based Encryption ivE scheme is a tuple $\Psi := (\mathcal{K}, \mathcal{N}, \mathcal{M}, \mathsf{Enc}, \mathsf{Dec})$. Encryption algorithm Enc takes a key $K \in \mathcal{K}$ and a message $M \in \mathcal{M}$ and returns $(\mathsf{iv}, C) = \mathsf{Enc}(K, M)$, where $\mathsf{iv} \in \mathcal{N}$ is the initialization vector and $C \in \mathcal{M}$ is the ciphertext. Decryption algorithm Dec takes K, iv, C and returns $M = \mathsf{Dec}(K, \mathsf{iv}, C)$. Correctness condition says that for all $K \in \mathcal{K}$ and $M \in \mathcal{M}$ $\mathsf{Dec}(K, \mathsf{Enc}(K, M)) = M$. The Priv\$ advantage [14,52–54] of $\mathcal{A}$ is defined as

$$\mathbf{Adv}_{\mathsf{ivE}}^{\mathsf{priv\$}}(\mathcal{A}) := \left| \Pr_{\mathsf{K}} \left[\mathcal{A}^{\mathsf{Enc}_\mathsf{K}} = 1 \right] - \Pr_{\Gamma} \left[\mathcal{A}^{\Gamma} = 1 \right] \right|$$

where $\mathsf{K} \leftarrow_\$ \mathcal{K}$ and Γ is a random function from $\mathcal{M} \to \mathcal{N} \times \mathcal{M}$. The Priv\$ security of ivE, is defined as

$$\mathbf{Adv}_{\mathsf{ivE}}^{\mathsf{priv\$}}(q, t) := \max_{\mathcal{A}} \mathbf{Adv}_{\mathsf{ivE}}^{\mathsf{priv\$}}(\mathcal{A}). \tag{3}$$

(NONCE-BASED) AUTHENTICATED ENCRYPTION WITH ASSOCIATED DATA: A (nonce-based) authenticated encryption with associated data or NAEAD scheme

$\mathfrak{A}$ consists of a key space $\mathcal{K}$, a (possibly empty) nonce space $\mathcal{N}$, a message space $\mathcal{M}$, an associated data space $\mathcal{A}$, and a tag space $\mathcal{T}$, along with two functions $\mathsf{Enc} : \mathcal{K} \times \mathcal{N} \times \mathcal{A} \times \mathcal{M} \to \mathcal{M} \times \mathcal{T}$, and $\mathsf{Dec} : \mathcal{K} \times \mathcal{N} \times \mathcal{A} \times \mathcal{M} \times \mathcal{T} \to \mathcal{M} \cup \{\bot\}$, with the correctness condition that for any $K \in \mathcal{K}, N \in \mathcal{N}, A \in \mathcal{A}, M \in \mathcal{M}$, we must have $\mathsf{Dec}(K, N, A, \mathsf{Enc}(M)) = M$. When the nonce space is empty, we call the AE scheme a deterministic AE or DAE scheme.

Following the security definition in [14,52–54], we define the NAEAD (DAE for deterministic AE) advantage of $\mathcal{A}$ as

$$\mathbf{Adv}^{\mathsf{ae}}_{\mathfrak{A}}(\mathcal{A}) := \left| \Pr_{K}\left[\mathcal{A}^{\mathsf{Enc}_K, \mathsf{Dec}_K} = 1\right] - \Pr_{\Gamma}\left[\mathcal{A}^{\Gamma, \bot} = 1\right] \right|,$$

where $K \leftarrow_\$ \mathcal{K}$ and Γ is a random function from $\mathcal{N} \times \mathcal{A} \times \mathcal{M} \to \mathcal{M} \times \mathcal{T}$, and $\bot$ is the reject oracle that takes (N, A, C, T) as input and returns the reject symbol $\bot$. The NAEAD/DAE security of $\mathfrak{A}$, is defined as

$$\mathbf{Adv}^{\mathsf{ae}}_{\mathfrak{A}}(q, t) := \max_{\mathcal{A}} \mathbf{Adv}^{\mathsf{ae}}_{\mathfrak{A}}(\mathcal{A}). \tag{4}$$

3 The Elastic-Tweak Framework

In this section, we introduce the Elastic-Tweak framework (illustrated in Fig. 1) on SPN based block ciphers that allows one to efficiently design tweakable block ciphers with short tweaks. As the name suggests, Elastic-Tweak refers to elastic expansion of short tweaks and we typically consider tweaks of size less than or equal to 16 bits. Using this framework, one can convert a block cipher to a short tweak tweakble block cipher denoted by tBC. We briefly recall the SPN structure on which this framework would be applied. An SPN block cipher iterates for rnd many rounds, where each round consists of three operations:

(a) SubCells (divides the state into cells and substitutes each cell by an s-bit S-box which is always non-linear),
(b) LinLayer (uses a linear mixing layer over the full state to create diffusion), and
(c) AddRoundKey (add a round keys to the state).

The basic idea of the framework is to expand a small tweak (of size t) using a suitable linear code of high distance and then the expanded tweak (of size t_e) is injected (i.e. xored) to the internal block cipher state affecting a certain number of S-boxes (say, tic). We apply the same process after every gap number of rounds. An important feature of tBC is that it is implemented using very low tweak state and without any tweak schedule (only tweak expansion). In the following, we describe the linear code to expand the tweak and how to inject the tweak into the underlying block cipher state. If BC denotes the underlying SPN block cipher, we denote the tweakable block cipher as Twe BC $[t, t_e, \mathsf{tic}, \mathsf{gap}]$ where $t, t_e, \mathsf{tic}, \mathsf{gap}$ are suitable parameters as described above.

3.1 Exp: Expanding the Tweak

In this section, we describe our method to expand the tweak T of t bits to an expanded tweak T_e of t_e bits. We need the parameters to satisfy the following conditions:

(a) t_e is divisible by $2t$ and tic. Let $w := t_e/\text{tic}$, the underlying word size.
(b) w divides t and $w \leq s$.

The tweak expansion, called Exp, follows an "Expand then (optional) Copy" style as follows:

(i) Let $\tau := t/w$, and we view $T = (T_1, \ldots, T_\tau)$ as a $1 \times \tau$ vector of elements from $\mathbb{F}_{2^w}$. We expand T by applying a $[2\tau, \tau, \tau]$-linear code[3] over $\mathbb{F}_{2^w}$ with the generating matrix $G_{\tau \times 2\tau} = [I_\tau : I_\tau \oplus J_\tau]$, where I_τ is the identity matrix of dimension τ and J is the all 1 square matrix of dimension τ over $\mathbb{F}_{2^w}$. Let $T' = T \cdot G$ be the resultant code. Note that, T' can be computed as $S \oplus T_1 \| \cdots \| S \oplus T_\tau$ where $S = T_1 \oplus \cdots \oplus T_\tau$.

(ii) Finally, we compute the expanded tweak by concatenating $t_e/2t$ many copies of T' i.e.

$$T_e = T' \| \cdots \| T'.$$

Note that, T_e can be viewed as an application of $[\text{tic}, \tau, \text{tic}/2]$-linear code on T. The main rationale behind the choice of this expansion function is that it generates high distance codes (which is highly desired from the cryptanalysis point of view) with a low cost (only $(2\tau - 1)$ addition over $\mathbb{F}_{2^w}$ is required).

Tweak Expansion and Injection

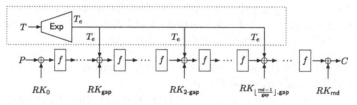

Fig. 1. Elastic-Tweak construction.

3.2 Injecting Expanded Tweak into Round Functions

Note that the expanded tweak can be viewed as $T_{e,1} \| \cdots \| T_{e,\text{tic}}$ where each $T_{e,i}$ is of size w-bits and $w \leq s$. Now we xor these tweak in addition to the round keys in tic number of S-boxes. The exact choices of S-box would be design specific so that the diffusion due to tweak difference is high.

The tweak injection is optional for each round, the tweak injection starts from round start and it is injected at an interval of gap rounds and stops at

---

[3] An $[n, k, d]$-linear code over a field $\mathbb{F}$ is defined by a $k \times n$ matrix G called the *generator* matrix over $\mathbb{F}$ such that for all nonzero vectors $v \in \mathbb{F}^k$, $v \cdot G$ has at least d many nonzero elements.

Function $\mathsf{Exp}[t_e, w](T)$

1. $\tau \leftarrow \frac{|T|}{w}$
2. $T_e \leftarrow \phi$
3. $(T_1, T_2, \ldots, T_\tau) \xleftarrow{w} T$
4. $T' \leftarrow T \| (T \oplus T \cdot J_\tau)$
5. **for** $i = 1$ **to** $t_e/2t$
6. $T_e \leftarrow T_e \| T'$
7. **return** T_e

Algorithm $\mathsf{tBC}\ [t_e, \mathsf{tic}, \mathsf{gap}](X, K, T)$

1. $w \leftarrow t_e/\mathsf{tic}$
2. $T_e \leftarrow \mathsf{Exp}[t_e, w](T)$
3. **for** $i = 1$ **to** rnd
4. $X \leftarrow \mathsf{SubCells}(X)$
5. $X \leftarrow \mathsf{LinLayer}(X)$
6. $(K, X) \leftarrow \mathsf{AddRoundKey}(K, X, i)$
7.   **if** i % gap $= 0$ and $i <$ rnd
8. $\mathsf{AddTweak}[\mathsf{tic}](X, T_e)$
9. **return** X

Fig. 2. Function Exp and tBC. Here, $\mathsf{AddTweak}[\mathsf{tic}](X, T_e)$ represents the xoring tweak in to the state of the block cipher.

round end. To be precise, we inject tweak at the round number start, start $+$ gap, start $+$ 2.gap, $\ldots$, end. To have a uniformity in the tweak injection rounds, we typically choose start $=$ gap and inject the tweaks at an interval of gap rounds. This implicitly sets end $=$ gap.$\lfloor \frac{\mathsf{rnd}-1}{\mathsf{gap}} \rfloor$ (Fig. 2).

REQUIREMENTS FROM Twe BC. We must ensure Twe BC should have same security level as the underlying block cipher.

From the performance point of view, our target is to obtain the above mentioned security.

    "minimizing t_e (signifies the area) and $t_e.\lfloor \frac{\mathsf{rnd}-1}{\mathsf{gap}} \rfloor$ (signifies the energy)."

FEATURES OF Twe BC.

1. Our tBC is applied to any SPN based block ciphers.
2. Due to linear expansion of tweak, tBC with zero tweak turns out to be same as the underlying block cipher (note that we keep same number of rounds as the block cipher). This feature would be useful to reduce overhead due to nonzero tweak. Later we see some applications (e.g., application on FCBC) where the nonzero tweaks is only applied to process the last block.

3.3 Tweakable GIFT and AES

In this section, we provide various instantiation of tBC built upon the two popular block ciphers GIFT and AES. We are primarily interested on tweak size $4, 8, 16$, and hence considered $t \in \{4, 8, 16\}$.

Instantiation of tBC with 4 Bit Tweak. All the recommendations with 4-bit tweaks have extremely low overhead over the original block cipher and they can be ideal for reducing multiple keys scheme to an equivalent single key scheme instance with a minuscule loss in efficiency. Detailed description can be found in Sect. 4.

(i) GIFT-64[4, 16, 16, 4]. In this case the tweak is expanded from 4 bits to 16 bits and the expanded tweak is injected at bit positions $4i + 3$, for $i = 0, \ldots, 15$.

(ii) GIFT-128[4, 32, 32, 5]. Here we expand the 4 bit tweak to 32 bits and the expanded tweak is injected at bit positions $4i + 3$, for $i = 0, \ldots, 31$.

(iii) AES[4, 8, 8, 2]. Here we expand the 4 bit tweak to 8 bits and the expanded tweak is injected at the least-significant bits of each of the 8 S-Boxes in the top two rows.

Instantiation of tBC with 8 and 16 Bit Tweak. tBC with tweak size of 8/16-bits are ideal for replacing the length counter bits (or masking) used in many constructions. Detailed description can be found in Sect. 4.

(i) AES[8, 16, 8, 2]. For 8 bit tweak, we only use AES. The tweak is first extended to 16 bits and the tweak is injected at the two least-significant bits of each of the 8 S-Boxes in the top two rows.

(ii) GIFT-128[16, 32, 32, 4]. Here we expand the 16 bit tweak to 32 bits and the expanded tweak is injected at bit positions $4i + 3$, for $i = 0, \ldots, 31$.

(iii) AES[16, 32, 8, 2]. Here we expand the 16 bit tweak to 32 bits and expanded tweak is injected at the four least-significant bits of each of the 8 S-Boxes in the top two rows.

CRYPTANALYSIS OF THE PROPOSED CANDIDATES: A detailed security analysis of all the proposed candidates is given in Sect 4 in the full version [51]. We remark that several of these candidates have already been analyzed in [47–50].

PERFORMANCE: Sect 3.4 and Appendix C in the full version [51] summarize the hardware and software performance of all the proposed candidates.

4   Applications of Short-Tweak Tweakable Block Ciphers

In this section, we present some use cases where an efficient tBC would be beneficial.

4.1   Reducing the Key Size in Multi-keyed Modes of Operation

Several block cipher based modes of operation employ a block cipher with multiple independently sampled keys. In general, this is done either to boost the security, or to simplify the analysis of the overall construction. The number of keys can be naturally reduced to a single key by replacing the multi-keyed block cipher with a single keyed tBC where distinct tweaks are used to simulate independent block cipher instantiations. Proposition 1 below gives the theoretical justification for this remedy. The proof is obvious from the definitions of (tweakable) random permutation.

Proposition 1. *For some fixed $t \in \mathbb{N}$, and $k \in [2^t]$. Let $(\Pi_1, \ldots, \Pi_k)$ $\leftarrow_\$ (\mathsf{Perm}[n])^k$ and $\widetilde{\Pi} \leftarrow_\$ \mathsf{TPerm}[t, n]$. Let $\mathcal{O}_{\Pi;k}$ and $\mathcal{O}_{\widetilde{\Pi};k}$ be two oracles giving bidirectional access to $(\Pi_1, \ldots, \Pi_k)$, and $(\widetilde{\Pi}^1, \ldots, \widetilde{\Pi}^k)$, respectively. Then, for all distinguisher $\mathcal{A}$, we have*

$$\Delta_\mathcal{A}(\mathcal{O}_{\Pi;k}; \mathcal{O}_{\widetilde{\Pi};k}) := \left| \Pr[\mathcal{A}^{\mathcal{O}_{\Pi;k}} = 1] - \Pr[\mathcal{A}^{\mathcal{O}_{\widetilde{\Pi};k}} = 1] \right| = 0.$$

Now, we demonstrate the utility of this idea through some examples.

FCBC MAC: FCBC mode is a 3-key message authentication code, by Black and Rogaway [16], which is defined as follows:

$$\Sigma := \mathsf{E}_{K_0}\Big(M_{m-1} \oplus \mathsf{E}_{K_0}\big(M_{m-2} \oplus \mathsf{E}_{K_0}\big(\cdots \oplus (M_2 \oplus \mathsf{E}_{K_0}(M_1)) \big) \big) \Big),$$

$$\mathsf{FCBC}[\mathsf{E}](M) := \mathsf{E}_{K_t}(\Sigma \oplus \mathsf{ozp}(M_m)), \text{ where } t \leftarrow (|M_m| = n)?\ 1 : 2.$$

FCBC has not received much appreciation in its existing 3-key form, even though it offers better security, $O(q^2/2^n + q\ell^2/2^n + q^2\ell^4/2^{2n})$ in [17,18, Theorem 3 and Remark 5], than CMAC [4,55], $O(q^2\ell/2^n + q^2\ell^4/2^{2n})$ in [19, Theorem 4.6]. Quantitatively, the number of queries per key increases from $2^{3n/8}$ to $2^{n/2}$ for message lengths up to $2^{n/4}$ blocks. This is mainly due to presence of three keys which not only costs keys size of the algorithm but it requires to run three key scheduling algorithms. Keeping these in mind, we define Twe-FCBC, as follows:

$$\Sigma := \widetilde{\mathsf{E}}_K^0 \Big(M_{m-1} \oplus \widetilde{\mathsf{E}}_K^0 \big(M_{m-2} \oplus \widetilde{\mathsf{E}}_K^0 \big(\cdots \oplus (M_2 \oplus \widetilde{\mathsf{E}}_K^0(M_1)) \big) \big) \Big),$$

$$\mathsf{Twe\text{-}FCBC}[\widetilde{\mathsf{E}}](M) := \widetilde{\mathsf{E}}_K^t(\Sigma \oplus \mathsf{ozp}(M_m)), \text{ where } t \leftarrow (|M_m| = n)?\ 1 : 2.$$

It is clear that Twe-FCBC is a variant of FCBC, that follows the principle established in Proposition 1, and replaces the 3 block ciphers $\mathsf{E}_{K_0}, \mathsf{E}_{K_1}, \mathsf{E}_{K_2}$ with $\widetilde{\mathsf{E}}_K^0$, $\widetilde{\mathsf{E}}_K^1$ and $\widetilde{\mathsf{E}}_K^2$, respectively. Using Proposition 1 and [18, Theorem 3 and Remark 5], we get the PRF security for Twe-FCBC in a straightforward manner in Proposition 2.

Proposition 2. *Assuming all queries are of length $\ell \leq 2^{n/4}$, and $\sigma \leq q\ell$, we have*

$$\mathbf{Adv}^{\mathsf{prf}}_{\mathsf{Twe\text{-}FCBC}[\widetilde{\mathsf{E}}]}(t, q, \sigma) \leq \mathbf{Adv}^{\mathsf{tprp}}_{\widetilde{\mathsf{E}}}(t', \sigma) + O\left(\frac{q^2}{2^n}\right).$$

Clearly, Twe-FCBC has two major advantages over CMAC- (i) no need to hold an additional state for final message block masking, (ii) security bound is free of length factor for all reasonably sized messages (close to 6 Gigabyte for a 128-bit block cipher). In addition, Twe-FCBC can also avoid the additional block cipher call used to generate the masking. Due to backward compatibility, except the last block we have used the original block cipher. So the performance overhead due to nonzero tweak only applies to the last block cipher call. This features ensures to get similar performance (or even better) for long message.

DOUBLE BLOCK HASH-THEN-SUM: The very basic version of Double-block Hash-then-Sum or DbHtS [56], is defined as below

$$\mathsf{DbHtS}(M) := \mathsf{E}_{K_1}(\Sigma) \oplus \mathsf{E}_{K_2}(\Theta),$$

where H is a $2n$-bit output hash function, $(\Sigma, \Theta) := \mathsf{H}_L(M)$, and L, K_1, K_2 are all sampled independently. DbHtS is a generic design paradigm that captures several popular BBB secure MACs such as PMAC_Plus, LightMAC_Plus, SUM_ECBC and 3kf9. Using a tBC, the two block cipher keys can now simply be replaced by a single tweakable block cipher key and two distinct tweaks. Formally, we define Twe-DbHtS as follows

$$\mathsf{Twe\text{-}DbHtS}(M) := \widetilde{\mathsf{E}}_K^1(\Sigma) \oplus \widetilde{\mathsf{E}}_K^2(\Theta).$$

Moreover, one can also generate the dedicated hash key using the tweakable block cipher key itself. Suppose the hash function is block cipher based, then the tBC key can be used along with a different tweak to replace the dedicated hash key. In all other cases, the hash key can be derived as $L := (\widetilde{\mathsf{E}}_K^0(0) \| \widetilde{\mathsf{E}}_K^0(1) \| \cdots \| \widetilde{\mathsf{E}}_K^0(h-1))$, where $|L| = hn$. Since $\widetilde{\mathsf{E}}_K^0(i)$'s are sampled in without replacement manner, this adds an additional factor of $\frac{h^2}{2^n}$ due to the PRP-PRF switching, which can be ignored for small h. One can easily verify that due to Proposition 1, the result on DbHtS [56, Theorem 2.(iii)] also applies to Twe-DbHtS. Formally, the security of Twe-DbHtS is given by Proposition 3.

Proposition 3.

$$\mathbf{Adv}_{\mathsf{Twe\text{-}DbHtS}[\mathsf{H},\widetilde{\mathsf{E}}]}^{\mathsf{prf}}(q,\ell,t) \leq 2\mathbf{Adv}_{\widetilde{\mathsf{E}}}^{\mathsf{tprp}}(2q,t') + \mathbf{Adv}_{C_3^*[H,\pi_0,\pi_1,\pi_2]}^{\mathsf{prf}}(q,\ell,t).$$

In this way, we have one-key versions of different well known designs PMAC_Plus, LightMAC_Plus, SUM_ECBC, 3kf9 etc. We note that one key version of PMAC_Plus based on solely block cipher has been proposed [57]. However, one key version of the other designs either are not known or it can be shown to be secure up to the birthday bound.[4]

SUM OF PERMUTATIONS: The sum of permutations is a popular approach of constructing an n-bit length preserving PRF. Given 2 independent instantiations, E_{K_0} and E_{K_1}, of a secure block cipher over $\{0,1\}^n$, the sum of permutations, denoted XOR2, is defined by the mapping $x \mapsto \mathsf{E}_{K_0}(x) \oplus \mathsf{E}_{K_1}(x)$. The XOR2 construction has been proved to be n-bit secure [11]. There is a single key variant of XOR2, but it sacrifices one bit (i.e. defined from $\{0,1\}^{n-1}$ to $\{0,1\}^n$) for domain separation. Instead, we can use a tBC to simply replace the two block cipher keys with one tBC key and two distinct tweaks. We define $\mathsf{Twe\text{-}XOR2}(x) := \widetilde{\mathsf{E}}_K^0(x) \oplus \widetilde{\mathsf{E}}_K^1(x)$. Again combining Proposition 1 with [11, Theorem 4], we obtain

---

[4] 1kf9 is proposed in the ePrint version [58], which later found to be attacked in birthday complexity [59].

Proposition 4. *For* $q \leq 2^{n-4}$,

$$\mathbf{Adv}_{\text{Twe-XOR2}}^{\text{prf}}(t, q) \leq \mathbf{Adv}_{\widetilde{\mathsf{E}}}^{\text{tprp}}(t', q) + (q/2^n)^{1.5}.$$

TWEAKING VARIOUS OTHER CONSTRUCTIONS: In the following list, we apply similar technique as above to several other constructions with multiple keys. The security of all the tBC-based variants is similar to the multi-key original constructions, so we skip their explicit security statements.

1. **Encrypted Davis Meyer (EDM)** [12]: EDM uses two keys and obtains BBB PRF security. We define the tBC-based variant as follows:

$$\text{Twe-EDM}(x) := \widetilde{\mathsf{E}}_K^1(\widetilde{\mathsf{E}}_K^0(x) \oplus x).$$

2. **Encrypted Wegman Carter Davis Meyer (EWCDM)** [12]: EWCDM is a nonce-based BBB secure MAC that requires two block cipher keys and a hash key. The tBC-based variant of EWCDM is defined as:

$$\text{Twe-EWCDM}(N, M) := \widetilde{\mathsf{E}}_K^2\left(\widetilde{\mathsf{E}}_K^1(N) \oplus N \oplus H_{\widetilde{\mathsf{E}}_K^0(0)}(M)\right).$$

3. **Chained LRW2 (CLRW2)** [13]: The CLRW2 construction is a TBC that achieves BBB TSPRP security using two independent block cipher keys and two independent hash keys. We define a tBC-based variant of CLRW2 as follows:

$$\text{Twe-CLRW2}(M, T) := \widetilde{\mathsf{E}}_K^2\left(\widetilde{\mathsf{E}}_K^1(M \oplus h_{L_1}(T)) \oplus h_{L_1}(T) \oplus h_{L_2}(T)\right) \oplus h_{L_2}(T),$$

where L_1 and L_2 can be easily derived using $\widetilde{\mathsf{E}}$ with dedicated independent tweaks. It is easy to see that one can easily extend the idea to obtain single keyed CLRWr [60] using r distinct tweaks.

4. **GCM-SIV-2** [14]. GCM-SIV-2 is an MRAE scheme with $2n/3$-bit security. However, it requires 6 independent block cipher keys along with 2 independent hash keys. We can easily make it single keyed using a tBC:

$$V_1 := H_{\widetilde{\mathsf{E}}_K^0(0)}(N, A, M), \quad V_2 := H_{\widetilde{\mathsf{E}}_K^0(1)}(N, A, M)$$

$$T_1 := \widetilde{\mathsf{E}}_K^1(V_1) \oplus \widetilde{\mathsf{E}}_K^2(V_2), \quad T_2 := \widetilde{\mathsf{E}}_K^3(V_1) \oplus \widetilde{\mathsf{E}}_K^4(V_2),$$

$$C_i := M_i \oplus \widetilde{\mathsf{E}}_K^5(T_1 \oplus i) \oplus \widetilde{\mathsf{E}}_K^6(T_2 \oplus i).$$

Extending the same approach, one can get a single keyed version of GCM-SIV-r as well.

5. **The Benes Construction** [15]: The Benes construction is a method to construct $2n$-bit length preserving PRF construction with n-bit security that uses 8 independent n bit to n bit PRFs. Formally,

$$L' := f_1(L) \oplus f_2(R)$$

$$R' := f_3(L) \oplus f_4(R)$$

$$\mathsf{Benes}(L, R) := (f_5(L') \oplus f_6(R'), f_7(L') \oplus f_8(R')).$$

Now these f_i functions can be constructed using sum of two permutations, however that would essentially require 16 block cipher keys. With a tBC, we can reduce the number of keys to one by instantiating $f_i := \widetilde{\mathsf{E}}_K^{2i} \oplus \widetilde{\mathsf{E}}_K^{2i+1}$ for each $i \in [8]$.

4.2 Efficient Processing for Short Messages

In energy constrained environments, reducing the number of primitive invocations is crucial, as for short messages, this reduction leads to efficient energy consumption. The tBC framework can be used to reduce the number of primitive invocations for many existing constructions such as LightMAC_Plus [61].

LightMAC_Plus is a counter-based PMAC_Plus in which $\langle i \rangle_m \| M_i$ is input to the i-th keyed block cipher call, where $\langle i \rangle_m$ is the m-bit binary representation of i and M_i is the i-th message block of $n - m$ bits. The counters ensure that there is no input collision, which indirectly helps in negating the influence of ℓ. LightMAC_Plus has been shown to have $O(q^3/2^{2n})$ PRF security. However, it has two shortcomings: (i) it requires 3 keys, and (ii) it has rate $1 - m/n$ which increases the number of block cipher calls. This is highly undesirable in low memory and energy constrained scenarios

To resolve these shortcomings specifically for short to moderate length messages (slightly less than 1 Megabyte), we propose Twe-LightMAC_Plus, which can be viewed as an amalgamation of LightMAC_Plus [61] and PMACx [33]. The key idea is to use the block counters as tweak in hash layer, while having distinct tweaks for the finalization. The pictorial description of the algorithm is given in Fig. 3. It is easy to see that Twe-LightMAC_Plus is single-keyed and it achieves rate 1. This reduces the number of block cipher calls by up to 50% for short messages, which has direct effect on reducing the energy consumption. We claim that Twe-LightMAC_Plus is as secure as LightMAC_Plus. Formally, we have the following security result. We note that similar improvements can also be applied to PMAC, PMAC_Plus.

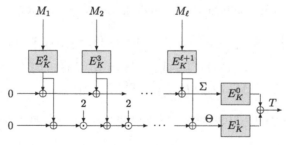

Fig. 3. Twe-LightMAC construction.

Proposition 5. *For* $q \leq 2^{n-1}$,

$$\mathbf{Adv}^{\mathsf{prf}}_{\mathsf{Twe\text{-}LightMAC\_Plus}[\widetilde{\mathsf{E}}]}(t, q, \ell) \leq \mathbf{Adv}^{\mathsf{tprp}}_{\widetilde{\mathsf{E}}}(t', q\ell) + O\left(\frac{q^3}{2^{2n}}\right).$$

Proof. Twe-LightMAC_Plus is an instance of Twe-DbHtS, and hence offers similar security. The security bound of Twe-DbHtS includes a term

$$\mathbf{Adv}^{\mathrm{prf}}_{C_3^*[H,\pi_0,\pi_1,\pi_2]}(q,\ell,t)$$

from [56]. One can verify from [56, Proof of Theorem 2.(iii)], that this term is predominantly bounded by two probabilities:

1. $\Pr[\exists$ distinct i,j,k such that $\Sigma_i = \Sigma_j, \Theta_i = \Theta_k]$.
2. $\Pr[\exists$ distinct i,j such that $\Sigma_i = \Sigma_j, \Theta_i = \Theta_j]$.

Now the hash layer of Twe-LightMAC_Plus is exactly same as the PHASHx of [33]. Using similar arguments as in [33, Proof of Theorem 1] it can be shown that 1. is upper bounded by $O(q^3/2^{2n})$, and 2. is upper bounded by $O(q^2/2^{2n})$. The result follows by combining 1 and 2. □

4.3 A Note on tBC's Advantages over XE and XEX

The XE and XEX modes, by Rogaway [36], are two reasonably efficient ways of converting a block cipher into a tweakable block cipher. These methods are widely used in various modes such as PMAC [44], OCB [45], COPA [29], ELmD [46] etc. The XE scheme to generate a TBC $\widetilde{\mathsf{E}}$ from a BC E is defined as

$$\mathsf{XE}: \quad \widetilde{\mathsf{E}}^{i_1,\cdots,i_t}_K(M) := \mathsf{E}_K(\Delta \oplus M)$$

where $\Delta = \alpha_1^{i_1} \cdots \alpha_t^{i_t} \cdot L$. Here L is generally an n-bit secret state, which is generated using block cipher call.[5] It is sufficient for us to compare XE and tBC, as XEX is much similar to XE. Now one may think of using XE instead of tBC to convert multi-keyed modes to single-keyed mode, as above. But in comparison to tBC, XE lacks two important features:

1. DEGRADATION TO BIRTHDAY BOUND SECURITY: XE (and XEX) is proved to be birthday bound secure TBC mode. This is not a big issue for birthday secure multi-keyed modes. In fact, the CMAC mode can be viewed as an example that uses the XE mode, much in the same way as Twe-FCBC uses tBC. However, if we use XE in multi-keyed applications such as DbHtS or XOR2, the security of these constructions would degrade to birthday bound. So, we cannot use XE or XEX, in a black box fashion, to instantiate the tweakable variants, without a significant degradation in the security of the modified mode. In contrast, tBC directly works on the block cipher level, and hence does not suffer from such degradation unless the block cipher is itself weak.
2. ADDITIONAL COMPUTATIONAL AND STORAGE OVERHEADS: The XE mode requires, precomputation of the secret state L, (ii) an additional block cipher invocation to generate L, and (iii) an additional storage to store L. This

---

[5] Alternative constructions to define Δ can be found in [62,63].

cannot be neglected in constrained computation and communication environments, as mentioned earlier. On the other hand, the tBC framework incurs far less overheads. In this respect, one can easily define simple tBC-variants of PMAC [36] (based on XE), COPE [29] (based on XEX), COLM [64] (XE like processing) etc. much along the same line as Twe-LightMAC_Plus.

5   Simplification of Authenticated Encryption Schemes

In this section, we demonstrate some AE schemes that achieve a combination of advantages discussed in Sect. 4.

5.1   Twe-CLOC and Twe-SILC

We propose tBC variant for CLOC and SILC, called Twe-CLOC and Twe-SILC, respectively. CLOC and SILC are nonce-based authentication encryption (NAEAD) modes, which aim to optimize the implementation overhead beyond the block cipher calls, the precomputation complexity, and the memory requirement. CLOC is suitable for uses in embedded processors, and SILC aims to optimize hardware implementation cost. Our choices of CLOC and SILC are motivated by two factors (see Subsect. 5.2 below): design simplification and reduction in block cipher calls.

The three tBC variants are described in Fig. 4. We have made minimal changes in the original schemes. CLOC and SILC employ Encrypt-then-PRF paradigm and use a variant of CFB [3] mode in its encryption part and a variant of FCBC in the authentication part.

$\mathsf{CFB}(V, M, t)$	$\mathsf{ivFCBC}(T, D, t_0, t_1, t_2)$
1. $M_1 \| \cdots \| M_m \leftarrow M$	1. $D_1 \| \cdots \| D_d \leftarrow D$
2. $C_1 \leftarrow V \oplus M_1$	2. **for** $i = 1$ **to** $d - 1$
3. **for** $i = 2$ **to** m	3. $T \leftarrow \widetilde{\mathscr{E}}_K^{t_0}(T \oplus D_i)$
4. $C_i \leftarrow \lfloor \widetilde{\mathscr{E}}_K^t(C_{i-1}) \rfloor_{|M_i|} \oplus M_i$	4. $t \leftarrow (|D_d| = n)?\ t_1 : t_2$
5. **return** $(C_1 \| \cdots \| C_m)$	5. $T \leftarrow \widetilde{\mathscr{E}}_K^t(T \oplus \mathsf{pad}(D_d))$
	6. **return** T
$\mathsf{Twe\text{-}SILC}_K(N, A, M)$	$\mathsf{Twe\text{-}CLOC}_K(N, A, M)$
1. $T \leftarrow \mathsf{ivFCBC}(0^n, N\|A, 0, 0\|1, \mathsf{Len}\|1)$	1. $T \leftarrow \mathsf{ivFCBC}(T, A\|N, 0, 1, 2)$
2. $C \leftarrow \mathsf{CFB}(T, M, 0\|2)$	2. $C \leftarrow \mathsf{CFB}(T, M, 3)$
3. $T \leftarrow \mathsf{ivFCBC}(0, C, 1, 0\|3, \mathsf{Len}\|0)$	3. $T \leftarrow \mathsf{ivFCBC}(0, C, 4, 5, 6)$
4. **return** (C, T)	4. **return** (C, T)

Fig. 4. Encryption and algorithm of Twe-SILC and Twe-CLOC. pad uses 10^* padding for Twe-CLOC and 0^* padding for Twe-SILC.

5.2   Features of the Proposed AE Schemes

The proposed tBC-based AE schemes offer two added features over the existing block cipher based schemes.

DESIGN SIMPLIFICATION: Twe-CLOC and Twe-SILC simplifies their respective original algorithms very efficiently. CLOC and SILC require several linear functions (f, g_1, g_2, h_1, h_2 for CLOC and g for SILC) for domain separations and bit fixing operations. Twe-CLOC and Twe-SILC perform all the domain separations by using distinct tweaks, which significantly simplifies the design.

Table 1. Comparison between the number of (tweakable) block cipher invocations for original CLOC and SILC, and their tBC counterparts. Here a, and m denote the length of associated data and plaintext, respectively.

Modes	No. of BC calls		No. of tBC calls	
	$a \neq 0$	$a = 0$	$a \neq 0$	$a = 0$
CLOC	$a + 2m + 1$	$2m + 2$	$a + 2m$	$2m$
SILC	$a + 2m + 3$	$2m + 2$	$a + 2m$	$2m$

ENERGY EFFICIENT FOR SHORT INPUTS: Apart from the simplification of the original designs, the proposed AE schemes offer another advantage over the non-tweaked versions. They require lesser number of block cipher calls for shorter/empty AD or message processing, which essentially makes them more efficient in terms of energy consumption. The number of block cipher invocations required to process an associated data of a blocks and message of m blocks are given in Table 1. As seen from the table, SILC requires 4 block cipher calls to process 1 block AD and empty message, Twe-SILC requires only 1 block cipher call.

5.3   Security of the Proposed AE Schemes

Twe-CLOC and Twe-SILC are in essence just the multi-key variants of CLOC and SILC, respectively. So, intuitively they should be at least as secure as the original modes, and the security argument for these schemes is relatively easier than the original schemes. We show in Proposition 6 that our intuitions are correct to a large extent. For the sake of simplicity, we refrain from giving exact bounds, and instead give the asymptotic expressions.

We first look at the abstract design paradigm behind Twe-CLOC and Twe-SILC, which is the so-called Encrypt-then-PRF, or EtPRF.

THE EtPRF PARADIGM: EtPRF [53, Construction A5] is a design paradigm to construct NAEAD schemes. It is composed of three stages (illustrated in Fig. 5): a random IV generator, G that generates iv using the nonce N and (possibly) the AD A; an IV-based encryption phase, ivE that generates the ciphertext C using iv as the random IV; and a tag-generation phase, F that generates the tag on the input N, A, C. Formally, for key space $\mathcal{K} \times \mathcal{L}$ the encryption algorithm of EtPRF is defined by the following mapping

$$(K, L, N, A, M) \mapsto \mathsf{ivE}(K, N, A, M) \,\|\, \mathsf{F}(L, N, A, \mathsf{ivE}(K, N, A, M)),$$

for all $(L, K, N, A, M) \in \mathcal{L} \times \mathcal{K} \times \mathcal{A} \times \mathcal{M}$. Here, $C := \mathsf{ivE}(K, N, A, M) \in \mathcal{M}$, and $T := \mathsf{F}(L, N, A, C) \in \mathcal{M}$. Note that, for the sake of simplicity we subsumed the G function within the ivE phase. In [53], Namprempre et al. showed that the NAEAD security of an EtPRF scheme, $\mathfrak{A}$, given by:

$$\mathbf{Adv}_{\mathfrak{A}}^{\mathsf{ae}}(q, \ell, \sigma) \le \mathbf{Adv}_{\mathsf{F}}^{\mathsf{prf}}(q, \ell, \sigma) + \mathbf{Adv}_{\mathsf{G}}^{\mathsf{prf}}(q, \ell, \sigma) + \mathbf{Adv}_{\mathsf{ivE}}^{\mathsf{priv\$}}(q, \ell, \sigma), \quad (5)$$

where PRIV denotes the Priv\$ security (see Sect. 2.1).

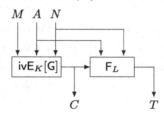

Fig. 5. The EtPRF paradigm based on an IV-based encryption scheme ivE for the encryption phase, and a PRF F for the tag generation phase. The [G] denotes that ivE internally uses G to generate the random IV.

In case of both Twe-CLOC and Twe-SILC, G and F are variants of Twe-FCBC, and hence can be shown to have $O(\sigma^2/2^n)$ PRF security [16]. ivE phase is an instance of the CFB mode with random IV, which has been shown to have $O(\sigma^2/2^n)$ security in [65]. Hence, by substituting the relevant bounds in Eq. (5), we get the following security result for Twe-CLOC and Twe-SILC.

Proposition 6. *The security of Twe-CLOC and Twe-SILC is given by:*

$$\mathbf{Adv}^{\mathsf{ae}}_{\mathsf{Twe\text{-}CLOC[\widetilde{E}]}}(t, q, \ell, \sigma) \le \mathbf{Adv}^{\mathsf{tprp}}_{\widetilde{\mathsf{E}}}(t', q\ell) + O(\frac{\sigma^2}{2^n}),$$

$$\mathbf{Adv}^{\mathsf{ae}}_{\mathsf{Twe\text{-}SILC[\widetilde{E}]}}(t, q, \ell, \sigma) \le \mathbf{Adv}^{\mathsf{tprp}}_{\widetilde{\mathsf{E}}}(t', q\ell) + O(\frac{\sigma^2}{2^n}).$$

where t, q, ℓ, σ denote the computational time, query bound, maximum query length, and the total number of tBC calls across all encryption and decryption queries, respectively.

Remark 1. The security of CLOC and SILC do not follow from Eq. (5), in a straightforward way, as the tag generation and encryption share the same key.

6   Further Applications and Future Directions

We think that tBC can have several other applications. For instance, consider a scenario where two multiple algorithms are running on the same platform, sharing the same secret key. We could find several examples where such an arrangement could be vulnerable. For example, consider a scenario where AES-GCM and AES-CMAC are running on the same device, sharing the same secret key. Now, it is easy to see that, an adversary can trivially forge a tag for AES-CMAC using an encryption query on AES-GCM. tBC can efficiently take care of such problems by separating these algorithms using different tweak values, i.e. unique tweak values for each of these algorithms.

We have defined the Elastic-Tweak framework for SPN based block ciphers. Extending this further for ARX based constructions could be an interesting problem. Also, it would be interesting to see designs for short-tweak tweakable public permutations, which might have strong impact on the simplification of permutation based constructions such as Sponge, Beetle, Minalpher etc.

Acknowledgement. The authors would like to thank all the anonymous reviewers of Indocrypt 2021 for their valuable comments. Prof. Mridul Nandi is supported by the project "Study and Analysis of IoT Security" by NTRO under the Government of India at R.C.Bose Centre for Cryptology and Security, Indian Statistical Institute, Kolkata. Dr. Ashwin Jha's work was carried out in the framework of the French-German-Center for Cybersecurity, a collaboration of CISPA and LORIA.

References

1. NIST: Data Encryption Standard (AES). FIPS Publication (Withdrawn) 46-3 (1999)
2. 197, N.F.: Advanced Encryption Standard (AES). Federal Information Processing Standards Publication 197 (2001)
3. Dworkin, M.: Recommendation for Block Cipher Modes of Operation: Methods and Techniques. NIST Special Publication 800-38A, National Institute of Standards and Technology (2001)
4. Dworkin, M.: Recommendation for Block Cipher Modes of Operation - Methods and Techniques. NIST Special Publication 800-38A, National Institute of Standards and Technology, U.S. Department of Commerce (2001)
5. Dworkin, M.: Recommendation for Block Cipher Modes of Operation: The CCM Mode for Authentication and Confidentiality. NIST Special Publication 800-38C, National Institute of Standards and Technology (2004)
6. Matsui, M.: Linear cryptanalysis method for DES cipher. In: Helleseth, T. (ed.) EUROCRYPT 1993. LNCS, vol. 765, pp. 386–397. Springer, Heidelberg (1994). https://doi.org/10.1007/3-540-48285-7_33
7. Biham, E., Shamir, A.: Differential cryptanalysis of DES-like cryptosystems. In: Menezes, A.J., Vanstone, S.A. (eds.) CRYPTO 1990. LNCS, vol. 537, pp. 2–21. Springer, Heidelberg (1991). https://doi.org/10.1007/3-540-38424-3_1
8. Dworkin, M.: Recommendation for Block Cipher Modes of Operation: Galois/Counter Mode (GCM) and GMAC. NIST Special Publication 800-38D, National Institute of Standards and Technology (2007)
9. Banik, S., Pandey, S.K., Peyrin, T., Sasaki, Yu., Sim, S.M., Todo, Y.: GIFT: a small present. In: Fischer, W., Homma, N. (eds.) CHES 2017. LNCS, vol. 10529, pp. 321–345. Springer, Cham (2017). https://doi.org/10.1007/978-3-319-66787-4_16

10. Patarin, J.: Security in $O(2^n)$ for the Xor of two random permutations - proof with the standard H technique -. IACR Cryptology ePrint Archive **2013**, 368 (2013)
11. Dai, W., Hoang, V.T., Tessaro, S.: Information-theoretic indistinguishability via the chi-squared method. In: Katz, J., Shacham, H. (eds.) CRYPTO 2017, Part III. LNCS, vol. 10403, pp. 497–523. Springer, Cham (2017). https://doi.org/10.1007/978-3-319-63697-9_17
12. Cogliati, B., Seurin, Y.: EWCDM: an efficient, beyond-birthday secure, nonce-misuse resistant MAC. In: Robshaw, M., Katz, J. (eds.) CRYPTO 2016, Part I. LNCS, vol. 9814, pp. 121–149. Springer, Heidelberg (2016). https://doi.org/10.1007/978-3-662-53018-4_5
13. Landecker, W., Shrimpton, T., Terashima, R.S.: Tweakable blockciphers with beyond birthday-bound security. In: Safavi-Naini, R., Canetti, R. (eds.) CRYPTO 2012. LNCS, vol. 7417, pp. 14–30. Springer, Heidelberg (2012). https://doi.org/10.1007/978-3-642-32009-5_2
14. Iwata, T., Minematsu, K.: Stronger security variants of GCM-SIV. IACR Cryptology ePrint Archive **2016**, 853 (2016)
15. Patarin, J.: A proof of security in $O(2^n)$ for the Benes scheme. In: Vaudenay, S. (ed.) AFRICACRYPT 2008. LNCS, vol. 5023, pp. 209–220. Springer, Heidelberg (2008). https://doi.org/10.1007/978-3-540-68164-9_14
16. Black, J., Rogaway, P.: CBC MACs for arbitrary-length messages: the three-key constructions. J. Cryptol. **18**(2), 111–131 (2005). https://doi.org/10.1007/s00145-004-0016-3
17. Jha, A., Nandi, M.: Revisiting structure graphs: applications to CBC-MAC and EMAC. J. Math. Cryptol. **10**(3–4), 157–180 (2016)
18. Jha, A., Nandi, M.: Revisiting structure graph and its applications to CBC-MAC and EMAC. IACR Cryptology ePrint Archive **2016**, 161 (2016)
19. Nandi, M.: Improved security analysis for OMAC as a pseudorandom function. J. Math. Cryptol. **3**(2), 133–148 (2009)
20. Iwata, T., Minematsu, K., Guo, J., Morioka, S., Kobayashi, E.: CLOC and SILC. Submission to CAESAR (2016). https://competitions.cr.yp.to/round3/clocsilcv3.pdf
21. Karlof, C., Sastry, N., Wagner, D.: TinySec: a link layer security architecture for wireless sensor networks. In: Proceedings of Embedded Networked Sensor Systems, SenSys 2004, pp. 162–175. ACM (2004)
22. 11898, I.: CAN FD Standards and Recommendations. https://www.can-cia.org/news/cia-in-action/view/can-fd-standards-and-recommendations/2016/9/30/
23. EPCglobal: Electronic Product Code (EPC) Tag Data Standard (TDS). Technical Report. http://www.epcglobalinc.org/standards/tds/
24. Banik, S., Bogdanov, A., Luykx, A., Tischhauser, E.: SUNDAE: small universal deterministic authenticated encryption for the Internet of Things. IACR Trans. Symmetric Cryptol. **2018**(3), 1–35 (2018)
25. Luykx, A., Preneel, B., Tischhauser, E., Yasuda, K.: A MAC mode for lightweight block ciphers. In: Peyrin, T. (ed.) FSE 2016. LNCS, vol. 9783, pp. 43–59. Springer, Heidelberg (2016). https://doi.org/10.1007/978-3-662-52993-5_3
26. Schroeppel, R.: The Hasty Pudding Cipher. Submitted candidate for AES (1998)
27. Liskov, M., Rivest, R.L., Wagner, D.: Tweakable block ciphers. In: Yung, M. (ed.) CRYPTO 2002. LNCS, vol. 2442, pp. 31–46. Springer, Heidelberg (2002). https://doi.org/10.1007/3-540-45708-9_3
28. Krovetz, T., Rogaway, P.: The software performance of authenticated-encryption modes. In: Joux, A. (ed.) FSE 2011. LNCS, vol. 6733, pp. 306–327. Springer, Heidelberg (2011). https://doi.org/10.1007/978-3-642-21702-9_18

29. Andreeva, E., Bogdanov, A., Luykx, A., Mennink, B., Tischhauser, E., Yasuda, K.: AES-COPA, vol 2. Submission to CAESAR (2015). https://competitions.cr.yp.to/round2/aescopav2.pdf

30. Jean, J., Nikolić, I., Peyrin, T.: Deoxys v1.41. Submission to CAESAR (2016). https://competitions.cr.yp.to/round3/deoxysv141.pdf

31. Iwata, T., Minematsu, K., Peyrin, T., Seurin, Y.: ZMAC: a fast tweakable block cipher mode for highly secure message authentication. In: Katz, J., Shacham, H. (eds.) CRYPTO 2017, Part III. LNCS, vol. 10403, pp. 34–65. Springer, Cham (2017). https://doi.org/10.1007/978-3-319-63697-9_2

32. Cogliati, B., Lampe, R., Seurin, Y.: Tweaking Even-Mansour ciphers. In: Gennaro, R., Robshaw, M. (eds.) CRYPTO 2015, Part I. LNCS, vol. 9215, pp. 189–208. Springer, Heidelberg (2015). https://doi.org/10.1007/978-3-662-47989-6_9

33. List, E., Nandi, M.: ZMAC+ - an efficient variable-output-length variant of ZMAC. IACR Trans. Symmetric Cryptol. **2017**(4), 306–325 (2017)

34. Crowley, P.: Mercy: a fast large block cipher for disk sector encryption. In: Goos, G., Hartmanis, J., van Leeuwen, J., Schneier, B. (eds.) FSE 2000. LNCS, vol. 1978, pp. 49–63. Springer, Heidelberg (2001). https://doi.org/10.1007/3-540-44706-7_4

35. Ferguson, N., et al.: The skein hash function family. Submission to NIST (Round 3) **7**(7.5), 3 (2010)

36. Rogaway, P.: Efficient instantiations of tweakable blockciphers and refinements to modes OCB and PMAC. In: Lee, P.J. (ed.) ASIACRYPT 2004. LNCS, vol. 3329, pp. 16–31. Springer, Heidelberg (2004). https://doi.org/10.1007/978-3-540-30539-2_2

37. Jha, A., List, E., Minematsu, K., Mishra, S., Nandi, M.: XHX - a framework for optimally secure tweakable block ciphers from classical ciphers and universal hashing. IACR Cryptology ePrint Archive **2017**, 1075 (2017)

38. Jean, J., Nikolić, I., Peyrin, T.: Tweaks and keys for block ciphers: the TWEAKEY framework. In: Sarkar, P., Iwata, T. (eds.) ASIACRYPT 2014, Part II. LNCS, vol. 8874, pp. 274–288. Springer, Heidelberg (2014). https://doi.org/10.1007/978-3-662-45608-8_15

39. Jean, J., Nikolić, I., Peyrin, T.: KIASU v1. Submission to CAESAR (2016). https://competitions.cr.yp.to/round1/kiasuv1.pdf

40. Beierle, C., et al.: The SKINNY family of block ciphers and its low-latency variant MANTIS. In: Robshaw, M., Katz, J. (eds.) CRYPTO 2016, Part II. LNCS, vol. 9815, pp. 123–153. Springer, Heidelberg (2016). https://doi.org/10.1007/978-3-662-53008-5_5

41. Dobraunig, C., Eichlseder, M., Mendel, F.: Square attack on 7-Round Kiasu-BC. In: Manulis, M., Sadeghi, A.-R., Schneider, S. (eds.) ACNS 2016. LNCS, vol. 9696, pp. 500–517. Springer, Cham (2016). https://doi.org/10.1007/978-3-319-39555-5_27

42. Dobraunig, C., List, E.: Impossible-differential and boomerang cryptanalysis of round-reduced Kiasu-BC. In: Handschuh, H. (ed.) CT-RSA 2017. LNCS, vol. 10159, pp. 207–222. Springer, Cham (2017). https://doi.org/10.1007/978-3-319-52153-4_12

43. Tolba, M., Abdelkhalek, A., Youssef, A.M.: A meet in the middle attack on reduced round Kiasu-BC. IEICE Trans. **99-A**(10), 1888–1890 (2016)

44. Black, J., Rogaway, P.: A block-cipher mode of operation for parallelizable message authentication. In: Knudsen, L.R. (ed.) EUROCRYPT 2002. LNCS, vol. 2332, pp. 384–397. Springer, Heidelberg (2002). https://doi.org/10.1007/3-540-46035-7_25

45. Rogaway, P., Bellare, M., Black, J.: OCB: a block-cipher mode of operation for efficient authenticated encryption. ACM Trans. Inf. Syst. Secur. **6**(3), 365–403 (2003)

46. Datta, N., Nandi, M.: Proposal of ELmD v2.1. Submission to CAESAR (2015). https://competitions.cr.yp.to/round2/elmdv21.pdf
47. Chakraborti, A., Datta, N., Jha, A., Mancillas-López, C., Nandi, M., Sasaki, Y.: INT-RUP secure lightweight parallel AE modes. IACR Trans. Symmetric Cryptol. **2019**(4), 81–118 (2019)
48. Chakraborti, A., Datta, N., Jha, A., Mancillas-López, C., Nandi, M., Sasaki, Y.: ESTATE: a lightweight and low energy authenticated encryption mode. IACR Trans. Symmetric Cryptol. **2020**(S1), 350–389 (2020)
49. Chakraborti, A., Datta, N., Jha, A., Mancillas-López, C., Nandi, M., Sasaki, Y.: LOTUS-AEAD and LOCUS-AEAD. Submission to NIST LwC Standardization Process (Round 2) (2019)
50. Chakraborti, A., Datta, N., Jha, A., Mancillas-López, C., Nandi, M., Sasaki, Y.: ESTATE. Submission to NIST LwC Standardization Process (Round 2) (2019)
51. Chakraborti, A., Datta, N., Jha, A., López, C.M., Nandi, M., Sasaki, Y.: Elastic-tweak: a framework for short tweak tweakable block cipher. IACR Cryptology ePrint Archive 440 (2019)
52. Gueron, S., Lindell, Y.: GCM-SIV: full nonce misuse-resistant authenticated encryption at under one cycle per byte. In: Proceedings of the ACM SIGSAC Conference on Computer and Communications Security 2015, pp. 109–119 (2015)
53. Namprempre, C., Rogaway, P., Shrimpton, T.: Reconsidering generic composition. In: Nguyen, P.Q., Oswald, E. (eds.) EUROCRYPT 2014. LNCS, vol. 8441, pp. 257–274. Springer, Heidelberg (2014). https://doi.org/10.1007/978-3-642-55220-5_15
54. Rogaway, P., Shrimpton, T.: A provable-security treatment of the key-wrap problem. In: Vaudenay, S. (ed.) EUROCRYPT 2006. LNCS, vol. 4004, pp. 373–390. Springer, Heidelberg (2006). https://doi.org/10.1007/11761679_23
55. Iwata, T., Kurosawa, K.: OMAC: one-key CBC MAC. In: Johansson, T. (ed.) FSE 2003. LNCS, vol. 2887, pp. 129–153. Springer, Heidelberg (2003). https://doi.org/10.1007/978-3-540-39887-5_11
56. Datta, N., Dutta, A., Nandi, M., Paul, G.: Double-block hash-then-sum: a paradigm for constructing BBB Secure PRF. IACR Trans. Symmetric Cryptol. **2018**(3), 36–92 (2018)
57. Datta, N., Dutta, A., Nandi, M., Paul, G., Zhang, L.: Single key variant of PMAC_Plus. IACR Trans. Symmetric Cryptol. **2017**(4), 268–305 (2017)
58. Datta, N., Dutta, A., Nandi, M., Paul, G., Zhang, L.: Single key variant of PMAC_Plus. IACR Cryptology ePrint Archive **2017**, 848 (2017)
59. Leurent, G., Nandi, M., Sibleyras, F.: Generic attacks against beyond-birthday-bound MACs. In: Shacham, H., Boldyreva, A. (eds.) CRYPTO 2018, Part I. LNCS, vol. 10991, pp. 306–336. Springer, Cham (2018). https://doi.org/10.1007/978-3-319-96884-1_11
60. Lampe, R., Seurin, Y.: Tweakable blockciphers with asymptotically optimal security. In: Moriai, S. (ed.) FSE 2013. LNCS, vol. 8424, pp. 133–151. Springer, Heidelberg (2014). https://doi.org/10.1007/978-3-662-43933-3_8
61. Naito, Y.: Blockcipher-based MACs: beyond the birthday bound without message length. In: Takagi, T., Peyrin, T. (eds.) ASIACRYPT 2017, Part III. LNCS, vol. 10626, pp. 446–470. Springer, Cham (2017). https://doi.org/10.1007/978-3-319-70700-6_16
62. Chakraborty, D., Sarkar, P.: A general construction of tweakable block ciphers and different modes of operations. IEEE Trans. Inf. Theory **54**(5), 1991–2006 (2008)

63. Granger, R., Jovanovic, P., Mennink, B., Neves, S.: Improved masking for tweakable blockciphers with applications to authenticated encryption. In: Fischlin, M., Coron, J.-S. (eds.) EUROCRYPT 2016, Part I. LNCS, vol. 9665, pp. 263–293. Springer, Heidelberg (2016). https://doi.org/10.1007/978-3-662-49890-3_11

64. Andreeva, E., et al.: COLM v1. Submission to CAESAR (2016). https://competitions.cr.yp.to/round3/colmv1.pdf

65. Wooding, M.: New proofs for old modes. IACR Cryptology ePrint Archive **2008**, 121 (2008)

Lightweight Cryptography

Three Input Exclusive-OR Gate Support for Boyar-Peralta's Algorithm

Anubhab Baksi[1]($\boxtimes$), Vishnu Asutosh Dasu[2], Banashri Karmakar[3],
Anupam Chattopadhyay[1], and Takanori Isobe[4]

[1] Nanyang Technological University, Singapore, Singapore
anubhab001@e.ntu.edu.sg, anupam@ntu.edu.sg
[2] TCS Research and Innovation, Bangalore, India
vishnu.dasu1@tcs.com
[3] Indian Institute of Technology, Bhilai, India
banashrik@iitbhilai.ac.in
[4] University of Hyogo, Kobe, Japan
takanori.isobe@ai.u-hyogo.ac.jp

Abstract. The linear layer, which is basically a binary non-singular matrix, is an integral part of cipher construction in a lot of private key ciphers. As a result, optimising the linear layer for device implementation has been an important research direction for about two decades. The Boyar-Peralta's algorithm (SEA'10) is one such common algorithm, which offers significant improvement compared to the straightforward implementation. This algorithm only returns implementation with XOR2 gates, and is deterministic. Over the last couple of years, some improvements over this algorithm has been proposed, so as to make support for XOR3 gates as well as make it randomised. In this work, we take an already existing improvement (Tan and Peyrin, TCHES'20) that allows randomised execution and extend it to support three input XOR gates. This complements the other work done in this direction (Banik et al., IWSEC'19) that also supports XOR3 gates with randomised execution. Further, noting from another work (Maximov, Eprint'19), we include one additional tie-breaker condition in the original Boyar-Peralta's algorithm. Our work thus collates and extends the state-of-the-art, at the same time offers a simpler interface. We show several results that improve from the lastly best-known results.

Keywords: Implementation · Block cipher · Linear layer

1 Introduction

With the rapid growth of lightweight cryptography in recent times, it becomes essential to reduce the cost of the cipher components. The linear layer is responsible for spreading the diffusion to the entire state in a lot of modern ciphers,

---

This paper combines and extends from [5,6,10]. An extended version of this paper is available at [3]. The first author would like to thank Sylvain Guilley (Télécom-Paris; Secure-IC) for providing the gate costs in the STM 130 nm (ASIC4) library.

A. Adhikari et al. (Eds.): INDOCRYPT 2021, LNCS 13143, pp. 141–158, 2021.
https://doi.org/10.1007/978-3-030-92518-5_7

thus constituting an integral part in cipher construction. Indeed, together with an SBox, it constitutes the unkeyed permutation of a cipher, which is then analysed against the common classical attacks (like differential, linear, algebraic etc.). Without loss of generality, a linear layer can be expressed as a binary non-singular matrix (e.g., `AES MixColumn` can be expressed as a 32×32 binary non-singular matrix), it can be implemented using assignment operations (software) or wiring (hardware) with XOR gates only.

While finding the naïve XOR implementation (the so-called d-XOR representation, see Definition 1), finding an optimal implementation using XOR gates is a complex problem. The Boyar-Peralta's algorithm [13] is an important step in this direction, which aims at finding efficient implementation of a given linear layer by using XOR2 gates only. The original version is presented over two decades ago, but there is a renewed interest as can be seen from a number of recent follow-ups [10,21,24].

The main motivation for this work comes from an observation made in [10] that using higher input XOR gates may lead to reduced area in certain ASIC libraries. In particular, the authors in [10] make a randomised variation to the original Boyar-Peralta's algorithm and do a post-processing to the output to fit XOR3 gates.

Continuing in this line, we show a dynamic higher input XOR support to a randomised variation atop the original Boyar-Peralta's algorithm (this variation is taken from [24] and is referred to as RNBP). This allows us for native support for XOR3, XOR4 etc. gates, while taking care of the individual costs for each gate. This extends from the XOR3 support in [10] as this modification does not take into consideration the costs for the XOR3 and XOR2 gates, meaning it will return the same implementation no matter the costs of the XOR2 and XOR3 gates.

Contribution

In a nutshell, we present the first open-source[1] work to support higher input XOR gates that allows for efficient implementation for the linear layer. As far we know, this is the first and so-far only available project (other open-source projects like [20,24,25]) only consider XOR2 operation; and the source-code for [10] is not public).

Several considerations and design choices are made in our implementation. The following major changes mark our contribution:

1. We take into account all the patches/updates made to the Boyar-Peralta's algorithm [13], namely [10,21,24]. We implement our version of the algorithm on top of taking ideas from all of those.
   (a) It is reported in [21] that, a tie-breaker inside the original Boyar-Peralta's algorithm [13] picks only that case which maximises certain condition (see Sect. 3 for more details), does not (always) result in the lowest cost. It is

---

[1] Available at https://bitbucket.org/vdasu_edu/boyar-peralta-xor3/.

suggested to use that case which minimises certain condition instead in [21]. We use both the maximisation and minimisation variants.

(b) In the original Boyar-Peralta's algorithm, the tie cases are broken based on lexicography. It results in a deterministic execution, meaning the exact same representation is returned all the time. Two randomised variations are presented, in [24] and in [10]. We use the fastest implementation, called RNBP, from [24] (as the source code is public) and use the randomisation described in [10] on top of it (the corresponding source code is not public).

2. We adopt the XOR3 support in Boyar-Peralta's algorithm in [10] and provide a native interface for it in our implementation[2]. In addition, we propose a support for higher input XOR gates (which can directly work with XOR3, XOR4 etc.). The new higher input XOR support that we present is dynamic in the sense that it takes into account the exact cost for each gates. This is not the case for [10], where the same XOR3 implementation is given disregarding the cost for XOR3 gates.

With our implementation, we present several results that improve the state-of-the-art bounds with {XOR2, XOR3} gates. In total, we show the costs for five libraries, namely gate count (GC), STM 90 nm (ASIC1), STM 65 nm (ASIC2), TSMC 65 nm (ASIC3) and STM 130 nm (ASIC4), see Sect. 2.4 for the respective costs for the gates in the library. More details on the results can be found in Sect. 5, here we mention a few which set the new state-of-the-art. For AES MixColumn, we get the least cost in b_2 (see Definition 6) for GC (59 with depth 4, down from 67 with depth 6) and for ASIC4 (258.98 GE). For the TWOFISH [22] and JOLTIK-BC [16] linear layers, we either touch or improve the benchmarks for all the five libraries.

2   Background and Prerequisite

2.1   Notions of XOR Count

Three notions for XOR count are mentioned in the literature; namely d-XOR, s-XOR, and g-XOR [17–19,25]. Those names are shorthand notations for 'direct XOR', 'sequential XOR', and 'general XOR', respectively. As our aim is to support higher input XOR gates, we need to generalise the definitions.

In order to do that, first we present the respective definitions in Definitions 1, 2 and 3. Then we extend the definitions of by an additional parameter ϵ. Instead of the term general XOR (introduced in [25]), we use the term branch XOR (b-XOR for short) instead. Since we are generalising the pre-existing definitions, we argue it sounds better to call 'generalised branch XOR' than 'generalised general XOR'. The term 'branch' indicates that there can be branches (i.e., feed-forward paths) in this implementation.

---

[2] The algorithm in [10], with the kind permission from the authors, is available within our implementation (the relevant source-code is written by us).

Definition 1 (d-XOR Count). *The d-XOR count of the binary matrix $M^{m \times n}$ is defined as $d(M) = \mathrm{HW}(M) - m$, where $\mathrm{HW}(\cdot)$ denotes the Hamming weight. The corresponding implementation is referred to as the d-XOR representation.*

Definition 2 (s-XOR Count). *A binary non-singular matrix $M^{n \times n}$, can be implemented by a sequence of in-place XOR operations of the form: $x_i \leftarrow x_i \oplus x_j$ for $0 \leq i, j \leq n-1$. The s-XOR count is defined as the minimum number of XOR operations of this form. Any representation that conforms to this implementation is referred to a s-XOR representation.*

Definition 3 (g-XOR Count). *A given binary $M^{m \times n}$ matrix can be implemented as a sequence of equations either of the form: $a_i \leftarrow b_i \oplus c_i$ (1 XOR operation is needed), or $a_i \leftarrow b_i$ (no XOR operation is needed). The representation is called a g-XOR representation and the minimum number of XOR operations needed is referred to as the g-XOR count of M.*

The definitions for s-XOR (to s_ϵ-XOR) and g-XOR (to b_ϵ-XOR) are given subsequently in Definitions 5 and 6. To facilitate the definition for s_ϵ-XOR, we define the 'ϵ-addition matrix' in Definition 4. Note that the case for $\epsilon = 1$ is referred to as the 'addition matrix' in the literature [19].

Definition 4 (ϵ-addition Matrix). *Let $I^{n \times n}$ be the identity matrix and $E_{i,j}^{n \times n}$ be null matrix except for $E[i,j] = 1$ for some i, j over $\mathbb{F}_2$. Then $A_\epsilon = I + E_{i,j_1} + \cdots + E_{i,j_\epsilon}$ for distinct $\{i, j_1, \ldots, j_\epsilon\}$, is defined an ϵ-addition matrix where $\epsilon \geq 1$.*

Definition 5 (s_ϵ-XOR Count). *Given a cost vector $c = [c_0, c_1, \ldots, c_\epsilon]$ where $\epsilon \geq 1$ and $c_i \geq 0$ $\forall i$, the s_ϵ-XOR count, of the non-singular matrix $M^{n \times n}$ over $\mathbb{F}_2$, is defined as*

$$\min\left(c_0 + c_1 e_1 + \cdots + c_\epsilon e_\epsilon\right),$$

provided M can be expressed as a product of the factor matrices from the multiset (with the given multiplicity) in any order:

$$[P, \underbrace{A_1, \ldots, A_1}_{e_1 \text{ times}}, \ldots, \underbrace{A_\epsilon, \ldots, A_\epsilon}_{e_\epsilon \text{ times}}],$$

where $A_\epsilon^{n \times n}$'s are ϵ-addition matrices, and $P^{n \times n}$ is a permutation matrix. Here c_0 is the cost for P, and equals to 0 if P is identity.

The s_ϵ-XOR notion coincides with s-XOR when $\epsilon = 1$ and the cost vector is $[0, 1]$. Since this is the most common cost vector, it is assumed intrinsically unless mentioned otherwise. The permutation matrix P can be implemented as a wire in hardware, which effectively takes zero area, but it can take few clock cycles in software. Thus to generalize, we consider a non-negative cost for P.

Definition 6 (b_ϵ-XOR Count). *Given a cost vector $c = [c_0, c_1, \ldots, c_\epsilon]$ where $\epsilon \geq 1$ and $c_i \geq 0$ $\forall i$, the b_ϵ-XOR count of the matrix $M^{m \times n}$ over $\mathbb{F}_2$ is defined as*

$$\min\left(c_0 e_0 + c_1 e_1 + \cdots + c_\epsilon e_\epsilon\right),$$

given M can be expressed by using equations of the following types (with the frequency for each type as mentioned) in any order:

$$t_i = t_{j_0} \qquad\qquad\qquad\qquad\qquad \} \ e_0 \ times,$$
$$t_i = t_{j_0} \oplus t_{j_1} \qquad\qquad\qquad\qquad \} \ e_1 \ times,$$
$$\vdots$$
$$t_i = t_{j_0} \oplus t_{j_1} \oplus t_{j_2} \oplus \cdots \oplus t_{j_\epsilon} \qquad \} \ e_\epsilon \ times.$$

The notion of b_ϵ-XOR coincides with that of general XOR or the g-XOR for short [25] when $\epsilon = 1$. Similar to the case of s_ϵ, the cost for the assignment operation can be taken as zero in hardware, but it is likely not zero in software.

Example 1. Consider the binary matrix, $M^{5\times5} = \begin{pmatrix} 1 & 0 & 0 & 0 & 0 \\ 0 & 1 & 0 & 0 & 0 \\ 1 & 1 & 1 & 0 & 0 \\ 1 & 1 & 0 & 1 & 0 \\ 1 & 1 & 0 & 0 & 1 \end{pmatrix}$.

With the modelling in [7, Section 3], we confirm that the s_1-XOR count of M is 5 with one addition matrix having multiplicity of 2. Here, $d(M) = 6$, $s_1(M) = 5$ and $b_1(M) = 4$ (obtained using the Boyar-Peralta's algorithm [24]. Hence for this case, $b_1(M) < s_1(M) < d(M)$.

It may be noted that the notion of b_ϵ covers that of d-XOR as well as s_ϵ, thus $b_\epsilon(M) \leq \min(d(M), s_\epsilon(M))$. Moreover, s_ϵ is undefined if the matrix is singular or rectangular. While we are not aware of use of a singular matrix, rectangular matrices are used in coding theory, which has application to cryptography.

On the other hand, s_ϵ allows to implement in-place [25]. Also, the best known result on the AES MixColumn takes 92 XOR2 gates (a b_1 representation by [21]), but one s_1 representation is also available at the same cost, thanks to [25]. Later, the authors of [20] manage to reduce the cost to 91 with a b_1 representation.

Further, implementations that follow the s_ϵ representation will be useful in the context of reversible computing (this includes quantum computing). There have been a few research works regarding reversible (including quantum) implementation of symmetric key ciphers recently, like [4,15].

As for the application of the d-XOR count, one may note that this is the simplest among all the notions and the fastest to compute. Ergo, it may be useful when finding the cost for a large number of linear layers with an automated tool.

Results on AES MixColumn. With regard to the state-of-the-art progress on the AES linear layer (i.e., MixColumn), it can be stated that the Boyar-Peralta's algorithm [13] and its variants such as [10,21,24] attempt to find b_1 (i.e., returns a solution in the b_1 representation). The FSE'20 paper [25] attempts to find an s_1 representation (best known result in this category); and the CT-RSA'21 paper [20] uses a b_1 representation to get a cost of 91 (also the best known result in this category). Additionally, the authors of [10] implement the AES MixColumn using XOR2 and XOR3 gates, which falls into the realm of b_2 representation with the associated cost vectors $[0, 2, 3.25]$ for STM 90 nm and $[0, 1.981, 3.715]$ for STM 65 nm CMOS libraries, respectively (these libraries are indicated as ASIC1 and ASIC2 respectively in this work). An overview of notable works in recent times that implement AES MixColumn, including our own results, can be found in Table 1.

Table 1. Summary of recent AES MixColumn implementations

	Representation	# XOR2	# XOR3	Depth	GC
Banik, Funabiki, Isobe [10]	b_1	95	–	6	95
(Available within this work)	b_2	39	28	6	67
Tan, Peyrin [24]	b_1	94	–	9	94
Maximov [21]	b_1	92	–	6	92
Xiang, Zeng, Lin, Bao, Zhang [25]	s_1	92	–	6	92
Lin, Xiang, Zeng, Zhang [20]	b_1	91	–	7	91
Exclusively in this work	b_2	12	47	4	59

2.2 Straight Line Program (SLP)

The implementation of the linear circuits is generally shown as a sequence of operations where every step is of the form: $u \leftarrow \bigoplus_{i=1}^{\epsilon} \lambda_i v_i$ where $\lambda_i \in \{0, 1\} \ \forall i$ are constants and rest are variables. Note that, it inherently captures multi-input XOR gates. This definition is captured from [13] (it introduces the Boyar-Peralta's algorithm). Note that it coincides with the g-XOR representation given $\epsilon = 1$ (Definition 3), or with the b_ϵ-XOR representation (Definition 6).

Not clear why, but an agreed-upon terminology appears to be non-existent. The original paper that presents the Boyar-Peralta's algorithm [13] uses the term, 'linear straight line program'; the IWSEC'19 paper [10] uses the term, 'shortest linear program'; the TCHES'20 paper [24] uses the term 'short linear program' in the title. We use the term 'straight line program' (adopting from [13]) and 'SLP' as its abbreviation.

2.3 Depth

The depth of a logical circuit can be defined as the number of combinational logic gates along the longest path of the circuit. The input variables are at depth 0; and for an SLP, depth can be computed as the maximum of depths for the variables in RHS plus 1.

For example, our b_2 implementation of Fig. 1 of AES MixColumn has the depth of 4. The variables at equal depth are shown column-wise from left to right, the left-most column has depth of 0. The variables $y_{25}, y_1, y_{15}, y_{31}, y_{30}, y_{14}$ (see Sect. 5 for the interpretation/details) are at depth 4, making the entire implementation of depth 4.

2.4   Logic Libraries

A total of five logic libraries are used in this paper for benchmarking the implementations. Shown in Table 2, the libraries contain XOR2 and XOR3 gates.

The gate count library simply counts the number of gates. The first two ASIC libraries are adopted from [10]. The third ASIC library is the same as the one used in [8]. The fourth ASIC library is the 130 nm process from STMicroelectronics, HCMOS9GP.

Table 2. Logic libraries with gates and corresponding cost

Gate \ Library	Gate Count (GC)	STM 90nm (ASIC1)	STM 65nm (ASIC2)	TSMC 65nm (ASIC3)	STM 130nm (ASIC4)
XOR2	1	2.00 GE	1.981 GE	2.50 GE	3.33 GE
XOR3	1	3.25 GE	3.715 GE	4.20 GE	4.66 GE

3   Boyar-Peralta's Algorithm and Its Variants

Before proceeding further, we describe the basic work-flow of the Boyar-Peralta's algorithm [13] (Sect. 3.1). Over the years, multiple variants of this algorithm are proposed, a summary of which is given thereafter (Sect. 3.2).

3.1   Basic Work-Flow of Boyar-Peralta's Algorithm

The original Boyar-Peralta's algorithm [13] attempts to implement b_1 with the cost vector $[0, 1]$ for the binary matrix $M^{m \times n}$. The algorithm works as follows. Initially, two vectors called the *Base* vector of size n and *Dist* vector of size m are created. The *Dist* vector is initially assigned one less than the Hamming weight of each row and the *Base* vector contains all the input variables, i.e., $x_1, x_2, \ldots, x_n$. At any given point, the *Dist* vector for a given row represents the number of elements from the *Base* vector that need to be combined to generate the implementation of that particular row and the *Base* vector contains the implementations that have been generated so far. The following steps are then performed until the sum of all elements of the *Dist* vector are 0.

1. Generate all $\binom{n}{2}$ combinations of the *Base* vector elements and compute their sum. Create a copy of the *Dist* vector for each combination. This will be called *DistC* for each combination.

2. For each combination, determine whether it is possible to reduce $DistC[i]$ by 1, where $i \in [1, m]$. To put it explicitly, determine whether it is possible to implement the sum of the ith row of M and the combination using $DistC[i] - 1$ elements of the $Base$ vector. If it is possible to do so, set $DistC[i]$ to $DistC[i] - 1$. If it is not possible, leave $DistC[i]$ as is.

3. Determine the most suitable combination (based on a defined heuristic) to be added to the $Base$ vector. Set the $Dist$ vector with the $DistC$ vector of the selected combination.

4. If any element $Dist[i] = 1$, this means that the ith row of M can be implemented by adding two elements of the $Base$ vector. Check every pair of elements in the $Base$ vector to determine which pair when summed will be equal to the ith row of M. Once this pair has been found, set $Dist[i]$ to 0.

5. Repeat until $Dist[i] = 0$ for all i.

Remark 1. $Dist[i] + 1$ at each step of the Boyar-Peralta's algorithm contains the number of elements of the $Base$ vector which need to be summed to equal to the ith row of M.

Choice of Heuristic. In Step 3 of Boyar-Peralta's algorithm, a heuristic is to be chosen to break the tie among multiple candidates which give the equal cost reduction. In the original Boyar-Peralta's algorithm [13], maximisation of Euclidean norm on $Dist$ vector is taken (we skip the justification given in [13] for brevity). Therefore, for multiple $Dist$ vectors which equal sum, the algorithm picks that one which maximises the Euclidean norm.

This maximisation heuristic is followed as-is in [10,24]. However, it is argued in [21] that the minimisation of the same will work just fine. Following this, we run both the maximisation and minimisation variants in our algorithm independently of one another.

Role of `reachable()` Function. The existing literature [10,13,24] tend to overly explain the initial part of the Boyar-Peralta's algorithm (up to the maximisation of Euclidean norm), whereas the later part that contains the `reachable()` function seems to be overlooked in the textual description. The concept of `reachable()` is arguably more difficult. So, we present a short description here for the sake of completeness and better understanding of the algorithm.

The `reachable()` function of the Boyar-Peralta's algorithm determines whether its possible to implement the ith row of a binary matrix with a new pair of $Base$ vector elements using $Dist[i] - 1$ XOR2 operations. For example, consider the following from the first row of the AES MixColumn matrix (following the encoding used in, e.g., [10]): $y_0 \leftarrow x_7 \oplus x_8 \oplus x_{15} \oplus x_{16} \oplus x_{24}$ The initial $Base$ vector contains 32 elements, i.e., $x_0, \ldots, x_{31}$; and the distance of the first row is 4 since it can be trivially implemented using 4 XOR2 gates. Given a new pair $t_0 \leftarrow x_7 \oplus x_8$ of the $Base$ vector, the `reachable()` function returns true since the first row can be implemented with three XOR2 gates: $y_0 \leftarrow t_0 \oplus x_{15} \oplus x_{16} \oplus x_{24}$. However, the `reachable()` returns false for the pair $t_1 \leftarrow x_1 \oplus x_3$ since the number of XOR2 gates required to implement the row does not reduce if this pair is chosen. Once the new distance corresponding to all possible $\binom{n}{2}$ pairs of the initial *Base* vector is computed, the optimal candidates that are to be added to the augmented *Base* vector is determined using the chosen heuristic (like RNBP [24]).

3.2 Variants of Boyar-Peralta's Algorithm

In the last couple of years, three variants of the original Boyar-Peralta's algorithm are proposed in the literature [10,21,24]. The authors of [10] use random row and column permutations of the target matrix before feeding to the original Boyar-Peralta's algorithm. They report a b_1 cost of 95. In another direction, the authors of [24] proposed three types of randomisation, all are internal to the algorithm and the least b_1 cost reported is 94^3. The best implementation using the Boyar-Peralta's algorithm family is reported in [21] with a b_1 cost of 92.

4 XOR3 (b_2) Support for Boyar-Peralta's Algorithm

To the best of our knowledge, the only attempt on b_2 is reported in [10], where the authors use a post processing on the output of the algorithm that returns XOR2 implementation. This algorithm (see Sect. 4.1 for a concise description), with some amendments is implemented in the overall open-source package we deliver.

4.1 Modelling for XOR3 (Adopted)

The basic idea of XOR3 support in the IWSEC'19 paper by Banik, Funabiki, Isobe [10] can be thought of as a post-processing to the original Boyar-Peralta's algorithm. It can be concisely described as follows.

Start with the sequence of SLPs returned by the original Boyar-Peralta's algorithm (the matrix is fed to the algorithm after the rows and columns are given random permutations). Then look for an instance where a t or y variable has the fan-out of 1. For example, assume a snippet of a sequence of SLPs looks like this:

```
1   t4 = x0 + x6 // t4 has fan-out of 1
2   t20 = x1 + t4 // t20 is the only variable that uses t4
```

Then, it can be rewritten by introducing an XOR3 operation as:

```
1   // t4 = x0 + x6 (omitted)
2   t20 = x1 + x0 + x6 // t4 is substituted, t20 uses an XOR3 operation
```

---

[3] It may be stated that, we are unable to reduce the cost of AES MixColumn from 95 XOR2 gates by using the source-code for all the three variants (RNBP, A1, A2) presented in [24], despite dedicated efforts. Apparently, the case of 94 XOR2 gates reported in [24] happens with a low probability.

Therefore, one SLP is omitted where the LHS variable has fan-out of 1. The other variable which uses the variable is now substituted with the RHS of the omitted SLP, thereby introducing an XOR3 operation. In this way, multiple (if not all) such variables with 1 fan-out can be substituted. As it can be seen, it does not take into account the cost vector for XOR2, XOR3. Thus, it is going to give the same implementation no matter the costs for XOR2 and XOR3.

One thing to note, it may not be always possible to substitute SLPs just like that. For instance, consider the following snippet:

```
1   t84 = t0 + t13 // t84 has fan-out of 1
2   t85 = x13 + t10 // t85 has fan-out of 1
3   y7 = t84 + t85 // Either t84 or t85 (but not both) can be substituted
```

Here, either of the t variables can be substituted, but not both (substituting both would lead to an XOR4 operation). Either of the implementation will result in equal cost, but the depth may vary. In our source-code that implements this algorithm, we explore both cases and pick the one with the least depth (tie is broken arbitrarily).

4.2   Modelling for XOR3 (New)

Suppose a cost vector with costs for XOR2 and XOR3 is given. Initialization of the $Base$ vector and $Dist$ vector is identical to the original algorithm (described in Sect. 3.1). The following steps highlight the changes made:

1. Generate all $\binom{n}{2}$ pairs and $\binom{n}{3}$ triplets of the $Base$ vector elements and compute the XOR. The pairs represent XOR2 combinations and the triplets represent XOR3 combinations. For each combination, assign the corresponding cost from the cost vector.
2. For each of the XOR2 combinations, determine whether it is possible to reduce $DistC[i]$ by 1. Similarly, for each of the XOR3 combinations, first check it is possible to reduce $DistC[i]$ by 2; if it is not, then check if $DistC[i]$ can be reduced by 1. If $DistC[i]$ cannot be changed, leave it as-is.
3. Based on the defined heuristic, determine the most suitable combination to be included to the $Base$ vector. Unlike the original Boyar-Peralta's algorithm, the heuristic would account for the distance vector, $DistC$; and the cost of the combination.
4. If $Dist[i] = 1$ or $Dist[i] = 2$, then the ith row of M can be implemented by adding two or three elements of the $Base$ vector respectively, i.e., either XOR2 or XOR3 operations. Check every pair/triplet of the $Base$ vector to determine the elements which sum to $M[i]$. Once these elements have been found, set $Dist[i]$ to 0, and include $M[i]$ to the $Base$ vector.
5. Repeat until $Dist[i] = 0$ for all i.

Remark 2. The Boyar-Peralta's algorithm assumes that the cost of XOR2 gates is 1. Therefore, to incorporate XOR3 support, XOR3 cost needs to be taken relative to XOR2 (so that the cost for XOR2 remains at 1).

Remark 3. Because of the way the `EasyMove()` function in Boyar-Peralta's algorithm is implemented, an additional hard check (that allows any XOR3 gate only if its cost is less than or equal to $2\times$ XOR2 gate) would possibly be required. Otherwise, if the Hamming weight of a row is 2, the algorithm would always pick an XOR3 gate even if it costs more than $2\times$ XOR2 gate. In our current implementation, a warning is given if XOR3 is greater than $2\times$ XOR2.

Remark 4. In a similar way, it is possible to extend the support for XOR4 (and even higher input XOR gates). This is an interesting research direction, but we skip it here for brevity. Also, support for higher input XOR gates would make the program taking considerably longer time.

As the source code for [24] is available online[4], we decide to implement our approach (which is described in Sect. 4.2) on top of it. We choose the RNBP variant due to its efficiency over the other variants proposed in [24].

4.3 Other Aspects Considered

In addition to the incorporation of two types of XOR3 support, the following amendments are incorporated in our source-code:

- We make continuous numbering for the temporary variables. This appears not to be the case for the previous works [10,13,24].
- Due to the way the Boyar-Peralta's algorithm is implemented, it skips the rows of the given matrix if the Hamming weight is 1 (as the XOR2 implementation is trivial in this case). While the justification is correct, it leads to a wrong SLP sequence in this case. We fix this issue.
- As already noted, we make the following enhancements:
  - Make use of the randomisation inside the algorithm (namely, RNBP) which is proposed in [24], as well as the row-column permutation of the matrix before feeding it to the algorithm which is proposed in [10].
  - Instead of only the tie-breaker based on maximisation of the Euclidean norm (which is the case for [10,13,24]); we also implement the same but with minimisation, following [21].
  - XOR3 support which is proposed in [10] is available as a native interface (with our implementation of the algorithm, as the source-code for [10] is not publicly available). Aside from that, we implement the minimisation tie-breaker. Also we check for depth for all possible implementations with the same cost (see Sect. 4.1 for more details).
- We provide an easy-to-use Python interface to generate SLPs and the entire package is available as an open-source project. The user is notified when a least cost is obtained and all the relevant results are stored in separate files. The maximum and minimum tie-breakers are internally supported with two threads in the program.

---

[4] At https://github.com/thomaspeyrin/XORreduce.

5   Results

In this part, we present a summary of the experimental results. Here x's and y's are the Boolean variables which respectively indicate the input variables and the output variables. An arbitrary number of temporary variables, t's, are created on-the-fly (those are required since this is not an in-place algorithm) to produce the SLP. So, the RHS can contain all variables while the LHS can only have the t and y variables. Given the binary matrix $M^{m \times n}$, $X^{n \times 1}$ = vector of x's, $Y^{m \times 1}$ = vector of y's, then it holds that $Y = MX$. In all the examples that follow, we only take square matrices, i.e., $m = n$. Least costs with respect to the five libraries (described in Sect. 2.4) and depth (described in Sect. 2.3) are given hereafter.

5.1   16 × 16 Matrices

In general, the execution for the binary 16 × 16 matrices is quite fast in our implementation. Table 3 shows consolidated results for few well-known ciphers. All the results reported can be obtained by our implementation, though some are already reported in [10]. The highlighted entries mark the least cost in the respective category, which are reported for the first time in the literature.

Table 3. Implementations of few 16 × 16 matrices in b_2

Matrix	GC	ASIC1	ASIC2	ASIC3	ASIC4
JOLTIK-BC [16]	28 (6, 22)	83.0 (9, 20)	91.14 (16, 16)	106.5 (9, 20)	122.50 (6, 22)
MIDORI [9]	16 (0, 16)	45.0 (16, 4)	46.56 (16, 4)	56.8 (16, 4)	71.92 (16, 4)
PRINCE M_0, M_1 [12]	16 (0, 16)	45.0 (16, 4)	46.56 (16, 4)	56.8 (16, 4)	71.92 (16, 4)
PRIDE $L_0 - L_3$ [1]	16 (0, 16)	45.0 (16, 4)	46.56 (16, 4)	56.8 (16, 4)	71.92 (16, 4)
QARMA-64 [2]	16 (0, 16)	45.0 (16, 4)	46.56 (16, 4)	56.8 (16, 4)	71.92 (16, 4)
SMALLSCALE-AES [14]	24 (0, 24)	78.0 (0, 24)	85.93 (19, 13)	100.8 (0, 24)	111.84 (0, 24)

Number of (XOR2, XOR3) gates are given within parenthesis

The algorithm for XOR3 support in [10] (Sect. 4.1) only allows for a fixed implementation disregarding the costs for XOR2 and XOR3 gates. In contrast, the new idea we present here takes into account the relative costs and returns various implementations. One such example is given, which is the case of the JOLTIK-BC linear layer in Codes 1.1 and 1.2 each as a sequence of SLPs (both are indicated in Table 3). The former implementation has the least cost so far for ASIC1 (83.0 GE, with 9 XOR2 and 20 XOR3), and has the depth of 5; the latter gives the least cost so far for GC (28) and ASIC4 (122.50 GE, with 6 XOR2 and 22 XOR3), and has the depth of 7.

Code 1.1. JOLTIK-BC linear layer in b_2 (83.0 GE in ASIC1) in SLP format

```
 1   t0 = x8 + x13 + x12      11   t10 = x4 + x2 + t4      21   t20 = x11 + t12
 2   y3 = x5 + x3 + t0        12   y4 = x10 + t10          22   y2 = x12 + t10 + t20
 3   t2 = x0 + x4 + x1        13   t12 = x7 + t4           23   y11 = t7 + y7 + t20
 4   y15 = x9 + x15 + t2      14   y7 = x13 + x1 + t12     24   y14 = x8 + t18 + t20
 5   t4 = x9 + t0             15   y9 = x15 + t5 + t12     25   t24 = y3 + y12 + t10
 6   t5 = x14 + x2 + t0       16   t15 = x6 + x13 + x10    26   y10 = y15 + t24
 7   y5 = x11 + y3 + t5       17   y13 = x3 + x11 + t15    27   t26 = x15 + t4 + t15
 8   t7 = x5 + t2             18   y8 = t5 + y12 + t15     28   y6 = x1 + t24 + t26
 9   t8 = x2 + x10 + x12      19   t18 = x14 + x0 + t4     29   y1 = y7 + t26
10   y12 = t7 + t8            20   y0 = x6 + t18
```

Code 1.2. JOLTIK-BC linear layer in b_2 (28 GC, 122.50 GE in ASIC4) in SLP format

```
 1   t0 = x5 + x4 + x0        11   y3 = x3 + t5 + t8       21   y5 = y11 + y3 + t18
 2   y11 = x13 + x11 + t0     12   t11 = x14 + x9 + x2     22   y2 = x5 + y14 + t18
 3   t2 = x8 + x9 + x12       13   y9 = x15 + x7 + t11     23   t22 = y15 + t13 + t16
 4   y7 = x1 + x7 + t2        14   t13 = x14 + x6          24   y6 = y3 + t22
 5   t4 = x1 + t0             15   y0 = x0 + t5 + t13      25   t24 = t6 + t8
 6   t5 = x13 + t2            16   y8 = x8 + t4 + t13      26   y1 = x7 + y15 + t24
 7   t6 = x10 + x6 + t0       17   t16 = x14 + y0 + y8     27   y10 = t2 + y6 + t24
 8   y13 = x3 + y11 + t6      18   y14 = y11 + y7 + t16    28   y4 = t11 + y0 + t24
 9   t8 = x5 + x9             19   t18 = t0 + t2 + t11
10   y15 = x15 + t4 + t8      20   y12 = t6 + y8 + t18
```

5.2   32 × 32 Matrices

Similar to the 16 × 16 matrices, we now show the summarised results for the 32 × 32 binary matrices in Table 4, while the results reported for the first time are highlighted (the rest are the state-of-the-art results and reported in [10]). It is to be noted that, we achieve improvement for GC for all the matrices we experiment with.

Table 4. Implementations of few 32×32 matrices in b_2

Matrix	GC	ASIC1	ASIC2	ASIC3	ASIC4
AES	59 (12, 47)	169.0 (39, 28)	181.28 (39, 28)	215.1 (39, 28)	258.98 (12, 47)
ANUBIS [11]	62 (11, 51)	185.0 (60, 20)	193.16 (60, 20)	234.0 (60, 20)	274.29 (11, 51)
CLEFIA M_0 [23]	62 (13, 49)	185.0 (60, 20)	193.16 (60, 20)	234.0 (60, 20)	271.63 (13, 49)
CLEFIA M_1 [23]	65 (3, 62)	193.0 (38, 36)	209.00 (38, 36)	246.2 (38, 36)	294.30 (38, 36)
TWOFISH [22]	73 (17, 56)	215.5 (20, 54)	240.23 (20, 54)	276.8 (20, 54)	317.57 (17, 56)

Number of (XOR2, XOR3) gates are given within parenthesis

In terms of the AES MixColumn matrix (with encoding compatible to that of [24]), our best result is of 59 GC (12 XOR2 and 47 XOR3 gates), depth 4; which is given in Code 1.3. This improves from the 67 GC, depth 6 implementation of [10] (all the implementations obtained have a depth of 6). Note that the same implementation also gives the least known cost for ASIC4 (258.98 GE, which is an improvement from [10]). A graphical representation for this implementation grouping variables at same depth in the same column is given in Fig. 1. Further, an improved implementation of TWOFISH [22] linear layer is given in Code 1.4; which incurs a GC cost of 73, ASIC4 cost of 317.57 GE, and depth of 9.

Code 1.3. AES MixColumn in b_2 with 59 GC/depth 4 in SLP format

```
 1   t0 = x8 + x16              21   t20 = x22 + x5 + x29        41   y31 = t29 + t38
 2   t1 = x24 + x0              22   y21 = x13 + x30 + t20       42   t41 = x17 + x16 + t1
 3   t2 = x28 + x24 + x16       23   y13 = x14 + x21 + t20       43   y16 = x25 + t0 + t41
 4   t3 = x12 + x8 + x0         24   t23 = x18 + x1 + x25        44   y8 = x9 + t41
 5   t4 = x22 + x14 + x7        25   y9 = x10 + x17 + t23        45   t44 = x1 + x0 + t0
 6   t5 = x23 + x6 + x30        26   y17 = x9 + x26 + t23        46   y0 = x9 + t1 + t44
 7   t6 = x20 + x27 + x3        27   t26 = x6 + x21 + x29        47   y24 = x25 + t44
 8   y19 = x11 + t2 + t6        28   y29 = x22 + y21 + t26       48   t47 = t1 + y6 + y7
 9   t8 = x11 + x4 + x19        29   y5 = x13 + x14 + t26        49   y30 = t5 + t47
10   y3 = x27 + t3 + t8         30   t29 = x24 + x16 + x31       50   t49 = x4 + x21 + t10
11   t10 = x13 + x20 + x28      31   y23 = x7 + x15 + t29        51   y12 = t0 + t49
12   y4 = x5 + t3 + t10         32   y22 = x14 + t5 + t29        52   t51 = x19 + t0 + t6
13   t12 = x12 + x4 + x29       33   t32 = x2 + y9 + y17         53   y11 = x12 + t51
14   y20 = x21 + t2 + t12       34   y25 = x10 + x1 + t32        54   t53 = x20 + x5 + t1
15   t14 = x18 + x26 + x11      35   y1 = x26 + x25 + t32        55   y28 = t12 + t53
16   y2 = x10 + x3 + t14        36   t35 = x8 + x15 + x0         56   t55 = x28 + x3 + t1
17   y10 = x2 + x19 + t14       37   y6 = x30 + t4 + t35         57   y27 = t8 + t55
18   t17 = x18 + x10 + x27      38   y7 = x23 + x31 + t35        58   t57 = t0 + y23 + y22
19   y18 = x11 + y10 + t17      39   t38 = x23 + t1 + y23        59   y14 = t4 + t57
20   y26 = x3 + x2 + t17        40   y15 = t35 + t38
```

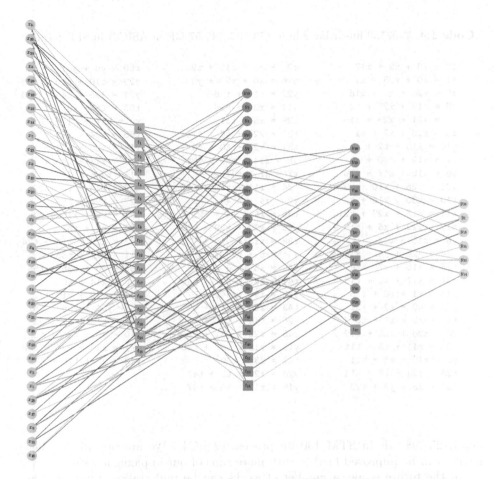

Fig. 1. AES linear layer (MixColumn) in b_2 with 59 GC/depth 4 in graphical form

6   Conclusion

With the renewed interest in the Boyar-Peralta's algorithm [13] in the last couple of years, our work combines existing ideas about the algorithm atop our own idea of incorporating XOR3 support in it. We take an open-source implementation of the algorithm (provided by the authors of [24]), make several changes to reflect the state-of-the-art observations [10,21], and finally deliver a complete package as an easy-to-use and versatile open-source project (that contains our algorithm for XOR3 support).

Our work achieves the best known results in terms of a logic library comprising of {XOR2, XOR3} gates, several of which are reported for the first time (the rest results that are reported here are tied with [10]). For instance, we present an implementation of the AES MixColumn matrix with 59 gate count/4

Code 1.4. TWOFISH linear layer in b_2 (73 GC, 317.57 GE in ASIC4) in SLP format

```
 1   t0  = x8 + x9 + x17        26   t25 = x9 + t12 + t23       51   t50 = y6 + y31
 2   t1  = x0 + x25 + x1        27   t26 = x0 + x23 + y6        52   y29 = t10 + t29 + t50
 3   t2  = x24 + x8 + x16       28   y22 = t15 + t26            53   y21 = x25 + t45 + t50
 4   t3  = x19 + x27 + t2       29   y14 = x24 + t26            54   t53 = t5 + y8
 5   t4  = x31 + x23 + x15      30   t29 = x5 + t11             55   y0  = x17 + t1 + t53
 6   t5  = x26 + x2 + t1        31   t30 = x27 + t8 + t14       56   t55 = x24 + x21
 7   y16 = x10 + t2 + t5        32   t31 = x25 + t0 + t4        57   y19 = x20 + t24 + t55
 8   t7  = x12 + x20 + x0       33   y5  = x14 + t29 + t31      58   t57 = x11 + t43 + t53
 9   t8  = x18 + x17 + y16      34   y7  = x7 + t31             59   y1  = t2 + t57
10   y24 = x25 + x10 + t8       35   t34 = x11 + t19 + t23      60   t59 = x13 + t2 + t24
11   t10 = x30 + x14 + t2       36   y2  = x4 + t34             61   y27 = x28 + t59
12   t11 = x13 + x29 + x21      37   t36 = x5 + t1 + t25        62   t61 = x8 + x15 + t26
13   t12 = x22 + x6 + t10       38   y20 = x22 + x29 + t36      63   y30 = x7 + t61
14   y6  = x15 + t12            39   t38 = x13 + y15 + t25      64   t63 = x29 + t14 + t24
15   t14 = x28 + x4 + x16       40   y4  = x6 + y23 + t38       65   y11 = x12 + t63
16   t15 = x16 + x7 + t4        41   t40 = x3 + t0 + t5         66   t65 = t0 + t36 + t55
17   y31 = x17 + t1 + t15       42   t41 = x27 + x11 + t40      67   y28 = x14 + t65
18   y15 = x1 + t0 + t15        43   y17 = x24 + t41            68   t67 = x12 + y16 + t34
19   y23 = t0 + t2 + y31        44   t43 = x26 + x18 + t3       69   y9  = y24 + y26 + t67
20   t19 = x9 + x1 + t8         45   y25 = t40 + t43            70   t69 = x19 + t1 + y2
21   y8  = x26 + x25 + t19      46   t45 = x22 + x31 + y5       71   y10 = x0 + t14 + t69
22   t21 = x11 + t3 + t11       47   y13 = y15 + t31 + t45      72   y71 = x30 + x21 + t38
23   y3  = x12 + x3 + t21       48   t47 = x3 + t30             73   y12 = x9 + t15 + t71
24   t23 = x24 + t7 + t14       49   y26 = x20 + t3 + t47
25   t24 = x5 + y3 + t23        50   y18 = x12 + t0 + t47
```

depth/258.98 GE in STM 130 nm process (ASIC4). We are optimistic, these results can be improved further with more runs of our implementation.

In the future scope, a number of works can be undertaken. First, we may consider the XNOR gates in the library. Higher input XOR gates (XOR4 and beyond) can be incorporated. It may be of interest to optimise the depth for the implementation, as far we know there is no dedicated work in the literature for studying this metric. The cost for inverse of the matrices for the given libraries may be an interesting direction to study as well. One may also be interested in finding a reversible implementation together with XOR3 support.

References

1. Albrecht, M.R., Driessen, B., Kavun, E.B., Leander, G., Paar, C., Yalçın, T.: Block ciphers – focus on the linear layer (feat. PRIDE). In: Garay, J.A., Gennaro, R. (eds.) CRYPTO 2014. LNCS, vol. 8616, pp. 57–76. Springer, Heidelberg (2014). https://doi.org/10.1007/978-3-662-44371-2_4

2. Avanzi, R.: The QARMA block cipher family. Almost MDS matrices over rings with zero divisors, nearly symmetric Even-Mansour constructions with non-involutory central rounds, and search heuristics for low-latency s-boxes. IACR Trans. Symmetric Cryptol. **2017**(1), 4–44 (2017). https://doi.org/10.13154/tosc.v2017.i1.4-44

3. Baksi, A., Dasu, V.A., Karmakar, B., Chattopadhyay, A., Isobe, T.: Three input exclusive-or gate support for Boyar-Peralta's algorithm (extended version). Cryptology ePrint Archive, Report 2021/1400 (2021). https://ia.cr/2021/1400

4. Baksi, A., Jang, K., Song, G., Seo, H., Xiang, Z.: Quantum implementation and resource estimates for rectangle and knot. Cryptology ePrint Archive, Report 2021/982 (2021). https://ia.cr/2021/982

5. Baksi, A., Karmakar, B., Dasu, V.A.: POSTER: optimizing device implementation of linear layers with automated tools. In: Zhou, J., et al. (eds.) ACNS 2021. LNCS, vol. 12809, pp. 500–504. Springer, Cham (2021). https://doi.org/10.1007/978-3-030-81645-2_30

6. Baksi, A., Karmakar, B., Dasu, V.A., Saha, D., Chattopadhyay, A.: Further insights on implementation of the linear layer. In: SILC Workshop-Security and Implementation of Lightweight Cryptography (2021)

7. Baksi, A., Karmakar, B., Dasu, V.A., Saha, D., Chattopadhyay, A.: Further insights on implementation of the linear layer. In: SILC Workshop - Security and Implementation of Lightweight Cryptography (2021). https://www.esat.kuleuven.be/cosic/events/silc2020/wp-content/uploads/sites/4/2020/10/Submission1.pdf

8. Baksi, A., Pudi, V., Mandal, S., Chattopadhyay, A.: Lightweight ASIC implementation of AEGIS-128, pp. 251–256 (2018). https://doi.org/10.1109/ISVLSI.2018.00054

9. Banik, S., et al.: Midori: a block cipher for low energy (extended version). Cryptology ePrint Archive, Report 2015/1142 (2015). https://eprint.iacr.org/2015/1142

10. Banik, S., Funabiki, Y., Isobe, T.: More results on shortest linear programs. Cryptology ePrint Archive, Report 2019/856 (2019). https://eprint.iacr.org/2019/856

11. Barreto, P.S.L.M., Rijmen, V.: The Anubis block cipher (2000). Submission to NESSIE project. https://www.cosic.esat.kuleuven.be/nessie/workshop/submissions/anubis.zip

12. Borghoff, J., et al.: PRINCE – a low-latency block cipher for pervasive computing applications. In: Wang, X., Sako, K. (eds.) ASIACRYPT 2012. LNCS, vol. 7658, pp. 208–225. Springer, Heidelberg (2012). https://doi.org/10.1007/978-3-642-34961-4_14

13. Boyar, J., Peralta, R.: A new combinational logic minimization technique with applications to cryptology. In: Festa, P. (ed.) SEA 2010. LNCS, vol. 6049, pp. 178–189. Springer, Heidelberg (2010). https://doi.org/10.1007/978-3-642-13193-6_16

14. Cid, C., Murphy, S., Robshaw, M.J.B.: Small scale variants of the AES. In: Gilbert, H., Handschuh, H. (eds.) FSE 2005. LNCS, vol. 3557, pp. 145–162. Springer, Heidelberg (2005). https://doi.org/10.1007/11502760_10

15. Dasu, V.A., Baksi, A., Sarkar, S., Chattopadhyay, A.: LIGHTER-R: optimized reversible circuit implementation for s-boxes. In: 32nd IEEE International System-on-Chip Conference, SOCC 2019, Singapore, 3–6 September 2019, pp. 260–265 (2019). https://doi.org/10.1109/SOCC46988.2019.1570548320

16. Jean, J., Nikolić, I., Peyrin, T.: Joltik v1.3 (2015). Submission to the CAESAR competition. http://www1.spms.ntu.edu.sg/~syllab/Joltik

17. Jean, J., Peyrin, T., Sim, S.M., Tourteaux, J.: Optimizing implementations of lightweight building blocks. IACR Trans. Symmetric Cryptol. **2017**(4), 130–168 (2017). https://doi.org/10.13154/tosc.v2017.i4.130-168

18. Khoo, K., Peyrin, T., Poschmann, A.Y., Yap, H.: FOAM: searching for hardware-optimal SPN structures and components with a fair comparison. In: Batina, L., Robshaw, M. (eds.) CHES 2014. LNCS, vol. 8731, pp. 433–450. Springer, Heidelberg (2014). https://doi.org/10.1007/978-3-662-44709-3_24

19. Kölsch, L.: XOR-counts and lightweight multiplication with fixed elements in binary finite fields. In: Ishai, Y., Rijmen, V. (eds.) EUROCRYPT 2019. LNCS, vol. 11476, pp. 285–312. Springer, Cham (2019). https://doi.org/10.1007/978-3-030-17653-2_10

20. Lin, D., Xiang, Z., Zeng, X., Zhang, S.: A framework to optimize implementations of matrices. In: Paterson, K.G. (ed.) CT-RSA 2021. LNCS, vol. 12704, pp. 609–632. Springer, Cham (2021). https://doi.org/10.1007/978-3-030-75539-3_25

21. Maximov, A.: AES mixcolumn with 92 XOR gates. Cryptology ePrint Archive, Report 2019/833 (2019). https://eprint.iacr.org/2019/833

22. Schneier, B., Kelsey, J., Whiting, D., Wagner, D., Hall, C., Ferguson, N.: Twofish: a 128-bit block cipher (1998). https://www.schneier.com/academic/paperfiles/paper-twofish-paper.pdf

23. Shirai, T., Shibutani, K., Akishita, T., Moriai, S., Iwata, T.: The 128-bit blockcipher CLEFIA (extended abstract). In: Biryukov, A. (ed.) FSE 2007. LNCS, vol. 4593, pp. 181–195. Springer, Heidelberg (2007). https://doi.org/10.1007/978-3-540-74619-5_12

24. Tan, Q.Q., Peyrin, T.: Improved heuristics for short linear programs. Cryptology ePrint Archive, Report 2019/847 (2019). https://eprint.iacr.org/2019/847

25. Xiang, Z., Zeng, X., Lin, D., Bao, Z., Zhang, S.: Optimizing implementations of linear layers. Cryptology ePrint Archive, Report 2020/903 (2020). https://eprint.iacr.org/2020/903

Pushing the Limits: Searching for Implementations with the Smallest Area for Lightweight S-Boxes

Zhenyu Lu[1,2], Weijia Wang[1,2], Kai Hu[1,2], Yanhong Fan[1,2], Lixuan Wu[1,2], and Meiqin Wang[1,2(✉)]

[1] School of Cyber Science and Technology, Shandong University, Qingdao 266237, Shandong, China
[2] Key Laboratory of Cryptologic Technology and Information Security, Ministry of Education, Shandong University, Qingdao 266237, Shandong, China
{luzhenyu,hukai,fanyh,lixuanwu}@mail.sdu.edu.com,
{wjwang,mqwang}@sdu.edu.cn

Abstract. The area is one of the most important criteria for an S-box in hardware implementation when designing lightweight cryptography primitives. The area can be well estimated by the number of gate equivalent (GE). However, to our best knowledge, there is no efficient method to search for an S-box implementation with the least GE. Previous approaches can be classified into two categories, one is a heuristic that aims at finding an implementation with a satisfying but not necessarily the smallest GE number; the other one is SAT-based focusing on only the smallest number of gates while it ignored that the areas of different gates vary. Implementation with the least gates would usually not lead to the smallest number of GE.

In this paper, we propose an improved SAT-based tool targeting optimizing the number of GE of an S-box implementation. Given an S-box, our tool can return the implementation of this S-box with the smallest number of GE. We speed up the search process of the tool by bit-sliced technique. Additionally, our tool supports 2-, 3-, and 4-input gates, while the previous tools cover only 2-input gates. To highlight the strength of our tool, we apply it to some 4-bit and 5-bit S-boxes of famous ciphers. We obtain a better implementation of RECTANGLE's S-box with the area of 18.00GE. What's more, we prove that the implementations of S-boxes of PICCOLO, SKINNY, and LBLOCK in the current literature have been optimal. When using the DC synthesizer on the circuits produced by our tool, the area are much better than the circuits converted by DC synthesizers from the lookup tables (LUT). At last, we use our tool to find implementations of 5-bit S-boxes, such as those used in KECCAK and ASCON.

Keywords: Lightweight ciphers · S-box implementations · Gate equivalent complexity · SAT-solvers

© Springer Nature Switzerland AG 2021
A. Adhikari et al. (Eds.): INDOCRYPT 2021, LNCS 13143, pp. 159–178, 2021.
https://doi.org/10.1007/978-3-030-92518-5_8

1   Introduction

Lightweight cryptographic primitives are deployed more and more in the source-constraint devices that manipulate sensitive data. The National Institute of Standards and Technology (NIST) has initiated a competition to call for a new lightweight cryptography standard for constrained environments [12]. The designer of lightweight cryptography needs to consider both the security property and implementation performance. The hardware implementation performance includes many criteria, e.g., throughput, area, energy, power, and latency, where the area is a crucial criterion for the implementation of lightweight ciphers.

Since the area cost of different gates depends on the technology library, measuring and comparing the area cost of implementations requires a standard unit. A gate equivalent usually stands for the unit of measure which allows specifying manufacturing-technology-independent complexity of digital electronic circuits. Practically, the NAND constitutes the unit area commonly referred to as a gate equivalent while the GE of other gates are measured based on the NAND gates. For example, in the library of UMC 180nm [8], the GE of some gates are listed in Table 1.

Table 1. Area cost of typical cell gates under UMC 180nm library [8]. The values are given in GE.

Techniques	AND	NOT	NAND	XOR	NAND3	XOR3	MAOI1	MOAI1
	OR		NOR	XNOR	NOR3	XNOR3		
UMC 180nm	1.33	0.67	1.00	3.00	1.33	4.67	2.67	2.00

To predict the area of a hardware implementation of a given S-box, we commonly compute the number of GE of this implementation. As a result, to find an optimal implementation of an S-box with the smallest area, we need to find the optimal combination of a set of gates whose number of GE is the smallest.

Before this work, no approach is suitable to find the implementation of an S-box with the smallest area directly. Here we briefly introduce two main-stream methods to find the implementation of an S-box.

Heuristic Search. In the domain of logic synthesis, several heuristic algorithms provide satisfactory solutions, such as BOOM [7] and ESPRESSO [13] which are probably implemented in many commercial synthesizers. An automated tool LIGHTER proposed by Jean et al. [9] uses a graph-based meet-in-the-middle search algorithm under the assumption that every instructions is invertible. Despite of the efficiency and practical applicability for different S-boxes, these algorithms rely on some heuristics and are infeasible to prove that their results are optimal implementation of S-box circuits.

SAT-Based Search. At FSE 2016, Stoffelen models the problem of finding an efficient implementation of a lightweight S-box as a SAT problem [15]. Then with a SAT solver, this tool can find the implementation of S-box with the smallest number of gates. However, as Table 1 shows, the area costs of different gates are different. The smallest number of gates will still lead to a large number of GE.

Our Contributions. In this paper, we give the first method to search for the optimal area implementation of small S-boxes by SAT solver. The main contributions are shown below.

A New Searching Algorithm. Based on the SAT method [15], we propose an algorithm to find the optimal implementation of a lightweight S-box focusing on the area. We reduce the search space by a pre-computed algorithm. This algorithm first searches for the optimal implementation in the terms of number of gates, then it calculates the lower and upper bounds of the number of gates and area.

Within this range, we find out the optimal implementation by querying the SAT solver. The number of variables in the SAT model has a great dependence on the types and the number of gates. As the number of variables increases, the efficiency would be lower. Consequently, we use the bit-sliced technique to reduce the number of variables and then speed up the model.

A Generalization to 2-, 3-, 4-input Gates. In [1], the authors have shown that replacing several simple gates with two inputs complex gates with multiple inputs can save the area significantly. Insipred by this, on the basis of the 2-input gate model [15], our model includes complex gates. Our model gives a unified expression that can describe gates with 2 inputs, 3 inputs (e.g., XOR3, XNOR3, OR3, NOR3, AND3, and NAND3) and 4 inputs (e.g., MOAI1 and MAOI1).

Better S-box Implementations. We apply our method to many 4- and 5-bit S-boxes of popular ciphers such as RECTANGLE [17], PICCOLO [14], SKINNY [2], LBLOCK [16], KECCAK [3] and ASCON [5].

We manage to find an improved circuit of RECTANGLE's S-box with 18.00 GE cost which is better than LIGHTER's and we can verify that the circuits of PICCOLO, SKINNY and LBLOCK's S-boxes have the optimal area cost under the 2-, 3- and 4-input gates we considered. In addition, due to the bit-sliced technique, our model is also useful in finding the implementation of the 5-bit S-boxes.

Organization of the Paper. In Sect. 2, we first introduce some preliminary notions and recall some previous works on the implementation of S-box. We introduce our new model with the pre-computed algorithm and bit-sliced technique to search the optimal area implementation of an S-box in Sect. 3. In Sect. 4, we provide an comparison between our results and previous works. At the end, we conclude the paper in Sect. 5.

2   Preliminaries

In this section, we first present some definitions and notions used in this paper. Then, we briefly recall Stoffelen's SAT-based tool in [15].

2.1   Notations

Table 2. List of Boolean operators implemented by standard cell gates from the libraries. $\wedge, \vee, \oplus, \neg$ stand for logical and, or, exclusive or, not [9], respectively.

Operation	Function	Operation	Function
NAND	$(a,b) \rightarrow \neg(a \wedge b)$	XOR	$(a,b) \rightarrow a \oplus b$
NOR	$(a,b) \rightarrow \neg(a \vee b)$	XNOR	$(a,b) \rightarrow \neg(a \oplus b)$
AND	$(a,b) \rightarrow a \wedge b$	NAND3	$(a,b,c) \rightarrow \neg(a \wedge b \wedge c)$
OR	$(a,b) \rightarrow (a \vee b)$	NOR3	$(a,b) \rightarrow \neg(a \vee b \vee c)$
NOT	$a \rightarrow \neg a$	XOR3	$(a,b,c) \rightarrow (a \oplus b \oplus c)$
MAOI1	$(a,b,c,d) \rightarrow \neg((a \wedge b) \vee (\neg(c \vee d)))$	XNOR3	$(a,b,c) \rightarrow \neg(a \oplus b \oplus c)$
MOAI1	$(a,b,c,d) \rightarrow \neg((a \vee b) \wedge (\neg(c \wedge d)))$		

The combinatorial cell gates implement classical Boolean operations, whose functional behavior is shown in Table 2. In this paper, we use *logical connectives* to denote the types of operations, i.e., let $\wedge$, $\vee$, $\oplus$, $\neg$ denote AND, OR, XOR, NOT, respectively, and let $\uparrow$, $\downarrow$, $\leftrightarrow$ denote NAND, NOR, XNOR, respectively. The notations used in this paper are listed in Table 3.

2.2   Stoffelen's SAT-based Tool

The Boolean satisfiability problem (SAT) is the problem of determining whether there exists an evaluation for the binary variables such that the value of the given Boolean formula equals one. Through translating a problem into a SAT problem, we could then take the off-the-shelf solvers to solve this SAT problem, and finally get the corresponding answer to the original problem.

Since our tool can be regarded as an improved version of Stoffelen's SAT-based tool [15] that aims at finding the implementation with smallest number of GE rather than only the number of gates, we introduce the basic methods used in his tool. In [15], Stoffelen explores the feasibility of applying SAT solvers to optimize implementations of small S-boxes for the criteria including of the number of gates. He proposed a binary model to solve the following decision problem: *Is there a circuit that implements an S-box $S : \mathbb{F}_2^n \rightarrow \mathbb{F}_2^m$ and that uses at most K logic operations?*

Table 3. List of notations in this paper.

Notations	Definitions
K	K represents the number of gates
G	G represents the area cost of a circuit
x_i (resp. y_j)	Boolean variables, represent S-box inputs (resp. outputs)
q_{2i}	The i-th gate input , $q_{2i} \in \mathbb{F}_2$
t_i	The i-th gate output, $t_i \in \mathbb{F}_2$
a_i	Coefficient variables $a_i \in \mathbb{F}_2$ represent wiring between gates. (More details can refer to example 1.)
b_i	Variables $b_i \in \mathbb{F}_2$ determine the types of gates. (More details can refer to example 1.)
$Cost[i]$	The array $Cost[i]$ represents the cost of different gate operations

He uses a method in [4,11] to transform the decision problem into a model. This model encodes each gate as an Algebraic Normal Form (ANF) equation and can judge the existence of solutions when given the number of gates. To get the smallest number of gates, it should exhaust K until finding the smallest one that there exists an implementation of an S-box.

As an example, we give a model of a decision problem whether there is a circuit implements an 2-bit toy S-box with 2 gates.

Example 1. Given a 2-bit S-box in Table 4 and we encode the model of this S-box as follows.

Table 4. Lookup table of the 2-bit S-box.

x	0	1	2	3
$S(x)$	3	2	0	1

Encode the Input and Output of the S-box. We encode the S-box as Boolean variables x_i and y_i.

$$x_0 = 0, \ x_1 = 0, \ y_0 = 1, \ y_1 = 1; \quad //denote\ S(0) = 3$$
$$x_2 = 0, \ x_3 = 1, \ y_2 = 1, \ y_3 = 0; \quad //denote\ S(1) = 2$$
$$x_4 = 1, \ x_5 = 0, \ y_4 = 0, \ y_5 = 0; \quad //denote\ S(2) = 0$$
$$x_6 = 1, \ x_7 = 1, \ y_6 = 0, \ y_7 = 1; \quad //denote\ S(3) = 1$$

Then, for each x and $S(x)$, this model needs one set of equations as follows to represent a circuit with K gates and there are a total of 2^2 sets.

Encode a Decision of Choosing Two Inputs of a Gate. The Boolean variables q_i represent the inputs of a gate. For example, q_0 and q_1 are two inputs of the gate t_0, while q_2 and q_3 are two inputs of the gate t_1.

$$q_0 = a_0 \cdot x_0 + a_1 \cdot x_1$$
$$q_1 = a_2 \cdot x_0 + a_3 \cdot x_1$$
$$q_2 = a_4 \cdot x_0 + a_5 \cdot x_1 + a_6 \cdot t_0$$
$$q_3 = a_7 \cdot x_0 + a_8 \cdot x_1 + a_9 \cdot t_0$$

One q_i must come from one of the S-box's inputs or the output of a previous gate. This constraint can be described as that only one of the variables a_i in an equation can be equal to 1.

$$a_0 \cdot a_1 = 0.$$
$$a_2 \cdot a_3 = 0.$$
$$a_4 \cdot a_5 = 0 \; AND \; a_4 \cdot a_6 = 0 \; AND \; a_5 \cdot a_6 = 0.$$
$$a_7 \cdot a_8 = 0 \; AND \; a_7 \cdot a_9 = 0 \; AND \; a_8 \cdot a_9 = 0.$$

Encode the Decision of Choosing a Type of Gate. The variables b_i determine what kind of gate the t_i will represent, as can be seen in Table 5. When the value of the pattern $b_{3i}||b_{3i+1}||b_{3i+2}$ is different, t_i represents different kind of gate, such as AND, OR, XOR, NAND, NOR, and XNOR.

$$t_0 = b_0 \cdot q_0 \cdot q_1 + b_1 \cdot q_0 + b_1 \cdot q_1 + b_2$$
$$t_1 = b_2 \cdot q_2 \cdot q_3 + b_3 \cdot q_2 + b_3 \cdot q_3 + b_4$$

There are a total of K variables t_i to represent K different gates.

Encode the decision of choosing the output of the circuit. The Boolean variables y_i also represent the outputs of the circuit.

$$y_0 = a_{18} \cdot x_0 + a_{19} \cdot x_1 + a_{20} \cdot t_0 + a_{21} \cdot t_1$$
$$y_0 = a_{22} \cdot x_0 + a_{23} \cdot x_1 + a_{24} \cdot t_0 + a_{25} \cdot t_1$$

Similar to q_i, one y_i must come from one of the S-box's inputs or the output of a gate. This constraint can be described as that only one of the variables a_i in an equation can be equal to 1 too.

3   Optimizing Implementations for S-Boxes

We measure the gate sizes in terms of Gate Equivalent (GE), which is a normalized ratio using the area of a 2-input NAND gate as a common reference.

Table 5. Encoding of different types of gates.

$b_{3i}\|b_{3i+1}\|b_{3i+2}$	Operations	Gate function
0 0 0	0	0
0 0 1	1	1
0 1 0	XOR	$q_{2i} \oplus q_{2i+1}$
0 1 1	XNOR	$q_{2i} \leftrightarrow q_{2i+1}$
1 0 0	AND	$q_{2i} \wedge q_{2i+1}$
1 0 1	NAND	$q_{2i} \uparrow q_{2i+1}$
1 1 0	OR	$q_{2i} \vee q_{2i+1}$
1 1 1	NOR	$q_{2i} \downarrow q_{2i+1}$

3.1 Main Idea of Our Model

In this section, we introduce how to improve Stoffelen's tool for optimizing the area of an S-box. Stoffelen's model can produce an implementation with a set of K gates and we denote this set as $\mathcal{I}$. We can add the cost of each gate up to obtain the area of this implementation. Let G denote the area of the implementation, we have

$$G = \sum_{g_i \in I} Cost_{g_i}, \tag{1}$$

where $Cost_{g_i}$ is the area of the gate g_i in $\mathcal{I}$. Since we want to search for an implementation of the S-box with G area, Eq. 1 is naturally the objective function of our new model together with all equations in Stoffelen's model. This model can determine whether a circuit can implement an S-box with K gates and G area.

However, even if there exists a circuit, the area is not the smallest one. It needs to exhaust K and G and encode the corresponding decision problem to find the smallest area implementation by querying the SAT solver.

In this term, there are three limitations of Stoffelen's tool. Firstly, the NOT operation is not considered, because in his model a NOT gate is always redundant for it can always be incorperated into a new combinatorial gate. For example, a NOT gate and an AND gate can be combined into a NAND gate. However, if we want to consider the area, our model cannot ignore the NOT gate. In addition, his tool only covers 2-inputs gates, while the complex gates such as 3- and 4-inputs gates have a great effect on implementations. Secondly, the area costs of different gates are different and his model could not find the smallest number of GE of an S-box's implementation. Finally, as the number of gates increases, Stoffelen's model needs more variables, which results in a lower efficiency and the model does not work for 5-bit S-boxes and even some 4-bit S-boxes.

To overcome these limitations, we first re-encode the ANF equation of an gate including the NOT gate and 2-, 3-, 4-input gates. Then, we propose a new decision problem: *is there a circuit that implements an S-box so that the area cost at most G?* To solve this problem, we set an array to denote the area cost of different gates and give an algorithm to determine the upper and lower bounds of the K and G. In the end, we use a technique called bit-sliced to reduce the variables in our model and speed up the search.

3.2   Encode the NOT Gate and Complex Gates

In this section, we re-encode the equation of a gate to include the NOT gate and 2-, 3-, 4-input gates. The 3-input gates include the AND3, OR3, XOR3, NAND3, NOR3 and XNOR3 gates while the MAOI1 and MOAI1 gates are two 4-input gates.

NOT Gate. Firstly, we re-encode the gates equation from Stoffelen's model as follows to add the NOT gate.

$$t = b_0 \cdot q_0 \cdot q_1 + b_1 \cdot q_0 + b_1 \cdot q_1 + \mathbf{b_2} \cdot \mathbf{q_0} + b_3 \tag{2}$$

In this equation, when $b_2 = 0$, the patterns $b_0||b_1||b_3$ represent the same gates to the patterns Stoffelen's model, which can be seen in Table 6.

Table 6. Improve the encoding of different types of gates.

$b_0||b_1||b_2||b_3$	Operations	Gate function
0 0 1 1	**NOT**	$\neg q_0$
0 1 0 0	XOR	$q_0 \oplus q_1$
0 1 0 1	XNOR	$q_0 \leftrightarrow q_1$
0 1 1 1	**NOT**	$\neg q_1$
1 0 0 0	AND	$q_0 \wedge q_1$
1 0 0 1	NAND	$q_0 \uparrow q_1$
1 1 0 0	OR	$q_0 \vee q_1$
1 1 0 1	NOR	$q_0 \downarrow q_1$

From Table 6, the patterns $b_0||b_1||b_2||b_3$ do not cover the whole space of $\mathbb{F}_2^4$. For example, when b_2 equals to 1, b_3 should equal to 1 and b_0 equal to 0. We describe this case as a constraint in our model to make sure that each pattern is corresponding to one gate.

$$Cst_1 = \{b_3 = 1 \text{ and } b_0 = 0 | b_2 = 1\}.$$

However, more complex gates, such as 3-input and 4-input operations have a great effect on the number of GE. For example, two consecutive XOR gates can be replaced by a XOR3 gate and the XOR3 gate cost 4.67 GE which is smaller than two XOR gates.

3-Input Gates. We improve the Equation (2) to add the 3-input gates, such as AND3, NAND3, OR3, NOR3, XOR3, and XNOR3.

$$t = b_0 \cdot q_0 \cdot q_1 \cdot q_2 + b_1 \cdot q_0 \cdot q_1 + b_1 \cdot q_0 \cdot q_2 + b_1 \cdot q_1 \cdot q_2 +$$
$$b_1 \cdot q_0 + b_1 \cdot q_1 + b_1 \cdot q_2 + b_2 \cdot q_0 + b_2 \cdot q_1 + b_2 \cdot q_2 + \qquad (3)$$
$$b_3 \cdot q_0 \cdot q_1 + b_4 \cdot q_0 + b_4 \cdot q_1 + b_5 \cdot q_0 + b_6.$$

This equation adds three b_i and one q_i to encode the 3-input gates. We propose the detail of the gate in Table 7.

Table 7. Encoding of different types of 2-input and 3-input gates.

$b_0\|b_1\|b_2\|b_3\| b_4\|b_5\|b_6$	Operations	Gate function
0 0 0 0 0 1 1	NOT	$\neg q_0$
0 0 0 0 1 0 0	XOR	$q_0 \oplus q_1$
0 0 0 0 1 0 1	XNOR	$q_0 \leftrightarrow q_1$
0 0 0 0 1 1 1	NOT	$\neg q_1$
0 0 0 1 0 0 0	AND	$q_0 \wedge q_1$
0 0 0 1 0 0 1	NAND	$q_0 \uparrow q_1$
0 0 0 1 1 0 0	OR	$q_0 \vee q_1$
0 0 0 1 1 0 1	NOR	$q_0 \downarrow q_1$
1 0 0 0 0 0 0	AND3	$q_0 \wedge q_1 \wedge q_2$
1 0 0 0 0 0 1	NAND3	$\neg(q_0 \wedge q_1 \wedge q_2)$
1 1 0 0 0 0 0	OR3	$q_0 \vee q_1 \vee q_2$
1 1 0 0 0 0 1	NOR3	$\neg(q_0 \vee q_1 \vee q_2)$
0 0 1 0 0 0 0	XOR3	$q_0 \oplus q_1 \oplus q_2$
0 0 1 0 0 0 1	XNOR3	$\neg(q_0 \oplus q_1 \oplus q_2)$

Similarly, the patterns $b_0\|b_1\|b_2\|b_3\|b_4\|b_5\|b_6$ of this equation do not cover the whole space of $\mathbb{F}_2^7$. When $b_0 = b_1 = b_2 = 0$, the patterns $b_3\|b_4\|b_5\|b_6$ represent the gates are the same as the 2-input ones. To make sure each pattern represents one gate, we add the following constraints in our model.

$$Cst_1 = \{b_6 = 1 \ and \ b_3 = 0 | b_5 = 1\}.$$
$$Cst_2 = \{b_2 = b_3 = b_4 = b_5 = 0 | b_0 = 1\}.$$
$$Cst_3 = \{b_0 = 1 | b_1 = 1\}.$$
$$Cst_4 = \{b_0 = b_1 = b_3 = b_4 = b_5 = 0 | b_2 = 1\}.$$

4-Input Gates. The gate functions of the MAOI1 and MOAI1 4-input gates are listed in Table 8. It is easy to know that $MAOI1(a, b, c, d) = \neg MOAI1(a, b, c, d)$.

We further improve Equation (3) to add the 4-input gates into our model. Firstly, we decompose the function of MAOI1 gate as follows

$$
\begin{aligned}
&MAOI1(a,b,c,d)\\
&= \neg((a \wedge b) \vee (\neg(c \vee d)))\\
&= (\neg(a \wedge b)) \wedge (c \vee d)\\
&= (b_0 \cdot a \cdot b + b_0) \cdot (b_1 \cdot c \cdot d + b_1 \cdot c + b_1 \cdot d)\\
&= b_0 b_1 \cdot abcd + b_0 b_1 \cdot abc + b_0 b_1 \cdot abd + b_0 b_1 \cdot cd + b_0 b_1 \cdot c + b_0 b_1 \cdot d\\
&= b_* \cdot abcd + b_* \cdot abc + b_* \cdot abd + b_* \cdot cd + b_* \cdot c + b_* \cdot d.
\end{aligned}
\tag{4}
$$

Then, we add one b_i and one q_i to encode all 2-, 3- and 4-input gates.

$$
\begin{aligned}
t = &\, b_0 \cdot q_0 \cdot q_1 \cdot q_2 \cdot q_3 + b_0 \cdot q_0 \cdot q_1 \cdot q_2 +\\
&\, b_0 \cdot q_0 \cdot q_1 \cdot q_3 + b_0 \cdot q_2 \cdot q_3 + b_0 \cdot q_2 + b_0 \cdot q_3 +\\
&\, b_1 \cdot q_0 \cdot q_1 \cdot q_2 + b_2 \cdot q_0 \cdot q_1 + b_2 \cdot q_0 \cdot q_2 + b_2 \cdot q_1 \cdot q_2 +\\
&\, b_2 \cdot q_0 + b_2 \cdot q_1 + b_2 \cdot q_2 + b_3 \cdot q_0 + b_3 \cdot q_1 + b_3 \cdot q_2 +\\
&\, b_4 \cdot q_0 \cdot q_1 + b_5 \cdot q_0 + b_5 \cdot q_1 + b_6 \cdot q_0 + b_7.
\end{aligned}
\tag{5}
$$

In Table 8, we propose the details of the 4-input gate. Besides, to make sure each pattern represents one gate, we add one more constraint in our model.

Table 8. Encoding of different types of 4-inputgates.

$b_0 \,\|\, b_1\|b_2\|b_3\|\, b_4\|b_5\|b_6\|b_7$	Operations	Gate function
1 0 0 0 0 0 0 0	MAOI1	$\neg((q_0 \wedge q_1) \vee (\neg(q_2 \vee q_3)))$
1 0 0 0 0 0 0 1	MOAI1	$\neg((q_0 \vee q_1) \wedge (\neg(q_2 \wedge q_3)))$

$$
Cst_5 = \{b_1 = b_2 = b_3 = b_4 = b_5 = b_6 = 0 | b_0 = 1\}.
$$

In summary, Fig. 1 gives the framework of our model and the number of the input variables q_i corresponding to each gate t_i in the model has become to 4 and a set of equations has a total of $4K$ inputs variables q_i.

We also use the decision problem whether there is a circuit implements an 2-bit toy S-box and that uses at most 3 logic operations as an example. The set of the equation re-encode as

$$
\begin{aligned}
q_0 &= a_0 \cdot x_0 + a_1 \cdot x_1\\
q_1 &= a_2 \cdot x_0 + a_3 \cdot x_1\\
q_2 &= a_4 \cdot x_0 + a_5 \cdot x_1\\
q_3 &= a_6 \cdot x_0 + a_7 \cdot x_1
\end{aligned}
$$

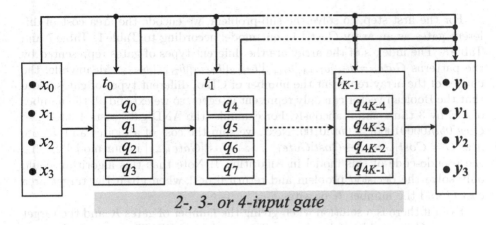

Fig. 1. Illustration of our model.

$$t_0 = b_0 \cdot q_0 \cdot q_1 \cdot q_2 \cdot q_3 + b_0 \cdot q_0 \cdot q_1 \cdot q_2 +$$
$$b_0 \cdot q_0 \cdot q_1 \cdot q_3 + b_0 \cdot q_2 \cdot q_3 + b_0 \cdot q_2 + b_0 \cdot q_3 +$$
$$b_1 \cdot q_0 \cdot q_1 \cdot q_2 + b_2 \cdot q_0 \cdot q_1 + b_2 \cdot q_0 \cdot q_2 + b_2 \cdot q_1 \cdot q_2 +$$
$$b_2 \cdot q_0 + b_2 \cdot q_1 + b_2 \cdot q_2 + b_3 \cdot q_0 + b_3 \cdot q_1 + b_3 \cdot q_2 +$$
$$b_4 \cdot q_0 \cdot q_1 + b_5 \cdot q_0 + b_5 \cdot q_1 + b_6 \cdot q_0 + b_7.$$

$$\cdots$$

$$y_0 = a_{36} \cdot x_0 + a_{37} \cdot x_1 + a_{38} \cdot t_0 + a_{39} \cdot t_1 + a_{40} \cdot t_2$$
$$y_1 = a_{41} \cdot x_0 + a_{42} \cdot x_1 + a_{43} \cdot t_0 + a_{44} \cdot t_1 + a_{45} \cdot t_2$$

It can be seen from the set of equations, the number of variables including a_i, q_i and b_i which has grown a lot.

3.3   Searching for the Implementation with the Smallest Area

As mentioned before, we propose a new decision problem: is there a circuit that implements an S-box with the area cost at most G GE? At first glance, it seems easy to solve this problem by slightly adjusting Stoffelen's tool. However, Stoffelen's SAT-based model needs to encode the problem based on a determined K. It could not determine the number of variables in a set of equations without knowing the K. On the other hand, it is simple to solve a sub-problem, whether a circuit can implement an S-box that uses determined K logic operations with G GE.

In this section, we first solve this sub-problem by Algorithm 1. Then we propose Algorithm 2 to determine the range of the search space to find the smallest number of GE step by step.

For the first step, to solve the sub-problem, we encode the area cost of different gates as an array $Cost[]$ in our model according to Table 1, Table 7 and Table 8. The indexes of the array are the different types of gates represented by the patterns $Gate_i = b_{7i}||b_{7i+1}||b_{7i+2}||b_{7i+3}||b_{7i+4}||b_{7i+5}||b_{7i+6}$. Meanwhile, the entries of the array represent the number of GE of different types of gates. Note that the Boolean vector can only represent integers, so we expand all the number of GE by 3 times simultaneously. For example, the AND gate costs 1.33GE, so $Cost[0bin00001000] = 0bin0100$. Next, we sum the cost of all gates and denote it as $G = Cost[Gate_0] + Cost[Gate_1] + ... + Cost[Gate_{K-1}]$ in our model. Seeing the pseudo-code of this model in Algorithm 1. Note that this algorithm could only solve the decision problem and return 0 or 1 when given the target area cost G and the number K of gates.

Even if there is a solution when giving the number of gates K and the target area cost G, it could not be the smallest number of GE. The second step is to determine the search space $\mathcal{V}(K, G)$ where the (K_{opt}, G_{opt}) of the global optimal implementation lie in. We can use the model in Sect. 3.2 to find an implementation with the smallest number of gates K_{low}, then we give a proposition.

Proposition 1. K_{low} represents the smallest number of gates of an S-box's implementation. We set the area cost G_{up} of this implementation as the upper bound of the number of GE. Then, the range of $\mathcal{V}(K, G)$ is $K_{low} \leq K \leq G_{up}/1.00GE$ and $1.00GE \times K_{low} \leq G \leq G_{up}$.

Proof. 1.00GE represents the lower area cost of the non-linear operation (e.g. NAND). Every implementation of an S-box needs several non-linear operations. Assuming that all K_{low} gates of an implementation are NAND, the area of this implementation must be the smallest one. Thus, the lower bound of G is $1.00GE \times K_{low}$. In the same way, if the number of gates in an implementation exceeds $G_{up}/1.00GE$, its area must be greater than G_{up}. $\square$

Finally, we propose Algorithm 2 and utilize the Proposition 1 to find a circuit implementing an S-box with the smallest number of GE.

3.4   Bit-Sliced Technique

Bit-sliced techniques are widely used in the implementation and optimization of cryptographic primitives [2,5,6,10,17]. We transplanted the idea of bit-sliced into our model and provide a natural way to optimally encode the relation between inputs and outputs of the S-boxes.

As can be seen from Example 1, our model needs 2^n sets of equations to encode each input x and output $S(x)$ for an n-bit S-box. Although the coefficient variables a and b of each set of equations are the same, which determine the implementation circuit, more intermediate variables q and t are needed. To reduce the number of variables and then speed up our model, we use the bit-sliced technique as follows.

Algorithm 1: Solve the sub-problem: whether a circuit can implement an S-box uses determined (K) logic operations with (G) GE.

Input: K : Number of gates

G : Target area cost

$Sbox[]$: an n-bit to n-bit S-box

Output: If the sub-problem has a solution, it returns "1" and the implementation of this S-box or other case returns "0".

1 //Encode this sub-problem as an SAT-model with equtions.

2 $Counter_q \leftarrow 2K \cdot 2^n$

3 $Counter_t \leftarrow K \cdot 2^n$

4 $Counter_a \leftarrow 2 \times (n + (n + K - 2)) \times K/2 + n^2 + n \cdot K$

5 $Counter_b \leftarrow 4K$

6 $Cost[2^4] \leftarrow$ each area cost of operations in Table 1

7 **for** $x \leftarrow 0$ *to* $2^n - 1$ **do**

8 $\quad$ $x = x_0||x_1||...||x_{n-1}$;

9 $\quad$ $y = S(x) = y_0||y_1||...||y_{n-1}$;

10 $\quad$ **for** $i \leftarrow 0$ *to* $K - 1$ **do**

11 $\quad\quad$ $q_{2i} \leftarrow$ one of S-box's inputs or outputs of previous gates;

12 $\quad\quad$ $q_{2i+1} \leftarrow$ one of S-box's inputs or outputs of previous gates;

13 $\quad\quad$ $q_{2i+2} \leftarrow$ one of S-box's inputs or outputs of previous gates;

14 $\quad\quad$ $q_{2i+3} \leftarrow$ one of S-box's inputs or outputs of previous gates;

15 $\quad\quad$ $t_i = ...$;

16 $\quad$ **end**

17 $\quad$ **for** $i \leftarrow 0$ *to* $n - 1$ **do**

18 $\quad\quad$ $y_i \leftarrow$ only one of S-box inputs or outputs of previous gates t;

19 $\quad$ **end**

20 **end**

21 $total_{cost} \leftarrow$ sum of all the gates' area cost;

22 //Here is the end of the model.

23 **if** *Solve the model by STP, it returns "No Solution"* **then**

24 $\quad$ **return** *0;*

25 **end**

26 **else**

27 $\quad$ **return** *1 and the implementations of this S-box;*

28 **end**

Example 2. We give RECTANGLE's S-box and its corresponding truth table in Table 9.

Firstly, we re-encode every variables as a 16-bit Boolean vectorial variables instead of Boolean variables. For example, we use $x_0, x_1, \ldots, x_{63}$ to encode the inputs of the S-box and $y_0, y_1, \ldots, y_{63}$ to encode the outpus of the S-box in our original model. We re-encode them and only use 8 variables as

$$X_0 = 0\text{x}00\text{ff},\ X_1 = 0\text{x}0\text{f}0\text{f},\ X_2 = 0\text{x}3333,\ X_3 = 0\text{x}5555;$$

$$Y_0 = 0\text{x}369\text{c},\ Y_1 = 0\text{xe}616,\ Y_2 = 0\text{x}96\text{c}5,\ Y_3 = 0\text{x}4\text{bb}4;$$

Algorithm 2: find the implementation of an S-box with the smallest number of GE.

Input: K_{low} : Gates' number of the optimal gate complexity implementation.
G_{up} : Total area cost of the optimal gate complexity implementation.
$Sbox[]$: an n-bit to n-bit S-box.

Output: The optimal GEC implementation and its area cost.

1 $K_{up} \leftarrow G_{up}$
2 $G_{low} \leftarrow K_{low}$
3 **for** $K \leftarrow K_{low}$ to K_{up} **do**
4 | **for** $G \leftarrow G_{up}$ to G_{low} **do**
5 | | **if** *call the Algorithm 1 return 0 with the input (K,G,S)* **then**
6 | | | $G_{up} = G + 1$
7 | | | $K_{up} = G_{up}$
8 | | | break;
9 | | **end**
10 | **end**
11 **end**
12 **return** (K_{up}, G_{up})

Table 9. Truth table of RECTANGLE S-box.

x	0	1	2	3	4	5	6	7	8	9	10	11	12	13	14	15	Hex
$S(x)$	6	5	12	10	1	14	7	9	11	0	3	13	8	15	4	2	–
x_0	0	0	0	0	0	0	0	0	1	1	1	1	1	1	1	1	0x00ff
x_1	0	0	0	0	1	1	1	1	0	0	0	0	1	1	1	1	0x0f0f
x_2	0	0	1	1	0	0	1	1	0	0	1	1	0	0	1	1	0x3333
x_3	0	1	0	1	0	1	0	1	0	1	0	1	0	1	0	1	0x5555
y_0	0	0	1	1	0	1	0	1	1	0	0	1	1	1	0	0	0x369c
y_1	1	1	1	0	0	1	1	0	0	0	0	1	0	1	1	0	0xe616
y_2	1	0	0	1	0	1	1	0	1	0	1	0	0	1	0	1	0x96c5
y_3	0	1	0	0	1	0	1	1	1	0	1	1	0	1	0	0	0x4bb4

Then, we also use 16-bit vectorial Boolean variables A_i, Q_i, B_i and T_i to re-encode the Boolean variables a_i, q_i, b_i and t_i.

$$Q_0 = A_0 \cdot X_0 + A_1 \cdot X_1 + A_2 \cdot X_2 + A_3 \cdot X_3$$
$$Q_1 = A_4 \cdot X_0 + A_5 \cdot X_1 + A_6 \cdot X_2 + A_7 \cdot X_3$$
$$Q_2 = A_8 \cdot X_0 + A_9 \cdot X_1 + A_{10} \cdot X_2 + A_{11} \cdot X_3$$
$$Q_3 = A_{12} \cdot X_0 + A_{13} \cdot X_1 + A_{14} \cdot X_2 + A_{15} \cdot X_3$$

$$T_0 = B_0 \cdot Q_0 \cdot Q_1 \cdot Q_2 \cdot Q_3 + Q_0 \cdot Q_0 \cdot Q_1 \cdot Q_2 +$$
$$B_0 \cdot Q_0 \cdot Q_1 \cdot Q_3 + B_0 \cdot Q_2 \cdot Q_3 + B_0 \cdot Q_2 + B_0 \cdot Q_3 +$$
$$B_1 \cdot Q_0 \cdot Q_1 \cdot Q_2 + B_2 \cdot Q_0 \cdot Q_1 + B_2 \cdot Q_0 \cdot Q_2 + B_2 \cdot Q_1 \cdot Q_2 +$$
$$B_2 \cdot Q_0 + B_2 \cdot Q_1 + B_2 \cdot Q_2 + B_3 \cdot Q_0 + B_3 \cdot Q_1 + B_3 \cdot Q_2 +$$
$$B_4 \cdot Q_0 \cdot Q_1 + B_5 \cdot Q_0 + B_5 \cdot Q_1 + B_6 \cdot Q_0 + B_7.$$

. . .

In this set of equations, we add more constraints on coefficient variables A_i and B_i as follows

$$A_i \in 0x0000 \, , \, 0x1111,$$
$$B_i \in 0x0000 \, , \, 0x1111.$$

In conclusion, we only need 1 set of equations to encode RECTANGLE's S-box instead of 2^4 sets of equations in our original model above. The bit-sliced technique would immediately reduce the number of Q_i, T_i, X_i, and Y_i by a factor of 2^n and speed up the search. For more details about our model before and after the re-encoding, please refer to the code which are available online at https://github.com/Zhenyulu-cyber/Sample_implementation.

4   Applications to Lightweight S-Boxes

We now give our results related to small S-boxes. Our goal is to find the smallest circuits implementing those S-boxes with respect to the overall area. All of our experiments are running on AMD EPYC 7302 CPU 3.0Hz with 8-core. We use our tool and provide the details on the implementation of RECTANGLE's S-box in Table 10. In addition, some implementations of 4-bit and 5-bit S-boxes from well-known ciphers, such as PICCOLO, SKINNY, LBLOCK, KECCAK, and ASCON, are listed in Appendix A.

To highlight the strength of our tool, we compare our results with previous works in [9] and [15] under the UMC 180nm library which is a technology used in [9]. In Table 11, it can be seen that all of our results are better than Stoffelen's and this is expected as Stoffelen's tool simply minimizes the number of gate. Meanwhile, we find a circuit of RECTANGLE's S-box with 18.00GE cost which is better than LIGHTER's and we can verify that the circuits of PICCOLO, SKINNY and LBLOCK's S-boxes have the optimal area cost under the 2-, 3- and 4-input gates we considered. In addition, due to the bit-sliced technique, our model can be used to find the implementation of 5-bit S-box. However, due to the expansion of the search space, we cannot guarantee that the searched implementation of 5-bit S-box is the optimal one.

Moreover, we also use the state-of-the-art synthesis tool Synopsys Design Compiler (DC) to synthesize lookup table (LUT) based implementation and equation based implementation circuits from three tools (e.g. ours, Stoffelen's [15] and LIGHTER [9]). We set the compiler being specifically instructed to

Table 10. The implementation of RECTANGLE's S-box.

a	b	c	d	Operations
$q_0 = x_0$;	$q_1 = x_1$;	$q_2 = 0$;	$q_3 = 0$;	$t_0 = NOR(a, b)$;
$q_4 = x_3$;	$q_5 = t_0$;	$q_6 = x_3$;	$q_7 = t_0$;	$t_1 = MOAI1(a, b, c, d)$;
$q_8 = x_2$;	$q_9 = t_1$;	$q_{10} = 0$;	$q_{11} = 0$;	$t_2 = NOR(a, b)$;
$q_{12} = x_0$;	$q_{13} = t_2$;	$q_{14} = x_0$;	$q_{15} = t_2$;	$t_3 = MOAI1(a, b, c, d)$;
$q_{16} = x_1$;	$q_{17} = t_3$;	$q_{18} = x_1$;	$q_{19} = t_3$;	$t_4 = MOAI1(a, b, c, d)$;
$q_{20} = x_1$;	$q_{21} = x_2$;	$q_{22} = x_1$;	$q_{23} = x_2$;	$t_5 = MOAI1(a, b, c, d)$;
$q_{24} = t_1$;	$q_{25} = t_5$;	$q_{26} = 0$;	$q_{27} = 0$;	$t_6 = AND(a, b)$
$q_{28} = t_5$;	$q_{29} = t_1$;	$q_{30} = t_5$;	$q_{31} = t_1$;	$t_7 = MOAI1(a, b, c, d)$;
$q_{32} = t_4$;	$q_{33} = t_7$;	$q_{34} = 0$;	$q_{35} = 0$;	$t_8 = NAND(a, b)$;
$q_{36} = t_6$;	$q_{37} = t_3$;	$q_{38} = t_6$;	$q_{39} = t_3$;	$t_9 = MOAI1(a, b, c, d)$;
$q_{40} = t_8$;	$q_{41} = t_1$;	$q_{42} = t_8$;	$q_{43} = t_1$;	$t_{10} = MOAI1(a, b, c, d)$;
$y_0 = t_7$;	$y_1 = t_9$;	$y_2 = t_4$;	$y_3 = t_{10}$;	GEC = 18.00GE

optimize the circuit for area under the TSMC 90nm library. By comparing the output results of these algorithms, we measure the quality of the synthesis in the setting where area only should be minimized. We list the results in Table 12.

When using the DC synthesizer on the circuits produced by our tool (equation based implementation), the area is much better than the circuits produced by Stoffelen's tool (equation based implementation) and the circuits converted by DC synthesizers from the LUT. Especially the performance on RECTANGLE's S-box, the results from our tool is much better than LIGHTER.

Note that the choice of standard cell libraries used is almost irrelevant for our work as we are mainly interested in the quality of the area-optimized synthesis itself.

Table 11. Comparison of area-optimized on the UMC 180nm.

Sbox	LIGHTER	[15]	Ours			
	Area	Area	Area	Gate number	Optimal	Time
PICCOLO	13.00GE	16.66GE	13.00GE	8	$\checkmark$	1 min
SKINNY	13.33GE	16.33GE	13.33GE	8	$\checkmark$	3 min
RECTANGLE	18.33GE	25.66GE	18.00GE	11	–	43 min
LBLOCK S_0	16.33GE	23GE	16.33GE	10	$\checkmark$	12 min
KECCAK	–	–	17.66GE	13	–	6.66 h
ASCON	–	–	30.00GE	15	–	4.66 h

Table 12. Comparison of area-optimized on the TSMC 90nm.

Sbox	TSMC 90nm Logic Process			
	DC (from LUT)	DC (from Ours)	DC (from [15])	DC (from LIGHTER)
PICCOLO	18.25GE	11.25GE	11.25GE	11.25GE
SKINNY	23.00GE	11.00GE	11.00GE	11.00GE
RECTANGLE	23.00GE	16.25GE	18.25GE	18.00GE
LBLOCK S_0	17.50GE	14.25GE	14.75GE	14.25GE
KECCAK	17.00GE	16.50GE	–	–
ASCON	27.75GE	27.00GE	–	–

5   Conclusion and Future Work

In this article, we have described a new method to improve the implementation of lightweight cipher S-boxes. Our tool based on SAT-model could search for the optimal area implementation with 2, 3, and 4 inputs gates. It is very practical for cryptographic designers. There are still some weakness and future works that deserve to consider. For example, our tool can only apply to small S-boxes, e.g., 4-bit and 5-bit S-boxes. When the implementation of an S-box is complex, it is difficult to find the optimal implementation. The efficiency of our tool depends heavily on the size and complexity of S-boxes. So, a future work is to reduce the search space and speed up finding the optimal implementation.

Acknowledgement. We thank the anonymous reviewers for their valuable comments and suggestions to improve the quality of the paper. This work is supported by the National Natural Science Foundation of China (Grant No. 62032014), the National Key Research and Development Program of China (Grant No. 2018YFA0704702), the Major Scientific and Technological Innovation Project of Shandong Province, China (Grant No. 2019JZZY010133), the Major Basic Research Project of Natural Science Foundation of Shandong Province, China (Grant No. ZR202010220025), the Program of Qilu Young Scholars (Grant No. 61580082063088) of Shandong University, and National Natural Science Foundation of China (Grant No. 62002204).

Appendix A   Implementation of Some S-boxes

In this section, we give the implementations of several Sboxes mapped on the UMC 180nm standard cell libraries used in this paper (Tables 13, 14, 15 and 16).

Table 13. The implementation of PICCOLO's S-box.

a	b	c	d	Operations
$q_0 = x_2$;	$q_1 = x_3$;	$q_2 = 0$;	$q_3 = 0$;	$t_0 = OR(a,b)$;
$q_4 = x_0$;	$q_5 = t_0$;	$q_6 = x_0$;	$q_7 = t_0$;	$t_1 = MOAI1(a,b,c,d)$;
$q_8 = x_1$;	$q_9 = t_1$;	$q_{10} = 0$;	$q_{11} = 0$;	$t_2 = NOR(a,b)$;
$q_{12} = x_1$;	$q_{13} = x_2$;	$q_{14} = 0$;	$q_{15} = 0$;	$t_3 = OR(a,b)$;
$q_{16} = x_2$;	$q_{17} = t_2$;	$q_{18} = x_2$;	$q_{19} = t_2$;	$t_4 = MOAI1(a,b,c,d)$;
$q_{20} = x_3$;	$q_{21} = t_3$;	$q_{22} = x_3$;	$q_{23} = t_3$;	$t_5 = MOAI1(a,b,c,d)$;
$q_{24} = t_1$;	$q_{25} = t_5$;	$q_{26} = 0$;	$q_{27} = 0$;	$t_6 = OR(a,b)$
$q_{28} = x_1$;	$q_{29} = t_6$;	$q_{30} = x_1$;	$q_{31} = t_6$;	$t_7 = MOAI1(a,b,c,d)$;
$y_0 = t_7$;	$y_1 = t_4$;	$y_2 = t_5$;	$y_3 = t_1$;	GEC = 13.00GE

Table 14. The implementation of SKINNY's S-box.

a	b	c	d	Operations
$q_0 = x_2$;	$q_1 = x_3$;	$q_2 = 0$;	$q_3 = 0$;	$t_0 = OR(a,b)$;
$q_4 = x_1$;	$q_5 = x_2$;	$q_6 = 0$;	$q_7 = 0$;	$t_1 = OR(a,b)$;
$q_8 = x_3$;	$q_9 = t_1$;	$q_{10} = x_3$;	$q_{11} = t_1$;	$t_2 = MOAI1(a,b,c,d)$;
$q_{12} = x_0$;	$q_{13} = t_0$;	$q_{14} = x_0$;	$q_{15} = t_0$;	$t_3 = MOAI1(a,b,c,d)$;
$q_{16} = x_1$;	$q_{17} = t_3$;	$q_{18} = 0$;	$q_{19} = 0$;	$t_4 = OR(a,b)$;
$q_{20} = t_2$;	$q_{21} = t_3$;	$q_{22} = 0$;	$q_{23} = 0$;	$t_5 = OR(a,b)$;
$q_{24} = x_1$;	$q_{25} = t_5$;	$q_{26} = x_1$;	$q_{27} = t_5$;	$t_6 = MOAI1(a,b,c,d)$;
$q_{28} = x_2$;	$q_{29} = t_4$;	$q_{30} = x_2$;	$q_{31} = t_4$;	$t_7 = MOAI1(a,b,c,d)$;
$y_0 = t_6$;	$y_1 = t_7$;	$y_2 = t_2$;	$y_3 = t_3$;	GEC = 13.33GE

Table 15. The implementation of LBLOCK's S-box.

a	b	c	d	Operations
$q_0 = x_2$;	$q_1 = x_3$;	$q_2 = 0$;	$q_3 = 0$;	$t_0 = OR(a,b)$;
$q_4 = x_0$;	$q_5 = t_0$;	$q_6 = x_0$;	$q_7 = t_0$;	$t_1 = MOAI1(a,b,c,d)$;
$q_8 = x_1$;	$q_9 = t_1$;	$q_{10} = x_1$;	$q_{11} = t_1$;	$t_2 = MOAI1(a,b,c,d)$;
$q_{12} = x_2$;	$q_{13} = t_2$;	$q_{14} = 0$;	$q_{15} = 0$;	$t_3 = NAND(a,b)$;
$q_{16} = x_0$;	$q_{17} = t_3$;	$q_{18} = x_0$;	$q_{19} = t_3$;	$t_4 = MOAI1(a,b,c,d)$;
$q_{20} = x_3$;	$q_{21} = t_4$;	$q_{22} = x_3$;	$q_{23} = t_4$;	$t_5 = MOAI1(a,b,c,d)$;
$q_{24} = t_2$;	$q_{25} = t_5$;	$q_{26} = 0$;	$q_{27} = 0$;	$t_6 = NOR(a,b)$
$q_{28} = x_3$;	$q_{29} = t_6$;	$q_{30} = x_3$;	$q_{31} = t_6$;	$t_7 = MOAI1(a,b,c,d)$;
$q_{32} = t_5$;	$q_{33} = t_7$;	$q_{34} = 0$;	$q_{35} = 0$;	$t_8 = NAND(a,b)$;
$q_{36} = x_2$;	$q_{37} = t_8$;	$q_{38} = x_2$;	$q_{39} = t_8$;	$t_9 = MOAI1(a,b,c,d)$;
$y_0 = t_2$;	$y_1 = t_5$;	$y_2 = t_9$;	$y_3 = t_7$;	GEC = 16.33GE

Table 16. The implementation of KECCAK's S-box.

a	b	c	d	Operations
$q_0 = x_2$;	$q_1 = 0$;	$q_2 = 0$;	$q_3 = 0$;	$t_0 = NOT(a)$;
$q_4 = x_4$;	$q_5 = 0$;	$q_6 = 0$;	$q_7 = 0$;	$t_1 = NOT(a)$;
$q_8 = x_1$;	$q_9 = 0$;	$q_{10} = 0$;	$q_{11} = 0$;	$t_2 = NOT(a)$;
$q_{12} = x_3$;	$q_{13} = t_1$;	$q_{14} = 0$;	$q_{15} = 0$;	$t_3 = OR(a, b)$;
$q_{16} = x_2$;	$q_{17} = t_3$;	$q_{18} = x_2$;	$q_{19} = t_3$;	$t_4 = MOAI1(a, b, c, d)$;
$q_{20} = x_3$;	$q_{21} = t_0$;	$q_{22} = 0$;	$q_{23} = 0$;	$t_5 = NAND(a, b)$;
$q_{24} = x_0$;	$q_{25} = t_2$;	$q_{26} = 0$;	$q_{27} = 0$;	$t_6 = OR(a, b)$
$q_{28} = x_4$;	$q_{29} = t_6$;	$q_{30} = x_4$;	$q_{31} = t_6$;	$t_7 = MOAI1(a, b, c, d)$;
$q_{32} = x_1$;	$q_{33} = t_5$;	$q_{34} = x_1$;	$q_{35} = t_5$;	$t_8 = MOAI1(a, b, c, d)$;
$q_{36} = x_2$;	$q_{37} = t_2$;	$q_{38} = 0$;	$q_{39} = 0$;	$t_9 = NAND(a, b)$;
$q_{40} = x_0$;	$q_{41} = t_9$;	$q_{42} = x_0$;	$q_{43} = t_9$;	$t_{10} = MOAI1(a, b, c, d)$;
$q_{44} = x_0$;	$q_{45} = t_1$;	$q_{46} = 0$;	$q_{47} = 0$;	$t_{11} = NAND(a, b)$;
$q_{48} = x_3$;	$q_{49} = t_{11}$;	$q_{50} = x_3$;	$q_{51} = t_{11}$;	$t_{12} = MOAI1(a, b, c, d)$;
$y_0 = t_{10}$;	$y_1 = t_8$;	$y_2 = t_4$;	$y_3 = t_{12}$; $y_4 = t_7$;	GEC = 17.66GE

References

1. Banik, S., Funabiki, Y., Isobe, T.: More results on shortest linear programs. Cryptology ePrint Archive, Report 2019/856 (2019). https://ia.cr/2019/856
2. Beierle, C., et al.: The SKINNY family of block ciphers and its low-latency variant MANTIS. In: Robshaw, M., Katz, J. (eds.) CRYPTO 2016. LNCS, vol. 9815, pp. 123–153. Springer, Heidelberg (2016). https://doi.org/10.1007/978-3-662-53008-5_5
3. Bertoni, G., Daemen, J., Peeters, M., Van Assche, G.: Keccak. In: Johansson, T., Nguyen, P.Q. (eds.) EUROCRYPT 2013. LNCS, vol. 7881, pp. 313–314. Springer, Heidelberg (2013). https://doi.org/10.1007/978-3-642-38348-9_19
4. Courtois, N., Mourouzis, T., Hulme, D.: Exact logic minimization and multiplicative complexity of concrete algebraic and cryptographic circuits. Int. J. Adv. Intell. Syst. 6(3), 165–176 (2013)
5. Dobraunig, C., Eichlseder, M., Mendel, F., Schläffer, M.: Ascon v1. 2. Submission to the CAESAR Competition (2016)
6. Goudarzi, D., et al.: Pyjamask: Block cipher and authenticated encryption with highly efficient masked implementation. IACR Trans. Symmetric Cryptol. 2020(S1), 31–59 (2020). https://doi.org/10.13154/tosc.v2020.iS1.31-59
7. Hlavicka, J., Fiser, P.: Boom-a heuristic Boolean minimizer. In: IEEE/ACM International Conference on Computer Aided Design. ICCAD 2001. IEEE/ACM Digest of Technical Papers (Cat. No.01CH37281), pp. 439–442 (2001). https://doi.org/10.1109/ICCAD.2001.968667
8. Virtual Silicon Inc.: 0.18μm VIP standard cell library tape out ready, part number: UMCL18G212T3, process: UMC logic 0.18 μm generic ii technology: 0.18μm, July 2004

9. Jean, J., Peyrin, T., Sim, S.M., Tourteaux, J.: Optimizing implementations of lightweight building blocks. IACR Trans. Symmetric Cryptol. **2017**(4), 130–168 (2017). https://doi.org/10.13154/tosc.v2017.i4.130-168
10. Kwon, H., Koleva, B., Schnädelbach, H., Benford, S.: "it's not yet A gift": understanding digital gifting. In: Lee, C.P., Poltrock, S.E., Barkhuus, L., Borges, M., Kellogg, W.A. (eds.) Proceedings of the 2017 ACM Conference on Computer Supported Cooperative Work and Social Computing, CSCW 2017, Portland, OR, USA, 25 February–1 March 2017, pp. 2372–2384. ACM (2017). https://doi.org/10.1145/2998181.2998225
11. Mourouzis, T.: Optimizations in algebraic and differential cryptanalysis. Ph.D. thesis, UCL (University College London) (2015)
12. NIST.: Submission requirements and evaluation criteria for the lightweight cryptography standardization process (2018). https://csrc.nist.gov/projects/lightweight-cryptography
13. Rudell, R.L.: Multiple-valued logic minimization for PLA synthesis. Technical report. UCB/ERL M86/65, EECS Department, University of California, Berkeley, June 1986. http://www2.eecs.berkeley.edu/Pubs/TechRpts/1986/734.html
14. Shibutani, K., Isobe, T., Hiwatari, H., Mitsuda, A., Akishita, T., Shirai, T.: *Piccolo*: an ultra-lightweight blockcipher. In: Preneel, B., Takagi, T. (eds.) CHES 2011. LNCS, vol. 6917, pp. 342–357. Springer, Heidelberg (2011). https://doi.org/10.1007/978-3-642-23951-9_23
15. Stoffelen, K.: Optimizing S-box implementations for several criteria using SAT solvers. In: Peyrin, T. (ed.) FSE 2016. LNCS, vol. 9783, pp. 140–160. Springer, Heidelberg (2016). https://doi.org/10.1007/978-3-662-52993-5_8
16. Wu, W., Zhang, L.: LBlock: a lightweight block cipher. In: Lopez, J., Tsudik, G. (eds.) ACNS 2011. LNCS, vol. 6715, pp. 327–344. Springer, Heidelberg (2011). https://doi.org/10.1007/978-3-642-21554-4_19
17. Zhang, W., Bao, Z., Lin, D., Rijmen, V., Yang, B., Verbauwhede, I.: RECTANGLE: a bit-slice lightweight block cipher suitable for multiple platforms. Sci. China Inf. Sci. **58**(12), 1–15 (2015)

Quantum Resource Estimation for FSR Based Symmetric Ciphers and Related Grover's Attacks

Ravi Anand[1(✉)], Arpita Maitra[2], Subhamoy Maitra[3],
Chandra Sekhar Mukherjee[4], and Sourav Mukhopadhyay[5]

[1] RC Bose CCS, Indian Statistical Institute Kolkata, Kolkata, India
[2] TCG CREST Kolkata, Kolkata, India
[3] Applied Statistics Unit, Indian Statistical Institute, Kolkata, India
subho@isical.ac.in
[4] Indian Statistical Institute, Kolkata, India
[5] Indian Institute of Technology Kharagpur, Kharagpur, India

Abstract. Several studies on the resource estimation of quantum key search attack exploiting Grover on different symmetric ciphers have been studied in state-of-the-art cryptology research. In this paper, we consider the popular Feedback Shift Register (FSR) based ciphers like Grain-128-AEAD, TinyJAMBU, LIZARD, Grain-v1 and study their implementations in different quantum environments. To evaluate with respect to NIST's depth restriction (MAXDEPTH), we design reversible quantum circuits for these ciphers and provide the QISKIT implementations with total gate counts. Our results show that quantum cryptanalysis is possible with gate counts less than $2^{170}/$MAXDEPTH. Our results provide a clear view of the exact status of quantum cryptanalysis against FSR-based symmetric ciphers.

Keywords: Quantum cryptanalysis · Grover's algorithm · FSR based ciphers · QISKIT implementation

1 Introduction

In recent times there has been an extensive study on the impact of Grover's search algorithm [8] on block ciphers, especially on AES [5,7,15,22]. Some of the existing works have shown that classically secure ciphers can be broken with quantum algorithms [13,16,17,20,21]. Some works also show that the quantum algorithm can be used to speed up classical attacks [12,18,27]. At the same time, there are many results on symmetric ciphers in the quantum framework which suggests that analyzing the ciphers using Grover for the post-quantum world is necessary. One part of symmetric cipher is stream cipher and most of the hardware stream ciphers are Feedback Shift Register (FSR) based. In this paper we look at the FSR based stream ciphers and try to see certain implementation issues if an adversary is going to explore the quantum attacks on these ciphers.

© Springer Nature Switzerland AG 2021
A. Adhikari et al. (Eds.): INDOCRYPT 2021, LNCS 13143, pp. 179–198, 2021.
https://doi.org/10.1007/978-3-030-92518-5_9

There has been no detailed previous study to evaluate the security of stream ciphers in the quantum framework. Wu, in his thesis [31], commented that: "The threat of Grover's algorithm on stream ciphers can be simply eliminated by doubling the key size". Though doubling the key length seems to be a good solution, a more accurate analysis is called for. The structure of a stream cipher is different from block ciphers and so requires a different analysis in the quantum framework. As a starting point in this work, we present the application of Grover's algorithm for key search on FSR based ciphers. The ciphers Grain-128-AEAD and Tiny-JAMBU are finalists of NIST's Lightweight Crypto Standardization [24].

However, the question here is why do we need to implement ciphers in a quantum domain: the first requirement is whenever there will be any quantum attack then we need to prepare the quantum circuit. Corresponding to each cipher we need to implement a quantum circuit and we check the resources required of the quantum circuit. One very standard attack on the symmetric ciphers is the Grover's attack and it requires running several loops of the cipher. Added to this we also have to run the cipher for several loops to generate the keystream. Since in quantum circuits there is no concept of loops, i.e., we cannot feedback the output in the same circuit [23, p. 23], due to the limitations of the implementation of the quantum circuit, the only option we have is to repeat the circuit and so this requires a huge amount of resource. After we create the circuit for the ciphers, we compute the cost for implementation of the cipher. We also check the implementation in IBMQ interface and compute the number of gates and the depth of the circuit. To verify that the circuit gate count and depth estimates computed were correct we implemented these circuits in Microsoft's Q# and observed that the values were matching in both the implementations.

Since quantum computers are still in a primary stage, it is difficult to decide the exact cost for each gate. Most of the previous works had focused on reducing the number of T gates and the number of qubits in their circuit construction. This work is more inclined towards reducing the depth and the number of quantum gates used in the circuit to study the security of a cipher under NISTs MAXDEPTH constraint [25, pp. 16–18] at the cost of a few qubits.

1.1 Contribution and Organization

We mainly focus on FSR based stream ciphers but have included TinyJAMBU because its state gets updated by a non-linear feedback shift register and so a similar technique could be used to construct its circuit.

In Sect. 3, we have presented reversible quantum circuits for Grain-128-AEAD, TinyJAMBU, LIZARD, and Grain-v1 and applied Grover's search algorithm for key recovery on these ciphers. We estimate the cost of applying Grover for key recovery in Table 3 and then estimate it under the NISTs MAXDEPTH constraint in Table 4. We find that implementing Grover's on ciphers Grain-128-AEAD and TinyJAMBU is possible with gate count complexity $1.569 \cdot 2^{123}$ and $1.155 \cdot 2^{125}$, respectively, when MAXDEPTH $= 2^{40}$.

In Sect. 4 we show how the correctness of our resource estimates were verified by implementing the circuits in IBMQ's Qiskit as well as Microsoft's Q#. As an example we provide the code for TinyJAMBU's permutation P_n, $n = 1$ for independent verification. We conclude in Sect. 5. The QISKIT codes for all the circuits are provided in [33].

1.2   Related Works

Since the publication of quantum circuit of AES by Grassl et al. [7], a lot of research on quantum implementation of symmetric key primitives as well as the resource estimation required for implementing Grover's search algorithm on those ciphers have been published. The readers may refer to, for example, AES [5,6,15,22,32], SIMON [1], GIMLI [28], SPECK [2,14], RECTANGLE and KNOT [4]. It is interesting to note here that all the previous works were dedicated only towards block ciphers.

In this work, we try to construct quantum circuits for FSR-based (stream) ciphers. As we know that in quantum circuits there is no concept of loops, i.e., we cannot feedback the output in the same circuit, it becomes difficult to design an optimized circuit for these ciphers. Every FSR-based cipher makes use of feedback functions that are used to update the internal state. The naive approach is to compute the feedback value in an ancilla and use it to update the internal state. This, however, means we require at least 2 CNOT gates (1 for uncomputation) which when multiplied by $2^{k/2}$, where k is the key size, amounts to a very large value.

However, a very simple solution to this problem exists in how the FSRs operate. Consider a FSR of size n, denote its content as $S = [s_0, s_1, \cdots, s_{n-1}]$ and let f_i be the feedback value at i^{th} clocking. Then at the ith clocking the state gets updated as:

$$\text{for } 0 \leq j \leq (n-2) : s_j = s_{j+1}$$
$$s_{n-1} = f_i$$

Then we observe that after n clockings we have $s_0 = f_0, s_1 = f_1, \cdots, s_{n-1} = f_{n-1}$, i.e. we can store the value of the feedback f_0 in s_0 and this qubit will not be operated for the next $n - 1$ clockings. We use this observation to construct circuits without use of any ancilla to store the value of the feedback.

2   Preliminaries

2.1   Key Search Using Grover's Algorithm

Grover's algorithm searches through the space of N elements, and finds the marked element in only $O(\sqrt{N})$ iterations. For simplicity, we restrict $N = 2^k$, where k is the size of the key to be searched. The input to the algorithm is the superposition $|\psi\rangle = 2^{-\frac{k}{2}} \sum_{x \in \{0,1\}^k} |x\rangle$, which is held in a register of k qubits. It makes use of an operator U_f for evaluating a Boolean function $f : \{0,1\}^k \rightarrow \{0,1\}$ which marks $f(x_0) = 1$ if and only if x_0 is the required key.

When we apply the Grover oracle U_f to a state $|x\rangle |y\rangle$, where $|x\rangle$ is a k-qubit state and $|y\rangle$ is a single qubit then it acts as $U_f : |x\rangle |y\rangle \rightarrow |x\rangle |y \oplus f(x)\rangle$ in the computational basis. If $|y\rangle$ is chosen to be $|\phi\rangle = \frac{1}{\sqrt{2}}(|0\rangle - |1\rangle)$, then we have

$$U_f : |x\rangle \frac{1}{\sqrt{2}}(|0\rangle - |1\rangle) \rightarrow (-1)^{f(x)} |x\rangle \frac{1}{\sqrt{2}}(|0\rangle - |1\rangle)$$

The Grover's algorithm consists of repeatedly applying the operation G to the initial state $|\psi\rangle |\phi\rangle$, where G is defined as

$$G = (2|\psi\rangle \langle\psi| - I)U_f.$$

G is called the Grover's iteration, an operation that consists of the oracle U_f followed by the operator $2|\psi\rangle \langle\psi| - I$ and can be viewed as an inversion about the mean amplitude. Overall G has to be applied a number of $O(2^{\frac{k}{2}})$ times to obtain an element x_0 such that $f(x_0) = 1$ with a high probability.

Key Search for a Stream Cipher. Let for any key $K = \{0,1\}^k$ and initialization vector $IV = \{0,1\}^m$, denote by $\mathcal{S}_{K,IV} = ks$, the stream cipher which generates the keystream ks under the key K and initialization vector IV. Since the initialization vectors are generally assumed to known, thus let $\mathcal{S}_K = ks$. We now aim to apply Grover's algorithm to find the unknown secret key. The Boolean function f for the Grover's oracle U_f, which takes the key K as input is defined as

$$f(K) = \begin{cases} 1 & \text{if } \mathcal{S}_K = ks \\ 0 & \text{otherwise} \end{cases}$$

Key Search for a Block Cipher. Let C be a block cipher with block length n; for any key $K = \{0,1\}^k$ denote by $C_K(m) = c$, the encryption of a plaintext m under the key K. If we are given r plaintext-ciphertext pairs (m_i, c_i), we aim to apply Grover's algorithm to find the unknown secret key. The Boolean function f for the Grover's oracle U_f, which takes the key K as input is defined as

$$f(K) = \begin{cases} 1 & \text{if } C_K(m_i) = c_i, \ 0 \le i \le (r-1) \\ 0 & \text{otherwise} \end{cases}$$

2.2   Uniqueness of the Recovered Key

It is possible that there exists other keys which generates the same keystream (or in case of TinyJambu (block cipher) encrypt the known plaintexts to the same ciphertexts). So, to increase the success probability of the attack we need to extend the search for more keystream (or plaintext-ciphertext pairs). Interestingly, the corresponding increase in the circuit size is different for block ciphers and stream ciphers.

Let us first discuss the scenario for a block cipher. We assume a block cipher that has been initialized with a key K of size k and has a block size of k bits to be a pseudo random permutation (PRP) $C_K : \{0,1\}^k \rightarrow \{0,1\}^k$ that takes a message M of size k bit and outputs a cipher text of the same size. Then if we generate t-blocks of cipher-text corresponding to a message, then we have the following collision probability

$$\Pr_{K \neq K'} \left(C_K(M_1)|| \cdots ||C_K(M_t) = C_{K'}(M_1)|| \cdots ||C_{K'}(M_t) \right) \approx (2^k - 1) \prod_{i=1}^{t} \frac{1}{2^k - i - 1}.$$

Even if we set $t = 2$ then we have a negligibly low probability of collision $\mathcal{O}\left(2^{-k}\right)$. However, note that in this case we need to evaluate the cipher to generate $2k$ bits of cipher text in each application of the Grover oracle which adds to the circuit size.

In this regard, an adversary can get an advantage in terms of the circuit size when applying Grover's oracle for stream ciphers. Suppose a stream cipher has a key of size k bits. Then we can design the following function $\hat{C}_\rho(K) : \{0,1\}^k \rightarrow \{0,1\}^\rho$ which takes in the key K and outputs ρ bits of keystream. Then we can safely assume

$$\Pr_{K \neq K'} (\hat{C}_\rho(K) = \hat{C}_\rho(K')) \approx \frac{2^k - 1}{2^\rho}.$$

Even if we set $\rho = k + c$ for some constant c, the collision probability is approximately $\mathcal{O}\left(2^{-c}\right)$. Then even for $c = 10$ we have a very low probability of collision and thus less false positives. However, in this case there is an advantage in terms of the circuit size as we can design the Grover oracle to only generate $k + c$ bits of keystream each round.

2.3   Grover's Oracle

As explained above to implement the Grover's search algorithm we need to design an oracle that generates ρ-bit keystreams under the same key and then computes a Boolean value which determines if the resulting keystream is equal to the given available keystream. The target qubit will be flipped if the keystreams match. This is called Grover's oracle. The construction of oracle for the stream ciphers and TinyJAMBU is slightly different and we discuss these constructions in detail below.

We denote by $\mathcal{ENC}$, the quantum circuit of the cipher and by $\mathcal{ENC}^\dagger$ the uncomputation of the cipher circuit, which is constructed by performing the quantum gates of the circuit $\mathcal{ENC}$ in reverse to restore the initial input state.

Grover's Oracle for the Stream Ciphers. To construct the oracle for the stream ciphers we construct the circuit for the cipher which generates $\rho = k + c = (k + 10)$-bit long keystream and then this keystream is matched with the given keystream. The target qubit will be flipped if the keystreams match. The construction of such an oracle is given in Fig. 1.

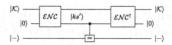

Fig. 1. Grover oracle for stream ciphers. The (=) operator compares the output of the $\mathcal{ENC}$ with the given keystreams and flips the target qubit if they are equal.

Grover's Oracle for TinyJAMBU. Consider that we are given two plaintext-ciphertext pairs $(M_1, C_1), (M_2, C_2)$. The oracle is then constructed so that the given plaintexts are encrypted under the same key and then computes a Boolean value which determines if all the resulting ciphertexts are equal to the given available ciphertexts. This can be done by running two encryption circuits in parallel and then the resultant ciphertexts are compared with the given ciphertexts. The target qubit will be flipped if the ciphertexts match. In Fig. 2, the construction of such an oracle is described.

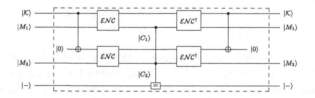

Fig. 2. Grover oracle using two blocks for TinyJAMBU.

2.4   Circuit Design and Resource Estimation

The circuits described in this work operates on qubits and are composed of commonly used universal fault-tolerant gate set Clifford (NOT and CNOT) + T gates. These gates allow us to fully simulate the circuits classically. In this work the only source of T gates are the Toffoli gates used in the construction of the circuits.

The NOT gate, also known as flip gate, maps $|0\rangle \rightarrow |1\rangle$ or $|1\rangle \rightarrow |0\rangle$. The CNOT (or controlled-X) gate can be described as the gate that maps $|a, b\rangle \rightarrow |a, a \oplus b\rangle$. The Toffoli gate can be described as the gate which maps $|a, b, c\rangle \rightarrow |a, b, c \oplus ab\rangle$.

Resource Estimation. It is well known that if a circuit can be implemented in the classical domain with a polynomial number of gates with respect to its inputs, then the circuit can be implemented in the quantum domain also with a polynomial number of quantum gates In the present initiative, we consider the ciphers whose classical hardware is feasible and try to estimate the resources for quantum hardware. We construct reversible circuits for implementation of all the ciphers. We then provide the resource estimates for these construction in terms of number of qubits, T gates, CNOT gates, NOT gates, and depth of the circuit in Table 1.

We have assumed full parallelism while constructing the circuits, i.e., any number of gates can be applied in the circuit simultaneously if these gates act on disjoint sets of qubits. We decompose the Toffoli gates into the set of Clifford+T gates using the decomposition provided by [3] that requires 7 T gates and 8 Clifford gates, a T depth of 4 and total depth 8.

We estimate the cost of constructing the Grover's oracle in terms of number of Clifford and T gates, T depth and the full depth (D). The total number of Clifford gates is computed as

1. for the stream ciphers

$$2 \times \text{ Clifford gates in } (\mathcal{ENC}) \tag{1}$$

2. for TinyJAMBU

$$2 \times k + 4 \times \text{ Clifford gates in } (\mathcal{ENC}) \tag{2}$$

Now in case of the stream ciphers, the grover oracle consists of comparing $\rho = k + c$ bits of keystream, which can be done using ρ-controlled CNOT gates.

For a block cipher, the grover oracle consists of comparing the k-bit outputs of the r cipher instances with the given k-bit ciphertexts, where k is the key-size,. This can be done using $(k \times r)$-controlled CNOT gates (we neglect some NOT gates which depend on the given ciphertexts). Following [30], we estimate the number of T gates required to implement a n-fold controlled CNOT gates as $(32 \times n - 84)$. Since we have assumed $r = 2$, so the total number of T gates is computed as

1. for the stream ciphers

$$(32 \times (k + 10) - 84) + 2 \times T \text{ gates in } (\mathcal{ENC}) \tag{3}$$

2. for TinyJAMBU

$$(32 \times (k \times 2) - 84) + 4 \times T \text{ gates in } (\mathcal{ENC}) \tag{4}$$

To estimate the full depth and the T-depth we only consider the depths of the cipher instances. Since we have assumed full parallelism, it can be seen in Fig. 2 that both cipher instances can be implemented simultaneously as they use disjoint sets of qubits, and so for both oracles we have

$$\text{the depth of the oracle} = 2 \times (\text{Depth of } \mathcal{ENC}) \tag{5}$$

These estimates are presented in Table 2.

The cost of running the complete Grover's key search algorithm can be computed by iterating the oracle $\frac{\pi}{4} 2^{\frac{k}{2}}$ times, where k is the key size and is presented in Table 3.

2.5   Resource Estimation Under a Depth Limit

In this work we are focused on estimating the cost of implementing Grover's search algorithm under NIST's MAXDEPTH. Grover's full algorithm parallelizes very badly. So, we use the inner parallelization as described by Kim, Han, and Jeong [19]. In inner parallelization the search space is divided into disjoint subsets and each subset is assigned to a different machine. Since, each machine's search space is smaller, the required number of iterations is smaller.

The original search space has size 2^k, where k is the key size. Let us assume that we use a Grover's oracle $\mathcal{O}$ such that a single Grover's iteration costs $\mathcal{O}_g$ gates and has a depth $\mathcal{O}_d$. Also, assume that $M = 2^m$ be the number of machines that are used in parallel by dividing the search space into M disjoint sets.

Since the search space is now reduced to 2^{k-m} for each machine, hence we can expect that one of the machines will recover the correct key after approximately $\imath_m = \frac{\pi}{4}2^{\frac{k-m}{2}}$ iterations, with a very high success probability. Then, the total depth of $\imath_m$ Grover iterations will be

$$D_m = \imath_m \times \mathcal{O}_d \approx \frac{\pi}{4}2^{\frac{k-m}{2}}\mathcal{O}_d \tag{6}$$

Each of the M machines will be using $\imath_m \times \mathcal{O}_g$ gates for $\imath_m$ iterations and thus the total gate cost over all M machines will be

$$G_m = 2^m \imath_m \times \mathcal{O}_g \approx \frac{\pi}{4}2^{\frac{k+m}{2}}\mathcal{O}_g \tag{7}$$

Now let us fix the depth limit to MAXDEPTH. Then from Eq. 6, we will have

$$\mathsf{MAXDEPTH} = \frac{\pi}{4}2^{\frac{k-m}{2}}\mathcal{O}_d$$

$$\implies M = 2^m = \left(\frac{\pi}{4}\right)^2 2^k \frac{\mathcal{O}_d^2}{\mathsf{MAXDEPTH}^2} \tag{8}$$

Using this value in Eq. 7, we obtain the total gate cost under the MAXDEPTH restriction as

$$G_{MD} = \left(\frac{\pi}{4}\right)^2 2^k \frac{\mathcal{O}_g\mathcal{O}_d}{\mathsf{MAXDEPTH}} \tag{9}$$

We will use these values to compute the cost of implementing Grover's search on the ciphers under NISTs MAXDEPTH limit in Table 4.

3   Estimating Resources for Applying Grover on Grain-128-AEAD, TinyJAMBU, LIZARD, and Grain-V1

In this section, we provide detailed description of how to construct a reversible quantum circuit of ciphers Grain-128-AEAD, TinyJAMBU, LIZARD, and Grain-v1. For detailed description of the ciphers, readers are referred to [9–11, 29].

3.1   Quantum Circuit for Grain-128-AEAD

In Grain-128-AEAD, the state is of size 256-bits and the length of key is 128, so we require 256 qubits for the state and 128 qubits for the key. At any time t, the update function of LFSR denoted by $f(S_t)$, the update function of the NFSR, $g(B_t)$, and the pre-output function $y(t)$ can be implemented as described below.

Algorithm 1: Quantum Circuit for Grain-128-AEAD

```
/* QUANTUM CIRCUIT FOR f(St)                                                */
```
1   **for** $i \leftarrow \{7, 38, 70, 81, 96\}$ **do**
2   $\quad$ CNOT $(s_{(i+t)\%128}, s_{t\%128})$

```
/* QUANTUM CIRCUIT FOR g(Bt)                                                */
```
3   CNOT $(s_{(t)\%128}, b_{t\%128})$
4   **for** $i \leftarrow \{26, 56, 91, 96\}$ **do**
5   $\quad$ CNOT $(b_{(i+t)\%128}, b_{t\%128})$
6   $l = [3, 11, 17, 27, 40, 61, 68], m = [67, 13, 18, 59, 48, 65, 84]$
7   **for** $i \leftarrow \{0, 6\}$ **do**
8   $\quad$ Toffoli $(b_{(l[i]+t)\%128}, b_{(m[i]+t)\%128}, b_{t\%128})$
9   toffoli3$(b_{(22+t)\%128}, b_{(24+t)\%128}, b_{(25+t)\%128}, ge0_0, ge0_1, b_{t\%128})$
10 toffoli3$(b_{(70+t)\%128}, b_{(78+t)\%128}, b_{(82+t)\%128}, ge1_0, ge1_1, b_{t\%128})$
11 toffoli4$(b_{(82+t)\%128}, b_{(92+t)\%128}, b_{(93+t)\%128}, b_{(95+t)\%128}, ge2_0, ge2_1, ge2_2, b_{t\%128})$

```
/* QUANTUM CIRCUIT FOR y(t)                                                 */
```
12 $l = [12, 13, 95, 60], m = [8, 20, 42, 79]$
13 **for** $i \leftarrow 0, 3$ **do**
14 $\quad$ Toffoli $(b_{(l[i]+t)\%128}, s_{(m[i]+t)\%128}, y_t)$
15 toffoli3$(b_{(12+t)\%128}, b_{(95+t)\%128}, s_{(94+t)\%128}, ye_0, ye_1, y_t)$
16 CNOT $(s_{(93+t)\%128}, y_t)$
17 **for** $i = 2, 15, 36, 45, 64, 73, 89$ **do**
18 $\quad$ CNOT $(b_{(i+t)\%128}, y_t)$

The functions toffoli3 and toffoli4 used above are *compute-copy-uncompute* method for implementing Toffoli gates on 3 and 4 qubits respectively. These functions are described in Fig. 3a and Fig. 3b respectively.

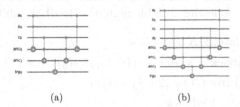

(a)   (b)

Fig. 3. The circuit for **(a)** toffoli3. **(b)** toffoli4

Now, using the quantum circuits for $f(S_t), f(B_t)$, and $y(t)$ we can construct the circuit for full Grain-128-AEAD. The complete Grain-128-AEAD can be divided into two phases: the initialization phase and the key generation phase. In the keystream generation phase we generate ρ keystream bits for which we require to clock the cipher $2 \times \rho$ times. The keystream is stored in the qubits $y_t, (0 \leq t \leq \rho)$. The circuit is constructed as described in Algorithm 2.

Algorithm 2: Quantum circuit of initialization and key generation phase

```
/* INITIALIZATION                                                    */
1  for i ← {0, 127} do
2  |    CNOT (k_i, b_i)

3  for i ← {0, 95} do
4  |    if iv_i ← 1 then
5  |    |    NOT (s_i)

6  for i ← {96, 127} do
7  |    NOT (s_i)

8  for j ← {0, 1} do
9  |    for i ← {0, 127} do
10 |    |    Implement y(t) replacing y_t by s_(0+t)%128
11 |    |    Implement g(B_t)
12 |    |    Implement f(S_t)

13 for i ← {0, 127} do
14 |    Implement g(B_t)
15 |    CNOT (k_i, s_i)
16 |    Implement f(S_t)

/* KEY GENERATION                                                    */
17 for j ← {0, 1} do
18 |    for i ← {0, ρ} do
19 |    |    Implement y(t)
20 |    |    Implement g(B_t)
21 |    |    Implement f(S_t)
```

3.2   Circuit for TinyJAMBU

In TinyJAMBU the state is updated using the permutation P_n as described below. The permutation P_n consists of n rounds and in the ith round the state is updated using the following 128-bit nonlinear feedback shift register:

$$\text{StateUpdate}(S, K, i):$$
$$\text{feedback} = s_0 \oplus s_{47} \oplus (\sim (s_{70} \& s_{85})) \oplus s_{91} \oplus k_{i \bmod k}$$
$$\text{for } j \text{ from } 0 \text{ to } 126: s_j = s_{j+1}$$
$$s_{127} = \text{feedback}$$
$$end$$

where $k = \{128, 192, 256\}$ is the key length.

This permutation P_n can be implemented as a quantum circuit as described in Algorithm 3.

Algorithm 3: Quantum circuit of permutation P_n

```
/* PERMUTATION Pn                                                        */
1  for j ← {0, (n/128)} do
2  |   for i ← {0, 127} do
3  |   |   CNOT (k((128*j+i)%klen), s(0+i)%128)
4  |   |   CNOT (s(47+i)%128, s(0+i)%128)
5  |   |   Toffoli (s(70+i)%128, s(85+i)%128, anc0)
6  |   |   CNOT (anc0, s(0+i)%128)
7  |   |   Toffoli (s(70+i)%128, s(85+i)%128, anc0)
8  |   |   CNOT (s(91+i)%128, s(0+i)%128)
```

Now we show the implementation of the three steps (for the cipher with key size = 128, implementations for other key sizes is similar). We need 128 qubits for the state all initialized to 0, 128 qubits for the keys and 1 ancilla initialized to 1 required for the implementation of P_n. For our work we assume associated data of length 96-bits.

Algorithm 4: Quantum circuit TinyJAMBU

```
/* KEY AND NONCE SETUP                                                   */
1   Update the state using P1024
2   for i ← 0, 2 do
3   |   NOT (s36)
4   |   Update the state using P640
5   |   for j ← 0, 31 do
6   |   |   if nonce(32i+j) ← 1 then
7   |   |   |   NOT (sj+96)

/* PROCCESSING ASSOCIATED DATA                                           */
8   for i ← 0, 2 do
9   |   NOT (s36), NOT (s37)
10  |   Update the state using P640
11  |   for j ← 0, 31 do
12  |   |   if ad(32i+j) ← 1 then
13  |   |   |   NOT (sj+96)

/* ENCRYPTION                                                            */
14  for j ← 0, 3 do
15  |   NOT (s36), NOT (s38)
16  |   Update the state using P1024
17  |   for i ← 0, 31 do
18  |   |   CNOT (pt32*j+i, s96+i)
19  |   for i ← 0, 31 do
20  |   |   CNOT (s64+i, pt32*j+i)
```

3.3   Quantum Circuit for LIZARD

The state size of LIZARD is 121, so we need 121 qubits for the state, 31 for NFSR1 (denoted as $n1$) and 90 for NFSR2 (denoted as $n2$). The key size is 120 and the key is used twice in the state initialization phase so we need 120 qubits for keys.

We first describe the implementation of the feedback functions of the two ciphers and the output function in Algorithm 5. The gates toffoli3, toffoli4, toffoli5, toffoli6 and toffoli7 can be constructed following the circuits described in Fig. 3 and $anc[i], 0 \leq i \leq 9$ are ancillae.

Algorithm 5: Quantum circuit for output function at time t

```
/* OUTPUT FUNCTION                                                      */
1  for i = 7, 11, 30, 40, 45, 54, 71, 5 do
2  ⌊   CNOT ((n2[(i + t)%90], y[t])

3  l = [4, 9, 18, 44, 8]
4  m = [21, 52, 37, 76, 82]
5  for i ← 0, 4 do
6  ⌊   Toffoli (n2[(l[i] + t)%90], n2[(m[i] + t)%90], y[t])

7  toffoli3(n2[(34 + t)%90], n2[(67 + t)%90], n2[(73 + t)%90], y[t])
8  toffoli4(n2[(2 + t)%90], n2[(28 + t)%90], n2[(41 + t)%90],
9        n2[(65 + t)%90], y[t])
10 toffoli5(n2[(13 + t)%90], n2[(29 + t)%90], n2[(50 + t)%90],
11       n2[(64 + t)%90], n2[(75 + t)%90], y[t])
12 toffoli6(n2[(6 + t)%90], n2[(14 + t)%90], n2[(26 + t)%90],
13       n2[(32 + t)%90],
14       n2[(47 + t)%90], n2[(61 + t)%90], y[t])
15 toffoli7(n2[(1 + t)%90], n2[(19 + t)%90], n2[(27 + t)%90],
16       n2[(43 + t)%90], n2[(57 + t)%90], n2[(66 + t)%90], n2[(78 + t)%90], y[t])
17 CNOT ((n1[(23 + t)%31], y[t])
18 Toffoli (n1[(3 + t)%31], n1[(16 + t)%31], y[t])
19 toffoli3(n1[(9 + t)%31], n1[(13 + t)%31], n1[(48 + t)%31], y[t])
20 toffoli4(n1[(1 + t)%31], n1[(24 + t)%31], n2[(38 + t)%90], n2[(63 + t)%90], y[t])
```

Using the procedures defined in Algorithm 5 and 6 the circuit for full LIZARD can be constructed. as described below:

– Circuit for Phase 1: The state is initialized by the values of key and IV by using CNOT gates to copy the values of key to the state and then adequate number of NOT gates to initialize the state with IV bits. So in this step we require 120 CNOT gates and a maximum of 66 NOT gates, considering that IV is all $1's$.
– Circuit for Phase 2: This phase mixes the state in the same way as Grain family of ciphers. This phase requires 7808 CNOT gates, 12032 Toffoli gates and 512 NOT gates.
– Circuit for Phase 3: In this phase the key is XORed into the state which can be implemented using 120 CNOT gates and 1 NOT gate.
– Circuit for Phase 4: This final phase is similar to Phase 2 with the exception that the feedback is discarded. This phase requires 7552 CNOT gates, 12032 Toffoli gates and 512 NOT gates.
– Circuit for key generation: This step is same as Phase 4, where the keystream are stored instead of discarding it.

Algorithm 6: Quantum circuit for feedback functions at time t

---

```
   /* FEEDBACK FUNCTION OF NFSR1                                              */
 1 for i = 2, 5, 6, 15, 17, 18, 20, 25 do
 2  └ CNOT (n1[(i + t)%31], n1[(t)%31])

 3 Toffoli (n1[(14 + t)%31], n1[(19 + t)%31], anc[0])
 4 Toffoli (n1[(17 + t)%31], n1[(21 + t)%31], anc[0])
 5 CNOT (anc[0], n1[(0 + t)%31])
 6 Toffoli (n1[(17 + t)%31], n1[(21 + t)%31], anc[0])
 7 Toffoli (n1[(14 + t)%31], n1[(19 + t)%31], anc[0])
 8 CNOT (n1[(21 + t)%31], anc[1])
 9 NOT (anc[1])
10 Toffoli (n1[(20 + t)%31], n1[(22 + t)%31], anc[1])
11 CNOT (anc[1], n1[(0 + t)%31])
12 Toffoli (n1[(20 + t)%31], n1[(22 + t)%31], anc[1])
13 NOT (anc[1])
14 l = [21, 4, 19],  m = [1, 3, 3]
15 for i ← 0, 2 do
16  └ CNOT (n1[(l[i] + t)%31], anc[m[i]])

17 CNOT (anc[3], anc[2])
18 Toffoli (n1[(12 + t)%31], n1[(22 + t)%31], anc[2])
19 CNOT (anc[2], n1[(0 + t)%31])
20 Toffoli (n1[(12 + t)%31], n1[(22 + t)%31], anc[2])
21 CNOT (anc[3], anc[2])
22 CNOT (n1[(7 + t)%31], anc[4])
23 CNOT (n1[(22 + t)%31], anc[4])
24 Toffoli (anc[3], anc[4], anc[5])
25 NOT (anc[5])
26 Toffoli (n1[(12 + t)%31], n1[(21 + t)%31], anc[5])
27 CNOT (anc[5], n1[(0 + t)%31])
28 Toffoli (n1[(12 + t)%31], n1[(21 + t)%31], anc[5])
29 NOT (anc[5])
30 Toffoli (anc[3], anc[4], anc[5])
31 l = [22, 7, 19, 4, 18, 20],  m = [4, 4, 3, 3, 6, 6]
32 for i ← 0, 5 do
33  └ CNOT (n1[(l[i] + t)%31], anc[m[i]])

34 Toffoli (n1[(8 + t)%31], anc[6], anc[7])
35 CNOT (anc[7], n1[(0 + t)%31])
36 CNOT (n1[(7 + t)%31], anc[8])
37 CNOT (n1[(22 + t)%31], anc[8])
38 Toffoli (n1[(21 + t)%31], anc[8], anc[9])
39 CNOT (n1[(22 + t)%31], anc[9])
40 Toffoli (anc[9], anc[7], n1[(0 + t)%31])
41 CNOT (n1[(22 + t)%31], anc[9])
42 Toffoli (n1[(21 + t)%31], anc[8], anc[9])
43 CNOT (n1[(22 + t)%31], anc[8])
44 CNOT (n1[(7 + t)%31], anc[8])
45 Toffoli (n1[(8 + t)%31], anc[6], anc[7])
46 CNOT (n1[(20 + t)%31], anc[6])
47 CNOT (n1[(18 + t)%31], anc[6])

   /* FEEDBACK FUNCTION OF NFSR2                                              */
48 for i = 24, 49, 79, 84 do
49  └ CNOT ((n2[(i + t)%90], n2[(t)%90])

50 l = [3, 10, 15, 25, 35, 55, 60] m = [59, 12, 16, 53, 42, 58, 74]
51 for i ← 0, 6 do
52  └ Toffoli ((n2[(l[i] + t)%90], n2[(m[i] + t)%90], n2[(t)%90])

53 toffoli3(n2[(20 + t)%90], n2[(22 + t)%90], n2[(23 + t)%90], n2[(t)%90])
54 toffoli3(n2[(62 + t)%90], n2[(68 + t)%90], n2[(78 + t)%90], n2[(t)%90])
55 toffoli4(n2[(77 + t)%90], n2[(80 + t)%90], n2[(81 + t)%90], n2[(83 + t)%90], n2[(t)%90])
```

3.4   Circuit to Implement Grain-V1

In Grain-v1, the state is of size 160-bits and the length of key is 80, so we require 160 qubits for the state (80 for LFSR denoted by s and 80 for NFSR denoted by b) and 80 qubits for the key. As a keystream of length 128 is sufficient to obtain a unique key, so we need 128 qubits for the keystream. Using the Algorithms 7 the complete circuit for Grain-v1 can be constructed following the process used while constructing Grain-128-AEAD.

Algorithm 7: Quantum circuit for output and feedback functions at any time t

---

/* OUTPUT FUNCTION   */

1 Toffoli $s[(46 + t)\%80], b[(63 + t)\%80], ye[0])$
2 Toffoli $s[(3 + t)\%80], s[(46 + t)\%80], ye[1])$
3 **for** $i = 25, 64$ **do**
4 $\quad$ ⌊ CNOT $(s[i\%80], ye[2])$

5 **for** $i = 3, 46, 64$ **do**
6 $\quad$ ⌊ CNOT $(s[i\%80], ye[3])$

7 Toffoli $ye[2], ye[0], s[(t)\%80])$, Toffoli $ye[2], ye[1], s[(t)\%80])$
8 Toffoli $ye[3], s[(64 + t)\%80], s[(t)\%80])$
9 NOT $(ye[1])$, CNOT $(ye[1], z[t])$
10 CNOT $(b[(63 + t)\%80], z[t])$, NOT $(ye[1])$
11 **for** $i = 64, 46, 3$ **do**
12 $\quad$ ⌊ CNOT $(s[i\%80], ye[3])$

13 **for** $i = 64, 25$ **do**
14 $\quad$ ⌊ CNOT $(s[i\%80], ye[2])$

15 Toffoli $s[(3 + t)\%80], s[(46 + t)\%80], ye[1])$
16 Toffoli $s[(46 + t)\%80], b[(63 + t)\%80], ye[0])$
17 **for** $i = 1, 2, 4, 31, 43, 56$ **do**
18 $\quad$ ⌊ CNOT $(b[i + t], z[t])$

/* UPDATE FUNCTION OF LFSR   */

19 **for** $i = 13, 23, 38, 51, 62$ **do**
20 $\quad$ ⌊ Apply CNOT $(s_{(i+t)\%80}, s_{t\%80})$

/* UPDATE FUNCTION OF NFSR   */

21 CNOT $(s_{(t)\%80}, b_{t\%80})$
22 **for** $i = 9, 14, 21, 28, 33, 37, 45, 52, 60, 63$ **do**
23 $\quad$ ⌊ CNOT $(b_{(i+t)\%80}, b_{t\%80})$

24 $l = [63, 37, 15], \ m = [60, 33, 9]$
25 **for** $i \leftarrow 0, 2$ **do**
26 $\quad$ ⌊ Toffoli $b[(l[i] + t)\%80], b[(m[i] + t)\%80], b[(t)\%80])$

27 toffoli3$(b[(60 + t)\%80], b[(52 + t)\%80], \ b[(45 + t)\%80], ge0[0], ge0[1], b[(t)\%80])$
28 toffoli3$(b[(33 + t)\%80], b[(28 + t)\%80], b[(21 + t)\%80], ge1[0], ge1[1], b[(t)\%80])$
29 toffoli4$(b[(63 + t)\%80], b[(45 + t)\%80],$
$\quad b[(28 + t)\%80], b[(9 + t)\%80], ge2[0], ge2[1], ge2[2], b[(t)\%80])$
30 toffoli4$(b[(60 + t)\%80], b[(52 + t)\%80],$
$\quad b[(37 + t)\%80], b[(33 + t)\%80], ge2[0], ge2[1], ge2[2], b[(t)\%80])$
31 toffoli4$(b[(63 + t)\%80], b[(60 + t)\%80],$
$\quad b[(21 + t)\%80], b[(15 + t)\%80], ge2[0], ge2[1], ge2[2], b[(t)\%80])$
32 toffoli5$(b[(63 + t)\%80], b[(60 + t)\%80], \ b[(52 + t)\%80], b[(45 + t)\%80], b[(37 + t)\%80], b[(t)\%80])$
33 toffoli5$(b[(33 + t)\%80], b[(28 + t)\%80], b[(21 + t)\%80], b[(15 + t)\%80], b[(9 + t)\%80], b[(t)\%80])$
34 toffoli6$(b[(52 + t)\%80], b[(45 + t)\%80],$
$\quad b[(37 + t)\%80], b[(33 + t)\%80], b[(28 + t)\%80], b[(21 + t)\%80], b[(t)\%80])$

3.5   Resource Estimation

Cost of Implementing the Ciphers. We estimate the cost of the stream ciphers when the cipher produces $\rho = k + c$ bits keystream, where k is the key size and $c = 10$, and the cost of implementing TinyJAMBU when it encrypts 128 bits of plaintext with 96 bits of nonce and associated data each. In our estimates we assume that the nonce and the associated data is known. Table 1 gives the cost estimates of implementing the ciphers.

Table 1. Cost of implementing the ciphers

Cipher	Clifford gates	T gates	T-depth	Full depth	qubits
Grain-128-AEAD	158679	126812	72464	75951	531
TinyJAMBU ($k = 128$)	148817	103936	59392	126209	385
TinyJAMBU ($k = 192$)	161617	112896	64512	137089	449
TinyJAMBU ($k = 256$)	174417	121856	69632	147969	513
LIZARD ($k = 120/80$)	314897	253988	145136	210993	392
Grain-v1 ($k = 80$)	135410	108500	62000	74886	346

Cost of Grover Oracle. Using Eqs. 1, 2, 3, 4, 5 the cost estimates of Grover's oracle for all ciphers are presented in Table 2. $\mathcal{O}_g$ is the sum of Clifford gates and T gates.

Table 2. Cost of Grover oracle.

Cipher	Clifford gates	T gates	Gate Cost($\mathcal{O}_g$)	T-depth	Full depth($\mathcal{O}_d$)	qubits
Grain-128-AEAD	317358	257956	575314	144928	151902	532
TinyJAMBU ($k = 128$)	595524	423852	1019376	118784	252418	771
TinyJAMBU ($k = 192$)	646852	463788	1110640	129024	274178	899
TinyJAMBU ($k = 256$)	698180	503724	1201904	139264	295938	1027
LIZARD ($k = 120/80$)	629794	512052	1141846	290272	421986	393
Grain-v1 ($k = 80$)	270820	219796	490616	124000	149772	347

Cost of Exhaustive Key Search. Using the estimates in Table 2 of the Grover oracle for the various variants, we provide the cost estimates for the full exhaustive key search Table 3. We consider $\frac{\pi}{4}2^{k/2}$ iterations of the Grover oracle, where k is the key size. The gate cost G is the sum of the Clifford gates and T gates.

Table 3. Cost estimates of Grover's algorithm with $\frac{\pi}{4}2^{k/2}$ oracle iterations

Cipher	Clifford gates	T gates	Gate Cost (G)	T-depth	Full depth (D)	qubits
Grain-128-AEAD	$1.902 \cdot 2^{81}$	$1.546 \cdot 2^{81}$	$1.724 \cdot 2^{82}$	$1.737 \cdot 2^{80}$	$1.820 \cdot 2^{80}$	523
TinyJAMBU $(k = 128)$	$1.784 \cdot 2^{82}$	$1.270 \cdot 2^{82}$	$1.527 \cdot 2^{83}$	$1.423 \cdot 2^{80}$	$1.513 \cdot 2^{81}$	771
TinyJAMBU $(k = 192)$	$1.938 \cdot 2^{114}$	$1.390 \cdot 2^{114}$	$1.664 \cdot 2^{115}$	$1.546 \cdot 2^{112}$	$1.642 \cdot 2^{113}$	889
TinyJAMBU $(k = 256)$	$1.046 \cdot 2^{147}$	$1.509 \cdot 2^{146}$	$1.800 \cdot 2^{147}$	$1.669 \cdot 2^{144}$	$1.773 \cdot 2^{145}$	1027
LIZARD $(k = 120/80)$	$1.887 \cdot 2^{78}$	$1.534 \cdot 2^{78}$	$1.711 \cdot 2^{79}$	$1.739 \cdot 2^{77}$	$1.264 \cdot 2^{78}$	393
Grain-v1 $(k = 80)$	$1.623 \cdot 2^{57}$	$1.317 \cdot 2^{57}$	$1.470 \cdot 2^{58}$	$1.486 \cdot 2^{56}$	$1.795 \cdot 2^{55}$	347

3.6   Cost of Grover Search Under NISTs MAXDEPTH Limit

In this work we have assumed that an adversary is bounded by a constraint on the depth of the circuit that (s)he can use for Grover. NIST suggests a parameter MAXDEPTH as such a bound and the plausible values range from 2^{40} to 2^{96}. From [25]:

1. In, Page 16, it is stated: "In particular, NIST will define a separate category for each of the following security requirements (listed in order of increasing strength): 1) Any attack that breaks the relevant security definition must require computational resources comparable to or greater than those required for key search on a block cipher with a 128-bit key (e.g. AES128)."
2. In Page 18, it is stated: "NIST provides the estimates for optimal key recovery for AES128 as 2^{170}/MAXDEPTH."

In Table 4 we provide the gate counts for Grover's search on both the ciphers under the constraint of MAXDEPTH. These counts are computed using Eq. 9.

Table 4. Cost of Grover search on the ciphers under MAXDEPTH, the final column provides the product of the gate counts in each cell by MAXDEPTH.

k		G_{MD} for MAXDEPTH			
		2^{40}	2^{64}	2^{96}	$G_{MD} \times$ MAXDEPTH
128	NIST[25]	2^{130}	2^{106}	2^{74}	2^{170}
	Grain-128-AEAD	$1.569 \cdot 2^{123}$	$1.569 \cdot 2^{99}$	$1.724 \cdot 2^{82*}$	$1.569 \cdot 2^{163}$
	TinyJAMBU	$1.154 \cdot 2^{125}$	$1.154 \cdot 2^{101}$	$1.527 \cdot 2^{83*}$	$1.154 \cdot 2^{165}$
	AES[15]	$1.07 \cdot 2^{117}$	$1.07 \cdot 2^{93}$	$1.34 \cdot 2^{83*}$	$\approx 2^{157}$
192	NIST[25]	2^{193}	2^{169}	2^{137}	2^{233}
	TinyJAMBU	$1.367 \cdot 2^{189}$	$1.367 \cdot 2^{165}$	$1.367 \cdot 2^{133}$	$1.367 \cdot 2^{229}$
	AES[15]	$1.09 \cdot 2^{181}$	$1.09 \cdot 2^{157}$	$1.09 \cdot 2^{126}$	$\approx 2^{221}$
256	NIST[25]	2^{258}	2^{234}	2^{202}	2^{298}
	TinyJAMBU	$1.596 \cdot 2^{253}$	$1.596 \cdot 2^{229}$	$1.596 \cdot 2^{197}$	$1.596 \cdot 2^{293}$
	AES[15]	$1.39 \cdot 2^{245}$	$1.39 \cdot 2^{221}$	$1.39 \cdot 2^{190}$	$\approx 2^{285}$
120/80	LIZARD	$1.081 \cdot 2^{118}$	$1.081 \cdot 2^{94}$	$1.711 \cdot 2^{79*}$	$1.081 \cdot 2^{158}$
80	Grain-v1	$1.319 \cdot 2^{75}$	$1.470 \cdot 2^{58*}$	$1.470 \cdot 2^{58*}$	$1.319 \cdot 2^{115}$

Note that * denotes a special case as the attack does not require any parallelization and the approximation underestimates the cost.

Remark 1. The best known quantum implementation of AES results in a attack
with complexity 2^{157}/MAXDEPTH [15], instead of 2^{170}/MAXDEPTH as initially
estimated by NIST. The values of gate count by NIST was computed based on
the resources estimated by Grassl [7]. The resource estimate obtained in [7] has
been improved several times, the best being the one obtained in [15].

4   Experience over Different Quantum Simulators

To check the correctness of our computation of resource estimates we implemented our circuits in IBMQ's Qiskit as well as in Microsoft's Q#. We observed
that the values of the gate count and the depth of the circuit were same in both
these implementations.

As an example we describe here the circuit of TinyJAMBU's permutation
P_1, i.e., the permutation P_n for $n = 1$ in IBMQ's Qiskit as well as in Microsoft's
Q# for independent verification by the readers.

```
1   #Importing the required classes and modules
2   from qiskit import QuantumCircuit, QuantumRegister, AER
3
4   def permut(qc,round):
5     for r in range(round):
6       for i in range(128):
7         qc.cx(k[((128*r+i)%klen)],q[(0+i)%128])
8         qc.cx(q[(47+i)%128],q[(0+i)%128])
9         qc.ccx(q[(70+i)%128],q[(85+i)%128],anc[0])
10        qc.cx(anc[0],q[(0+i)%128])
11        qc.ccx(q[(70+i)%128],q[(85+i)%128],anc[0])
12        qc.cx(q[(91+i)%128],q[(0+i)%128])
13
14  q = QuantumRegister(128) #128 qubits for  state
15  k = QuantumRegister(128) #128 qubits for  key
16  anc = QuantumRegister(1) # 1 ancilla needed to implement
      NAND gate
17
18  qc = QuantumCircuit(q,k,anc)
19  rounds = 1
20  permut(qc,rounds)
21
22  #Estimating resources
23  print (qc.count_ops())
24  print (qc.width())
25  print (qc.depth())
```

Listing 1.1. Qiskit code for TinyJAMBU permutation P_1

```
1   #Importing the required classes and modules
2   open Microsoft.Quantum.Math;
3   open Microsoft.Quantum.Intrinsic;
4   open Microsoft.Quantum.Canon;
5   open Microsoft.Quantum.Measurement;
6   open Microsoft.Quantum.Arrays;
7   open Microsoft.Quantum.Convert;
8   open Microsoft.Quantum.Diagnostics;
9
10  operation permutation(rounds:Int, qs : Qubit[], anc :
       Qubit[]) : Unit {
11    for(r in 0 .. rounds-1){
12      for(i in 0 .. 128-1){
13        CNOT(qs[47],qs[0]);
14        CCNOT(qs[70],qs[85],anc[0]);
15        CNOT(anc[0],qs[0]);
16        CCNOT(qs[70],qs[85],anc[0]);
17        CNOT(qs[91],qs[0]);
18      }
19    }
20  }
21
22  operation main() : Unit {
23  using ((qubit,anc) = ( Qubit[128], Qubit[1])){
24    X (anc[0]);
25    let rounds = 1;
26    permutation(rounds,qubit,anc);
27  }
28  }
29
30  #Estimating resources
31  %estimate main
```

Listing 1.2. Q# code for TinyJAMBU permutation P_1

Implementing these two circuits, results in the same values of the gate counts and circuit depth.

5   Conclusion

In this work we study quantum cryptanalysis of FSR based symmetric ciphers, along with the FSR based block cipher TinyJAMBU. We construct compact reversible quantum circuits for popular Feedback Shift Register (FSR) based ciphers such as Grain-128-AEAD, TinyJAMBU, LIZARD, and Grain-v1. We study the cost of implementing Grover's key search algorithm on these ciphers under the NISTs MAXDEPTH constraint and find that all these ciphers fail to satisfy the security constraints. We observe that the increase in circuit size to reduce chances of getting a false positive is lesser for stream ciphers compared to block ciphers, although the difference is that of a constant factor ≈ 2.

References

1. Anand, R., Maitra, A., Mukhopadhyay, S.: Grover on SIMON. Quant. Inf. Proces. **19**(9), 1–17 (2020)
2. Anand, R., Maitra, A., Mukhopadhyay, S.: Evaluation of quantum cryptanalysis on SPECK. In: Bhargavan, K., Oswald, E., Prabhakaran, M. (eds.) INDOCRYPT 2020. LNCS, vol. 12578, pp. 395–413. Springer, Cham (2020). https://doi.org/10. 1007/978-3-030-65277-7_18
3. Amy, M., Maslov, D., Mosca, M., Roetteler, M.: A meet-in-the-middle algorithm for fast synthesis of depth-optimal quantum circuits. IEEE Trans. Comput.-Aid. Des. Integr. Circut. Syst. **32**(6), 818–830 (2013)
4. Baksi, A., Jang, K., Song, G., Seo, H., Xiang, Z.: Quantum implementation and resource estimates for RECTANGLE and KNOT. Cryptology ePrint Archive (2021)
5. Bonnetain, X., Naya-Plasencia, M., Schrottenloher, A.: Quantum security analysis of AES. IACR Trans. Symm. Cryptol. **2019**(2), 55–93 (2019)
6. Davenport, J.H., Pring, B.: Improvements to Quantum Search Techniques for Block-Ciphers, with Applications to AES. In: Dunkelman, O., Jacobson, Jr., M.J., O'Flynn, C. (eds.) SAC 2020. LNCS, vol. 12804, pp. 360–384. Springer, Cham (2021). https://doi.org/10.1007/978-3-030-81652-0_14
7. Grassl, M., Langenberg, B., Roetteler, M., Steinwandt, R.: Applying Crover's algorithm to AES: quantum resource estimates. In: Takagi, T. (ed.) PQCrypto 2016. LNCS, vol. 9606, pp. 29–43. Springer, Cham (2016). https://doi.org/10.1007/978-3-319-29360-8_3
8. Grover, L.K.: A fast quantum mechanical algorithm for database search. In Proceedings of the Twenty-Eighth Annual ACM Symposium on Theory of Computing, pp. 212–219, July 1996
9. Hell, M., Johansson, T., Meier, W.: Grain-a stream cipher for constrained environments. eSTREAM, ECRYPT Stream Cipher (2005). http://www.ecrypt.eu.org/stream
10. Hell, M., Johansson, T., Meier, W., Sönnerup, J., Yoshida, H.: Grain-128 aead-a lightweight aead stream cipher. Lightweight Cryptography (LWC) Standardization (2019)
11. Hamann, M., Krause, M., Meier, W.: LIZARD-A lightweight stream cipher for power-constrained devices. IACR Trans. Symm. Cryptol. **2017**(1), 45–79 (2017)
12. Hosoyamada, A., Sasaki, Yu.: Cryptanalysis against symmetric-key schemes with online classical queries and offline quantum computations. In: Smart, N.P. (ed.) CT-RSA 2018. LNCS, vol. 10808, pp. 198–218. Springer, Cham (2018). https://doi.org/10.1007/978-3-319-76953-0_11
13. Hosoyamada, A., Sasaki, Y.: Quantum Demiric-Selçuk meet-in-the-middle attacks: applications to 6-round generic feistel constructions. In: Catalano, D., De Prisco, R. (eds.) SCN 2018. LNCS, vol. 11035, pp. 386–403. Springer, Cham (2018). https://doi.org/10.1007/978-3-319-98113-0_21
14. Jang, K., Choi, S., Kwon, H., Seo, H.: Grover on SPECK: quantum resource estimates. IACR Cryptol. ePrint Arch. **2020**, 640 (2020)
15. Jaques, S., Naehrig, M., Roetteler, M., Virdia, F.: Implementing Grover oracles for quantum key search on AES and LowMC. Adv. Cryptol.-EUROCRYPT **2020**(12106), 280 (2020)
16. Kaplan, M.: Quantum attacks against iterated block ciphers (). arXiv preprint arXiv:1410.1434 (2014)

17. Kaplan, M., Leurent, G., Leverrier, A., Naya-Plasencia, M.: Breaking symmetric cryptosystems using quantum period finding. In: Annual International Cryptology Conference, pp. 207–237. Springer, Berlin, Heidelberg , August 2016
18. Leurent, G., Kaplan, M., Leverrier, A., Naya-Plasencia, M.: March. Quantum differential and linear cryptanalysis. In: FSE 2017-Fast Software Encryption, March 2017
19. Kim, P., Han, D., Jeong, K.C.: Time-space complexity of quantum search algorithms in symmetric cryptanalysis: applying to AES and SHA-2. Quant. Inf. Process. **17**(12), 1–39 (2018)
20. Kuwakado, H., Morii, M.: Security on the quantum-type Even-Mansour cipher. In: 2012 International Symposium on Information Theory and Its Applications, pp. 312–316. IEEE, October 2012
21. Leander, G., May, A.: Grover meets Simon – quantumly attacking the FX-construction. In: Takagi, T., Peyrin, T. (eds.) ASIACRYPT 2017. LNCS, vol. 10625, pp. 161–178. Springer, Cham (2017). https://doi.org/10.1007/978-3-319-70697-9_6
22. Langenberg, B., Pham, H., Steinwandt, R.: Reducing the cost of implementing the advanced encryption standard as a quantum circuit. IEEE Trans. Quant. Eng. **1**, 1–12 (2020)
23. Nielsen, M.A., Chuang, I.L.: Quantum Computation and Quantum Information: 10th Anniversary edn., Cambridge University Press (2011)
24. NIST: Lightweight crypto standardization. https://csrc.nist.gov/Projects/lightweight-cryptography/round-2-candidates
25. NIST: Submission requirements and evaluation criteria for the post-quantum cryptography standardization process (2016). https://csrc.nist.gov/CSRC/media/Projects/Post-Quantum-Cryptography/documents/call-for-proposals-final-dec-2016.pdf
26. QISKIT. https://qiskit.org/
27. Santoli, T., Schaffner, C.: Using Simon's algorithm to attack symmetric-key cryptographic primitives. arXiv preprint arXiv:1603.07856 (2016)
28. Schlieper, L.: In-place implementation of Quantum-Gimli. arXiv preprint arXiv:2007.06319 (2020)
29. Wu, H., Huang, T.: TinyJAMBU: A Family of Lightweight Authenticated Encryption Algorithms. the NIST Lightweight Cryptography (LWC) Standardization project (A Round-2 Candidate) (2019)
30. Wiebe, N., Roetteler, M.: Quantum arithmetic and numerical analysis using repeat-until-success circuits. Quant. Inf. Process. **16**(1&2), 134–178 (2016)
31. Wu, H., Preneel, B.: Cryptanalysis and design of stream ciphers. Ph.D. thesis of Katholieke Universiteit Leuven, Belgium (2008). https://www.esat.kuleuven.be/cosic/publications/thesis-167.pdf
32. Zou, J., Wei, Z., Sun, S., Liu, X., Wu, W.: Quantum circuit implementations of AES with fewer qubits. In: Moriai, S., Wang, H. (eds.) ASIACRYPT 2020. LNCS, vol. 12492, pp. 697–726. Springer, Cham (2020). https://doi.org/10.1007/978-3-030-64834-3_24
33. https://github.com/raviro/FSR_quant

Side-Channel Attacks

Analyzing Masked Ciphers Against Transition and Coupling Effects

Siemen Dhooghe[✉] [iD]

imec-COSIC, ESAT, KU Leuven, Leuven, Belgium
siemen.dhooghe@esat.kuleuven.be

Abstract. This paper discusses how to analyze the probing security of masked symmetric primitives against the leakage effects from Faust *et al.* in CHES 2018; glitches, transitions, and coupling effects. This is illustrated on several architectures of ciphers like PRESENT, AES, and ASCON where we transform glitch-extended probing secure maskings into transition and/or coupling secure ones. The analysis uses linear cryptanalytic methods and the diffusion layers of the cipher to efficiently protect against the advanced leakage effects.

Keywords: Hardware · Linear cryptanalysis · Masking · Robust probing security · Side-channel analysis

1 Introduction

From the moment a symmetric primitive is implemented on a physical device, it becomes susceptible to side-channel attacks. The most well-known attack in this line is differential power analysis where the power consumption of the device is correlated to its processed secrets [29]. Masking methods form a popular countermeasure against these attacks. Here each secret variable is split into multiple random shares. A masking method allows for algorithmic protection aiming to catch vulnerabilities before production. This algorithmic protection is based on security models trying to capture realistic attacks. The most popular model is the probing model originally proposed by Ishai *et al.* [27]. In the dth-order and single-shot variant of this model, it is stated that any set of d intermediate values in the computation of a symmetric key primitive need to be independent of any secret value.

While the probing model is a good step towards finding reliable algorithmic countermeasures against side-channel attacks, it does not capture all realistic leakage effects in hardware. Faust *et al.* [22] formalizes some realistic effects which are not captured in the probing model and effectively extends the security model. The three effects discussed are glitches, transitions, and coupling effects. The extension of the formal probing model allows designers to find effective maskings to protect hardware implementations even against more advanced leakages.

© Springer Nature Switzerland AG 2021
A. Adhikari et al. (Eds.): INDOCRYPT 2021, LNCS 13143, pp. 201–223, 2021.
https://doi.org/10.1007/978-3-030-92518-5_10

We currently succeed in protecting hardware maskings against glitches thanks to the non-completeness property introduced by Nikova *et al.* [33]. However, it still remains an open problem how to efficiently protect against transition or coupling leakage and, more importantly, against a combination of leakage sources. While the work from Faust *et al.* provides a model how to capture these effects, it remains an open problem how to analyze the security of a masking in this new model.

In Asiacrypt 2020, Beyne *et al.* [5] introduced a security analysis based on linear cryptanalysis. The work shows that by analyzing linear trails through the masking, where the probed values form the start and end of the trail, one can show the security of the design. This analysis makes it particularly easy to analyze leakage on a courser granularity where, for example, the adversary gets information from different rounds of a cipher. As a result, the security analysis is particularly useful for the robust probing model where the adversary will get non-complete information from multiple cells in the computation of the symmetric primitive. In this work, we investigate the application of the theory from Beyne *et al.* to analyze the robust probing security of a masking.

Contributions. This paper introduces an analysis technique to assess the transition and coupling-extended probing security defined by Faust *et al.* [22]. The analysis is based on the work by Beyne *et al.* [5] and extends it for the advanced leakage effects. In essence the method transforms a glitch-extended probing secure masking to a transition and coupling secure one as follows:

- Take a glitch-extended probing secure implementation of a symmetric primitive. For example, using threshold implementations [33] or a masking created using glitch-extended SNI or PINI secure gates [9,22].
- Use the work by Faust *et al.* [22] and analyze the architecture of the masking to determine what an adversary can view. For example, via memory recombinations an adversary can view the output of two different masked S-boxes.
- Use the work by Beyne *et al.* [5] and determine whether there are trails between the observed values. In case zero-correlation approximations are found between the probed values, the countermeasure is deemed secure.

In this work we go over the theoretical analysis of several symmetric primitives and over various architectures a designer can use to implement the primitive. The primitives PRESENT, AES, and ASCON are taken as case studies. As similar primitives would have similar security arguments, these case studies represent a large class of primitives. The analysis is made as general as possible by considering black box masked S-boxes. Meaning that our analysis applies to *any* masking of the considered primitives as long as that masking is glitch-extended probing secure. For example, one can apply the analysis to the state of the art first-order masked architecture of the AES to make it secure against transition-extended probes using additional randomness.

We explicitly use the diffusion properties of the symmetric primitive to minimize the cost of protecting against transition or coupling leakage. We show that one typically requires only a total few random bits to protect a masking against these effects. This should be compared to the current state of the art where there is an area and randomness overhead per shared multiplication like the work by Dhooghe and Nikova [19] and by Cassiers and Standaert [10, Table 2]. In particular, the work by Cassiers and Standaert [10, Table 2] requires several additional thousands of bits of randomness to secure a first-order glitch-resistant PRESENT against transition leakage. Instead, our analysis shows their glitch-resistant masking (for any of their proposed architectures) can be made secure against transition leakage using at most a single additional random bit.

2 Preliminaries

This work uses the tools of linear cryptanalysis to analyze the security of masking implementations against probing adversaries which are extended to view advanced leakage such as glitches, transitions, and couplings. In this section, we recall the basics of hardware, the probing model, threshold implementations, and linear cryptanalysis over masked variables.

2.1 The Physical World

This section recalls the basics of hardware and side-channel attacks.

Synchronous Circuits. A synchronous circuit consists of combinatorial gates (AND, XOR, etc.) and sequential logic (memory, registers). When the circuit is powered on, all registers, gates, and wires are powered too at which point they all carry a digital value. There is a clock synchronizing the operations of different circuit elements. A clock cycle is the time between two clock ticks. During each clock cycle the combinatorial logic is re-evaluated and results are stored in the registers.

Registers. A register (or memory cell) has one input and one output and its functionality is controlled by the clock. Registers release a signal by opening its "out-line" while the "input-line" is closed (only one is open at a time). The register out-line stays open until the signal in the logic becomes stable, after that it stores the newly computed value - hence the register closes the output-line and opens the input-line.

Logical Gates. Logical gates perform simple Boolean operations. They have several wires as input and a single wire as output. Each gate can have a different time to propagate a signal from its inputs to its output and each gate can have a different power consumption. A change of its inputs causes re-evaluation of the gate and hence may change the output value.

2.2 The Bounded-Query Probing Model

This section recalls the bounded-query probing model, its expansion considering the effect of glitches, its security analysis, and a note on key schedules. Later on, the probing model is further expanded to capture transition and coupling effects.

Threshold Probing. A dth-order probing adversary $\mathcal{A}$, as first proposed by Ishai *et al.* [27], can view up to d gates or wires in a circuit per query. This circuit encodes an operation, such as a cipher call, and consists of gates, such as AND or XOR gates, and wires. The adversary $\mathcal{A}$ is computationally unbounded, and must specify the location of the probes before querying the circuit. However, the adversary can change the location of the probes over multiple circuit queries. The adversary's interaction with the circuit is mediated through encoder and decoder algorithms, neither of which can be probed.

In the bounded query model, the security of a circuit C with input k against a dth-order probing adversary is quantified by means of the left-or-right security game. The challenger picks a random bit b and provides an oracle $\mathcal{O}^b$, to which adversary $\mathcal{A}$ is given query access. The adversary queries the oracle by choosing up to d wires to probe – we denote this set of probe positions by $\mathcal{P}$ – and sends it to the oracle along with chosen inputs k_0 and k_1. The oracle responds with the probed wire values of $C(k_b)$. After a total of q queries, the adversary responds to the challenger with a guess for b. For $b \in \{0, 1\}$, denote the result of the adversary after interacting with the oracle $\mathcal{O}^b$ using q queries by $\mathcal{A}^{\mathcal{O}^b}$. The left-or-right advantage of the adversary $\mathcal{A}$ is then as defined as

$$\text{Adv}_{\text{-thr}}(\mathcal{A}) = |\Pr[\mathcal{A}^{\mathcal{O}^0} = 1] - \Pr[\mathcal{A}^{\mathcal{O}^1} = 1]|.$$

Modeling Glitches. Let us consider "basic" combinatorial logic, namely the logic which connects two layers of registers. When a cycle starts, the output signals of the registers are inputs for the basic logic and these signals will start propagating through the wires and the gates until they reach the output registers. Gate evaluation may happen several times until the signals (and hence the gate) become stable. This can be due to many reasons, we list three of them: a) the wire signals propagate with different speed; b) the wires have different length; and c) each gate has different propagation time. We will refer to these value changes on the wires and gates as glitches.

In a cycle there are two main phases. The first phase is one in which the wires and gates do not have a stable value. This phase is followed by one in which all values are stable. The power consumption at a time sample is the sum of the power consumption of the wires, gates, and registers belonging to this simple logic. For CMOS technologies, the power consumption during the first phase is higher and more apt to change because of glitches compared to the second phase. We stress that glitches occur in the logic between two memory gates and are stopped by registers. In other words, glitches do not propagate through memory gates.

Glitches can result in significant leakage that is not accounted for by the standard probing model, see for example the attacks of Mangard *et al.* on several masked AES implementations [31]. Consequently, it is necessary to extend the capabilities of threshold probing adversaries in order to capture the physical effect of glitches on a hardware platform. Whereas one of the adversary's probes normally results in the value of a single wire, a glitch-extended probe allows obtaining the values of all wires in a bundle. This extension of the probing

model has been discussed by several authors, here we give the definition from
Faust *et al.* [22] who describes it as follows:

"Specific Model for Glitches. For any ϵ-input circuit gadget G, combinatorial
recombinations (aka glitches) can be modeled with specifically ϵ-extended probes
so that probing any output of the function allows the adversary to observe all
its ϵ inputs".

Security Analysis. The main theoretical result of [5] is that the bounded-query
probing security of a masked cipher can be related to its linear cryptanalysis.
The first step towards this result is provided by Theorem 1 below, which relates
the security of the masked cipher to the Fourier transform of the probability distribution of wire values obtained by probing. The link with linear cryptanalysis
will be developed in detail in Sect. 2.4.

The Fourier transform of a function $V \to \mathbb{C}$, where V is a subspace of $\mathbb{F}_2^n$,
can be defined as in Definition 1 below. For the purposes of this section, only
probability mass functions on $\mathbb{F}_2^n$ need be considered. Despite this, Definition 1
considers more general functions on an arbitrary subspace $V \subseteq \mathbb{F}_2^n$. Since any
vector space over $\mathbb{F}_2$ is isomorphic to $\mathbb{F}_2^n$ for some n, this generalization is mostly
a matter of notation. Nevertheless, this extended notation will be convenient in
Sect. 2.4.

Definition 1 ([5], §2.1). *Let $V \subseteq \mathbb{F}_2^n$ be a vector space and $f : V \to \mathbb{C}$ a
complex-valued function on V. The Fourier transformation of f is a function
$\widehat{f} : \mathbb{F}_2^n/V^\perp \to \mathbb{C}$ defined by*

$$\widehat{f}(u) = \sum_{x \in V} (-1)^{u^\top x} f(x),$$

*where we write u for $u + V^\perp$. Equivalently, $\widehat{f}$ is the representation of f in the
basis of functions $x \mapsto (-1)^{u^\top x}$ for $u \in \mathbb{F}_2^n/V^\perp$.*

Recall that the orthogonal complement $V^\perp$ of a subspace V of $\mathbb{F}_2^n$ is the
vector space $V^\perp = \{x \in \mathbb{F}_2^n \mid \forall v \in V : v^\top x = 0\}$. The quotient space $\mathbb{F}_2^n/V^\perp$
is by definition the vector space of cosets of $V^\perp$. For convenience, an element
$x + V^\perp \in \mathbb{F}_2^n/V^\perp$ will simply be denoted by x. For $x \in \mathbb{F}_2^n/V^\perp$ and $v \in V$, the
expression $x^\top v$ is well-defined. Consequently, the above definition is proper.

The main theorem on the advantage of an adversary in the bounded-query
probing model can now be stated. It relies on the observation that, for a bounded-
query probing secure circuit, all probed wire values either closely resemble uniform randomness or reveal nothing about the secret input.

Theorem 1 ([5], §4). *Let $\mathcal{A}$ be a t-threshold-probing adversary for a circuit
C. Assume that for every query made by $\mathcal{A}$ on the oracle $\mathcal{O}^b$, there exists a
partitioning (depending only on the probe positions) of the resulting wire values
into two random variables $\mathbf{x}$ ('good') and $\mathbf{y}$ ('bad') such that*

1. *The conditional probability distribution $p_{\mathbf{y}|\mathbf{x}}$ satisfies $\mathbb{E}_{\mathbf{x}} \|\widehat{p}_{\mathbf{y}|\mathbf{x}} - \delta_0\|_2^2 \le \varepsilon$ with
   δ_0 the Kronecker delta function,*

2. *Any t-threshold-probing adversary for the same circuit C and making the same oracle queries as $\mathcal{A}$, but which only receives the 'good' wire values (i.e. corresponding to $\mathbf{x}$) for each query, has advantage zero.*

The advantage of $\mathcal{A}$ can be upper bounded as

$$\mathrm{Adv}_{t\text{-thr}}(\mathcal{A}) \leq \sqrt{2\,q\,\varepsilon}\,,$$

where q is the number of queries to the oracle $\mathcal{O}^b$.

This work only considers a 1-threshold-probing adversary, but extends the probing model such that one probe can provide multiple shares even over different rounds. Furthermore, we consider the effect of transitions and couplings which typically provide shares over two consecutive rounds. As a result, we use the above theorem only for the 'bad' values. Moreover, in this work we are only interested to find out whether the 2-norm $\|\widehat{p}_{\mathbf{z}} - \delta_0\|_2$ is zero or not. As potential trails have to be short, the correlation is bound to be high. Thus, we are interested to see whether the diffusion layers of a masked cipher allow for zero-correlation approximations.

Key Schedule. This work focuses on the state function of a cipher and considers the (masked) key to be constant. This focus is based on two reasons.

– To create security arguments independent of the used mode of operation. Since in some modes the key input can be public, one cannot rely on entropy coming from the key schedule.
– In practice, the masked key of a block cipher is not frequently re-masked with fresh randomness. Over several queries, the masked key is thus without fresh entropy.

The key is thus labeled a 'good' variable. Depending on the use case, the designer can nevertheless opt to include the key schedule for a more in-depth analysis.

2.3 Boolean Masking and Threshold Implementations

In this section, we recall Boolean masking and threshold implementations as countermeasures against side-channel analysis. We specifically recall threshold implementations since we require the maskings of the S-box in our case studies to be uniform and we need the property of non-completeness to protect against glitches.

Boolean masking, as originally proposed by Goubin and Patarin [23] and Chari *et al.* [11], has become a popular countermeasure against side-channel analysis. Intuitively, each sensitive variable is split in multiple pieces such that the adversary is forced to recombine those, exponentially increasing the noise on the data in the number of pieces. Formally, a secret sharing scheme is used. For Boolean masking, each secret x is split in the variables $\bar{x} = (x^1, x^2, \ldots, x^{s_x})$ such that $x = \sum_{i=1}^{s_x} x^i$ where the sum is taken over a binary finite field K. We call a random Boolean masking of a fixed secret uniform if all sharings of that secret are equally likely.

A masking countermeasure shares each intermediate variable of a primitive such that at no point in time a secret value is directly processed. There are several methods how to achieve this given in the literature. In this work, we focus on the method of threshold implementations as introduced by Nikova *et al.* [33]. A threshold implementation consists of several layers of Boolean functions. Each layer is calculated in one clock cycle and stores its output in registers.

Let $\bar{F}$ be a layer in the threshold implementation corresponding to a part of the circuit $F : \mathbb{F}_2^n \to \mathbb{F}_2^m$. For example, F might be the linear layer of a block cipher. The function $\bar{F} : \mathbb{F}_2^{ns_x} \to \mathbb{F}_2^{ms_y}$, where we assume s_x shares per input bit and s_y shares per output bit, will be called a *sharing* of F. A share of a function is denoted by $F^i : \mathbb{F}_2^{ns_x} \to \mathbb{F}_2^m$, for $i \in \{1, .., s_y\}$. The main properties of threshold implementations are summarized in Definition 2.

Definition 2 (Properties of a threshold implementation [33]). *Let $F : \mathbb{F}_2^n \to \mathbb{F}_2^m$ be a function and $\bar{F} : \mathbb{F}_2^{ns_x} \to \mathbb{F}_2^{ms_y}$ a sharing of F. The sharing $\bar{F}$ is said to be*

1. *correct if $\sum_{i=1}^{s_y} F^i(x^1, \ldots, x^{s_x}) = F(x)$ for all $x \in \mathbb{F}_2^n$ and for all shares $x^1, \ldots, x^{s_x} \in \mathbb{F}_2^n$ such that $\sum_{i=1}^{s_x} x^i = x$,*
2. *non-complete if any component function F^i depends on at most $s_x - 1$ input shares,*
3. *uniform if $\bar{F}$ maps a uniform random sharing of any $x \in \mathbb{F}_2^n$ to a uniform random sharing of $F(x) \in \mathbb{F}_2^m$.*

Recall glitch-extended probes as introduced in Sect. 2.2. Since each component function in a threshold implementation works on a non-complete set of shares and since each function is walled-off by registers, a threshold implementation is secure even in face of glitch effects. The glitch-extended probing security of a threshold implementation has been formally proven by Dhooghe *et al.* [20]. Also we recall from [20, Sect. 4] that every SNI secure gadget is also uniform. Thus, the secure analysis requirement for a uniform masked S-box is achieved by most maskings in the literature.

2.4   Linear Cryptanalysis of Threshold Implementations

As discussed in Sect. 2.2, Theorem 1 allows proving the security of higher-order threshold implementations given an upper bound on the Fourier coefficients of probability distributions of wire values obtained by probing. This section shows how such an upper bound can be obtained using linear cryptanalysis.

For any linear masking scheme, there exists a vector space $\mathbb{V} \subset \mathbb{F}_2^\ell$ of valid sharings of zero. More specifically, an $\mathbb{F}_2$-linear secret sharing scheme is an algorithm that maps a secret $x \in \mathbb{F}_2^n$ to a random element of a corresponding coset of the vector space $\mathbb{V}$. Let $\rho : \mathbb{F}_2^n \to \mathbb{F}_2^\ell$ be a map that sends secrets to their corresponding coset representative. For convenience, we denote $\mathbb{V}_a = a + \mathbb{V}$.

Let $\bar{G}$ be a correct sharing of a function $G : \mathbb{F}_2^n \to \mathbb{F}_2^n$ in the sense of Definition 2. Fix any $x \in \mathbb{F}_2^n$ and let $a = \rho(x)$ and $b = \rho(G(x))$. The correctness property implies that $\bar{G}(\mathbb{V}_a) \subseteq \mathbb{V}_b$. It follows that the restriction $F : \mathbb{V}_a \to \mathbb{V}_b$ of $\bar{G}$ defined by $F(x) = \bar{G}(x)$ is a well defined function.

Linear cryptanalysis is closely related to the propagation of the Fourier transformation of a probability distribution under a function $F : \mathbb{V}_a \to \mathbb{V}_b$. This leads to the notion of correlation matrices due to Daemen *et al.* [13]. The action of F on probability distributions can be described by a linear operator. The coordinate representation of this operator with respect to the standard basis $\{\delta_x\}_{x \in V}$ may be called the *transition matrix* of F. Following [4], the correlation matrix of F is then the same operator expressed with respect to the Fourier basis. The correlation matrix of a sharing can be defined as follows. Note that it only depends on the spaces $\mathbb{V}_a$ and $\mathbb{V}_b$, not on the specific choice of the representatives a and b.

Definition 3 (Correlation matrix). *For a subspace $\mathbb{V} \subseteq \mathbb{F}_2^\ell$, let $F : \mathbb{V}_a \to \mathbb{V}_b$ be a function. The correlation matrix C^F of F is a real $|\mathbb{V}_b| \times |\mathbb{V}_a|$ matrix with coordinates indexed by elements $u, v \in \mathbb{F}_2^n/\mathbb{V}^\perp$ and equal to*

$$C_{v,u}^F = \frac{1}{|\mathbb{V}|} \sum_{x \in \mathbb{V}_a} (-1)^{u^\top x + v^\top F(x)} \, .$$

The relation between Definition 3 and linear cryptanalysis is as follows: the coordinate $C_{v,u}^F$ is equal to the correlation of a linear approximation over F with input mask u and output mask v. That is, $C_{v,u}^F = 2 \Pr[v^\top F(\mathbf{x}) = u^\top \mathbf{x}] - 1$ for $\mathbf{x}$ uniform random on $\mathbb{V}_a$. An important difference with ordinary linear cryptanalysis is that, for shared functions, the masks u and v correspond to equivalence classes. This formalizes the intuitive observation that masks which differ by a vector orthogonal to the space $\mathbb{V}$ lead to identical correlations.

From this point on, we restrict to second-order probing adversaries. The description of the link with linear cryptanalysis presented in [5], is completed by Theorem 2 below. It shows that the coordinates of $\widehat{p}_{\mathbf{z}}$ are entries of the correlation matrix of the state-transformation between the specified probe locations. In Theorem 2, the restriction of $x \in \mathbb{V}_a$ to an index set $I = \{i_1, \ldots, i_m\}$ is denoted by $x_I = (x_{i_1}, \ldots, x_{i_m}) \in \mathbb{F}_2^{|I|}$. This definition depends on the specific choice of the representative a, but the result of Theorem 2 does not.

Theorem 2 ([5], §5.2). *Let $F : \mathbb{V}_a \to \mathbb{V}_b$ be a function with $\mathbb{V} \subset \mathbb{F}_2^\ell$ and $I, J \subset \{1, \ldots, \ell\}$. For $\mathbf{x}$ uniform random on $\mathbb{V}_a$ and $\mathbf{y} = F(\mathbf{x})$, let $\mathbf{z} = (\mathbf{x}_I, \mathbf{y}_J)$. The Fourier transformation of the probability mass function of $\mathbf{z}$ then satisfies*

$$|\widehat{p}_{\mathbf{z}}(u, v)| = |C_{\widetilde{v}, \widetilde{u}}^F|,$$

where $\widetilde{u}, \widetilde{v} \in \mathbb{F}_2^\ell/\mathbb{V}^\perp$ are such that $\widetilde{u}_I = u$, $\widetilde{u}_{[\ell] \setminus I} = 0$, $\widetilde{v}_J = v$ and $\widetilde{v}_{[\ell] \setminus J} = 0$.

Theorem 2 relates the linear approximations of F to $\widehat{p}_{\mathbf{z}}(u)$ and hence provides a method to upper bound $\|\widehat{p}_{\mathbf{z}} - \delta_0\|_2$ based on linear cryptanalysis. Upper bounding the absolute correlations $|C_{\tilde{v},\,\tilde{u}}^F|$ is nontrivial in general. However, the piling-up principle [32,35] can be used to obtain heuristic estimates.

Importantly, Theorem 2 relates to linear cryptanalysis with respect to $\mathbb{V}$ rather than $\mathbb{F}_2^\ell$. The differences are mostly minor, but there is a subtle difference in relation to the important notion of 'activity'. In standard linear cryptanalysis, an S-box is said to be active if its output mask is nonzero. The same definition applies for linear cryptanalysis with respect to $\mathbb{V}$, but one must take into account that the mask is now an element of the quotient space $\mathbb{F}_2^\ell/\mathbb{V}^\perp$. In particular, if the mask corresponding to the shares of a particular bit can be represented by an all-one vector $(1,1,\ldots,1)^\top$, it may be equivalently represented by the zero vector. It is still true that a valid linear approximation for a permutation must have either both input masks equivalent to zero or neither equivalent to zero. More generally, this condition is ensured by any uniform sharing.

3   Analyzing Transition Leakage

This section studies the effect of transition leakage. Consider registers as recalled in Sect. 2.1. When the register input is open to store the incoming value, the new value has to overwrite the so far stored value. If these are different values then the attacker can measure a peak in the power consumption compared to the case when the values are the same – this is called transition leakage. Similar to registers, if a new value different from the wire current value starts propagating through a wire then the power consumption will differ compared to the case when the new and the current value are the same.

As a result, if in a memory cell the element x is erased and instead y is stored, transitions can leak both x and y. We integrate such leakage effects in the probing model following the work by Faust et al. [22]. There the model is described as follows.

"Specific Model for Transitions. For a memory cell m, memory recombinations (aka transitions) can be modeled with specifically 2-extended probes so that probing m allows the adversary to observe any pair of values stored in 2 of its consecutive invocations."

As mentioned above, transition leakage does not only occur in memory elements. Thus, we extend the description such that the extended leakage is viewed in any gate or wire.

The work by Ishai et al. [27] and the publications that followed considered a circuit model that represents a deterministic circuit as a directed acyclic graph whose vertices are combinatorial gates and its edges are wires carrying elements from a finite field. However such a simplification of the circuit model does not take into account the circuit topology. While the leakage of glitches does not depend on the circuit architecture/topology, for the transitions and the wire coupling models the leakage is mainly influenced by the circuit's architecture. As a result, we study circuits with loops and a notion of time and consider particular architectures when discussing the side-channel security of symmetric primitives.

Finally, we consider the combined effect of glitches and transition leakage. According to Faust *et al.* [22] probing a memory gate is equivalent to probe the sole input (i.e. the wire) to it which can be considered also as output of the particular simple logic which ends up with the considered memory gate. In that regard, leakage caused by glitches might seem stronger than the leakage caused by transitions. However, in practice the two leakages can manifest differently in the time interval representing a single cycle, namely the glitches and the logic transitions will occur in the beginning while the memory transition will occur only at the end. As illustrated by Faust *et al.*, there could be a time window between the computational and the storage phases.

We apply the extended probing model to arbitrary glitch-extended probing secure masking of several architectures of PRESENT, AES, and ASCON to investigate how to best protect the masked primitives. In our analysis we consider a black box masking of the S-box to make the analysis more general. We just assume the linear layers are masked share-wise and that the masked S-boxes do not share inputs such as recycled randomness.

3.1 PRESENT

We recall the PRESENT cipher from the work of Bogdanov *et al.* [7]. The input to PRESENT is a 64-bit plaintext m. Each round comprises an XOR with the round key, a substitution layer, and a permutation layer. The substitution layer consists of 16 applications of a four-bit cubic S-box. The permutation layer of PRESENT is a bit permutation which is depicted in Fig. 1. The following arguments are also applicable to the GIFT cipher [1].

Round-Based Architectures Require Extra Protection. We first consider a glitch-extended probing secure masking (such as a threshold implementation) in a round-based architecture. In such an architecture each masked S-box in the round function is implemented separately on the device. When an adversary places a transition-extended probe in an S-box of a round-based architecture, it can view the computation of the same implemented S-box in two consecutive rounds. In this architecture, the diffusion layer of PRESENT allows for some weak points concerning transition leakage. More specifically, bits $0, 21, 42$ and 63 are mapped to the same position. As a result, transition leakage from the $0, 5, 10$ or 15th masked S-box could reveal information. An example activity pattern is indicated in dotted blue in Fig. 1. The weakness can be resolved by re-masking the bits which remain fixed through the diffusion layer. This randomness can be re-used every round and can be the same over the bits $0, 21, 42$ and 63. For the previously mentioned sharing of the S-box this countermeasure would cost a total of two random bits for the entire masked cipher.

So far we assumed the shared S-box $\bar{S}$ was implemented as a rolled-out circuit on the device. However, the typical threshold implementation of the PRESENT S-box consists of two degree two maps $\bar{G}$, this sharing is given in Appendix A. A designer could implement $\bar{G}$ and evaluate it twice to compute an S-box. We denote the two parts of the shared S-box by $\bar{S}_1$ and $\bar{S}_2$. If an adversary uses a transition-extended probe on the shared S-box it can view the computation of both $\bar{S}_1$ and $\bar{S}_2$. This is depicted in blue in Fig. 2.

We give an example that the above explained weakness can constitute a probing attack for a particular sharing of the S-box. In particular, we consider the blue activity pattern from Fig. 2. Considering the sharing of the S-box from Appendix A. Consider, for a secret x, the shares x^1, x^2, x^3 such that $\sum_{i=1}^{3} x^i = x$. An adversary placing a glitch and transition-extended probe $\mathcal{P}$ in the first component of $\bar{S}_1(\bar{x}, \bar{y}, \bar{z}, \bar{w})$ is given back the shares $x^1, y^1, y^2, z^1, z^2, w^1$, and w^2. However, from the second part of the shared S-box $\bar{S}_2$ the adversary views the input values (equivalently $\bar{S}_1$'s output values)

$$\bar{S}_1^1 = w^1 + x^1 y^1 + x^1 y^2 + x^2 y^1,$$
$$\bar{S}_1^2 = w^2 + x^2 y^2 + x^2 y^3 + x^3 y^2.$$

Thus, $\mathcal{P} = \{\bar{S}_1^1, \bar{S}_1^2, x^1, y^1, y^2, z^1, z^2, w^1, w^2\}$. Consider random secrets x, y, z, w, then we find that

$$I(x; \mathcal{P}) = H(x) - H(x|\mathcal{P}) \neq 0,$$

with I the mutual information and H the Shannon entropy. In other words, a glitch- and transition-extended probing adversary can break the design.

As a conclusion, a straightforward round-based architecture of PRESENT could be vulnerable to transition leakage and thus extra costs would be required to secure the architecture.

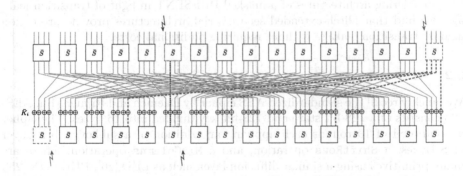

Fig. 1. An activity pattern caused by transition leakage in PRESENT. In dotted blue lines, we find harmful transition leakage using a round-based architecture. In dashed red lines, we find no such leakage using a serial architecture. (Color figure online)

Serial Architectures are Secure. As a second example, we consider a glitch-extended probing secure masking in an S-box serial architecture. In this architecture only one shared S-box is implemented on the device and each S-box in the cipher is computed in series. Following Fig. 1, the architecture computes the S-boxes from left to right. Transition leakage from such a design occurs either

Fig. 2. Transition leakage in the calculation of the shared S-box divided in $\bar{S}_1$ and $\bar{S}_2$. The dotted blue lines denote leakage in a round-based architecture. The dashed red lines denote leakage in a serial architecture. (Color figure online)

between two S-boxes in the same round or between the last and first S-box of two consecutive rounds. Assuming the shared S-boxes are uniform, the former case never constitutes a weakness. The latter case is harmless thanks to the linear layer of PRESENT as indicated in red in Fig. 1. We see, no matter which input or output mask is chosen, the resulting hull will always be a zero-correlation linear approximation. Thus, no extra precautions need to be made to ensure security against transition leakage.

In case the shared S-box is calculated over two cycles using the same resources, the architecture can be secured against transition leakage if all $\bar{S}_1$ are first calculated from left to right and before calculating the $\bar{S}_2$. A transition-extended probe either only views two separate $\bar{S}_1$ (similarly $\bar{S}_2$) in the same cycle or it views the parts as depicted in red in Fig. 2. It is clear that in no case the adversary can break the masking using transition leakage.

Considering architectures of a masked PRESENT in light of transition leakage, we find that glitch-extended secure serial architectures provide protection against transition leakage without requiring additional costs.

3.2   AES

We quickly recall the standardized AES cipher by Daemen and Rijmen [14]. AES-128 consists of a 128-bit state and 128-bit key divided into 16 bytes. The cipher is composed of 10 rounds each applying an addition of a subkey, a bricklayer of S-Boxes, a `ShiftRows` operation, and a `MixColumns` operation. There are many primitives using a similar diffusion layer such as LED [26], PHOTON [25], PRINCE [8], SKINNY [2], etc. The security analysis considered here applies to all these primitives.

Every Architecture Requires Extra Protection. For a glitch-extended probing secure AES, we find that architectures are vulnerable against transition leakage in the application of the `MixColumns` operation. First, notice that no matter the architecture, transition leakage from the computation of an S-box is never usable for an adversary due to the branch number of the `MixColumns`. An example of such an activity pattern is depicted in Fig. 3. However, during the computation of the `MixColumns` and due to the effect of glitches, the adversary can view the input of the operation and place a mask such that only one output byte is active. This active byte can only shift over the state, causing the adversary to also observe the computation of the following MixColumns due to transition leakages. An activity pattern for a round-based architecture is shown in Fig. 4. Even by changing the order of the MixColumns harmful activity patterns can always be found.

One can prevent this leakage by re-masking some cells (for example, the top row for the round-based architecture) of the AES state. This randomness cost is low as the same randomness can be used for every round and for every cell. More specifically, considering a two-shared threshold implementation, a total of eight random bits are needed to prevent any transition leakage from occurring.

Another countermeasure is based on the verification of the Linear Approximation Table (LAT) of the shared AES S-box using the definitions from Sect. 2.4. More specifically, note that a masking of a linear operation works share-wise. As a result, a transition-extended probe on the AES diffusion layer only views one share each of two MixColumns operations and thus one input and one output share of the shared S-box. Given an s-sharing of the AES S-box $\bar{S}$ and $\mathbb{V} = \bigoplus_{i=1}^{s} \mathbb{V}^i$ such that each mask $u \in \mathbb{F}_2^{8s}/\mathbb{V}^\perp$ can be decomposed in $(u^1, ..., u^s)$ with $u^i \in \mathbb{F}_2^8/(\mathbb{V}^i)^\perp$ then the linear approximation between the observed values is only harmful if

$$\forall \alpha, \beta \in \mathbb{F}_2^{8s}/\mathbb{V}^\perp : \ C_{\alpha,\beta}^{\bar{S}} = 0 \text{ when } \mathrm{wt}(\alpha) = 1, \mathrm{wt}(\beta) = 1.$$

In words, the sharing is secure if the masked S-box has nontrivial diffusion between the shares. A sharing using randomness, for example the sharing of the AES S-box by De Cnudde et al. [17], typically has this property. Currently there exists no uniform sharing of the AES S-box and thus every AES S-box sharing (except those using changing of the guards as explained later) uses randomness. However, applying the above property to sharings of primitives such as LED or PRINCE could be interesting future work.

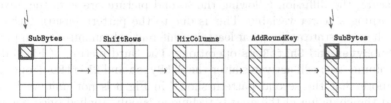

Fig. 3. Activity patterns between the top left S-boxes of rounds i and $i + 1$ of a masked AES. The figure denotes in blue what the adversary can observe and hatched cells denote active cells. (Color figure online)

Using Changing of the Guards. Currently, the AES S-box has no known uniform sharing. As a result, designers typically use the changing of the guards technique

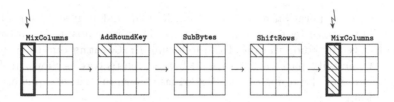

Fig. 4. An activity pattern caused by transition leakage following the AES diffusion layers. The figure denotes in blue what the adversary can observe and hatched cells denote active cells. (Color figure online)

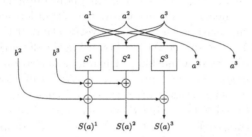

Fig. 5. The "Changing of the Guards" method to make a sharing uniform.

by Daemen [12] to ensure uniformity. The technique adds input shares of one S-box to the output of another in order to embed the sharing in a permutation similar to the Feistel construction. The method is depicted in Fig. 5. Since the technique chains S-boxes, extra diffusion is added to the round function. A depiction of such an example is given in the left picture of Fig. 6. The figure shows which inputs (start of an arrow) are used to "re-mask" a shared S-box (end of an arrow). When this technique is used with care, one might use it to strengthen the masking against transition leakage. For example, while the diffusion following the left picture still allows for harmful transition leakage in a round-based architecture, the diffusion following the second picture prevents the adversary from learning a secret variable. This is due to the pattern ensuring that each active cell in the state activates at least one different column after the application of the SubBytes and ShiftRows operations. The third picture of Fig. 6 depicts which column each cell activates after the SubBytes and ShiftRows operations.

We note that the second pattern shown in Fig. 6 is not unique. It is also assumed the changing of the guards technique is only applied once per round. If it is applied multiple times (such as in the work by Wegener *et al.* [36] or by Sugawara [34]), different patterns should be used to secure the cipher against transition leakage.

3.3   ASCON

ASCON [21] consists of a mode of operation which uses a specific permutation. In this work, we focus on the permutation. The substitution layer is the parallel

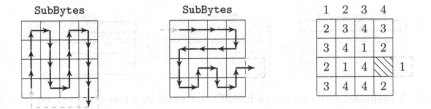

Fig. 6. Two example diffusion patterns using the changing of the guards technique. In gray we denote the added extra cells. The left pattern combined with the AES diffusion layers is vulnerable to transition leakage, the right provides resistance. The third figure shows the activation of columns of the second pattern combined with ShiftRows.

column-wise application of 64 5-bit S-boxes which are an affine transformation of the χ mapping of Keccak [3]. These S-boxes have linear branch number three. The linear layer consists of five row-wise applications of a linear function Σ. Each Σ function has linear branch number four and uses different rotation values depending on the row to optimize diffusion over several rounds.

Every Architecture is Secure. Consider again an arbitrary glitch-extended probing secure masking of ASCON. We investigate whether we can transform this masking to be transition-extended probing secure. First, while the S-box of ASCON has a nontrivial linear branch number, its sharing might not have a similar property. Denoting the ASCON S-box by S. While S has a correlation zero transition between its first input bit x and first output bit z, the sharing of S can allow for such a transition. Meaning that one can place a nontrivial mask on the sharing of x and on the sharing of z and still find nonzero correlation. The sharing of the S-box given in Appendix B has been verified to still have a nontrivial linear branch number over the bits. More specifically, given that $\mathbb{V} = \bigoplus_{i=1}^{5} \mathbb{V}_i$ such that each mask $u \in \mathbb{F}_2^{20}/\mathbb{V}^\perp$ can be decomposed in $(u_1, u_2, u_3, u_4, u_5)$ with $u_i \in \mathbb{F}_2^4/(\mathbb{V}_i)^\perp$ then

$$\min_{\alpha,\beta\in\mathbb{F}_2^{20}/\mathbb{V}^\perp, C_{\alpha,\beta}^S \neq 0} \{wt(\alpha) + wt(\beta)\} = 3 \,.$$

By adding linear correction terms, we can cycle through other non-complete sharings of the ASCON S-box. Via this search method we found sharings which were uniform but did not attain the above property.

In case the sharing of the ASCON S-box has a nontrivial branch number, a round-based implementation is automatically secure against any harmful transition leakage. A typical simplified activity pattern is shown in Fig. 7. Moreover, the same applies for other architectures like a bit-serial implementation. In other words, except for some trivial share-serial approaches, the round function of ASCON requires no additional care to prevent any harmful transition leakage.

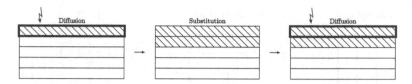

Fig. 7. A simplified activity pattern in ASCON caused by a transition-extended probe.

4   Analyzing Coupling Leakage

We consider a leakage effect originating from coupling capacitors between circuit wires, and between circuit wires and ground which are influenced by the switching activity on that wire causing recombinations of the wire values. Effectively when observing leakage from one wire, one can observe leakage from nearby coupled wires. De Cnudde *et al.* [15] has shown that the security of masked hardware implementations can be affected due to coupling effects. These effects are integrated into the probing model following the work by Faust *et al.* [22].

"**Specific Model for Couplings.** For any set of adjacent wires $\{w_1, ..., w_d\}$, routing recombinations (aka couplings) can be modeled with c-extended probes so that probing one wire w_i allows the adversary to observe c wires adjacent to w_i."

Defending against the above model is not straightforward as two wires carrying different shares of a secret can be coupled. The work by De Cnudde *et al.* [16] discusses three potential solutions to "separate" logic.

- To perform sequential operations instead of parallelism where the implementation processes a non-complete set of shares at each clock cycle. While this provides security this reduces the throughput and avoids making use of the full parallelism feature of hardware.
- Via the use of embedded voltage regulators (VRM) inside the chip, which are already used in commercial smart cards. However, it remains unclear whether electromagnetic signals exhibit potential issues.
- Via the chip having separate Vdd lines to supply functions associated to each share independently. However, it is still an open problem how to supply nonlinear functions which operate on sets of shares and prove the security of the countermeasure.

In this work, we assume one of the above countermeasures has been applied to the masking. To that end, we assume the masking is "domain non-complete" meaning that each domain processes only a non-complete set of shares per cycle. An example is shown in Fig. 8. As a result, a coupling-extended probe (for any c in the above definition) does not yield all the shares of a secret. This non-completeness property alone is sufficient to protect an implementation against coupling-extended probes. However, a more detailed security analysis is needed when combining multiple leakage effects together.

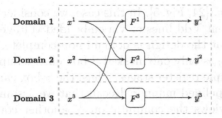

Fig. 8. Separation into domains of a layer of masked Boolean functions.

5   Analyzing Glitches, Transitions, and Couplings

For the final analysis, we study maskings which are secure against all combined effects described by Faust *et al.* [22], *i.e.* glitches, transitions, and coupling leakage. Considering coupling effects, we study the effect when $c = 1$ following the definition above. That means the adversary is capable of observing the probed wire along with one coupled wire. Recall that we consider that a coupling-extended probe can not view all shares of a secret in one cycle. Combining coupling effects with glitches and transitions, using a single probe, the adversary observes all inputs to the probed wire, the previous values which flowed through those resources, and glitches and transition leakage from a coupled operation. We revisit the case studies from Sect. 3.

5.1   PRESENT: Serial Architecture

We revisit the masking of PRESENT from Sect. 3.1. More specifically, we consider a glitch-extended probing secure masking in an S-box serial architecture which we showed was secure against the combined effect of glitches and transitions. We adapt the architecture to work share-serial meaning that each cycle one share of one S-box (or quadratic function in the S-box) is calculated. In particular, such an architecture is domain non-complete.

In this case, glitch effects already include the effect of couplings as only one operation per cycle is calculated. When the architecture would calculate two shares of the same S-box consecutively, transitions could leak the input secret of the S-box. Instead, we interleave computation on shares of a secret with the computation of other parts of the state. Thus, the architecture would first calculate the ith share of each S-box before calculating a $(i + 1)^{\text{th}}$ share. This secures from harmful transition leakage. The activity patterns are the same as before, given in red in Fig. 1.

5.2   AES: Serial Architecture

We consider a glitch-extended probing secure masking in a serial architecture where only one S-box and MixColumns is implemented. This is a popular architecture for maskings, examples can be found in the works by De Meyer *et al.* [18,

Fig. 6] and Gross *et al.* [24, Fig. 5]. In this case, we consider that a domain separation through different Vdd lines or via embedded voltage regulators has been implemented such that the design is domain non-complete.

Even though there is only one masked S-box on the implementation, it typically consists of multiple register stages. Thus, the S-box can compute on several bytes at once in a pipelined manner. Recall that we assume that $c = 1$, thus a probe on an S-box views the computation of another coupled S-box. Due to transition leakage, the adversary can view the two S-boxes over two consecutive cycles. Due to the MixColumns having branch number five, this leakage can never reveal a secret. However, there is still leakage from the calculation of the MixColumns as noted in Sect. 3.2. Finally, there can be coupling leakage between the MixColumns and an S-box (from a different column). However, these cases do not add extra harmful activity patterns. Thus, as explained in Sect. 3.2, we only require adding one cell of extra randomness to secure against the combined effect of glitches, transitions, and couplings.

5.3   ASCON: Round-Based Architecture

Finally, we consider a glitch-extended probing secure masking with a round-based architecture for ASCON. Again, we consider the case where $c = 1$ meaning that a probe can observe an additional operation in that cycle and we consider domain non-complete maskings where there is some countermeasure ensuring coupling leakage alone does not reveal all shares of a secret.

Due to the combined effect of transitions and couplings, a probed S-box gives information on two S-boxes over two consecutive rounds. Previously, we argued ASCON was secure when probing an S-box due to the nontrivial branch number of the linear layer. This argument no longer holds as the linear layer only has branch number four. However, the case remains secure as the layer does not allow for transitions of two active input bits to two active output bits. This can be verified on sight from the equations of the Σ function:

$$\Sigma_{\alpha,\beta}(x) = x \oplus (x \ggg \alpha) \oplus (x \ggg \beta),$$

with $\ggg$ the right circular shift and $\alpha, \beta \in \mathbb{N}$ constants specific for ASCON.

When the adversary probes the linear layer, it can potentially activate two input and two output bits of a shared S-box. The diffusion of the S-box is not sufficient to prevent harmful leakage. However, we observe that the probe returns bits from the same share, e.g. both from the first share of the input and first share of the output. Thus, one can protect the implementation when the shared S-box $\bar{S}$ has the following property. Given an s-sharing $\bar{S}$ and $\mathbb{V} = \bigoplus_{i=1}^{s} \mathbb{V}^i$ such that each mask $u \in \mathbb{F}_2^{5s}/\mathbb{V}^\perp$ can be decomposed in $(u^1, ..., u^s)$ with $u^i \in \mathbb{F}_2^5/(\mathbb{V}^i)^\perp$ then for $i \in \{1, ..., s\}$

$$\forall \alpha, \beta \in \mathbb{F}_2^{5s}/\mathbb{V}^\perp \ : \ C_{\alpha,\beta}^{\bar{S}} = 0 \text{ when } \alpha = (0, ..., \alpha^i, ..., 0), \beta = (0, ..., \beta^i, ..., 0).$$

A similar property was explored in Sect. 3.2 on diffusion between shares. Since the S-box is quadratic, one can easily find non-complete sharings of the entire

S-box. This non-completeness can be used to argue that the ith share of the input and output of the S-box do not reveal any secret information. An example sharing with the above property is given in Appendix B. For example, the first bit of the second output share is

$$\chi_1^2 = x_1^2 + x_3^2 + (x_2^2 + x_2^3 + x_2^4)(x_3^2 + x_3^3 + x_3^4).$$

Together with the second input shares x_i^2 for $i \in \{1, 2, 3, 4, 5\}$, one always misses the first input shares x_i^1 to retrieve an input secret.

6 Conclusion

This work discussed the security of masked symmetric primitives against the combined leakage effects of glitches, transitions, and couplings. This was done using the standard tools from linear cryptanalysis and on case studies of symmetric primitives. The case studies were made considering black box glitch-extended probing secure maskings. Moreover, we covered case studies on PRESENT, AES, and ASCON to show our analysis is applicable to a wide range of primitives.

Interesting future work would be transform our analysis method (which currently is only done by hand) into a tool which can verify netlists on potential transition leakage using the linear cryptanalytic properties of basic gates such as ANDs and XORs. We also did not investigate methods to analyze transition leakage when re-using randomness between S-boxes or transition leakage inside a single S-box. However, for such cases, brute-force verification is possible allowing for extensions of existing tools such as SILVER [28]. Finally, we noted a lack of theory concerning correlation matrices of masked functions together with interesting examples which indicate that bounds on the maximum absolute correlation or branch number of a masking might be difficult to find. More research on this topic could improve the security and efficiency of masked designs.

Acknowledgements. I thank Vincent Rijmen, Svetla Nikova, Venci Nikov, Tim Beyne, and Adrián ranea for the interesting discussions and their advice. Siemen Dhooghe is supported by a PhD Fellowship from the Research Foundation – Flanders (FWO).

A   Three Sharing of the PRESENT S-Box

This appendix provides a decomposition of the PRESENT S-box and a three sharing of the S-box. We denote by (x, y, z, w) the input nibble from most significant to least significant bit.

Following the work by Kutzner et al. [30], the PRESENT S-box S can be decomposed as follows

$$S(x, y, z, w) = B'(G(G(G(C'(x, y, z, w) + d)) + e).$$

In the above, the nonlinear function $G(x, y, z, w)$ is given as

$$G_1 = x + yz + yw \qquad G_2 = w + xy \qquad G_3 = y \qquad G_4 = z + yw.$$

When implemented, the above function is computed over two register stages. We denote $S_1(x, y, z, w) = G(C'(x, y, z, w) + d)$ and $S_2(x, y, z, w) = B'(G(x, y, z, w) + e)$ for each stage.

This permutation G is shared using a direct balanced sharing. More specifically, for each share $i \in \{1, 2, 3\}$

$$
\begin{aligned}
G_1^i &= x^i + y^i z^i + y^i z^{i+1} + y^{i+1} z^i + y^i w^i + y^i w^{i+1} + y^{i+1} w^i, \\
G_2^i &= w^i + x^i y^i + x^i y^{i+1} + x^{i+1} y^i, \\
G_3^i &= y^i, \\
G_4^i &= z^i + y^i w^i + y^i w^{i+1} + y^{i+1} w^i,
\end{aligned}
$$

where the convention is used that superscripts wrap around at three. The linear layers are masked share-wise.

B   Uniform Sharing of the ASCON S-Box

This appendix provides a uniform four-sharing of the ASCON S-box. Recall that the ASCON S-box is affine equivalent to the Keccak S-box. More specifically, for the Keccak S-box χ and the ASCON S-box S we have that

$$S(x) = B(\chi(B(x))) + c,$$

with A, B linear transformations and c a constant.

Denoting the five input bits by $\{x_1, x_2, x_3, x_4, x_5\}$ going from least significant to most significant bit. A uniform sharing of the Keccak S-box χ using four shares was given by Bilgin et $al.$ [6]. For $i = 1, 2, 3, 5$ we have

$$
\begin{aligned}
\chi_i^1 &= x_i^1 + x_{i+2}^1, \\
\chi_i^2 &= x_i^2 + x_{i+2}^2 + (x_{i+1}^2 + x_{i+1}^3 + x_{i+1}^4)(x_{i+2}^2 + x_{i+2}^3 + x_{i+2}^4), \\
\chi_i^3 &= x_i^3 + x_{i+2}^3 + x_{i+1}^1(x_{i+2}^3 + x_{i+2}^4) + x_{i+2}^1(x_{i+1}^3 + x_{i+1}^4) + x_{i+1}^1 x_{i+2}^1, \\
\chi_i^4 &= x_i^4 + x_{i+2}^4 + x_{i+1}^1 x_{i+2}^2 + x_{i+2}^1 x_{i+1}^2,
\end{aligned}
$$

where the convention is used that subscripts wrap around at five. For the remaining fourth coordinate function we have

$$
\begin{aligned}
\chi_4^1 &= x_4^1. \\
\chi_4^2 &= x_4^2 + x_1^2 + x_1^3 + x_1^4 + (x_5^2 + x_5^3 + x_5^4)(x_1^2 + x_1^3 + x_1^4), \\
\chi_4^3 &= x_4^3 + x_1^1 + x_5^1(x_1^3 + x_1^4) + x_1^1(x_5^3 + x_5^4) + x_1^1 x_5^1, \\
\chi_4^4 &= x_4^4 + x_5^1 x_1^2 + x_1^1 x_5^2,
\end{aligned}
$$

References

1. Banik, S., Pandey, S.K., Peyrin, T., Sasaki, Yu., Sim, S.M., Todo, Y.: GIFT: a small present - towards reaching the limit of lightweight encryption. In: Fischer, W., Homma, N. (eds.) CHES 2017. LNCS, vol. 10529, pp. 321–345. Springer, Cham (2017). https://doi.org/10.1007/978-3-319-66787-4_16

2. Beierle, C., et al.: The SKINNY family of block ciphers and its low-latency variant MANTIS. In: Robshaw, M., Katz, J. (eds.) CRYPTO 2016, Part II. LNCS, vol. 9815, pp. 123–153. Springer, Heidelberg (2016). https://doi.org/10.1007/978-3-662-53008-5_5

3. Bertoni, G., Daemen, J., Peeters, M., Van Assche, G.: The Keccak reference. http://keccak.noekeon.org/

4. Beyne, T.: Block cipher invariants as eigenvectors of correlation matrices. In: Peyrin, T., Galbraith, S. (eds.) ASIACRYPT 2018, Part I. LNCS, vol. 11272, pp. 3–31. Springer, Cham (2018). https://doi.org/10.1007/978-3-030-03326-2_1

5. Beyne, T., Dhooghe, S., Zhang, Z.: Cryptanalysis of masked ciphers: a not so random idea. In: Moriai, S., Wang, H. (eds.) ASIACRYPT 2020, Part I. LNCS, vol. 12491, pp. 817–850. Springer, Cham (2020). https://doi.org/10.1007/978-3-030-64837-4_27

6. Bilgin, B., Daemen, J., Nikov, V., Nikova, S., Rijmen, V., Van Assche, G.: Efficient and first-order DPA resistant implementations of Keccak. In: Francillon, A., Rohatgi, P. (eds.) CARDIS 2013. LNCS, vol. 8419, pp. 187–199. Springer, Cham (2014). https://doi.org/10.1007/978-3-319-08302-5_13

7. Bogdanov, A., et al.: PRESENT: an ultra-lightweight block cipher. In: Paillier, P., Verbauwhede, I. (eds.) CHES 2007. LNCS, vol. 4727, pp. 450–466. Springer, Heidelberg (2007). https://doi.org/10.1007/978-3-540-74735-2_31

8. Borghoff, J., et al.: PRINCE – a low-latency block cipher for pervasive computing applications - extended abstract. In: Wang, X., Sako, K. (eds.) ASIACRYPT 2012. LNCS, vol. 7658, pp. 208–225. Springer, Heidelberg (2012). https://doi.org/10.1007/978-3-642-34961-4_14

9. Cassiers, G., Standaert, F.: Trivially and efficiently composing masked gadgets with probe isolating non-interference. IEEE Trans. Inf. Forensics Secur. **15**, 2542–2555 (2020)

10. Cassiers, G., Standaert, F.: Provably secure hardware masking in the transition- and glitch-robust probing model: Better safe than sorry. IACR Trans. Cryptogr. Hardw. Embed. Syst. **2021**(2), 136–158 (2021). https://doi.org/10.46586/tches.v2021.i2.136-158

11. Chari, S., Jutla, C.S., Rao, J.R., Rohatgi, P.: Towards sound approaches to counteract power-analysis attacks. In: Wiener, M. (ed.) CRYPTO 1999. LNCS, vol. 1666, pp. 398–412. Springer, Heidelberg (1999). https://doi.org/10.1007/3-540-48405-1_26

12. Daemen, J.: Changing of the guards: a simple and efficient method for achieving uniformity in threshold sharing. In: Fischer, W., Homma, N. (eds.) CHES 2017. LNCS, vol. 10529, pp. 137–153. Springer, Cham (2017). https://doi.org/10.1007/978-3-319-66787-4_7

13. Daemen, J., Govaerts, R., Vandewalle, J.: Correlation matrices. In: Preneel, B. (ed.) FSE 1994. LNCS, vol. 1008, pp. 275–285. Springer, Heidelberg (1995). https://doi.org/10.1007/3-540-60590-8_21

14. Daemen, J., Rijmen, V.: Advanced Encryption Standard (AES). National Institute of Standards and Technology (NIST), FIPS PUB 197, U.S. Department of Commerce, November 2001

15. De Cnudde, T., Bilgin, B., Gierlichs, B., Nikov, V., Nikova, S., Rijmen, V.: Does coupling affect the security of masked implementations? In: Guilley, S. (ed.) COSADE 2017. LNCS, vol. 10348, pp. 1–18. Springer, Cham (2017). https://doi.org/10.1007/978-3-319-64647-3_1

16. De Cnudde, T., Ender, M., Moradi, A.: Hardware masking, revisited. IACR TCHES **2018**(2), 123–148 (2018). https://doi.org/10.13154/tches.v2018.i2.123-148. https://tches.iacr.org/index.php/TCHES/article/view/877

17. De Cnudde, T., Reparaz, O., Bilgin, B., Nikova, S., Nikov, V., Rijmen, V.: Masking AES with d+1 shares in hardware. In: Gierlichs, B., Poschmann, A.Y. (eds.) CHES 2016. LNCS, vol. 9813, pp. 194–212. Springer, Heidelberg (2016). https://doi.org/10.1007/978-3-662-53140-2_10

18. De Meyer, L., Reparaz, O., Bilgin, B.: Multiplicative masking for AES in hardware. IACR TCHES **2018**(3), 431–468 (2018). https://doi.org/10.13154/tches.v2018.i3.431-468. https://tches.iacr.org/index.php/TCHES/article/view/7282

19. Dhooghe, S., Nikova, S.: Let's tessellate: tiling for security against advanced probe and fault adversaries. IACR Cryptol. ePrint Arch. **2020**, 1146 (2020). https://eprint.iacr.org/2020/1146

20. Dhooghe, S., Nikova, S., Rijmen, V.: Threshold implementations in the robust probing model. In: Bilgin, B., Petkova-Nikova, S., Rijmen, V. (eds.) Proceedings of ACM Workshop on Theory of Implementation Security Workshop, TIS@CCS 2019, London, UK, 11 November 2019, pp. 30–37. ACM (2019). https://doi.org/10.1145/3338467.3358949

21. Dobraunig, C., Eichlseder, M., Mendel, F., Schläffer, M.: ASCON v1.2. https://ascon.iaik.tugraz.at/files/asconv12-nist.pdf

22. Faust, S., Grosso, V., Pozo, S.M.D., Paglialonga, C., Standaert, F.X.: Composable masking schemes in the presence of physical defaults & the robust probing model. IACR TCHES **2018**(3), 89–120 (2018). https://doi.org/10.13154/tches.v2018.i3.89-120. https://tches.iacr.org/index.php/TCHES/article/view/7270

23. Goubin, L., Patarin, J.: DES and differential power analysis (the "duplication" method). In: Koç, Ç.K., Paar, C. (eds.) CHES 1999. LNCS, vol. 1717, pp. 158–172. Springer, Heidelberg (1999). https://doi.org/10.1007/3-540-48059-5_15

24. Groß, H., Mangard, S., Korak, T.: Domain-oriented masking: compact masked hardware implementations with arbitrary protection order. In: Bilgin, B., Nikova, S., Rijmen, V. (eds.) Proceedings of the ACM Workshop on Theory of Implementation Security, TIS@CCS 2016 Vienna, Austria, October 2016, p. 3. ACM (2016). https://doi.org/10.1145/2996366.2996426

25. Guo, J., Peyrin, T., Poschmann, A.: The PHOTON family of lightweight hash functions. In: Rogaway, P. (ed.) CRYPTO 2011. LNCS, vol. 6841, pp. 222–239. Springer, Heidelberg (2011). https://doi.org/10.1007/978-3-642-22792-9_13

26. Guo, J., Peyrin, T., Poschmann, A., Robshaw, M.: The LED block cipher. In: Preneel, B., Takagi, T. (eds.) CHES 2011. LNCS, vol. 6917, pp. 326–341. Springer, Heidelberg (2011). https://doi.org/10.1007/978-3-642-23951-9_22

27. Ishai, Y., Sahai, A., Wagner, D.: Private circuits: securing hardware against probing attacks. In: Boneh, D. (ed.) CRYPTO 2003. LNCS, vol. 2729, pp. 463–481. Springer, Heidelberg (2003). https://doi.org/10.1007/978-3-540-45146-4_27

28. Knichel, D., Sasdrich, P., Moradi, A.: SILVER – statistical independence and leakage verification. In: Moriai, S., Wang, H. (eds.) ASIACRYPT 2020, Part I. LNCS, vol. 12491, pp. 787–816. Springer, Cham (2020). https://doi.org/10.1007/978-3-030-64837-4_26

29. Kocher, P., Jaffe, J., Jun, B.: Differential power analysis. In: Wiener, M. (ed.) CRYPTO 1999. LNCS, vol. 1666, pp. 388–397. Springer, Heidelberg (1999). https://doi.org/10.1007/3-540-48405-1_25

30. Kutzner, S., Nguyen, P.H., Poschmann, A., Wang, H.: On 3-share threshold implementations for 4-Bit S-boxes. In: Prouff, E. (ed.) COSADE 2013. LNCS, vol. 7864, pp. 99–113. Springer, Heidelberg (2013). https://doi.org/10.1007/978-3-642-40026-1_7

31. Mangard, S., Pramstaller, N., Oswald, E.: Successfully attacking masked AES hardware implementations. In: Rao, J.R., Sunar, B. (eds.) CHES 2005. LNCS, vol. 3659, pp. 157–171. Springer, Heidelberg (2005). https://doi.org/10.1007/11545262_12

32. Matsui, M.: Linear cryptanalysis method for DES cipher. In: Helleseth, T. (ed.) EUROCRYPT 1993. LNCS, vol. 765, pp. 386–397. Springer, Heidelberg (1994). https://doi.org/10.1007/3-540-48285-7_33

33. Nikova, S., Rechberger, C., Rijmen, V.: Threshold implementations against side-channel attacks and glitches. In: Ning, P., Qing, S., Li, N. (eds.) ICICS 2006. LNCS, vol. 4307, pp. 529–545. Springer, Heidelberg (2006). https://doi.org/10.1007/11935308_38

34. Sugawara, T.: 3-share threshold implementation of AES S-box without fresh randomness. IACR TCHES 2019(1), 123–145 (2018). https://doi.org/10.13154/tches.v2019.i1.123-145. https://tches.iacr.org/index.php/TCHES/article/view/7336

35. Tardy-Corfdir, A., Gilbert, H.: A known plaintext attack of FEAL-4 and FEAL-6. In: Feigenbaum, J. (ed.) CRYPTO 1991. LNCS, vol. 576, pp. 172–182. Springer, Heidelberg (1992). https://doi.org/10.1007/3-540-46766-1_12

36. Wegener, F., Moradi, A.: A first-order SCA resistant AES without fresh randomness. In: Fan, J., Gierlichs, B. (eds.) COSADE 2018. LNCS, vol. 10815, pp. 245–262. Springer, Cham (2018). https://doi.org/10.1007/978-3-319-89641-0_14

A Lightweight Implementation of Saber Resistant Against Side-Channel Attacks

Abubakr Abdulgadir[✉], Kamyar Mohajerani, Viet Ba Dang, Jens-Peter Kaps, and Kris Gaj

Cryptographic Engineering Research Group, George Mason University, Fairfax, VA, USA
{aabdulga,mmohajer,vdang6,jkaps,kgaj}@gmu.edu

Abstract. The field of post-quantum cryptography aims to develop and analyze algorithms that can withstand classical and quantum cryptanalysis. The NIST PQC standardization process, now in its third round, specifies ease of protection against side-channel analysis as an important selection criterion. In this work, we develop and validate a masked hardware implementation of Saber key encapsulation mechanism, a third-round NIST PQC finalist. We first design a baseline lightweight hardware architecture of Saber and then apply side-channel countermeasures. Our protected hardware implementation is significantly faster than previously reported protected software and software/hardware co-design implementations. Additionally, applying side-channel countermeasures to our baseline design incurs approximately 2.9× and 1.4× penalty in terms of the number of LUTs and latency, respectively, in modern FPGAs.

Keywords: Post-quantum cryptography · Lattice-based · Key encapsulation mechanism · Hardware · FPGA · Side-channel analysis

1 Introduction

The accelerating development of post-quantum computing threatens the security of our current public-key infrastructure, based on traditional public-key cryptosystems, such as RSA and Elliptic Curve Cryptography (ECC). This threat motivates Post-Quantum Cryptography (PQC) research and development, aiming to produce and analyze algorithms that can withstand quantum and classical attacks and, at the same time, run on traditional computing platforms. The NIST PQC standardization process, currently in its third round, aims to coordinate the development and analysis of PQC algorithms to eventually select a few of them as new American Federal Information Processing Standards (FIPS).

Side-channel analysis (SCA), including Differential Power Analysis (DPA) [12], is a significant threat to the successful deployment of cryptographic solutions. Lightweight applications with limited or no physical security are even more susceptible to such attacks since adversaries can easily collect side-channel information. Consequently, the NIST PQC standardization process specifies ease

© Springer Nature Switzerland AG 2021
A. Adhikari et al. (Eds.): INDOCRYPT 2021, LNCS 13143, pp. 224–245, 2021.
https://doi.org/10.1007/978-3-030-92518-5_11

of protection against side-channel attacks as a desirable feature of candidates. Among the most urgent tasks in the evaluation process is developing SCA-resistant implementations of third-round finalists and assessing their comparative cost of protection against SCA. All the range of target platforms from pure software to full hardware and hybrid platforms need consideration since leakage patterns differ from one platform to another. For example, architectural leakage stemming from processor architecture can affect the software, while glitches, dependent on basic combinational and sequential circuit building blocks, affect hardware implementations.

NIST has selected Saber, a lattice-based key encapsulation mechanism (KEM), as a third-round finalist in July 2020. Previous works on applying SCA countermeasures to Saber concentrated on software [4] and software/hardware co-design [8].

In this work, we develop and evaluate SCA-resistant full hardware implementations of Saber. Our hardware design is significantly faster compared to previously reported SW, and SW/HW masked implementations of Saber. Additionally, our masked design uses approximately $2.9\times$ more lookup tables (LUTs) while incurring $1.4\times$ performance penalty compared to the unprotected baseline design when implemented in Xilinx Artix-7 FPGAs. Our results show the possibility of producing efficient masked hardware implementations of Saber that are significantly faster than SW and SW/HW designs. The source code of our implementation is publicly available at https://github.com/GMUCERG/SABER-SCA.

2   Previous Work

PQC algorithm side-channel resistance is an active research field with several open problems. Developing efficient countermeasures suitable for PQC algorithms and assessing the comparative cost of protection are critical for a fair comparison of NIST PQC third-round candidates. The community has made progress towards these goals, but many open questions remain.

In [16], Reparaz et al. proposed a masked implementation for ring-Learning-With-Errors (ring-LWE). The main idea is to split the secret polynomial s into two shares s_0 and s_1 such that $s = s_0 + s_1$. Multiplying the shared version of s by an unshared polynomial is a linear operation so, it can be done on each share separately. The result of the polynomial multiplication is fed to a custom threshold decoder. The decoder uses a masked lookup table. However, to simplify the function calculated by the table, the authors use a set of rules to reduce the number of inputs to the lookup table. The main disadvantage of this decoder is that it increases the decryption failure rate and has a large performance overhead due to the need to repeatedly check the set of rules. The hardware crypto-processor reported in [16] is 20% larger and requires $2.6\times$ more cycles to perform decryption compared to the unprotected design.

Many real-wold applications require the use of schemes that resists chosen-ciphertext attacks (CCA) and adaptive chosen-ciphertext attacks (CCA2). Oder et al. investigated masked implementations for CCA2-secured ring-LWE schemes in [15]. The authors developed a unit (MDecode) that receives the arithmetically shared polynomial coefficients, converts them to Boolean sharing, and outputs the decoded version. However, their design requires 5.7× more clock cycles compared to the unprotected implementation.

A first-order SCA resistant software implementation of Saber was introduced by Beirendonck et al. in [4], building on work started by Verhulst [19]. The reported overhead of this work is 2.52× in terms of clock cycles compared to the unprotected software. This low overhead is due to Saber's power-of-two moduli and the reliance on rounding for noise generation. A significant contribution of this work is a unit that performs logical shifting on arithmetic shares, based on arithmetic-to-Boolean algorithms by Coron and Debraiz [5,7]. Their binomial sampler is based on the bit-sliced masked binomial sampler by Schneider et al. [17].

In April 2021, Fritzmann et al. reported a masked SW/HW co-design that supports Saber and Kyber [8]. Their design is based on an open-source RISC-V implementation, in which they added accelerators and instruction-set extensions for PQC algorithms. The accelerators reported are used to speed up hashing, binomial sampling, polynomial multiplication, Arithmetic-to-Boolean (A2B), and Boolean-to-Arithmetic (B2A) operations. The authors report a 2.63× performance overhead for Saber compared to unprotected implementations.

3 Background

3.1 Saber

Saber is a lattice-based KEM that depends on the hardness of the Module Learning With Rounding (MLWR) problem [18]. KEMs use a public and private key pair to generate and securely exchange keys between communication parties. Specifically, Alice generates a key pair, keeps the private key, and distributes the public key. Bob provides Alice's public key to the encapsulation algorithm to generate a secrete key K and ciphertext c. The ciphertext can now be transmitted to Alice. Alice feeds her private key and the ciphertext to the decapsulation algorithm to generate the secret key K.

We concentrate on the SCA protection of the CCA-Secure decapsulation algorithm, Saber.KEM.Decaps, since it uses the long-term private key. The Saber.KEM.Decaps algorithm is based on the CPA-secure algorithms Saber.PKE.Enc and Saber.PKE.Dec. These algorithms are shown in Algorithms 1–3 for reference. Detailed specification can be found at [18].

Saber uses power-of-two moduli, and the primary operation performed is polynomial multiplication. Other significant operations include hashing, an extendable output function, and Binomial sampling.

3.2 Masking

In this work, we utilize masking as an SCA countermeasure. Masking is a well-researched countermeasure that provides a basis for constructing provably secure

---

Algorithm 1. Saber.PKE.Enc [18]

Require: $(pk := (seed_A, b), m \in R_2; r)$
Ensure: $c := (c_m, b')$
1: $A = \text{gen}(seed_\mathbf{A}) \in R_q^{l \times l}$
2: $s' = \beta_\mu(R_q^{l \times 1}; r)$
3: $b' = ((A^T s' + h) \bmod q) \gg (\epsilon_q - \epsilon_p) \in R_p^{l \times 1}$
4: $v' = b^T (s' \bmod p) \in R_p$
5: $c_m = (v' + h_1 - 2^{\epsilon_p - 1} m \bmod p) \gg (\epsilon_q - \epsilon_T) \in R_T$

Algorithm 2. Saber.PKE.Dec [18]

Require: $(s, c := (c_m, b'))$
Ensure: m'
1: $v = b^T (s \bmod p) \in R_p$
2: $m' = ((v - 2^{\epsilon_p - \epsilon_T} c_m + h_2) \bmod p) \gg (\epsilon_p - 1) \in R_2$

Algorithm 3. Saber.KEM.Decaps [18]

Require: $(sk := (z, pkh, pk, s), c)$
Ensure: K
1: $m' = \text{Saber.PKE.Dec}(s, c)$
2: $(r', \hat{K}') = \mathcal{G}(pkh, m')$
3: $c' = \text{Saber.PKE.Enc}(pk, m'; r')$
4: **if** $c = c'$ **then**
5:     $K = \mathcal{H}(\hat{K}, c)$
6: **else**
7:     $K = \mathcal{H}(z, c)$
8: **end if**

---

systems provided that certain assumptions hold. In general, two components define a masking scheme: 1) the method used to split the data into shares, 2) the method used to perform computations on these shares.

For example, in Boolean masking, each sensitive variable x is split into n shares $x_0, x_1, \ldots, x_{n-1}$ such that $\bigoplus x_i = x$. A commonly used way to achieve this is by generating $n - 1$ random masks $m_0, m_1, \ldots, m_{n-2}$, setting $x_0 = m_0, x_1 = m_1, \ldots, x_{n-2} = m_{n-2}$, and computing $x_{n-1} = x \oplus m_0 \oplus m_1 \oplus \cdots \oplus m_{n-2}$. On the other hand, in arithmetic masking, a variable a is split into n shares $a_0, a_1, \ldots, a_{n-1}$ such that $\sum a_i \bmod q = a$. This can be achieved by generating $n - 1$ random masks $m_0, m_1, \ldots, m_{n-2}$, setting $a_0 = m_0, a_1 = m_1, \ldots, a_{n-2} = m_{n-2}$, and computing $a_{n-1} = (a - m_0 - m_1 - m_{n-2}) \bmod q$.

The computation on the shares should be performed such that all intermediate values are statistically independent of the unshared sensitive variables.

Masking linear functions is trivial. The same function is duplicated, with each instance taking one share of each input variable and producing one share of each output variable. Non-linear functions require much more care to make sure the implementation is correct and secure.

3.3 Domain Oriented Masking

Domain Oriented Masking (DOM) [11], introduced by Gross et al., provides security against SCA attacks in the presence of glitches. It also allows building circuits that can be synthesized for an arbitrary protection order. Similar to classical Boolean masking, variables are split into shares. For example, x is split into x_0 and x_1 such that $x = x_0 \oplus x_1$.

DOM uses the concept of share domains, where every share of each variable is associated with a domain. For example, x_0 and y_0 can be associated with *Domain0*.

In DOM, calculations are done so that data in different domains are kept independent of each other. In case data from two domains must be combined, steps are taken to preserve this independence. Linear functions are trivial to calculate since they require shares from each domain to be used separately. In non-linear functions, however, shares from different domains must be mixed.

4 Methodology

To study the impact of applying SCA countermeasures on the hardware implementations of Saber, we start by developing a baseline lightweight hardware implementation. This allows us to reuse components from the unprotected design, enabling meaningful comparison and evaluation of the cost of protection. At the same time, some components remain unchanged in the protected implementations. We choose a lightweight (LW) implementation because LW applications are especially vulnerable to SCA attacks. In many cases, LW applications have limited or no physical security, allowing easy collection of side-channel information by adversaries. We utilize the Register-Transfer-Level (RTL) methodology to construct our hardware. RTL provides granular control over operations, which simplifies countermeasure application. Additionally, hardware implementations provide performance and power efficiency, which are helpful in many applications. We primarily use VHDL for hardware description, except for the SHA-3 core, which is written using Chisel.

The baseline Saber implementation is then protected against DPA using masking countermeasures, adapting protection schemes to hardware when necessary. Furthermore, we design flexible hardware that has performance and area trade-offs. Doing that results in a highly configurable implementation that can be adapted to a wide range of applications.

The security of our design has been experimentally verified using the Test Vector Leakage Assessment methodology [9]. Finally, we benchmark our design on widely used state-of-the-art FPGA devices to quantify the resource utilization and performance to evaluate the effect of applying the countermeasures on Saber. The results are compared to masked software and software/hardware co-design implementations of Saber.

5   Baseline Lightweight Saber Implementation

The datapath of our hardware implementation of Saber, capable of performing encapsulation and decapsulation, is shown in Fig. 1. The figure omits control signals for clarity. The design uses a FIFO-based interface with one input port and one output port. This interface facilitates connecting the design as an accelerator to processors using similar interfaces such as AXI stream [2]. We use memory to store all data, including keys. We choose a memory width of 16 bits to read/write one polynomial coefficient in one clock cycle since the largest coefficient size is 13 bits, and our lightweight units for polynomial arithmetic receive/produce at most one coefficient per clock cycle. All data kept in memory is in byte-string format. This approach allows data to be kept in a compact, memory-saving form. We utilize *width converters* to perform unpacking byte-strings into polynomials before feeding them into arithmetic units and packing the resulting polynomials into byte-strings before memory write-back on the fly. The central control unit implements the sequencing of operations needed to perform encapsulation and decapsulation. The user of the core uses pre-defined opcodes to select one of the two operations.

Data flow from memory to arithmetic units and back to memory, or from memory to SHA3/Sampling units and back to memory. Combining this simple data flow and utilizing width converters simplify our control logic since width converters adjust the width of data with minimal control signals from the central controller, and the simple data flow minimizes control signals to the datapath.

The general operation of the core is as follows: the core pulls input data via the din port and interprets the first word as an opcode to select between encapsulation or decapsulation. If encapsulation was selected, the core loads the public key and the random message from the input port and computes the ciphertext and the secret key. If the operation specified in the opcode is decapsulation, the core loads the public key, the private key, and the ciphertext and computes the secret key. In both cases, the dout port is used to output results. Below, we discuss the significant units used in the design in detail.

5.1   Polynomial Arithmetic Units

One of the most intensively used operations in Saber and other lattice-based algorithms is polynomial multiplication. Our design goal is to minimize resource utilization of this operation, which comes at the expense of clock cycles.

We developed a flexible schoolbook multiplier and accumulation unit *Poly-MAC* with a configurable rolling factor $ROLL$, which can be set at synthesis time. We define a multiplier with $ROLL = 1$ as a multiplier capable of performing n coefficient multiplications simultaneously. Here, n is the number of coefficients in a polynomial which is equal to 256 in Saber. Our multiplier multiplies $n/ROLL$ coefficients in one clock cycle, and it needs $n \cdot ROLL$ clock cycles to perform the multiplication of two polynomials. Furthermore, it needs roughly $2n$ clock cycles for input and output. This configuration allows us to have a performance-area trade-off yielding a highly flexible design.

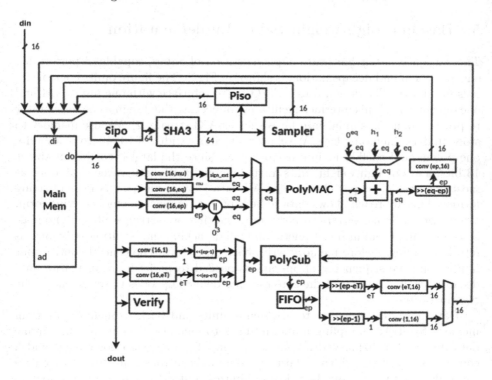

Fig. 1. Lightweight Saber datapath

The *PolyMAC* unit is shown in Fig. 2 and it operates as follows. The multiplier receives the first polynomial *poly1* via the **di** port and stores it internally in a two-dimensional circular input buffer as shown in the left part of Fig. 2. The coefficients of *poly1* are organized into columns that can rotate from left to right. *PolyMAC* then receives the second polynomial *poly2* one coefficient at a time via the **di** port and multiplies it by all coefficients of *poly1*. To do the multiplication by all coefficients of *poly1*, the right-most column of the input buffer is multiplied by the current *poly2* coefficient, and the result is stored in the left-most columns of the 2D circular output buffer (shown to the right of the MAC units). The columns of the input and output buffer rotate until all coefficients of *poly1* have been multiplied. The multiplier then pulls the next coefficient of *poly2* until all coefficients are consumed. The result of the polynomial multiplication is stored internally, and the multiplier is ready to output the result or accept another two polynomials to multiply and accumulate to the previous result. This is useful to implement vector-by-vector multiplication. After any multiplication, the result can be cleared using a control signal.

The other polynomial arithmetic operation in Saber is polynomial subtraction. This operation is much less time-intensive and has a small effect on the overall execution time of the algorithm. To implement this operation, we developed the *PolySub* unit shown in Fig. 3. *PolySub* instantiates a single subtractor

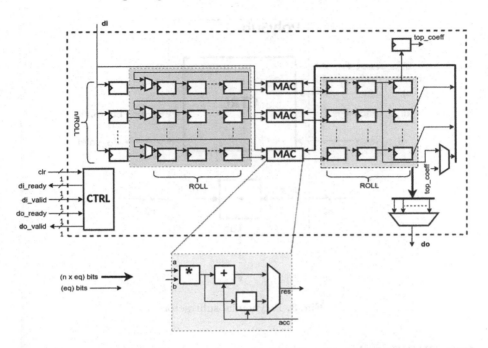

Fig. 2. Configurable schoolbook polynomial multiplier. Input circular buffer high-lighted in green and output circular buffer highlighted in blue (Color figure online)

capable of subtracting two coefficients at a time. This unit is purely combinational. However, we use control signals for handshaking to make sure that the unit consumes two coefficients from the source before providing the corresponding coefficient of the result at the output. Constants h_1 and h_2 are added using a simple adder at the output of the *PolyMAC* unit, capable of adding two coefficients together in one clock cycle.

5.2 SHA3 Unit

We have developed a flexible SHA-3 unit that can be configured to process a configurable number of state slices to provide performance/area trade-off. Additionally, the IO width of the module is configurable. The core user can select between SHA3-256, SHA3-512, and SHAKE128 functions using a command word. All of these functions are required by Saber. This core has been written in Chisel to exploit its capability to generate highly configurable hardware.

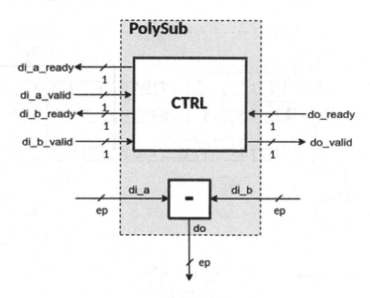

Fig. 3. Polynomial subtractor

5.3 CBD Sampler

Saber.KEM.Decaps uses Centered Binomial Distribution (CBD) to sample the polynomial vector s'. To generate one binomial sample, our sampler takes two $\mu/2$ bit-wide uniform samples x and y and calculates the CBD sample as $HW(x) - HW(y)$, where $HW(.)$ is the Hamming weight function. Figure 4 shows the sampler unit. It receives 64 bits of uniform randomness generated by SHA-3 and converts it into eight binomial samples in two clock cycles.

5.4 Width Converter Unit

Saber uses many polynomial coefficient sizes. For example, Saber uses polynomials with coefficient sizes of eq, ep, and eT, which are equal to 13, 10, and 4 bits, respectively. To avoid designing separate packing and unpacking units for each size, we developed a flexible width converter with arbitrary input and output width. This unit is essentially an asymmetric FIFO. In Fig. 1, width converters are labeled conv(WI,WO), where WI and WO are the input width and output width (in bits), respectively.

Figure 5 shows the internal structure of this unit. We use asymmetric RAM to briefly store the input data and allow it to be read via the output port. Control logic is needed to keep track of pointers to locations for the next read and write and the number of bits stored in the width converter. Utilizing such a unit simplifies data packing and unpacking since the central controller delegates this task to the width converters and only enables the proper width converters for the current transaction. At the inputs of polynomial arithmetic units, we instantiated width converters to convert from memory width to the coefficient

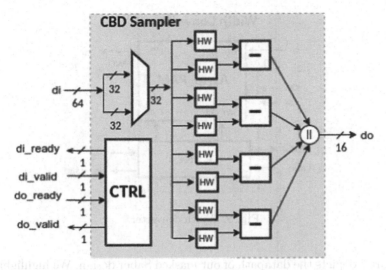

All buses are 4 bit-wide unless explicitly specified

Fig. 4. CBD sampler

sizes processed by the unit. At the output, we instantiate width converters to pack the data into the memory words on the fly.

5.5 Other Units

The ciphertext verification is done using a comparator that compares two memory locations in two clock cycles. If the contents of the two locations are not equal, we set a flag to indicate the inequality. Regardless of the comparison outcome, we go through all the ciphertext c and the re-encryption ciphertext c' to ensure that our implementation runs in constant time, which is necessary to resist timing attacks. The left-shift operations, which are used for rounding, are free in hardware.

6   Masked Saber Implementation

Contrary to encapsulation, the decapsulation process utilizes the long-term private key, which makes it vulnerable to side-channel analysis. We implement a masked full hardware implementation of Saber.KEM.Decaps based on our lightweight hardware design. We adapt general ideas presented in [4] for hardware. The data flow of our masked Saber.KEM.Decaps is shown in Fig. 6. All operations that are dependent on the private key are highlighted in grey. SCA attacks could target any intermediate value processed in these units.

Polynomial multiplication of an unshared polynomial by a shared polynomial is a linear operation when utilizing arithmetic masking. Hence, multiplication can be done by performing it for each share separately.

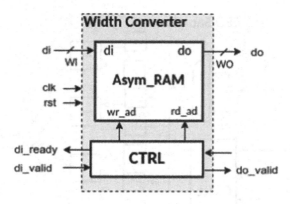

Fig. 5. Width converter

Figure 7 depicts the datapath of our masked Saber design. We highlight operations that can be done separately for each of the two shares in green and blue. Hashing using SHA-3, CBD sampling, and rounding include non-linear operations, and both shares mix at some stage in these operations. We highlight these units in red. Eventually, these units produce two shares of data that can be safely consumed in destination domains. In Fig. 7, data generally flows from the two memories inward through linear polynomial arithmetic units, then through non-linear rounding units in the center of the figure, and back to main memories. Also, data can flow from the memories to the SHA-3/Sampling units in the middle of the figure and back to memory.

The linear units in the masked design are the same units used in the baseline design. We duplicated these units for each of the two shares. However, non-linear units were re-implemented. We perform constant addition of h_1 and h_2 constants to one of the shares only.

In the following subsections, we describe the hardware implementation of the primary units of the protected design in detail.

6.1   Polynomial Arithmetic Units

Polynomial multiplication is done using the approach used previously by Reparaz et al. in [16]. Since polynomial multiplication is linear for arithmetic masking, secret polynomials are split into two arithmetic shares (coefficient-wise). For a polynomial s, two polynomials s_0 and s_1 are generated such that $s = s_0 + s_1$. Now, multiplication of the shared version of s by another unshared polynomial w is performed as $w * s_0 + w * s_1$. Polynomial addition/subtraction of an unshared polynomial is performed on only one share.

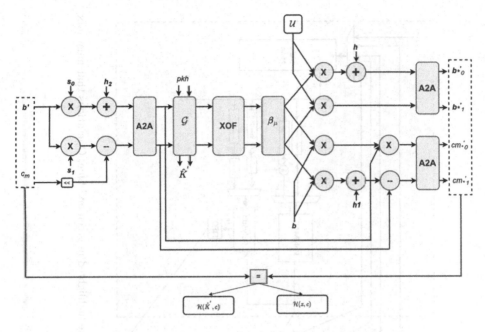

Fig. 6. Masked Saber decapsulation data flow [4]

6.2   SHA3 Unit

We utilize Domain-Oriented Masking (DOM) [11] to develop a first-order protected implementation of our SHA3 core based on [3]. As the input of the Keccak core comes from a uniformly random distribution, we can use uncorrelated state bits to provide for the randomness required for the non-linear χ operation [3].

6.3   CBD Sampler

As shown in Fig. 6, the CBD sampler in Saber must be protected against SCA. This sampler should securely compute a CBD sample as the difference between the Hamming weights of two uniform samples x and y as discussed previously.

The masked sampler takes Boolean shares from SHAKE as input. However, the subsequent operations (i.e., polynomial multiplication) use arithmetic shares.

We implemented a masked CBD sampler per Algorithm 4 which was introduced by Schneider et al. [17]. $\mathbf{x}$ and $\mathbf{y}$ are two μ-bit numbers in Boolean sharing representation. The output $\mathbf{A}$ is an arithmetic sharing representation of $HW(x) - HW(y)$, i.e., $\sum A_i = HW(x) - HW(y)$. This task is accomplished by converting one bit at a time of $\mathbf{x}$ and $\mathbf{y}$ from Boolean to arithmetic representation. The generated arithmetic shares are added to compute the Hamming weight of x and y, and finally, a subtraction is performed to compute the binomial sample.

We utilized Goubin's method [10] for Boolean-to-Arithmetic conversion B2A. In this conversion, $x = x_p \oplus r$ is converted to arithmetic masking in the form

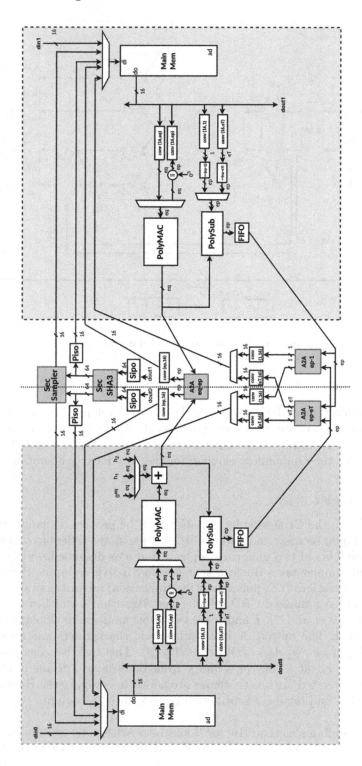

Fig. 7. Protected Saber datapath. Operations performed on only one share are highlighted in green and blue. Operations that must mix shares (non-linear operations) are highlighted in red. (Color figure online)

Algorithm 4. SecSampler1 [17]

Require: $\mathbf{x} = (x_i)_{1 \leq i \leq n} \in \mathbb{F}_{2^\mu}, \mathbf{y} = (y_i)_{1 \leq i \leq n} \in \mathbb{F}_{2^\mu}$, such that $\bigoplus_i x_i = x$ and $\bigoplus_i y_i = y$

Ensure: $\mathbf{A} = (A_i)_{1 \leq i \leq n} \in \mathbb{F}_q$ such that $\sum_i A_i = HW(x) - HW(y) \mod q$

1: $(A_i)_{1 \leq i \leq n} \leftarrow 0$
2: **for** $i = 0$ **to** $\mu - 1$ **do**
3:     $(A_i)_{1 \leq i \leq n} \leftarrow 0$
4:     $\mathbf{B} \leftarrow B2A((\mathbf{x} >> i \wedge 1))$
5:     $\mathbf{C} \leftarrow B2A((\mathbf{y} >> i \wedge 1))$
6:     $\mathbf{A} \leftarrow \mathbf{A} + \mathbf{B} \mod q$
7:     $\mathbf{A} \leftarrow \mathbf{A} - \mathbf{C} \mod q$
8: **end for**

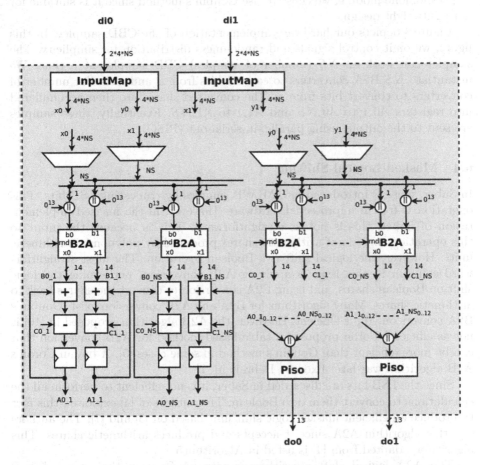

Fig. 8. Masked CBD sampler

$x = A + r \mod 2^K$ where $K \geq 1$. In this method, the share r is kept as is and A is calculated from the Boolean shares and a random value γ as follows:

$$A = [(x' \oplus \gamma) - \gamma] \oplus x' \oplus [(x' \oplus (r \oplus \gamma)) - (r \oplus \gamma)] \tag{1}$$

Goubin's B2A conversion is efficient and lightweight. Additionally, it works a power-of-two modulus, which makes it suitable for Saber. We used synchronization registers to prevent mixing intermediates that depend on both Boolean shares in our hardware implementation.

The SW/HW design in [8] uses B2A and A2B conversion algorithms from [6]. Both algorithms utilize secure addition over Boolean shares. This enables them to use the same adder to accelerate both operations. In our case, since the sampler is a standalone module, we chose to use Goubin's method since it is suitable for our lightweight design.

Figure 8 depicts our hardware implementation of the CBD sampler. In this figure, we omit control signals and randomness distribution for simplicity. The sampler can work on NS (number of samples) CBD samples at a time. We instantiate NS B2A converters to convert bits from x and a similar number of converters to convert bits from y. The converted shares are then accumulated into registers $A0\_1$ to $A0\_NS$ and $A1\_1$ to $A1\_NS$. Eventually, these samples are sent to the output using parallel-in-serial-out (PISO).

6.4   Masked Logical Shifting

In Saber, noise is introduced into MLWR samples by truncating LSB bits. This operation is free in unprotected hardware. However, in the masked implementation of Saber, this is not as straightforward. This is because the input to this operation consists of arithmetic shares produced by polynomial arithmetic units. However, the logical shift is a Boolean operation. The most straightforward solution to this issue is applying A2B conversion, performing the logic shift on Boolean shares, and using B2A conversion to convert the shares back to arithmetic shares. Many algorithms for B2A and A2B conversion exist. Goubin's B2A conversion [10] is efficient. However, the A2B algorithm proposed in [10] is not as efficient. Coron proposed a table-based method for A2B conversion that can be more efficient than Goubin's method in some cases [5]. A bug in Coron's A2B algorithm was later fixed by Debraiz in [7].

Since the LSB bits are discarded in Saber, it is not efficient to perform all the calculations to convert them into Boolean. The authors of [4] exploited this fact to produce an efficient masked logic shift unit based on [5] and [7]. The authors call this algorithm A2A since it accepts and produces arithmetic shares. This algorithm, adapted from [4] is listed in Algorithm 5.

The A2A logical shift algorithm accepts (A, R) such that $x = A + R \mod s^{m+n \cdot k}$ and returns (A, R) such that $x >> (n \cdot k) = A + R \mod 2^m$, which is the shifted version of x in arithmetic shares. The shifts in Saber are $>> 9, >> 6$ and $>> 3$. Our hardware implementation of the A2A algorithm

is shown in Fig. 9. We use registers to store the values of the algorithm intermediates. Since the algorithm requires various synchronization stages, we use
registers to stop glitch propagation in hardware. We adopt the (m, n, k) values
used in [4]. Specifically we set $(m, n, k) = (1, 3, 3), (4, 2, 3)$ and $(10, 1, 3)$ for the
$\gg 9, \gg 6$ and $\gg 3$ shifts, respectively. The operation of this module is as follows:
first, the module is initialized and it pre-computes the value Γ and the table T.
The hardware to compute this step is not shown in Fig. 9 for simplicity. Once
the module is initialized, it can accept the shares (A, R), and return the shifted
version in arithmetic shares via the Aout and Rout ports.

7   Leakage Assessment

We performed a non-specific fixed-vs-random Test Vector Leakage Assessment
(TVLA) [9] to test the first-order leakage of the design. We instantiated the
design-under-test (DUT) in the NewAE CW305 target board, which is an Artix-
7-based board. The DUT power consumption is measured at the output of the
CW305's onboard amplifier, which amplifies the voltage drop across the onboard
$0.1\,\Omega$ resistor. The DUT was clocked at 12.5 MHz, and a USB3-based oscilloscope
(Picoscope 5000) was used to collect traces at a sampling rate of 125 MS/s, and 8-
bit sample resolution. We utilized the Flexible Opensource workBench fOr Side-
channel analysis (FOBOS) [1] platform to control test-vector communication
and trace capture from the oscilloscope. The fixed test vectors are formed by
generating fresh sharing of a fixed private key, and the random test vectors are
generated using a completely random private key. In both cases, the rest of the
test vector consists of fixed ciphertext and public key.

To validate our experimental setup, we performed a TVLA test with the
PRNG output set to zero. This disables the countermeasures since they depend
on randomness generated from the PRNG. The result of this test is shown in
Fig. 10. As expected, significant leakage is detected. This can be observed even
at 2,000 traces.

To test the protected version, we enabled the PRNG to activate the countermeasures. The TVLA result after analyzing 100,000 traces is shown in Fig. 11.
The right-most spike is related to comparing the hash of the input ciphertext
and the ciphertext generated by the re-encryption process. This leakage does not
provide any useful side-channel information to an attacker, as discussed in [4].
All other points in the TVLA result are below the threshold, indicating that our
countermeasures are effective.

Although the protected version shows significant leakage reduction, it can
still be vulnerable to fault attacks as well as profiling and deep learning-based
attacks such as [13, 14]. We leave protection against these attacks for future work.

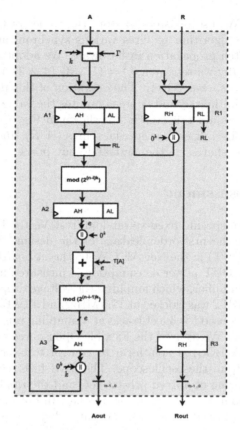

Fig. 9. A2A logical shift unit

Algorithm 5. A2A Logical Shift [4]

Require: (A, R) such that $x = A + R \mod 2^{m+n\cdot k}$, T, r, γ
Ensure: (A, R) such that $x >> (n \cdot k) = A + R \mod 2^m$
  /*Let $A = (A_h || A_l), R = (R_h, R_l)$ where A_l, R_l the k LSB bits.*/
1: $\Gamma \leftarrow \sum_{i=1}^{n} 2^{i \cdot k} \cdot \gamma \mod 2^{m+n\cdot k}$
2: $P \leftarrow \sum_{i=0}^{n-1} 2^{i \cdot k} \cdot r \mod 2^{m+n\cdot k}$
3: $A \leftarrow A - P \mod 2^{m+n\cdot k}$
4: $A \leftarrow A - \Gamma \mod 2^{m+n\cdot k}$
5: **for** $i = 0$ **to** $n - 1$ **do**
6:    $A \leftarrow A + R_l \mod 2^{m+(n-i)\cdot k}$
7:    $A_h \leftarrow A_h + T[A_l] \mod 2^{m+(n-i-1)\cdot k}$
8:    $A \leftarrow A_h$
9:    $R \leftarrow R_h$
10: **end for**

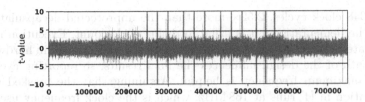

Fig. 10. TVLA result with PRNG disabled (2,000 traces)

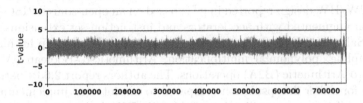

Fig. 11. TVLA result with PRNG enabled (100,000 traces)

8   Results and Comparison

To quantify the cost and performance of our baseline and masked Saber designs, we benchmark them on Xilinx Artix-7 FPGA. Resource utilization in terms of lookup tables (LUTs), flip-flops (FFs), and the number of DSP units is provided. We also provide latency information in clock cycles, maximum frequency, and encapsulation and decapsulation time. These information are shown in Tables 1 and 2.

Saber-r8 refers to our baseline design with *PolyMAC* rolling factor, ROLL, set to 8, so it can perform $n/8 = 32$ coefficient multiplications in one clock cycle. This is the variant that we report in Tables 1 and 2. Saber-r8 has a low area footprint and requires only 6,713 LUTs and 32 DSPs. On the other hand, Saber-r8-masked, the corresponding masked design, uses 19,299 LUTs and 64 DSPs. That is 2.9× more LUTs and exactly 2× more DSP units compared to the baseline unprotected variant. Since our baseline design has a small footprint, we decided to duplicate the logic and process shares simultaneously in the masked design. Another option is to use the same hardware resources and process the shares sequentially at the expense of latency. The protected design needs twice as many DSP units because it uses two *PolyMAC* units, the only unit that uses DSPs.

Our masked design performs decapsulation in 576 µs, assuming keys are already loaded. This is 1.36× the baseline unprotected variant.

To evaluate how our designs compare to previously reported masked implementations of Saber on various platforms, we summarize all results in Table 1 and 2.

In [4], the authors report a masked software implementation of Saber.KEM.Decaps and benchmarking results on STM32F407-DISCOVERY board featuring an ARM Cortex-M4 processor. The decapsulation time reported is 2,833,348 clock cycles, 2.52× more than the unprotected decapsulation. For software implementations, it is usual to report cycle count. Execution time can be calculated after knowing the processor clock speed. However, in hardware, the critical path of the design influences the final results, so reporting cycle count and the maximum frequency is helpful. Assuming that the masked software decapsulation in [4] runs at 168 MHz, which is the clock frequency used in the STM32F407-DISCOVERY board, protected decapsulation will take 16,865 μs. In this case, our hardware implementation can provide a speedup of 29×.

The SW/HW design reported in [8] is based on an open-source RISC-V implementation augmented with accelerators and instruction-set extensions that can support Saber and Kyber. The accelerators are used to speed up hashing, binomial sampling, polynomial multiplication, Arithmetic-to-Boolean (A2B), and Boolean-to-Arithmetic (B2A) operations. The authors report 2.63× performance overhead for Saber decapsulation compared to unprotected implementations. In Table 2, we list resource utilization of this SW/HW design. It uses block RAM (BRAMs) while our design does not. However, our designs use more DSP units. In terms of decapsulation time, the protected SW/HW design needs 15,398 μs when run at the reported maximum frequency of 58.8 MHz. Consequently, our full hardware design, Saber-r8-masked, provides a speedup of 26×.

A breakdown of component area (in LUTs) for Saber-r8 and Saber-r8-masked is depicted in Fig. 12. The combinations of SHA3, *PolyMAC*, and main memory utilize 88% and 61% for baseline and masked variants, respectively. Width converters that perform packing and unpacking occupy around 7% and 5% in the baseline and masked variants, respectively. In Saber-r8, other components include CBD sampler, *PolySub*, control logic, and other units. These units account for only 4.7%. On the other hand, in Saber-r8-masked, the CBD sampler requires 21% of the LUTs, and other components need 13%. This breakdown shows that further area improvements of both masked and baseline variants will benefit from more area-efficient SHA3 and polynomial multiplication units. A smaller CBD sampler will improve resource utilization of the masked variant.

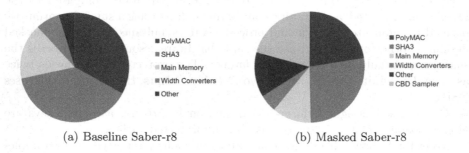

(a) Baseline Saber-r8   (b) Masked Saber-r8

Fig. 12. Resource utilization per unit

Table 1. Comparison between masked Saber implementations in the literature and designs in this work. Notation: U - unprotected, P - protected.

	Type	Platform	Protection	Freq MHz
This work	HW	FPGA-Artix7	U	125
				125
			P	125
[4]	SW	ARM Cortex-M4	U	168
			P	168
[8]	SW/HW	RISC-V+ Acc.	U	62.5
				62.5
			P	58.8

Table 2. Comparison between resource utilization and latency of masked Saber implementations in the literature and in this work. Notation: U - unprotected, P - protected.

	Protection	Resource utilization					Latency			
		LUTs	FFs	Slices	DSPs	BRAMs	Operation	Cycles	us	Ratio
This work	U	6,713	7,363	2,631	32	0	Encaps	46,705	373.1	-
							Decaps	52,758	422.1	1.00
	P	19,299	21,977	7,036	64	0	Decaps	72,005	576.0	1.36
[4]	U	-	-	-	-	-	Decaps	1,123,280	6,686.2	1.00
	P						Decaps	2,833,348	16,865.2	2.52
[8]	U	20,697	11,833	6,852	13	36.5	Encaps	308,430	4,934.9	-
							Decaps	347,323	5,557.2	1.00
	P	29,889	17,152	9,641	13	52.5	Decaps	905,395	15,397.9	2.77

9   Conclusions and Future Work

In this work, we report an SCA-resistant hardware implementation of Saber. We have started with a baseline lightweight hardware design and applied side-channel countermeasures to resist DPA attacks. Our masked hardware implementation offers 29× and 26× speedup over previously reported protected software and software/hardware co-design implementations, respectively. Also, our design occupies around 2.9× the number of LUTs and requires 1.4× the latency compared to our baseline design when benchmarked on modern FPGAs. Interesting future work includes investigating resistance against fault and deep learning-based attacks. Reducing resource utilization and improving the performance of hardware implementations of Saber and other finalists in the NIST PQC standardization process will also be helpful.

References

1. Abdulgadir, A., Diehl, W., Kaps, J.-P.: An open-source platform for evaluation of hardware implementations of lightweight authenticated ciphers. In: 2019 International Conference on ReConFigurable Computing and FPGAs (ReConFig), Cancun, Mexico, pp. 1–5. IEEE, December 2019. https://doi.org/10.1109/ReConFig48160.2019.8994788. ISBN 978-1-72811-957-1
2. ARM. AMBA AXI Protocol Specification (2003). https://developer.arm.com/docs/ihi0022/b/amba-axi-protocol-specification-v10
3. Arribas, V., Bilgin, B., Petrides, G., Nikova, S., Rijmen, V.: Rhythmic Keccak: SCA security and low latency in HW. IACR Trans. Cryptogr. Hardware Embedded Syst. 269–290, February 2018. https://doi.org/10.46586/tches.v2018.i1.269-290. ISSN 2569-2925
4. Van Beirendonck, M., D'anvers, J.-P., Karmakar, A., Balasch, J., Verbauwhede, I.: A side-channel-resistant implementation of SABER. ACM J. Emerging Technol. Comput. Syst. **17**(2), 1–26 (2021). https://doi.org/10.1145/3429983. ISSN 1550-4832, 1550-4840
5. Coron, J.-S., Tchulkine, A.: A new algorithm for switching from arithmetic to boolean masking. In: Walter, C.D., Koç, Ç.K., Paar, C. (eds.) CHES 2003. LNCS, vol. 2779, pp. 89–97. Springer, Heidelberg (2003). https://doi.org/10.1007/978-3-540-45238-6_8
6. Coron, J.-S., Großschädl, J., Vadnala, P.K.: Secure conversion between boolean and arithmetic masking of any order. In: Batina, L., Robshaw, M. (eds.) CHES 2014. LNCS, vol. 8731, pp. 188–205. Springer, Heidelberg (2014). https://doi.org/10.1007/978-3-662-44709-3_11
7. Debraize, B.: Efficient and provably secure methods for switching from arithmetic to boolean masking. In: Prouff, E., Schaumont, P. (eds.) CHES 2012. LNCS, vol. 7428, pp. 107–121. Springer, Heidelberg (2012). https://doi.org/10.1007/978-3-642-33027-8_7
8. Fritzmann, T.: Masked accelerators and instruction set extensions for postquantum cryptography. Cryptology ePrint Archive 2021/479, April 2021
9. Goodwill, G., Jun, B., Jaffe, J., Rohatgi, P.: A testing methodology for side-channel resistance validation. In: NIST Non-invasive Attack Testing Workshop, Nara, Japan (2011)
10. Goubin, L.: A sound method for switching between boolean and arithmetic masking. In: Koç, Ç.K., Naccache, D., Paar, C. (eds.) CHES 2001. LNCS, vol. 2162, pp. 3–15. Springer, Heidelberg (2001). https://doi.org/10.1007/3-540-44709-1_2
11. Gross, H., Mangard, S., Korak, T.: Domain-oriented masking: compact masked hardware implementations with arbitrary protection order. In: Proceedings of the 2016 ACM Workshop on Theory of Implementation Security - TIS 2016, Vienna, Austria, p. 3. ACM Press (2016). https://doi.org/10.1145/2996366.2996426. ISBN 978-1-4503-4575-0
12. Kocher, P., Jaffe, J., Jun, B.: Differential power analysis. In: Wiener, M. (ed.) CRYPTO 1999. LNCS, vol. 1666, pp. 388–397. Springer, Heidelberg (1999). https://doi.org/10.1007/3-540-48405-1_25
13. Ngo, K., Dubrova, E., Guo, Q., Johansson, T.: A side-channel attack on a masked IND-CCA secure Saber KEM implementation. IACR Trans. Cryptogr. Hardware Embedded Syst. 676–707, August 2021. https://doi.org/10.46586/tches.v2021.i4.676-707. ISSN 2569-2925

14. Ngo, K., Dubrova, E., Johansson, T.: Breaking masked and shuffled CCA secure Saber KEM. Cryptology ePrint Archive 2021/902, July 2021
15. Oder, T.: Efficient and side-channel resistant implementation of lattice-based cryptography. Doctoral thesis, Ruhr-Universität Bochum, January 2020
16. Reparaz, O., Bilgin, B., Nikova, S., Gierlichs, B., Verbauwhede, I.: Consolidating masking schemes. In: Gennaro, R., Robshaw, M. (eds.) CRYPTO 2015. LNCS, vol. 9215, pp. 764–783. Springer, Heidelberg (2015). https://doi.org/10.1007/978-3-662-47989-6_37
17. Schneider, T., Paglialonga, C., Oder, T., Güneysu, T.: Efficiently masking binomial sampling at arbitrary orders for lattice-based crypto. In: Lin, D., Sako, K. (eds.) PKC 2019. LNCS, vol. 11443, pp. 534–564. Springer, Cham (2019). https://doi.org/10.1007/978-3-030-17259-6_18
18. Saber Submission Team: Round 2 Submissions - Saber candidate submission package. https://www.esat.kuleuven.be/cosic/pqcrypto/saber/resources.html, April 2019
19. Verhulst, K.: Power analysis and masking of Saber. Master's thesis, KU Leuven (2019)

Improving First-Order Threshold Implementations of SKINNY

Andrea Caforio[1($\boxtimes$)], Daniel Collins[1], Ognjen Glamočanin[2],
and Subhadeep Banik[1]

[1] LASEC, Ecole Polytechnique Fédérale de Lausanne, Lausanne, Switzerland
{andrea.caforio,daniel.collins,subhadeep.banik}@epfl.ch
[2] PARSA, Ecole Polytechnique Fédérale de Lausanne, Lausanne, Switzerland
ognjen.glamocanin@epfl.ch

Abstract. Threshold Implementations have become a popular generic technique to construct circuits resilient against power analysis attacks. In this paper, we look to devise efficient threshold circuits for the lightweight block cipher family SKINNY. The only threshold circuits for this family are those proposed by its designers who decomposed the 8-bit S-box into four quadratic S-boxes, and constructed a 3-share byte-serial threshold circuit that executes the substitution layer over four cycles. In particular, we revisit the algebraic structure of the S-box and prove that it is possible to decompose it into (a) three quadratic S-boxes and (b) two cubic S-boxes. Such decompositions allow us to construct threshold circuits that require three shares and executes each round function in three cycles instead of four, and similarly circuits that use four shares requiring two cycles per round. Our constructions significantly reduce latency and energy consumption per encryption operation. Notably, to validate our designs, we synthesize our circuits on standard CMOS cell libraries to evaluate performance, and we conduct leakage detection via statistical tests on power traces on FPGA platforms to assess security. (For reproducibility's sake, we provide a public repository containing the source code to all proposed schemes together with a script to run the SILVER verification suite [8].)

Keywords: DPA · Masking · SKINNY · Threshold Implementation

1 Introduction

Side-channel attacks have been widely successful at efficiently attacking implementations of cryptosystems. Power analysis has been particularly effective in part due to the relatively low cost of the requisite equipment. In differential power analysis [17] (DPA) and its generalizations [6,18], an attacker observes the power consumption of a cryptographic primitive over time and applies statistical analysis to infer the underlying secret key. An attacker can perform a d-th order attack, e.g., by probing up to d internal wires of the circuit at once [15].

© Springer Nature Switzerland AG 2021
A. Adhikari et al. (Eds.): INDOCRYPT 2021, LNCS 13143, pp. 246–267, 2021.
https://doi.org/10.1007/978-3-030-92518-5_12

In an attempt to mitigate the damaging effects of side-channel attacks, the development of countermeasures has proliferated. Masking is one such approach which uses secret sharing to randomize input and intermediate values within a circuit. To standardise the error-prone and often ad-hoc process of designing secure masked circuits, Threshold Implementations (TI) were introduced which provide provable security with respect to side-channel attacks [4,10,20]. When implemented in hardware, a TI is secure even in the presence of glitches, an inherent side effect not considered in earlier schemes [15].

A correct TI must satisfy so-called non-completeness and uniformity to ensure security. Satisfying these properties for linear components of a given circuit is relatively straight-forward. Non-linear components are less trivial; a t-degree function must be split into at least $(td + 1)$ coordinate functions in the canonical higher-order TI [4] to provide d-th order security guarantees. Approaches to reduce this complexity like adding additional randomness exist [3], but there is an inherent trade-off between area, randomness requirements and latency when designing a TI of a given circuit. Unsurprisingly, TI schemes for AES and Keccak have enjoyed the most attention the literature. Recent works include [25,27,29] and [1,28] respectively.

1.1 SKINNY

SKINNY is a lightweight family of tweakable block ciphers designed by Beierle et al. [2]. The cipher performs extremely well on both software and hardware platforms, and is the core encryption primitive used in the authenticated encryption scheme Romulus [14] which is a finalist in the NIST lightweight cryptography competition [26]. Moreover, a criterion for the competition is the efficiency of protected circuit implementations. In the 64-bit block size versions of SKINNY, the underlying S-box defined over four bits. Designing Threshold Implementations for 4-bit S-boxes is a well-studied problem [5], and so in this work we focus on the 128-bit block size versions of SKINNY which use an 8-bit S-box, hereafter denoted by S.

S is very lightweight and uses only sixteen cross-connected two-input logic gates. Using the fact that S can be decomposed in the form $I \circ H \circ G \circ F$ (hereafter denoted by S_{2222}[1]) where each sub-function is quadratic, the designers of SKINNY proposed a first-order TI of SKINNY using a byte-serial circuit. However, when this decomposition is used to construct a TI of a round-based circuit, a single S-box layer takes four cycles to execute. This increases the latency and hence energy consumption per encryption operation in the circuit, as was shown in [7].

1.2 Contributions and Organization

In this paper, we take a closer look at first-order Threshold Implementations of the 8-bit substitution box of round-based SKINNY instantiations. As previously

---

[1] Note that throughout this paper we use the notation $S_{i_1 \dots i_k}$ to denote decompositions of the same S-box S into k component S-boxes of algebraic degrees $i_1 \dots i_k$.

mentioned, the only in-depth analysis and indeed proposal of such a masked circuit is that of S_{2222} which appeared in the design paper [2] for the byte-serial variant of SKINNY. This 3-share scheme is likely the optimal choice for a first-order secure realization in the byte-serial setting when it comes to area, latency and power/energy consumption. However, for round-based circuits, this assertion does not hold true anymore. In fact, we propose two novel decompositions that eclipse the existing variant in both latency, power and energy consumption without significantly increasing the circuit area. More specifically, our contributions are summarized as follows:

1. We devise an approach that exploits the simple 4×4 cross-connected structure of S and automatizes the search for decompositions and thus Threshold Implementations.
2. The proposed technique is then used as a gateway to efficiently decompose S into three quadratic functions $S_{222} = H \circ G \circ F$ that is computed over three cycles. The resulting 3-share masked circuit exhibits a similar area footprint to S_{2222} but cuts the number of required cycles for an encryption by one quarter and consumes around 30% less energy across different clock frequencies and cell libraries.
3. In a second step, by extending the previous technique, we propose a decomposition of S into two cubic functions $S_{33} = G \circ F$ that is thus computed in two cycles. The corresponding 4-share TI halves the number of encryption cycles and consumes 30% less energy while moderately increasing the circuit area relative to S_{2222}. We emphasise that neither of the above circuits require additional randomness beyond the initial plaintext masking.
4. We provide an extensive suite of synthesis measurements on both ASIC and FPGA targets for all investigated schemes showcasing the advantages of both S_{222} and S_{33}.
5. The proposed schemes are proven sound via the SILVER verification framework [16] that performs its analysis on ASIC netlists, which in our case are generated by the NanGate 45 nm standard cell library. In addition, we perform practical leakage assessments using the TVLA methodology [12,24] by taking power traces on FPGA targets.

The paper unfolds as follows: Sect. 2 reiterates some preliminaries regarding masking and Threshold Implementations. Subsequently in Sect. 3, we detail the derivation of S_{222} and S_{33}. Synthesis results are given in Sect. 4 and leakage assessment is performed in Sect. 5. Finally, we conclude in Sect. 6.

2   Preliminaries

Masked hardware implementations of cryptographic algorithms use the secret sharing methodology in which key-related, intermediate values x_i are split into s independent shares $x_{i,0}, x_{i,1}, \ldots, x_{i,s-1}$ such that $\sum_{j=0}^{s-1} x_{i,j} = x_i$. In practice, sharing variables implies that each function $f(x_{n-1}, \ldots, x_0) = z$ within an algorithm needs to be decomposed into functions $f_i(\cdot) = z_i$ adhering to the same correctness requirement $\sum_{i=0}^{s-1} f_i = f$.

In the following, we assume that an attacker is capable of probing individual wires of a circuit and can extract their intermediate values during the computation [15]. More specifically, we consider d-th order security, where information of any d wires can be gathered and processed. Different d-th order security properties can be defined and satisfied by a given design [9], the most natural being d-*probing* security which is satisfied given that any observation made on up to d wires is statistically independent of the secret [15]. Security properties are further considered with respect to a leakage model. Two such models of interest are the *standard* model, where a circuit without any glitching or unintended behaviour is assumed, and the *glitch-robust* model [10,11] which accounts for such behaviour. Hereafter, we say that a masked implementation in a given leakage model is d-th order secure if it is d-probing secure. There is a correspondence between d-probing security and security against d-th order differential power analysis (hereafter DPA), where the latter is implied by d-th glitch-robust probing security [3].

Threshold Implementation. The task of designing d-th order secure masking schemes has spawned various approaches, of which Threshold Implementations have crystallized themselves as one of the most adopted strategies. First introduced by Nikova et al. [4,19] Threshold Implementations provide some d-th order security guarantees against DPA in the presence of hardware glitches that are inherent to any CMOS circuit. We note that higher-order TI as defined below does not necessarily ensure d-th order security without additional measures [22,23]. Nonetheless, in the first-order setting, our setting of interest in this work, a first-order Threshold Implementation achieves first-order security in the glitch-robust model [10].

The decomposition of an n-variable Boolean function $f(x_{n-1}, \ldots, x_0) = z$ into a set of s functions $f_0, \ldots, f_{s-1}$ such that $\sum_{i=0}^{s-1} f_i = f$ is a d-th order Threshold Implementation if and only if the following conditions are met:

1. *Non-Completeness.* The functions $f_0, \ldots, f_{s-1}$ are d-th order non-complete, if any combination of at most d functions is independent of at least one input share.
2. *Uniformity.* For all x such that $f(x) = z$, the input masking is said to be uniform if each set of valid input shares of x (i.e., those sum to x) have equal probability of occurring. If this holds, the shared implementation of f is said to be uniform if each valid output share also have equal probability of occurring.

The number of input shares s_{in} respectively output shares s_{out} required to achieve a non-complete and uniform sharing of a function of algebraic degree t is given by the below bounds [4]:

$$s_{in} \geq td + 1, \quad s_{out} \geq \binom{td + 1}{t}.$$

Note that a first-order TI of a quadratic function can thus be obtained with $s_{in} = s_{out} = 3$. In this work, we will bootstrap the sharing of an arbitrary quadratic function via the canonical direct sharing of the function $f(x_2, x_1, x_0) = x_0 + x_1 x_2$, i.e.,

$$f_0 = x_{0,1} + x_{1,1} x_{2,1} + x_{1,1} x_{2,2} + x_{1,2} x_{2,1}$$
$$f_1 = x_{0,2} + x_{1,0} x_{2,0} + x_{1,2} x_{2,0} + x_{1,0} x_{2,2}$$
$$f_2 = x_{0,0} + x_{1,0} x_{2,0} + x_{1,1} x_{2,0} + x_{1,0} x_{2,1}.$$

We use an analogous direct sharing for cubic terms.

2.1 SKINNY-128 Substitution Box

As Threshold Implementations of linear functions are obtained by simple decompositions, the crux lies in finding efficient sharings for non-linear mappings. In our case, this involves the 8-bit substitution box of the 128-bit block size variants of SKINNY with different tweakey sizes which we denote by SKINNY-128, SKINNY-256 and SKINNY-384 given by the iterative mapping

$$\Pi' \circ T \circ [\Pi \circ T]^3 (x_7, x_6, x_5, x_4, x_3, x_2, x_1, x_0) = (z_7, z_6, z_5, z_4, z_3, z_2, z_1, z_0),$$

composed of a transformation T and two bitwise permutations Π, Π' such that

$$T(x_7, \ldots, x_1, x_0) = (x_7, x_6, x_5, x_4 + (x_7 \bar{\vee} x_6), x_3, x_2, x_1, x_0 + (x_3 \bar{\vee} x_2))$$
$$\Pi(x_7, \ldots, x_1, x_0) = (x_2, x_1, x_7, x_6, x_4, x_0, x_3, x_5)$$
$$\Pi'(x_7, \ldots, x_1, x_0) = (x_7, x_6, x_5, x_4, x_3, x_1, x_2, x_0).$$

Here, $\bar{\vee}$ denotes the logical NOR gate, i.e., $x \bar{\vee} y = xy + x + y + 1$. A graphical depiction of the 8-bit S-box circuit is given in Fig. 1a. Note that the highest algebraic degree of six is reached in output term z_0. The full expression of each term is given in Appendix A.

3 Partitioning the S-Box S

In [21], the authors showed how to decompose the S-box S_P of the PRESENT block cipher into two quadratic S-boxes F, G such that $S_P = G \circ F$. This enabled the authors to construct a 3-share TI of PRESENT by constructing Threshold Implementations of F and G separately with a register bank in between which suppresses and thus prevents the glitches produced by the F layer from propagating to the G layer. This however means that every evaluation of the shared S-box requires two cycles to complete. However, this is compensated by the fact that the construction requires only three shares and thus the total silicon area required for the circuit is minimal. The approach used by the authors to obtain the decomposition can be summarized as follows:

1. Evaluate all quartets of 4-bit vectorial Boolean functions f_0, f_1, f_2, f_3 such that all the f_i's are quadratic. There are 2^{11} quadratic functions in 4 bits and so a total of 2^{44} such quartets are possible.

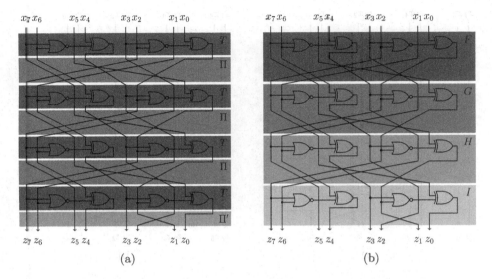

Fig. 1. (a) Definition of the 8-bit SKINNY-128 substitution box given the transformation T and two permutations Π, Π'. (b) TI decomposition proposed in [2] using four quadratic functions F, G, H and I.

2. Of the above list only filter for the quartets such that the function F : $\{0,1\}^4 \to \{0,1\}^4$ with $F(x_0, x_1, x_2, x_3) = (f_0, f_1, f_2, f_3)$ is a bijective S-box.
3. For all such F check if $G = S_P \circ F^{-1}$ is also a quadratic S-box. If so, output the pair of S-boxes (G, F).

It was later shown in [5] that S_P belongs to the affine equivalence class $\mathcal{C}_{266}$ of 4-bit S-boxes. All S-boxes in this class allows decomposition into two quadratic S-boxes. The above approach can not be extended to 8-bit S-boxes even considering the authors' suggested optimisations. To begin with there are 2^{37} quadratic functions over 8 bits, and therefore the number of octets of the form $f_0, f_1, \ldots, f_7$ will be $2^{37 \times 8} = 2^{296}$.

3.1 The Techniques

As done with PRESENT our goal lies in finding decompositions of the 8-bit SKINNY S-box S that allow for efficient Threshold Implementations in terms of circuit area, latency and energy consumption. In turn, this implies finding an appropriate balance between the number of shares, coordinate functions, and their degrees and gate complexity. To obtain a similar decomposition of S let us first state the following definitions:

Definition 1 (*i*-representable). *A Boolean function B has AND-complexity n, if its circuit can be constructed with a total of n 2-input AND gates or fewer. Its AND-depth is i (or equivalently it is i-representable) if there exists a circuit in which the AND gates can be arranged in i distinct levels in the following*

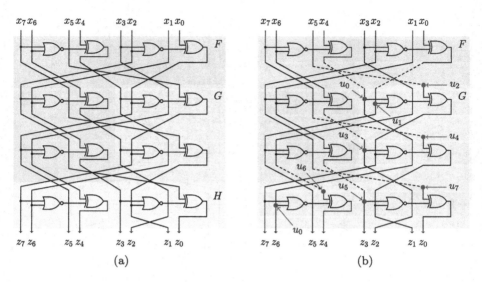

Fig. 2. (a) $S_{232} = H \circ G \circ F$ decomposition with $\deg(F) = \deg(H) = 2$ and $\deg(G) = 3$. (b) $S_{24} = G \circ F$ decomposition with $\deg(F) = 2$ and $\deg(G) = 4$. We later introduce the terminology S_{Blue} and S_{Red} to denote F, G respectively in (b). (Color figure online)

sense: all quadratic functions are 1-representable of some order, and a function B_i is i-representable if it can be expressed as $B_i = Q(t_0, t_1, \ldots, t_{m-1})$ where Q is quadratic and the functions $t_0, t_1, \ldots, t_{m-1}$ are each k-representable of some order for $k \le (i - 1)$. B is i-representable of order n if there exists a circuit which constructs it with AND-depth i and AND-complexity n.

Thus a function which is i-representable of order n can be necessarily implemented by n or a smaller number of 2-input AND gates (connected such that the total AND-depth is at most i) along with other linear gates. Thus all four coordinate functions of S_P are 2-representable of some fixed order, which allows a 3-share TI over two clock cycles.

Regarding S, the eight output functions $z_0, z_1, \ldots, z_7$ are of different algebraic degrees. z_2, z_3, z_5, z_6 are themselves quadratic and their algebraic expressions contain only one quadratic term and hence are 1-representable of order one. z_4, z_7 have algebraic degree four: the fact that z_7 is 2-representable of order three can be easily deduced from Fig. 3a: the paths from the input bits to the z_7 node go through exactly three NOR gates arranged so that the depth is two. We have $z_4 = z_7 \bar{\vee} z_6 + x_3$. Hence z_4 is at most 3-representable (in fact we will later prove that it is 2-representable too). z_0 and z_1 have algebraic degree six and five respectively: they can not be 2-representable since the set of all 2-representable functions contains members of degree four or less.

3.2   Exhaustive Partition Search

As mentioned, the byte-serial scheme presented in the SKINNY design paper [2], and later adapted to round-based setting in [7], considers a three-share decomposition into four functions of degree two which we denote by S_{2222}. As a consequence, the S-box operation is performed in a pipelined fashion over four clock cycles which incurs a large latency thus energy penalty, i.e., a single encryption of a plaintext takes four times the number of rounds when implemented as a round-based circuit.

Since z_0 and z_1 are not 2-representable, the decomposition of S into quadratic S-boxes $F_i \circ F_{i-1} \circ \cdots \circ F_1$ is not possible for $i \leq 2$. Consequently, we aim to decompose every coordinate Boolean function of S into 3-representable functions of low order. Given that S can be realized in only 16 logical two-input gates, a natural approach to obtain efficient decompositions is by partitioning the circuit into connected sub-circuits. For example, the S_{2222} decomposition corresponds to making three horizontal cuts after each row of gates. The number of possible partitions of 16 gates into n sets is n^{16}, however among those, only a small fraction of those partitions respect functional correctness. Hence, if $n = 3$, it is feasible to enumerate all correct partitions. Although this procedure does not admit a 3-representable decomposition of each coordinate function, we found many decompositions of the form $S = H \circ G \circ F$ where $\deg(F) = \deg(H) = 2$ and $\deg(G) = 3$. One such example denoted by S_{232} is shown in Fig. 2a.

3.3   A Deeper Dive

As noted above, all coordinate functions of S except z_0 and z_1 are 3-representable. If we can argue that z_0 and z_1 are also 3-representable, then it becomes straightforward to decompose S into three quadratic S-boxes. z_1 is clearly 3-representable of order five as can be deduced from Fig. 3b. The set of all paths from the input bits to z_1 traverses exactly five NOR gates arranged in three levels and so the result follows (they are marked in red in Fig. 3b).

z_0 is of algebraic degree 6 and from Fig. 1 it is at least 4-representable of order 7. This is because all but one of the 8 NOR gates are used to produce the z_0 bit and they are clearly arranged in 4 levels. However the question is: *Is z_0 also 3-representable of a suitable low order?* If yes, a 3-share first-order TI which evaluates the S-box in only three cycles is possible.

In this part we will show that z_0 is indeed 3-representable of order 8. Note that since the algebraic expression for z_0 is very complex, we avoid directly working with it to prove 3-representability: it would be very difficult to keep the AND-complexity down to a suitable value. Instead, consider the function $\pi(x, y, z) = (x \bar{\vee} y) + z$, whose algebraic expression is given by $xy + x + y + z + 1$. Note that π is completely linear in the last input z. In Fig. 4, π is represented by a green circular node, and the figure represents the circuit graph for z_0. The figure itself is redrawn by isolating the circuit path for z_0 as in Fig. 1, and will help us prove the 3-representability of z_0. Note that Fig. 4 also makes it clear that z_0 is 4-representable of order 7.

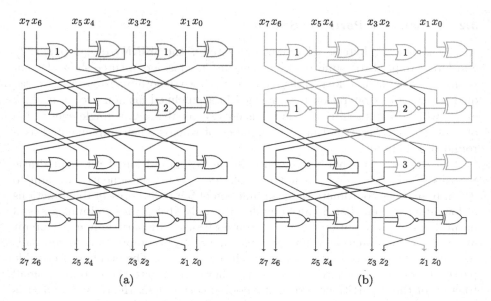

Fig. 3. (a) The path up to z_7 is marked in blue. There are 3 NOR gates, whose levels are marked inside. There is a single NOR gate at level 2, which takes inputs from the 2 other level 1 NOR gates in the first row. (b) The path up to z_1 is marked in red. There are 5 NOR gates, whose levels are marked inside. There is a single NOR gate at level 3, which takes inputs from the level 2 NOR gate and another level 1 NOR gate in the second row. (Color figure online)

Lemma 1. *It is possible to transform the circuit graph for z_0 according to the transformation (a) $\rightarrow$ (b) shown in Fig. 5.*

Proof. This transformation is easy to prove: consider the nodes labeled in darker green in Fig. 5a. The output bit $e = \pi(b, x_3, x_1)$ is given by the following algebraic expression:

$$
\begin{aligned}
e = \pi(b, x_3, x_1) &= \pi(\pi(x_2, x_3, x_0), x_3, x_1) \\
&= \pi(x_2 x_3 + x_2 + x_3 + x_0 + 1, x_3, x_1) \\
&= x_3(x_2 x_3 + x_2 + x_3 + x_0 + 1) + x_3 + (x_2 x_3 + x_2 + x_3 + x_0 + 1) + x_1 + 1 \\
&= x_0 x_3 + x_2 x_3 + x_2 + x_0 + x_1 \\
&= x_3(x_0 + x_2) + (x_0 + x_2) + x_3 + (x_1 + x_3 + 1) + 1 \\
&= \pi(x_0 + x_2, x_3, x_1 + x_3 + 1)
\end{aligned}
$$

Lemma 2. *It is possible to transform the circuit graph for z_0 according to the transformation (a) $\rightarrow$ (b) shown in Fig. 6. Thus, z_0 is 3-representable of order eight.*

Proof. The proof for this transformation is slightly more involved. Consider again the gates labeled in dark green in Fig. 6a. They lie entirely in levels 3 and 4 of

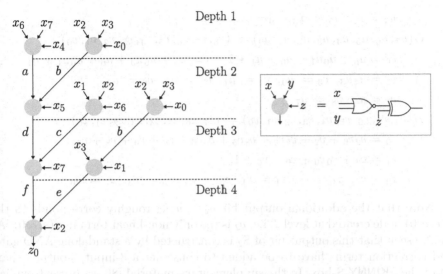

Fig. 4. Circuit graph for z_0. Its AND-complexity is 7 (note the gate $\pi(x_2, x_3, x_0)$ is shown twice for a clearer representation). (Color figure online)

the circuit graph, and takes as input the signals d, c, e, x_7, x_2 and produces z_0 as output. The expression can be written as:

$$
\begin{aligned}
z_0 &= \pi(f, e, x_2) = \pi(\pi(d, c, x_7), e, x_2) \\
&= \pi(dc + d + c + x_7 + 1, e, x_2) \\
&= e(dc + d + c + x_7 + 1) + e + (dc + d + c + x_7 + 1) + x_2 + 1 \\
&= edc + ed + ec + ex_7 + dc + d + c + x_7 + x_2 \\
&= d(ec + e + c + 1) + ec + ex_7 + c + x_7 + x_2 \\
&= d(\pi(e, c, 0)) + (ec + e + c + 1) + d + (d + e + 1 + ex_7 + x_7 + x_2) \\
&= d(\pi(e, c, 0)) + \pi(e, c, 0) + d + (ex_7 + e + x_7 + x_2 + 1 + d) \\
&= \pi\Big(\pi(e, c, 0), d, d + \pi(e, x_7, x_2)\Big)
\end{aligned}
$$

This completes the proof of the transformation. Figure 6 also proves that z_0 can be constructed with a AND-depth of 3 and so it is 3-representable.

This allows us to decompose the S-box into $H \circ G \circ F = S_{222}$, where $F : \{0, 1\}^8 \to \{0, 1\}^8$, $G : \{0, 1\}^8 \to \{0, 1\}^9$ and $H : \{0, 1\}^9 \to \{0, 1\}^8$ are each quadratic S-boxes. The algebraic expressions are as follows:

$$
\begin{aligned}
F(x_7, x_6, x_5, x_4, x_3, x_2, x_1, x_0) &= (u_7, u_6, u_5, u_4, u_3, u_2, u_1, u_0) \\
u_0 = x_4 + x_6 x_7 + x_6 + x_7 + 1, \quad u_1 &= x_0 + x_2 x_3 + x_2 + x_3 + 1 \\
u_2 = x_0 x_3 + x_0 + x_1 + x_2 x_3 + x_2, \quad u_3 &= x_1 x_2 + x_1 + x_2 + x_6 + 1
\end{aligned}
$$

$$u_4 = x_2, \; u_5 = \; x_3, \; u_6 = \; x_5, \; u_7 = \; x_7$$

$$G(u_7, u_6, u_5, u_4, u_3, u_2, u_1, u_0) = \; (v_8, v_7, v_6, v_5, v_4, v_3, v_2, v_1, v_0)$$

$$v_0 = u_6 + u_0 u_1 + u_0 + u_1 + 1, \; v_1 = u_5 + u_6 u_0 + u_6 + u_0 u_1 + u_1$$

$$v_2 = u_2 u_3, \; v_3 = \; u_0, \; v_4 = \; u_1, \; v_5 = \; u_2, \; v_6 = \; u_3,$$

$$v_7 = u_4, \; v_8 = \; u_7$$

$$H(v_8, v_7, v_6, v_5, v_4, v_3, v_2, v_1, v_0) = \; (z_7, z_6, z_5, z_4, z_3, z_2, z_1, z_0)$$

$$z_0 = v_2 v_0 + v_2 + v_5 v_0 + v_8 v_5 + v_6 v_0 + v_6 + v_0 + v_8 + v_7,$$

$$z_1 = v_8 + v_0 v_6 + v_0 + v_6 + 1,$$

$$z_2 = v_6, \; z_3 = \; v_5, \; z_4 = \; v_1, \; z_5 = \; v_4, \; z_6 = \; v_3, \; z_7 = \; v_0$$

Note that the additional output bit $v_2 = u_2 u_3$ roughly corresponds to the $\pi(e, c, 0)$ node created at level 2, i.e. v_2 is the only non-linear term in $\pi(e, c, 0)$. As can be seen that this output bit of S_2 is constructed by a standalone AND gate, and correction terms have to be added to construct a 3-input/3-output share TI of the SKINNY S-box. In the supplementary material [8], we present explicit algebraic expressions for all 3 shares of the S-boxes F, G and H. While non-completeness and correctness are easy to argue, we additionally argue uniformity of our construction too.

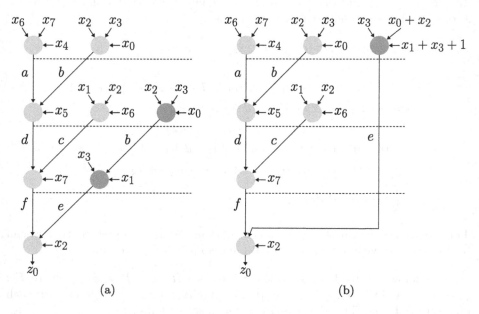

Fig. 5. Transformation (a)→(b) of the circuit graph of z_0 for Lemma 1. (Color figure online)

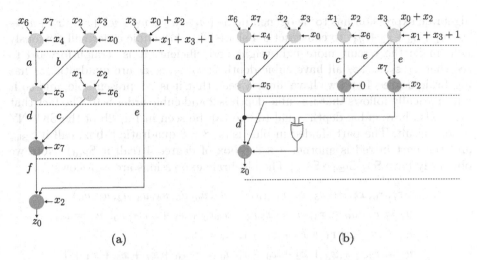

Fig. 6. Transformation (a)→(b) of the circuit graph of z_0 for Lemma 2, proving that z_0 is 3-representable of order 8 (right).(Color figure online)

3.4 Decomposition into Two Cubic S-Boxes

Note that it is straightforward to decompose S into two S-boxes of degree 4 each. For example from $S_{2222} = I \circ H \circ G \circ F$, both $G \circ F$ and $I \circ H$ are degree 4 S-boxes. A first order TI of degree 4 S-box requires 5 shares. So by using the above decomposition we can implement a circuit that evaluates the shared S-box in only 2 clock cycles but requires 5 shares. Suppose we were able to decompose S into two cubic S-boxes: if this were so then a first order TI would need only 4 shares. Such a circuit would require smaller circuit area and hence consume less power on account of the reduced number of shares and also consume less energy to encrypt a plaintext on account of the reduced power consumption. So in principle it is an interesting exercise to see if this decomposition is at all possible.

In order to decompose S into two cubic S-boxes, we can again mount an exhaustive search on all partitions of two sets as done in Sect. 3.3. This procedure does not yield such a decomposition but many of the form $S = G \circ F$ where $\deg(F) = 2$ and $\deg(G) = 4$ or vice-versa as shown in Fig. 2b. However, we can follow a similar strategy as in detailed in the previous section. We begin with the following definition:

Definition 2. *A Boolean function B is said to have cubic depth 2, if it can be expressed as $B = C(c_1, c_2, \ldots, c_n)$ where $C, c_1, c_2, \ldots, c_n$ are each either cubic Boolean functions or functions of algebraic degree strictly less than 3. The cubic order of such a function is said to be i, if the total number cubic terms in the algebraic expressions of $C, c_1, c_2, \ldots, c_n$ combined is i.*

Note that lower cubic depth allows us to construct a TI of the given function lower number of cycles using only 4 shares. Since every cubic term wxy in the algebraic expression has to be opened up as $(w_1 + w_2 + w_3 + w_4)(x_1 + x_2 + x_3 + x_4)(y_1 + y_2 + y_3 + y_4)$ to construct a 4 share TI, a low cubic order will obviously help make the circuit more lightweight and efficient. It is straightforward to see that $z_1, z_2, \ldots, z_7$ all have cubic depth 2: z_2, z_3, z_5, z_6 are quadratic. z_7 has algebraic degree 4 and we have already seen that it is 2-representable, and so it automatically follows that its cubic depth is 2 and cubic order is 0. The fact that z_1, z_4 also have cubic depth equal to two can be seen in Fig. 2b of the SKINNY S-box circuit. The part shaded in blue is an 8×8 quadratic S-box, call it S_{Blue} and the part in red is another 8×8 S-box of degree 4 (call it S_{Red}). Note we obviously have $S = S_{\mathsf{Red}} \circ S_{\mathsf{Blue}}$. The algebraic expressions are as follows:

$$S_{\mathsf{Blue}}(x_7, x_6, x_5, x_4, x_3, x_2, x_1, x_0) = (u_7, u_6, u_5, u_4, u_3, u_2, u_1, u_0)$$
$$u_7 = x_2, \ u_6 = x_3, \ u_5 = x_3 x_2 + x_3 x_0 + x_2 + x_1 + x_0, \ u_4 = x_7,$$
$$u_3 = x_6 + x_2 x_1 + x_2 + x_1 + 1, \ u_2 = x_5,$$
$$u_1 = x_3 x_2 + x_3 + x_2 + x_0 + 1, \ u_0 = x_7 x_6 + x_7 + x_6 + x_4 + 1$$
$$S_{\mathsf{Red}}(u_7, u_6, u_5, u_4, u_3, u_2, u_1, u_0) = (z_7, z_6, z_5, z_4, z_3, z_2, z_1, z_0)$$
$$z_7 = u_2 + u_1 u_0 + u_1 + u_0 + 1, \ z_6 = u_0, \ z_5 = u_1$$
$$z_4 = u_6 + u_2 u_0 + u_2 + u_1 u_0 + u_1, \ z_3 = u_5, \ z_2 = u_3,$$
$$z_1 = u_4 + u_3 u_2 + u_3 u_1 u_0 + u_3 u_1 + u_3 u_0 + u_2 + u_1 u_0 + u_1 + u_0,$$
$$z_0 = u_7 + u_5 u_4 + u_5 u_3 u_2 + u_5 u_3 u_1 u_0 + u_5 u_3 u_1 + u_5 u_3 u_0 + u_5 u_2$$
$$+ u_5 u_1 u_0 + u_5 u_1 + u_5 u_0 + u_5 + u_4 + u_3 u_2 + u_3 u_1 u_0$$
$$+ u_3 u_1 + u_3 u_0 + u_2 + u_1 u_0 + u_1 + u_0 + 1$$

From the expression we can see that z_1 as the output of S_{Red} is a cubic function with only a single cubic term. And since the u_i's are at most quadratic this follows that the cubic depth of z_1 is 2 and its cubic order is 1. Also the expression for z_4 is quadratic in S_{Red}, which proves that not only is its cubic depth 2 and cubic order 0, but it is also 2-representable. It is elementary to verify that its AND-complexity is 3.

The only problematic part is proving that z_0 also has cubic depth 2 of some suitably low order, since it is not clear from this decomposition. Note that there is only one degree 4 term $u_5 u_3 u_1 u_0$ in the expression of z_0. Also $u_5 u_1 = x_3 x_2 x_1 + x_3 x_1 + x_1 + x_1 x_2 + x_0 x_1$ is a cubic expression in the x_i's. Therefore, we construct the following S-box $S'_{\mathsf{Blue}} : \{0, 1\}^8 \to \{0, 1\}^9$ where

$$S'_{\mathsf{Blue}}(x_7, x_6, x_5, x_4, x_3, x_2, x_1, x_0) = (u_8, u_7, u_6, u_5, u_4, u_3, u_2, u_1, u_0)$$

such that $u_8 = x_3 x_2 x_1 + x_3 x_1 + x_1 + x_1 x_2 + x_0 x_1$ and the other u_i's are as defined for S_{Blue}. Correspondingly we define $S'_{\mathsf{Red}} : \{0, 1\}^9 \to \{0, 1\}^8$ where

$$S'_{\mathsf{Red}}(u_8, u_7, u_6, u_5, u_4, u_3, u_2, u_1, u_0) = (z_7, z_6, z_5, z_4, z_3, z_2, z_1, z_0)$$

such that $z_0 = u_7 + u_5 u_4 + u_5 u_3 u_2 + u_8 u_3 u_0 + u_5 u_3 u_1 + u_5 u_3 u_0 + u_5 u_2 + u_5 u_1 u_0 + u_5 u_1 + u_5 u_0 + u_5 + u_4 + u_3 u_2 + u_3 u_1 u_0 + u_3 u_1 + u_3 u_0 + u_2 + u_1 u_0 + u_1 + u_0 + 1$ and the other z_i's are as defined for S_{Red}. Since both S'_{Blue} and S'_{Red} are cubic

S-boxes this proves that the cubic depth of z_0 is also 2. It is easy to count that there are 5 cubic terms in the modified expression of z_0 and one cubic term in the expression for u_8, which implies that the cubic order of z_0 is 6. Since we also have that $S = S'_{Red} \circ S'_{Blue}$, this also gives us the cubic decomposition required to construct a first order TI using 4 input/output shares that can evaluate the shared S-box in just 2 cycles. In the supplementary material [8], we present explicit algebraic expressions for all 4 shares of the S-boxes S'_{Red}, S'_{Blue}, where we additionally argue uniformity of our construction too.

4   Implementation

After decomposing the S-box into quadratic and cubic component functions, we use the direct sharing approach to obtain the algebraic expressions for each of the individual shares of the masked S-box. In all cases, except for S_{2222}, correction terms were required to ensure uniform sharing (all the algebraic expressions for the individual shares can be found in [8]).

All the investigated schemes in this work have been synthesized on both ASIC and FPGA platforms. In particular, we used Synopsys Design Vision v2019.03 to synthesize the hardware description into a netlist via the `compile_ultra -no_autoungroup` directive that respects entity boundaries and thus prevents the optimizer from potentially interfering with the threshold properties of the circuit. Additionally, the power figures were obtained using back annotation of the switching activity onto the netlist performed by the Synopsys Power Compiler. In order to obtain a comprehensive set of measurements, our circuits were synthesized using three standard cell libraries of different sizes, namely the low-leakage TSMC 28 nm and UMC 65 nm libraries and the high-leakage NanGate 45 nm process.

In Table 1, we detail the measurements for the investigated S-box circuits and note that both in latency and power, S_{222} as well as S_{33} eclipse the other variants. This trend is amplified when the entire SKINNY circuit is implemented as shown in Table 2. We denote by $SKINNY_{i_1...i_k}$ the full SKINNY circuit using the S-box $S_{i_1...i_k}$.

The schemes have also been implemented on a 65 nm Xilinx Virtex-5 FPGA and a 45 nm Xilinx Spartan-6 FPGA using the Xilinx ISE synthesis and implementation tool. To prevent optimisations that might break the masking scheme, `DONT_TOUCH`, `KEEP`, and `KEEP_HIERARCHY` constraints have been added to the HDL source files. The resulting measurements are tabulated in Table 3.

5   Leakage Assessment

SILVER [16] is a formal verification tool for masking countermeasures. For a given security property [9], the tool exhaustive evaluates the input netlist using reduced-ordered binary decision diagrams. We compile the netlist for the S_{222} and S_{33} S-boxes using the NanGate 45 nm standard cell library and verified that both netlists satisfied first-order probing security in the standard and robust

Table 1. ASIC synthesis measurements for the investigated substitution boxes.

Scheme	Library	Latency (Cycles)	Area (GE)	Timing (ns)	Power (μW)	
					10 MHz	100 MHz
S_{2222}	TSMC 28 nm	4	550.3	0.20	4.880	45.32
	NanGate 45 nm	4	584.3	0.24	43.81	157.1
	UMC 65 nm	4	597.9	1.15	5.735	56.14
S_{232}	TSMC 28 nm	3	922.0	0.50	6.490	59.17
	NanGate 45 nm	3	915.3	1.11	86.15	166.2
	UMC 65 nm	3	941.3	3.82	7.986	77.86
S_{222}	TSMC 28 nm	3	598.9	0.24	4.561	42.03
	NanGate 45 nm	3	600.6	0.31	46.77	154.4
	UMC 65 nm	3	616.5	1.73	5.395	52.63
S_{33}	TSMC 28 nm	2	1995	0.72	11.12	99.49
	NanGate 45 nm	2	1906	1.21	159.7	553.7
	UMC 65	2	1924	4.79	14.35	139.1

probing models as well as uniformity. A script together and the corresponding netlist files are given in the auxiliary repository [8].

5.1 t-Tests

The TVLA methodology [12, 24] provides a set of best-practice guidelines for performing non-invasive leakage detection on a device under test (DUT). To verify the security of our designs, we follow this approach using Welch's t-test and the min-p strategy for null hypothesis rejection. In particular, we perform non-specific fixed versus random t-tests, where we aim to determine the validity of the null hypothesis that *encryptions with a fixed and uniformly sampled plaintext admit the same mean power consumption* (i.e., are indistinguishable under first-order statistical analysis). Following the state of the art [1, 24, 30], we set a threshold $|t| > 4.5$ for any t-value to reject the null hypothesis.

To perform t-tests, power traces of SKINNY$_{222}$ and SKINNY$_{33}$ were measured using the Sakura-X and Sasebo-GII power side-channel leakage evaluation boards. These boards contain a core FPGA target on which a cryptographic circuit can be programmed, allowing the evaluation of custom hardware implementations of cryptographic primitives. To reduce noise, the boards contain an additional FPGA for communication with the host PC, which is used to send keys and plaintexts and read ciphertexts. Moreover, these boards contain direct connectors for oscilloscope probes, facilitating the acquisition of the power supply voltage traces for the side-channel evaluation. The encryption FPGA has

Table 2. ASIC synthesis figures for all investigated schemes for three cell libraries.

Scheme	Library	Latency (Cycles)	Area (GE)	Critical Path (ns)	Power (μW)		Energy (nJ/128 bits)	
					10 MHz	100 MHz	10 MHz	100 MHz
SKINNY-128$_{2222}$	TSMC 28 nm	872	4461	0.31	21.91	186.2	1.911	1.623
Byte-Serial	NanGate 45 nm	872	5039	0.51	100.6	343.5	8.772	2.995
	UMC 65 nm	872	4989	1.59	25.82	244.5	2.251	2.132
SKINNY-256$_{2222}$	TSMC 28 nm	1040	5280	0.33	25.90	219.6	2.694	2.284
Byte-Serial	NanGate 45 nm	1040	5993	0.52	120.7	420.8	12.55	4.376
	UMC 65 nm	1040	5876	1.64	30.33	287.3	3.154	2.988
SKINNY-384$_{2222}$	TSMC 28 nm	1208	6122	0.35	26.97	222.5	3.258	2.688
Byte-Serial	NanGate 45 nm	1208	6949	0.57	140.3	496.4	16.94	5.993
	UMC 65 nm	1208	6782	1.69	34.98	333.1	4.226	4.024
SKINNY-128$_{2222}$	TSMC 28 nm	160	13671	0.35	80.01	707.0	1.280	1.131
	NanGate 45 nm	160	14637	0.47	917.3	2199	14.68	3.518
	UMC 65 nm	160	15116	2.03	93.57	898.7	1.497	1.438
SKINNY-256$_{2222}$	TSMC 28 nm	192	15197	0.36	88.13	776.9	1.692	1.491
	NanGate 45 nm	192	16315	0.47	1041	2490	19.98	4.781
	UMC 65 nm	192	16735	2.12	103.1	990.3	1.979	1.901
SKINNY-384$_{2222}$	TSMC 28 nm	224	16641	0.38	95.98	844.8	2.149	1.892
	NanGate 45 nm	224	17991	0.47	1166	2774	26.12	6.213
	UMC 65 nm	224	18357	2.12	113.4	1088	2.538	2.437
SKINNY-128$_{222}$	TSMC 28 nm	120	14452	0.44	77.58	683.3	0.931	0.819
	NanGate 45 nm	120	14899	0.66	474.9	1890	5.699	2.268
	UMC 65 nm	120	15413	3.40	93.05	892.7	1.156	1.071
SKINNY-256$_{222}$	TSMC 28 nm	144	15975	0.44	86.74	761.1	1.249	1.095
	NanGate 45 nm	144	16576	0.66	501.5	2010	7.222	2.894
	UMC 65 nm	144	17031	3.51	104.0	997.1	1.497	1.436
SKINNY-384$_{222}$	TSMC 28 nm	168	17484	0.44	95.51	838.7	1.604	1.410
	NanGate 45 nm	168	18253	0.66	632.1	2298	10.62	3.861
	UMC 65 nm	168	18654	3.51	115.6	1109	1.942	1.863
SKINNY-128$_{33}$	TSMC 28 nm	80	24375	0.66	114.7	988.5	0.917	0.791
	NanGate 45 nm	80	23954	0.88	980.1	3200	7.841	2.560
	UMC 65 nm	80	24923	4.13	139.1	1391	1.113	1.113
SKINNY-256$_{33}$	TSMC28 nm	96	26192	0.66	126.3	1090	1.212	1.046
	NanGate 45 nm	96	25888	0.87	1109	3678	10.64	3.531
	UMC 65 nm	96	26767	4.23	159.3	1542	1.529	1.480
SKINNY-384$_{33}$	TSMC 28 nm	112	27964	0.66	137.5	1190	1.540	1.333
	NanGate 45 nm	112	27820	0.87	1382	4001	15.48	4.481
	UMC 65 nm	112	28621	4.24	147.7	1636	1.654	1.832

direct connections to header pins on the board, allowing easy synchronisation using a dedicated trigger signal.

The Sakura-X board contains a more recent FPGA from the Xilinx 7-Series (Kintex-7, XC7K160T), while the Sasebo-GII board contains an older FPGA from the 5-Series (Virtex-5, XC5VLX30) architecture. To prevent unwanted optimizations during the FPGA toolchain synthesis and implementation, DONT_TOUCH, KEEP_HIERARCHY, and KEEP constraints are added. The clock frequency of our designs is constrained to a low 3 MHz on both boards. All power measurements are performed using a Tektronix MDO3104 oscilloscope with a sampling rate of 1 GS/s and AC coupling; we take 10000 sample points per trace with 1 μs horizontal graduations.

Table 3. Xilinx Virtex-5 and Spartan-6 substitution and cipher synthesis results.

Scheme	Target	Slices	Flip-Flops	Lookup Tables	Max. Frequency (MHz)
S_{2222}	Virtex-5	35	72	24	600
	Spartan-6	41	72	32	375
S_{222}	Virtex-5	30	51	46	472
	Spartan-6	42	51	52	316
S_{33}	Virtex-5	106	36	296	278
	Spartan-6	178	36	300	202
SKINNY-128$_{2222}$	Virtex-5	1348	1672	1514	280
	Spartan-6	2204	1672	928	194
SKINNY-128$_{222}$	Virtex-5	956	1337	1689	250
	Spartan-6	791	1328	1619	105
SKINNY-128$_{33}$	Virtex-5	2883	1224	5834	180
	Spartan-6	2640	1216	5641	110

To perform non-specific t-tests, all encryptions were performed with a fixed key. The cryptographic primitive was reset before every encryption to ensure identical initial conditions for both the fixed and random traces. Consequently, this allowed us to record traces for t-tests in a deterministic interleaving fashion, where a random plaintext preceded a fixed plaintext and vice-versa, reducing bias in any one dataset from potential variation in noise and environmental conditions over time. To avoid leakage arising from generating random masks on the DUT itself, we sent pre-masked plaintext shares to the FPGA.

In order to verify the soundness of our experimental setup, we first ran t-tests in the *masks off* setting by setting all but one share of the plaintext to the zero vector. We perform the masks off t-tests on 10000 traces for each design. Figures 10a and 10b plot a sample trace for the two designs. Note that we take traces corresponding to 10 rounds of an encryption operation in each experiment. Recall that executing a round of SKINNY with S_{33} uses two cycles, rather than three like with S_{222}. The encryption operation for the SKINNY$_{33}$ experiments only begins after a few thousand data points, whereas we record from the beginning of an encryption for the SKINNY$_{222}$ experiments.

The results in Figs. 7a and 8a indicate that there is potentially exploitable leakage with just 10000 traces, even with measurements with low SNR taken on the Sakura-X board. We then record 1 million traces with randomly generated masks to assess the first-order security of our designs (Figs. 7b and 8b). Our results indicate that the threshold of 4.5 is not crossed in any of the trace samples, and that no leakage is detected with this number of traces. Since Threshold Implementations are well-studied, we expect these results to hold with a larger number of traces also.

To demonstrate that our Threshold Implementation of SKINNY$_{222}$ is secure even on a smaller FPGA with a higher SNR (lower noise), we also performed t-tests with both randomly generated and zero masks using the Sasebo-II side-channel evaluation board. Figure 10c shows a sample trace taken during the experiments, where the power consumption from the encryption operation in

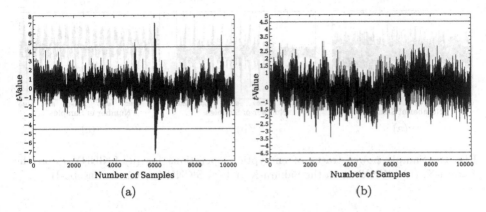

Fig. 7. t-test results for SKINNY$_{222}$ on the Sakura-X with (a) 10000 traces and masks off and (b) one million traces and masks on.

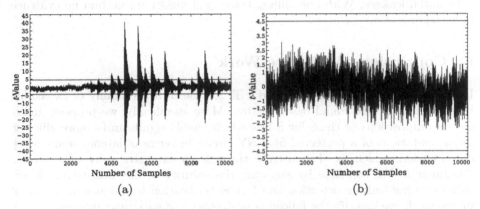

Fig. 8. t-test results for SKINNY$_{33}$ on the Sakura-X with (a) 10000 traces and masks off and (b) one million traces and masks on.

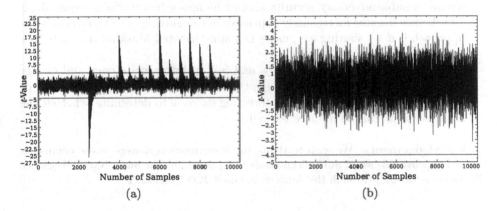

Fig. 9. t-test results for SKINNY$_{222}$ on the Sasebo-II with (a) 10000 traces and masks off and (b) one million traces and masks on.

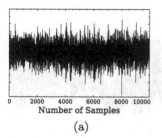 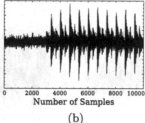 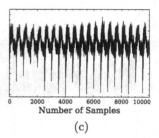

(a)   (b)   (c)

Fig. 10. Sample power traces of encryption operations for (a) SKINNY$_{222}$ on the Sakura-X, (b) SKINNY$_{33}$ on the Sakura-X and (c) SKINNY$_{222}$ on the Sasebo-II.

each clock cycle is clearly visible. Figure 9 shows the t-values obtained for the power traces. As before, with 10000 traces in the masks off setting, we note substantial leakage. With one million traces and masks on, we find no evidence of leakage.

6   Conclusion and Future Work

In this work, we re-envision first-order TI for the SKINNY family of tweakable block ciphers in the round-based setting. More specifically, we propose different decompositions of the 8-bit S-box which enable significantly more efficient implementations of a protected SKINNY circuit in terms of latency and energy consumption, which we demonstrate through an extensive suite of synthesis benchmarks. We conclude by assessing the security of our designs via leveraging existing leakage detection and formal verification techniques. In terms of future work, we identify the following problems as of particular interest:

- *Higher-Order Schemes.* This paper covers first-order realizations but against a more capable adversary, security against higher-order attacks is required. As TI schemes become increasingly expensive in this setting, a suitable candidate approach is $d+1$ sharing e.g., using Domain-Oriented Masking [13] to reduce the number of required shares.
- *Area Optimizations.* Although S$_{222}$ and S$_{33}$ optimize for latency and energy consumption in comparison to S$_{2222}$, their circuit area is roughly the same or moderately larger. It is thus an interesting exercise to determine whether the area footprint can be reduced as well.

Acknowledgements. We wish to thank the anonymous reviewers whose comments helped improve this work. Subhadeep Banik is supported by the Swiss National Science Foundation (SNSF) through the Ambizione Grant PZ00P2_179921.

A Algebraic Expressions for **SKINNY** S-box S

$$z_0 = x_7x_6x_3x_2x_1x_0 + x_7x_6x_3x_2x_0 + x_7x_6x_3x_2 + x_7x_6x_3x_1x_0 + x_7x_6x_2x_1 +$$
$$x_7x_6x_1x_0 + x_7x_3x_2x_1x_0 + x_7x_3x_2x_0 + x_7x_3x_1x_0 + x_7x_3x_0 + x_7x_2x_1 +$$
$$x_7x_2 + x_7x_1x_0 + x_7x_1 + x_7x_0 + x_7 + x_6x_5x_3x_2 + x_6x_5x_3x_0 + x_6x_5x_2 +$$
$$x_6x_5x_1 + x_6x_5x_0 + x_6x_5 + x_6x_4x_3x_2x_1 + x_6x_4x_3x_1 + x_6x_4x_3x_0 +$$
$$x_6x_4x_3 + x_6x_4x_2x_1 + x_6x_4x_1x_0 + x_6x_3x_2x_1x_0 + x_6x_3x_2x_1 + x_6x_3x_2x_0 +$$
$$x_6x_3x_1x_0 + x_6x_3x_1 + x_6x_3 + x_6x_2 + x_6x_1 + x_6x_0 + x_6 + x_5x_3x_2x_1x_0 +$$
$$x_5x_3x_2x_0 + x_5x_3x_2 + x_5x_3x_1x_0 + x_5x_2x_1x_0 + x_5x_2x_1 + x_5x_2x_0 +$$
$$x_5x_1x_0 + x_4x_3x_2x_1x_0 + x_4x_3x_2x_0 + x_4x_3x_2 + x_4x_3x_1x_0 + x_4x_2x_1 +$$
$$x_4x_1x_0 + x_3x_2x_1x_0 + x_3x_2x_0 + x_3x_1x_0 + x_3x_0 + x_2x_1x_0 + x_2x_1 +$$
$$x_2x_0 + x_1x_0 + x_1 + x_0 + 1$$

$$z_1 = x_7x_6x_3x_2x_1 + x_7x_6x_3x_1 + x_7x_6x_2x_1x_0 + x_7x_6x_2x_0 + x_7x_6x_2 +$$
$$x_7x_6x_1x_0 + x_7x_3x_2x_1 + x_7x_3x_1 + x_7x_2x_1x_0 + x_7x_2x_0 + x_7x_2 +$$
$$x_7x_1x_0 + x_7 + x_6x_5 + x_6x_4x_3x_2 + x_6x_4x_3 + x_6x_4x_2 + x_6x_4x_0 +$$
$$x_6x_3x_2x_1 + x_6x_3x_2 + x_6x_3x_1 + x_6x_3 + x_6x_2x_1x_0 + x_6x_2x_0 +$$
$$x_6x_1x_0 + x_6x_0 + x_6 + x_5x_2x_1 + x_5x_2 + x_5x_1 + x_4x_3x_2x_1 + x_4x_3x_1 +$$
$$x_4x_2x_1x_0 + x_4x_2x_0 + x_4x_2 + x_4x_1x_0 + x_2x_1 + x_2 + x_1$$

$$z_2 = x_6 + x_2x_1 + x_2 + x_1 + 1, \quad z_3 = x_3x_2 + x_3x_0 + x_2 + x_1 + x_0$$

$$z_4 = x_7x_6x_5 + x_7x_6x_3x_2 + x_7x_6x_3 + x_7x_6x_2 + x_7x_6x_0 + x_7x_6 + x_7x_5 +$$
$$x_7x_3x_2 + x_7x_3 + x_7x_2 + x_7x_0 + x_7 + x_6x_5 + x_6x_3x_2 + x_6x_3 + x_6x_2 +$$
$$x_6x_0 + x_6 + x_5x_4 + x_4x_3x_2 + x_4x_3 + x_4x_2 + x_4x_0 + x_4 + x_3$$

$$z_5 = x_3x_2 + x_3 + x_2 + x_0 + 1, \quad z_6 = x_7x_6 + x_7 + x_6 + x_4 + 1$$

$$z_7 = x_7x_6x_3x_2 + x_7x_6x_3 + x_7x_6x_2 + x_7x_6x_0 + x_7x_3x_2 + x_7x_3 + x_7x_2 +$$
$$x_7x_0 + x_6x_3x_2 + x_6x_3 + x_6x_2 + x_6x_0 + x_5 + x_4x_3x_2 + x_4x_3 +$$
$$x_4x_2 + x_4x_0$$

References

1. Arribas, V., Bilgin, B., Petrides, G., Nikova, S., Rijmen, V.: Rhythmic Keccak: SCA security and low latency in HW. IACR Trans. Cryptogr. Hardware Embed. Syst. **2018**(1), 269–290 (2018). https://doi.org/10.13154/tches.v2018.i1.269-290
2. Beierle, C., et al.: The SKINNY family of block ciphers and its low-latency variant MANTIS. In: Robshaw, M., Katz, J. (eds.) CRYPTO 2016. LNCS, vol. 9815, pp. 123–153. Springer, Heidelberg (2016). https://doi.org/10.1007/978-3-662-53008-5_5
3. Bilgin, B.: Threshold implementations: as countermeasure against higher-order differential power analysis. Ph.D. thesis, University of Twente, Netherlands, May 2015. https://doi.org/10.3990/1.9789036538916

4. Bilgin, B., Gierlichs, B., Nikova, S., Nikov, V., Rijmen, V.: Higher-order threshold implementations. In: Sarkar, P., Iwata, T. (eds.) ASIACRYPT 2014. LNCS, vol. 8874, pp. 326–343. Springer, Heidelberg (2014). https://doi.org/10.1007/978-3-662-45608-8_18

5. Bilgin, B., Nikova, S., Nikov, V., Rijmen, V., Stütz, G.: Threshold implementations of All 3×3 and 4×4 S-Boxes. In: Prouff, E., Schaumont, P. (eds.) CHES 2012. LNCS, vol. 7428, pp. 76–91. Springer, Heidelberg (2012). https://doi.org/10.1007/978-3-642-33027-8_5

6. Brier, E., Clavier, C., Olivier, F.: Correlation power analysis with a leakage model. In: Joye, M., Quisquater, J.-J. (eds.) CHES 2004. LNCS, vol. 3156, pp. 16–29. Springer, Heidelberg (2004). https://doi.org/10.1007/978-3-540-28632-5_2

7. Caforio, A., Balli, F., Banik, S.: Energy analysis of lightweight AEAD circuits. In: Krenn, S., Shulman, H., Vaudenay, S. (eds.) CANS 2020. LNCS, vol. 12579, pp. 23–42. Springer, Cham (2020). https://doi.org/10.1007/978-3-030-65411-5_2

8. Caforio, A., Collins, D., Glamocanin, O., Banik, S.: Improving first-order threshold implementations of SKINNY (Repository), October 2021. https://github.com/qantik/skinny-dipping

9. De Meyer, L., Bilgin, B., Reparaz, O.: Consolidating security notions in hardware masking. IACR Trans. Cryptogr. Hardware Embed. Syst. **2019**(3), 119–147 (2019). https://doi.org/10.13154/tches.v2019.i3.119-147

10. Dhooghe, S., Nikova, S., Rijmen, V.: Threshold implementations in the robust probing model. In: Bilgin, B., Petkova-Nikova, S., Rijmen, V. (eds.) Proceedings of ACM Workshop on Theory of Implementation Security Workshop, TIS@CCS 2019, London, UK, 11 November 2019, pp. 30–37. ACM (2019). https://doi.org/10.1145/3338467.3358949

11. Faust, S., Grosso, V., Pozo, S.M.D., Paglialonga, C., Standaert, F.X.: Composable masking schemes in the presence of physical defaults & the robust probing model. IACR Trans. Cryptogr. Hardware Embed. Syst. **2018**(3), 89–120 (2018). https://doi.org/10.13154/tches.v2018.i3.89-120

12. Gilbert Goodwill, B.J., Jaffe, J., Rohatgi, P., et al.: A testing methodology for side-channel resistance validation. In: NIST Non-invasive Attack Testing Workshop, vol. 7, pp. 115–136 (2011)

13. Groß, H., Mangard, S., Korak, T.: Domain-oriented masking: compact masked hardware implementations with arbitrary protection order. In: Bilgin, B., Nikova, S., Rijmen, V. (eds.) Proceedings of the ACM Workshop on Theory of Implementation Security, TIS@CCS 2016 Vienna, Austria, October 2016, p. 3. ACM (2016). https://doi.org/10.1145/2996366.2996426

14. Guo, C., Iwata, T., Khairallah, M., Minematsu, K., Peyrin, T.: Romulus v1.3. Technical report (2021)

15. Ishai, Y., Sahai, A., Wagner, D.: Private circuits: securing hardware against probing attacks. In: Boneh, D. (ed.) CRYPTO 2003. LNCS, vol. 2729, pp. 463–481. Springer, Heidelberg (2003). https://doi.org/10.1007/978-3-540-45146-4_27

16. Knichel, D., Sasdrich, P., Moradi, A.: SILVER – statistical independence and leakage verification. In: Moriai, S., Wang, H. (eds.) ASIACRYPT 2020. LNCS, vol. 12491, pp. 787–816. Springer, Cham (2020). https://doi.org/10.1007/978-3-030-64837-4_26

17. Kocher, P., Jaffe, J., Jun, B.: Differential power analysis. In: Wiener, M. (ed.) CRYPTO 1999. LNCS, vol. 1666, pp. 388–397. Springer, Heidelberg (1999). https://doi.org/10.1007/3-540-48405-1_25

18. Moradi, A., Standaert, F.X.: Moments-correlating DPA. In: Proceedings of the 2016 ACM Workshop on Theory of Implementation Security, pp. 5–15 (2016)

19. Nikova, S., Rechberger, C., Rijmen, V.: Threshold implementations against side-channel attacks and glitches. In: Ning, P., Qing, S., Li, N. (eds.) ICICS 2006. LNCS, vol. 4307, pp. 529–545. Springer, Heidelberg (2006). https://doi.org/10.1007/11935308_38

20. Nikova, S., Rijmen, V., Schläffer, M.: Secure hardware implementation of nonlinear functions in the presence of glitches. J. Cryptol. 24(2), 292–321 (2011). https://doi.org/10.1007/s00145-010-9085-7

21. Poschmann, A., Moradi, A., Khoo, K., Lim, C.W., Wang, H., Ling, S.: Side-channel resistant crypto for less than 2,300 GE. J. Cryptol. 24(2), 322–345 (2011). https://doi.org/10.1007/s00145-010-9086-6

22. Reparaz, O.: A note on the security of higher-order threshold implementations. Cryptology ePrint Archive, Report 2015/001 (2015). https://eprint.iacr.org/2015/001

23. Reparaz, O., Bilgin, B., Nikova, S., Gierlichs, B., Verbauwhede, I.: Consolidating masking schemes. In: Gennaro, R., Robshaw, M. (eds.) CRYPTO 2015. LNCS, vol. 9215, pp. 764–783. Springer, Heidelberg (2015). https://doi.org/10.1007/978-3-662-47989-6_37

24. Schneider, T., Moradi, A.: Leakage assessment methodology. In: Güneysu, T., Handschuh, H. (eds.) CHES 2015. LNCS, vol. 9293, pp. 495–513. Springer, Heidelberg (2015). https://doi.org/10.1007/978-3-662-48324-4_25

25. Shahmirzadi, A.R., Božilov, D., Moradi, A.: New first-order secure AES performance records. IACR Trans. Cryptogr. Hardware Embed. Syst. 2021(2), 304–327 (2021). https://doi.org/10.46586/tches.v2021.i2.304-327

26. Sönmez Turan, M., et al.: Status report on the second round of the NIST lightweight cryptography standardization process. Technical report, National Institute of Standards and Technology (2021)

27. Sugawara, T.: 3-share threshold implementation of AES s-box without fresh randomness. IACR Trans. Cryptogr. Hardware Embed. Syst. 2019(1), 123–145 (2018). https://doi.org/10.13154/tches.v2019.i1.123-145

28. Wegener, F., Baiker, C., Moradi, A.: Shuffle and mix: on the diffusion of randomness in threshold implementations of KECCAK. In: Polian, I., Stöttinger, M. (eds.) COSADE 2019. LNCS, vol. 11421, pp. 270–284. Springer, Cham (2019). https://doi.org/10.1007/978-3-030-16350-1_15

29. Wegener, F., De Meyer, L., Moradi, A.: Spin me right round rotational symmetry for FPGA-specific AES: extended version. J. Cryptol. 33(3), 1114–1155 (2020). https://doi.org/10.1007/s00145-019-09342-y

30. Zarei, S., Shahmirzadi, A.R., Soleimany, H., Salarifard, R., Moradi, A.: Low-latency Keccak at any arbitrary order. IACR Trans. Cryptogr. Hardware Embed. Syst. 2021, 388–411 (2021)

Fault Attacks

Differential Fault Attack on Espresso

Bhagwan Bathe[1], Siddhartha Tiwari[2], Ravi Anand[3($\boxtimes$)] (iD), Dibyendu Roy[2], and Subhamoy Maitra[4]

[1] Bhabha Atomic Research Centre (CI), Homi Bhabha National Institute,
Mumbai, India
bathebn@barc.gov.in
[2] Indian Institute of Information Technology Vadodara (Gandhinagar Campus),
Vadodara, India
{201851127,dibyendu.roy}@iiitvadodara.ac.in
[3] RC Bose Centre for Cryptology and Security, Indian Statistical Institute,
Kolkata, India
[4] Applied Statistics Unit, Indian Statistical Institute, Kolkata, India
subho@isical.ac.in

Abstract. In this paper we analyze the 5G standard cipher Espresso against differential fault attack. The attack outcome results in a complete internal state recovery by injecting only 4 random faults into the state of the keystream generation phase of Espresso. Since the round update function of Espresso is reversible it allows recovery of the secret key just by doing the inverse key-IV initialization process. To the best of our knowledge this is the first differential fault attack analysis of Espresso which finds the secret key of the cipher with a very minimal number of fault injection. We also provide a hardware implementation of the cipher to support our software implemented results.

Keywords: Espresso · 5G · Differential fault attack · Signatures

1 Introduction

With the growth of Internet of Things (IoT) applications, demand for lightweight ciphers in the IoT industry has increased manifold. Lightweight ciphers are required to offer the users a high level of security, while running in devices with constrained resources. Hence, besides being implemented in IoT devices that usually have limited computing power and strict power constraints, lightweight ciphers should also offer low propagation delays in implementation. Additionally, with the rise of 5G networks, traffic volume is estimated to increase by approximately 1000 times [11]. This advent of very fast 5G networks, efficient stream ciphers with low hardware cost are much in need. Espresso [6] is one of such ciphers, that not just decreases the average execution speed of the encryption, but also have a relatively easier hardware implementation.

When it comes to implementing any cryptosystem on hardware, security of the cipher becomes a primary concern. The adversary can always take advantage

© Springer Nature Switzerland AG 2021
A. Adhikari et al. (Eds.): INDOCRYPT 2021, LNCS 13143, pp. 271–286, 2021.
https://doi.org/10.1007/978-3-030-92518-5_13

of the cipher implementation by disturbing the normal operation mode of the cipher, and then trying to find the secrets of the cipher by restricting its computationally expensive search space to a smaller domain. By disturbing normal modes of operation of a cipher we mean causing glitches in the clock input, using focused laser beams to introduce bit flips, exposing the hardware to severe environments like high temperatures, over-voltage or anything that can change the internal state of the cipher. Once the changes are incorporated into the cipher and faulty ciphertexts are produced, the differences between fault-free and faulty ciphertexts are noted and we try to deduce the internal state of the cipher, and if possible, the secret key too. Since Boneh et al. [3] used fault attacks against an implementation of RSA, fault attacks have been widely used against many encryption algorithms, including DES [4] and AES [5].

Fault attacks study the robustness of a cryptosystem in a setting that is weaker than its original or expected mode of operation. Though optimistic, this model of attack can successfully be employed against a number of proposals. In a practical setting, it is indeed possible to mount such an attack when the number of faults is very low and we do not require precise controls over fault injection, both in terms of exact register locations as well as timing. In this paper we achieve these goals and present a first differential fault attack on Espresso.

Espresso is a non-linear feedback register based stream cipher. The cipher contains the NFSR in Galois configuration instead of Fibonacci configuration, as used in many ciphers. This reduces the size of feedback functions, thus decreasing the propogational delay of its hardware implementation. The NFSR has a non-linear output function with 20 variables. The cipher runs in two phases, the first one is Key and IV Initialization phase which takes a 128-bit key and 96-bit IV and uses it to initialize the state. After that the cipher runs for 256 times and the output bit is XORed with two state bits in each round. No keystream bits are generated in this round. The second phase is the keystream generation phase, where each clock gives a keystream bit.

The primary reason behind the design of Espresso is to provide a very efficient stream cipher that uses as few hardware resources as possible. This ensures Espresso to be used in various IOT technologies, where the hardware resources provided to run the encryption algorithm are very limited. Due to its very efficient implementation, Espresso is also used in 5G, which requires a very low latency.

Contribution and Organization. In this work we have presented a differential fault attack on 5G standard cipher Espresso. In Sect. 2, we describe the design of Espresso. In Sect. 3 we describe in detail the differential fault attack, how the faults are located using signatures. Our main contributions are as follows:

– In Sect. 4 we illustrate our attack on Espresso. We show that the secret key of the Espresso stream cipher can be recovered by injecting only 4 faults into the state of the cipher in the keystream generation phase. To describe our attack we first show that if we inject fault at random location then that location can be identified by doing statistical analysis on the normal and fault affected keystream bits. After detecting the location of the fault we generate 200 many normal and faulty keystream bits. Using these keystream bits we recover the state of the cipher in approximately 400 s on a laptop with Intel i5 processor and 8 GB ram. As the key-IV initialization phase of Espresso is reversible thus it yields a successful key recovery attack on Espresso.

- As Espresso needs to be implemented in the hardware terminal of a mobile (IOT) device, we further implement our attack on hardware to check its correctness. In Sect. 5 we illustrate the hardware implementation.

We conclude in Sect. 6.

2 Design Description of Espresso

Espresso [6] is a stream cipher based on 256-bit NFSR in the Galois Configuration, with key size 128-bit and IV size 96-bit. The state of the cipher is denoted by $(x_0, x_1, \ldots, x_{256})$, the key is denoted by $(k_0, k_1, \ldots, k_{127})$ and the IV is denoted by $(iv_0, iv_1, \ldots, iv_{95})$. There are feedback functions for each of the state bits, and the functions are denoted by $f_i \forall i \in 0, 1, \ldots, 255$. The cipher runs in two phases, the first one is the Initialization phase, in which the key along with the IV is used to initialize the starting state of the cipher. Then the cipher runs for 256 rounds, and in each round the output bits are XORed with the state bits x_{255} and x_{217}. This first phase is described in the Algorithm 1.

Algorithm 1. Key and IV Initialization Phase

1: $(s_0, s_1, \ldots, s_{127}) \leftarrow (k_0, k_1, \ldots, k_{127})$;
2: $(s_{128}, s_{129}, \ldots, s_{223}) \leftarrow (iv_0, iv_1, \ldots, iv_{95})$;
3: $(s_{224}, s_{225}, \ldots, s_{254}) \leftarrow (1, 1, \ldots, 1)$;
4: $s_{255} \leftarrow 0$;
5: **for** $i = 1$ to 256 **do**
6:     $z \leftarrow x_{80} \oplus x_{99} \oplus x_{137} \oplus x_{227} \oplus x_{222} \oplus x_{187} \oplus x_{243}x_{217} \oplus x_{247}x_{231} \oplus x_{213}x_{235} \oplus x_{255}x_{251}$
        $\oplus x_{181}x_{239} \oplus x_{174}x_{44} \oplus x_{164}x_{29} \oplus x_{255}x_{247}x_{243}x_{213}x_{181}x_{174}$;
7:     $f_{255} = x_0 \oplus x_{41}x_{70} \oplus z$; $f_{217} = x_{218} \oplus x_3x_{32} \oplus z$;
8:     $f_{213} = x_{214} \oplus x_4x_{45}$; $f_{209} = x_{210} \oplus x_6x_{64}$;
9:     $f_{205} = x_{206} \oplus x_5x_{80}$; $f_{201} = x_{202} \oplus x_8x_{103}$;
10:    $f_{197} = x_{198} \oplus x_{29}x_{52}x_{72}x_{99}$; $f_{193} = x_{194} \oplus x_{12}x_{121}$;
11:    $f_{251} = x_{252} \oplus x_8 \oplus x_{42}x_{83}$;
12:    $f_{247} = x_{248} \oplus x_{40} \oplus x_{44}x_{102}$;
13:    $f_{243} = x_{244} \oplus x_{103} \oplus x_{43}x_{118}$;
14:    $f_{239} = x_{240} \oplus x_{117} \oplus x_{46}x_{141}$;
15:    $f_{235} = x_{236} \oplus x_{67}x_{90}x_{110}x_{117}$;
16:    $f_{231} = x_{232} \oplus x_{189} \oplus x_{50}x_{159}$;
17:    $(x_0, x_1, \ldots x_{254}) \leftarrow (x_1, x_2, \ldots x_{255})$;
18:    $(x_{193}, x_{197}, x_{201}, x_{205}, x_{209}, x_{213}, x_{217}, x_{231}, x_{235}, x_{239}, x_{243}, x_{247}, x_{251}, x_{255}) \leftarrow$
        $(f_{193}, f_{197}, f_{201}, f_{205}, f_{209}, f_{213}, f_{217}, f_{231}, f_{235}, f_{239}, f_{243}, f_{247}, f_{251}, f_{255})$;
19: **end for**

The second phase is the keystream generation phase, in which the output bits are taken as the keystream bits. This phase is described in the Algorithm 2.

Algorithm 2. Keystream Generation Phase

1: **for** $i = 0$ to $n - 1$ **do**
2:    $z_i \leftarrow x_{80} \oplus x_{99} \oplus x_{137} \oplus x_{227} \oplus x_{222} \oplus x_{187} \oplus x_{243}x_{217} \oplus x_{247}x_{231} \oplus x_{213}x_{235} \oplus x_{255}x_{251}$
       $\oplus x_{181}x_{239} \oplus x_{174}x_{44} \oplus x_{164}x_{29} \oplus x_{255}x_{247}x_{243}x_{213}x_{181}x_{174};$ ▷This is the keystream bit
3:    $f_{255} = x_0 \oplus x_{41}x_{70}; \ f_{217} = x_{218} \oplus x_3x_{32};$
4:    $f_{213} = x_{214} \oplus x_4x_{45}; \ f_{209} = x_{210} \oplus x_6x_{64};$
5:    $f_{205} = x_{206} \oplus x_5x_{80}; \ f_{201} = x_{202} \oplus x_8x_{103};$
6:    $f_{197} = x_{198} \oplus x_{29}x_{52}x_{72}x_{99}; \ f_{193} = x_{194} \oplus x_{12}x_{121};$
7:    $f_{251} = x_{252} \oplus x_8 \oplus x_{42}x_{83};$
8:    $f_{247} = x_{248} \oplus x_{40} \oplus x_{44}x_{102};$
9:    $f_{243} = x_{244} \oplus x_{103} \oplus x_{43}x_{118};$
10:   $f_{239} = x_{240} \oplus x_{117} \oplus x_{46}x_{141};$
11:   $f_{235} = x_{236} \oplus x_{67}x_{90}x_{110}x_{117};$
12:   $f_{231} = x_{232} \oplus x_{189} \oplus x_{50}x_{159};$
13:   $(x_0, x_1, \ldots x_{254}) \leftarrow (x_1, x_2, \ldots x_{255});$
14:   $(x_{193}, x_{197}, x_{201}, x_{205}, x_{209}, x_{213}, x_{217}, x_{231}, x_{235}, x_{239}, x_{243}, x_{247}, x_{251}, x_{255}) \leftarrow$
       $(f_{193}, f_{197}, f_{201}, f_{205}, f_{209}, f_{213}, f_{217}, f_{231}, f_{235}, f_{239}, f_{243}, f_{247}, f_{251}, f_{255});$
15: **end for**

---

3   The Differential Fault Attack

When it comes to implementing any cryptosystem on hardware, security of the cipher becomes a primary concern. The adversary can always take advantage of the cipher implementation by disturbing the normal operation mode of the cipher, and then trying to find the secrets of the cipher by restricting its computationally expensive search space to a smaller domain. Disturbing normal modes of operation of a cipher seems to be a daunting task, and can possibly corrupt the data, or even worse, damage the cipher. Certainly, these can be performed in very harsh environments, and in normal use, the cipher still stays safe.

When we say introducing a disturbance in the cipher, we mean causing glitches in the clock input, using focused laser beams to introduce bit flips, exposing the hardware to severe environments like high temperatures, over-voltage or anything that can change the internal state of the cipher. The most popular method is using focused laser beams to flip some bits of the internal state. The precision of the laser beam - w.r.t. time and position of the injected fault - can be quite flexible according to some fault models, while some works assume the same. Once the changes are incorporated into the cipher and faulty ciphertexts are produced, the differences between fault-free and faulty ciphertexts are noted and we try to deduce the internal state of the cipher, and if possible, the secret key too.

When we assume that an adversary can inject faults into the cipher, it is a very strong assumption. Similarly, if the fault attack model assumes that the adversary can inject faults with precise location and timing, it is an another strong assumption. Hence, before we discuss mounting of a fault attack, we briefly mention the various assumptions made while mounting a fault attack:

1. has the required tool for injecting the fault.
2. can inject multiple faults at the exact timings during the execution.
3. can restart the cipher multiple times with the same key and IV.
4. can introduce controlled number of faults. If the number of faults is higher, injecting faults will have adverse effects on the encryption device.

Locating Faults Using Signatures. Consider a fault has been injected into some unknown location f of the state of the cipher. We have access to λ keystream bits, for every fault injected into the cipher. The entire process of identifying a fault can be divided into two parts - the offline phase, and the online phase.

First, we will define a vector of λ length which we would refer to as a *signature*, corresponding to a known fault location f.

$$S^{(f)} = \{s_0^{(f)}, s_1^{(f)}, \ldots, s_{\lambda-1}^{(f)}\}. \tag{1}$$

where $s_i^{(f)}$ is set as:

$$s_i^{(f)} = \frac{1}{2} - Pr(z_i \neq z_i^{(f)}). \tag{2}$$

Here z_i represents the keystream bits obtained without injecting any fault; whereas $z_i^{(f)}$ represents the keystream bits obtained by injecting a fault in a known location f. The probability that the fault-free keystream and fault affected keystreams will be unequal is calculated over some number of trials, say 2^{20}, for different possible states with faults injected in the same known location f. The calculated value of $s_i^{(f)}$ will fall between -0.5 and 0.5.

So the adversary does the following during the offline phase. For each possible location f of the state of the cipher, the adversary calculates $S^{(f)}$ for some value of λ, which is recommended to be taken comparable to the state size of the cipher, over some large number of trials and stores it in a table. The calculated fault signature is said to be strong if the value,

$$\sigma(S^{(f)}) = 2 \cdot \Sigma_{i=1}^{\lambda-1} \cdot \frac{|s_i^{(f)}|}{\lambda}$$

is close to 1. More sharp is the signature, better are the chances of identifying the fault location.

Now, the adversary performs ω many trials and injects a fault in the cipher in each trial, such that ω is large enough to solve equations and derive the state of the cipher (and if possible the key), as we will discuss in Sect. 4.2. The adversary notes down the original keystream $z_0, z_1, \ldots, z_{\lambda-1}$. Now the adversary uses the assumption of resetting the cipher to the original state, re-keying the cipher with the same key and IV. Then the adversary injects a fault in an unknown location γ and records the corresponding keystream $z_0^{(\gamma)}, z_1^{(\gamma)}, \ldots, z_{\lambda-1}^{(\gamma)}$. The process is repeated ω many times and the adversary has now access to $\omega + 1$ keystream sequences.

Next, the adversary computes a trail vector for each unknown fault γ:

$$\tau^{(\gamma)}[i] = \begin{cases} \frac{1}{2}, & \text{if } z_i = z_i^{(\gamma)} \\ \frac{-1}{2}, & \text{if } z_i \neq z_i^{(\gamma)} \end{cases} \tag{3}$$

for $i = 0, 1, 2, \ldots, \lambda - 1$.

The fault location f for which the fault signature $\mathcal{S}^{(f)}$ matches the trail $\tau^{(\gamma)}$ (for some unknown γ) the best would ideally be the correct fault location. To attain the best matching, we use correlation coefficient to match a trail with a corresponding signature. Pearson's correlation coefficient lies between -1 to 1, and the better the correlation, we consider it a better match. To improve matching, we consider the correlation coefficient $\mu(\mathcal{S}^{(f)}, \tau^{(\gamma)}) = -1$ if there is a complete mismatch between the two, i.e. $S_i^{(f)} = \frac{1}{2}, \tau_i^{(\gamma)} = \frac{-1}{2}$ or $S_i^{(f)} = \frac{-1}{2}, \tau_i^{(\gamma)} = \frac{1}{2}$.

For each γ, the adversary calculates the correlation coefficient between $\tau^{(\gamma)}$ and $\mathcal{S}^{(f)}$ for each possible fault location f and creates a list of fault indices $\mathcal{L}_\gamma$ sorted with reducing correlation coefficient. The adversary has to construct ω such lists, $\mathcal{L}_0, \mathcal{L}_1, \ldots, \mathcal{L}_{\omega-1}$. Now, the adversary considers a set of fault locations $\rho_0, \rho_1, \ldots, \rho_{\omega-1}$, where each $\rho_i \in \mathcal{L}_i$ and choosen from $\mathcal{L}_i$ in the increasing order of rank in the list, and tries solving equations. After solving equations and recovering state, the adversary obtains a $2n$-length keystream from the state and checks it with the available keystream. In case of a miss, the adversary repeats the solving of equations with the next best set of locations $\rho_0, \rho_1, \ldots, \rho_{\omega-1}$, chosen in the increasing order of rank in the list.

4   Differential Fault Attack on Espresso

In this section we demonstrate our proposed attack on Espresso. We follow a transient single bit-flip model of attack here. It is *transient*, because the injected fault propagates to other locations with further encryption rounds. It is different from other fault attack models like *hard faults*, where a fault is *permanent* and sticks to a certain position. Moreover, hard faults can damage the device and prevent its re-usability.

As we discussed earlier, the attack model we employ here has been inspired from Differential Fault Attack on Stream Ciphers. Note that our fault attack model assumes a flip of a single bit from $1 \to 0$ or $0 \to 1$. We assume that the adversary has the technology to inject a single laser beam of wavelength not bigger than the target cell itself, i.e., only a single bit will be affected. The adversary must have the ability to reset the cipher with the original key and plaintext. Since the faults are not permanent, such assumptions are considered to be feasible in literature.

We also assume that the location of the fault is not known to the adversary. For this purpose, we explain below how we identify the location of the injected fault.

4.1   Offline Phase

In this section we describe the Offline phase of DFA on Espresso. First we prepare the signature, and then for each location find out trail and the correlation between trail and the signature. The signatures are prepared for 100 keystream bits. The signature is plotted in the Fig. 1, It can be seen from the Fig. 1 that

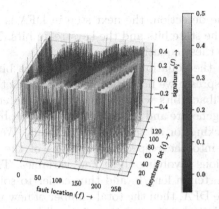

Fig. 1. Signature of Espresso

the signature lies close to 0.5 for most of the locations and keystream bits. This indicates that the correlation between trail and signature obtained will be closer to 1.0 for the same fault location, thus making the identification of the fault location easier. This is indeed verified by the plot of maximum correlation of each location in Fig. 2. The rank comes out to be 0 for every fault location. Looking at the plots, it is clear that the fault location can easily be inferred from the correlation.

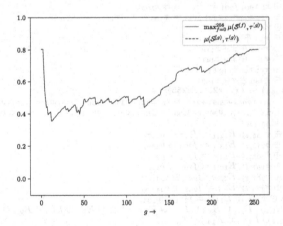

Fig. 2. Blue line shows $\mu(\mathcal{S}^{(g)}, \tau^{(g)})$, $\max_{f=0}^{100} \mu(\mathcal{S}^{(g)}, \tau^{(g)})$ is represented by the red line. (Color figure online)

4.2 Online Phase

The Online phase of DFA consists of injecting the fault and then detecting the fault location. By following the above discussion, this detection is easy to do in Espresso. After the detection, the next step in DFA is to create a system of equations involving the state bits and the keystream bits. This section describes the process to create these equations.

We first generate the equations for the keystreams bits without fault. But from the design of Espresso we note that it contains exactly 14 non-linear feedback bits. These feedback bits will gradually make the equations lengthy and almost impossible to generate and solve. To tackle this problem we introduce new variables in each clocking for all the 14 feedback bits. We use these keystream bits to feed it back into the respective positions of the state bits, and form another set of equations involving these new variables. Thus all the equations generated will be shorter in length, and thus easier to solve. If we are using n keystream bits for the DFA, then the total number of new variables required will be $14n$. Also, for the initial state each state bit will be represented by a different variable. Hence, the total number of variables used for generating the equations related to the normal keystream bits is $14n + 256$. This technique is described in the Algorithm 3.

Algorithm 3. Generation of Equations for keystream bits without fault

1: $Eq = \phi$;   ▷ This is the set of equations formed
2: **for** $i = 0$ to $n - 1$ **do**
3:    $eqo \leftarrow x_{80} \oplus x_{99} \oplus x_{137} \oplus x_{227} \oplus x_{222} \oplus x_{187} \oplus x_{243}x_{217} \oplus x_{247}x_{231} \oplus x_{213}x_{235}$
       $\oplus x_{255}x_{251} \oplus x_{181}x_{239} \oplus x_{174}x_{44} \oplus x_{164}x_{29} \oplus x_{255}x_{247}x_{243}x_{213}x_{181}x_{174}$;
4:    $E_{1,i} \leftarrow eqo \oplus z_i$;   ▷ z_i is the ith keystream bit, known beforehand.
5:    $f_{255} = x_0 \oplus x_{41}x_{70}$; $f_{217} = x_{218} \oplus x_3x_{32}$;
6:    $f_{213} = x_{214} \oplus x_4x_{45}$; $f_{209} = x_{210} \oplus x_6x_{64}$;
7:    $f_{205} = x_{206} \oplus x_5x_{80}$; $f_{201} = x_{202} \oplus x_8x_{103}$;
8:    $f_{197} = x_{198} \oplus x_{29}x_{52}x_{72}x_{99}$; $f_{193} = x_{194} \oplus x_{12}x_{121}$;
9:    $f_{251} = x_{252} \oplus x_8 \oplus x_{42}x_{83}$;
10:   $f_{247} = x_{248} \oplus x_{40} \oplus x_{44}x_{102}$;
11:   $f_{243} = x_{244} \oplus x_{103} \oplus x_{43}x_{118}$;
12:   $f_{239} = x_{240} \oplus x_{117} \oplus x_{46}x_{141}$;
13:   $f_{235} = x_{236} \oplus x_{67}x_{90}x_{110}x_{117}$;
14:   $f_{231} = x_{232} \oplus x_{189} \oplus x_{50}x_{159}$;
15:   $(x_0, x_1, \ldots x_{254}) \leftarrow (x_1, x2, \ldots x255)$;
16:   $(x_{193}, x_{197}, x_{201}, x_{205}, x_{209}, x_{213}, x_{217}, x_{231}, x_{235}, x_{239}, x_{243}, x_{247}, x_{251}, x_{255}) \leftarrow$
        $(v_{193,i}, v_{197,i}, v_{201,i}, v_{205,i}, v_{209,i}, v_{213,i}, v_{217,i}, v_{231,i}, v_{235,i}, v_{239,i}, v_{243,i}, v_{247,i},$
        $v_{251,i}, v_{255,i})$;
17:   $E_{2,i} = f_{255} \oplus v_{255,i}$; $E_{12,i} = f_{217} \oplus v_{217,i}$;
18:   $E_{3,i} = f_{213} \oplus v_{213,i}$; $E_{13,i} = f_{209} \oplus v_{209,i}$;
19:   $E_{4,i} = f_{205} \oplus v_{205,i}$; $E_{14,i} = f_{201} \oplus v_{201,i}$;
20:   $E_{5,i} = f_{197} \oplus v_{197,i}$; $E_{15,i} = f_{193} \oplus v_{193,i}$;
21:   $E_{6,i} = f_{251} \oplus v_{251,i}$; $E_{7,i} = f_{247} \oplus v_{247,i}$;
22:   $E_{9,i} = f_{239} \oplus v_{239,i}$; $E_{8,i} = f_{243} \oplus v_{243,i}$;
23:   $E_{10,i} = f_{235} \oplus v_{235,i}$; $E_{11,i} = f_{231} \oplus v_{231,i}$;
24:   $Eq = Eq \cup E_{1,i} \cup E_{2,i} \cup E_{3,i} \cup E_{4,i} \cup E_{5,i} \cup E_{6,i} \cup E_{7,i} \cup E_{8,i} \cup E_{9,i} \cup E_{10,i} \cup E_{11,i}$
        $\cup E_{12,i} \cup E_{13,i} \cup E_{14,i} \cup E_{15,i}$;
25: **end for**

Now, we inject random faults in the cipher to generate fault affected keystream bits. These faults are injected just after the key scheduling phase of the cipher. For the fault affected keystream bits, we have to choose new variables for each feedback bits again. But in this case we can also do another tweak to ensure that the equations formed are very short in length. This is done by forming difference equations for the fault affected bits.

Consider the fact that if a fault is injected at f in the state of the cipher, then the change in the value of state bits is 0 for all other locations except at f which will be 1. Thus $\Delta x_i = 0 \ \forall x_i \in \{0, 1, \ldots, f-1, f+1, \ldots 255\}$ when the fault is injected at location f. The delta represents the difference between initial and final values of some parameter. Also, note that for any two boolean variables a and b, the following basic propositions are true:

$$\Delta(a \oplus b) = (\Delta a) \oplus (\Delta b)$$
$$\Delta(a.b) = ((\Delta a).b) \oplus ((\Delta b).a) \oplus (\Delta a.\Delta b) \tag{4}$$

Following these propositions we can create a more generalized equation of difference for multiple boolean values. These values are derived in the equations below ($+$ is equivalent to $\oplus$ and is used only for brevity):

$$
\begin{aligned}
\Delta(a \cdot b \cdot c) &= (\Delta(a \cdot b)) \cdot c + (\Delta c)a \cdot b + (\Delta(a \cdot b))\Delta c \\
&= ((\Delta a) \cdot b + (\Delta b) \cdot a + \Delta a \cdot \Delta b) \cdot c \\
&\quad + ((\Delta a) \cdot b + (\Delta b) \cdot a + \Delta a \cdot \Delta b)\Delta c + (\Delta c)a \cdot b \\
&= a \cdot b \cdot \Delta c + a \cdot \Delta b \cdot c + a \cdot \Delta b \cdot \Delta c + \Delta a \cdot b \cdot c \\
&\quad + \Delta a \cdot b \cdot \Delta c + \Delta a \cdot \Delta b \cdot c + \Delta a \cdot \Delta b \cdot \Delta c
\end{aligned}
\tag{5}
$$

For four, five and six variables these difference equations can be generated in a similar sense, and are given in the Eqs. 6 and 7.

$$
\begin{aligned}
\Delta(a \cdot b \cdot c \cdot d) &= a \cdot b \cdot c \cdot \Delta d + a \cdot b \cdot d \cdot \Delta c + a \cdot c \cdot d \cdot \Delta b + b \cdot c \cdot d \cdot \Delta a \\
&\quad + a \cdot b \cdot \Delta c \cdot \Delta d + a \cdot d \cdot \Delta b \cdot \Delta c + b \cdot d \cdot \Delta a \cdot \Delta c + a \cdot c \cdot \Delta b \cdot \Delta d \\
&\quad + c \cdot d \cdot \Delta a \cdot \Delta b + b \cdot c \cdot \Delta a \cdot \Delta d + a \cdot \Delta b \cdot \Delta c \cdot \Delta d + b \cdot \Delta a \cdot \Delta c \cdot \Delta d \\
&\quad + c \cdot \Delta a \cdot \Delta b \cdot \Delta d + d \cdot \Delta a \cdot \Delta b \cdot \Delta c + \Delta a \cdot \Delta b \cdot \Delta c \cdot \Delta d
\end{aligned}
\tag{6}
$$

$$
\begin{aligned}
\Delta(a \cdot b \cdot c \cdot d \cdot e) &= a \cdot b \cdot c \cdot d \cdot \Delta e + a \cdot b \cdot c \cdot e \cdot \Delta d + a \cdot b \cdot d \cdot e \cdot \Delta c + a \cdot c \cdot d \cdot e \cdot \Delta b \\
&\quad + b \cdot c \cdot d \cdot e \cdot \Delta a + a \cdot b \cdot c \cdot \Delta d \cdot \Delta e + a \cdot b \cdot e \cdot \Delta c \cdot \Delta d + a \cdot c \cdot e \cdot \Delta b \cdot \Delta d \\
&\quad + b \cdot c \cdot e \cdot \Delta a \cdot \Delta d + a \cdot b \cdot d \cdot \Delta c \cdot \Delta e + a \cdot d \cdot e \cdot \Delta b \cdot \Delta c + b \cdot d \cdot e \cdot \Delta a \cdot \Delta c \\
&\quad + a \cdot c \cdot d \cdot \Delta b \cdot \Delta e + c \cdot d \cdot e \cdot \Delta a \cdot \Delta b + b \cdot c \cdot d \cdot \Delta a \cdot \Delta e + a \cdot b \cdot \Delta c \cdot \Delta d \cdot \Delta e \\
&\quad + a \cdot c \cdot \Delta b \cdot \Delta d \cdot \Delta e + b \cdot c \cdot \Delta a \cdot \Delta d \cdot \Delta e + a \cdot d \cdot \Delta b \cdot \Delta c \cdot \Delta e + b \cdot d \cdot \Delta a \\
&\quad \cdot \Delta c \cdot \Delta e + c \cdot d \cdot \Delta a \cdot \Delta b \cdot \Delta e + a \cdot e \cdot \Delta b \cdot \Delta c \cdot \Delta d + b \cdot e \cdot \Delta a \cdot \Delta c \cdot \Delta d \\
&\quad + c \cdot e \cdot \Delta a \cdot \Delta b \cdot \Delta d + d \cdot e \cdot \Delta a \cdot \Delta b \cdot \Delta c + a \cdot \Delta b \cdot \Delta c \cdot \Delta d \cdot \Delta e + b \cdot \Delta a \cdot \Delta c \\
&\quad \cdot \Delta d \cdot \Delta e + c \cdot \Delta a \cdot \Delta b \cdot \Delta d \cdot \Delta e + d \cdot \Delta a \cdot \Delta b \cdot \Delta c \cdot \Delta e + e \cdot \Delta a \cdot \Delta b \cdot \Delta c \cdot \Delta d \\
&\quad + \Delta a \cdot \Delta b \cdot \Delta c \cdot \Delta d \cdot \Delta e
\end{aligned}
\tag{7}
$$

Using these equations for transforming the feedback functions, the difference in feedback functions will look like as in set of Eq. 8.

$$\Delta f_{255} = \Delta x_0 + \Delta x_{41} \cdot x_{70} + x_{41} \cdot \Delta x_{70} + \Delta x_{41} \cdot \Delta x_{70}$$

$$\Delta f_{251} = \Delta x_{252} + \Delta x_{42} \cdot x_{83} + x_{42} \cdot \Delta x_{83} + \Delta x_{42} \cdot \Delta x_{83} + \Delta x_8$$

$$\Delta f_{247} = \Delta x_{248} + \Delta x_{44} \cdot x_{102} + x_{44} \cdot \Delta x_{102} + \Delta x_{44} \cdot \Delta x_{102} + \Delta x_{40}$$

$$\Delta f_{243} = \Delta x_{244} + \Delta x_{43} \cdot x_{118} + x_{43} \cdot \Delta x_{118} + \Delta x_{43} \cdot \Delta x_{118} + \Delta x_{103}$$

$$\Delta f_{239} = \Delta x_{240} + \Delta x_{46} \cdot x_{141} + x_{46} \cdot \Delta x_{141} + \Delta x_{46} \cdot \Delta x_{141} + \Delta x_{117}$$

$$\begin{aligned}
\Delta f_{235} = {}& \Delta x_{236} + \Delta x_{67} \cdot x_{90} \cdot x_{110} \cdot x_{137} + x_{67} \cdot \Delta x_{90} \cdot x_{110} \cdot x_{137} + x_{67} \cdot x_{90} \cdot \Delta x_{110} \cdot x_{137} \\
& + x_{67} \cdot x_{90} \cdot x_{110} \cdot \Delta x_{137} + \Delta x_{67} \cdot \Delta x_{90} \cdot x_{110} \cdot x_{137} + \Delta x_{67} \cdot x_{90} \cdot \Delta x_{110} \cdot x_{137} \\
& + \Delta x_{67} \cdot x_{90} \cdot x_{110} \cdot \Delta x_{137} + x_{67} \cdot \Delta x_{90} \cdot \Delta x_{110} \cdot x_{137} + x_{67} \cdot \Delta x_{90} \cdot x_{110} \cdot \Delta x_{137} \\
& + x_{67} \cdot x_{90} \cdot \Delta x_{110} \cdot \Delta x_{137} + \Delta x_{67} \cdot \Delta x_{90} \cdot \Delta x_{110} \cdot x_{137} + \Delta x_{67} \cdot \Delta x_{90} \cdot x_{110} \cdot \Delta x_{137} \\
& + \Delta x_{67} \cdot x_{90} \cdot \Delta x_{110} \cdot \Delta x_{137} + x_{67} \cdot \Delta x_{90} \cdot \Delta x_{110} \cdot \Delta x_{137} + \Delta x_{67} \cdot \Delta x_{90} \cdot \Delta x_{110} \cdot \Delta x_{137}
\end{aligned}$$

$$\Delta f_{231} = \Delta x_{232} + \Delta x_{50} \cdot x_{159} + x_{50} \cdot \Delta x_{159} + \Delta x_{50} \cdot \Delta x_{159} + \Delta x_{189}$$

$$\Delta f_{217} = \Delta x_{218} + \Delta x_3 \cdot x_{32} + x_3 \cdot \Delta x_{32} + \Delta x_3 \cdot \Delta x_{32}$$

$$\Delta f_{213} = \Delta x_{214} + \Delta x_4 \cdot x_{45} + x_4 \cdot \Delta x_{45} + \Delta x_4 \cdot \Delta x_{45}$$

$$\Delta f_{209} = \Delta x_{210} + \Delta x_6 \cdot x_{64} + x_6 \cdot \Delta x_{64} + \Delta x_6 \cdot \Delta x_{64}$$

$$\Delta f_{205} = \Delta x_{206} + \Delta x_5 \cdot x_{80} + x_5 \cdot \Delta x_{80} + \Delta x_5 \cdot \Delta x_{80}$$

$$\Delta f_{201} = \Delta x_{202} + \Delta x_8 \cdot x_{103} + x_8 \cdot \Delta x_{103} + \Delta x_8 \cdot \Delta x_{103}$$

$$\begin{aligned}
\Delta f_{197} = {}& \Delta x_{198} + \Delta x_{29} \cdot x_{52} \cdot x_{72} \cdot x_{99} + x_{29} \cdot \Delta x_{52} \cdot x_{72} \cdot x_{99} + x_{29} \cdot x_{52} \cdot \Delta x_{72} \cdot x_{99} \\
& + x_{29} \cdot x_{52} \cdot x_{72} \cdot \Delta x_{99} + \Delta x_{29} \cdot \Delta x_{52} \cdot x_{72} \cdot x_{99} + \Delta x_{29} \cdot x_{52} \cdot \Delta x_{72} \cdot x_{99} \\
& + \Delta x_{29} \cdot x_{52} \cdot x_{72} \cdot \Delta x_{99} + x_{29} \cdot \Delta x_{52} \cdot \Delta x_{72} \cdot x_{99} + x_{29} \cdot \Delta x_{52} \cdot x_{72} \cdot \Delta x_{99} \\
& + x_{29} \cdot x_{52} \cdot \Delta x_{72} \cdot \Delta x_{99} + \Delta x_{29} \cdot \Delta x_{52} \cdot \Delta x_{72} \cdot x_{99} + \Delta x_{29} \cdot \Delta x_{52} \cdot x_{72} \cdot \Delta x_{99} \\
& + \Delta x_{29} \cdot x_{52} \cdot \Delta x_{72} \cdot \Delta x_{99} + x_{29} \cdot \Delta x_{52} \cdot \Delta x_{72} \cdot \Delta x_{99} + \\
& \Delta x_{29} \cdot \Delta x_{52} \cdot \Delta x_{72} \cdot \Delta x_{99}
\end{aligned}$$

$$\Delta f_{193} = \Delta x_{194} + \Delta x_{12} \cdot x_{121} + x_{12} \cdot \Delta x_{121} + \Delta x_{12} \cdot \Delta x_{121}$$

$$(8)$$

A similar change will also happen in the non-linear output function. The function has a degree of 6, so the difference equation will be quite lengthy to write here. The difference equation of this non-linear output function, along with other details to form the equations related to fault affected keystream bits is given in Algorithm 4. Note that this algorithm generates equations for a single fault. For multiple faults it can be repeated accordingly.

Algorithm 4. Keystream Bits Difference Equation Generation

1:   $Eq = \phi$;

2:   $(\Delta x_0, \Delta x_1, \ldots, \Delta x_{255}) \leftarrow (0, 0, \ldots, 0)$

3:   $\Delta x_f \leftarrow 1$ ▷ f is the fault location

4:   **for** $i = 0$ to $n - 1$ **do**

5:      $\Delta z_i = \Delta x_{80} + \Delta x_{99} + \Delta x_{137} + \Delta x_{227} + \Delta x_{222} + \Delta x_{187} + \Delta x_{243} \cdot x_{217} + x_{243} \cdot \Delta x_{217} + \Delta x_{243} \cdot \Delta x_{217}$
$+ \Delta x_{247} \cdot x_{231} + x_{247} \cdot \Delta x_{231} + \Delta x_{247} \cdot \Delta x_{231} + \Delta x_{213} \cdot x_{235} + x_{213} \cdot \Delta x_{235} + \Delta x_{213} \cdot \Delta x_{235}$
$+ \Delta x_{255} \cdot x_{251} + x_{255} \cdot \Delta x_{251} + \Delta x_{255} \cdot \Delta x_{251} + \Delta x_{181} \cdot x_{239} + x_{181} \cdot \Delta x_{239} + \Delta x_{181} \cdot \Delta x_{239}$
$+ \Delta x_{174} \cdot x_{44} + x_{174} \cdot \Delta x_{44} + \Delta x_{174} \cdot \Delta x_{44} + \Delta x_{164} \cdot x_{29} + x_{164} \cdot \Delta x_{29} + \Delta x_{164} \cdot \Delta x_{29}$
$+ \Delta x_{255} \cdot x_{247} \cdot x_{243} \cdot x_{213} \cdot x_{181} \cdot x_{174} + x_{255} \cdot \Delta x_{247} \cdot x_{243} \cdot x_{213} \cdot x_{181} \cdot x_{174}$
$+ x_{255} \cdot x_{247} \cdot \Delta x_{243} \cdot x_{213} \cdot x_{181} \cdot x_{174} + x_{255} \cdot x_{247} \cdot x_{243} \cdot \Delta x_{213} \cdot x_{181} \cdot x_{174}$
$+ \Delta x_{255} \cdot \Delta x_{247} \cdot x_{243} \cdot x_{213} \cdot x_{181} \cdot x_{174} + \Delta x_{255} \cdot x_{247} \cdot \Delta x_{243} \cdot x_{213} \cdot x_{181} \cdot x_{174}$
$+ \Delta x_{255} \cdot x_{247} \cdot x_{243} \cdot \Delta x_{213} \cdot x_{181} \cdot x_{174} + \Delta x_{255} \cdot x_{247} \cdot x_{243} \cdot x_{213} \cdot \Delta x_{181} \cdot x_{174}$
$+ \Delta x_{255} \cdot x_{247} \cdot x_{243} \cdot x_{213} \cdot x_{181} \cdot \Delta x_{174} + x_{255} \cdot \Delta x_{247} \cdot \Delta x_{243} \cdot x_{213} \cdot x_{181} \cdot x_{174}$
$+ x_{255} \cdot \Delta x_{247} \cdot x_{243} \cdot \Delta x_{213} \cdot x_{181} \cdot x_{174} + x_{255} \cdot \Delta x_{247} \cdot x_{243} \cdot x_{213} \cdot \Delta x_{181} \cdot x_{174}$
$+ x_{255} \cdot \Delta x_{247} \cdot x_{243} \cdot x_{213} \cdot x_{181} \cdot \Delta x_{174} + x_{255} \cdot x_{247} \cdot \Delta x_{243} \cdot \Delta x_{213} \cdot x_{181} \cdot x_{174}$
$+ \Delta x_{255} \cdot \Delta x_{247} \cdot \Delta x_{243} \cdot \Delta x_{213} \cdot x_{181} \cdot x_{174} + \Delta x_{255} \cdot x_{247} \cdot x_{243} \cdot \Delta x_{213} \cdot \Delta x_{181} \cdot x_{174}$
$+ \Delta x_{255} \cdot x_{247} \cdot x_{243} \cdot \Delta x_{213} \cdot x_{181} \cdot \Delta x_{174} + \Delta x_{255} \cdot x_{247} \cdot x_{243} \cdot x_{213} \cdot \Delta x_{181} \cdot x_{174}$
$+ \Delta x_{255} \cdot x_{247} \cdot x_{243} \cdot x_{213} \cdot \Delta x_{181} \cdot x_{174} + x_{255} \cdot \Delta x_{247} \cdot \Delta x_{243} \cdot x_{213} \cdot x_{181} \cdot x_{174}$
$+ x_{255} \cdot x_{247} \cdot \Delta x_{243} \cdot x_{213} \cdot \Delta x_{181} \cdot x_{174} + x_{255} \cdot x_{247} \cdot x_{243} \cdot \Delta x_{213} \cdot x_{181} \cdot x_{174}$
$+ x_{255} \cdot x_{247} \cdot x_{243} \cdot \Delta x_{213} \cdot \Delta x_{181} \cdot x_{174} + x_{255} \cdot x_{247} \cdot x_{243} \cdot x_{213} \cdot \Delta x_{181} \cdot \Delta x_{174}$
$+ \Delta x_{255} \cdot \Delta x_{247} \cdot \Delta x_{243} \cdot \Delta x_{213} \cdot \Delta x_{181} \cdot x_{174} + \Delta x_{255} \cdot \Delta x_{247} \cdot x_{243} \cdot x_{213} \cdot \Delta x_{181} \cdot x_{174}$
$+ \Delta x_{255} \cdot x_{247} \cdot \Delta x_{243} \cdot \Delta x_{213} \cdot x_{181} \cdot x_{174} + \Delta x_{255} \cdot x_{247} \cdot x_{243} \cdot x_{213} \cdot x_{181} \cdot x_{174}$
$+ \Delta x_{255} \cdot x_{247} \cdot x_{243} \cdot \Delta x_{213} \cdot x_{181} \cdot x_{174} + x_{255} \cdot \Delta x_{247} \cdot \Delta x_{243} \cdot \Delta x_{213} \cdot x_{181} \cdot x_{174}$
$+ x_{255} \cdot \Delta x_{247} \cdot x_{243} \cdot x_{213} \cdot x_{181} \cdot x_{174} + x_{255} \cdot x_{247} \cdot \Delta x_{243} \cdot \Delta x_{213} \cdot x_{181} \cdot x_{174}$
$+ x_{255} \cdot x_{247} \cdot x_{243} \cdot \Delta x_{213} \cdot x_{181} \cdot x_{174} + x_{255} \cdot x_{247} \cdot x_{243} \cdot x_{213} \cdot \Delta x_{181} \cdot x_{174}$
$+ x_{255} \cdot \Delta x_{247} \cdot \Delta x_{243} \cdot \Delta x_{213} \cdot x_{181} \cdot \Delta x_{174} + x_{255} \cdot \Delta x_{247} \cdot \Delta x_{243} \cdot x_{213} \cdot \Delta x_{181} \cdot x_{174}$
$+ x_{255} \cdot \Delta x_{247} \cdot x_{243} \cdot \Delta x_{213} \cdot \Delta x_{181} \cdot x_{174} + \Delta x_{255} \cdot x_{247} \cdot \Delta x_{243} \cdot x_{213} \cdot \Delta x_{181} \cdot x_{174}$
$+ \Delta x_{255} \cdot \Delta x_{247} \cdot x_{243} \cdot x_{213} \cdot x_{181} \cdot \Delta x_{174} + x_{255} \cdot \Delta x_{247} \cdot \Delta x_{243} \cdot x_{213} \cdot x_{181} \cdot \Delta x_{174}$
$+ \Delta x_{255} \cdot \Delta x_{247} \cdot \Delta x_{243} \cdot \Delta x_{213} \cdot x_{181} \cdot \Delta x_{174} + \Delta x_{255} \cdot x_{247} \cdot \Delta x_{243} \cdot x_{213} \cdot \Delta x_{181} \cdot x_{174}$
$+ \Delta x_{255} \cdot \Delta x_{247} \cdot \Delta x_{243} \cdot \Delta x_{213} \cdot x_{181} \cdot x_{174}$
$+ \Delta x_{255} \cdot \Delta x_{247} \cdot \Delta x_{243} \cdot \Delta x_{213} \cdot \Delta x_{181} \cdot x_{174} + \Delta x_{255} \cdot \Delta x_{247} \cdot \Delta x_{243} \cdot \Delta x_{213} \cdot \Delta x_{181} \cdot \Delta x_{174}$

6:      $\Delta f_{255} = \Delta x_0 + \Delta x_{41} \cdot x_{70} + x_{41} \cdot \Delta x_{70} + \Delta x_{41} \cdot \Delta x_{70}$;

7:      $\Delta f_{251} = \Delta x_{252} + \Delta x_{42} \cdot x_{83} + x_{42} \cdot \Delta x_{83} + \Delta x_{42} \cdot \Delta x_{83} + \Delta x_8$;

8:      $\Delta f_{247} = \Delta x_{248} + \Delta x_{44} \cdot x_{102} + x_{44} \cdot \Delta x_{102} + \Delta x_{44} \cdot \Delta x_{102} + \Delta x_{40}$;

9:      $\Delta f_{243} = \Delta x_{244} + \Delta x_{43} \cdot x_{118} + x_{43} \cdot \Delta x_{118} + \Delta x_{43} \cdot \Delta x_{118} + \Delta x_{103}$;

10:     $\Delta f_{239} = \Delta x_{240} + \Delta x_{46} \cdot x_{141} + x_{46} \cdot \Delta x_{141} + \Delta x_{46} \cdot \Delta x_{141} + \Delta x_{117}$;

11:     $\Delta f_{235} = \Delta x_{236} + \Delta x_{67} \cdot x_{90} \cdot x_{110} \cdot x_{137} + x_{67} \cdot \Delta x_{90} \cdot x_{110} \cdot x_{137} + x_{67} \cdot x_{90} \cdot \Delta x_{110} \cdot x_{137}$
$+ x_{67} \cdot x_{90} \cdot x_{110} \cdot \Delta x_{137} + \Delta x_{67} \cdot \Delta x_{90} \cdot x_{110} \cdot x_{137} + \Delta x_{67} \cdot x_{90} \cdot \Delta x_{110} \cdot x_{137}$
$+ \Delta x_{67} \cdot x_{90} \cdot x_{110} \cdot \Delta x_{137} + x_{67} \cdot \Delta x_{90} \cdot \Delta x_{110} \cdot x_{137} + x_{67} \cdot \Delta x_{90} \cdot x_{110} \cdot \Delta x_{137}$
$+ x_{67} \cdot x_{90} \cdot \Delta x_{110} \cdot \Delta x_{137} + \Delta x_{67} \cdot \Delta x_{90} \cdot \Delta x_{110} \cdot x_{137} + \Delta x_{67} \cdot \Delta x_{90} \cdot x_{110} \cdot \Delta x_{137}$
$+ \Delta x_{67} \cdot x_{90} \cdot \Delta x_{110} \cdot \Delta x_{137} + x_{67} \cdot \Delta x_{90} \cdot \Delta x_{110} \cdot \Delta x_{137} + \Delta x_{67} \cdot \Delta x_{90} \cdot \Delta x_{110} \cdot \Delta x_{137}$;

12:     $\Delta f_{231} = \Delta x_{232} + \Delta x_{50} \cdot x_{159} + x_{50} \cdot \Delta x_{159} + \Delta x_{50} \cdot \Delta x_{159} + \Delta x_{189}$;

13:     $\Delta f_{217} = \Delta x_{218} + \Delta x_3 \cdot x_{32} + x_3 \cdot \Delta x_{32} + \Delta x_3 \cdot \Delta x_{32}$;

14:     $\Delta f_{213} = \Delta x_{214} + \Delta x_4 \cdot x_{45} + x_4 \cdot \Delta x_{45} + \Delta x_4 \cdot \Delta x_{45}$;

15:     $\Delta f_{209} = \Delta x_{210} + \Delta x_6 \cdot x_{64} + x_6 \cdot \Delta x_{64} + \Delta x_6 \cdot \Delta x_{64}$;

16:     $\Delta f_{205} = \Delta x_{206} + \Delta x_5 \cdot x_{80} + x_5 \cdot \Delta x_{80} + \Delta x_5 \cdot \Delta x_{80}$;

17:     $\Delta f_{201} = \Delta x_{202} + \Delta x_8 \cdot x_{103} + x_8 \cdot \Delta x_{103} + \Delta x_8 \cdot \Delta x_{103}$;

18:     $\Delta f_{197} = \Delta x_{198} + \Delta x_{29} \cdot x_{52} \cdot x_{72} \cdot x_{99} + x_{29} \cdot \Delta x_{52} \cdot x_{72} \cdot x_{99} + x_{29} \cdot x_{52} \cdot \Delta x_{72} \cdot x_{99}$
$+ x_{29} \cdot x_{52} \cdot x_{72} \cdot \Delta x_{99} + \Delta x_{29} \cdot \Delta x_{52} \cdot x_{72} \cdot x_{99} + \Delta x_{29} \cdot x_{52} \cdot \Delta x_{72} \cdot x_{99}$
$+ \Delta x_{29} \cdot x_{52} \cdot x_{72} \cdot \Delta x_{99} + x_{29} \cdot \Delta x_{52} \cdot \Delta x_{72} \cdot x_{99} + x_{29} \cdot \Delta x_{52} \cdot x_{72} \cdot \Delta x_{99}$
$+ x_{29} \cdot x_{52} \cdot \Delta x_{72} \cdot \Delta x_{99} + \Delta x_{29} \cdot \Delta x_{52} \cdot \Delta x_{72} \cdot x_{99} + \Delta x_{29} \cdot \Delta x_{52} \cdot x_{72} \cdot \Delta x_{99}$
$+ \Delta x_{29} \cdot x_{52} \cdot \Delta x_{72} \cdot \Delta x_{99} + x_{29} \cdot \Delta x_{52} \cdot \Delta x_{72} \cdot \Delta x_{99} + \Delta x_{29} \cdot \Delta x_{52} \cdot \Delta x_{72} \cdot \Delta x_{99}$;

19:     $\Delta f_{193} = \Delta x_{194} + \Delta x_{12} \cdot x_{121} + x_{12} \cdot \Delta x_{121} + \Delta x_{12} \cdot \Delta x_{121}$;

20:     $I = \Delta z_i \oplus z_i \oplus z_i^f$ ▷ z_i^f is the ith-bit of fault affected keystream

21:     $Eq = Eq \cup I$

22:     $(\Delta x_0, \Delta x_1, \ldots \Delta x_{254}) \leftarrow (\Delta x_1, \Delta x_2, \ldots \Delta x_{255})$;

23:     $(\Delta x_{193}, \Delta x_{197}, \Delta x_{201}, \Delta x_{205}, \Delta x_{209}, \Delta x_{213}, \Delta x_{217}, \Delta x_{231}, \Delta x_{235}, \Delta x_{239}, \Delta x_{243},$
$\Delta x_{247}, \Delta x_{251}, \Delta x_{255}) \leftarrow (\Delta f_{193}, \Delta f_{197}, \Delta f_{201}, \Delta f_{205}, \Delta f_{209}, \Delta f_{213}, \Delta f_{217},$
$\Delta f_{231}, \Delta f_{235}, \Delta f_{239}, \Delta f_{243}, \Delta f_{247}, \Delta f_{251}, \Delta f_{255})$;

24:     $(x_0, x_1, \ldots x_{254}) \leftarrow (x_1, x_2, \ldots x_{255})$;   ▷ State bits are updated as in Algorithm 3

25:     $(x_{193}, x_{197}, x_{201}, x_{205}, x_{209}, x_{213}, x_{217}) \leftarrow$
$\left(v_{193,i}, v_{197,i}, v_{201,i}, v_{205,i}, v_{209,i}, v_{213,i}, v_{217,i} \right)$;

26:     $(x_{231}, x_{235}, x_{239}, x_{243}, x_{247}, x_{251}, x_{255}) \leftarrow$
$\left(v_{231,i}, v_{235,i}, v_{239,i}, v_{243,i}, v_{247,i}, v_{251,i}, v_{255,i} \right)$;

27: **end for**

Using the idea described above we implemented the attack in SageMath 9.0 [14] and SAT solver, and tried various different configurations of fault locations. Wo observed that if we inject four random faults the Sat Solver is able to find the values of all the state bits correctly. As an example, we injected faults at locations {212, 33, 155, 3}, which were selected randomly, and generated a system of equations as described in Algorithm 4 for 200 keystreams. These system of equations were then fed to the SAT solver. The SAT solver solves the system of equations and returns the state bits. This experiment took approximately 400 s. All these experiments were performed on a system with a 2208 Mhz processor, 8 GB RAM running on Ubuntu-20.04 operating system.

5   Hardware Implementation of Espresso

In this section, we describe the hardware implementation of Espresso. Espresso is based on Non linear Feedback Shift Register (NLFSR) in Galois configuration. The size of the NLFSR is $256 - bit$. The state of the cipher is denoted by $(x_0, x_1, \ldots, x_{255})$, the key is denoted by $(k_0, k_1, \ldots, k_{127})$ and the IV is denoted by $(iv_0, iv_1, \ldots, iv_{95})$. The output bit of espresso is denoted by z.

Figure 3 shows the implementation details for the cipher. The state register is $256 - bit$ and is updated using Non linear feedback functions. The Output is generated by non linear output function operating on 20 bits from the state register. In each clock the state register is shifted by one bit position.

Espresso has two phases, key scheduling phase and pseudorandom bit generation phase. In key scheduling phase, state register x is initialized by using key and IV as follows:

$$(x_0, x_1, \ldots, x_{127}) \leftarrow (k_0, k_1, \ldots, k_{127})$$
$$(x_{128}, x_{129}, \ldots, x_{223}) \leftarrow (iv_0, iv_1, \ldots, iv_{95})$$
$$(x_{224}, x_{225}, \ldots, x_{254}) \leftarrow (1, 1, \ldots, 1)$$
$$(x_{255}) \leftarrow 0$$

After initialization, the state register is updated using non-linear feedback function for 256 clocks. In most of the stream ciphers designs based on feedback shift registers only LSB is updated using nonlinear or linear update function. In Espresso, 14 bits of state register are updated using different nonlinear feedback functions as follows:

$$x_{213} \leftarrow x_{214} \oplus x_4 x_{45}$$
$$x_{209} \leftarrow x_{210} \oplus x_6 x_{64}$$
$$x_{205} \leftarrow x_{206} \oplus x_5 x_{80}$$
$$x_{201} \leftarrow x_{202} \oplus x_8 x_{103}$$
$$x_{197} \leftarrow x_{198} \oplus x_{29} x_{52} x_{72} x_{99}$$
$$x_{193} \leftarrow x_{194} \oplus x_{12} x_{121}$$
$$x_{251} \leftarrow x_{252} \oplus x_8 \oplus x_{42} x_{83}$$

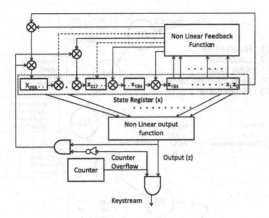

Fig. 3. Design of Espresso

$$x_{247} \leftarrow x_{248} \oplus x_{40} \oplus x_{44}x_{102}$$

$$x_{243} \leftarrow x_{244} \oplus x_{103} \oplus x_{43}x_{118}$$

$$x_{239} \leftarrow x_{240} \oplus x_{117} \oplus x_{46}x_{141}$$

$$x_{235} \leftarrow x_{236} \oplus x_{67}x_{90}x_{110}x_{117}$$

$$x_{231} \leftarrow x_{232} \oplus x_{189} \oplus x_{50}x_{159}$$

$$x_{255} \leftarrow x_0 \oplus x_{41}x_{70} \oplus z$$

$$x_{217} \leftarrow x_{218} \oplus x_3x_{32} \oplus z$$

Output bit z is generated as:

$$z \leftarrow x_{80} \oplus x_{99} \oplus x_{137} \oplus x_{227} \oplus x_{222} \oplus x_{187} \oplus x_{243}x_{217} \oplus x_{247}x_{231} \oplus x_{213}x_{235} \oplus$$
$$x_{255}x_{251} \oplus x_{181}x_{239} \oplus x_{174}x_{44} \oplus x_{164}x_{29} \oplus x_{255}x_{247}x_{243}x_{213}x_{181}x_{174}$$

The output z generated during initialization phase is also used to update x_{255} and x_{217}. In pseudorandom bit generation phase the one output bit is generated per clock. The output z generated during this phase is not used to update x_{255} and x_{217}.

State machine is used to control operation of Espresso. Details of state machine are shown in Fig. 4. In each state, state machine generates control signals required for controlling the different functions of operation. In Reset state $S1$, state register x and control signals are set to zero. In Loading state $S2$, State register is loaded with Key and IV as described above. In key scheduling state $S3$, the state register is updated for 256 clocks. After 256 clocks the cipher enters the fault injection state $S4$. In state $S4$, a particular bit/bits in a state register x is flipped without shifting the state register. In pseudo random generations state $S5$, the cipher starts generation of Key stream. One key stream bit is generated per clock. The keystream bit generated during this state is transferred to computer using buffered FIFO.

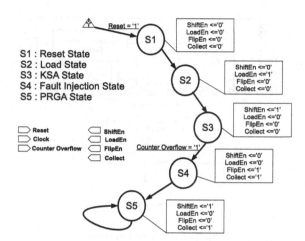

Fig. 4. Control finite state machine

Functional simulation of Espresso is carried out using Aldec ActiveHDL 10.1. Figure 5 gives details of various waveforms generated during the cipher operations.

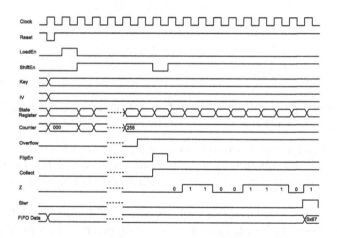

Fig. 5. Functional simulation result

On Reset signal, state register and control signals become zero. LoadEn signal loads the state register x. On ShiftEn signal, state register is updated and shifted by one bit position on each rising edge of the clock. On FlipEn signal an appropriate bit in state register x is flipped and keystream generation starts from the next clock cycles. The faulty keystream is collected in a 8 bit register using collect signal and transferred to computer using buffered FIFO.

Above circuit is synthesized using Xilinx ISE design suite. Our hardware setup consists of Xilinx Sparton 3 FPGA (Spartan3S50AN) which is interfaced with computer using buffered FIFO. Device resource utilization after implementation of the circuit is provided in Table 1.

Table 1. Device utilization summary

Logic utilization	Used	Available	Utilization
# Slice Flip Flops	294	1408	20%
# 4 Input LUTs	318	1408	22%
# Occupied Slices	184	704	26%
# Slices Containing Only Related Logic	184	184	100%
# Slices Containing Unrelated Logic	0	184	0%
Total # 4 Input LUTs	329	1408	23%
Number Used as Logic	318		
Number Used as a Route-thru	11		
# Bounded IOBs	16	108	14%
# BUFGMUXs	1	24	4%
Average Fanout of Non-Clock Nets	5.28		

Steps in Generation of Differential Data

1. Initialize the Key and IV with random values.
2. Generate the bit file.
3. Download bit file to FPGA.
4. Reset the FPGA and start keystream generation.
5. Collect the keystream in computer.
6. Repeat the step 1 to 5 for bit difference at locations from the set $\{3, 33, 155, 212\}$.
7. Use the output generated from FPGA for further analysis using Sage.

After getting the fault-free and faulty keystream bits, we generate a system of equations involving the internal state bits of Espresso in SageMath software. The details of how these equations are generated for the software is explained in Sect. 4. The SAT solver returns the correct solution which matches with the internal state. Since the state update of Espresso is invertible the internal state recovery implies key recovery. We have validated our result with the software simulation described in Sect. 4 of our main article.

6   Conclusion

In this paper we demonstrate a differential fault attack on Espresso. The designers of the cipher have not performed any security analysis of Espresso against fault attacks. We show that an adversary can retrieve complete internal state using DFA and which then can reversed to reveal the secret key. Precisely we require only 4 random faults and approximately 200 keystreams to recover the complete internal state in a practical time of approximately 400 s.

Acknowledgements. We would like to thank the anonymous reviewers for their constructive comments and suggestions, which considerably improved the editorial and technical quality of our paper.

References

1. Banik, S., Maitra, S.: A differential fault attack on MICKEY 2.0. In: Bertoni, G., Coron, J.-S. (eds.) CHES 2013. LNCS, vol. 8086, pp. 215–232. Springer, Heidelberg (2013). https://doi.org/10.1007/978-3-642-40349-1_13
2. Biham, E., Dunkelman, O.: Differential cryptanalysis in stream ciphers. https://eprint.iacr.org/2007/218.pdf
3. Boneh, D., DeMillo, R.A., Lipton, R.J.: On the importance of checking cryptographic protocols for faults. In: Fumy, W. (ed.) EUROCRYPT 1997. LNCS, vol. 1233, pp. 37–51. Springer, Heidelberg (1997). https://doi.org/10.1007/3-540-69053-0_4
4. Biham, E., Shamir, A.: Differential fault analysis of secret key cryptosystems. In: Kaliski, B.S. (ed.) CRYPTO 1997. LNCS, vol. 1294, pp. 513–525. Springer, Heidelberg (1997). https://doi.org/10.1007/BFb0052259
5. Blömer, J., Seifert, J.-P.: Fault based cryptanalysis of the advanced encryption standard (AES). In: Wright, R.N. (ed.) FC 2003. LNCS, vol. 2742, pp. 162–181. Springer, Heidelberg (2003). https://doi.org/10.1007/978-3-540-45126-6_12
6. Dubrova, E., Hell, M.: Espresso: a stream cipher for 5G wireless communication systems. Cryptogr. Commun. **9**(2), 273–289 (2017). https://doi.org/10.1007/s12095-015-0173-2
7. Hoch, J.J., Shamir, A.: Fault analysis of stream ciphers. In: Joye, M., Quisquater, J.-J. (eds.) CHES 2004. LNCS, vol. 3156, pp. 240–253. Springer, Heidelberg (2004). https://doi.org/10.1007/978-3-540-28632-5_18
8. Hojsík, M., Rudolf, B.: Differential fault analysis of trivium. In: Nyberg, K. (ed.) FSE 2008. LNCS, vol. 5086, pp. 158–172. Springer, Heidelberg (2008). https://doi.org/10.1007/978-3-540-71039-4_10
9. Hojsík, M., Rudolf, B.: Floating fault analysis of trivium. In: Chowdhury, D.R., Rijmen, V., Das, A. (eds.) INDOCRYPT 2008. LNCS, vol. 5365, pp. 239–250. Springer, Heidelberg (2008). https://doi.org/10.1007/978-3-540-89754-5_19
10. Maitra, S., Siddhanti, A., Sarkar, S.: A differential fault attack on plantlet. IEEE Trans. Comput. **66**(10), 1804–1808 (2017)
11. Olsson, M., Cavdar, C., Frenger, P., Tombaz, S., Sabella, D., Jantti, R.: 5GrEEn: towards green 5G mobile networks. In: 2013 IEEE 9th International Conference on Wireless and Mobile Computing, Networking and Communications (WiMob), pp. 212–216. IEEE (2013)
12. Sarkar, S., Dey, P., Adhikari, A., Maitra, S.: Probabilistic signature based generalized framework for differential fault analysis of stream ciphers. Cryptogr. Commun. **9**(4), 523–543 (2017). https://doi.org/10.1007/s12095-016-0197-2
13. Siddhanti, A., Sarkar, S., Maitra, S., Chattopadhyay, A.: Differential fault attack on grain v1, ACORN v3 and lizard. In: Ali, S.S., Danger, J.-L., Eisenbarth, T. (eds.) SPACE 2017. LNCS, vol. 10662, pp. 247–263. Springer, Cham (2017). https://doi.org/10.1007/978-3-319-71501-8_14
14. SageMath: A free open-source mathematics software. https://www.sagemath.org/

Differential Fault Attack on Montgomery Ladder and in the Presence of Scalar Randomization

Andy Russon[1,2]([✉])

[1] Orange, Applied Crypto Group, Cesson-Sévigné, France
[2] Univ Rennes, CNRS, IRMAR - UMR 6625, 35000 Rennes, France
andy.russon@univ-rennes1.fr

Abstract. Differential fault attacks are powerful techniques to break a cryptographic primitive, where the adversary disrupts the execution of a calculation to find a secret key. Those attacks have been applied in Elliptic Curve Cryptography under various types of faults, and there exists several protection mechanisms to prevent them.

In this paper, we present a new differential fault attack on the Montgomery ladder algorithm for scalar multiplication. We further present that such attacks can be applied when specific point additions formulas are used and when different scalar blinding techniques to randomize the computation are present.

Keywords: Differential fault attack · Elliptic curve · Montgomery ladder · Scalar blinding · Scalar splitting

1 Introduction

Differential Fault Analysis (DFA) was first introduced on block ciphers [4] and RSA [7]. In these attacks, a fault is induced and modifies the behavior of the execution resulting in an erroneous output. The effects of the fault on the output are compared with the correct one to compromise the full secret key.

The efficiency of Elliptic Curve Cryptography (ECC) makes it popular for embedded devices due mainly to the small parameter size for high-security level, thus it is necessary to protect against physical attacks such as fault attacks. In this paper, we are interested in several unexplored paths for DFA on the scalar multiplication which is the main operation of ECC.

The first main contribution is a new attack on the Montgomery ladder algorithm [22]. Its most sensitive part as implemented in cryptographic libraries is a conditional swap, and we extend the analysis of DFA when a fault affects this operation. In particular, we look at the use of specific point addition formulas that do not use all point coordinates. Those are specific to the Montgomery ladder algorithm and often used in libraries outside of the classical formulas. Furthermore, we show that point validation or loop invariant verification are not sound measures to protect against our attack.

© Springer Nature Switzerland AG 2021
A. Adhikari et al. (Eds.): INDOCRYPT 2021, LNCS 13143, pp. 287–310, 2021.
https://doi.org/10.1007/978-3-030-92518-5_14

Our second main contribution is to show that scalar blinding methods do not prevent DFA if the randomizer is too small. Those are the first Coron counter-measure [13] that adds a random multiple of the group order to blind the secret scalar, and the others are methods that separate in several shares the scalar with a multiplicative or Euclidean splitting [12,38]. We consider the attack in the context of the ECDSA signature scheme, as it is well suited for DFA and can be exploited for key recovery using lattice techniques [25]. Finally, our attack was experimented on several simulations.

The paper is organized as follows. In Sect. 2 we introduce notations on elliptic curves and ECDSA. Then, Sect. 3 describes our DFA attack on the Montgomery ladder algorithm, followed in Sect. 4 on how the scalar blinding and scalar split-ting methods can also be attacked. We give in Sect. 5 a practical evaluation of the implementation of the ladder algorithm in cryptographic libraries, how the attack can be achieved under the skip instruction fault model or with a random fault in a register, and results from several simulations. Finally, we discuss in Sect. 6 past proposed countermeasures to protect against DFA and the limita-tions of some against our attack, and we conclude in Sect. 7. The construction of the lattices adapted for each case considered in the paper is presented in Appendix A.

1.1   Related Works

The first report of DFA with elliptic curves was presented in [3]. The target of the fault injection is a point coordinate during a scalar multiplication resulting in a point that does not belong to the original elliptic curve. The algorithm is run backward with the correct and erroneous outputs by making guesses on the bits of the secret scalar processed after the fault was made. The comparison with the correct value is used to check which guess is the correct one. This attack makes the points leave the curve, and a classical countermeasure is to validate them using the curve equation before releasing an output.

Another DFA was proposed in [6], with the advantage that a point validation does not detect the fault. Indeed this *sign-change fault* attack only modifies the sign of a point, so it still satisfies the curve equation. An example is given to realize such an effect with a fault during the calculation of the NAF represen-tation of the secret scalar, and the paper claims that it could be adapted to the Montgomery ladder algorithm in the case the y-coordinate is used.

In the same line of work, DFA where point validation cannot detect the fault were presented in [32] and [33] on the Montgomery ladder algorithm. The faults considered are a skip of one or several operations of the algorithm such that one bit is not processed in the first paper, or with a skip of one multiplication or one squaring when used with RSA in the second paper (but compatible with elliptic curves if one replaces the operations with point doublings and point additions). Then, it is possible to recover the bits of the scalar processed after or before the fault occurred.

Our attack is akin to the previous DFA on the Montgomery ladder algorithm, where the fault does not make the points leave the elliptic curve. But it shares similarities to the *sign-change fault* attack, as the goal is to change the sign of the implicit loop invariant of the algorithm.

There are other recent fault attacks on ECC, but those are either a DFA against a wNAF algorithm for scalar multiplication [11], or target specifically deterministic signature scheme such as the determinist variant of ECDSA or EdDSA [1, 26, 29, 30] that cover well the subject.

2   Preliminaries

In this section, we introduce notations of elliptic curves, followed by a description of ECDSA and why it is useful for a DFA attack.

2.1   Elliptic Curves over Prime Fields

An elliptic curve E defined over a field $\mathbf{F}_p$ with p a prime greater than 5 is the set of points $(x, y) \in (\mathbf{F}_p)^2$ that satisfy an equation of the form

$$y^2 = x^3 + Ax + B, \quad A, B \in \mathbf{F}_p, \tag{1}$$

with $\Delta = 4A^3 + 27B^2 \neq 0$, and an additional point $\mathcal{O}$, alongside an operation that makes the curve an abelian group. This operation is the point addition, where the identity is $\mathcal{O}$, and the inverse of a point $P = (x_P, y_P)$ is $-P = (x_P, -y_P)$.

For an integer k, the operation called scalar multiplication is the repeated addition of a point P that appears k times and is noted $[k]P$. For all points P, there exists a smallest positive integer k such that $[k]P = \mathcal{O}$ and is called the order of the point.

Given Q a point in the subgroup of prime order q generated by P, then there exists an integer k such that $Q = [k]P$ and is called the discrete logarithm of Q in base P. The security of ECC is based upon the hardness of finding the discrete logarithm, and the best algorithms are Baby Step-Giant Steps (BSGS) [35] and Pollard's *rho* algorithms with complexity $O(\sqrt{q})$. In the case k is known to lie in a relatively small interval $[a, b]$, then it can be found in complexity $O(\sqrt{b-a})$ with BSGS or Pollard's kangaroo algorithm [27].

2.2   ECDSA

This is an elliptic curve-based signature scheme [24]. Its domain parameters are an elliptic curve E and a base point P of prime order q that belongs to the curve.

Given a private key α in $[1, q - 1]$ and a hashing function H, signing a message M is done according to Algorithm 1, and the pair (r, s) forms the signature.

The verification process consists of computing the point

$$\widetilde{Q} = [\mathrm{H}(M)s^{-1}]P + [rs^{-1}]P_{\mathrm{pub}} \tag{2}$$

where $P_{\mathrm{pub}} = [\alpha]P$ is the public key of the signer, and the signature is valid if r is equal to the x-coordinate of $\widetilde{Q}$ (lifted as an integer, then reduced modulo q).

Algorithm 1. ECDSA signature generation.

Require: message M, private key α, point P of order q on an elliptic curve
Ensure: signature (r, s) of the message M under the private key α

1: **repeat**
2:     $k \leftarrow$ random integer in $[1, q-1]$
3:     $Q \leftarrow [k]P$
4:     $r \leftarrow x_Q \bmod q$
5:     $s \leftarrow k^{-1}(\mathrm{H}(M) + \alpha r) \bmod q$
6: **until** $r \neq 0$ and $s \neq 0$
7: **return** (r, s)

Faulty Signature. The differential fault attack of this paper results in the production of a faulty signature. If a fault is made during the scalar multiplication such that the output is Q', then the resulting signature (r', s') is

$$\begin{cases} r' = x_{Q'} & \bmod q \\ s' = k^{-1}(\mathrm{H}(M) + \alpha r') & \bmod q. \end{cases}$$

It is not possible to recover the full signature (r, s) from the faulty signature, but the point Q from which r is derived can be reconstructed using the public point of the signer from the relation that is used for signature verification:

$$[\mathrm{H}(M)s'^{-1}]P + [r's'^{-1}]P_{\mathrm{pub}} = [k]P = Q.$$

The point Q' can also be obtained by lifting the integer r' as a point on the elliptic curve. However, the value $x_{Q'}$ has been reduced modulo the prime q. It has been shown that outside of Q' there are only a few possible points [2]. Since the prime q is generally the curve cardinality and is very close to the field order, there are likely only two possible points, Q' and $-Q'$.

Therefore, an attacker can obtain both Q and Q', which is a major part of a DFA attack.

2.3   Hidden Number Problem

The attack presented in this paper allows an attacker to retrieve partial knowledge of the nonce in an ECDSA signature. This can be turned into an instance of the Hidden Number Problem, and solve it using lattices to recover the private key [8,25].

By injecting the partial information of nonces in the linear equations of n signatures, it can be rewritten as a linear system of n equations and $(n + 1)$ variables:

$$u_i X + v_i \equiv Y_i, \quad (\bmod q), \quad 1 \leq i \leq n. \tag{3}$$

The unknowns are X (the private key α) and $Y_1, \ldots, Y_n$ (the unknown parts of the nonces). The Hidden Number Problem is finding X when the variables Y_i are known to belong in a relatively small interval.

The simplest case is when the most significant bits (respectively least) of the nonces are known, thus the variables Y_i consist of their least significant bits (respectively most). The number of signatures to collect depends on the leak obtained on each nonce. We can get a rough idea with a rule of thumb: with a t-bit curve and ℓ bits leaked per nonce, we can expect around t/ℓ signatures for the lattice attack to succeed. For instance, with 5 least significant bits leaked on a 256-bit curve, an average of 54 signatures are generally sufficient. Therefore, this step in the attack has a negligible cost from a few milliseconds up to a few seconds.

Explanation and construction of lattices for each situation are detailed in Appendix A.

3   DFA on Montgomery Ladder

In this section, we present the Montgomery ladder algorithm, then we describe our attack.

3.1   The Montgomery Ladder Algorithm

One advantage of the Montgomery ladder algorithm for computing $Q = [k]P$ is that the same elliptic curve operations are executed for each bit processed: the algorithm has a regular behavior.

This is done by using two variable points R_0 and R_1 that satisfy the invariant $R_1 - R_0 = P$ in each loop. Let $k = (k_{n-1}, \ldots, k_0)_2$ the binary representation of the scalar k, and suppose the leading bits $\widehat{k}$ down to k_j are already processed, meaning that $R_0 = [\widehat{k}]P$ and $R_1 = [\widehat{k}+1]P$. The state of the Montgomery ladder algorithm is updated depending on the current bit k_{j-1} as follows:

$$(R_0, R_1) = \begin{cases} ([2]R_0, R_0 + R_1) & \text{if } k_{j-1} = 0, \\ (R_0 + R_1, [2]R_1) & \text{if } k_{j-1} = 1. \end{cases} \tag{4}$$

As a consequence, at the end of the step, we have $R_0 = [2\widehat{k} + k_{j-1}]P$, and the relation $R_1 - R_0 = P$ still holds. The process goes on until the last bit, and the final state gives $R_0 = [k]P$.

To avoid branch conditions, a conditional swap with bitwise masking techniques is commonly used in implementations so the point doubling is executed with the correct value, and a second time after the operations to restore R_0 and R_1 (see Algorithm 2).

Remark 1. There is also a padding method to avoid a leak of the bit length of its input given in [10], using the group order q of bit length t: the scalar k is replaced with $k+\varepsilon q$ with $\varepsilon \in \{1, 2\}$ that makes the new scalar exactly a $(t+1)$-bit integer. Since q is the order of the base point, the final result of the scalar multiplication is unchanged. We suppose in the following that this countermeasure is implicitly used.

Algorithm 2. Montgomery ladder

Require: $k = (k_{n-1}, \ldots, k_0)_2$, P, $k_{n-1} = 1$
Ensure: $Q = [k]P$

1: $R_0 \leftarrow P$
2: $R_1 \leftarrow [2]P$
3: **for** $i = n - 2$ **down to** 0 **do**
4:      conditional_swap(k_i, R_0, R_1)
5:      $R_1 \leftarrow R_0 + R_1$
6:      $R_0 \leftarrow [2]R_0$
7:      conditional_swap(k_i, R_0, R_1)
8: **return** R_0

3.2 New Attack: Invariant Sign-Change Fault

We consider a fault that inverts the state of the ladder algorithm after the processing of the bit k_j (see Sect. 5 for examples of how it can be achieved):

$$\begin{cases} R_0 = [\widehat{k}]P \\ R_1 = [\widehat{k} + 1]P \end{cases} \xrightarrow[\text{fault}]{\notslash} \begin{cases} R_0 = [\widehat{k} + 1]P \\ R_1 = [\widehat{k}]P \end{cases} \tag{5}$$

The value R_0 for processing the next bit is $R' = [\widehat{k} + 1]P$ and the invariant for the remainder of the algorithm is the point $I = -P$. Thus, the resulting point of the scalar multiplication is

$$Q' = [2^j]R' + [\overline{k}]I = [(\widehat{k} + 1)2^j - \overline{k}]P, \tag{6}$$

where $\overline{k} = (k_{j-1}, \ldots, k_0)_2$ are the least significant bits following the bit processed when the fault was made.

Then, the following difference is a point that depends only on the j least significant bits of k:

$$Q - Q' = [2\overline{k} - 2^j]P. \tag{7}$$

Those j bits can be found with an exhaustive search. An alternative is to calculate the sum

$$Q + Q' = [\widehat{k}2^{j+1} + 2^j]P, \tag{8}$$

that depends only on the most significant bits of k.

While this type of fault is undetectable with a point validation, a check of the invariant reveals that a wrong calculation occurred. This is true for classical formulas such as affine point addition or their projective equivalent (including the complete formulas of [28]). However, there are specific formulas that do not use all point coordinates which has an impact on the previous description and makes the fault undetectable by a check of the invariant, and it is covered below.

Remark 2. In the particular case of $\overline{k} = 2^{j-1}$ the points Q and Q' are equal, so it is impossible to distinguish with the cases where the fault has no impact on the swap operation.

x-only Formulas. The particularity of those formulas is that the y-coordinates of the points are not used to compute either a point doubling or a point addition [9,18]. Let $P_1 = (x_1, y_1)$ and $P_2 = (x_2, y_2)$. Given x_1 and x_2, and the auxiliary value x_P the x-coordinate of $P_1 - P_2$, then those formulas compute the x-coordinate of $P_1 + P_2$. No auxiliary data is needed for the point doubling (outside of the elliptic curve parameters). Those formulas are well adapted for the Montgomery ladder algorithm since the point addition occurs between two points whose difference is invariant and equal to the input of the scalar multiplication.

The invariant is replaced by $-P$ in our attack. Its x-coordinate is the same as P, so the point additions in the following steps are correctly calculated, and the differential analysis can be done.

The interesting side-effect happens for the reconstruction of the missing coordinate y of the resulting faulty point, since it uses formulas involving the two coordinates of the invariant (see Appendix B for the formula). In this case, the invariant has changed from (x_P, y_P) to $(x_P, -y_P)$, and the code might use the original invariant directly, stored in registers and not modified by the execution. The sign difference only impacts the y-coordinate of the output Q' which is the same as in Eq. (6) with a sign change (so it passes a point validation test). However, the attack on ECDSA needs to construct candidates for Q' which also includes $-Q'$ so it makes no difference in the analysis.

Furthermore, a check of the invariant would not detect the fault. Indeed, the points R_0 and R_1 will be reconstructed as $R'_0 = -R_0$ and $R'_1 = -R_1$ as explained above, so the difference

$$R'_1 - R'_0 = -(R_1 - R_0) = P$$

would yield the invariant P as if no fault occurred.

Co-Z Formulas. We look now at the co-Z formulas based on Jacobian projective representation of the points: a point (x, y) is represented by $(X : Y : Z)$ with $x = X/Z^2$ and $y = Y/Z^3$. The particularity of those formulas is the requirement that the two points share the third projective coordinate Z. We consider the variant that does not use this coordinate in the formulas [17].

Instead of a regular point doubling and point addition in a ladder step, it is composed of two additions, XYcoZ-ADDC and XYcoZ-ADD, such that the two inputs share the same Z-coordinate, and give two outputs with the same property:

$$\text{XYcoZ-ADDC} : (P_1, P_2) \mapsto (P_1 + P_2, P_1 - P_2)$$
$$\text{XYcoZ-ADD} : (P_1, P_2) \mapsto (P_1 + P_2, P_1).$$

A formula for the recovery of the missing coordinate Z is necessary at the end of the scalar multiplication during the processing of the last bit to get the affine form.

The formulas are correct as long as the points share the Z-coordinate, and this property is not impacted by the attack. What remains to observe is the effect on the Z-coordinate recovery. The original invariant (x_P, y_P) might be used instead of the new one $(x_P, -y_P)$ following the fault for the same reason as with the x-only formulas, and the consequence is the appearance of a factor -1 in the reconstructed coordinate Z of the points R_0 and R_1 (see Appendix B for details). But it only changes the sign of the affine coordinate y due to the Jacobian coordinates. So the erroneous output Q' is a valid point of the elliptic curve.

Finally, as with the x-only formulas, a check of the invariant would not detect the fault. Indeed, we have $R_1 - R_0 = -P$ after the fault, and the points are reconstructed as $R'_0 = -R_0$ and $R'_1 = -R_1$ so the difference $R'_1 - R'_0$ would yield the correct invariant.

Remark 3. An alternative view for the x-only and co-Z formulas is that the invariant of the algorithm is not the full point P anymore, but only its x-coordinate which stays intact during the attack.

Unknown Step. The differential points in Eq. (7) and (8) do not depend only on the least or most significant bits of the secret scalar, but also on the step where the fault was made. This could result in several candidates if several steps j are considered during the analysis.

Conservative choices can be made to lift this indeterminacy, at the cost of losing a few bits of the scalar. Suppose we retrieved the discrete logarithm $d = 2\bar{k} - 2^j$ of the differential point of Eq. (7), but the step j is unknown. We can compute $d/2 \bmod 2^i$ for an integer i that we expect to be smaller than j (say 5 for i against 10 for j), then the i least significant bits are retrieved.

The loss of precision is not impactful as the lattice attack on ECDSA can still be successful from a few bits per nonce.

4   DFA with Scalar Randomization

In this section, we present how differential fault attacks might still be applicable when the scalar is randomized with scalar blinding methods in the context of ECDSA.

4.1   Scalar Blinding with Group Order

This is the most classical measure proposed in [13]. The secret scalar k is replaced with
$$k^\star = k + mq,$$
where m is a random integer of λ bits. Since q is the order of the base point P, then we have
$$Q = [k^\star]P = [k]P + [mq]P = [k]P.$$

Write $k^\star = \widehat{k^\star}2^j + \overline{k}^\star$ where $\overline{k}^\star$ are the j least significant bits, and $\widehat{k^\star}$ the most significant bits. Suppose that a DFA reveals $\overline{k}^\star$ (as in our attack on Montgomery ladder), then the unknown part satisfies the inequality

$$\frac{q - \overline{k}^*}{2^j} \leq \widehat{k}^* < \frac{q + 2^\lambda q - \overline{k}^*}{2^j}, \tag{9}$$

which is an interval of width $q/2^{j-\lambda}$. Then, it is necessary to have $j > \lambda$ for the unknown to be in an interval of width less than q, a necessity for exploitation in a lattice attack on ECDSA as described in Appendix A.

Cost. Suppose that we get a point whose discrete logarithm depends on the $j = \lambda + \varepsilon$ least significant bits of the blinded scalar for a nonnegative ε. An exhaustive search on those bits is expensive in this case, so a discrete logarithm algorithm such as BSGS and Pollard's kangaroo might be used to find the bits more efficiently in complexity $O(2^{(\lambda+\varepsilon)/2})$. For example, if λ is 20 (as was originally suggested in [13]), then a fault on the step $j = 24$ would make the discrete logarithm easy to find, and a small ε is sufficient to attack ECDSA as can be attested in our simulation tools. Therefore, the cost depends essentially on λ which has to be chosen quite large to prevent the attack or to make it impractical.

4.2   Euclidean Splitting

This method was proposed in [12] to protect against side-channel attacks as an alternative for scalar blinding. The secret scalar k is rewritten as

$$k = am + b,$$

where m is a random integer of λ bits with $a = \lfloor k/m \rfloor$ and $b = k \bmod m$. Then, the scalar multiplication $Q = [k]P$ can be computed as $Q = [m]([a]P) + [b]P$ using three individual scalar multiplications and a point addition.

   We show here how to recover the random divisor (or one of its factors) and the remainder of the Euclidean division of a secret scalar k from a single fault. This can be used in ECDSA for a lattice attack, and on a fixed scalar with the Chinese Remainder Theorem.

   We start by giving the general principle. Let $R = [a]P$ the scalar multiplication with the quotient, so the output is given by

$$Q = [m]R + [b]P.$$

If the point R is known, then the BSGS algorithm can be applied to find m and b. It consists of computing a first list of possible values for $[b]P$ (the *baby steps*), then a second list of possible points for $Q - [m]R$ (the *giant steps*) until a collision with the first list occurs, revealing the values m and b.

   The first list depends only on the base point, so it can be computed once and stored for reuse. Since both m and b are less than 2^λ, both the time and space complexities of the algorithm are $O(2^\lambda)$.

The proposed target is the scalar multiplication $[m]R$ with the random divisor. We suppose a fault has been made such that the effective calculation is $[m']R$ where the difference $\delta = m - m'$ belongs to a set of size T. Then the result of the whole scalar multiplication $Q = [m]R + [b]P$ is altered in a point $Q' = [m']R + [b]P$, and their difference is

$$Q - Q' = [\delta]R.$$

A candidate for R is constructed from each candidate $\tilde{\delta}$ for δ:

$$\widetilde{R} = [1/\tilde{\delta}](Q - Q').$$

The BSGS strategy is applied to get candidates $(\tilde{m}, \tilde{b})$ that satisfy the equality

$$Q - [\tilde{m}]\widetilde{R} = [\tilde{b}]P.$$

Cost. There are T possible values for δ and the BSGS algorithm runs in $O(2^\lambda)$ steps, so the overall cost is $O(2^\lambda T)$. So it is practical only for a small parameter λ (the only library implementing this technique that we found uses a parameter λ of 32 bits so the time and memory constraints are low enough). In particular, the memory constraints of BSGS should make the attack infeasible for $\lambda = 64$.

Several Candidates. Eventually, several candidates for (m, b) can be found, but we can still salvage valuable information on the scalar k. Let $(\tilde{m}, \tilde{b})$ a candidate alongside the corresponding value $\tilde{\delta}$. The correct values (m, b) and δ are also amongst the candidates.

We start with the case $b \neq \tilde{b}$. Since $(\tilde{m}, \tilde{b})$ is a candidate, we have

$$[\tilde{m}]\widetilde{R} + [\tilde{b}]P = [m]R + [b]P, \tag{10}$$

from which we derive the relation

$$a \equiv \tilde{\delta}(\tilde{b} - b)(m\tilde{\delta} - \tilde{m}\delta)^{-1} \pmod{q}. \tag{11}$$

The quotient a is recovered, so the scalar k can be fully reconstructed and verified with the relation $Q = [k]P$. This case seems unlikely to happen.

In the case the candidates are $(\tilde{m}_1, b), \ldots, (\tilde{m}_N, b)$, then we can pose $d = \gcd(\tilde{m}_1, \ldots, \tilde{m}_N)$, and we get the relation $k \equiv b \pmod{d}$.

Example with the Invariant Sign-Change Fault. We apply the attack of Sect. 3.2 when no specific formulas are used. After a fault on the scalar multiplication $[m]R$, then the result is $[m']R$ with $m' = (\hat{m} + 1)2^j - \overline{m}$. The difference with the correct output Q is

$$Q - Q' = [2\overline{m} - 2^j]R,$$

and the value $\delta = 2\overline{m} - 2^j$ depends only on the least significant bits of m. Therefore, the BSGS part of the attack only needs to run an exhaustive search on the most significant bits of m. If the *baby steps* are precomputed, then the complexity is $O(2^\lambda)$.

4.3   Multiplicative Splitting

This technique was proposed in [38]. A random value m of λ bits is randomly generated, and γ is defined such that we have the relation

$$k \equiv m\gamma \pmod{q}.$$

The scalar multiplication $Q = [k]P$ is computed in two successive scalar multiplications as $R = [m]P$ and $Q = [\gamma]R$.

The differential fault attack can be applied with a fault in the second scalar multiplication. We suppose a fault has been made such that the effective calculation is $[\gamma']R$ where the difference $\delta = \gamma - \gamma'$ belongs to a set of size T. Then the result of the whole scalar multiplication $Q = [\gamma m]P$ is altered in a point $Q' = [\gamma'm]P$, and their difference is

$$Q - Q' = [\delta m]P.$$

The value δm can be found by running through all possible values for δ, and then computing the discrete logarithm of the point $[m]P$ in base P with BSGS or Pollard's kangaroo algorithms.

Cost. Since m is a positive integer less than 2^λ the overall cost is $O(2^{\lambda/2}T)$. The cost is similar to the attack on the blinding with the group order, so it is tractable for small λ (such as 20 or 32).

Example with the Invariant Sign-Change Fault. In certain cases, a single discrete logarithm is sufficient when δ represents a small value. For example, if we consider the fault of Sect. 3.2 during the processing of the bit γ_j, then the difference with the result of the whole scalar multiplication is

$$Q - Q' = [(2\overline{\gamma} - 2^j)m]P.$$

We obtain a point whose discrete logarithm in base P is less than $2^{\lambda+j}$ (in absolute value), so the complexity to find it is $O(2^{(\lambda+j)/2})$. Again, this is practical when λ is relatively small (as was suggested in the paper that proposed this method), then the discrete logarithm can be found in a matter of seconds or minutes.

This discrete logarithm is useful for lattice attacks on ECDSA. Indeed, we have the relation

$$\frac{k - m\overline{\gamma}}{m2^j} \equiv \widehat{\gamma} \pmod{q}, \tag{12}$$

where $\widehat{\gamma}$ is a relatively small integer compared to the order q (at least j bits less). When it is possible to distinguish m from $2\overline{\gamma} - 2^j$ in the discrete logarithm (if m is prime for instance), then a lattice attack can be applied.

Table 1. Overview of Montgomery ladder in several cryptographic libraries.

Library	Init	Swap variant	Formulas	Remarks
Weierstrass curves				
OpenSSL 1.1.1k	$(P, 2P)$	Algorithm 3*	x-only	
LibreSSL 3.2.4	$(P, 2P)$	Algorithm 3*	Jacobian	
CoreCrypto (Apple)	$(P, 2P)$	Algorithm 3	Co-Z	Point valid., Eucl. split
Montgomery curves				
SymCrypt	$(\mathcal{O}, P)$	Algorithm 3	x-only	
Mbed TLS	$(\mathcal{O}, P)$	Algorithm 2	x-only	
libsodium †	$(\mathcal{O}, P)$	Algorithm 3	x-only	

*The source code is slightly different but the compiled code corresponds to Algorithm 3.
†ref10 implementation of Curve25519 present in other libraries.

Algorithm 3. Processing of the bit k_i in the Montgomery ladder variants with merged swaped.

1: pbit ← pbit $\oplus$ k_i
2: conditional_swap(pbit, R_0, R_1)
3: $R_1 \leftarrow R_0 + R_1$
4: $R_0 \leftarrow [2]R_0$
5: pbit ← k_i

5   Practical Evaluation

In this section, we consider the practicality of the attack and present evidence on how it can be achieved on several cryptographic libraries, with simulated experiments to validate our claims that are publicly available[1].

5.1   Montgomery Ladder in Libraries

In most cryptographic libraries, the second swap in the loop is merged with the first swap of the next step to avoid an unnecessary swap: the swap is effective only if the scalar bit differs from the previous one. This variant is presented in Algorithm 3.

We list in Table 1 the variant used for several libraries that implement the Montgomery ladder algorithm for the elliptic curve scalar multiplication. Elliptic curves in Montgomery form such as Curve25519 are also present in the table, though those are not used for ECDSA, the attack might still be applicable in situations where the attacker can obtain the correct and erroneous outputs.

It shall be noted that in some cases side-channel attacks could be sufficient, but those are inherent to how the actual swap is implemented. There is the

---

[1] https://github.com/orangecertcc/dfa-ladder.

binary masking technique, where the swap is made using a mask with its bits all set to 0 or 1, and a template attack was applied where the leak comes from the AND binary operator [23]. In the case of Mbed TLS, the multiplication by 0 or 1 is used to swap the values, and is also vulnerable to a template attack [21]. In both cases, a single trace could reveal the whole scalar.

Assuming that an implementation is protected against these attacks, then a fault attack becomes relevant. In the following we present a strategy to perform our attack with the variant of Algorithm 3.

5.2 Realization of the Fault Attack

Physical access to the device is necessary, and the attacker must be able to disturb the calculation at a specific point in time and location.

Skip Instruction. The first model considered is the skip instruction that was applied successfully in practice on RSA exponentiation with a spike injection on a microcontroller to skip a squaring [31]. It was also recently applied in the elliptic curve point decompression algorithm to make a point lie on weak curve [5,36].

The effects described in Sect. 3.2 can be achieved if line 1 of Algorithm 3 is omitted during one iteration of the algorithm. Indeed, the variable pbit at the beginning of the loop refers to the previous scalar bit, and keeps track of the current state of the couple (R_0, R_1) such that the loop invariant is

$$R_{1-\text{pbit}} - R_{\text{pbit}} = P.$$

So, if the line "pbit $\leftarrow$ pbit $\oplus k_i$" is not executed and the bit k_i is 1, then the variable pbit is not updated:

- If pbit was 0, then we have $R_1 - R_0 = P$, the points are not switched, so we still have $R_1 - R_0 = P$;
- If pbit was 1, then we have $R_0 - R_1 = P$, the points are switched, so we have now $R_1 - R_0 = P$.

In both cases, the variable pbit gets the value 1 at the end of the loop, so starting from the next iteration we have

$$R_{1-\text{pbit}} - R_{\text{pbit}} = R_0 - R_1 = -P,$$

and the sign of the loop invariant has changed for the remainder of the algorithm.

One alternative is to target the line "pbit $\leftarrow k_i$". If this line is skipped and the bit k_i differs from the value in the variable pbit, then it will not be consistent with the current state or (R_0, R_1), but starting from the processing of the next loop iteration.

Remark 4. Of course, in half of the cases, skipping one of these instructions will not have an effect and result in a correct output (and it is discarded in our attack).

Algorithm 4. Constant-time conditional swap of two values with binary operators (comments: alternative version)

Require: (w_0, w_1), bit b
Ensure: (w_b, w_{1-b})
  mask $\leftarrow (b, \ldots, b)_2$
  tmp $\leftarrow$ mask $\wedge (w_0 \oplus w_1)$ $\triangleright$ tmp $\leftarrow w_0$
  $w_0 \leftarrow w_0 \oplus$ tmp $\triangleright w_0 \leftarrow (w_0 \wedge \neg \text{mask}) \vee (w_1 \wedge \text{mask})$
  $w_1 \leftarrow w_1 \oplus$ tmp $\triangleright w_1 \leftarrow (w_1 \wedge \neg \text{mask}) \vee (\text{tmp} \wedge \text{mask})$
  return (w_0, w_1)

Fault in a Register. A common method for the conditional swap is to use binary masks as presented in Algorithm 4. The interesting part is the construction of the binary mask. It is generally done using the binary representation of -1 in a machine-word with all bits set to 1. So the value $-b$ gives a null mask if b is 0, and a binary mask with all bits set to 1 if b is 1.

However, there are other ways to construct such masks, where any nonzero b ends up with a binary mask with bits set to 1. Let N the bit length of machine-words, then the two equivalent following formulas give an example of such construction (the first one is present in Mbed TLS and the second in OpenSSL) where "$\gg$" is the bitwise shift right operator:

$$-\big((b \vee (-b)) \gg (N-1)\big) \quad \text{or} \quad \big((\neg b \wedge (b-1)) \gg (N-1)\big) - 1.$$

A fault that randomly modifies the register that contains the bit b will have the desired effect and swaps the points if the original value of b is 0. This can be achieved with a random fault on a register.

5.3   Simulations

Simulations were used to put in practice our attack and evaluate the other different cases of the paper. The first one uses the GNU Debugger GDB to simulate faults according to the fault models presented above in the OpenSSL implementation of the Montgomery ladder algorithm. The second is based on the Unicorn engine[2] to test the effect of faults wrongly injected with the skip instruction fault model. Finally, other cases with the randomization methods were also simulated in Python and the lattice attack used the fpylll library [37].

GDB Simulation. We give in Listing 1.1 part of the assembly code related to the loop of the Montgomery ladder algorithm in OpenSSL version 1.1.1k (compiled on a Raspberry Pi device model 4B).

The instruction on address 0xdd208 corresponds to the line "pbit $\leftarrow$ pbit $\oplus$ k_i" that needs to be ignored in the skip instruction fault model. The second fault model can be achieved with a modification of register r6 after this same

---

[2] https://www.unicorn-engine.org/.

```
dd1e8:    mov     r1, r8
dd1ec:    ldr     r0, [sp, #8]
dd1f0:    bl      8b440 <BN_is_bit_set>      ; r0 <- current bit k_i
dd1f4:    ldr     r6, [sp, #12]              ; r6 <- pbit
dd1f8:    mov     r3, r9
dd1fc:    ldr     r2, [fp, #8]
dd200:    ldr     r1, [r7, #8]
dd204:    sub     r8, r8, #1
dd208:    eor     r6, r6, r0                 ; r6 <- pbit XOR k_i
dd20c:    mov     sl, r0
dd210:    mov     r0, r6
dd214:    bl      8b554 <BN_consttime_swap>  ; swap X if r0 = 1
dd218:    mov     r0, r6
dd21c:    mov     r3, r9
dd220:    ldr     r2, [fp, #12]
dd224:    ldr     r1, [r7, #12]
dd228:    str     sl, [sp, #12]              ; pbit <- k_i
dd22c:    bl      8b554 <BN_consttime_swap>  ; swap Y if r0 = 1
dd230:    mov     r0, r6
dd234:    mov     r3, r9
dd238:    ldr     r2, [fp, #16]
dd23c:    ldr     r1, [r7, #16]
dd240:    bl      8b554 <BN_consttime_swap>  ; swap Z if r0 = 1
```

Listing 1.1. Excerpt of assembly code of the function ec_scalar_mul_ladder in OpenSSL 1.1.1k.

instruction. Indeed, this variable is only used thereafter for the conditional swap on each point coordinates.

It is easy to instrument these faults with GDB, and has been automatized with two scripts. In both cases the analysis on the signatures followed by the lattice attack resulted in a successful private key recovery.

Unicorn Simulation. Unicorn is CPU framework emulator and we used it through the Rainbow tool[3] that makes it easy to trace the execution of all instructions of a binary. It can be stopped at any moment and the next instruction can be read. Then the skip instruction fault model can be instrumented as follows: we read the next instruction, and it is skipped by resuming the execution at the following instruction using the size of the skipped instruction.

The constant-time big integer modular arithmetic of the secp256r1 curve written in assembly was chosen (taken from the OpenSSL project). It has no external dependency which makes it easier to work with the emulator. Two binaries were created to implement the Montgomery ladder variant of Algorithm 3: the first with Jacobian projective coordinates, and the second with co-Z formulas.

The instructions related to the lines "pbit ← pbit ⊕ k_i" and "pbit ← k_i" are present in the assembly code of both binaries. When one of those is skipped during an iteration of the main loop, then the analysis of Sect. 3.2 is successful and the least significant bits of the scalar are recovered.

---

[3] https://github.com/Ledger-Donjon/rainbow.

However, we found a false positive situation with both binaries when the fault skips one instruction in the function that extracts one bit of the scalar. What happens is that the extracted bit is incorrect: the bit k_j is replaced with $1 - k_j$, but the remaining of the scalar multiplication is done correctly. This is equivalent to a bitflip of the scalar, and as a consequence we have

$$Q - Q' = \begin{cases} [-2^j]P & \text{if } k_j = 0, \\ [2^j]P & \text{if } k_j = 1. \end{cases}$$

If we look at Eq. (7), this might wrongly reveal that the least significant bits of the scalar are only composed of zero bits. Therefore, to avoid a wrong signature in the lattice attack against ECDSA, it might be better to discard this case (say j is 16, then there would be one out 65536 scalars on average where the 16 least significant bit are indeed set to 0 so discarding a correct result would be rare).

Another false positive was observed with the Jacobian projective formulas: after a specific instruction skip in the point addition function, one of the points is not loaded correctly and the addition happens with the same point: the doubling function is called instead, and the analysis catches a wrong value.

For the co-Z binary, we included the invariant check at the end of the scalar multiplication as a countermeasure [39]. We adapted the XYcoZ-ADD function such that it computes the difference of the inputs (the invariant) instead. Once the missing Z-coordinate is recovered and the points are converted to their affine representation, the calculated invariant I is XORed with P, the correct invariant, and the output Q:

$$Q \oplus I \oplus P.$$

If the calculated invariant is correct, it should be canceled by P. As was expected from Sect. 3.2, I is indeed correctly calculated as P. The output is a valid point and it does not prevent our attack.

6 Countermeasures

As with other works where the fault does not make the elliptic curve point leave the curve, a point validation cannot detect the fault, even in the case of x-only or co-Z formulas (for the former it was suggested in [15] to recover the missing coordinate and perform the verification, but in the context of the attack of [16], and would not be able to prevent our attack).

Verification of the Montgomery ladder invariant was proposed in [14,39] against fault attacks. As we have seen in Sect. 3.2, it should work in general because the invariant is changed, except in the cases of the x-only and co-Z formulas (the reconstructed invariant would be the correct one) as was experimented in Sect. 5.3.

There is another idea from [14] to prevent our attack with the x-only and co-Z formulas. It is a variant of the point blinding countermeasure from [13] adapted to Montgomery ladder: the algorithm is initialized as $R_0 = P + R$ and $R_1 = [2]P + R$ for a random point R, and the invariant $R_1 - R_0$ is still the input P. At the end of the scalar multiplication we have $R_0 = [k]P + [2^{n-1}]R$, so a subtraction by $S = [2^{n-1}]P$ is needed to get the correct output. In our attack, the points R_0 and R_1 are inverted and the invariant becomes $-P$:

$$\begin{cases} R_0 = [k']P + [2^{n-1}]R \\ R_1 = R_0 - P. \end{cases}$$

We have seen that it changes the sign of the reconstructed point after the recovery of the missing coordinate. Therefore, subtracting the blinded point to get the output would give

$$Q' = -R_0 - [2^{n-1}]R = -[k']P - [2^n]R,$$

and without the knowledge of the point R, the output is useless for an attacker. However, this is true as long as R is randomly selected at each new execution, and it was originally proposed to update R by replacing it with the point $[(-1^\beta)2]R$ with $\beta \in \{0,1\}$ chosen randomly. With faults successfully injected in consecutive runs, it might be possible to deduce the point R, and then the differential analysis could be done.

Classic countermeasures such as repeating the operations twice and check consistency can be applied against our attack. To reduce the cost, it was proposed in [6] to make the second computation on an elliptic curve $E_{p'}$ over a smaller prime field $\mathbf{F}_{p'}$, and the first on an elliptic curve $E_{pp'}$ over the integer ring $\mathbf{Z}/pp'\mathbf{Z}$. On one hand, the reduction modulo p of the result gives the expected calculation, and on the other hand, the reduction modulo p' is checked with the calculation on $E_{p'}$.

A variant of the previous method was proposed in [19,32] where the second computation is done on an auxiliary group glued together with the elliptic curve operation. For instance, it can be done by adding an integer to point coordinates which keeps track of the current discrete logarithm of the points using the following rules:

$$(P_1, \ell_1) + (P_2, \ell_2) = (P_1 + P_2, \ell_1 + \ell_2), \quad [2](P, \ell) = ([2]P, 2\ell).$$

If no fault occurred the resulting point should be $([k]P, k)$ with k the secret scalar. This method should detect the fault in our attack since the auxiliary value is consistent with the point, so a change in the point affects the value too.

Finally, in the case of an attack on ECDSA, it is always possible to verify the signature at the end of the calculation.

7   Conclusion

In this paper, we presented a new differential fault attack on Elliptic Curve Cryptography with the Montgomery ladder algorithm. We showed that an attacker can switch two points with either a skip instruction or a random fault in a

register. With this modification in the program flow, the least (or most) significant bits of the secret scalar can be determined from the difference between the
correct and erroneous outputs.

Furthermore, this attack bypasses some of past countermeasures against fault
attacks on ECC. A consequence is that particular care is necessary to choose
the right measures to protect an implementation when protection against fault
attacks is part of the threat model.

Finally, we presented evidence that scalar randomization with common methods is not enough to thwart differential fault attacks. It requires that the randomizer is small enough for the attack to be practical. However, it is generally
suggested in the papers that proposed such methods to choose them small to
reduce the extra cost.

Future work could explore further ways to achieve the effects of our attack
using other fault models or targeting other instructions, or investigate other
randomization methods.

A   Lattice Attack

In this appendix, we present the lattice construction to solve the Hidden Number
Problem, then we give the values for the particular cases met in the paper.

A.1   Lattice Construction

First we introduce the notation $| \cdot |_q$ defined as

$$|z|_q = \min_{y \in \mathbf{Z}} |z - yq|,$$

for any real z, which is a reduction modulo q in the range $[-q/2, q/2]$ followed
by an absolute value.

Let $uX + v \equiv Y \bmod q$ a linear equation in the variables X and Y, where an
approximation viewed as an integer of Y is known:

$$B_1 \leq Y < B_2,$$

where B_1 and B_2 are two integers with $(B_2 - B_1) < q/L$ for a positive integer L.
The width of the interval can be reduced by centering around 0. Let $C = (B_1 + B_2)/2$ be the center of the interval, and we get the bound

$$|Y - C| < q/(2L).$$

Therefore, noting $v' = C - v$, we have $|uX - v'|_q = |Y - C|_q = |Y - C|$, since
we know that $(Y - C)$ is in $[-q/2, q/2]$. Then, using the bound on it, we obtain
the inequality

$$|uX - v'|_q < q/(2L), \tag{13}$$

whose meaning is that when seen modulo q, the value v' is close to a multiple of
the hidden number X.

Given n inequalities of the form $|u_i X - v_i'|_q < q/(2L_i)$ derived from equations where X is a common variable, we construct the lattice generated by this integer matrix:

$$\begin{bmatrix} 2L_1q & & & & & \\ & 2L_2q & & & & \\ & & \ddots & & & \\ & & & 2L_nq & & \\ 2L_1u_1 & 2L_2u_2 & \cdots & 2L_nu_n & 1 & 0 \\ 2L_1v_1' & 2L_2v_2' & \cdots & 2L_nv_n' & 0 & q \end{bmatrix}.$$

Denoting $\mathbf{m}_i$ the i-th line of the matrix, and

$$\begin{cases} \mathbf{u} = (2L_1u_1, \ldots, 2L_nu_n, 1, 0) \\ \mathbf{v} = (2L_1v_1', \ldots, 2L_nv_n', 0, q), \end{cases}$$

the vectors from the last two lines of the matrix, there exists integers λ_i such that the vector $X\mathbf{u} - \mathbf{v} + \sum_{i=1}^{n} \lambda_i \mathbf{m}_i$ is a short vector of the lattice according to the inequalities, since each coordinate is bounded by q.

Applying a lattice basis reduction algorithm such as LLL [20] or BKZ [34], there is a possibility that one of the vectors of the reduced basis is the one we are looking for. By construction, this short vector has the hidden number X as its penultimate coordinate. In the different settings, it corresponds with a private key and can be easily checked with the public key.

A.2   Application to ECDSA

First, we recall that a signature (r, s) can be rewritten:

$$k \equiv \alpha r/s + \mathrm{H}(M)/s \pmod{q}.$$

The hidden number X is the private key α, while the unknown variable Y corresponds partially to the ephemeral value k in various ways depending on each of the following cases.

Case 1. Let $k = am + b$ the Euclidean division of k by an integer m. This case concerns the attack on the Euclidean splitting in Sect. 4.2, but also cases when the ℓ least significant bits are known by setting $m = 2^\ell$. If m and b are known, then we have

$$\begin{cases} Y = a, \\ u = r/(sm) \bmod q, \\ v = \mathrm{H}(M)/(sm) - b/m \bmod q. \end{cases}$$

With the padding method applied on k beforehand, we have $2^t \leq k < 2^t + q$ so the unknown a is bounded by

$$\frac{2^t - b}{m} \leq a < \frac{2^t + q - b}{m},$$

of width q/m. When the blinding method of Sect. 4.1 is used instead of a padding, we have the inequality in Eq. (9) when the ℓ least significant bits are known.

Case 2. Instead, if a and m are known in the Euclidean division of k by m, then we have

$$\begin{cases} Y = b, \\ u = r/s \bmod q, \\ v = \mathrm{H}(M)/s - am \quad \bmod q. \end{cases}$$

The unknown b is a non-negative integer less than m. This case corresponds to the most significant bits of k known. Suppose that we know the $(\ell + 1)$ most significant bits (including one from the padding), then $m = 2^{t-\ell}$ (which can be approximated to $q/2^\ell$ when q is very close to 2^t for some standardized elliptic curves).

Case 3. This is the situation of Sect. 4.3 where k is randomized by an integer m of at most λ bits, and is rewritten as $k \equiv m\gamma \bmod q$. If m and the ℓ least significant bits $\overline{\gamma}$ of γ are known, we can write

$$k \equiv m\widehat{\gamma}2^\ell + m\overline{\gamma} \pmod{q},$$

where the unknown is $\widehat{\gamma}$ (the most significant bits of γ). We have

$$\begin{cases} Y = \widehat{\gamma}, \\ u = r/(ms2^\ell) \bmod q, \\ v = \mathrm{H}(M)/(sm2^\ell) - \overline{\gamma}/2^\ell \bmod q. \end{cases}$$

If no padding was applied on the scalar multiplication with γ, then the unknown is bounded by $0 \le \widehat{\gamma} < q/2^\ell$, and if a padding is applied then the bound on the unknown is

$$\frac{2^t - \overline{\gamma}}{2^\ell} \le \widehat{\gamma} < \frac{2^t + q - \overline{\gamma}}{2^\ell},$$

both of them of width $q/2^\ell$.

B   Coordinates Recovery

In this appendix, we give more details on the recovery of the missing coordinates for the x-only and co-Z formulas.

B.1 x-only Formulas

Those are based on the homogeneous projective coordinates: a point (x, y) is represented as $[X : Z]$ where $x = X/Z$ for a nonzero Z.

The missing coordinate can be recovered in the case of the Montgomery ladder algorithm. Let $[X_0 : Z_0]$ and $[X_1 : Z_1]$ the representations of two points R_0 and R_1, and $P = (x_P, y_P)$ the point such that $R_1 - R_0 = P$. The formula to recover the affine y-coordinate of R_0 is

$$y_0 = \frac{2BZ_0^2Z_1 + Z_1(AZ_0 + x_PX_0)(x_PZ_0 + X_0) - X_1(x_PZ_0 - X_0)^2}{2y_PZ_0^2Z_1} \tag{14}$$

Algorithm 5. Recovery of the missing coordinate with co-Z formulas in the last step of the Montgomery ladder algorithm.

1: $R_{1-k_0}, R_{k_0} \leftarrow \text{XYcoZ-ADDC}(R_{k_0}, R_{1-k_0})$
2: $Z \leftarrow (X(R_1) - X(R_0)) x_P Y(R_{k_0})/y_P X(R_{k_0})$
3: $R_{k_0}, R_{1-k_0} \leftarrow \text{XYcoZ-ADD}(R_{1-k_0}, R_{k_0})$
4: $Q = (X(R_0)/Z^2, Y(R_0)/Z^3)$

If the invariant sign-change fault attack of Sect. 3.2 is successful, then we have $R_1 - R_0 = -P = (x_P, -y_P)$. A correct reconstruction of R_0 should use $-y_P$ instead of y_P in Eq. (14). On the contrary, it will introduce a factor -1 in the computation of y_0, so the reconstructed point will be $R'_0 = -R_0$. A similar formula can be derived for R_1 and the reconstruction would give $R'_1 = -R_1$. So the difference $R'_1 - R'_0$ would still be equal to the original invariant.

B.2   Co-Z Formulas

Those formulas are based on the Jacobian projective coordinates: a point (x, y) is represented by $(X : Y : Z)$ with $x = X/Z^2$ and $y = Y/Z^3$. The variant considered does not use the third coordinate Z in calculation.

The missing coordinate is mandatory to get the affine representation. Let $P = (X : Y : Z)$ with the coordinate Z unknown, and (x, y) its known affine representation, then we have

$$Z = \frac{x \cdot Y}{y \cdot X}. \tag{15}$$

On the last step of the Montgomery ladder algorithm, the XYcoZ-ADDC operation computes the difference of the points R_0 and R_1, so the invariant P appears in Jacobian projective form. The above formula allows the reconstruction of its missing Z-coordinate which is common to R_0 and R_1. This is given in Algorithm 5 (another factor is present in line 2 to take into account the final XYcoZ-ADD operation).

If the invariant sign-change fault attack of Sect. 3.2 is successful, then the invariant becomes $-P$ which introduces a factor -1 in Eq. (15) since the affine coordinates of P will be used. As a consequence, the missing coordinate reconstructed in line 2 of Algorithm 5 will be $-Z$. Let $R_0 = (X_0 : Y_0 : Z)$ and $R_1 = (X_1 : Y_1 : Z)$ the two points at the end of the Montgomery ladder algorithm. Then using $-Z$ instead of Z to get the affine form will result in

$$R'_i = \left(\frac{X_i}{(-Z)^2}, \frac{Y_i}{(-Z)^3} \right) = (x_i, -y_i) = -R_i, \quad i \in \{0, 1\}.$$

So the difference $R'_1 - R'_0$ would still be equal to the original invariant.

References

1. Ambrose, C., Bos, J.W., Fay, B., Joye, M., Lochter, M., Murray, B.: Differential attacks on deterministic signatures. In: Smart, N.P. (ed.) CT-RSA 2018. LNCS, vol. 10808, pp. 339–353. Springer, Cham (2018). https://doi.org/10.1007/978-3-319-76953-0_18
2. Barenghi, A., Bertoni, G.M., Breveglieri, L., Pelosi, G., Sanfilippo, S., Susella, R.: A fault-based secret key retrieval method for ECDSA: analysis and countermeasure. ACM J. Emerg. Technol. Comput. Syst. **13**(1), 8:1–8:26 (2016). https://doi.org/10.1145/2767132
3. Biehl, I., Meyer, B., Müller, V.: Differential fault attacks on elliptic curve cryptosystems. In: Bellare, M. (ed.) CRYPTO 2000. LNCS, vol. 1880, pp. 131–146. Springer, Heidelberg (2000). https://doi.org/10.1007/3-540-44598-6_8
4. Biham, E., Shamir, A.: Differential fault analysis of secret key cryptosystems. In: Kaliski, B.S. (ed.) CRYPTO 1997. LNCS, vol. 1294, pp. 513–525. Springer, Heidelberg (1997). https://doi.org/10.1007/BFb0052259
5. Blömer, J., Günther, P.: Singular curve point decompression attack. In: Homma, N., Lomné, V. (eds.) FDTC 2015, pp. 71–84. IEEE Computer Society (2015). https://doi.org/10.1109/FDTC.2015.17
6. Blömer, J., Otto, M., Seifert, J.-P.: Sign change fault attacks on elliptic curve cryptosystems. In: Breveglieri, L., Koren, I., Naccache, D., Seifert, J.-P. (eds.) FDTC 2006. LNCS, vol. 4236, pp. 36–52. Springer, Heidelberg (2006). https://doi.org/10.1007/11889700_4
7. Boneh, D., DeMillo, R.A., Lipton, R.J.: On the importance of checking cryptographic protocols for faults. In: Fumy, W. (ed.) EUROCRYPT 1997. LNCS, vol. 1233, pp. 37–51. Springer, Heidelberg (1997). https://doi.org/10.1007/3-540-69053-0_4
8. Boneh, D., Venkatesan, R.: Hardness of computing the most significant bits of secret keys in Diffie-Hellman and related schemes. In: Koblitz, N. (ed.) CRYPTO 1996. LNCS, vol. 1109, pp. 129–142. Springer, Heidelberg (1996). https://doi.org/10.1007/3-540-68697-5_11
9. Brier, É., Joye, M.: Weierstraß elliptic curves and side-channel attacks. In: Naccache, D., Paillier, P. (eds.) PKC 2002. LNCS, vol. 2274, pp. 335–345. Springer, Heidelberg (2002). https://doi.org/10.1007/3-540-45664-3_24
10. Brumley, B.B., Tuveri, N.: Remote timing attacks are still practical. In: Atluri, V., Diaz, C. (eds.) ESORICS 2011. LNCS, vol. 6879, pp. 355–371. Springer, Heidelberg (2011). https://doi.org/10.1007/978-3-642-23822-2_20
11. Cao, W., et al.: Two lattice-based differential fault attacks against ECDSA with wNAF algorithm. In: Kwon, S., Yun, A. (eds.) ICISC 2015. LNCS, vol. 9558, pp. 297–313. Springer, Cham (2016). https://doi.org/10.1007/978-3-319-30840-1_19
12. Ciet, M., Joye, M.: (Virtually) free randomization techniques for elliptic curve cryptography. In: Qing, S., Gollmann, D., Zhou, J. (eds.) ICICS 2003. LNCS, vol. 2836, pp. 348–359. Springer, Heidelberg (2003). https://doi.org/10.1007/978-3-540-39927-8_32
13. Coron, J.-S.: Resistance against differential power analysis for elliptic curve cryptosystems. In: Koç, Ç.K., Paar, C. (eds.) CHES 1999. LNCS, vol. 1717, pp. 292–302. Springer, Heidelberg (1999). https://doi.org/10.1007/3-540-48059-5_25
14. Dominguez-Oviedo, A., Hasan, M.A.: Algorithm-Level error detection for Montgomery ladder-based ECSM. J. Cryptogr. Eng. **1**(1), 57–69 (2011). https://doi.org/10.1007/s13389-011-0003-1

15. Ebeid, N.M., Lambert, R.: Securing the elliptic curve Montgomery ladder against fault attacks. In: Breveglieri, L., Koren, I., Naccache, D., Oswald, E., Seifert, J. (eds.) FDTC 2009, pp. 46–50. IEEE Computer Society (2009). https://doi.org/10.1109/FDTC.2009.35

16. Fouque, P., Lercier, R., Réal, D., Valette, F.: Fault attack on elliptic curve Montgomery ladder implementation. In: Breveglieri, L., Gueron, S., Koren, I., Naccache, D., Seifert, J. (eds.) FDTC 2008, pp. 92–98. IEEE Computer Society (2008). https://doi.org/10.1109/FDTC.2008.15

17. Goundar, R.R., Joye, M., Miyaji, A., Rivain, M., Venelli, A.: Scalar multiplication on Weierstraß elliptic curves from co-Z arithmetic. J. Cryptogr. Eng. 1(2), 161–176 (2011). https://doi.org/10.1007/s13389-011-0012-0

18. Izu, T., Takagi, T.: A fast parallel elliptic curve multiplication resistant against side channel attacks. In: Naccache, D., Paillier, P. (eds.) PKC 2002. LNCS, vol. 2274, pp. 280–296. Springer, Heidelberg (2002). https://doi.org/10.1007/3-540-45664-3_20

19. Joye, M.: A method for preventing "skipping" attacks. In: IEEE Symposium on Security and Privacy Workshops, pp. 12–15. IEEE Computer Society (2012). https://doi.org/10.1109/SPW.2012.14

20. Lenstra, A.K., Lenstra, Hendrik W., J., Lovász, L.: Factoring polynomials with rational coefficients. Mathematische Annalen 261, 515–534 (1982). https://doi.org/10.1007/BF01457454

21. Loiseau, A., Lecomte, M., Fournier, J.J.A.: Template attacks against ECC: practical implementation against Curve25519. In: HOST 2020, pp. 13–22. IEEE (2020). https://doi.org/10.1109/HOST45689.2020.9300261

22. Montgomery, P.L.: Speeding the Pollard and elliptic curve methods of factorization. Math. Comput. 48, 243–264 (1987). https://doi.org/10.1090/S0025-5718-1987-0866113-7

23. Nascimento, E., Chmielewski, Ł, Oswald, D., Schwabe, P.: Attacking embedded ECC implementations through cmov side channels. In: Avanzi, R., Heys, H. (eds.) SAC 2016. LNCS, vol. 10532, pp. 99–119. Springer, Cham (2017). https://doi.org/10.1007/978-3-319-69453-5_6

24. National Institute of Standards and Technology: FIPS PUB 186-4 Digital Signature Standard (DSS) (2013)

25. Nguyen, P.Q., Shparlinski, I.E.: The insecurity of the elliptic curve digital signature algorithm with partially known nonces. Des. Codes Cryptogr. 30(2), 201–217 (2003). https://doi.org/10.1023/A:1025436905711

26. Poddebniak, D., Somorovsky, J., Schinzel, S., Lochter, M., Rösler, P.: Attacking deterministic signature schemes using fault attacks. In: EuroS&P 2018, pp. 338–352. IEEE (2018). https://doi.org/10.1109/EuroSP.2018.00031

27. Pollard, J.M.: Monte Carlo methods for index computation (mod p). Math. Comput. 32, 918–924 (1978)

28. Renes, J., Costello, C., Batina, L.: Complete addition formulas for prime order elliptic curves. In: Fischlin, M., Coron, J.-S. (eds.) EUROCRYPT 2016. LNCS, vol. 9665, pp. 403–428. Springer, Heidelberg (2016). https://doi.org/10.1007/978-3-662-49890-3_16

29. Romailler, Y., Pelissier, S.: Practical fault attack against the Ed25519 and EdDSA signature schemes. In: FDTC 2017, pp. 17–24. IEEE Computer Society (2017). https://doi.org/10.1109/FDTC.2017.12

30. Samwel, N., Batina, L.: Practical fault injection on deterministic signatures: the case of EdDSA. In: Joux, A., Nitaj, A., Rachidi, T. (eds.) AFRICACRYPT 2018. LNCS, vol. 10831, pp. 306–321. Springer, Cham (2018). https://doi.org/10.1007/978-3-319-89339-6_17

31. Schmidt, J., Herbst, C.: A practical fault attack on square and multiply. In: Breveglieri, L., Gueron, S., Koren, I., Naccache, D., Seifert, J. (eds.) FDTC 2008, pp. 53–58. IEEE Computer Society (2008). https://doi.org/10.1109/FDTC.2008.10

32. Schmidt, J., Medwed, M.: A fault attack on ECDSA. In: Breveglieri, L., Koren, I., Naccache, D., Oswald, E., Seifert, J. (eds.) FDTC 2009, pp. 93–99. IEEE Computer Society (2009). https://doi.org/10.1109/FDTC.2009.38

33. Schmidt, J.-M., Medwed, M.: Fault attacks on the Montgomery powering ladder. In: Rhee, K.-H., Nyang, D.H. (eds.) ICISC 2010. LNCS, vol. 6829, pp. 396–406. Springer, Heidelberg (2011). https://doi.org/10.1007/978-3-642-24209-0_26

34. Schnorr, C., Euchner, M.: Lattice basis reduction: improved practical algorithms and solving subset sum problems. Math. Program. **66**, 181–199 (1994). https://doi.org/10.1007/BF01581144

35. Shanks, D.: Class number, a theory of factorization, and genera. In: Proceedings of Symposium Mathematical Society, vol. 20, pp. 415–440 (1971). https://doi.org/10.1090/pspum/020

36. Takahashi, A., Tibouchi, M.: Degenerate fault attacks on elliptic curve parameters in OpenSSL. In: EuroS&P 2019, pp. 371–386. IEEE (2019). https://doi.org/10.1109/EuroSP.2019.00035

37. The FPLLL development team: fpylll, a Python wraper for the fplll lattice reduction library, Version: 0.5.6 (2021). https://github.com/fplll/fpylll

38. Trichina, E., Bellezza, A.: Implementation of elliptic curve cryptography with built-in counter measures against side channel attacks. In: Kaliski, B.S., Koç, K., Paar, C. (eds.) CHES 2002. LNCS, vol. 2523, pp. 98–113. Springer, Heidelberg (2003). https://doi.org/10.1007/3-540-36400-5_9

39. Vasyltsov, I., Saldamli, G.: Fault detection and a differential fault analysis countermeasure for the Montgomery power ladder in elliptic curve cryptography. Math. Comput. Model. **55**(1–2), 256–267 (2012). https://doi.org/10.1016/j.mcm.2011.06.017

Fault-Enabled Chosen-Ciphertext Attacks on Kyber

Julius Hermelink[1,2](✉), Peter Pessl[1], and Thomas Pöppelmann[1]

[1] Infineon Technologies AG, Munich, Germany
{peter.pessl,thomas.poeppelmann}@infineon.com
[2] Research Institute CODE, Universität der Bundeswehr München,
Munich, Germany
julius.hermelink@unibw.de

Abstract. NIST's PQC standardization process is in the third round, and a first final choice between one of three remaining lattice-based key-encapsulation mechanisms is expected by the end of 2021. This makes studying the implementation-security aspect of the candidates a pressing matter. However, while the development of side-channel attacks and corresponding countermeasures has seen continuous interest, fault attacks are still a vastly underdeveloped field.

In fact, a first practical fault attack on lattice-based KEMs was demonstrated just very recently by Pessl and Prokop. However, while their attack can bypass some standard fault countermeasures, it may be defeated using shuffling, and their use of skipping faults makes it also highly implementation dependent. Thus, the vulnerability of implementations against fault attacks and the concrete need for countermeasures is still not well understood.

In this work, we shine light on this problem and demonstrate new attack paths. Concretely, we show that the combination of fault injections with chosen-ciphertext attacks is a significant threat to implementations and can bypass several countermeasures. We state an attack on Kyber which combines ciphertext manipulation–flipping a single bit of an otherwise valid ciphertext–with a fault that "corrects" the ciphertext again during decapsulation. By then using the Fujisaki-Okamoto transform as an oracle, i.e., observing whether or not decapsulation fails, we derive inequalities involving secret data, from which we may recover the private key. Our attack is not defeated by many standard countermeasures such as shuffling in time or Boolean masking, and the fault may be introduced over a large execution-time interval at several places. In addition, we improve a known recovery technique to efficiently and practically recover the secret key from a smaller number of inequalities compared to the previous method.

1 Introduction

The emerging threat of large-scale quantum computers to asymmetric cryptography drives the research on quantum-secure schemes. The standardization

© Springer Nature Switzerland AG 2021
A. Adhikari et al. (Eds.): INDOCRYPT 2021, LNCS 13143, pp. 311–334, 2021.
https://doi.org/10.1007/978-3-030-92518-5_15

process on Post-Quantum cryptography (PQC) of the National Institute of Standards and Technology (NIST) [Natb] is in the third round, and as the process slowly reaches its (preliminary) end, the topic of implementation security of PQC schemes is receiving increased attention. While for classical public-key cryptography, implementation security has seen decades of research and threats are relatively well understood, the situation is much less clear for quantum-secure algorithms.

In this regard, lattice-based key-encapsulation mechanisms (KEMs) are of particular interest. These schemes offer comparably small key- and ciphertext sizes and high speeds. Therefore, they are especially well-suited for embedded devices, which are highly susceptible to implementation attacks. Also, NIST expects to pick one of the three third-round lattice KEMs for standardization by the end of 2021, thereby making the study of side-channel and fault attacks and possible mitigations a pressing matter [Nata].

In fact, the side-channel aspect has already seen some analysis. Especially single-trace (or more generally, profiled) attacks appear to be a focal point of research, in, e.g., [PPM17,PP19,ACLZ20,PH16]. Another emerging topic is the combination of side-channel analysis with chosen-ciphertext attacks as shown in [RRCB20] and [HHP+21]. Almost all finalist KEMs in the NIST process use some variant of the Fujisaki-Okamoto (FO) transform [FO99,HHK17] to achieve CCA security. However, chosen ciphertexts are still highly useful when combined with side-channel leakage from the re-encryption step involved in this transform [RRCB20,RBRC20,GJN20,BDH+21]. There also exist works on side-channel secured implementations [OSPG18,BDH+21,HP21,RRVV15, RRdC+16].

Fault attacks against these systems, however, are a comparably underdeveloped topic. A potential reason is that the FO transform closes many attack paths through its re-encryption step and ciphertext-equality test. One already well documented attack option is to skip the equality test and thereby re-enabling chosen-ciphertext attacks [VOGR18,OSPG18,BGRR19,XIU+21]. Very recently, however, Pessl and Prokop [PP21] showed that other parts of the decapsulation can also be sensitive to fault injections. By skipping over certain instructions and then observing if the device still computes the correct shared secret (ineffective fault) or not (effective fault), they can gather information on the secret key. After faulting many decapsulation calls and accumulating said information, they can solve for the key. While their attack is practical, it does not come without caveats. For instance, instructions-skip attacks typically require a certain level of knowledge on the used implementation, and they presume that the attacker can find the selected instruction in the execution time. Also, since the shuffling countermeasure randomizes the time of execution, the specific attack by Pessl and Prokop might be already defeated by this relatively cheap technique. Thus, it is unknown whether such standard countermeasures might already suffice when used on an FO-transformed KEM. It is also unclear what algorithm steps and intermediates require protection, and if more general data corruption can also be used for attacks.

Our Contribution. In this work, we explore these open questions and show that fault-enabled CCA-attacks are a powerful attack tool capable of bypassing many standard fault countermeasures. We also demonstrate that in these scenarios public data (the ciphertext) needs to be secured against manipulation. To show this, we present such a fault-enabled attack on Kyber, but instead of faulting the equality test within the FO-transformation, we exploit it as an oracle. We flip a single selected bit in an otherwise honestly generated ciphertext. This ciphertext is sent to the device under attack. The device decrypts and then re-encrypts the message before comparing the re-encrypted ciphertext to the sent ciphertext. Anytime between the initial unpacking and the final comparison of the ciphertexts, we correct the induced flip on either the sent or the recomputed ciphertext using a fault and observe whether the following comparison fails. From this, linear inequalities involving the secret key can be derived, akin to the attack by Pessl and Prokop [PP21]. We further improve upon their key-recovery; our belief propagation based recovery technique significantly reduces the amount of memory required and recovers the secret key using far fewer faults.

Our fault can, e.g., be introduced in memory during virtually the entire decapsulation, or at more specific locations in registers during re-encryption. That is, our attack is flexible in its target choice. Securing the equality check of the FO-transform does not protect against our attack. Several countermeasures, such as shuffling (which protects against [PP21]) and also Boolean masking, can be bypassed. In addition, our fault is introduced in public data only, making fault profiling easier. We thereby stress the importance of not only securing certain operations but also to protect the integrity of both secret and public data over most of the execution time. In addition, we show that countermeasures such as first-order masking, as presented e.g. in [OSPG18], on CCA2-secured LWE-based schemes are not sufficient to protect against fault attacks. Our results in this regard are similar to and in line with the results of [BDH+21] but in a more general setting and not reliant on a faulty comparison. In addition, compared to their approach, we provide a drastically improved key-recovery algorithm.

While we demonstrate our attack on Kyber, related attacks likely apply to conceptually similar schemes, such as Saber [DKRV18], FrodoKEM [ABD+21], or NewHope [AAB+19].

Outline. We first, in Sect. 2, give a short overview over necessary preliminaries, focusing on the Kyber [BDK+18] algorithm for reference in the later sections. We also give a short introduction to the belief propagation algorithm and the prior work of [PP21]. In Sect. 3, we describe the basic idea of our attack, leading to a description of the practical implementation and simulation in Sect. 4 and then give and discuss the results of our simulations. In Sect. 5, we explore possible countermeasures against our attack.

2   Preliminaries

2.1   Kyber

Kyber [BDK+18] is an IND-CCA2-secure key exchange mechanism (KEM) and a finalist in the NIST standardization process [Natb]. Kyber relies on the hardness of the Module Learning with Errors (MLWE) problem [LS15] and thus belongs to the field of lattice-based cryptography. Three parameter sets are currently specified: Kyber512, Kyber768, and Kyber1024. Kyber internally uses a CPA-secure public-key encryption scheme (PKE) which can be seen as a descendant of the LPR scheme [LPR13]. From the PKE, a CCA-secure KEM is derived by using a variant of the Fujisaki-Okamoto (FO) transform [FO99,HHK17]. We now describe (simplified) versions of the KEM and the internally used PKE.

Kyber PKE. Computations in Kyber take place in R_q and R_q^k, with $R_q = \mathbb{Z}_q[x]/(x^n + 1)$ with $q = 3329$, $n = 256$, and $k \in \{2, 3, 4\}$ (depending on the parameter set). Sample$_{\mathsf{Uniform}}$ performs coefficient-wise sampling from a uniform distribution over $\mathbb{Z}_q$, Sample$_{\mathsf{Binom},\eta}$ denotes coefficient-wise sampling from a centered binomial distribution defined over $\{-\eta, -\eta + 1, \ldots, \eta\}$, where $\eta \in \{\eta_1, \eta_2\}$. Sampling is deterministic and depends on a seed which is incremented after each call. The functions compress and decompress are given by

$$\mathsf{compress}(x, d) = \left\lceil \frac{2^d}{q} \cdot x \right\rfloor \bmod 2^d$$
$$\mathsf{decompress}(x, d) = \left\lceil \frac{q}{2^d} \cdot x \right\rfloor$$

where d is either set to d_u or d_v. The concrete values of all parameters are given in Table 1. The functions Encode and Decode[1] interpret a bitstream as polynomial and vice-versa. Decode therefor multiplies each bit of a message m by $\frac{q}{2}$. $\lceil \cdot \rfloor$ denotes rounding to the nearest integer and mod q maps an integer x to an element $x' \in \{0, 1 \ldots, q - 1\}$ such that $x \equiv x' \bmod q$. Elements a under the number theoretic transform (NTT) are denoted by $\hat{a} = \mathrm{NTT}(a)$, and the symbol $\circ$ denotes pointwise multiplication. Vectors and matrices, i.e. elements in R_q^k and $R_q^{(k \times k)}$, are denoted in bold lowercase and uppercase letters, respectively. For an element $\mathbf{a} \in R_q^k$, $\mathrm{NTT}(\mathbf{a})$ is defined as applying the NTT component-wise to its components.

Table 1. Kyber parameter sets

Parameter set	q	n	k	(η_1, η_2)	(d_u, d_v)
Kyber512	3329	256	2	(3, 2)	(10, 4)
Kyber768	3329	256	3	(2, 2)	(10, 4)
Kyber1024	3329	256	4	(2, 2)	(11, 5)

Key generation (Algorithm 1) uniformly samples a matrix $\mathbf{A}$ using a seed ρ and samples vectors $\mathbf{s}, \mathbf{e}$ from a binomial distribution using a seed σ. The public key is then calculated as $\mathbf{t} = \mathbf{As} + \mathbf{e}$, the secret key is $\mathbf{s}$.

---

[1] In earlier works, the names of Encode and Decode were sometimes switched. We use them according to Kyber's specification.

Encryption (Algorithm 2) reconstructs $\mathbf{A}$, samples $\mathbf{r}, \mathbf{e_1}, e_2$ from the binomial distribution, and computes $\mathbf{u} = \mathbf{A}^T\mathbf{r} + \mathbf{e_1}$ and $v = \mathbf{t}^T\mathbf{r} + e_2 + \mathsf{Decode}(m)$. The compressed $\mathbf{u}$ and v are returned as ciphertext. The decryption, depicted in Algorithm 3, computes an approximate version (due to compression being ignored here) of

$$
\begin{aligned}
v &- \mathbf{s}^T\mathbf{u} \\
&= \mathbf{t}^T\mathbf{r} + e_2 + \mathsf{Decode}(m) - \mathbf{s}^T\mathbf{A}^T\mathbf{r} - \mathbf{s}^T\mathbf{e_1} \\
&= \mathbf{s}^T\mathbf{A}^T\mathbf{r} + \mathbf{e}^T\mathbf{r} + e_2 - \mathbf{s}^T\mathbf{A}^T\mathbf{r} - \mathbf{s}^T\mathbf{e_1} + \mathsf{Decode}(m) \\
&= \mathsf{Decode}(m) + \mathbf{e}^T\mathbf{r} + e_2 - \mathbf{s}^T\mathbf{e_1}
\end{aligned}
\tag{1}
$$

and as $\mathbf{e}$, $\mathbf{r}$, e_2, $\mathbf{s}$, and $\mathbf{e_1}$ are sufficiently small (due to being sampled from a narrow binomial distribution), the above gives m when encoded[2].

Algorithm 1. PKE.KeyGen (simplified)

Input: Seeds ρ, σ
Output: Public key pk, secret key sk
1: $\hat{\mathbf{A}} \in R_q^{k \times k} \leftarrow \mathsf{Sample_{Uniform}}(\rho)$ ▷ Generate uniform $\hat{\mathbf{A}}$ in NTT domain
2: $\mathbf{s}, \mathbf{e} \in R_q^k \leftarrow \mathsf{Sample_{Binom,\eta_1}}(\sigma)$ ▷ Sample from binomial distribution
3: $\hat{\mathbf{s}} \leftarrow \mathsf{NTT}(\mathbf{s})$ ▷ NTT for efficient multiplication
4: $\hat{\mathbf{t}} \leftarrow \hat{\mathbf{A}} \circ \hat{\mathbf{s}} + \mathsf{NTT}(\mathbf{e})$ ▷ $\mathbf{t} := \mathbf{As} + \mathbf{e}$
5: **return** $(pk := (\hat{\mathbf{t}}, \rho), sk := \hat{\mathbf{s}})$

Algorithm 2. PKE.Encrypt (simplified)

Input: Public key $pk = (\hat{\mathbf{t}}, \rho)$, message m, seed τ
Output: Ciphertext ct
1: $\hat{\mathbf{A}} \leftarrow \mathsf{Sample_{Uniform}}(\rho) \in R_q^{k \times k}$
2: $\mathbf{r} \in R_q^k \leftarrow \mathsf{Sample_{Binom,\eta_1}}(\tau)$
3: $\mathbf{e_1} \in R_q^k, e_2 \in R_q \leftarrow \mathsf{Sample_{Binom,\eta_2}}(\tau)$ ▷ Sample from binomial distribution
4: $\mathbf{u} \leftarrow \mathsf{NTT}^{-1}(\hat{\mathbf{A}}^T \circ \mathsf{NTT}(\mathbf{r})) + \mathbf{e_1}$ ▷ $\mathbf{u} = \mathbf{A}^T\mathbf{r} + \mathbf{e_1}$
5: $v \leftarrow \mathsf{NTT}^{-1}(\hat{\mathbf{t}}^T \circ \mathsf{NTT}(\mathbf{r})) + e_2 + \mathsf{Decode}(m)$ ▷ $v = \mathbf{t}^T\mathbf{r} + e_2 + \mathsf{Decode}(m)$
6: $\mathbf{c_1}, c_2 \leftarrow \mathsf{Compress}(\mathbf{u}, v)$ ▷ Lossy compression
7: **return** $c := (\mathbf{c_1}, c_2)$

Kyber KEM. To transform the PKE to a KEM using the FO-transform, two distinct hash functions H and G are required. The key generation of the KEM (Algorithm 4) corresponds mostly to that of the PKE. In the encapsulation (Algorithm 5) the shared secret K is derived from the hash of a uniform message m, the public key and the ciphertext c under PKE.Encrypt of the message,

---

[2] The function $\mathsf{Encode}(\mathsf{Compress}(\cdot))$ is often called Decoder by previous works.

Algorithm 3. PKE.Decrypt (simplified)

Input: Secret key $sk = \hat{\mathbf{s}}$, ciphertext $c = (\mathbf{c}_1, c_2)$
Output: Message m
1: $\mathbf{u}, v \leftarrow \mathsf{Decompress}(\mathbf{c}_1, c_2)$ ▷ Decompress ciphertext
2: $m \leftarrow \mathsf{Encode}(\mathsf{Compress}(v - \mathsf{NTT}^{-1}(\hat{\mathbf{s}}^T \circ \mathsf{NTT}(\mathbf{u}))))$ ▷ Retrieve m
3: **return** m

---

with seed τ depending on the message and the public key. The decapsulation (Algorithm 6) decrypts the ciphertext using PKE.Decrypt and re-encrypts the message using the randomness retrieved from the message and the public-key hash $H(pk)$. If the re-encrypted ciphertext c' matches the received ciphertext c, the shared secret is returned, otherwise, the secret value z is used for an implicit rejection.

Algorithm 4. Kyber-KEM Key Generation (simplified)

Output: Public key $pk = pk_{pke}$, secret key $sk = (sk_{pke}||pk||H(pk)||z)$
1: $z, \rho, \sigma \leftarrow \mathsf{Sample}_{\mathsf{Uniform}}$
2: $pk_{pke}, sk_{pke} \leftarrow \mathsf{PKE.KeyGen}(\rho, \sigma)$
3: **return** $(pk := pk_{pke}, sk := (sk_{pke}||pk||H(pk)||z))$

Algorithm 5. Kyber-KEM Encapsulation (simplified)

Input: Public key $pk = (\hat{\mathbf{t}}, \rho)$
Output: Ciphertext c, shared key K
1: $m, \tau \leftarrow \mathsf{Sample}_{\mathsf{Uniform}}$ ▷ Uniformly sample a message and a seed
2: $(\bar{K}, \tau) \leftarrow \mathsf{G}(m||H(pk))$
3: $c \leftarrow \mathsf{PKE.Encrypt}(pk, m, \tau)$ ▷ CPA encryption with seed τ
4: $K \leftarrow \mathsf{KDF}(\bar{K}||H(c))$ ▷ Derive shared key from ct, m, and pk
5: **return** (c, K)

2.2 Belief Propagation

Since the belief propagation algorithm is an important part of our attack, we now give a brief introduction based on the description of MacKay [Mac03, Chapter 26]. For random variables $\{x_i\}_{i \in \{1,...,N\}} = \mathbf{x}$ on a set X with joint mass function

$$p(\mathbf{x}) = \prod_{k=1}^{K} f_k(\mathbf{x}_{I_k}), x \in X$$

Algorithm 6. Kyber-KEM Decapsulation (simplified)

Input: Secret key $sk = (\hat{\mathbf{s}}, pk, z)$, ciphertext $ct = (\mathbf{c}_1, c_2)$
Output: Shared key K
1: $m \leftarrow$ PKE.Decrypt(sk, ct)
2: $(\bar{K}, \tau) \leftarrow$ G$(m \| H(pk))$ ▷ Retrieve seed for re-encryption
3: $c' \leftarrow$ PKE.Encrypt(pk, m, τ) ▷ Re-encrypt
4: **if** $c = c'$ **then**
5:     $K \leftarrow$ KDF$(\bar{K} \| H(c))$ ▷ Derive shared key on successful re-encryption
6: **else**
7:     $K \leftarrow$ KDF$(z \| H(c))$ ▷ Implicit rejection on failure
8: **return** K

---

with $I_k \subseteq \{1, \ldots, N\}$ and f_k functions mapping $\mathbf{x}_{I_k} = \{x_i\}_{i \in I_k}$ to $[0,1]$, belief propagation aims on efficiently computing all

$$Z_n(x) = \sum_{\mathbf{x}, \mathbf{x}_n = x} p(\mathbf{x})$$

which are proportional to the marginal distributions of x_n. Naïvely computing Z_n is often computationally infeasible. Belief propagation exploits the factorisation of p to significantly reduce the complexity of computing the marginals.

To compute the Z_n, and thereby the marginal distributions of x_n, for all n, the $x_1, \ldots, x_N$ are interpreted as *variable nodes*, which are connected to *factor nodes* given by $f_1, ..., f_K$, where the connections are described by the index sets $I_1, ..., I_K$. In each step, either variable nodes or factor nodes send messages to connected nodes. Messages at a variable node (with index) $i \in \{1, \ldots, N\}$ to factor node $j \in \{1, \ldots, K\}$ are computed as

$$m_{i,j}(x) \leftarrow \prod_{k \neq j} m'_{k,i}(x)$$

where $m'_{k,i}$ are the messages that were sent to the i-th node in the previous iteration. Messages from a factor node j to a variable node i are computed as

$$m_{j,i}(x) \leftarrow \sum_{\mathbf{x}, \mathbf{x}_i = x} f_j(\mathbf{x}) \prod_{k \neq i} m'_{k,j}(x).$$

Belief propagation consists of the repeated computation and passing of messages from variable to factor nodes and vice-versa. For an acyclic graph, the product of the messages at the n-th variable node converges against Z_n. Belief propagation on cyclic graphs is called *loopy belief propagation* and often gives useful approximations, even graphs might not converge or, in the context of key recovery, retrieve the correct result.

Belief propagation has proven to be a powerful tool for side-channel analysis of a wide variety of schemes [VGS14, PPM17, GRO18, PP19, KPP20, GGSB20], recently also in combination with chosen-ciphertext attacks [HHP+21].

In this work, we use belief propagation to find the most likely solution in a linear system of inequalities. This is similar to the usage of belief propagation for decoding, e.g., low density parity check (LDPC) codes [Mac03], where one aims at solving a system of (possibly erroneous) linear equations. In our case, every variable node has a so called *prior* distribution, which is set to the distribution the corresponding unknown variable was sampled from. In every iteration, either all variable nodes process messages and pass them to factor nodes or vice-versa. A *full iteration* is the combination of iterations from variable to factor nodes and vice-versa.

2.3 The Fault Attack of Pessl and Prokop

In [PP21], Pessl and Prokop introduced an instruction-skipping fault in the Decompress/Decode method of Algorithm 3. They thereby provided proof that the equality check of the FO-transform is not the only critical operation for fault attacks.

By introducing said fault and observing whether the re-encryption comparison in Algorithm 6 fails (by testing if the device still returns the correct shared secret K), they obtain a linear inequality involving the decryption error polynomial (c.f. Eq. (1)). In the j-th fault introduction, this error polynomial is given by

$$\mathbf{e}^T \mathbf{r}_j - \mathbf{s}^T (\mathbf{e}_{1j} + \Delta \mathbf{u}_j) + e_{2j} + \Delta v_j \tag{2}$$

for $j \in \{0, ..., l-1\}$ where l is the total number of faults introduced, and where $\Delta \mathbf{u}_j$ and Δv_j denote the compression error introduced to $\mathbf{u}_j$ and v_j, respectively, by applying compression and decompression. Note that $\mathbf{r}, \mathbf{e}_1, e_2, \Delta \mathbf{u}, \Delta v$, as well as the true shared secret K are all known to the attacker, assuming he honestly performs encapsulation.

Denoting the t-th component of a vector of polynomials by $\mathbf{r}^{(t)}$, by writing out Eq. (2), we get that the i-th coefficient of the error term polynomial is given by

$$\sum_{t=0}^{k-1} \sum_{h=0}^{n} \sigma(h, i) \mathbf{e}_h^{(t)} \mathbf{r}_{j, \tau(h,i)}^{(t)}$$

$$+ \sum_{t=0}^{k-1} \sum_{h=0}^{n} \sigma(h, i) \mathbf{s}_h^{(t)} (\mathbf{e}_{1 j, \tau(h,i)}^{(t)} + \Delta \mathbf{u}_{j, \tau(h,i)}^{(t)})$$

$$+ e_{2j,i} + \Delta v_{j,i},$$

where $\tau(h, i) = i - h \mod n$, and $\sigma(h, i)$ returning 1 if $i - h \geq 0$ and -1 otherwise. Using the notation $(\cdot)_i$ to encapsulate all involved sign flips and index shifts, we can restate the above using dot products:

$$\langle (\mathbf{r}_j)_i, \mathbf{e} \rangle + \langle (\mathbf{e}_{1,j} + \Delta \mathbf{u}_j)_i, \mathbf{s} \rangle + e_{2j,i} + \Delta v_{j,i}$$

Assuming that i is constant over all injections, the inequalities, involving the error polynomial, may thus be written in matrix-vector form as $Ax \lesseqgtr -b$ where

$$A = \begin{pmatrix} (\mathbf{r}_0)_i & (\mathbf{e}_{10} + \Delta\mathbf{u}_0)_i \\ (\mathbf{r}_1)_i & (\mathbf{e}_{11} + \Delta\mathbf{u}_1)_i \\ \vdots & \\ (\mathbf{r}_{l-1})_i & (\mathbf{e}_{1l-1} + \Delta\mathbf{u}_{l-1})_i \end{pmatrix},$$

$$x = \begin{pmatrix} \mathbf{e} \\ \mathbf{s} \end{pmatrix}, \text{ and } b = \begin{pmatrix} e_{20,i} + \Delta v_{0,i} \\ e_{21,i} + \Delta v_{1,i} \\ \cdots \\ e_{2l-1,i} + \Delta v_{l-1,i} \end{pmatrix}.$$

Note that these inequalities hold over $\mathbb{Z}$ as due to all polynomials involved being small, no reduction modulo q happens.

Each coefficient of each polynomial of $\mathbf{e}$ and $\mathbf{s}$ was sampled from a known binomial distribution with small support. To recover the key from the inequalities above, Pessl and Prokop initialize a $2n$ vector of probability distributions using said distribution. This vector is successively updated in each iteration according to the information given by the system of inequalities represented by A and b.

As previously mentioned, the attack is highly implementation specific and requires a high level of synchronisation, as one needs to skip over a very specific instruction. Also, the attack can likely be prevented by simple shuffling. Hence, the true potential of fault attacks is still unclear.

3   Enabling Chosen-Ciphertext Attacks with Faults

In this section, present an attack that improves on the mentioned weaknesses of [PP21]. Concretely, we explain how to use a fault to enable a chosen-ciphertext attack on Kyber. Instead of faulting the decoder, we assume an attacker to be able to introduce a single-bit fault. Sending a manipulated ciphertext and then correcting it back to a valid ciphertext after the decryption step using a fault yields inequalities, similar to [PP21]. This is due to the fact that the success of decapsulation implies that decrypting the manipulated ciphertext yields the original message used to create the valid ciphertext. This means, our attack consists of

1. manipulating the polynomial v (in Algorithm 2) of a valid ciphertext during encapsulation in Algorithm 5 by flipping a single bit in the compressed ciphertext,
2. sending the manipulated ciphertext to the device under attack,
3. correcting the ciphertext during decapsulation (Algorithm 6) using a one-bit fault,

4. observing whether a valid shared secret is established,
5. deriving inequalities from repeating the above steps (one inequality per fault),
6. and recovering the secret key from those inequalities.

As shown in Fig. 5, being able to introduce one-bit faults anywhere in the red phases enables our attack. Decompression and compression methods are depicted here, even though they belong to the decryption and the re-encryption, as they prevent an earlier manipulation of c'. The incoming ciphertext c is manipulated and either c or c' need to be "corrected" using a fault. That is, either c is faulted such that it matches the unaltered ciphertext, or c' is faulted such that it matches the manipulated ciphertext. Introducing a fault in c can be done by e.g. flipping a bit in RAM, while manipulation of c' would likely be done using a fault against a value in a register, as values generated during the re-encryption might not be stored RAM, or only for a shorter duration and possibly varying addresses. The decryption/re-encryption corresponds to lines 1 to 3 in Algorithm 6, the compression and decompression methods correspond to lines 5 and 1 of Algorithm 2 and Algorithm 3 which are called from lines 1 and 3 of Algorithm 6, respectively.

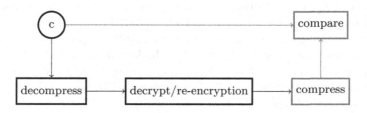

Fig. 1. Visualisation of the FO-transforms re-encryption check including decompression and compression. Being able to introduce one-bit faults anywhere in the red (light) phases enables our attack. (Color figure online)

3.1 Manipulating and Correcting the Ciphertext

The PKE ciphertext consists of the result of compressing a polynomial v (to get c_2) and of compressing a vector of polynomials $\mathbf{u}$ (to get c_1). The decrypt functions decompresses both c_1 and c_2, retrieves approximate versions of $\mathbf{u}$ and v, and computes and approximate version of $v - \mathbf{u}^T\mathbf{s}$, given by

$$rec = \mathbf{e}^T\mathbf{r} - \mathbf{s}^T(\mathbf{e_1} + \Delta\mathbf{u}) + e_2 + \Delta v + \text{Decode}(m)$$

where each coefficient is reduced to the range $\{0, ..., q-1\}$ and the Δ-terms denote the difference introduced by first compressing and then decompressing a (vector of) polynomial(s). The message is then recovered by mapping the coefficients of rec, $rec[i]$ for $i \in \{0, \ldots, n-1\}$, to a 0-bit if $rec[i]$ is closer to 0 or q than to

$q/2$ and to a 1-bit, otherwise; i.e. the function mapping a coefficient, reduced to $\{0, ..., q - 1\}$, to a bit is given by

$$\phi : \{0, ..., q - 1\} \rightarrow \{0, 1\}$$

$$a \mapsto \begin{cases} 0, & \text{if } \min(|a - q|, |a|) < q/4 \\ 1, & \text{else.} \end{cases}$$

For an honestly generated ciphertext, this yields the message m with high probability as the error polynomial d, given by

$$d = \mathbf{e}^T \mathbf{r} - \mathbf{s}^T (\mathbf{e_1} + \Delta \mathbf{u}) + e_2 + \Delta v,$$

is small.

Decoding of Manipulated Ciphertexts. By adding $q/4$ to $rec[i]$, we in some cases change the i-th bit m_i of the decoded message m. If m_i is 0, $rec[i]$ is "closer" to 0 mod q, i.e., 0 or q, than to $q/2$. In the first case ($rec[i]$ is close to 0), adding $q/4$ changes the decoding result to 1, as the result is now closer to $q/2$. In the second case ($rec[i]$ is close to q) $rec[i] + q/4$ will still be decoded to 0 (the result is now closer to 0 than to $q/2$). Analogously, if m_i is 1, then adding $q/4$ to $rec[i]$ changes the result of decoding to 0 if $rec[i] < q/2$.

Hence, observing if decoding $rec[i] + q/4$ still results in the same message m allows to retrieve information about the error polynomial d. By modularly mapping the coefficients of d to $\{-\lfloor \frac{q}{2} \rfloor, ..., \lfloor \frac{q}{2} \rfloor\}$ and ignoring rounding, this may be as expressed as

$$rec[i] + \frac{q}{4} \text{ decodes to } m_i \text{ if, and only if, } d[i] < 0.$$

We are using this property of ϕ to manipulate ciphertexts and introduce faults such that we may derive a system of inequalities involving the secret key.

Correct vs. Incorrect Message. Recall that during decapsulation (Algorithm 6), the randomness τ used for re-encryption is derived by hashing the message m with the hash of the public key. Hence, flipping just a single bit in m yields a completely random c'. However, if the correct m is still computed, then c' will be equal to the original (non manipulated) ciphertext and thus only differs in a single bit from the sent ciphertext.

Introducing and Correcting an Error. The above observations lead to the following method. In the encapsulation step, we first create a valid ciphertext $c = (v, \mathbf{u})$ where $v = \sum_{i=0}^{n-1} v_i x^i$. We then replace v by $v' = v + \frac{q}{4} x^i$ and compress it to obtain a manipulated ciphertext c', which is sent to the device under attack. The attacked device decompresses c', retrieves a message m', re-encrypts the message to a ciphertext c'' and compares c' against c''. Before the comparison, we introduce a fault, flipping a bit of c', such that $c' = c$. Thereby, we achieve that the attacker performs the decryption on the manipulated ciphertext c' but effectively compares against the honestly generated ciphertext c. Observing whether a shared secret is established then tells us if the decryption of the manipulated ciphertext c' resulted in the original message m which was used to generate c. We note that this approach (manipulating a single coefficient of v and then testing if a decryption failure occurs) bares some resemblance to the side-channel attack of [BDH+21] on (flawed) algorithms for masked comparison [OSPG18,BPO+20].

Retrieving Information from Observing Encryption Failures. In the decryption step of the decapsulation routine, replacing c by the manipulated ciphertext c' results in the message being recovered from

$$v' - \mathbf{s}^T \mathbf{u} = v - \mathbf{s}^T \mathbf{u} + \left\lfloor \frac{q}{4} \right\rfloor x^i = rec + \left\lfloor \frac{q}{4} \right\rfloor x^i.$$

The manipulation therefore only affects the i-th message bit m_i and does not produce the same message and thus prevents a failed shared secret from being established if $d[i] > 0$ and $m_i = 0$ or $d[i] \geq 0$ and $m_i = 1^3$. The probability of an error occurring not introduced by the manipulated ciphertext is those of a decryption failure and can be ignored for this attack.

Restricting to Single-Bit Differences. If c and c' differ by more than one bit, we do not use that ciphertext and re-try with new randomness. Otherwise, single-bit faults would not be sufficient. This may take a few tries, but as ciphertexts can be pre-computed and are not sent to the device, we do not regard this as a limitation. Note that allowing multi-bit differences would also result in slightly different inequalities as in these cases, compression changes the error added to v.

Fault Location and Profiling. A single-bit fault model at a specific time in execution is realistic but requires profiling or good understanding of the implementation of software as well as hardware [RSDT13,OGM17]. However, in our case, the fault may be introduced over a time interval spanning almost the whole execution time and on different intermediates and methods, e.g. against a value in memory or in a register, as depicted in Fig. 1. Note that the attacker knows the value of the bit to be flipped and may discard ciphertexts with an undesired value of the targeted bit. Thus, a bit flip can be achieved if the attacker is being able to either set or reset bits, which is a more realistic attacker assumption compared to straight-up flipping [RSDT13,OGM17]. If a Boolean-masked value is targeted, then setting/resetting a bit is ineffective with a probability of 50 %, even if the plain value is known. Still, if we observe a successful decapsulation (no decryption failure), then we can infer that the bit was actually flipped. As we cannot further distinguish the cause of a decapsulation failure (decryption failure or ineffective fault injection), we have to ignore injections yielding this result. Therefore, in this case, the number of required faults is approximately quadrupled.

---

^{3} The difference in strictness arises from rounding to integers.

In addition, the observed outcome of the FO can be used for profiling, i.e., finding the correct faulting position in memory. The sent manipulated ciphertext will always be rejected unless properly corrected using a fault. This means that one can sweep over faulting positions and accept the one which leads to a correct decapsulation.[4] Even after finding a proper position, discarding inequalities resulting from observed decapsulation failures allows to filter out fault injections which did not produce the desired effect.

We finally note that the fault target (the ciphertext c) is public. Using, e.g., power analysis, one can find the point in time at which c is written into memory. This can aid in finding its address and physical location in RAM.

3.2 Obtaining Inequalities

To obtain inequalities in $\mathbf{e}$ and $\mathbf{s}$, we apply the procedure described in the previous section l times, where in the j-th step we obtain an inequality involving the i-th coefficient of the error polynomial, denoted d_j. As described before, in case of the decapsulation failing, we have $d_j[i] \geq 0$ and otherwise $d_j[i] \leq 0$[5]. The polynomial d_j is given by

$$
\begin{aligned}
d_j &= \psi(v_j) - \mathbf{s}^T \psi(\mathbf{u_j}) \\
&= (v + \Delta v) - \mathbf{s}^T \mathbf{u_j} - \mathbf{s}\Delta\mathbf{u} \\
&= \mathbf{e}^T \mathbf{r}_j - \mathbf{s}^T(\mathbf{e_{1j}} + \Delta\mathbf{u}_j) + e_{2j} + \Delta v_j + \mathrm{Decode}(m),
\end{aligned}
$$

where ψ denotes Decompress(Compress($\cdot$)). This means our inequalities are of the form

$$
(\mathbf{e}^T \mathbf{r}_j - \mathbf{s}^T(\mathbf{e_{1j}} + \Delta\mathbf{u}_j))[i] \lesseqgtr (e_{2j} + \Delta v_j)[i],
$$

where i is the coefficient we are manipulating/faulting, j is the index of the current step/fault, and all variables except for $\mathbf{e}$ and $\mathbf{s}$ are known. As the inequalities are clearly linear in $\mathbf{e}$ and $\mathbf{s}$, we may write those equations as $Ax \lesseqgtr -b$ where each row of the matrix A, together with the corresponding row of b and the information whether this row corresponds to a smaller or a greater sign, gives a check node as described in the next section. The construction of A and b is analogue to the construction in Sect. 2.3, x is the vector consisting of the entries of $\mathbf{e}$ and $\mathbf{s}$. In contrast to [PP21], we are not directly using the matrix structure. As described in the next section, each inequality, i.e. each row of A and b, are represented by a check node in a belief propagation graph.

---

[4] By first adding, e.g., only $q/8$ instead of $q/4$ to one coefficient of v, the chance that $m = m'$ and thus the probability of acceptance after a successful fault is drastically increased. This allows finding neighboring bits in memory more easily, which can then be used to find the actual targeted bit.

[5] By taking the i-th message bit into consideration, one may derive strict inequalities.

3.3   Recovering the Secret Key

To recover the secret key from inequalities, we use belief propagation. Our belief propagation graph consists of *variable nodes*, representing each unknown coefficient of **e** and **s**, and factor nodes, which inspired by decoding algorithms we call *check nodes*, representing an inequality. Check nodes are connected to all variable nodes. In each iteration, the check nodes send messages to the variable nodes or vice-versa. A message represents a probability distribution over $\{-\eta_1, \ldots, \eta_1\}$ of a key coefficient, where we interpret the key as consisting of **e** and **s** and denote the key vector as x. In each step the messages are combined according to the inequalities represented by the respective check node, from which probability distributions for each key coefficient are derived. Figure 2 shows a simplified example with four unknown variables (represented by x_0, x_1, x_2, x_3) and five inequalities (represented by *Check 0, ..., Check 4*).

The variable nodes are initialized with the distribution **e** and **s** were sampled from in Algorithm 1, this is called the prior distribution and in the following denoted by *prior*. In the first step, the prior distributions, now called *messages*, are sent to the check nodes. The check nodes update the distributions according to the inequality they represent. For an unknown coefficient i, all other messages are combined according to the represented inequality and the resulting probability distribution is used to derive a distribution for the i-th coefficient. To be precise, for each input with index i every check node computes the distribution of the sum in the inequality, leaving out i. This means a check node with index j, corresponding to an inequality

$$\sum_i a_{ji} x_i \lesseqgtr b_j$$

receiving messages $m_0, \ldots, m_{2n-1}$ (m_i belongs the i-th key coefficient) computes distributions

$$D_i = \sum_{i \neq j} a_{ji} m_i \text{ for } i \in \{0 \ldots 2n\} \tag{3}$$

where addition corresponds to computing the distribution of the sum of the corresponding random variables, i.e. convolution of the m_i (see Sect. 4), and sends the messages

$$x \mapsto P_{D_i}(x \lesseqgtr b_j) \text{ for } i \in \{0 \ldots 2n\}, \; x \in \{-\eta_1, \ldots, \eta_1\}$$

to the i-th variable node. As described in Sect. 4, for efficiency reasons, the computations of Eq. (3) are carried out in the Fourier domain.

The variable nodes combine incoming messages by computing the product with one index left out. For incoming messages $m_0, \ldots, m_l$ (m_j is the message coming from the j-th check node/inequality), the (normalized) product

$$x \mapsto \frac{\prod_{i \neq j} m_i(x)}{\sum_y \prod_{i \neq j} m_i(y)}, \; x \in \{-\eta_1, \ldots, \eta_1\}$$

is sent to the j-th check node.

Sending messages from variable nodes to factor nodes or vice-versa is called an *iteration*; sending messages from variable nodes to factor nodes and vice-versa is called a *full iteration*. After each full iteration, we may compute the current resulting probability distributions for the i-th coefficient, by multiplying and normalizing the incoming messages at the i-th node. That is, we compute the distribution

$$x \mapsto \frac{\prod_j m_j(x)}{\sum_y \prod_j m_j(y)}, \; x \in \{-\eta_1, \ldots, \eta_1\}$$

and use this as (preliminary) result for the i-th coefficient. We do not use an equivalent of the clustering method used in [PP21].

Note that this process is also related to decoding Low-density parity-check codes using belief propagation [Mac03]. In our setting, the implied code is not low-density, instead, all variable nodes are connected to all factor nodes.

The belief propagation varies with the parameters k and η_1, depending on the parameter set as described in Table 1, and l. The parameter k determines the number of variable nodes, given by $2nk$; the size of a message is $2\eta_1 + 1$ probabilities. Each of the l observations corresponds to a check node.

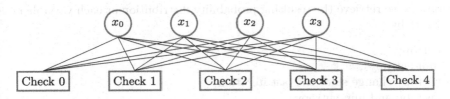

Fig. 2. A belief propagation graph with four variable nodes and five check nodes corresponding to four unknown coefficients and five inequalities.

4 Attack Implementation and Simulation

We implemented the simulation of the attack in Python and Rust where we rely on a modified version of PQClean [PQC]. We obtain inequalities by calling the Kyber implementation from Python, process them, and use a Rust implementation of belief propagation to recover the secret key from those inequalities. As single-bit faults are an established fault model and can be achieved e.g. using a laser, we solely rely on a simulation. The implementation is available at https://github.com/juliusjh/fault_enabled_cca.

4.1 Introducing Faults

To simulate our attack, we first fix a secret key on the assumed device. The simulated attacker then generates ciphertexts, checking for each ciphertext if the manipulation described in Sect. 3.1 only affects a single bit in the compressed ciphertext. If this is the case, we call a manipulated decapsulation function, correcting the manipulated ciphertext before the comparison of the ciphertext with the re-encrypted ciphertext. This function corresponds to a call to the device under attack during which we flip one bit of the ciphertext. By observing whether the correct shared secret is returned, we retrieve an inequality as described in Sect. 3.2. These steps are repeated until a sufficient number of inequalities have been extracted. Note that ciphertexts that differ in more than one bit are not sent to the device but are discarded before any communication happens.

For our simulation, we assume a perfect bit-flipping fault. As mentioned in Sect. 3.1, this assumption can be relaxed at the expense of having to send more manipulated ciphertexts to the device under attack. Depending on the fault model, it might be favorable to allow the manipulated ciphertext to differ in multiple bits, e.g. in a pattern matching some property of the expected introduced fault.

4.2 Belief Propagation

For each coefficient of $\mathbf{e}$ and $\mathbf{s}$, we initialize a variable node and for each inequality, we initialize a check node. We then propagate for a maximum of 80 full iterations, i.e. from variable to factor nodes and vice-versa, and, after each full iteration, we retrieve the resulting probability distribution at each variable node and sort by

- entropy,
- min-entropy[6],
- entropy change since the last iteration,
- entropy and min-entropy.

If the first n coefficients are correct in any ordering, we can find the other n coefficients by solving the public key equation $\mathbf{b} = \mathbf{As} + \mathbf{e}$ using linear algebra. In this case, the belief propagation is aborted and counted as a success. To minimize the runtime for obtaining statistics, we also abort if after 5 full iterations, the number of correct coefficients has not improved.

To compute the distributions D_i, described in Sect. 3.3, Eq. (3), for each variable node i, the convolution of $n-1$ messages has to be computed. Naïvely, this results in having to compute $(n-1)n$ convolutions of distributions (with growing support) at each check node in every full iteration. To avoid inefficient re-computations when computing partial products in check nodes, we are using the binary tree algorithm described by Pessl and Prokop in [PP21]. Using an upwardly constructed and a downwardly constructed tree, we are avoiding recomputations and may compute all D_i at once. This is similar to the classical two-directional pass to compute partial products.

To construct the upward tree, we first initialize leaf nodes with $\hat{y}_i$. Every following layer then consists of the product of two nodes of the previous layer up until the $\log(2n) - 1$-th layer having two nodes. The downward tree is then

---

[6] The negative logarithm of the probability of the most likely value.

initialized by swapping the values of the last layer of the upward tree. Every other layer of the downward tree is computed by multiplying the node of the layer above with the sibling from the upward tree. Thus, each node of the downward tree is the product of all nodes except its child nodes. The algorithm is also used for variable nodes. As the number of inequalities is not always a power of two, we add an additional node to a layer if the number nodes in the previous layer is not even. This additional node is equal to the last node of the previous layer, i.e. we implicitly add a node with the value of the multiplicative neutral element to each uneven layer.

Algorithm 7. Computations at a check node representing a less-equal inequality given by $a_0, \ldots a_{2n-1}$, a value b, and set of possible values V. Messages m map a 16-bit signed value to a probability represented as 64-bit float by the $[\cdot]$ operator. The i-th messages represents the variable x_i corresponding to the coefficient a_i in the inequality.

Input: Incoming messages $m_0, \ldots, m_{2n-1}$
Output: Outgoing messages $m'_0, \ldots, m'_{2n-1}$
1: **for all** $i \in \{0, \ldots, 2n-1\}$ **do**
2:      **for all** $v \in V$ **do**
3:          $mm_i[a_i \cdot v] \leftarrow m_i[x]$ ▷ Distribution of $a_i x_i$
4:      $\widehat{mm}_i \leftarrow \mathsf{FFT}(mm_i)$
5: downtree $\leftarrow$ BinaryTrees.compute$(\widehat{mm}_0, \ldots, \widehat{mm}_{2n-1})$ ▷ Multiply leaving one out
6: **for all** $i \in \{0, \ldots, 2n-1\}$ **do**
7:      $\widehat{mp}_i \leftarrow$ downtree.leaf(i) ▷ downtree.leaf$(i) = \prod_{j \neq i} \widehat{mm}_j$
8:      $mp \leftarrow \mathsf{FFT}^{-1}(\widehat{mp}_i)$ ▷ Holds distribution of $\sum_{j \neq i} a_j x_j$
9:      **for all** $v \in V$ **do**
10:         $m'_i[v] \leftarrow mp_i.\mathsf{sum\_lesseq\_than}(b - v)$ ▷ $m'_i[v] = P(\sum_{j \neq i} a_j x_j \leq b - v)$
11: **return** $m'_0, \ldots, m'_{2n-1}$

4.3   Results

We ran our simulations for all three Kyber parameter sets to determine the number of inequalities and thus faulted decapsulations necessary to retrieve the secret key. We first determined the range of inequalities from which on a key recovery is possible. We than tested different numbers of inequalities with a step-size of 250, 500, and 1000 inequalities depending on the rate of change in the recovered coefficients in that range. For every number of inequalities, we ran 20 experiments, the success rate is then calculated as the number of successful runs divided by the total number of runs. The number of recovered coefficients is the average number of recovered coefficients.

Abort Criteria. We abort if the key is found or after at most 80 full iterations. To check for a successful recovery, an attacker would use the ordering described in Sect. 4.2 and the public key equation. To obtain statistics, we simply abort if at least n of the coefficients in any of the orderings are correct. In addition, we abort early if there is no improvement after 20 steps.

Success Rate. Figure 3 shows the success rate of our experiments. In our simulations, our approach recovered the secret key in all cases starting with 5750 inequalities for Kyber512, 6750 inequalities for Kyber768, and 8500 inequalities for Kyber1024. Each inequality corresponds to one manipulated key exchange (and therefore one fault) with the device. More inequalities gave a higher success rate in all experiments. Succeeding runs usually occur starting with 5000 inequalities for Kyber512, 5750 inequalities for Kyber768, and 7250 inequalities for Kyber1024.

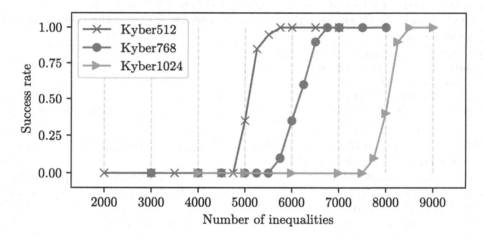

Fig. 3. Success rate depending on the number of inequalities/introduced faults.

Recovered Coefficients. In failing cases, we often recover a high number of coefficients that might be sufficient to retrieve the key, using standard lattice reduction algorithms such as [CN11]. We count recovered coefficients as the longest chain of correct coefficients in one of the orderings described in Sect. 4.2 after any step. As the number of correct coefficients might decrease after further iterations, especially in corner cases, an attacker should test if the key can be recovered using the public key equations after every step. If additional lattice reduction techniques are used, those should also be applied to intermediate results. Figure 4 shows the average number of recovered coefficients. Given that the number of recovered inequalities rises quickly after obtaining more than a certain threshold of inequalities, we assume that additional lattice reduction techniques are only useful for cases where obtaining further inequalities is very difficult or expensive. In all other cases where lattice reduction techniques may yield a correct result, retrieving more inequalities should quickly increase the success rate to 1.

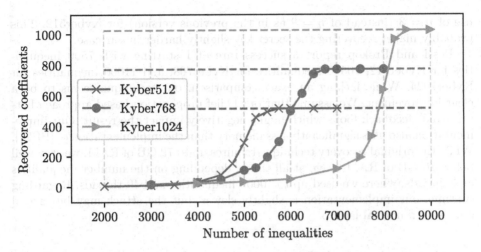

Fig. 4. Average number of recovered coefficients. The dashed lines mark 512, 768, and 1024 coefficients.

Runtime. Our implementation is in large parts multithreaded with the ability to utilize as many cores as the number of inequalities used. The runtime strongly depends on the number of inequalities as each inequality is represented by a factor node.

Our attack runs on widely available hardware. For example, on a standard laptop, one full iteration for Kyber768 and with 7000 inequalities takes about 15 min using a single thread of an Intel(R) Core(TM) i7-10510U CPU. Table 2 shows the average number of full iterations and the runtime in minutes for successful runs with 32 and 8 threads on a Intel(R) Xeon(R) Gold 6242 CPU with 16 cores.

Table 2. Runtimes in minutes on a Intel(R) Xeon(R) Gold 6242 with 32 and 8 threads.

Parameter set	Iterations	32 threads	8 threads
Kyber512 (6000 inequalities)	6.8	3.25	9.3
Kyber768 (7000 inequalities)	6.75	6.7	18.6
Kyber1024 (9000 inequalities)	9	16.9	39.25

Comparison with Previous Work. The work of Pessl and Prokop, presented in [PP21], uses a different attack (especially regarding the fault model) to obtain similar inequalities. Their technique to recover the secret key from those inequalities is different, but in a way related to ours.

Note that they analyzed an older version of Kyber. The main difference between the versions, in the context of key recovery from inequalities, is the use of $\eta = 3$ (instead of $\eta = 2$ as in the previous version) for Kyber512. This probably makes recovering the secret key slightly harder in our case.

Pessl and Prokop report a success rate of 1 starting with 7500 inequalities for Kyber512, 10500 inequalities for Kyber768, and 11000 inequalities for Kyber1024. While lacking an exact comparison, our technique seems to be a clear improvement. We assume that our belief propagation based approach better avoids feedback loops which might negatively impact the result. Our implementation also uses significantly less memory than the implementation of [PP21]. While the original recovery technique requires up to 79 GB of RAM, we stay well below 10 GB of RAM usage at all times, depending on the number inequalities and threads, where we used up to 10000 inequalities and 40 threads. Regarding runtime, our implementation is slightly slower, but the attack may be carried out using a normal laptop.

5   Conclusion and Countermeasures

In the previous sections, we presented a realistic attack by combining a chosen-ciphertext attack with a fault injection and introduced an improved recovery technique for linear inequalities involving the secret key. The fault may be injected over a long execution-time interval and on different variables which hold public data. Our attack depends on the result of computations and not the computational steps itself. Therefore, securing computations and Boolean masking of inputs does not prevent our attack. We thereby highlighted the importance to protect seemingly non-sensitive, public data as well as operations over the whole execution time and to implement additional countermeasures to protect against fault-enabled chosen-ciphertext attacks. In addition, we give another exemplary usage of the belief propagation algorithm for key recovery and provide further evidence for the importance of the belief propagation algorithm for side-channel analysis. While we targeted Kyber, we conjecture that variants of this attacks are applicable to conceptually similar schemes such as Saber [DKRV18], FrodoKEM [ABD+21], or NewHope [AAB+19]. In this section, we provide an overview over standard countermeasures and if and how they defend against our attack.

Shuffling. In contrast to [PP21], our attack may not be mitigated by shuffling the decoder. They introduce a fault in the decoder and need to know which bit has been faulted to extract correct inequalities, which explains the usefulness of shuffling. Shuffling in time, however, does not affect the physical location of c in RAM, which is why manipulation of this value is not prevented. Still, a second attack path, namely manipulating c' during re-encryption (cf. Fig. 1), becomes more difficult to exploit. When only using successful decapsulations–they can only occur when the correct coefficient was faulted–the number of required faults is approximately multiplied by the number of shuffling positions.

Redundancy. Introducing redundancy in the storage of c, as depicted in Fig. 5, might drastically increase the effort and abilities required by an attacker. For that, a hash of c is computed directly after receiving the ciphertext. Right after the comparison check of the re-encryption, c is again hashed and compared against the previously computed hash. This mainly protects against faults introduced in c while it is stored in RAM. A manipulation during compression of c' is still possible, therefore the attack is not fully prevented but significantly harder to carry out.

The combination of introducing redundancy, shuffling the decoder, together with a secured comparison (via, e.g., double computation) likely prevents our attack with high probability. Additional security can be achieved by randomising the memory layout, e.g. by storing coefficients in a permuted order, and shuffling the compression function.

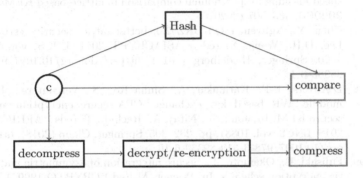

Fig. 5. Visualisation of the FO-transforms re-encryption check including decompression and compression with an additional countermeasure. Being able to introduce one-bit faults anywhere in the red (light) phases enables our attack. Introducing redundancy drastically reduces the attack surface. (Color figure online)

Acknowledgments. This work has been supported by the German Federal Ministry of Education and Research (BMBF) under the project "PQC4MED" (16KIS1041), as well as by the European Union's Horizon 2020 research and innovation program under grant agreement No 830927. We would like to thank the anonymous reviewers for their helpful comments which improved this work.

References

[AAB+19] Alkim, E., et al.: NewHope - Submission to the NIST post-quantum project (2019). https://newhopecrypto.org/data/NewHope_2019_07_10.pdf

[ABD+21] Alkim, E., et al.: FrodoKEM Learning With Errors Key Encapsulation (2021). https://frodokem.org/files/FrodoKEM-specification-20210604.pdf

[ACLZ20] Amiet, D., Curiger, A., Leuenberger, L., Zbinden, P.: Defeating NEWHOPE with a single trace. In: Ding, J., Tillich, J.-P. (eds.) PQCrypto 2020. LNCS, vol. 12100, pp. 189–205. Springer, Cham (2020). https://doi.org/10.1007/978-3-030-44223-1_11

[BDH+21] Bhasin, S., D'Anvers, J.-P., Heinz, D., Pöppelmann, T., Van Beirendonck, M.: Attacking and defending masked polynomial comparison for lattice-based cryptography. IACR Cryptology ePrint Archive **2021**, 104 (2021)

[BDK+18] Bos, J.W., et al.: CRYSTALS - Kyber: a CCA-secure module-lattice-based KEM. In: 2018 IEEE European Symposium on Security and Privacy, EuroS&P 2018, London, UK, 24–26 April 2018, pp. 353–367. IEEE (2018)

[BGRR19] Bauer, A., Gilbert, H., Renault, G., Rossi, M.: Assessment of the key-reuse resilience of NewHope. In: Matsui, M. (ed.) CT-RSA 2019. LNCS, vol. 11405, pp. 272–292. Springer, Cham (2019). https://doi.org/10.1007/978-3-030-12612-4_14

[BPO+20] Bache, F., Paglialonga, C., Oder, T., Schneider, T., Güneysu, T.: High-speed masking for polynomial comparison in lattice-based KEMs. TCHES **2020**(3), 483–507 (2020)

[CN11] Chen, Y., Nguyen, P.Q.: BKZ 2.0: better lattice security estimates. In: Lee, D.H., Wang, X. (eds.) ASIACRYPT 2011. LNCS, vol. 7073, pp. 1–20. Springer, Heidelberg (2011). https://doi.org/10.1007/978-3-642-25385-0_1

[DKRV18] D'Anvers, J.-P., Karmakar, A., Sinha Roy, S., Vercauteren, F.: Saber: module-LWR based key exchange, CPA-secure encryption and CCA-secure KEM. In: Joux, A., Nitaj, A., Rachidi, T. (eds.) AFRICACRYPT 2018. LNCS, vol. 10831, pp. 282–305. Springer, Cham (2018). https://doi.org/10.1007/978-3-319-89339-6_16

[FO99] Fujisaki, E., Okamoto, T.: Secure integration of asymmetric and symmetric encryption schemes. In: Wiener, M. (ed.) CRYPTO 1999. LNCS, vol. 1666, pp. 537–554. Springer, Heidelberg (1999). https://doi.org/10.1007/3-540-48405-1_34

[GGSB20] Guo, Q., Grosso, V., Standaert, F.-X., Bronchain, O.: Modeling soft analytical side-channel attacks from a coding theory viewpoint. IACR TCHES **2020**(4), 209–238 (2020)

[GJN20] Guo, Q., Johansson, T., Nilsson, A.: A key-recovery timing attack on post-quantum primitives using the Fujisaki-Okamoto transformation and its application on FrodoKEM. IACR Cryptology ePrint Archive **2020**, 743 (2020)

[GRO18] Green, J., Roy, A., Oswald, E.: A systematic study of the impact of graphical models on inference-based attacks on AES. In: Bilgin, B., Fischer, J.-B. (eds.) CARDIS 2018. LNCS, vol. 11389, pp. 18–34. Springer, Cham (2019). https://doi.org/10.1007/978-3-030-15462-2_2

[HHK17] Hofheinz, D., Hövelmanns, K., Kiltz, E.: A modular analysis of the Fujisaki-Okamoto transformation. In: Kalai, Y., Reyzin, L. (eds.) TCC 2017. LNCS, vol. 10677, pp. 341–371. Springer, Cham (2017). https://doi.org/10.1007/978-3-319-70500-2_12

[HHP+21] Hamburg, M., et al.: Chosen ciphertext k-trace attacks on masked CCA2 secure kyber. IACR Cryptology ePrint Archive **2021**, 956 (2021)

[HP21] Heinz, D., Pöppelmann, T.: Combined fault and DPA protection for lattice-based cryptography. IACR Cryptology ePrint Archive **2021**, 101 (2021)

[KPP20] Kannwischer, M.J., Pessl, P., Primas, R.: Single-trace attacks on Keccak. TCHES **2020**(3), 243–268 (2020)

[LPR13] Lyubashevsky, V., Peikert, C., Regev, O.: On ideal lattices and learning with errors over rings. J. ACM **60**(6), 43:1-43:35 (2013)

[LS15] Langlois, A., Stehlé, D.: Worst-case to average-case reductions for module lattices. Des. Codes Crypt. **75**(3), 565–599 (2014). https://doi.org/10.1007/s10623-014-9938-4

[Mac03] MacKay, D.J.C.: Information Theory, Inference, and Learning Algorithms. Cambridge University Press, Cambridge (2003)

[Nata] National Institute of Standards and Technology. NIST Status Update on the 3rd Round. https://csrc.nist.gov/CSRC/media/Presentations/status-update-on-the-3rd-round/images-media/session-1-moody-nist-round-3-update.pdf

[Natb] National Institute of Standards and Technology. Post-Quantum Cryptography Standardization. https://csrc.nist.gov/Projects/Post-Quantum-Cryptography/Post-Quantum-Cryptography-Standardization

[OGM17] Ordas, S., Guillaume-Sage, L., Maurine, P.: Electromagnetic fault injection: the curse of flip-flops. J. Cryptogr. Eng. **7**(3), 183–197 (2016). https://doi.org/10.1007/s13389-016-0128-3

[OSPG18] Oder, T., Schneider, T., Pöppelmann, T., Güneysu, T.: Practical CCA2-secure and masked Ring-LWE implementation. TCHES **2018**(1), 142–174 (2018)

[PH16] Park, A., Han, D.-G.: Chosen ciphertext Simple Power Analysis on software 8-bit implementation of Ring-LWE encryption. In: 2016 IEEE Asian Hardware-Oriented Security and Trust, AsianHOST 2016, Yilan, Taiwan, 19–20 December 2016, pp. 1–6. IEEE Computer Society (2016)

[PP19] Pessl, P., Primas, R.: More practical single-trace attacks on the number theoretic transform. In: Schwabe, P., Thériault, N. (eds.) LATINCRYPT 2019. LNCS, vol. 11774, pp. 130–149. Springer, Cham (2019). https://doi.org/10.1007/978-3-030-30530-7_7

[PP21] Pessl, P., Prokop, L.: Fault attacks on CCA-secure lattice KEMs. TCHES **2021**(2), 37–60 (2021)

[PPM17] Primas, R., Pessl, P., Mangard, S.: Single-trace side-channel attacks on masked lattice-based encryption. In: Fischer, W., Homma, N. (eds.) CHES 2017. LNCS, vol. 10529, pp. 513–533. Springer, Cham (2017). https://doi.org/10.1007/978-3-319-66787-4_25

[PQC] Contributors to PQClean. PQClean. https://github.com/PQClean/PQClean

[RBRC20] Ravi, P., Bhasin, S., Roy, S.S., Chattopadhyay, A.: Drop by Drop you break the rock - Exploiting generic vulnerabilities in Lattice-based PKE/KEMs using EM-based Physical Attacks. IACR Cryptology ePrint Archive, p. 549 (2020)

[RRCB20] Ravi, P., Roy, S.S., Chattopadhyay, A., Bhasin, S.: Generic side-channel attacks on CCA-secure lattice-based PKE and KEMs. TCHES **2020**(3), 307–335 (2020)

[RRdC+16] Reparaz, O., Roy, S.S., de Clercq, R., Vercauteren, F., Verbauwhede, I.: Masking Ring-LWE. J. Cryptogr. Eng. **6**(2), 139–153 (2016)

[RRVV15] Reparaz, O., Sinha Roy, S., Vercauteren, F., Verbauwhede, I.: A masked Ring-LWE implementation. In: Güneysu, T., Handschuh, H. (eds.) CHES 2015. LNCS, vol. 9293, pp. 683–702. Springer, Heidelberg (2015). https://doi.org/10.1007/978-3-662-48324-4_34

[RSDT13] Roscian, C., Sarafianos, A., Dutertre, J.-M., Tria, A.: Fault model analysis of laser-induced faults in SRAM memory cells. In: Fischer, W., Schmidt, J.-M. (eds.) 2013 Workshop on Fault Diagnosis and Tolerance in Cryptography, Los Alamitos, CA, USA, 20 August 2013, pp. 89–98. IEEE Computer Society (2013)

[VGS14] Veyrat-Charvillon, N., Gérard, B., Standaert, F.-X.: Soft analytical side-channel attacks. In: Sarkar, P., Iwata, T. (eds.) ASIACRYPT 2014. LNCS, vol. 8873, pp. 282–296. Springer, Heidelberg (2014). https://doi.org/10.1007/978-3-662-45611-8_15

[VOGR18] Valencia, F., Oder, T., Güneysu, T., Regazzoni, F.: Exploring the vulnerability of R-LWE encryption to fault attacks. In: Goodacre, J., Luján, M., Agosta, G., Barenghi, A., Koren, I., Pelosi, G. (eds.) Proceedings of the Fifth Workshop on Cryptography and Security in Computing Systems, CS2 2018, Manchester, UK, 24 January 2018, pp. 7–12. ACM (2018)

[XIU+21] Xagawa, K., Ito, A., Ueno, R., Takahashi, J., Homma, N.: Fault-injection attacks against NIST's post-quantum cryptography round 3 KEM candidates. IACR Cryptology ePrint Archive 2021, 840 (2021)

Post-Quantum Cryptography

DeCSIDH: Delegating Isogeny Computations in the CSIDH Setting

Robi Pedersen[(✉)][ⓘ]

imec-COSIC KU Leuven, Kasteelpark Arenberg 10 Bus 2452, 3001 Leuven, Belgium
robi.pedersen@esat.kuleuven.be

Abstract. Delegating heavy computations to auxiliary servers, while keeping the inputs secret, presents a practical solution for computationally limited devices to use resource-intense cryptographic protocols, such as those based on isogenies, and thus allows the deployment of post-quantum security on mobile devices and in the internet of things. We propose two algorithms for the secure and verifiable delegation of isogeny computations in the CSIDH setting. We then apply these algorithms to different instances of CSIDH and to the signing algorithms SeaSign and CSI-FiSh. Our algorithms present a communication-cost trade-off. Asymptotically (for high communication), the cost for the delegator is reduced by a factor 9 for the original CSIDH-512 parameter set and a factor 30 for SQALE'd CSIDH-4096, while the relative cost of SeaSign vanishes. Even for much lower communication cost, we come close to these asymptotic results. Using the knowledge of the class group, the delegation of CSI-FiSh is basically free (up to element generation) already at a very low communication cost.

Keywords: Post-quantum cryptography · Isogeny-based cryptography · CSIDH · Secure computation outsourcing · Lightweight cryptography

1 Introduction

Delegation of Computations. The last decade has witnessed an immense surge in mobile devices, including RFID-cards, tiny sensor nodes, smart phones and a myriad of devices in the internet of things. Since such mobile devices are usually computationally limited or have other constraints such as low battery life, the delegation of their computations to external, more powerful devices, has become an active area of research. While delegation allows to relieve these devices of their most heavy computations, it comes at a certain risk, such as potentially malicious servers trying to extract sensitive data or returning wrong results for these computations. Mitigating these threats is especially important when delegating cryptographic protocols, where such servers might try to extract private keys. The necessary properties for secure and verifiable delegation were first formalized in a security model introduced by Hohenberger and Lysyanskaya [15]

© Springer Nature Switzerland AG 2021
A. Adhikari et al. (Eds.): INDOCRYPT 2021, LNCS 13143, pp. 337–361, 2021.
https://doi.org/10.1007/978-3-030-92518-5_16

in the context of group exponentiations. Their model lets the delegator shroud sensitive data before sending it to the server and then verify and de-shroud the server's output. The operations performed by the delegator should still be efficient enough for the delegation to be worthwhile.

Isogeny-based Cryptography. Isogeny-based cryptography goes back to the works of Couveignes [12] and Rostovtsev and Stolbunov [24] and is based on the difficulty of finding an explicit isogeny linking two given isogenous elliptic curves defined over a finite field. While the original proposal uses ordinary elliptic curves, recent quantum attacks [11,18,23], which use the commutativity of the endomorphism ring, push the secure parameter size to the realm of prohibitively inefficient protocols. In response, two new approaches using supersingular elliptic curves have been introduced. The first one, commonly referred to as SIDH (supersingular isogeny Diffie-Hellman) was proposed by Jao and De Feo [16] and uses the fact that supersingular elliptic curves over $\mathbb{F}_{p^2}$ have a non-commutative endomorphism ring, so that the previously discussed attacks are not applicable. The second one, called CSIDH [7] (commutative SIDH), uses the structure of supersingular elliptic curves to immensely reduce the computational cost of the originally proposed protocols back to the realm of usability. We note that while CSIDH closely follows the line of the original Couveignes-Rostovtsev-Stolbunov scheme, SIDH uses a different approach that is more closely related to the cryptographic hash function proposed by Charles, Goren and Lauter [8].

Motivation and Related Work. While isogeny-based protocols profit from the lowest key sizes of any of the current post-quantum standardization proposals [1, 7,16,19,26], they are still among the slowest. This might be tolerable for specific applications, but given the immense surge in low-power mobile devices in recent years, there is a strong need for easily deployable and computationally cheap, yet secure cryptographic protocols. It is of particular interest for these limited devices to profit from post-quantum security in order to allow them to remain secure in the long term. While there have been many proposals for the delegation of group exponentiations and pairings [15,29], the delegation of post-quantum cryptographic protocols is a very new topic. In 2019, Pedersen and Uzunkol [20] proposed the first delegation algorithms for isogeny computations and improved upon their work with a follow-up paper in 2021 [21]. Their approach is applied to SIDH-type protocols, i.e. supersingular isogeny protocols over $\mathbb{F}_{p^2}$, and is based on the outsource security model from [15]. The question of delegating isogenies in the CSIDH setting has been proposed as a direction of future research by [21] and will be the main focus of this work. While we will also use the outsource security model from [15], we stress that we cannot simply use or translate the previously proposed isogeny delegation schemes in the SIDH setting to the CSIDH setting. The main reason is that cryptographic protocols in these two schemes use very different descriptions and are not related to one another in an obvious way.

Our Contribution. The purpose of this work is to propose the first isogeny delegation algorithms in the CSIDH setting, which are secure and provide high verifiability guarantees. More precisely,

1. We introduce and analyze ShrVec, an algorithm that allows transforming a uniform vector into three vectors, two of which are uniform, and the third one being small. This allows to shroud secret keys in the CSIDH protocol [7].
2. We define two new algorithms based on the outsource-security description of Hohenberger and Lysyanskaya [15]:
   - The (commutative) *isogeny computation algorithm* CIso, which allows to delegate the computation of an isogeny, while keeping the kernel hidden from the auxiliary servers, and
   - The *hidden isogeny computation algorithm* HIso, which allows to delegate the computation of an isogeny, while keeping both the kernel and the isogeny codomain hidden from the auxiliary servers.

   We present both algorithms in the *one-malicious two untrusted program* (OMTUP) assumption defined in [15] and in the newly introduced *two honest-but-curious* (2HBC) assumption. All of our algorithms work in two rounds of communication.
3. We apply our delegation algorithms to different protocols in the CSIDH setting and compare the reduced cost of the delegator to the full, local computation. Most of our algorithms allow a trade-off between computational and communication cost. Asymptotically (for large communication cost), we reduce the computational cost of CSIDH-512 [7] to below 12% of the local cost of the full protocol, while the SQALE'd CSIDH-4096 [9] protocol can be reduced to about 3.5% of the local cost. Also for lower communication costs, the gain of the delegator quickly approaches the asymptotic values. The gains for signatures are even better: The relative cost of delegating SeaSign asymptotically vanishes and can be easily reduced to a few percent at low communication cost, while CSI-FiSh, by using knowledge of the class group structure, can be made virtually free at low communication cost.

Naming. Following the *fishy name trend* of commutative supersingular isogeny protocols, we refer to their delegation as DeCSIDH (**De**legated **CSIDH**) and pronounce it *deckside*. The reader is free to imagine a fisher with limited resources being helped by a more powerful (yet potentially malicious) fishing boat.

2   Elliptic Curves and Isogenies

Isogeny-based cryptography is based on the good mixing properties of isogeny graphs, i.e. graphs of isomorphism classes of elliptic curves over finite fields connected by isogenies. Isogenies are surjective homomorphisms between elliptic curves that are also algebraic maps. Separable isogenies are uniquely defined by their kernel. While it is easy to compute an isogeny from a given kernel, it is in general difficult to find the kernel, given two isogenous elliptic curves.

The original protocols by Couveignes [12] and Rostovtsev and Stolbunov [24, 27] used ordinary elliptic curves, defined over a prime field $\mathbb{F}_p$, while the later CSIDH protocol by Castryck, Lange, Martindale, Panny and Renes [6] uses supersingular elliptic curves over $\mathbb{F}_p$ for efficiency reasons. These curves have

Frobenius trace $t = 0$ and their $\mathbb{F}_p$-rational endomorphism rings are orders $\mathcal{O}$ in a quadratic imaginary field $\mathbb{Q}(\sqrt{-p})$. A key observation of these protocols is that the ideals in the class group $\mathrm{Cl}(\mathcal{O})$ uniquely define subgroups via their kernel and therefore uniquely define isogenies, i.e. for a given elliptic curve $E/\mathbb{F}_p$ and ideal $\mathfrak{a} \in \mathrm{Cl}(\mathcal{O})$, we have a separable isogeny $E \to E/\mathfrak{a}$ with kernel $\bigcap_{\alpha \in \mathfrak{a}} \ker \alpha$. As a result, the ideal-class group $\mathrm{Cl}(\mathcal{O})$ acts freely and transitively on the set of $\mathbb{F}_p$-isomorphism classes of these elliptic curves via isogenies [12] and this group action is generally written as $E \to \mathfrak{a} * E$.

In the CSIDH protocol [7], the underlying prime field $\mathbb{F}_p$ is defined via $p = 4 \prod_{i=1}^{n} \ell_i - 1$, where the ℓ_i are small primes. Since $\#E(\mathbb{F}_p) = p + 1$, the chosen structure of p implies that $\ell_i \mathcal{O}$ decomposes as the product of two prime ideals $\mathfrak{l}_i = (\ell_i, \pi - 1)$ and $\mathfrak{l}_i^{-1} = (\ell_i, \pi + 1)$, where π corresponds to the Frobenius endomorphism. The action of these ideals on the set of (isomorphism classes of) elliptic curves over $\mathbb{F}_p$ can then be computed with the standard Vélu formulae [30] and are efficient for small ℓ_i. Given the structure of p, ideals can generally be expressed as $\mathfrak{a} = \prod_{i=1}^{n} \mathfrak{l}_i^{a_i}$, where positive exponents a_i correspond to the action of $\mathfrak{l}_i$, while negative exponents correspond to the action of $\mathfrak{l}_i^{-1}$. Ideals can then be simply expressed by representative vectors, e.g. $\mathbf{a} = (a_1, \ldots, a_n)$ would correspond to the action of $\mathfrak{a}$ as defined above. The order of the application of the prime ideals $\mathfrak{l}_i$ of $\mathfrak{a}$ does not matter and its dual is simply $\mathfrak{a}^{-1}$ represented by $-\mathbf{a}$. Note that $\mathfrak{a}_1 \mathfrak{a}_2$ corresponds to $\mathbf{a}_1 + \mathbf{a}_2$.

Isogenies can be computed using Algorithm 2 of [7]. We denote by $\mathcal{I}(\mathfrak{a})$ the generic cost of computing an isogeny defined by the ideal $\mathfrak{a}$.

The Class Group. While the class group has asymptotic size $\#\mathrm{Cl}(\mathcal{O}) \approx 2\sqrt{p}$ [25], computing its exact structure is a difficult task for large p [3,17]. The original proposal of CSIDH-512 [7] circumvented this problem by choosing $n = 74$ small primes (the 73 smallest odd primes and $\ell_{74} = 587$) and sampling the elements a_i of $\mathbf{a}$ from a range $\{-5, \ldots, 5\}$ of size 11. As such, $11^n \approx 2^{256}$, which should cover most of the class group without knowing its exact structure. In 2019, Beullens, Kleinjung and Vercauteren [3] computed the class group structure and the relation lattice for the CSIDH-512 parameter set and found a cyclic class group of order $\#\mathrm{Cl}(\mathcal{O}) \approx 2^{257}$. This knowledge allows to sample random elements from $\mathbb{Z}_{\#\mathrm{Cl}(\mathcal{O})} = \mathbb{Z}/\#\mathrm{Cl}(\mathcal{O})\mathbb{Z}$ and transform them into vectors $\mathbf{a}$ by solving easy instances of the closest vector problem using the relation lattice. This guarantees uniform coverage of the entire class group, while also allowing efficient computation via low-degree isogenies. Unfortunately, class group computations for larger parameter sets than CSIDH-512 seem currently out of reach.

Notation. We use "←" as the assignment operator: If the right hand side is an algorithm, the left hand side represents the variables to which its output is assigned. If the right hand side is a set, we assume the left hand side to represent a randomly sampled value from this set. We will write $[start, end]$ as a shorthand for the set of integers ranging from $start \in \mathbb{Z}$ to $end \in \mathbb{Z}$. We define as $\mathbb{B}(N) \subset \mathbb{Z}^n$ any set of the form $\mathbb{B} = \mathbb{B}_1 \times \cdots \times \mathbb{B}_n$, where $\mathbb{B}_i \subset \mathbb{Z}$ are intervals of length $d_i = \#\mathbb{B}_i$, and such that $\#\mathbb{B}(N) = \prod_{i=1}^{n} d_i \approx N$. As an example, for

CSIDH-512, we use $\mathbb{B}(2^{256}) = [-5,5]^n$. Ideals in $\mathrm{Cl}(\mathcal{O})$ can then be represented by vectors $\mathbf{a} \in \mathbb{B}(N)$, where typically $N \leq \#\mathrm{Cl}(\mathcal{O})$. Intervals $\mathbb{B}_i$ are of the types $[-B_i, B_i]$ or $[0, B_i]$ for $B_i \in \mathbb{N}$ (see e.g. [5,7,9]). Throughout this work, we will use the former case for simplicity, for which it holds $d_i = 2B_i + 1$. The case $[0, B_i]$ follows completely analogously.

We write ideals in $\mathrm{Cl}(\mathcal{O})$ in the fraktur font (e.g. $\mathfrak{a}, \mathfrak{b}, \mathfrak{s}, \dots$) while the corresponding vectors in $\mathbb{B}(N)$ are written in bold font (e.g. $\mathbf{a}, \mathbf{b}, \mathbf{s}, \dots$). If the class group is known, we write elements from $\mathbb{Z}_{\#\mathrm{Cl}(\mathcal{O})}$ in the standard font (e.g. $a, b, s, \dots$). We assume $\mathrm{Cl}(\mathcal{O})$ to be cyclic with publicly known generator $\mathfrak{g}$.[1] We always see elements using the same letters as related, e.g. $a \in \mathbb{Z}_{\#\mathrm{Cl}(\mathcal{O})}$ and $\mathbf{a} \in \mathbb{B}(N)$ will always represent $\mathfrak{a} \in \mathrm{Cl}(\mathcal{O})$, while the same holds for $(b, \mathbf{b}, \mathfrak{b})$, $(s, \mathbf{s}, \mathfrak{s})$ etc. Let $\mathbf{a} = (a_1, \dots, a_n)$, then we can express this relation as follows:

$$\mathfrak{a} = \prod_{i=1}^{n} \mathfrak{l}_i^{a_i} = \mathfrak{g}^a.$$

Note that vector entries are also written in the standard font. Their distinction from elements in $\mathbb{Z}_{\#\mathrm{Cl}(\mathcal{O})}$ will always be clear from context.

It is useful to note that multiplications between elements in $\mathrm{Cl}(\mathcal{O})$ naturally translate to additions in $\mathbb{Z}_{\#\mathrm{Cl}(\mathcal{O})}$ and $\mathbb{B}(N)$, while divisions translate to subtractions. As an example, $\mathfrak{a}\mathfrak{b}^{-1}$ can be represented by $a - b$ or by $\mathbf{a} - \mathbf{b}$.

Security. Security of CSIDH and related protocols is generally based on the following hard problem.

Definition 1 (Group action inverse problem (GAIP)). *[7] Given two supersingular elliptic curves E, E' over $\mathbb{F}_p$ with the same $\mathbb{F}_p$-rational endomorphism ring $\mathcal{O}$, find an ideal $\mathfrak{a} \in Cl(\mathcal{O})$ such that $E' = \mathfrak{a} * E$.*

Classical security is based on a meet-in-the-middle attack. The query complexity of this attack is $O(\sqrt{\#\mathrm{Cl}(\mathcal{O})})$. Quantum security of CSIDH is still subject to scrutiny. For current estimates of the quantum security, we refer the reader to [4,7,9] and [22]. We will use these estimates for later assessment of our schemes and always refer to the source in question. We write $\lambda(N)$ for a generic quantum security parameter for a class group of size approximately N.

3   Secure and Verifiable Delegation

3.1   Security Model by Hohenberger and Lysyanskaya

The secure delegation model of Hohenberger and Lysyanskaya [15] is defined around three central entities: a delegator $\mathcal{T}$, a set of auxiliary servers $\mathcal{U}$ and the

---

[1] Throughout this work, we will only consider the known class group established in [3]. In any other case, where $\mathrm{Cl}(\mathcal{O})$ would not be cyclic, we can always assume to work in a cyclic subgroup. For simplicity, we will still refer to it as the class group and write $\mathrm{Cl}(\mathcal{O})$.

environment $\mathcal{E}$. The delegator interacts with the servers, denoted as $\mathcal{T}^{\mathcal{U}}$, so that they jointly implement an algorithm Alg at a lower computational cost for $\mathcal{T}$, than if $\mathcal{T}$ would run Alg itself. The environment represents any third party, that might observe the interaction or that might later (or previously) interact with $\mathcal{T}$ itself. Most notably, $\mathcal{E}$ includes the manufacturer of the service provided by $\mathcal{U}$. A key assumption of the model is that after $\mathcal{T}$ starts using $\mathcal{U}$, there is no more direct channel between $\mathcal{U}$ and $\mathcal{E}$ or between the different servers in $\mathcal{U}$. The rationale behind this, is that $\mathcal{T}$ has access to $\mathcal{U}$ only through a firewall. Yet, these entities can still try to communicate indirectly. Thus, this interaction has multiple threats to mitigate: First, $\mathcal{T}$ has to make sure that neither $\mathcal{E}$ nor $\mathcal{U}$ gain any sensitive information from $\mathcal{T}$'s interaction with $\mathcal{U}$ (and possibly later with $\mathcal{E}$). In general, this means that $\mathcal{T}$ has to find a way to shroud sensitive data before passing it on to $\mathcal{U}$ and be able to recover its desired result (i.e. the output of Alg) from whatever $\mathcal{U}$ returns. Secondly, to be able to do so, $\mathcal{T}$ also needs a way to verify that the output of $\mathcal{U}$ is indeed correct. This is generally achieved by checking that the outputs fulfill some verification conditions that adversarily produced outputs could only fulfill with a low probability.

The following definition summarizes the security assumptions used throughout this work and includes the reduction in computational cost α that $\mathcal{T}$ profits from, when compared to the local computation, as well as the degree of certainty β that the outputs of the servers are correct.

Definition 2 $((\alpha, \beta)$**-outsource-security).** *[15] Let* Alg *be an algorithm with the following outsource input/output specification: We distinguish* secret, protected *and* unprotected *inputs and outputs, depending on whether only $\mathcal{T}$ has access, only $\mathcal{T}$ and $\mathcal{E}$ have access, or all parties have access, respectively. The non-secret inputs are further subdivided into* honest *and* adversarial, *depending on whether they originate from a trusted source or not. Then, the pair $(\mathcal{T}, \mathcal{U})$ constitutes an (α, β)-outsource-secure implementation of* Alg *if:*

- **Correctness:** *$\mathcal{T}^{\mathcal{U}}$ is a correct implementation of* Alg.
- **Security:** *For all PPT adversaries $\mathcal{A} = (\mathcal{E}, \mathcal{U})$, there exist PPT simulators $(\mathcal{S}_1, \mathcal{S}_2)$ that can simulate the views of $\mathcal{E}$ and $\mathcal{U}$ indistinguishable from the real process. If $\mathcal{U}$ consists of multiple servers $\mathcal{U}_i$, then there is a PPT-simulator $\mathcal{S}_{2,i}$ for each of their views. We formalize this with the following pairs:*
  - **Pair One:** *$\mathcal{E}VIEW_{real} \sim \mathcal{E}VIEW_{ideal}$: $\mathcal{E}$ learns nothing about the secret inputs and outputs.*
  - **Pair Two:** *$\mathcal{U}VIEW_{real} \sim \mathcal{U}VIEW_{ideal}$: $\mathcal{U}$ learns nothing about the secret and (honest/adversarial) protected inputs and outputs.*
  For a more formal description of these experiments, we refer the reader to Definition 2.2 of [15].
- *for all inputs x, the running time of $\mathcal{T}$ is at most an α-multiplicative factor of the running time of* Alg(x) *(i.e. $Time(\mathcal{T}) \leq \alpha\, Time(Alg))$,*
- *for all inputs x, if $\mathcal{U}$ deviates from its advertised functionality during the execution of $\mathcal{T}^{\mathcal{U}}(x)$, then $\mathcal{T}$ will detect the error with probability $\geq \beta$.*

We call α the *cost reduction function* and β the *verifiability* of a delegation algorithm. Many adversarial models for $\mathcal{U}$ have been proposed in the literature, differing along the number of servers and their adversarial powers. In this work, we will use the OMTUP and 2HBC assumptions, the latter being based on the one-server honest-but-curious assumption from [10].

Definition 3 (OMTUP [15]). *The* one-malicious version of a two untrusted program model *defines the adversary as* $\mathcal{A} = (\mathcal{E}, (\mathcal{U}_1, \mathcal{U}_2))$ *and assumes that at most one of the two servers* $\mathcal{U}_1$ *or* $\mathcal{U}_2$ *deviates from its advertised functionality (for a non-negligible fraction of the inputs), while* $\mathcal{T}$ *does not know which one.*

Definition 4 (2HBC). *The* two honest-but-curious program model *defines the adversary as* $\mathcal{A} = (\mathcal{E}, (\mathcal{U}_1, \mathcal{U}_2))$, *where* $\mathcal{U}_1$ *and* $\mathcal{U}_2$ *are servers that always return correct results, but may try to extract sensitive data.*

3.2 Advertised Server Functionality

For our purposes throughout this work, we assume that as input, we give the servers multiple pairs $(\mathfrak{a}_1, E_1), \ldots, (\mathfrak{a}_k, E_k)$ consisting of ideals $\mathfrak{a}_i$ and associated elliptic curves E_i. The servers then generate and return the codomain curves $\mathfrak{a}_i * E_i$ for each $i = 1, \ldots, k$. We write

$$(\mathfrak{a}_1 * E_1, \ldots, \mathfrak{a}_k * E_k) \leftarrow \mathcal{U}((\mathfrak{a}_1, E_1), \ldots, (\mathfrak{a}_k, E_k)).$$

We assume that the input elements are always given in a random order as to avoid distinguishability of the elements. We define two ways for the delegator to transmit ideals to the server:

- In the case where $\mathrm{Cl}(\mathcal{O})$ is known with generator $\mathfrak{g}$, we assume that we can give an element $a \in \mathbb{Z}_{\#\mathrm{Cl}(\mathcal{O})}$ to the server, which represents the ideal $\mathfrak{a} = \mathfrak{g}^a$. The server can efficiently compute a short representation of $\mathfrak{a}$ using the relation lattice by applying the procedure described in [3].
- Otherwise, the delegator can give a vector $\mathbf{a} \in \mathbb{B}$, representing $\mathfrak{a} = \prod_{i=1}^{n} \mathfrak{l}_i^{a_i}$, to the servers.

4 Shrouding and Splitting

Before we present implementations for our delegation algorithms, we discuss how to shroud ideals. The basic idea is to split the secret $\mathfrak{s}$ into a pair of random-looking ideals $(\mathfrak{a}_1, \mathfrak{a}_2)$, so that $\mathfrak{a}_1 * (\mathfrak{a}_2 * E) = \mathfrak{s} * E$. In the case where $\mathrm{Cl}(\mathcal{O})$ is known, we can simply generate $(a, s - a)$ for $a \leftarrow \mathbb{Z}_{\#\mathrm{Cl}(\mathcal{O})}$. If $\mathrm{Cl}(\mathcal{O})$ is unknown, on the other hand, we cannot simply generate $(\mathbf{a}, \mathbf{s} - \mathbf{a})$ for a random vector $\mathbf{a} = (a_1, \ldots, a_n) \in \mathbb{B}$ since $\mathbf{s} - \mathbf{a}$ would no longer be in $\mathbb{B}$ and leak information about the secret [28]. A similar problem was addressed in [13] using rejection sampling: taking vector elements $a_i \leftarrow [-(\delta_i + 1)B_i, (\delta_i + 1)B_i]$ for integers $\delta_i \geq 1$, so that $s_i - a_i \in [-\delta_i B_i, \delta_i B_i]$ for all $i \in \{1, \ldots, n\}$ makes $\mathbf{s} - \mathbf{a}$ look uniform. On the other hand, $\mathbf{a}$ is then no longer uniformly distributed in $\mathbb{B}(N)$, since e.g. $s_i = -B$ would exclude the values of $a_i > (\delta - 1)B$. This is not an issue in [13], since $\mathbf{a}$ is never directly revealed. In our case, however, we also want to delegate the computation of the isogeny defined by $\mathbf{a}$, and currently this would reveal information about the secret. We circumvent this problem in Algorithm 1 by splitting up $\mathbf{s}$ into three vectors $\mathbf{r_0}, \mathbf{r_1}, \mathbf{r}^*$, so that the first two are uniform, while the third one contains extra information about $\mathbf{s}$ that the delegator computes itself. To make $\mathbf{r_0}$ and $\mathbf{r_1}$ uniform, $\mathbf{r}^*$ is in general non-zero. The goal of the algorithm is to minimize the Hamming weight of $\mathbf{r}^*$. We define by $\chi(k)$ the uniform distribution in $[-k, k]$ and let $\delta\mathbb{B}(N) = [-\delta_1 B_1, \delta_1 B_1] \times \cdots \times [-\delta_n B_n, \delta_n B_n]$. We further present Algorithm 2, which allows to split a vector $\mathbf{s}$ into two vectors $\mathbf{s}'$ and $\mathbf{s}^*$, so that $\mathbf{s}^*$ has a given Hamming weight.

Input : secret $\mathbf{s} = (s_1, \ldots, s_n) \in \mathbb{B}$ and parameters $\delta = (\delta_1, \ldots, \delta_n)$
Output: $\mathbf{r_0}, \mathbf{r_1} \in \delta\mathbb{B}$ uniform, $\mathbf{r}^* \in \mathbb{B}$ small, such that $\mathbf{r_0} + \mathbf{r_1} + \mathbf{r}^* = \mathbf{s}$

1 **for** $i = 1, \ldots, n$ **do**
2   **repeat**
3        $r_{0,i} \leftarrow \chi((\delta_i + 1)B_i)$
4        $r_{1,i} = s_i - r_{0,i}$
5   **until** $|r_{0,i}| \leq \delta_i B_i$ or $|r_{1,i}| \leq \delta_i B_i$
6     $b \leftarrow \{0,1\}$
7   **if** $|r_{0,i}| > \delta_i B_i$ **then**
8   **if** $b == 0$ **then** $r_{1,i} \leftarrow \chi(\delta_i B_i)$
9        $r_{0,i} = -r_{1,i}$
10       $r_i^* = s_i$
11   **else if** $|r_{1,i}| > \delta_i B_i$ **then**
12   **if** $b == 0$ **then** $r_{0,i} \leftarrow \chi(\delta_i B_i)$
13       $r_{1,i} = -r_{0,i}$
14       $r_i^* = s_i$
15   **else** $r_i^* = 0$
16 **end**
17 **return** $\mathbf{r_0} = (r_{0,1}, \ldots, r_{0,n})$, $\mathbf{r_1} = (r_{1,1}, \ldots, r_{1,n})$, $\mathbf{r}^* = (r_1^*, \ldots, r_n^*)$.

Algorithm 1: ShrVec: Shrouding a vector in $\mathbb{B}$.

We write the invocation of these algorithms as $(\mathbf{r_0}, \mathbf{r_1}, \mathbf{r}^*) \leftarrow \mathsf{ShrVec}_\delta(\mathbf{s})$ and $(\mathbf{s}^*, \mathbf{s}') \leftarrow \mathsf{Split}(\mathbf{s}, k)$, respectively. We generally omit δ in the index if it is clear from the context or not explicitly needed. In Sect. A of the supporting material, we prove correctness of our algorithms and the two Lemmas below. We further show, that the expected value of r^* vanishes for $\delta \to \infty$.[2] These lemmas imply that $\mathbf{r_0}$ and $\mathbf{r_1}$ do not contain any information about $\mathbf{s}$.

---

[2] This also follows intuitively from the fact, that the interval $[-(\delta+1)B, -\delta B - 1] \cup [\delta B + 1, (\delta+1)B]$ is constant in size, while $[-\delta B, \delta B]$ grows with increasing δ, making it less and less probable for r_0, r_1 to be sampled from the former.

Input : secret $\mathbf{s} = (s_1, \ldots, s_n) \in \mathbb{B}$, and parameter k
Output: $\mathbf{s}', \mathbf{s}^* \in \mathbb{B}$, such that $\mathbf{s}^*$ has Hamming weight $\leq k$ and $\mathbf{s}' + \mathbf{s}^* = \mathbf{s}$.
1 Sample a uniform subset $C^* \leftarrow \{1, \ldots, n\}$ of size k.
2 **for** $i = 1, \ldots, n$ **do**
3   **if** $i \in C^*$ **then** $(s_i^*, s_i') = (s_i, 0)$
4   **else** $(s_i^*, s_i') = (0, s_i)$
5 **end**
6 **return** $\mathbf{s}^* = (s_1^*, \ldots, s_n^*), \mathbf{s}' = (s_1', \ldots, s_n')$.

Algorithm 2: Split: Splitting a vector in $\mathbb{B}$.

Lemma 1. *If* $\mathbf{s}$ *is uniformly distributed in* $\mathbb{B}(N)$, *the outputs* $\mathbf{r}_0$ *and* $\mathbf{r}_1$ *of Algorithm 1 are uniformly distributed in* $\delta\mathbb{B}(N)$.

Lemma 2. *Let* $(\mathbf{s}^*, \mathbf{s}') \leftarrow \mathsf{Split}(\mathbf{s}, k)$ *where* $\mathbf{s} \leftarrow \mathbb{B}(N)$ *uniform and let* $(\mathbf{r}_0, \mathbf{r}_1, \mathbf{r}^*) \leftarrow \mathsf{ShrVec}_\delta(\mathbf{s}')$. *Then, the outputs* $\mathbf{r}_0$ *and* $\mathbf{r}_1$ *of Algorithm 1 are uniformly distributed in* $\delta\mathbb{B}(N)$.

5 Delegation Algorithms

In this section, we present two delegation algorithms and their implementation under different assumptions. In both algorithms we want to delegate the computation of $\mathfrak{s} * E$ from $(\mathfrak{s}, E)$. The first algorithm, Clso keeps $\mathfrak{s}$ hidden from the servers, while the second algorithm Hlso, keeps $\mathfrak{s}$ and $\mathfrak{s} * E$ hidden from the servers. For the efficiency reasons discussed in [7], we assume that there is a short representation $\mathbf{s} = (s_1, \ldots, s_n) \in \mathbb{B}(N)$ of $\mathfrak{s} = \prod_{i=1}^n \mathfrak{l}^{s_i}$. In the case where $\mathrm{Cl}(\mathcal{O})$ is known, we further assume that $s \in \mathbb{Z}_{\#\mathrm{Cl}(\mathcal{O})}$ is known by the delegator, such that $\mathfrak{s} = \mathfrak{g}^s$. We define the two algorithms below, using the formalism from [15].

Definition 5 (Clso and Hlso). *The isogeny computation algorithm* Clso *and the hidden isogeny computation algorithm* Hlso *take as inputs a supersingular elliptic curve* $E/\mathbb{F}_p$ *and an ideal* $\mathfrak{s}$, *either as an element in* $\mathbb{Z}_{\#\mathrm{Cl}(\mathcal{O})}$ *or a vector in* $\mathbb{B}(N)$, *then return the elliptic curve* $\mathfrak{s} * E$. *The input* E *is (honest/adversarial) unprotected, while* $\mathfrak{s}$ *is secret or (honest/adversarial) protected. The output* $\mathfrak{s} * E$ *of* Clso *is unprotected, while it is protected in the case of* Hlso. *We write*

$$\mathfrak{s} * E \leftarrow \mathsf{Clso}(\mathfrak{s}, E) \quad and \quad \mathfrak{s} * E \leftarrow \mathsf{Hlso}(\mathfrak{s}, E).$$

Below, we present implementations for both Clso and Hlso in the OMTUP and 2HBC assumptions (Definitions 3 and 4). Both work in two rounds of delegation.

5.1 Clso: Unprotected Codomain

Our general approach to hide $\mathfrak{s}$ from the servers is to split it up into two ideals $\mathfrak{a}_1, \mathfrak{a}_2$, such that the consecutive application of both yields $\mathfrak{a}_1 * (\mathfrak{a}_2 * E) = \mathfrak{a}_2 * (\mathfrak{a}_1 * E) = \mathfrak{s} * E$, i.e. that we can compute the desired codomain in two rounds of delegation. In the 2HBC case, this can be implemented more or less straight-forwardly. If, however, one of the servers is malicious, it could simply return a wrong codomain. Thus in the OMTUP case we want to be able to verify these computations. Unfortunately, unlike in the DLOG setting (e.g. see [15]), we can not compose elliptic curves in order to verify correctness, so we have to resort to comparisons, i.e. let two servers compute the same curve and check if they are the same. Note that simply going two different paths to $\mathfrak{s} * E$ and comparing the results is also not possible, since the malicious server would take part in the computation of both of them and could simply apply another isogeny defined by an ideal $\mathfrak{r}$ to its result in both rounds yielding the result $\mathfrak{r} * (\mathfrak{s} * E)$ in both cases.

The goal of the verification is that the servers do not return an incorrect codomain without the delegator realizing (up to a certain probability). Note that we need to be able to verify intermediate results as well. We resort to direct comparisons, i.e. giving both servers common queries whose output we can directly compare. In the first round, we have the starting curve at our disposal, which easily allows to make the same queries to both servers. The second round becomes more tricky, however, since all the curves at our disposal are the starting curve and the curves generated by the servers in the first round, potentially maliciously. Reusing the starting curve in some queries while not in others makes the queries distinguishable. One obvious possibility would be to generate curves ourselves, which would however defeat the purpose of delegating in the first place. An alternative would be to work with lookup-tables analogous to the DLOG setting, but since we can not combine multiple elliptic curves, elements of the form $(\mathfrak{a}, \mathfrak{a} * E)$ could only be used individually. Again, using such sets ends up defeating the need for delegation. Therefore our algorithm in the OMTUP case resorts to delegating sets of extra curves in order to increase verifiability.

To this end, we generate a set $\mathcal{S}$ of ideal tuples $(\mathfrak{c}_1, \mathfrak{c}_2, \mathfrak{d}_1, \mathfrak{d}_2)$ that satisfy $\mathfrak{c}_1\mathfrak{c}_2 = \mathfrak{d}_1\mathfrak{d}_2$. If we work over $\mathbb{Z}_{\#\mathrm{Cl}(\mathcal{O})}$, this is straightforward. If we work with elements in $\delta\mathbb{B}(N)$, we can implement this as follows: for $i = 1, \ldots, n$, generate $c_{1,i}, c_{2,i}, d_{1,i} \leftarrow \chi(\delta_i B_i)$ and define $d_{2,i} = c_{1,i} + c_{2,i} - d_{1,i}$ until $d_{2,i} \in [-\delta_i B_i, \delta_i B_i]$. Note that this approach might yield some information about $c_{1,i} + c_{2,i}$ (at most that it is positive or negative) given $c_{1,i}$ only, but we do not really need to care about that, since this is not enough information to be able to distinguish $d_{2,i}$ from a random value (mainly because $d_{1,i}$ remains unknown), so this will neither reduce the security nor the verifiability of the scheme. In the first round, we further delegate the computation of a second set $\mathcal{R}$ of ideals applied to the starting curve and directly compare between the servers to increase verifiability.

We present our approach for the 2HBC assumption in Fig. 1 and our approach for the OMTUP assumption in Fig. 2. We analyze these protocols and discuss secure parameter sizes in Sect. 5.3. Note that the case (a) corresponds to the delegation algorithm presented in [15] with unprotected base element.

5.2   HIso: Hidden Codomain

Next to keeping $\mathfrak{s}$ hidden, HIso also does not disclose the codomain curve to the auxiliary servers. The idea works similar to CIso, but rather than shrouding and

---

CIso: 2HBC case.

Input   : Ideal s, elliptic curve E.
Output : Elliptic curve $s * E$ or $\perp$.

1. Generate the ideals $\mathfrak{a}_1, \mathfrak{a}_2$ as follows.
   (a) If $\mathrm{Cl}(\mathcal{O})$ is known, generate $\mathfrak{a}_1 \leftarrow \mathbb{Z}_{\#\mathrm{Cl}(\mathcal{O})}$ uniformly and compute $\mathfrak{a}_2 = s - \mathfrak{a}_1$.
   (b) If $\mathrm{Cl}(\mathcal{O})$ is not known, generate $(\mathfrak{a}_1, \mathfrak{a}_2, \mathfrak{a}^*) \leftarrow \mathsf{ShrVec}(s)$.
2. Delegate the computation of $E_1 \leftarrow \mathcal{U}_1((\mathfrak{a}_1, E))$.
3. In the case where $\mathrm{Cl}(\mathcal{O})$ is not known, compute $E_1 \leftarrow \mathfrak{a}^* * E_1$ locally.
4. Delegate the computation of $E_2 \leftarrow \mathcal{U}_2((\mathfrak{a}_2, E_1))$.
5. Return E_2.

Fig. 1. Implementation of CIso in the 2HBC assumption.

delegating the computation of the isogeny generated by some secret ideal s, we do the same for an ideal s' to yield a codomain $s' * E$ that can be known to the servers. The goal is to choose s', so that $s' * E$ is close enough to $s * E$, that the path can be efficiently computed by the delegator, while searching the space of potential curves is too large to reasonably allow an attacker to find $s * E$ by walking from $s' * E$. We call the remaining path $s^* = ss'^{-1}$, so that $s^* * (s' * E) = s * E$.

To be able to assess path lengths, we work with ideals only in their vector representation in $\mathbb{B}(N)$. In the case where the class group $\mathrm{Cl}(\mathcal{O})$ is known, this is achieved by working modulo the relation lattice [3].[3] We then call $\widetilde{\mathbb{B}}(N) \subseteq \mathbb{B}(N)$ the subset from which s^* is sampled. We can achieve this splitting of s using the Split-procedure (Algorithm 2). The protocol then uses CIso as a subroutine with s' as the secret argument. It is summarized in Fig. 3. Note that the protocol has the same description in the 2HBC and OMTUP assumptions, and that CIso is called with the appropriate assumption.

5.3   Analysis

Size of k. Assume we work with a class group of size approximately N, which has an associated quantum security level $\lambda(N)$ with respect to GAIP (Definition 1). Let $D = \#\mathbb{B}(N)$ denote the number of possible vectors in $\mathbb{B}(N)$. The basic idea is to define a subset $\widetilde{\mathbb{B}}(N) \subseteq \mathbb{B}(N)$ of size $\widetilde{D} = \#\widetilde{\mathbb{B}}(N)$, that is big enough that searching the entire space is at least as hard as breaking a GAIP instance. Since the servers are only given $s'*E$, they cannot resort to a meet-in-the-middle attack to find information about $s * E$, but rather have to resort to a database search of size $\widetilde{D}$ to find it. We assume that they would be able to identify the correct

---

[3]   Note that $\mathbb{B}(N)$ does not necessarily contain a representation for all elements in $\mathrm{Cl}(\mathcal{O})$. We ignore this case and assume we can delegate such elements using simple heuristics, such as computing the "overshoot" locally, or simply by resampling.

Clso: OMTUP case.

Input : Ideal $\mathfrak{s}$, elliptic curve E.
Output : Elliptic curve $\mathfrak{s} * E$ or $\perp$.

1. Generate the ideals $\mathfrak{a}_1, \mathfrak{a}_2, \mathfrak{b}_1, \mathfrak{b}_2$ as follows.
   (a) If $\mathrm{Cl}(\mathcal{O})$ is known, generate two random elements $a_1, b_1 \leftarrow \mathbb{Z}_{\#\mathrm{Cl}(\mathcal{O})}$ and compute $a_2 = s - a_1$ and $b_2 = s - b_1$.
   (b) If $\mathrm{Cl}(\mathcal{O})$ is not known, generate $(\mathbf{a_1}, \mathbf{a_2}, \mathbf{a}^*) \leftarrow \mathsf{ShrVec}(s)$ and $(\mathbf{b_1}, \mathbf{b_2}, \mathbf{b}^*) \leftarrow \mathsf{ShrVec}(s)$.
   Further, generate a set of random ideals $\mathcal{R} = \{\mathfrak{e} \mid \mathfrak{e} \leftarrow \mathrm{Cl}(\mathcal{O})\}$ and a set of random ideal tuples $\mathcal{S} = \{(\mathfrak{c}_1, \mathfrak{c}_2, \mathfrak{d}_1, \mathfrak{d}_2) \leftarrow \mathrm{Cl}(\mathcal{O})^4 \mid \mathfrak{c}_1\mathfrak{c}_2 = \mathfrak{d}_1\mathfrak{d}_2\}$, where all the ideals are generated using $\mathbb{Z}_{\#\mathrm{Cl}(\mathcal{O})}$ or $\delta\mathbb{B}(N)$, respectively.
2. Delegate the computation of

$$E_{\mathfrak{a}_1}, \{E_{\mathfrak{c}_1}\}, \{E_{\mathfrak{e}}\} \leftarrow \mathcal{U}_1\Big((\mathfrak{a}_1, E), \{(\mathfrak{c}_1, E) \mid \mathfrak{c}_1 \in \mathcal{S}\}, \{(\mathfrak{e}, E) \mid \mathfrak{e} \in \mathcal{R}\}\Big),$$

$$E_{\mathfrak{b}_1}, \{E_{\mathfrak{d}_1}\}, \{E_{\mathfrak{e}}'\} \leftarrow \mathcal{U}_2\Big((\mathfrak{b}_1, E), \{(\mathfrak{d}_1, E) \mid \mathfrak{d}_1 \in \mathcal{S}\}, \{(\mathfrak{e}, E) \mid \mathfrak{e} \in \mathcal{R}\}\Big).$$

3. Verify if $E_{\mathfrak{e}} \stackrel{?}{=} E_{\mathfrak{e}}'$ for $\mathfrak{e} \in \mathcal{R}$. If not, return $\perp$, otherwise continue.
4. In the case with $\mathrm{Cl}(\mathcal{O})$ unknown, locally compute

$$E_{\mathfrak{a}_1} \leftarrow \mathfrak{a}^* * E_{\mathfrak{a}_1}, \quad E_{\mathfrak{b}_1} \leftarrow \mathfrak{b}^* * E_{\mathfrak{b}_1}.$$

5. Delegate the computation of

$$E_s, \{E_{\mathfrak{d}}\} \leftarrow \mathcal{U}_1\Big((\mathfrak{b}_2, E_{\mathfrak{b}_1}), \{(\mathfrak{d}_2, E_{\mathfrak{d}_1}) \mid \mathfrak{d}_2 \in \mathcal{S}\}\Big),$$

$$E_s', \{E_{\mathfrak{c}}\} \leftarrow \mathcal{U}_2\Big((\mathfrak{a}_2, E_{\mathfrak{a}_1}), \{(\mathfrak{c}_2, E_{\mathfrak{c}_1}) \mid \mathfrak{c}_2 \in \mathcal{S}\}\Big).$$

6. Verify if $E_s \stackrel{?}{=} E_s'$ and if all $E_{\mathfrak{d}} \stackrel{?}{=} E_{\mathfrak{c}}$. If not, return $\perp$, otherwise return E_s.

Fig. 2. Implementation of Clso in the OMTUP assumption.

curve once found (e.g. by being able to decrypt a given ciphertext). The best known quantum algorithm for this database search is Grover's algorithm [14], which runs in $O(\widetilde{D}^{1/2})$. Thus in order to ensure a quantum security level of λ, we choose $\widetilde{D} = 2^{2\lambda}$. We can therefore define $\widetilde{\mathbb{B}}(N)$ analogously to $\mathbb{B}(N)$, i.e. $\widetilde{\mathbb{B}}(N) = \widetilde{\mathbb{B}}_1 \times \cdots \times \widetilde{\mathbb{B}}_n$, where $\widetilde{\mathbb{B}}_i \in \{[0,0], \mathbb{B}_i\}$ of size $\widetilde{d}_i \in \{1, d_i\}$, such that $\widetilde{D} = \prod_{i=1}^n \widetilde{d}_i \approx 2^{2\lambda}$.

The input parameter k of Split determines the number of non-zero $\widetilde{\mathbb{B}}_i$. Thus, we need to choose k large enough such that an adversary's search space is approximately $2^{2\lambda}$. We note that due to Lemma 2, the adversary can not distinguish in which entries $\mathbf{s}'$ is zero and can therefore not know the subset C^*. Thus, the size of the search space can be determined by searching through any k-out-of-n subsets and running through all permutations in these subsets. Therefore, we have to choose k, such that

---

HIso: General case

Input   : Ideal $\mathfrak{s}$, elliptic curve E, parameter k.
Output : Elliptic curve $\mathfrak{s} * E$ or $\perp$.

1. Compute $(\mathfrak{s}^*, \mathfrak{s}') \leftarrow \mathsf{Split}(\mathfrak{s}, k)$.
2. Delegate $E' \leftarrow \mathsf{CIso}(\mathfrak{s}', E)$.
3. Compute $E_s = \mathfrak{s}^* * E'$ locally.
4. Return E_s.

Fig. 3. Implementation of HIso for both 2HBC and OMTUP assumptions.

$$\binom{n}{k} \prod_{i \in C^*} d_i \approx 2^{2\lambda}. \tag{1}$$

Verifiability in the OMTUP Case. In the OMTUP case, the servers successfully cheat if all of the verification conditions succeed but the output is wrong, i.e. $E_s \neq s * E$. Let us assume $\mathcal{U}_1$ is the malicious server. In order to be successful, $\mathcal{U}_1$ needs to correctly identify the query $(\mathfrak{a}_1, E)$ in the first round and $(\mathfrak{b}_2, E_{\mathfrak{b}_1})$ in the second round. Note that $\mathcal{U}_1$ can also change the elements in $\mathcal{S}$, as long as it does so consistently in both rounds. The elements in $\mathcal{R}$ have to be returned correctly, since they are directly compared to $\mathcal{U}_2$'s results.

Let $m_s = \#\mathcal{S}$ and $m_r = \#\mathcal{R}$. By choosing a random subset of size $\kappa \in \{1, \ldots, 1 + m_s\}$ among the queries of the first round, the probability of choosing a set that includes $\mathfrak{a}_1$ (or $\mathfrak{b}_1$) and no elements of $\mathcal{R}$ is given by $\binom{m_s}{\kappa-1} / \binom{1+m_s+m_r}{\kappa}$. Furthermore, in the second round, the malicious server has to identify the *same* subset, which it achieves with probability $1 / \binom{1+m_s}{\kappa}$, yielding the full success probability for the adversary of

$$Pr[success] = \frac{\binom{m_s}{\kappa-1}}{\binom{1+m_s+m_r}{\kappa}\binom{1+m_s}{\kappa}} = \frac{\kappa}{1+m_s} \frac{\kappa!(m_s + m_r + 1 - \kappa)!}{(m_s + m_r + 1)!}. \tag{2}$$

If $m_r = 0, 1, 2$, this probability is maximal for $\kappa = 1 + m_s$, while for $m_r \geq 3$, we find $\kappa = 1$ to be optimal. In the latter case, the upper probability simplifies to $Pr[success \mid m_r \geq 3] = [(1 + m_s)(1 + m_s + m_r)]^{-1}$. Since this probability decreases quadratically with bigger m_s, we minimize the overall set sizes (and thus communication cost) by fixing $m_r = 3$ and choosing m_s to yield the desired verifiability. We thus find the verifiability

$$\beta(m_s) = 1 - Pr[success \mid m_r = 3] = \frac{m_s^2 + 5m_s + 3}{m_s^2 + 5m_s + 4}. \tag{3}$$

Security Proofs. We prove security of Clso and Hlso.

Theorem 1. *Figure 1 is an outsource-secure implementation of* Clso *in the 2HBC assumption.*

Proof. Correctness follows immediately from $a_1 + a_2 = s$ or from the correctness of ShrVec, respectively. We prove security by proposing the following simulators:

- Environment $\mathcal{E}$: If s is not secret, both simulators behave as in the real execution of the protocol. Otherwise, in each round, $\mathcal{S}_1$ generates random ideals u_1, u_2 either as elements in $\mathbb{Z}_{\#Cl(\mathcal{O})}$ (case (a)) or as vectors in $\delta\mathbb{B}(N)$ (case (b)). In the second case, $\mathcal{S}_1$ further generates $\mathbf{u}^* \leftarrow \mathbb{B}(N)$. Then $\mathcal{S}_1$ makes the query $E_1 \leftarrow \mathcal{U}_1((u_1, E))$, computes $E_1 \leftarrow \mathbf{u}^* * E_1$ if applicable, then makes the query $E_2 \leftarrow \mathcal{U}_2((u_2, E_1))$. $\mathcal{S}_1$ returns E_2 and saves its own state and those of the servers. In any round, the input values u_1, u_2 are indistinguishable from a_1, a_2. In case (b), this is given by Lemma 1.
- Servers $\mathcal{U}_1, \mathcal{U}_2$: For any s, the simulator $\mathcal{S}_2$ proceeds exactly as the simulator $\mathcal{S}_1$ for a secret s. $UVIEW_{real} \sim UVIEW_{ideal}$ is guaranteed by the indistinguishability of $u_1, u_2, \mathbf{u}^*$ and a_1, a_2, a^*. Note that applying $a^* * E_1$ between the two queries has the advantage that neither server will see both the domain and the codomain of this isogeny and therefore cannot recover a^*.   □

Theorem 2. *Figure 2 is an outsource-secure implementation of* Clso *in the OMTUP assumption.*

Proof. Correctness of the output follows again from the definition of s. Concerning the verification conditions, correctness of $E_c \stackrel{?}{=} E_{\mathfrak{d}}$ follows from the definition of $\mathcal{S}$. The other verification conditions are simple comparison operations between both servers. We prove security by proposing the following simulators:

- Environment $\mathcal{E}$: If s is not secret, both simulators behave as in the real execution of the protocol. Otherwise, in each round, $\mathcal{S}_1$ generates random ideals u_1, u_2, v_1, v_2 and in case (b) further $\mathbf{u}^*, \mathbf{v}^*$ as vectors in $\mathbb{B}(N)$. $\mathcal{S}_1$ further generates two random sets of ideals $\mathcal{M}_1, \mathcal{M}_2$ of size m_r and four sets of ideals $\mathcal{N}_1, \mathcal{N}_2, \mathcal{N}_3, \mathcal{N}_4$ of size m_s, such that for $(n_1, n_2, n_3, n_4)_i \in \mathcal{N}_1 \times \mathcal{N}_2 \times \mathcal{N}_3 \times \mathcal{N}_4$, it holds that $n_1 n_4 = n_2 n_3$, pairwise for $i = 1, \ldots, m_s$. Then $\mathcal{S}_1$ makes the queries

$$E_{u_1}, \{E_{n_1}\}, \{E_{m_1}\} \leftarrow \mathcal{U}_1\Big((u_1, E), \{(n_1, E) \mid n_1 \in \mathcal{N}_1\}, \{(m_1, E) \mid m_1 \in \mathcal{M}_1\}\Big),$$

$$E_{v_1}, \{E_{n_2}\}, \{E_{m_2}\} \leftarrow \mathcal{U}_2\Big((v_1, E), \{(n_2, E) \mid n_2 \in \mathcal{N}_2\}, \{(m_2, E) \mid m_2 \in \mathcal{M}_2\}\Big).$$

$\mathcal{S}_1$ verifies the results. If either of the elements in $\{E_{m_1}\}$ or $\{E_{m_2}\}$ are incorrect, then $\mathcal{S}_1$ returns $\bot$, otherwise it continues. In case (b), $\mathcal{S}_1$ computes $E_{u_1} \leftarrow \mathbf{u}^* * E_{u_1}$ and $E_{v_1} \leftarrow \mathbf{v}^* * E_{v_1}$. Then, in the second round, $\mathcal{S}_1$ makes the queries

$$E_{v_2}, \{E_{n_3}\}, \leftarrow \mathcal{U}_1\Big((v_2, E_{v_1}), \{(n_3, E_{n_2}) \mid n_3 \in \mathcal{N}_3\}\Big),$$

$$E_{u_2}, \{E_{n_4}\}, \leftarrow \mathcal{U}_2\Big((u_2, E_{u_1}), \{(n_4, E_{n_1}) \mid n_4 \in \mathcal{N}_4\}\Big).$$

Again, S_1 verifies the results. If $\nexists \mathfrak{x} : E_{\mathfrak{u}_2} = (\mathfrak{r}\mathfrak{u}_1\mathfrak{u}_2) * E \wedge E_{\mathfrak{v}_2} = (\mathfrak{r}\mathfrak{v}_1\mathfrak{v}_2) * E$, S_1 returns $\perp$. Otherwise, let κ be the number of pairs $(E_{\mathfrak{n}_3}, E_{\mathfrak{n}_4})$ for which there doesn't exist such an $\mathfrak{r}$. Then with probability $1 - Pr[success]$ (as given in Eq. (2)), S_1 returns E_s, otherwise S_1 returns $\perp$. S_1 saves the appropriate states. In any round of the simulation, the input tuple $(\mathfrak{u}_1, \mathfrak{u}_2, \mathfrak{u}^*, \mathfrak{v}_1, \mathfrak{v}_2, \mathfrak{v}^*, \mathcal{M}_1, \mathcal{M}_2, \mathcal{N}_1, \mathcal{N}_2, \mathcal{N}_3, \mathcal{N}_4)$ is indistinguishable from the tuple $(\mathfrak{a}_1, \mathfrak{a}_2, \mathfrak{a}^*, \mathfrak{b}_1, \mathfrak{b}_2, \mathfrak{b}^*, \mathcal{R}, \mathcal{R}, \{\mathfrak{c}_1 \in S\}, \{\mathfrak{d}_1 \in S\}, \{\mathfrak{d}_2 \in S\}, \{\mathfrak{c}_2 \in S\})$, due to uniform sampling or because of Lemma 1. If a server cheats, S_1 outputs a wrong result with probability $Pr[success]$, otherwise it returns $\perp$, as in the real execution of the protocol. It follows $\mathcal{EVIEW}_{\text{real}} \sim \mathcal{EVIEW}_{\text{ideal}}$.

– Servers $\mathcal{U}_1, \mathcal{U}_2$: For any $\mathfrak{s}$, the simulator S_2 proceeds exactly as the simulator S_1 for a secret $\mathfrak{s}$, except for the verification procedure after the second round, which is not necessary. $\mathcal{UVIEW}_{\text{real}} \sim \mathcal{UVIEW}_{\text{ideal}}$ is guaranteed by the indistinguishability of the tuple described above. $\square$

Theorem 3. *Figure 3 is an outsource-secure implementation of* HIso *in both the 2HBC and OMTUP assumptions.*

Proof. Correctness of the output follows from the correctness of Split and CIso. Security follows from the outsource-security of CIso and the appropriate choice of the parameter k as determined by Eq. (1).

Remark 1. Note that Definition 4 implies that $\mathcal{U}_1$ and $\mathcal{U}_2$ might try to collude. Yet, since their outputs are honestly generated, their indirect communication channel through T is in fact non-existent. For example, E_1, output by $\mathcal{U}_1$ and input to $\mathcal{U}_2$, is honestly generated and can therefore not contain any auxiliary information that $\mathcal{U}_2$ could use to learn any information about $\mathfrak{a}_1$. Definition 3 implies that at least one of the two servers is honest, so that collusion is not possible in the OMTUP case.

Communication Cost. We want to express the communication cost between the delegator and the server. We do this by looking at the information content of the exchanged elements in bits. We establish the following maximal costs.

Element of	Maximal cost in bits
$\mathbb{Z}_{\#\mathrm{Cl}(\mathcal{O})}$	$\lceil \log_2 \#\mathrm{Cl}(\mathcal{O}) \rceil$
$\delta\mathbb{B}(N)$	$\sum_{i=1}^{n} \log_2 (2\delta_i B_i + 1)$
$\mathbb{F}_p$	$\lceil \log_2 p \rceil$

Note that elliptic curves in Montgomery form are encoded by a single curve parameter in $\mathbb{F}_p$. The actual average communication cost of elements in $\mathbb{B}$ and $\delta\mathbb{B}$ is smaller than the maximal cost if the individual vector entries are expressed using the minimal amount of bits. This representation considerably lowers the communication cost, especially for large δ_i. We can estimate the communication costs by establishing the minimal number of bits of an element uniformly sampled from $\delta\mathbb{B}$ as

$$\mathsf{Ex}_I(\delta\mathbb{B}) := \sum_{i=1}^{n} \frac{1}{2\delta_i B_i + 1} \sum_{y=-\delta_i B_i}^{\delta_i B_i} \lceil \log_2(2|y|+1) \rceil .$$

We can now establish the communication cost for the delegation of CIso and HIso, which are the same. In the 2HBC case, the delegator uploads one element from either $\mathbb{Z}_{\#\mathrm{Cl}(\mathcal{O})}$ or $\delta\mathbb{B}(N)$ and downloads one elliptic curve from each server, defined by a parameter in $\mathbb{F}_p$. In the OMTUP case, the delegator uploads $2 + 2m_s + m_r$ elements from either $\mathbb{Z}_{\#\mathrm{Cl}(\mathcal{O})}$ or $\delta\mathbb{B}(N)$ to each server and downloads the same amount of elliptic curves. We define the upload and download costs per server in the 2HBC ($b = 0$) and OMTUP ($b = 1$) case:

$$Up(x) = \begin{cases} (1 + (2m_s + m_r + 1)b)\lceil \log_2 \#\mathrm{Cl}(\mathcal{O}) \rceil, & x = \mathrm{Cl}(\mathcal{O}), \\ (1 + (2m_s + m_r + 1)b)\mathsf{Ex}_I(\delta\mathbb{B}), & x = \delta\mathbb{B}, \end{cases} \quad (4)$$

$$Down = (1 + (2m_s + m_r + 1)b)\lceil \log_2 p \rceil,$$

Cost Reduction Functions. Ignoring the costs of comparison operations, element generation and ShrVec, as they are negligible in comparison to isogeny computations, we get the following cost reduction functions for CIso and HIso

$$\alpha_{\mathsf{CIso}}(\delta, B, n, b) = \frac{(1+b)\mathcal{I}(r^*)}{\mathcal{I}(s)}, \quad \alpha_{\mathsf{HIso}}(\delta, B, n, k, b) = \frac{(1+b)\mathcal{I}(r^*) + \mathcal{I}(s^*)}{\mathcal{I}(s)}, \quad (5)$$

where the parameter $b \in \{0,1\}$ distinguishes between the 2HBC and OMTUP cases, respectively, and where s, r^*, s^* and r relate to the outputs of Split and ShrVec. Note that the isogeny cost functions all depend on B and n. Further, the size of r^* (thus $\mathcal{I}(r^*)$) depends on δ and the size of s^* (thus $\mathcal{I}(s^*)$) on k. Remember that in the case, where the class group and relation lattice are known, we do not need to use ShrVec, so that, effectively, $\mathcal{I}(r^*) = 0$. Similarly, since the expected value of r^* vanishes for $\delta \to \infty$, we can identify

$$\alpha_{\mathsf{CIso}}^{\mathrm{Cl}(\mathcal{O})}(B, n) = \lim_{\delta \to \infty} \alpha_{\mathsf{CIso}}(\delta, B, n, b) = 0,$$

$$\alpha_{\mathsf{HIso}}^{\mathrm{Cl}(\mathcal{O})}(B, n, k) = \lim_{\delta \to \infty} \alpha_{\mathsf{HIso}}(\delta, B, n, k, b) = \frac{\mathcal{I}(s^*)}{\mathcal{I}(s)}. \quad (6)$$

In this case the cost also becomes independent of b, i.e. of the underlying server assumption. Each server, on the other hand, has to compute $(2m_s + m_r + 1)b + 1$ isogenies of cost given by $\mathcal{I}(r)$. We therefore find the relative cost per server of

$$\alpha_{\mathcal{U}}(\delta, B, n, b) = \frac{((2m_s + m_r + 1)b + 1)\mathcal{I}(r)}{\mathcal{I}(s)}$$

where the size of r also depends on δ. Note that we generally have $\alpha_{\mathcal{U}}(\delta, B, n, b) \geq 1$. We will still refer to this as the cost reduction function.

6 Applications

In this section we discuss how to apply our delegation algorithm to some of the isogeny-based protocols in the CSIDH setting and benchmark our delegation algorithms using the *VeluSqrt* implementation in MAGMA,[4] introduced in [2]. All benchmarks were done in Magma v2.25-6 on an Intel(R) Xeon(R) CPU E5-2630 v2 @ 2.60GHz with 128 GB memory.[5] We note that our benchmarks support our assumption that ShrVec is negligible as its cost generally constitutes less than 0.01% of the cost of the delegator in terms of CPU cycles.

6.1 Delegating the CSIDH Key Exchange Protocol

We briefly revisit the CSIDH key exchange protocol in this section and then show how to delegate it. CSIDH uses a prime $p = 4 \prod_{i=1}^{n} \ell_i - 1$ of appropriate size and defines the starting curve as $E_0 : y^2 = x^3 + x$ over $\mathbb{F}_p$. Further, CSIDH uses symmetric boxes around 0, all of equal size, i.e. $\mathbb{B}(N) = [-B, B]^n$.

- *Key generation*: Alice's private key is a vector $\mathsf{s} \in \mathbb{B}(N)$ representing $\mathfrak{s}$ and her public key is $E_A = \mathfrak{s} * E_0$.
- *Key exchange*: Using Bob's public key E_B, Alice can compute the shared secret $\mathfrak{s} * E_B$.

In terms of the input/output specifications from Definition 2, we consider $\mathfrak{s}$ as a secret input, $\mathfrak{s} * E_0$ as an unprotected output, and $\mathfrak{s} * E_B$ as a secret or protected output. Note that we have to consider E_B as honestly generated, which can always be achieved by authenticating the public key. We can then use CIso to delegate the key generation step and HIso for the key exchange step as follows:

- *Key generation*: Delegate $E_A \leftarrow \mathsf{CIso}(\mathfrak{s}, E_0)$.
- *Key exchange*: Delegate $\mathfrak{s} * E_B \leftarrow \mathsf{HIso}(\mathfrak{s}, E_B)$.

We can easily see that the cost reduction function for the delegation of CSIDH can be expressed as $\alpha_{\mathrm{CSIDH}}(\delta, B, n, k, b) = \frac{1}{2}(\alpha_{\mathsf{CIso}}(\delta, B, n, b) + \alpha_{\mathsf{HIso}}(\delta, B, n, k, b))$, while for the server, we have $\alpha_{\mathcal{U},\mathrm{CSIDH}}(\delta, B, n, b) = \alpha_{\mathcal{U}}(\delta, B, n, b)$.

Instantiations. We look at specific instantiations of CSIDH. While the security is still subject of scrutiny, we go on a limb and make certain assumptions in this section, which the reader should take with caution. Our estimates for λ are mainly based on the results in [4, Table 8], [9, Table 3] and [22, Fig. 1].

CSIDH-512. The original proposal from [7] uses the following parameters: $n = 74$, $\log_2 p \approx 512$, $B = 5$, so that $D = \#\mathbb{B}(N) = (2B + 1)^{74} \approx 2^{256}$. For the key exchange round, we have to define k such that Eq. (1) is fulfilled. Looking at the different security assessments found in the literature, we take the lower estimate of $\lambda \approx 58$ from [22, Fig. 1], which corresponds to $k = 18$. The benchmark results are summarized in Table 1.

---

[4] https://velusqrt.isogeny.org/software.html.
[5] Our implementation can be found here: https://github.com/gemeis/DeCSIDH.

Table 1. Benchmarks for CSIDH-512: In the left table are the benchmarked cost reduction functions for the delegator, while the right table shows the relative cost of the server. For the latter, we chose $m_r = 3$ and compare the cases $m_s = 0$ ($\beta = 75\%$) and $m_s = 8$ ($\beta = 99\%$). Different m_r and m_s do not impact the delegator cost. Note that the case for $\delta \to \infty$ corresponds to the cost of delegating CSIDH if the class group structure and relation lattice are known (cf. Eq. (6)). For the CSIDH-512 parameter set this is indeed the case as the class group has been computed in [3].

α_{CSIDH}	$\delta = 1$	5	10	100	$\to \infty$
2HBC	0.462	0.253	0.213	0.134	0.113
OMTUP	0.877	0.391	0.322	0.159	0.113

$\alpha_{\mathcal{U},\text{CSIDH}}$	$\delta = 1$	5	10	100
2HBC	0.971	4.59	8.84	91.9
OMTUP ($m_s = 0$)	4.83	20.5	42.1	395
OMTUP ($m_s = 8$)	19.1	80.5	170	1376

Communication Cost. The communication cost of the full protocol is four times the cost from Eq. (4), since CIso is invoked twice with two servers each time. The total costs are summarized in Table 2. The OMTUP case is strongly dependent on m_r, m_s. But even if we want high verifiability and low cost in the OMTUP case, the communication cost is manageable, e.g. assuming $m_r = 3$ and setting $\delta = 100$ and $m_s = 100$, we find $33kB$ of upload and $13kB$ of download.

Table 2. Communication costs of CSIDH-512 in the 2HBC and OMTUP assumptions. In the OMTUP case, we choose $m_r = 3$ and compare the cases $m_s = 0$ ($\beta = 75\%$) and $m_s = 8$ ($\beta = 99\%$). We compare different values of δ and the case where the class group and relation lattice are known.

	Upload					Download
	$\text{Cl}(\mathcal{O})$	$\delta = 1$	5	10	100	
2HBC	129 B	108 B	180 B	215 B	333 B	256 B
OMTUP ($m_s = 0$)	645 B	539 B	900 B	1074 B	1663 B	1280 B
OMTUP ($m_s = 8$)	2.63 kB	2.21 kB	3.69 kB	4.40 kB	6.82 kB	5.25 kB

CSIDH-1792 and SQALE'd CSIDH-4096. As a comparison to CSIDH-512, we also consider the larger parameter set for CSIDH-1792 proposed and analyzed in [4] as well as the SQALE'd CSIDH-4096 proposal from [9]. The former has $\log_2 p \approx 1792$, $n = 209$, $B = 10$, and we find $k = 24$ taking the value $\lambda = 104$ from [4, Table 8]. CSIDH-4096 uses $n = 417$, $\log_2 p \approx 4096$ and $B = 1$, such that $\#\mathbb{B}(N) \approx 2^{661} \ll \#\text{Cl}(\mathcal{O})$. Using $\lambda = 124$ as an estimate (cf. [9, Table 3]) yields $k = 40$. The results are summarized in Table 3. It is interesting to note that the gains in CSIDH-4096 are not considerably larger than for CSIDH-1792. This is mainly due to the fact, that the authors of [9] chose a key set that covers only a subset of the class group, such that the relative cost of local computations is lower than if the full group would be covered, resulting in a lower overall gain for the delegator.

Table 3. Benchmarked cost reduction functions for different δ, representing CSIDH-1792 from [4] and SQALE'd CSIDH-4096 from [9], respectively, in the 2HBC and OMTUP assumptions. The case $\delta \to \infty$ again represents the cost in case class group structure and relation lattice are known.

$\alpha_{\text{CSIDH}}^{1792}$	$\delta = 1$	5	10	100	$\to \infty$	$\alpha_{\text{CSIDH}}^{4096}$	$\delta = 1$	5	10	100	$\to \infty$
2HBC	0.331	0.123	0.103	0.067	0.042	2HBC	0.312	0.101	0.076	0.055	0.033
OMTUP	0.614	0.209	0.165	0.085	0.043	OMTUP	0.577	0.179	0.132	0.079	0.036

6.2   Signature Protocols

SeaSign. SeaSign is a signature protocol based on Fiat-Shamir with aborts [13] for cases where the class group is unknown. During the signature process, the signer needs to compute t isogenies $\mathfrak{b}_1, \ldots, \mathfrak{b}_t$ as commitments, where t is a security parameter that depends amongst others on the public key size 2^s. Secure instantiations require $st \geq \lambda$. The exponents $\mathbf{b}_i$ that define these isogenies are sampled from $\mathbb{B}(N) = [-(nt+1)B, (nt+1)B]^n$ in order to guarantee a reasonable success probability. Further steps are the typical hashing and response computation, which we assume to have negligible cost. The verification has the same average computational cost as the signing process, as the commitments are verified using response vectors in $\mathbb{B}(N)$. Delegation can be achieved by using t instances of CIso (possibly in parallel). The delegator is left with computing the $\mathfrak{r}^*$-part of each of these delegations, we therefore find

$$\alpha_{\text{SeaSign}}(\delta, B, n, t, b) = \frac{(1+b)\mathcal{I}(r^*)}{\mathcal{I}(s)},$$

choosing the same δ for each step. We note that while r^* and s are sampled from the larger set $\mathbb{B}(N) = [-(nt+1)B, (nt+1)B]^n$, the cost difference between different $t \in \{1, \ldots, 128\}$ is negligible, so that we find $\alpha_{\text{SeaSign}}(\delta, B, n, t, b) \approx \alpha_{\text{CIso}}(\delta, B, n, b)$. The instantiation in [13] uses the parameter set from CSIDH-512 [7]. We show the cost reduction for different values of δ in the top of Table 4. Because of the size of the set $\mathbb{B}$, the communication costs of delegating SeaSign become more expensive. In the OMTUP case, since we repeat the protocol throughout many rounds, we choose $m_r = 3$ and $m_s = 0$ for our assessment of the communication costs, which are summarized in the bottom of Table 4.

CSI-FiSh. One the main results of the CSI-FiSh paper [3] is the computation of the class group structure and relation lattice for the CSIDH-512 parameter set. Using the knowledge of $\text{Cl}(\mathcal{O})$, the authors construct a signature scheme in the random oracle model based on the original identification protocol from Rostovtsev and Stolbunov [24, 27]. The main computational effort of the signature process comes, analogous to SeaSign, from the fact that the signer needs to compute t isogenies given by $\mathfrak{b}_1, \ldots, \mathfrak{b}_t$, depending on the public key size 2^s. In contrast to SeaSign however, these elements can simply be sampled from $\mathbb{Z}_{\#\text{Cl}(\mathcal{O})}$ and then translated into short vectors using the relation lattice. A verifier has to compute the same amount of isogenies and therefore has the same computational cost as the signer. Both the prover and verifier can delegate these isogenies using Clso, but knowing $Cl(\mathcal{O})$ has now the advantage of not having to resort to ShrVec, and therefore not needing to compute the $\mathfrak{r}^*$ part of the isogeny. This means that from the point of view of the delegator, the signature and its verification are basically free, up to element generation in $\mathbb{Z}_{\#Cl(\mathcal{O})}$ and comparison operations. The communication costs for CSI-FiSh, again assuming $m_r = 3$ and $m_s = 0$ amount to $64.25t$ bytes upload and $128t$ bytes download in the 2HBC case and $321.25t$ bytes upload and $640t$ bytes download in the OMTUP case.

Table 4. Top: Benchmarked cost reduction function for different δ. Bottom: Communication cost (assuming unknown $Cl(\mathcal{O})$) in the 2HBC and OMTUP assumptions. We compare the cases $t = 32$ and $t = 128$.

α_{SeaSign}	$\delta = 1$	5	10	100	$\rightarrow \infty$
2HBC	0.393	0.162	0.120	0.031	0.003
OMTUP	0.809	0.315	0.226	0.057	0.003

	Upload				Download
	$\delta = 1$	5	10	100	
2HBC, $t = 32$	7.87 kB	9.19 kB	9.77 kB	11.7 kB	4.0 kB
2HBC, $t = 128$	36.1 kB	41.4 kB	43.7 kB	51.4 kB	16.0 kB
OMTUP, $t = 32$	39.4 kB	45.9 kB	48.8 kB	58.5 kB	20.0 kB
OMTUP, $t = 128$	181 kB	207 kB	218 kB	257 kB	80.0 kB

7   Conclusion

This work presents a first approach of securely and verifiably delegating isogeny computations to potentially untrusted servers in the CSIDH setting. We presented two algorithms and showed their application to different instances of CSIDH [4,7,9] and to the signature schemes SeaSign [13] and CSI-FiSh [3]. Our algorithms present a communication-cost trade-off. In terms of the cost reduction function, we reduced the delegator's cost asymptotically (for large communication cost) down to 11.3% and about 3.5% of the cost of the local computation for CSIDH-512 and SQALE'd CSIDH-4096, respectively, while the cost of SeaSign reduces to a few percent and asymptotically vanishes. Using the known class group of CSI-FiSh, its delegated cost reduces to element generation in $\mathbb{Z}_{\#Cl(\mathcal{O})}$.

Our protocols work in two rounds of delegation and use either the OMTUP or the 2HBC server assumptions. It is of interest to try to reduce delegation to a single round. The tools developed in this work do not seem to allow delegation to only malicious servers. We therefore leave it open to develop delegation schemes that work in the *two untrusted* or *one untrusted program model* presented in [15].

We leave it as an open question to apply delegation to other post-quantum cryptographic paradigms, such as lattice-based and code-based cryptography.

Acknowledgments. This work was supported in part by the European Research Council (ERC) under the European Union's Horizon 2020 research and innovation programme (Grant agreement No. 101020788 - Adv-ERC-ISOCRYPT), the Research Council KU Leuven grant C14/18/067, and by CyberSecurity Research Flanders with reference number VR20192203. The author would like to thank Frederik Vercauteren and Osmanbey Uzunkol, as well as the anonymous reviewers for valuable feedback regarding this work.

A   Proving Lemmas 1 and 2

Distributions of ShrVec and Split. We first analyze the properties of Algorithm 1. Since they hold for any $i \in \{1, \ldots, n\}$, we will omit the index. Correctness holds, since after the repeat loop, we have $r_0 + r_1 = s$ and $r^* = 0$. If either of the if-conditions succeed, then $r_0 + r_1 = 0$ and $r^* = s$. In either case, $r_0 + r_1 + r^* = s$ holds. Before proving Lemma 1, we first introduce some notation. We define the discrete rectangular function $\Theta_x[x_{\text{start}}, x_{\text{end}}]$ which is 1, if $x \in \{x_{\text{start}}, \ldots, x_{\text{end}}\}$ and 0 otherwise. We also write $f(x)\big|_{x_{\text{start}}}^{x_{\text{end}}} = f(x)\Theta_x[x_{\text{start}}, x_{\text{end}}]$ as a shorthand. For further conciseness, we introduce

$$c_k = (\delta + k)B \quad , \quad \Delta_k = 2c_k + 1 \quad \text{and} \quad d = 2B + 1.$$

In general, we denote the distribution of a value by the corresponding capital letter, e.g. $S(x)$ represents the distribution of s etc. Finally, we write convolutions as $f(x) * g(x) = \sum_{y=-\infty}^{\infty} f(y)g(x - y)$. As an example for our notation, consider the trapezoidal distribution

$$\chi(c_0) \star \chi(B) = (d\Delta_0)^{-1} \left((x + c_1 + 1)\big|_{-c_1}^{-c_{-1}-1} + d\big|_{-c_{-1}}^{c_{-1}} + (-x + c_1 + 1)\big|_{c_{-1}+1}^{c_1} \right).$$

We further denote by $H_n = \sum_{i=1}^{n} \frac{1}{i}$ the n-th harmonic number. We establish expected values for elements sampled from the distributions surrounding ShrVec. Since all of these distributions will turn out be symmetric, we define the expected values in terms of the absolute values of the elements. The expected absolute value of an element from a distribution $F(x)$ is thus

$$\mathsf{Ex}_F := \sum_{y=-\infty}^{\infty} |y| F(y).$$

As an example, consider the uniform distribution $\chi(x)$ for which we find $\mathsf{Ex}_\chi(x) = \frac{x(x+1)}{2x+1}$. This allows us to determine the expected values of elements from e.g. $S(x)$ and $R(x)$:

$$\mathsf{Ex}_S(B) := \mathsf{Ex}_\chi(B) = \frac{1}{d}B(B + 1) \quad \text{and} \quad \mathsf{Ex}_R(\delta, B) := \mathsf{Ex}_\chi(c_0) = \frac{1}{\Delta_0}c_0(c_0 + 1) \quad (7)$$

In order to prove Lemma 1, we analyze how the distribution of s and of r_0 and r_1 change throughout the algorithm. We define different instances of the distributions with different subscripts [i].

1. We first analyze what happens in the **repeat**-loop. In order to fulfill the condition at the end of the loop, we distinguish two possible cases for r_0:
   - $r_0 \in [-c_0, c_0]$: The **until**-condition always succeeds and we have

$$R_1^{(0)}(x) = \frac{\Theta_x[-c_0, c_0]}{\Delta_1} * \chi(B) = (d\Delta_1)^{-1} \begin{cases} x + c_1 + 1, & x \in [-c_1, -c_{-1}], \\ d, & x \in [-c_{-1}, c_{-1}], \\ -x + c_1 + 1, & x \in [c_{-1}, c_1]. \end{cases}$$

   - $r_0 \in [-c_1, -c_0 - 1] \cup [c_0 + 1, c_1]$: In this case, we have

$$R_1'^{(0)}(x) = (d\Delta_1)^{-1} \begin{cases} -|x| + c_2 + 1 & x \in [-c_2, -c_1 - 1] \cup [c_1 + 1, c_2], \\ B & x \in [-c_1, -c_0 - 1] \cup [c_0 + 1, c_1], \\ |x| - c_{-1} & x \in [-c_0, -c_{-1}] \cup [c_{-1}, c_0]. \end{cases}$$

At the end of the **repeat**-loop, the distribution of r_1 is simply the average of these two cases, excluding $|r_0|, |r_1| > c_0$ because of the **until**-condition (and changing the normalization appropriately). We note that

$$(x + c_1 + 1)\big|_{-c_1}^{-c_{-1}} + (-x - c_{-1})\big|_{-c_0}^{-c_{-1}} = (x + c_1 + 1)\big|_{-c_1}^{-c_0 - 1} + d\big|_{-c_0}^{-c_{-1}},$$
$$(-x + c_1 + 1)\big|_{c_{-1}}^{c_1} + (x - c_{-1})\big|_{c_{-1}}^{c_0 - 1} = d\big|_{c_{-1}}^{c_0} + (-x + c_1 + 1)\big|_{c_0 + 1}^{c_1},$$

so that finally we find

$$R^{(1)}(x) = K^{-1} \begin{cases} -|x| + c_1 + 1, & x \in [-c_1, -c_0 - 1] \cup [c_0 + 1, c_1], \\ d, & x \in [-c_0, c_0], \end{cases}$$

where $K = B(B + 1) + d\Delta_0$ is the normalization constant, guaranteeing that $\sum_{y=-\infty}^{\infty} R^{(1)}(y) = 1$. Note that exchanging the roles of r_0 and r_1 within the **repeat**-clause yields the same distributions after fulfillment of the **until**-condition. $R^{(1)}(x)$ thus describes the distribution of either after the **repeat**-loop. We establish the probability of either r_0 or r_1 being outside $[-c_0, c_0]$:

$$P^* := Pr\left[|r| > c_0 \Big| r \leftarrow R^{(1)}(x)\right] = \frac{B(B + 1)}{B(B + 1) + d\Delta_0} \tag{8}$$

2. In the second part of the algorithm, whenever $|r_0| > c_0$ or $|r_1| > c_0$, these values are reassigned to $[-c_0, c_0]$. For simplicity, we consider only the case $|r_0| > c_0$. Note that if this is the case, then since $r_1 = s - r_0$, $s \in \chi(B)$ and $|r_1| \leq c_0$, the counterpart to $|r_0| > c_0$ is the "flipped"

$$r_1 \in F(x) = K^{-1} \left((-x - c_{-1})\big|_{-c_0}^{-c_{-1} - 1} + (x - c_{-1})\big|_{c_{-1} + 1}^{c_0} \right).$$

We distinguish two cases, depending on the random parameter b.
   - If $b = 1$, we simply redefine $r_0 = -r_1$, which amounts to $R_1^{(2)}(x) = R_0^{(1)}(x)\big|_{-c_0}^{c_0} + F(x) = dK^{-1}\Theta_x[-c_0, c_0] + F(x)$.

- If $b = 0$, r_1 is first resampled from $\chi(c_0)$, then we redefine $r_0 = -r_1$, which means $F(x)$ is subtracted from $\chi(c_0)$, then resampled from $\chi(c_0)$. In terms of the distributions, this implies $R_1'^{(2)}(x) = (1+P^*)\chi(c_0) - F(x)$. Averaging over both cases, we get the uniform distribution

$$R^{(3)}(x) = \frac{1}{2}\left(R^{(2)}(x) + R'^{(2)}(x)\right) = \Delta_0^{-1}\Theta_x[-c_0, c_0],$$

which holds for both r_0 and r_1 and thus proves the lemma.

Distribution and Expected Value of r^*. We analyze how r^* is distributed at the end of Algorithm 1. Since r^* either takes the value of s or is zero, we first establish the probability of non-zero r^* for a given s. With the same considerations as in the proof of Lemma 1, we find that after the repeat-loop, the probability of r_0 or r_1 being outside $[-c_0, c_0]$ is $P_s^* = \frac{|s|}{\Delta_0 + |s|}$, for fixed s. Since either r_0 or r_1 can be outside $[-c_0, c_0]$, r^* has probability $2P_s^*$ of taking the value of s and probability $1 - 2P_s^*$ of being zero. Averaging over all possible s, we find

$$R^*(x) = \frac{1}{d}\left(\frac{2|x|}{\Delta_0 + |x|}\Theta_x[-B, B] + \left(4\Delta_0(H_{\Delta_0+B} - H_{\Delta_0}) - 2B + 1\right)\Theta_x[0,0]\right).$$

The second term represents the case $r^* = 0$, when $|r_0|, |r_1| \leq c_0$, computed as $\frac{\Theta_x[0,0]}{d}\sum_{y=-B}^{B}\left(1 - \frac{2|y|}{\Delta_0+|y|}\right)$. We can now compute the expected value of $|r^*|$ as

$$\mathsf{Ex}_{R^*}(\delta, B) = \frac{1}{d}\sum_{y=-B}^{B}\frac{2|y|^2}{\Delta_0 + |y|} = \frac{1}{d}\left(2B(B+1) + 4\Delta_0(-B + \Delta_0(H_{\Delta_0+B} - H_{\Delta_0}))\right). \quad (9)$$

We analyze the asymptotic dependency of $\mathsf{Ex}_{R^*}(\delta, B)$ on δ. The first term of (9) is an offset, while the second term $T := 4\Delta_0(-B + \Delta_0(H_{\Delta_0+B} - H_{\Delta_0})$ strongly depends on $\Delta_0 = 2\delta B + 1$. Using $\Delta_0(H_{\Delta_0+B} - H_{\Delta_0}) = \sum_{y=1}^{B}\frac{1}{1+y\Delta_0^{-1}}$, we find

$$\lim_{\delta\to\infty} T = \lim_{\delta\to\infty} -4\sum_{y=1}^{B}\frac{y}{1+y\Delta_0^{-1}} = -4\sum_{y=1}^{B}y = -2B(B+1),$$

which is exactly the offset, thus $\lim_{\delta\to\infty}\mathsf{Ex}_{R^*}(\delta, B) \to 0$. For δ small, the behavior is dominated by the difference of the harmonic numbers.

Finally, Eq. (8) also allows us to express the estimated Hamming weight of the full vector r^* simply as $2nP^*$, since we have $2n$ values $r_{0,i}, r_{1,i}$.

Split and Lemma 2. Correctness of Split is straightforward, since $s_i^* + s_i' = s_i$ is always guaranteed. We analyze how the outputs are distributed. We again drop the indices i and indicate distributions by the corresponding capital letters. Since $\#C^* = k$, we have $Pr[i \in C^*] = \frac{k}{n}$ for $i \in \{1, \ldots, n\}$. It immediately follows

$$S^*(x) = \frac{k}{dn}\Theta_x[-B, B] + \frac{n-k}{n}\Theta_x[0,0], \quad S'(x) = \frac{n-k}{dn}\Theta_x[-B, B] + \frac{k}{n}\Theta_x[0,0].$$

We can determine the expected value of s^* as

$$\mathsf{Ex}_{S^*}(B, n, k) = \frac{k}{dn}B(B+1) = \frac{k}{n}\mathsf{Ex}_S(B). \tag{10}$$

From Algorithm 2, it immediately follows that an entry s_i' is either uniform in $[-B_i, B_i]$ or zero. Following Lemma 1, the first case results in $r_{0,i}$ and $r_{1,i}$ being uniform. If $s_i' = 0$ this also immediately follows from the first `repeat`-loop in Algorithm 1, thus proving Lemma 2.

References

1. Azarderakhsh, R., et al.: Supersingular isogeny key encapsulation. Submission to the NIST Post-Quantum Standardization project (2017)
2. Bernstein, D., De Feo, L., Leroux, A., Smith, B.: Faster computation of isogenies of large prime degree. arXiv preprint arXiv:2003.10118 (2020)
3. Beullens, W., Kleinjung, T., Vercauteren, F.: CSI-FiSh: efficient isogeny based signatures through class group computations. In: Galbraith, S.D., Moriai, S. (eds.) ASIACRYPT 2019. LNCS, vol. 11921, pp. 227–247. Springer, Cham (2019). https://doi.org/10.1007/978-3-030-34578-5_9
4. Bonnetain, X., Schrottenloher, A.: Quantum security analysis of CSIDH. In: Canteaut, A., Ishai, Y. (eds.) EUROCRYPT 2020. LNCS, vol. 12106, pp. 493–522. Springer, Cham (2020). https://doi.org/10.1007/978-3-030-45724-2_17
5. Castryck, W., Decru, T.: CSIDH on the surface. In: Ding, J., Tillich, J.-P. (eds.) PQCrypto 2020. LNCS, vol. 12100, pp. 111–129. Springer, Cham (2020). https://doi.org/10.1007/978-3-030-44223-1_7
6. Castryck, W., Galbraith, S.D., Farashahi, R.R.: Efficient arithmetic on elliptic curves using a mixed Edwards-Montgomery representation. IACR Cryptol. ePrint Arch. **2008**, 218 (2008)
7. Castryck, W., Lange, T., Martindale, C., Panny, L., Renes, J.: CSIDH: an efficient post-quantum commutative group action. In: Peyrin, T., Galbraith, S. (eds.) ASIACRYPT 2018. LNCS, vol. 11274, pp. 395–427. Springer, Cham (2018). https://doi.org/10.1007/978-3-030-03332-3_15
8. Charles, D.X., Lauter, K.E., Goren, E.Z.: Cryptographic hash functions from expander graphs. J. Cryptol. **22**(1), 93–113 (2009)
9. Chávez-Saab, J., Chi-Domınguez, J.J., Jaques, S., Rodrıguez-Henrıquez, F.: The SQALE of CSIDH: Square-root Vélu quantum-resistant isogeny action with low exponents. Technical report, Cryptology ePrint Archive, Report 2020/1520 (2020)
10. Chevalier, C., Laguillaumie, F., Vergnaud, D.: Privately outsourcing exponentiation to a single server: cryptanalysis and optimal constructions. In: Askoxylakis, I., Ioannidis, S., Katsikas, S., Meadows, C. (eds.) ESORICS 2016. LNCS, vol. 9878, pp. 261–278. Springer, Cham (2016). https://doi.org/10.1007/978-3-319-45744-4_13
11. Childs, A., Jao, D., Soukharev, V.: Constructing elliptic curve isogenies in quantum subexponential time. J. Math. Cryptol. **8**(1), 1–29 (2014)
12. Couveignes, J.M.: Hard homogeneous spaces. IACR Cryptol. ePrint Arch. **2006**, 291 (2006)
13. De Feo, L., Galbraith, S.D.: SeaSign: compact isogeny signatures from class group actions. In: Ishai, Y., Rijmen, V. (eds.) EUROCRYPT 2019. LNCS, vol. 11478, pp. 759–789. Springer, Cham (2019). https://doi.org/10.1007/978-3-030-17659-4_26

14. Grover, L.K.: A fast quantum mechanical algorithm for database search. In: Proceedings of the Twenty-eighth Annual ACM Symposium on Theory of Computing, pp. 212–219 (1996)
15. Hohenberger, S., Lysyanskaya, A.: How to securely outsource cryptographic computations. In: Kilian, J. (ed.) TCC 2005. LNCS, vol. 3378, pp. 264–282. Springer, Heidelberg (2005). https://doi.org/10.1007/978-3-540-30576-7_15
16. Jao, D., De Feo, L.: Towards quantum-resistant cryptosystems from supersingular elliptic curve isogenies. In: Yang, B.-Y. (ed.) PQCrypto 2011. LNCS, vol. 7071, pp. 19–34. Springer, Heidelberg (2011). https://doi.org/10.1007/978-3-642-25405-5_2
17. Kleinjung, T.: Quadratic sieving. Math. Comput. **85**(300), 1861–1873 (2016)
18. Kuperberg, G.: A subexponential-time quantum algorithm for the dihedral hidden subgroup problem. SIAM J. Comput. **35**(1), 170–188 (2005)
19. NIST: NIST post-quantum cryptography, round 3 submissions (2020). https://csrc.nist.gov/projects/post-quantum-cryptography/round-3-submissions
20. Pedersen, R., Uzunkol, O.: Secure delegation of isogeny computations and cryptographic applications. In: Proceedings of the 2019 ACM SIGSAC Conference on Cloud Computing Security Workshop, pp. 29–42 (2019)
21. Pedersen, R., Uzunkol, O.: Delegating supersingular isogenies over $\mathbb{F}_{p^2}$ with cryptographic applications. IACR Cryptol. ePrint Arch. **2021**, 506 (2021)
22. Peikert, C.: He gives C-sieves on the CSIDH. In: Canteaut, A., Ishai, Y. (eds.) EUROCRYPT 2020. LNCS, vol. 12106, pp. 463–492. Springer, Cham (2020). https://doi.org/10.1007/978-3-030-45724-2_16
23. Regev, O.: A subexponential time algorithm for the dihedral hidden subgroup problem with polynomial space. arXiv preprint quant-ph/0406151 (2004)
24. Rostovtsev, A., Stolbunov, A.: Public-key cryptosystem based on isogenies. IACR Cryptol. ePrint Arch. **2006**, 145 (2006)
25. Siegel, C.: Über die classenzahl quadratischer zahlkörper. Acta Arith **1**(1), 83–86 (1935)
26. SIKE: Supersingular Isogeny Key Encapsulation (2018). https://sike.org
27. Stolbunov, A.: Constructing public-key cryptographic schemes based on class group action on a set of isogenous elliptic curves. Adv. Math. Commun. **4**(2), 215 (2010)
28. Stolbunov, A.: Cryptographic schemes based on isogenies. Norges teknisk-naturvitenskapelige universitet (2012)
29. Uzunkol, O., Rangasamy, J., Kuppusamy, L.: Hide the modulus: a secure non-interactive fully verifiable delegation scheme for modular exponentiations via CRT. In: Chen, L., Manulis, M., Schneider, S. (eds.) ISC 2018. LNCS, vol. 11060, pp. 250–267. Springer, Cham (2018). https://doi.org/10.1007/978-3-319-99136-8_14
30. Vélu, J.: Isogénies entre courbes elliptiques. CR Acad. Sci. Paris Sér. A **273**, 305–347 (1971)

Key-Oblivious Encryption from Isogenies with Application to Accountable Tracing Signatures

Surbhi Shaw$^{(\boxtimes)}$ and Ratna Dutta

Department of Mathematics, Indian Institute of Technology Kharagpur,
Kharagpur 721302, India
surbhi_shaw@iitkgp.ac.in, ratna@maths.iitkgp.ac.in

Abstract. *Key-oblivious encryption* (KOE) is a promising cryptographic primitive that randomizes the public keys of an encryption scheme in an oblivious manner. It has applications in designing *accountable tracing signature* (ATS) that facilitates the group manager to revoke the anonymity of traceable users in a group signature while preserving the anonymity of non-traceable users. KOE is an independent primitive and may serve as a technical building block in designing privacy preserving protocols.

In this work, we introduce the *first isogeny-based* KOE *scheme*. Isogeny-based cryptography is a fairly young post-quantum cryptography with sophisticated algebraic structures and unique security properties. Our KOE scheme is resistant to quantum attacks and derives its security from *Commutative Supersingular Decisional Diffie-Hellman* (CSSDDH), which is an isogeny-based hard problem. More concretely, we show that our construction exhibits *key randomizability, plaintext indistinguishability under key randomization* and *key privacy under key randomization* in the *standard model* adapting the security framework of [12]. Furthermore, we have manifested an *instantiation* of our scheme from cryptosystem based on *Commutative Supersingular Isogeny Diffie-Hellman* (CSIDH-512) [3] parameter set. Additionally, we demonstrate the utility of our KOE scheme by leveraging it to construct an *isogeny-based* ATS scheme preserving anonymity under tracing, traceability, non-frameability, anony-mity with accountability and trace obliviousness in the random oracle model following the security framework of [14].

Keywords: Post-quantum cryptography · Isogenies · Key-oblivious encryption · Key privacy · Provable security

1 Introduction

Key-oblivious encryption (KOE) is not a newly developed primitive, but rather cryptographic folklore. Ling et al. have recently renewed interest in KOE in his work [14]. The core concept in KOE is to enable randomization of a large set of

© Springer Nature Switzerland AG 2021
A. Adhikari et al. (Eds.): INDOCRYPT 2021, LNCS 13143, pp. 362–386, 2021.
https://doi.org/10.1007/978-3-030-92518-5_17

public keys related to the same secret key. This randomization generates related keys and the relation remains oblivious as long as the knowledge of the secret key and the randomness used are hidden.

How is KOE Different from PKE? KOE is nontrivial and useful particularly when key privacy is at prime concern apart from data privacy. The traditional security prerequisite of any *public key encryption* (PKE) scheme is to provide privacy of the encrypted data only. There exist encryption schemes that are able to meet *indistinguishability under chosen-ciphertext attack* (IND-CCA), which is the most potent form of data privacy, but do not provide key privacy. KOE captures this data privacy requirement by the security attribute *plaintext indistinguishability under key randomization*. Besides data privacy, KOE seeks to provide two key privacy requirements and is formalized by *key randomizability* and *key privacy under key randomization*. Key randomizability requires that an adversary cannot distinguish between the original public key and a randomized public key without having the secret key. In contrast, key privacy under key randomization requires anonymity from the adversary's point of view. An adversary in possession of a ciphertext is unable to tell which particular key from a set of adversarially randomized public keys is used to create the ciphertext. These notions are a variant of standard key privacy requirements introduced in [2].

Applications. KOE has interesting applications in accountable tracing signature (ATS) [12] and anonymous credential systems [6] described below.

- Recent interest in designing a KOE is because of its application in developing a framework for ATS. ATS is an enhanced variant of group signature. In the traditional group signature scheme, the group manager (GM) is allowed to randomly revoke the anonymity of any signer to avoid the misuse of anonymity of the signer. The GM is trusted blindly and there is no means to check his accountability. On the other hand, the GM is kept accountable for his actions in an ATS scheme. Once a user enrolls in the group, the GM determines the category of the user. The traceable users are the suspected users and their anonymity can be revoked by the GM. For non-traceable users, anonymity remains preserved and even the GM cannot trace the signatures generated by them. The GM then issues a certificate corresponding to his choice (traceable/non-traceable) to the user. Later the GM reveals his choice of category to enforce his accountability.
- Another application of KOE was put forward in [6] which showed how the key privacy notions can be used to realise anonymous credential systems, a primitive that enable users to control the dissemination of information about themselves. Their construction make use of a *verifiable circular key-oblivious encryption* scheme.

A variant of key privacy property of KOE has surfaced in various different aspects in the past and found several applications as in searchable encryption [1], bid secrecy and verifiability in auction protocols [17], anonymous broadcast encryption schemes [13] and many more. As the goals of data privacy and key privacy are orthogonal, designing KOE with the above stated security requirements is not only indispensable but challenging as well.

Our Contributions. KOE is an independent primitive and may serve as a technical building block in designing privacy preserving protocols. However, due to lack of comprehensive treatment we believe it is worthwhile to develop such a primitive in the isogeny world and bring its application to light. Considering its limited development in the literature, we devote this paper in designing KOE from isogenies that withstands quantum attacks. The only two existing KOE constructions so far are [12] and [14]. The KOE scheme presented in [12] relies on the *Decisional Diffie-Hellman* (DDH) assumption but is insecure in the presence of a quantum machine due to Shor's algorithm [18]. San Ling et al. [14] introduced KOE in the lattice settings which is secure under the hardness of *Ring Learning With Errors* (RLWE) assumption. In a nutshell, our contribution in this paper is twofold and can be summed up as follows:

- *Firstly*, we initiate the study of KOE in the isogeny world. We have developed the first isogeny-based KOE and named it as *Commutative Supersingular Isogeny Key-Oblivious Encryption* (CSIKOE). We provide concrete security analysis and have shown that our scheme satisfies *key randomizability, plaintext indistinguishability under key randomization* and *key privacy under key randomization* in the standard model (Sect. 4). Unlike [12], our security proof for plaintext indistinguishability under key randomization is not a straight forward reduction. Instead, our proof comprises of a sequence of games to achieve the desired security notion.
- *Secondly*, we have manifested an instantiation of our CSIKOE scheme from cryptosystem based on *Commutative Supersingular Isogeny Diffie-Hellman* (CSIDH-512) parameter set. We refer to it as CSIKOE-512 (Sect. 5).
- *Finally*, to address the application of our KOE scheme, we exploit our CSIKOE-512 scheme to develop an *isogeny-based* ATS *scheme* to make the group manager accountable in a group signature scheme (Sect. 7).

In 2019, Castryck et al. gave the non-interactive key exchange based on isogeny, named as CSIDH [7]. The ElGamal-like PKE based on CSIDH without using hash functions is not *indistinguishability under chosen-plaintext attack* (IND-CPA) secure [15]. Thus, we construct our CSIKOE scheme leveraging the PKE from CSIDH based on hash function which is IND-CPA secure. We believe our CSIKOE scheme enjoys efficiency in terms of storage and communication cost. For a security parameter λ, our CSIKOE scheme features user public key, user secret key and ciphertext size of $O(\lambda)$ each. Our CSIKOE can be instantiated with any of the three sets of CSIDH parameters that have been introduced till now (CSIDH-512, CSIDH-1024, and CSIDH-1792). However, we emphasize that our CSIKOE scheme derived from the CSIDH-512 parameter set turns out to be more efficient. We provide a detailed security analysis and arrived at the following result:

Theorem 1. *Under the* CSSDDH *assumption, our isogeny-based* CSIKOE *scheme satisfies key randomizability, plaintext indistinguishability under key randomization and key privacy under key randomization in the standard model.*

To address the rising concern for tracing mechanism in group signatures to ensure user accountability, we extend our KOE scheme to develop the first ATS scheme from isogenies. We integrate the *Commutative Supersingular Isogeny based Fiat-Shamir* (CSI-FiSh) signature scheme [3] and a zero-knowledge argument system (Sect. 2.2) in our CSIKOE-512 scheme in a suitable manner to yield an ATS scheme. We have arrived at the following theorem:

Theorem 2. *Our isogeny-based* ATS *scheme satisfies anonymity under tracing, traceability, non-frameability, anonymity with accountability and trace obliviousness in the random oracle model following the security framework of [14] as* CSI-FiSh *signature scheme is strongly unforgeable,* CSIKOE-512 *scheme satisfies key randomizability, plaintext indistinguishability under key randomization and key privacy under key randomization and under the assumption that* Π *is zero-knowledge simulation-extractable argument system.*

Technical Overview of our ATS Scheme. The main idea behind our ATS scheme is that here a trusted party generates a public key $pk^{(0)}$ using the key generation algorithm of our CSIKOE-512 scheme. He sends the public key $pk^{(0)}$ to the GM as a part of group parameter gp. Its corresponding secret key $sk^{(0)}$ is discarded and not known to anyone. Similarly, the GM generates another public key $pk^{(1)}$ using our CSIKOE-512 scheme. He publishes both the public keys $pk^{(0)}$ and $pk^{(1)}$ as a part of his group public key gpk and keeps the secret key $sk^{(1)}$ secret to himself. Each user sets his user public key upk and user secret key usk to be the verification and signing key of the CSI-FiSh signature, respectively. At the time of enrolment of a user to a group, the GM uses the randomize algorithm of our CSIKOE-512 scheme to randomize one of the public keys $pk^{(0)}$ (for non-traceable users) or $pk^{(1)}$ (for traceable users) and generates the randomized public key epk. It may be the case where a dishonest GM sends malicious randomness to the user and later blames the user for modifying epk. By this, the GM may claim a traceable user to be non-traceable. In order to guarantee non-repudiation, the GM needs to generate a signature σ_{cert} on his randomized public key epk along with his user public key upk using the CSI-FiSh signature. He sends the randomized public key epk and the signature as a certificate to the user's enrolment and keeps the randomness involved to generate epk as a witness. By the key randomizability property of our CSIKOE-512 scheme, the users have no idea whether they are traceable to the GM or not. Next, to sign a message the user generates a CSI-FiSh verification key, generates a CSI-FiSh signature σ_u on it, encrypts the signature along with his user public key upk using our CSIKOE-512 scheme and finally generates a zero-knowledge proof π to proof the knowledge of (upk, epk, $\sigma_{\text{cert}}, \sigma_u$). As $sk^{(0)}$ is not known to the GM, he will only be able to decrypt the ciphertext and retrieve the identity of a traceable user using his secret key $\mathsf{sk}^{(1)}$. Anonymity of the user remains preserved for non-traceable users. In a later phase, the GM proves his accountability using his stored witness, which follows from the correctness of our CSIKOE-512 scheme.

2   Preliminaries

Notation. Throughout this paper, we use the following notations: Let $\lambda \in \mathbb{N}$ denote the security parameter. We use #S to denote the cardinality of the set S. The residue class ring is denoted by $\mathbb{Z}/q\mathbb{Z}$. A function $\mu(\cdot)$ is negligible if for every integer c, there exists an integer k such that for all $\lambda > k$, $|\mu(\lambda)| < 1/\lambda^c$.

Elliptic Curves and Isogenies [9,19]. Let K be a finite field and $\overline{K}$ be its algebraic closure. An elliptic curve E over K is a non-singular, projective, cubic curve having genus one with a special point O, called the point at infinity. The set of K-rational points of the elliptic curve E form an additive abelian group with O as the identity element. A *Montgomery elliptic curve* E is of the form $E : By^2 = x^3 + Ax^2 + x$ where $B(A^2 - 4) \neq 0$ for some $A, B \in K$.

Let E_1 and E_2 be two elliptic curves over a field K. An *isogeny* from E_1 to E_2 is a non-constant morphism $\phi : E_1 \longrightarrow E_2$ over $\overline{K}$ preserving the point at infinity O. The *degree* of the isogeny ϕ, denoted by $\mathsf{deg}(\phi)$ is its degree as a rational map. A non-zero isogeny ϕ is called *separable* if and only if $\mathsf{deg}(\phi) = \#\mathsf{ker}(\phi)\,(= \phi^{-1}(O_{E_2}))$.

Endomorphism Ring. The set of all isogenies from E to itself defined over $\overline{K}$ forms a ring under pointwise addition and composition. This ring is called the *endomorphism ring* of the elliptic curve E and is denoted by $\mathsf{End}(E)$. By $\mathsf{End}_K(E)$, we mean the set of all isogenies from E to itself defined over K. If $\mathsf{End}(E)$ is isomorphic to an order in a quaternion algebra, the curve E is said to be *supersingular*. On the other hand, if $\mathsf{End}(E)$ is isomorphic to an order in an imaginary quadratic field, we say the curve E is *ordinary*.

Theorem 3 [21]. *Let E_1 be a curve and G be its finite subgroup. Then there is a unique elliptic curve E_2 and a separable isogeny $\phi : E_1 \longrightarrow E_2$ with $\mathsf{ker}(\phi) = G$ such that $E_2 \cong E_1/G$ which can be computed using Vélu's formulae [20].*

Ideal Class Group [15]. Let F be a number field, and $\mathcal{O}$ be an order in F. A fractional ideal $\mathfrak{a}$ of $\mathcal{O}$ is a finitely generated $\mathcal{O}$-submodule of F. Let $\mathcal{I}(O)$ be a set of invertible fractional ideals of $\mathcal{O}$. Then $\mathcal{I}(\mathcal{O})$ is an abelian group derived from the multiplication of ideals with the identity $\mathcal{O}$. Let $\mathcal{P}(\mathcal{O})$ be a subgroup of $\mathcal{I}(\mathcal{O})$ defined by $\mathcal{P}(\mathcal{O}) = \{\mathfrak{a}|\mathfrak{a} = \alpha\mathcal{O} \text{ for some } \alpha \in F \setminus \{0\}\}$. The abelian group $\mathsf{Cl}(\mathcal{O})$ defined by $\mathcal{I}(\mathcal{O})/\mathcal{P}(\mathcal{O})$ is called the *ideal class group* of $\mathcal{O}$. An element of $\mathsf{Cl}(\mathcal{O})$ denoted by $[\mathfrak{a}]$ is an equivalence class of $\mathfrak{a}$.

The Class Group Action. Let $\mathsf{Ell}_p(\mathcal{O})$ denote the set of $\mathbb{F}_p$-isomorphic classes of supersingular curves E, whose $\mathbb{F}_p$-endomorphism ring $\mathsf{End}_{\mathbb{F}_p}(E) \cong \mathcal{O} = \mathbb{Z}[\sqrt{-p}]$. The ideal class group $\mathsf{Cl}(\mathcal{O})$ acts freely and transitively on $\mathsf{Ell}_p(\mathcal{O})$. For the curve $E \in \mathsf{Ell}_p(\mathcal{O})$, the *action* $*$ of $[\mathfrak{a}] \in \mathsf{Cl}(\mathcal{O})$ on E is defined as follows:

- Consider all the endomorphisms α in $\mathfrak{a}$.
- Compute the subgroup $E[\mathfrak{a}] = \bigcap_{\alpha \in \mathfrak{a}} \ker(\alpha)$.
- Compute the elliptic curve $E/E[\mathfrak{a}]$ and an isogeny $\phi_{\mathfrak{a}} : E \longrightarrow E/E[\mathfrak{a}]$ using Velu's formula. (See Theorem 3) and returns the elliptic curve $E/E[\mathfrak{a}]$.

Henceforth, we shall use the notation $[\mathfrak{a}]E$ instead of $[\mathfrak{a}] * E$ to denote the elliptic curve $E/E[\mathfrak{a}]$. The next theorem suggests that since the curves in $\mathsf{Ell}_p(\mathcal{O})$ where $\mathcal{O} = \mathbb{Z}[\sqrt{-p}]$ can be uniquely represented by their Montgomery coefficient.

Theorem 4 [7]. *Let $p \geq 5$ be a prime such that $p \equiv 3 \pmod{8}$ and E be a supersingular elliptic curve over $\mathbb{F}_p$. Then $\mathsf{End}_{\mathbb{F}_p}(E) = \mathbb{Z}[\sqrt{-p}]$ if and only if there exists $A_{mg} \in \mathbb{F}_p$ such that E is $\mathbb{F}_p$-isomorphic to the Montgomery curve $E_{A_{mg}} : y^2 = x^3 + A_{mg}x^2 + x$. Moreover, if such an A_{mg} exists then it is unique.*

2.1 CSIDH: a Non-interactive Key Exchange Based on Isogeny [7]

The non-interactive key exchange scheme $\mathsf{CSIDH} = (\mathsf{Setup}, \mathsf{KeyGen}, \mathsf{KeyExchange})$ consists of polynomial-time algorithms with the following requirements:

$\mathsf{Setup}(1^\lambda) \to \mathsf{pp}$: A trusted authority runs this probabilistic polynomial-time (PPT) algorithm on input a security parameter 1^λ and proceed as follows:

- Chooses a large prime p of the form $p = 4\,l_1 l_2 \ldots l_n - 1$, where l_i's are small distinct odd primes.
- Picks an integer m and selects a base elliptic curve $E_0 : y^2 = x^3 + x \in \mathsf{Ell}_p(\mathcal{O})$ over $\mathbb{F}_p$ with endomorphism ring $\mathcal{O} = \mathbb{Z}[\sqrt{-p}]$.
- Defines $M_C : \mathsf{Ell}_p(\mathcal{O}) \to \mathbb{F}_p$, a function that maps isomorphism classes of elliptic curve to its Montgomery coefficient. (See Theorem 4)
- Sets the public parameter $\mathsf{pp} = (p, l_1, l_2, \ldots, l_n, m, E_0, M_C)$.

$\mathsf{KeyGen}(\mathsf{pp}) \to (\mathsf{pk}, \mathsf{sk})$: A user, say U on input the public parameter pp runs this randomized algorithm by executing the following steps and generate its public key pk and secret key sk.

- Samples an integer vector $\mathfrak{u} = (u_1, \ldots, u_n)$ randomly where $u_i \in [-m, m]$, $i = 1, \ldots, n$ and defines $[\mathfrak{u}] \in \mathsf{Cl}(\mathcal{O})$ as $[\mathfrak{u}] = [\mathfrak{l}_1^{u_1} \cdots \mathfrak{l}_n^{u_n}]$, where $\mathfrak{l}_i = <l_i, \pi - 1>$. Here $<,>$ denotes the ideal generated by multiplication by l_i map and $\pi - 1$ where π is the Frobenius endomorphism that maps (x, y) to (x^p, y^p).
- Computes the action of $[\mathfrak{u}] \in \mathsf{Cl}(\mathcal{O})$ on $E_0 \in \mathsf{Ell}_p(\mathcal{O})$ to get the curve $[\mathfrak{u}]E_0$. Computes the unique Montgomery coefficient $U_{mg} = M_C([\mathfrak{u}]E_0) \in \mathbb{F}_p$ of the elliptic curve $[\mathfrak{u}]E_0 : y^2 = x^3 + U_{mg}x^2 + x$.
- Sets its public key $\mathsf{pk} = U_{mg}$ and secret key $\mathsf{sk} = \mathfrak{u}$.

$\mathsf{KeyExchange}$: Key exchange between users A and B who want to agree upon a common secret is depicted in Fig. 1.

Correctness. Correctness of CSIDH follows immediately from the commutativity of the class group $\mathsf{Cl}(\mathcal{O})$ and Theorem 4.

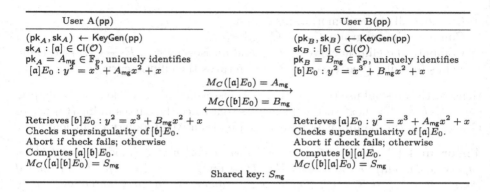

Fig. 1. KeyExchange protocol of CSIDH between Alice and Bob

Remark 1. We dwell upon few important aspects of CSIDH.

- As the cardinality of the class group is asymptotically $\#\mathsf{Cl}(\mathcal{O}) \sim \sqrt{\Delta}$, it is computationally infeasible to compute the structure of the class group $\mathsf{Cl}(\mathcal{O})$, where Δ stands for discriminant of class group. Thus [7] opts for heuristic arguments assuming that $\mathfrak{l}_i$ do not have very small order and are uniformly distributed in the class group, two ideals $\mathfrak{l}_1^{a_1} \cdots \mathfrak{l}_n^{a_n}$ for small a_i will occasionally lie in the same class group. The exponents a_i's are preferred to be sampled from a short range $\{-m, \ldots, m\}$ for some integer m such that $2m + 1 \geq \sqrt[n]{\#\mathsf{Cl}(\mathcal{O})}$.
- Choosing prime p of the form $4\, l_1 l_2 \ldots l_n - 1$, establishes an association of the fractional ideal $\mathfrak{l}_i = <l_i, \pi - 1>$ to each l_i. The action of these $\mathfrak{l}_i$ can be computed efficiently by finding an $\mathbb{F}_p$-rational point and hence a unique subgroup of $E_0(\mathbb{F}_p)$ of order l_i and applying Velu's formulas [20].

Theorem 5. *The non-interactive key exchange protocol* CSIDH *is secure under the Commutative Supersingular Decisional Diffie-Hellman* (CSSDDH) *assumption as defined in Definition 1.*

Definition 1 (Commutative Supersingular Decisional Diffie-Hellman assumption). *Let p be a large prime of the form $p = 4\, l_1 l_2 \ldots l_n - 1$, where l_i's are small distinct odd primes and E_0 be the base curve given by $y^2 = x^3 + x$ over $\mathbb{F}_p$. The Commutative Supersingular Decisional Diffie-Hellman (CSSDDH) advantage of any PPT adversary denoted by $\mathsf{Adv}_{\mathcal{A}}^{\mathsf{CSSDDH}}(\lambda)$ is defined as:*

$$\mathsf{Adv}_{\mathcal{A}}^{\mathsf{CSSDDH}}(\lambda) = |\Pr[\mathcal{A}(E_0, [\mathfrak{a}]E_0, [\mathfrak{b}]E_0, [\mathfrak{a}][\mathfrak{b}]E_0) = 1 \mid \mathfrak{a}, \mathfrak{b} \leftarrow \mathsf{Cl}(\mathcal{O})]$$
$$-\Pr[\mathcal{A}(E_0, [\mathfrak{a}]E_0, [\mathfrak{b}]E_0, [\mathfrak{c}]E_0) = 1] \mid \mathfrak{a}, \mathfrak{b}, \mathfrak{c} \leftarrow \mathsf{Cl}(\mathcal{O})|.$$

We say that the CSSDDH *assumption holds if the* CSSDDH *advantage of any PPT adversary $\mathcal{A}$ is negligible.*

Definition 2 (Entropy Smoothing). *Let $\mathcal{H} := \{H_k\}_{k \in K}$ be a family of keyed hash functions where each H_k maps from group G to $\{0,1\}^l$. Let $\mathcal{A}$ be an* *algorithm that on input an element of key space K and an element of $\{0,1\}^l$ and outputs a bit. We say $\mathcal{H} := \{H_k\}_{k \in K}$ is entropy smoothing if the advantage:*

$$\mathsf{Adv}_{\mathcal{A}}^{\mathsf{ES}}(\lambda) = |\Pr[\, k \leftarrow K, g \leftarrow G \,|\, \mathcal{A}(k, H_k(g)) = 1\,]$$
$$-\Pr[\, k \leftarrow K, h \leftarrow \{0,1\}^l \,|\, \mathcal{A}(k, h) = 1\,]\,|$$

of any PPT adversary $\mathcal{A}$ is negligible.

2.2   Non-interactive Zero-Knowledge [4]

Syntax. A Non-Interactive Zero-Knowledge (NIZK) argument system $\Pi =$ (Setup, Prove, Verify, $\mathcal{S} = (\mathcal{S}_1, \mathcal{S}_2)$) for a language $\mathcal{L} \in \mathsf{NP}$ with witness relation $\mathcal{R}$ specifies the following PPT algorithms:

Setup$(1^\lambda) \rightarrow crs$: A trusted party runs this randomized algorithm taking input the security parameter 1^λ and generates a common reference string crs.

Prove$(crs, x, w) \rightarrow \pi$: To prove the statement $x \in \mathcal{L}$ with witness w, the prover runs this randomized algorithm taking the crs and generates a proof π.

Verify$(crs, x, \pi) \rightarrow \{0,1\}$: This is a deterministic algorithm run by a verifier that takes input the crs, a statement x and a proof π and returns 1 if the proof π is valid, else returns 0.

A NIZK argument system has the following three requirements: *Completeness, Soundness* and *Zero-Knowledge* which are explicitly described below.

Definition 3 (Completeness). *A NIZK argument system Π for a language $\mathcal{L}$ $\in \mathsf{NP}$ with witness relation $\mathcal{R}$ is complete if for all x, w such that $\mathcal{R}(x, w) = 1$ and all $crs \leftarrow \mathsf{Setup}(1^\lambda)$, it must hold that $\mathsf{Verify}(crs, x, \mathsf{Prove}(crs, x, w)) = 1$.*

Definition 4 (Soundness). *A NIZK argument system Π for a language $\mathcal{L} \in$ NP with witness relation $\mathcal{R}$ is sound if the advantage of any PPT adversary $\mathcal{A}$ given by $\mathsf{Adv}_{\Pi,\mathcal{R},\mathcal{A}}^{\mathsf{SnD}}(\lambda) = \Pr[\mathsf{Exp}_{\Pi,\mathcal{R},\mathcal{A}}^{\mathsf{SnD}}(\lambda) = 1]$ is negligible where the experiment $\mathsf{Exp}_{\Pi,\mathcal{R},\mathcal{A}}^{\mathsf{SnD}}(\lambda)$ is specified in Fig. 2.*

Definition 5 (Zero-knowledge). *A NIZK argument system Π for a language $\mathcal{L} \in \mathsf{NP}$ with witness relation $\mathcal{R}$ is zero-knowledge if the advantage of any PPT adversary $\mathcal{A}$ given by $\mathsf{Adv}_{\Pi,\mathcal{R},\mathcal{A}}^{\mathsf{ZoK}}(\lambda) = \Pr[\mathsf{Exp}_{\Pi,\mathcal{R},\mathcal{A}}^{\mathsf{ZoK}}(\lambda) = 1]$ is negligible where $\mathcal{S}_1, \mathcal{S}_2$ in the experiment $\mathsf{Exp}_{\Pi,\mathcal{R},\mathcal{A}}^{\mathsf{ZoK}}(\lambda)$ specified in Fig. 2 stands for the simulator.*

Definition 6 (NIZK argument of knowledge). *A NIZK argument system Π for a language $\mathcal{L} \in \mathsf{NP}$ with witness relation $\mathcal{R}$ is an argument of knowledge if there exists a PPT extractor $\mathsf{E} = (\mathsf{E}_1, \mathsf{E}_2)$ such that the advantage of any PPT adversary $\mathcal{A}$ given by $\mathsf{Adv}_{\Pi,\mathcal{R},\mathcal{A}}^{\mathsf{ExT}}(\lambda) = \Pr[\mathsf{Exp}_{\Pi,\mathcal{R},\mathcal{A}}^{\mathsf{ExT}}(\lambda) = 1]$ is negligible, where trap refers to a trapdoor in the experiment $\mathsf{Exp}_{\Pi,\mathcal{R},\mathcal{A}}^{\mathsf{ExT}}(\lambda)$ specified in Fig. 2.*

$$\begin{array}{|ll|}
\hline
\mathsf{Exp}^{\mathsf{SnD}}_{\Pi,\mathcal{R},\mathcal{A}}(\lambda) & \\
\hline
\end{array}$$

$\mathsf{Exp}^{\mathsf{SnD}}_{\Pi,\mathcal{R},\mathcal{A}}(\lambda)$	$\mathsf{Exp}^{\mathsf{ZoK}}_{\Pi,\mathcal{R},\mathcal{A}}(\lambda)$
$crs \leftarrow \mathsf{Setup}(1^\lambda)$	
$(x,\pi) \leftarrow \mathcal{A}(crs)$	$crs_1 \leftarrow \mathsf{Setup}(1^\lambda)$
if $(x \notin \mathcal{L} \wedge \mathsf{Verify}(crs,x,\pi))$	$(crs_0, trap) \leftarrow \mathcal{S}_1(1^\lambda)$
$\quad$ return 1	$b' \leftarrow \mathcal{A}^{\mathsf{Prove}}(crs_b)$
else return 0.	if $(b = b')$
	$\quad$ return 1
$\mathsf{Exp}^{\mathsf{ExT}}_{\Pi,\mathcal{R},\mathcal{A}}(\lambda)$	else return 0.
$crs \leftarrow \mathsf{Setup}(1^\lambda)$	**Oracle** $\mathsf{Prove}(x,w)$
$(crs, trap) \leftarrow \mathsf{E}_1(1^\lambda)$	
$(x,\pi) \leftarrow \mathcal{A}(crs)$	if $\mathcal{R}(x,w) = 0$, return $\perp$
$w \leftarrow \mathsf{E}_2(crs, trap, x, \pi)$	if $b = 1$ then $\pi \leftarrow \mathsf{Prove}(crs_1, x, w)$
if $(\mathcal{R}(x,w) = 0 \wedge \mathsf{Verify}(crs,x,\pi))$	else $\pi \leftarrow \mathcal{S}_2(crs_0, x, trap)$
$\quad$ return 1	return π.
else return 0.	

Fig. 2. Experiment defining soundness, zero-knowledge, NIZK argument of knowledge

3   Key-Oblivious Encryption (KOE)

Syntax. A key-oblivious encryption is a tuple $\mathsf{KOE} = (\mathsf{Setup}, \mathsf{KeyGen}, \mathsf{KeyRand}, \mathsf{Enc}, \mathsf{Dec})$ of five polynomial-time algorithms with the following requirements:

$\mathsf{Setup}(1^\lambda) \rightarrow \mathsf{pp}$: This is a randomized algorithm run by a trusted authority that on input the security parameter 1^λ outputs the public parameter pp.

$\mathsf{KeyGen}(\mathsf{pp}) \rightarrow (\mathsf{pk}, \mathsf{sk})$: A user runs this randomized algorithm on input the public parameter pp and generates a key pair $(\mathsf{pk}, \mathsf{sk})$. The public key pk is published while the key sk is kept secret to the user.

$\mathsf{KeyRand}(\mathsf{pp}, \mathsf{pk}; r) \rightarrow \mathsf{pk}'$: Any entity can randomize pk using the public parameter pp and some randomness r to produce a new public key pk' for the same secret key sk.

$\mathsf{Enc}(\mathsf{pp}, \mathsf{pk}, m) \rightarrow \mathsf{ct}$: This randomized algorithm is executed by an encryptor who uses the public parameter pp, the public key pk of the recipient to encrypt a message m and outputs a ciphertext ct.

$\mathsf{Dec}(\mathsf{pp}, \mathsf{ct}, \mathsf{sk}) \rightarrow m'$: This is a deterministic algorithm run by the decryptor taking input the public parameter pp, the secret key sk, the ciphertext ct and outputs the decrypted message m'.

Correctness. A KOE scheme is said to be correct if for all security parameter λ, all $\mathsf{pp} \leftarrow \mathsf{Setup}(1^\lambda)$, all $(\mathsf{pk}, \mathsf{sk}) \leftarrow \mathsf{KeyGen}(\mathsf{pp})$, all $\mathsf{pk}' \leftarrow \mathsf{KeyRand}(\mathsf{pp}, \mathsf{pk}; r)$, all m, it must hold that $\mathsf{Dec}(\mathsf{pp}, \mathsf{Enc}(\mathsf{pp}, \mathsf{pk}', m), \mathsf{sk}) = m$.

Security Models. We describe the three security requirements for KOE scheme: (i) *Key randomizability* (KR): This property demands that no adversary should be able to figure out how the public keys are related to each other without the secret key and randomness used. This is formalized by means of the experiment $\mathsf{Exp}^{\mathsf{KR}}_{\mathsf{KOE},\mathcal{A}}(\lambda)$ between an adversary $\mathcal{A}$ and a challenger $\mathcal{C}$ described in Fig. 3.

---

1. The challenger $\mathcal{C}$ performs the following steps to generate (pp, pk, pk_b) and sends it to $\mathcal{A}$.
   - pp ← KOE.Setup(1^λ)
   - (pk, sk) ← KOE.KeyGen(pp)
   - pk_0 ← KOE.KeyRand(pp, pk; r)
   - (pk_1, sk_1) ← KOE.KeyGen(pp)
   - b ← $\{0, 1\}$
2. The adversary $\mathcal{A}$ eventually outputs a guess bit b' ← $\mathcal{A}$(pk, pk_b) where $b' \in \{0, 1\}$.
3. The challenger $\mathcal{C}$ returns 1 if $b = b'$ and 0 otherwise.

Fig. 3. The key randomizability experiment $\mathsf{Exp}^{\mathsf{KR}}_{\mathsf{KOE}, \mathcal{A}}$

Definition 7 (Key randomizability). *A KOE scheme is key randomizable if the advantage* $\mathsf{Adv}^{\mathsf{KR}}_{\mathsf{KOE}, \mathcal{A}}(\lambda) = |\Pr[\mathsf{Exp}^{\mathsf{KR}}_{\mathsf{KOE}, \mathcal{A}}(\lambda) = 1] - \frac{1}{2}|$ *of any PPT adversary* $\mathcal{A}$ *is negligible.*

(ii) *Plaintext indistinguishability under key randomization* (INDr): This security notion requires that no adversary can differentiate the ciphertexts corresponding to messages of its choice even though the adversary is allowed to randomize the public key. This is formalized in the experiment $\mathsf{Exp}^{\mathsf{INDr}}_{\mathsf{KOE}, \mathcal{A}}(\lambda)$ given in Fig. 4.

---

1. The challenger $\mathcal{C}$ generates (pp, pk) by performing the following steps and sends it to $\mathcal{A}$.
   - pp ← KOE.Setup(1^λ)
   - (pk, sk) ← KOE.KeyGen(pp)
2. The adversary $\mathcal{A}$ randomizes pk using randomness r to produce a randomized public key pk′ ← KOE.KeyRand(pp, pk; r). He chooses two equal-length messages m_0, m_1 and sends (pk′, r, m_0, m_1, st) ← $\mathcal{A}$(pp, pk) to the challenger $\mathcal{C}$, where st is the state information.
3. Challenger $\mathcal{C}$ performs the following steps and sends ct to $\mathcal{A}$.
   - if pk′ $\neq$ KOE.KeyRand(pp, pk; r) then return ⊥
   - b ← $\{0, 1\}$
   - ct ← KOE.Enc(pp, pk′, m_b)
4. The adversary $\mathcal{A}$ eventually outputs a guess bit b' ← $\mathcal{A}$(ct, st), where $b' \in \{0, 1\}$.
5. The challenger $\mathcal{C}$ returns 1 if $b = b'$ and 0 otherwise.

Fig. 4. The plaintext indistinguishability experiment $\mathsf{Exp}^{\mathsf{INDr}}_{\mathsf{KOE}, \mathcal{A}}(\lambda)$

Definition 8 (Plaintext indistinguishability under key randomization). *A KOE scheme is plaintext indistinguishable under key randomization if the advantage* $\mathsf{Adv}^{\mathsf{INDr}}_{\mathsf{KOE}, \mathcal{A}}(\lambda) = |\Pr[\mathsf{Exp}^{\mathsf{INDr}}_{\mathsf{KOE}, \mathcal{A}}(\lambda) = 1] - \frac{1}{2}|$ *of any PPT adversary* $\mathcal{A}$ *is negligible.*

(iii) *Key privacy under key randomization* (KPr): This feature requires that no adversary can distinguish between ciphertexts of a particular message under adversarially randomized public keys. This is formally modelled by the experiment $\mathsf{Exp}^{\mathsf{KPr}}_{\mathsf{KOE}, \mathcal{A}}(\lambda)$ between an adversary $\mathcal{A}$ and a challenger $\mathcal{C}$ in Fig. 5.

Definition 9 (Key privacy under key randomization). *A KOE scheme is key private under key randomization if the advantage of any PPT adversary* $\mathcal{A}$ *given by* $\mathsf{Adv}^{\mathsf{KPr}}_{\mathsf{KOE}, \mathcal{A}}(\lambda) = |\Pr[\mathsf{Exp}^{\mathsf{KPr}}_{\mathsf{KOE}, \mathcal{A}}(\lambda) = 1] - \frac{1}{2}|$ *is negligible.*

---

1. The challenger $\mathcal{C}$ generates (pp, pk_0, pk_1) performing the following steps and sends it to $\mathcal{A}$.
   - $pp \leftarrow$ KOE.Setup(1^λ)
   - $(pk_0, sk_0) \leftarrow$ KOE.KeyGen(pp)
   - $(pk_1, sk_1) \leftarrow$ KOE.KeyGen(pp)
2. The adversary $\mathcal{A}$ randomizes pk_0 and pk_1 using randomness r_0 and r_1 respectively, to generate randomized public keys $pk'_0 \leftarrow$ KeyRand$(pp, pk_0; r_0)$ and $pk'_1 \leftarrow$ KeyRand$(pp, pk_1; r_1)$. He chooses a message m and sends $(pk'_0, r_0, pk'_1, r_1, m, st) \leftarrow \mathcal{A}(pp, pk_0, pk_1)$ to $\mathcal{C}$.
3. Challenger $\mathcal{C}$ performs the following steps and sends ciphertext ct to $\mathcal{A}$:
   - if $pk'_i \neq$ KOE.KeyRand$(pp, pk_i; r_i)$ for some $i \in \{0, 1\}$ then return $\perp$
   - $b \leftarrow \{0, 1\}$
   - ct $\leftarrow$ KOE.Enc(pp, pk'_b, m)
4. The adversary $\mathcal{A}$ eventually outputs a guess bit $b' \leftarrow \mathcal{A}(ct, st)$, where $b' \in \{0, 1\}$.
5. The challenger $\mathcal{C}$ returns 1 if $b = b'$ and 0 otherwise.

Fig. 5. The key privacy under key randomization experiment $\mathsf{Exp}^{\mathsf{KPr}}_{\mathsf{KOE}, \mathcal{A}}(\lambda)$

4   Our Key-Oblivious Encryption from Isogenies

In this section, we explain our proposed isogeny-based KOE scheme and we call it as *Commutative Supersingular Isogeny Key-Oblivious Encryption* (CSIKOE). For convenience we adapt the following notational framework from [11]:

- $[\mathfrak{a}]E$ will be replaced by $[\mathsf{a}]E$, where $[\mathfrak{a}] = [\mathfrak{l}_1^{a_1} \cdots \mathfrak{l}_n^{a_n}] \in \mathsf{Cl}(\mathcal{O})$ is determined by its exponent vector $\mathsf{a} = (a_1, \ldots, a_n)$.
- $[\mathfrak{a}][\mathfrak{b}]E$ will be replaced by $[\mathsf{a}+\mathsf{b}]E$ where $[\mathfrak{a}], [\mathfrak{b}] \in \mathsf{Cl}(\mathcal{O})$ and $\mathsf{a} = (a_1, \ldots, a_n)$, $\mathsf{b} = (b_1, \ldots, b_n) \in \mathbb{Z}^n$ represents exponent vectors of $[\mathfrak{a}]$ and $[\mathfrak{b}]$ respectively.

Setup$(1^\lambda) \rightarrow$ pp: A trusted authority runs this algorithm on input a security parameter 1^λ and performs the following steps:

- Chooses a large prime p of the form $p = 4\,l_1 l_2 \ldots l_n - 1$, where l_i's are small distinct odd primes. Picks an integer m such that $2m + 1 \geq \sqrt[n]{\#\mathsf{Cl}(\mathcal{O})}$ and selects a base elliptic curve $E_0 : y^2 = x^3 + x \in \mathsf{Ell}_p(\mathcal{O})$ over $\mathbb{F}_p$ with endomorphism ring $\mathcal{O} = \mathbb{Z}[\sqrt{-p}]$.
- Defines $M_C : \mathsf{Ell}_p(\mathcal{O}) \rightarrow \mathbb{F}_p$, a function that maps isomorphism classes of elliptic curve to its Montgomery coefficient.
- Samples a family of hash function $\mathcal{H} := \{H_k\}_{k \in K}$ where $H_k : \mathbb{F}_p \rightarrow \{0, 1\}^\lambda$ for each $k \in K$, where K is the key space and message space $\mathcal{M} = \{0, 1\}^\lambda$.
- Sets the public parameter pp $= (p, l_1, l_2, \ldots, l_n, m, E_0, M_C, \mathcal{H} := \{H_k\}_{k \in K})$.

KeyGen$(pp) \rightarrow (pk, sk)$: This is a randomized algorithm run by a user on input the public parameter pp $= (p, l_1, l_2, \ldots, l_n, m, E_0, M_C, \mathcal{H} := \{H_k\}_{k \in K})$ to generate his public key pk and secret key sk. The user proceeds as follows:

- Samples randomly two n-tuple integer vectors $\mathsf{a} = (a_1, \ldots, a_n)$, $\mathsf{r} = (r_1, \ldots, r_n)$ where $a_i, r_i \in [-m, m]$ for $i = 1, \ldots, n$. These integer vectors define the ideal classes $[\mathfrak{a}] = [\mathfrak{l}_1^{a_1} \cdots \mathfrak{l}_n^{a_n}]$ and $[\mathfrak{r}] = [\mathfrak{l}_1^{r_1} \cdots \mathfrak{l}_n^{r_n}] \in \mathsf{Cl}(\mathcal{O})$ respectively, where $\mathfrak{l}_i = \langle l_i, \pi - 1 \rangle$ and π is the Frobenius endomorphism.
- Computes the elliptic curves $E_1 = [\mathsf{a}]E_0$, $E_2 = [\mathsf{r}]E_1 = [\mathsf{r} + \mathsf{a}]E_0$ and returns the public key pk $= (E_1, E_2)$ and keeps sk $= \mathsf{r}$ secret.

KeyRand(pp, pk; r') → pk': This randomized algorithm takes input the public parameter pp, public key pk = (E_1, E_2) and randomize it to obtain pk'. The steps involved are as follows:

- Samples randomly an n-tuple integer vector r' = $(r'_1, \ldots, r'_n)$ where $r'_i \in [-m, m]$ for $i = 1, \ldots, n$. This integer vector r' defines the ideal class [r'] = $[\mathfrak{l}_1^{r'_1} \cdots \mathfrak{l}_n^{r'_n}] \in Cl(\mathcal{O})$.
- Computes the curves $E'_1 = [r']E_1$, $E'_2 = [r']E_2$ and outputs the randomized public key pk' = (E'_1, E'_2).

Enc(pp, pk, m) → ct: An encryptor takes input the public parameter pp, the public key pk = (E_1, E_2), a message m and performs the following steps:

- Samples randomly an n-tuple vector c = $(c_1, \ldots, c_n)$ of integers, where $c_i \in [-m, m]$ for $i = 1, \ldots, n$, which defines the ideal class [c] = $[\mathfrak{l}_1^{c_1} \cdots \mathfrak{l}_n^{c_n}]$.
- Computes $ct_1 = [c]E_1$, $ct_2 = H_k(M_C([c]E_2)) \oplus m$ and returns ct = (ct_1, ct_2).

Dec(pp, ct, sk) → m: This a deterministic algorithm run by a decryptor that takes input the public parameter pp, the secret key sk = r and the ciphertext ct = (ct_1, ct_2) where $ct_1 = [c]E_1$, $ct_2 = H_k(M_C([c]E_2)) \oplus m$. The decryptor retrieves the plaintext m by computing $ct_2 \oplus H_k(M_C([r]ct_1))$.

Correctness. The correctness of the CSIKOE protocol follows from:

$$
\begin{aligned}
ct_2 \oplus H_k(M_C([r]ct_1)) &= H_k(M_C([c]E'_2)) \oplus m \oplus H_k(M_C([r]ct_1)) \\
&= H_k(M_C([c][r'][r + a]E_0)) \oplus m \oplus H_k(M_C([r][c][r']E_1)) \\
&= m.
\end{aligned}
$$

Parameter Setting. The system parameters must be set in such a way that no polynomial-time adversary can guess the private key with non-negligible probability. Note that the private key is an n-tuple vector of integers with each co-ordinates chosen randomly from $[-m, m]$. Therefore the private key space is $(2m + 1)^n$ and $(2m + 1)^n \geq 2^{3\lambda} \Rightarrow n \log(2m + 1) \geq 3\lambda$ needs to be satisfied to provide a secure key space, with the goal that no polynomial-time attacker can guess the private key [10]. Considering the best-known threats, three sets of parameters were recommended for CSIDH under three NIST security levels - CSIDH-512, CSIDH-1024 and CSIDH-1792. The parameters of CSIDH-512 were fully specified in practice ($n = 74$, $m = 5$, $l_{73} = 373$, $l_{74} = 587$) corresponding to the NIST level 1 and achieves 127-bit classical and 64-bit quantum security.

Remark 2. Castryck et al. [8] pointed out that the CSSDDH problem is easy if we work with supersingular elliptic over $\mathbb{F}_p$ with $p \equiv 1 \pmod 4$. It is noteworthy that CSIDH is secure as it relies on supersingular elliptic curves over $\mathbb{F}_p$ with $p \equiv 3 \pmod 4$. Consequently, our CSIKOE construction is secure as for our setting the CSSDDH assumption is conjectured to be hard.

Efficiency. We now analyse the efficiency of our CSIKOE scheme in terms of security parameter λ. The size of public key pk is of $O(\log p) = O(\lambda)$. The secret key sk has $n \log(2m+1)$ bits. Since $n \log(2m+1) \geq 3\lambda$, thus the size of the secret key sk is $O(\lambda)$. In Table 1, we provide a theoretical comparison of our CSIKOE with other proposed KOE.

Table 1. Comparative summary of communication bandwidth and storage overhead of KOE

Scheme	Quantum secure	Storage		Communication	Computation		Security
		|pk|	|sk|	|ct|	Encryption	Decryption	
[12]	No	$2\|\mathbb{G}\|$	$\|\mathbb{Z}_q\|$	$2\|\mathbb{G}\|$	2 exponentiation 1 multiplication	1 exponentiation 1 inversion	DDH
[14]	Yes	$2nl$	n-tuple vector over $\mathbb{Z}$	$2nl$	2 scalar multiplication 1 Ternary decomposition	1 modular division 1 matrix multiplication	RLWE
Ours	Yes	$2\log p$	$n\log(2m+1)$	$2\log p$	2 group actions 1 XOR operation	1 group action 1 XOR operation	CSSDDH

pk = Public key, sk = Secret key, ct = Ciphertext For [12], $\mathbb{G}$ is a group of prime order q. For [14], $n = \mathcal{O}(\lambda)$ is a power of 2, $l = \lfloor \log \frac{q-1}{2} \rfloor + 1$ and $q = \widetilde{\mathcal{O}}(n^4)$.

4.1   Security Analysis

Theorem 6. *Under the* CSSDDH *assumption as defined in Definition 1 of Sect. 2, the isogeny-based* CSIKOE *scheme presented in Sect. 4 satisfies key randomizability* (KR) *as per Definition 7.*

Proof. Let us assume that there exists a PPT adversary $\mathcal{A}$ and a non-negligible function $\mu(\cdot)$ such that $\Pr[\mathsf{Exp}_{\mathsf{KOE}, \mathcal{A}}^{\mathsf{KR}}(\lambda) = 1] \geq \frac{1}{2} + \mu(\lambda)$, where $\mathsf{Exp}_{\mathsf{KOE}, \mathcal{A}}^{\mathsf{KR}}(\lambda)$ is defined in Fig. 3 of Sect. 3. We will prove that we can design a PPT distinguisher $\mathcal{D}$ which can solve any CSSDDH instance, i.e., distinguishes between (E_0, $X = [\mathsf{x}]E_0$, $Y = [\mathsf{y}]E_0$, $Z_1 = [\mathsf{x}+\mathsf{y}]E_0$) and (E_0, $X = [\mathsf{x}]E_0$, $Y = [\mathsf{y}]E_0$, $Z_0 = [\mathsf{z}]E_0$) with non-negligible probability where $E_0 \in \mathsf{Ell}_p(\mathcal{O})$ and $\mathsf{x} = (x_1, \ldots, x_n)$, $\mathsf{y} = (y_1, \ldots, y_n)$, $\mathsf{z} = (z_1, \ldots, z_n)$ are integer vectors such that $x_i, y_i, z_i \in [-m, m]$ for $i = 1, \ldots, n$. Given a CSSDDH challenge (E_0, $X = [\mathsf{x}]E_0$, $Y = [\mathsf{y}]E_0$, Z_b) where $b \in \{0, 1\}$, the reduction is straight forward and proceeds as described in Fig. 6.

---

1. The Distinguisher $\mathcal{D}$ uses the CSSDDH instance (E_0, X, Y, Z_b) where $b \in \{0, 1\}$, from the CSSDDH challenger, generates (pk, pk_b) and sends it to $\mathcal{A}$.
   - Sets $\mathsf{pp} = (p, E_0, l_1, l_2, \ldots, l_n, m, M_C, \mathcal{H} := \{H_k\}_{k \in K})$ where p, E_0 are extracted from the CSSDDH instance and the parameters are defined as in our CSIKOE construction.
   - Samples an integer vector $\mathsf{r} = (r_1, \ldots, r_n)$ such that $r_i \in [-m, m]$ for $i = 1, \ldots, n$.
   - Sets $\mathsf{pk} = ([\mathsf{r}]E_0, [\mathsf{r}]X)$, $\mathsf{pk}_b = ([\mathsf{r}]Y, [\mathsf{r}]Z_b)$.
2. The adversary $\mathcal{A}$ eventually outputs a bit $b \leftarrow \mathcal{A}(\mathsf{pk}, \mathsf{pk}_b)$, where $b \in \{0, 1\}$.
3. The distinguisher returns the bit b to the CSSDDH challenger.

Fig. 6. Distinguisher $\mathcal{D}$ for the KR security of CSIKOE

For the instance when $b = 1$, i.e., $(X = [x]E_0, Y = [y]E_0, Z_1 = [x+y]E_0)$ is a CSSDDH triple, the view of the adversary $\mathcal{A}$ is identical to experiment $\mathsf{Exp}^{\mathsf{KR}}_{\mathsf{KOE},\mathcal{A}}(\lambda)$. As the adversary receives original public key $\mathsf{pk} = ([r]E_0, [r]X)$ $= ([r]E_0, [x+r]E_0)$ and the subsequent public key $\mathsf{pk}_1 = ([r]Y, [r]Z_1)) = ([y][r]E_0, [y][x+r]E_0)$, a re-randomization of the original key pk using y. On the other hand, when $b = 0$, i.e., $(X = [x]E_0, Y = [y]E_0, Z_0 = [z]E_0)$, the second key $\mathsf{pk}_0 = ([r]Y, [r]Z_0)) = ([y][r]E_0, [z+r]E_0)$ is a complete randomized key. Thus, if $\mathcal{A}$ correctly distinguishes between a real or random key with a non-negligible advantage, the distinguisher $\mathcal{D}$ breaks CSSDDH with the same non-negligible advantage as that of $\mathcal{A}$. More formally, the probability of $\mathcal{D}$ winning in the distinguishability game $= \Pr[\mathsf{Exp}^{\mathsf{KR}}_{\mathsf{KOE},\mathcal{A}}(\lambda) = 1] \geqslant \frac{1}{2} + \mu(\lambda)$. $\qquad\square$

Theorem 7. *The isogeny-based* CSIKOE *scheme presented in Sect. 4 satisfies plaintext indistinguishability under key randomization* (INDr) *as per Definition 8 under* CSSDDH *assumption as defined in Definition 1 and the assumption that $\mathcal{H} := \{H_k\}_{k \in K}$ is "entropy smoothing" as defined in Definition 2.*

Proof. We prove the plaintext indistinguishability under key randomization (INDr) of our CSIKOE scheme using the following sequence of games G_0, G_1, G_2, under CSSDDH assumption and the presumption that $\mathcal{H}$ is entropy smoothing.

Game G_0. We start with game G_0 which is the true INDr experiment $\mathsf{Exp}^{\mathsf{INDr}}_{\mathsf{KOE},\mathcal{A}}(\lambda)$ and is explicitly described in Fig. 7.

---

1. The challenger $\mathcal{C}$ begins the experiment by computing (pp, pk) and sends it to $\mathcal{A}$.
   - pp $\leftarrow$ KOE.Setup(1^λ) where pp $= (p, E_0, l_1, l_2, \ldots, l_n, m, M_C, \mathcal{H} := \{H_k\}_{k \in K})$.
   - Samples two integer vector r $= (r_1, \ldots, r_n)$, a $= (a_1, \ldots, a_n)$ such that r_i, $a_i \in [-m, m]$ for $i = 1, \ldots, n$.
   - (pk $= (E_1 = [a]E_0, E_2 = [r+a]E_0)$, sk $= r) \leftarrow$ KOE.KeyGen(pp)
2. The adversary $\mathcal{A}$ randomizes pk $= (E_1, E_2)$ using randomness r$'$ to produce a randomized public key pk$'$ $\leftarrow$ KOE.KeyRand(pp, pk; r$'$). He chooses two equal-length messages m_0, m_1 and sends (pk$'$, r$'$, m_0, m_1, st) $\leftarrow \mathcal{A}$(pp, pk) to $\mathcal{C}$, where pk$'$ $= (E_1' = [r']E_1, E_2' = [r']E_2)$.
3. Challenger $\mathcal{C}$ performs the following steps and sends ciphertext ct to the adversary $\mathcal{A}$.
   - if pk$'$ $\neq$ KOE.KeyRand(pp, pk; r$'$) then return $\bot$
   - $b \leftarrow \{0, 1\}$
   - Samples an integer vector c $= (c_1, \ldots, c_n)$ such that $c_i \in [-m, m]$ for $i = 1, \ldots, n$.
     - For game G_0, ct $\leftarrow$ KOE.Enc(pp, pk$'$, m_b), where ct $= (\mathsf{ct}_1 = [c]E_1', \mathsf{ct}_2 = H_k(M_C([c]E_2')) \oplus m_b)$
     - For game G_1, ct $= (\mathsf{ct}_1 = [c]E_1', \mathsf{ct}_2 = H_k(M_C([z]E_2')) \oplus m_b)$ where z $= (z_1, \ldots, z_n)$ is an integer vector such that $z_i \in [-m, m]$ for $i = 1, \ldots, n$.
     - For game G_2, ct $= (\mathsf{ct}_1 = [c]E_1', \mathsf{ct}_2 = h \oplus m_b)$ where $h \leftarrow \{0, 1\}^\lambda$.
4. The adversary $\mathcal{A}$ eventually outputs a guess bit $b' \leftarrow \mathcal{A}$(ct, st), where $b' \in \{0, 1\}$.
5. The challenger $\mathcal{C}$ returns 1 if $b = b'$ and 0 otherwise.

Fig. 7. Game G_i for $i = 0, 1, 2$ in the proof of Theorem 7

Game G_1. It is the same as game G_0, but with a small tweak. In this game, the challenger sets the targeted ciphertext ct $= (\mathsf{ct}_1 = [c]E_1', \mathsf{ct}_2 = H_k(M_C([z]E_2')) \oplus m_b)$ where z $= (z_1, \ldots, z_n)$ is an integer vector sampled randomly such that $z_i \in [-m, m]$ for $i = 1, \ldots, n$.

For Game G_i for $i = 0, 1, 2$, let T_i be the event associated with $b = b'$. We first prove the following claim.

Claim: For the event T_i in game G_i where $i = 0, 1$, we have $|\Pr[T_0] - \Pr[T_1]| = \epsilon_{cssddh}$ where ϵ_{cssddh} is the CSSDDH-advantage of any PPT adversary, which is negligible.

Proof of Claim. To prove that $|\Pr[T_0] - \Pr[T_1]|$ is negligible, one argues that there exists a distinguishing algorithm $\mathcal{D}$ that interpolates between game G_0 and game G_1, so that when given $(E_0, X = [x]E_0, Y = [y]E_0, Z_1 = [x+y]E_0)$ as input, $\mathcal{D}$ outputs 1 with probability $\Pr[T_0]$ and when given $(E_0, X = [x]E_0, Y = [y]E_0, Z_0 = [z]E_0)$ as input, $\mathcal{D}$ outputs 1 with probability $\Pr[T_1]$. The CSSDDH indistinguishability assumption then implies that $|\Pr[T_0] - \Pr[T_1]|$ is negligible. Our distinguisher $\mathcal{D}$ is precisely described in Fig. 8.

---

1. The Distinguisher $\mathcal{D}$ uses the CSSDDH instance $(E_0, X = [x]E_0, Y = [y]E_0, Z_\delta)$ where $\delta \in \{0, 1\}$ from the CSSDDH challenger, generates (pp, pk) and sends it to $\mathcal{A}$.
   - Sets $pp = (p, E_0, l_1, l_2, \ldots, l_n, m, M_C, \mathcal{H} = \{H_k\}_{k \in K})$ where p, E_0 are extracted from the CSSDDH instance and the parameters are defined as in our CSIKOE construction.
   - Samples an integer vector $a = (a_1, \ldots, a_n)$ such that $a_i \in [-m, m]$ for $i = 1, \ldots, n$.
   - $pk \leftarrow ([a]E_0, [a]X)$.
2. The adversary $\mathcal{A}$ randomizes pk using randomness r' to produce a randomized public key pk' $\leftarrow$ KOE.KeyRand(pp, pk; r'). He chooses two equal-length messages m_0, m_1 and sends (pk', r', m_0, m_1, st) $\leftarrow \mathcal{A}$(pp, pk) to the distinguisher $\mathcal{D}$, where $pk' = ([r'][a]E_0, [r'][a+x]E_0)$.
3. The distinguisher $\mathcal{D}$ performs the following steps and sends ciphertext ct to the adversary $\mathcal{A}$.
   - if $pk' \neq ([r'][a]E_0, [r'][a]X)$ then return $\perp$
   - $b \leftarrow \{0, 1\}$
   - $ct \leftarrow ([a+r']Y, H_k(M_C([a+r']Z_\delta)) \oplus m_b)$
4. Adversary $\mathcal{A}$ taking the ciphertext ct eventually outputs a bit $b' \leftarrow \mathcal{A}$(ct, st), where $b' \in \{0, 1\}$.
5. The distinguisher $\mathcal{D}$ outputs 1 if $b = b'$ or else outputs 0.

Fig. 8. Distinguisher $\mathcal{D}$ for the INDr security of CSIKOE

If the input to $\mathcal{D}$ is of the form $(E_0, X = [x]E_0, Y = [y]E_0, Z_1 = [x+y]E_0)$, then computation proceeds just as in game G_0, and therefore

$$\Pr[x, y \leftarrow [-m, m]^n | \mathcal{D}(E_0, X, Y, Z_1 = [x+y]E_0) = 1] = \Pr[T_0].$$

On the other hand, if the input to $\mathcal{D}$ is of the form $(E_0, X = [x]E_0, Y = [y]E_0, Z_0 = [z]E_0)$, then computation proceeds as in game G_1, and therefore

$$\Pr[x, y \leftarrow [-m, m]^n | \mathcal{D}(E_0, X, Y, Z_0 = [z]E_0) = 1] = \Pr[T_1].$$

Thus we have, $\text{Adv}_{\mathcal{D}}^{\text{CSSDDH}}(\lambda)$

$$= |\Pr[x, y \leftarrow [-m, m]^n | \mathcal{D}(E_0, X = [x]E_0, Y = [y]E_0, Z_1 = [x+y]E_0) = 1]$$
$$- \Pr[x, y \leftarrow [-m, m]^n | \mathcal{D}(E_0, X = [x]E_0, Y = [y]E_0, Z_0 = [z]E_0) = 1]|$$
$$= |\Pr[T_0] - \Pr[T_1]|$$

From this, it follows that the CSSDDH-advantage of $\mathcal{D}$ is equal to $|\Pr[T_0] - \Pr[T_1]|$, which completes the proof of the Claim.

Game G_2. Game G_2 is identical to game G_1, except that the challenger sets ct $= (ct_1 = [c]E_1', ct_2 = h \oplus m_b)$ by choosing $h \in \{0, 1\}^\lambda$ uniformly at random.

Then from the entropy smoothing assumption of the family of hash functions $\mathcal{H}$ as defined in Definition 2, we have $|\Pr[T_1] - \Pr[T_2]| = \epsilon_{es}$, where ϵ_{es} is the entropy smoothing advantage of any PPT algorithm, which is negligible. Also, note that as h behaves like a one-time pad in game G_2. Thus, $\Pr[T_2] = \frac{1}{2}$. Thus,

$$\mathsf{Adv}^{\mathsf{INDr}}_{\mathsf{KOE}, \mathcal{A}}(\lambda) = |\Pr[\mathsf{Exp}^{\mathsf{INDr}}_{\mathsf{KOE}, \mathcal{A}}(\lambda) = 1] - \frac{1}{2}|$$

$$= |\Pr[T_0] - \Pr[T_2]|$$

$$\leq |\Pr[T_0] - \Pr[T_1]| + |\Pr[T_1] - \Pr[T_2]|$$

$$= \epsilon_{cssddh} + \epsilon_{es}$$

which is negligible since both ϵ_{cssddh} and ϵ_{es} are negligible. $\qquad\square$

Theorem 8. *Under the CSSDDH assumption as defined in Definition 1 of Sect. 2, the isogeny based CSIKOE scheme presented in Sect. 4 satisfies key private under key randomization (KPr) as per Definition 9.*

Proof. On the contrary, let us assume that there exists a PPT adversary $\mathcal{A}$ and a non-negligible function $\mu(\cdot)$ such that $\Pr[\mathsf{Exp}^{\mathsf{KPr}}_{\mathsf{KOE}, \mathcal{A}}(\lambda) = 1] \geq \frac{1}{2} + \mu(\lambda)$. Now we shall prove that we can design a PPT distinguisher $\mathcal{D}$ which distinguishes between $(E_0, X = [\mathsf{x}]E_0, Y = [\mathsf{y}]E_0, Z_1 = ([\mathsf{x}+\mathsf{y}]E_0)$ and $(E_0, X = [\mathsf{x}]E_0, Y = [\mathsf{y}]E_0, Z_0 = ([\mathsf{z}]E_0)$ with non negligible probability where $E_0 \in \mathsf{Ell}_p(\mathcal{O})$ and $\mathsf{x} = (x_1, \ldots, x_n)$, $\mathsf{y} = (y_1, \ldots, y_n)$, $\mathsf{z} = (z_1, \ldots, z_n)$ are integer vectors such that $x_i, y_i, z_i \in [-m, m]$ for $i = 1, \ldots, n$. Given a CSSDDH challenge (E_0, X, Y, Z_δ), where $\delta \in \{0, 1\}$ the reduction is given in the Fig. 9.

---

1. The Distinguisher $\mathcal{D}$ uses the CSSDDH instance $(E_0, X = [\mathsf{x}]E_0, Y = [\mathsf{y}]E_0, Z_\delta)$, where $\delta \in \{0, 1\}$ and proceed as follows to generate $(\mathsf{pp}, \mathsf{pk}_0, \mathsf{pk}_1)$ and sends it to $\mathcal{A}$.
   - Sets $\mathsf{pp} = (p, E_0, l_1, l_2, \ldots, l_n, m, M_C, \mathcal{H} := \{H_k\}_{k \in K})$ where p, E_0 are extracted from the CSSDDH instance and the parameters are defined as in our CSIKOE construction.
   - Samples each of the integer vectors α, β, r_0, r_1 from $[-m, m]^n$.
   - $X_0 = X$; $Y_0 = Y$; $S_0 = Z_\delta$
   - $X_1 = [\alpha]X$; $Y_1 = [\beta]Y$; $S_1 = [\alpha + \beta]Z_\delta$
   - $\mathsf{pk}_0 = ([r_0]E_0, [r_0]Y_0)$, $\mathsf{pk}_1 = ([r_1]E_0, [r_1]Y_1)$
2. The adversary $\mathcal{A}$ randomizes the public key pk_0, pk_1 using randomness v_0, v_1 respectively and generates $\mathsf{pk}'_0 = ([v_0 + r_0]E_0, [v_0 + r_0]Y_0)$, $\mathsf{pk}'_1 = ([v_1 + r_1]E_0, [v_1 + r_1]Y_1)$ and sends $(\mathsf{pk}'_0, \mathsf{pk}'_1, v_0, v_1, m, st) \leftarrow \mathcal{A}(\mathsf{pp}, \mathsf{pk}_0, \mathsf{pk}_1)$ to the distinguisher $\mathcal{D}$.
3. The distinguisher $\mathcal{D}$ performs the following steps and sends ciphertext ct to the adversary $\mathcal{A}$.
   - if $\mathsf{pk}'_0 \neq ([v_0][r_0]E_0, [v_0][r_0]Y_0) \lor \mathsf{pk}'_1 \neq ([v_1][r_1]E_0, [v_1][r_1]Y_1)$ return $\perp$
   - $b \leftarrow \{0, 1\}$
   - Computes $\mathsf{ct} = (\mathsf{ct}_1, \mathsf{ct}_2)$ where $\mathsf{ct}_1 = [r_b + v_b]X_b$, $\mathsf{ct}_2 = H_k(M_C([r_b + v_b]S_b)) \oplus m$.
4. Adversary $\mathcal{A}$ taking the ciphertext ct outputs a bit $b' \leftarrow \mathcal{A}(\mathsf{ct}, st)$, where $b' \in \{0, 1\}$
5. The distinguisher $\mathcal{D}$ outputs 1 if $b = b'$ or else outputs 0.

Fig. 9. Distinguisher $\mathcal{D}$ for the KPr security of CSIKOE

Observe that if X_0, Y_0, S_0 is a CSSDDH triple, then so is X_1, Y_1, S_1. Moreover, the two triples are identically distributed and generates proper distributions of keys in CSIKOE. For the instance when $\delta = 1$, $(X_b = [\mathsf{x}_b]E_0, Y_b = [\mathsf{y}_b]E_0, S_b = [\mathsf{x}_b + \mathsf{y}_b]E_0)$ is a CSSDDH triple, the view of the adversary $\mathcal{A}$ is identical to experiment $\mathsf{Exp}^{\mathsf{KPr}}_{\mathsf{KOE}, \mathcal{A}}(\lambda)$, where $\mathsf{x}_0 = \mathsf{x}$, $\mathsf{x}_1 = \mathsf{x} + \alpha$, $\mathsf{y}_0 = \mathsf{y}$, $\mathsf{y}_1 = \mathsf{y} + \beta$.

Indeed, $[r_b + v_b]S_b = [r_b + v_b][x_b + y_b]E_0 = [y_b]([r_b + v_b]X_b) = [y_b]\mathsf{ct}_1$. On the other hand, when $\delta = 0$, S_b is a random element, then the challenge ciphertext provided to $\mathcal{A}$ contains no information. Hence $\mathcal{A}$'s advantage at guessing the bit is negligible. Thus, if $\mathcal{A}$ has a non-negligible advantage in experiment $\mathsf{Exp}^{\mathsf{KPr}}_{\mathsf{KOE}, \mathcal{A}}(\lambda)$, $\mathcal{D}$ breaks CSSDDH with the same non-negligible advantage as that of $\mathcal{A}$. Thus, the probability of $\mathcal{D}$ winning in the distinguishability game $= \Pr[\mathsf{Exp}^{\mathsf{KPr}}_{\mathsf{KOE}, \mathcal{A}}(\lambda) = 1] \geqslant \frac{1}{2} + \mu(\lambda)$. This completes the proof. $\qquad\square$

5 Instantiation of CSIKOE from CSIDH-512

We now show an instantiation of our CSIKOE scheme based on the CSIDH-512 parameter set and name it as CSIKOE-512. The structure of the class group $\mathsf{Cl}(\mathcal{O})$ where $\mathcal{O} = \mathbb{Z}[\sqrt{-p}]$ is computed by Beullens et al. [3]. They have shown that $\mathsf{Cl}(\mathcal{O})$ is a cyclic group and $\mathfrak{g} = <3, \pi - 1>$ is a generator of this class group. The class number of this ideal class group is given by N, where

$$N = \#\mathsf{Cl}(\mathcal{O}) = 37 \times 1407181 \times 51593604295295867744293584889$$
$$\times 31599414504681995853008278745587832204909.$$

For simplicity we can consider $\mathsf{Cl}(\mathcal{O})$ to be $\mathbb{Z}_N$ and use the following notation:

- $[\mathfrak{a}]E$ will be replaced by $[a]E$ for any element $[\mathfrak{a}] \in \mathsf{Cl}(\mathcal{O})$ which can be written as $[\mathfrak{g}^a]$ for some $a \in \mathbb{Z}_N$.
- $[\mathfrak{a}][\mathfrak{b}]E$ will be replaced by $[a + b]E$ where $[\mathfrak{a}], [\mathfrak{b}] \in \mathsf{Cl}(\mathcal{O})$ and $[\mathfrak{a}]E = [\mathfrak{g}^a]E$, $[\mathfrak{b}]E = [\mathfrak{g}^b]E$ for some $a, b \in \mathbb{Z}_N$.

$\mathsf{Setup}(1^\lambda) \rightarrow \mathsf{pp}$: A trusted authority runs this algorithm on input a security parameter 1^λ and performs the following steps:

- Chooses a large prime p of the form $p = 4\, l_1 l_2 \ldots l_n - 1$, where the l_i are small distinct odd primes with $n = 74$, $l_1 = 3$, $l_{73} = 373$, and $l_{74} = 587$.
- Sets the generator of the ideal class group $\mathcal{G} = \mathsf{Cl}(\mathcal{O})$ to be $\mathfrak{g} = <3, \pi - 1>$ with class number N.
- Selects a base elliptic curve $E_0 : y^2 = x^3 + x$, a function $M_C : \mathsf{Ell}_p(\mathcal{O}) \rightarrow \mathbb{F}_p$ and a family of keyed hash function $\mathcal{H} := \{H_k\}_{k \in K}$ where $H_k : \mathbb{F}_p \rightarrow \{0, 1\}^\lambda$ for each $k \in K$ same as in our CSIKOE construction.
- Sets the public parameter $\mathsf{pp} = (p, \mathfrak{g}, N, E_0, M_C, \mathcal{H})$.

$\mathsf{KeyGen}(\mathsf{pp}) \rightarrow (\mathsf{pk}, \mathsf{sk})$: This is a randomized algorithm run by a user to generate his corresponding pair of public and secret keys. The user samples two elements $[\mathfrak{a}] = [\mathfrak{g}^a]$ and $[\mathfrak{r}] = [\mathfrak{g}^r] \in \mathcal{G}(\cong \mathbb{Z}_N)$ for some a, r in $\mathbb{Z}_N$. Computes the elliptic curves $E_1 = [a]E_0$, $E_2 = [r]E_1 = [r + a]E_0$ and returns the public key $\mathsf{pk} = (E_1, E_2)$ and keeps $\mathsf{sk} = r$ secret.

$\mathsf{KeyRand}(\mathsf{pp}, \mathsf{pk}; r') \rightarrow \mathsf{pk}'$: This is a randomized algorithm run by any entity taking input a public key pk and randomize it to obtain pk'. For this he samples $[\mathfrak{r}'] = [\mathfrak{g}^{r'}] \in \mathcal{G}(\cong \mathbb{Z}_N)$ for some r' in $\mathbb{Z}_N$. Computes the elliptic curves $E_1' = [r']E_1$, $E_2' = [r']E_2$ and outputs the randomized public key $\mathsf{pk}' = (E_1', E_2')$.

Enc(pp, pk, m) → ct: The encryptor samples $[\mathfrak{c}] = [\mathfrak{g}^c] \in \mathcal{G}(\cong \mathbb{Z}_N)$ for some c in $\mathbb{Z}_N$. Computes $\mathsf{ct}_1 = [c]E_1$ and $\mathsf{ct}_2 = H_k(M_C([\mathfrak{c}]E_2)) \oplus m$ using the input public key pk $= (E_1, E_2)$ and returns the ciphertext ct $= (\mathsf{ct}_1, \mathsf{ct}_2)$, which is the encryption of the message $m \in \{0,1\}^\lambda$.

Dec(pp, ct, sk) → m: Given the secret key sk $= r$ and the ciphertext ct $=$ ($\mathsf{ct}_1, \mathsf{ct}_2$) where $\mathsf{ct}_1 = [c]E_1$ and $\mathsf{ct}_2 = H_k(M_C([c]E_2)) \oplus m$, the decryptor returns the message $m = \mathsf{ct}_2 \oplus H_k(M_C([r]\mathsf{ct}_1))$.

Remark 3. The recent quantum security analysis of CSIDH-512 in [5, 16] corresponding to NIST category 1 reveals that CSIDH-512 is broken by 40 bit quantum memory and 2^{16} quantum oracle queries, thereby reducing the expected quantum security level of CSIDH-512. But the quantum circuit for the group operations of CSIDH is expensive. Taking a note of such external overheads of circuits in addition to his evaluation, CSIDH appears to be safe in reality.

6 Accountable Tracing Signature

Syntax. An accountable tracing signature (ATS) scheme is a tuple ATS = (Setup, GrKeyGen, UsKeyGen, Enroll, Sign, Verify, Open, Judge, Account) of nine polynomial-time algorithms with the following requirements:

Setup(1^λ) → gp: This is a randomized algorithm run by a trusted authority that on input the security parameter λ and outputs the group parameter gp.

GrKeyGen(gp) → (gpk, gsk): The GM runs this randomized algorithm on input the group parameter gp and generates the group public key gpk which includes gp and group secret key gsk $=$ (isk, opk) where isk is the issue key and opk is the opening key.

UsKeyGen(gp) → (upk, usk): This is a randomized algorithm run by a user that takes input the group parameter gp and generates its user public key upk and user secret key usk. The user public key upk is published while the user secret key usk is kept secret to the user.

Enroll(gp, gpk, isk, upk, tr) → (cert, w^{escrw}): The GM runs this randomized algorithm taking inputs the group parameter gp, the group public key gpk, a user public key upk, issue key isk and a trace bit tr $\in \{0,1\}$. For tr $= 0$, the anonymity of the user is preserved whereas for tr $= 1$, the user is traceable. Based on the choice of bit tr, the GM produces a certificate cert including upk and witness w^{escrw}. The GM sends the certificate cert to the user and keeps the witness w^{escrw} secret to himself.

Sign(gp, gpk, cert, usk, msg) → σ: This randomized algorithm is executed by a user that takes inputs the group parameter gp, the group public key gpk, a user secret key usk, user certificate cert and generates a signature σ on the message msg.

Verify(gp, gpk, msg, σ) → $\{0,1\}$: Given the group parameter gp, the group public key gpk, a message msg and a signature σ, the verifier runs this deterministic algorithm and outputs 1 if σ is a valid signature on msg, else outputs 0.

Open(gp, gpk, opk, msg, σ) $\rightarrow$ (upk, Prf): This is a deterministic algorithm run by the GM which takes inputs the group parameter gp, the group public key gpk, the opening key opk, a message msg and a signature σ. The algorithm outputs the user public key upk and a proof Prf which ensures that the signature σ on the message msg is indeed generated by the user with public key upk. In case of upk $= \perp$, Prf $= \perp$.

Judge(gp, gpk, msg, σ, (upk, Prf)) $\rightarrow$ \{0, 1\}: This is a deterministic algorithm that takes inputs the group parameter gp, the group public key gpk, a message msg, a signature σ, a user public key upk and a proof Prf and outputs 1 if the proof Prf guarantees that the signature σ on the message msg is indeed generated by the user public key upk, else outputs 0.

Account(gp, gpk, cert, w^{escrw}, tr) $\rightarrow$ \{0, 1\}: This is a deterministic algorithm run by the GM taking inputs the group parameter gp, the group public key gpk, a certificate cert, witness w^{escrw}, trace bit tr and outputs 1 if the witness confirms the choice of tr, else outputs 0.

Correctness. For a traceable user (tr $= 1$), an ATS scheme is said to be correct if for all security parameter λ, all gp $\leftarrow$ Setup(1^λ), all (gpk, gsk) $\leftarrow$ GrKeyGen(gp), all (upk, usk) $\leftarrow$ UsKeyGen(gp), all (cert, w^{escrw}) $\leftarrow$ Enroll(gp, gpk, isk, upk, tr $= 1$), all $\sigma \leftarrow$ Sign(gp, gpk, cert, usk, msg) it must hold that

$$\text{Verify}(gp, gpk, msg, \sigma) = 1$$
$$\text{Judge}(gp, gpk, msg, \sigma, \text{Open}(gp, gpk, opk, msg, \sigma)) = 1$$
$$\text{Account}(gp, gpk, cert, w^{escrw}, 1) = 1$$

For a non-traceable user (tr $= 0$), an ATS scheme is said to be correct if for all security parameter λ, all gp $\leftarrow$ Setup(1^λ), all (gpk, gsk) $\leftarrow$ GrKeyGen(gp), all (upk, usk) $\leftarrow$ UsKeyGen(gp), all (cert, w^{escrw}) $\leftarrow$ Enroll(gp, gpk, isk, upk, tr $= 0$), all $\sigma \leftarrow$ Sign(gp, gpk, cert, usk, msg) it must hold that

$$\text{Verify}(gp, gpk, msg, \sigma) = 1$$
$$\text{Account}(gp, gpk, cert, w^{escrw}, 0) = 1$$

7   Our Accountable Tracing Signature from Isogenies

In this section we show the concrete construction of our ATS-scheme from isogenies. The main ingredients for our ATS scheme are: the CSI-FiSh signature scheme [3], our CSIKOE-512 scheme described in Sect. 5 and a zero-knowledge argument system described in Sect. 2.2.

Setup(1^λ) $\rightarrow$ gp: A trusted authority runs this algorithm on input a security parameter 1^λ and proceeds as follows to generate the group parameter gp.

– Sets the public parameter $pp = (p, \mathfrak{g}, N, E_0, M_C, H_k, H')$ where the parameters are defined exactly as in CSIKOE-512. Additionally, pp also includes a hash functions $H' : \{0, 1\}^* \rightarrow [-(S-1), (S-1)]^t$.

- Samples two elements $[\mathfrak{a}] = [\mathfrak{g}^a]$ and $[\mathfrak{r}] = [\mathfrak{g}^r] \in \mathcal{G}$ for some $a, r \in \mathbb{Z}_N$. Computes the curves $E_1^{(0)} = [a]E_0$ and $E_2^{(0)} = [a + r]E_0$ and sets the public key $\mathsf{pk}^{(0)} = (E_1^{(0)}, E_2^{(0)})$. Generates $crs \leftarrow \Pi.\mathsf{Setup}(1^\lambda)$ (See Sect. 2.2) and finally sets the group parameter $\mathsf{gp} = (pp, \mathsf{pk}^{(0)} = (E_1^{(0)}, E_2^{(0)}), crs)$.

$\mathsf{GrKeyGen}(\mathsf{gp}) \to (\mathsf{gpk}, \mathsf{gsk})$: The GM runs this randomized algorithm to generate the group public key gpk and group secret key gsk in the following manner:

- Extracting $\mathfrak{g}, N, E_0$ from $\mathsf{gp}.pp$, samples $S - 1$ elements $[\mathfrak{m}_i] = [\mathfrak{g}^{m_i}] \in \mathcal{G}$ for some $m_i \in \mathbb{Z}_N$, computes the elliptic curve $E_i = [m_i]E_0$ for $i = 1, \ldots, S - 1$ and sets $vk = \{E_1, \ldots, E_{S-1}\}$.
- Samples two elements $[\mathfrak{b}] = [\mathfrak{g}^b]$ and $[\mathfrak{s}] = [\mathfrak{g}^s] \in \mathcal{G}$ for some $b, s \in \mathbb{Z}_N$, computes the curves $E_1^{(1)} = [b]E_0$ and $E_2^{(1)} = [b + s]E_0$, sets the public key $\mathsf{pk}^{(1)} = (E_1^{(1)}, E_2^{(1)})$ and the secret key $\mathsf{sk}^{(1)} = s$. The GM publishes $\mathsf{gpk} = (\mathsf{gp} = (pp, \mathsf{pk}^{(0)} = (E_1^{(0)}, E_2^{(0)}), crs), vk, \mathsf{pk}^{(1)} = (E_1^{(1)}, E_2^{(1)}))$ and keeps $\mathsf{gsk} = (isk = (m_1, \ldots, m_{S-1}), opk = s)$ secret to himself.

$\mathsf{UsKeyGen}(\mathsf{gp}) \to (\mathsf{upk}, \mathsf{usk})$: This is a randomized algorithm run by a user that takes input the group parameter $\mathsf{gp} = (pp = (p, \mathfrak{g}, N, E_0, M_C, H_k, H'), \mathsf{pk}^{(0)} = (E_1^{(0)}, E_2^{(0)}), crs)$ and generates its user public key upk and user secret key usk.

- Samples $S - 1$ elements $[\mathfrak{n}_i] = [\mathfrak{g}^{n_i}] \in \mathcal{G}$ for some $n_i \in \mathbb{Z}_N$, computes the elliptic curve $E_i' = [n_i]E_0$ for $i = 1, \ldots, S - 1$ where $\mathfrak{g}, N, E_0$ are extracted from $\mathsf{gp}.pp$. Sets $\mathsf{upk} = \{E_1', \ldots, E_{S-1}'\}$ and $\mathsf{usk} = (n_1, \ldots, n_{S-1})$.

$\mathsf{Enroll}(\mathsf{gp}, \mathsf{gpk}, isk, \mathsf{upk}, tr) \to (cert, w^{\mathsf{escrw}})$: The GM runs this algorithm taking inputs the group parameter $\mathsf{gp} = (pp, \mathsf{pk}^{(0)} = (E_1^{(0)}, E_2^{(0)}), crs)$, the group public key $\mathsf{gpk} = (\mathsf{gp}, vk, \mathsf{pk}^{(1)} = (E_1^{(1)}, E_2^{(1)}))$, a user public key $\mathsf{upk} = \{E_1', \ldots, E_{S-1}'\}$, an issue key $isk = (m_1, \ldots, m_{S-1})$ and a value of trace bit $tr \in \{0, 1\}$. He produces a certificate - witness pair $(cert, w^{\mathsf{escrw}})$ to the bit tr as follows:

- Randomizes the public key $\mathsf{pk}^{(tr)} = (E_1^{(tr)}, E_2^{(tr)})$ and generates a new public key epk by sampling $[\mathfrak{r}'] = [\mathfrak{g}^{r'}] \in \mathcal{G}$ for some $r' \in \mathbb{Z}_N$, computing the curves $E_1'^{(tr)} = [r']E_1^{(tr)}$ and $E_2'^{(tr)} = [r']E_2^{(tr)}$ and setting $\mathsf{epk} = (E_1'^{(tr)}, E_2'^{(tr)})$.
- Generates a CSI-FiSh signature σ_{cert} on $\mathsf{upk}\|\mathsf{epk}$ $= E_1'\|\ldots\|E_{S-1}'\|E_1'^{(tr)}\|E_2'^{(tr)}$ using the issue key $isk = (m_1, \ldots, m_{S-1})$ by setting $m_0 \leftarrow 0$, sampling $[\mathfrak{m}_i'] = [\mathfrak{g}^{m_i'}] \in \mathcal{G}$ for some $m_i' \in \mathbb{Z}_N$, computing t commitment elliptic curves $\widehat{E}_i = [m_i']E_0$ for $i = 1, \ldots, t$ and generating the challenge string of length t over $[-(S - 1), (S - 1)]$ as follows:

$$(ch_1, \ldots, ch_t) = H'(\widehat{E}_1\|\cdots\|\widehat{E}_t\|\mathsf{upk}\|\mathsf{epk}).$$

The GM computes the response $z_i = m_i' - \mathsf{sgn}(ch_i)m_{|ch_i|} \pmod{N}$ using issue key isk and sets the signature $\sigma_{\mathsf{cert}} = (ch_1, \ldots, ch_t, z_1, \ldots, z_t)$, where $\mathsf{sgn}(ch_i)$ denotes the sign of ch_i. He finally sends the certificate $cert = (\mathsf{upk} = \{E_1', \ldots, E_{S-1}'\}, \mathsf{epk} = (E_1'^{(tr)}, E_2'^{(tr)}), \sigma_{\mathsf{cert}} = (ch_1, \ldots, ch_t, z_1, \ldots, z_t))$ to the user and keeps secret $w^{\mathsf{escrw}} = r'$.

Sign(gp, gpk, cert, usk, msg) $\to \sigma$: This randomized algorithm is run by a user to generate a signature σ on a message $msg \in \{0,1\}^\lambda$ using the group parameter gp $= (pp = (p, \mathfrak{g}, N, E_0, M_C, H_k, H'), \mathsf{pk}^{(0)} = (E_1^{(0)}, E_2^{(0)}), crs)$, the group public key gpk $= (\mathsf{gp}, vk, \mathsf{pk}^{(1)} = (E_1^{(1)}, E_2^{(1)}))$, a user certificate cert $=$ (upk $= \{E_1', \ldots, E_{S-1}'\}$, epk $= (E_1'^{(\mathsf{tr})}, E_2'^{(\mathsf{tr})})$, $\sigma_{\mathsf{cert}} = (ch_1, \ldots, ch_t, z_1, \ldots, z_t))$ and a user secret key usk $= (n_1, \ldots, n_{S-1})$ in the following manner:

- Samples $S-1$ elements $[\mathfrak{e}_i] = [\mathfrak{g}^{e_i}] \in \mathcal{G}$ for some $e_i \in \mathbb{Z}_N$, computes the elliptic curve $E_i'' = [e_i]E_0$ for $i = 1, 2, \ldots, S-1$ and sets $pk = \{E_1'', \ldots, E_{S-1}''\}$ and $sk = (e_1, \ldots, e_{S-1})$.
- Computes a signature σ_u on the message $pk = \{E_1'', \ldots, E_{S-1}''\}$ using usk $= (n_1, \ldots, n_{S-1})$ as the signing key. For which the user sets $n_0 \leftarrow 0$, samples $[\mathfrak{n}_i'] = [\mathfrak{g}^{n_i'}] \in \mathcal{G}$ for some $n_i' \in \mathbb{Z}_N$, computes t commitment curves $\widetilde{E}_i = [n_i']E_0$, the challenge string of length t over $[-(S-1), (S-1)]$ given by:

$$(ch_1', \ldots, ch_t') = H'(\widetilde{E}_1|| \cdots ||\widetilde{E}_t||pk),$$

the response $z_i' = n_i' - \text{sign}(ch_i') \, n_{|ch_i'|} \pmod{N}$ for $i = 1, \ldots, t$ and sets the signature $\sigma_u = (ch_1', \ldots, ch_t', z_1', \ldots, z_t')$.
- Encrypts the message $\gamma = \text{bin}(M_C(E_1'))|| \cdots ||\text{bin}(M_C(E_{S-1}'))||\text{bin}(ch_1')|| \cdots ||$ $\text{bin}(ch_t')||\text{bin}(z_1')|| \cdots ||\text{bin}(z_t')$ using randomized public key epk $= (E_1'^{(\mathsf{tr})}, E_2'^{(\mathsf{tr})})$ extracted from cert to generate the ciphertext $ct = (ct_1, ct_2)$. For which the user samples $[\mathfrak{q}] = [\mathfrak{g}^q] \in \mathcal{G}$ for some $q \in \mathbb{Z}_N$ and sets $ct_1 = [q]E_1'^{(\mathsf{tr})}$, $ct_2 = H_k(M_C([q]E_2'^{(\mathsf{tr})})) \oplus \gamma$ and the encryption randomness $rand = q$. This encryption is same as the CSIKOE-512 scheme described in Sect. 5.
- Generates a proof $\pi \leftarrow \Pi.\text{Prove}(crs, \text{stmt}, \text{wit})$ (Sect. 2.2) using crs for the following relation $\mathcal{R}$ to prove knowledge of (upk, epk, $\sigma_{\mathsf{cert}}, \sigma_u$) where the statement stmt $= (ct = (ct_1, ct_2), pk = \{E_1'', \ldots, E_{S-1}''\}, vk = \{E_1, \ldots, E_{S-1}\})$ and witness wit $= ($upk $= \{E_1', \ldots, E_{S-1}'\}$, epk $= (E_1'^{(\mathsf{tr})}, E_2'^{(\mathsf{tr})})$, $\sigma_{\mathsf{cert}} = (ch_1, \ldots, ch_t, z_1, \ldots, z_t)$, $\sigma_u = (ch_1', \ldots, ch_t', z_1', \ldots, z_t')$, $rand = q)$. We say that (stmt, wit)$\in \mathcal{R}$ if and only if the following three relations hold:

1. The ciphertext $ct = (ct_1, ct_2)$ must be a correct encryption of message $\gamma = \text{bin}(M_C(E_1'))|| \cdots ||\text{bin}(M_C(E_{S-1}'))||\text{bin}(ch_1')|| \cdots ||\text{bin}(ch_t')||\text{bin}(z_1')|| \cdots ||$ $\text{bin}(z_t')$ under the public key epk with encryption randomness $rand = q$ satisfying:

$$ct_1 = [q]E_1'^{(\mathsf{tr})}, \quad ct_2 = H_k(M_C([q]E_2'^{(\mathsf{tr})})) \oplus \gamma$$

2. The CSI-FiSh signature σ_u on the message pk must be a valid signature under the verification key upk satisfying

$$(ch_1', \ldots, ch_t') = H'(\widetilde{E}_1|| \cdots ||\widetilde{E}_t|| pk)$$

where $\widetilde{E}_i = [n_i']E_0$ is recovered by computing $[z_i']E_{ch_i'}'$ for $i = 1, \ldots, t$.

3. The CSI-FiSh signature σ_{cert} on upk||epk must be a valid signature under the verification key vk satisfying:

$$(ch_1, \ldots, ch_t) = H'(\widehat{E}_1|| \cdots ||\widehat{E}_t||\text{upk}||\text{epk})$$

where $\widehat{E}_i = [m'_i]E_0$ is recovered by computing $[z_i]E_{ch_i}$ for $i = 1, \ldots, t$.

– Generates a CSI-FiSh signature σ_0 on the message $msg \, || \, ct \, || \, pk \, || \, vk \, || \, \pi$, i.e.,

$$msg||ct_1||ct_2||E''_1|| \cdots ||E''_{S-1}||E_1|| \cdots ||E_{S-1}||\pi$$

taking $sk = (e_1, \ldots, e_{S-1})$ as the signing key. For which the user sets $e_0 \leftarrow 0$, samples $[\mathfrak{e}'_i] = [\mathfrak{g}^{e'_i}] \in \mathcal{G}$ for some $e'_i \in \mathbb{Z}_N$. Computes t elliptic curves $\overline{E}_i = [e'_i]E_0$, the challenge string of length t over $[-(S-1), (S-1)]$ given by:

$$(ch''_1, \ldots, ch''_t) = H'(\overline{E}_1|| \cdots ||\overline{E}_t|| msg||ct||pk||vk||\pi)$$

and the response $z''_i = e'_i$ - $\text{sign}(ch''_i) \, e_{| ch''_i |}$ (mod N) for $i = 1, \ldots, t$. Sets the signature $\sigma_0 = (ch''_1, \ldots, ch''_t, z''_1, \ldots, z''_t)$.
– Finally, outputs the signature $\sigma = (\sigma_0, pk, ct = (ct_1, ct_2), \pi)$ on msg.

Verify(gp, gpk, msg, σ) $\rightarrow \{0,1\}$: This is a deterministic algorithm that verifies the signature $\sigma = (\sigma_0 = (ch''_1, \ldots, ch''_t, z''_1, \ldots, z''_t), pk = \{E''_1, \ldots, E''_{S-1}\}, ct = (ct_1, ct_2), \pi)$ on the message $msg \in \{0,1\}^\lambda$ by performing the following steps using the group parameter gp $= (pp, \text{pk}^{(0)} = (E_1^{(0)}, E_2^{(0)}), crs)$ and the group public key gpk $= (\text{gp}, vk, \text{pk}^{(1)} = (E_1^{(1)}, E_2^{(1)}))$.

– Parse $\sigma_0 = (ch''_1, \ldots, ch''_t, z''_1, \ldots, z''_t)$. Defines $E_{-i} = E_i^t$ for $i = 1, \ldots, S-1$, where E_i^t is the twist[1] of the elliptic curve E_i. Recovers t elliptic curves $\overline{E}_i = [z''_i]E_{ch''_i}$ for $i = 1, \ldots, t$. If $(ch''_1, \ldots, ch''_t) = H'(\overline{E}_1|| \cdots ||\overline{E}_t||msg||ct||pk||vk||\pi)$ returns 1, else returns 0.
– Runs Π.Verify(crs, stmt, π) (See Sect. 2.2) taking input the statement stmt $= (ct, pk, vk)$ and crs to verify π, where pk, ct are extracted from σ and vk is obtained from gpk. If all the checks succeed, returns 1, else returns 0.

Open(gp, gpk, opk, msg, σ) $\rightarrow$ (upk, Prf): This is a deterministic algorithm run by the GM which takes inputs the group parameter gp $= (pp, \text{pk}^{(0)} = (E_1^{(0)}, E_2^{(0)}), crs)$, the group public key gpk$= (\text{gp}, vk, \text{pk}^{(1)} = (E_1^{(1)}, E_2^{(1)}))$, the opening key opk $= s$, a message $msg \in \{0,1\}^\lambda$ and a signature $\sigma = (\sigma_0, pk, ct = (ct_1, ct_2), \pi)$ and outputs the user public key upk and a proof Prf in the following manner:

– Runs Verify(gp, gpk, msg, σ) and aborts if it fails.
– Extracts the ciphertext $et = (ct_1, ct_2)$ from the signature σ and recovers the message $\gamma = \text{bin}(M_C(E'_1))|| \cdots ||\text{bin}(M_C(E'_{S-1}))||\text{bin}(ch'_1)|| \cdots ||\text{bin}(ch'_t)||\text{bin}(z'_1)|| \ldots ||\text{bin}(z'_t)$ using the opening key opk $= s$ by evaluating $ct_2 \oplus H_k(M_C([s]ct_1))$ and finally computing upk $= \{E'_1, E'_2, \ldots, E'_{S-1}\}$ and $\sigma_u = (ch'_1, \ldots, ch'_t, z'_1, \ldots, z'_t)$ from γ.

---

[1] The quadratic twist of an elliptic curve $E : y^2 = f(x)$ defined over a field K is given by $E^t : dy^2 = f(x)$ where $d \in K$ has Legendre symbol value -1.

– Outputs $\mathsf{upk} = \{E'_1, \ldots, E'_{S-1}\}$ and $\mathsf{Prf} = \sigma_u$.

$\mathsf{Judge}(\mathsf{gp}, \mathsf{gpk}, \mathsf{upk}, \mathsf{Prf}, msg, \sigma) \to \{0, 1\}$: This is a deterministic algorithm that takes inputs the group parameter $\mathsf{gp} = (pp, \mathsf{pk}^{(0)} = (E_1^{(0)}, E_2^{(0)}), crs)$, the group public key $\mathsf{gpk} = (\mathsf{gp}, vk, \mathsf{pk}^{(1)} = (E_1^{(1)}, E_2^{(1)}))$, a message msg, a signature $\sigma = (\sigma_0, pk, ct = (ct_1, ct_2), \pi)$, a user public key $\mathsf{upk} = \{E'_1, E'_2, \ldots, E'_{S-1}\}$ and a proof $\mathsf{Prf} = \sigma_u$ and outputs 0 or 1 by executing the below steps:

– Runs $\mathsf{Verify}(\mathsf{gp}, \mathsf{gpk}, msg, \sigma)$ and aborts if it fails.
– Parse $\sigma_u = (ch'_1, \ldots, ch'_t, z'_1, \ldots, z'_t)$. Defines $E_{-i} = E_i^t$ for $i = 1, \ldots, S-1$. Recovers t elliptic curves $\widetilde{E}_i = [n'_i]E_0$ by computing $[z'_i]E'_{ch'_i}$ for $i = 1, \ldots, t$. If $(ch'_1, \ldots, ch'_t) = H'(\widetilde{E}_1 || \cdots || \widetilde{E}_t || pk)$ returns 1 or else returns 0.
– If all the checks succeed returns 1, or else returns 0.

$\mathsf{Account}(\mathsf{gp}, \mathsf{gpk}, \mathsf{cert}, w^{\mathsf{escrw}}, \mathsf{tr}) \to \{0, 1\}$: This is a deterministic algorithm run by the GM taking inputs the group parameter $\mathsf{gp} = (pp, \mathsf{pk}^{(0)} = (E_1^{(0)}, E_2^{(0)}), crs)$, the group public key $\mathsf{gpk} = (\mathsf{gp}, vk, \mathsf{pk}^{(1)} = (E_1^{(1)}, E_2^{(1)}))$, a certificate $\mathsf{cert} = (\mathsf{upk} = \{E'_1, \ldots, E'_{S-1}\}, \mathsf{epk} = (E_1'^{(\mathsf{tr})}, E_2'^{(\mathsf{tr})}), \sigma_{\mathsf{cert}} = (ch_1, \ldots, ch_t, z_1, \ldots, z_t))$, witness $w^{\mathsf{escrw}} = r'$, trace bit tr and checks if the equality $([r']E_1^{(\mathsf{tr})}, [r']E_2^{(\mathsf{tr})}) = (E_1'^{(\mathsf{tr})}, E_2'^{(\mathsf{tr})})$ holds. If the verification succeeds return 1, else return 0.

Correctness. The correctness of our ATS scheme is an immediate consequence of the correctness of our CSIKOE-512 scheme, completeness of zero-knowledge argument system and the correctness of the CSI-FiSh signature scheme.

Efficiency. Since our ATS scheme is the first isogeny based accountable tracing signature scheme, we do not compare the efficiency of our scheme with other works. The key and signature size of our scheme grows as S grows and thus it is not very reasonable. But that can be reduced somewhat using the Merkle tree technique and other optimizations stated in [3]. From the efficiency point of view, our ATS scheme is not up to the mark and needs a lot more optimization. However, we believe that it will open avenues for more research in this direction. The following theorem follows from Theorem 12 of [12].

Theorem 9. *Our isogeny-based ATS scheme satisfies anonymity under tracing, traceability, non-frameability, anonymity with accountability and trace-obliviousness in the random oracle model following the security framework of [14] as CSI-FiSh [3] signature scheme is strongly unforgeable under chosen-message attack, CSIKOE-512 scheme (Sect. 5) satisfies KR, INDr and KPr and under the assumption that Π is zero-knowledge simulation-extractable argument system (Sect. 2.2).*

References

1. Abdalla, M., et al.: Searchable encryption revisited: consistency properties, relation to anonymous IBE, and extensions. In: Shoup, V. (ed.) CRYPTO 2005. LNCS, vol. 3621, pp. 205–222. Springer, Heidelberg (2005). https://doi.org/10.1007/11535218_13

2. Bellare, M., Boldyreva, A., Desai, A., Pointcheval, D.: Key-privacy in public-key encryption. In: Boyd, C. (ed.) ASIACRYPT 2001. LNCS, vol. 2248, pp. 566–582. Springer, Heidelberg (2001). https://doi.org/10.1007/3-540-45682-1_33
3. Beullens, W., Kleinjung, T., Vercauteren, F.: CSI-FiSh: efficient isogeny based signatures through class group computations. In: Galbraith, S.D., Moriai, S. (eds.) ASIACRYPT 2019. LNCS, vol. 11921, pp. 227–247. Springer, Cham (2019). https://doi.org/10.1007/978-3-030-34578-5_9
4. Blum, M., De Santis, A., Micali, S., Persiano, G.: Noninteractive zero-knowledge. SIAM J. Comput. **20**(6), 1084–1118 (1991)
5. Bonnetain, X., Schrottenloher, A.: Quantum security analysis of CSIDH. In: Canteaut, A., Ishai, Y. (eds.) EUROCRYPT 2020. LNCS, vol. 12106, pp. 493–522. Springer, Cham (2020). https://doi.org/10.1007/978-3-030-45724-2_17
6. Camenisch, J., Lysyanskaya, A.: An efficient system for non-transferable anonymous credentials with optional anonymity revocation. In: Pfitzmann, B. (ed.) EUROCRYPT 2001. LNCS, vol. 2045, pp. 93–118. Springer, Heidelberg (2001). https://doi.org/10.1007/3-540-44987-6_7
7. Castryck, W., Lange, T., Martindale, C., Panny, L., Renes, J.: CSIDH: an efficient post-quantum commutative group action. In: Peyrin, T., Galbraith, S. (eds.) ASIACRYPT 2018. LNCS, vol. 11274, pp. 395–427. Springer, Cham (2018). https://doi.org/10.1007/978-3-030-03332-3_15
8. Castryck, W., Sotáková, J., Vercauteren, F.: Breaking the decisional Diffie-Hellman problem for class group actions using genus theory. In: Micciancio, D., Ristenpart, T. (eds.) CRYPTO 2020. LNCS, vol. 12171, pp. 92–120. Springer, Cham (2020). https://doi.org/10.1007/978-3-030-56880-1_4
9. De Feo, L.: Mathematics of isogeny based cryptography. arXiv preprint arXiv:1711.04062 (2017)
10. De Feo, L., Galbraith, S.D.: SeaSign: compact isogeny signatures from class group actions. In: Ishai, Y., Rijmen, V. (eds.) EUROCRYPT 2019. LNCS, vol. 11478, pp. 759–789. Springer, Cham (2019). https://doi.org/10.1007/978-3-030-17659-4_26
11. De Feo, L., Meyer, M.: Threshold schemes from isogeny assumptions. IACR Cryptology ePrint Archive **2019**, 1288 (2019)
12. Kohlweiss, M., Miers, I.: Accountable metadata-hiding escrow: a group signature case study. Proc. Privacy Enhancing Technol. **2015**(2), 206–221 (2015)
13. Libert, B., Paterson, K.G., Quaglia, E.A.: Anonymous broadcast encryption: adaptive security and efficient constructions in the standard model. In: Fischlin, M., Buchmann, J., Manulis, M. (eds.) PKC 2012. LNCS, vol. 7293, pp. 206–224. Springer, Heidelberg (2012). https://doi.org/10.1007/978-3-642-30057-8_13
14. Ling, S., Nguyen, K., Wang, H., Xu, Y.: Accountable tracing signatures from lattices. In: Matsui, M. (ed.) CT-RSA 2019. LNCS, vol. 11405, pp. 556–576. Springer, Cham (2019). https://doi.org/10.1007/978-3-030-12612-4_28
15. Moriya, T., Onuki, H., Takagi, T.: SiGamal: a supersingular isogeny-based PKE and its application to a PRF. In: Moriai, S., Wang, H. (eds.) ASIACRYPT 2020. LNCS, vol. 12492, pp. 551–580. Springer, Cham (2020). https://doi.org/10.1007/978-3-030-64834-3_19
16. Peikert, C.: He gives C-Sieves on the CSIDH. In: Canteaut, A., Ishai, Y. (eds.) EUROCRYPT 2020. LNCS, vol. 12106, pp. 463–492. Springer, Cham (2020). https://doi.org/10.1007/978-3-030-45724-2_16
17. Sako, K.: An auction protocol which hides bids of losers. In: Imai, H., Zheng, Y. (eds.) PKC 2000. LNCS, vol. 1751, pp. 422–432. Springer, Heidelberg (2000). https://doi.org/10.1007/978-3-540-46588-1_28

18. Shor, P.W.: Polynomial-time algorithms for prime factorization and discrete logarithms on a quantum computer. SIAM Rev. **41**(2), 303–332 (1999)
19. Silverman, J.H.: The Arithmetic of Elliptic Curves. GTM, vol. 106. Springer, New York (2009). https://doi.org/10.1007/978-0-387-09494-6
20. Vélu, J.: Isogénies entre courbes elliptiques. CR Acad. Sci. Paris, Séries A **273**, 305–347 (1971)
21. Waterhouse, W.C.: Abelian varieties over finite fields. In: Annales scientifiques de l'École Normale Supérieure, vol. 2, pp. 521–560 (1969)

Identity-Based Signature and Extended Forking Algorithm in the Multivariate Quadratic Setting

Sanjit Chatterjee, Akansha Dimri, and Tapas Pandit[✉]

Department of Computer Science and Automation, Indian Institute of Science,
Bangalore, India
{sanjit,akanshadimri,tapas}@iisc.ac.in

Abstract. We propose a provably secure Identity-Based Signature (IBS) scheme in the multivariate quadratic (MQ) setting. Our construction utilizes the 3-pass identification scheme (IDS) and salted-UOV scheme (of Sakumoto et al. Crypto 2011, PQCrypto 2011). The main technical tool in our security reduction is a further generalization of the Forking Lemma of Bellare and Neven (CCS 2006). The forking algorithm of Bellare-Neven cannot be directly applied to our context, as it requires simulating two random oracles one of which needs to be suitably programmed to embed the challenge supplied in the problem instance. Our formulation of forking algorithm involves an encoding technique that satisfies all the requirements of the security reduction. To the best of our knowledge, the algorithm introduced here is the first formulation of forking in a nonlinear setting. This abstraction is likely of independent interest, particularly to argue security of signature schemes in the MQ-setting.

Keywords: Identity-based signature · Multivariate cryptography · Forking algorithm · Post-quantum security

1 Introduction

In 1984, Shamir [Sha84] in his landmark paper introduced the concept of ID-based cryptography as an alternative to the complex certificate management process of public key infrastructure. In the same work, he proposed an Identity-Based Signature (IBS) scheme in the RSA setting. Since then several concrete IBS schemes have been proposed in various other settings such as discrete-log and pairing [Hes02, Pat02, CC03]. Such IBS schemes find application in practical cryptosystems such as in MANET [KCC05].

In [BNN04, BNN09], Bellare et al. proposed two generic constructions of IBS. Their certificate-based IBS utilizes a base signature scheme (SS) at two levels. During key-generation for an identity id, a random key-pair $(\mathsf{pk}, \mathsf{sk})$ of SS is chosen and a signature σ_{id} is generated on $(\mathsf{pk}, \mathsf{id})$ using the private key generator's master secret key for the same SS and the user is issued the key $\mathsf{sk}_{\mathsf{id}} = \mathsf{sk}$ and

© Springer Nature Switzerland AG 2021
A. Adhikari et al. (Eds.): INDOCRYPT 2021, LNCS 13143, pp. 387–412, 2021.
https://doi.org/10.1007/978-3-030-92518-5_18

a certificate $\mathsf{cert_{id}} = (\sigma_{id}, \mathsf{pk})$. A signature in IBS scheme on (M, id) has two components, a signature on M generated using $\mathsf{sk_{id}}$ and the certificate $\mathsf{cert_{id}}$.

Their second construction uses a standard identification (SI) (along with trapdoor sampleable relation (TSR)) and works in two steps. First, convert (SI, TSR) to an identity-based identification (IBI) and then convert it to an IBS through Fiat-Shamir transformation [FS86]. In two-step reduction, they showed that their IBS is EUF-CMA secure in the random oracle model, provided the underlying SI and TSR satisfy certain security properties (see Corollary 4.10 in [BNN09]). The paper also describes several instantiations of their frameworks while noting that not all identification schemes are amenable to their framework, Schnorr identification [Sch89] being one such prominent example.

We are interested in the question of constructing provably secure IBS in the post-quantum setting, where the hash functions will be treated as classical random oracles. Unlike the traditional (or classical) setting like RSA or discrete-logarithm, the cryptosystems in the post-quantum setting such as lattices, codes, multivariate-quadratic (MQ) polynomials etc., are expected to be secure against both classical and quantum adversaries. Recently, signature schemes in the multi-variate quadratic setting have gained a lot of attention in the crypto community. In fact, four multivariate signatures Rainbow, LUOV, GeMSS and MQDSS were shortlisted for the second round of evaluation for NIST standardization project [NIS19] of which Rainbow is one of the finalists while GeMSS is being considered as an alternative candidate [NIS20].

Shen et al. [STX13] were the first to propose an IBS in the MQ-setting. Their construction is nothing but a concrete instantiation of the certificate-based IBS of Bellare et al. [BNN09] mentioned earlier. They suggested UOV [KPG99] as the base signature scheme. As noted by Lyuen [Luy19], the UOV considered in their proposal is not known to be provably secure, so the security of the IBS cannot be formally argued. The same paper [Luy19] proposed a provably secure Rainbow as the base SS in a similar certificate-based IBS construction. A limitation of this proposal is that the final signature contains the Rainbow public-key which is quite large.

In [CLND19], the authors proposed an IBS from Rainbow using a new technique. At high-level, their construction works as follows. The pp and msk of their IBS are the Rainbow public-key and secret key respectively. Note that in general, the underlying polynomials of the key-pair are expressed by some collection of coefficients (basically constants) over a field $\mathbb{F}$. But, in this proposal, the authors considered the coefficients of each polynomial in pp and msk to be linear functions in $\mathsf{id} = (z_1, \cdots, z_d) \in \mathbb{F}^d$ for some integer $d > 0$. For an identity id, the key $\mathsf{sk_{id}}$ is extracted by evaluating each polynomial in msk at id. In addition, some randomly chosen matrices have to be properly embedded in the key structure to prevent trivial attacks. Their scheme is very efficient, in fact, the size of the signature is the same as that of Rainbow. However, we noticed an issue in the correctness of their proposal, namely, the affine transformations involved in $\mathsf{sk_{id}}$ cannot be guaranteed to be invertible. Further, the proposal does not have any formal security reduction.

Our Result. In this paper, we construct a provably secure IBS scheme in the MQ-setting. In order to argue its security, we propose a novel extension of the General Forking Lemma of Bellare-Neven [BN06]. The extended Forking Lemma proposed here is likely to find further applications in the MQ-setting.

The main building blocks of our IBS are a 3-pass identification scheme proposed in [SSH11b] and a salted version of UOV signature scheme proposed in [SSH11a] along with the Fiat-Shamir transformation (in short, FST) [FS86]. At a high level, it works as follows.

- The secret key sk_{id} for an identity id is generated by running the sign algorithm of the salted-UOV on id. Here sk_{id} has the form (x, s) such that $\mathcal{P}(x) = \omega$, where $\mathcal{P} : \mathbb{F}^n \to \mathbb{F}^m$ is the UOV-public map, $\omega = \mathcal{H}(id, s)$, $\mathcal{H}$ is a cryptographic hash function and, s is called salt.
- The IBS signature on (M, id) is generated by running r-parallel rounds of the underlying 3-pass IDS (which we refer to as IDS^r) using $(x, (\mathcal{P}, \omega))$ as key-pair followed by FST which essentially commits M.

We note that the generic framework of [BNN09] is not directly applicable on the building blocks of the IBS proposed here. Also, there are two subtle structural differences with our construction. The first one is that in [BNN09], no salt is involved in the computation of ω and the second one is that we consider nested hashing, i.e., first, we compute $\omega = \mathcal{H}(id, s)$ and then compute the challenge as a hash of (M, ω, ct), instead of (id, M, ct), where ct is the commitment used in the underlying SI. The rationale for these differences will be clearer in our security proof. Also see Sect. 4 where we further comment on the differences with the generic framework of [BNN09].

The sizes of the public parameters pp and master secret key msk of the IBS are the same as the public-key pk and secret key sk of the underlying UOV-scheme respectively. For an identity id, the size of its secret key sk_{id} is the same as that of salted-UOV [SSH11a]. The signature size of the IBS is roughly the same as that of the 3-pass version of MQDSS [CHR+16].

The security of our IBS is argued in a modular fashion. First, we show a reduction of *existential unforgeability under no-message attack* (EUF-NMA) security without giving access to the key-extraction and signature oracle. We then show how to simulate the key-extraction queries by manipulating the random oracle involved in the salted-UOV. Finally, we give a reduction of EUF-CMA security by showing how to simulate the signature queries. This step involves a novel application of partitioning technique originally introduced in [Cor00] to consistently respond to the signature queries.

The first reduction is the most technically involved one and requires running the adversary multiple times on related inputs. This technique, called rewinding the adversary, was originally introduced in [PS96] to argue security of discrete log based (blind) signature schemes. In [BN06], Bellare and Neven proposed an abstraction of rewinding in the form of a general forking algorithm. Informally speaking, the forking algorithm supplies the problem instance to a wrapper algorithm as input along with a set of random values. The wrapper, in turn, runs the adversary using the problem instance to construct the public key of the underlying signature scheme while the supplied random values serve to simulate the random oracle.

However, the forking algorithm as abstracted by Bellare and Neven (or, for that matter, the rewinding strategy of [PS96]) cannot be directly applied in our context. The main reason for that is, unlike [BN06], we have to simulate two random oracles and one of them needs to be appropriately programmed to embed the challenge supplied as part of the MQ-problem instance. Also, the forking algorithm of [BN06] models rewinding the adversary once while we need to rewind the adversary twice. We, therefore, need to extend the original forking algorithm and related analysis of [BN06].

Firstly, we introduce an appropriate encoding technique which enables our wrapper algorithm to answer both types of random oracle queries made by the adversary using only a single set of random values. The encoding technique essentially involves some functions that map from a common index set to the ranges of the respective hash functions and satisfy regularity, thereby ensuring the uniformity in the random oracle outputs. In addition, the encoding also ensures that the random oracles can be programmed at any suitable index, if necessary.

Secondly, we partition the problem instance into two parts, $(\mathsf{inst}_1, \mathsf{inst}_2)$, where inst_1 corresponds to the underlying one-way function and inst_2 to the given target that needs to be inverted under inst_1. We use inst_2 in programming of the random oracles via the corresponding encoding function. Further, we use the trick of nested hashing mentioned earlier in the context of our scheme design to ensure that the hash value programmed by inst_2 is not modified in the process of rewinding the adversary.

In the MQ-setting, there are a few schemes, e.g., [PBB13, CHR+16] that claimed to invoke the rewinding style argument of [PS96] without providing any details. The security reduction of 5-pass MQDSS [CHR+16] includes an application of the original Pointcheval-Stern rewinding technique [PS96]. That reduction considers rewinding the adversary thrice, but neither does it involve more than one random oracle nor is there any need to embed the problem instance in the random oracle response.

All the exiting results that we are aware of which either use the forking algorithm of Bellare-Neven [BN06] or generalize it as in [HKL19] have implicitly or explicitly considered the setting of linear functions like RSA or discrete log. To the best of our knowledge, the extended forking algorithm introduced here is the first abstraction of general forking in a non-linear setting. This abstraction is likely to find other applications, for example to argue security of blind signature in the MQ-setting.

2   Preliminaries

The basic notations, the background of multivariate quadratic polynomials and some hardness assumptions are defined in this section. The syntax and security definitions of IBS and 3-pass IDS are also provided in this section. Further, the 3-pass IDS of [SSH11b] and related results are reproduced here.

2.1   Notations and Background

Notations. For a set S, the notation $x \xleftarrow{\$} S$ denotes that x is drawn uniformly at random from S. For an algorithm A and its input x, the notation $y \xleftarrow{\$} A(x)$ denotes that when A is run on x, it chooses its internal coin ρ uniformly at random from the coin space Λ and outputs y. This essentially says that A is a randomized algorithm. When ρ is supplied to A in addition to x, then A will behave deterministically and will be denoted by $y \longleftarrow A(x; \rho)$. For $a, b \in \mathbb{N} \cup \{0\}$, define $[a, b] = \{x \in \mathbb{N} \cup \{0\} : a \le x \le b\}$ and when $b \in \mathbb{N}$, define $[b] = [1, b]$.

Multivariate Quadratic Polynomials. Let v, m and n be three positive integers with $n = v + m$ and let these integers be called the number of vinegar variables, the number of oil variables and the total number of variables respectively. Without loss of generality, we assume that out of n variables, the first v variables are vinegar variables and the remaining m variables are oil variables. If $\boldsymbol{x} = (x_1, \dots, x_v, x_{v+1}, \dots, x_{v+m})$, then we write $\boldsymbol{x} = (\boldsymbol{x}_v, \boldsymbol{x}_o)$, where $\boldsymbol{x}_v = (x_1, \dots, x_v)$ and $\boldsymbol{x}_o = (x_{v+1}, \dots, x_{v+m})$. The same integer m also represents the number of polynomials in the context of system of equations.

By a quadratic polynomial map $\mathcal{F} : \mathbb{F}^n \to \mathbb{F}^m$ of *oil-vinegar* type, we mean $\mathcal{F} = (f^{(1)}, \dots, f^{(m)})$ and each $f^{(k)} : \mathbb{F}^n \to \mathbb{F}$ is a quadratic polynomial of oil-vinegar type, i.e., of the form:

$$f^{(k)}(x_1, \dots, x_n) = \sum_{i=1}^{v} \sum_{j=i}^{n} \alpha_{ij}^{(k)} \cdot x_i x_j + \sum_{i=1}^{n} \beta_i^{(k)} \cdot x_i + \gamma^{(k)} \tag{1}$$

where $\mathbb{F}$ is a field and $\alpha_{ij}^{(k)}, \beta_i^{(k)}, \gamma^{(k)} \in \mathbb{F}$ for $k \in [m]$. The above map $\mathcal{F} : \mathbb{F}^n \to \mathbb{F}^m$ is called the central map of oil-vinegar type. When $v \approx 2 \cdot m$, then $f^{(i)}$ would be called quadratic map of *unbalanced oil-vinegar* (UOV) type [KPG99] and $\mathcal{F} : \mathbb{F}^n \to \mathbb{F}^m$ would be called the central map of UOV-type.

By invertible affine map, we mean $\mathcal{T} = (A, \boldsymbol{a}) \in \mathsf{GL}_n(\mathbb{F}) \times \mathbb{F}^n$, where $\mathsf{GL}_n(\mathbb{F})$ denotes the set of all $n \times n$ non-singular matrices over $\mathbb{F}$. For $\boldsymbol{x} \in \mathbb{F}^n$, define $\mathcal{T}(\boldsymbol{x}) := A\boldsymbol{x} + \boldsymbol{a}$. So, $\mathcal{T}$ is a map from $\mathbb{F}^n$ onto $\mathbb{F}^n$. We use the notation $\mathsf{invAff}(\mathbb{F}^n, \mathbb{F}^n)$ to denote the set of all affine invertible maps from $\mathbb{F}^n$ onto $\mathbb{F}^n$.

Let $\mathcal{F}_{\mathsf{uov}}(\mathbb{F}^n, \mathbb{F}^m)$ be the collection of all quadratic polynomial maps $\mathcal{F} : \mathbb{F}^n \to \mathbb{F}^m$ of UOV-type. Define $\mathcal{P}_{\mathsf{uov}}(\mathbb{F}^n, \mathbb{F}^m) = \{\mathcal{F} \circ \mathcal{T} : \mathcal{F} \in \mathcal{F}_{\mathsf{uov}}(\mathbb{F}^n, \mathbb{F}^m) \wedge \mathcal{T} \in \mathsf{invAff}(\mathbb{F}^n, \mathbb{F}^n)\}$. Let $\mathcal{P}(\mathbb{F}^n, \mathbb{F}^m)$ be the collection of all quadratic polynomial maps $\mathcal{P} : \mathbb{F}^n \to \mathbb{F}^m$. Obviously, $\mathcal{P}_{\mathsf{uov}}(\mathbb{F}^n, \mathbb{F}^m)$ is a subset of $\mathcal{P}(\mathbb{F}^n, \mathbb{F}^m)$.

For a quadratic map $\mathcal{P} : \mathbb{F}^n \to \mathbb{F}^m$, its polar form $\mathsf{G} : \mathbb{F}^n \times \mathbb{F}^n \to \mathbb{F}^m$ is defined by

$$\mathsf{G}(\boldsymbol{x}, \boldsymbol{y}) = \mathcal{P}(\boldsymbol{x} + \boldsymbol{y}) - \mathcal{P}(\boldsymbol{x}) - \mathcal{P}(\boldsymbol{y}) + \mathcal{P}(\boldsymbol{0})$$

where $\boldsymbol{x}, \boldsymbol{y} \in \mathbb{F}^n$. One can easily show that it is a bilinear map in each variable.

The signature scheme based on UOV central map (called UOV-signature) was studied in [KPG99]. But, no formal security proof was known until the work of [SSH11a]. The main difficulty is perhaps non-uniformity of output signatures. In [SSH11a], Sakumoto et al. considered a random salt in the signing process to make the output signature uniform and then argued the security following the FDH-style [BR93] of security reduction.

2.2   Hardness Assumption

The multivariate quadratic (MQ)-problem is one of the central problems in multivariate public-key cryptography and proven to be NP-hard. Further, it is widely believed that solving random instances of the MQ-problem (with $m \approx n$) is a hard task. Note that the security parameter κ defines several sets of parameters consisting of the number of variables, the number of equations and the size of the underlying field. Let (n, m, q) be one such set of parameters. For simplicity of the security reduction, we assume that security parameter κ uniquely defines the corresponding parameter set. For ease of exposition, we may drop κ from the following hardness assumptions.

Definition 1 (MQ-problem [SSH11b]).   *Given* $(\mathcal{P}, \boldsymbol{y}^*) \in \mathcal{P}(\mathbb{F}^n, \mathbb{F}^m) \times \mathbb{F}^m$, *find an* $\boldsymbol{x}^* \in \mathbb{F}^n$ *such that* $\boldsymbol{y}^* = \mathcal{P}(\boldsymbol{x}^*)$. *The advantage* $\mathsf{Adv}_{\mathcal{A}}^{\mathrm{MQ}}(\kappa)$ *of an algorithm* $\mathcal{A}$ *in breaking the MQ-problem is defined by*

$$\Pr\left[\mathcal{P}(\boldsymbol{x}^*) = \boldsymbol{y}^* : \; (\mathcal{P}, \boldsymbol{y}^*) \xleftarrow{\$} \mathcal{P}(\mathbb{F}^n, \mathbb{F}^m) \times \mathbb{F}^m; \; \boldsymbol{x}^* \leftarrow \mathcal{A}(\mathcal{P}, \boldsymbol{y}^*)\right].$$

We say the MQ-problem is intractable, if for every quantum PPT algorithm $\mathcal{A}$, *the advantage* $\mathsf{Adv}_{\mathcal{A}}^{\mathrm{MQ}}(\kappa)$ *is a negligible function in* κ.

Now, consider a special case of the MQ-problem which we call the WMQ-problem. The authors [SSH11a] considered this problem for proving security of their salted version of UOV-signature.

Definition 2 (WMQ-problem [SSH11a]).   *Given* $(\mathcal{P}, \boldsymbol{y}^*) \in \mathcal{P}_{\mathsf{uov}}(\mathbb{F}^n, \mathbb{F}^m) \times \mathbb{F}^m$, *find an* $\boldsymbol{x}^* \in \mathbb{F}^n$ *such that* $\boldsymbol{y}^* = \mathcal{P}(\boldsymbol{x}^*)$. *The advantage* $\mathsf{Adv}_{\mathcal{A}}^{\mathrm{WMQ}}(\kappa)$ *of an algorithm* $\mathcal{A}$ *in breaking the WMQ-problem is defined by*

$$\Pr\left[\mathcal{P}(\boldsymbol{x}^*) = \boldsymbol{y}^* : \; (\mathcal{P}, \boldsymbol{y}^*) \xleftarrow{\$} \mathcal{P}_{\mathsf{uov}}(\mathbb{F}^n, \mathbb{F}^m) \times \mathbb{F}^m; \; \boldsymbol{x}^* \leftarrow \mathcal{A}(\mathcal{P}, \boldsymbol{y}^*)\right].$$

We say the WMQ-problem is intractable if for every quantum PPT algorithm $\mathcal{A}$, *the advantage* $\mathsf{Adv}_{\mathcal{A}}^{\mathrm{WMQ}}(\kappa)$ *is a negligible function in* κ.

Let us fix the parameter set and the underlying field $\mathbb{F}$ of the WMQ-problem to be (n, m, q) and $\mathbb{F}$ respectively. This means, all the instances of the problem will have the same parameter set and the underlying field as above. Following Definition 2, we can express any instance $(\mathcal{P}, \boldsymbol{y}^*)$ of the problem into two parts, viz., the one-way function $\mathcal{P}$ and the target $\boldsymbol{y}^* \in \mathbb{F}^m$. Let Wmq denote the set of all instances of the WMQ-problem. Then, we can always write Wmq as $\mathsf{Wmq}_1 \times \mathsf{Wmq}_2$, and a random instance inst of the WMQ-problem can be written as $(\mathsf{inst}_1, \mathsf{inst}_2)$, where inst_1 and inst_2 are uniformly distributed over Wmq_1 and Wmq_2 respectively. Notice that here $\mathsf{Wmq}_2 = \mathbb{F}^m$.

2.3   Commitment and IBS Schemes

A non-interactive commitment scheme has three PPT algorithms - CSetup, Commit and Open. CSetup generates a public commitment key ck, Commit on input (ck, M) returns a commitment-decommitment pair (ct, dct) and Open outputs M on input (ck, ct, dct). If the randomness τ used in Commit is supplied from outside, we can write $(ct, dct) \longleftarrow$ Commit$(ck, M; \tau)$. In our construction, we do not use Open, rather given (ct, M, τ), we simply check whether ct $\overset{?}{=}$ Commit$(ck, M; \tau)$. Further, throughout this paper, we neither explicitly mention ck nor the random coin τ as part of the input of Commit.

Definition 3 (IBS Scheme). *It consists of four PPT algorithms - IBS.Setup, IBS.KeyGen, IBS.Sign and IBS.Ver.*

- IBS.Setup: *It takes as input a security parameter κ and outputs public parameters and master secret key pair (pp, msk).*
- IBS.KeyGen: *It takes as input public parameters pp, master secret key msk and an identity id $\in \mathcal{ID}$, where $\mathcal{ID}$ is the identity space, and outputs a signing key sk_{id}.*
- IBS.Sign: *It takes as input public parameters pp, a message $M \in \mathcal{M}$, where $\mathcal{M}$ is the message space, and a secret key sk_{id} and outputs a signature σ.*
- IBS.Ver: *It takes as input public parameters pp, a message M, a signature σ and an identity id. It outputs a value 1, if σ is a valid signature for (M, id), else it outputs 0.*

Correctness: For all $(pp, msk) \overset{\$}{\longleftarrow}$ IBS.Setup(1^κ), for all id $\in \mathcal{ID}$, $sk_{id} \overset{\$}{\longleftarrow}$ IBS.KeyGen(pp, msk, id) and for all $M \in \mathcal{M}$, it is required that

$$\mathsf{IBS.Ver}(pp, M, \mathsf{IBS.Sign}(pp, M, sk_{id}), id) = 1.$$

Next, we define a security notion of IBS against adaptive identity existential unforgeability under chosen-key attack (CKA) and chosen-message attack (CMA). In the literature [BNN04], this security notion is often referred to as EUF-CMA. Formally, it is defined as follows.

Definition 4 (EUF-CMA). *An IBS scheme is said to be EUF-CMA secure, if for all PPT algorithms $\mathcal{A}$, the advantage*

$$\mathsf{Adv}_{\mathcal{A}}^{\mathrm{EUF\text{-}CMA}}(\kappa) := \Pr\left[\mathsf{Exp}_{\mathcal{A}}^{\mathrm{EUF\text{-}CMA}}(\kappa) = 1\right]$$

in $\mathsf{Exp}_{\mathcal{A}}^{\mathrm{EUF\text{-}CMA}}(\kappa)$ defined in Fig. 1 is a negligible function in κ, where $\mathcal{A}$ is provided access to signature oracle $\mathcal{O}_{\mathsf{Sign}}$ and key-gen oracle $\mathcal{O}_{\mathsf{Key}}$ at most polynomial number of times, and Q_{key} is the set of identities on which key-gen queries were made and Q_{sign} is the set of message-identity pairs on which signature queries were made.

$\mathsf{Exp}_{\mathcal{A}}^{\text{EUF-CMA}}(\kappa):$

1. $(\mathsf{pp}, \mathsf{msk}) \xleftarrow{\$} \mathsf{IBS.Setup}(1^{\kappa})$
2. $(M^*, \mathsf{id}^*, \sigma^*) \longleftarrow \mathcal{A}^{\{\mathcal{O}_{\text{Key}}, \mathcal{O}_{\text{Sign}}\}}(\mathsf{pp})$
3. return 0, if $\mathsf{id}^* \in \mathsf{Q}_{\text{key}}$ or $(M^*, \mathsf{id}^*) \in \mathsf{Q}_{\text{sign}}$ or $\mathsf{IBS.Ver}(\mathsf{pp}, M^*, \sigma^*, \mathsf{id}^*) = 0$
4. return 1

Fig. 1. Experiments for EUF-CMA of IBS scheme

2.4 Identification Scheme

For the abstract definition of identification scheme (IDS), knowledge error and statistical honest verifier zero-knowledge (HVZK), the reader may consult [CHR+16]. In general for practical use of IDS, we want the knowledge error μ to be $\mathsf{negl}(\kappa)$. If μ is non-negligible in κ, then by running IDS r-times in parallel (denoted by IDS^r), we can make the knowledge error to be μ^r, which is negligible by considering r sufficiently large.

Definition 5 (3-Pass IDS). *A canonical three pass identification scheme (3-pass IDS) consists of three PPT algorithms - KeyGen, P and V together with a challenge space* ChS.

- KeyGen: *It takes as input a security parameter κ and outputs a public and private key pair* $(\mathsf{pk}, \mathsf{sk})$.
- Identification: *The execution of* $P(\mathsf{pk}, \mathsf{sk})$ *and* $V(\mathsf{pk})$ *is illustrated in the following order.*
  1. *The prover* P *first sends a commitment* ct *to* V.
  2. *The verifier* V *then picks* ch $\xleftarrow{\$}$ ChS *and sends it to* P.
  3. *In the final pass,* P *sends a response* rs *to* V.
  4. *Finally,* V *decides to accept or reject based on* pk *and* π, *where* $\pi = (\mathsf{ct}, \mathsf{ch}, \mathsf{rs})$ *is called transcript.*

Remark 1. We often refer to sk and pk as witness and statement respectively. Note that for a statement, there could be more than one witness.

Definition 6 (3-Special Soundness). *A 3-pass identification scheme* $\mathsf{IDS} = (\mathsf{KeyGen}, \mathsf{P}, \mathsf{V})$ *with* $|\mathsf{ChS}| \geq 3$ *and public-key* pk *is said to satisfy 3-special soundness, if there exists an extractor* Extr *such that given any three accepted transcripts of the form* $\pi = (\mathsf{ct}, \mathsf{ch}, \mathsf{rs})$, $\pi' = (\mathsf{ct}, \mathsf{ch}', \mathsf{rs}')$ *and* $\pi'' = (\mathsf{ct}, \mathsf{ch}'', \mathsf{rs}'')$ *with* $\mathsf{ch} \neq \mathsf{ch}' \neq \mathsf{ch}'' \neq \mathsf{ch}$, *it can efficiently compute a witness* sk.

2.5 3-Pass IDS of Sakumoto et al.

Described here is the 3-pass identification scheme of Sakumoto et al. [SSH11b]. Choose $(\mathcal{P}, s) \xleftarrow{\$} \mathcal{P}(\mathbb{F}^n, \mathbb{F}^m) \times \mathbb{F}^n$ and set $v = \mathcal{P}(s)$. The public key and secret

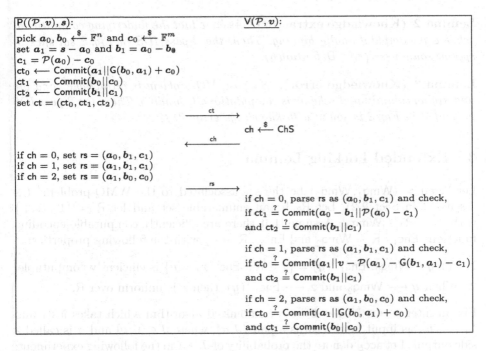

$P((\mathcal{P}, v), s)$:

pick $a_0, b_0 \xleftarrow{\$} \mathbb{F}^n$ and $c_0 \xleftarrow{\$} \mathbb{F}^m$
set $a_1 = s - a_0$ and $b_1 = a_0 - b_0$
$c_1 = \mathcal{P}(a_0) - c_0$
$ct_0 \longleftarrow \mathsf{Commit}(a_1 || G(b_0, a_1) + c_0)$
$ct_1 \longleftarrow \mathsf{Commit}(b_0 || c_0)$
$ct_2 \longleftarrow \mathsf{Commit}(b_1 || c_1)$
set $ct = (ct_0, ct_1, ct_2)$

$\xrightarrow{\quad ct \quad}$

$V(\mathcal{P}, v)$:

$ch \xleftarrow{\$} \mathsf{ChS}$

$\xleftarrow{\quad ch \quad}$

if $ch = 0$, set $rs = (a_0, b_1, c_1)$
if $ch = 1$, set $rs = (a_1, b_1, c_1)$
if $ch = 2$, set $rs = (a_1, b_0, c_0)$

$\xrightarrow{\quad rs \quad}$

if $ch = 0$, parse rs as (a_0, b_1, c_1) and check,
  if $ct_1 \stackrel{?}{=} \mathsf{Commit}(a_0 - b_1 || \mathcal{P}(a_0) - c_1)$
  and $ct_2 \stackrel{?}{=} \mathsf{Commit}(b_1 || c_1)$

if $ch = 1$, parse rs as (a_1, b_1, c_1) and check,
  if $ct_0 \stackrel{?}{=} \mathsf{Commit}(a_1 || v - \mathcal{P}(a_1) - G(b_1, a_1) - c_1)$
  and $ct_2 \stackrel{?}{=} \mathsf{Commit}(b_1 || c_1)$

if $ch = 2$, parse rs as (a_1, b_0, c_0) and check,
  if $ct_0 \stackrel{?}{=} \mathsf{Commit}(a_1 || G(b_0, a_1) + c_0)$
  and $ct_1 \stackrel{?}{=} \mathsf{Commit}(b_0 || c_0)$

Fig. 2. Illustration of 3-pass IDS of Sakumoto et al. [SSH11b].

key pair is given by $pk = (\mathcal{P}, v)$ and $sk = s$. Let $G : \mathbb{F}^n \times \mathbb{F}^n \to \mathbb{F}^m$ be the polar form of $\mathcal{P}$ and let $\mathsf{ChS} = \{0, 1, 2\}$. The interaction between a prover P and V is shown in Fig. 2.

The following three lemmas play a crucial role in the formal security argument of our IBS (see Lemmas 5, 6 and 7). The proofs of Lemmas 2 and 3 more or less follow [SSH11b] and are omitted from here due to space constraints.

Lemma 1 (Statistical HVZK). *The above 3-pass IDS is statistical HVZK, if the underlying commitment scheme has statistical hiding property.*

Proof. First, notice that whatever be the challenge $ch \in \mathsf{ChS}$, the components involved in the corresponding response rs are always uniformly distributed over their respective domains. We construct a PPT simulator Simu which generates proofs as follows. It chooses $ch \xleftarrow{\$} \mathsf{ChS}$ and a fake secret $s' \in \mathbb{F}^n$. Then, $ct = (ct_0, ct_1, ct_2)$ and rs are generated exactly in similar manner as in the original execution (but using the fake secret s') except, when $ch = 1$. If $ch = 1$, then ct_1 is computed as it is computed during verification, i.e., $ct_1 = \mathsf{Commit}(a_1 || v - \mathcal{P}(a_1) - G(b_1, a_1) - c_1)$. Since, the underlying commitment scheme is statistical hiding, so ct does not leak any information related to the fake secret s' and the corresponding response rs. Therefore, the original proof and the simulated proof are indistinguishable from any adversary.

Lemma 2 (Knowledge extractor). *Assume that the underlying commitment scheme is computationally binding. Then, the 3-pass IDS in Fig. 2 satisfies 3-special soundness (c.f., Definition 6).*

Lemma 3 (Knowledge error). *Suppose MQ-problem is intractable[1] and the underlying commitment scheme is computationally binding. Then, the 3-pass IDS presented in Fig. 2 is sound with knowledge error 2/3.*

3   Extended Forking Lemma

Let $\mathsf{Wmq} = (\mathsf{Wmq}_1, \mathsf{Wmq}_2)$ be the set associated to the WMQ-problem[2] (as discussed in Sect. 2.2). Let R_2 be an enumerable set and let $\mathsf{R} = \{1, \ldots, \varphi\}$ with $\varphi = |\mathsf{R}_2| \cdot |\mathsf{Wmq}_2|$. Assume that there are efficiently computable encoding functions $\mathsf{Enc}_1 : \mathsf{R} \to \mathsf{Wmq}_2$ and $\mathsf{Enc}_2 : \mathsf{R} \to \mathsf{R}_2$ with the following properties:

1. For $\boldsymbol{y} \in \mathsf{Wmq}_2$, $\mathsf{Enc}_1^{-1}(\boldsymbol{y}) = \{x \in \mathsf{R} : \mathsf{Enc}_1(x) = \boldsymbol{y}\}$ is efficiently computable.
2. When $\boldsymbol{y} \xleftarrow{\$} \mathsf{Wmq}_2$ and $x \xleftarrow{\$} \mathsf{Enc}_1^{-1}(\boldsymbol{y})$, then x is uniform over R.

Fix an integer $\nu \in \mathbb{N}$. Let $\mathcal{B}$ be a randomized algorithm which takes inst_1 and $h_1, \ldots, h_\nu$ as input, and returns a pair (J, σ), where $J \in [0, \nu]$ and σ is called a side output. Let $\mathsf{acc}_{\mathcal{B}}$ denote the probability of $J \geq 1$ in the following experiment:

$$(\mathsf{inst}_1, \boldsymbol{h}) \xleftarrow{\$} \mathsf{Wmq}_2 \times \mathsf{R}^\nu; \quad (J, \sigma) \xleftarrow{\$} \mathcal{B}(\mathsf{inst}_1, \boldsymbol{h}).$$

Let Λ be the domain from which $\mathcal{B}$ picks its random coins. Next, define a forking algorithm $\mathsf{ExtF}_{\mathcal{B}}$ (given as Algorithm 1) associated to $\mathcal{B}$, a randomized algorithm which extends the forking algorithm of Bellare-Neven [BN06]. Further, it provides room to embed the challenge of the problem instance in the random oracle via the respective encoding function (see steps 2 to 4). The algorithm takes $(\mathsf{inst}_1, \mathsf{inst}_2) \in \mathsf{Wmq}_1 \times \mathsf{Wmq}_2$ as input and runs $\mathcal{B}$ thrice on related inputs to get 3 signatures on the same message, but associated with three different random values of R.

Proposition 1. *Let the forking probability of $\mathsf{ExtF}_{\mathcal{B}}$ be defined by*

$$\mathsf{frk} = \Pr\left[b = 1 : \ (\mathsf{inst}_1, \mathsf{inst}_2) \xleftarrow{\$} \mathsf{Wmq}; \ (b, \sigma, \sigma', \sigma'') \longleftarrow \mathsf{ExtF}_{\mathcal{B}}(\mathsf{inst}_1, \mathsf{inst}_2)\right].$$

Then

$$\mathsf{frk} \geq \mathsf{acc}_{\mathcal{B}} \left(\frac{\mathsf{acc}_{\mathcal{B}}^2}{\nu^2} - \frac{3}{\varphi} \right). \tag{2}$$

---

[1] If the public map $\mathcal{P}$ (involved in the 3-pass IDS) is considered to be UOV-public map, then this lemma will rely on WMQ-problem.

[2] For the sake of concreteness, we present the extended forking algorithm using only the instance of the WMQ-problem. The same algorithm also works for a similar kind of problem instance. It would be interesting to find some applications that rely on problems other than the WMQ-problem.

Algorithm 1. Extended Forking

1: **procedure** $\mathsf{ExtF}_\mathcal{B}(\mathsf{inst}_1, \mathsf{inst}_2)$
2:　　pick $\theta \xleftarrow{\$} [\nu]$
3:　　pick $\hbar \xleftarrow{\$} \mathsf{Enc}_1^{-1}(\mathsf{inst}_2)$
4:　　choose $\boldsymbol{h} \xleftarrow{\$} R^\nu$ such that $h_\theta = \hbar$
5:　　pick random coin $\rho \xleftarrow{\$} \Lambda$ for $\mathcal{B}$
6:　　$(J, \sigma) \longleftarrow \mathcal{B}(\mathsf{inst}_1, \boldsymbol{h}; \rho)$
7:　　**if** $J = 0$ **then**
8:　　　　**return** $(0, \epsilon, \epsilon, \epsilon)$
9:　　**end if**
10:　　pick $h'_J, \ldots, h'_\nu \xleftarrow{\$} R$
11:　　$\boldsymbol{h}' \leftarrow (h_1, \ldots, h_{J-1}, h'_J, \ldots, h'_\nu)$
12:　　$(J', \sigma') \longleftarrow \mathcal{B}(\mathsf{inst}_1, \boldsymbol{h}'; \rho)$
13:　　**if** $J \neq J'$ or $h_J = h'_J$ **then**
14:　　　　**return** $(0, \epsilon, \epsilon, \epsilon)$
15:　　**end if**
16:　　pick $h''_J, \ldots, h''_\nu \xleftarrow{\$} R$
17:　　$\boldsymbol{h}'' \leftarrow (h_1, \ldots, h_{J-1}, h''_J, \ldots, h''_\nu)$
18:　　$(J'', \sigma'') \longleftarrow \mathcal{B}(\mathsf{inst}_1, \boldsymbol{h}''; \rho)$
19:　　**if** $J' = J''$ and $h_J \neq h''_J$ and
　　　　$h'_J \neq h''_J$ **then**
20:　　　　**return** $(1, \sigma, \sigma', \sigma'')$
21:　　**end if**
22:　　**return** $(0, \epsilon, \epsilon, \epsilon)$
23: **end procedure**

Proof. We start by stating the following results which are important for calculating the forking probability.

Lemma 4. *Let* X *be a non-negative real-valued random variable. Then*

$$\mathbf{E}\left[\mathsf{X}^3\right] \geq \mathbf{E}\left[\mathsf{X}\right]^3.$$

The proof of the lemma is omitted here as it is an immediate consequence of Jensen's inequality [Jen06] with the underlying convex function being X^3 for $\mathsf{X} \geq 0$.

Corollary 1. *Let* $a \geq 1$ *be an integer and* $x_1, \ldots, x_a \geq 0$ *be real numbers. Then*

$$\sum_{i=1}^{a} x_i^3 \geq \frac{1}{a^2}\left(\sum_{i=1}^{a} x_i\right)^3.$$

Proof. Let X be a random variable which takes x_i with probability $1/a$ for $i \in [a]$. Then, we can write

$$\mathbf{E}\left[\mathsf{X}^3\right] = \frac{1}{a}\sum_{i=1}^{a} x_i^3 \text{ and } \mathbf{E}\left[\mathsf{X}\right]^3 = \frac{1}{a^3}\left(\sum_{i=1}^{a} x_i\right)^3.$$

The proof is concluded following Lemma 4.

For $\mathsf{inst}_1 \in \mathsf{Wmq}_1$, define

$$\mathsf{frk}(\mathsf{inst}_1) = \Pr\left[b = 1 : \mathsf{inst}_2 \xleftarrow{\$} \mathsf{Wmq}_2; (b, \sigma, \sigma', \sigma'') \longleftarrow \mathsf{ExtF}_\mathcal{B}(\mathsf{inst}_1, \mathsf{inst}_2)\right].$$

Then, we can write

$$\mathsf{frk} = \frac{1}{|\mathsf{Wmq}_1|}\sum_{\mathsf{inst}_1 \in \mathsf{Wmq}_1} \mathsf{frk}(\mathsf{inst}_1) = \mathop{\mathbf{E}}_{\mathsf{inst}_1}\left[\mathsf{frk}(\mathsf{inst}_1)\right]. \tag{3}$$

For $\text{inst}_1 \in \text{Wmq}_1$, let

$$\text{acc}_\mathcal{B}(\text{inst}_1) = \Pr\left[J \geq 1: \; \boldsymbol{h} \xleftarrow{\$} \mathsf{R}^\nu; \; (J,\sigma) \xleftarrow{\$} \mathcal{B}(\text{inst}_1, \boldsymbol{h})\right].$$

Therefore, we can write

$$\text{acc}_\mathcal{B} = \frac{1}{|\text{Wmq}_1|} \sum_{\text{inst}_1 \in \text{Wmq}_1} \text{acc}_\mathcal{B}(\text{inst}_1) = \mathop{\mathbf{E}}_{\text{inst}_1} \left[\text{acc}_\mathcal{B}(\text{inst}_1)\right]. \tag{4}$$

Now, for $\text{inst}_1 \in \text{Wmq}_1$ we compute

$$
\begin{aligned}
\text{frk}(\text{inst}_1) &= \Pr\left[b = 1: \; \text{inst}_2 \xleftarrow{\$} \text{Wmq}_2; \; (b,\sigma,\sigma',\sigma'') \longleftarrow \text{ExtF}_\mathcal{B}(\text{inst}_1, \text{inst}_2)\right] \\
&= \Pr\left[J = J' = J'' \wedge J \geq 1 \wedge h_J \neq h'_J \wedge h'_J \neq h''_J \wedge h_J \neq h''_J\right] \\
&\geq \Pr\left[J = J' = J'' \wedge J \geq 1\right] - \Pr\left[J \geq 1 \wedge h_J = h'_J = h''\right] \\
&= \Pr\left[J = J' = J'' \wedge J \geq 1\right] - \Pr\left[J \geq 1\right](3/\varphi - 2/\varphi^2) \\
&\geq \underbrace{\Pr\left[J = J' = J'' \wedge J \geq 1\right]}_{\Upsilon} - 3 \cdot \Pr\left[J \geq 1\right]/\varphi \\
&= \Upsilon - 3 \cdot \text{acc}_\mathcal{B}(\text{inst}_1)/\varphi. \tag{5}
\end{aligned}
$$

For calculating $\Pr\left[J = J' = J'' \wedge J \geq 1\right]$, we will discuss some machinery (as considered in [BN06]) as follows. For $j \in [\nu]$, define $\Delta_j := \Lambda \times \mathsf{R}^{j-1}$. For each $j \in [\nu]$, define a random variable $\mathsf{X}_j : \Delta_j \to [0,1]$ as follows. For $t = (\rho, \boldsymbol{h}_1) \in \Delta_j$, where $\boldsymbol{h}_1 = (h_1, \ldots, h_{j-1}) \in \mathsf{R}^{j-1}$, define

$$\mathsf{X}_j(t) = \Pr\left[J = j: \; \boldsymbol{h}_2 \xleftarrow{\$} \mathsf{R}^{\nu-j+1}; \; \boldsymbol{h} \leftarrow (\boldsymbol{h}_1, \boldsymbol{h}_2); \; (J,\sigma) \longleftarrow \mathcal{B}(\text{inst}_1, \boldsymbol{h}; \rho)\right].$$

Regard X_j as a random variable having uniform distribution on its domain. So, we can write

$$\mathbf{E}\left[\mathsf{X}_j\right] = \sum_{t \in \Delta_j} \frac{1}{|\Delta_j|} \cdot \mathsf{X}_j(t) \tag{6}$$

$$\mathbf{E}\left[\mathsf{X}_j^3\right] = \sum_{t \in \Delta_j} \frac{1}{|\Delta_j|} \cdot \mathsf{X}_j^3(t). \tag{7}$$

For $\text{inst}_1 \in \text{Wmq}_1$, we have

$$
\begin{aligned}
\text{acc}_\mathcal{B}(\text{inst}_1) &= \Pr\left[J \geq 1: \; \boldsymbol{h} \xleftarrow{\$} \mathsf{R}^\nu; \; (J,\sigma) \longleftarrow \mathcal{B}(\text{inst}_1, \boldsymbol{h})\right] \\
&= \sum_{j=1}^{\nu} \sum_{t \in \Delta_j} \Pr\left[J = j: \; \boldsymbol{h} \xleftarrow{\$} \mathsf{R}^\nu; \; (J,\sigma) \longleftarrow \mathcal{B}(\text{inst}_1, \boldsymbol{h}) \big| t \xleftarrow{\$} \Delta_j\right] \cdot \\
&\quad \Pr\left[t \xleftarrow{\$} \Delta_j\right] \\
&= \sum_{j=1}^{\nu} \sum_{t \in \Delta_j} \frac{1}{|\Delta_j|} \cdot \mathsf{X}_j(t) \overset{\text{Eqn } 6}{=} \sum_{j=1}^{\nu} \mathbf{E}\left[\mathsf{X}_j\right]. \tag{8}
\end{aligned}
$$

Now, calculate the following

$$\Upsilon = \Pr\left[J = J' = J'' \wedge J \geq 1\right]$$

$$= \sum_{j=1}^{\nu} \sum_{t \in \Delta_j} \Pr\left[J = J' = J'' \wedge J \geq 1 \Big| J = j \wedge t \xleftarrow{\$} \Delta_j\right] \cdot \Pr\left[J = j \wedge t \xleftarrow{\$} \Delta_j\right]$$

$$= \sum_{j=1}^{\nu} \sum_{t \in \Delta_j} \Pr\left[J' = j \Big| t \xleftarrow{\$} \Delta_j\right] \cdot \Pr\left[J'' = j \Big| t \xleftarrow{\$} \Delta_j\right] \cdot$$

$$\Pr\left[J = j \Big| t \xleftarrow{\$} \Delta_j\right] \cdot \Pr\left[t \xleftarrow{\$} \Delta_j\right]$$

$$= \sum_{j=1}^{\nu} \sum_{t \in \Delta_j} \frac{1}{|\Delta_j|} \cdot \mathsf{X}_j^3(t) \overset{\text{Eqn } 7}{=} \sum_{j=1}^{\nu} \mathbf{E}\left[\mathsf{X}_j^3\right] \overset{\text{Lem } 4}{\geq} \sum_{j=1}^{\nu} \mathbf{E}\left[\mathsf{X}_j\right]^3$$

$$\overset{\text{Cor } 1}{\geq} \frac{1}{\nu^2} \cdot \left(\sum_{j=1}^{\nu} \mathbf{E}\left[\mathsf{X}_j\right]\right)^3 \overset{\text{Eqn } 8}{=} \frac{1}{\nu^2} \cdot (\mathsf{acc}_\mathcal{B}(\mathsf{inst}_1))^3. \tag{9}$$

Using Eqs. 5 and 9, we can write

$$\mathsf{frk}(\mathsf{inst}_1) \geq \frac{1}{\nu^2} \cdot (\mathsf{acc}_\mathcal{B}(\mathsf{inst}_1))^3 - \frac{3}{\varphi} \cdot \mathsf{acc}_\mathcal{B}(\mathsf{inst}_1). \tag{10}$$

Therefore, we can write

$$\mathsf{frk} \overset{\text{Eqn } 3}{=} \underset{\mathsf{inst}_1}{\mathbf{E}}\left[\mathsf{frk}(\mathsf{inst}_1)\right] \overset{\text{Eqn } 10}{\geq} \underset{\mathsf{inst}_1}{\mathbf{E}}\left[\frac{1}{\nu^2} \cdot (\mathsf{acc}_\mathcal{B}(\mathsf{inst}_1))^3 - \frac{3}{\varphi} \cdot \mathsf{acc}_\mathcal{B}(\mathsf{inst}_1)\right]$$

$$\geq \frac{1}{\nu^2} \cdot \underset{\mathsf{inst}_1}{\mathbf{E}}\left[\mathsf{acc}_\mathcal{B}(\mathsf{inst}_1)\right]^3 - \frac{3}{\varphi} \cdot \underset{\mathsf{inst}_1}{\mathbf{E}}\left[\mathsf{acc}_\mathcal{B}(\mathsf{inst}_1)\right]$$

$$\overset{\text{Eqn } 4}{=} \frac{1}{\nu^2} \cdot \mathsf{acc}_\mathcal{B}^3 - \frac{3}{\varphi} \cdot \mathsf{acc}_\mathcal{B} = \mathsf{acc}_\mathcal{B}\left(\frac{\mathsf{acc}_\mathcal{B}^2}{\nu^2} - \frac{3}{\varphi}\right).$$

4   Identity-Based Signature

In this section, we present an identity-based signature scheme based on salted-UOV scheme [SSH11a] and the 3-pass IDS[3] of [SSH11b]. The key-generation algorithm of IBS utilizes the sign algorithm of the salted-UOV signatures. The

---

[3] In [SSH11b], authors also proposed a 5-pass IDS whose knowledge error is remarkably less than its 3-pass variant. So, the number of parallel rounds required to construct any signature scheme based on that 5-pass IDS is expected to be significantly less than its 3-pass counterpart. This, in turn, implies that a signature based on 5-pass IDS would be more efficient than its 3-pass variant. However, the authors in [KZ20] showed a forgery on MQDSS [CHR+16] (a signature scheme based on this 5-pass IDS). To compensate for this attack, one has to go for larger values of parameters, which essentially means that 5-pass IDS is no more efficient than its 3-pass variant for the same security level. On the other hand, the 3-pass IDS is well understood and structurally simpler and thus appears to be a better choice.

signature generation of IBS follows the style of MQDSS, i.e., it runs the 3-pass variant of IDS^r followed by FST [FS86]. More formally, our IBS construction is given as follows.

IBS.Setup(κ). Let (v, m, q) be a set of parameters defined by the security parameter κ, where v, m and q denote the number of vinegar variables, the number of oil variables and the size of the field respectively. Set $n = v + m$ and let $\mathbb{F}$ be a field of size q. Let $\mathcal{M}$ and $\mathcal{ID}$ be the message space and identity space respectively. Let $\mathsf{SaltSp} = \{0, 1\}^\ell$ be salt space, where $\ell \in \mathbb{N}$. Let $\mathcal{H}_1 : \mathcal{ID} \times \mathsf{SaltSp} \to \mathbb{F}^m$ and $\mathcal{H}_2 : \{0, 1\}^* \to \{0, 1, 2\}^r$ be cryptographic hash functions. Let $\mathcal{C} = (\mathsf{CSetup}, \mathsf{Commit}, \mathsf{Open})$ be an efficient commitment scheme. The following steps are remaining part of the setup algorithm.

1. choose $r \in \mathbb{N}$ such that $(2/3)^r = \mathsf{negl}(\kappa)$, where r denotes the number of rounds
2. pick $\mathcal{F} \xleftarrow{\$} \mathcal{F}_{\mathsf{uov}}(\mathbb{F}^n, \mathbb{F}^m)$ and $\mathcal{T} \xleftarrow{\$} \mathsf{invAff}(\mathbb{F}^n, \mathbb{F}^n)$
3. set $\mathcal{P} = \mathcal{F} \circ \mathcal{T}$
4. run $\mathsf{ck} \xleftarrow{\$} \mathsf{CSetup}(\kappa)$
5. set $\mathsf{pp} = (\mathcal{P}, \mathcal{H}_1, \mathcal{H}_2, \mathsf{ck}, r)$ and $\mathsf{msk} = (\mathcal{F}, \mathcal{T})$.

IBS.KeyGen($\mathsf{pp}, \mathsf{msk}, \mathsf{id}$). The key-generation for the identity id consists of the following steps:

1. choose $\boldsymbol{x}_v' \xleftarrow{\$} \mathbb{F}^v$
2. $\boldsymbol{s} \xleftarrow{\$} \mathsf{SaltSp}$
3. $\boldsymbol{\omega} = \mathcal{H}_1(\mathsf{id}||\boldsymbol{s})$
4. if $\{\boldsymbol{x}_m \in \mathbb{F}^m : \mathcal{F}(\boldsymbol{x}_v', \boldsymbol{x}_m) = \boldsymbol{\omega}\} = \emptyset$, go to step 2
5. $\boldsymbol{x}_o' \xleftarrow{\$} \{\boldsymbol{x}_m \in \mathbb{F}^m : \mathcal{F}(\boldsymbol{x}_v', \boldsymbol{x}_m) = \boldsymbol{\omega}\}$
6. $\boldsymbol{x} = \mathcal{T}^{-1}(\boldsymbol{x}_v', \boldsymbol{x}_o')$
7. return $\mathsf{sk}_{\mathsf{id}} = (\mathsf{id}, \boldsymbol{x}, \boldsymbol{s})$.

IBS.Sign($\mathsf{pp}, M, \mathsf{sk}_{\mathsf{id}}$). Parse $\mathsf{sk}_{\mathsf{id}}$ as $(\mathsf{id}, \boldsymbol{x}, \boldsymbol{s})$. Here the signature is generated using the 3-pass IDS of Sakumoto et al. [SSH11b]. Note that the signer knows the witness $\boldsymbol{x}$ for the statement $(\mathcal{P}, \boldsymbol{\omega})$, where $\boldsymbol{\omega} = \mathcal{H}_1(\mathsf{id}||\boldsymbol{s})$. The steps are given as follows:

1. let G be the polar form of the system $\mathcal{P} : \mathbb{F}^n \to \mathbb{F}^m$
2. pick $\boldsymbol{a}_{0,i}, \boldsymbol{b}_{0,i} \xleftarrow{\$} \mathbb{F}^n$ and $\boldsymbol{c}_{0,i} \xleftarrow{\$} \mathbb{F}^m$ for $i \in [r]$
3. set $\boldsymbol{a}_{1,i} = \boldsymbol{x} - \boldsymbol{a}_{0,i}$, $\boldsymbol{b}_{1,i} = \boldsymbol{a}_{0,i} - \boldsymbol{b}_{0,i}$ and $\boldsymbol{c}_{1,i} = \mathcal{P}(\boldsymbol{a}_{0,i}) - \boldsymbol{c}_{0,i}$ for $i \in [r]$
4. for each $i \in [r]$, compute the following.
   (a) $\mathsf{ct}_{0,i} \longleftarrow \mathsf{Commit}(\boldsymbol{a}_{1,i}, \mathsf{G}(\boldsymbol{b}_{0,i}, \boldsymbol{a}_{1,i}) + \boldsymbol{c}_{0,i})$
   (b) $\mathsf{ct}_{1,i} \longleftarrow \mathsf{Commit}(\boldsymbol{b}_{0,i}||\boldsymbol{c}_{0,i})$
   (c) $\mathsf{ct}_{2,i} \longleftarrow \mathsf{Commit}(\boldsymbol{b}_{1,i}||\boldsymbol{c}_{1,i})$
5. set $\mathbf{ct} = (\mathsf{ct}_{0,1}, \mathsf{ct}_{1,1}, \mathsf{ct}_{2,1}, \ldots, \mathsf{ct}_{0,r}, \mathsf{ct}_{1,r}, \mathsf{ct}_{2,r})$ and compute $\mathbf{ch} = \mathcal{H}_2(M, \boldsymbol{\omega}, \mathbf{ct})$
6. parse $\mathbf{ch}$ as $(\mathsf{ch}_1, \ldots, \mathsf{ch}_r)$
7. for each $i \in [r]$, do the following.
   (a) if $\mathsf{ch}_i = 0$, set $\mathsf{rs}_i = (\boldsymbol{a}_{0,i}, \boldsymbol{b}_{1,i}, \boldsymbol{c}_{1,i})$
   (b) if $\mathsf{ch}_i = 1$, set $\mathsf{rs}_i = (\boldsymbol{a}_{1,i}, \boldsymbol{b}_{1,i}, \boldsymbol{c}_{1,i})$
   (c) if $\mathsf{ch}_i = 2$, set $\mathsf{rs}_i = (\boldsymbol{a}_{1,i}, \boldsymbol{b}_{0,i}, \boldsymbol{c}_{0,i})$

8. set $\mathbf{rs} = (\mathbf{rs}_1, \ldots, \mathbf{rs}_r)$ and return $\sigma = (s, \mathbf{ct}, \mathbf{rs})$

IBS.Ver(pp, M, σ, id). It consists of the following steps.

1. parse σ as $(s, \mathbf{ct}, \mathbf{rs})$, where $\mathbf{ct} = (\mathsf{ct}_{0,1}, \mathsf{ct}_{1,1}, \mathsf{ct}_{2,1}, \ldots, \mathsf{ct}_{0,r}, \mathsf{ct}_{1,r}, \mathsf{ct}_{2,r})$
   and $\mathbf{rs} = (\mathbf{rs}_1, \ldots, \mathbf{rs}_r)$
2. compute $\omega = \mathcal{H}_1(\mathsf{id}, s)$ and $\mathbf{ch} = \mathcal{H}_2(M, \omega, \mathbf{ct})$
3. for each $i \in [r]$, do the following:
   (a) if $\mathsf{ch}_i = 0$, parse rs_i as $(a_{0,i}, b_{1,i}, c_{1,i})$ and check, if
   $$\mathsf{ct}_{1,i} \overset{?}{=} \mathsf{Commit}(a_{0,i} - b_{1,i} \| \mathcal{P}(a_{0,i}) - c_{1,i}) \ \& \ \mathsf{ct}_{2,i} \overset{?}{=} \mathsf{Commit}(b_{1,i} \| c_{1,i})$$

   (b) if $\mathsf{ch}_i = 1$, parse rs_i as $(a_{1,i}, b_{1,i}, c_{1,i})$ and check, if
   $$\mathsf{ct}_{0,i} \overset{?}{=} \mathsf{Commit}(a_{1,i} \| \omega - \mathcal{P}(a_{1,i}) - \mathsf{G}(b_{1,i}, a_{1,i}) - c_{1,i}) \ \& \ \mathsf{ct}_{2,i} \overset{?}{=}$$
   $$\mathsf{Commit}(b_{1,i} \| c_{1,i})$$

   (c) if $\mathsf{ch}_i = 2$, parse rs_i as $(a_{1,i}, b_{0,i}, c_{0,i})$ and check, if
   $$\mathsf{ct}_{0,i} \overset{?}{=} \mathsf{Commit}(a_{1,i} \| \mathsf{G}(b_{0,i}, a_{1,i}) + c_{0,i}) \ \& \ \mathsf{ct}_{1,i} \overset{?}{=} \mathsf{Commit}(b_{0,i} \| c_{0,i})$$

   (d) return 0, if any of the above checks fail
4. return 1

Correctness. It follows from the correctness of the underlying salted-UOV signature and 3-pass IDS. Also to note that the signature component response rs_i implicitly contains the random coin used in Commit. This is used in the signature verification algorithm for the commitment equations involved in Eqs. 3(a), 3(b) and 3(c) as mentioned in the discussion of commitment scheme in Sect. 2.3.

Remark 2. Following our construction, one can build an IBS using a two-layers salted version of Rainbow [DS05] and its security can be argued similarly as done in Sect. 5.

Remark 3. Sometimes, we consider the following form of signature: $\sigma = (s, \mathbf{ct}, \mathbf{ch}, \mathbf{rs})$, where $\omega = \mathcal{H}_1(\mathsf{id}, s)$, and $\mathbf{ch} = \mathcal{H}_2(M, \omega, \mathbf{ct})$ which, further, can be written as $\sigma = \left(s, \{\mathsf{ct}_i, \mathsf{ch}_i, \mathsf{rs}_i\}_{i \in [r]}\right)$.

Comparison with [BNN09]. Note that the security of the 3-pass version of IDS^r [SSH11b] relies on the intractability of the MQ-problem. This IDS^r can be a possible instantiation of SI required for the construction of IBS following the modular approach of [BNN09], if an instantiation of trapdoor sampleable relation (TSR) is available such that SI and TSR together satisfy the necessary security properties. Also, note that ω is computed as $\omega = \mathcal{H}_1(\mathsf{id})$ as part of the public-key of the underlying SI in [BNN09]. Therefore, the salted UOV-signature (even if we treat this as the right candidate of TSR in the MQ-setting) does not exactly fit in their modular approach. Another possible candidate of TSR in the MQ-setting could be (plain) UOV-signature [KPG99]. In either of the two approaches outlined above, we cannot prove the security of the IBS following the proof-strategy of [BNN09] as it is not known whether the underlying candidates, the IDS^r and (salted or plain) UOV-signature satisfy the requirement of Corollary 4.10 in [BNN09][4]. For the sake of discussion, let us assume (i) IDS^r

---

[4] Note that this is not something unique for the MQ-setting as [BNN09] itself observed that their framework does not encompass all possible candidate schemes.

and UOV-signature fulfill the security properties mentioned in [BNN09] and (ii) the security of the UOV relies on the intractability of the WMQ-problem. Then, following [BNN09] for the corresponding IBS we would get a reduction from WMQ-problem. From [BNN09, Corollary 4.10] and the passive-attack version of [SSH11b, Lemma 8], one can show that the degradation factor in the security reduction is roughly ν^6. On the other hand, the degradation factor of our reduction (see Eq. 17) is roughly $\nu^3 \cdot \nu_{key}^3$, where ν and ν_{key} are the number of queries to the random oracles and key-gen oracle respectively. Since in practice ν and ν_{key} are roughly 2^{60} and 2^{30} respectively, our reduction is tighter than the one following [BNN09].

5   Security of the Proposed IBS

In this section, we prove EUF-CMA-security of our proposed IBS scheme. Note that in EUF-CMA-security model (c.f., Definition 4), an adversary is provided access to both, the signature oracle $\mathcal{O}_{Sign}$ and key-gen oracle $\mathcal{O}_{Key}$. We also consider two weaker security models, *existential unforgeability under chosen-key attack* (EUF-CKA) and *existential unforgeability under no-message attack* (EUF-NMA), where the adversary is not provided access to $\mathcal{O}_{Sign}$-oracle and $(\mathcal{O}_{Sign}, \mathcal{O}_{Key})$-oracles respectively.

In Lemma 5, we first show a reduction of EUF-NMA-security of the IBS scheme (c.f., Sect. 4) from WMQ-problem and computational binding property of the underlying commitment scheme in the random oracle model. Then, in Lemmas 6 and 7 we show reductions of EUF-CKA-security from EUF-NMA-security and EUF-CMA-security from EUF-CKA-security respectively in the random oracle model. Finally, in Corollary 2, we prove EUF-CMA security of the IBS scheme from WMQ-problem and computational binding and statistical hiding properties of the underlying commitment scheme. We start with the following proposition which will be used in Lemma 5.

Proposition 2. *Assume that $\mathcal{H}_2$ (involved in the IBS construction in Sect. 4) is a random oracle. Then, given any three signatures $\sigma = (s, ct, ch, rs)$, $\sigma' = (s, ct, ch', rs')$ and $\sigma'' = (s, ct, ch'', rs'')$ with $ch \neq ch' \neq ch'' \neq ch$, we can find with probability $1 - (7/9)^r$ an $i \in [r]$ such that $ch_i \neq ch'_i \neq ch''_i \neq ch_i$.*

Proof. For each $i \in [r]$, let $Event_i$ denote $ch_i \neq ch'_i \neq ch''_i \neq ch_i$. By simple counting argument, we can write $Pr[Event_j] = 6/27 = 2/9$. Now, the probability of its complement is given by

$$Pr[\neg Event_j] = Pr[ch_i = ch'_i \vee ch_i = ch''_i \vee ch'_i = ch''_i]$$
$$= 1 - Pr[Event_j] = 7/9.$$

Since challenge components are chosen uniformly at random from $\{0, 1, 2\}$, we can write

$$Pr[\exists i \in [r] \ s.t \ Event_i = true] = 1 - Pr[\neg Event_1 \wedge \cdots \wedge \neg Event_r] = 1 - (7/9)^r.$$

Lemma 5. *If the WMQ-problem (c.f., Definition 2) is intractable and the underlying commitment scheme is computationally binding, then our proposed IBS scheme described in Sect. 4 is* EUF-NMA-*secure in the random oracle model.*

Proof. Recall that there are two hash functions $\mathcal{H}_1 : \mathcal{ID} \times \mathsf{SaltSp} \to \mathbb{F}^m$ and $\mathcal{H}_2 : \{0,1\}^* \to \{0,1,2\}^r$. We model both the hash functions as random oracles. Note that here the ranges of the hash functions are enumerable sets and hence, the values in the ranges can be uniquely and efficiently determined by their indices in the corresponding enumerations. We assume that the index of an element in each range set starts with 1. Wlog, we can use the element of a range set and its index interchangeably.

We denote the ranges of $\mathcal{H}_1$ and $\mathcal{H}_2$ by R_1 and R_2 respectively. So, $|\mathsf{R}_1| = q^m = |\mathsf{Wmq}_2|$ and $|\mathsf{R}_2| = 3^r$. Let $\mathsf{R} = \{1, 2, \ldots, \varphi\}$, where $\varphi = 3^r q^m$. We would call R as common range which is basically an index set. Now, we define two encoding functions $\mathsf{Enc}_1 : \mathsf{R} \to \mathsf{R}_1$ and $\mathsf{Enc}_2 : \mathsf{R} \to \mathsf{R}_2$ as follows: for $x \in \mathsf{R}$, define

$$\mathsf{Enc}_1(x) = \left\lceil \frac{x}{3^r} \right\rceil \text{ and } \mathsf{Enc}_2(x) = \left\lceil \frac{x}{q^m} \right\rceil.$$

It is easy to check that the above encoding functions satisfy the following properties:

1. Each $\mathsf{Enc}_i : \mathsf{R} \to \mathsf{R}_i$ is efficiently computable.
2. If $x \xleftarrow{\$} \mathsf{R}$, then $\mathsf{Enc}_i(x)$ is uniform over R_i for $i = 1, 2$.
3. For $y \in \mathbb{F}^m$, the preimage set[5] $\mathsf{Enc}_1^{-1}(y) = \{3^r \cdot (y - 1) + 1, 3^r \cdot (y - 1) + 2, \ldots, 3^r \cdot y\}$ is efficiently computable and $|\mathsf{Enc}_1^{-1}(y)| = 3^r$.
4. When $y \xleftarrow{\$} \mathsf{Wmq}_2$ and $x \xleftarrow{\$} \mathsf{Enc}_1^{-1}(y)$, then x is uniform over R.

Items (3) and (4) implies that Enc_1 fulfills all the requirements of the forking algorithm $\mathsf{ExtF}_{\mathcal{B}}$ (Algorithm 1) defined in Sect. 3.

Our proof strategy is in the similar line as in [BN06] which is described as follows:

(a) Given an EUF-NMA-attacker $\mathcal{A}_0$, we first show that with non-negligible probability, $\mathcal{A}_0$ can be rewound with the same random tape but different oracles to generate three signatures for the same message-identity pair (M, id).
(b) From these 3 signatures, we extract out three transcripts of the underlying 3-pass IDS with three different challenges.
(c) Then, we extract the witness using the 3-special soundness property of the 3-pass IDS.

To proceed along the above strategy, we first construct a wrapper algorithm $\mathcal{B}$ which will create an environment for $\mathcal{A}_0$ and thereby, outputs the associated forking-index of $\mathcal{H}_2$-oracle in addition to the forgery. Knowing this forking-index is important for rewinding $\mathcal{B}$ with the same random tape but different random values of $\mathcal{H}_2$-oracle. Let the numbers of queries made by $\mathcal{A}_0$ to $\mathcal{H}_1$ and $\mathcal{H}_2$-oracles be ν_1 and ν_2 respectively. Let $\nu = \nu_1 + \nu_2$. Our wrapper algorithm $\mathcal{B}$

---

[5] Recall that y is considered here as an index, i.e., a positive integer.

Algorithm 2. Wrapper

1: **procedure** $\mathcal{B}(\text{inst}_1, h)$ ▷ Compute a signature σ and the corresponding forking-index J

2:    run ck $\xleftarrow{\$}$ CSetup(κ)

3:    pick $r \in \mathbb{N}$ s.t $(2/3)^r = \text{negl}(\kappa)$

4:    List $\leftarrow \emptyset$ and ctr $\leftarrow 0$ ▷ List stores the tuples of the form $(\text{ctr}, i, \text{arg}, \mathcal{H}_i(\text{arg}))$ for $i \in [2]$

5:    $(M, \text{id}, (s, \text{ct}, \text{rs})) \xleftarrow{\$} \mathcal{A}_0^{\{\mathcal{O}_{\mathcal{H}_1}, \mathcal{O}_{\mathcal{H}_2}\}}(\text{inst}_1, \text{ck}, r)$ ▷ the oracles $\mathcal{O}_{\mathcal{H}_i}$ for $i = 1, 2$ are defined after "end procedure"

6:        $\omega \leftarrow \mathcal{O}_{\mathcal{H}_1}(\text{id}, s)$

7:        ch $\leftarrow \mathcal{O}_{\mathcal{H}_2}(M, \omega, \text{ct})$

8:        set $\sigma = (s, \text{ct}, \text{ch}, \text{rs})$

9:        **if** IBS.Ver(pp, $M, \sigma, \text{id}) = 0$ **then**

10:            **return** $(0, \epsilon)$ ▷ abort

11:        **end if**

12:        **return** (J, σ) such that tuple $(J, 2, M\|\omega\|\text{ct}, \text{ch}) \in$ List

13: **end procedure**

$\mathcal{O}_{\mathcal{H}_i}(\text{arg})$: // for $i = 1, 2$

    if $(*, i, \text{arg}, \mathcal{H}_i(\text{arg})) \notin$ List **then**

        ctr $\leftarrow$ ctr $+ 1$

        $\mathcal{H}_i(\text{arg}) \leftarrow \text{Enc}_i(h_{\text{ctr}})$ ▷ $\mathcal{H}_i$ is programmed via encoding Enc_i and the property defined in item 2 ensures the uniformity of $\mathcal{H}_i(\text{arg})$

        List $\leftarrow$ List $\cup \{(\text{ctr}, i, \text{arg}, \mathcal{H}_i(\text{arg}))\}$

    end if

    return $\mathcal{H}_i(\text{arg})$

(described as Algorithm 2) takes $(\text{inst}_1, h) \in \text{Wmq}_1 \times \text{R}^\nu$ as input and returns a pair (J, σ). Note that $\mathcal{B}$ handles both types of random oracle queries perfectly using the supplied ν-many random indices from R and the encoding functions described above. The acceptance probability $\text{acc}_\mathcal{B}$ of $\mathcal{B}$ is negligibly close[6] to $\text{Adv}_{\mathcal{A}_0}^{\text{EUF-NMA}}(\kappa)$.

Finally, we design an WMQ-problem solver which will make use of the extended forking algorithm $\text{ExtF}_\mathcal{B}$ (Algorithm 1 in Sect. 3) and solves the given problem instance. Let $(\mathcal{P}, y^*) \in \text{Wmq}_1 \times \text{Wmq}_2$ be the given random instance of WMQ-problem. Then, the WMQ-problem solver algorithm Solver is described as Algorithm 3.

The probability that we can reach to step 12 of Algorithm 3 without abort is $\text{frk} \cdot (1 - (7/9)^r)$ (using Proposition 2). Notice that the witness x^* computed in step 12 always satisfies the following identity

$$\mathcal{P}(x^*) = \omega = \mathcal{H}_1(\text{id}, s) \tag{11}$$

as π, π' and π'' being the accepted transcripts for the statement $(\mathcal{P}, \omega)$. Now, the quantity in the RHS of Eq. 11 cannot equal y^* in general, unless $\mathcal{H}_1$ is programmed accordingly. So, the witness computed in step 12 cannot provide a correct solution of the given problem instance.

To extract out the correct solution, we guess an index $\theta \in [\nu]$, where (id, s) will appear as a query to the oracle $\mathcal{H}_1$ (see step 2 of Algorithm 1). So, $\mathcal{H}_1(\text{id}, s)$

---

[6] This probability does not include any non-negligible advantage due to the knowledge error $(2/3)^r$ (c.f., Lemma 3) of the underlying IDS^r as $(2/3)^r = \text{negl}(\kappa)$ by the choice of r. Otherwise, the forking algorithm would fail to provide sufficient information about the underlying witness.

Algorithm 3. WMQ Solver

1: **procedure** Solver($\mathcal{P}, \boldsymbol{y}^*$)   ▷ Output $\boldsymbol{x}^*$ such that $\mathcal{P}(\boldsymbol{x}^*) = \boldsymbol{y}^*$
2:    $(b, \sigma, \sigma', \sigma'') \xleftarrow{\$} \mathsf{ExtF}_\mathcal{B}(\mathcal{P}, \boldsymbol{y}^*)$ ▷ run $\mathsf{ExtF}_\mathcal{B}(\mathsf{inst}_1, \mathsf{inst}_2)$, where $\mathsf{inst}_1 = \mathcal{P}$ and $\mathsf{inst}_2 = \boldsymbol{y}^*$
3:    **if** $b = 0$ **then**
4:        abort
5:    **end if**
6:    parse σ, σ' and σ'' as $\sigma = (\boldsymbol{s}, \mathsf{ct}, \mathsf{ch}, \mathsf{rs})$, $\sigma' = (\boldsymbol{s}, \mathsf{ct}, \mathsf{ch}', \mathsf{rs}')$ and $\sigma'' = (\boldsymbol{s}, \mathsf{ct}, \mathsf{ch}'', \mathsf{rs}'')$
7:    find an $i \in [r]$ such that $\mathsf{ch}_i \neq \mathsf{ch}'_i \neq \mathsf{ch}''_i \neq \mathsf{ch}_i$
8:    **if** such i is not found **then**
9:        abort
10:   **end if**
11:   set $\pi = (\mathsf{ct}_i, \mathsf{ch}_i, \mathsf{rs}_i)$, $\pi' = (\mathsf{ct}_i, \mathsf{ch}'_i, \mathsf{rs}'_i)$ and $\pi'' = (\mathsf{ct}_i, \mathsf{ch}''_i, \mathsf{rs}''_i)$
12:   $\boldsymbol{x}^* \longleftarrow \mathsf{Extr}(\pi, \pi', \pi'')$ ▷ Extr is involved in Lemma 2
13:   **if** $\mathcal{P}(\boldsymbol{x}^*) \neq \boldsymbol{y}^*$ **then**
14:       abort
15:   **else**
16:       **return** $\boldsymbol{x}^*$
17:   **end if**
18: **end procedure**

---

gets the programmed value $\mathsf{Enc}_1(h_\theta) = \boldsymbol{y}^*$ with probability $1/\nu$ (see steps 3 and 4 of Algorithm 1). Further, the nested hashing ensures that the $\mathcal{H}_1$-value at $(\mathsf{id}, \boldsymbol{s})$ will remain unchanged, once it is programmed by $\boldsymbol{y}^*$. Therefore, $\boldsymbol{x}^*$ is a solution of the given problem instance. Due to the above guess, the success probability of finding correct solution becomes

$$\mathsf{Adv}_\mathsf{Solver}^\mathsf{WMQ}(\kappa) \geq \frac{\mathsf{frk}}{\nu} \cdot \left(1 - \left(\frac{7}{9}\right)^r\right) \overset{\mathrm{Eqn\ 2}}{\geq} \frac{\mathsf{acc}_\mathcal{B}}{\nu} \left(\frac{\mathsf{acc}_\mathcal{B}^2}{\nu^2} - \frac{3}{\varphi}\right) \cdot \left(1 - \left(\frac{7}{9}\right)^r\right)$$

$$\approx \frac{1}{\nu^3} \cdot \left(\mathsf{Adv}_{\mathcal{A}_0}^\mathsf{EUF\text{-}NMA}(\kappa)\right)^3 \cdot \left(1 - \left(\frac{7}{9}\right)^r\right). \tag{12}$$

Lemma 6. *Suppose there exists an adversary $\mathcal{A}_1$ who can break EUF-CKA-security of the proposed IBS scheme described in Sect. 4 in the random oracle model, where $\mathcal{H}_1$ and $\mathcal{H}_2$ are treated as random oracles. Then using $\mathcal{A}_1$ as a subroutine, we can create an algorithm $\mathcal{A}_0$ for breaking EUF-NMA-security of the same IBS with advantage*

$$\mathsf{Adv}_{\mathcal{A}_0}^\mathsf{EUF\text{-}NMA}(\kappa) \approx \left(1 - \frac{\nu_1 \cdot \nu_\mathsf{key}}{2^\ell}\right) \cdot \mathsf{Adv}_{\mathcal{A}_1}^\mathsf{EUF\text{-}CKA}(\kappa) \tag{13}$$

where ν_1 and ν_key are the number of $\mathcal{H}_1$ queries and the number of signature queries respectively, and ℓ is the size of a salt.

Proof. We construct an EUF-NMA-attacker $\mathcal{A}_0$ (described as Algorithm 4) using the EUF-CKA-attacker $\mathcal{A}_1$ of the proposed IBS as subroutine. The EUF-NMA-attacker $\mathcal{A}_0$ gets access to two random oracles $\mathcal{O}_{\mathcal{H}_1}$ and $\mathcal{O}_{\mathcal{H}_2}$ from its challenger and at the end, it returns a forgery. Here the main challenging part is to answer key-gen queries of $\mathcal{A}_1$ without having access to any external key-gen oracle $\mathcal{O}_\mathsf{Key}$.

First note that all the oracle queries are answered perfectly, except those answers of $\mathcal{H}_1$-queries which are programmed locally by $\mathcal{A}_0$ (see step 5 of the

Algorithm 4. EUF-NMA-Attacker

1: **procedure** $\mathcal{A}_0^{\{\mathcal{O}_{\mathcal{H}_1}, \mathcal{O}_{\mathcal{H}_2}\}}(\mathcal{P}, \mathsf{ck}, r)$ ▷ Return a forgery
2:     $\mathsf{List}_1 \leftarrow \emptyset$ ▷ List_1 stores the pairs of the form $((\mathsf{id}, s), \mathcal{H}_1(\mathsf{id}, s))$
3:     $(M^*, \mathsf{id}^*, (s^*, \mathbf{ct}^*, \mathbf{rs}^*)) \xleftarrow{\$} \mathcal{A}_1^{\{\widetilde{\mathcal{O}_{\mathcal{H}_1}}, \mathcal{O}_{\mathcal{H}_2}, \widetilde{\mathcal{O}_{\mathsf{Key}}}\}}(\mathcal{P}, \mathsf{ck}, r)$ ▷ the oracles $\widetilde{\mathcal{O}_{\mathcal{H}_1}}$ and
       $\widetilde{\mathcal{O}_{\mathsf{Key}}}$ are defined in Figure 3
4:         $\omega^* \leftarrow \mathcal{O}_{\mathcal{H}_1}(\mathsf{id}^*, s^*)$
5:         $\mathbf{ch}^* \leftarrow \mathcal{O}_{\mathcal{H}_2}(M^*, \omega^*, \mathbf{ct}^*)$
6:         set $\sigma^* = (s^*, \mathbf{ct}^*, \mathbf{ch}^*, \mathbf{rs}^*)$
7:         **if** $\boxed{\mathsf{IBS.Ver}(\mathsf{pp}, M^*, \sigma^*, \mathsf{id}^*) = 0}$ **then**
8:             **return** $(0, \epsilon, \epsilon, \epsilon)$ ▷ abort
9:         **end if**
10:        **return** $(1, M^*, \mathsf{id}^*, \sigma^*)$ ▷ forgery produced by $\mathcal{A}_0$
11: **end procedure**

$\widetilde{\mathcal{O}_{\mathcal{H}_1}}(\mathsf{arg})$:
1: **if** $(\mathsf{arg}, *) \notin \mathsf{List}_1$ **then**
2:     $\omega \leftarrow \mathcal{O}_{\mathcal{H}_1}(\mathsf{arg})$
3:     $\mathsf{List}_1 \leftarrow \mathsf{List}_1 \cup \{(\mathsf{arg}, \omega)\}$
4: **end if**
5: **return** ω ▷ such that $(\mathsf{arg}, \omega) \in \mathsf{List}_1$

$\widetilde{\mathcal{O}_{\mathsf{Key}}}(\mathsf{id})$:
1: $(\boldsymbol{x}, \boldsymbol{s}) \xleftarrow{\$} \mathbb{F}^n \times \mathsf{SaltSp}$
2: **if** $\boxed{((\mathsf{id}, \boldsymbol{s}), *) \in \mathsf{List}_1}$ **then**
3:     **return** $(\epsilon, \epsilon, \epsilon)$ ▷ abort
4: **end if**
5: $\mathsf{List}_1 \leftarrow \mathsf{List}_1 \cup \{((\mathsf{id}, \boldsymbol{s}), \mathcal{P}(\boldsymbol{x}))\}$ ▷
   $\mathcal{H}_1(\mathsf{id}, \boldsymbol{s})$ is programmed as $\mathcal{P}(\boldsymbol{x})$
6: **return** $\mathsf{sk}_{\mathsf{id}} = (\mathsf{id}, \boldsymbol{x}, \boldsymbol{s})$

Fig. 3. Description of the oracles $\widetilde{\mathcal{O}_{\mathcal{H}_1}}$ and $\widetilde{\mathcal{O}_{\mathsf{Key}}}$ involved in EUF-NMA-Attacker (Algorithm 4).

key-gen oracle $\widetilde{\mathcal{O}_{\mathsf{Key}}}$ in Fig. 3), i.e., $\mathcal{H}_1(\mathsf{id}, \boldsymbol{s}) = \mathcal{P}(\boldsymbol{x})$. It suffices to show that $\mathcal{P}(\boldsymbol{x})$ is uniform over $\mathbb{F}^m$. Since $\mathcal{P}$ is random UOV-public map, we can assume that for a uniform choice of $\boldsymbol{x} \in \mathbb{F}^n$, $\mathcal{P}(\boldsymbol{x})$ will be uniform over $\mathbb{F}^m$. The same assumption was implicitly considered in the security proof of salted UOV-scheme [SSH11a]. Further, note that the $\mathcal{H}_1$-oracle value involved in the forgery produced by $\mathcal{A}_1$ (in step 3 of Algorithm 4) is consistent with external oracle $\mathcal{O}_{\mathcal{H}_1}$ as $\mathcal{A}_0$ locally programs only at $(\mathsf{id}, *)$ such that $\mathsf{id} \neq \mathsf{id}^*$. Therefore, the probability of a valid forgery produced by $\mathcal{A}_0$ is

$$\mathsf{Adv}_{\mathcal{A}_0}^{\mathsf{EUF\text{-}NMA}}(\kappa) = \Pr\left[b = 1 : (b, M^*, \mathsf{id}^*, \sigma^*) \xleftarrow{\$} \mathcal{A}_0^{\{\mathcal{O}_{\mathcal{H}_1}, \mathcal{O}_{\mathcal{H}_2}\}}(\mathcal{P}, \mathsf{ck}, r)\right]$$

$$= \left(1 - \frac{\nu_1}{2^\ell}\right)^{\nu_{\mathsf{key}}} \cdot \mathsf{Adv}_{\mathcal{A}_1}^{\mathsf{EUF\text{-}CKA}}(\kappa) \tag{14}$$

$$\approx \left(1 - \frac{\nu_1 \cdot \nu_{\mathsf{key}}}{2^\ell}\right) \cdot \mathsf{Adv}_{\mathcal{A}_1}^{\mathsf{EUF\text{-}CKA}}(\kappa)$$

where the first and last factors of the RHS of Eq. 14 are due to the probabilities that step 2 of the routine $\widetilde{\mathcal{O}_{\mathsf{Key}}}$ and step 7 of Algorithm 4 will not hold (highlighted by bounded box) respectively. This concludes the lemma.

Lemma 7. *Assume that the underlying commitment scheme is statistically hiding. Suppose there exists an adversary $\mathcal{A}_2$ who can break EUF-CMA-security of the proposed IBS scheme described in Sect. 4 in the random oracle model, where $\mathcal{H}_1$ and $\mathcal{H}_2$ are treated as random oracles. Then using $\mathcal{A}_2$ as a subroutine, we can create an algorithm $\mathcal{A}_1$ for breaking EUF-CKA-security of the same IBS with advantage*

$$\mathsf{Adv}_{\mathcal{A}_1}^{\mathsf{EUF\text{-}CKA}}(\kappa) \approx \mathsf{Adv}_{\mathcal{A}_2}^{\mathsf{EUF\text{-}CMA}}(\kappa)/\nu_{\mathsf{key}} \tag{15}$$

where ν_{key} is the number of key-gen queries.

Proof. We construct an EUF-CKA-attacker $\mathcal{A}_1$ using the EUF-CMA-attacker $\mathcal{A}_2$ of the proposed IBS as subroutine in the random oracle model. The EUF-CKA-attacker $\mathcal{A}_1$ gets access to two random oracles $\mathcal{O}_{\mathcal{H}_1}$ and $\mathcal{O}_{\mathcal{H}_2}$ and access to the key-gen oracle $\mathcal{O}_{\mathsf{Key}}$ from its challenger and at the end, it returns a forgery.

Here, the main challenging part is to answer signature queries of $\mathcal{A}_2$ without having access to any external signature oracle $\mathcal{O}_{\mathsf{Sign}}$. One might think that each signature query would be answered using the simulator for the HVZK of the underlying 3-pass IDS. But, it is not possible for the following reason. First, notice that the secret key $\mathsf{sk}_{\mathsf{id}}$ and a signature on (M, id) have some common ingredient, namely, the salt $\mathbf{s}$. Just consider the following situation: $\mathcal{A}_2$ first asks a signature query on (M, id) and gets the simulated signature $\sigma = (\mathbf{s}, \mathbf{ct}, \mathbf{rs})$, where $\mathbf{s}$ is uniform over SaltSp. Later, if $\mathcal{A}_2$ asks for a key-gen query on the same identity id, then with high probability the salt part in $\mathsf{sk}_{\mathsf{id}}$ will be different and hence, violates the environment of the real execution.

To tackle the above issue, we adapt Coron's partitioning technique [Cor00], where the identity space $\mathcal{ID}$ is partitioned into $\mathcal{ID}_\lambda$ and $\mathcal{ID} \setminus \mathcal{ID}_\lambda$ based on a biased coin with probability of head being λ (λ will be chosen later). In fact, for each $\mathsf{id} \in \mathcal{ID}$, toss the biased coin, and let η be the outcome of the toss (note that $\Pr[\eta = 1] = \lambda$). Then, assign id to $\mathcal{ID}_\lambda$ if $\eta = 1$, otherwise assign to $\mathcal{ID} \setminus \mathcal{ID}_\lambda$. The following proof strategy ensures that the aforementioned issue will never arise.

1. If a query identity id of $\mathcal{O}_{\mathsf{Key}}$ belongs to $\mathcal{ID}_\lambda$, then abort.
2. For a signature query on (M, id), we do the following:
   (a) If $\mathsf{id} \in \mathcal{ID}_\lambda$, then we answer using Simu (defined in the proof of Lemma 1) for the HVZK of the underlying 3-pass IDS. In this case, we program $\mathcal{H}_2$ locally at some points (see step 9 of the oracle $\mathcal{O}_{\mathsf{hvzk}}$ in Fig. 4).
   (b) Else, generate signature according to IBS.Sign using $\mathsf{sk}_{\mathsf{id}}$.
3. If the challenge $\mathsf{id}^* \notin \mathcal{ID}_\lambda$, then abort.

The EUF-CKA-attacker $\mathcal{A}_1$ is formally described as Algorithm 5, where the queries of $\mathcal{A}_2$ to the oracles may appear in an interleaved manner. The queries to $\mathcal{H}_1$ and key-gen oracles are handled by forwarding to its external oracles $\mathcal{O}_{\mathcal{H}_1}$ and $\mathcal{O}_{\mathsf{Key}}$. However, for answering signature queries, we maintain two lists List_2 and $\mathsf{List}_{\mathsf{key}}$ which respectively store the pairs of the form $(\mathsf{arg}, \mathcal{H}_2(\mathsf{arg}))$ and $(\mathsf{id}, \boldsymbol{x}, \mathbf{s})$, where $\boldsymbol{x} \in \mathbb{F}^n \cup \{\bot\}$. The list List_2 is updated while answering signature queries

Algorithm 5. EUF-CKA-Attacker

1: **procedure** $\mathcal{A}_1^{\{\mathcal{O}_{\mathcal{H}_1}, \mathcal{O}_{\mathcal{H}_2}, \mathcal{O}_{\mathsf{Key}}\}}(\mathcal{P}, \mathsf{ck}, r)$ ▷ Return a forgery

2:     $\mathsf{List}_2 \leftarrow \emptyset$ and $\mathsf{List}_{\mathsf{key}} \leftarrow \emptyset$

3:     $(M^*, \mathsf{id}^*, (s^*, \mathbf{ct}^*, \mathbf{rs}^*)) \xleftarrow{\$} \mathcal{A}_2^{\{\mathcal{O}_{\mathcal{H}_1}, \widetilde{\mathcal{O}_{\mathcal{H}_2}}, \widetilde{\mathcal{O}_{\mathsf{Key}}}, \mathcal{O}_{\mathsf{Sign}}\}}(\mathcal{P}, \mathsf{ck}, r)$ ▷ the oracles $\widetilde{\mathcal{O}_{\mathcal{H}_2}}$, $\widetilde{\mathcal{O}_{\mathsf{Key}}}$ and $\mathcal{O}_{\mathsf{Sign}}$ are defined in Figure 4

4:     $\omega^* \leftarrow \mathcal{O}_{\mathcal{H}_1}(\mathsf{id}^*, s^*)$

5:     $\mathsf{ch}^* \leftarrow \mathcal{O}_{\mathcal{H}_2}(M^*, \omega^*, \mathbf{ct}^*)$

6:     set $\sigma^* = (s^*, \mathbf{ct}^*, \mathsf{ch}^*, \mathbf{rs}^*)$

7:     **if** $\boxed{\mathsf{id}^* \notin \mathcal{ID}_\lambda}$ or $\boxed{\mathsf{IBS.Ver}(\mathsf{pp}, M^*, \sigma^*, \mathsf{id}^*) = 0}$ **then**

8:         **return** $(0, \epsilon, \epsilon, \epsilon)$ ▷ abort

9:     **end if**

10:     **return** $(1, M^*, \mathsf{id}^*, \sigma^*)$ ▷ forgery produced by $\mathcal{A}_1$

11: **end procedure**

$\widetilde{\mathcal{O}_{\mathcal{H}_2}}(\mathsf{arg})$:

1: **if** $(\mathsf{arg}, *) \notin \mathsf{List}_2$ **then**
2:     $\mathsf{ch} \leftarrow \mathcal{O}_{\mathcal{H}_2}(\mathsf{arg})$
3:     $\mathsf{List}_2 \leftarrow \mathsf{List}_2 \cup \{(\mathsf{arg}, \mathsf{ch})\}$
4: **end if**
5: **return** ch ▷ such that $(\mathsf{arg}, \mathsf{ch}) \in \mathsf{List}_2$

$\mathcal{O}_{\mathsf{Sign}}(M, \mathsf{id})$:

1: **if** $(\mathsf{id}, *, *) \notin \mathsf{List}_{\mathsf{key}}$ **then**
2:     **if** $\mathsf{id} \notin \mathcal{ID}_\lambda$ **then**
3:         $\mathsf{sk}_{\mathsf{id}} \leftarrow \mathcal{O}_{\mathsf{Key}}(\mathsf{id})$
4:         $\mathsf{List}_{\mathsf{key}} \leftarrow \mathsf{List}_{\mathsf{key}} \cup \{\mathsf{sk}_{\mathsf{id}}\}$
5:     **else**
6:         $s \xleftarrow{\mathsf{U}} \mathsf{SaltSp}$
7:         $\mathsf{List}_{\mathsf{key}} \leftarrow \mathsf{List}_{\mathsf{key}} \cup \{(\mathsf{id}, \perp, s)\}$
8:     **end if**
9: **end if**
10: **if** $(\mathsf{id}, \perp, s) \in \mathsf{List}_{\mathsf{key}}$ **then**
11:     $\sigma \leftarrow \mathcal{O}_{\mathsf{hvzk}}(M, \mathsf{id}, s)$
12: **else**
13:     $\sigma \leftarrow \mathsf{IBS.KeyGen}(\mathsf{pp}, M, \mathsf{sk}_{\mathsf{id}})$
14: **end if**
15: **return** σ

$\widetilde{\mathcal{O}_{\mathsf{Key}}}(\mathsf{id})$:

1: **if** $\boxed{\mathsf{id} \in \mathcal{ID}_\lambda}$ **then**
2:     **return** $(\epsilon, \epsilon, \epsilon)$ ▷ abort
3: **end if**
4: **if** $(\mathsf{id}, x, s) \in \mathsf{List}_{\mathsf{key}}$ for some $(x, s) \in \mathbb{F}^n \times \mathsf{SaltSp}$ **then**
5:     set $\mathsf{sk}_{\mathsf{id}} = (\mathsf{id}, x, s)$
6: **else**
7:     $\mathsf{sk}_{\mathsf{id}} \leftarrow \mathcal{O}_{\mathsf{Key}}(\mathsf{id})$
8:     $\mathsf{List}_{\mathsf{key}} \leftarrow \mathsf{List}_{\mathsf{key}} \cup \{\mathsf{sk}_{\mathsf{id}}\}$
9: **end if**
10: **return** $\mathsf{sk}_{\mathsf{id}}$

$\mathcal{O}_{\mathsf{hvzk}}(M, \mathsf{id}, s)$:

1: $\omega \leftarrow \mathcal{O}_{\mathcal{H}_1}(\mathsf{id}, s)$
2: $(\pi_1, \ldots, \pi_r) \leftarrow \mathsf{Simu}^r(\mathcal{P}, \omega)$, where $\pi_i = (\mathbf{ct}_i, \mathsf{ch}_i, \mathbf{rs}_i)$
3: $\mathbf{ct} \leftarrow (\mathbf{ct}_1, \ldots, \mathbf{ct}_r)$
4: $\mathsf{ch} \leftarrow (\mathsf{ch}_1, \ldots, \mathsf{ch}_r)$
5: $\mathbf{rs} \leftarrow (\mathbf{rs}_1, \ldots, \mathbf{rs}_r)$
6: **if** $\boxed{((M, \omega, \mathbf{ct}), *) \in \mathsf{List}_2}$ **then**
7:     **return** $(\epsilon, \epsilon, \epsilon)$ ▷ abort
8: **else**
9:     $\mathsf{List}_2 \leftarrow \mathsf{List}_2 \cup \{((M, \omega, \mathbf{ct}), \mathsf{ch})\}$
10: **end if**
11: **return** $(s, \mathbf{ct}, \mathbf{rs})$

Fig. 4. Description of the oracles $\widetilde{\mathcal{O}_{\mathcal{H}_2}}$, $\widetilde{\mathcal{O}_{\mathsf{Key}}}$ and $\mathcal{O}_{\mathsf{Sign}}$ involved in EUF-CKA-Attacker (Algorithm 5). The notation $\mathsf{Simu}^r(\mathcal{P}, \omega)$ involved in the routine $\mathcal{O}_{\mathsf{hvzk}}$ indicates that the simulator of the underlying IDS is run r-times on the same input $(\mathcal{P}, \omega)$ to generate transcripts $\pi_1, \ldots, \pi_r$.

with underlying identity $\mathsf{id} \in \mathcal{ID}_\lambda$ and $\mathcal{H}_2$-queries, whereas the list $\mathsf{List}_{\mathsf{key}}$ is updated while answering key-gen and signature queries. Wlog, we assume that for an identity id, at most one secret key $\mathsf{sk}_{\mathsf{id}} = (\mathsf{id}, x, s)$ will be issued to $\mathcal{A}_2$ and the same will be stored in $\mathsf{List_{key}}$[7]. While answering signature query on (M, id), if $\mathsf{id} \in \mathcal{ID}_\lambda$, then $(\mathsf{id}, \perp, s)$ is stored in $\mathsf{List_{key}}$, where $s \xleftarrow{\$} \mathsf{SaltSp}$. Therefore, for each identity id involved in the queries, there will be at most one entry in $\mathsf{List_{key}}$ containing id. We do not need to store the outcome η of the biased coin to each query identity id as the 2nd-entry of $\mathsf{List_{key}}$ can decide η. How the lists $\mathsf{List_2}$ and $\mathsf{List_{key}}$ are exactly updated via the queries to $\widetilde{\mathcal{O}_{\mathcal{H}_2}}$, $\widetilde{\mathcal{O}_{\mathsf{Key}}}$ and $\mathcal{O}_{\mathsf{Sign}}$ made by $\mathcal{A}_2$ are shown in Fig. 4.

Note that all the random oracle queries and key-gen queries are handled perfectly. Also, the signature queries are answered properly thanks to Simu for the HVZK of the underlying 3-pass IDS. Therefore, the probability of valid forgery produced by $\mathcal{A}_1$ is

$$\mathsf{Adv}^{\mathsf{EUF\text{-}CKA}}_{\mathcal{A}_1}(\kappa) = \Pr\left[b = 1 : (b, M^*, \mathsf{id}^*, \sigma^*) \xleftarrow{\$} \mathcal{A}_1^{\{\mathcal{O}_{\mathcal{H}_1}, \mathcal{O}_{\mathcal{H}_2}, \mathcal{O}_{\mathsf{Key}}\}}(\mathcal{P}, \mathsf{ck}, r)\right]$$

$$\geq (1-\lambda)^{\nu_{\mathsf{key}}} \cdot \left(1 - \frac{\nu_2 + \nu_{\mathsf{sign}}}{q^m \cdot 2^{3 \cdot r \cdot \zeta}}\right)^{\nu_{\mathsf{sign}}} \cdot \lambda \cdot \mathsf{Adv}^{\mathsf{EUF\text{-}CMA}}_{\mathcal{A}_2}(\kappa) \quad (16)$$

$$\approx (1-\lambda)^{\nu_{\mathsf{key}}} \cdot \lambda \cdot \mathsf{Adv}^{\mathsf{EUF\text{-}CMA}}_{\mathcal{A}_2}(\kappa) \quad \text{as} \quad \left(1 - \frac{\nu_2 + \nu_{\mathsf{sign}}}{q^m \cdot 2^{3 \cdot r \cdot \zeta}}\right)^{\nu_{\mathsf{sign}}} \approx 1$$

$$\approx \frac{1}{e} \cdot \frac{1}{\nu_{\mathsf{key}}} \cdot \mathsf{Adv}^{\mathsf{EUF\text{-}CMA}}_{\mathcal{A}_2}(\kappa) \approx \mathsf{Adv}^{\mathsf{EUF\text{-}CMA}}_{\mathcal{A}_2}(\kappa)/\nu_{\mathsf{key}}.$$

Each factor appears in Eq. 16 due to the non-abort probability of Algorithm 5, where the abort cases are highlighted by the bounded boxes in the algorithm as well as in the associated oracles defined in Fig. 4. In particular, the probability that abort will not occur in step 6 of the oracle $\mathcal{O}_{\mathsf{hvzk}}$ for each call is at least $(1 - \frac{\nu_2 + \nu_{\mathsf{sign}}}{q^m \cdot 2^{3 \cdot r \cdot \zeta}})$, where ν_2 and ν_{sign} are the number of queries to $\mathcal{O}_{\mathcal{H}_2}$ and $\mathcal{O}_{\mathsf{Sign}}$ oracles respectively, and ζ is the collision entropy of the underlying commitment scheme. Note that the quantity $(1 - \lambda)^{\nu_{\mathsf{key}}} \cdot \lambda$ attains the maximum value $1/(e \cdot \nu_{\mathsf{key}})$ when $\lambda = 1/(1 + \nu_{\mathsf{key}})$. Therefore, the last expression is guaranteed by setting $\lambda = 1/(1 + \nu_{\mathsf{key}})$. This concludes the lemma.

Corollary 2. *Suppose WMQ-problem (c.f., Definition 2) is intractable and the underlying commitment scheme is computationally binding and statistically hiding. Then, the proposed IBS scheme described in Sect. 4 is EUF-CMA secure in the random oracle model.*

Proof. Let ν_1, ν_2 and ν_{key} be the numbers of queries to $\mathcal{H}_1$, $\mathcal{H}_2$ and key-gen oracles respectively and let $\nu = \nu_1 + \nu_2$. Let $\mathcal{A}_2$ be an EUF-CMA-attacker, i.e., EUF-CMA attacker of the proposed IBS scheme. Let Solver be the WMQ-problem solver. Then, using Lemmas 5, 6 and 7, the advantage of Solver is given by:

---

[7] This consideration is for an easy exposition of the reduction. Otherwise, we can allow asking multiple key-gen queries for an identity. In this case, we can keep a counter for each queried identity and even allow $\mathcal{A}_2$ to choose a particular secret key for the same identity by specifying the counter to answer the signature queries.

$$\text{Adv}_{\text{Solver}}^{\text{WMQ}}(\kappa) \geq \frac{1}{\nu^3} \cdot \frac{1}{\nu_{\text{key}}^3} \cdot \left(\text{Adv}_{\mathcal{A}_2}^{\text{EUF-CMA}}(\kappa)\right)^3 \cdot \left(1 - \left(\frac{7}{9}\right)\right)^r \qquad (17)$$

This completes the corollary.

6   Conclusion

We have proposed a provably secure IBS scheme in the MQ-setting. To achieve the security of our construction, we have developed a new forking technique by extending the existing forking algorithm of Bellare-Neven. To the best of our knowledge, our forking related result is the first to apply in the MQ-setting. The forking algorithm is likely to be applicable in the security reduction of other primitives such as blind signature in the MQ-setting.

Acknowledgement. We would like to thank Dr. Subhabrata Samajder and the anonymous reviewers of Indocrypt 2021 for their comments and suggestions that helped us in polishing the technical and editorial content of this paper. This work is supported by the Ministry of Electronics and Information Technology, Government of India through its grants for the Center for Excellence in Quantum Technology at IISc, Bangalore.

References

[BN06]   Bellare, M., Neven, G.: Multi-signatures in the plain public-key model and a general forking lemma. In: 13th ACM Conference on Computer and Communications Security, pp. 390–399. Association for Computing Machinery, New York (2006)

[BNN04] Bellare, M., Namprempre, C., Neven, G.: Security proofs for identity-based identification and signature schemes. In: Cachin, C., Camenisch, J.L. (eds.) EUROCRYPT 2004. LNCS, vol. 3027, pp. 268–286. Springer, Heidelberg (2004). https://doi.org/10.1007/978-3-540-24676-3_17

[BNN09] Bellare, M., Namprempre, C., Neven, G.: Security proofs for identity-based identification and signature schemes. J. Cryptol. **22**(1), 1–61 (2009). https://doi.org/10.1007/s00145-008-9028-8

[BR93]   Bellare, M., Rogaway, P.: Random oracles are practical: a paradigm for designing efficient protocols. In: 1st ACM Conference on Computer and Communications Security, pp. 62–73. SIAM (1993)

[CC03]   Choon, J.C., Hee Cheon, J.: An identity-based signature from gap Diffie-Hellman groups. In: Desmedt, Y.G. (ed.) PKC 2003. LNCS, vol. 2567, pp. 18–30. Springer, Heidelberg (2003). https://doi.org/10.1007/3-540-36288-6_2

[CHR+16] Chen, M.-S., Hülsing, A., Rijneveld, J., Samardjiska, S., Schwabe, P.: From 5-pass $\mathcal{MQ}$-based identification to $\mathcal{MQ}$-based signatures. In: Cheon, J.H., Takagi, T. (eds.) ASIACRYPT 2016. LNCS, vol. 10032, pp. 135–165. Springer, Heidelberg (2016). https://doi.org/10.1007/978-3-662-53890-6_5

[CLND19] Chen, J., Ling, J., Ning, J., Ding, J.: Identity-based signature schemes for multivariate public key cryptosystems. Comput. J. **62**(8), 1132–1147 (2019)

[Cor00]   Coron, J.-S.: On the exact security of full domain hash. In: Bellare, M. (ed.) CRYPTO 2000. LNCS, vol. 1880, pp. 229–235. Springer, Heidelberg (2000). https://doi.org/10.1007/3-540-44598-6_14

[DS05]   Ding, J., Schmidt, D.: Rainbow, a new multivariable polynomial signature scheme. In: Ioannidis, J., Keromytis, A., Yung, M. (eds.) ACNS 2005. LNCS, vol. 3531, pp. 164–175. Springer, Heidelberg (2005). https://doi.org/10.1007/11496137_12

[FS86]   Fiat, A., Shamir, A.: How to prove yourself: practical solutions to identification and signature problems. In: Odlyzko, A.M. (ed.) CRYPTO 1986. LNCS, vol. 263, pp. 186–194. Springer, Heidelberg (1987). https://doi.org/10.1007/3-540-47721-7_12

[Hes02]   Hess, F.: Efficient identity based signature schemes based on pairings. In: Nyberg, K., Heys, H. (eds.) SAC 2002. LNCS, vol. 2595, pp. 310–324. Springer, Heidelberg (2003). https://doi.org/10.1007/3-540-36492-7_20

[HKL19]   Hauck, E., Kiltz, E., Loss, J.: A modular treatment of blind signatures from identification schemes. In: Ishai, Y., Rijmen, V. (eds.) EUROCRYPT 2019. LNCS, vol. 11478, pp. 345–375. Springer, Cham (2019). https://doi.org/10.1007/978-3-030-17659-4_12

[Jen06]   Jensen, J.L.W.V.: Sur les fonctions convexes et les inégalités entre les valeurs moyennes. Acta Math. 30, 175–193 (1906). https://doi.org/10.1007/BF02418571

[KCC05]   Kurkowski, S., Camp, T., Colagrosso, M.: MANET simulation studies: the incredibles. ACM SIGMOBILE Mobile Comput. Commun. Rev. 9(4), 50–61 (2005)

[KPG99]   Kipnis, A., Patarin, J., Goubin, L.: Unbalanced oil and vinegar signature schemes. In: Stern, J. (ed.) EUROCRYPT 1999. LNCS, vol. 1592, pp. 206–222. Springer, Heidelberg (1999). https://doi.org/10.1007/3-540-48910-X_15

[KZ20]   Kales, D., Zaverucha, G.: An attack on some signature schemes constructed from five-pass identification schemes. In: Krenn, S., Shulman, H., Vaudenay, S. (eds.) CANS 2020. LNCS, vol. 12579, pp. 3–22. Springer, Cham (2020). https://doi.org/10.1007/978-3-030-65411-5_1

[Luy19]   Van Luyen, L.: An improved identity-based multivariate signature scheme based on rainbow. Cryptography 3(1), 8 (2019)

[NIS19]   National Institute of Standards and Technology: Post-quantum crypto project (Second Round) (2019). https://csrc.nist.gov/Projects/post-quantum-cryptography/round-2-submissions. Accessed 04 Sept 2021

[NIS20]   National Institute of Standards and Technology: Post-quantum crypto project (Third Round) (2020). https://csrc.nist.gov/publications/detail/nistir/8309/final. Accessed 04 Sept 2021

[Pat02]   Paterson, K.G.: Id-based signatures from pairings on elliptic curves. Electron. Lett. 38(18), 1025–1026 (2002)

[PBB13]   Petzoldt, A., Bulygin, S., Buchmann, J.: A multivariate based threshold ring signature scheme. Appl. Algebra Eng. Commun. Comput. 24(3–4), 255–275 (2013). https://doi.org/10.1007/s00200-013-0190-3

[PS96]   Pointcheval, D., Stern, J.: Security proofs for signature schemes. In: Maurer, U. (ed.) EUROCRYPT 1996. LNCS, vol. 1070, pp. 387–398. Springer, Heidelberg (1996). https://doi.org/10.1007/3-540-68339-9_33

[Sch89]   Schnorr, C.P.: Efficient identification and signatures for smart cards. In: Brassard, G. (ed.) CRYPTO 1989. LNCS, vol. 435, pp. 239–252. Springer, New York (1990). https://doi.org/10.1007/0-387-34805-0_22

[Sha84] Shamir, A.: Identity-based cryptosystems and signature schemes. In: Blakley, G.R., Chaum, D. (eds.) CRYPTO 1984. LNCS, vol. 196, pp. 47–53. Springer, Heidelberg (1985). https://doi.org/10.1007/3-540-39568-7_5

[SSH11a] Sakumoto, K., Shirai, T., Hiwatari, H.: On provable security of UOV and HFE signature schemes against chosen-message attack. In: Yang, B.-Y. (ed.) PQCrypto 2011. LNCS, vol. 7071, pp. 68–82. Springer, Heidelberg (2011). https://doi.org/10.1007/978-3-642-25405-5_5

[SSH11b] Sakumoto, K., Shirai, T., Hiwatari, H.: Public-key identification schemes based on multivariate quadratic polynomials. In: Rogaway, P. (ed.) CRYPTO 2011. LNCS, vol. 6841, pp. 706–723. Springer, Heidelberg (2011). https://doi.org/10.1007/978-3-642-22792-9_40

[STX13] Shen, W., Tang, S., Xu, L.: IBUOV, a provably secure identity-based UOV signature scheme. In: IEEE 16th International Conference on Computational Science and Engineering, pp. 388–395. IEEE (2013)

Public Key Encryption and Protocols

Identity-Based Matchmaking Encryption Without Random Oracles

Danilo Francati[1] , Alessio Guidi[2], Luigi Russo[3](✉) , and Daniele Venturi[2]

[1] Aarhus University, Aarhus, Denmark
dfrancati@cs.au.dk
[2] Sapienza University of Rome, Rome, Italy
venturi@di.uniroma1.it
[3] EURECOM, Sophia Antipolis, Biot, France
russol@eurecom.fr

Abstract. Identity-based matchmaking encryption (IB-ME) is a generalization of identity-based encryption where the sender and the receiver can both specify a target identity: If both the chosen target identities match the one of the other party, the plaintext is revealed, and otherwise the sender's identity, the target identity, and the plaintext remain hidden. Previous work showed how to construct IB-ME in the random oracle model. We give the first construction in the plain model, based on standard assumptions over bilinear groups.

Keywords: Identity-based encryption · Matchmaking encryption · Plain model

1 Introduction

Identity-based encryption (IBE) [6] extends the standard concept of public-key encryption to a setting where the receiver's public key is an arbitrary string representing its identity. This allows a sender to encrypt a message while specifying the identity rcv $\in \{0,1\}^*$ of the intended receiver. A receiver with identity $\rho \in \{0,1\}^*$ obtains a decryption key dk_ρ from an authority, which allows to correctly decrypt the ciphertext so long as $\rho = \mathsf{rcv}$.

Identity-based matchmaking encryption (IB-ME) [2] is a generalization of IBE in which the sender's identity $\sigma \in \{0,1\}^*$ can also be embedded in the ciphertext. The receiver can now additionally specify a target sender's identity snd $\in \{0,1\}^*$ on the fly, and obtain the message so long as there is a match in both directions (*i.e.*, $\rho = \mathsf{rcv}$ and $\sigma = \mathsf{snd}$). An IB-ME should satisfy two main security properties:

- *Privacy:* In case of mismatch (*i.e.*, either $\rho \neq \mathsf{rcv}$ or $\sigma \neq \mathsf{snd}$) both the sender's identity and the plaintext remain hidden.
- *Authenticity:* The sender obtains from the authority an encryption key ek_σ associated to its identity, with the guarantee that it should be hard to forge a valid ciphertext embedding σ without knowing such a key.

© Springer Nature Switzerland AG 2021
A. Adhikari et al. (Eds.): INDOCRYPT 2021, LNCS 13143, pp. 415–435, 2021.
https://doi.org/10.1007/978-3-030-92518-5_19

IB-ME finds applications in settings where IBE with strong anonymity guarantees is required. For instance, Ateniese *et al.* [2] show how to use IB-ME in order to construct a privacy-preserving bulletin board that can be used by newspapers and organizations to collect information from anonymous sources.

1.1   Our Contribution

The work of Ateniese *et al.* [2] shows how to construct IB-ME under the Bilinear Diffie-Hellman assumption. This leaves the following open problem:

Can we construct IB-ME in the plain model?

We answer the above question to the positive by providing the first construction of IB-ME without random oracles (see Sect. 4). On a high level, our result is obtained in two steps:

- First, we give a construction of an IB-ME satisfying privacy based on the Decisional Augmented Bilinear Diffie-Hellman Exponent assumption over bilinear groups. Our scheme builds upon the anonymous IBE of Gentry [4]. Very roughly, we add the functionality that the receiver can decrypt a ciphertext only if it knows (or guesses) the sender's identity. This is achieved by adding a second layer of encryption using a one-time pad derived from the sender's identity via a randomness extractor. While it seems that this idea can be applied generically to any anonymous IBE, our security analysis crucially relies on specific properties of Gentry's scheme (e.g., homomorphism).
- Second, we exhibit a generic transform taking as input any private IB-ME and outputting an IB-ME satisfying both privacy and authenticity. The main idea is to let ek_σ consist of a signature over the sender's identity σ (computed using the authority's master secret key). Hence, the sender encrypts the message using the underlying IB-ME but additionally proves in zero knowledge that it knows a valid signature of the string representing its identity. Privacy follows by the privacy property of the underlying IB-ME along with the zero knowledge property; authenticity follows by knowledge soundness.

An additional contribution of our work is to significantly strengthen the definition of privacy for IB-ME. In particular, the previous definition only guarantees privacy when the receiver's identity ρ does not match the target identity rcv specified by the sender. We give a stronger definition that allows to characterize privacy in a meaningful way also in case the target identity snd chosen by the receiver does not match the identity σ of the sender. We refer the reader to Sect. 3 for more details.

1.2   Related Work

Ateniese *et al.* [2] define the more general concept of ME, in which both the sender and the receiver (each with its own attributes) can specify policies the other party must satisfy in order for the message to be revealed. Differently than IB-ME, the policy chosen by the receiver cannot be chosen on the fly, but is associated to a secret key that is generated by the authority.

As pointed out in [2], the general concept of ME implies both (anonymous) ciphertext-policy and key-policy attribute-based encryption [5,7]. The implication holds in the identity-based setting too: IB-ME can be seen as a more expressive version of (anonymous) IBE [1], in which both the sender and the receiver can specify a target communicating entity (in a privacy-preserving way).

2 Preliminaries

2.1 Notation

We use the notation $[n] \stackrel{\text{def}}{=} \{1, \ldots, n\}$. Capital boldface letters (such as $\mathbf{X}$) are used to denote random variables, small letters (such as x) to denote concrete values, calligraphic letters (such as $\mathcal{X}$) to denote sets, and serif letters (such as A) to denote algorithms. All of our algorithms are modeled as (possibly interactive) Turing machines; if algorithm A has oracle access to some oracle O, we write $\mathcal{Q}_\mathsf{O}$ and $\mathcal{O}_\mathsf{O}$ for the set of queries asked by A to O and for the set of outputs returned by O, respectively.

For a string $x \in \{0,1\}^*$, we let $|x|$ be its length; if $\mathcal{X}$ is a set, $|\mathcal{X}|$ represents the cardinality of $\mathcal{X}$. When x is chosen randomly in $\mathcal{X}$, we write $x \leftarrow_\$ \mathcal{X}$. If A is an algorithm, we write $y \leftarrow_\$ \mathsf{A}(x)$ to denote a run of A on input x and output y; if A is randomized, y is a random variable and $\mathsf{A}(x; r)$ denotes a run of A on input x and (uniform) randomness r. An algorithm A is *probabilistic polynomial-time* (PPT) if A is randomized and for any input $x, r \in \{0,1\}^*$ the computation of $\mathsf{A}(x; r)$ terminates in a polynomial number of steps (in the input size).

Negligible Functions. We denote by $\lambda \in \mathbb{N}$ the security parameter and we implicitly assume that every algorithm takes as input the security parameter (written in unary). A function $\nu : \mathbb{N} \to [0,1]$ is called *negligible* in the security parameter λ if it vanishes faster than the inverse of any polynomial in λ, i.e. $\nu(\lambda) \in O(1/p(\lambda))$ for all positive polynomials $p(\lambda)$. We sometimes write $\mathsf{negl}(\lambda)$ (resp., $\mathsf{poly}(\lambda)$) to denote an unspecified negligible function (resp., polynomial function) in the security parameter.

Unpredictability and Indistinguishability. The min-entropy of a random variable $\mathbf{X} \in \mathcal{X}$ is $\mathbb{H}_\infty(\mathbf{X}) \stackrel{\text{def}}{=} -\log \max_{x \in \mathcal{X}} \mathbb{P}[X = x]$, and it measures the best chance to predict $\mathbf{X}$ (by a computationally unbounded algorithm). We say that $\mathbf{X}$ and $\mathbf{Y}$ are *computationally* indistinguishable, denoted $\mathbf{X} \approx_c \mathbf{Y}$, if for all PPT distinguishers D we have $\Delta_\mathsf{D}(\mathbf{X}; \mathbf{Y}) \in \mathsf{negl}(\lambda)$, where

$$\Delta_\mathsf{D}(\mathbf{X}; \mathbf{Y}) \stackrel{\text{def}}{=} \left| \mathbb{P}\left[\mathsf{D}(1^\lambda, \mathbf{X}) = 1\right] - \mathbb{P}\left[\mathsf{D}(1^\lambda, \mathbf{Y}) = 1\right] \right|.$$

2.2 Signature Schemes

A signature scheme with message space $\mathcal{M}$ is made of the following polynomial-time algorithms.

$\mathsf{KGen}(1^\lambda)$: Upon input the security parameter 1^λ, the randomized key generation algorithm outputs a secret and a public key $(\mathsf{sk}, \mathsf{pk})$.

$\mathsf{Sign}(\mathsf{sk}, m)$: Upon input the secret key sk and the message $m \in \mathcal{M}$, the deterministic signing algorithm produces a signature s.

$\mathsf{Ver}(\mathsf{pk}, m, s)$: Upon input the public key pk, the message $m \in \mathcal{M}$, and the signature s, the deterministic verification algorithm returns a decision bit.

A signature scheme should satisfy two properties. The first property says that honestly generated signatures always verify correctly. The second property, called unforgeability, says that it should be hard to forge a signature on a fresh message, even after seeing signatures on polynomially many messages.

Definition 1 (Correctness of signatures). *A signature scheme $\Pi = (\mathsf{KGen}, \mathsf{Sign}, \mathsf{Ver})$ with message space $\mathcal{M}$ is correct if $\forall \lambda \in \mathbb{N}$, $\forall (\mathsf{sk}, \mathsf{pk})$ output by $\mathsf{KGen}(1^\lambda)$, and $\forall m \in \mathcal{M}$, the following holds:* $\mathbb{P}[\mathsf{Ver}(\mathsf{pk}, m, \mathsf{Sign}(\mathsf{sk}, m)) = 1] = 1$.

Definition 2 (Unforgeability of signatures). *A signature scheme $\Pi = (\mathsf{KGen}, \mathsf{Sign}, \mathsf{Ver})$ is existentially unforgeable under chosen-message attacks (EUF-CMA) if for all PPT adversaries A:*

$$\mathbb{P}\left[\mathbf{G}^{\mathsf{euf}}_{\Pi,\mathsf{A}}(\lambda) = 1\right] \leq \mathsf{negl}(\lambda),$$

where $\mathbf{G}^{\mathsf{euf}}_{\Pi,\mathsf{A}}(\lambda)$ is the following experiment:

- $(\mathsf{sk}, \mathsf{pk}) \leftarrow_\$ \mathsf{KGen}(1^\lambda)$.
- $(m, s) \leftarrow_\$ \mathsf{A}^{\mathsf{Sign}(\mathsf{sk}, \cdot)}(1^\lambda, \mathsf{pk})$
- *If $m \notin \mathcal{Q}_{\mathsf{Sign}}$, and $\mathsf{Ver}(\mathsf{pk}, m, s) = 1$, output 1, else output 0.*

2.3 Non-interactive Zero Knowledge

Let R be a relation, corresponding to an NP language L. A non-interactive zero-knowledge (NIZK) proof system for R is a tuple of polynomial-time algorithms $\Pi = (\mathsf{I}, \mathsf{P}, \mathsf{V})$ specified as follows. (i) The randomized algorithm I takes as input the security parameter and outputs a common reference string ω; (ii) The randomized algorithm $\mathsf{P}(\omega, (y, x))$, given $(y, x) \in R$ outputs a proof π; (iii) The deterministic algorithm $\mathsf{V}(\omega, (y, \pi))$, given an instance y and a proof π outputs either 0 (for "reject") or 1 (for "accept"). We say that a NIZK for relation R is *correct* if for all $\lambda \in \mathbb{N}$, every ω output by $\mathsf{I}(1^\lambda)$, and any $(y, x) \in R$, we have that $\mathsf{V}(\omega, (y, \mathsf{P}(\omega, (y, x)))) = 1$.

We define two properties of a NIZK proof system. The first property, called adaptive multi-theorem zero knowledge, says that honest proofs do not reveal anything beyond the fact that $y \in L$. The second property, called knowledge soundness, requires that every adversary creating a valid proof for some statement, must know the corresponding witness.

Definition 3 (Adaptive multi-theorem zero-knowledge). *A NIZK Π for a relation R satisfies adaptive multi-theorem zero-knowledge if there exists a PPT simulator $\mathsf{Z} := (\mathsf{Z}_0, \mathsf{Z}_1)$ such that the following holds:*

- *Algorithm Z_0 outputs ω and a simulation trapdoor ζ.*
- *For all PPT distinguishers D, we have that*

$$\left| \mathbb{P}\left[\mathsf{D}^{\mathsf{P}(\omega,(\cdot,\cdot))}(\omega) = 1 : \ \omega \leftarrow_{\$} \mathsf{I}(1^\lambda) \right] \right.$$
$$\left. - \mathbb{P}\left[\mathsf{D}^{\mathsf{O}(\zeta,(\cdot,\cdot))}(\omega) = 1 : \ (\omega,\zeta) \leftarrow_{\$} \mathsf{Z}_0(1^\lambda) \right] \right| \leq \mathsf{negl}(\lambda),$$

where the oracle $\mathsf{O}(\zeta, (\cdot, \cdot))$ takes as input a pair (y, x) and returns $\mathsf{Z}_1(\zeta, y)$ if $(y, x) \in R$ (and $\perp$ otherwise).

Definition 4 (Knowledge soundness). *A NIZK Π for a relation R satisfies knowledge soundness if there exists a PPT extractor $\mathsf{K} = (\mathsf{K}_0, \mathsf{K}_1)$ such that the following holds:*

- *Algorithm K_0 outputs ω and an extraction trapdoor ξ, such that the distribution of ω is computationally indistinguishable to that of $\mathsf{I}(1^\lambda)$.*
- *For all PPT adversaries A, we have that*

$$\mathbb{P}\left[\begin{array}{c} \mathsf{V}(\omega, (y, \pi)) = 1 \wedge \\ (y, x) \notin R \end{array} : \begin{array}{c} (\omega, \xi) \leftarrow_{\$} \mathsf{K}_0(1^\lambda) \\ (y, \pi) \leftarrow_{\$} \mathsf{A}(\omega) \\ x \leftarrow_{\$} \mathsf{K}_1(\xi, y, \pi) \end{array} \right] \leq \mathsf{negl}(\lambda).$$

2.4 Reusable Computational Extractors

A computational extractor is a polynomial time algorithm $\mathsf{Ext} : \mathcal{S} \times \mathcal{X} \to \mathcal{Y}$ that on input a seed $s \in \mathcal{S}$ and a value $x \in \mathcal{X}$ outputs $\mathsf{Ext}_s(x) = y \in \mathcal{Y}$. The security of computational extractors guarantees that $y \in \mathcal{Y}$ is pseudorandom when the seed is sampled at random from $\mathcal{S}$ and x is sampled from an input distribution $\mathbf{X}$ (defined over the input space $\mathcal{X}$) of min-entropy $\mathbb{H}_\infty(\mathbf{X}) \geq k$, even if the seed is made public. In this work, we will rely on so-called *reusable* [3], computational extractors, that produce random looking outputs even if evaluated multiple times on the same input. The formal definition is provided below.

Definition 5 (Reusable computational extractors). *An algorithm $\mathsf{Ext} : \mathcal{S} \times \mathcal{X} \to \mathcal{Y}$ is a (k, q)-reusable-extractor if for all random variables $\mathbf{X} \in \mathcal{X}$ such that $\mathbb{H}_\infty(\mathbf{X}) \geq k$, and for all PPT distinguishers D, it holds that*

$$\Delta_\mathsf{D}((s_1, \ldots, s_q, \mathsf{Ext}_{s_1}(x), \ldots, \mathsf{Ext}_{s_q}(x)); (s_1, \ldots, s_q, y_1, \ldots, y_q)) \leq \mathsf{negl}(\lambda),$$

where $x \leftarrow_{\$} \mathbf{X}$, $s_i \leftarrow_{\$} \mathcal{S}$, and $y_i \leftarrow_{\$} \mathcal{Y}$ (for all $i \in [q]$).

2.5 Augumented Bilinear Diffie-Hellman Exponent Assumption

Our IB-ME construction is based on the hardness of the decisional truncated ABDHE assumption, which we recall below.

Definition 6 (Decisional truncated q-ABDHE assumption). *Let $\mathbb{G}$ and $\mathbb{G}_T$ be two groups of prime order p. Let $e : \mathbb{G} \times \mathbb{G} \to \mathbb{G}_T$ be an admissible bilinear map, and let g, g' be generators of $\mathbb{G}$. The decisional truncated q-ABDHE problem is hard in $(\mathbb{G}, \mathbb{G}_T, e)$ if for every PPT adversary A:*

$$\left| \mathbb{P}\left[\mathsf{A}(g', g'_{q+2}, g, g_1, \ldots, g_q, e(g_{q+1}, g')) = 0\right] \right.$$
$$\left. - \mathbb{P}\left[\mathsf{A}(g', g'_{q+2}, g, g_1, \ldots, g_q, Z) = 0\right] \right| \leq \mathsf{negl}(\lambda),$$

where $g_i = g^{(\alpha^i)}$, $g, g' \leftarrow_{\$} \mathbb{G}$, $\alpha \leftarrow_{\$} \mathbb{Z}_p$ and $Z \in \mathbb{G}_T$.

3 Identity-Based Matchmaking Encryption

We recall below the definition of IB-ME presented in [2]. In IB-ME (i.e., ME in the identity-based setting), attributes and policies are treated as binary strings. We denote with rcv and snd the target identities (i.e., policies) chosen by the sender and the receiver, respectively. We say that a match (resp. mismatch) occurs when $\sigma = \mathsf{snd}$ and $\rho = \mathsf{rcv}$ (resp. $\sigma \neq \mathsf{snd}$ or $\rho \neq \mathsf{rcv}$). The receiver can choose the target identity snd on the fly.

3.1 Syntax

More formally, an IB-ME scheme is composed of the following 5 polynomial-time algorithms:

Setup(1^λ): Upon input the security parameter 1^λ, the randomized setup algorithm outputs the master public key mpk and the master secret key msk. We implicitly assume that all other algorithms take mpk as input.

SKGen(msk, σ): Upon input the master secret key msk, and identity σ, the randomized sender-key generator outputs an encryption key ek_σ for σ.

RKGen(msk, ρ): Upon input the master secret key msk, and identity ρ, the randomized receiver-key generator outputs a decryption key dk_ρ for ρ.

Enc(ek_σ, rcv, m): Upon input the encryption key ek_σ for identity σ, a target identity rcv, and a message $m \in \mathcal{M}$, the randomized encryption algorithm produces a ciphertext c linked to both σ and rcv.

Dec(dk_ρ, snd, c): Upon input the decryption key dk_ρ for identity ρ, a target identity snd, and a ciphertext c, the deterministic decryption algorithm outputs either a message m or $\bot$.

Correctness. Correctness of IB-ME simply says that in case of a match the receiver obtains the plaintext.

Definition 7 (Correctness of IB-ME). *An IB-ME Π = (Setup, SKGen, RKGen, Enc, Dec) is correct if $\forall \lambda \in \mathbb{N}$, $\forall (\text{mpk}, \text{msk})$ output by $\text{Setup}(1^\lambda)$, $\forall m \in \mathcal{M}$, $\forall \sigma, \rho, \text{rcv}, \text{snd} \in \{0, 1\}^*$ such that $\sigma = \text{snd}$ and $\rho = \text{rcv}$:*

$$\mathbb{P}[\text{Dec}(\text{dk}_\rho, \text{snd}, \text{Enc}(\text{ek}_\sigma, \text{rcv}, m)) = m] \geq 1 - \text{negl}(\lambda),$$

where $\text{ek}_\sigma \leftarrow_\$ \text{SKGen}(\text{msk}, \sigma)$ *and* $\text{dk}_\rho \leftarrow_\$ \text{RKGen}(\text{msk}, \rho)$.

3.2 Security

We now define privacy and authenticity of IB-ME. Recall that privacy captures secrecy of the sender's inputs (σ, rcv, m). This is formalized by asking the adversary to distinguish between $\text{Enc}(\text{ek}_{\sigma_0}, \text{rcv}_0, m_0)$ and $\text{Enc}(\text{ek}_{\sigma_1}, \text{rcv}_1, m_1)$ where $(m_0, m_1, \sigma_0, \sigma_1, \text{rcv}_0, \text{rcv}_1)$ are chosen by the attacker.

$\mathbf{G}_{\Pi,\mathsf{A}}^{\text{ib-priv}}(\lambda)$	$\mathbf{G}_{\Pi,\mathsf{A}}^{\text{ib-auth}}(\lambda)$
$(\text{mpk}, \text{msk}) \leftarrow_\$ \text{Setup}(1^\lambda)$	$(\text{mpk}, \text{msk}) \leftarrow_\$ \text{Setup}(1^\lambda)$
$(m_0, m_1, \text{rcv}_0, \text{rcv}_1, \sigma_0, \sigma_1, \alpha) \leftarrow_\$ \mathsf{A}_1^{\mathsf{O}_1, \mathsf{O}_2}(1^\lambda, \text{mpk})$	$(c, \rho, \text{snd}) \leftarrow_\$ \mathsf{A}^{\mathsf{O}_1, \mathsf{O}_2}(1^\lambda, \text{mpk})$
$b \leftarrow_\$ \{0, 1\}$	$\text{dk}_\rho \leftarrow_\$ \text{RKGen}(\text{msk}, \rho)$
$\text{ek}_{\sigma_b} \leftarrow_\$ \text{SKGen}(\text{msk}, \sigma_b)$	$m = \text{Dec}(\text{dk}_\rho, \text{snd}, c)$
$c \leftarrow_\$ \text{Enc}(\text{ek}_{\sigma_b}, \text{rcv}_b, m_b)$	If $\forall \sigma \in \mathcal{Q}_{\mathsf{O}_1} : (\sigma \neq \text{snd}) \wedge (m \neq \bot)$
$b' \leftarrow_\$ \mathsf{A}_2^{\mathsf{O}_1, \mathsf{O}_2}(1^\lambda, c, \alpha)$	**return 1**
If $(b' = b)$ **return 1**	Else **return 0**
Else **return 0**	

Fig. 1. Games defining CPA-privacy and CPA-authenticity security of IB-ME. Oracles O_1, O_2 are implemented by $\text{SKGen}(\text{msk}, \cdot)$, $\text{RKGen}(\text{msk}, \cdot)$.

Definition 8 (Privacy of IB-ME [2]). *We say that an IB-ME Π satisfies privacy if for all valid PPT adversaries $\mathsf{A} = (\mathsf{A}_1, \mathsf{A}_2)$:*

$$\left| \mathbb{P}\left[\mathbf{G}_{\Pi,\mathsf{A}}^{\text{ib-priv}}(\lambda) = 1\right] - \frac{1}{2} \right| \leq \text{negl}(\lambda),$$

where game $\mathbf{G}_{\Pi,\mathsf{A}}^{\text{ib-priv}}(\lambda)$ *is defined in Fig. 1. Adversary $\mathsf{A} = (\mathsf{A}_1, \mathsf{A}_2)$ is called valid if $\forall \rho \in \mathcal{Q}_{\mathsf{O}_2}$ it satisfies the following invariant:*

$$\rho \neq \text{rcv}_0 \wedge \rho \neq \text{rcv}_1 \tag{1}$$

Note that, when a match occurs, IB-ME reveals all the inputs of the encryption algorithm (as the sender's and receiver's identities match). Hence, the above definition only guarantees privacy when a match does not occur (mismatch case). However, as discussed in [2], since the receiver can choose a target identity snd on the fly during the decryption process, we need to restrict privacy only to the case when the adversary holds a decryption key dk_ρ for an identity ρ that does not satisfy both target identities rcv_0 and rcv_1 (see Eq. (1)). This is because otherwise an adversary can submit a challenge $(m, m, \sigma_0, \sigma_1, rcv, rcv)$ such that $\sigma_0 \neq \sigma_1$, and then ask for the decryption key dk_ρ for the identity $\rho = rcv$ (i.e., the adversary's identity satisfies the sender's policy). Then, the adversary can retrieve the challenge bit b by simply decrypting the challenge ciphertext c under the target identity snd_0.

The definition of authenticity intuitively says that an adversary cannot compute a valid ciphertext under the identity σ, if it does not hold the corresponding encryption key ek_σ produced by the authority.

Definition 9 (Authenticity of IB-ME [2]). *We say that an IB-ME Π satisfies* authenticity *if for all PPT adversaries* A:

$$\mathbb{P}\left[\mathbf{G}_{\Pi,A}^{\text{ib-auth}}(\lambda) = 1\right] \leq \text{negl}(\lambda),$$

where game $\mathbf{G}_{\Pi,A}^{\text{ib-auth}}(\lambda)$ *is defined in Fig. 1.*

Note that the secret encryption key ek_σ is needed only when authenticity is required. For applications where authenticity is not required, we can simply let $ek_\sigma = \sigma = \text{SKGen}(msk, \sigma)$ and $\text{Enc}(ek_\sigma, rcv, m) = \text{Enc}(\sigma, rcv, m)$. We also observe that Definition 9 is slightly stronger than the definition of authenticity given in [2]. In particular, the adversary is allowed to obtain the decryption key dk_σ for the identity $\sigma = snd$ where snd is the receiver's target identity included in the forgery (c, ρ, snd).

3.3   A Stronger Flavor of Privacy

As we argue below, the above definition of privacy provides an unsatisfactory level of security and does not match the intuitive privacy guarantee of matchmaking encryption. In particular, Definition 8 guarantees privacy only when the receiver does not hold a decryption key dk_ρ for an identity ρ that allows to decrypt the challenge ciphertext. This is reminiscent of anonymous IBE (where anonymity refers to secrecy of the sender's identity). Indeed, we can use an anonymous IBE $\Pi' = (\text{Setup}', \text{KGen}', \text{Enc}', \text{Dec}')$ to build an IB-ME $\Pi_{\text{bad}} = (\text{Setup}, \text{SKGen}, \text{RKGen}, \text{Enc}, \text{Dec})$ as follows:

1. The IB-ME encryption algorithm $\text{Enc}(ek_\sigma, rcv, m)$ produces a ciphertext $c \leftarrow_\$ \text{Enc}'(rcv, m\|\sigma)$ where $ek_\sigma = \sigma$ and $(msk, mpk) \leftarrow_\$ \text{Setup}(1^\lambda) = \text{Setup}'(1^\lambda)$.
2. The IB-ME decryption algorithm $\text{Dec}(dk_\rho, snd, c)$ computes $m\|\sigma = \text{Dec}(dk_\rho, c)$ where $dk_\rho \leftarrow_\$ \text{RKGen}(msk, \rho) = \text{KGen}'(msk, \rho)$. Finally, it outputs m if $\sigma = snd$. Otherwise, it returns $\perp$.

It is easy to see that the above IB-ME satisfies privacy as per Definition 8, as security of the anonymous IBE Π' implies that $\mathsf{Enc}(\mathsf{ek}_{\sigma_0}, \mathsf{rcv}_0, m_0) = \mathsf{Enc}'(\mathsf{rcv}_0, m_0 || \sigma_0) \approx_c \mathsf{Enc}'(\mathsf{rcv}_1, m_1 || \sigma_1) = \mathsf{Enc}(\mathsf{ek}_{\sigma_1}, \mathsf{rcv}_1, m_1)$. However, Π_{bad} does not meet the intuitive privacy guarantee of IB-ME. Suppose a receiver, holding an identity ρ, tries to decrypt a ciphertext c computed as $\mathsf{Enc}'(\mathsf{rcv}, m || \sigma)$ where $\rho = \mathsf{rcv}$. Regardless of the selected target identity snd, the receiver will learn the sender's identity σ by simply decrypting c using the decryption key dk_ρ.

This gap is due to the fact that Definition 8 does not take into account the case in which the receiver's target identity snd is not satisfied by σ. Unfortunately, this seems inherent in that when σ_0 and σ_1 are chosen by the adversary, the attacker can simply try to decrypt the challenge ciphertext by choosing on the fly a target identity $\mathsf{snd} = \sigma_0 \neq \sigma_1$. Ateniese et al. [2, Remark 1] noticed this gap and informally argued that their IB-ME construction hides the message and the sender's identity to an honest receiver that uses an invalid target identity snd. For readers familiar with [2], the latter follows by the fact that their construction leverages a random oracle to derive a one-time key from the sender's identity σ. Intuitively, this allows to hide σ to an honest receiver that does not evaluate the random oracle on the same input $\mathsf{snd} = \sigma$ (i.e., to a receiver that does not choose the correct target identity $\mathsf{snd} = \sigma$).

A Stronger Definition of Privacy. We introduce a stronger flavor of privacy, which we dub *enhanced* privacy. Enhanced privacy captures privacy of IB-ME according to every possible mismatch condition for the receiver. The main challenge is to capture the scenario in which the adversary wants to leak information from a ciphertext $c \leftarrow_\$ \mathsf{Enc}(\mathsf{ek}_{\sigma_b}, \mathsf{rcv}_b, m_b)$ while holding a decryption key dk_ρ such that $\rho = \mathsf{rcv}_b$ for $b \in \{0, 1\}$. As explained in [2, Section 5], an adversary that matches the target identity chosen by the sender, can always choose on the fly a target identity snd such that $\mathsf{snd} = \sigma_0 \neq \sigma_1$ and leak the bit b by decrypting the challenge ciphertext. In order to rule out the above trivial attack, our definition of enhanced privacy modifies the mismatch condition in such a way that the sender's identities σ_0, σ_1 are hidden when the adversary holds a decryption key dk_ρ for the identity $\rho = \mathsf{rcv}$. This does not allow the attacker to choose $\mathsf{snd} = \sigma_0 \neq \sigma_1$, since σ_0, σ_1 are kept secret.

More formally, the security game for enhanced privacy (see Fig. 2) is identical to that of privacy (see Fig. 1) except that the challenge sender's attributes σ_0 and σ_1 are replaced with two adversarial distributions $\mathbf{ID}_0$ and $\mathbf{ID}_1$. The challenger privately samples $(\sigma_0, \sigma_1) \leftarrow_\$ \mathbf{ID}_0 \times \mathbf{ID}_1$ and proceeds as usual by computing $c \leftarrow_\$ \mathsf{Enc}(\mathsf{ek}_{\sigma_b}, \mathsf{rcv}_b, m_b)$ for $b \leftarrow_\$ \{0, 1\}$. To capture secrecy of σ_i for $i \in \{0, 1\}$, and avoid trivial attacks when the adversary holds dk_ρ such that $\rho = \mathsf{rcv}_i$, we require the distributions $\mathbf{ID}_i$ to have a non-trivial amount of min-entropy $\mathbb{H}_\infty(\mathbf{ID}_i) \geq \omega(\log(\lambda))$. In particular, an adversary is considered valid if for every identity ρ for which it knows the corresponding decryption key dk_ρ: (i) Either $\rho \neq \mathsf{rcv}_0$ and $\rho \neq \mathsf{rcv}_1$, or (ii) the distributions $\mathbf{ID}_0$ and $\mathbf{ID}_1$ have a non-trivial amount of min-entropy $\mathbb{H}_\infty(\mathbf{ID}_i) \geq \omega(\log(\lambda))$ for $i \in \{0, 1\}$, or (iii) $\rho \neq \mathsf{rcv}_0$ and

$$
\begin{array}{|l|}
\hline
\mathbf{G}_{\Pi,\mathsf{A}}^{\mathsf{ib\text{-}priv}^+}(\lambda) \\
\hline
(\mathsf{mpk}, \mathsf{msk}) \leftarrow_\$ \mathsf{Setup}(1^\lambda) \\
(m_0, m_1, \mathsf{rcv}_0, \mathsf{rcv}_1, \mathbf{ID}_0, \mathbf{ID}_1, \alpha) \leftarrow_\$ \mathsf{A}_1^{\mathsf{O}_1, \mathsf{O}_2}(1^\lambda, \mathsf{mpk}) \\
\sigma_0 \leftarrow_\$ \mathbf{ID}_0, \sigma_1 \leftarrow_\$ \mathbf{ID}_1 \\
\mathsf{ek}_{\sigma_0} \leftarrow_\$ \mathsf{SKGen}(\mathsf{msk}, \sigma_0), \mathsf{ek}_{\sigma_1} \leftarrow_\$ \mathsf{SKGen}(\mathsf{msk}, \sigma_1) \\
b \leftarrow_\$ \{0, 1\} \\
c \leftarrow_\$ \mathsf{Enc}(\mathsf{ek}_{\sigma_b}, \mathsf{rcv}_b, m_b) \\
b' \leftarrow_\$ \mathsf{A}_2^{\mathsf{O}_1, \mathsf{O}_2, \{\mathsf{O}_3^i\}_{i \in \{0,1\}}}(1^\lambda, c, \alpha) \\
\text{If } (b' = b) \\
\quad \textbf{return } 1 \\
\text{Else } \textbf{return } 0 \\
\hline
\end{array}
$$

Fig. 2. Games defining enhanced privacy of IB-ME. Oracles O_1, O_2 are implemented by $\mathsf{SKGen}(\mathsf{msk}, \cdot)$, $\mathsf{RKGen}(\mathsf{msk}, \cdot)$. Oracle $\mathsf{O}_3^i(m, \mathsf{rcv})$ is implemented by $\mathsf{Enc}(\mathsf{ek}_{\sigma_i}, \mathsf{rcv}, m)$ for $i \in \{0, 1\}$.

$\mathbf{ID}_1$ has a non-trivial amount of min-entropy $\mathbb{H}_\infty(\mathbf{ID}_1) \geq \omega(\log(\lambda))$, or (iv) $\rho \neq \mathsf{rcv}_1$ and $\mathbf{ID}_0$ has a non-trivial amount of min-entropy $\mathbb{H}_\infty(\mathbf{ID}_0) \geq \omega(\log(\lambda))$.

Definition 10 (Enhanced privacy of IB-ME). *We say that an IB-ME Π satisfies* enhanced privacy *if for all valid PPT adversaries* $\mathsf{A} = (\mathsf{A}_1, \mathsf{A}_2)$:

$$
\left| \mathbb{P}\left[\mathbf{G}_{\Pi,\mathsf{A}}^{\mathsf{ib\text{-}priv}^+}(\lambda) = 1 \right] - \frac{1}{2} \right| \leq \mathsf{negl}(\lambda),
$$

where game $\mathbf{G}_{\Pi,\mathsf{A}}^{\mathsf{ib\text{-}priv}^+}(\lambda)$ *is depicted in Fig. 2. Adversary* $\mathsf{A} = (\mathsf{A}_1, \mathsf{A}_2)$ *is called* valid *if* $\forall \rho \in \mathcal{Q}_{\mathsf{O}_2}$ *it satisfies the following invariant:*

$$
(\rho \neq \mathsf{rcv}_0 \wedge \rho \neq \mathsf{rcv}_1) \vee (\mathbb{H}_\infty(\mathbf{ID}_0), \mathbb{H}_\infty(\mathbf{ID}_1) \geq \omega(\log(\lambda))) \tag{2}
$$
$$
\vee\ (\rho \neq \mathsf{rcv}_0 \wedge \mathbb{H}_\infty(\mathbf{ID}_1) \geq \omega(\log(\lambda)))
$$
$$
\vee\ (\rho \neq \mathsf{rcv}_1 \wedge \mathbb{H}_\infty(\mathbf{ID}_0) \geq \omega(\log(\lambda))).
$$

Note that, in the second query phase, the adversary has oracle access to $\mathsf{Enc}(\mathsf{ek}_{\sigma_0}, \cdot, \cdot)$ and $\mathsf{Enc}(\mathsf{ek}_{\sigma_0}, \cdot, \cdot)$. This is crucial in order to give the attacker the possibility to obtain ciphertexts under arbitrary messages and target identities when the identity σ_i is unknown (i.e., $\mathbb{H}_\infty(\mathbf{ID}_i) \geq \omega(\log(\lambda))$).

Remark 1. Observe that enhanced privacy (cf. Definition 10) is stronger than privacy (cf. Definition 8). Indeed, enhanced privacy rules out all the adversaries that choose two constant distributions $\mathbf{ID}_0 = \sigma_0$ and $\mathbf{ID}_1 = \sigma_1$ and always play the security experiment with respect to the first mismatch condition ($\rho \neq \mathsf{rcv}_0 \wedge \rho \neq \mathsf{rcv}_1$) of Eq. (2). Those are all the adversaries ruled out by Definition 8.

Remark 2. The contrived IB-ME Π_{bad} described at the beginning of Sect. 3.3 does not satisfy enhanced privacy. To see this, consider the adversary that plays the experiment $\mathbf{G}^{\mathsf{ib\text{-}priv}^+}_{\Pi_{\mathsf{bad}},\mathsf{A}}(\lambda)$ of Fig. 2 with respect to the second mismatch condition $(\mathbb{H}_\infty(\mathbf{ID}_0) \geq \omega(\log(\lambda) \wedge \mathbb{H}_\infty(\mathbf{ID}_1) \geq \omega(\log(\lambda)))$ of Eq. (2) as follows:

- Output a challenge $(m, m, \mathsf{rcv}, \mathsf{rcv}, \mathbf{ID}_0, \mathbf{ID}_1)$ such that $\mathbf{ID}_0$, $\mathbf{ID}_1$ have an empty intersection (i.e., there does not exist an identity σ that is output by both distributions) and $\mathbb{H}_\infty(\mathbf{ID}_0) \geq \omega(\log(\lambda))$, $\mathbb{H}_\infty(\mathbf{ID}_1) \geq \omega(\log(\lambda))$.
- Ask to $\mathsf{O}_2(\cdot) = \mathsf{RKGen}(\mathsf{msk}, \cdot) = \mathsf{KGen}'(\mathsf{msk}, \cdot)$ the decryption key dk_ρ for $\rho = \mathsf{rcv}$ (observe that this is a valid query when $\mathbb{H}_\infty(\mathbf{ID}_0) \geq \omega(\log(\lambda))$ and $\mathbb{H}_\infty(\mathbf{ID}_1) \geq \omega(\log(\lambda))$).
- Decrypt the challenge ciphertext c by executing $m||\sigma = \mathsf{Dec}'(\mathsf{dk}_\rho, c)$ using the decryption algorithm of the underlying IBE, and output $b' = 0$ if $\sigma \in \mathbf{ID}_0$. Otherwise, output $b' = 1$.

Since the encryption algorithm $\mathsf{Enc}(\mathsf{ek}_\sigma, \mathsf{rcv}, m)$ of Π_{bad} encrypts a ciphertext by running $\mathsf{Enc}'(\mathsf{rcv}, m||\sigma)$ (see Item 1 in the description of Π_{bad}) where Enc' is the encryption algorithm of the underlying IBE, the above adversary outputs $b' = b$ with overwhelming probability.

4   Construction Without Random Oracles

In this section, we describe our constructions of IB-ME and prove their security. We start by giving a direct construction of an IB-ME satisfying enhanced privacy in the plain model. Hence, we show how to add authenticity generically via a generic transform (while preserving enhanced privacy).

4.1   Achieving Privacy

Our construction is based on the anonymous IBE of Gentry [4]. At a high level, in this scheme one encrypts a message m under the target identity rcv by computing $m \cdot g^s$ where s is sampled at random. During decryption, a receiver holding the correct decryption key dk_ρ for $\rho = \mathsf{rcv}$ is able to compute the inverse g^{-s} of g^s (by leveraging auxiliary information included in the ciphertext) and therefore obtain the message. Our IB-ME leverages the homomorphic properties of the IBE scheme to encrypt the message as $m \cdot g^s \cdot g_\sigma$, where g_σ is output by a reusable extractor $\mathsf{Ext}_x(\sigma)$. This way, a receiver also needs to choose the correct target identity $\mathsf{snd} = \sigma$ to recompute g_σ and recover m. Since our construction will not meet authenticity directly, we will assume that $\sigma = \mathsf{ek}_\sigma = \mathsf{SKGen}(\mathsf{msk}, \sigma)$ and $\mathsf{Enc}(\mathsf{ek}_\sigma, \mathsf{rcv}, m) = \mathsf{Enc}(\sigma, \mathsf{rcv}, m)$.

Construction 1. *Let $\mathbb{G}$ and $\mathbb{G}_T$ be groups of order p, and let $e : \mathbb{G} \times \mathbb{G} \to \mathbb{G}_T$ be a symmetric pairing, and let $\mathsf{Ext} : \mathcal{S} \times \mathbb{Z}_p \to \mathbb{G}_T$.*

$\mathsf{Setup}(1^\lambda)$: *Sample random generators $g \in \mathbb{G}$ and $\alpha, y \leftarrow_\$ \mathbb{Z}_p$. Compute $g_\alpha = g^\alpha \in \mathbb{G}$, and $h = g^y$. Output $\mathsf{mpk} = (g, g_\alpha, h)$ and $\mathsf{msk} = (\alpha, y)$.*

SKGen(msk, σ): *Upon input* msk $= (\alpha, y)$ *and* $\sigma \in \{0,1\}^*$, *return* ek$_\sigma = \sigma$.

RKGen(msk, ρ): *Upon input* msk $= (\alpha, y)$ *and* $\rho \in \mathbb{Z}_p$, *sample* $r_\rho \in \mathbb{Z}_p$ *and output* dk$_\rho = (h_\rho, r_\rho)$, *where* $h_\rho = g^{\frac{y - r_\rho}{\alpha - \rho}}$. *If an indentity* $\rho \in \mathbb{Z}_p$ *is queried multiple times, we require* RKGen *to use the same value* r_ρ *(this can be accomplished by leveraging a PRF).*

Enc(ek$_\sigma$, rcv, m): *Upon input* ek$_\sigma = \sigma \in \{0,1\}^*$, rcv $\in \mathbb{Z}_p$, *and* $m \in \mathbb{G}_T$, *sample* $s \leftarrow_\$ \mathbb{Z}_p$, $x \leftarrow_\$ \mathcal{S}$, *compute* $g_\sigma = \mathsf{Ext}_x(\sigma)$, *and return* $c = (c_1, c_2, c_3, c_4)$ *where*

$$c_1 = (g_\alpha \cdot g^{-\mathsf{rcv}})^s, \quad c_2 = e(g, g)^s, \quad c_3 = x, \quad c_4 = m \cdot e(g, h)^{-s} \cdot g_\sigma.$$

Dec(dk$_\rho$, snd, c): *Upon input* dk$_\rho = (h_\rho, r_\rho)$, snd $\in \{0,1\}^*$, *and* $c = (c_1, c_2, c_3, c_4)$, *return* $m = c_4 \cdot e(c_1, h_\rho) \cdot c_2^{r_\rho} \cdot g_\mathsf{snd}^{-1}$ *where* $g_\mathsf{snd} = \mathsf{Ext}_{c_3}(\mathsf{snd})$.

Correctness (cf. Definition 7) follows because $\forall \sigma, \mathsf{rcv}, \rho, \mathsf{snd} \in \mathbb{Z}_p$, $(h_\rho, r_\rho) =$ dk$_\rho \leftarrow_\$ $ RKGen(msk, ρ) such that snd $= \sigma$ and rcv $= \rho$, we have:

$$g_\mathsf{snd} = \mathsf{Ext}_{c_3}(\mathsf{snd}) = \mathsf{Ext}_x(\sigma) = g_\sigma, \text{ and}$$

$$e(c_1, h_\rho) \cdot c_2^{r_\rho} = e(g^{s(\alpha - \rho)}, g^{\frac{y - r_\rho}{\alpha - \rho}}) \cdot e(g, g)^{s \cdot r_\rho} = e(g, h)^s.$$

The theorem below says that the above scheme satisfies enhanced privacy. The proof of security leverages both the homomorphic properties and the ciphertext structure of Gentry's scheme. For this reason, our technique does not extend directly to any anonymous IBE scheme.

Theorem 1. *Assuming that* Ext *is an* $(\omega(\log(\lambda)), q_\mathsf{ext})$-*reusable-extractor, and that the truncated decisional* q_abdhe-*ABDHE problem is hard, then the IB-ME Π from Construction 1 satisfies enhanced privacy, so long as* $q_\mathsf{abdhe} = q_{\mathcal{O}_2} + 1$ *and* $q_\mathsf{ext} = \max\{q_{\mathcal{O}_3^0}, q_{\mathcal{O}_3^1}\} + 1$ *(where* $q_\mathcal{O}$ *is the number of queries submitted to oracle* $\mathcal{O}$ *in the game of Fig. 2).*

Proof. For brevity, let $\mathbf{G}_{\Pi,\mathsf{A}}^{\mathsf{ib\text{-}priv}^+}(\lambda) = \mathbf{G}(\lambda)$ be the experiment of Fig. 2. Recall that, in order to be valid, the adversary A must satisfy at least one of the four mismatch conditions given in Eq. (2); we define the events corresponding to each condition below:

$$\mathbf{Mismatch}_1 : \forall \rho \in \mathcal{Q}_{\mathcal{O}_2}, \rho \neq \mathsf{rcv}_0 \wedge \rho \neq \mathsf{rcv}_1 \tag{3}$$

$$\mathbf{Mismatch}_2 : \mathbb{H}_\infty(\mathbf{ID}_0), \mathbb{H}_\infty(\mathbf{ID}_1) \geq \omega(\log(\lambda)) \tag{4}$$

$$\mathbf{Mismatch}_3 : \forall \rho \in \mathcal{Q}_{\mathcal{O}_2}, \rho \neq \mathsf{rcv}_0 \wedge \mathbb{H}_\infty(\mathbf{ID}_1) \geq \omega(\log(\lambda)) \tag{5}$$

$$\mathbf{Mismatch}_4 : \forall \rho \in \mathcal{Q}_{\mathcal{O}_2}, \rho \neq \mathsf{rcv}_1 \wedge \mathbb{H}_\infty(\mathbf{ID}_0) \geq \omega(\log(\lambda)). \tag{6}$$

Lemma 1. $\left| \mathbb{P}\left[\mathbf{G}_{\Pi,\mathsf{A}}^{\mathsf{ib\text{-}priv}^+}(\lambda) = 1 \middle| \mathbf{Mismatch}_1 \right] - \frac{1}{2} \right| \leq \mathsf{negl}(\lambda)$.

Proof. We consider a sequence of hybrid experiments. For the rest of this proof, we think of the experiments as conditioned on the event $\mathbf{Mismatch}_1$ of Eq. (3).

$\mathbf{H}_1(\lambda)$: This is identical to $\mathbf{G}(\lambda)$. Without loss of generality we assume the adversary A does not make any query to oracles $\{O_3^i\}$ for $i \in \{0, 1\}$. This is because, according to Eq. (3), A can choose two constant distributions $\sigma_0 = \mathsf{ID}_0, \sigma_1 = \mathsf{ID}_1$ and simulate the oracle $O_3^i(m, \mathsf{rcv})$ as $\mathsf{Enc}(\mathsf{ek}_{\sigma_i}, \mathsf{rcv}, m)$ where $\mathsf{ek}_{\sigma_i} \leftarrow\!\!{\scriptstyle\$}\, O_1(1^\lambda, \sigma_i)$, for $i \in \{0, 1\}$.

$\mathbf{H}_2(\lambda)$: Same as $\mathbf{H}_1(\lambda)$, except that, after receiving the challenge $(m_0, m_1, \mathsf{rcv}_0, \mathsf{rcv}_1, \sigma_0 = \mathsf{ID}_0, \sigma_1 = \mathsf{ID}_1)$ from the adversary (recall we assume that $\mathsf{ID}_0, \mathsf{ID}_1$ are constant distributions), the challenger produces the challenge ciphertext $c^* = (c_1^*, c_2^*, c_3^*, c_4^*)$ where c_4^* is computed as

$$c_4^* = (m_b \cdot g_{\sigma_b}^*)/(e(c_1^*, h_{\mathsf{rcv}_b}) \cdot c_2^{* r_{\mathsf{rcv}_b}^*}) \tag{7}$$

for $(h_{\mathsf{rcv}_b}^*, r_{\mathsf{rcv}_b}^*) \leftarrow\!\!{\scriptstyle\$}\, \mathsf{RKGen}(\mathsf{msk}, \mathsf{rcv}_b)$ and $g_{\sigma_b}^* = \mathsf{Ext}_{c_3^*}(\sigma_b)$. Observe that the value $1/(e(c_1^*, h_{\mathsf{rcv}_b}) \cdot c_2^{* r_{\mathsf{rcv}_b}^*})$ in Eq. (7) can be computed by running $e(g, h)^{-s}$ as in the decryption algorithm.

$\mathbf{H}_3(\lambda)$: Same as $\mathbf{H}_2(\lambda)$, except for the following differences.

Setup: The challenger samples a random polynomial $f(x) \leftarrow\!\!{\scriptstyle\$}\, \mathbb{Z}_p[x]$ of degree $q = q_{\mathsf{abdhe}}$, $\alpha \leftarrow\!\!{\scriptstyle\$}\, \mathbb{Z}_p$, and sets $g_\alpha = g^\alpha$ and $h = g^{f(\alpha)}$. Then, it returns $\mathsf{mpk} = (g, g_\alpha, h)$ and keeps $\mathsf{msk} = (\alpha, y)$ where $y = f(\alpha)$.

RKGen $= O_2$: On input $\rho \in \mathbb{Z}_p$ for $\mathsf{RKGen} = O_2$, the challenger defines the polynomial $F_\rho(x) = (f(x) - f(\rho))/(x - \rho)$ of degree $q - 1$ and computes $h_\rho = g^{F_\rho(\alpha)}$ and $r_\rho = f(\rho)$. Finally, it returns $\mathsf{dk}_\rho = (h_\rho, r_\rho)$.

Challenge: The challenger receives the challenge $(m_0, m_1, \mathsf{rcv}_0, \mathsf{rcv}_1, \sigma_0 = \mathsf{ID}_0, \sigma_1 = \mathsf{ID}_1)$. It samples $b \leftarrow\!\!{\scriptstyle\$}\, \{0, 1\}$ and it defines the degree $q + 1$ polynomial

$$F^*(x) = \frac{x^{q+2} - \mathsf{rcv}_b^{q+2}}{x - \mathsf{rcv}_b} = \sum_{i=0}^{q+1} F_i^* \cdot x^i,$$

where F_i^* is the i-th coefficient of F^*. It computes the challenge ciphertext $c^* = (c_1^*, c_2^*, c_3^*, c_4^*)$ as $c_1^* = g'^{\alpha^{q+2}} \cdot g'^{-\mathsf{rcv}_b^{q+2}}$ and $c_2^* = e(g', g)^{\alpha^{q+2}} \cdot e(g', \prod_{i=0}^q (g^{\alpha^i})^{F_i^*})$, where $g' \leftarrow\!\!{\scriptstyle\$}\, \mathbb{G}$, and c_3^*, c_4^* are computed as described in experiment $\mathbf{H}_2(\lambda)$.

$\mathbf{H}_4(\lambda)$: Same as $\mathbf{H}_3(\lambda)$, except that the challenger generates c_1^* and c_2^* in the challenge ciphertext using different randomness. In more details, the challenger computes $c_1^* = (g_\alpha \cdot g^{\mathsf{rcv}_b})^{s_1}$ and $c_2^* = e(g, g)^{s_2}$ for $s_1 \leftarrow\!\!{\scriptstyle\$}\, \mathbb{Z}_p$ and $s_2 \leftarrow\!\!{\scriptstyle\$}\, \mathbb{Z}_p \backslash \{s_1\}$.

Claim. $\{\mathbf{H}_1(\lambda)\}_{\lambda \in \mathbb{N}} \equiv \{\mathbf{H}_2(\lambda)\}_{\lambda \in \mathbb{N}}$.

Proof. The difference between $\mathbf{H}_1(\lambda)$ and $\mathbf{H}_2(\lambda)$ is purely conceptional. Hence, the claim follows.

Claim. $\{\mathbf{H}_2(\lambda)\}_{\lambda \in \mathbb{N}} \equiv \{\mathbf{H}_3(\lambda)\}_{\lambda \in \mathbb{N}}$.

Proof. We show that $\mathbf{H}_2(\lambda)$ and $\mathbf{H}_3(\lambda)$ are identically distributed. The distribution of mpk and msk in $\mathbf{H}_3(\lambda)$ is perfectly simulated since f is a random polynomial. The challenger evaluates the polynomial $f(x)$ on points $\mathcal{I} =$

$\{\alpha, \mathsf{rcv}_b\} \cup \mathcal{Q}_{\mathsf{O}_2}$. Let $q = q_{\mathsf{abdhe}}$. Since $|\mathcal{I}| \leq q+1$ and f are random polynomials of degree q, we have that $\{f(i)\}_{i \in \mathcal{I}}$ are uniform and independent as in $\mathbf{H}_2(\lambda)$.

As for the challenge ciphertext, note that c_3^*, c_4^* are computed in the same way in both experiments. Hence, we focus on c_1^*, c_2^*. In $\mathbf{H}_3(\lambda)$ we can write c_1^* and c_2^* as follows

$$c_1^* = (g'^{\alpha^{q+2}} \cdot g'^{-\mathsf{rcv}_b^{q+2}}) = g^{t(\alpha - \mathsf{rcv}_b)F^*(\alpha)}$$

$$c_2^* = e(g', g)^{\alpha^{q+2}} \cdot e(g', \prod_{i=0}^{q}(g^{\alpha^i})^{F_i^*}) = e(g^t, g^{F^*(\alpha)})$$

where $g' = g^t$. By setting the randomness $s = t \cdot F^*(\alpha)$ (note that s is random since g' is random) we obtain that c_1^*, c_2^* of $\mathbf{H}_3(\lambda)$ are identically distributed to the ones of $\mathbf{H}_2(\lambda)$. This concludes the proof.

Claim. $\{\mathbf{H}_3(\lambda)\}_{\lambda \in \mathbb{N}} \approx_c \{\mathbf{H}_4(\lambda)\}_{\lambda \in \mathbb{N}}$.

Proof. For the sake of clarity, let $q = q_{\mathsf{abdhe}}$. Assume there exists a distinguisher D that is able to distinguish between $\mathbf{H}_3(\lambda)$ and $\mathbf{H}_4(\lambda)$ with non-negligible advantage. We build an adversary A that solves the q-ABDHE problem. A receives as input $(g', g'^{\alpha^{q+2}}, g, g^{\alpha}, \ldots, g^{\alpha^q}, Z)$ and proceeds as in $\mathbf{H}_3(\lambda)$ except for the following differences.

- At setup, it samples a random polynomial $f(x) \leftarrow_\$ \mathbb{Z}_p[x]$ of degree q and sets $h = g^{f(\alpha)}$. Note that h can be computed without knowing α using the values $g, g^{\alpha}, \ldots, g^{\alpha^q}$. Send $\mathsf{mpk} = (g, g_\alpha = g^{\alpha}, h)$ to D. Note that the distribution of mpk is perfectly simulated and this implicitly defines the secret key $\mathsf{msk} = (\alpha, y)$ where $y = f(\alpha)$.
- On input $\rho \in \mathbb{Z}_p$ for $\mathsf{RKGen} = \mathsf{O}_2$, it answers as in $\mathbf{H}_3(\lambda)$ except that $h_\rho = g^{F_\rho(\alpha)}$ is computed without knowing α using $g, g^{\alpha}, \ldots, g^{\alpha^q}$. Note that dk_ρ is a correctly simulated decryption key.
- During the challenge phase, it receives $(m_0, m_1, \mathsf{rcv}_0, \mathsf{rcv}_1, \sigma_0 = \mathbf{ID}_0, \sigma_1 = \mathbf{ID}_1)$. Hence, A samples $b \leftarrow_\$ \{0,1\}$ and defines the degree $q+1$ polynomial

$$F^*(x) = \frac{x^{q+2} - \mathsf{rcv}_b^{q+2}}{x - \mathsf{rcv}_b} = \sum_{i=0}^{q+1} F_i^* \cdot x^i$$

as in $\mathbf{H}_3(\lambda)$. Finally, A computes the challenge ciphertext $c^* = (c_1^*, c_2^*, c_3^*, c_4^*)$ as in $\mathbf{H}_3(\lambda)$ except that it sets $c_1^* = g'^{\alpha^{q+2}} \cdot g'^{-\mathsf{rcv}_b^{q+2}}$ and $c_2^* = Z \cdot e(g', \prod_{i=0}^{q}(g^{\alpha^i})^{F_i^*})$. Note that c_1^*, c_2^* can be computed using the input for the q-ABDHE problem.

As in the proof of the previous claim, if c_1^*, c_2^* are correctly distributed, so are c_3^*, c_4^*. We write c_1^* as $c_1^* = g'^{\alpha^{q+2}} \cdot g'^{-\mathsf{rcv}_b^{q+2}} = g^{t(\alpha - \mathsf{rcv}_b)F^*(\alpha)} = g^{(\alpha - \mathsf{rcv}_b)s_1}$, for $s_1 = t \cdot F^*(\alpha)$. Note that s_1 is random since g' is a random generator of $\mathbb{G}$. If

$Z = e(g', g)^{\alpha^{q+1}}$, the ciphertext c^* is distributed as in $\mathbf{H_3}(\lambda)$ since c_1^* and c_2^* are computed using the same randomness. Indeed, we have

$$c_2^* = Z \cdot e(g', \prod_{i=0}^{q} (g^{\alpha^i})^{F_i^*}) = e(g^t, g^{F^*(\alpha)}) = e(g, g)^{s_1}.$$

On the other hand, if $Z \leftarrow_{\$} \mathbb{G}_T$ so is c_2^* as in $\mathbf{H_4}(\lambda)$. This concludes the proof.

In the last experiment, c_1^*, c_2^*, and c_3^* look like three random elements in $\mathbb{G}$, $\mathbb{G}_T$, and $\mathcal{S}$, respectively. Since c_1^* and c_2^* are random, the inequalities $c_2^* \neq e(c_1^*, g)^{\frac{1}{\alpha - \mathsf{rcv}_0}}$ and $c_2^* \neq e(c_1^*, g)^{\frac{1}{\alpha - \mathsf{rcv}_1}}$ hold with overwhelming probability. When the above inequalities hold, the value $e(c_1^*, h_{\mathsf{rcv}_b}^*) \cdot (c_2^*)^{r_{\mathsf{rcv}_b}^*}$ (used to compute c_4^*) is uniformly distributed in $\mathbb{G}_T$ since $r_{\mathsf{rcv}_b}^*$ is random and independent from the A's view (since A can not ask for decryption key $\mathsf{dk}_{\mathsf{rcv}_0}$ and $\mathsf{dk}_{\mathsf{rcv}_1}$). As a consequence, the tuple $c^* = (c_1^*, c_2^*, c_3^*, c_4^*)$ does not leak any information about b (except with negligible probability). Hence, Lemma 1 follows by combining the above claims.

Lemma 2. $\left| \mathbb{P}\left[\mathbf{G}_{\Pi,\mathsf{A}}^{\mathsf{ib\text{-}priv}^+}(\lambda) = 1 \middle| \mathbf{Mismatch_2} \right] - \frac{1}{2} \right| \leq \mathsf{negl}(\lambda).$

Proof. Without loss of generality, assume $q_{\mathsf{O}_3^b} \geq q_{\mathsf{O}_3^{1-b}}$. Hence, we have $q_{\mathsf{ext}} = q_{\mathsf{O}_3^b} + 1$. We consider a sequence of hybrid experiments. For the rest of this proof, we think of the experiments as conditioned on the event $\mathbf{Mismatch_2}$ of Eq. (4).

$\mathbf{H_1}(\lambda)$: This is identical to $\mathbf{G}(\lambda)$.

$\mathbf{H_2}(\lambda)$: Same as $\mathbf{H_1}(\lambda)$, except that the challenger changes how it produces the challenge and the answers of oracles O_3^0 and O_3^1 for $i \in \{0, 1\}$. Let $\mathcal{L}_0$ and $\mathcal{L}_1$ be two empty sets:
  - When computing the challenge $c^* = (c_1^*, c_2^*, c_3^*, c_4^*)$ for bit b, the challenger adds c_3^* to $\mathcal{L}_b$.
  - On input (m, rcv) for O_3^i, the challenger computes $c = (c_1, c_2, c_3, c_4)$ as in $\mathbf{H_1}(\lambda)$. Then, if $c_3 \in \mathcal{L}_i$, the challenger aborts. Otherwise, it adds c_3 to $\mathcal{L}_i$ and proceeds as in $\mathbf{H_1}(\lambda)$.

$\mathbf{H_3}(\lambda)$: Same as $\mathbf{H_2}(\lambda)$, except that the challenger changes how it produces the challenge and the answers of oracles O_3^b where b is the challenge bit.
  - When computing the challenge $c^* = (c_1^*, c_2^*, c_3^*, c_4^*)$ for bit b, the challenger samples $g_{\sigma_b}^*$ at random from $\mathbb{G}_T$.
  - On input (m, rcv) for O_3^b, the challenger samples $s \leftarrow_{\$} \mathbb{Z}_p$ and computes (c_1, c_2, c_3) under the randomness s (note that c_1, c_2, c_3 are computed as usual). Then, it samples $g_{\sigma_b} \leftarrow_{\$} \mathbb{G}_T$ and it computes $c_4 = m \cdot e(g, h)^{-s} \cdot g_{\sigma_b}$.

$\mathbf{H_4}(\lambda)$: Same as $\mathbf{H_3}(\lambda)$, except that the challenger changes the answers of oracles O_3^{1-b} where b is the challenge bit.
  - On input (m, rcv) for O_3^{1-b}, the challenger samples $s \leftarrow_{\$} \mathbb{Z}_p$ and computes (c_1, c_2, c_3) under the randomness s (note that c_1, c_2, c_3 are computed as usual). Then, it samples $g_{\sigma_{1-b}} \leftarrow_{\$} \mathbb{Z}_p$ and it computes $c_4 = m \cdot e(g, h)^{-s} \cdot g_{\sigma_{1-b}}$.

$\mathbf{H}_5(\lambda)$: Same as $\mathbf{H}_4(\lambda)$, except that, after receiving the challenge $(m_0, m_1, \mathsf{rcv}_0,$ $\mathsf{rcv}_1, \mathbf{ID}_0, \mathbf{ID}_1)$ from the adversary, the challenger produces the challenge ciphertext $c^* = (c_1^*, c_2^*, c_3^*, c_4^*)$ where c_4^* is computed as

$$c_4^* = (m_b \cdot g_{\sigma_b}^*)/(e(c_1^*, h_{\mathsf{rcv}_b}^*) \cdot c_2^{* r_{\mathsf{rcv}_b}^*}), \tag{8}$$

where $(h_{\mathsf{rcv}_b}^*, r_{\mathsf{rcv}_b}^*) \leftarrow_{\$} \mathsf{RKGen}(\mathsf{msk}, \mathsf{rcv}_b)$ and $g_{\sigma_b}^* \leftarrow_{\$} \mathbb{G}_T$. Note that the value $1/(e(c_1^*, h_{\mathsf{rcv}_b}^*) \cdot c_2^{* r_{\mathsf{rcv}_b}^*})$ in Eq. (8) can be computed by running $e(g, h)^{-s}$ in the decryption algorithm. The same approach is used to answer the queries submitted to O_3^0 and O_3^1. On input (m, rcv) for O_3^i for $i \in \{0, 1\}$, the challenger computes $c = (c_1, c_2, c_3, c_4)$ except that c_4 is computed as $c_4 = (m \cdot g_{\sigma_i})/(e(c_1, h_{\mathsf{rcv}}) \cdot c_2^{r_{\mathsf{rcv}}})$, where $(h_{\mathsf{rcv}}, r_{\mathsf{rcv}}) \leftarrow_{\$} \mathsf{RKGen}(\mathsf{msk}, \mathsf{rcv})$ and $g_{\sigma_i} \leftarrow_{\$} \mathbb{G}_T$

$\mathbf{H}_6(\lambda)$: Same as $\mathbf{H}_5(\lambda)$, except for the following differences.

Setup: The challenger samples a random polynomial $f(x) \leftarrow_{\$} \mathbb{Z}_p[x]$ of degree $q = q_{\mathsf{abdhe}}$, $\alpha \leftarrow_{\$} \mathbb{Z}_p$, and sets $g_\alpha = g^\alpha$ and $h = g^{f(\alpha)}$. It returns $\mathsf{mpk} = (g, g_\alpha, h)$ and keeps $\mathsf{msk} = (\alpha, y)$ where $y = f(\alpha)$.

$\mathsf{RKGen}(1^\lambda, \cdot) = \mathsf{O}_2(\cdot)$: On input $\rho \in \mathbb{Z}_p$ for $\mathsf{RKGen} = \mathsf{O}_2$, the challenger defines the polynomial $F_\rho(x) = (f(x) - f(\rho))/(x - \rho)$ of degree $q - 1$ and computes $h_\rho = g^{F_\rho(\alpha)}$ and $r_\rho = f(\rho)$ Finally, it returns $\mathsf{dk}_\rho = (h_\rho, r_\rho)$.

Challenge: The challenger receives the challenge $(m_0, m_1, \mathsf{rcv}_0, \mathsf{rcv}_1, \mathbf{ID}_0,$ $\mathbf{ID}_1)$. It samples $b \leftarrow_{\$} \{0, 1\}$ and it defines the degree $q + 1$ polynomial

$$F^*(x) = \frac{x^{q+2} - \mathsf{rcv}_b^{q+2}}{x - \mathsf{rcv}_b} = \sum_{i=0}^{q+1} F_i^* \cdot x^i,$$

where F_i^* is the i-th coefficient of F^*. It computes the challenge ciphertext $c^* = (c_1^*, c_2^*, c_3^*, c_4^*)$ as $c_1^* = g'^{\alpha^{q+2}} \cdot g'^{-\mathsf{rcv}_b^{q+2}}$ and $c_2^* = e(g', g)^{\alpha^{q+2}} \cdot e(g', \prod_{i=0}^{q} (g^{\alpha^i})^{F_i^*})$, where $g' \leftarrow_{\$} \mathbb{G}$, and c_3^*, c_4^* are computed as described in experiment $\mathbf{H}_5(\lambda)$.

$\mathsf{Enc}(\mathsf{ek}_{\sigma_i}, \cdot, \cdot) = \mathsf{O}_3^i(\cdot, \cdot)$: On input (m, rcv) for $\mathsf{Enc} = \mathsf{O}_3^i$, the challenger generates the decryption key $\mathsf{dk}_{\mathsf{rcv}} = (h_{\mathsf{rcv}}, r_{\mathsf{rcv}}) \leftarrow_{\$} \mathsf{O}_2(1^\lambda, \mathsf{rcv})$ and computes $c = (c_1, c_2, c_3, c_4)$ as in $\mathbf{H}_5(\lambda)$, i.e.

$$c_1 = (g_\alpha \cdot g^{-\mathsf{rcv}})^s, \quad c_2 = e(g, g)^s, \quad c_3 = x$$
$$c_4 = (m \cdot g_{\sigma_i})/(e(c_1, h_{\mathsf{rcv}}) \cdot c_2^{r_{\mathsf{rcv}}}),$$

where $s \leftarrow_{\$} \mathbb{Z}_p$, $g_{\sigma_i} \leftarrow_{\$} \mathbb{G}_T$.

$\mathbf{H}_7(\lambda)$: Same as $\mathbf{H}_6(\lambda)$, except that the challenger generates c_1^* and c_2^* in the challenge ciphertext using different randomness. More in details, the challenger compute $c_1^* = (g_\alpha \cdot g^{\mathsf{rcv}_b})^{s_1}$ and $c_2^* = e(g, g)^{s_2}$ for $s_1 \leftarrow_{\$} \mathbb{Z}_p$ and $s_2 \leftarrow_{\$} \mathbb{Z}_p \backslash \{s_1\}$.

Claim. $\{\mathbf{H}_1(\lambda)\}_{\lambda \in \mathbb{N}} \approx_c \{\mathbf{H}_2(\lambda)\}_{\lambda \in \mathbb{N}}$.

Proof. The claim follows by simply observing that each time c_3 is sampled at random. Hence, since the adversary submits at most a polynomial number of queries to oracles O_3^0 and O_3^1, the probability that $c_3 \in \mathcal{L}_0$ or $c_3 \in \mathcal{L}_1$ is negligible.

Claim. $\{\mathbf{H}_2(\lambda)\}_{\lambda \in \mathbb{N}} \approx_c \{\mathbf{H}_3(\lambda)\}_{\lambda \in \mathbb{N}}$.

Proof. Assume there exists D telling apart the two experiments with non-negligible advantage. We build an adversary A that breaks the security of the reusable extractor.

1. A proceeds as in experiment $\mathbf{H}_2(\lambda)$ until the challenge phase.
2. During the challenge phase, it receives $(m_0, m_1, \mathsf{rcv}_0, \mathsf{rcv}_1, \mathbf{ID}_0, \mathbf{ID}_1)$. Hence, A samples $b \leftarrow_\$ \{0, 1\}$ and sends $\mathbf{ID}_b$ to the challenger. It receives $(x_1, \ldots, x_{q_{\mathrm{ext}}}, g_1, \ldots, g_{q_{\mathrm{ext}}})$, where A has to determine if $g_i = \mathsf{Ext}_{x_i}(\sigma_b)$ for $\sigma_b \leftarrow_\$ \mathbf{ID}_b$. Hence:
   - It samples $\sigma_{1-b} \leftarrow_\$ \mathbf{ID}_{1-b}$ and it creates an empty set $\mathcal{L}_b$.
   - It computes $c^* = (c_1^*, c_2^*, c_3^*, c_4^*)$ as in $\mathbf{H}_2(\lambda)$ except that $c_3^* = x_1$ and $c_4^* = m_b \cdot e(g, h)^{s^*} \cdot g_1$, where s^* is the randomness used to compute c_1^* and c_2^*.
3. During the second query phase, the adversary answers to the queries submitted as usual except for O_3^b:
   - On input the i-th query (m, rcv) for O_3^b, the adversary computes $c = (c_1, c_2, c_3, c_4)$ as in $\mathbf{H}_2(\lambda)$ except that $c_3 = x_i$ and $c_4 = m \cdot e(g, h)^{-s} \cdot g_i$, where s is the randomness used to compute c_1 and c_2.

Note that $q_{\mathrm{ext}} = q_{\mathsf{O}_3^b}$ and $\mathbb{H}_\infty(\mathbf{ID}_b) \geq \omega(\log(\lambda))$. It is easy to see that if $(g_1, \ldots, g_{q_{\mathrm{ext}}}) = (\mathsf{Ext}_{x_1}(\sigma_b), \ldots, \mathsf{Ext}_{x_{q_{\mathrm{ext}}}}(\sigma_b))$ then A perfectly simulates experiment $\mathbf{H}_2(\lambda)$. On the other hand, if $(g_1, \ldots, g_{q_{\mathrm{ext}}})$ are random elements, then A perfectly simulates $\mathbf{H}_3(\lambda)$. Hence, A breaks the security of the reusable extractors with the same advantage of D. This concludes the proof.

Claim. $\{\mathbf{H}_3(\lambda)\}_{\lambda \in \mathbb{N}} \approx_c \{\mathbf{H}_4(\lambda)\}_{\lambda \in \mathbb{N}}$.

Proof. Identical to the analogous step in the proof of Lemma 1, and therefore omitted.

Claim. $\{\mathbf{H}_4(\lambda)\}_{\lambda \in \mathbb{N}} \equiv \{\mathbf{H}_5(\lambda)\}_{\lambda \in \mathbb{N}}$.

Proof. The difference between the two hybrids is purely conceptional. Hence, the claim follows.

Claim. $\{\mathbf{H}_5(\lambda)\}_{\lambda \in \mathbb{N}} \equiv \{\mathbf{H}_6(\lambda)\}_{\lambda \in \mathbb{N}}$.

Proof. Similarly to the proof of a previous claim, we have that the setup phase, the challenge phase, and the queries to oracle O_2 are perfectly simulated. It follows that the answers returned by O_3^i in $\mathbf{H}_5(\lambda)$ are identical to the ones in $\mathbf{H}_6(\lambda)$, for $i \in \{0, 1\}$. This concludes the proof.

Claim. $\{\mathbf{H}_6(\lambda)\}_{\lambda \in \mathbb{N}} \approx_c \{\mathbf{H}_7(\lambda)\}_{\lambda \in \mathbb{N}}$.

Proof. Similar to the proof of the corresponding step in Lemma 1. The only differences are that oracles O_3^i must be simulated as defined in $\mathbf{H}_5(\lambda)$ and that the challenge ciphertext $c = (c_1^*, c_2^*, c_3^*, c_4^*)$ can be simulated by sampling $g_{\sigma_b}^*$ uniformly at random from $\mathbb{G}_T$ as in $\mathbf{H}_5(\lambda)$.

In the last experiment, c_1^*, c_2^*, c_3^* are random elements in $\mathbb{G}$, $\mathbb{G}_T$, and $\mathcal{S}$, respectively. Moreover, since $g_{\sigma_b}^*$ (used to compute c_4^*) is sampled at random, we conclude that the tuple $c^* = (c_1^*, c_2^*, c_3^*, c_4^*)$ does not leak any information about b (except with negligible probability). Hence, Lemma 2 follows by combining the above claims.

Lemma 3. $\left| \mathbb{P}\left[\mathbf{G}_{\Pi,\mathsf{A}}^{\mathsf{ib\text{-}priv}^+}(\lambda) = 1 \,\middle|\, \mathbf{Mismatch}_3 \right] - \frac{1}{2} \right| \leq \mathsf{negl}(\lambda)$.

Proof. As in the proof of Lemma 2, we assume $q_{\mathsf{O}_3^b} \geq q_{\mathsf{O}_3^{1-b}}$. Hence, we have $q_{\mathsf{ext}} = q_{\mathsf{O}_3^b} + 1$. We consider a sequence of hybrid experiments, where $\mathbf{H}^b(\lambda)$ is the experiment with challenge bit is $b \in \{0,1\}$. For the rest of this proof, we think of the experiments as conditioned on the event $\mathbf{Mismatch}_3$ of Eq. (5).

$\mathbf{H}_1^0(\lambda)$: This is identical to $\mathbf{G}(\lambda)$ with challenge bit $b = 0$. Without loss of generality we assume the adversary A does not make any query to oracles O_3^0. Similarly to $\mathbf{H}_1(\lambda)$ in the proof of Lemma 1, according to Eq. (5), the adversary A can choose a constant distribution $\sigma_0 = \mathbf{ID}_0$ and simulate the oracle $\mathsf{O}_3^0(m, \mathsf{rcv})$ as $\mathsf{Enc}(\mathsf{ek}_{\sigma_0}, \mathsf{rcv}, m)$ where $\mathsf{ek}_{\sigma_0} \leftarrow\!\!{}_\$ \mathsf{O}_1(1^\lambda, \sigma_0)$. Observe that $\mathbf{H}_1^0(\lambda)$ is identical to $\mathbf{H}_1(\lambda)$ in the proof of Lemma 1, except that we fix the challenge bit $b = 0$ and we assume only $\sigma_0 = \mathbf{ID}_0$ as constant distribution.

$\mathbf{H}_i^0(\lambda)$, **for** $i \in \{2,3,4\}$: Each hybrid $\mathbf{H}_i^0(\lambda)$ is defined as $\mathbf{H}_i(\lambda)$ in the proof of Lemma 1 for $i \in \{2,3,4\}$ except that we fix the bit $b = 0$ and, similarly to $\mathbf{H}_1^0(\lambda)$ we assume only $\sigma_0 = \mathbf{ID}_0$ is constant (and thus there are no queries submitted to O_3^0).

$\mathbf{H}_5^0(\lambda)$: Same as $\mathbf{H}_4^0(\lambda)$ except that the challenger changes how it produces the answers of oracle O_3^1. Let $\mathcal{L}_1$ be an empty set:
  - On input (m, rcv) for O_3^1, the challenger computes $c = (c_1, c_2, c_3, c_4)$ as in $\mathbf{H}_1^0(\lambda)$. Then, if $c_3 \in \mathcal{L}_1$, the challenger aborts. Otherwise, it adds c_3 to $\mathcal{L}_1$ and proceeds as in $\mathbf{H}_4^0(\lambda)$.

Note that $\mathbf{H}_5^0(\lambda)$ is defined similarly to $\mathbf{H}_2(\lambda)$ in the proof of Lemma 2.

$\mathbf{H}_6^0(\lambda)$: Same as $\mathbf{H}_5^0(\lambda)$ except that the challenger changes the answers of oracles O_3^1 as follows.
  - On input (m, rcv) for O_3^1, the challenger computes (c_1, c_2, c_3, c_4) as in $\mathbf{H}_5^0(\lambda)$ except that $g_{\sigma_1} \leftarrow\!\!{}_\$ \mathbb{G}_T$ (note that g_{σ_1} is used to compute c_4).

Note that $\mathbf{H}_6^0(\lambda)$ is defined similarly to $\mathbf{H}_4(\lambda)$ in the proof of Lemma 2.

$\mathbf{H}_i^1(\lambda)$, **for** $i \in \{7,8,9,10,11,12,13\}$: Each hybrid $\mathbf{H}_i^1(\lambda)$ is defined as $\mathbf{H}_{i-4}(\lambda)$ in the proof of Lemma 2 except that we fix the bit $b = 0$ and, similarly to $\mathbf{H}_1^0(\lambda)$ we assume only $\sigma_0 = \mathbf{ID}_0$ is constant (and thus there are no queries submitted to O_3^0). Note that $\mathbf{H}_5^1(\lambda)$ is identical to $\mathbf{G}(\lambda)$ with challenge bit $b = 1$.

Claim. $\{\mathbf{H}_1^0(\lambda)\}_{\lambda \in \mathbb{N}} \approx_c \{\mathbf{H}_4^0(\lambda)\}_{\lambda \in \mathbb{N}}$.

Proof. Identical to the proof of a previous claim, except that we set the challenge bit $b = 0$ and we simulate O_3^1 as defined in Construction 1. In particular, one can show:

$$\mathbf{H}_1^0(\lambda) \equiv \mathbf{H}_2^0 \equiv \mathbf{H}_3^0(\lambda) \approx_c \mathbf{H}_4^0(1^\lambda).$$

Claim. $\{\mathbf{H}_7^1(\lambda)\}_{\lambda \in \mathbb{N}} \approx_c \{\mathbf{H}_{13}^1(\lambda)\}_{\lambda \in \mathbb{N}}.$

Proof. Identical to the proof of a previous claim, except that we set the challenge bit $b = 1$. In particular, one can show:

$$\mathbf{H}_7^1(1^\lambda) \approx_c \mathbf{H}_8^1 \approx_c \mathbf{H}_9^1(1^\lambda) \approx_c \mathbf{H}_{10}^1(1^\lambda) \equiv \mathbf{H}_{11}^1(1^\lambda) \equiv \mathbf{H}_{12}^1(1^\lambda) \approx_c \mathbf{H}_{13}^1(1^\lambda).$$

Claim. $\{\mathbf{H}_4^0(\lambda)\}_{\lambda \in \mathbb{N}} \approx_c \{\mathbf{H}_5^0(\lambda)\}_{\lambda \in \mathbb{N}}.$

Proof. Similar to the proof of a previous claim and therefore omitted.

Claim. $\{\mathbf{H}_5^0(\lambda)\}_{\lambda \in \mathbb{N}} \approx_c \{\mathbf{H}_6^0(\lambda)\}_{\lambda \in \mathbb{N}}.$

Proof. Similar to the proof of a previous claim and therefore omitted.

Claim. $\{\mathbf{H}_6^0(\lambda)\}_{\lambda \in \mathbb{N}} \equiv \{\mathbf{H}_{13}^1(\lambda)\}_{\lambda \in \mathbb{N}}.$

Proof. By leveraging the same argument used at the end of the proof of Lemma 1 and Lemma 2, we conclude that in both experiments $\mathbf{H}_6^0(\lambda)$ and $\mathbf{H}_{13}^1(\lambda)$ the challenge ciphertext $c^* = (c_1^*, c_3^*, c_3^*, c_4^*)$ is uniform in $\mathbb{G}_1 \times \mathbb{G}_2 \times \mathcal{S} \times \mathbb{G}_T$ to the eyes of the adversary. Hence, the two hybrid experiments are identically distributed. This concludes the proof.

Lemma 4. $\left| \mathbb{P}\left[\mathbf{G}_{\Pi,\mathsf{A}}^{\mathsf{ib\text{-}priv}^+}(\lambda) = 1 \middle| \mathsf{Mismatch}_4 \right] - \frac{1}{2} \right| \leq \mathsf{negl}(\lambda).$

Proof. The proof is symmetrical to that of Lemma 3, and therefore omitted.

Theorem 1 now follows by combining the above lemmas.

4.2 Adding Authenticity

We show how to add authenticity to any IB-ME scheme satisfying enhanced privacy. Without loss of generality, we assume that the encryption keys ek_σ of the underlying IB-ME are defined as in Construction 1.

Construction 2. *Let* $\Pi = (\mathsf{Setup}, \mathsf{SKGen}, \mathsf{RKGen}, \mathsf{Enc}, \mathsf{Dec})$ *be an IB-ME with encryption keys* ek_σ *of the form* $\mathsf{ek}_\sigma = \sigma$, $\Pi' = (\mathsf{KGen}, \mathsf{Sign}, \mathsf{Ver})$ *be a signature scheme and* $\Pi'' = (\mathsf{I}, \mathsf{P}, \mathsf{V})$ *be a NIZK argument for the following NP relation:*

$$R = \left\{ ((\mathsf{mpk}, \mathsf{pk}, c), (\sigma, s)) : \begin{array}{c} \exists \mathsf{rcv}, m, r, \ s.t. \\ c = \mathsf{Enc}(\mathsf{mpk}, \sigma, \mathsf{rcv}, m; r) \wedge \mathsf{Ver}(\mathsf{pk}, \sigma, s) = 1 \end{array} \right\}.$$

Consider the following IB-ME $\Pi^* = (\mathsf{Setup}^*, \mathsf{SKGen}^*, \mathsf{RKGen}^*, \mathsf{Enc}^*, \mathsf{Dec}^*).$

$\mathsf{Setup}^*(1^\lambda)$: *Output* $\mathsf{msk}^* = (\mathsf{msk}, \mathsf{sk})$ *and* $\mathsf{mpk}^* = (\mathsf{mpk}, \omega, \mathsf{pk})$ *where* $(\mathsf{msk}, \mathsf{mpk}) \leftarrow_\$ \mathsf{Setup}(1^\lambda)$, $(\mathsf{sk}, \mathsf{pk}) \leftarrow_\$ \mathsf{KGen}(1^\lambda)$ *and* $\omega \leftarrow_\$ \mathsf{I}(1^\lambda).$

$\mathsf{SKGen}^*(\mathsf{msk}, \sigma)$: *Upon input* $\mathsf{msk}^* = (\mathsf{msk}, \mathsf{sk})$ *and* $\sigma \in \{0, 1\}^*$, *return* $\mathsf{ek}_\sigma = (s, \sigma)$ *where* $s = \mathsf{Sign}(\mathsf{sk}, \sigma).$

$\mathsf{RKGen}^*(\mathsf{msk}, \rho)$: *Upon input* $\mathsf{msk}^* = (\mathsf{msk}, \mathsf{sk})$ *and* $\rho \in \{0,1\}^*$, *return* $\mathsf{dk}_\rho \leftarrow_\$ \mathsf{RKGen}(\mathsf{msk}, \rho)$.

$\mathsf{Enc}^*(\mathsf{ek}_\sigma, \mathsf{rcv}, m)$: *Upon input* $\mathsf{ek}_\sigma = (s, \sigma)$, $\mathsf{rcv} \in \{0,1\}^*$, *and* $m \in \{0,1\}^*$, *output* $c^* = (c, \pi)$ *where* $c \leftarrow_\$ \mathsf{Enc}(\sigma, \mathsf{rcv}, m)$ *and* $\pi \leftarrow_\$ \mathsf{P}(\omega, (\mathsf{mpk}, \mathsf{pk}, c), (\sigma, s))$.

$\mathsf{Dec}^*(\mathsf{dk}_\rho, \mathsf{snd}, c)$: *Upon input* dk_ρ, $\mathsf{snd} \in \{0,1\}^*$, *and* $c^* = (c, \pi)$, *output* $m = \mathsf{Dec}(\mathsf{dk}_\rho, \mathsf{snd}, c)$ *if* $\mathsf{V}(\omega, (\mathsf{mpk}, \mathsf{pk}, c), \pi) = 1$. *Otherwise, return* $\bot$.

Correctness is immediate. As for security, we establish the following results.

Theorem 2. *If Π satisfies enhanced privacy and Π'' satisfies adaptive multi-theorem zero knowledge, then the IB-ME scheme Π^* from Construction 2 satisfies enhanced privacy.*

Proof. Consider the following hybrid experiments.

$\mathbf{H}_0(\lambda)$: This is identical to the experiment $\mathbf{G}^{\mathsf{ib\text{-}priv}^+}_{\Pi^*, \mathsf{A}^*}(\lambda)$.

$\mathbf{H}_1(\lambda)$: Same as $\mathbf{H}_0(\lambda)$ but now the challenger uses the simulator $\mathsf{Z} = (\mathsf{Z}_0, \mathsf{Z}_1)$ to generate the CRS and to compute the proofs. Formally, the challenger runs $(\omega, \zeta) \leftarrow_\$ \mathsf{Z}_0(1^\lambda)$ at the beginning of the experiment; when the adversary outputs the challenge $(m_0, m_1, \mathsf{rcv}_0, \mathsf{rcv}_1, \mathbf{ID}_0, \mathbf{ID}_1)$, the challenger generates the ciphertext $c^* = (c, \pi)$, where $c \leftarrow_\$ \mathsf{Enc}^*(\sigma_b, \mathsf{rcv}_b, m_b)$, $\sigma_b \leftarrow_\$ \mathbf{ID}_b$, and $\pi \leftarrow_\$ \mathsf{Z}_1(\zeta, (\mathsf{mpk}, \mathsf{pk}, c))$.

Claim. $\{\mathbf{H}_0(\lambda)\}_{\lambda \in \mathbb{N}} \approx_c \{\mathbf{H}_1(\lambda)\}_{\lambda \in \mathbb{N}}$

Proof. The claim follows from the adaptive multi-theorem zero-knowledge property of the NIZK. The reduction is standard, and therefore omitted.

Claim. $|\Pr[\mathbf{H}_1(\lambda) = 1] - \frac{1}{2}| \leq \mathsf{negl}(\lambda)$.

Proof. The claim follows from the enhanced privacy property of the IB-ME. The reduction is standard, and therefore omitted.

By combining the above claims, Construction 2 satisfies enhanced privacy.

Theorem 3. *If Π' is EUF-CMA and Π'' satisfies knowledge soundness, then the IB-ME scheme Π^* from Construction 2 satisfies authenticity.*

Proof. Assume that Construction 2 does not satisfy authenticity, i.e., there exists a PPT attacker A^* that has a non negligible advantage in experiment $\mathbf{G}^{\mathsf{ib\text{-}auth}}_{\Pi^*, \mathsf{A}^*}(\lambda)$. We build an attacker A' that breaks the EUF-CMA security of the signature scheme Π'. Attacker A' proceeds as follows:

1. Upon receiving pk from the challenger, generate $(\mathsf{msk}, \mathsf{mpk}) \leftarrow_\$ \mathsf{Setup}(1^\lambda)$, $(\omega, \xi) \leftarrow_\$ \mathsf{K}_0(1^\lambda)$ and forward $\mathsf{mpk}^* = (\mathsf{mpk}, \mathsf{pk}, \omega)$ to A^*.
2. A' answers to the incoming queries as follows:
   - On input $\sigma \in \{0,1\}^*$ for $\mathsf{O}_1^* = \mathsf{SKGen}^*$, forward the query σ to the signing oracle in order to obtain a valid signature s. Finally, return to A^* the key $\mathsf{ek}_\sigma = (s, \sigma)$.

- On input $\rho \in \{0,1\}^*$ for $O_2^* = \mathsf{RKGen}^*$, return $\mathsf{dk}_\rho \leftarrow_\$ \mathsf{RKGen}(\mathsf{msk}, \rho)$ to A^*.

3. Upon receiving the forgery $(c^* = (c, \pi), \rho^*, \mathsf{snd}^*)$ check whether $\mathsf{V}(\omega, (\mathsf{mpk}, \mathsf{pk}, c), \pi) = 0$ or $\mathsf{Dec}(\mathsf{dk}_{\rho^*}, \mathsf{snd}^*, c) = \bot$ where $\mathsf{dk}_\rho^* \leftarrow_\$ \mathsf{RKGen}(\mathsf{msk}, \rho^*)$. If true, abort. Otherwise, extract $(s^*, \sigma^*) \leftarrow_\$ \mathsf{K}_1(\xi, (\mathsf{mpk}, \mathsf{pk}, c), \pi)$ and return (σ^*, s^*) as forgery to the challenger.

Except with negligible probability, the oracle queries of A^* are perfectly simulated by A'. This is because the CRS ω is computed via K_0 in the reduction, which yields a CRS that is computationally close to an honestly generated CRS. This means that with non-negligible probability the ciphertext $c^* = (c, \pi)$ returned by A^* as a forgery for snd^* is valid. Now, by knowledge soundness of the underlying NIZK proof, except with negligible probability, we must have that s^* is a valid signature for σ^* (note that $\sigma^* = \mathsf{snd}^*$) with respect to the public key pk sampled by the challenger. Furthermore, this is a valid forgery because A^* never queried O_1 on the identity σ^* which implies that A' has never asked for a signature of σ^* to the challenger. Hence, (σ^*, s^*) is a valid forgery for the EUF-CMA game. This concludes the proof.

Acknowledgements. The first author was partially supported by the Carlsberg Foundation under the Semper Ardens Research Project CF18-112 (BCM). The last author was supported by Sapienza University of Rome under the grant SPECTRA.

References

1. Abdalla, M., et al.: Searchable encryption revisited: consistency properties, relation to anonymous IBE, and extensions. In: Shoup, V. (ed.) CRYPTO 2005. LNCS, vol. 3621, pp. 205–222. Springer, Heidelberg (2005). https://doi.org/10.1007/11535218_13
2. Ateniese, G., Francati, D., Nuñez, D., Venturi, D.: Match me if you can: matchmaking encryption and its applications. In: Boldyreva, A., Micciancio, D. (eds.) CRYPTO 2019. LNCS, vol. 11693, pp. 701–731. Springer, Cham (2019). https://doi.org/10.1007/978-3-030-26951-7_24
3. Dodis, Y., Kalai, Y.T., Lovett, S.: On cryptography with auxiliary input. In: Mitzenmacher, M. (ed.) 41st ACM STOC, pp. 621–630. ACM Press, May/June 2009
4. Gentry, C.: Practical identity-based encryption without random oracles. In: Vaudenay, S. (ed.) EUROCRYPT 2006. LNCS, vol. 4004, pp. 445–464. Springer, Heidelberg (2006). https://doi.org/10.1007/11761679_27
5. Goyal, V., Pandey, O., Sahai, A., Waters, B.: Attribute-based encryption for fine-grained access control of encrypted data. In: Juels, A., Wright, R.N., De Capitani di Vimercati, S. (eds.) ACM CCS 2006, pp. 89–98. ACM Press, October/November 2006. Available as Cryptology ePrint Archive Report 2006/309
6. Shamir, A.: Identity-based cryptosystems and signature schemes. In: Blakley, G.R., Chaum, D. (eds.) CRYPTO 1984. LNCS, vol. 196, pp. 47–53. Springer, Heidelberg (1985). https://doi.org/10.1007/3-540-39568-7_5
7. Waters, B.: Ciphertext-policy attribute-based encryption: an expressive, efficient, and provably secure realization. In: Catalano, D., Fazio, N., Gennaro, R., Nicolosi, A. (eds.) PKC 2011. LNCS, vol. 6571, pp. 53–70. Springer, Heidelberg (2011). https://doi.org/10.1007/978-3-642-19379-8_4

Forward-Secure Public Key Encryption Without Key Update from Proof-of-Stake Blockchain

Seiya Nuta[1]($\boxtimes$), Jacob C. N. Schuldt[2], and Takashi Nishide[1]

[1] University of Tsukuba, Tsukuba, Japan
nuta@cipher.risk.tsukuba.ac.jp, nishide@risk.tsukuba.ac.jp
[2] National Institute of Advanced Industrial Science and Technology, Tokyo, Japan
jacob.schuldt@aist.go.jp

Abstract. A forward-secure public-key encryption (PKE) scheme prevents eavesdroppers from decrypting past ciphertexts in order to mitigate the damage caused by a potential secret key compromise. In prior works, forward security in a non-interactive setting, such as forward-secure PKE, is achieved by constantly updating (secret) keys. In this paper, we formalize the notion of blockchain-based forward-secure PKE and show the feasibility of constructing a forward-secure PKE scheme without key update (i.e. both the public key and the secret key are immutable), assuming the existence of a proof-of-stake blockchain with the distinguishable forking property introduced by Goyal *et al.* (TCC 2017). Our construction uses the proof-of-stake blockchain as an *immutable decryption log* and witness encryption by Garg *et al.* (STOC 2013) to ensure that the same ciphertext cannot be decrypted twice, thereby rendering a compromised secret key useless with respect to decryption of past ciphertext the legitimate user has already decrypted.

Keywords: Public-key encryption · Forward security · Blockchain

1 Introduction

Forward security for public-key encryption is a security notion that ensures that a secret key compromise does not affect the confidentiality of past ciphertexts. More specifically, even if Alice's long-term secret key sk_A is compromised by an eavesdropper Eve, who observed and recorded ciphertexts sent to Alice in the past, forward security guarantees that Eve does not learn the secrets required for decrypting these *past* ciphertexts (i.e. sk_A is insufficient to decrypt).

While forward security in an interactive setting (e.g. key exchange protocols), can be achieved relatively easily by generating *ephemeral* secrets that are erased when no longer needed, this is harder in a non-interactive setting. However, one strategy for achieving forward security in a non-interactive setting, is to constantly update or erasing long term secrets. For example, a naïve approach to obtaining forward-secure PKE is generating a series of *one-time* public/secret

© Springer Nature Switzerland AG 2021
A. Adhikari et al. (Eds.): INDOCRYPT 2021, LNCS 13143, pp. 436–461, 2021.
https://doi.org/10.1007/978-3-030-92518-5_20

key pairs; once a key pair has been used, erase the secret key as soon as possible to ensure that an adversary cannot learn this key in a potential future compromise. The disadvantage of this approach is that a sender needs to update Alice's public key if all of the key pairs have been used, and furthermore needs to be aware of which keys Alice has already used and erased. This makes the naïve approach impractical, but more practical approaches to forward security have been developed, which we will briefly outline below.

Canetti et al. [8] formally introduced forward-secure PKE by extending the definition of PKE with a key update algorithm. In their scheme, the encryption algorithm takes as input a time period along with the receiver's public key and a message. The ciphertext is associated with the specified time period. The key update algorithm takes as input a secret key sk and outputs an updated secret key sk' (the public key pk remains the same). Even if an adversary compromises sk', they cannot decrypt ciphertexts in the prior periods (and thus provides forward security).

Green et al. [16] presented a fine-grained forward-secure (aka. absolute forward security [6]) encryption scheme called puncturable encryption. It introduces a key update algorithm similar to [8], but allows revoking a specific ciphertext, that is, the key update algorithm outputs an updated secret key which can be used to decrypt ciphertexts except the ciphertext given to the algorithm.

While interactive by definition, the recent work [2,11,18] on ensuring forward security of 0-RTT key exchange involves techniques that can be used to implement forward security for non-interactive primitives such as PKE. The idea behind 0-RTT key exchange, introduced in such as TLS 1.3 [22], is to enable clients to send encrypted data in their first message using pre-shared secrets. This essentially corresponds to a non-interactive encryption for the server, and to provide forward security of this data, is almost equivalent to constructing a forward-secure PKE (e.g. see the bloom filter encryption in [11]).

To the best of our knowledge, forward security in a non-interactive setting such as PKE, has only been achieved by introducing key update [2,8,11,16, 18,21]. This seems natural, since in an ordinary PKE, if an eavesdropper Eve compromises the secret key sk, she can decrypt any ciphertext c by simply running the decryption algorithm Dec to obtain $m \leftarrow \mathsf{Dec}(sk, c)$. Hence, in order to achieve forward security, it is natural to prevent Eve from compromising an unmodified secret key. In the key update approach, we update or partially break the secret key $sk^{(i)}$ to derive a new secret key $sk^{(i+1)}$ which cannot be used for decrypting past (or already decrypted) ciphertexts, and then erase the old key $sk^{(i)}$.

1.1 Our Contribution

In this paper, we give a feasibility result of a forward-secure encryption scheme without key update, i.e. both the public key and the secret key remain unchanged like ordinary (non-forward-secure) PKE. To achieve this, we allow the PKE scheme to make use of a blockchain for encryption and decryption of messages.

Firstly, we note that the standard definitions of correctness and (forward) security are insufficient for capturing a setting in which the PKE scheme depends on a blockchain. This is due to the ability of an adversary to observe any information posted to the blockchain when encrypting or decrypting messages, and the ability to post maliciously crafted blocks to the blockchain, which might prevent an honest user from correctly decrypting a ciphertext. Hence, we appropriately extend these definitions. Our forward security notions are obtained by extending the standard IND-CPA security notion for ordinary PKE with two additional oracles. The first oracle, Leak, captures secret key leakage that happens after the honest user decrypts the challenge ciphertext. The second oracle, HonestDec, captures the information leakage an adversary can observe on the blockchain when an honest user decrypts a ciphertext. For the full details of our security definition, see Sect. 4.

Our construction of a forward-secure PKE without key update, assumes the existence of a proof-of-stake blockchain which satisfies properties described in [14]. We combine this with witness encryption, which in general allows a plaintext to be encrypted under an NP statement instead of a public encryption key, and anyone in possession of a witness for the statement, will be able to decrypt. In our construction, we use witness encryption to tie a ciphertext to information posted by the decryptor to the blockchain, and thereby turn the blockchain into an *immutable decryption log* that only allows a ciphertext to be decrypted once. In other words, like puncturable encryption [16], our construction implements fine-grained forward security which removes the ability to decrypt on a ciphertext-by-ciphertext basis, as opposed to the (standard) more coarse approach of revoking the ability to decrypt any ciphertext constructed in the time period between key updates (we discuss security further in Sect. 4). Note that while encryptor and decryptor are required to interact with the blockchain protocol to obtain an updated view of the blockchain, the communication between the two remains non-interactive: once the encryptor has created a ciphertext based on his current view of the blockchain, no further communication is required on his part and he can go offline without affecting the decryptor's ability to decrypt.

Specifically, the pair of public key and secret key in our construction is simply that of a digital signature scheme. The encryption algorithm uses witness encryption to encrypt a message for an NP statement capturing that a certain type of message signed by the receiver has been posted to the blockchain. The decryption algorithm generates an ephemeral secret esk, posts a signed message associated with esk to the blockchain, which will allow the decryption of the ciphertext using the relevant sequence of blocks on the blockchain and esk as a witness (decryption key). Immediately after decryptions, the decryption algorithm erases esk which ensures that an adversary compromising the secret key, will not be able to decrypt as they don't know esk.

Since our construction uses a simple key pair of a digital signature scheme and these are immutable, the size of the keys is obviously independent of the number of time periods or decryptions unlike existing forward-secure PKE schemes [8,16]. Fixed immutable keys are furthermore an interesting property from an application point of view. For example, it is undesirable to use a fine-grained forward-secure PKE scheme with key updates in a scenario where the decryption key is used by multiple devices, such as laptops and smartphones, as keys would have to be synchronized to maintain fine-grained forward security. This concern is alleviated by fixed immutable secret keys. Lastly, we note that our construction enjoys some interesting security properties in addition to forward security, such as secret key leakage detection and a variant of post-compromise security [9]. We will discuss these benefits in detail in Sect. 5.

2 Preliminaries

In this section, we introduce building blocks and their security definitions. Besides the primitives defined below, we make use of an EUF-CMA secure signature scheme $\mathsf{Sig} = (\mathsf{Sig.KGen}, \mathsf{Sig.Sign}, \mathsf{Sig.Ver})$, and a one-way hash function $H : \{0,1\}^n \to \{0,1\}^m$. Due to space limitations, we do not include the standard definitions of these, but defer these to the full version of the paper.

2.1 Witness Encryption

Witness Encryption is a type of encryption introduced by Garg et al. [12]. Instead of a pair of public and private keys, in witness encryption, a plaintext is encrypted with respect to an NP statement x and the ciphertext can be decrypted with the corresponding witness w.

Definition 1 (Witness Encryption [12]). *A witness encryption scheme* WE *for NP language L (with witness relation R) is a tuple of algorithms* (WE.Enc, WE.Dec).

- $c \leftarrow$ WE.Enc$(1^\lambda, x, m)$: *The encryption algorithm* WE.Enc *takes as input a string x, and a message m, and outputs a ciphertext c.*
- $m/\bot \leftarrow$ WE.Dec(c, w): *The decryption algorithm* WE.Dec *takes as input a ciphertext c, and a string w, and outputs a message m or the symbol $\bot$.*

A witness encryption scheme WE *is required to satisfy correctness: for all security parameters λ, all strings x and w for which $R(x, w)$ holds, for all m, it holds that* WE.Dec(WE.Enc$(1^\lambda, x, m), w) = m$.

For a witness encryption scheme, we will use the security notion *extractability*, first proposed in [13], which informally requires that, for all adversaries able to distinguish between encryptions of different messages for a statement x, there exists an extractor that can extract a witness w from the adversary, such that $R(x, w)$ holds. We use the adaptive definition by Bellare et al. [5] in which $\mathcal{A}$ is allowed to specify x.

Definition 2 (Extractability). *A witness encryption scheme with witness relation R is extractable if for every security parameter λ, every PPT adversary*

$\mathcal{A} = (\mathcal{A}_1, \mathcal{A}_2)$ *with a random tape* r, *there exists a corresponding PPT algorithm* $\mathcal{E}$ *(the extractor) such that:*

$$\left| \Pr \left[b' = b \wedge \neg R(x, w) \,\middle|\, \begin{array}{l} (x, m_0, m_1, st) \leftarrow \mathcal{A}_1(1^\lambda; r); \\ b \xleftarrow{\$} \{0, 1\}; \\ c \leftarrow \mathsf{WE.Enc}(1^\lambda, x, m_b); \\ b' \leftarrow \mathcal{A}_2(st, c); \\ w \leftarrow \mathcal{E}(1^\lambda, r); \end{array} \right] - \frac{1}{2} \right| \leq neg(\lambda)$$

The above definition ensures that if an adversary $\mathcal{A}$ with non-negligible advantage $\varepsilon(\lambda)$ in distinguishing the ciphertexts of two messages exists, an extractor $\mathcal{E}$ with success probability $\varepsilon(\lambda) - neg(\lambda)$ must also exist.

Instantiating Witness Encryption. Witness encryption is a strong cryptographic primitive and efficiently instantiating this remains a work in progress. Recent interesting results include constructions by Barta *et al.* [3] based on the generic group model, and Bartusek *et al.* [4] based on affine determinant programs, with the latter claimed to be the first construction sufficiently efficient to be implementable. However, these works do not consider extractability, and it is unclear whether efficient extractors can be obtained for these construction.

Goldwasser *et al.* [13] proposed a candidate extractable witness encryption scheme but without a formal security reduction. Liu *et al.* [20] proposed a construction based on multi-linear maps, which can be instantiated from indistinguishability obfuscation (iO) [1], which in turn can be obtained from well-founded assumptions [19], leading to a theoretical instantiation. A different approach was taken by Goyal *et al.* [15] who show how the functionality of extractable witness encryption can be implemented efficiently on a blockchain. This approach is especially appealing in relation to our work due to the obtained efficiency and that our construction already makes use of a blockchain. Note that [15] requires the miners maintaining the blockchain to implement additional functionality i.e. smaller changes would have to be made to existing blockchain protocols to achieve the desired functionality, and to maintain forward security, the communication between miners and the decryptor must be forward secure (e.g. by using TLS 1.3 [22]). Furthermore, due to the dependency on a blockchain, [15] does not follow the standard definition of witness encryption. However, in this work, we will make use of the standard definitions above.

2.2   Blockchain Protocol

In general, a blockchain protocol is a multi-party distributed protocol that maintains an ordered sequence of blocks (*blockchain*) without a trusted third party. The blockchain is continuously extended by parties called *miners* under a consensus algorithm and forging sufficiently old blocks is considered difficult based on underlying hardness assumptions. A *Proof-of-Stake* blockchain uses a consensus algorithm in which a party with more stake (e.g. number of coins) is more likely to succeed in mining a new block. Below, we recall the abstract definition of blockchain protocols used in [14].

Definition 3 (Blockchain Protocol). *A blockchain protocol* BLC_V *with validity predicate* V *is a tuple of algorithms* (BLC_V.UpdateState, BLC_V.GetRecords, BLC_V.Broadcast).

- BLC_V.UpdateState(1^λ): *It is a stateful algorithm that takes as input the security parameter* λ *and maintains the local state* st. *It has no output.*
- $\mathbf{B} \leftarrow \mathsf{BLC}_V$.GetRecords($1^\lambda$, st): *It takes as input the security parameter* λ *and a local state* st, *and outputs the longest ordered sequence of blocks* $\mathbf{B}$ *(the blockchain) contained in* st.
- BLC_V.Broadcast(1^λ, m): *It takes as input the security parameter* λ *and a message* m, *and spreads the message* m *over the blockchain network. It outputs nothing.*

In the above, V is a predicate which takes a sequence of blocks $\mathbf{B}$ and outputs 1 if $\mathbf{B}$ is valid. The definition of "validity" varies with the blockchain protocol; details of how V is defined will not be important for our purpose.

Blockchain Execution. At a high level, the execution of the blockchain protocol corresponds to the participants running UpdateState, which will continuously update their state according to messages broadcast using Broadcast e.g. a miner might broadcast a new successfully mined block. Each participant can access his current view of the blockchain via GetRecords. We assume that (honest) miners will include any record broadcast via Broadcast in the blocks they attempt to mine, which allows all participating parties to have records added to the blockchain (e.g. in cryptocurrencies, a user might wish to add a transaction).

In [14], the execution of a blockchain protocol is formally modeled in the UC-framework [7], and is directed by the environment $\mathcal{Z}$, which initially activates all participants as either honest or corrupt (as in [14], we only consider static corruptions). All corrupt parties are controlled by an adversary $\mathcal{A}$. The execution starts by all honest users running UpdateState on an empty state, and proceeds in rounds. In each round, an honest user might receive a record from $\mathcal{Z}$ which it will attempt to add to the blockchain, as well as messages from the other parties. The user may then perform any computation, broadcast a message via Broadcast, and update its local state. $\mathcal{A}$ is responsible for delivering all messages between parties, and may delay or reorder these, but is not allowed to modify them. $\mathcal{Z}$ can communicate with $\mathcal{A}$ and access the local view of the blockchain obtained via GetRecords of any honest party. For a more detailed discussion of the blockchain execution, see [14].

We will let $\mathsf{EXEC}^{\mathsf{BLC}_V}[\mathcal{A}, \mathcal{Z}, 1^\lambda]$ denote the above execution, and view $\leftarrow \mathsf{EXEC}^{\mathsf{BLC}_V}[\mathcal{A}, \mathcal{Z}, 1^\lambda]$ denote the joint view of all parties in the execution. The latter fully determines the former.

Blockchain Properties. We will now define several blockchain properties introduced in [14], which our construction will be based on. In these definition, we make use of the *unique stake fraction* of the last ℓ blocks of a blockchain $\mathbf{B}$, which we denote u-stakefrac$(\mathbf{B}, \ell)$, and which is defined to be the combined stake of all miners who mined at least one of the last ℓ blocks in $\mathbf{B}$ divided by the total amount of stake for the blockchain. Additionally, we will use the notation $\mathbf{B}^{\lceil \ell}$ to denote $\mathbf{B}$ with the last ℓ blocks removed, and $\mathbf{B} \preceq \tilde{\mathbf{B}}$ to denote that $\mathbf{B}$ is a prefix of $\tilde{\mathbf{B}}$.

The blockchain properties are defined based on the following predicates: blockchain consistency (consistent), which captures that all honest participants in the blockchain protocol agrees upon all except the last ℓ blocks; sufficient stake contribution (suf-stake), which captures that all blockchains of length ℓ has a unique stake fraction of at least β; and bounded stake forking (bd-stake-fork), which captures that all maliciously constructed forks of the blockchain has unique stake fraction less than α. Formally, these predicates are defined as:

- consistent$^{\ell}$(view) $= 1$ iff for all rounds $r \leq \tilde{r}$ and honest parties i, j in view with blockchain $\mathbf{B}$ in round r and $\tilde{\mathbf{B}}$ in round $\tilde{r}$, respectively, it holds that $\mathbf{B}^{\lceil \ell} \preceq \tilde{\mathbf{B}}$.
- suf-stake$^{\ell}$(view, β) $= 1$ iff for every round $r \geq \ell$, and each honest party i with blockchain $\mathbf{B}$ at round r, it holds that u-stakefrac$(\mathbf{B}, \ell) \geq \beta$.
- bd-stake-fork$^{(\ell_1, \ell_2)}$(view, α) $= 1$ iff for all rounds $r \geq \tilde{r}$, each honest party i with blockchain $\mathbf{B}$ at round r, each corrupt party j with blockchain $\tilde{\mathbf{B}}$ at round $\tilde{r}$, if there exists $\ell' \geq \ell_1 + \ell_2$ such that $\tilde{\mathbf{B}}^{\lceil \ell'} \preceq \mathbf{B}$ and for all $\tilde{\ell} < \ell'$, $\tilde{\mathbf{B}}^{\lceil \tilde{\ell}} \npreceq \mathbf{B}$, then u-stakefrac$(\tilde{\mathbf{B}}, \ell' - \ell_1) \leq \alpha$.

Based on the consistency and sufficient stake contribution predicates, we define the corresponding blockchain properties.

Definition 4 (Chain Consistency). *A blockchain protocol* BLC_V *satisfies* ℓ_0-*consistency for adversary* $\mathcal{A}$ *in environment* $\mathcal{Z}$, *if for every* $\ell > \ell_0$

$$\Pr\left[\text{consistent}^{\ell}(\text{view}) \mid \text{view} \leftarrow \mathsf{EXEC}^{\mathsf{BLC}_V}[\mathcal{A}, \mathcal{Z}, 1^{\lambda}]\right] \geq 1 - neg(\lambda)$$

Definition 5 (Sufficient Stake Contribution). *A blockchain protocol* BLC_V *satisfies* (ℓ_0, β)-*sufficient stake contribution for adversary* $\mathcal{A}$ *in environment* $\mathcal{Z}$, *if for every* $\ell > \ell_0$

$$\Pr\left[\text{suf-stake}^{\ell}(\text{view}, \beta) \mid \text{view} \leftarrow \mathsf{EXEC}^{\mathsf{BLC}_V}[\mathcal{A}, \mathcal{Z}, 1^{\lambda}]\right] \geq 1 - neg(\lambda)$$

Lastly, we consider a property called distinguishable forking which requires that sufficient stake contribution and bounded stake forking properties hold simultaneously. Note that when this is the case (and $\alpha < \beta$), it is possible to distinguish an honestly created extension of the blockchain from an adversarially created fork by examining the unique stake fraction shown in the extension or fork.

Definition 6 (Distinguishable Forking). *A blockchain protocol* BLC_V *satisfies* $(\alpha, \beta, \ell_1, \ell_2)$-*distinguishable forking for adversary* $\mathcal{A}$ *in environment* $\mathcal{Z}$, *if for every* $\ell > \ell_1$ *and* $\tilde{\ell} \geq \ell_2$

$$\Pr\left[\begin{array}{c} \alpha + neg_1(\lambda) < \beta \wedge \\ \mathsf{suf\text{-}stake}^\ell(\mathsf{view}, \beta) = 1 \wedge \\ \mathsf{bd\text{-}stake\text{-}fork}^{(\ell,\tilde{\ell})}(\mathsf{view}, \alpha + neg_1(\lambda)) = 1 \end{array} \;\middle|\; \mathsf{view} \leftarrow \mathsf{EXEC}^{\mathsf{BLC}_V}[\mathcal{A}, \mathcal{Z}, 1^\lambda]\right]$$

$$\geq 1 - neg_2(\lambda)$$

Goyal *et al.* showed in [14] that *Snowwhite*, a Proof-of-Stake based blockchain protocol proposed by Daian *et al.* [10], satisfies all of the above properties.

Proof-of-Work Blockchain. The above properties, which will be used as a basis for the security of our construction, are all stated with respect to a blockchain based on Proof-of-Stake. It might be considered whether it would be possible to instead rely on a blockchain based on *Proof-of-Work* in which the blockchain is extended by miners solving computational puzzles (i.e. relying on the computational power of the miners). This, however, seems difficult. More specifically, in the typical Proof-of-Work setting, an adversary can locally compute a valid fork in realistic time by solving the required puzzles and ignoring input from honest miners. This would break the distinguishable forking property which our construction crucially depends on. In contrast, this property can be achieved in a Proof-of-Stake blockchain because we assume, as in [14], that the adversary controls only a minority stake and cannot forge digital signatures of other miners controlling a majority stake.

Additional Blockchain Notation. Each block of a blockchain $\mathbf{B}$ contains a list of records. A record is a set of fields and a field is an arbitrary string. We denote the i-th block of $\mathbf{B}$ as $\mathbf{B}_{[i]}$, the number of records in the i-th block as $|\mathbf{B}_{[i]}|$, the j-th record in the i-th block as $\mathbf{B}_{[i][j]}$, and each field in a record r as $r.\mathsf{name}$. We use the notation $r \in \mathbf{B}$ if there exists i, j such that $\mathbf{B}_{[i][j]} = r$, and $r \notin \mathbf{B}$ when this is not the case.

Also, we overload the consistency predicate, and define $\mathsf{consistent}^\ell(\mathbf{B}_{\mathsf{prefix}}, \mathbf{B})$ to hold for two sequences of blocks, $\mathbf{B}_{\mathsf{prefix}}$ and $\mathbf{B}$, if and only if $\mathbf{B}_{\mathsf{prefix}}^{\lceil \ell} \preceq \mathbf{B}$ i.e. $\mathbf{B}_{\mathsf{prefix}}$ with the last ℓ blocks truncated is a prefix of $\mathbf{B}$. Finally, for a blockchain satisfying $(\alpha, \beta, \ell_1, \ell_2)$-distinguishable forking, we introduce a predicate $\mathsf{ext\text{-}suf\text{-}stk}^{(\beta, \ell_1, \ell_2)}(\mathbf{B}, i)$ (short for "extended with sufficient stake"), which takes a sequence of blocks $\mathbf{B}$ and index i where $i \geq 0$, and holds if and only if the number of blocks after the i-th block is larger than $\ell_1 + \ell_2$ and at least β fraction of stake is proved in the last ℓ_2 blocks. Intuitively, $\mathsf{ext\text{-}suf\text{-}stk}$ determines whether the i-th block looks honestly created, assuming stakes of adversaries are bounded by α (where $\alpha < \beta$).

3   Forward-Secure PKE Without Key Update

In this section, we give definitions and the construction of our forward-secure PKE scheme without key update. In contrast to existing forward-secure PKE schemes[8,16], both pk and sk are immutable, and since we don't employ key update to achieve forward security, the syntax looks much closer to the traditional non-forward-secure PKE schemes except we allow the encryption and decryption algorithm to make use of a blockchain protocol.

Specifically, we assume that both encryptor and decryptor are participants in a blockchain protocol, and will allow the encryption and decryption algorithms direct access to the state of the encryptor and decryptor, respectively. Note that this does not necessarily require that the encryptor or decryptor have any stake in the blockchain, but that they have the ability to broadcast messages across the blockchain network, and can extract, from their local state, their current view of the blockchain. It is assumed that both encryptor and decryptor will maintain their state by running UpdateState of the blockchain protocol, and that the encryption and decryption algorithms will have access to the most recent state when extracting the current view of the blockchain via GetRecords. In other words, we treat the input state st to the encryption and decryption algorithms as a reference to the most current state (as opposed to the value of the state at the time the algorithms are called), which will allow, for example, the algorithms to broadcast a message, and wait for this message to be included in the blockchain, before continuing execution.

The syntax of our forward-secure PKE scheme is as follows:

Definition 7 (FSPKE). *A forward-secure public-key encryption scheme without key update under the existence of a blockchain protocol* BLC$_V$ *is a tuple of algorithms* (FSPKE.KGen, FSPKE.Enc, FSPKE.Dec).

- $(pk, sk) \leftarrow$ FSPKE.KGen(1^λ): *The key generation algorithm* FSPKE.KGen *takes as input the security parameter λ. It outputs a key pair (pk, sk).*
- $c \leftarrow$ FSPKE.Enc(st, pk, m): *The encryption algorithm* FSPKE.Enc *takes as input a reference to a blockchain state* st, *a public key pk and a message m. It outputs a ciphertext c.*
- $m/\bot \leftarrow$ FSPKE.Dec(st, sk, c): *The decryption algorithm* FSPKE.Dec *takes as input a reference to a blockchain state* st, *a secret key sk and a ciphertext c. It outputs a message m or the symbol $\bot$.*

3.1   Correctness

Unlike ordinary (forward-secure) PKE, the correctness of a PKE scheme dependent on a blockchain is non-trivial. Specifically, when decryption is dependent on information obtained from or posted to the blockchain, we need to consider potential adversarial interference from other entities with access to the blockchain. Firstly, malicious miners can potentially prevent correct decryption by simply not including any information required for decryption in the

$$\begin{array}{l|l}
\mathsf{G}^{\mathsf{Corr}}_{\mathcal{A},\mathcal{Z},\mathsf{FSPKE},m,i,j}: & \mathsf{Enc}(): \\
(pk, sk) \leftarrow \mathsf{FSPKE.KGen}(1^\lambda); & c^* \leftarrow \mathsf{FSPKE.Enc}(\mathsf{st}_i, pk, m); \\
\mathsf{EXEC}^{\mathsf{BLC}_V}[\mathcal{A}^{\mathsf{Enc},\mathsf{Dec}}(pk), \mathcal{Z}, 1^\lambda]; & \mathbf{return}\ c^* \\
\mathbf{output}\ m' = m & \\
\hline
& \mathsf{Dec}(): \\
& m' \leftarrow \mathsf{FSPKE.Dec}(\mathsf{st}_j, sk, c^*); \\
& \mathbf{return}\ m'
\end{array}$$

Fig. 1. Game defining correctness.

blockchain. Secondly, since the basic premise of the use of the blockchain is that anyone can post a block, and by doing so, any malicious user might be able to interfere with the decryption by honest users. We capture this aspect of the use of a blockchain, by considering a correctness definition similar to a security game, in which the adversary attempts to prevent decryption of an honestly constructed ciphertext. Note that besides controlling corrupt parties, the adversary in our definition can make honestly mined blocks contain maliciously generated messages by simply broadcasting these, since we assume that all honest miners will include messages received via the broadcast functionality of the blockchain.

We define correctness via the security game shown in Fig. 1 in which the adversary can instruct two honest users to encrypt and decrypt any time during the execution of the blockchain protocol via the Enc and Dec oracles. Note that for the correctness definition to be meaningful, we will only consider adversaries that query these oracles once in that order. We refer to such adversaries as *correctness-admissible*. Furthermore, note that additional restrictions on the adversary and the execution of the blockchain are likely to be required for correctness to hold for any scheme that makes meaningful use of the blockchain. In particular, the delay an adversary might introduce for messages sent to honest parties might have to be limited, and the execution of the blockchain protocol might be required to extend the blockchain. However, we will not include such restrictions or guarantees in the definition below, but introduce appropriate assumptions when showing correctness of our concrete scheme.

Definition 8 (Correctness). *We say that* FSPKE *with access to blockchain protocol* BLC_V *satisfies correctness for adversary* $\mathcal{A}$ *in environment* $\mathcal{Z}$ *if for every plaintext* m, *every pair of honest users* i *and* j *in* $\mathcal{Z}$, *there exists a negligible function* $\varepsilon(\cdot)$ *such that the following holds:*

$$\Pr\left[\ \mathsf{G}^{\mathsf{Corr}}_{\mathcal{A},\mathcal{Z},\mathsf{FSPKE},m,i,j} = 1\ \right] \geq 1 - \varepsilon(\lambda)$$

3.2   Security

We will now define a security notion capturing forward security for a PKE scheme FSPKE based on a blockchain. Like in the case of correctness, the definition is non-standard due to the ability of an adversary to observe and manipulate the blockchain. Our security notion, which we denote fs-IND-CPA security, is based on the standard IND-CPA security notion for ordinary PKE, in which the adversary is challenged to distinguish between the encryption c^* of two adversarially chosen messages, m_0 and m_1. However, we allow the adversary to access two new oracles: Leak and HonestDec. The first oracle, Leak, captures the notion of a key compromise. When it's invoked, it will return the secret key to the adversary, but before doing so, it ensures that the challenge ciphertext has been decrypted by running $m^* \leftarrow$ FSPKE.Dec(st, sk, c^*). In previous forward security notions, this oracle would correspond to an oracle that updates the secret key and returns the new (updated) key to the adversary.

The second oracle, HonestDec(c), captures potential information leakage from records posted on the blockchain by honest users in the decryption process[1]. Specifically, in the blockchain setting, an honest user might be required to post information related to a ciphertext c or their secret key sk, in order to be able to decrypt c. Since the blockchain is public, an adversary will be able to obtain this information just by monitoring the blockchain. To capture this, the oracle HonestDec allows the adversary to submit any ciphertext c, which the oracle will decrypt as $m \leftarrow$ FSPKE.Dec(st, sk, c). However, as we consider a CPA security notion, the decryption result m will not be returned to the adversary (he will only be able to observe any information posted to the blockchain in the decryption process). Our definition can be extended to a CCA notion, simply by returning m and restricting the adversary from submitting c^*. Note that in our definition below, no restrictions are placed on c submitted to HonestDec.

Finally, note that the fs-IND-CPA definition *itself* is generic: it does not place any assumptions on the adversary in terms of adversarial control of the blockchain (e.g. the amount of stake held by the adversary). For our concrete scheme, which will be presented in Sect. 3.3, we will show that fs-IND-CPA security holds, assuming the stake controlled by the adversary is sufficiently small as in [14].

Security is defined via the game shown in Fig. 2. We say that an adversary fs-IND-CPA $\mathcal{A}$ is *admissible* if $\mathcal{A}$ queries the challenge oracle Chal once with messages m_0 and m_1 of equal length, and only queries the Leak oracle after Chal has been queried (without loss of generality, we can assume any $\mathcal{A}$ always queries both oracles).

Definition 9 (fs-IND-CPA). *Let* BLC_V *be a blockchain protocol with the validity predicate V, and let* FSPKE $=$ (FSPKE.KGen, FSPKE.Enc, FSPKE.Dec) *be a public-key encryption scheme with access to* BLC_V*. We define the advantage* $\mathsf{Adv}_{\mathcal{A},\mathsf{FSPKE}}^{\mathsf{fs\text{-}IND\text{-}CPA}}(\lambda)$ *of an adversary $\mathcal{A}$ against the fs-IND-CPA security of* FSPKE *as*

$$\mathsf{Adv}_{\mathcal{A},\mathsf{FSPKE}}^{\mathsf{fs\text{-}IND\text{-}CPA}}(\lambda) := \left| \Pr\left[\mathsf{G}_{\mathcal{A},\mathcal{Z},\mathsf{FSPKE},i,j}^{\mathsf{fs\text{-}IND\text{-}CPA}} = 1 \right] - \frac{1}{2} \right|$$

---

[1] Note that encryption might likewise require information being posted to the blockchain, but this is already captured by running the encryption algorithm when constructing the challenge ciphertext c^*.

$G^{\text{fs-IND-CPA}}_{\mathcal{A},\mathcal{Z},\text{FSPKE},i,j}$:

$(pk, sk) \leftarrow \text{FSPKE.KGen}(1^\lambda)$;

$b \xleftarrow{\$} \{0,1\}$;

$\text{EXEC}^{\text{BLC}_V}[\mathcal{A}^{\text{HonestDec}(\cdot),\text{Chal}(\cdot,\cdot),\text{Leak}}(pk), \mathcal{Z}, 1^\lambda]$;

$b' \leftarrow \mathcal{A}$;

output $b' = b$

$\text{HonestDec}(c)$:

$m \leftarrow \text{FSPKE.Dec}(\text{st}_j, sk, c)$;

return $\perp$

$\text{Chal}(m_0, m_1)$:

$c^* \leftarrow \text{FSPKE.Enc}(\text{st}_i, pk, m_b)$;

return c^*

$\text{Leak}()$:

$m^* \leftarrow \text{FSPKE.Dec}(\text{st}_j, sk, c^*)$;

return sk

Fig. 2. Security game defining fs-IND-CPA security.

where the security game $G^{\text{fs-IND-CPA}}_{\mathcal{A},\mathcal{Z},\text{FSPKE},i,j}$ is defined in Fig. 2. We say that FSPKE is fs-IND-CPA secure against an admissible adversary $\mathcal{A}$ in environment $\mathcal{Z}$ if for all honest users i and j in $\mathcal{Z}$, $\text{Adv}^{\text{fs-IND-CPA}}_{\mathcal{A},\text{FSPKE}}(\lambda)$ is negligible in λ.

Note that similar to puncturable encryption [16], the above security notion guarantees fine-grained forward security i.e. the scheme must support removing the ability to decrypt just a single ciphertext. This improves upon the notion for standard forward-secure schemes based on key update, in which the ability to decrypt all ciphertexts constructed between two key updates is lost in the second key update. Note that adjusting the time period between key updates in this type of scheme is a challenging task; frequent updates implies that the ability to decrypt any ciphertext the decryptor cannot immediately access and decrypt will be lost, whereas infrequent updates implies that any adversary gaining access to the decryption key will have the ability to decrypt a potentially large number of previous ciphertexts i.e. any ciphertext constructed within the current time period (as well as future ciphertexts). In contrast, fine-grained forward security does not require a notion of time, and any ciphertext not yet decrypted by the decryptor will remain decryptable. In this sense, a fine-grained forward-secure scheme provides a functionality closer to ordinary non-forward-secure encryption, while still providing strong security guarantees in the case of key compromise. It should be noted, however, that standard fine-grained forward-secure schemes inherently do not protect against a particular type of message suppression attack [6]. In Sect. 5, we discuss the details of this as well as how our particular construction allows this type of attack to be mitigated.

3.3 Construction

Our construction is inspired by the idea behind the construction of one-time programs using a proof-of-stake blockchain presented by Goyal *et al.* [14], in particular, the use of a proof-of-stake blockchain in combination with a witness encryption scheme[2]. In our construction, a message is encrypted under an NP statement requiring that a certain type of record associated to an ephemeral secret to be signed by the receiver and posted to the blockchain. Here, the signing key is the receiver's long-term secret. The decryption algorithm, which has access to the signing key, constructs and signs such a record, posts this to the blockchain, and waits until the blockchain has been sufficiently extended. Then, using the ephemeral secret and the blockchain containing the corresponding record as a witness, the decryption algorithm is able to decrypt the message.

Note that the ephemeral secret is the only secret required to construct a valid witness required for decryption as the blockchain is assumed to be public. Hence, neither the record posted to the blockchain nor a key compromise must leak this. The former is ensured by using a one-way hash function (and high-entropy ephemeral secrets), and the latter is ensured by deleting the ephemeral secret once decryption has been completed. Note also, that an attacker without access to the long-term signing key will be unable to construct an appropriate record that can be used for decryption, assuming the signature scheme is secure.

The key to making this construction forward secure is to require the NP relation to check that the record used in the witness is the *first* record in the blockchain that allows decryption. This will prevent an attacker from creating a valid witness for a given ciphertext once this has been decrypted by the receiver, even if the attacker gains access to the long-term signing key.

The above assumes that the attacker cannot manipulate the blockchain itself. To ensure the security extends to attackers with a minority stake in the blockchain, we rely on the distinguishable forking property (Definition 6). More specifically, the distinguishable forking property guarantees that honestly created blockchain extensions can be distinguished from adversarially constructed forks by examining the unique stake in blockchain. Hence, by letting the NP relation additionally check that blockchain used in the witness is of sufficient length and has sufficient stake, we can ensure that the attacker cannot decrypt by constructing a fork of the blockchain.

Let WE be a witness encryption scheme for the NP relation R_{FSPKE} (defined in Fig. 3), BLC_V a blockchain protocol with the validity predicate V, Sig a public key signature scheme, and H a one-way hash function. We present our construction, FSPKE, of a forward-secure public-key encryption scheme without key update in Fig. 4. Note that the scheme depends on a set of parameters $\mathsf{par} = (\beta, \ell_c, \ell_1, \ell_2)$ which should be set according to the properties of the underlying blockchain protocol.

---

[2] As a one-time program is a powerful primitive, it might be considered to base the construction of a forward-secure encryption scheme directly on this (besides additional appropriate primitives). However, we note that it is not clear whether such a construction will be able to meet our security notions (e.g. [14] does not consider correctness against malicious adversaries whereas we do), and any potential construction will be much more complicated due to the generality of one-time programs based on garbled circuits. Hence, we focus on a direct construction based on a proof-of-stake blockchain.

A pair of NP instance $x = (\mathbf{B} \,\|\, \mathrm{id} \,\|\, pk)$ and a witness $w = (\mathbf{B}' \,\|\, esk)$ satisfies R_{FSPKE} if and only if the following properties are satisfied:

$$R_{\mathsf{FSPKE}}(\mathbf{B} \,\|\, \mathrm{id} \,\|\, pk, \mathbf{B}' \,\|\, esk) := R_{\mathsf{ValidBlocks}}(\mathbf{B}, \mathbf{B}') \wedge R_{\mathsf{ValidEsk}}(pk, \mathrm{id}, \mathbf{B}', esk)$$

$$\wedge\, \mathsf{consistent}^{\ell_c}(\mathbf{B}, \mathbf{B}')$$

where

$$R_{\mathsf{ValidBlocks}}(\mathbf{B}, \mathbf{B}') := V(\mathbf{B}) = 1 \wedge V(\mathbf{B}') = 1$$

$$R_{\mathsf{ValidEsk}}(pk, \mathrm{id}, \mathbf{B}', esk) := \exists i^*, \exists j^*,$$

$$\mathsf{ext\text{-}suf\text{-}stk}^{(\beta, \ell_1, \ell_2)}(\mathbf{B}', i^*)$$

$$\wedge\, R_{\mathsf{DecAttempt}}(\mathrm{id}, pk, \mathbf{B}'_{[i^*][j^*]})$$

$$\wedge\, R_{\mathsf{NotYetDecrypted}}(\mathbf{B}', i^*, j^*, \mathrm{id}, pk)$$

$$\wedge\, R_{\mathsf{KnowsEsk}}(\mathbf{B}', i^*, j^*, esk)$$

$$R_{\mathsf{DecAttempt}}(\mathrm{id}, pk, r) := (r.\mathrm{id} = \mathrm{id}) \wedge (\mathsf{Sig.Ver}(pk, r.\mathrm{id} \,\|\, r.\sigma, r.\mathsf{cert}) = 1)$$

$$R_{\mathsf{NotYetDecrypted}}(\mathbf{B}', i^*, j^*, \mathrm{id}, pk) := (\forall 0 \le j < j^*, \neg R_{\mathsf{DecAttempt}}(\mathrm{id}, pk, \mathbf{B}'_{[i^*][j]}))$$

$$\wedge\, (\forall 0 \le i < i^*, \forall 0 \le j < |\mathbf{B}'_{[i]}|,$$

$$\neg R_{\mathsf{DecAttempt}}(\mathrm{id}, pk, \mathbf{B}'_{[i][j]}))$$

$$R_{\mathsf{KnowsEsk}}(\mathbf{B}', i^*, j^*, esk) := H(esk) = \mathbf{B}'_{[i^*][j^*]}.\sigma$$

Fig. 3. An NP relation R_{FSPKE} based on the blockchain protocol BLC_V with validity predicate V and parameters $\mathsf{par} = (\beta, \ell_c, \ell_1, \ell_2)$, Sig is a public key signature scheme, and H is a one-way hash function.

On the Relation R_{FSPKE}. The relation R_{FSPKE} used in WE and defined in Fig. 3 -relations. We discuss the intuition of these in the following. $R_{\mathsf{ValidBlocks}}$ ensures that both sequences of blocks satisfy blockchain-protocol-specific requirements i.e. it denies malformed inputs. R_{ValidEsk} ensures that the ciphertext has not yet been decrypted. It requires that the given esk is valid for the *first* record on the blockchain which satisfies $R_{\mathsf{DecAttempt}}$. $\mathsf{ext\text{-}suf\text{-}stk}$ used in R_{ValidEsk} ensures the i^*-th block is honestly created with all but negligible probability. $R_{\mathsf{DecAttempt}}$ is true if the given record r contains a decryption attempt for the ciphertext associated with id. $R_{\mathsf{NotYetDecrypted}}$ ensures that before the j^*-th record in the i^*-th block in $\mathbf{B}'$, there're no valid decryption attempts for the ciphertext associated with id. This relation guarantees that the ciphertext can be decrypted only once. R_{KnowsEsk} ensures that the party who is trying to decrypt knows the ephemeral secret key esk for the first decryption attempt.

3.4   Proof of Correctness

Before showing correctness of our scheme, we will introduce mild assumptions regarding the execution of the blockchain. Firstly, we will restrict our attention

---

$(pk, sk) \leftarrow \text{FSPKE.KGen}(1^\lambda)$

1. $(pk, sk) \leftarrow \text{Sig.KGen}(1^\lambda)$.
2. Output (pk, sk).

$c \leftarrow \text{FSPKE.Enc}(st, pk, m)$

1. $\mathbf{B} \leftarrow \text{BLC}_V.\text{GetRecords}(1^\lambda, st)$.
2. $\text{id} \xleftarrow{\$} \{0,1\}^\lambda$.
3. $x := (\mathbf{B} \,\|\, \text{id} \,\|\, pk)$.
4. $CT \leftarrow \text{WE.Enc}(1^\lambda, x, m)$.
5. Output $c := (\text{id}, CT)$.

$m \leftarrow \text{FSPKE.Dec}(st, sk, c)$

1. Parse c as (id, CT).
2. $esk \xleftarrow{\$} \{0,1\}^\lambda$.
3. $\sigma \leftarrow H(esk)$.
4. $\text{cert} \leftarrow \text{Sig.Sign}(sk, \text{id} \,\|\, \sigma)$.
5. $r := (\text{id} \,\|\, \sigma \,\|\, \text{cert})$.
6. $\text{BLC}_V.\text{Broadcast}(1^\lambda, r)$.
7. $\mathbf{B} \leftarrow \text{BLC}_V.\text{GetRecords}(1^\lambda, st)$.
8. While $r \notin \mathbf{B}^{\lceil(\ell_1+\ell_2)}$:
9. $\mathbf{B} \leftarrow \text{BLC}_V.\text{GetRecords}(1^\lambda, st)$.
10. $w := (\mathbf{B} \,\|\, esk)$.
11. $m \leftarrow \text{WE.Dec}(CT, w)$.
12. Erase esk and then output m.

Fig. 4. A construction of FSPKE where WE is a witness encryption scheme for the NP relation R_{FSPKE} (defined in Fig. 3), BLC_V is a blockchain protocol with the validity predicate V and parameters $\text{par} = (\beta, \ell_c, \ell_1, \ell_2)$, Sig is a public key signature scheme, and H is a one-way hash function.

to blockchain executions that lead to a sufficient growth of the blockchain. More specifically, we will refer to a blockchain execution as *ℓ-growth respecting* if the blockchain of all honest parties is extended with at least ℓ blocks following a broadcast by an honest party. Finally, we restrict the delay in terms of growth of the blockchain, an adversary might introduce for messages broadcast by honest parties. Specifically, we refer to a blockchain execution as *$\tilde{\ell}$-delay respecting*, if the blockchain of any honest users is extended with at most $\tilde{\ell}$ blocks between an honest user broadcasting a message and this is delivered to all other honest users.

Theorem 1. *Assume the signature scheme* Sig *is EUF-CMA secure and that the blockchain protocol* BLC_V *provides ℓ_c-consistency, and (ℓ_2, β)-sufficient stake for all PPT adversaries with stake at most α' in environment $\mathcal{Z}$. Then the construction described in Fig. 4 with parameters $\text{par} = (\beta, \ell_c, \ell_1, \ell_2)$ satisfies correctness for any PPT correctness-admissible adversary $\mathcal{A}$ in $\mathcal{Z}$ with stake at most $\alpha < \min(\alpha', \beta)$ in blockchain executions that are $\tilde{\ell}$-delay and $(\tilde{\ell}+\ell_1+2\ell_2)$-growth respecting.*

Proof (Theorem 1). Firstly note that the definition of ℓ_c-consistency directly implies that for blockchain $\mathbf{B}$ used in the encryption performed in the Enc oracle and the blockchain $\mathbf{B}'$ used in the decryption in the Dec oracle, $\text{consistent}^{\ell_c}(\mathbf{B}, \mathbf{B}')$ holds with overwhelming probability.

Secondly, since the execution is $(\tilde{\ell}+\ell_1+2\ell_2)$-growth respecting, the blockchain $\mathbf{B}'$ contained in st_j used in the decryption must be extended with $\tilde{\ell} + \ell_1 + 2\ell_2$ blocks after the broadcast of r in line 6 of the decryption algorithm. Since the execution is also $\tilde{\ell}$-delay respecting, r must have been delivered to all honest miners before $\mathbf{B}'$ has been extended with $\tilde{\ell}$ blocks, and due to the (ℓ_2, β)-sufficient stake property and $\alpha < \beta$, the next ℓ_2 blocks must contain an honestly mined block (which must include r unless r has already been posted) with overwhelming probability. Hence, there must be at least $\ell_1 + \ell_2$ blocks after the block containing r, and again due to the (ℓ_2, β)-sufficient stake property, the ℓ_2 last blocks of these will have stake at least β. This implies that ext-suf-stk$^{(\beta, \ell_1, \ell_2)}(\mathbf{B}', i^*)$ is satisfied, where i^* is the index of the block containing r.

Combined with the observation that r is honestly constructed, the above implies that the witness $\mathbf{B}' \| esk$ constructed in the decryption is a valid witness *unless* $R_{\text{NotYetDecrypted}}$ does not hold. This happens only if $\mathbf{B}'$ contains a block with index less than i^* with a record r' for which $r'.\sigma \neq r.\sigma$ but which satisfies $R_{\text{DecAttempt}}(\text{id}, pk, r')$ for the id used in the encryption. This in turn implies that $r'.$cert is a valid signature on $r'.\text{id} \| r'.\sigma$. However, if $\mathcal{A}$ can cause such a record to be added to $\mathbf{B}'$, we can construct a PPT algorithm $\mathcal{B}$ which breaks the EUF-CMA of the digital signature scheme. $\mathcal{B}$ simply plays the correctness game with $\mathcal{A}$ simulating all honest parties, and using his signing oracle to obtain $r.$cert corresponding to a signature on $r.\text{id} \| r.\sigma$. After the game finishes, it searches $\mathbf{B}' \leftarrow \mathsf{GetRecords}(1^\lambda, \text{st}_j)$ for a valid record r' (posted by $\mathcal{A}$) such that $\mathsf{Sig.Ver}(pk, r'.\text{id} \| r'.\sigma, r'.\text{cert}) = 1$ holds. Lastly, it outputs the pair $(r'.\text{id} \| r'.\sigma, r'.\text{cert})$ in the EUF-CMA security game.

Since the signature scheme is assumed to be secure, we conclude that $\mathcal{B}$ will only succeed with negligible probability, and hence, that $R_{\text{NotYetDecrypted}}$ will hold with overwhelming probability. Thus the theorem holds. (Theorem 1) $\square$

Note that in the above, we assume that WE does not impose a length bound on the used witness. If the maximum witness length of the witness encryption is bounded, we additionally need to assume that the number of records posted to the blockchain by $\mathcal{A}$ for a certain period is bounded for correctness to hold. In other words, we would require the honest user is able to decrypt before $\mathcal{A}$ posts so many blocks to the blockchain such that it cannot be used as a witness due to the length bound being exceeded. A similar assumption is necessary in the framework of [14].

Lastly, we note that correctness would still hold even if the encryptor bases his encryption on a previously obtained version of the blockchain as opposed to the most recent up-to-date version. This is because our construction (Fig. 3) only requires the blockchain $\mathbf{B}$ used in encryption to be a prefix of and be consistent (w.r.t. consistent$^\ell$ as defined in Sect. 2.2) with the decryptor's blockchain $\mathbf{B}'$. However, note again that if the witness encryption only supports witnesses of bounded size, the difference in terms of blocks between the versions of the blockchain used by encryptor and decryptor cannot exceed this bound, as decryption would otherwise fail[3].

---

[3] For ease of notation, as in [14], we use the entire blockchain $\mathbf{B}'$ as part of the witness w. However, we note that essentially only the blocks appended to the blockchain after encryption suffice as part of the witness w.

3.5 Efficiency

The efficiency of our construction essentially follows from the efficiency of the underlying signature scheme, witness encryption scheme, and blockchain. We emphasize that neither encryptor nor decryptor are required to participate in the blockchain protocol itself, but are only required to be able to access an up-to-date version of the blockchain, and in case of the decryptor, be able to post a message to the blockchain e.g. by requesting a miner to do so. Depending on the premise of the blockchain protocol execution, the latter might involve an additional cost to the decryptor (e.g. paying a fee to the miner).

In more detail, key generation and public/private key size correspond to that of the signature scheme, and the computational encryption cost and the ciphertext size correspond to that of the witness encryption scheme, assuming accessing the blockchain does not involve any computational requirements. Decryption firstly requires the decryptor to post a signed message to the blockchain. Note that he will not be able to immediately decrypt once this has been posted, but must wait for the blockchain to grow sufficiently to satisfy distinguishable forking (Definition 6). Once this happens, he will invoke the decryption of the witness encryption scheme, which will most likely dominate the computational decryption cost (compared to signing). We refer the reader to Sect. 2.1 for a discussion of potential witness encryption instantiations.

Finally, we note that the relation in Fig. 3, which is required to be implemented by the witness encryption, is relatively complex, which could be an efficiency concern as ciphertext size and encryption/decryption cost typically scale with the size and complexity of the encryption statement and witness[4][5]. However, as noted in [20], this can be addressed by the use of succinct non-interactive arguments of knowledge (SNARKs) (e.g. see [17]). In our construction, the decryptor could include a SNARK common reference string in his public key[6], allowing the relation in Fig. 3 to be proved using the SNARK and the witness encryption to only rely on the verification and succinct witness from the SNARK. This would alleviate concerns regarding encryption cost and ciphertext size.

4 Security Analysis

The following theorem establishes the security of our construction.

---

[4] Note that in our construction, the lower bound of the witness size would be $\ell_1 + \ell_2 + \ell_d$ blocks where ℓ_1 and ℓ_2 are blockchain-specific parameters from the distinguishable forking property (see Sect. 2.2), and ℓ_d is the difference in the number of blocks between the blockchain obtained by encryptor and decryptor.

[5] We note the approach by Goyal et al. [15] allows efficient encryption and only requires the decryptor to perform a potentially heavy computation related to the relevant statement and witness.

[6] To maintain forward security, the randomness and trapdoor for this common reference string must be securely erased by the key pair holder after key generation.

Theorem 2. *Assume* WE *is an extractable witness encryption scheme for the NP relation R_{FSPKE},* Sig *is an EUF-CMA-secure signature scheme, H is a one-way hash function, and* BLC_V *is a blockchain protocol satisfying $(\alpha, \beta, \ell_1, \ell_2)$-distinguishable forking property for any PPT adversary with stake fraction at most α in environment $\mathcal{Z}$. Then the construction described in Fig. 4 is fs-IND-CPA secure for any admissible PPT adversary $\mathcal{A}$ in $\mathcal{Z}$ with at most α stake fraction.*

4.1   Proof of Theorem 2

Simulation of the Blockchain. Theorem 2 is with respect to an adversary $\mathcal{A}$ who controls at most an α stake fraction of the blockchain. With the exception of Claim 3, our security reduction will simulate the parties holding the remaining stake fraction for $\mathcal{A}$, by honestly executing the blockchain protocol BLC_V. We do not include an explicit simulation of this in the following proof.

Proof (Theorem 2). Let FORGE be the event that $\mathcal{A}$ causes honest user j to add a maliciously constructed record r^* to the blockchain contained in st_j that can be used to decrypt the challenge ciphertext c^*. More precisely, FORGE denotes that r^* is the first record in sequence of blocks $\mathbf{B} \leftarrow \mathsf{GetRecords}(1^\lambda, \mathsf{st}_j)$ satisfying $\mathsf{Sig.Ver}(pk, r^*.\mathsf{id} \,\|\, r^*.\sigma, r^*.\mathsf{cert}) = 1$. Note that since the Leak oracle will add a valid record to the blockchain contained in st_j for decryption of c^*, $\mathcal{A}$ needs to compute $r^*.\mathsf{cert}$ and post r^* *before* Leak does so (i.e. without sk) for FORGE to occur. That is, intuitively speaking, posting r^* means that $\mathcal{A}$ can forge a valid signature $r^*.\mathsf{cert}$. In the following lemma, we formalize this intuition.

Lemma 1. *Assume that* Sig *is an EUF-CMA secure signature scheme. Then* $\Pr[\mathsf{FORGE}] < neg(\lambda)$.

Proof (Lemma 1). If FORGE occurs, we can construct an adversary $\mathcal{B}_{\mathsf{Sig}}$ which breaks EUF-CMA security of Sig. $\mathcal{B}_{\mathsf{Sig}}$ simulates the role of a challenger in the fs-IND-CPA game for $\mathcal{A}$, and is defined as follows:

1. Upon receiving pk in the EUF-CMA game, $\mathcal{B}_{\mathsf{Sig}}$ forwards pk to $\mathcal{A}$. When running, $\mathcal{B}_{\mathsf{Sig}}$ simulates all honest parties in the blockchain and executes the blockchain protocols honestly. If $\mathsf{HonestDec}(c)$ is called where $c = (\mathsf{id}, CT)$, $\mathcal{B}_{\mathsf{Sig}}$ performs the decryption operations as described in Fig. 4 except it computes cert using the signing oracle of the EUF-CMA game. Lastly, $\mathcal{B}_{\mathsf{Sig}}$ adds $(\mathsf{id} \,\|\, \sigma)$ to a set Σ. When $\mathcal{A}$ calls Leak, $\mathcal{B}_{\mathsf{Sig}}$ aborts $\mathcal{A}$ after decryption of c^*, before the secret key sk is returned.
2. When $\mathcal{A}$ finishes its execution (or is terminated by $\mathcal{B}_{\mathsf{Sig}}$ due to a call to Leak), $\mathcal{B}_{\mathsf{Sig}}$ searches the blockchain $\mathbf{B} \leftarrow \mathsf{GetRecords}(1^\lambda, \mathsf{st}_j)$ for a valid record r^* such that $(r^*.\mathsf{id} \,\|\, r^*.\sigma) \notin \Sigma$, and outputs $(r^*.\mathsf{id} \,\|\, r^*.\sigma, r^*.\mathsf{cert})$ if such a record is found.

From the above description, it should be clear that $\mathcal{B}_{\mathsf{Sig}}$ provides a perfect simulation for $\mathcal{A}$ up until abortion, and that, assuming FORGE occurs, $\mathcal{B}_{\mathsf{Sig}}$ returns a valid forgery.   (Lemma 1) $\square$

Let S be the event that the adversary $\mathcal{A}$ wins the fs-IND-CPA game. In the following lemma, we consider the case $\mathcal{A}$ wins the game without causing a valid maliciously constructed record to the blockchain of honest user j that can be used for decrypting the challenge ciphertext, i.e. without FORGE occurring.

Lemma 2. *Assume* WE *is an extractable witness encryption scheme, H is a one-way hash function, and the blockchain protocol* BLC_V *satisfies* $(\alpha, \beta, \ell_1, \ell_2)$-*distinguishable forking property in* $\mathcal{Z}$. *Then* $|\Pr[S|\neg FORGE] - \frac{1}{2}| \le neg(\lambda)$

Proof (Lemma 2). Assume there exists an fs-IND-CPA attacker $\mathcal{A}$ with non-negligible advantage $\varepsilon = |\Pr[S|\neg FORGE] - \frac{1}{2}|$. From $\mathcal{A}$, we construct an attacker $\mathcal{A}^{WE}$ against WE as follows. Firstly, we choose random $esk \leftarrow \{0,1\}^n$, and compute $y \leftarrow H(esk)$. The value y will be hardcoded into $\mathcal{A}^{WE}$, and we use the notation $\mathcal{A}_y^{WE}$ to denote this. Hardcoding y into $\mathcal{A}^{WE}$ is needed, as below, we will consider a value y given by an external one-way challenger for H, and hence, $\mathcal{A}^{WE}$ cannot generate y internally.

$\mathcal{A}_y^{WE}$ will simulate the fs-IND-CPA game for $\mathcal{A} = (\mathcal{A}_1, \mathcal{A}_2)$ as follows:

1. $\mathcal{A}_y^{WE}$ generates a FSPKE key pair as $(pk, sk) \leftarrow$ FSPKE.KGen(1^λ).
2. $\mathcal{A}_y^{WE}$ sends pk to $\mathcal{A}_1$ and forwards its output m_0, m_1 and $x = (\mathbf{B} \| id \| pk)$ as the challenge instance in the extractability game, where $\mathbf{B}$ and id are computed as $\mathbf{B} \leftarrow$ BLC$_V$.GetRecords$(1^\lambda, st_i)$ and $id \overset{\$}{\leftarrow} \{0,1\}^\lambda$ respectively.
3. Upon receiving the challenge ciphertext c^*, $\mathcal{A}_y^{WE}$ forwards c^* to $\mathcal{A}_2$.
   - If HonestDec oracle is called by $\mathcal{A}$, $\mathcal{A}_y^{WE}$ executes step 1 to 5 of the decryption algorithm for the given ciphertext c, as defined in the construction, except it replaces σ with the hardcoded value y if c is the challenge ciphertext[7].
   - If the Leak oracle is called by $\mathcal{A}$, $\mathcal{A}_y^{WE}$ responds in the same way as in HonestDec, and then returns sk.
4. Lastly, $\mathcal{A}_2$ outputs b, and $\mathcal{A}_y^{WE}$ forwards this as its own response in the extractability game.

From the above description, it should be clear that the view of $\mathcal{A}$ is identical to the fs-IND-CPA game, and that if $\mathcal{A}$ successfully distinguishes the encryption of m_0 and m_1, so will $\mathcal{A}_y^{WE}$ in the extractable witness encryption game. Since WE is extractable, there exists a PPT extractor $\mathcal{E}$ for $\mathcal{A}_y^{WE}$, and assuming we can show that $\mathcal{A}_y^{WE}$ successfully distinguishes with a non-negligible advantage, $\mathcal{E}$ will likewise be able to compute a valid witness with non-negligible advantage. However, here a subtle issue arises: from the assumption that the advantage of $\mathcal{A}$ is ε, it only follows that $\mathcal{A}_y^{WE}$ has advantage ε when the choice of y is considered part of the probability space defining the advantage. For a fixed value of y, even if this is correctly distributed, we can no longer draw the conclusion that $\mathcal{A}_y^{WE}$ has advantage ε. Nevertheless, the following claim shows that, with probability $\varepsilon/2$ over the choice of y, $\mathcal{A}_y^{WE}$ will have an advantage larger than $\varepsilon/2$.

---

[7] Note that $\mathcal{A}_y^{WE}$ cannot fully decrypt the challenge ciphertext c^*, as it does not know the preimage of the hardcoded value y, which is required to construct a witness for decryption.

Claim 1. *Let b' denote the bit output by $\mathcal{A}_y^{WE}$, let b denote the challenge bit in the extractability game, and let Good_y denote the event that $\Pr[b = b'] \geq \varepsilon/2 + 1/2$. Then, $\Pr[\mathsf{Good}_y] \geq \varepsilon/2$, where the probability is taken over a random choice of $esk \leftarrow \{0,1\}^n$ and $y \leftarrow H(esk)$.*

Proof (Claim 1). Let Succ denote the event $b' = b$ when $esk \leftarrow \{0,1\}^n$ is picked at random and $y \leftarrow H(esk)$. From the construction of $\mathcal{A}_y^{WE}$ and the assumption that the advantage of $\mathcal{A}$ is ε, we have that $\Pr[\mathsf{Succ}] = \varepsilon + 1/2$. Hence,

$$\varepsilon + \frac{1}{2} = \Pr[\mathsf{Succ}|\mathsf{Good}_y]\Pr[\mathsf{Good}_y] + \Pr[\mathsf{Succ}|\neg\mathsf{Good}_y]\Pr[\neg\mathsf{Good}_y]$$
$$\leq \Pr[\mathsf{Good}_y] + \Pr[\mathsf{Succ}|\neg\mathsf{Good}_y]$$
$$\leq \Pr[\mathsf{Good}_y] + \frac{\varepsilon}{2} + \frac{1}{2}$$

where the last inequality follows by the definition of $\neg\mathsf{Good}_y$. Rearranging the terms, we obtain $\Pr[\mathsf{Good}_y] \geq \varepsilon/2$. (Claim 1) □

The above claim allows us to conclude that we can extract a valid witness for x specified by $\mathcal{A}_y^{WE}$ (including its internal fs-IND-CPA attacker $\mathcal{A}$) with non-negligible probability, despite invoking the extractor $\mathcal{E}$ with $\mathcal{A}_y^{WE}$ for a fixed (but randomly chosen) y. This can be seen as follows. Let w denote the witness extracted by $\mathcal{E}$ from $\mathcal{A}_y^{WE}$. Then we have that

$$\Pr[R_{\mathsf{FSPKE}}(x,w)] \geq \Pr[b = b' \wedge R_{\mathsf{FSPKE}}(x,w)]$$
$$\geq \Pr[\mathsf{Good}_y] \cdot \Pr[b = b' \wedge R_{\mathsf{FSPKE}}(x,w)|\mathsf{Good}_y]$$
$$\geq \varepsilon/2 \cdot \Pr[b = b' \wedge R_{\mathsf{FSPKE}}(x,w)|\mathsf{Good}_y]. \qquad (1)$$

By definition, Good_y ensures that the advantage of $\mathcal{A}_y^{WE}$ is greater than $\varepsilon/2$, and we obtain that

$$\varepsilon/2 \leq \Pr[b = b'|\mathsf{Good}_y] - \frac{1}{2}$$
$$\leq \Pr[b = b' \wedge R_{\mathsf{FSPKE}}(x,w)|\mathsf{Good}_y] + \Pr[b = b' \wedge \neg R_{\mathsf{FSPKE}}(x,w)|\mathsf{Good}_y] - \frac{1}{2}$$
$$\leq \Pr[b = b' \wedge R_{\mathsf{FSPKE}}(x,w)|\mathsf{Good}_y] + neg(\lambda)$$

where the last inequality follows from the extractability of WE (note that extractability requires a successful extractor exists for all successful adversaries, including any adversary $\mathcal{A}_y^{WE}$ for values of y such that Good_y is satisfied). Rearranging the terms yields that

$$\Pr[b = b' \wedge R_{\mathsf{FSPKE}}(x,w)|\mathsf{Good}_y] \geq \frac{\varepsilon}{2} - neg(\lambda)$$

and combining this with (1) we obtain that

$$\Pr[R_{\mathsf{FSPKE}}(x,w)] \geq \frac{\varepsilon}{2} \cdot (\frac{\varepsilon}{2} - neg(\lambda)).$$

Note that if ε is non-negligible, then so is $\Pr[R_{\mathsf{FSPKE}}(x, w)]$. In other words, with non-negligible probability, we obtain a valid witness w for x specified by $\mathcal{A}_y^{\mathsf{WE}}$ via the extractor $\mathcal{E}$.

In the following, we will show that if a valid witness can be extracted, we can either break the onewayness of the hash function H, or the distinguishable forking property of BLC_V.

Let HONEST be the event that $\mathcal{E}$ outputs a sequence of blocks $\mathbf{B}'$ containing the record r^* honestly constructed in the first decryption query of the challenge ciphertext c^* (either a query to Dec or Leak) as the first valid record that allows decryption of c^*. We have that

$$
\begin{aligned}
\Pr[R_{\mathsf{FSPKE}}(x, w)] &= \Pr[R_{\mathsf{FSPKE}}(x, w)|\mathsf{HONEST}] \cdot \Pr[\mathsf{HONEST}] \\
&\quad + \Pr[R_{\mathsf{FSPKE}}(x, w)|\neg\mathsf{HONEST}] \cdot \Pr[\neg\mathsf{HONEST}] \\
&\leq \Pr[R_{\mathsf{FSPKE}}(x, w)|\mathsf{HONEST}] \\
&\quad + \Pr[R_{\mathsf{FSPKE}}(x, w)|\neg\mathsf{HONEST}]
\end{aligned}
\tag{2}
$$

Claim 2. *If* $\Pr[R_{\mathsf{FSPKE}}(x, w)|\mathsf{HONEST}]$ *is non-negligible, there exists an adversary* $\mathcal{B}_{\mathsf{OW}}$ *against the onewayness of* H *with non-negligible advantage.*

Proof (Claim 2). $\mathcal{B}_{\mathsf{OW}}$ is constructed as follows. Given a challenge y^*, $\mathcal{B}_{\mathsf{OW}}$ simply constructs $\mathcal{A}_{y^*}^{\mathsf{WE}}$ as described above, but using y^* as the embedded y value. Note that as $\mathcal{B}_{\mathsf{OW}}$'s challenge is constructed as $y^* = H(esk^*)$ for a randomly chosen esk^*, the construction of $\mathcal{A}_{y^*}^{\mathsf{WE}}$ is identical to the above description. $\mathcal{B}_{\mathsf{OW}}$ then runs $\mathcal{E}$ for $\mathcal{A}_{y^*}^{\mathsf{WE}}$ to obtain a witness w, and forwards $w.esk$ as the solution in the onewayness game. Since HONEST occurs, $\mathcal{E}$ outputs a witness w corresponding to the honestly created record r^* for the challenge ciphertext c^* i.e. r^* must have been posted by the HonestDec or the Leak oracle. Furthermore, it must hold that $H(w.esk) = r^*.\sigma$, and due to the construction of $\mathcal{A}_{y^*}^{\mathsf{WE}}$, $r^*.\sigma = y^*$. Thus the obtained value $w.esk$ satisfies $w.esk = H^{-1}(y^*)$, and $\mathcal{B}_{\mathsf{OW}}$ therefore successfully wins the onewayness game. (Claim 2) $\square$

Claim 3. *If* $\Pr[R_{\mathsf{FSPKE}}(x, w)|\neg\mathsf{HONEST}]$ *is non-negligible, there exists an adversary* $\mathcal{B}_{\mathsf{BLC}}$ *breaking the* $(\alpha, \beta, \ell_1, \ell_2)$-*distinguishable forking property of the blockchain with non-negligible advantage.*

Proof (Claim 3). The construction of $\mathcal{B}_{\mathsf{BLC}}$ is straightforward: $\mathcal{B}_{\mathsf{BLC}}$ simply runs $\mathcal{E}$, and returns its output $\mathbf{B}'$. Note, however, that $\mathcal{B}_{\mathsf{BLC}}$ plays the role of an adversary against the distinguishable forking property of the blockchain, and therefore must abide by the rules for this type of adversary. In particular, $\mathcal{B}_{\mathsf{BLC}}$ cannot control the honest parties participating in the blockchain protocol. Nevertheless, the simulation remains straightforward: $\mathcal{B}_{\mathsf{BLC}}$ simply corrupts the parties required by the underlying adversary $\mathcal{A}$, who will have a total stake fraction at most α, and forwards any messages to honest parties over the blockchain network as dictated by $\mathcal{A}$.

Since HONEST is assumed not to occur, the first valid record r' in $\mathbf{B}'$ allowing decryption of c^* does not correspond to the honestly generated record r^* in a Dec or Leak upon submission of c^* (recall that $\mathbf{B}'$ from a valid witness is required to contain a valid record allowing decryption of c^*). Furthermore, since FORGE is also assumed not to occur, r' cannot occur before r^* in the honest blockchain $\mathbf{B}'' \leftarrow \mathsf{GetRecords}(1^\lambda, \mathsf{st}_j)$ held by the honest user j. This implies that from the block in $\mathbf{B}'$ in which r' occurs, $\mathbf{B}'$ cannot be a prefix of $\mathbf{B}''$. Additionally, witness correctness implies that there are at least $\ell' = \ell_1 + \ell_2$ blocks after the block in which r' occurs, and that the last $\ell' - \ell_1$ blocks of these contain a combined stake fraction more than β. Hence, $\mathbf{B}'$ contradicts the $(\alpha, \beta, \ell_1, \ell_2)$-distinguishable forking property, which requires these blocks to contain a stake fraction less than $\alpha < \beta$. (Claim 3) $\square$

Combining the above observations, we conclude that the existence of an adversary $\mathcal{A}$ with non-negligible advantage implies $\Pr[R_{\mathsf{FSPKE}}(x, w)]$ being non-negligible, which in turn implies that either the onewayness of H or the distinguishable forking property of BLC_V can be broken with non-negligible advantage due to (2) in combination with Claim 2 and Claim 3. This contradicts the assumption that H and BLC_V are secure, and we hence conclude that all $\mathcal{A}$ must have negligible advantage. Hence, Lemma 2 follows. (Lemma 2) $\square$

Putting Lemma 1 and Lemma 2 together, we obtain:

$$\mathsf{Adv}^{\mathsf{fs\text{-}IND\text{-}CPA}}_{\mathcal{A},\mathsf{FSPKE}}(\lambda) = \left| \Pr[S] - \frac{1}{2} \right|$$

$$= \left| \Pr[S|\mathsf{FORGE}] \Pr[\mathsf{FORGE}] + \Pr[S|\neg\mathsf{FORGE}] \Pr[\neg\mathsf{FORGE}] - \frac{1}{2} \right|$$

$$\leq \left| \Pr[S|\neg\mathsf{FORGE}] \Pr[\neg\mathsf{FORGE}] - \frac{1}{2} \right| + \Pr[\mathsf{FORGE}]$$

$$\leq \left| \Pr[S|\neg\mathsf{FORGE}](1 - \Pr[\mathsf{FORGE}]) - \frac{1}{2} \right| + \Pr[\mathsf{FORGE}]$$

$$\leq neg(\lambda) + neg(\lambda) = neg(\lambda)$$

Hence, Theorem 2 follows. (Theorem 2) $\square$

5 Discussion

Besides forward security, our construction provides several interesting properties which lead to advantages compared to existing approaches as well as additional security guarantees, but also impacts aspects such as decryption privacy. In the following, we discuss these in further detail.

Fixed Immutable Secret Keys. The unique feature of our construction is that forward security is achieved without key updates, and secret keys are short and immutable. This property provides several advantages.

Firstly, while the size of secret keys in most previous works [8, 16] depends on the number of key updates, our construction achieves a constant size secret key and furthermore does not impose a predetermined maximum number of possible key updates (such as Bloom filter encryption [11]).

Secondly, fixed immutable keys are interesting from an application point of view. For example, a fixed secret key can be embedded in secure read-only memory, which would provide an additional hardware-based defense against key compromise. Note that in our construction, the secret key is only required for signature generation, which is a standard functionality supported by most trusted platform modules (TPMs), and that the remaining part of decryption can be done without direct access to the secret key. In contrast, providing similar protection for a dynamically changing secret key of non-constant size is a harder task requiring a more advanced trusted execution environment, which in turn is more difficult and expensive to implement securely.

Lastly, a fixed secret key allows the key to be distributed among several independent devices or servers without introducing security concerns due to a potential lack of synchronization. Key distribution might be desirable e.g. if the same user uses several different devices or several servers are used to implement load balancing (here the servers look like one server from the outside). In this case, security concerns might arise for schemes implementing fine-grained forward security based on key update. For example, if a device decrypts a ciphertext c, the local key of that device will be rendered useless for future decryptions of c to ensure forward security. However, unless the keys stored by all other devices are updated with respect to c, an adversary will still be able to decrypt c by compromising a device with a key that has not yet been updated. Hence, this creates a potentially significant synchronization problem. On the other hand, this problem is completely eliminated by a scheme with fixed secret keys, as there is no need to update keys to ensure security.

Decryption Privacy and Key Compromise Detection. Our construction requires the decryptor to post an appropriate message to the blockchain to decrypt a ciphertext. Specifically, Alice (holding the key pair pk_A and sk_A) is required to post a record r to the blockchain such that $\mathsf{Sig}.\mathsf{Ver}(pk_A, r.\mathsf{id} \,\|\, r.\sigma, r.\mathsf{cert}) = 1$ holds to be able to decrypt a ciphertext $c = (\mathsf{id}, CT)$.

Note that as $r.\mathsf{cert}$ is publicly verifiable with respect to Alice's public key pk_A and id uniquely identifies c, anyone monitoring the blockchain, which is assumed to be publicly accessible, will be able to tell when Alice decrypts a specific ciphertext i.e. the construction does not provide Alice with privacy regarding decryption.

On the other hand, this gives the construction a unique security property not provided by existing schemes. More precisely, by monitoring the blockchain, Alice can detect if someone else is trying to decrypt a ciphertext using her private key. Hence, it is possible for Alice to detect a key compromise if the compromised key is ever attempted to be used for decryption. This property is not achievable if decryption can be done without any information being made public.

One-Time Decryption. In existing fine-grained encryption schemes without interaction [11,16,18], a ciphertext can be decrypted only once even by a legitimate user because an updated secret key cannot be used for decrypting past ciphertexts; the same limitation applies to our construction. Note that one-time decryption is an inherent property of fine-grained forward security.

Message Suppression Attacks and Mitigation. As we mentioned in Sect. 3.2, a standard fine-grained forward-secure scheme with perfect correctness inherently does not protect against message suppression attacks [6]. A message suppression attack is a man-in-the-middle attack where the attacker is assumed to control the communication between encryptor and decryptor and simply does not deliver a given ciphertext c. Then, if the attacker is allowed to compromise the secret key, he will be able to decrypt c due to the perfect correctness of the scheme and the fact that c has not been attempted to decrypt by the decryptor[8].

To mitigate the attack in our construction, we can introduce *decryption expiration* (similar to eventual forward security [6]) by checking in the witness relation $R_{\mathsf{FSPKE}}(x, w)$ that the number of blocks in $w.\mathbf{B}'$ extended from $x.\mathbf{B}$ is less than a predefined expiration threshold. This ensures that if the adversary does not compromise the secret key before the extension of the blockchain passes the threshold, he will not be able to decrypt the intercepted ciphertext. However, this will also require the legitimate decryptor to decrypt the ciphertext before the expiration, as he would otherwise lose the ability to do so. Finally note that this change does not interfere with the property that once the decryptor has decrypted a ciphertext, this can no longer be decrypted by an adversary compromising the decryption key i.e. fine-grained forward security is maintained.

Acknowledgments. This work was supported in part by JSPS KAKENHI Grant Number 20K11807.

References

1. Albrecht, M.R., Farshim, P., Han, S., Hofheinz, D., Larraia, E., Paterson, K.G.: Multilinear maps from obfuscation. J. Cryptol. **33**(3), 1080–1113 (2020)
2. Aviram, N., Gellert, K., Jager, T.: Session resumption protocols and efficient forward security for TLS 1.3 0-RTT. In: Ishai, Y., Rijmen, V. (eds.) EUROCRYPT 2019. LNCS, vol. 11477, pp. 117–150. Springer, Cham (2019). https://doi.org/10.1007/978-3-030-17656-3_5
3. Barta, O., Ishai, Y., Ostrovsky, R., Wu, D.J.: On succinct arguments and witness encryption from groups. In: Micciancio, D., Ristenpart, T. (eds.) CRYPTO 2020. LNCS, vol. 12170, pp. 776–806. Springer, Cham (2020). https://doi.org/10.1007/978-3-030-56784-2_26

---

[8] In a scheme based on periodical key updates, this type of attack does not work assuming the key has been updated after the ciphertext was constructed and the attacker compromises this updated key. However, schemes based on periodical key updates only achieve coarse-grained forward security (eventual forward security [6]) and are still vulnerable to the attack until the key is updated.

4. Bartusek, J., Ishai, Y., Jain, A., Ma, F., Sahai, A., Zhandry, M.: Affine determinant programs: a framework for obfuscation and witness encryption. In: Vidick, T. (ed.) 11th Innovations in Theoretical Computer Science Conference, ITCS 2020. LIPIcs, vol. 151, pp. 82:1–82:39 (2020)

5. Bellare, M., Hoang, V.T.: Adaptive witness encryption and asymmetric password-based cryptography. In: Katz, J. (ed.) PKC 2015. LNCS, vol. 9020, pp. 308–331. Springer, Heidelberg (2015). https://doi.org/10.1007/978-3-662-46447-2_14

6. Boyd, C., Gellert, K.: A modern view on forward security. Comput. J. **64**, 639–652 (2020)

7. Canetti, R.: Universally composable security: a new paradigm for cryptographic protocols. In: Proceedings 42nd IEEE Symposium on Foundations of Computer Science, pp. 136–145. IEEE (2001)

8. Canetti, R., Halevi, S., Katz, J.: A forward-secure public-key encryption scheme. In: Biham, E. (ed.) EUROCRYPT 2003. LNCS, vol. 2656, pp. 255–271. Springer, Heidelberg (2003). https://doi.org/10.1007/3-540-39200-9_16

9. Cohn-Gordon, K., Cremers, C., Garratt, L.: On post-compromise security. In: 2016 IEEE 29th Computer Security Foundations Symposium (CSF), pp. 164–178 (2016)

10. Daian, P., Pass, R., Shi, E.: Snow White: robustly reconfigurable consensus and applications to provably secure proof of stake. In: Goldberg, I., Moore, T. (eds.) FC 2019. LNCS, vol. 11598, pp. 23–41. Springer, Cham (2019). https://doi.org/10.1007/978-3-030-32101-7_2

11. Derler, D., Jager, T., Slamanig, D., Striecks, C.: Bloom filter encryption and applications to efficient forward-secret 0-RTT key exchange. In: Nielsen, J.B., Rijmen, V. (eds.) EUROCRYPT 2018. LNCS, vol. 10822, pp. 425–455. Springer, Cham (2018). https://doi.org/10.1007/978-3-319-78372-7_14

12. Garg, S., Gentry, C., Sahai, A., Waters, B.: Witness encryption and its applications. In: Proceedings of the Forty-Fifth Annual ACM Symposium on Theory of Computing, STOC 2013, pp. 467–476 (2013)

13. Goldwasser, S., Kalai, Y.T., Popa, R.A., Vaikuntanathan, V., Zeldovich, N.: How to run turing machines on encrypted data. In: Canetti, R., Garay, J.A. (eds.) CRYPTO 2013. LNCS, vol. 8043, pp. 536–553. Springer, Heidelberg (2013). https://doi.org/10.1007/978-3-642-40084-1_30

14. Goyal, R., Goyal, V.: Overcoming cryptographic impossibility results using blockchains. In: Kalai, Y., Reyzin, L. (eds.) TCC 2017. LNCS, vol. 10677, pp. 529–561. Springer, Cham (2017). https://doi.org/10.1007/978-3-319-70500-2_18

15. Goyal, V., Kothapalli, A., Masserova, E., Parno, B., Song, Y.: Storing and Retrieving Secrets on a Blockchain. IACR Cryptol. ePrint Arch, p. 504 (2020)

16. Green, M.D., Miers, I.: Forward secure asynchronous messaging from puncturable encryption. In: Proceedings of the 2015 IEEE Symposium on Security and Privacy, SP 2015, pp. 305–320 (2015)

17. Groth, J.: On the size of pairing-based non-interactive arguments. In: Fischlin, M., Coron, J.-S. (eds.) EUROCRYPT 2016. LNCS, vol. 9666, pp. 305–326. Springer, Heidelberg (2016). https://doi.org/10.1007/978-3-662-49896-5_11

18. Günther, F., Hale, B., Jager, T., Lauer, S.: 0-RTT key exchange with full forward secrecy. In: Coron, J.-S., Nielsen, J.B. (eds.) EUROCRYPT 2017. LNCS, vol. 10212, pp. 519–548. Springer, Cham (2017). https://doi.org/10.1007/978-3-319-56617-7_18

19. Jain, A., Lin, H., Sahai, A.: Indistinguishability obfuscation from well-founded assumptions. In: STOC 2021: 53rd Annual ACM SIGACT Symposium on Theory of Computing, Virtual Event, Italy, 21–25 June 2021, pp. 60–73 (2021)

20. Liu, J., Jager, T., Kakvi, S.A., Warinschi, B.: How to build time-lock encryption. Des. Codes Crypt. **86**(11), 2549–2586 (2018)
21. Pointcheval, D., Sanders, O.: Forward secure non-interactive key exchange. In: Security and Cryptography for Networks, pp. 21–39 (2014)
22. Rescorla, E.: The Transport Layer Security (TLS) Protocol Version 1.3, RFC8446

Cryptanalysis of the Privacy-Preserving Ride-Hailing Service TRACE

Deepak Kumaraswamy[1]($\boxtimes$) and Srinivas Vivek[2]

[1] National Institute of Technology Karnataka, Mangalore, India
[2] International Institute of Information Technology Bangalore, Bengaluru, India
srinivas.vivek@iiitb.ac.in

Abstract. In a typical ride-hailing service, the service provider (RS) matches a customer (RC) with the closest vehicle (RV) registered to this service. Ride-hailing services have gained tremendous popularity over the past years, and several works have been proposed to ensure privacy of riders and drivers during ride-matching. TRACE is an efficient privacy-preserving ride-hailing service proposed by Wang et al. (IEEE Trans. Vehicular Technology 2018). TRACE uses masking along with other cryptographic techniques to ensure efficient and accurate ride-matching. RS computes a (secret) spatial division of a region into quadrants. The RS uses masked location information to match RCs and RVs within a quadrant without obtaining their exact locations, thus ensuring privacy. Additionally, an RC only gets to know location of the closest RV finally matched to it, and not of other responding RVs in the region.

In this work, we disprove the privacy claims in TRACE by showing the following: a) RCs and RVs can identify the secret spatial division maintained by RS (this reveals information about the density of RVs in the region and other potential trade secrets), and b) the RS can identify exact locations of RCs and RVs (this violates location privacy). Prior to exchanging encrypted messages in the TRACE protocol, each entity masks the plaintext message with a secret unknown to others. Our attack allows other entities to recover this plaintext from the masked value by exploiting shared randomness used across different messages, that eventually leads to a system of linear equations in the unknown plaintexts. This holds even when all the participating entities are honest-but-curious. We implement our attack and demonstrate its efficiency and high success rate. For the security parameters recommended for TRACE, an RV can recover the spatial division in less than a minute, and the RS can recover the location of an RV in less than a second on a commodity laptop.

Keywords: Location privacy · Privacy-preserving protocols · Ride-hailing services · Cryptanalysis · Random masking

1 Introduction

Ride-hailing services such as Uber and Lyft have become a popular choice of transportation in the past decade [9]. By offering convenience and reliability

A. Adhikari et al. (Eds.): INDOCRYPT 2021, LNCS 13143, pp. 462–484, 2021.
https://doi.org/10.1007/978-3-030-92518-5_21

to its customers, these services are well suited for intra-city commutes. A ride-hailing service usually consists of three entities: the ride-hailing server (RS), riders or customers (RCs) and drivers or vehicles (RVs). The RS is primarily responsible for hosting the ride-hailing service publicly. Drivers can register to this service and become identified as certified RVs. A customer who wishes to make use of this service can sign up as an RC and request for a ride. Depending on the pick-up and destination locations, the RS smartly forwards this ride request from RC to suitable RVs in the region. A list of nearby available RVs is revealed to the RC along with their reputations, who then makes a suitable choice.

However, revealing locations of RCs/RVs to other entities can have severe consequences. A pick-up location could correspond to the residential address of an RC, which can be used for stalking/kidnapping. There have also been instances when RVs registered to a particular ride-hailing service have been targeted by regular taxi drivers or targeted for theft [4,14]. Preserving privacy of sensitive users' locations has become a primary concern in ride-hailing services. Generally, the RS is assumed to be *honest-but-curious*. This means that RS tries to learn as much information as possible without maliciously deviating from the ride-hailing protocol. Such a model is reasonable to assume since the RS wishes to preserve its reputation among the public. But it is still dangerous for the RS to learn locations of RCs and RVs, in case the RS later turns malicious or becomes a victim of cyberattacks [3,8].

In the past few years, there have been many works that focus on ensuring location privacy of RCs and RVs in the context of ride-hailing services. Section 5 contains an overview of recent papers in this area. These works use cryptographic primitives to hide sensitive location information from the RS, while trying to ensure efficiency and ride-matching accuracy.

In this paper, we focus on TRACE [16], proposed by Wang et al. in 2018. TRACE is a privacy-preserving solution to ride-hailing services. Here, the RS first spatially divides each city into quadrants. RCs and RVs mask their sensitive location information using randomness and then forward it to RS. The RS then identifies the quadrant in which RCs and RVs lie, without finding out their exact locations. To ensure efficiency and accuracy, the ride request from an RC is forwarded only to RVs that are in the same quadrant as RC. The RC then makes a choice among RVs that lie in its vicinity to finalize ride establishment. Since the RS knows the distribution of RVs in different quadrants, it can periodically change its spatial division of the city to optimize bandwidth usage, reduce waiting time and improve accuracy.

TRACE uses masking with random secrets to prevent other entities of the protocol from learning the underlying message. At a high level, a large prime p is chosen and the plaintext is multiplied with a random integer in $\mathbb{Z}_p$. These masked messages are encrypted using shared keys to prevent external eavesdroppers from gaining any useful information. Since TRACE uses lightweight cryptographic techniques and simple modular arithmetic, it is efficient in practice. The security guarantees for TRACE state that RS cannot learn about the exact locations of

RCs and RVs apart from the quadrant they are in. Additionally, RCs and RVs cannot learn about the secret spatial division maintained by RS, since this could reveal the density of drivers across the city, among other proprietary information and trade secrets of RS.

1.1   Our Contribution

We propose an attack on TRACE and disprove the above security claims by showing that the RS can indeed retrieve the exact locations of all RCs and RVs. Secondly, we show that RCs and RVs can learn the secret spatial division information maintained by RS. These attacks constitute a total break of the privacy objectives of TRACE. The underlying idea behind our attack is to eliminate the (unknown) randomness shared across different messages when other entities mask their location values. This allows one to efficiently obtain an overdetermined system of linear (modular) equations in the unknown plaintext locations. We stress that this attack is purely algebraic, and does not make any geometric assumptions about the region. Our attack is efficient (runs in time quadratic in the security parameters) and holds even when all entities are honest-but-curious. For instance, with the recommended security parameters from [16], an RV can recover the quadtree maintained by RS in under a minute (see Table 2) and the RS can recover the exact location of an RV in under a second (see Table 3).

The rest of our paper is organized as follows. In Sect. 2, we describe relevant steps of the TRACE protocol from [16]. The first attack in Sect. 3.1 describes how RCs and RVs can recover the secret quadtree maintained by RS. The second attack in Sect. 3.2 describes how the RS can recover exact locations of RCs and RVs. We briefly discuss a modification to the TRACE protocol that prevents only the first attack, and argue that the second attack (which is more severe than the first) is hard to thwart. Algorithms 1 and 2 summarize the above two attacks. Section 4 provides details about our experimental setup and evaluates the efficiency and success rate of our attack in practice (refer Tables 2 and 3). Section 5 gives an overview of recent works in the area of privacy-preserving ride-hailing services. We conclude our paper and provide remarks about future work in Sect. 6.

2   Overview of TRACE

This section contains a high level overview of the TRACE protocol [16]. Details that are not directly relevant to our attack will be omitted. For more information the reader is referred to the original paper.

2.1   Preliminaries

A quadtree $\{N_1, \ldots, N_m\}$ with m nodes is a data structure used to represent the partition of a 2-D space into quadrants and subquadrants. Each node N_i in the tree is associated with four (x, y) coordinates denoting corners of the quadrant represented by that node. Every non-leaf node in the quadtree has four children denoting the division of that quadrant into four subquadrants. An example is presented in Fig. 1.

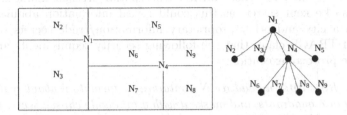

Fig. 1. Example of a quadtree

Given a point $P = (x, y)$ and a quadrant $\{(x_j, y_j)\}$ with $j = 1, \ldots, 4$, we can easily check if P lies within the quadrant by doing the following [16, Section III]. For each j compute

$$S_j = (xy_j + yx_{j'} + x_j y_{j'}) - (xy_{j'} + yx_j + x_{j'} y_j) \tag{1}$$

where $j' = (j \bmod 4) + 1$. If all $S_j \geq 0$, then P lies within the quadrant, otherwise it does not. Given a quadtree, this idea can be extended to find the quadrant/node of the tree in which P lies. Starting at the root, among its four children, find that quadrant/node in which P lies; then recurse on its children until a leaf is encountered.

2.2 System Design and Security Goals

System Design. The three primary entities in the TRACE protocol are the ride-hailing server/service provider (RS), the customer/rider (RC) and the vehicle/driver (RV). All of the aforementioned entities are assumed to be honest-but-curious. This means that they wish to learn as much information as they can about the other entities without violating any protocol steps.

RS is mainly responsible for forwarding requests/responses between RCs and RVs. As part of the protocol, RS maintains a spatial division of the city into quadrants and uses it to identify regions in which RCs and RVs lie. It does so in such a way that RCs and RVs do not learn any information about the spatial division, while RS does not learn the exact locations of RCs and RVs. The RC can choose a pick-up point and send a ride-hailing request to RS, who then forwards it to the RVs that lie in close vicinity of RC. RVs submit their masked location information to RS at regular intervals, allowing the RS to have an idea of distribution of RVs in the city. Depending on the density of RVs, RS can periodically optimize its space division to improve ride-matching accuracy.

Threat Model. We assume the same threat model that is considered in TRACE. All entities are assumed to be honest-but-curious, that is, they follow the protocol specification but may infer additional data from the observed transcripts. RS does not collude with RCs and RVs (to try and obtain information about customers), since it has an incentive to maintain high reputation.

Security Goals. It is essential to ensure that location information of RCs and RVs is not revealed to other entities. The spatial division maintained by RS should also be kept secret, as this could reveal information about density of drivers in a city and other proprietary information/trade secrets of RS. The authors of TRACE claim that the following security requirements are satisfied during the protocol execution.

Claim 1. *RS creates a quadtree N containing information about spatial divison of the city into quadrants, and masks it with a randomly chosen secret to compute EN. Given EN, RCs and RVs do not learn anything about N.*

Claim 2. *RS can only learn the quadrants in which RCs lie. RS does not obtain any other information about the exact pick-up locations of RCs.*

Claim 3. *RS can only learn the quadrants in which RVs lie. RS does not obtain any other information about the exact locations of RVs.*

2.3   TRACE Protocol

This section describes the execution of the TRACE protocol. Figure 2 gives a summarized view of the messages exchanged between different entities. RS acts as a central entity for forwarding messages between RCs and RVs. It establishes shared keys with RCs and RVs through the Diffie-Hellman key exchange. All messages exchanged between RS and RCs, RVs are encrypted using a symmetric encryption scheme. The authentication of entities is ensured by signing these messages using the BLS signature scheme [1]. The notations used in the TRACE protocol and their descriptions are provided in Table 1.

For convenience, the remainder of this paper shall refer to subscripts $(\cdot)_{i,j}$ and $(\cdot)_{i,j,l}$ as simply $(\cdot)_{ij}$ and $(\cdot)_{ijl}$, respectively.

Step 0. RS publishes details about different system parameters (for example, the group and its generator used in the signature scheme, public key of RS, choice of symmetric encryption). RCs and RVs also establish their public keys. RS announces security parameters k_1, k_2, k_3, k_4. As we shall see subsequently, they specify the size of different randomness used when masking location information. Step 3 elaborates on the constraint that should exist among these four parameters to ensure correctness of the protocol.

RS chooses two large public primes p and α (of size k_1 bits and k_2 bits, respectively) and a random secret $s \in \mathbb{Z}_p^*$ known only to itself.

Step 1. RS divides the two-dimensional space into squares or rectangles represented by a quadtree

$$N = \{N_1, N_2, \ldots, N_m\}$$

with m nodes. The i-th quadrant N_i has four corners $\{N_{ij} = (x_{Nij}, y_{Nij})\}$ where $j = 1, \ldots, 4$. RS wishes to learn the quadrant in which each RV lies without

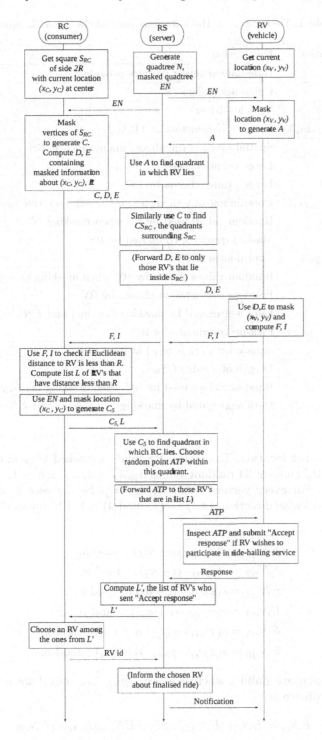

Fig. 2. Overview of TRACE protocol

Table 1. Description of the notations used in the TRACE protocol.

Notation	Description
RS	Ride-hailing server (service provider)
RC	Customer (rider)
RV	Vehicle (driver)
k_1, k_2, k_3, k_4	Security parameters of TRACE
N	Spatial division (quadtree) maintained by RS
α, p	Large primes chosen by RS
α', p'	Large primes chosen by RC
(x_{Nij}, y_{Nij})	Coordinates of j-th vertex in the i-th quadtree node N_i
s, a_{jh}	Random values used by RS when masking N
EN	Masked quadtree computed by RS
(x_V, y_V)	Coordinates of RV
r_{ij}	Random values chosen by RV when masking (x_V, y_V)
$\pi(\cdot)$	Random permutation chosen by RV
A	Data aggregated by masking (x_V, y_V) and EN
(x_{CP}, y_{CP})	Pick-up coordinates of RC
S_{RC}	Square with (x_{CP}, y_{CP}) at its center
R	Length of a side of S_{RC}
s', d_i	Random values used by RC when masking (x_{CP}, y_{CP})
$C_1, \ldots, C_5$	Data aggregated by masking (x_{CP}, y_{CP}) and EN

learning its exact location. To do this, RS sends a masked version of N_i to RV. Concretely, RS chooses 24 random values a_{jh} ($j = 1, \ldots, 4; h = 1, \ldots, 6$) of size k_3 bits each. For every vertex N_{ij} of N_i, let $N_{ij'}$ be the vertex adjacent to it in the anticlockwise direction, i.e. $j' = (j \bmod 4) + 1$. RS masks this vertex by computing

$$
\begin{aligned}
EN_{ij1} &= s(x_{Nij} \cdot \alpha + a_{j1}) \quad \bmod p, \\
EN_{ij2} &= s(y_{Nij} \cdot \alpha + a_{j2}) \quad \bmod p, \\
EN_{ij3} &= s(x_{Nij'} \cdot \alpha + a_{j3}) \quad \bmod p, \\
EN_{ij4} &= s(y_{Nij'} \cdot \alpha + a_{j4}) \quad \bmod p, \\
EN_{ij5} &= s(x_{Nij} \cdot y_{Nij'} \cdot \alpha + a_{j5}) \quad \bmod p, \\
EN_{ij6} &= s(x_{Nij'} \cdot y_{Nij} \cdot \alpha + a_{j6}) \quad \bmod p.
\end{aligned}
$$

The values α, p are public, whereas s, x_{Nij}, y_{Nij} are only known to RS. The masked coordinate is

$$
EN_{ij} = EN_{ij1} \| EN_{ij2} \| EN_{ij3} \| EN_{ij4} \| EN_{ij5} \| EN_{ij6},
$$

where $\|$ denotes concatenation. Next, RS computes the masked quadrant

$$EN_i = EN_{i1}\|EN_{i2}\|EN_{i3}\|EN_{i4},$$

for $i = 1, \ldots, m$, to get the masked quadtree

$$EN = \{EN_1, EN_2, \ldots, EN_m\}.$$

It then encrypts EN and forwards it to RV.

Step 2. RV decrypts this message and uses EN along with its own randomness to mask its location (x_V, y_V). For $i = 1, \ldots, m; j = 1 \ldots, 4$, RV chooses a fresh random number r_{ij} (each k_4 bits long) and computes

$$A_{ij1} = r_{ij} \cdot \alpha(x_V \cdot EN_{ij4} + y_V \cdot EN_{ij1} + EN_{ij6}) \mod p,$$
$$A_{ij2} = r_{ij} \cdot \alpha(x_V \cdot EN_{ij2} + y_V \cdot EN_{ij3} + EN_{ij5}) \mod p,$$
$$A_{ij} = A_{ij1}\|A_{ij2}.$$

RV chooses a random permutation $\pi(\cdot)$ to reorder the j-indices for each A_i. That is,

$$A_i = A_{i\pi(1)}\|A_{i\pi(2)}\|A_{i\pi(3)}\|A_{i\pi(4)},$$
$$A = \{A_1, \ldots, A_m\}.$$

The order within each $A_{i\pi(j)}$ is still preserved, that is,

$$A_{i\pi(j)} = A_{i\pi(j)1}\|A_{i\pi(j)2}.$$

RV encrypts A and forwards it to RS.

Step 3. RS obtains A that contains the masked location of each RV, and does the following computations to identify the quadrant/node N_i of the quadtree in which RV lies.

$$
\begin{aligned}
B_{ij1} &= s^{-1} \cdot A_{ij1} \mod p \\
&= s^{-1} \cdot r_{ij} \cdot \alpha(x_V \cdot EN_{ij4} + y_V \cdot EN_{ij1} + EN_{ij6}) \mod p \\
&= s^{-1} \cdot r_{ij} \cdot s[\alpha^2(x_V \cdot y_{Nij'} + y_V \cdot x_{Nij} + x_{Nij'} \cdot y_{Nij}) \\
&\quad + \alpha(x_V \cdot a_{j4} + y_V \cdot a_{j1} + a_{j6})] \mod p. \\
B'_{ij1} &= \frac{B_{ij1} - (B_{ij1} \mod \alpha^2)}{\alpha^2} \\
&= r_{ij}(x_V \cdot y_{Nij'} + y_V \cdot x_{Nij} + x_{Nij'} \cdot y_{Nij}).
\end{aligned}
$$

Similarly,

$$B_{ij2} = s^{-1} \cdot A_{ij2} \mod p,$$

$$B'_{ij2} = \frac{B_{ij2} - (B_{ij2} \mod \alpha^2)}{\alpha^2}$$

$$= r_{ij}(x_V \cdot y_{Nij} + y_V \cdot x_{Nij'} + x_{Nij} \cdot y_{Nij'}).$$

Next, RS computes the difference

$$B_{ij} = B'_{ij2} - B'_{ij1}$$

$$= r_{ij}[(x_V \cdot y_{Nij} + y_V \cdot x_{Nij'} + x_{Nij} \cdot y_{Nij'})$$

$$- (x_V \cdot y_{Nij'} + y_V \cdot x_{Nij} + x_{Nij'} \cdot y_{Nij})].$$

Compare this to Eq. (1). Since r_{ij} is always positive, RS can identify whether RV lies in N_i by checking if B_{ij} is positive for all $j = 1, \ldots, 4$. Using the method described in Sect. 2.1, RS can query the quadtree to identify the exact quadrant where RV lies.

Note that it was necessary to remove the modulus with respect to p when obtaining B'_{ij1} and B'_{ij2}, otherwise those values would always be positive irrespective of whether RV was inside the quadrant N_i or not. To remove this modulus it is sufficient if the following is always true during the computation of B_{ij1} (a similar condition exists for B_{ij2}).

$$r_{ij}[\alpha^2(x_V \cdot y_{Nij'} + y_V \cdot x_{Nij} + x_{Nij'} \cdot y_{Nij})$$

$$+ \alpha(x_V \cdot a_{j4} + y_V \cdot a_{j1} + a_{j6})] < p,$$

$$r_{ij} \cdot \alpha(x_V \cdot a_{j4} + y_V \cdot a_{j1} + a_{j6}) < \alpha^2,$$

$$r_{ij} \cdot \alpha(x_V \cdot a_{j2} + y_V \cdot a_{j3} + a_{j5}) < \alpha^2.$$

Let $\langle \cdot \rangle$ denote the bit length of a non-negative integer. Recall that $\langle p \rangle = k_1, \langle \alpha \rangle = k_2, \langle a_{jh} \rangle = k_3, \langle r_{ij} \rangle = k_4$. To ensure the above conditions hold, the parameters are chosen such that

$$k_4 + 2k_2 < k_1,$$

$$k_2 + k_3 < k_1,$$

$$k_3 + k_4 < k_2. \tag{2}$$

Moreover, the size of location coordinates are assumed to be negligible compared to these security parameters. In [16], the above values are set as $k_1 = 512, k_2 = 160, k_3 = 75, k_4 = 75$.

Step 4. RC receives EN from RS. Now the RC tries to mask its location with respect to the quadtree and send it to RS. Suppose the pick-up point of RC is (x_{CP}, y_{CP}). RC chooses a square S_{RC} of side $2R$ (where R is $\geq 1\,\mathrm{km}$) with this pickup point at its center. Let the vertices of this square be $\{(x_{S1}, y_{S1}),$ $(x_{S2}, y_{S2}), (x_{S3}, y_{S3}), (x_{S4}, y_{S4})\}$. Recall that in Step 2, each RV masked its location (x_V, y_V) with respect to EN and computed A. RC also does an equivalent computation here; after receiving EN from RS, it computes a masking for each of the four vertices of S_{RC} to obtain $C = C_1 \| C_2 \| C_3 \| C_4$.

Next, RC chooses a public prime p' of size k_1 bits, a public prime α' of k_2 bits, a secret $s' \in \mathbb{Z}_{p'}^*$ and 4 random values d_i of k_4 bits each. It computes

$$D_1 = s'(x_{CP} \cdot \alpha' + d_1) \mod p',$$
$$D_2 = s'(y_{CP} \cdot \alpha' + d_2) \mod p',$$
$$D_3 = s' \cdot d_3 \mod p',$$
$$D_4 = s' \cdot d_4 \mod p',$$
$$D = D_1 \| D_2 \| D_3 \| D_4,$$
$$E = x_{CP}^2 + y_{CP}^2 - R^2.$$

RC encrypts C, D, E and sends it to RS.

Step 5. The goal here is to convey the masked location information from RC to RVs that are "nearby" to it. RS decrypts the message from RC to get C, D, E. Similar to Step 3, for each of C_1, C_2, C_3, C_4, RS obtains the quadrant in which the vertex represented by C_i (i.e. (x_{Si}, y_{Si})) lies. With this RS knows the quadrants in which the corners of square S_{RC} lies. RS can construct a region CS_{RC} enclosing S_{RC}. From Step 3, RS also knows the quadrants in which each RV lies. RS encrypts D, E and sends it to those RVs that lie in CS_{RC} (call these RVs as SRVs).

Step 6. SRV receives D, E from RS and tries to add in masked information about its own location (x_{SV}, y_{SV}) to these values. It chooses three random r_i's of k_4 bits each and computes

$$F_1 = x_{SV} \cdot \alpha' \cdot D_1 \mod p',$$
$$F_2 = y_{SV} \cdot \alpha' \cdot D_2 \mod p',$$
$$F_3 = r_1 \cdot D_3 \mod p',$$
$$F_4 = r_2 \cdot D_4 \mod p',$$
$$F = r_3(F_1 + F_2 + F_3 + F_4),$$
$$I = r_3(x_{SV}^2 + y_{SV}^2 + E).$$

SRV encrypts and sends I, F to RC via RS.

Step 7. RC uses I, F (that contain masked information of RC's and SRVs' locations) to check if that SRV is within distance R.

$$J = s'^{-1} \cdot F \mod p'$$
$$= s'^{-1} \cdot s' \cdot r_3[\alpha'^2(x_{CP} \cdot x_{SV} + y_{CP} \cdot y_{SV})$$
$$+ \alpha'(x_{SV} \cdot d_1 + y_{SV} \cdot d_2) + r_1 \cdot d_3 + r_2 \cdot d_4] \mod p',$$
$$J' = \frac{J - (J \mod \alpha'^2)}{\alpha'^2} = r_3(x_{CP} \cdot x_{SV} + y_{CP} \cdot y_{SV}),$$
$$K = I - 2J'$$
$$= r_3[x_{CP}^2 + y_{CP}^2 + x_{SV}^2 + y_{SV}^2$$
$$- 2(x_{CP} \cdot x_{SV} + y_{CP} \cdot y_{SV}) - R^2]$$
$$= r_3[(x_{CP} - x_{SV})^2 - (y_{CP} - y_{SV})^2 - R^2].$$

When $K \leq 0$, the SRV is within the circle query range C_{RC} of radius R around RC. Call such SRVs as CRVs.

Once again (similar to Step 3) we need to eliminate the modulus with respect to p' (otherwise K would always be positive even if the SRV had distance $> R$). With the relationship imposed on the security parameters (Eq. (2) in Step 3), the following condition holds and the modulus is removed.

$$r_3[\alpha'^2(x_{CP} \cdot x_{SV} + y_{CP} \cdot y_{SV})$$
$$+ \alpha'(x_{SV} \cdot d_1 + y_{SV} \cdot d_2) + r_1 \cdot d_3 + r_2 \cdot d_4] < p',$$
$$r_5[\alpha'(x_{SV} \cdot d_1 + y_{SV} \cdot d_2) + r_1 \cdot d_3 + r_2 \cdot d_4] < \alpha'^2.$$

Step 8. RC masks its take-off point (x_{CT}, y_{CT}) using EN (similar to Step 2) to create C_5, and forwards C_5 along with the list of CRVs to RS. (The take-off point usually lies very close to the RC's pick-up point from Step 4). Similar to Step 3, RS uses C_5 to identify the subregion in which the take-off point lies. RS chooses a random location ATP in this subregion and forwards it to CRVs. Each CRV inspects ATP to make a decision on whether to accept this ride-hailing request from RC. The CRVs who decide to accept send an "Accept Response" to RS. RS forwards the list of ready and available CRVs to RC. RC chooses a suitable CRV from this list, and this CRV is informed about the same by RS. Later, the RC and the chosen CRV proceed with ride establishment by negotiating a shared session key and by exchanging information such as location, phone number, reputation, etc.

3   Attack on TRACE

This section presents two attacks which (with high empirical probability) disprove the following privacy claims made about TRACE. First, in Sect. 3.1, we show that RCs and RVs can obtain the secret spatial division (quadtree) information maintained by RS (violation of Claim 1). We also discuss a modification to the TRACE protocol, as a countermeasure for this attack. Secondly, in Sect. 3.2, we show how the RS can identify exact locations of all RCs and RVs (violation of Claims 2, 3). We also briefly argue why this attack is not straightforward to thwart. In both attacks, the entities recover location coordinates modulo prime p. This is same as recovering the actual integer values since p is a very large prime and the coordinate values are negligibly small compared to p.

Steps from the TRACE protocol described in Sect. 2.3 will be referred as and when needed. In Sect. 4, we shall experimentally evaluate the success probability of our attacks.

3.1   RCs, RVs Obtain Quadtree

After an RV receives the masked quadtree EN computed by RS (Step 2), we show how it can recover all underlying vertices x_{Nij}, y_{Nij} of the quadtree's nodes. This same principle allows an RC to obtain information about the quadtree as well (recall that each RC receives EN from RS in Step 4).

Intuition. Intuitively, our attack works as follows. Each quadtree node N_i is masked by the RS using random values s, α, a_{jh}, resulting in EN_i. When an RV receives $EN_1, \ldots, EN_m$, it knows p, α but does not know s, a_{jh}. For a single EN_i, the number of equations involved is $4 \times 6 = 24$ (since there is one equation for each EN_{ijh}, $j = 1, \ldots, 4; h = 1, \ldots, 6$). The number of unknowns involved in EN_i is $1 + 24 + 8 = 33$ (s, a_{jh}'s and quadrant vertices x_{Nij}, y_{Nij}, $j = 1, \ldots, 4; h = 1, \ldots, 6$). A key observation is that if one considers EN_i along with a different $EN_{i'}$, the number of equations is $24 + 24 = 48$. However the number of unknowns involved is $1 + 24 + 8 + 8 = 41$ (s, a_{jh}'s and quadrant vertices $x_{Nij}, y_{Nij}, x_{Ni'j}, y_{Ni'j}$, where $j = 1, \ldots, 4; h = 1, \ldots, 6$). That is, considering an additional $EN_{i'}$ gives 24 new equations but introduces only 8 new variables. This would allow RV to solve this system of modular equations and obtain the secrets s along with quadrant vertices of N_i and $N_{i'}$.

Formal Attack. Without loss of generality, we show how an RV can recover vertices of quadrants N_1, N_2 when given EN_1, EN_2 (i.e. $i = 1, i' = 2$). The first task is to eliminate the unknown randomness a_{jh}, $j = 1, \ldots, 4; h = 1, \ldots, 6$. This can be done by subtracting EN_{2jh} from EN_{1jh}. For $h = 1, \ldots, 6$, we get the following equations.

$$EN_{1j1} - EN_{2j1} = s\alpha(x_{N1j} - x_{N2j}) \mod p, \tag{3}$$

$$EN_{1j2} - EN_{2j2} = s\alpha(y_{N1j} - y_{N2j}) \mod p, \tag{4}$$

$$EN_{1j3} - EN_{2j3} = s\alpha(x_{N1j'} - x_{N2j'}) \mod p, \tag{5}$$

$$EN_{1j4} - EN_{2j4} = s\alpha(y_{N1j'} - y_{N2j'}) \mod p, \tag{6}$$

$$EN_{1j5} - EN_{2j5} = s\alpha(x_{N1j}y_{N1j'} - x_{N2j}y_{N2j'}) \mod p, \tag{7}$$

$$EN_{1j6} - EN_{2j6} = s\alpha(x_{N1j'}y_{N1j} - x_{N2j'}y_{N2j}) \mod p. \tag{8}$$

Here $j' = (j \mod 4) + 1$. The parameters s, α are unknown to RV along with the 16 variables $x_{N1j}, y_{N1j}, x_{N2j}, y_{N2j}, \; j = 1, \ldots, 4$. RV can obtain linear (modular) equations in these variables by eliminating s, α as follows.

Compare (3) $\times \, y_{N1j'} + $ (6) $\times \, x_{N2j}$ and (7):

$$
\begin{aligned}
(EN_{1j1} &- EN_{2j1}) \times y_{N1j'} + (EN_{1j4} - EN_{2j4}) \times x_{N2j} \\
&= s\alpha(x_{N1j}y_{N1j'} - x_{N2j}y_{N1j'} + y_{N1j'}x_{N2j} - y_{N2j'}x_{N2j}) \\
&= s\alpha(x_{N1j}y_{N1j'} - x_{N2j}y_{N2j'}) \\
&= (EN_{1j5} - EN_{2j5}) \mod p.
\end{aligned}
\tag{9}
$$

Compare (3) $\times \, y_{N2j'} + $ (6) $\times \, x_{N1j}$ and (7):

$$
\begin{aligned}
(EN_{1j1} &- EN_{2j1}) \times y_{N2j'} + (EN_{1j4} - EN_{2j4}) \times x_{N1j} \\
&= s\alpha(x_{N1j}y_{N2j'} - x_{N2j}y_{N2j'} + y_{N1j'}x_{N1j} - y_{N2j'}x_{N1j}) \\
&= s\alpha(x_{N1j}y_{N1j'} - x_{N2j}y_{N2j'}) \\
&= (EN_{1j5} - EN_{2j5}) \mod p.
\end{aligned}
\tag{10}
$$

Compare (4) $\times \, x_{N1j'} + $ (5) $\times \, y_{N2j}$ and (8):

$$
\begin{aligned}
(EN_{1j2} &- EN_{2j2}) \times x_{N1j'} + (EN_{1j3} - EN_{2j3}) \times y_{N2j} \\
&= s\alpha(y_{N1j}x_{N1j'} - y_{N2j}x_{N1j'} + x_{N1j'}y_{N2j} - x_{N2j'}y_{N2j}) \\
&= s\alpha(x_{N1j'}y_{N1j} - x_{N2j'}y_{N2j}) \\
&= (EN_{1j6} - EN_{2j6}) \mod p.
\end{aligned}
\tag{11}
$$

Compare (4) $\times \, x_{N2j'} + $ (5) $\times \, y_{N1j}$ and (8):

$$
\begin{aligned}
(EN_{1j2} &- EN_{2j2}) \times x_{N2j'} + (EN_{1j3} - EN_{2j3}) \times y_{N1j} \\
&= s\alpha(y_{N1j}x_{N2j'} - y_{N2j}x_{N2j'} + x_{N1j'}y_{N1j} - x_{N2j'}y_{N1j}) \\
&= s\alpha(x_{N1j'}y_{N1j} - x_{N2j'}y_{N2j}) \\
&= (EN_{1j6} - EN_{2j6}) \mod p.
\end{aligned}
\tag{12}
$$

Compare (3) and (4):

$$
\begin{aligned}
(EN_{1j1} &- EN_{2j1}) \times s\alpha(y_{N1j} - y_{N2j}) \\
&= (EN_{1j2} - EN_{2j2}) \times s\alpha(x_{N1j} - x_{N2j}) \mod p, \\
\Rightarrow (EN_{1j2} &- EN_{2j2})(x_{N1j} - x_{N2j}) \\
&- (EN_{1j1} - EN_{2j1})(y_{N1j} - y_{N2j}) = 0 \mod p.
\end{aligned}
\tag{13}
$$

Similarly, compare (4) and (5), and (5) and (6):

$$
\begin{aligned}
(EN_{1j3} &- EN_{2j3})(y_{N1j} - y_{N2j}) \\
&- (EN_{1j2} - EN_{2j2})(x_{N1j'} - x_{N2j'}) = 0 \mod p,
\end{aligned}
\tag{14}
$$

$$
\begin{aligned}
(EN_{1j4} &- EN_{2j4})(x_{N1j'} - x_{N2j'}) \\
&- (EN_{1j3} - EN_{2j3})(y_{N1j'} - y_{N2j'}) = 0 \mod p.
\end{aligned}
\tag{15}
$$

Consider Eqs. (9)—(15) for all $j = 1, \ldots, 4$; $j' = (j \mod 4) + 1$. There are 28 linear (modular) equations in the 16 unknowns $(x_{N1j}, y_{N1j}), (x_{N2j}, y_{N2j})$; $j = 1, \ldots, 4$. This can be treated as a linear system of equations with elements from the field $\mathbb{Z}_p$, and standard techniques from linear algebra such as Gaussian Elimination can be applied to find solutions for X in $\mathbb{Z}_p$.

Existence of a Unique Solution. Suppose we represent Eqs. (9)—(15) using matrix notation as $PX = Q$, where $dim(P) = 28 \times 16$, $dim(X) = 16 \times 1$, $dim(Q) = 28 \times 1$, and vector X represents the 16 unknown quadrant vertices of N_1, N_2. We observed that $rank(P) \leq 13 < 16$, and the RV cannot obtain unique solutions for X from this system.

Hence we propose a modification to our attack such that $rank(P)$ equals the number of unknowns. Previously, considering only N_1, N_2 gave us 28 equations and $8 \times 2 = 16$ unknowns. If we instead consider N_1, N_2, N_3 and take $\binom{3}{2} = 3$ pairwise combinations, we end up with $28 \times 3 = 84$ equations and $8 \times 3 = 24$ unknowns (which is slightly better). But we observed that in some cases, the resulting 84×24 matrix P had rank $23 < 24$. Next, considering N_1, N_2, N_3, N_4 and taking $\binom{4}{2} = 6$ pairwise combinations gives us $28 \times 6 = 168$ equations and $8 \times 4 = 32$ unknowns. We observed (from experiments described in Sect. 4) that the corresponding 168×32 matrix P always had rank 32, and an RV can therefore solve this system to get the unique values (in $\mathbb{Z}_p$) of quadrant vertices for $N_1, \ldots, N_4$. One can proceed further and consider more N_i, but that would be redundant since rank already equals the number of unknowns.

We now formalize the above idea. Let the linear system defined by Eqs. (9)—(15) (for vertices of N_1, N_2) be denoted by

$$\left[P_{N1N2} \mid P_{N2N1} \right] \left[\begin{array}{c} X_{N1} \\ \hline X_{N2} \end{array} \right] = \left[Q_{N1N2} \right]. \tag{16}$$

Here P_{N1N2}, X_{N1} and P_{N2N1}, X_{N2} are submatrices corresponding to unknown vertices of N_1 and N_2, respectively. Note that $dim(P_{N1N2}) = dim(P_{N2N1}) = 28 \times 8$, $dim(X_{N1}) = dim(X_{N2}) = 8 \times 1$, $dim(Q_{N1N2}) = 28 \times 1$. In the same manner, take all $\binom{4}{2} = 6$ pairwise combinations $N_i, N_{i'}$; $1 \leq i < i' \leq 4$ from N_1, N_2, N_3, N_4 and compute $P_{NiN i'}, X_{Ni}, P_{Ni'Ni}, X_{Ni'}, Q_{NiNi'}$. Define a linear system that considers all the above systems simultaneously.

$$PX = Q,$$

$$\begin{bmatrix} P_{N1N2} & P_{N2N1} & 0 & 0 \\ P_{N1N3} & 0 & P_{N3N1} & 0 \\ P_{N1N4} & 0 & 0 & P_{N4N1} \\ 0 & P_{N2N3} & P_{N3N2} & 0 \\ 0 & P_{N2N4} & 0 & P_{N4N2} \\ 0 & 0 & P_{N3N4} & P_{N4N3} \end{bmatrix} \begin{bmatrix} X_{N1} \\ X_{N2} \\ X_{N3} \\ X_{N4} \end{bmatrix} = \begin{bmatrix} Q_{N1N2} \\ Q_{N1N3} \\ Q_{N1N4} \\ Q_{N2N3} \\ Q_{N2N4} \\ Q_{N3N4} \end{bmatrix}. \tag{17}$$

Algorithm 1: RV recovers quadtree

Input : Size of quadtree m, masked quadtree $EN = (EN_1, \ldots, EN_m)$
Output: Underlying quadrant vertices $N = (N_1, \ldots, N_m)$
Procedure `Recover_Quadtree`$(m,\ EN)$:

   while `size`$(EN) > 0$ **do**

      Pick four random entries EN_a, EN_b, EN_c, EN_d and delete them from EN

      for each of the $\binom{4}{2}$ pairwise combinations (i, i') from a, b, c, d **do**

         Obtain a linear system in the unknown vertices of N_i, N_i' using equations similar to (9)—(15)

         Let the corresponding matrices be $P_{N_iN_{i'}}, X_{N_i}, P_{N_{i'}N_i}, X_{N_{i'}}$, $Q_{N_iN_{i'}}$ similar to (16)

      end

      Using the above matrices, define the system $PX = Q$ similar to (17)

      Solve this system to obtain quadrant vertices corresponding to N_a, N_b, N_c, N_d

   end

   Output: $(N_1, \ldots, N_m)$

Here 0 denotes the zero matrix of dimension 28×8, $dim(P) = 168 \times 32$, $dim(X) = 32 \times 1$, $dim(Q) = 168 \times 1$ and $rank(P)$ is experimentally observed to be 32. The RV can solve this system to obtain unique solutions for X (i.e. quadrant vertices of $N_1, \ldots, N_4$) in $\mathbb{Z}_p$.

Note that there is no restriction here to use equations for the first four quadrants $N_1, \ldots, N_4$. The RV can consider equations corresponding to any four distinct N_i and find their underlying vertices. The above steps are repeated for other quadrants as well, until all of them are recovered. We summarize the attack in Algorithm 1. The same idea also allows an RC to recover the quadtree, when it receives EN from RS.

We remark that this attack is purely algebraic and does not make any assumptions about geometry of the region. The same attack would still work even if quadrants in the spatial division were not restricted to rectangles/squares.

Complexity. The linear system of equations represented by $PX = Q$, where $dim(P) = 168 \times 32, dim(X) = 32 \times 1, dim(Q) = 168 \times 1$, and all operations are in the field $\mathbb{Z}_p$, can be solved in time $O((\log p)^2) = O(k_1^2)$ [2]. We need to repeatedly solve such a system $\lceil m/4 \rceil$ times to recover vertices of all m quadrants. The total asymptotic complexity of this attack is $O(k_1^2 m)$. Our attack is efficient in practice, and Table 2 shows the average time taken to recover quadrant vertices for varying tree sizes and security parameters.

Remark. The aforementioned attack mainly relies on the fact that TRACE uses the same set of 24 random values $a_{jh}, j = 1, \ldots, 4; h = 1, \ldots, 6$ throughout all $EN_i, i = 1, \ldots, m$ (refer to Step 1 of the TRACE protocol in Sect. 2.3). However, upon careful observation, one can see that the correctness of the TRACE protocol would still hold if different set of values of a_{jh} were used for each EN_i. That is, sample $24 \times m$ independent random values $a_{ijh}, i = 1, \ldots, m; j = 1, \ldots, 4; h =$

$1, \ldots, 6$ and mask EN_{ijh} with a_{ijh}. In the TRACE protocol, these random values are involved only when computing B_{ij1} and B_{ij2} (Step 3). Correctness still holds since these values cancel each other out when computing $B_{ij1} - (B_{ij1} \mod \alpha^2)$.

Therefore, one can modify the TRACE protocol by using a new random a_{ijh} each time when computing EN_{ijh}. This is a countermeasure to prevent RCs and RVs from obtaining the secret quadtree because, EN_{ijh} is masked by fresh randomness each time and no information can be obtained about (x_{Nij}, y_{Nij}) given the EN_i values (similar to a one-time pad). This simple observation leads to the following lemma.

Lemma 1. *The above modification to TRACE provides information-theoretic security against any passive adversary who wishes to obtain additional information about the quadtree maintained by RS.*

However, as we shall see in Sect. 3.2, this modification does not prevent the RS in obtaining locations of RCs and RVs. We will also later see that a similar countermeasure does not exist for the latter attack. Trying to use fresh randomness there will violate the correctness of the protocol.

3.2   RS Obtains Locations of RCs, RVs

RS Finds Location of RVs. In Step 3, RS receives $A_i = A_{i\pi(1)} \| A_{i\pi(2)} \| A_{i\pi(3)} \| A_{i\pi(4)}$, $i = 1, \ldots, m$, from each RV, that contains masked information about (x_V, y_V). RS knows EN_{ij} but does not know r_{ij} and the random permutation π used on the four A_{ij} values. Since there can only be 24 possible choices for π, the RS can enumerate all of them to try and find π.

For each i, RS initializes an empty set S_i. For each choice of permutation ρ (among the set of all permutations on four elements), RS permutes the four components of A_i according to ρ. That is, RS computes

$$A_i' = A_{i\rho(\pi(1))} \| A_{i\rho(\pi(2))} \| A_{i\rho(\pi(3))} \| A_{i\rho(\pi(4))}$$
$$= A_{i1}' \| A_{i2}' \| A_{i3}' \| A_{i4}'. \tag{18}$$

A_i' corresponds to the original value $A_{i1} \| A_{i2} \| A_{i3} \| A_{i4}$ computed by RV only when $\rho = \pi^{-1}$. To see if the current choice ρ equals π^{-1}, RS can do the following: eliminate r_{ij}, α from A_{ij1}' and A_{ij2}' to get a linear equation in the unknowns x_V, y_V:

$$A_{ij1}'(x_V \cdot EN_{ij2} + y_V \cdot EN_{ij3} + EN_{ij5})$$
$$= A_{ij2}'(x_V \cdot EN_{ij4} + y_V \cdot EN_{ij1} + EN_{ij6}) \mod p. \tag{19}$$

In this way, RS can obtain four linear equations for $j = 1, \ldots, 4$, in the two unknowns x_V, y_V. Two of these equations can be used to solve and find x_V, y_V (if a solution does not exist, move to the next choice of ρ). The remaining two equations can be used to check if the values of x_V, y_V previously obtained are consistent. If so, then with high probability RS can infer that $\rho = \pi^{-1}$; add this

---

Algorithm 2: RS recovers location of an RV

Input : $(A_1, \ldots, A_m)$ representing masked information about an RV's location
Output: RV's location (x_V, y_V)
Procedure Recover_Location$(A_1, \ldots, A_m)$:

  for $i = 1, \ldots, m$ do
    $S_i = \phi$
    $\mathcal{P}$ = set of all permutations on 4 elements
    for $\rho \in \mathcal{P}$ do
      /* Permute the 4 components of A_i using ρ */
      Compute A_i' according to (18)
      Obtain a linear system in the unknowns x_V, y_V by substituting
        $j = 1, 2$ in (19)
      if *this system does not have a unique solution* **then**
        | continue
      end
      /* Solve this system and check if the unique solution (x, y) also
        satisfies the two equations obtained when substituting $j = 3, 4$ in
        (19) */
      if (x, y) *satisfies the consistency check* **then**
        | $S_i = S_i \cup \{(x, y)\}$
      end
      /* Note that $\forall i, (x_V, y_V) \in S_i$ */
    end
    /* With high probability, we have $|\cap_{i=1}^{m} S_i| = 1$ */
    $\{(x_V, y_V)\} = \cap_{i=1}^{m} S_i$
  end
  Output: (x_V, y_V)

---

solution to set S_i. If it is not consistent discard it and check the next permutation choice for ρ. Note that S_i always contains the original x_V, y_V chosen by RV since this solution satisfies the consistency checks when $\rho = \pi^{-1}$. In rare cases it could be possible that a false positive also passes these consistency checks for a different ρ and is added to S_i.

The above procedure is discussed only for one value of i. There are m such A_i's received by RS (in general $30 \leq m \leq 100$ [16, Section VI]), and the original x_V, y_V is present in each S_i. Moreover, it is highly unlikely that the same false positive appears in every S_i. Therefore, it is very likely that there is only one common element present in all S_i (this probability increases with m), and that would be the required location of RV. Once again, there are no assumptions made regarding geometry of the spatial region. We summarize the attack in Algorithm 2.

Complexity. For each $i = 1, \ldots, m$, RS enumerates over all 24 possible permutations. In each choice of permutation, RS solves a system of equations in two variables (with all elements being in $\mathbb{Z}_p$) and checks for consistency with two other equations to finally obtain the set S_i. The size of each S_i is at most 24. RS later computes the intersection of all S_i to determine the RV's coordinates. All these operations can be done in time $O(k_1^2 m)$. Table 3 shows the average time taken to recover (x_V, y_V) for varying tree size and security parameters.

RS Finds Location of RCs. In Step 5, RS receives $C_1 \| C_2 \| C_3 \| C_4$ from RC. Recall that RC chooses a square S_{RC} of side $2R$ with its pick-up location at the center. Each C_j corresponds to one vertex of that square, masked in a manner similar to how RV masked its location as A (refer to Step 2). Since we just saw an attack where RS can recover the original underlying location when given such a masking, RS can obtain the 4 vertices corresponding to S_{RC}. The center of this square directly gives the pick-up location of RC.

RS can also find the take-off location of RC. In Step 8, RS receives C_5 from RC, which is a masking of RC's take-off location using EN similar to what we have seen in Step 2. Using the same attack as for RV, RS can directly recover RCs location from C_5. Note that, in practice, the pick-up and the take-off points are quite close.

Remark. In Sect. 3.1 we saw that using fresh randomness for each encrypted quadtree term EN_i did not violate correctness of the protocol. If we try to apply the same argument here, then in Step 2 of the TRACE protocol, A_{ij1} and A_{ij2} have to be masked with different (and fresh) randomness, say r_{ij1} and r_{ij2}, respectively (currently, they are both masked by the same r_{ij}). But in Step 3 of the TRACE protocol, this would mean B'_{ij1} is masked with r_{ij1}, and B'_{ij2} is masked with r_{ij2}. Hence $B_{ij} = B'_{ij1} - B'_{ij2}$ would not have a common factor r_{ij}, and one cannot infer whether the RV lies inside the quadrant N_i just by checking the sign of B_{ij}. Therefore, this approach will violate the correctness of the TRACE protocol, and we believe that other countermeasures for this attack are not straightforward to come up with.

4 Experimental Results

In this section, we discuss the experimental setup and other implementation aspects of the attacks[1] mentioned in Sect. 3. Our experiments were implemented using SageMath [13] and run on an Intel Core i5-8250U CPU @ 1.60 GHz with 8 GB RAM running Ubuntu 20.04 LTS.

4.1 Setup

The TRACE paper [16] states that setting $(k_1, k_2, k_3, k_4) = (512, 160, 75, 75)$ should be sufficient to ensure that Claims 1, 2, 3 hold. We also initialize these security parameters with the same values. In addition, we demonstrate the robustness of our attack by performing another set of experiments with larger values $(2048, 1000, 400, 400)$ satisfying Eq. (2). Note that our attack is clearly independent of the security of encryption schemes/digital signatures used in TRACE.

---

[1] The implementation can be accessed at https://github.com/deepakkavoor/rhs-atta
ck/tree/trace-attack.

The implementation of TRACE protocol from [16] does not give any reference to the dataset that was used to create spatial divisions. So, we simulate the creation of an arbitrary quadtree by first choosing an outermost rectangular quadrant, followed by picking a random center and dividing it into four sub-quadrants. We repeat this for the smaller quadrants until the number of nodes in the tree is m. The TRACE implementation in [16] varies m between 28 and 84; we set $m = 50$ and $m = 100$ in our experiments. The attack indeed works for any value of m (recall $m \geq 4$) and its success probability increases with m.

Integer modular arithmetic is used in all computations. Since the sizes of location coordinates are negligible compared to the security parameters $k_1, \ldots, k_4$, the vertices of the outermost quadrant are randomly chosen in the range $[0, 2^{20} - 1]$ (for $(k_1, k_2, k_3, k_4) = (512, 160, 75, 75)$) and in $[0, 2^{50} - 1]$ (for $(k_1, k_2, k_3, k_4) = (2048, 1000, 400, 400)$).

4.2   RCs, RVs Recover Quadtree

RS computes the encrypted quadtree EN and sends it to an RV as described in Sect. 2.3. Next, RV carries out the attack described in Sect. 3.1. We perform 20 iterations of this attack, and in each iteration, the RS generates a fresh random quadtree (as described in Sect. 4.1) and computes EN accordingly. We observed that in *all* iterations, RV was able to recover the exact values of *all* quadrant vertices every time. We repeat the same for different choices of m and security parameters, and tabulate the average time taken to recover the quadtree in Table 2. Since the same attack allows an RC to recover the quadtree, similar experimental statistics can be expected in this case.

Table 2. Time taken (in seconds) for an RV to recover quadtree, averaged over 30 iterations.

Security parameters (k_1, k_2, k_3, k_4)	Size of quadtree m	
	50	100
$(512, 160, 75, 75)$	55.686	108.566
$(2048, 1000, 400, 400)$	2341.836	4771.549

4.3   RS Recovers Locations of RCs and RVs

The location (x_V, y_V) of an RV is randomly chosen within the outermost quadrant. We simulate the exchange of messages between RS and this particular RV, following the steps of TRACE protocol (Sect. 2.3). Next, RS carries out the attack described in Sect. 3.2. We perform 30 iterations of the attack with freshly generated (random) values for quadtree and (x_V, y_V) in each iteration. We observed that in *all* iterations, RS was able to recover the exact location of the RV. That is, $|\cap_{i=1}^{m} S_i|$ was exactly 1, and the recovered coordinate was same as the RV's location in all iterations (refer Algorithm 2). We repeat the same for

Table 3. Time taken (in seconds) for RS to recover an RV's location, averaged over 30 iterations.

Security parameters (k_1, k_2, k_3, k_4)	Size of quadtree m	
	50	100
$(512, 160, 75, 75)$	0.206	0.402
$(2048, 1000, 400, 400)$	7.461	14.778

different choices of m and security parameters, and tabulate the average time taken to recover RV's location in Table 3.

The attack to recover an RC's location is exactly the same as that for an RV. Since we assume the distribution of RC's location to be random as well, the same statistics also hold true when RS recovers the location of an RC.

5   Related Work

We briefly mention the prior works in privacy-preserving ride-hailing services. Since these works use fundamentally different ideas (such as homomorphic encryption, garbled circuits) compared to TRACE (which relies on random masking), our attack does not directly apply to these works.

PrivateRide by Pham et al. [11] is the first work that provides a practical solution towards privacy in ride-hailing systems. The locations and identities of riders are hidden using cloaked regions and anonymous credentials. They use efficient cryptographic primitives to ensure privacy of sensitive information. *ORide* by Pham et al. [10] offers accountability guarantees and secure payments along with privacy of riders and drivers. They use homomorphic encryption to compute the Euclidean distance and identify the closest driver in a zone. [5] proposes a modification to ORide to ensure location privacy of responding drivers in the region with respect to a rider.

Zhao et al. [20] conduct a study on leakage of sensitive data in ride-hailing services. They analyze APIs in non-privacy preserving apps provided to drivers by Uber and Lyft.

pRide by Luo et al. [7] proposes a privacy-preserving solution involving two non-colluding servers, one of them being the RS and the other a third-party Crypto Provider (CP). They use road network embedding in a higher dimension to approximate shortest distance over road networks. The homomorphically computed (approximate) distances are compared using a garbled circuit. Their scheme provides higher ride-matching accuracy than *ORide* while being computationally efficient. *lpRide* by Yu et al. [19] improves upon *pRide* by eliminating the need for a second Crypto Provider. They use a modified version of Paillier cryptosystem for encrypting locations of riders and drivers. However, [15] proposed an attack on the modified Paillier scheme used in lpRide, allowing the service provider to recover locations of all riders and drivers in the region.

EPRide by Yu et al. [18] uses an efficient approach to compute the exact shortest road distance using road network hypercube embedding. They use somewhat homomorphic encryption over packet ciphertexts to achieve high ride-matching accuracy and efficiency, reporting significant improvements over *ORide* and *pRide*. Xie et al. [17] improve upon *pRide* by combining the idea of road network embedding with cryptographic constructs such as Property-preserving Hash. They eliminate the need for a trusted third-party server to compute shortest distances.

Lu et al. [6] proposed a protocol for Privacy-Preserving Scalar Product (PP-SP) in 2013, which allows two parties P_0 and P_1 (having input vectors $\vec{a}$ and $\vec{b}$, respectively) to jointly compute the scalar product $\vec{a} \cdot \vec{b}$ such that no information about P_i's input is revealed to P_{1-i} (other than what is revealed by the output itself), for $i \in \{0, 1\}$. Their protocol was claimed to achieve information-theoretic security using random masking, and does not make use of any computational assumptions. However, in 2019, [12] proposed an attack on the PP-SP protocol of Lu et al. and showed that it is impossible to construct a PP-SP protocol without the use of computational hardness assumptions. These attacks are based on constructing distinguishers that leak additional information about the other party's secrets than what the output should reveal. While the TRACE protocol is motivated by the designs of the PP-SP protocols of Lu et al., we would like to stress that the application context, i.e., privacy-preserving ride-hailing services, is different in our setting, and hence the privacy requirements differ too. The main goal of our attacks on the TRACE protocol is the complete recovery of secret locations rather than just distinguishing them from uniform random values, and hence the attack techniques are also different. Note that the anonymity of users' locations is the main requirement for a PP-RHS, and not just indistinguishability from uniform random values. Hence, the attack in [12] does not necessarily imply our results, though it certainly provides the motivation for a deeper investigation such as our work.

Also, the impossibility result of [12] does not necessarily imply that a PP-RHS cannot be constructed without computational hardness assumptions. For instance, in Sect. 3.1, we showed that our modification to the TRACE protocol, where fresh random values are used for each invocation, prevents RCs and RVs from obtaining the secret quadtree (this is based on an information-theoretic argument similar to that of a one-time pad). Hence, impossibility results for the PP-SP setting do not necessarily translate to the PP-RHS setting.

6   Conclusion and Future Work

In this work we proposed an attack on the privacy-preserving ride-hailing service TRACE. We disproved several privacy claims about TRACE in an honest-but-curious setting. We showed how riders (RCs) and drivers (RVs) can recover the secret spatial division information maintained by the ride-hailing server (RS). We also showed how the RS can recover the exact locations of RCs and RVs. We implemented our attack and evaluated the success probability for different security parameters. In the future, it would be interesting to propose a modified protocol for TRACE in which all the aforementioned privacy claims hold.

Acknowledgements. This work was partially funded by the Infosys Foundation Career Development Chair Professorship grant for Srinivas Vivek.

References

1. Boneh, D., Lynn, B., Shacham, H.: Short signatures from the weil pairing. In: Boyd, C. (ed.) ASIACRYPT 2001. LNCS, vol. 2248, pp. 514–532. Springer, Heidelberg (2001). https://doi.org/10.1007/3-540-45682-1_30
2. Eberly, W., Giesbrecht, M., Giorgi, P., Storjohann, A., Villard, G.: Solving sparse integer linear systems. CoRR abs/cs/0603082 (2006). http://arxiv.org/abs/cs/0603082
3. EconomicTimes: Bengaluru techie arrested for data theft from Aadhaar website (2017). https://economictimes.indiatimes.com/small-biz/security-tech/security/ola-employee-arrested-for-data-theft-from-aadhaar-website/articleshow/59909079.cms?from=mdr. Accessed 17 June 2021
4. Hurriyet Daily News: Istanbul taxi drivers hunt down, beat up Uber drivers as tensions rise (2018). https://www.hurriyetdailynews.com/istanbul-taxi-drivers-hunt-down-beat-up-uber-drivers-as-tensions-rise-128443. Accessed 17 June 2021
5. Kumaraswamy, D., Murthy, S., Vivek, S.: Revisiting driver anonymity in oride. CoRR abs/2101.06419 (2021). https://arxiv.org/abs/2101.06419, to appear in SAC 2021
6. Lu, R., Lin, X., Shen, X.: Spoc: a secure and privacy-preserving opportunistic computing framework for mobile-healthcare emergency. IEEE Trans. Parallel Distrib. Syst. **24**(3), 614–624 (2013). https://doi.org/10.1109/TPDS.2012.146
7. Luo, Y., Jia, X., Fu, S., Xu, M.: pRide: privacy-preserving ride matching over road networks for online ride-hailing service. IEEE Trans. Inf. Forensics Secur. **14**(7), 1791–1802 (2019). https://doi.org/10.1109/TIFS.2018.2885282
8. NortonLifeLock: Uber Announces New Data Breach Affecting 57 million Riders and Drivers (2020). https://us.norton.com/internetsecurity-emerging-threats-uber-breach-57-million.html. Accessed 17 June 2021
9. Pew Research Center: More Americans Are Using Ride-Hailing Apps (2019). https://www.pewresearch.org/fact-tank/2019/01/04/more-americans-are-using-ride-hailing-apps/. Accessed 17 June 2021
10. Pham, A., Dacosta, I., Endignoux, G., Troncoso-Pastoriza, J.R., Huguenin, K., Hubaux, J.: ORide: a privacy-preserving yet accountable ride-hailing service. In: Kirda, E., Ristenpart, T. (eds.) 26th USENIX Security Symposium, USENIX Security 2017, Vancouver, BC, Canada, 16–18 August 2017, pp. 1235–1252. USENIX Association (2017). https://www.usenix.org/conference/usenixsecurity17/technical-sessions/presentation/pham
11. Pham, A., et al.: PrivateRide: a privacy-enhanced ride-hailing service. PoPETs **2017**(2), 38–56 (2017). https://doi.org/10.1515/popets-2017-0015
12. Schneider, T., Treiber, A.: A comment on privacy-preserving scalar product protocols as proposed in SPOC. IEEE Trans. Parallel Distrib. Syst. **31**(3), 543–546 (2020). https://doi.org/10.1109/TPDS.2019.2939313
13. The Sage Developers: SageMath, the Sage Mathematics Software System (Version 9.0) (2021). https://www.sagemath.org

14. Thejournal.ie: West Dublin gang using hailing apps to target older taxi drivers (2019). https://www.thejournal.ie/west-dublin-taxi-robbery-4420178-Jan2019/. Accessed 17 June 2021

15. Vivek, S.: Attacks on a privacy-preserving publish-subscribe system and a ride-hailing service. CoRR abs/2105.04351 (2021). https://arxiv.org/abs/2105.04351, to appear in IMACC 2021

16. Wang, F., et al.: Efficient and privacy-preserving dynamic spatial query scheme for ride-hailing services. IEEE Trans. Veh. Technol. **67**(11), 11084–11097 (2018)

17. Xie, H., Guo, Y., Jia, X.: A privacy-preserving online ride-hailing system without involving a third trusted server. IEEE Trans. Inf. Forensics Secur. **16**, 3068–3081 (2021). https://doi.org/10.1109/TIFS.2021.3065832

18. Yu, H., Jia, X., Zhang, H., Shu, J.: Efficient and privacy-preserving ride matching using exact road distance in online ride hailing services. IEEE Trans. Serv. Comput. 1 (2020). https://doi.org/10.1109/TSC.2020.3022875

19. Yu, H., Shu, J., Jia, X., Zhang, H., Yu, X.: lpride: lightweight and privacy-preserving ride matching over road networks in online ride hailing systems. IEEE Trans. Veh. Technol. **68**(11), 10418–10428 (2019). https://doi.org/10.1109/TVT.2019.2941761

20. Zhao, Q., Zuo, C., Pellegrino, G., Lin, Z.: Geo-locating drivers: a study of sensitive data leakage in ride-hailing services. In: 26th Annual Network and Distributed System Security Symposium, NDSS 2019, San Diego, California, USA, 24–27 February 2019. The Internet Society (2019). https://www.ndss-symposium.org/ndss-paper/geo-locating-drivers-a-study-of-sensitive-data-leakage-in-ride-hailing-services/

Cryptographic Constructions

Cryptographic Construction

Exipnos: An Efficient Verifiable Dynamic Symmetric Searchable Encryption Scheme with Forward and Backward Privacy

Najwa Aaraj, Chiara Marcolla[✉], and Xiaojie Zhu

Technology Innovation Institute, Abu Dhabi, UAE
{najwa,chiara.marcolla,xiaojie.zhu}@tii.ae

Abstract. Multiple approaches have been developed to address data privacy concerns, as cloud services increasingly gain traction. One of these methods is Searchable Encryption (SE), which enables a user to search over encrypted data. When applied to a dynamic dataset, it is important that SE achieves two essential properties upon updating a dynamic dataset: (1) *Forward Privacy*, which guarantees that an updated document would not be linked to previous searches and (2) *Backward Privacy*, which prevents information leakage from deleted data.

In this paper, we propose an efficient Verifiable Dynamic Symmetric Searchable Encryption (VDSSE) scheme, achieving forward and backward privacy. The scheme is designed based on the principle of additive secret sharing, where each keyword is assigned a secret and each document containing the keyword is assigned a share of the secret to hide its entry. To support a dynamic update, the last secret share, which is stored only on the client-side, is recursively shared. Each secret share is applied to reconstruct the secret. If the secret is reconstructed correctly, a search result is considered correct. We formally prove the security of the proposed VDSSE scheme and show its practicality by conducting a large number of experiments over a publicly available dataset 20 *Newsgroups*. Experimental results show that it takes less than 1 microsecond (µs) - on average - to retrieve a document from an encrypted dataset.

Keywords: Dynamic searchable encryption · Forward privacy · Backward privacy · Verifiability

1 Introduction

Remote cloud storage services have gained popularity over the past decade. However, privacy concerns that cloud services inherently carry are still not resolved.

Searchable Encryption (SE) [30] is one of the promising techniques proposed to address privacy challenges. It allows data owners to efficiently outsource their data to the Cloud Service Provider (CSP) and retrieve and/or update the targeted dataset without privacy violation while bearing a reasonable overhead in terms of computation and communication.

© Springer Nature Switzerland AG 2021
A. Adhikari et al. (Eds.): INDOCRYPT 2021, LNCS 13143, pp. 487–509, 2021.
https://doi.org/10.1007/978-3-030-92518-5_22

In the last years, researchers focused on *Dynamic Symmetric Searchable Encryption* (DSSE) schemes, which support modifications to the encrypted dataset such as document insertion or deletion. Developing a secure and efficient DSSE scheme is still an open challenge due to additional information that document updates disclose to the CSP. The following aspects remain to be addressed.

Secure Search: SE is susceptible to information leakage resulting from the search functionality. Oblivious RAM (ORAM) [32] hides access patterns but requires a large amount of local and remote storage and extra communication between clients and the CSP. Private information retrieval (PIR) [12] achieves the same goal but demands a high computational power from the CSP.

Verifiable Search Result: A CSP conducting search operations is able to provide to the user incorrect search results. It could intentionally change search results in order to save computational resources. System and network faults could also impact search results. SE may not work correctly in such scenarios.

Secure Insert: As new data gets added into a dataset stored on the CSP, information gets exposed to the CSP, potentially revealing the timestamp of a new record's addition, memory address of an inserted record, etc. Moreover, if the CSP records previous queries and observes states before and after insertion, it may be able to link the document to a specific keyword. To prevent such attacks, *forward privacy* [11] has become an essential property for DSSE schemes.

Secure Delete: Exposed data during a delete operation could potentially reveal deletion time, the memory address of a deleted record, and a deleted record could easily be linked to a keyword w by analyzing the search process before and after deletion. In order to address such attacks, *backward privacy* [31] is proposed and can be divided into three levels. The highest level reveals the timestamp of matched inserted files, the total number of updates, and matching documents associated with w. The second level additionally reveals updates' timestamp. The lowest level additionally reveals the type of updates, i.e., insert or delete (Ref. Sect. 3.5).

In addition to the challenges above, *efficiency* is an important factor in designing a DSSE scheme. In this paper, we propose a *Verifiable Dynamic Symmetric Searchable Encryption* (VDSSE) scheme, secure against an active adversary, and achieving both forward and backward privacy, while providing an optimal Efficiency - Security tradeoff under the lowest configuration requirements on the client side.

High-Level Overview of our Methodology. Our scheme is based on the principle of additive secret sharing. A keyword is assigned a secret, which is then split into a number of shares equal to the total number of data records containing the keyword plus one. Namely, broadly speaking, we use a share r_{id} of a secret to *obfuscate* a document-index id and thus the secret (related to the keyword w) can be reconstructed starting from the (obfuscated) list formed by all indexes of the documents containing w. More in details, we first assign a secret to a keyword w and split it into n shares, where $n - 1$ is the number of documents containing the keyword w. Thus, $s = r_{\mathrm{id}_1} \oplus \cdots \oplus r_{\mathrm{id}_{n-1}} \oplus r$ where $\oplus$ denotes the Exclusive Or (XOR) operation, s represents a secret, r and r_{id_i} represent a share for $1 \leq i \leq n - 1$. The first $n - 1$ shares can be random, while the last share needs to match $r = s \oplus r_{\mathrm{id}_1} \oplus \cdots \oplus r_{\mathrm{id}_{n-1}}$. We can further modify the above equation into $r \oplus s = r_{\mathrm{id}_1} \oplus \cdots \oplus r_{\mathrm{id}_{n-1}}$. Particularly,

- For each keyword w, the scheme builds the (obfuscated) list T which does *not* contain the last share r and it is stored on the CSP. Note that each document containing the keyword holds one share from which it is impossible to reconstruct the initial secret without all other shares.
- For each document, the server also stores the encrypted document identifier Encrypt(id) which is linked with the share r_{id}.
- The client saves (only) the last share r, in order to prevent the CSP from reconstructing the secret.
- In the *Search phase*, the client sends r (and some auxiliary information, i.e., a key K) to the server. The server, with a simple operation, recovers the previous obfuscated document-index, i.e., $r_{\mathrm{id}_{n-1}}$. Using this share, the server retrieves the corresponding encrypted document identifier Encrypt(id_{n-1}). Repeating recursively these operations, it is able to recover all the (encrypted) document-indexes.
  Note that, the search token is constant-sized since it consists only of the share r (plus the key K) and so it does not increase with the frequency of the queried keyword.
- A similar method is used during the *Update phase* where the scheme updates the obfuscated list T for the CSP and the last share r. As before, the client holds the last share r locally and the random shares (i.e. the obfuscated document-indexes $r_{\mathrm{id}_1}, \ldots, r_{\mathrm{id}_{n+1}}$) are submitted to the CSP.

To verify the efficiency of our proposed scheme, we run our experiments over 20 *Newsgroups* [1] - a common dataset in the area of information retrieval (2,579,597 keyword/document pairs). Results show that the proposed scheme takes less than 1 μs to retrieve a document. We compare our results with $\sum o\phi o\varsigma$ [5], which is the most efficient existing scheme to achieve forward privacy through the lowest requirements at the client side. Our experimental results show that our scheme is 10x to 20x faster than $\sum o\phi o\varsigma$ in searching keywords contained in documents. We also compare our scheme against MITRA that requires the least search computations from the CSP and achieves forward and type 2 backward privacy (formally defined in Sect. 3.5). However, MITRA's query generation mechanism can be more than 4500 times slower than our scheme when the number of matching documents is larger than 10,000 (Ref. Sect. 8).

2   Related Work

The first practical SE scheme was presented in 2000 by Song *et al.* [30]. Three years later, Goh introduced the secure index-based search, where an index is built per document [21]. In 2006, the first index-based SSE construction achieving sublinear search complexity was proposed by Curtmola *et al.* [13]. While, previous schemes are only suitable for static datasets, in 2012, Kamara *et al.* [25] introduced a dynamic and sublinear search scheme, which was later improved in [24]. In 2013, Cash *et al.* [9] developed a highly-scalable SSE scheme with support for boolean queries. One year later, Cash *et al.* [8] developed a dynamic scheme optimized for large datasets. Stefanov *et al.* [31] introduced the notion of *forward* and *backward privacy* for dynamic schemes. The formal definition of forward security was proposed in 2016 by Bost [5] and one year later refined by Kamara *et al.* [23]. Bost *et al.* [7] classify backward privacy into the three types. Zuo *et al.* [38] introduce a non-conventional intermediate level backward privacy, called *type* 1^-. This kind of backward privacy, to one side, does not protect access pattern (unlike type 1) but it is stronger than type 2, since it leaks only the history of updates.

The concept of forward and backward privacy was almost not discussed in literature until 2016, when Zhang *et al.* [36] proposed a powerful version of injection attacks, proving that an adversary can obtain the content of a past query by inserting only 10 new documents. After this work, many forward privacy schemes were proposed, e.g. [2,5–7,10,16,17,19,26,29,33,34,38] but only some of them (e.g., [7,10,16,33,34,38]) also provide backward privacy. The most popular scheme to achieve forward privacy is $\sum o\phi o\varsigma$, proposed by Bost in [5]. $\sum o\phi o\varsigma$ claims to achieve the optimal point of the privacy/performance trade-off for SSE. Lai *et al.* in [29] construct secure DSSE schemes over labeled bipartite graphs, used to model the relationship between keywords and files. They propose a parallelizable dynamic encrypted data structure, which offers parallelism and efficient update and search operations. In 2018, Etemad *et al.* proposed a parallel structure to improve efficiency [19] and Chamani *et al.* offloaded computational tasks from a server to a client to reduce computations on the server [10]. Although they lower the search time, overheads are incurred by local storage and increased bandwidth. Sun *et al.* [34] proposed a DSSE scheme based on symmetric puncturable encryption [22] that can revoke a server's searching ability on deleted data. In a very recent work, Sun *et al.* present a type 2 backward private DSSE scheme [33], where deletions are made oblivious to the server.

Previous schemes assume that the server is honest-but-curious. However, there are scenarios where the server can be malicious. *Verifiable* SSE schemes were proposed (e.g., [6,27,28,35,37]). The first verifiable SSE scheme is given by Kurosawa *et al.* [27], and, one year later, it was extended to the dynamic setting by the same authors [28]. After this scheme, several VDSSE schemes achieving forward security have been proposed. Bost [5] proposed a verifiable version of $\sum o\phi o\varsigma$, called $\sum o\phi o\varsigma\text{-}\epsilon$, at the cost of increasing client's storage; Bost *et al.* [6] introduced a scheme based on Verifiable Hash Tables; Yoneyama *et al.* [35] solved the problem of $\sum o\phi o\varsigma\text{-}\epsilon$ extra client storage cost and Zhang *et al.* [37] proposed a scheme which can simultaneously achieve verifiability of search results and forward security. To the best of our knowledge, all the VDSSE schemes achieving forward security proposed so far, do *not* offer backward privacy.

Table 1. Performance comparison of DSSE schemes. Notation: $D = \#$ documents, $|\mathbf{W}| = \#$ keywords, $N = \#$ keyword/document pairs, $a_w = \#$ times queried keyword w was added to the database, $d_w = \#$ deleted entries for w, $p = \#$ processors, $n_w = \#$ documents matching w, i.e., $n_w = a_w - d_w$, $d = \max_w d_w \cdot n_w$ is the size of search result matching w, $-$ = much larger than other listed schemes. RT is roundtrip. Here, we assume two rounds of result-hiding scheme is equal to one round of result-revealing scheme. FP is forward privacy, BP is backward privacy. $\widetilde{O}$ notation hides polylogarithmic factors.

Scheme		Computation			Communication			Client	Security		Verifiability
		Query	Search	Update	Search	Update	RT	Storage	FP	BP	
Π^{dyn}	[8]	$O(1)$	$O(a_w)$	$O(1)$	$O(n_w)$	$O(1)$	1	$O(1)$	✗	✗	✗
$\sum o\phi o\varsigma$	[5]	$O(1)$	$O(a_w)$	$O(1)$	$O(n_w)$	$O(1)$	1	$O(|\mathbf{W}|\log D)$	✓	✗	✗
MONETA	[7]	$-$	$\widetilde{O}(a_w \log N + \log^3 N)$	$\widetilde{O}(\log^2 N)$	$\widetilde{O}(a_w \log N + \log^3 N)$	$\widetilde{O}(\log^3 N)$	3	$O(1)$	✓	Type 1	✗
FIDES		$O(a_w)$	$O(a_w)$	$O(1)$	$O(a_w)$	$O(1)$	2	$O(|\mathbf{W}|\log D)$	✓	Type 2	✗
DIANA		$O(\log a_w)$	$O(a_w)$	$O(\log a_w)$	$O(n_w + \log a_w)$	$O(1)$	1	$O(|\mathbf{W}|\log D)$	✓	✗	✗
DIANA$_{del}$		$O(d_w \log a_w)$	$O(a_w)$	$O(\log a_w)$	$O(n_w + d_w \log a_w)$	$O(1)$	2	$O(|\mathbf{W}|\log D)$	✓	Type 3	✗
JANUS		$O(1)$	$O(n_w d_w)$	$O(1)$	$O(n_w)$	$O(1)$	1	$O(|\mathbf{W}|\log D)$	✓	Type 3	✗
Scheme	[19]	$O(n_w)$	$O(a_w/p)$	$O(1)$	$O((a_w + n_w)/p)$	$O(1)$	2	$O(|\mathbf{W}| + D)$	✓	✗	✗
ORION	[10]	$-$	$O(n_w \log^2 N)$	$O(\log^2 N)$	$O(n_w \log^2 N)$	$O(\log^2 N)$	$O(\log N)$	$O(1)$	✓	Type 1	✗
MITRA		$O(a_w)$	$O(a_w)$	$O(1)$	$O(a_w)$	$O(1)$	2	$O(|\mathbf{W}|\log D)$	✓	Type 2	✗
HORUS		$-$	$O(n_w \log d_w \log N)$	$O(\log^2 N)$	$O(n_w \log d_w \log N)$	$O(\log^2 N)$	$O(\log d_w)$	$O(|\mathbf{W}|\log D)$	✓	Type 3	✗
SD$_a$	[15]	$-$	$O(a_w + \log N)$	$O(\log N)$	$O(a_w + \log N)$	$O(\log N)$	2	$O(1)$	✓	Type 2	✗
SD$_d$		$-$	$O(a_w + \log N)$	$O(\log^3 N)$	$O(a_w + \log N)$	$O(\log N)$	2	$O(1)$	✓	Type 2	✗
JANUS++	[34]	$O(\log D)$	$O(n_w d)$	$O(d)$	$O(n_w)$	$O(1)$	1	$O(|\mathbf{W}|\log D)$	✓	Type 3	✗
AURA	[33]	$O(\log D)$	$O(n_w)$	$O(1)$	$O(n_w)$	$O(1)$	1	$O(|\mathbf{W}|D)$	✓	Type 2	✗
FB-DSSE	[38]	$O(1)$	$O(a_w)$	$O(1)$	$O(n_w)$	$O(n_w)$	1	$O(|\mathbf{W}|\log D)$	✓	Type 1^-	✗
VSPS	[6]	$O(1)$	$O(m \log^3 N)$	$O(\log^2 N)$	$O(n_w)$	$O(1)$	1	$O(|\mathbf{W}|D)$	✓	✗	✓
VFSSE	[37]	$O(1)$	$O(a_w)$	$O(1)$	$O(n_w)$	$O(1)$	1	$O(|\mathbf{W}|\log D)$	✓	✗	✓
Our scheme		$O(1)$	$O(a_w)$	$O(1)$	$O(a_w)$	$O(1)$	1	$O(|\mathbf{W}|\log D)$	✓	Type 2	✓

Beyond State of the Art: Table 1 compares our scheme with prior work.

Our scheme provides the same time complexity of search and update with Π^{dyn} and $\sum o\phi o\varsigma$. However, Π^{dyn} does not offer forward nor backward privacy, while $\sum o\phi o\varsigma$ provides forward privacy. FIDES, MITRA and AURA attempt to bridge the gap between $\sum o\phi o\varsigma$ and backward privacy. All achieve type 2 backward privacy. However, their approach increases the time to generate a query or client storage. The query generation complexity of AURA is $O(\log D)$, and of FIDES and MITRA is $O(a_w)$, where a_w is the number of updates related to keyword w. In comparison, as we already mention, our scheme has a complexity of $O(1)$, namely, our search token is constant-sized.

ORION and MONETA (relying on ORAM), provide the strongest notion of backward privacy. However, communication is largely increased and efficiency is impacted. Etemal *et al.*'s scheme [19] presents the most efficient search through parallel programming, however, it sacrifices backward privacy and incurs a large amount of local storage. VSPS [6] and VFSSE [37] achieve verifiability, but *not* backward privacy.

Our scheme achieves an optimal tradeoff between privacy (forward and backward), verifiability, and efficiency, without shifting the workload to the client. It achieves better search efficiency than $\sum o\phi o\varsigma$ and provides a more efficient query generation mechanism than MITRA. In addition, our scheme achieves the security level of type 2 backward privacy.

3 Preliminaries

3.1 Notations

In the rest of the paper, we will use the following notations:

- $\xleftarrow{\$}$ is used to represent a uniform random selection;
- $|\ |$ denotes the size of an object or the number of elements in a set;
- $\|$ and $\oplus$ represent concatenation and bitwise exclusive (XOR), respectively;
- λ is the security parameter, while $negl(\lambda)$ is a negligible function in λ;
- w is a keyword; id is a document identifier; and r_{id} is a random string selected for document id;
- DB is a database, while $DB[w]$ is a tupla of n data entries associated to keyword w: $DB[w]=(id_{i_1}, \cdots, id_{i_n})$;
- T is a T-Dic in the form $T[key] = value$; where T-Dic is a tuple dictionary;
- Π_w is a random string for keyword w;
- W is a T-Dic stored in the form $W[w] = \Pi_w$;
- F is a pseudorandom function (PRF);
- H is a collision resistant hash function;
- S and Φ are sets storing ciphertexts and ids, respectively; and
- $\mathcal{L}$ is a leakage function

3.2 DSSE Scheme and VDSSE Scheme

A DSSE scheme Σ is composed of one algorithm $Setup$ and two protocols ($Search$ and $Update$) between a client and a server [5].

- $Setup(\text{DB})$ takes as input a dataset DB. It outputs a pair (EDB, K, σ) where K is a secret key, EDB the encrypted database, and σ the client's state.
- $Search(K, q, \sigma, \text{EDB}) = (Search_C(K, q, \sigma), Search_S(\text{EDB}))$ is a protocol between the client with input the key K, its state σ, and a search query q, and the server with input EDB.
- $Update(K, \sigma, op, in, \text{EDB}) = (Update_C(K, \sigma, op, in), Update_S(\text{EDB}))$ is a protocol between the client with input the key K, the state σ, an operation op and an input in parsed as the index id and the keyword w, and the server with input EDB. The update operations are taken from the set $\{add, del\}$ (addition and deletion of a document/keyword pair).

A VDSSE scheme is an extension of DSSE scheme, providing verifiability. Specifically, an algorithm $Verify$ is implemented with input of retrieved result. If the result is correct, then the $Verify$ returns $True$, otherwise $False$.

3.3 Data Structure

In our scheme, we propose a primitive made up of a tuple dictionary (referred to as T-Dic), which is built from T-Set, a set of tuples, proposed in [9]. Each T-Set associates a list of fixed-sized data tuples to each keyword in the database (e.g., an inverted index [3], where the keyword is used to retrieve a list of document identifiers, is a T-Set).

A T-Dic is designed to store and associate pairwise fixed-sized elements, e.g., (w, Π_w). Each pairwise element consists of two parts: the first part is unique, referred to as key, and the second part is the associated information, referred to as value. Note that T-Dic is designed to store pairwise elements, which is different from T-set suitable for element-list structure. T-Dic consists of two algorithms: *Insert* and *Get*. *Insert* adds a pair of key and value into the T-Dic. If the operation is executed successfully, a boolean value *True* is returned, else, *False* is returned. We will denote by $T[k]$ the value associated with key k in the T-Dic T. The *Get* function, on an input key, returns the corresponding value if the corresponding key exists in T-Dic. Otherwise, no value is returned. In the following sections, to be brief, we only use an arrow that starts from T-Dic to represent *Get* function and that ends at T-Dic to represent *Insert* function.

3.4   Information Leakage Analysis

We consider the leakage of size pattern, search pattern, and access pattern in our analysis. Informally, *size pattern* leakage includes the size of encrypted data learnt by the CSP, the *search pattern* leakage is the record of the queries sent to the CSP, and the *access pattern* leakage reveals the history of data access.

Definition 1 (Ciphertext Size Pattern). *Let T be a T-Dic containing pairs that consist of the ith key t_i and the corresponding value v_i, i.e., $v_i \leftarrow T[t_i]$. The ciphertext size pattern α is defined as $\alpha = \{|T|, (|t_i|, |v_i|), 0 \leq i < |T|\}$, where $|T|$ represents the total number of records in T, and $|t_i|$ and $|v_i|$ represent the size of t_i and v_i respectively.*

Definition 2 (Search Pattern). *Let M_{sp} be a two dimensional binary matrix. The first dimension represents the search token observed as a query result by the CSP and the second dimension represents the time at which the query was received. The value inside M_{sp} is either 1 or 0: 1 representing the fact that a query was performed on a keyword at a given time. For a set of queries, $Q_0, \ldots, Q_q$, the search pattern can be defined as $\beta = \{M_{sp}, |Q_0|, \ldots, |Q_q|\}$.*

Definition 3 (Access Pattern). *Let M_{ac} be a two dimensional matrix. The first dimension represents the keyword observed as a query by the CSP and the second dimension is the encrypted document identifier observed as ciphertext by the CSP. The value of the matrix is either 1 or 0. For a set of queries, $Q_0, \ldots, Q_q$ on encrypted data T, which resulted in the retrieved values $v_i, \ldots, v_j$ ($i \leq j \leq |T|$), the access pattern γ is defined as $\gamma = \{M_{ac}, |Q_0|, \ldots, |Q_q|, |v_i|, \ldots, |v_j|\}$.*

In our scheme, keys and values have the same size due to the T-Dic structure and the query size is uniform. Moreover, the the two values of the T-Dic T are, roughly speaking, (i) the *obfuscated* list of all document-indexes except the last index (needed to reconstruct the secret) and (ii) the encrypted document identifiers.

Therefore, we can simplify the above definitions. The size pattern is reformulated as $\alpha = \{|T|\}$, since T is sent to the server during the *Setup* and *Update* phases. The search pattern leakage is the time of when the query was received, namely, $\beta = \{M_{sp}\}$. The access pattern is $\gamma = \{M_{ac}\}$, that is, the encrypted document identifiers observed by the server during the *Setup* (and *Update*) phase. Finally, the leakage function of the proposed scheme is defined as $\mathcal{L} = \alpha \cup \beta \cup \gamma = \{|T|, M_{sp}, M_{ac}\}$.

3.5   Privacy Definition

In our privacy definition, we do not want the CSP to learn anything related to client data beyond some explicit leakage, which is typically captured by using *real world* and *ideal world* formalisation [14,25]. In the *real world* SSE_{real}, the SSE scheme is executed honestly and the CSP observes the transcript of each operation. In the *ideal world* SSE_{ideal}, the CSP is given a simulated transcript that is generated by a simulator *Sim* using the leaked information. The leaked information is given by leakage function $\mathcal{L}$ (defined in Sect. 3.4) that describes what the CSP is able to learn. If these two worlds are indistinguishable, the SSE scheme is *secure*. To formalise the above description, we present the following definition of adaptive security of SSE schemes:

Definition 4 (Adaptive security of SSE schemes [7]). *An SSE scheme $\Sigma = \{Setup, QueryGen, Search, Update$ and $Decrypt\}$ is $\mathcal{L}$-adaptively-secure, with respect to a leakage function $\mathcal{L}$, if for any polynomial-time adversary $\mathcal{A}$ issuing a polynomial number of queries q, there exists a PPT simulator Sim such that*

$$\left| P[\mathsf{SSE}_{real,\mathcal{A}}^{\Sigma}(\lambda,q) = 1] - P[\mathsf{SSE}_{ideal,(\mathcal{A},Sim,\mathcal{L})}^{\Sigma}(\lambda,q) = 1] \right| \leq negl(\lambda).$$

In our analysis, we consider forward privacy and backward privacy. Formally, we have the following definitions [7]:

Definition 5 (Forward privacy). *A $\mathcal{L}$-adaptively-secure SSE is forward-private iff the insert operation leakage function $\mathcal{L}$ can be written as: $\mathcal{L} = \{op\}$, where op is the current operation type, i.e., insert or delete.*

Definition 6 (Backward privacy - type 1). *A $\mathcal{L}$-adaptively-secure SSE scheme achieves type 1 backward privacy iff the leakage function can be written as: $\mathcal{L} = \{DB[w], \Psi[DB[w]], |\Phi[w]|, op\}$ where $|\Phi[w]|$ records the total number of operations over keyword w, $\Psi[DB[w]]$ records the insert timestamp of all the matching documents, and op is the insert operation.*

Definition 7 (Backward privacy - type 2). *A $\mathcal{L}$-adaptively-secure SSE scheme achieves type 2 backward privacy iff the leakage function can be written as: $\mathcal{L} = \{DB[w], \Psi[w], op\}$, where $\Psi[w]$ records the timestamp of all operations over keyword w and op is the insert operation.*

Definition 8 (Backward privacy - type 3). *A $\mathcal{L}$-adaptively-secure SSE scheme achieves type 3 backward privacy iff the leakage function can be written as: $\mathcal{L} = \{DB[w], \Psi[w], H[w]\}$, where $\Psi[w]$ records the timestamp of all operations over keyword w and $H[w]$ records all operations over keyword w.*

Our scheme aims to achieve forward privacy and *type* 2 backward privacy. By obfuscating access patterns, it could also achieve type 1 backward privacy. However, obfuscation techniques are far from practical applications [20, 32].

4   Models

We now introduce the system, query, and threat models for our proposed scheme.

4.1   System Model

The proposed system consists of two parties, the client and the CSP. Initially, the client extracts keywords from its documents and builds an inverted index [3]. Then, the client encrypts the index and documents before outsourcing them to the CSP. Once data is uploaded to the CSP, the client is capable of generating a request and send it to the CSP for searching or updating (i.e., performing an insert and delete operation) the encrypted documents. Upon receiving the request, the CSP processes the request and sends the result back to the client.

4.2   Query Model

The proposed system supports search and update requests. The search request is used to search for documents based on a keyword, while the update request is designed for inserting or deleting specific documents. The search (query) process can be further split into two steps. The first step is to retrieve a target document identifier and the second step is to retrieve a document based on the identifier. Our paper focuses on the first step, since completion of the second step is trivial given a correct output from the first step. Similarly, for the update request, we emphasize on the index update instead of uploading/deleting documents. For protecting the security of the second step, we could apply many techniques to prevent the CSP from getting access to the content of the updated document or any information related to it (e.g., uploading fake documents to obfuscate the updated documents or delaying and grouping updated documents).

A search request requires three inputs: (i) a target keyword; (ii) a client's secret key; and (iii) a T-Dic where the key is the keyword and value is a string (i.e. the *obfuscated* list that we introduced in Sect. 1) corresponding to the keyword (see Sect. 3.3 for the definition of a T-Dic). Specifically, a client first inputs a target keyword and a secret key to generate two sub-keys. The first sub-key is sent in the clear to the CSP, while the second sub-key is privately stored by the client within a specific keychain. In addition, the client reads the value from the T-Dic and sends it to the CSP along with the first sub-key (see Sect. 5.1 for details). Based on the key and value sent from the client, the CSP can search over the encrypted data and return the encrypted identifiers of documents containing the keyword.

The update request takes five input parameters: (i) a keyword, which is supposed to be included in the target document; (ii) a secret key, only known to the client; (iii) an identifier of the target document; (iv) an operation type, which specifies either an insert or a delete operation; and (v) a T-Dic, which stores the keywords and corresponding strings.

Similarly to the query request, a client first generates two sub-keys through inputting the target keyword and its secret key. Then the client reads the value from T-Dic where the key is the target keyword. To hide the operation type and updated document identifier, the client encrypts the operation type (insertion or deletion) and target document identifier. Based on the above result, the client constructs two key-value pairs (see Sect. 5.1 for details) and sends them to the CSP. The CSP updates the stored data by adding the two uploaded pairs.

4.3   Threat Model

In our work, we first consider the semi-honest model and then we extend it to malicious model [6], providing the verifiable variant of our scheme. In the semi-honest model, the CSP is assumed to be semi-honest, which means the CSP honestly follows the protocol but could try to launch passive attacks by analyzing available data. Under this assumption, the CSP is able to examine the ciphertext and try to infer the plaintext. Moreover, it keeps a record of the queries submitted by the client and tries to analyze their content. We, specifically, consider the following attacks.

1) Ciphertext Analysis: Uploaded data is stored on the CSP, which can perform analyses and inference on the ciphertext. For instance, the CSP could deduce information such as the size of the ciphertext and the number of records.
2) Query Analysis: Clients send encrypted queries to the CSP, which executes queries and tries to infer their content and link documents to specific keywords.
3) Update Analysis: Update requests are sent to the CSP, which diligently addresses them. The CSP is capable of observing the whole process and tries to deduce the update type, its content, and target documents.
In the malicious model, the CSP could exhibit following malicious behaviors:
1) Incomplete Search Result: The CSP may try to save resources by not running the query over the whole dataset. As a result, only a part of the requested data is returned.
2) Incorrect Search Result: The CSP may intentionally change search results so that the content deliberately misleads the client into making a wrong decision.

5   Proposed Scheme

We provide a detailed explanation of the components of our scheme (verifiability will be introduced in Sect. 7). We also provide a proof of the correctness.

5.1   Details of the Proposed Scheme

The proposed DSSE construction inspired by the additive secret sharing scheme differs from traditional schemes as follows:

1. **Secret Generation and Assignment.** Given a set of documents, keywords are first extracted. A generator creates and assigns a secret to each keyword.
2. **Secret Shares Generation and Assignment.** Let $n_w - 1$ be the number of documents containing keyword w, and s_w be a secret value associated with w. Each secret Π_w is split into n_w same-sized shares $s_{w,id}$ ($1 \leq id \leq n_w$) by randomly selecting $n_w - 1$ shares and selecting the last one share such that $\Pi_w = \sum_{id=1}^{n_w} s_{w,id}$. Note that in Algorithm 1 we denoted $s_{w,id}$ as r_{id}. Afterwards, each document containing the keyword will be assigned a share.
3. **Index Construction.** Tuples consist of a keyword, a secret share, and a document identifier and are applied to construct a secure index.

The proposed scheme consists of five modules: *Initialization*, *Query Generation*, *Search*, *Decrypt*, and *Update*.

Initialization. The client pre-processes documents by extracting keywords and storing them into database DB as an inverted index: $\{w, (id_1, \ldots, id_n)\}$. After DB construction (Algorithm 1), the client builds two T-Dic T and W as follows:

1. A secret key K is first drawn uniformly at random from $\{0,1\}^\lambda$. This key K is known only to the client and is never exposed to the CSP.
2. For each keyword w inside DB, the client calls PRF F with two inputs: w and K. The output is split into K_1 and K_2. K_1 is a key sent to the CSP during search phase while K_2 is a key stored locally and is used for decryption.
3. The client initialises a string Π_w with all ones of size λ,
4. For each document identifier id belonging to $DB(w)$, a uniformly random string r_{id} is selected from $\{0,1\}^\lambda$.
5. Π_w is XORed with r_{id}. The result is stored back to Π_w.
6. Π_w is XORed with K_1 and passed into a collision-resistant hash function H. The outcome is a key of the T-Dic T, denoted as t_1. The corresponding value v is obtained by computing the XOR of r_{id} and $H(\Pi_w)$.
7. Another key t_2 of T is constructed by calling the hash function H: the result of K_1 XOR r_{id} is an input into H.
8. The value of $T[t_2]$ is a ciphertext which is generated by invoking a symmetric encryption, with inputs as key K_2 and $op||id$ op represents the type of operation (*insert* or *delete*). We use one bit to express op: 1 represents *insertion* and 0 *deletion*. Note that the op bit is set to one in the initialization phase.
9. After all document identifiers belonging to $DB(w)$ have been processed, value Π_w is stored into the T-Dic W with key w.
10. T-Dic T and W are built. T is sent to the CSP, W is stored locally.

Query Generation. Once the T-Dic T is stored on the CSP, the client is allowed to generate a query locally with a specified keyword and send it to the CSP to search for target document identifiers. As shown in Algorithm 2, the client first calls the PRF F with the input of its secret key K and keyword w. The output of F consists of two keys, K_1 and K_2. Subsequently, the value Π_w of $W[w]$ is read. Finally, the string Π_w and K_1 are sent to the CSP while K_2 is stored locally.

Search. The CSP seeks document identifiers that match a search query and returns them to the client. Specifically, CSP receives Π_w and K_1 from the client and initializes a list S, used to store identifiers. If Π_w contains at least one zero (not the initial state), the following is executed, otherwise, an empty list S is returned. The first operation is an XOR of Π_w with K_1 followed by a hash of the result. The outcome t_1 is a key of T. The corresponding value r_{id} is computed by executing $T[t_1] \oplus H(\Pi_w)$. Afterwards, $K_1 \oplus r_{id}$ is hashed with H. The computed result t_2 is another key of T. Value c of $T[t_2]$ is a ciphertext generated using symmetric encryption and added into S. Subsequently, Π_w is replaced with value $\Pi_w \oplus r_{id}$. The above process is recursively executed until Π_w contains only ones (initial state). Search operation is presented in Algorithm 3.

Algorithm 1: Setup

Client:

Input: λ, DB
Output: T, W, K
$K \xleftarrow{\$} \{0,1\}^\lambda$
for $w \in DB$ **do**
    $K_1 \| K_2 \leftarrow F(K, w)$
    $\Pi_w \leftarrow 1^\lambda$
    for $id \in DB(w)$ **do**
        $r_{id} \xleftarrow{\$} \{0,1\}^\lambda$
        $\Pi_w \leftarrow \Pi_w \oplus r_{id}$
        $t_1 \leftarrow H(\Pi_w \oplus K_1)$
        $v \leftarrow r_{id} \oplus H(\Pi_w)$
        $T[t_1] \leftarrow v$
        $t_2 \leftarrow H(K_1 \oplus r_{id})$
        $T[t_2] \leftarrow Enc(K_2, op\|id)$
    $W[w] \leftarrow \Pi_w$

Algorithm 2: QueryGen

Client:

Input: K, w, W
Output: Π_w, K_1, K_2
$K_1 \| K_2 \leftarrow F(K, w)$
$\Pi_w \leftarrow W[w]$
send Π_w and K_1 to CSP
store K_2 locally

Algorithm 3: Search

CSP:

Input: Π_w, K_1, T
Output: S
$S \leftarrow [\ \ ]$
while $\Pi_w \neq 1^\lambda$ **do**
    $t_1 \leftarrow H(\Pi_w \oplus K_1)$
    $v \leftarrow T[t_1]$
    $r_{id} \leftarrow v \oplus H(\Pi_w)$
    $t_2 \leftarrow H(K_1 \oplus r_{id})$
    $c \leftarrow T[t_2]$
    $S \leftarrow S \cup c$
    $\Pi_w \leftarrow \Pi_w \oplus r_{id}$

Decrypt. (Ref. Algorithm 4) Once a retrieval result is received from the CSP, the client has to decrypt them in order to recover the plaintext. The client first initializes a set Φ used to store document identifiers. For all ciphertexts inside S, the client sequentially decrypts them following a Late In First Out (LIFO) strategy, thus, keeping the order of operations. With key K_2 and ciphertext c, the decryption algorithm Dec is invoked and the plaintext of op and id is extracted. If op is equal to zero, id is removed from Φ, otherwise the id is added into Φ. The above is recursively executed until all the ciphertexts of S are deciphered.

Update. Upon an update operation (insertion or deletion), T-Dic T is updated. The update process is split in two phases (Ref. Algorithm 5). In the first phase, the client generates an update request; the CSP responds in the second phase. The client initially calls the PRF F with secret key K and keyword w. The client then tries to read the value Π_w from W with key w. If the key w does not exist inside W, then w is inserted into W and the corresponding Π_w is set to all ones. Subsequently, a string r_{id} is randomly selected from $\{0,1\}^\lambda$. The result of $\Pi_w \oplus r_{id}$ is stored back into Π_w and the newly generated Π_w is stored into W with key w. In addition, two new (key, value) pairs of T are computed. The first new key t_1 is computed by calling hash H with input $\Pi_w \oplus K_1$, where value v is computed as $r_{id} \oplus H(\Pi_w)$. The second key is t_2 that is computed by invoking $H(K_1 \oplus r_{id})$. The associated value c is generated by running encryption algorithm with inputs: K_2 and $op||id$. At the end of phase 1, the two (key, value) pairs are sent to the CSP. Upon receiving the uploaded content, the CSP starts to update T. More precisely, the CSP puts the value v into $T[t_1]$ and c into $T[t_2]$.

Algorithm 4: Decrypt

Client:
Input: S, K_2
Output: Φ
$\Phi \leftarrow \phi$
for $c \in S$ **do**
   $(op, id) \leftarrow Dec(K_2, c)$
   if $op=0$; /* delete if op =
   0,otherwise insert */
   then
     | $\Phi \leftarrow \Phi \setminus id$
   else
     $\llcorner$ $\Phi \leftarrow \Phi \cup id$

Algorithm 5: Update

Client:
Input: w, id, op, K, W
Output: θ
$K_1||K_2 \leftarrow F(K, w)$
$\Pi_w \leftarrow W[w]$
if $\Pi =\perp$ **then**
   $\llcorner$ $\Pi_w \leftarrow 1^\lambda$
$r_{id} \xleftarrow{\$} \{0,1\}^\lambda$
$\Pi_w \leftarrow \Pi_w \oplus r_{id}$
$W[w] \leftarrow \Pi_w$
$t_1 \leftarrow H(\Pi_w \oplus K_1)$
$v \leftarrow H(\Pi_w) \oplus r_{id}$
$t_2 \leftarrow H(K_1 \oplus r_{id})$
$c \leftarrow Enc(K_2, op||id)$
$\theta \leftarrow (t_1, v) \cup (t_2, c)$
CSP:
Input: θ, T
Output: True/False
$(t_1, v), (t_2, c) \leftarrow \theta$
$T[t_1] \leftarrow v$
$T[t_2] \leftarrow c$

5.2   Proof of Correctness

We prove here that our scheme correctly retrieves all existing documents that contain a specific input keyword and excludes documents inserted then deleted.

Correctness of Search: The input of the search algorithm is Π_w, K_1 and T. Based on the *Setup* procedure, T is a list of pairs. Keys in T are generated by either $H(\Pi_w \oplus K_1)$ or $H(r_{id} \oplus K_1)$, where K_1 is the key generated from input keyword w, and r_{id} is the random string associated with w. During search, for key generation, CSP constructs the first key t_1 by calling $H(\Pi_w \oplus K_1)$ and computes the value r_{id} through $T[t_1] \oplus H(\Pi_w)$. Then, the ciphertext c can be read from $T[t_2]$ with key $t_2 = H(r_{id} \oplus K_1)$. To retrieve all documents containing w, the recursive process is controlled through Π_w. In *Setup*, for each document id, an r_{id} is selected and the value Π_w of $W[w]$ is equal to $1^\lambda \oplus_{id \in \Phi} r_{id}$, where Φ is the set of documents that contain w.

During the *Search* process, the value of Π_w is read from $W[w]$ and recursively updated as $\Pi_w \leftarrow \Pi_w \oplus r_{id}$, for each r_{id} in the set Φ, until Π_w is equal to 1^λ. Thus, the search procedure is performing the inverse operations of *Setup*, which proves the correctness of the search process.

Correctness of Decryption: Inputs consists of search result and decryption key K_2. K_2 is the same as the encryption key, so decryption is executed correctly. Decryption is also consistent with the order of operations over the ciphertext.

Correctness of Update: If input keyword w already exists in W, *Update* procedure reads string Π_w from W with w and conducts an XOR operation with a randomly selected string r_{id}. Otherwise, the Π_w of the keyword w is set to the initial string (1^λ), which is same as the *Setup*. The second difference is that the newly generated pairs of keys and values are sent to the CSP instead of updating T locally. In *Setup*, the client holds T while in the context of *Update*, T is stored in the CSP. Hence, the client sends the change of T to the CSP, which directly stores the submitted (key,value) pairs into T without any further operation. The result is the same as the *Setup* operation and thus *Update* is correct.

6   Privacy Analysis

In this section, we formally prove that our scheme is $\mathcal{L}$-adaptively-secure where $\mathcal{L}$ matches the requirements of forward and type 2 backward privacy. We prove Theorem 1 through the *real/ideal* world game of SSE (Ref. in Sect. 3.5).

Theorem 1. *If the output of PRF (F) is indistinguishable from a random function, the collision resistant hash function H is modeled as a random oracle and the applied symmetric encryption algorithm is semantically secure, then our scheme is $\mathcal{L}$-adaptively-secure, where $\mathcal{L} = \{DB[w], \Psi[w], op\}$.*

Proof Sketch: If an adversary has significant advantage in breaking the scheme, it is capable to break either pseudorandom function, or collision resistant hash function or applied semantically secure encryption.

Game G_0: G_0 is the same as the proposed scheme.

Game G_1: Instead of calling F when generating K_1 and K_2 with inputs w and K, G_1 randomly selects two strings, k_1^*, k_2^*, with the same size and stores them in a table T_k, that is, $T_k[w] \leftarrow (k_1^*, k_2^*)$. If an adversary can distinguish G_1 from G_0, then the adversary is able to distinguish F from a random function. The advantage can be formalized as follows: $Adv_F^{PRF} = |P[G_0 = 1] - P[G_1 = 1]|$.

Game G_2: In G_2, in *Setup*, random oracle H is programmed and outputs random strings for the original hash function. Change details are presented in Algorithms 6, 7, 8, and 9. An adversary trying to distinguish G_2 from G_1 is to set *conflict* to be *true*. If the adversary is able to distinguish $G2$ from $G1$ in significant advantage, the adversary is able to break the collision resistant hash function in significant advantage. The advantage can be formalized as follows: $Adv_H^{PRF} = |P[G_0 = 1] - P[G_1 = 1]|$.

Game G_3: The difference of G_3 over G_2 is that all updates over w are recorded and the Oracle of H is reprogrammed. Moreover, a random string is selected as the encryption output. The timestamp is represented by ts, which starts at 0 and increases by 1 for each new operation. We use $\Psi[w]$ to record all the updates of w and corresponding timestamps. Algorithms 10 and 11 detail the modifications.

Game G_4: The difference over G_3 is that only the first update over w is recorded.

Game G_5: The difference over G_4 is that all the updates are randomly generated.

Comparing G_3 with G_2, we observe that update operations in both cases have the same distribution since both output random strings. For the search operation, in G_2, the search result is the ciphertext generated from a symmetric encryption algorithm, while in G_3, the search result is a random string.

Assuming a semantically secure symmetric encryption algorithm, the ciphertext can only be distinguished from a random string with a negligible advantage. Therefore, we have $Adv_{enc} = |P[G_2 = 1] - P[G_3 = 1]| \leq negl(\lambda)$.

The difference between G_4 and G_3 is that G_4 only records the first *insert* operation while G_3 records all the operations. In G_5, operations are not recorded. From G_3, we learn that all operations are encrypted. Thus, the output of G_5 is indistinguishable from G_4 and G_3.

From the above analysis, we deduce that G_5 is the same as the ideal world of SSE, which can be simulated by a simulator Sim with leaked information $\mathcal{L}$. Since Sim only needs to simulate the process on the client-side, we only give the corresponding simulation details, as shown in Algorithms 12, 13 and 14.

Combining all aforementioned games, we can conclude that the advantage in distinguishing the game in the real world from the game in the ideal world is negligible. Let Δ represent the proposed scheme. Formally, we have $Adv_\Delta \leq Adv_F^{PRF} + Adv_H + Adv_{enc} \leq negl(\lambda)$. Thus we proved Theorem 1.

Algorithm 6: Setup*

Client:

Input: λ, DB

Output: T, W

conflict $\leftarrow$ false

for $w \in DB$ **do**

$\quad K_1^* \leftarrow \{0,1\}^\lambda$

$\quad K_2^* \leftarrow \{0,1\}^\lambda$

$\quad T_k[w] \leftarrow (K_1^*, K_2^*)$

$\quad \Pi_w \leftarrow 1^\lambda$

$\quad$ **for** $id \in DB(w)$ **do**

$\quad\quad r_{id} \xleftarrow{\$} \{0,1\}^\lambda$

$\quad\quad \Pi_w \leftarrow \Pi_w \oplus r_{id}$

$\quad\quad r_1 \leftarrow \{0,1\}^\lambda$

$\quad\quad \boxed{H(\Pi_w) \leftarrow r_1}$

$\quad\quad r_2 \leftarrow \{0,1\}^\lambda$

$\quad\quad \boxed{H(\Pi_w \oplus K_1^*) \leftarrow r_2}$

$\quad\quad r_3 \leftarrow \{0,1\}^\lambda$

$\quad\quad \boxed{H(r_{id} \oplus K_1^*) \leftarrow r_3}$

$\quad\quad t_1 \leftarrow H(\Pi_w \oplus K_1^*)$

$\quad\quad v \leftarrow r_{id} \oplus H(\Pi_w)$

$\quad\quad T[t_1] \leftarrow v$

$\quad\quad t_2 \leftarrow H(K_1^* \oplus r_{id})$

$\quad\quad T[t_2] \leftarrow Enc(K_2^*, op||id)$

$\quad W[w] \leftarrow \Pi_w$

Algorithm 7: Search*

CSP:

Input: Π_w, K_1^*, T

Output: S

$S \leftarrow \phi$

while $\Pi_w \neq 1^\lambda$ **do**

$\quad t_1 \leftarrow H(\Pi_w \oplus K_1^*)$

$\quad v \leftarrow T[t_1]$

$\quad r_{id} \leftarrow v \oplus H(\Pi_w)$

$\quad t_2 \leftarrow H(K_1^* \oplus r_{id})$

$\quad c \leftarrow T[t_2]$

$\quad S \leftarrow S \cup c$

$\quad \Pi_w \leftarrow \Pi_w \oplus r_{id}$

Algorithm 8: Query generation*

Client:

Input: w, W

Output: Π_w, K_1^*, K_2^*

$K_1^*||K_2^* \leftarrow T_k(w)$

$\Pi_w \leftarrow W[w]$

send Π_w and K_1^* to cloud

Algorithm 9: Update*

Client:

Input: w, id, op, K, W

Output: θ

$\Pi_w \leftarrow W[w]$

if $\Pi_w = \bot$ **then**

$\quad \Pi_w \leftarrow 1^\lambda$

if $T_k[w] = \bot$ **then**

$\quad K_1^* \leftarrow \{0,1\}^\lambda$

$\quad K_2^* \leftarrow \{0,1\}^\lambda$

$\quad T_k[w] \leftarrow (K_1^*, K_2^*)$

$\quad$ **if** $\Pi_w \notin H$ **then**

$\quad\quad r_1 \leftarrow \{0,1\}^\lambda$

$\quad\quad \boxed{H(\Pi_w) \leftarrow r_1}$

$\quad$ **if** $\Pi_w \oplus K_1^* \notin H$ **then**

$\quad\quad r_2 \leftarrow \{0,1\}^\lambda$

$\quad\quad \boxed{H(\Pi_w \oplus K_1^*) \leftarrow r_2}$

$\quad$ **else**

$\quad\quad$ conflict $\leftarrow$ true

$\quad$ **if** $r \oplus K_1^* \notin H$ **then**

$\quad\quad r_3 \leftarrow \{0,1\}^\lambda$

$\quad\quad \boxed{H(r \oplus K_1^*) \leftarrow r_3}$

$\quad$ **else**

$\quad\quad$ conflict $\leftarrow$ true

$r_{id} \xleftarrow{\$} \{0,1\}^\lambda$

$\Pi_w \leftarrow \Pi_w \oplus r_{id}$

$W[w] \leftarrow \Pi_w$

$t_1 \leftarrow H(\Pi_w \oplus K_1^*)$

$v \leftarrow H(\Pi_w) \oplus r_{id}$

$t_2 \leftarrow H(K_1^* \oplus r_{id})$

$c \leftarrow Enc(K_2^*, op||id)$

$\theta \leftarrow (t_1, v) \cup (t_2, c)$

CSP:

Input: θ, T

Output: True/False

$(t_1, v), (t_2, c) \leftarrow \theta$

$T[t_1] \leftarrow v$

$T[t_2] \leftarrow c$

Algorithm 10: Update**

Client:
Input: w, id, op, W
Output: θ
$ts \leftarrow ts + 1$
$t_1^* \leftarrow \{0,1\}^{(\lambda)}$
$v^* \leftarrow \{0,1\}^{(\lambda)}$
$t_2^* \leftarrow \{0,1\}^{(\lambda)}$
$\boxed{c^* \leftarrow \{0,1\}^{(\lambda)}}$
$\theta^* \leftarrow (t_1^*, v^*) \cup (t_2^*, c^*)$
$\boxed{\Phi[w] \ appends \ (ts, \theta^*)}$
CSP:
Input: θ^*, T
Output: True/False
$(t_1^*, v^*), (t_2^*, c^*) \leftarrow \theta^*$
$T[t_1^*] \leftarrow v^*$
$T[t_2^*] \leftarrow c^*$

Algorithm 11: Query generation**

Client:
Input: w, W
Output: Π_w, K_1^*, K_2^*
$(K_1^*, K_2^*) \leftarrow T_k(w)$
$\Pi_w^* \leftarrow 1^\lambda$
$\boxed{\theta_1^* \cdots \theta_c^* \leftarrow \Phi[w]}$
for *ts from 1 to c* **do**
$\quad r_{id} \xleftarrow{\$} \{0,1\}^\lambda$
$\quad t_1^*, v^*, t_2^* \leftarrow \theta_{st}^*$
$\quad \Pi_w^* \leftarrow \Pi_w^* \oplus r_{id}$
$\quad H(\Pi_w^* \oplus K_1^*) \leftarrow t_1^*$
$\quad H(\Pi_w^*) \leftarrow v^* \oplus r_{id}$
$\quad H(K_1^* \oplus r_{id}) \leftarrow t_2^*$
send Π_w^* and K_1^* to CSP

Algorithm 12: Setup-Sim

Client:
Input: λ, $\mathcal{L}$
Output: T^*, W^*
$K^* \xleftarrow{\$} \{0,1\}^\lambda$
$W^*, T^* \leftarrow \mathcal{L}$
$ts \leftarrow 0$

Algorithm 13: Update-Sim

Client:
Input: $\mathcal{L}$
Output: θ^*
$ts \leftarrow ts + 1$
$t_1^* \leftarrow \{0,1\}^\lambda$
$v^* \leftarrow \{0,1\}^\lambda$
$t_2^* \leftarrow \{0,1\}^\lambda$
$c^* \leftarrow \{0,1\}^\lambda$
$\theta^* \leftarrow (t_1^*, v^*) \cup (t_2^*, c^*)$
send θ^* to CSP

Algorithm 14: Query generation-Sim

Client:
Input: W^*, $\mathcal{L}$, Φ
Output: Π_w^*, K_1^*
$w^* \leftarrow \mathcal{L}$
$K_1^* \leftarrow 1^\lambda$
$\Pi_w^* \leftarrow 1^\lambda$
$\iota[w^*] \leftarrow \Pi_w^*$
$\theta_1^* \cdots \theta_c^* \leftarrow \Phi[w^*]$
for *st from 1 to c* **do**
$\quad r_{id} \xleftarrow{\$} \{0,1\}^\lambda$
$\quad t_1^*, v^*, t_2^* \leftarrow \theta_{st}^*$
$\quad \Pi_w^* \leftarrow \Pi_w^* \oplus r_{id}$
$\quad H(\Pi_w^* \oplus K_1^*) \leftarrow t_1^*$
$\quad H(\Pi_w^*) \leftarrow v^* \oplus r_{id}$
$\quad H(K_1^* \oplus r_{id}) \leftarrow t_2^*$
send Π_w^* and K_1^* to CSP

7   Verifiability of Our Scheme

The scheme proposed in Sect. 5 is only secure against a semi-honest CSP. In order to extend the security of the current scheme against a malicious CSP, namely, turning our scheme into a verifiable SSE scheme, we force the CSP to provide proof that it correctly executed a specific request. We consider the two following types of malicious behavior:

- The search result is incomplete. The CSP may try to save resources by not running the query over the whole dataset. As a result, only a part of the requested data is returned.
- The CSP can send back an incorrect result. In such a case, the content may deliberately mislead the client into making a wrong decision.

To address above threats we modify the *Setup* algorithm to embed the random share into the retrieved result, enabling the client to bind the secret share with the document identifier (i.e., $id\|r_{id}$). Once a retrieved result is received, the client decrypts the result, verifies all shares (r_{id}), and consequently combines the locally stored share Π_w with all the shares r_{id} retrieved from the CSP: if all shares can recover the secret (1^λ), then the search is complete and correct. These modifications are formally described in Algorithms 15 and 16.

Algorithm 15: Setup

Client:

Input: λ, DB
Output: T, W
$K \xleftarrow{\$} \{0,1\}^\lambda$
for $w \in DB$ **do**
    $K_1\|K_2 \leftarrow F(K,w)$
    $\Pi_w \leftarrow 1^\lambda$
    for $id \in DB(w)$ **do**
        $r_{id} \xleftarrow{\$} \{0,1\}^\lambda$
        $\Pi_w \leftarrow \Pi_w \oplus r_{id}$
        $t_1 \leftarrow H(\Pi_w \oplus K_1)$
        $v \leftarrow r_{id} \oplus H(\Pi_w)$
        $T[t_1] \leftarrow v$
        $t_2 \leftarrow H(K_1 \oplus r_{id})$
        $\boxed{T[t_2] \leftarrow Enc(K_2, op\|id\|r_{id})}$
    $W[w] \leftarrow \Pi_w$

Algorithm 16: Decrypt

Client:

Input: S, Π_w, K_2
Output: Φ/False
$\Phi \leftarrow \phi$
for $c \in S$ **do**
    $(op, id, r_{id}) \leftarrow Dec(K_2, c)$
    $\boxed{\Pi_w \leftarrow \Pi_w \oplus r_{id}}$
    if $op=0$;   /* delete if op
    =0, otherwise insert */
    then
        $\Phi \leftarrow \Phi \setminus id$
    else
        $\Phi \leftarrow \Phi \cup id$
$\boxed{\textbf{if } \Pi_w = 1^\lambda \textbf{ then return } \Phi}$
return False

Note that in the Algorithms 15 the adopted encryption algorithm is an authenticated encryption algorithm [4,18] such that the adversary is not able to partially modify the retrieved result.

Proof of Correctness: To prove the correctness of our scheme and security against a malicious CSP, we prove that it can detect an incomplete search result and resist incorrect retrieval results. The proof of resisting incomplete search results is split into two cases. In the extreme case, the malicious CSP rejects to return any result. In such a case, the client can detect that because the local T-Dic W includes the keyword w and the corresponding Π_w of $W[w]$ is not equal to 1^λ, then there must exist at least a document containing the keyword.

Now let us focus on the case where the search operation provides only partial results. Since all retrieved results include random share r_{id}, which is encrypted in an authenticated encryption algorithm, the malicious CSP cannot observe that value. Therefore, the client can use all the shares, including the share that the client holds, to reconstruct 1^λ. If reconstruction fails, the search result remains incomplete.

The proof of the correctness of the search result is based on the above rationale. Indeed, since the document identifier is linked to the random share and both of them are encrypted in an authenticated encryption, the malicious CSP is not able to modify the ciphertext without being detected. Thus, if the secret share r_{id} is correct, the document identifier should also be correct. It remains to highlight that since all secret shares are correct - otherwise the correct secret could not be reconstructed - the search results are correct.

Note that the security proof of the VDSSE scheme is similar to the DSSE one. Since we only add the *Verify* function on the client side, the CSP is not able to learn any extra information. Therefore, the scheme is still $\mathcal{L}$-adaptively-secure.

8   Performance

In this section, we evaluate the performance of query generation (client side) and search (server side) of our scheme. We implement our scheme with C code on a laptop with a 2.6 GHz Intel Core i7 processor, 16 GB of RAM, and 500 GB flash storage. The security parameter is set to 128 bits. Meanwhile, AES is adopted as the applied symmetric encryption algorithm and 256-bit collision resistant hash function is adopted as the standard hash function. We use the well-known public dataset *20 Newsgroups* [1], which contains 61,187 keywords and 20,000 documents. The total number of keyword/document entries is 2,579,597. We repeat each experiment 10 times and report the average result. Specifically, in the experiments, we focus on comparing our scheme with $\sum o\phi o\varsigma$ and MITRA along the following dimensions: (i) Search Efficiency and (ii) Query Generation (MITRA only). Since our scheme has a similar Query Generation process as $\sum o\phi o\varsigma$, we skip the comparison of Query Generation with $\sum o\phi o\varsigma$. In order to demonstrate the scalability of our scheme, the total number of keyword/document entries is first set to 1,400,000 and then set to 2,579,597. In our scheme, the *Setup* algorithm of two different datasets costs 16.8 s and 30.7 s, respectively. The time cost of the update process is constant (regardless of the size of the dataset), requiring around 0.013 ms.

Figure 1 shows the average time cost (namely, the search time cost for *each* matching entry on average) required for searching a matching document. We can observe that our scheme takes on average 0.9 μs to retrieve a document, while $\sum o\phi o\varsigma$ needs 20 μs on average when the number of matching documents is less than 100. Nevertheless, with an increasing number of matching documents, $\sum o\phi o\varsigma$ reduces its average search time, eventually reaching around 7 μs

We can observe that, in our scheme, the average search time is almost constant, making it suitable to be deployed for use cases involving both large or

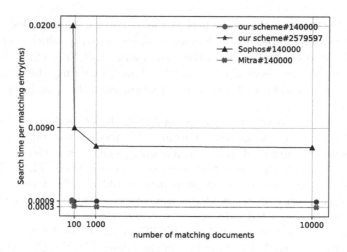

Fig. 1. Search: comparison with $\sum$οφος and MITRA

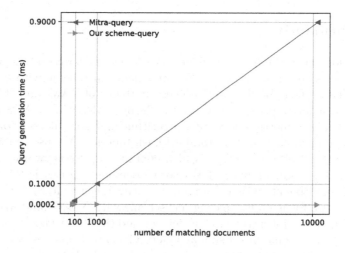

Fig. 2. Query generation: comparison with MITRA

small volumes of data. However, $\sum$οφος is sensitive to the number of matching documents. The reason behind this, is mainly caused by storage latency. More specific, we explain that because the cost of the storage latency and accessing the disk induces a certain amount of waiting. Since $\sum$οφος uses RSA operations during the search phase, we suppose that these RSA operations will not be fully interleaved with disk accesses and $\sum$οφος pays for the latency induced by mutexes and storage accesses.

Figure 1 shows that MITRA has a slightly better performance than our scheme in the search phase. However, in the Query Generation phase (Fig. 2), our scheme only needs 0.2 μs regardless of the number of matching documents while the time cost of MITRA's Query Generation increases linearly, reaching 900 μs when the number of matching documents reaches 10,000.

Hence, we conclude that our scheme is around 10x to 20x faster than $\sum o\phi o\varsigma$ during search phase. Our query generation could be more than 4500 times faster than MITRA when the number of matching documents is larger than 10,000.

9 Conclusion

In this paper, we propose a new approach based on additive secret sharing to construct SSE and we provide the first VDSSE scheme achieving both forward and backward privacy. Specifically, we construct a practical instance of VDSSE, achieving forward and type 2 backward privacy with the lowest configuration requirements on the client side. In addition, we present both theoretical and experimental comparisons between the proposed scheme and existing works. The comparison result shows that the proposed scheme is the most efficient scheme to achieve forward and type 2 backward privacy through the smallest client requirements. Our future research includes extensions where our scheme would benefit from further storage and communication optimization as well as an extension to support type 1 backward privacy.

Acknowledgement. This paper and the research behind it would not have been possible without the exceptional support of Florian Caullery. We appreciate all the effort made by Florian Caullery, especially the initial discussion, insightful comments, and long-term support.

We are also grateful for the meaningful and constructive comments offered by the anonymous peer reviewers.

References

1. 20newsgroups (2019). http://qwone.com/~jason/20Newsgroups/
2. Amjad, G., Kamara, S., Moataz, T.: Breach-resistant structured encryption. Priv. Enhancing Technol. **2019**(1), 245–265 (2019)
3. Baeza-Yates, R., Ribeiro-Neto, B., et al.: Modern information retrieval, vol. 463. ACM press, New York (1999)
4. Bogdanov, A., Mendel, F., Regazzoni, F., Rijmen, V., Tischhauser, E.: ALE: AES-based lightweight authenticated encryption. In: Moriai, S. (ed.) FSE 2013. LNCS, vol. 8424, pp. 447–466. Springer, Heidelberg (2014). https://doi.org/10.1007/978-3-662-43933-3_23
5. Bost, R.: $\Sigma o\varphi o\varsigma$: forward secure searchable encryption. In: ACM SIGSAC Conference on Computer and Communications Security, pp. 1143–1154. ACM (2016)
6. Bost, R., Fouque, P.A., Pointcheval, D.: Verifiable dynamic symmetric searchable encryption: Optimality and forward security. IACR Cryptology ePrint Arch. **2016**, 62 (2016)
7. Bost, R., Minaud, B., Ohrimenko, O.: Forward and backward private searchable encryption from constrained cryptographic primitives. In: ACM SIGSAC Conference on Computer and Communications Security, pp. 1465–1482. ACM (2017)

8. Cash, D., et al.: Dynamic searchable encryption in very-large databases: data structures and implementation. In: NDSS, vol. 14, pp. 23–26. Citeseer (2014)
9. Cash, D., Jarecki, S., Jutla, C., Krawczyk, H., Roşu, M.-C., Steiner, M.: Highly-scalable searchable symmetric encryption with support for Boolean queries. In: Canetti, R., Garay, J.A. (eds.) CRYPTO 2013. LNCS, vol. 8042, pp. 353–373. Springer, Heidelberg (2013). https://doi.org/10.1007/978-3-642-40041-4_20
10. Chamani, J.G., Papadopoulos, D., Papamanthou, C., Jalili, R.: New constructions for forward and backward private symmetric searchable encryption. In: ACM SIGSAC Conference on Computer and Communications Security, pp. 1038–1055 (2018)
11. Chang, Y.-C., Mitzenmacher, M.: Privacy preserving keyword searches on remote encrypted data. In: Ioannidis, J., Keromytis, A., Yung, M. (eds.) ACNS 2005. LNCS, vol. 3531, pp. 442–455. Springer, Heidelberg (2005). https://doi.org/10.1007/11496137_30
12. Chor, B., Goldreich, O., Kushilevitz, E., Sudan, M.: Private information retrieval. In: IEEE 36th Annual Foundations of Computer Science, pp. 41–50. IEEE (1995)
13. Curtmola, R., Garay, J., Kamara, S., Ostrovsky, R.: Searchable symmetric encryption: improved definitions and efficient constructions. In: CCS, pp. 79–88. ACM, New York (2006)
14. Curtmola, R., Garay, J., Kamara, S., Ostrovsky, R.: Searchable symmetric encryption: improved definitions and efficient constructions. J. Comput. Secur. 19(5), 895–934 (2011)
15. Demertzis, I., Chamani, J.G., Papadopoulos, D., Papamanthou, C.: Dynamic searchable encryption with small client storage. IACR Cryptology ePrint Arch. 2019, 1227 (2019)
16. Demertzis, I., Chamani, J.G., Papadopoulos, D., Papamanthou, C.: Dynamic searchable encryption with small client storage. In: 27th Annual Network and Distributed System Security Symposium, NDSS 2020, San Diego, California, USA, 23–26 February 2020. The Internet Society (2020)
17. Demertzis, L., Papadopoulos, S., Papapetrou, O., Deligiannakis, A., Garofalakis, M.: Practical private range search revisited. In: Proceedings of the 2016 International Conference on Management of Data, pp. 185–198. ACM (2016)
18. Diro, A., Reda, H., Chilamkurti, N., Mahmood, A., Zaman, N., Nam, Y.: Lightweight authenticated-encryption scheme for internet of things based on publish-subscribe communication. IEEE Access 8, 60539–60551 (2020)
19. Etemad, M., Küpçü, A., Papamanthou, C., Evans, D.: Efficient dynamic searchable encryption with forward privacy. Priv. Enhancing Technol. 1, 5–20 (2018)
20. Garg, S., Mohassel, P., Papamanthou, C.: TWORAM: efficient oblivious RAM in two rounds with applications to searchable encryption. In: Robshaw, M., Katz, J. (eds.) CRYPTO 2016. LNCS, vol. 9816, pp. 563–592. Springer, Heidelberg (2016). https://doi.org/10.1007/978-3-662-53015-3_20
21. Goh, E.J.: Secure indexes. IACR Cryptology ePrint Archive 2003, 216 (2003)
22. Green, M.D., Miers, I.: Forward secure asynchronous messaging from puncturable encryption. In: 2015 IEEE Symposium on Security and Privacy, pp. 305–320. IEEE (2015)
23. Kamara, S., Moataz, T.: Boolean searchable symmetric encryption with worst-case sub-linear complexity. In: Coron, J.-S., Nielsen, J.B. (eds.) EUROCRYPT 2017. LNCS, vol. 10212, pp. 94–124. Springer, Cham (2017). https://doi.org/10.1007/978-3-319-56617-7_4

24. Kamara, S., Papamanthou, C.: Parallel and dynamic searchable symmetric encryption. In: Sadeghi, A.-R. (ed.) FC 2013. LNCS, vol. 7859, pp. 258–274. Springer, Heidelberg (2013). https://doi.org/10.1007/978-3-642-39884-1_22
25. Kamara, S., Papamanthou, C., Roeder, T.: Dynamic searchable symmetric encryption. In: Proceedings of the 2012 ACM Conference on Computer and Communications Security, pp. 965–976. ACM (2012)
26. Kim, K.S., Kim, M., Lee, D., Park, J., Kim, W.H.: Forward secure dynamic searchable symmetric encryption with efficient updates. In: ACM SIGSAC Conference on Computer and Communications Security (2017)
27. Kurosawa, K., Ohtaki, Y.: UC-secure searchable symmetric encryption. In: Keromytis, A.D. (ed.) FC 2012. LNCS, vol. 7397, pp. 285–298. Springer, Heidelberg (2012). https://doi.org/10.1007/978-3-642-32946-3_21
28. Kurosawa, K., Ohtaki, Y.: How to update documents *verifiably* in searchable symmetric encryption. In: Abdalla, M., Nita-Rotaru, C., Dahab, R. (eds.) CANS 2013. LNCS, vol. 8257, pp. 309–328. Springer, Cham (2013). https://doi.org/10.1007/978-3-319-02937-5_17
29. Lai, R.W.F., Chow, S.S.M.: Forward-secure searchable encryption on labeled bipartite graphs. In: Gollmann, D., Miyaji, A., Kikuchi, H. (eds.) ACNS 2017. LNCS, vol. 10355, pp. 478–497. Springer, Cham (2017). https://doi.org/10.1007/978-3-319-61204-1_24
30. Song, D.X., Wagner, D., Perrig, A.: Practical techniques for searches on encrypted data. In: IEEE Symposium on Security and Privacy, pp. 44–55. IEEE (2000)
31. Stefanov, E., Papamanthou, C., Shi, E.: Practical dynamic searchable encryption with small leakage. In: NDSS, vol. 71, pp. 72–75 (2014)
32. Stefanov, E., et al.: Path oram: an extremely simple oblivious ram protocol. In: 2013 ACM SIGSAC Conference on Computer & Communications Security, pp. 299–310. ACM (2013)
33. Sun, S.F., et al.: Practical non-interactive searchable encryption with forward and backward privacy
34. Sun, S.F., et al.: Practical backward-secure searchable encryption from symmetric puncturable encryption. In: 2018 ACM SIGSAC Conference on Computer and Communications Security, pp. 763–780 (2018)
35. Yoneyama, K., Kimura, S.: Verifiable and forward secure dynamic searchable symmetric encryption with storage efficiency. In: Qing, S., Mitchell, C., Chen, L., Liu, D. (eds.) ICICS 2017. LNCS, vol. 10631, pp. 489–501. Springer, Cham (2018). https://doi.org/10.1007/978-3-319-89500-0_42
36. Zhang, Y., Katz, J., Papamanthou, C.: All your queries are belong to us: the power of file-injection attacks on searchable encryption. In: 25th {USENIX} Security Symposium ({USENIX} Security 16), pp. 707–720 (2016)
37. Zhang, Z., Wang, J., Wang, Y., Su, Y., Chen, X.: Towards efficient verifiable forward secure searchable symmetric encryption. In: Sako, K., Schneider, S., Ryan, P.Y.A. (eds.) ESORICS 2019. LNCS, vol. 11736, pp. 304–321. Springer, Cham (2019). https://doi.org/10.1007/978-3-030-29962-0_15
38. Zuo, C., Sun, S.-F., Liu, J.K., Shao, J., Pieprzyk, J.: Dynamic searchable symmetric encryption with forward and stronger backward privacy. In: Sako, K., Schneider, S., Ryan, P.Y.A. (eds.) ESORICS 2019. LNCS, vol. 11736, pp. 283–303. Springer, Cham (2019). https://doi.org/10.1007/978-3-030-29962-0_14

Smooth Zero-Knowledge Hash Functions

Behzad Abdolmaleki[1], Hamidreza Khoshakhlagh[2(✉)], and Helger Lipmaa[3]

[1] Max Planck Institute for Security and Privacy, Bochum, Germany
[2] Aarhus University, Aarhus, Denmark
hamidreza@cs.au.dk
[3] Simula UiB, Bergen, Norway

Abstract. We define smooth zero-knowledge hash functions (SZKHFs) as smooth projective hash functions (SPHFs) for which the completeness holds even when the language parameter lpar and the projection key hp were maliciously generated. We prove that blackbox SZKHF in the plain model is impossible even if lpar was honestly generated. We then define SZKHF in the registered public key (RPK) model, where both lpar and hp are possibly maliciously generated but accepted by an RPK server, and show that the CRS-model trapdoor SPHFs of Benhamouda *et al.* are also secure in the weaker RPK model. Then, we define and instantiate subversion-zero knowledge SZKHF in the plain model. In this case, both lpar and hp are completely untrusted, but one uses non-blackbox techniques in the security proof.

Keywords: Plain model · RPK model · SPHF · Trapdoor SPHF · Subversion zero-knowledge

1 Introduction

Smooth projective hash functions (SPHFs, [14]) for an NP language $\mathcal{L}_{\text{lpar}}$ (with corresponding relation $\mathcal{R}_{\text{lpar}}$ such that $\mathcal{L}_{\text{lpar}} = \{x : \exists w, (x, w) \in \mathcal{R}_{\text{lpar}}\}$), parametrized by a language parameter lpar, are cryptographic primitives with the following properties. Given lpar and a word x, one can compute a hash of x in two different ways: either (i) using a projection key hp (an analogue of a public key), and $(x, w) \in \mathcal{R}_{\text{lpar}}$, as $pH \leftarrow \text{projhash}(\text{lpar}; \text{hp}, x, w)$, or (ii) using a hashing key hk (an analogue of a secret key) and any x, as $H \leftarrow \text{hash}(\text{lpar}; \text{hk}, x)$. If $(x, w) \in \mathcal{R}_{\text{lpar}}$, then the *completeness* property guarantees that the two ways of computing the hash result in the same value, $pH = H$. If $x \notin \mathcal{L}_{\text{lpar}}$, then the *smoothness* property guarantees that, knowing hp but not hk, one cannot distinguish H from random. SPHFs are useful in many different applications, starting from constructing IND-CCA2 secure cryptosystems [14] and password-

H. Khoshakhlagh—Funded by the Concordium Foundation under Concordium Blockchain Research Center, Aarhus.

A. Adhikari et al. (Eds.): INDOCRYPT 2021, LNCS 13143, pp. 510–535, 2021.
https://doi.org/10.1007/978-3-030-92518-5_23

authenticated key exchange [20], and ending with honest-verifier zero knowledge [10], and non-interactive zero knowledge (NIZK, [1]).

Several varieties of SPHFs exist. In KV-SPHFs [24], hp is created first and then x can depend on hp. In GL-SPHFs [20], the order is opposite. In the current paper, we are primarily interested in the GL-SPHFs. Recent research [1,9,10] has shown how to construct efficient GL-SPHFs for a large variety of languages. In particular, it is known how to construct GL-SPHFs for the class of algebraic languages $\mathcal{L}_{\Gamma,\theta} := \{x : \exists w, \Gamma(x) \cdot w = \theta(x)\}$, where Γ and θ are x-dependent linear maps, [1,9,10]. Algebraic languages are quite powerful and include quadratic languages like the languages of the Elgamal encryption of bits, [10,13]. It is also known how to create GL-SPHFs for conjunction and disjunction of two algebraic languages [1,9,10]. On the other hand, assuming the polynomial hierarchy does not collapse, it is impossible to construct SPHF for NP-complete languages [9].

It is usually assumed that the creator of hp is honest; this explains, e.g., why the SPHF-based two-message zero-knowledge argument of [10] is honest-verifier only. Benhamouda et al. [10] defined *trapdoor SPHFs* (TSPHFs) as SPHFs where one can verify that the projection key has been generated correctly. Unfortunately, TSPHFs are defined in the strong common reference string (CRS) model, where everybody has to trust the same CRS creator. In many applications, such a universally trusted third party does not exist. This creates another avenue of subversion to which TSPHFs provide no answer: one obtains security against a malicious projection-key creator but not against a malicious CRS creator.

Several recent papers on zero-knowledge arguments [8], including succinct non-interactive arguments of knowledge (SNARKs [2,16]) and quasi-adaptive NIZKs (QA-NIZKs [4]), have shown how to achieve either soundness or zero-knowledge even when the public parameters, like the CRS or the public key, have been maliciously subverted. In the case of NIZK, many well-known (im)possibility results exist. E.g., one cannot achieve (say) blackbox or even auxiliary-string non-blackbox NIZK in the weak Bare Public Key (BPK, [12,28]; see also the full version [3]) model [22] while efficient no-auxiliary-string non-blackbox zero-knowledge (Sub-ZK) NIZK in the BPK model is possible [2,4,16]. Moreover, it is impossible to achieve NIZK that, at the same time, has the properties of subversion-resistant soundness and subversion-resistant zero-knowledge, [8].

We are not aware of similar positive or negative results for SPHFs in the case of trusted or untrusted hp, or of any previous research on the applications of non-blackbox assumptions to SPHF. We emphasize that in the case of SPHFs, this issue is even more critical than in the case of NIZKs: in SPHFs, hp is created by the verifier (who is by definition untrusted by the prover), while in NIZKs, the CRS creator *may* be honest, depending on the application.

Our Contributions. We study SPHFs with untrusted language-parameter and projection-key generator. We say that an SPHF HF is a *smooth zero-knowledge hash function* (SZKHF[1]) if

(i) smoothness holds even for a maliciously generated lpar (but honestly generated hp), and
(ii) zero-knowledge (i.e., completeness) holds even for a maliciously generated lpar and a maliciously generated hp, where lpar and hp are accepted respectively by a public lpar-verification algorithm verpar and a public hp-verification algorithm verhp.

First, we show that SZKHFs are impossible in the plain model. Second, we define SZKHFs in the RPK (registered public key) model, which is weaker than the CRS model. We show that SZKHFs exist in the RPK model. Third, we define Sub-ZK SZKHFs in the plain model, which are SZKHFs without any trust assumption, but similarly to Sub-ZK NIZKs, we use non-blackbox techniques to construct them and show that Sub-ZK GL-SZKHFs exist for all algebraic languages.

On the other hand, Sub-ZK NIZKs are only known in the bare public key model [12,28], which is in stark contrast to our results. In a parallel work, we motivate the difference by showing that Sub-ZK SZKHFs are equivalent to *Sub-ZK deterministic-prover quasi-adaptive two-message zero-knowledge arguments*.

Our Results and Techniques. First, we define blackbox SZKHFs in the plain model without any trust assumptions. Motivated by a classical impossibility result for blackbox two-round zero knowledge in the plain model [22], we prove that such SZKHFs are impossible for hard languages even if lpar is trusted. Thus, one has two options: either (i) allow SZKHFs to rely on non-blackbox assumptions, or (ii) construct SZKHFs in a trust model.

Second, we consider blackbox SZKHFs in the RPK [6] model, where each party $\mathcal{P}$ trusts *some* key-registration authority $\mathcal{R}$ and has registered her public key pk with $\mathcal{R}$. If $\mathcal{P}$ is honest, then the secret key sk can be extracted, and pk is correctly distributed. Otherwise, sk can be extracted, but there is no guarantee about its distribution. The RPK model is considerably weaker than the better known CRS model since, in the latter, one assumes that sk is always correctly distributed and that all parties trust the same CRS.

In this case, the zero-knowledge definition is similar to the soundness definition of trapdoor SPHFs (TSPHFs) in [10], except that the latter is given in the CRS model while we use the weaker RPK model. In addition, motivated by recent work on Sub-ZK QA-NIZK [4], we assume that lpar is also created in the RPK model, i.e., its trapdoor is extractable, but there is no guarantee

---

[1] We considered other terms. This notion corresponds to completeness/projectivity when lpar and hp are subverted, and thus it could be called *subversion-completeness/subversion-projectivity*. For trapdoor SPHFs, it was called *soundness* in [10] and, finally, *zero knowledge* in [9]. Zero-knowledge is the most intuitive term since in a typical application of HF; it guarantees that a malicious creator of hp does not learn anything new from seeing pH compared to when she sees H that does not depend on the witness.

about its distribution; this is in contrast to [10] that assumed that lpar is honestly generated. After appropriate tweaking, all known TSPHFs [10] will become computationally-smooth blackbox SZKHFs in the RPK model. Unfortunately, a TSPHF only shifts the subversion problem: instead of having to trust the generator of hp, one has to trust the generator of lpar and the RPK; however, in the RPK model, lpar and the RPK can be handled by different RPK authorities, and there is no need to assume that their trapdoors are correctly distributed.

Third, inspired by research on Sub-ZK NIZK [2,4,8,16], we define Sub-ZK SZKHF in the plain model. Motivated by an impossibility result about two-message zero-knowledge [22] and its use in [4], we prove that auxiliary-string non-blackbox SZKHF in the plain model is impossible for languages not in BPP, even if lpar is honestly generated. This impossibility result is strictly stronger than the impossibility result mentioned at the beginning of this subsection. Thus, as in [4], Sub-ZK corresponds to *no-auxiliary-string non-blackbox zero-knowledge*. Differently from Sub-ZK NIZK, where one assumes non-blackbox extraction of the secret key, we only require that one can extract $\kappa(\mathsf{hk})$, where κ can be a hard-to-invert bijection. Such a notion of κ-extractability emphasizes the fact that in many applications of SPHFs, it is not essential to extract hk; instead, it suffices to recover a related value $\kappa(\mathsf{hk})$ that can be used to verify efficiently that projhash was correctly computed.

More formally, let κ be an efficient algorithm, e.g., identity map or exponentiation/bilinear map. An SZKHF is κ-*extractable Sub-ZK* if it supports deterministic algorithms verpar (*language-parameter verification*), verhp (*projection-key verification*) and simhash (*subversion hash*), s.t. : for each PPT subverter $\mathcal{Z}$ that creates a verpar-accepted lpar and verhp-accepted hp, there exists a non-blackbox PPT extractor $\mathsf{Ext}_\mathcal{Z}$ that outputs $\kappa(\mathsf{hk})$, s.t. $\mathsf{simhash}(\mathsf{lpar}; \kappa(\mathsf{hk}), \mathsf{x}) = \mathsf{projhash}(\mathsf{lpar}; \mathsf{hp}, \mathsf{x}, \mathsf{w})$ for every $(\mathsf{x}, \mathsf{w}) \in \mathcal{R}_{\mathsf{lpar}}$. Importantly, compared to blackbox SZKHFs in the RPK model, a Sub-ZK SZKHF in the plain model does not rely on a trusted RPK, and thus, we get full subversion-resistance.

We construct a Sub-ZK SZKHF in the plain model based on SPHFs from DVSs (diverse vector spaces) [9,10]. Then, we give a construction of computationally smooth blackbox SZKHF in the RPK model based on DVS-based SPHFs. We also present a Sub-ZK SZKHF in the plain model and a blackbox SZKHF in the RPK model, both based on Benhamouda *et al.*'s TSPHFs [10] in the full version [3].

2   Preliminaries

For a matrix $\boldsymbol{A}$, colspace($\boldsymbol{A}$) is the subspace generated by its columns. Let PPT denote probabilistic polynomial-time. Let vect($\boldsymbol{A}$) be the vectorization of the matrix $\boldsymbol{A}$. The cokernel of $\boldsymbol{A}$ is defined as $\mathsf{coker}(\boldsymbol{A}) = \{\boldsymbol{a} : \boldsymbol{a}^\top \boldsymbol{A} = \boldsymbol{0}\}$. Let $\lambda \in \mathbb{N}$ be the security parameter. All adversaries will be stateful. For an algorithm $\mathcal{A}$, im($\mathcal{A}$) is the image of $\mathcal{A}$ (the set of valid outputs of $\mathcal{A}$), $\mathsf{RND}_\lambda(\mathcal{A})$ is the random tape of $\mathcal{A}$ (for a fixed choice of λ), and $r \leftarrow_\$ \mathsf{RND}_\lambda(\mathcal{A})$ denotes the random choice of r from $\mathsf{RND}_\lambda(\mathcal{A})$. By $y \leftarrow \mathcal{A}(\mathsf{x}; r)$ we denote that $\mathcal{A}$, given an input x and a randomizer r, outputs y. By $x \leftarrow_\$ \mathcal{D}$ we denote that x is sampled according to distribution $\mathcal{D}$ or uniformly randomly if $\mathcal{D}$ is a set. Let $\mathsf{negl}(\lambda)$ be an arbitrary negligible function. We write $a \approx_\lambda b$ if $|a - b| \leq \mathsf{negl}(\lambda)$. We follow Bellare et al. [8] by using "cryptographic" style in security definitions where all complexity (adversaries, algorithms, assumptions) is uniform, but the security (say, soundness) is quantified over all inputs chosen by the adversary.

A bilinear group generator $\mathsf{Pgen}(1^\lambda)$ returns $\mathsf{p} = (p, \mathbb{G}_1, \mathbb{G}_2, \mathbb{G}_T, \hat{e}, [1]_1, [1]_2)$, where $\mathbb{G}_1$, $\mathbb{G}_2$, and $\mathbb{G}_T$ are three additive cyclic groups of prime order p, $[1]_\iota$ is a generator of $\mathbb{G}_\iota$ for $\iota \in \{1, 2, T\}$ with $[1]_T = \hat{e}([1]_1, [1]_2)$, and $\hat{e} : \mathbb{G}_1 \times \mathbb{G}_2 \to \mathbb{G}_T$ is a non-degenerate efficiently computable bilinear pairing. We assume λ is implicitly described by p, and as in [8], we assume that p is a deterministic function of λ and thus cannot be subverted. (This is usually the case in practice.) We require the bilinear pairing to be Type-3 [18], that is, we assume that there is no efficient isomorphism between $\mathbb{G}_1$ and $\mathbb{G}_2$. We use the additive implicit notation of [15], that is, we write $[a]_\iota$ to denote $a[1]_\iota$ for $\iota \in \{1, 2, T\}$. We denote $\hat{e}([a]_1, [b]_2)$ by $[a]_1 \bullet [b]_2$. Thus, $[a]_1 \bullet [b]_2 = [ab]_T$. We freely use the bracket notation together with matrix notation; for example, if $\boldsymbol{AB} = \boldsymbol{C}$ then $[\boldsymbol{A}]_1 \bullet [\boldsymbol{B}]_2 = [\boldsymbol{C}]_T$. We also assume that $[\boldsymbol{A}]_2 \bullet [\boldsymbol{B}]_1 := ([\boldsymbol{B}]_1^\top \bullet [\boldsymbol{A}]_2^\top)^\top = [\boldsymbol{AB}]_T$.

Algebraic Languages. Let p be system parameters, including say the description of a bilinear group. Let $\mathtt{lpar} = (\boldsymbol{\Gamma}, \boldsymbol{\theta}, \boldsymbol{\lambda})$, where $\boldsymbol{\Gamma}, \boldsymbol{\theta}, \boldsymbol{\lambda}$ are all linear maps in their their inputs. More precisely, $\boldsymbol{\Gamma}(\mathbf{x})$ is an $n \times k$ matrix, $\boldsymbol{\theta}(\mathbf{x})$ is an n-dimensional vector, and $\boldsymbol{\lambda}(\mathbf{x}, \mathbf{w})$ is a k-dimensional vector. Moreover, different coefficients of $\boldsymbol{\theta}(\mathbf{x})$, $\boldsymbol{\Gamma}(\mathbf{x})$, and $\boldsymbol{\lambda}(\mathbf{x}, \mathbf{w})$ can belong to different algebraic structures (most commonly, given a bilinear group $\mathsf{p} = (p, \mathbb{G}_1, \mathbb{G}_2, \mathbb{G}_T, \hat{e})$, either to $\mathbb{Z}_p$, $\mathbb{G}_1$, $\mathbb{G}_2$, or $\mathbb{G}_T$ as long as the equation $\boldsymbol{\theta}(\mathbf{x}) = \boldsymbol{\Gamma}(\mathbf{x}) \cdot \boldsymbol{\lambda}(\mathbf{x}, \mathbf{w})$ is "well-typed". E.g., the equation $\begin{pmatrix} [\theta_1]_T \\ [\theta_2]_1 \end{pmatrix} = \begin{pmatrix} [\Gamma_{11}]_T & [\Gamma_{12}]_2 \\ [\Gamma_{21}]_1 & \Gamma_{22} \end{pmatrix} \begin{pmatrix} \lambda_1 \\ [\lambda_2]_1 \end{pmatrix}$ is well-typed. We omit the subscript $\mathtt{lpar}$ if it is clear from the context. Define

$$\mathcal{L}_{\mathtt{lpar}} = \{\mathbf{x} : \exists \mathbf{w}, \boldsymbol{\theta}(\mathbf{x}) = \boldsymbol{\Gamma}(\mathbf{x}) \cdot \boldsymbol{\lambda}(\mathbf{x}, \mathbf{w})\} \ . \tag{1}$$

Let $\mathcal{R}_\mathcal{L} = \{(\mathbf{x}, \mathbf{w}) : \boldsymbol{\theta}(\mathbf{x}) = \boldsymbol{\Gamma}(\mathbf{x}) \cdot \boldsymbol{\lambda}(\mathbf{x}, \mathbf{w})\}$ be the corresponding witness-relation. Languages of the form Eq. (1) have been studied at least since [10], and they called *algebraic*[2] in [13]. All linear languages are algebraic, but algebraic languages also include non-linear languages. E.g., the language of Elgamal encryptions of bits is algebraic [10]; in this case, $\boldsymbol{\Gamma}(\mathbf{x})$ depends on $\mathbf{x}$.

Projective Hash Functions. Let $\mathcal{L}_{\mathtt{lpar}} \subset \mathcal{X}_{\mathtt{lpar}}$ be a language parametrized by $\mathtt{lpar}$ (the language parameter), where $\mathcal{X}_{\mathtt{lpar}}$ is the underlying domain, e.g., a group. Let $\mathcal{R}_{\mathtt{lpar}}$ be the witness-relation defined by $\mathcal{L}_{\mathtt{lpar}} = \{\mathbf{x} : \exists \mathbf{w}, (\mathbf{x}, \mathbf{w}) \in \mathcal{R}_{\mathtt{lpar}}\}$. A projective hash function (PHF, [14]) for $\{\mathcal{L}_{\mathtt{lpar}}\}$ is a tuple of PPT algorithms $\mathsf{HF} = (\mathsf{Pgen}, \mathsf{setup.lpar}, \mathsf{hashkg}, \mathsf{projkg}, \mathsf{hash}, \mathsf{projhash})$, where

$\mathsf{Pgen}(1^\lambda)$: Takes a security parameter λ and generates the global parameters p.
$\mathsf{setup.lpar}(\mathsf{p})$: sets up the language parameters $\mathtt{lpar}$. $\mathtt{lpar}$ contains p and some public parameters specifying the relation (e.g., an encryption key).

---

[2] Couteau and Hartmann [13] considered $\boldsymbol{\lambda}(\mathbf{x}, \mathbf{w}) := \mathbf{w}$ only; however, one can just redefine the witness to contain all elements of $\boldsymbol{\lambda}(\mathbf{x}, \mathbf{w})$.

hashkg(lpar): Inputs a language parameter lpar. It generates and outputs a hashing key hk for $\mathcal{L}_{\text{lpar}}$.

projkg(lpar; hk, x): Inputs a language parameter lpar, a hashing key hk, and possibly a word $x \in \mathcal{X}_{\text{lpar}}$. It outputs deterministically a projection key hp.

hash(lpar; hk, x): Inputs a language parameter lpar, a hashing key hk, and a word $x \in \mathcal{X}_{\text{lpar}}$. It outputs deterministically a hash value H.

projhash(lpar; hp, x, w): inputs a language parameter lpar, a projection key hp, and $(x, w) \in \mathcal{R}_{\text{lpar}}$. It outputs deterministically a projected hash value pH.

The set of hash values is called the *range* of HF and is denoted by HashSet. We assume HashSet is an efficiently sampleable set that has size, exponential in λ. To shorten notation, we will denote the sequence "hk $\leftarrow$ hashkg(lpar); hp $\leftarrow$ projkg(lpar; hk, x)" by (hp, hk) $\leftarrow$ kgen(lpar; x).

A distribution $\mathcal{D}_p$ (e.g., the output distribution of setup.lpar(p)) on $\mathcal{L}_{\text{lpar}}$ is *witness-sampleable* [23] if there exists a PPT algorithm setup.ltrap(p) that outputs (lpar, ltrap) such that lpar is distributed according to $\mathcal{D}_p$, and membership of x in *the parameter language* $\mathcal{L}_{\text{lpar}}$ can be verified in PPT given ltrap. We always assume that lpar can be efficiently computed from ltrap. In SPHF-related research, $\mathcal{D}_p$ is often assumed to be witness-sampleable, even if it is not always necessary. Couteau and Hartmann [13] extended the definition of witness-sampleable languages to all algebraic languages.

HF is *perfectly complete* if for all lpar $\in$ im(setup.lpar(p)), $(x, w) \in \mathcal{R}_{\text{lpar}}$, and (hp, hk) $\in$ im(kgen(lpar; x)), hash(lpar; hk, x) = projhash(lpar; hp, x, w).

There are at least three types of smooth PHFs (SPHFs). Intuitively, in GL-SPHF [20], security is required even when hp maliciously depends on x. On the other hand, in KV-SPHF [24], security is required even when x can maliciously depend on hp. The third type is CS-SPHF, [14]; we will not discuss CS-SPHFs in what follows. See [9, Section 2.5] for more information.

A PHF HF for a language $\mathcal{L} \subseteq \mathcal{X}$ is *ε-GL-smooth (an ε-GL-SPHF)* if for any lpar and any word $x \in \mathcal{X}_{\text{lpar}} \setminus \mathcal{L}_{\text{lpar}}$, the following distributions are ε-close:

$$\{(\mathsf{hp}, \mathsf{H}) : (\mathsf{hp}, \mathsf{hk}) \leftarrow \mathsf{kgen}(\mathsf{lpar}; x); \mathsf{H} \leftarrow \mathsf{hash}(\mathsf{lpar}; \mathsf{hk}, x)\}$$
$$\{(\mathsf{hp}, \mathsf{H}) : (\mathsf{hp}, \mathsf{hk}) \leftarrow \mathsf{kgen}(\mathsf{lpar}; x); \mathsf{H} \leftarrow_{\$} \mathsf{HashSet}\}$$

A PHF is *GL-smooth* if it is ε-GL-smooth with ε negligible in λ.

HF for $\mathcal{L} \subseteq \mathcal{X}$ is *ε-KV-smooth (an ε-KV-SPHF)* if for any lpar and any (not necessarily computable in polynomial-time) function f from the set of possible projection keys hp to $\mathcal{X}_{\text{lpar}} \setminus \mathcal{L}_{\text{lpar}}$, the following distributions are ε-close:

$$\{(\mathsf{hp}, \mathsf{H}) : (\mathsf{hp}, \mathsf{hk}) \leftarrow \mathsf{kgen}(\mathsf{lpar}); \mathsf{H} \leftarrow \mathsf{hash}(\mathsf{lpar}; \mathsf{hk}, f(\mathsf{hp}))\}$$
$$\{(\mathsf{hp}, \mathsf{H}) : (\mathsf{hp}, \mathsf{hk}) \leftarrow \mathsf{kgen}(\mathsf{lpar}); \mathsf{H} \leftarrow_{\$} \mathsf{HashSet}\}$$

A PHF is *KV-smooth* if it is ε-KV-smooth with ε negligible in λ. Since projkg does not depend on x in this case, we often omit x as an argument for projkg.

For all (subset-membership-hard) algebraic languages, one can construct an efficient SPHF, [1, 9, 10], s.t. the hash value belongs to a source group, $\mathbb{G}_1$ or $\mathbb{G}_2$. Benhamouda [9, Section 2.5.3.2] remarks that one cannot construct GL-SPHF for an NP-complete language since then one can also to construct a witness encryption scheme for the same language [19] which would solve a long-standing open problem in the complexity theory.

3   Defining SZKHF

While completeness of SPHF, defined for honestly generated hp, is sufficient in many applications, it is natural to ask what happens if hp was generated maliciously. Consider, e.g., an application of SPHFs in the construction of zero-knowledge proof systems. One can use SPHFs to design two-message honest-verifier zero-knowledge proof systems [10] and non-interactive zero-knowledge (NIZKs) argument systems in the CRS model [1]. In the former case, the need to trust the hp generator translates to the need to trust the verifier who creates hp (hence, one gets honest-verifier zero-knowledge). While [10] showed how to obtain two-message zero-knowledge proof systems, they did it by introducing a trusted CRS generator. In this case and the case of SPHF-based NIZKs, [1], the need to trust the hp generator is transformed to the need to trust the CRS generator.

The CRS model [11] assumes the existence of a universally trusted CRS creator who creates the CRS from the correct distribution and does not leak any information. Unfortunately, NIZK in the plain model, and even auxiliary-string NIZK in the BPK [12,28] model, is impossible, [22]. One can construct efficient no-auxiliary-string non-blackbox zero-knowledge NIZK in the BPK model based on SNARKs and QA-NIZKs [2,4,16] assuming there exists a public BPK verification procedure PKV and, in the case of QA-NIZK [4], a public language parameter verification procedure verpar. No-auxiliary-string non-blackbox implies that, given the BPK pk is accepted by PKV, one can use an adversary-dependent extractor to extract the trapdoor of pk, and, in the case of QA-NIZK, lpar is accepted by verpar. For the extraction to succeed, it is required that the adversary has no auxiliary string since an auxiliary string could encode a pk for which she does not know the trapdoor.

Since SPHFs can be used to construct NIZKs [1], one can hope that some of the known (im)possibility results about NIZKs can be translated to the case of SPHFs. However, this is not evident, in particular since there is no prior work on non-blackbox SPHFs or SPHFs in different trust models, except [10] that only considers SPHFs in the CRS model. Thus, we need to use known (im)possibility results about *two-message* zero-knowledge argument systems.

We approach the question of untrusted lpar and hp systematically. We will define a stronger version of completeness (*zero-knowledge*) of an SPHF that guarantees that even if lpar and hp are created maliciously then either

(i) one detects that this is the case, or
(ii) if $(x, w) \in \mathcal{R}_{\mathcal{L}}$ then $\mathsf{hash}(\mathsf{lpar}; \mathsf{hk}, x) = \mathsf{projhash}(\mathsf{lpar}; \mathsf{hp}, x, w)$.

Additionally, we define a stronger version of smoothness, called *Sub-PAR smoothness* of an SPHF which guarantees that the smoothness holds even if lpar (but not hp) is created maliciously. A *smooth zero-knowledge hash function* (SZKHF) is an SPHF that satisfies zero-knowledge and Sub-PAR smoothness. The precise model (Sub-PAR smoothness and Sub-ZK) is motivated by the model used in [4] in the case of QA-NIZK. However, since SZKHFs are related not to QA-NIZK but to a flavour of two-message zero-knowledge argument systems, and thus the completeness of this model has to established separately in the case of SZKHFs.

We will consider SZKHFs in the following three models:

Blackbox zero-knowledge (ZK) in the plain model: ZK holds without the use of non-blackbox techniques or trust assumptions. We show that blackbox SZKHF in the plain model is impossible for languages not in BPP, even if lpar was honestly generated and auxiliary input is not allowed.[3]

Blackbox ZK in the RPK model: ZK holds without the use of non-blackbox techniques but one relies on the RPK model. In this case, SZKHF is a variant of the definition of TSPHFs from [10] that however were defined in the stronger CRS model. More precisely, both lpar and hp can be untrusted but they need to be accepted by an RPK server. (Thus, one can extract ltrap and td in the security proof.) On the other hand, [10] assumes that lpar and the CRS are correctly distributed. Known TSPHFs can be tweaked to be SZKHF in this sense but one still has the issue of the subversion of both lpar and the rpk.

Non-blackbox ZK in the plain model: ZK is proven by non-blackbox techniques in the plain model. Here, the SZKHF definiton is related to that of the subversion zero-knowledge (Sub-ZK) Sub-PAR smooth QA-NIZKs [4]. We show that auxiliary-string non-blackbox SZKHF in the plain model is impossible for languages not in BPP, even if lpar was honestly generated.

In all three cases, we will assume that there exist deterministic PPT algorithms verpar and verhp, such that correctness holds even if lpar and hp were maliciously constructed as long as verpar accepts lpar and verhp accepts (lpar; hp, x). (Note that verhp takes the input x only when we have a GL-SPHF.) We assume that verpar (resp., verhp) accepts all correctly generated language parameters (resp., projection keys). The existence of verhp for SPHFs was first postulated by Benhamouda *et al.* [10] who used it to obtain trapdoor SPHFs. An analogous algorithm CV for NIZKs was (independently) postulated for NIZKs in [2] and played a key part in their definition of Sub-ZK NIZK in the CRS model. We are not aware of any previous definition of verpar in the case of SPHFs; in the case of QA-NIZKs, it was first done in [4].

In the rest of the paper, we only consider GL-SZKHFs: security definitions in the case of GL-SZKHFs and KV-SZKHFs differ in small technical details that mostly just make it more difficult to parse the definitions.

3.1 Blackbox SZKHF in the Plain Model

We define blackbox GL-SZKHF in the plain model. We prove that, even if lpar was honestly generated, this definition can only be satisfied for languages

---

[3] In the case of blackbox ZK in the plain model, we will give the definition only for honestly generated lpar: since we will show that this definition is impossible to achieve, this will make our result only stronger.

$$\boxed{\mathsf{Complete}^{\mathsf{plain}}_{\mathsf{HF},\mathcal{A}}(\lambda)} \; / \; \underline{\underline{\mathsf{Complete}^{\mathsf{rpk}}_{\mathsf{HF},\mathcal{A}}(\lambda)}}$$

$\mathsf{p} \leftarrow \mathsf{Pgen}(1^\lambda); \underline{\mathsf{lpar} \leftarrow \mathsf{setup.lpar}(\mathsf{p})}; \underline{\underline{(\mathsf{lpar},\mathsf{ltrap}) \leftarrow \mathsf{setup.ltrap}(\mathsf{p})}};$

$\underline{\underline{(\mathsf{rpk},\mathsf{td}) \leftarrow \mathsf{K}_{\mathsf{rpk}}(\mathsf{lpar})}}; \; (\mathbf{x},\mathbf{w}) \leftarrow \mathcal{A}\left(\mathsf{lpar}\,\underline{,\mathsf{ltrap}};\underline{\underline{\mathsf{rpk}}}\right);$

$(\mathsf{hp},\mathsf{hk}) \leftarrow \mathsf{kgen}\left(\mathsf{lpar}\,\underline{\underline{,\mathsf{rpk}}};\mathbf{x}\right);$

$\text{if } \mathsf{verpar}(\mathsf{lpar}) = 1 \wedge \mathsf{verhp}\left(\mathsf{lpar}\,\underline{\underline{,\mathsf{rpk}}};\mathsf{hp},\mathbf{x}\right) = 1 \wedge$

$\quad ((\mathbf{x},\mathbf{w}) \notin \mathcal{R}_{\mathsf{lpar}} \vee \mathsf{hash}\left(\mathsf{lpar}\,\underline{\underline{,\mathsf{rpk}}};\mathsf{hk},\mathbf{x}\right) = \mathsf{projhash}(\mathsf{lpar}\,\underline{\underline{,\mathsf{rpk}}};\mathsf{hp},\mathbf{x},\mathbf{w}))$

$\quad \textbf{then return } 1; \textbf{else return } 0; \textbf{fi}$

Fig. 1. Completeness experiments in Definitions 1 to 3. The dashed-box/dotted-box part is only present in the dashed-boxed/dotted-boxed experiment.

$$\boxed{\mathsf{Smooth}^{\mathsf{bb\text{-}plain}}_{\mathsf{HF},\mathcal{A}}(\lambda)} \; / \; \underline{\mathsf{Smooth}^{\mathsf{bb\text{-}rpk}}_{\mathsf{HF},\mathcal{A}}(\lambda)} \; / \; \boxed{\mathsf{Smooth}^{\mathsf{nbb\text{-}plain}}_{\mathsf{HF},\mathcal{A}}(\lambda)}$$

$\mathsf{p} \leftarrow \mathsf{Pgen}(1^\lambda); \underline{(\mathsf{lpar},\mathsf{ltrap}) \leftarrow \mathsf{setup.ltrap}(\mathsf{p})}; \underline{\underline{(\mathsf{rpk},\mathsf{td}) \leftarrow \mathsf{K}_{\mathsf{rpk}}(\mathsf{lpar})}};$

$\left(\boxed{\mathsf{lpar}},\mathbf{x}\right) \leftarrow \mathcal{A}\left(\boxed{\mathsf{p}};\underline{\mathsf{lpar}};\underline{\underline{\mathsf{rpk}}}\right); (\mathsf{hp},\mathsf{hk}) \leftarrow \mathsf{kgen}\left(\mathsf{lpar}\underline{\underline{,\mathsf{rpk}}};\mathbf{x}\right);$

$\mathsf{H}_0 \leftarrow \mathsf{hash}\left(\mathsf{lpar}\underline{\underline{,\mathsf{rpk}}};\mathsf{hk},\mathbf{x}\right); \mathsf{H}_1 \leftarrow_{\$} \mathsf{HashSet}; b \leftarrow_{\$} \{0,1\}; b' \leftarrow \mathcal{A}(\mathsf{hp},\mathsf{H}_b);$

$\text{if } \boxed{\mathsf{verpar}(\mathsf{lpar}) = 1 \wedge} b' = b \wedge \neg(\exists \mathbf{w} : \mathcal{R}_{\mathsf{lpar}}(\mathbf{x},\mathbf{w}) = 1)$

$\quad \textbf{then return } 1; \textbf{else return } 0; \textbf{fi}$

Fig. 2. Smoothness experiments in Definitions 1 to 3. The boxed/dashed-box/dotted-box part is only present in the boxed/dashed-boxed/dotted-boxed experiment.

in BPP. In Definitions 1 to 3, we postulate the existence of a deterministic algorithm simhash, such that for any $(\mathbf{x},\mathbf{w}) \in \mathcal{R}_{\mathsf{lpar}}$, $\mathsf{projhash}(\mathsf{lpar};\mathsf{hp},\mathbf{x},\mathbf{w}) = \mathsf{simhash}(\mathsf{lpar};\mathsf{hp},\mathbf{x})$. Here, simhash does not get either the RPK trapdoor td or hk (or even $\kappa(\mathsf{hk})$, where κ is a possibly hard-to-invert bijection) as an input.

As in the case of TSPHFs [10], we assume only computational smoothness. Moreover, in the definition of smoothness, we only consider honestly generated lpar, and consider security in the case when $\mathcal{A}$ does not have access to ltrap (and thus the definition is not restricted to witness-sampleable languages). All these changes only make our impossibility result stronger.

A *GL-SZKHF in the plain model* is a PHF together with new deterministic algorithms verpar, verhp and simhash defined as follows:

- verhp($\mathsf{lpar};\mathsf{hp},\mathbf{x}$) outputs 1 if hp is a valid projection key and 0 otherwise.
- verpar(lpar): outputs 1 if lpar is well-formed and 0 otherwise.
- simhash($\mathsf{lpar};\mathsf{hp},\mathbf{x}$) returns the trapdoor hash value of $\mathbf{x}$, given hp.

Definition 1. *A GL-SZKHF* $\mathsf{HF} = (\mathsf{Pgen}, \mathsf{setup.ltrap}, \mathsf{hashkg}, \mathsf{projkg}, \mathsf{hash}, \mathsf{projhash}, \mathsf{verhp}, \mathsf{verpar}, \mathsf{simhash})$ *in the plain model satisfies the following properties, for the experiments depicted in Figs. 1 to 3.*

$$\boxed{\mathsf{ZK}^{\mathsf{bb\text{-}plain}}_{\mathsf{HF},\mathcal{Z},\mathcal{A}}(\lambda)} \ / \ \boxed{\mathsf{PZK}^{\mathsf{bb\text{-}rpk}}_{\mathsf{HF},\mathcal{Z},\mathcal{A}}(\lambda)}$$

$\mathsf{p} \leftarrow \mathsf{Pgen}(1^\lambda); \mathsf{lpar} \leftarrow \mathsf{setup.lpar}(\mathsf{p});$

$(\mathsf{lpar}, \mathsf{st}_{\mathcal{Z}}) \leftarrow \mathcal{Z}(\mathsf{p}); (\mathsf{rpk}, \mathsf{td}) \leftarrow \mathsf{K}^{\mathsf{adv}}_{\mathsf{rpk}}(\mathsf{lpar}); (\mathsf{x}, \mathsf{w}) \leftarrow \mathcal{A}\left(\mathsf{lpar}; \mathsf{rpk}; \mathsf{st}_{\mathcal{Z}}\right);$

$(\mathsf{hp}, \mathsf{st}_{\mathcal{Z}}) \leftarrow \mathcal{Z}(\mathsf{p}, \mathsf{lpar}; \mathsf{x}); \mathsf{H}_0 \leftarrow \mathsf{projhash}\left(\mathsf{lpar}, \mathsf{rpk}; \mathsf{hp}, \mathsf{x}, \mathsf{w}\right);$

$\mathsf{H}_1 \leftarrow \mathsf{simhash}\left(\mathsf{lpar}, \mathsf{td}; \mathsf{hp}, \mathsf{x}\right); b \leftarrow_{\$} \{0,1\}; b' \leftarrow \mathcal{A}(\mathsf{p}, \mathsf{st}_{\mathcal{Z}}, \mathsf{hp}, \mathsf{H}_b);$

if $\mathsf{verpar}(\mathsf{lpar}) = 1 \wedge (\mathsf{x}, \mathsf{w}) \in \mathcal{R}_{\mathsf{lpar}} \wedge \mathsf{verhp}(\mathsf{lpar}; \mathsf{hp}, \mathsf{x}) = 1 \wedge b' = b;$
then return 1; else return 0; fi

$$\boxed{\mathsf{ZK}^{\mathsf{nbb\text{-}plain}}_{\mathsf{HF},\mathsf{AUX},\mathcal{Z},\mathsf{Ext}_{\mathcal{Z}},\mathcal{A}}(\lambda)} \ / \ \boxed{\mathsf{PZK}^{\mathsf{nbb\text{-}plain}}_{\mathsf{HF},\mathsf{AUX},\mathcal{Z},\mathsf{Ext}_{\mathcal{Z}},\mathcal{A}}(\lambda)}$$

$\mathsf{p} \leftarrow \mathsf{Pgen}(1^\lambda); r \leftarrow_{\$} \mathsf{RND}_\lambda(\mathcal{Z});$

$(\mathsf{lpar}, \mathsf{ltrap}) \leftarrow \mathsf{setup.ltrap}(\mathsf{p}); (\mathsf{lpar}, \mathsf{st}_{\mathcal{Z}}) \leftarrow \mathcal{Z}(\mathsf{p}; r);$

$(\mathsf{x}, \mathsf{w}) \leftarrow \mathcal{A}\left(\mathsf{lpar}; \mathsf{st}_{\mathcal{Z}}\right); \mathsf{aux} \leftarrow \mathsf{AUX}(\mathsf{lpar}, \mathsf{x});$

$(\mathsf{hp}, \mathsf{st}_{\mathcal{Z}}) \leftarrow \mathcal{Z}\left(\mathsf{p}, \mathsf{lpar}; \mathsf{x}, \mathsf{aux}; r\right); \kappa(\mathsf{hk}) \leftarrow \mathsf{Ext}_{\mathcal{Z}}(\mathsf{p}, \mathsf{lpar}; \mathsf{x}, \mathsf{aux}; r);$

$\mathsf{H}_0 \leftarrow \mathsf{projhash}(\mathsf{lpar}; \mathsf{hp}, \mathsf{x}, \mathsf{w}); \mathsf{H}_1 \leftarrow \mathsf{simhash}(\mathsf{lpar}, \kappa(\mathsf{hk}); \mathsf{hp}, \mathsf{x});$

$b \leftarrow_{\$} \{0,1\}; b' \leftarrow \mathcal{A}(\mathsf{p}, \mathsf{st}_{\mathcal{Z}}, \mathsf{hp}, \mathsf{H}_b);$

if $\mathsf{verpar}(\mathsf{lpar}) = 1 \wedge (\mathsf{x}, \mathsf{w}) \in \mathcal{R}_{\mathsf{lpar}} \wedge \mathsf{verhp}(\mathsf{lpar}; \mathsf{hp}, \mathsf{x}) = 1 \wedge b' = b;$
then return 1; else return 0; fi

Fig. 3. (Persistent) zero-knowledge experiments in Definitions 1 to 3. The boxed/dashed-box/dotted-box part is only present in boxed/dashed-boxed/dotted-boxed experiments. Also, gray background marks differences compared to $\mathsf{ZK}^{\mathsf{bb\text{-}plain}}_{\mathsf{HF},\mathcal{Z},\mathcal{A}}(\lambda)$. (Color figure online)

Perfect completeness: *for all* λ, *PPT* $\mathcal{A}$, $\Pr[\mathsf{Complete}^{\mathsf{plain}}_{\mathsf{HF},\mathcal{A}}(\lambda) = 1] = 1$.

Computational (blackbox) smoothness: $\forall$ *PPT* $\mathcal{A}$, $\Pr[\mathsf{Smooth}^{\mathsf{bb\text{-}plain}}_{\mathsf{HF},\mathcal{A}}(\lambda) = 1] \approx_\lambda \frac{1}{2}$. *SZKHF* is statistically smooth *if this holds for all unbounded* $\mathcal{A}$.

Composable (blackbox) ZK: $\forall$ *PPT subverters* $\mathcal{Z}$, *unbounded* $\mathcal{A}$, $\Pr[\mathsf{ZK}^{\mathsf{bb\text{-}plain}}_{\mathsf{HF},\mathcal{Z},\mathcal{A}}(\lambda) = 1] \approx_\lambda \frac{1}{2}$.

(Recall that p is a deterministic function of λ.) Note that unbounded $\mathcal{A}$ creates (x, w) and only x is passed to bounded subverter $\mathcal{Z}$; this is necessary since in the case of GL-SZKHF, hp can depend on x. We do not allow $\mathcal{A}$ to transmit any other information. We consider $\mathcal{A}$ only to be successful if $(\mathsf{x}, \mathsf{w}) \in \mathcal{R}_{\mathsf{lpar}}$. Sadly, it is easy to show that Definition 1 can only be satisfied for $\mathcal{L}_{\mathsf{lpar}} \in \mathsf{BPP}$.

Lemma 1. *Let* HF *be a computationally smooth and composable ZK GL-SZKHF in the plain model for* $\mathcal{L}_{\mathsf{lpar}}$ *under blackbox assumptions. Then* $\mathcal{L}_{\mathsf{lpar}} \in \mathsf{BPP}$.

This lemma is a corollary of Theorem 1 from Sect. 5, but for the sake of completeness, we will next give a direct proof. A simple modification of the proof also shows the impossibility of KV-SZKHFs in the plain model.

Proof. Let HF be a computationally-smooth and composable ZK GL-SZKHF in the plain model for $\mathcal{L}_{1par}$. We describe $\mathcal{B}$, the BPP adversary for deciding $\mathcal{L}_{1par}$ as follows:

$$\boxed{\begin{array}{l} \mathcal{B}(1par, x) \\ \hline (hp, hk) \leftarrow kgen(1par; x); b_{\mathcal{A}} \leftarrow_\$ \{0,1\}; \\ H_0 \leftarrow hash(1par; hk, x); H_1 \leftarrow simhash(1par; hp, x); \\ \text{if } H_0 = H_1 \text{ then } b' \leftarrow 0; \text{else } b' \leftarrow 1; \text{fi} \\ \text{return } b'; \end{array}}$$

The challenger $\mathcal{C}$ of the BPP-decision game samples $p \leftarrow Pgen(1^\lambda)$, $1par \leftarrow$ setup.1par(p), $b \leftarrow_\$ \{0,1\}$, $x_0 \leftarrow_\$ \mathcal{L}_{1par}$, $x_1 \leftarrow_\$ \mathcal{X} \setminus \mathcal{L}_{1par}$. For $x \leftarrow x_b$, $\mathcal{C}$ sends $(1par; x)$ to $\mathcal{B}$ who returns b'.

The soundness of $\mathcal{B}$ follows directly from the computational-smoothness of HF. For any $x_b \notin \mathcal{L}_{1par}$, $\mathcal{B}$ will output $b' = 1$ with probability at least $1 - \varepsilon_{sm}$. Also, the Sub-ZK property of the HF guarantees the completeness of $\mathcal{B}$. Thus:

$$\begin{aligned} \Pr[b' = b] &= \left(\Pr[b' = 0 | b = 0] + \Pr[b' = 1 | b = 1]\right)/2 \\ &= \Pr[H_0 = H_1 | x = x_0]/2 + \Pr[H_0 \neq H_1 | x = x_1]/2 \\ &\geq \tfrac{1}{2} + \tfrac{1-\varepsilon_{sm}}{2} = 1 - \tfrac{\varepsilon_{sm}}{2} . \end{aligned}$$

Thus, $\mathcal{B}$ has non-negligible advantage in deciding $\mathcal{L}_{1par}$.   □

4   Blackbox SZKHF in the RPK Model

Since blackbox SZKHFs are impossible in the plain model, we will next consider blackbox SZKHFs in the RPK model [6]. The following definition combines the security definitions of Sub-PAR QA-NIZKs in the BPK model [4] with these of TSPHFs [10]. We will first give the new definition and then explain the difference between the new definition and the definitions of [4] and [10].

A SZKHF in the RPK model is defined together with new algorithms K_{rpk}, verpar, verhp and simhash as follows.

- Pgen, setup.1trap are as before, except that setup.1trap obeys the rules of the RPK model. (See the description of K_{rpk} below.)
- verpar(1par): outputs 1 if 1par is well-formed and 0 otherwise.
- K_{rpk}(1par): takes an input 1par generated by setup.1trap and outputs a public key rpk together with a secret key sk. K_{rpk} can either generate sk herself or can, alternatively, verify that the owner of sk knows the secret key corresponding to rpk, [6]. In the latter case, K_{rpk} can be implemented as a stand-alone interactive zero-knowledge protocol where a party registers her public key rpk with an authority by additionally proving the knowledge of td := sk. In a security proof, td is then extracted by using (say) rewinding.

If the creator of rpk is untrusted, rpk is well-formed and its underlying sk is returned; however, there is no guarantee about the distribution of rpk or sk. The setup.ltrap algorithm works similarly, but with rpk being replaced with lpar and sk being replaced with ltrap. Thus, if the creator of lpar is untrusted, lpar is well-formed and its underlying ltrap is returned; however, there is no guarantee about the distribution of lpar or ltrap.

- hashkg, projkg, hash, and projhash are as usual but also take rpk as an input. To shorten notation, we will denote "hk ← hashkg(lpar, rpk); hp ← projkg(lpar, rpk; hk, x)" by "(hp, hk) ← kgen(lpar, rpk; x)".
- verhp(lpar, rpk; hp, x): outputs 1 if hp is a valid projection key and 0 otherwise.
- simhash(lpar; td, hp, x): returns the simulated (trapdoor) hash value of x, given an RPK trapdoor td and hp.

In applications where K_{rpk} is not trusted (like the definition of zero-knowledge in the RPK model), we denote the untrusted K_{rpk} as K_{rpk}^{adv}. As above, the output of K_{rpk}^{adv} will be well-formed (in particular, it will return a correct sk) but there will be no assumption about the distribution of rpk and K_{rpk}^{adv} may leak information about sk to other adversaries.

Definition 2. *A blackbox GL-SZKHF* HF = (Pgen, setup.ltrap, hashkg, projkg, hash, projhash) *in the RPK model must satisfy the following properties for some PPT* K_{rpk}, *deterministic polynomial-time* verpar, verhp *and* simhash, *and the experiments depicted in Figs. 1 to 3.*

Perfect completeness: *for any* λ *and PPT* $\mathcal{A}$, $\Pr[\mathsf{Complete}_{HF,\mathcal{A}}^{rpk}(\lambda) = 1] = 1$.

Computational (blackbox) smoothness: *for any PPT* K_{rpk}^{adv} *and* $\mathcal{A}$, $\Pr[\mathsf{Smooth}_{HF,\mathcal{A}}^{bb\text{-}rpk}(\lambda) = 1] \approx_{\lambda} \frac{1}{2}$. *SZKHF is statistically smooth if the same holds for all unbounded adversaries.*

Composable (blackbox) persistent ZK in the RPK model: *For any PPT* $\mathcal{Z}$ *and unbounded* $\mathcal{A}$, $\Pr[\mathsf{PZK}_{HF,\mathcal{Z},\mathcal{A}}^{bb\text{-}rpk}(\lambda) = 1] \approx_{\lambda} \frac{1}{2}$.

Comparison with Previous Work. Differently from [4], the definitions are for SPHFs and not for QA-NIZKs. Our definition is in the RPK model for a trusted public key, without a non-blackbox extractor of the secret key.

Moreover, since we want to avoid non-blackbox techniques, in the definition of smoothness, we assume that also lpar is generated according to the rules of the RPK model (that is, setup.ltrap returns lpar with a corresponding ltrap). This is motivated by the fact that existing TSPHF constructions [10] are given for witness-sampleable distributions, where ltrap is used in the smoothness proofs explicitly. We modify the way the witness-sampleable distribution is used according to the model. In the RPK model, the RPK-model setup algorithm returns ltrap. In the non-blackbox plain model of Sect. 5, we will assume the existence of an extractor that can extract ltrap. In both cases, ltrap will be used in the smoothness and persistent ZK security proofs, and we do not assume that ltrap is correctly distributed. As in [4], persistent zero-knowledge means zero-knowledge in the case when lpar is maliciously constructed.

On the other hand, [10] defined TSPHFs in the CRS model (where there exists a universally trusted third party that creates a CRS), while we use the significantly weaker RPK model. More importantly, we consider the case of maliciously created lpar; this seems to be a first in the existing SPHF literature. More precisely, we assume that both lpar and rpk are constructed according to the rules of the RPK model. We only considered honest lpar in Definition 1 since there we gave an impossibility result. In the RPK model, we are interested in a possibility result; thus, following [4], we consider persistent ZK.[4] We also use a language that immediately guarantees composability of SZKHFs. Finally, [10] used different terminology: what we call zero-knowledge was called soundness in [10]; however, it was called zero-knowledge in [9].

Abdolmaleki *et al.* [4] showed that in the case of QA-NIZKs, while ZK (with honestly chosen lpar) sounds to be a weaker definition than persistent ZK (with maliciously chosen lpar), this is actually not the case. More precisely, they constructed a contrived QA-NIZK argument system Π_{leaky} where one need ltrap to be able to simulate. In the case of persistent ZK, one can use a knowledge extractor (the use of which is explicitly allowed by their definition of persistent ZK) to obtain ltrap and then use ltrap to simulate. However, Π_{leaky} does not achieve ZK since a simulator does not have access to ltrap. In our definition of persistent ZK in the RPK model, there is no extractor and thus ZK follows from the persistent ZK. However, we will use an extractor in Sect. 5 and thus there we will define ZK and persistent ZK separately.

Finally, we emphasize that persistent ZK holds in the case the RPK is honestly created (and thus simhash has access to the secret key td) but lpar and hp are subverted. Thus, like TSPHFs, SZKHFs in the RPK model provide only partial answer to the problem of subversion. To solve the latter, in Sect. 5, we define Sub-ZK SZKHF (in the plain model).

Constructions. We give two construction of computationally-smooth blackbox SZKHF in the RPK model. The first construction is from HF_{dvs} in Fig. 4, by defining $\mathsf{rpk} = [\tau]_2$ and $\mathsf{hpf} = (\mathsf{hp}, \mathsf{hp}_{ver})$ for $\mathsf{hp}_{ver} = [\tau\boldsymbol{\alpha}^\top]_2$, such that the Eq. (2) holds. The second construction is based on TSPHF [10]. Note that both constructions are computationally-smooth SZKHF under the DDH assumption for witness-sampleable languages. We defer the constructions and their security proofs to the full version [3].

5   Sub-ZK SZKHF in the Plain Model

In Sect. 4, we defined SZKHF in the RPK model and gave a construction of computationally smooth blackbox SZKHF in this model. Now, we consider the second direction of weakening Definition 1, namely, that of using non-blackbox techniques. To this end, we modify the Sub-ZK definition of QA-NIZKs by

---

[4] We emphasize that proving ZK in the case of subverted lpar and hp is paramount in applications where both lpar and hp are generated by the verifier (the party who checks that the values of hash and projhash are equal).

Abdolmaleki *et al.* [4] to the case of SPHFs. To facilitate reading by readers who come from the SPHF background, we will first motivate the security definition.

Briefly, [4] defines QA-NIZKs in the Bare Public Key (BPK) model, assuming that the public key pk and possibly lpar are created by a malicious subverter $\mathcal{Z}$. They define Sub-PAR soundness (soundness even if both lpar and pk are maliciously created), Sub-ZK (ZK, even if pk is maliciously created), and persistent Sub-ZK (ZK, even if both lpar and pk are maliciously created).

According to [8], independently of how lpar was generated, one cannot get at the same time Sub-SND (subversion-soundness, soundness if pk is maliciously generated) and Sub-ZK. [4] constructed a Sub-PAR sound and persistent Sub-ZK QA-NIZK. Moreover, [4] noted that Sub-ZK (QA-)NIZK in the CRS model is the same as *no-auxiliary-string non-blackbox* (QA-)NIZK in the weak BPK model. The Sub-ZK definition of [4] is motivated by the fact that blackbox [5,28] and even auxiliary-string non-blackbox [22] (see also [4,29]) NIZK in the BPK model is impossible.

More precisely, a Sub-ZK QA-NIZK in the BPK model [4] guarantees that if a malicious subverter $\mathcal{Z}$ creates lpar and pk that are accepted by a verpar (lpar-verification) and PKV (public-key verification), respectively, then there exists a non-blackbox extractor $\mathsf{Ext}_{\mathcal{Z}}$ that extracts the secret key sk that corresponds to pk. After that, sk can be used to run the original CRS-model simulator Sim that works in the case pk is generated honestly. Hence, one obtains non-blackbox ZK.

Next, we consider Sub-ZK SZKHFs *in the plain model* that are motivated by QA-NIZKs in the BPK model. In the case of SZKHF, we have a hp instead of the pk, hk instead of sk, verhp instead of PKV, projhash instead of the prover, and simhash instead of the simulator. Intuitively, since in many applications, hp is generated by the SZKHF verifier (the party who checks that hash and projhash results in the same values), a Sub-ZK SZKHF works in the plain model, i.e., without any trust assumptions at all. This is a fundamental difference compared to Sub-ZK SNARKs and QA-NIZKs where one has to rely on some trust assumption due to the use of the BPK.

As in [4], we define an efficient lpar-verification algorithm verpar (denoted by PARV in [4]) which checks whether lpar is well-formed. Following the definition of SZKHFs in the RPK model (see 4), we allow one to extract a function $\kappa(\mathsf{hk})$ of hk instead of hk itself. In general, κ may be the identity or a one-way function, e.g., $\kappa(\mathsf{hk}) = [\mathsf{hk}]_2$. In the latter case, it may not be possible to efficiently recover hk from $\kappa(\mathsf{hk})$. Due to this, we require that $\mathsf{simhash}(\mathsf{lpar}; \kappa(\mathsf{hk}), \mathsf{hp}, \mathsf{x}) = \mathsf{hash}(\mathsf{lpar}; \mathsf{hk}, \mathsf{x})$ for all lpar, hk, and x.

By analogy to [4], we obtain Definition 3. It is a variant of the definition of Sub-ZK QA-NIZKs, with syntactic differences caused by differences between SPHFs and NIZKs. On top of it, the definition is for GL-SZKHFs, which means that in the definition of ZK, a subverted hp can depend on input x chosen by the adversary before hp itself is chosen. In comparison, QA-NIZKs are related to KV-SZKHFs where x depends on hp. Sub-ZK NIZK is impossible in the plain model, [8]. On the other hand, as we will show in Sect. 6, Sub-ZK SZKHFs are possible in the plain model. We define separately auxiliary-string and no-auxiliary-string non-blackbox ZK in the plain model; this is motivated by Theorem 1 that states that the former is impossible for languages not in BPP. In the case of auxiliary-string non-blackbox ZK, we allow the auxiliary input to be generated by a PPT algorithm AUX called *auxiliary string machine* which takes the language parameter lpar as input and returns aux.

Definition 3. *A (no-)auxiliary-string non-blackbox zero knowledge GL-SZKHF* HF = (Pgen, setup.ltrap, hashkg, projkg, hash, projhash) *in the plain model satisfies the following properties for deterministic polynomial-time algorithms* verpar, verhp, simhash, κ, *and the experiments depicted in Figs. 1 to 3.*

Perfect completeness: *for any* λ, *PPT* $\mathcal{A}$, $\Pr[\mathsf{Complete}^{\mathsf{plain}}_{\mathsf{HF},\mathcal{A}}(\lambda) = 1] = 1$.

Computational Sub-PAR (non-blackbox) smoothness: *for any PPT* $\mathcal{A}$, $\Pr[\mathsf{Smooth}^{\mathsf{nbb\text{-}plain}}_{\mathsf{HF},\mathcal{A}}(\lambda) = 1] \approx_\lambda \frac{1}{2}$. *SZKHF is statistically Sub-PAR smooth if the same holds for any unbounded* $\mathcal{A}$.

Composable κ-extractable (no-)auxiliary-string non-blackbox ZK: *For any PPT subverter* $\mathcal{Z}$, *there exists a PPT extractor* $\mathsf{Ext}_\mathcal{Z}$, *s.t. for any PPT auxiliary string machine* AUX *and unbounded* $\mathcal{A}$, $\Pr[\mathsf{ZK}^{\mathsf{nbb\text{-}plain}}_{\mathsf{HF},\mathsf{AUX},\mathcal{Z},\mathsf{Ext}_\mathcal{Z},\mathcal{A}}(\lambda) = 1] \approx_\lambda \frac{1}{2}$. *In the no-auxiliary-string case,* AUX *always outputs* ϵ *(the empty string).*

Composable κ-extractable (no-)auxiliary-string non-blackbox persistent ZK: *For any PPT subverter* $\mathcal{Z}$, *there exists a PPT extractor* $\mathsf{Ext}_\mathcal{Z}$, *s.t. for any PPT auxiliary string machine* AUX *and unbounded* $\mathcal{A}$, $\Pr[\mathsf{PZK}^{\mathsf{nbb\text{-}plain}}_{\mathsf{HF},\mathsf{AUX},\mathcal{Z},\mathsf{Ext}_\mathcal{Z},\mathcal{A}}(\lambda) = 1] \approx_\lambda \frac{1}{2}$. *In the no-auxiliary-string case,* AUX *always outputs* ϵ.

HF is *extractable* if κ is the identity function; then, for $(\mathbf{x},\mathbf{w}) \in \mathcal{R}_{\mathsf{lpar}}$, simhash(lpar; hk, x) = projhash(lpar; hp, x, w). Differently from F-extractability [7] that limits applications compared to just extractability, we use κ-extractability only in the Sub-ZK proof and thus it has no negative effect.

Abdolmaleki *et al.* [4] defined separately ZK and persistent ZK for QA-NIZK, and showed that ZK does not follow from persistent ZK since in the latter one can use a knowledge assumption to extract ltrap that is not available in the former. The same problem holds in the case of SZKHFs, and thus in the security proofs, one has to prove separately that a Sub-ZK SZKHF satisfies both ZK and persistent ZK.

Motivated by applications in SNARKs, Abdolmaleki *et al.* [4] defined the notion of knowledge-soundness in the case $\mathcal{L}_{\mathsf{lpar}} = \mathcal{X}$ is the trivial language. One can similarly define knowledge-smoothness when $\mathcal{L}_{\mathsf{lpar}} = \mathcal{X}$; we decided not to do it since we already have too many new definitions.

Impossibility of Auxiliary-String SZKHF in the Plain Model. Goldreich and Oren [22, Thm. 4.4] proved that two-round non-uniform auxiliary-string computational zero-knowledge proof (and also argument) systems do not exist for languages outside BPP. We modify Thm. 4.4 of [22] to prove a similar result about GL-SZKHFs. Note that this result is strictly stronger than Lemma 1.

Motivated by this connection, we show in a parallel work that no-auxiliary-string non-blackbox GL-SZKHFs and quasi-adaptive two-message zero-knowledge (QA-2MZK) arguments are in one-to-one correspondence. A similar result holds in the case of blackbox and no-auxiliary-string non-blackbox GL-SZKHFs and QA-2MZK arguments. We omit further discussion.

Theorem 1. *Let* HF *be an auxiliary-string non-blackbox ZK GL-SZKHF in the plain model for* $\mathcal{L}_{\text{lpar}}$. *Then* $\mathcal{L}_{\text{lpar}} \in$ BPP *for all* lpar.

Proof. Let HF be a computationally-smooth κ-extractable auxiliary-string non-blackbox GL-SZKHF in the plain model for $\mathcal{L}_{\text{lpar}}$. The execution of HF can be seen as a question hp from the verifier, who has access to the randomness hk, and an answer pH $\leftarrow$ projhash(lpar; w, hp, x) by the prover. The prover's ability to provide an answer pH such that pH = hash(lpar; hk, x) is seen as a sufficient evidence that $x \in \mathcal{L}_{\text{lpar}}$. The perfect completeness property of HF ensures that if $x \in \mathcal{L}_{\text{lpar}}$ then the prover will be able to output pH for any hp $\leftarrow$ projkg(lpar; hk, x). The computational-smoothness guarantees that if $x \notin \mathcal{L}_{\text{lpar}}$ then given only hp $\leftarrow$ projkg(lpar; hk, x), no PPT prover can distinguish H $\leftarrow$ hash(lpar; hk, x) from random for any but a negligible fraction of the hk's.

The idea of the proof is to run the simhash algorithm as a means of generating pH. To be able to do it so that we could still rely on the computational-smoothness, it is essential to hide from the extractor Ext$_{\mathcal{Z}}$ the randomness used by the subverter $\mathcal{Z}$ when generating hp. This can be achieved by using the auxiliary string of the subverter as follows. Consider a subverter $\mathcal{Z}^*$ that, given a correctly generated projection key hpf as its auxiliary string, sets hp $\leftarrow$ hpf and outputs hp. Provided that the length of hpf is polynomial in the length of x, $\mathcal{Z}^*$ is clearly a PPT machine. Thus, by the ZK property, there exists an extractor Ext$_{\mathcal{Z}^*}$ that, given as input x and an auxiliary string hpf, outputs κ(hk) without knowing the randomness of hpf. Using Ext$_{\mathcal{Z}^*}$, we build a PPT adversary $\mathcal{B}$ that decides $\mathcal{L}_{\text{lpar}}$. On input x_b, $\mathcal{B}$ works as follows:

$\mathcal{B}(\text{lpar}; x_b)$ // $b = 0$ if $x \in \mathcal{L}_{\text{lpar}}$ and $b = 1$ if $x \notin \mathcal{L}_{\text{lpar}}$

---

hk $\leftarrow$ hashkg(lpar); hpf $\leftarrow$ projkg(lpar; hk, x_b);
$r \leftarrow_{\$} \text{RND}_\lambda(\mathcal{Z}^*)$; (hpf, st$_{\mathcal{Z}}$) $\leftarrow \mathcal{Z}^*$(ltrap; x_b, aux = hpf; r);
κ(hk) $\leftarrow$ Ext$_{\mathcal{Z}^*}$(ltrap; x_b, aux; r);
H $\leftarrow$ hash(lpar; hk, x_b); H$'$ $\leftarrow$ simhash(lpar, κ(hk); hpf, x_b);
if H = H$'$ **then** $b' \leftarrow 0$; **else** $b' \leftarrow 1$; **fi**
return b';

The soundness of $\mathcal{B}$ follows directly from the computational-smoothness of HF: if $x_b \notin \mathcal{L}_{\text{lpar}}$ and simhash is able to generate, with non-negligible probability, a hash value H$'$ such that H = H$'$, then a PPT adversary $\mathcal{A}$ using Ext$_{\mathcal{Z}^*}$ can trivially break the computational-smoothness property. Thus, for any $x_b \notin \mathcal{L}_{\text{lpar}}$, $\mathcal{B}$ will output $b' = 1$ with high probability $1 - \varepsilon_{sm}$. Also, the ZK property of the HF guarantees the completeness of $\mathcal{B}$. Thus:

$$\Pr[b = b'] = (\Pr[b' = 0|b = 0] + \Pr[b' = 1|b = 1])/2 = \tfrac{1}{2} + \tfrac{1 - \varepsilon_{sm}}{2} = 1 - \tfrac{\varepsilon_{sm}}{2} \ .$$

Thus, $\mathcal{B}$ has non-negligible advantage in deciding $\mathcal{L}_{1\text{par}}$. $\square$

6   Constructing SZKHF

In Sect. 3.1, we proved that blackbox SZKHFs in the plain model are restricted to languages in BPP. Thus, one must either use a preprocessing model (as defined in [10]) or rely on some non-blackbox technique (as defined in Sect. 5). As we already mentioned, the use of the CRS model as in [10] (or the weaker RPK model, as in 4) is not completely satisfactory since one essentially shifts the problem of protecting against a subverted hp-generator to the problem of protecting against a subverted crs/pk-generator. As always in cryptography, the end goal is not to have any trust at all whenever possible.

We first recall the notion of DVS and the construction of SPHF from DVS. Next, we construct a Sub-ZK SZKHF in the plain model based on DVS-based SPHFs and prove its security based on a new assumption. We also present a Sub-ZK SZKHF in the plain model based on Benhamouda *et al.*'s TSPHFs [10] in the full version [3].

6.1   Preliminaries: Diverse Vector Space (DVS)

A DVS [1,9,10] is essentially a representation of a language $\mathcal{L} \subseteq \mathcal{X}$ as a subspace $\hat{\mathcal{L}}$ of some vector space. Let $\mathcal{R}_{\mathcal{L}} = \{(\mathbf{x}, \mathbf{w})\}$ be a relation with $\mathcal{L} = \{\mathbf{x} : \exists \mathbf{w}, (\mathbf{x}, \mathbf{w}) \in \mathcal{R}_{\mathcal{L}}\}$. Let p be system parameters, including say the description of a bilinear group. Let $\boldsymbol{\Gamma}_{1\text{par}}(\mathbf{x})$ be an $n \times k$ matrix, $\boldsymbol{\theta}_{1\text{par}}(\mathbf{x})$ an n-dimensional vector, and $\boldsymbol{\lambda}_{1\text{par}}(\mathbf{x}, \mathbf{w})$ a k-dimensional vector. A (pairing-based) DVS $\mathcal{V}$ is equal to $\mathcal{V} = (\mathsf{p}, \mathcal{X}, \mathcal{L}, \mathcal{R}_{\mathcal{L}}, n, k, \boldsymbol{\Gamma}, \boldsymbol{\theta}, \boldsymbol{\lambda})$. The matrix $\boldsymbol{\Gamma}_{1\text{par}}(\mathbf{x})$ can depend on $\mathbf{x}$ (in this case, we say that we have a GL-DVS) or not (KV-DVS). Moreover, different coefficients of $\boldsymbol{\theta}_{1\text{par}}(\mathbf{x})$, $\boldsymbol{\Gamma}_{1\text{par}}(\mathbf{x})$, and $\boldsymbol{\lambda}_{1\text{par}}(\mathbf{x}, \mathbf{w})$ can belong to different algebraic structures (most commonly, given a bilinear group $\mathsf{p} = (p, \mathbb{G}_1, \mathbb{G}_2, \mathbb{G}_T, \hat{e})$, either to $\mathbb{Z}_p$, $\mathbb{G}_1$, $\mathbb{G}_2$, or $\mathbb{G}_T$) as long as the equation $\boldsymbol{\theta}_{1\text{par}}(\mathbf{x}) = \boldsymbol{\Gamma}_{1\text{par}}(\mathbf{x}) \cdot \boldsymbol{\lambda}_{1\text{par}}(\mathbf{x}, \mathbf{w})$ is "well-typed". That is, an equation like $\left(\begin{smallmatrix} [\theta_1]_T \\ [\theta_2]_1 \end{smallmatrix} \right) = \left(\begin{smallmatrix} [\Gamma_{11}]_T & [\Gamma_{12}]_2 \\ [\Gamma_{21}]_1 & \Gamma_{22} \end{smallmatrix} \right) \left(\begin{smallmatrix} \lambda_1 \\ [\lambda_2]_1 \end{smallmatrix} \right)$ holds. Note that $\mathcal{L}_{1\text{par}} = \{\mathbf{x} : \exists \boldsymbol{\lambda}, \boldsymbol{\theta}_{1\text{par}}(\mathbf{x}) = \boldsymbol{\Gamma}_{1\text{par}}(\mathbf{x}) \cdot \boldsymbol{\lambda}\}$. We omit the subscript 1par if it is clear from the context.

A DVS $\mathcal{V}$ satisfies the following properties [9]: (i) *coordinate-independence of groups:* the group in which each coordinate of $\boldsymbol{\theta}(\mathbf{x})$ lies is independent of $\mathbf{x}$. (ii) *perfect completeness:* for any $(\mathbf{x}, \mathbf{w}) \in \mathcal{R}_{\mathcal{L}}$, $\boldsymbol{\theta}(\mathbf{x}) = \boldsymbol{\Gamma}(\mathbf{x}) \cdot \boldsymbol{\lambda}(\mathbf{x}, \mathbf{w})$. (iii) *statistical ε-soundness:* $\forall \mathbf{x} \in \mathcal{X}_{1\text{par}} \setminus \mathcal{L}_{1\text{par}}$, $\Pr[\boldsymbol{\theta}(\mathbf{x}) \in \text{colspace}(\boldsymbol{\Gamma}(\mathbf{x}))] \leq \varepsilon$.

6.2   Preliminaries: DVS-Based SPHFs

Benhamouda *et al.* [9,10] defined diverse vector spaces (DVSs). We will not formally define DVSs (see 6.1), however, we need the following construction of DVS-based GL-SPHFs from [10]. Essentially, a DVS-based GL-SPHF is defined for any algebraic language (see Sect. 2) $\mathcal{L}_{1\text{par}}$, where $1\text{par} = (\boldsymbol{\Gamma}, \boldsymbol{\theta}, \boldsymbol{\lambda})$. Recall that in the case of GL-SPHFs, $\boldsymbol{\Gamma}$ and $\boldsymbol{\theta}$ are affine maps of $\mathbf{x}$, with $\boldsymbol{\Gamma}(\mathbf{x}) \in \mathbb{Z}_p^{n \times k}$, $n > k$. In a DVS-based GL-SPHF for $\mathcal{L}_{\mathtt{lpar}}$, one first samples a hashing key $\mathsf{hk} = \boldsymbol{\alpha} \leftarrow_{\mathtt{s}} \mathbb{Z}_p^n$ and then defines the projection key as $\mathsf{hp} = [\boldsymbol{\gamma}(\mathbf{x})]_1 \leftarrow \mathsf{projkg}(\mathtt{lpar}; \mathsf{hk}) = \boldsymbol{\alpha}^\top [\boldsymbol{\Gamma}]_1 \in \mathbb{G}_1^{1 \times k}$. For a witness $\mathbf{w} \in \mathbb{Z}_p^k$, the projection hash is $\mathsf{pH} \leftarrow \mathsf{projhash}(\mathtt{lpar}; \mathsf{hp}, \mathbf{x}, \mathbf{w}) = [\boldsymbol{\gamma}(\mathbf{x})]_1 \cdot \boldsymbol{\lambda}(\mathbf{x}, \mathbf{w}) = \boldsymbol{\alpha}^\top [\boldsymbol{\Gamma}(\mathbf{x})]_1 \boldsymbol{\lambda}(\mathbf{x}, \mathbf{w}) \in \mathbb{G}_1$. For an input $\mathbf{x} = [\boldsymbol{\theta}]_1 = [\boldsymbol{\Gamma}(\mathbf{x})]_1 \boldsymbol{\lambda}(\mathbf{x}, \mathbf{w}) \in \mathbb{G}_1^n$, the hash is $\mathsf{H} \leftarrow \mathsf{hash}(\mathtt{lpar}; \mathsf{hk}, \mathbf{x}) = \mathsf{hk}^\top \cdot \mathbf{x} = \boldsymbol{\alpha}^\top [\boldsymbol{\Gamma}(\mathbf{x})]_1 \boldsymbol{\lambda}(\mathbf{x}, \mathbf{w}) \in \mathbb{G}_1$. Thus, if $\mathbf{x} \in \mathcal{L}_{\mathtt{lpar}}$, then $\mathsf{H} = \mathsf{pH}$. See [9,10] for the proof of (information-theoretic) smoothness.

6.3   New DVS-Based SZKHF

Recall that a projection key hp is valid if there exists a hk such that $\mathsf{hp} = \mathsf{projkg}(\mathtt{lpar}; \mathsf{hk})$. Consider a DVS-based SPHF HF with $\mathsf{HashSet} = \mathbb{G}_1$ in the plain model, as defined in 6.1. Since $\boldsymbol{\Gamma}(\mathbf{x}) \in \mathbb{Z}_p^{n \times k}$ with $n > k$, it means that all hp-s are valid. Thus, we must add to the projection key an additional sub-key $\mathsf{hp}_{\mathsf{ver}}$ that corresponds to similar auxiliary data $\mathtt{crs}_{\mathsf{CV}}$ in [2], such that $\mathsf{hpf} = (\mathsf{hp}, \mathsf{hp}_{\mathsf{ver}})$ fixes uniquely the vector $\boldsymbol{\alpha} \in \mathbb{Z}_p^n$, such that $\mathsf{hp} = \boldsymbol{\alpha}^\top [\boldsymbol{\Gamma}(\mathbf{x})]_1$, and then make it possible to verify that $\mathsf{hp} = \boldsymbol{\alpha}^\top [\boldsymbol{\Gamma}(\mathbf{x})]_1$.

One has to be careful in defining $\mathsf{hp}_{\mathsf{ver}}$. For example, a simple approach is to set $\mathsf{hp}_{\mathsf{ver}} = [\boldsymbol{\alpha}]_2$; after that one can verify hp by just checking that $\mathsf{hp} \bullet [1]_2 = [\boldsymbol{\alpha}]_2^\top \bullet [\boldsymbol{\Gamma}(\mathbf{x})]_1$. Unfortunately, this breaks computational-smoothness, as anybody given an alleged hash H of $\mathbf{x}$, can check whether $\mathsf{H} \bullet [1]_2 = [\boldsymbol{\alpha}]_2^\top \bullet [\boldsymbol{\theta}(\mathbf{x})]_1 = \mathsf{pH} \bullet [1]_2 \in \mathbb{G}_T$. The latter can be done given only $\mathtt{lpar}$, $(\mathsf{hp}, \mathsf{hp}_{\mathsf{ver}})$ and $\mathbf{x}$. To overcome this issue, we use the idea from [10] to mask $[\boldsymbol{\alpha}]_2$ by multiplying it with a random integer $\tau \in \mathbb{Z}_p^*$. Intuitively, for the construction to be secure, τ has to be chosen so that from

$$\tau(\boldsymbol{\alpha}^\top \boldsymbol{\Gamma}(\mathbf{x}) - \boldsymbol{\gamma}) = \mathbf{0}_{1 \times k} \qquad (2)$$

it follows $\boldsymbol{\alpha}^\top \boldsymbol{\Gamma}(\mathbf{x}) = \boldsymbol{\gamma}$. This holds if $\tau \neq 0$. Differently from [10], we however add the corresponding elements to the projection key (chosen by a potentially malicious verifier) and not to the CRS (chosen by a universally trusted authority).

Moreover, differently from [10], we allow $\mathtt{lpar}$ to be chosen maliciously. Recall that for this, there must exist an efficient verpar algorithm that verifies that $\mathtt{lpar}$ is well-formed. Such efficient verpar exists only for certain distributions $\mathcal{D}_{\mathsf{p}}$; see [4] for discussion. In what follows, we assume that an efficient verpar exists.

The new Sub-ZK SZKHF $\mathsf{HF}_{\mathsf{dvs}}$ with $\mathsf{HashSet} = \mathbb{G}_T$ is depicted in Fig. 4. Next, we define the security assumptions needed to prove its security, and then follow with the security proof. While the construction is inspired by [10], the security assumptions and the proof are inspired by [4].

6.4   New Security Assumptions

In [10], the DDH adversary $\mathcal{B}$ defined in the computational-smoothness reduction for tsphf relies on the witness-sampleability of $\mathcal{D}_{\mathsf{p}}$ to obtain $([\boldsymbol{\Gamma}(\mathbf{x})]_1, \boldsymbol{\Gamma}(\mathbf{x}))$ sampled from $\mathcal{D}_{\mathsf{p}}'$. Since we prove Sub-PAR smoothness (i.e., smoothness even in the

setup.ltrap(p): return lpar ←$ HF.setup.lpar(p);
hashkg(lpar): return hk := α ←$ HF.hashkg(lpar);
projkg(lpar; hk, x): hp := $[\gamma]_1$ ← HF.projkg(lpar; hk, x); τ ←$ $\mathbb{Z}_p^*$; hp_{ver} ←
    $[\tau, \tau\alpha^\top]_2$; return hpf ← (hp, hp_{ver});   // $hp_{ver} \in \mathbb{G}_2^{n+1}$;
verpar(lpar = $[\Gamma(x)]_1$): check whether lpar is well-formed.
verhp(lpar = $[\Gamma(x)]_1$; hpf = (hp, hp_{ver}), x): check that $[\tau]_2 \in \mathbb{G}_2 \setminus \{1_{\mathbb{G}_2}\}$ and
    $[\tau\alpha^\top]_2 \bullet [\Gamma(x)]_1 = [\tau]_2 \bullet [\gamma]_1$.
hash(lpar; hk, x): return HF.hash(lpar; hk, x) $\bullet [1]_2$;
projhash(lpar; hpf = (hp, hp_{ver}), x, w): return HF.projhash(lpar; hp, x, w) $\bullet [1]_2$;
simhash(lpar; κ(hk) = $\kappa(\alpha)$), x = $[\theta]_1$): return $\chi(\kappa(\alpha))^\top \cdot [\theta]_1$;

Fig. 4. The GL-SZKHF HF_{dvs}. Here, HF is any DVS-based SPHF HF with HashSet = $\mathbb{G}_1$. We denote the procedures of HF by prepending their names with HF as in HF.hashkg. Moreover, $\chi(a) = [a]_2$ if $\kappa = id$ and $\chi(a) = a$ if $\kappa = [\cdot]_2$.

case $[\Gamma(x)]_1$ is maliciously generated), we cannot rely on witness-sampleability. Thus, we need an alternative way to extract $\Gamma(x)$. We follow an idea of [4]. Namely, in the proof of Sub-PAR smoothness, $\mathcal{B}$ obtains $[\Gamma(x)]_1 \leftarrow \mathcal{A}(p)$ and then uses a *non-adaptive* discrete logarithm (DL) oracle to extract $\Gamma(x)$. Hence, instead of the DDH assumption (together with witness-sampleability) that was used in [10], we prove (non-blackbox) Sub-PAR smoothness under the following new non-falsifiable, non-adaptive interactive DDH^{dl} assumption.

The DDH^{dl} assumption is an non-adaptive X^Y-type interactive assumption, where the assumption X is assumed to hold even if the adversary is given a non-adaptive (i.e., before the challenge X is chosen), access to an oracle that solves the assumption Y. Several X^Y assumptions are known in the literature, see, e.g., [4,21,26]. Some X^Y assumptions (e.g., the ones used in [26]) are falsifiable; however, DDH^{dl} is non-falsifiable.

Let $\iota \in \{1, 2\}$. The DDH$_{\mathbb{G}_\iota}^{dl}$ assumption states that DDH in $\mathbb{G}_\iota$ remains intractable even if the adversary is given a non-adaptive access to the DL oracle. More precisely, *the* DDH$_{\mathbb{G}_\iota}^{dl}$ *assumption* holds relative to Pgen, if $\forall$ PPT $\mathcal{A}$,

$$\Pr\left[\begin{array}{l} p \leftarrow \text{Pgen}(1^\lambda); st \leftarrow \mathcal{A}^{dl(\cdot)}(p); x, y, z \leftarrow_\$ \mathbb{Z}_p; w_0 \leftarrow xy; w_1 \leftarrow z; \\ b \leftarrow_\$ \{0, 1\}; b^* \leftarrow \mathcal{A}(p, st, [x, y, w_b]_\iota) : b = b^* \end{array}\right] \approx_\lambda 0 \ .$$

New knowledge assumptions. Let HF = HF_{dvs} be the new SZKHF. To prove ZK and persistent ZK properties in our construction, we need to rely on two new assumptions X-SZKHF-KE, for $X \in \{\mathcal{D}_p, \text{SUBPAR}\}$. We first define these assumptions. In Theorem 2, we prove they hold in the AGM [17]. The knowledge assumptions are to postulate that given a valid hpf, one can efficiently extract td = κ(hk). More precisely, SUBPAR-SZKHF-KE (resp., $\mathcal{D}_p$-SZKHF-KE) assumption is the core of the persistent ZK proof (resp., the ZK proof) of the DVS-based SZKHF construction in Theorem 3. There, we assume that if an adversary $\mathcal{A}$ outputs a language parameter lpar accepted by verpar and a hpf

$$\mathsf{Exp}_{\mathsf{HF},\mathcal{Z},\mathsf{Ext}_{\mathcal{Z}},\mathcal{A}}^{\mathcal{D}_\mathsf{p}\text{-}\mathsf{SZKHF\text{-}KE}}(\lambda) \;/\; \mathsf{Exp}_{\mathsf{HF},\mathcal{Z},\mathsf{Ext}_{\mathcal{Z}},\mathcal{A}}^{\mathsf{SUBPAR\text{-}SZKHF\text{-}KE}}(\lambda)$$

$\mathsf{p} \leftarrow \mathsf{Pgen}(1^\lambda); r \leftarrow_\$ \mathsf{RND}_\lambda(\mathcal{Z});$

$(\mathtt{lpar}, \mathtt{ltrap}) \leftarrow \mathsf{setup.lpar}(\mathsf{p}); (\mathtt{lpar}, \mathtt{st}_{\mathcal{Z}}) \leftarrow \mathcal{Z}(\mathsf{p}; r); (\mathbf{x}, \mathbf{w}) \leftarrow \mathcal{A}\left(\mathtt{lpar}; \mathtt{st}_{\mathcal{Z}}\right);$

$(\mathtt{hpf}, \mathtt{st}_{\mathcal{Z}}) \leftarrow \mathcal{Z}\left(\mathsf{p}, \mathtt{lpar}; \mathbf{x}, r\right); \kappa(\mathsf{hk}) \leftarrow \mathsf{Ext}_{\mathcal{Z}}\left(\mathsf{p}, \mathtt{lpar}; \mathbf{x}, r\right);$

if $\mathsf{verpar}(\mathtt{lpar}) = 1 \wedge \mathsf{verhp}(\mathtt{lpar}; \mathtt{hpf}, \mathbf{x}) = 1 \wedge (\mathbf{x}, \mathbf{w}) \in \mathcal{R}_{\mathtt{lpar}} \wedge$
  $\mathsf{simhash}(\mathtt{lpar}; \mathtt{hpf}, \mathbf{x}, \kappa(\mathsf{hk})) \neq \mathsf{projhash}(\mathtt{lpar}; \mathtt{hpf}, \mathbf{x}, \mathbf{w});$
then return 1; else return 0; fi

Fig. 5. SZKHF-KE experiments in Definition 4. The dotted-boxed/dashed-box part is only present in dotted-boxed/dashed-boxed experiments.

accepted by verhp, then there exists an extractor $\mathsf{Ext}_{\mathcal{A}}$ that by knowing the secret coins of $\mathcal{A}$, returns $\mathtt{td} = \kappa(\mathsf{hk})$ where hk was used to compute hpf.

Like KWKE [4] is a tautological knowledge assumption for the Kiltz-Wee QA-NIZK [25], X-SZKHF-KE is tautological knowledge assumption for $\mathsf{HF}_{\mathsf{dvs}}$. Nevertheless, KWKE has already found uses behind its original application in [4], and we hope the same will happen to X-SZKHF-KE.

Definition 4. *Let κ be a one-to-one map. Fix $n > k \geq 1$ and a distribution $\mathcal{D}_\mathsf{p}$. Let $\mathsf{HF} = \mathsf{HF}_{\mathsf{dvs}}$ be the new GL-SZKHF. The X-SZKHF-KE assumption for $X \in \{\mathcal{D}_\mathsf{p}, \mathsf{SUBPAR}\}$ holds relative to Pgen for any $\mathsf{p} \in \mathrm{im}(\mathsf{Pgen}(1^\lambda))$ and PPT adversary $\mathcal{A}$ and PPT subverter $\mathcal{Z}$, there exists a PPT extractor $\mathsf{Ext}_{\mathcal{Z}}$, such that $\Pr[\mathsf{Exp}_{\mathsf{HF},\mathcal{Z},\mathsf{Ext}_{\mathcal{Z}},\mathcal{A}}^{\mathsf{X\text{-}SZKHF\text{-}KE}}(\lambda) = 1] \approx_\lambda 0$, where $\mathsf{Exp}_{\mathsf{HF},\mathcal{Z},\mathsf{Ext}_{\mathcal{Z}},\mathcal{A}}^{\mathsf{X\text{-}SZKHF\text{-}KE}}(\lambda)$ is depicted in Fig. 5.*

Theorem 2 (Security of X-SZKHF-KE). *Let κ be a one-to-one map. Fix $n > k \geq 1$. Then SUBPAR-SZKHF-KE and $\mathcal{D}_\mathsf{p}$-SZKHF-KE hold relative to Pgen in the AGM.*

We refer to the full version [3] for a brief overview of the algebraic group model (AGM).

Proof. **(1: SUBPAR-SZKHF-KE.)** The proof is inspired by that of the KWKE assumption in [4]. However, the assumption itself is different. Moreover, we prove it in the standard AGM of [17] instead of the HAK assumptions introduced in [27]. This enables us to simplify the proof significantly.

Let $\mathcal{A}$ be a SUBPAR-SZKHF-KE adversary that, given public parameters p, and randomness $r \leftarrow_\$ \mathsf{RND}_\lambda(\mathcal{A})$ as input, outputs $\mathtt{lpar} = [\Gamma(\mathbf{x})]_1$ and hpf, s.t. with probability $\epsilon_{\mathcal{A}}$, $\mathsf{verhp}(\mathtt{lpar}; \mathtt{hpf}, \mathbf{x}) = 1$ and $\mathsf{verpar}(\mathtt{lpar}) = 1$. Denote $\Delta := \tau \alpha^\top \in \mathbb{Z}_p^{1 \times n}$. Let $\mathsf{verhp}(\mathtt{lpar}; \mathtt{hpf}, \mathbf{x}) = 1$, i.e., $[\Delta]_2 \bullet [\Gamma(\mathbf{x})]_1 = [\tau]_2 \bullet [\gamma]_1 \in \mathbb{G}_T^{1 \times k}$. Let $\mathsf{Ext}_{\mathcal{A}}^{\mathsf{agm}}$ be the extractor, existence of which is guaranteed by the AGM. Figure 6 depicts the extractor $\mathsf{Ext}_{\mathcal{A}}$, who also emulates the oracle answers $[q_{\iota i}]_\iota$ for $i > 0$ to $\mathcal{A}$ in $\mathbb{G}_\iota$. $\mathsf{Ext}_{\mathcal{A}}^{\mathsf{agm}}$ extracts N_ι, such that

$$\left[\begin{matrix} \mathrm{vect}(\Gamma) \\ \gamma \end{matrix}\right]_1 = N_1 \left[\begin{matrix} 1 \\ q_1 \end{matrix}\right]_1 \in \mathbb{G}_1^{nk+k}, \qquad \left[\begin{matrix} \tau \\ \mathrm{vect}(\Delta) \end{matrix}\right]_2 = N_2 \left[\begin{matrix} 1 \\ q_2 \end{matrix}\right]_2 \in \mathbb{G}_2^{n+1}.$$

$$\boxed{\begin{array}{l}
\mathsf{Ext}_{\mathcal{A}}(\mathsf{p};r) \\
\hline
\boldsymbol{q}_1 \leftarrow \emptyset; \boldsymbol{q}_2 \leftarrow \emptyset; \xi_1 \leftarrow 0; \xi_2 \leftarrow 0; \\
([\boldsymbol{\Gamma}]_1, \mathsf{hpf}) \leftarrow \mathcal{A}(\mathsf{p};r); \\
\mathbf{if} \ \mathsf{verpar}(\mathsf{lpar}) = 0 \lor \mathsf{verhp}(\mathsf{lpar};\mathsf{hpf},\mathbf{x}) = 0 \ \mathbf{then} \ \mathbf{return} \ \bot; \mathbf{fi} \ ; \\
(\boldsymbol{N}_1, \boldsymbol{N}_2) \leftarrow \mathsf{Ext}_{\mathcal{A}}^{\mathsf{agm}}(\mathsf{p};r); \text{Abort if this fails}; \\
\text{Compute } \tau, \boldsymbol{\Delta} \text{ from } \boldsymbol{N}_1, \boldsymbol{N}_2, \boldsymbol{q}_1, \boldsymbol{q}_2; \\
\mathbf{return} \ \boldsymbol{\alpha} \leftarrow \tau^{-1}\boldsymbol{\Delta}; \\
O(\iota) \\
\hline
\xi_\iota \leftarrow \xi_\iota + 1; q_{\iota\xi_\iota} \leftarrow_{\$} \mathbb{Z}_p; \mathbf{return} \ [q_{\iota\xi_\iota}]_\iota;
\end{array}}$$

Fig. 6. Extractors $\mathsf{Ext}_{\mathcal{A}}(\mathsf{p};r)$ in the proof of Theorem 3

Thus, e.g., $\tau = \sum_{t \geq 0}^{|q_2|+1} N_{2,1,t} \boldsymbol{q}_{2t}$. Given $\boldsymbol{N}_1, \boldsymbol{N}_2, \boldsymbol{q}_1$, and $\boldsymbol{q}_2$, one can efficiently compute $\boldsymbol{\Gamma} \in \mathbb{Z}_p^{n \times k}, \boldsymbol{\gamma} \in \mathbb{Z}_p^{1 \times k}, \tau \in \mathbb{Z}_p$ and $\boldsymbol{\Delta} \in \mathbb{Z}_p^{1 \times n}$.

We will now show that $\mathsf{Ext}_{\mathcal{A}}$ satisfies the requirements of the extractor in Eq. (2). Assume that $\mathcal{A}(\mathsf{p};r)$ was successful. We execute $\mathsf{Ext}_{\mathcal{A}}(\mathsf{p};r)$ and obtain either $\boldsymbol{\alpha}$ or $\bot$. From the fact that $[\boldsymbol{\Delta}]_2 \bullet [\boldsymbol{\Gamma}]_1 = [\tau]_2 \bullet [\boldsymbol{\gamma}]_1$, we get $\boldsymbol{\Delta\Gamma} = \tau\boldsymbol{\gamma} \in \mathbb{Z}_p^{1 \times k}$. Since $\tau \neq 0$, $\boldsymbol{\gamma} = \tau^{-1}\boldsymbol{\Delta\Gamma} \in \mathbb{Z}_p^{1 \times k}$. Clearly, $\boldsymbol{\alpha} := \tau^{-1}\boldsymbol{\Delta} \in \mathbb{Z}_p^n$ is a valid hk since $\boldsymbol{\alpha}^\top \boldsymbol{\Gamma} = \tau^{-1}\boldsymbol{\Delta\Gamma} = \boldsymbol{\gamma}$ and in particular $[\boldsymbol{\gamma}]_1 = \boldsymbol{\alpha}^\top[\boldsymbol{\Gamma}]_1$.

(2: $\mathcal{D}_p$-SZKHF-KE.) The proof is similar to the SUBPAR-SZKHF-KE proof with the difference that $\mathsf{lpar} = [\boldsymbol{\Gamma}]_1$ is honestly generated and so $\mathcal{A}$ is given $[\boldsymbol{\Gamma}]_1$ as additional input. $\qquad\square$

If $\kappa(\mathsf{hk}) = [\mathsf{hk}]_2$ then it suffices to extract $[\mathsf{hk}]_2$. Then, one can rewrite the proof so that the algebraic adversary only recovers the coefficients of $\tau(\boldsymbol{Q}_2)$ but not of $\boldsymbol{\Delta}(\boldsymbol{Q}_2)$. In that case, one can prove persistent ZK and Sub-ZK (see Theorem 3) under standard knowledge assumptions (instead relying on the AGM) by adding $[y\tau]_2$ to $\mathsf{hp}_{\mathsf{ver}}$, where $y \leftarrow_{\$} \mathbb{Z}_p$ is a knowledge trapdoor (i.e., only adding one additional group element to the projection key). Alternatively, one can define new tautological knowledge assumptions stating that given hpf as input, one can extract either hk or $\kappa(\mathsf{hk})$.

6.5   Security Proof

Theorem 3. *Let $\{\mathcal{L}_{\mathsf{lpar}}\}$ be a family of algebraic languages, such that there exists an efficient verpar algorithm. Let HF be a DVS-based GL-SPHF for $\{\mathcal{L}_{\mathsf{lpar}}\}$ and let $\mathsf{HF}_{\mathsf{dvs}}$ be the GL-SZKHF for $\{\mathcal{L}_{\mathsf{lpar}}\}$ depicted in Fig. 4.*

(i) If $\mathsf{DDH}_{\mathbb{G}_2}^{\mathsf{dl}}$ holds relative to Pgen, then $\mathsf{HF}_{\mathsf{dvs}}$ is a (non-blackbox) Sub-PAR computationally-smooth GL-SZKHF in the plain model.

(ii) Let $\kappa := a \mapsto [a]_2$ or $\kappa := \mathsf{id}$. The GL-SZKHF $\mathsf{HF}_{\mathsf{dvs}}$ is (a) auxiliary-string non-blackbox persistent ZK under SUBPAR-SZKHF-KE, and (b) no-auxiliary-string non-blackbox ZK under $\mathcal{D}_p$-SZKHF-KE, in the plain model.

$$\text{Smooth}_{\text{HF},\mathcal{A}}^{\text{nbb-plain}}(\lambda)$$

$\mathsf{p} \leftarrow \mathsf{Pgen}(1^\lambda);$
$(\mathtt{lpar} = [\boldsymbol{\Gamma}]_1, \mathbf{x}) \leftarrow \mathcal{A}(\mathsf{p});$
$(\mathsf{hpf} = (\mathsf{hp}, \mathsf{hp}_{\text{ver}}), \mathsf{hk} = \boldsymbol{\alpha}) \leftarrow \mathsf{kgen}([\boldsymbol{\Gamma}]_1; \mathbf{x});$
$\mathsf{H}_0 \leftarrow \mathsf{hash}([\boldsymbol{\Gamma}]_1; \boldsymbol{\alpha}, \mathbf{x}); \mathsf{H}_1 \leftarrow_{\$} \mathsf{HashSet}; b \leftarrow_{\$} \{0,1\}; b' \leftarrow \mathcal{A}(\mathsf{hpf}, \mathsf{H}_b);$
if $\mathsf{verpar}(\mathtt{lpar}) = 1 \wedge b' = b \wedge \neg(\exists \mathbf{w}: \mathbf{x} = [\boldsymbol{\Gamma}]_1 \mathbf{w})$
  then return 1; else return 0; fi

Fig. 7. Experiment $\text{Smooth}_{\text{HF},\mathcal{A}}^{\text{nbb-plain}}(\lambda)$

$$\mathsf{Exp}_{\mathcal{B}}^{\text{int}}(\mathsf{p})$$

$[\boldsymbol{\Gamma}]_1 \leftarrow \mathcal{B}(\mathsf{p});$
$\boldsymbol{\alpha} \leftarrow_{\$} \mathbb{Z}_p^n;$ // $\mathsf{hk} \leftarrow \mathsf{HF.hashkg}(\mathtt{lpar});$
$[\boldsymbol{\gamma}]_1 \leftarrow \boldsymbol{\alpha}^\top [\boldsymbol{\Gamma}]_1;$ // $\mathsf{hp} \leftarrow \mathsf{HF.projkg}(\mathtt{lpar}; \mathsf{hk});$
$\tau \leftarrow_{\$} \mathbb{Z}_p^*; \mathsf{hp}_{\text{ver}} \leftarrow [\tau, \tau\boldsymbol{\alpha}^\top]_2; \mathsf{hpf} \leftarrow (\mathsf{hp}, \mathsf{hp}_{\text{ver}});$
$b \leftarrow_{\$} \{0,1\};$
if $b = 0$ then $\boldsymbol{\beta} \leftarrow \boldsymbol{\alpha};$ else $\boldsymbol{\mu} \leftarrow_{\$} \mathsf{coker}(\boldsymbol{\Gamma}); \boldsymbol{\beta} \leftarrow \boldsymbol{\alpha} + \boldsymbol{\mu};$
  // $\boldsymbol{\beta}$ is either sk or sk+ random element of the cokernel
$b' \leftarrow \mathcal{B}(\mathsf{hpf}, [\boldsymbol{\beta}]_2);$
return $b = b';$

Fig. 8. Experiment $\mathsf{Exp}_{\mathcal{B}}^{\text{int}}(\mathsf{p})$ for the proof of Sub-PAR smoothness in Theorem 3

Proof. (**i: Sub-PAR smoothness**). First, recall that computational Sub-PAR (non-blackbox) smoothness says that for all PPT adversaries $\mathcal{A}$, $\Pr[\text{Smooth}_{\text{HF},\mathcal{A}}^{\text{nbb-plain}}(\lambda) = 1] \approx_\lambda 1/2$, where the experiment $\text{Smooth}_{\text{HF},\mathcal{A}}^{\text{nbb-plain}}(\lambda)$ is depicted in Fig. 7.

We first reduce the Sub-PAR smoothness to the following intermediate assumption: for all $\mathsf{p} \in \text{im}(\mathsf{Pgen}(1^\lambda))$, and stateful PPT adversaries $\mathcal{B}$, $\Pr[\mathsf{Exp}_{\mathcal{B}}^{\text{int}}(\mathsf{p}) = 1] \approx_\lambda 1/2$, where $\mathsf{Exp}_{\mathcal{B}}^{\text{int}}(\mathsf{p})$ is depicted in Fig. 8. Intuitively, this assumption states that for any PPT adversary (who is given the projection key hpf), it is hard to distinguish $[\mathsf{hk}]_2$ from $[\mathsf{hk}]_2 + \boldsymbol{\mu}$, where $\boldsymbol{\mu}$ is a random element of the cokernel of $[\boldsymbol{\Gamma}]_2$. That is, hpf does not contain sufficient information to decide which of the possible $|\text{coker}(\boldsymbol{\Gamma})|$ secret keys was used by the challenger. Note that since $\boldsymbol{\mu} \in \text{coker}(\boldsymbol{\Gamma})$, $(\boldsymbol{\alpha} + \boldsymbol{\mu})^\top \boldsymbol{\Gamma} = \boldsymbol{\alpha}^\top \boldsymbol{\Gamma}$.

Let $\mathcal{A}$ be a Sub-PAR smoothness adversary. We construct an adversary $\mathcal{B}$ against the intermediate problem that uses the help of $\mathcal{A}$. The idea is to let $\mathcal{B}$ play the role of the challenger in the smoothness experiment and feed $\mathcal{A}$ with values calculated based on the intermediate experiment. $\mathcal{B}(\mathsf{p})$ proceeds as follows:

1. $([\boldsymbol{\Gamma}]_1, \mathbf{x}) \leftarrow \mathcal{A}(\mathsf{p}).$
2. Return $[\boldsymbol{\Gamma}]_1$ to the challenger.
3. The challenger creates $(\mathsf{hpf}, [\boldsymbol{\beta}]_2)$ as in Fig. 8, and sends it to $\mathcal{B}$.
4. $\mathcal{B}$ computes $\mathsf{H}_b \leftarrow [\boldsymbol{\beta}]_2^\top \mathbf{x}.$

5. $b' \leftarrow \mathcal{A}(\mathsf{hpf}, \mathsf{H}_b)$.
6. Return b'.

Clearly, if $b = 0$ (i.e., $\boldsymbol{\beta} = \boldsymbol{\alpha}$), then $\mathsf{H}_b = \mathsf{H}(\mathtt{1par}; \mathsf{hk}, \mathbf{x})$. Otherwise (i.e., if $b = 1$), we have two cases:

– if $\mathbf{x} \notin \mathcal{L}_{\mathtt{1par}}$, then $\mathsf{H}_b = [\boldsymbol{\alpha} + \boldsymbol{\mu}]_2^\top \mathbf{x} = [\boldsymbol{\alpha}]_2^\top \mathbf{x} + [\boldsymbol{\mu}]_2^\top \mathbf{x}$ is uniformly random from the viewpoint of the adversary. This is because in this case, $\mathbf{x}$ is not in the column span of $[\boldsymbol{\Gamma}]_1$ and thus $\mathsf{H} = [\boldsymbol{\alpha}]_2^\top \mathbf{x}$ is uniformly random.
– if $\mathbf{x} \in \mathcal{L}_{\mathtt{1par}}$, then $\mathsf{H}_b = [\boldsymbol{\beta}]_2^\top \mathbf{x} = [\boldsymbol{\alpha}]_2^\top \mathbf{x} = \mathsf{H}(\mathtt{1par}; \mathsf{hk}, \mathbf{x})$.

Now assume that $\mathcal{A}$ breaks the Sub-PAR smoothness with non-negligible advantage. This means that with non-negligible probability, $\mathcal{A}$ outputs $b = 0$ in the case of receiving a real hash and outputs $b = 1$ in the case of receiving a random hash. Based on the above observation, this would be the same as the advantage of $\mathcal{B}$ in succeeding in $\mathsf{Exp}_{\mathcal{B}}^{\mathsf{int}}(\mathsf{p})$.

We now show that the intermediate assumption can be reduced to the $\mathsf{DDH}_{\mathbb{G}_2}^{\mathsf{dl}}$ problem. Let $\mathcal{D}$ be an adversary against the $\mathsf{DDH}_{\mathbb{G}_2}^{\mathsf{dl}}$ problem. Without loss of generality, we assume that the challenge given to $\mathcal{D}$ is of the form $[x, xy, z]_2$, where $x, y, z \in \mathbb{Z}_p$ and $z = y$ or random[5]. $\mathcal{D}$ plays the role of the challenger for $\mathcal{B}$ in the experiment $\mathsf{Exp}_{\mathcal{B}}^{\mathsf{int}}(\mathsf{p})$ in Fig. 8. Before describing the reduction, note that for all $[\boldsymbol{\gamma}]_1 \in \{[\boldsymbol{\gamma}']_1 \in \mathbb{G}_1^{1 \times k} : \exists \boldsymbol{\alpha} \in \mathbb{Z}_p^n \text{ s.t. } \boldsymbol{\gamma}' = \boldsymbol{\alpha}^\top \boldsymbol{\Gamma}\} \subseteq \mathbb{G}_1^{1 \times k}$, there exists $\boldsymbol{\Delta}_{\boldsymbol{\gamma}} \in \mathbb{Z}_p^{n \times (m+1)}$, with $m = n - k$, such that

$$\{\boldsymbol{\alpha} : \boldsymbol{\gamma} = \boldsymbol{\alpha}^\top \boldsymbol{\Gamma}\} = \{\boldsymbol{\Delta}_{\boldsymbol{\gamma}} \cdot \tilde{\boldsymbol{s}} : \tilde{\boldsymbol{s}} = (\begin{smallmatrix} s \\ 1 \end{smallmatrix}); \forall \boldsymbol{s} \in \mathbb{Z}_p^m\} \ .$$

In other words, the columns of $\boldsymbol{\Delta}_{\boldsymbol{\gamma}}$ form a basis for the solutions of equation $\boldsymbol{\gamma} = \boldsymbol{\alpha}^\top \boldsymbol{\Gamma}$ with unknown $\boldsymbol{\alpha}$[6]. By having this, the adversary $\mathcal{D}$ plays the role of the challenger for $\mathcal{B}$ as follows:

1. run $\mathcal{B}$ with input p and obtain $[\boldsymbol{\Gamma}]_1$.
2. call the DL oracle on input $[\boldsymbol{\Gamma}]_1$ and set $st := \boldsymbol{\Gamma} \in \mathbb{Z}_p^{n \times k}$.
3. given a challenge $\boldsymbol{C} = [x, xy, z]_2$, generate m DDH challenges $\boldsymbol{C} = \{[x, r_i xy, r_i z]_2\}_{i \in [m]}$ for $r_i \leftarrow_\$ \mathbb{Z}_p$ by using the self-randomizability of the DDH problem. To simplify the notation, we write $\boldsymbol{C} = [x, xy, z]_2$.
4. call $\mathcal{B}$ with input $([\tau, \boldsymbol{F}, \boldsymbol{G}]_2, [\boldsymbol{H}]_1)$ defined as $\tau = x$, $[\boldsymbol{F}]_2 = \boldsymbol{\Delta}_{\boldsymbol{\gamma}} \cdot x\tilde{\boldsymbol{y}} = x(\boldsymbol{\Delta}_{\boldsymbol{\gamma}} \cdot \tilde{\boldsymbol{y}})$, $[\boldsymbol{G}]_2 = \boldsymbol{\Delta}_{\boldsymbol{\gamma}} \cdot \tilde{\boldsymbol{z}}$ and $[\boldsymbol{H}]_1 = [\boldsymbol{\gamma}]_1$, where $\boldsymbol{\gamma} \leftarrow_\$ \mathbb{Z}_p^k$, $\tilde{\boldsymbol{y}} = (\begin{smallmatrix} y \\ 1 \end{smallmatrix})$, and $\tilde{\boldsymbol{z}} = (\begin{smallmatrix} z \\ 1 \end{smallmatrix})$.
5. return $\mathcal{B}$'s output.

Note that when $\boldsymbol{C} = [x, xy, z]_2$ is a vector of DDH tuples, then $z = y$ and $\mathcal{B}$ is given $([\tau, \tau\boldsymbol{\alpha}^\top, \boldsymbol{\alpha}]_2, \boldsymbol{\alpha}^\top [\boldsymbol{\Gamma}]_1)$ as input, where $\boldsymbol{\alpha} = \boldsymbol{\Delta}_{\boldsymbol{\gamma}} \cdot \tilde{\boldsymbol{y}}$. Thus $\mathcal{B}$ is expected to output $b' = 0$. On the other hand, if $\boldsymbol{C} = [x, xy, z]_2$ is not a vector of DDH

---

[5] Although this tuple is different from the usual DDH challenge $[x, y, z]_2$ where $z = xy$ or random, it is not hard to show they are two versions of the same hardness problem.
[6] The existence of $\boldsymbol{\Delta}_{\boldsymbol{\gamma}}$ comes from the parametric equations that describe all the solutions of the underlying system of equations.

$\mathcal{B}(\mathsf{p}; r_{\mathcal{Z}})$	$\mathsf{Ext}_{\mathcal{Z}}(\mathsf{p}; r_{\mathcal{Z}})$
$([\boldsymbol{\Gamma}]_1, \mathsf{hpf}, \mathsf{st}_{\mathcal{Z}}) \leftarrow \mathcal{Z}(\mathsf{p}; r_{\mathcal{Z}}); \mathbf{return} \ \mathsf{hpf};$	$\mathbf{return} \ \mathsf{Ext}_{\mathcal{B}}^2(\mathsf{p}; r_{\mathcal{Z}});$

Fig. 9. The extractor and the constructed adversary $\mathcal{B}$ from the persistent zero-knowledge proof of Theorem 3.

tuples, then z is a random vector different from y, but still such that $\Delta_{\gamma} \cdot \tilde{z} \in \{\alpha : \gamma = \alpha^{\top} \boldsymbol{\Gamma}\}$. This means that in this case, $\mathcal{B}$ is given $([\tau, \tau \alpha^{\top}, \boldsymbol{\beta}]_2, \alpha^{\top} [\boldsymbol{\Gamma}]_1)$ as input, where α and β are random vectors are solutions for $\{\alpha : \gamma = \alpha^{\top} \boldsymbol{\Gamma}\}$. This is $\mathcal{B}$'s input in Fig. 8 experiment for the case $b = 1$ and therefore, $\mathcal{B}$ is expected to output $b' = 1$. This completes the proof of Sub-PAR smoothness.

(ii-a: persistent ZK). Let $\mathcal{Z}$ be a subverter that breaks the auxiliary-string non-blackbox persistence ZK property. First, $\mathcal{Z}(\mathsf{p}; r_{\mathcal{Z}})$ outputs $([\boldsymbol{\Gamma}]_1, \mathsf{aux}_{\mathsf{hp}})$. Let $\mathcal{B}$ be the adversary from Fig. 9. Note that $\mathsf{RND}_{\lambda}(\mathcal{B}) = \mathsf{RND}_{\lambda}(\mathcal{Z})$. Under the SUBPAR-SZKHF-KE assumption, there exists an extractor $\mathsf{Ext}_{\mathcal{B}}^2$, such that if $\mathsf{verpar}([\boldsymbol{\Gamma}]_1) = 1$ and $\mathsf{verhp}([\boldsymbol{\Gamma}]_1, \mathsf{hpf}) = 1$ then $\mathsf{Ext}_{\mathcal{B}}^2(\mathsf{p}; r_{\mathcal{Z}})$ outputs α, such that $\gamma = \alpha^{\top} \boldsymbol{\Gamma}$. We construct a trivial extractor $\mathsf{Ext}_{\mathcal{Z}}(\mathsf{p}; r_{\mathcal{Z}})$ for $\mathcal{Z}$, as depicted in Fig. 9. Clearly, $\mathsf{Ext}_{\mathcal{Z}}$ returns $\mathsf{hk} = \alpha$, such that $\gamma = \alpha^{\top} \boldsymbol{\Gamma}$.

Fix concrete values of λ and $r_{\mathcal{Z}} \in \mathsf{RND}_{\lambda}(\mathcal{Z})$. Let $\mathsf{p} \leftarrow \mathsf{Pgen}(1^{\lambda})$, $(\mathsf{lpar} = [\boldsymbol{\Gamma}]_1, \mathsf{st}_{\mathcal{Z}}) \leftarrow \mathcal{Z}(\mathsf{p}; r_{\mathcal{Z}})$, $(\mathsf{x} = [y]_1, \mathsf{w} = w) \leftarrow \mathcal{A}(\mathsf{lpar}; \mathsf{st}_{\mathcal{Z}})$, $(\mathsf{hpf}, \mathsf{st}_{\mathcal{Z}}) \leftarrow \mathcal{Z}(\mathsf{p}; \mathsf{x}; r_{\mathcal{Z}})$, and run $\mathsf{Ext}_{\mathcal{Z}}(\mathsf{p}; r_{\mathcal{Z}})$ to obtain α.

It clearly suffices to show that if $\mathsf{verpar}(\mathsf{lpar}) = 1$, $\mathsf{verhp}(\mathsf{lpar}; \mathsf{hpf}, \mathsf{x}) = 1$ and $(\mathsf{x}, \mathsf{w}) \in \mathcal{R}_{\mathsf{lpar}}$, then $\mathsf{projhash}(\mathsf{lpar}; \mathsf{hpf}, \mathsf{x}, \mathsf{w}) = [\gamma]_1 w \bullet [1]_2$ and $\mathsf{simhash}(\mathsf{lpar}, \kappa(\mathsf{hk}) = \kappa(\alpha); \mathsf{hp}, \mathsf{x}) = \chi(\kappa(\alpha))^{\top} \mathsf{x}$ (for χ defined in Fig. 4) have the same distribution. Really, from $\mathsf{verhp}(\mathsf{lpar}; \mathsf{hpf}, \mathsf{x}) = 1$ it follows $\gamma = \alpha^{\top} \boldsymbol{\Gamma}$ and from $(\mathsf{x}, \mathsf{w}) \in \mathcal{R}_{\mathsf{lpar}}$ it follows $\mathsf{x} = \boldsymbol{\Gamma} w$. Thus, $\mathsf{projhash}(\mathsf{lpar}; \mathsf{hpf}, \mathsf{x}, \mathsf{w}) = [\gamma]_1 w \bullet [1]_2 = [\alpha^{\top} \boldsymbol{\Gamma} w]_1 \bullet [1]_2 = [\alpha]_2^{\top} \mathsf{x} = \mathsf{simhash}(\mathsf{lpar}, \kappa(\mathsf{hk}))$. Hence, $\mathsf{projhash}$ and $\mathsf{simhash}$ have the same distribution, and thus, $\mathsf{HF}_{\mathsf{dvs}}$ is persistent zero-knowledge under SUBPAR-SZKHF-KE assumption.

(ii-b: ZK). The proof can directly be captured from the proof in (ii-a) when $[\boldsymbol{\Gamma}]_1$ is picked honestly and $\mathcal{Z}$ gets it as an additional input. $\qquad \square$

References

1. Abdalla, M., Benhamouda, F., Pointcheval, D.: Disjunctions for Hash proof systems: new constructions and applications. In: Oswald, E., Fischlin, M. (eds.) EUROCRYPT 2015. LNCS, vol. 9057, pp. 69–100. Springer, Heidelberg (2015). https://doi.org/10.1007/978-3-662-46803-6_3

2. Abdolmaleki, B., Baghery, K., Lipmaa, H., Zając, M.: A subversion-resistant SNARK. In: Takagi, T., Peyrin, T. (eds.) ASIACRYPT 2017. LNCS, vol. 10626, pp. 3–33. Springer, Cham (2017). https://doi.org/10.1007/978-3-319-70700-6_1

3. Abdolmaleki, B., Khoshakhlagh, H., Lipmaa, H.: Smooth zero-knowledge hash functions. IACR Cryptol. ePrint Arch., 653 (2021)

4. Abdolmaleki, B., Lipmaa, H., Siim, J., Zając, M.: On QA-NIZK in the BPK model. In: Kiayias, A., Kohlweiss, M., Wallden, P., Zikas, V. (eds.) PKC 2020. LNCS, vol. 12110, pp. 590–620. Springer, Cham (2020). https://doi.org/10.1007/978-3-030-45374-9_20

5. Alwen, J., Persiano, G., Visconti, I.: Impossibility and feasibility results for zero knowledge with public keys. In: Shoup, V. (ed.) CRYPTO 2005. LNCS, vol. 3621, pp. 135–151. Springer, Heidelberg (2005). https://doi.org/10.1007/11535218_9

6. Barak, B., Canetti, R., Nielsen, J.B., Pass, R.: Universally composable protocols with relaxed set-up assumptions, pp. 186–195

7. Belenkiy, M., Chase, M., Kohlweiss, M., Lysyanskaya, A.: P-signatures and non-interactive anonymous credentials. In: Canetti, R. (ed.) TCC 2008. LNCS, vol. 4948, pp. 356–374. Springer, Heidelberg (2008). https://doi.org/10.1007/978-3-540-78524-8_20

8. Bellare, M., Fuchsbauer, G., Scafuro, A.: NIZKs with an untrusted CRS: security in the face of parameter subversion. In: Cheon, J.H., Takagi, T. (eds.) ASIACRYPT 2016. LNCS, vol. 10032, pp. 777–804. Springer, Heidelberg (2016). https://doi.org/10.1007/978-3-662-53890-6_26

9. Hamouda-Guichoux, F.B.: Diverse modules and zero-knowledge. Ph.D. Thesis, PSL Research University (2016)

10. Benhamouda, F., Blazy, O., Chevalier, C., Pointcheval, D., Vergnaud, D.: New techniques for SPHFs and efficient one-round PAKE protocols. In: Canetti, R., Garay, J.A. (eds.) CRYPTO 2013. LNCS, vol. 8042, pp. 449–475. Springer, Heidelberg (2013). https://doi.org/10.1007/978-3-642-40041-4_25

11. Blum, M., Feldman, P., Micali, S.: Non-interactive zero-knowledge and its applications (extended abstract), pp. 103–112

12. Canetti, R., Goldreich, O., Goldwasser, S., Micali, S.: Resettable zero-knowledge (extended abstract), pp. 235–244

13. Couteau, G., Hartmann, D.: Shorter non-interactive zero-knowledge arguments and ZAPs for algebraic languages. In: Micciancio, D., Ristenpart, T. (eds.) CRYPTO 2020. LNCS, vol. 12172, pp. 768–798. Springer, Cham (2020). https://doi.org/10.1007/978-3-030-56877-1_27

14. Cramer, R., Shoup, V.: Universal hash proofs and a paradigm for adaptive chosen ciphertext secure public-key encryption. In: Knudsen, L.R. (ed.) EUROCRYPT 2002. LNCS, vol. 2332, pp. 45–64. Springer, Heidelberg (2002). https://doi.org/10.1007/3-540-46035-7_4

15. Escala, A., Herold, G., Kiltz, E., Ràfols, C., Villar, J.: An algebraic framework for Diffie-Hellman assumptions. In: Canetti, R., Garay, J.A. (eds.) CRYPTO 2013. LNCS, vol. 8043, pp. 129–147. Springer, Heidelberg (2013). https://doi.org/10.1007/978-3-642-40084-1_8

16. Fuchsbauer, G.: Subversion-zero-knowledge SNARKs. In: Abdalla, M., Dahab, R. (eds.) PKC 2018. LNCS, vol. 10769, pp. 315–347. Springer, Cham (2018). https://doi.org/10.1007/978-3-319-76578-5_11

17. Fuchsbauer, G., Kiltz, E., Loss, J.: The algebraic group model and its applications. In: Shacham, H., Boldyreva, A. (eds.) CRYPTO 2018. LNCS, vol. 10992, pp. 33–62. Springer, Cham (2018). https://doi.org/10.1007/978-3-319-96881-0_2

18. Galbraith, S.D., Paterson, K.G., Smart, N.P.: Pairings for cryptographers. Discret. Appl. Math. **156**(16), 3113–3121 (2008)

19. Garg, S., Gentry, C., Sahai, A., Waters, B.: Witness encryption and its applications, pp. 467–476

20. Gennaro, R., Lindell, Y.: A framework for password-based authenticated key exchange. In: Biham, E. (ed.) EUROCRYPT 2003. LNCS, vol. 2656, pp. 524–543. Springer, Heidelberg (2003). https://doi.org/10.1007/3-540-39200-9_33
21. Gjøsteen, K.: A new security proof for damgård's ElGamal, pp. 150–158
22. Goldreich, O., Oren, Y.: Definitions and properties of zero-knowledge proof systems. J. Cryptology **7**, 1–32 (1994). https://doi.org/10.1007/BF00195207
23. Jutla, C.S., Roy, A.: Shorter quasi-adaptive NIZK proofs for linear subspaces, pp. 1–20
24. Katz, J., Vaikuntanathan, V.: Round-optimal password-based authenticated key exchange. In: Ishai, Y. (ed.) TCC 2011. LNCS, vol. 6597, pp. 293–310. Springer, Heidelberg (2011). https://doi.org/10.1007/978-3-642-19571-6_18
25. Kiltz, E., Wee, H.: Quasi-adaptive NIZK for linear subspaces revisited. In: Oswald, E., Fischlin, M. (eds.) EUROCRYPT 2015. LNCS, vol. 9057, pp. 101–128. Springer, Heidelberg (2015). https://doi.org/10.1007/978-3-662-46803-6_4
26. Lipmaa, H.: On the CCA1-security of Elgamal and Damgård's Elgamal. In: Lai, X., Yung, M., Lin, D. (eds.) Inscrypt 2010. LNCS, vol. 6584, pp. 18–35. Springer, Heidelberg (2011). https://doi.org/10.1007/978-3-642-21518-6_2
27. Lipmaa, H.: Simulation-Extractable ZK-SNARKs Revisited. Technical Report 2019/612, IACR (2019). https://eprint.iacr.org/2019/612, Accessed 13 July 2019
28. Micali, S., Reyzin, L.: Soundness in the public-key model. In: Kilian, J. (ed.) CRYPTO 2001. LNCS, vol. 2139, pp. 542–565. Springer, Heidelberg (2001). https://doi.org/10.1007/3-540-44647-8_32
29. Wee, H.: Lower bounds for non-interactive zero-knowledge. In: Vadhan, S.P. (ed.) TCC 2007. LNCS, vol. 4392, pp. 103–117. Springer, Heidelberg (2007). https://doi.org/10.1007/978-3-540-70936-7_6

Another Use of the Five-Card Trick: Card-Minimal Secure Three-Input Majority Function Evaluation

Kodai Toyoda[1]($\boxtimes$) , Daiki Miyahara[2,3]($\boxtimes$) , and Takaaki Mizuki[1,3]($\boxtimes$)

[1] Tohoku University, Sendai, Japan
kodai.toyoda.p1@dc.tohoku.ac.jp, mizuki+lncs@tohoku.ac.jp
[2] The University of Electro-Communications, Tokyo, Japan
daiki.miyahara.q4@alumni.tohoku.ac.jp
[3] National Institute of Advanced Industrial Science and Technology, Tokyo, Japan

Abstract. Starting from the five-card trick proposed by Den Boer (EUROCRYPT' 89), many card-based protocols performing secure multiparty computations with a deck of physical cards have been devised. However, the five-card trick is considered to be still the most elegant, easy-to-understand and practical protocol, which enables two players to securely evaluate the AND value of their private inputs using five cards. In other words, for more than thirty years, in the research area of card-based cryptography, we have not discovered any protocols that are as simple and beautiful as the five-card trick.

In this study, making use of the five-card trick, we design a novel easy-to-understand protocol which securely evaluates the three-input majority function using six cards. That is, by applying a simple shuffle, we reduce a secure three-input majority computation to evaluating the AND value. By virtue of a direct application of the five-card trick, our proposed majority protocol is extremely simple enough for lay-people to execute. In addition, one advantage is that ordinary people such as high school students will be able to learn the concept of logical AND/OR operations and the majority function as well as their relationship through our majority protocol, providing a nice tool of pedagogical significance. Thus, we believe that our new protocol is no less practical and beautiful than the five-card trick.

1 Introduction

To perform cryptographic tasks such as secure multiparty computations, *card-based cryptography* uses a deck of physical cards such as black ♣ and red cards ♡ where their backs are all identical ?. Using these cards, Boolean values are typically represented as follows:

$$\clubsuit\heartsuit = 0, \quad \heartsuit\clubsuit = 1. \tag{1}$$

When a one-bit value $x \in \{0, 1\}$ is encoded by two face-down cards according to the encoding rule (1) above, we call such a pair of cards a *commitment* to x, which is denoted by

© Springer Nature Switzerland AG 2021
A. Adhikari et al. (Eds.): INDOCRYPT 2021, LNCS 13143, pp. 536–555, 2021.
https://doi.org/10.1007/978-3-030-92518-5_24

$$\boxed{?}\boxed{?}.$$
$$\underbrace{}_{x}$$

This paper begins with introducing the first card-based protocol in history, called the *five-card trick*, designed by Den Boer [6].

1.1   The Five-Card Trick

Assume that Alice and Bob hold private input bits $x \in \{0,1\}$ and $y \in \{0,1\}$, respectively, and that each of them creates a commitment to his/her private bit. The five-card trick securely evaluates the AND value $x \wedge y$ of their private bits, given commitments to bits $x, y \in \{0,1\}$ along with an additional card $\boxed{\heartsuit}$:

$$\boxed{\heartsuit}\underbrace{\boxed{?}\boxed{?}}_{x}\underbrace{\boxed{?}\boxed{?}}_{y} \quad \rightarrow \quad \cdots \quad \rightarrow \quad x \wedge y.$$

The procedure is as follows. (Here, we slightly rearrange the order of cards from the original reference [6] for the sake of later explanation.)

1. By swapping the two cards constituting the commitment to y (which means the NOT computation), obtain a commitment to the negation $\bar{y}$, and turn over the additional card:

$$\underbrace{\boxed{\heartsuit}\boxed{?}\boxed{?}}_{x}\underbrace{\boxed{?}\boxed{?}}_{y} \quad \rightarrow \quad \underset{\heartsuit}{\boxed{?}}\underbrace{\boxed{?}\boxed{?}}_{x}\underbrace{\boxed{?}\boxed{?}}_{\bar{y}}.$$

Note that the three $\boxed{\heartsuit}$s are cyclically consecutive (i.e., the first, second, and fifth cards are red) if and only if $x \wedge y = 1$:

$$\underset{\heartsuit\,\clubsuit\,\heartsuit\,\clubsuit}{\boxed{?}\boxed{?}\boxed{?}\boxed{?}\boxed{?}} \quad \text{if } (x,y) = (0,0),$$

$$\underset{\heartsuit\,\clubsuit\,\heartsuit\,\clubsuit\,\heartsuit}{\boxed{?}\boxed{?}\boxed{?}\boxed{?}\boxed{?}} \quad \text{if } (x,y) = (0,1),$$

$$\underset{\heartsuit\,\heartsuit\,\clubsuit\,\heartsuit\,\clubsuit}{\boxed{?}\boxed{?}\boxed{?}\boxed{?}\boxed{?}} \quad \text{if } (x,y) = (1,0),$$

$$\underset{\heartsuit\,\heartsuit\,\clubsuit\,\clubsuit\,\heartsuit}{\boxed{?}\boxed{?}\boxed{?}\boxed{?}\boxed{?}} \quad \text{if } (x,y) = (1,1).$$

2. Apply a *random cut* to the sequence of five cards; a random cut, denoted by $\langle \cdot \rangle$, is a shuffling operation that cyclically shifts a sequence of cards at random without changing its order:

$$\langle \boxed{?}\boxed{?}\boxed{?}\boxed{?}\boxed{?} \rangle \quad \rightarrow \quad \boxed{?}\boxed{?}\boxed{?}\boxed{?}\boxed{?}.$$

Thus, the resulting sequence becomes one of the following five cases with the equal probability (i.e., $1/5$), where we attach a number to each card for convenience sake:

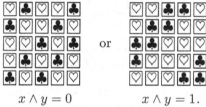

It is well-known that humans can securely implement a random cut easily so that nobody learns which case occurs [24].

3. Reveal all the five cards; then, we know the value of $x \wedge y$ depending on whether the three ♡s are cyclically consecutive:

$$x \wedge y = 0 \qquad x \wedge y = 1.$$

This is the five-card trick, whereby Alice and Bob can learn only the value of $x \wedge y$ without leaking any information about x and y more than necessary. As seen above, the five-card trick is extremely easy-to-understand: even lay-people can easily understand why this AND protocol works, and it is simple enough for non-experts such as high school students to execute without any difficulty.

1.2 Our Target

Since the invention of the five-card trick, many card-based protocols have been devised; refer to [9,14,23] for surveys. However, the five-card trick is considered to be still the most elegant, easy-to-understand, and practical protocol. The five-card trick provides a way of "secure dating" for two people [12] as well as it can be used for teaching the concept of secure multiparty computation to students [20,22].

While it is quite certain that the five-card trick is beautiful, many lay-people would consider that such a secure two-input AND computation may be somewhat useless because once Alice having a private bit of $x = 1$ knows that the result of the computation is $x \wedge y = 0$, she gets to know that Bob's bit is $y = 0$, implying that information about the other private input is leaked. Of course, this is inherent, but it would be worthwhile to find more suitable functions for educational purpose.

In this study, as a promising function, we consider the three-input majority function maj : $\{0,1\}^3 \rightarrow \{0,1\}$ defined as

$$\mathsf{maj}(a,b,c) = \begin{cases} 1 & \text{if } a+b+c \geq 2, \\ 0 & \text{if } a+b+c \leq 1. \end{cases} \tag{2}$$

That is, we solicit card-based protocols that securely evaluate $\mathsf{maj}(a, b, c)$; we call them *three-input majority protocols*. By using such a three-input majority protocol, Alice, Bob, and Carol can know only whether or not there are two or more players having 'Yes.' We believe that the three-input majority function is more convincing than the two-input AND function when teaching the concept of secure multiparty computation.

1.3   The Existing Protocols

There are several existing three-input majority protocols. Here, we review the history.

In 2013, Nishida et al. [17] presented for the first time a three-input majority protocol using eight cards. Their protocol takes commitments to bits $a, b, c \in \{0, 1\}$ along with two additional cards and outputs a commitment to the value of $\mathsf{maj}(a, b, c)$ using two shuffles:

Such a protocol is called a *committed-format* protocol (because it outputs a commitment). It has been an open problem to reduce the number of required additional cards (to 0 or 1).

In 2017, Nakai et al. [16] showed that the three-input majority function can be securely evaluated with four cards by introducing "private operations." Allowing private operations is a strong assumption[1] that a player may manipulate the cards privately, say behind their back, while making sure that the other players do not see the movement (cf. private PEZ protocols [1,5]). The protocol proposed by Nakai et al. includes a private rearranging operation and a private turning operation.

In 2018, Watanabe et al. [25] showed that the same task can be conducted with only three cards. Their protocol uses an oral response to reverse the value depending on the input value. In other words, this protocol uses a private negation.

In 2020, Yasunaga [26] proposed a protocol using six cards based on simple private operations. This protocol needs to reconstruct the input commitment to a in the middle. Yasunaga [26] also provided a protocol that does not use private operation by making a copy of the input commitment to a in advance, resulting in an eight-card protocol.

This paper focuses on protocols that do not rely on any private operation; hence, in our setting, all the previous works are the protocol by Nishida et al. [17] and the second protocol by Yasunaga [26], as shown in Table 1. The open problem mentioned above has not been resolved yet; we will close it by proposing "card-minimal" protocols, as explained below.

---

[1] Malicious behaviors during the private operations have been discussed in [2,11,18,19].

Table 1. The existing three-input majority protocols (without private operations) and our proposed protocols

	# Cards	# Shuf.	Committed format	Runtime
Nishida et al., 2013 [17]	8	2	✓	Finite
Yasunaga, 2020 [26]	8	3		Finite
Ours (Sect. 2)	6	2		Finite
Ours (Appendix A)	6	8 (exp.)	✓	Las Vegas

1.4   Our Contribution

In this paper, we construct two protocols using six cards that improve upon the existing three-input majority protocol proposed by Nishida et al. [16], as shown in Table 1.

Our first protocol is the main contribution of this paper: it securely evaluates $\mathsf{maj}(a, b, c)$ without any additional card:

$$\boxed{?}\boxed{?}\boxed{?}\boxed{?}\boxed{?}\boxed{?} \quad \rightarrow \quad \cdots \quad \rightarrow \quad \mathsf{maj}(a, b, c).$$
$$\underbrace{\quad}_{a} \underbrace{\quad}_{b} \underbrace{\quad}_{c}$$

Because any three-input majority protocol requires six cards due to three input commitments (in our setting) and our protocol needs no additional card, i.e., only three input commitments (consisting of six cards) suffice, our protocol is optimal in terms of the number of required cards under the encoding rules (1), i.e., it is *card-minimal*. Therefore, this is the first card-minimal protocol for the three-input majority function $\mathsf{maj}(a, b, c)$.

As seen later, our protocol makes use of the five-card trick [6]. That is, by applying a simple shuffle, we reduce the three-input majority computation to evaluating the AND value. Thus, our card-minimal protocol uses only a simple shuffle along with an execution of the five-card trick. As the five-card trick is famous for its brevity, our protocol is also simple enough for lay-people to execute.

As the second protocol, we will also provide a committed-format version, which we will present in Appendix A:

$$\boxed{?}\boxed{?}\boxed{?}\boxed{?}\boxed{?}\boxed{?} \quad \rightarrow \quad \cdots \quad \rightarrow \quad \boxed{?}\boxed{?} \quad .$$
$$\underbrace{\quad}_{a} \underbrace{\quad}_{b} \underbrace{\quad}_{c} \qquad\qquad \underbrace{\quad}_{\mathsf{maj}(a,b,c)}$$

This protocol is obtained by amending our first protocol using the idea behind the AND protocol proposed by Abe et al. [3]. Although the runtime of the protocol is Las Vegas, it is interesting to note that we can achieve the minimum number of cards without complex shuffling operations such as those required for the card-minimal AND protocol proposed by Koch et al. [10] and the one modified by Ruangwises and Itoh [21].

1.5   Outline

The outline of this paper is as follows. In Sect. 2, we present a simple and easy-to-understand three-input majority protocol which is card-minimal. In Sect. 3, we formally describe our protocol and give a formal proof for correctness and security. In Appendix A, we present a committed-format version of a card-minimal three-input majority protocol. We conclude this paper in Sect. 4.

2   Our Card-Minimal Majority Protocol

In this section, we design a three-input majority protocol without any additional card.

In our construction, we make use of the following simple fact on the three-input majority function $\mathsf{maj}(a, b, c)$ [16]:

$$\mathsf{maj}(a, b, c) = \begin{cases} b \wedge c & \text{if } a = 0, \\ b \vee c & \text{if } a = 1. \end{cases} \tag{3}$$

That is, we will reduce the computation of $\mathsf{maj}(a, b, c)$ to the computation of $b \wedge c$ or $b \vee c$. As we can compute $b \wedge c$ using the five-card trick shown in Sect. 1.1, let us consider how to compute $b \vee c$ in a similar manner, i.e., we first propose the five-card "OR" protocol by modifying the five-card trick slightly. We also describe variants of the five-card trick and the five-card OR protocol by replacing the additional red card $\heartsuit$ with a black card $\clubsuit$.

2.1   Variants of Five-Card Trick

In this subsection, based on the idea behind the five-card trick, we describe its four variants: the $\heartsuit$-based AND, $\heartsuit$-based OR, $\clubsuit$-based AND, and $\clubsuit$-based OR protocols.

The $\heartsuit$-based AND protocol is exactly the five-card trick itself because it uses $\heartsuit$ as an additional card and evaluates the AND value. We can obtain the $\heartsuit$-based OR protocol by modifying the rearrangements in the five-card trick. As for the $\clubsuit$-based protocols, let the output be 0 if three $\clubsuit$s are cyclically consecutive; otherwise, let the output be 1. (Note that this encoding is the opposite case where $\heartsuit$ is the additional card.) Then, we can have the $\clubsuit$-based AND and OR protocols, as seen below. For the sake of illustration, let us write commitments to x and y using x_0, x_1, y_0 and y_1 as

$$\underbrace{\boxed{?}\,\boxed{?}}_{x}\,\underbrace{\boxed{?}\,\boxed{?}}_{y},$$
$$\!\!\!\!\!\!\!\!\!x_0\,x_1\,y_0\,y_1$$

where x_0 and x_1 (y_0 and y_1) represent the two cards constituting the commitment to x (y). For example, if $x = 1$, x_0 is $\heartsuit$ and x_1 is $\clubsuit$.

The ♡-Based AND Protocol. This is exactly the same as the five-card trick presented in Sect. 1.1.

The ♡-Based OR Protocol

1. Arrange the five cards as follows:

$$\boxed{♡}\underbrace{\boxed{?}\boxed{?}}_{x}\underbrace{\boxed{?}\boxed{?}}_{y} \quad \rightarrow \quad \boxed{?}\underbrace{\boxed{?}\boxed{?}}_{x}\underbrace{\boxed{?}\boxed{?}}_{y}.$$
$$\hphantom{xxxxxx}♡$$

2. Rearrange the order of the sequence as

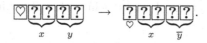

The resulting sequence of cards becomes

$$\underbrace{\boxed{?}\boxed{?}\boxed{?}\boxed{?}\boxed{?}}_{♡\ y_0\ x_1\ y_1\ x_0}.$$

Note that the three ♡s are cyclically consecutive if and only if $x \vee y = 1$.

3. Apply a random cut to the sequence of five cards:

$$\langle\boxed{?}\boxed{?}\boxed{?}\boxed{?}\boxed{?}\rangle \quad \rightarrow \quad \boxed{?}\boxed{?}\boxed{?}\boxed{?}\boxed{?}.$$

4. Reveal all the five cards. If the three red cards are cyclically consecutive $\boxed{♡}\boxed{♡}\boxed{♡}$, we have $x \vee y = 1$; otherwise, we have $x \vee y = 0$.

The ♣-Based AND Protocol

1. Perform Steps 1 and 2 of the ♡-based OR protocol where the additional card is $\boxed{♣}$ instead of $\boxed{♡}$. The resulting sequence of cards becomes

$$\boxed{♣}\underbrace{\boxed{?}\boxed{?}}_{x}\underbrace{\boxed{?}\boxed{?}}_{y} \quad \rightarrow \quad \underbrace{\boxed{?}\boxed{?}\boxed{?}\boxed{?}\boxed{?}}_{♣\ y_0\ x_1\ y_1\ x_0}.$$

Note that the three ♣s are *not* cyclically consecutive if and only if $x \wedge y = 1$.

2. Apply a random cut to the sequence of five cards:

$$\langle\boxed{?}\boxed{?}\boxed{?}\boxed{?}\boxed{?}\rangle \quad \rightarrow \quad \boxed{?}\boxed{?}\boxed{?}\boxed{?}\boxed{?}.$$

3. Reveal all the five cards. If the three black cards are cyclically consecutive $\boxed{♣}\boxed{♣}\boxed{♣}$, $x \wedge y = 0$; otherwise, $x \wedge y = 1$.

The ♣-Based OR Protocol

1. Perform Step 1 of the ♡-based AND protocol (namely, the five-card trick) where the additional card is ♣ instead of ♡. The resulting sequence of cards becomes

$$♣ \boxed{?}\boxed{?}\boxed{?}\boxed{?} \;\rightarrow\; \boxed{?}\boxed{?}\boxed{?}\boxed{?}\boxed{?}.$$
$$\underbrace{\quad}_{x}\;\underbrace{\quad}_{y} \qquad\qquad \underbrace{\quad}_{x}\;\underbrace{\quad}_{\tilde{y}}$$

   Note that the three ♣s are *not* cyclically consecutive if and only if $x \vee y = 1$.

2. Apply a random cut to the sequence of five cards:

$$\langle \boxed{?}\boxed{?}\boxed{?}\boxed{?}\boxed{?} \rangle \;\rightarrow\; \boxed{?}\boxed{?}\boxed{?}\boxed{?}\boxed{?}.$$

3. Reveal all the five cards. If the three black cards are cyclically consecutive $\boxed{♣}\boxed{♣}\boxed{♣}$, we have $x \vee y = 0$; otherwise, we have $x \vee y = 1$.

These four protocols satisfy the following relationship:

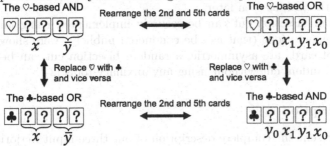

2.2   Idea

Here, we explain the idea behind our card-minimal three-input majority protocol. Consider an initial state

$$\boxed{?}\boxed{?}\boxed{?}\boxed{?}\boxed{?}\boxed{?}, \tag{4}$$
$$\underbrace{\quad}_{a}\;\underbrace{\quad}_{b}\;\underbrace{\quad}_{\bar{c}}$$

where we have a commitment to $\bar{c}$ by applying the NOT computation to a commitment to c. Let us apply a random cut to the second through sixth cards in this sequence; since the ♡-based AND will be applied (to the commitments to b and c) if $a = 0$ and the ♣-based OR will be applied if $a = 1$, we can derive the value of $\mathsf{maj}(a, b, c)$ because of the fact (3). However, depending on whether the output is ♡-based or ♣-based, the value of a will be leaked.

   To resolve this issue, using the aforementioned relationship between the four protocols, we "randomize" the state so that if $a = 0$, either the ♡-based AND or the ♣-based AND is applied with the equal probability, as follows. (Automatically, if $a = 1$, either the ♣-based OR or the ♡-based OR is applied in the same way.)

$$\boxed{?}\boxed{?}\boxed{?}\boxed{?}\boxed{?}\boxed{?} \rightarrow \begin{cases} \boxed{?}\boxed{?}\boxed{?}\boxed{?}\boxed{?}\boxed{?} & \text{with prob. } \tfrac{1}{2}, \\[4pt] \boxed{?}\boxed{?}\boxed{?}\boxed{?}\boxed{?}\boxed{?} & \text{with prob. } \tfrac{1}{2}. \end{cases} \tag{5}$$

It is easy to see that if we apply a random cut to the second through sixth cards in the above randomized state in (5), then either the $\heartsuit$- or $\clubsuit$-based AND is applied when $a = 0$ (with the equal probability) and either the $\heartsuit$- or $\clubsuit$-based OR is applied when $a = 1$; hence, the value of a cannot be leaked while the value of $\mathsf{maj}(a, b, c)$ can be derived.

To realize the randomization in (5), we introduce a practical shuffle, called a *random bisection cut*, invented by Mizuki and Sone [15]. It bisects a sequence of cards and swaps the two halves at random (denoted by $[\cdot|\cdot]$) as follows:

$$[\; \boxed{?}\boxed{?} \; | \; \boxed{?}\boxed{?} \;] \; \rightarrow \; \begin{cases} \boxed{?}\boxed{?} \; \boxed{?}\boxed{?} & \text{with prob. } \frac{1}{2}, \\ \boxed{?}\boxed{?} \; \boxed{?}\boxed{?} & \text{with prob. } \frac{1}{2}. \end{cases}$$

We will apply a random bisection cut to the commitment to a, the third card, and the sixth card, as seen later.

A random bisection cut can be securely implemented using familiar tools; a few implementations (that can be conducted publicly) were shown in [24]. If the backs of cards are asymmetric, a random bisection cut can be reduced to applying a random cut without using any auxiliary tools [24].

2.3   Description

Here, we present the complete description of our three-input majority protocol. This protocol starts with six cards of commitments to input bits a, b, and c.

1. Given commitments to a, b, and c, take the negation of the commitment to c:

$$\underbrace{\boxed{?}\boxed{?}}_{a}\underbrace{\boxed{?}\boxed{?}}_{b}\underbrace{\boxed{?}\boxed{?}}_{c} \; \rightarrow \; \underbrace{\boxed{?}\boxed{?}}_{a}\underbrace{\boxed{?}\boxed{?}}_{b}\underbrace{\boxed{?}\boxed{?}}_{\bar{c}}.$$

2. Apply a random bisection cut to the commitment to a, the third card, and the sixth card, and return the four cards, as follows:

$$\overset{1\;2\;3\quad\;\;6}{\boxed{?}\boxed{?}\boxed{?}\boxed{?}\boxed{?}\boxed{?}} \rightarrow [\; \overset{1\;3}{\boxed{?}\boxed{?}} | \overset{2\;6}{\boxed{?}\boxed{?}}] \overset{}{\boxed{?}\boxed{?}}$$

$$\rightarrow \overset{1\;2\;3\;4}{\boxed{?}\boxed{?}\boxed{?}\boxed{?}} \boxed{?}\boxed{?} \rightarrow \overset{1\quad 3\;2\quad\quad 4}{\boxed{?}\boxed{?}\boxed{?}\boxed{?}\boxed{?}\boxed{?}}.$$

Note that the state of the resulting sequence becomes what is in (5).
3. Apply a random cut to the second to sixth cards as follows:

$$\boxed{?} \; \langle\; \boxed{?}\boxed{?}\boxed{?}\boxed{?}\boxed{?} \;\rangle \rightarrow \boxed{?}\boxed{?}\boxed{?}\boxed{?}\boxed{?}\boxed{?}.$$

4. Reveal the first card.
   (a) If $\clubsuit$ appears, the result is $\heartsuit$-based. Reveal all the remaining five cards. If the three red cards are cyclically consecutive $\boxed{\heartsuit}\boxed{\heartsuit}\boxed{\heartsuit}$, we have

$\mathsf{maj}(a, b, c) = 1$; otherwise, we have $\mathsf{maj}(a, b, c) = 0$.

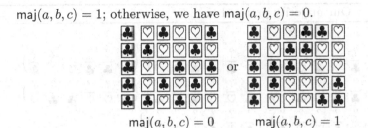

$$\mathsf{maj}(a, b, c) = 0 \qquad \mathsf{maj}(a, b, c) = 1$$

(b) If ♡ appears, the result is ♣-based. Reveal all the remaining five cards. If the three black cards are cyclically consecutive ♣♣♣, we have $\mathsf{maj}(a, b, c) = 0$; otherwise, we have $\mathsf{maj}(a, b, c) = 1$.

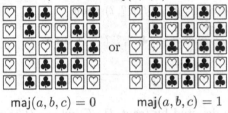

$$\mathsf{maj}(a, b, c) = 0 \qquad \mathsf{maj}(a, b, c) = 1$$

Thus, this protocol does not need any additional card, and uses only two shuffles. It is easy-to-understand as well as easy-to-implement.

We will provide a committed-format version as well in Appendix A.

3 Formal Treatment

In this section, we give a description of our majority protocol (presented in Sect. 2) in a formal way based on the computation model of card-based cryptography [13]. We also prove the correctness and security of our protocol by using the KWH-tree invented by Koch et al. [10].

3.1 Operations in Card-Based Cryptography

In card-based cryptography, there are three main operations performed on a sequence of cards, namely, permuting, turning, and shuffling. Below, we assume a sequence of n cards.

Permute. This is denoted by (perm, π) where π is a permutation applied to the sequence of cards as follows:

$$\underset{1\ 2\quad n}{\boxed{?}\boxed{?}\cdots\boxed{?}} \xrightarrow{(\mathsf{perm}, \pi)} \underset{\pi^{-1}(1)\ \pi^{-1}(2)\quad\ \pi^{-1}(n)}{\boxed{?}\ \boxed{?}\ \cdots\ \boxed{?}}.$$

Turn. This is denoted by (turn, T) where T is a set of indexes, indicating that the t-th card is turned over for every $t \in T$ as follows:

$$\underset{1\ 2\quad t\quad n}{\boxed{?}\boxed{?}\cdots\boxed{?}\cdots\boxed{?}} \xrightarrow{(\mathsf{turn}, T)} \underset{1\ 2\quad t \in T\quad n}{\boxed{?}\boxed{?}\cdots\boxed{\clubsuit}\cdots\boxed{?}}.$$

Algorithm 1 Our majority protocol

input set:

$$\left\{ \left(\frac{?}{\heartsuit}, \frac{?}{\clubsuit}, \frac{?}{\heartsuit}, \frac{?}{\clubsuit}, \frac{?}{\heartsuit}, \frac{?}{\clubsuit}\right), \left(\frac{?}{\heartsuit}, \frac{?}{\clubsuit}, \frac{?}{\heartsuit}, \frac{?}{\clubsuit}, \frac{?}{\clubsuit}, \frac{?}{\heartsuit}\right), \left(\frac{?}{\heartsuit}, \frac{?}{\clubsuit}, \frac{?}{\clubsuit}, \frac{?}{\heartsuit}, \frac{?}{\heartsuit}, \frac{?}{\clubsuit}\right), \right.$$

$$\left(\frac{?}{\heartsuit}, \frac{?}{\clubsuit}, \frac{?}{\clubsuit}, \frac{?}{\heartsuit}, \frac{?}{\clubsuit}, \frac{?}{\heartsuit}\right), \left(\frac{?}{\clubsuit}, \frac{?}{\heartsuit}, \frac{?}{\heartsuit}, \frac{?}{\clubsuit}, \frac{?}{\heartsuit}, \frac{?}{\clubsuit}\right), \left(\frac{?}{\clubsuit}, \frac{?}{\heartsuit}, \frac{?}{\heartsuit}, \frac{?}{\clubsuit}, \frac{?}{\clubsuit}, \frac{?}{\heartsuit}\right),$$

$$\left.\left(\frac{?}{\clubsuit}, \frac{?}{\heartsuit}, \frac{?}{\clubsuit}, \frac{?}{\heartsuit}, \frac{?}{\heartsuit}, \frac{?}{\clubsuit}\right), \left(\frac{?}{\clubsuit}, \frac{?}{\heartsuit}, \frac{?}{\clubsuit}, \frac{?}{\heartsuit}, \frac{?}{\clubsuit}, \frac{?}{\heartsuit}\right) \right\}$$

1. (perm, $(5\ 6)$)
2. (shuf, $\{id, (1\ 2)(3\ 6)\}$)
3. (shuf, $RC_{2,3,4,5,6}$)
4. (turn, $\{1\}$)
5. **if** visible sequence $= (\heartsuit, ?, ?, ?, ?, ?)$ **then**
6.   (result, $2, 3, 4, 5, 6$)
7. **else if** visible sequence $= (\clubsuit, ?, ?, ?, ?, ?)$ **then**
8.   (result, $2, 3, 4, 5, 6$)

Shuffle. This is denoted by (shuf, Π, $\mathcal{F}$) where Π is a permutation set and $\mathcal{F}$ is a probability distribution on Π, indicating that $\pi \in \Pi$ is drawn according to $\mathcal{F}$ and is applied to the sequence of cards as follows:

$$\underset{1\ \ 2\quad\ \ n}{\boxed{?}\boxed{?}\cdots\boxed{?}} \xrightarrow{(\text{shuf}, \Pi, \mathcal{F})} \underset{\pi^{-1}(1)\ \pi^{-1}(2)\qquad\ \pi^{-1}(n)}{\boxed{?}\quad\boxed{?}\ \cdots\ \boxed{?}}.$$

We note that nobody knows which permutation in Π was applied. If the probability distribution $\mathcal{F}$ is uniform, we may omit it.

3.2 Pseudocode

A pseudocode for our majority protocol is depicted in Algorithm 1, where we define

$$RC_{2,3,4,5,6} := \{id, (2\,3\,4\,5\,6), (2\,3\,4\,5\,6)^2, (2\,3\,4\,5\,6)^3, (2\,3\,4\,5\,6)^4\},$$

and (result, i, j, k, l, m) specifies output positions. The shuffle (shuf, $RC_{2,3,4,5,6}$) means that a random cut is applied to the second through sixth cards. The shuffle (shuf, $\{id, (1\,2)(3\,6)\}$) in Algorithm 1 represents the application of a random bisection cut in Step 2 shown in Sect. 2.3.

3.3 Correctness and Security

In this subsection, we verify the correctness and security of our non-committed-format majority protocol. A three-input majority protocol is said to be *correct* if, given input commitments to a, b and c, it always evaluates the value of $\mathsf{maj}(a, b, c)$

correctly. We say that such a protocol is *secure* if it leaks no information beyond the value of $\mathsf{maj}(a, b, c)$ for any run of the protocol.

To verify that our majority protocol is correct and secure, we make use of the *KWH-tree*, which is an excellent tool developed by Koch, Walzer, and Härtel [10]. That is, if one is able to write a KWH-tree satisfying some properties for a protocol, then it automatically implies that the protocol is correct and secure; see [8–10,14] for the details.

We describe the KWH-tree of our non-committed-format majority protocol in Fig. 1, following Chap. 7 of [9]. The first box in Fig. 1 corresponds to an initial sequence, consisting of three input commitments; X_{111}, X_{110}, X_{101}, X_{100}, X_{011}, X_{010}, X_{001}, and X_{000} represent the probabilities of $(a, b, c) = (1, 1, 1)$, $(a, b, c) = (1, 1, 0)$, $(a, b, c) = (1, 0, 1)$, $(a, b, c) = (1, 0, 0)$, $(a, b, c) = (0, 1, 1)$, $(a, b, c) = (0, 1, 0)$, $(a, b, c) = (0, 0, 1)$, and $(a, b, c) = (0, 0, 0)$, respectively. In the bottom boxes, we write X_1 instead of $X_{111} + X_{110} + X_{101} + X_{011}$ and write X_0 instead of $X_{100} + X_{010} + X_{001} + X_{000}$. A polynomial annotating a card sequence in a state, such as $1/2X_{111}$, represents the conditional probability that the current sequence is the one next to the polynomial, given the visible sequence trace observed so far on the table. From the two boxes at the bottom, one can see that $(\mathsf{turn}, \{2, 3, 4, 5, 6\})$ reveals the value of $\mathsf{maj}(a, b, c)$ definitively. Furthermore, in each box, the sum of all polynomials is equal to $X_{111} + X_{110} + X_{101} + X_{100} + X_{011} + X_{010} + X_{001} + X_{000}$, implying that no information about a, b and c leaks, i.e., the inputs and visible sequence trace are stochastically independent (before $(\mathsf{turn}, \{2, 3, 4, 5, 6\})$ is applied finally).

Thus, the KWH-tree in Fig. 1 guarantees that our proposed non-committed-format majority protocol is correct and secure.

4 Conclusion

In this paper, we constructed a three-input majority protocol using only six cards without depending on private operations. Therefore, this is the first card-minimal protocol for the three-input majority function $\mathsf{maj}(a, b, c)$. We also show that we can obtain a committed-format majority protocol with the minimum number of cards.

The former protocol is so simple that lay-people can easily execute it; see the pseudocode presented in Sect. 3.2 again to recall that the protocol is quite simple. Thus, we believe that our three-input majority protocol is no less practical and beautiful than the five-card trick. We even think that our majority protocol is better than the five-card trick in a sense: lay-people will be able to learn the concept of logical AND and OR operations and their relationship through our majority protocol (because our protocol is based on the nice property that $\mathsf{maj}(a, b, c)$ can be expressed simply using $b \wedge c$ and $b \vee c$, i.e., $\mathsf{maj}(a, b, c)$ is equal to one of the four variants of the five-card trick according to the value of c) while the five-card trick is just based on the fact that the three red cards are consecutive only when $x = y = 1$.

Our committed-format three-input majority protocol shown in Appendix A is not finite-runtime. Since there is no committed-format finite-runtime protocol

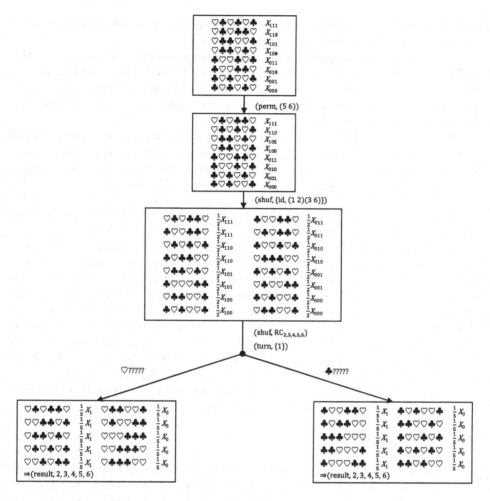

Fig. 1. The KWH-tree of our non-committed-format majority protocol

other than the eight-card protocol proposed by Nishida et al. [17], it is an interesting open problem to determine whether we can have a committed-format finite-runtime three-input majority protocol using less than eight cards. It is also interesting to investigate relationship between card-based general majority function protocols and Turing world computations (cf. [7]).

Acknowledgements. We thank the anonymous referees, whose comments have helped us improve the presentation of the paper. We would like to thank Hideaki Sone for his cooperation in preparing a Japanese draft version at an earlier stage of this work. This work was supported in part by JSPS KAKENHI Grant Numbers JP19J21153 and JP21K11881.

A   Transformation to Committed Format

In this section, we show how to transform our non-committed-format protocol proposed in Sect. 2 to a committed-format one. Subsequently, we give the description of the derived committed-format majority protocol.

A.1   How to Transform

The transformation is inspired by the five-card Las Vegas AND protocol proposed by Abe et al. [3]. Briefly, their protocol realizes to output a commitment to $x \wedge y$, by adding further manipulations to the five-card trick. Since the output in our proposed protocol is derived by using (the four variants of) the five-card trick, it is possible to obtain a commitment to $\mathsf{maj}(a, b, c)$ in a similar way to their protocol.

Here is the idea behind their protocol [3].

1. Perform Steps 1 to 3 of the five-card trick shown in Sect. 1.1:

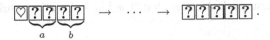

2. Turn over the center card; suppose that ♣ appears:

$$\boxed{?}\,\boxed{?}\,\boxed{?}\,\boxed{?}\,\boxed{?} \quad \rightarrow \quad \boxed{?}\,\boxed{?}\,\boxed{♣}\,\boxed{?}\,\boxed{?}\;.$$

At this time, the resulting sequence of cards is one of the following four cases:

(i)	♡♡♣♡♣	if $a \wedge b = 0$;
(ii)	♣♡♣♡♡	if $a \wedge b = 0$;
(iii)	♡♡♣♣♡	if $a \wedge b = 1$;
(iv)	♡♣♣♡♡	if $a \wedge b = 1$.

3. Turn the center card face down. For the sake of illustration, let us represent the sequence as follows:

$$\underbrace{\boxed{?}\,\boxed{?}}_{x}\,\underbrace{\boxed{?}\,\boxed{?}}_{y}\,\boxed{?}\;.$$

Observe that, in the cases (ii) and (iv), if we let the first and second cards be a commitment to $x \in \{0, 1\}$ and the third and fourth ones be a commitment to $y \in \{0, 1\}$, we have $x \oplus y = a \wedge b$. Therefore, by applying the committed-format XOR protocol [15] to them, one can obtain a commitment to $x \oplus y = a \wedge b$:

$$\underbrace{\boxed{?}\boxed{?}}_{x}\underbrace{\boxed{?}\boxed{?}}_{y}\boxed{?} \quad \to \quad \boxed{\clubsuit}\boxed{\heartsuit}\boxed{?}\boxed{?}\boxed{?} \text{ or } \boxed{\heartsuit}\boxed{\clubsuit}\boxed{?}\boxed{?}\boxed{?}.$$

$$\underset{a\wedge b}{} \qquad\qquad \underset{\overline{a\wedge b}}{}$$

Note that, even if it is the case (i) or (iii), one can still continue to execute the protocol without leaking information, as seen below.

In the next subsection, we present the description of our committed-format protocol using this idea.

A.2   Description

The following is our committed-format three-input majority protocol.

1. Perform Steps 1 to 3 of our non-committed-format protocol presented in Sect. 2.3:

2. Reveal the first card. Assume that it is black, i.e., the result will be $\heartsuit$-based:

(In the case where a red card is shown, it works by interchanging the black cards and the red cards.)
3. Reveal the fourth card. If $\boxed{\heartsuit}$ appears, turn it over and apply a random cut to the second through sixth cards; then, return to this step. If $\boxed{\clubsuit}$ appears, turn it over and go to the next step.
4. Apply the XOR protocol [15] to the second through fifth cards as follows.
   (a) Rearrange the order of the sequence as

   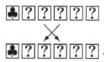

   (b) Apply a random bisection cut to the second through fifth cards:

   $$\boxed{\clubsuit}\left[\boxed{?}\boxed{?}\,\middle|\,\boxed{?}\boxed{?}\right]\boxed{?} \quad \to \quad \boxed{\clubsuit}\boxed{?}\boxed{?}\boxed{?}\boxed{?}\boxed{?}.$$

   (c) Rearrange the order of the sequence as

5. Reveal the second and third cards.
   (a) If ♣♡ or ♡♣ appears, we obtain a commitment to maj(a, b, c) as follows:

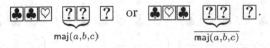

$$\text{maj}(a,b,c) \qquad \overline{\text{maj}(a,b,c)}$$

   In the latter case, by swapping the left and right cards, we obtain a commitment to $\overline{\text{maj}}(a, b, c)$.

   (b) If ♡♡ appears, then turn them over:

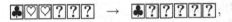

   and rearrange the order of the sequence as

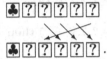

   Then, apply a random cut to the second through sixth cards and return to Step 3.

$$♣ \langle\, ?\,?\,?\,?\,? \,\rangle \rightarrow ♣\,?\,?\,?\,?\,?.$$

Let us find the number of required shuffles for this committed-format protocol. The AND protocol proposed by Abe et al. takes the average of seven shuffles to terminate [3]. Since we apply a random bisection cut first in our protocol, it terminates with the expected number of eight shuffles in total. (It should be noted that a recent technique presented in [4] will reduce the number of shuffles further).

A.3 Pseudocode

A pseudocode for our committed-format majority protocol is depicted in Algorithm 2.

Algorithm 2 Our committed-format majority protocol

---

input set:

$$
\left\{ \left(\frac{?}{\heartsuit}, \frac{?}{\clubsuit}, \frac{?}{\heartsuit}, \frac{?}{\clubsuit}, \frac{?}{\heartsuit}, \frac{?}{\clubsuit} \right), \left(\frac{?}{\heartsuit}, \frac{?}{\clubsuit}, \frac{?}{\heartsuit}, \frac{?}{\clubsuit}, \frac{?}{\clubsuit}, \frac{?}{\heartsuit} \right), \left(\frac{?}{\heartsuit}, \frac{?}{\clubsuit}, \frac{?}{\clubsuit}, \frac{?}{\heartsuit}, \frac{?}{\heartsuit}, \frac{?}{\clubsuit} \right), \right.
$$
$$
\left(\frac{?}{\heartsuit}, \frac{?}{\clubsuit}, \frac{?}{\clubsuit}, \frac{?}{\heartsuit}, \frac{?}{\clubsuit}, \frac{?}{\heartsuit} \right), \left(\frac{?}{\clubsuit}, \frac{?}{\heartsuit}, \frac{?}{\heartsuit}, \frac{?}{\clubsuit}, \frac{?}{\heartsuit}, \frac{?}{\clubsuit} \right), \left(\frac{?}{\clubsuit}, \frac{?}{\heartsuit}, \frac{?}{\heartsuit}, \frac{?}{\clubsuit}, \frac{?}{\clubsuit}, \frac{?}{\heartsuit} \right),
$$
$$
\left. \left(\frac{?}{\clubsuit}, \frac{?}{\heartsuit}, \frac{?}{\clubsuit}, \frac{?}{\heartsuit}, \frac{?}{\heartsuit}, \frac{?}{\clubsuit} \right), \left(\frac{?}{\clubsuit}, \frac{?}{\heartsuit}, \frac{?}{\clubsuit}, \frac{?}{\heartsuit}, \frac{?}{\clubsuit}, \frac{?}{\heartsuit} \right) \right\}
$$

1. (perm, (5 6))
2. (shuf, {id, (1 2)(3 6)})
3. (shuf, $RC_{2,3,4,5,6}$)
4. (turn, {1})
5. **if** visible sequence = $(\heartsuit, ?, ?, ?, ?, ?)$ **then**
6.   (turn, {4})
7.   **if** visible sequence = $(\heartsuit, ?, ?, \heartsuit, ?, ?)$ **then**
8.   (turn, {4})
9.   (shuf, $RC_{2,3,4,5,6}$)
10.   **go to 6**
11.   **else if** visible sequence = $(\heartsuit, ?, ?, \clubsuit, ?, ?)$ **then**
12.   (turn, {4})
13.   (shuf, {id, (2 3)(4 5)})
14.   (turn, {2, 3})
15.   **if** visible sequence = $(\heartsuit, \heartsuit, \heartsuit, ?, ?, ?)$ **then**
16.   (turn, {2, 3})
17.   (perm, (3 4 5 6))
18.   (shuf, $RC_{2,3,4,5,6}$)
19.   **go to 6**
20.   **else if** visible sequence = $(\heartsuit, \heartsuit, \clubsuit, ?, ?, ?)$ **then**
21.   (result, 4, 5)
22.   **else if** visible sequence = $(\heartsuit, \clubsuit, \heartsuit, ?, ?, ?)$ **then**
23.   (result, 5, 4)
24. **else if** visible sequence = $(\clubsuit, ?, ?, ?, ?, ?)$ **then**
25.   (turn, {4})
26.   **if** visible sequence = $(\clubsuit, ?, ?, \clubsuit, ?, ?)$ **then**
27.   (turn, {4})
28.   (shuf, $RC_{2,3,4,5,6}$)
29.   **go to 25**
30.   **else if** visible sequence = $(\clubsuit, ?, ?, \heartsuit, ?, ?)$ **then**
31.   (turn, {4})
32.   (shuf, {id, (2 3)(4 5)})
33.   (turn, {2, 3})
34.   **if** visible sequence = $(\clubsuit, \clubsuit, \clubsuit, ?, ?, ?)$ **then**
35.   (turn, {2, 3})
36.   (perm, (3 4 5 6))
37.   (shuf, $RC_{2,3,4,5,6}$)
38.   **go to 25**
39.   **else if** visible sequence = $(\clubsuit, \clubsuit, \heartsuit, ?, ?, ?)$ **then**
40.   (result, 4, 5)
41.   **else if** visible sequence = $(\clubsuit, \heartsuit, \clubsuit, ?, ?, ?)$ **then**
42.   (result, 5, 4)

A.4   Correctness and Security

To verify the correctness and security of our proposed committed-format majority protocol, we describe its KWH-tree in Fig. 2; it guarantees that our protocol is correct and secure.

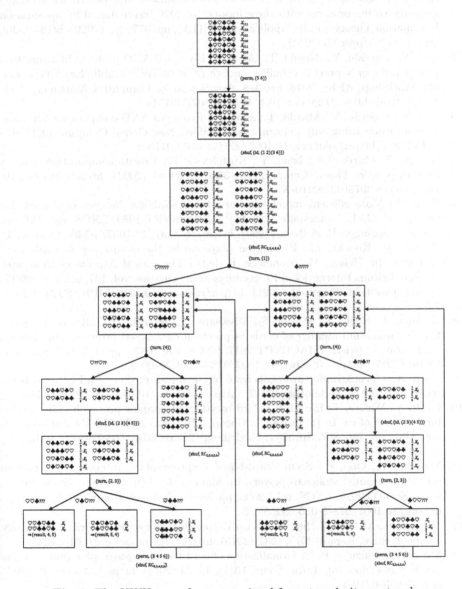

Fig. 2. The KWH-tree of our committed-format majority protocol

References

1. Abe, Y., Iwamoto, M., Ohta, K.: Efficient private PEZ protocols for symmetric functions. In: Hofheinz, D., Rosen, A. (eds.) TCC 2019. LNCS, vol. 11891, pp. 372–392. Springer, Cham (2019). https://doi.org/10.1007/978-3-030-36030-6_15

2. Abe, Y., Iwamoto, M., Ohta, K.: How to detect malicious behaviors in a card-based majority voting protocol with three inputs. In: 2020 International Symposium on Information Theory and Its Applications (ISITA), pp. 377–381 (2020). https://doi.org/10.34385/proc.65.C01-9

3. Abe, Y., Hayashi, Y., Mizuki, T., Sone, H.: Five-card AND protocol in committed format using only practical shuffles. In: 5th ACM on ASIA Public-Key Cryptography Workshop, APKC 2018, pp. 3–8. Association for Computing Machinery, New York (2018). https://doi.org/10.1145/3197507.3197510

4. Abe, Y., Hayashi, Y., Mizuki, T., Sone, H.: Five-card AND computations in committed format using only uniform cyclic shuffles. New Gener. Comput. **39**(1), 97–114 (2021). https://doi.org/10.1007/s00354-020-00110-2

5. Balogh, J., Csirik, J.A., Ishai, Y., Kushilevitz, E.: Private computation using a PEZ dispenser. Theor. Comput. Sci. **306**(1), 69–84 (2003). https://doi.org/10.1016/S0304-3975(03)00210-X

6. Boer, B.: More efficient match-making and satisfiability *the five card trick*. In: Quisquater, J.-J., Vandewalle, J. (eds.) EUROCRYPT 1989. LNCS, vol. 434, pp. 208–217. Springer, Heidelberg (1990). https://doi.org/10.1007/3-540-46885-4_23

7. Dvořák, P., Koucký, M.: Barrington plays cards: the complexity of card-based protocols. In: Bläser, M., Monmege, B. (eds.) Theoretical Aspects of Computer Science. Leibniz International Proceedings in Informatics, vol. 187, pp. 26:1–26:17. Schloss Dagstuhl, Dagstuhl (2021). https://doi.org/10.4230/LIPIcs.STACS.2021.26

8. Kastner, J., Koch, A., Walzer, S., Miyahara, D., Hayashi, Y., Mizuki, T., Sone, H.: The minimum number of cards in practical card-based protocols. In: Takagi, T., Peyrin, T. (eds.) ASIACRYPT 2017. LNCS, vol. 10626, pp. 126–155. Springer, Cham (2017). https://doi.org/10.1007/978-3-319-70700-6_5

9. Koch, A.: Cryptographic protocols from physical assumptions. Ph.D. thesis, Karlsruhe Institute of Technology (2019). https://doi.org/10.5445/IR/1000097756

10. Koch, A., Walzer, S., Härtel, K.: Card-based cryptographic protocols using a minimal number of cards. In: Iwata, T., Cheon, J.H. (eds.) ASIACRYPT 2015. LNCS, vol. 9452, pp. 783–807. Springer, Heidelberg (2015). https://doi.org/10.1007/978-3-662-48797-6_32

11. Manabe, Y., Ono, H.: Secure card-based cryptographic protocols using private operations against malicious players. In: Maimut, D., Oprina, A.-G., Sauveron, D. (eds.) SecITC 2020. LNCS, vol. 12596, pp. 55–70. Springer, Cham (2021). https://doi.org/10.1007/978-3-030-69255-1_5

12. Marcedone, A., Wen, Z., Shi, E.: Secure dating with four or fewer cards. Cryptology ePrint Archive, Report 2015/1031 (2015). https://eprint.iacr.org/2015/1031

13. Mizuki, T., Shizuya, H.: A formalization of card-based cryptographic protocols via abstract machine. Int. J. Inf. Secur. **13**(1), 15–23 (2013). https://doi.org/10.1007/s10207-013-0219-4

14. Mizuki, T., Shizuya, H.: Computational model of card-based cryptographic protocols and its applications. IEICE Trans. Fundam. Electron. Commun. Comput. Sci. **E100.A**(1), 3–11 (2017). https://doi.org/10.1587/transfun.E100.A.3

15. Mizuki, T., Sone, H.: Six-card secure AND and four-card secure XOR. In: Deng, X., Hopcroft, J.E., Xue, J. (eds.) FAW 2009. LNCS, vol. 5598, pp. 358–369. Springer, Heidelberg (2009). https://doi.org/10.1007/978-3-642-02270-8_36

16. Nakai, T., Shirouchi, S., Iwamoto, M., Ohta, K.: Four cards are sufficient for a card-based three-input voting protocol utilizing private permutations. In: Shikata, J. (ed.) ICITS 2017. LNCS, vol. 10681, pp. 153–165. Springer, Cham (2017). https://doi.org/10.1007/978-3-319-72089-0_9

17. Nishida, T., Mizuki, T., Sone, H.: Securely computing the three-input majority function with eight cards. In: Dediu, A.-H., Martín-Vide, C., Truthe, B., Vega-Rodríguez, M.A. (eds.) TPNC 2013. LNCS, vol. 8273, pp. 193–204. Springer, Heidelberg (2013). https://doi.org/10.1007/978-3-642-45008-2_16

18. Ono, H., Manabe, Y.: Card-based cryptographic protocols with the minimum number of cards using private operations. In: Zincir-Heywood, N., Bonfante, G., Debbabi, M., Garcia-Alfaro, J. (eds.) FPS 2018. LNCS, vol. 11358, pp. 193–207. Springer, Cham (2019). https://doi.org/10.1007/978-3-030-18419-3_13

19. Ono, H., Manabe, Y.: Card-based cryptographic logical computations using private operations. New Gener. Comput. **39**, 19–40 (2021). https://doi.org/10.1007/s00354-020-00113-z

20. Pass, R., Shelat, A.: A course in cryptography (2010). www.cs.cornell.edu/~rafael/

21. Ruangwises, S., Itoh, T.: AND protocols using only uniform shuffles. In: van Bevern, R., Kucherov, G. (eds.) CSR 2019. LNCS, vol. 11532, pp. 349–358. Springer, Cham (2019). https://doi.org/10.1007/978-3-030-19955-5_30

22. Salomaa, A.: Public-Key Cryptography. Texts in Theoretical Computer Science. An EATCS Series, Springer, Heidelberg (2013)

23. Shinagawa, K.: On the construction of easy to perform card-based protocols. Ph.D. thesis, Tokyo Institute of Technology (2020)

24. Ueda, I., Miyahara, D., Nishimura, A., Hayashi, Y., Mizuki, T., Sone, H.: Secure implementations of a random bisection cut. Int. J. Inf. Secur. **19**(4), 445–452 (2019). https://doi.org/10.1007/s10207-019-00463-w

25. Watanabe, Y., Kuroki, Y., Suzuki, S., Koga, Y., Iwamoto, M., Ohta, K.: Card-based majority voting protocols with three inputs using three cards. In: 2018 International Symposium on Information Theory and Its Applications (ISITA), pp. 218–222 (2018). https://doi.org/10.23919/ISITA.2018.8664324

26. Yasunaga, K.: Practical card-based protocol for three-input majority. IEICE Trans. Fundam. Electron. Commun. Comput. Sci. **E103.A**(11), 1296–1298 (2020). https://doi.org/10.1587/transfun.2020EAL2025

Blockchains

On Elapsed Time Consensus Protocols

Mic Bowman[1], Debajyoti Das[2(✉)], Avradip Mandal[3], and Hart Montgomery[3]

[1] Intel Labs, Santa Clara, USA
mic.bowman@intel.com
[2] imec-COSIC, KU Leuven, Leuven, Belgium
debajyoti.das@esat.kuleuven.be
[3] Fujitsu Laboratories of America, Sunnyvale, USA
{amandal,hhmontgomery}@fujitsu.com

Abstract. *Proof of Elapsed Time* (PoET) is a Nakamoto-style consensus algorithm where proof of work is replaced by a wait time randomly generated by a trusted execution environment (TEE). PoET was originally developed by Intel engineers and contributed to Hyperledger Sawtooth, but has never been formally defined or analyzed. In particular, PoET enables consensus on a bitcoin-like scale without having to resort to mining. *Proof of Luck* (PoL), designed by Milutinovic et al., is a similar (but not identical) protocol that also builds a Nakamoto-style consensus algorithm using a TEE. Like PoET, it also lacks a formal proof.

In this work, we formally define a simplified version of PoET and PoL, which we call *elapsed time consensus* (ET) with a trusted timer. We prove the security of our ET consensus with a trusted timer given an honest majority assumption in a model that generalizes the bitcoin backbone model proposed by Garay et al. which we call the *elapsed time backbone model*. Our model and protocol aim to capture the essence of PoET and PoL while ignoring some of the more practical difficulties associated with such protocols, such as bootstrapping and setting up the TEE.

The PoET protocol also contains a function called the z-test that limits the number of blocks a player can publish in any particular set of blocks of some (larger) size. Surprisingly, by improving this z-test we can prove the security of our ET consensus protocol *without* any TEEs with a (slightly stronger) honest majority assumption. This implies that Nakamoto-style consensus with rate limiting and no proofs of work can be used to obtain scalable consensus in a permissioned setting: in other words, "bitcoin without proofs of work" can be made secure without a TEE for private blockchains.

1 Introduction

In today's interconnected world, it is important to be able to share data widely but in a selective manner. Efficient distributed databases have been known for quite some time and continue to improve [48]. However, basic distributed

D. Das—This work was started during Debajyoti Das' internship at Fujitsu Laboratories of America and continued during the his PhD studies at Purdue.

© Springer Nature Switzerland AG 2021
A. Adhikari et al. (Eds.): INDOCRYPT 2021, LNCS 13143, pp. 559–583, 2021.
https://doi.org/10.1007/978-3-030-92518-5_25

databases have a core problem: they have absolutely no protection from malicious users. Since we do not live in a perfect world, we cannot expect database users to be angels [38], and this leads to many practical issues when using distributed databases: what happens when two people or entities that do not trust each other need to share data? What if some participants in the database are outright malicious?

Almost two decades ago, Castro and Liskov [18] came up with a clever solution to this problem: the practical byzantine fault tolerant (PBFT) consensus algorithm. PBFT was a clever and practical invention: it allowed people to use what were essentially distributed databases that tolerated up to a third of the users being malicious. This was a big improvement over basic distributed databases, but still did not allow for truly public databases. In addition, PBFT protocols require a large amount of communication between participants–$O\left(n^2\right)$, for n parties [25], which makes them very difficult to scale. So while PBFT protocols proved to be very useful for many applications of distributed computing, they did not fully solve the fundamental problem at hand.

In 2008, another new technology radically changed the state of distributed databases: bitcoin [41]. Someone using the pseudonym Satoshi Nakamoto designed what amounted to a new distributed database with some pretty incredible properties: the database is fully public, so anyone can participate, and (probabilistic) consensus in the optimistic case only requires $O\left(n\right)$ communication, meaning that it is easy for tens of thousands of users to participate in bitcoin at any given time. The ideas behind bitcoin have been further generalized: blockchains enabling smart contracts such as Ethereum constitute even more powerful types of distributed database.

But bitcoin and other proof of work-based systems have one major drawback: energy consumption. One source [1] reports that the power consumed for bitcoin proof-of-work in January 2019 was around 40TWh/year, comparable to the power use of a small country. In essence, the public trust that bitcoin guarantees is directly correlated to the energy consumption of the bitcoin miners. To put it differently, bitcoin's resiliency to attack is a direct result of consuming large amounts of power.

This brings us to a fundamental question in modern distributed databases: can we build systems with many of the good core properties of bitcoin–scalability and broadly decentralized trust—without the drawbacks associated with mining?

In an attempt to offer a low power but scalable alternative, Intel included in the Hyperledger Sawtooth [2] distributed ledger platform a form of Nakamoto consensus that replaced proof-of-work with an alternative called *proof of elapsed time (PoET)* [3], which utilizes the security properties provided by a trusted execution environment (TEE). Several academic works [21,47] point to the efficiency of PoET and its strong performance in large systems. However, PoET lacks any formal analysis, and we fill that gap in this paper.

1.1   Our Contributions

We generalize the PoET and Proof of Luck protocols into what we call *elapsed time (ET) consensus*, where we relax the PoET protocol to focus on the critical protocol itself and ignore some of the difficulties faced in practical implementations, such as bootstrapping, onboarding parties, and dynamic membership. We provide a formal description of our ET consensus protocol (as per our knowledge, there is no formal description of PoET available anywhere).

Our model can be considered as a generalization of the bitcoin backbone model [28, 29]—that might be of independent interest.

We focus on elapsed time consensus protocols with two main assumptions on the TEE: (1) The TEE has access to a trusted timer. (2) No TEEs are present, or TEEs can be easily compromised [32, 34, 36, 49].

ET Consensus with Trusted Timer. We first define a basic version of our protocol: *elapsed time consensus with a trusted timer*, where the TEE has access to a trusted timer.[1] This protocol captures the essence of PoET [3] and other related works like proof of luck [40] (which we discuss more later). We show that our ET consensus protocol with a trusted timer provides similar security guarantees as bitcoin with the same honest majority assumption.

Elapsed Time Consensus with a z-Test. We modify our basic ET consensus protocol and include a z-test to avoid the dependency on TEEs. However, our z-test is quite different than the one proposed by the Intel engineers, as theirs is not sufficient for our proof.[2] Instead of checking the proportion of the total number of blocks a player produces in a chain, we (essentially) restrict how many blocks a player can produce over a sliding window of time.

We prove that ET consensus with our z-test is secure in our (permissioned) model **without TEEs** and assuming that some constant fraction ($> \frac{2}{3}$) of the participants are Byzantine. In other words, we show that "bitcoin without mining" coupled with some clever rate-limiting (the z-test) is secure in a permissioned network without any hardware security guarantees, even if up to 33% parties are dishonest.

Until now, PoET, proof of luck, and other elapsed time based consensus systems have never (to our knowledge) been formally proven secure. Perhaps the most exciting implication of our proofs, though, is that we can ignore TEEs completely in these protocols and still maintain relatively good security with our z-test. This notion of "permissioned bitcoin without mining" will be very useful for future blockchain developments.

1.2 Related Work

The only current work of which we are aware on the security of PoET is [19]. This work shows how an adversary that is capable of compromising SGX can attack PoET up to the bounds of the z-test that PoET currently uses. Unfortunately, this paper does not offer any formal analysis in the other direction: it does not include a rigorous security proof that PoET is secure outside of these bounds. As

---

[1] Many TEEs, including SGX [4], have a trusted timer or equivalent functionality.

[2] Using the z-test given by the PoET specification would require much stronger parameter settings than for which we achieve provable security.

we have mentioned before, we note that Milutinovic et al. [40] define a consensus protocol called *proof of luck* (PoL) that functions very similarly to PoET, but do not offer a security analysis to their protocol or even a comparison to PoET. Additionally, the authors of [5] show a construction of a proof of stake protocol using TEEs, but this protocol also lacks a formal security proof.

Improved consensus algorithms and models with exciting new properties have proliferated recently. Some examples include Thunderella [45], the sleepy model of consensus [44], Snow White [22], Fruitchain [43], Ouroboros [24,31], Bitcoin-NG [27], Casper [15], Stellar [39], and ByzCoin [33]. Exciting new work in the space includes things like proofs of space and storage [9,20,26] and verifiable delay functions [12]. However, most of these protocols focus on public blockchains.

Comparatively, the academically-focused work on permissioned blockchains has been substantially less, but has notably included things like an analysis of Hyperledger Fabric [6,16] and the Tendermint consensus protocol [35]. Work on Byzantine fault tolerant consensus has also been done [11], including the recent an exciting development of [51]. There have also been a number of very useful papers that have analyzed these consensus protocols and their properties, including [10,17,30,42,50].

Several consensus protocols in past have leveraged different forms of trusted hardware. For example, MinBFT [46] proposes a trusted counter to reduce the number of nodes required from $3F + 1$ to $2F + 1$ for F faulty nodes. More recently, FastBFT [37] uses a trusted execution environment to aggregate messages for latency and throughput improvements. Other protocols use TEEs for the purposes of sharing on blockchains [23].

2   Elapsed Time Backbone Model

Our model can be considered as a generalization of [28]. Here we provide a summary and refer to our extended version [13] for a complete description.

2.1   Notations

We assume that the blockchain protocol has a fixed number n of players. We use $\mathcal{H} : \{0,1\}^* \rightarrow \{0,1\}^\kappa$ to represent a cryptographic hash function (modelled as a random oracle). A *block* is any tuple of the form $B = \langle s, x, \pi \rangle$, where $s \in \{0,1\}^\kappa$ is the hash of the previous block, $x \in \{0,1\}^*$ is the content of the block and $\pi \in \{0,1\}^*$ is the proof of block validity. validblock is the predicate that takes a block B and a chain $\mathcal{C}$ as input, checks validity of the content of B.

A *blockchain* or *chain* is a sequence of *blocks*. The (current) last block of a blockchain $\mathcal{C}$ is called the *head* of $\mathcal{C}$ and is denoted by $\mathcal{C}.head$. For an empty string or empty blockchain ε, we have $\varepsilon.head = \varepsilon$. The *length* of a chain is its number of blocks. A chain $\mathcal{C}$ can be extended by a block $B = \langle s, x, \pi \rangle$ if $s = \mathcal{H}(\mathcal{C}.head)$, ValidBlock$(B, \mathcal{C})$ is true and $B.\pi$ is a valid proof for the extended chain $\mathcal{C}' = \mathcal{C} \| B$. For the new chain $\mathcal{C}'$, we have $\mathcal{C}'.head = B$. For any chain $\mathcal{C} = (B_1, \cdots, B_\ell)$, $Length(\mathcal{C}) = \ell$ denotes the length of the chain. For any pair of integers $1 \leq i \leq j \leq \ell$, the chain $\tilde{\mathcal{C}} = (B_i, \cdots, B_j)$ is called a subchain of $\mathcal{C}$. $\mathcal{C}^{\lceil k}$ denotes the chain resulting from removing the k rightmost blocks, for a given non-negative integer k. If $k \geq \ell$, then $\mathcal{C}^{\lceil k} = \varepsilon$. For two chains $\mathcal{C}_1, \mathcal{C}_2$ the notation $\mathcal{C}_1 \preceq \mathcal{C}_2$ denotes that $\mathcal{C}_1$ is a prefix of $\mathcal{C}_2$.

2.2 Model and Structure

Our model assumes round-based protocols as in [7,28,29]. In our model we have three top level parameters: the total number of players n, the security parameter λ and honest parties' advantage δ. If t is the number of corrupt players then we require that $\frac{t}{n-t} \leq 1 - \delta$.

Adversary. We allow the adversary to see all of the *global variables* in the system, including the description of all of the algorithms in the protocol. The adversary can corrupt players at the beginning or during the protocol run, as long as the total number of corrupted players does not exceed t.

Model Rules. We model communication among protocol parties by having a global array of queues $PLAYER\_QUEUE[n]$ - where $PLAYER\_QUEUE[i]$ represents the queue associated with player i. We let each party send to other players' queues, but only read from their own queue.

2.3 Abstractions

In this work we use the following abstractions to simplify our protocol and proof.

Certifications. We use the *Cert* functionality (Fig. 1) instead of explicitly using digital signatures - they act as completely unforgeable, perfect digital signatures.

Cert$_u$ (Statement m): //certificate issued by u attesting validity of m

IsCertValid$_u$ (*Cert* $c_{u,m}$, **Statement** m):

   Return 1 if $c_{u,m}$ certifies statement m on behalf of user u and 0 otherwise.

Fig. 1. Certification functionality.

Trusted Execution Environment (TEE). In our model, a TEE is an unbreakable black box (a VBB obfuscator [8]) that runs some code in a way that completely hides the internals of the code—an adversary can only see the input and output values of the program being run by the TEE. We note that this is an idealistic model for a TEE since it presumes perfect security and no side channel attacks. We represent our abstraction of TEE in Fig. 2.

   In some protocols, we will give our TEE a trusted timer functionality. Since time is approximated by round number in our protocol, we will have the TEE return the current round number for this function. Additionally, we endow our TEE with a monotonic counter *TEE.Counter* which can never be decreased in value, *even if the TEE is reset.* We note that many modern TEEs like Intel's SGX have both trusted timer and monotonic counter functionalities [4].

TEE.$\alpha := null$; // Can be set to any program code.
TEE.$args := null$; // Arguments for $\alpha()$.
TEE.$Counter := 0$; // monotonic counter inside TEE.

TEE.GetCounterValue()
  Return TEE.Counter   // Just return the counter value.

TEE.CounterSet(x)
  if $TEE.Counter < x$ then $TEE.Counter \leftarrow x$ end if

TEE.Run($Prog, arguments$):
  // Run the program $Prog$ inside the TEE.
  // If there is any currently running program it aborts the current program.

  Abort(α); $\alpha \leftarrow Prog$; $args \leftarrow arguments$; Run $\alpha(args)$

TEE.Poll():
  // Can be called only after calling TEE.Run()
  if $\alpha = null$ then return $\perp$ end if
  if $\alpha()$ has completed running then
    $O \leftarrow$ output of $\alpha(args)$, **Return** $(O, \mathbf{Cert}_{TEE}(O||\alpha||args))$
  else return $Incomplete$ end if

Fig. 2. TEE functionality

2.4 Blockchain Properties

We next define three core blockchain properties: the common prefix property, the chain quality property, and the chain growth property. As argued in [28], these properties together essentially define what it means to be a functional and useful blockchain.

Definition 1. *Common Prefix Property*: *Suppose $\mathcal{C}_1$ is a chain which has been accepted by an honest party at round r_1 and $\mathcal{C}_2$ is another chain which has been accepted by some honest party at round $r_2 (\geq r_1)$. Then $\mathcal{C}_1^{\lceil k} \preceq \mathcal{C}_2$ holds for all integers $k \geq \ell_{cf}$, where ℓ_{cf} is the common prefix parameter.*

Definition 2. *Chain Quality Property*: *Suppose $\mathcal{C}$ is a chain that has been accepted by some honest party. Any subchain $\tilde{\mathcal{C}}$ of $\mathcal{C}$ of length $\tilde{\ell} \geq \ell_q$ must contain at least $\mu\tilde{\ell}$ many honest blocks. Here ℓ_q, μ are the chain quality parameters (Table 1).*

Table 1. Table of all parameters

n	:	Total number of players
t	:	Number of corrupted players
δ	:	Advantage of honest parties, $(\frac{t}{n-t} \leq 1 - \delta)$
p	:	Probability that an honest player creates a block in a given round
f	:	Probability at least one honest player creates a block in a given round
r_{end}	:	Total number of rounds in the security game
ϵ	:	A security parameter used to bound the "luckiness" of the adversary
		See the "typical execution" definition in Sect. 5.1
ϵ'	:	Quality of concentration for z-test (Definition 4)
λ	:	Security parameter
ℓ_{cf}	:	Minimum number of blocks in common prefix property
μ	:	Parameter in chain quality property
ℓ_q	:	Minimum number of blocks for which the chain quality property holds.
τ	:	Minimum number of blocks in chain growth property.
σ	:	Maximum number of blocks in chain growth property.
r_g	:	Minimum number of rounds for which the chain growth property holds

A block is an honest block, if it is created by an honest party.

Definition 3.   *Chain Growth Property: Suppose C_1 is a chain of length ℓ_1 which has been accepted by an honest party at round r_1 and C_2 is another chain of length ℓ_2 which has been accepted by some honest party at round r_2. If $r_2 - r_1 > r_g$, then $\ell_2 - \ell_1 \in [\tau(r_2 - r_1), \sigma(r_2 - r_1)]$. Here r_g, τ, σ are the chain growth parameters.*

Block.π:

π.timestamp   // Round of "mining."
π.WaitTime   // How many rounds until the block can be issued.
π.WaitCert   // Proof that a TEE generated the WaitTime properly.

Fig. 3. Block proof structure

3   Elapsed Time Consensus Protocol with Trusted Timer

Here we construct an elapsed time consensus protocol with a trusted timer. We start by defining the block validity proof π of a block in Fig. 3. The basic version of our ET protocol (with trusted timer), denoted by ET_{timer}, works in two phases: (1) Initialization phase and (2) Leader election phase.

Initialization Phase. In this phase, the challenger initializes the blockchain by calling *Genesis*() (refer to Fig. 4), which in turn creates the genesis block $B_{genesis}$ and initializes all the players.

Genesis(n, λ):

    generate the genesis block $B_{genesis}$
    $P :=$ Geometric Distribution with parameter p
    for $i = 1$ to n; i++ **do**
        $PLAYERS[i].Initialize(i, B_{genesis})$
    end for

Fig. 4. Initialization of the *Blockchain* for ET_{timer}

Leader Election Phase. In this phase, all the players compete with each other to be elected to generate the next block. Once a block is generated, they start a fresh competition and repeat the process [3]. We define the leader election protocol in the *RunPlayer*() routine defined in Fig. 5. For an honest user, the challenger runs *RunPlayer*() exactly once per round.

In every round, *RunPlayer*() checks if there are new chains in the input buffer of the player. These chains are generated in the previous round by other players. Our current player picks the best chain according to *PickChain*()

---

chain $\mathcal{C} := empty$; // A chain - an ordered list of blocks.
playerID; // denotes the index of the player provided by the challenger
TEE; // denotes the trusted execution environment specific to the player

Initialize(integer i, the genesis block $B_{genesis}$):

    $playerID \leftarrow i$; Add $B_{genesis}$ to $\mathcal{C}$;
    Initialize the TEE for player i
    $x \leftarrow$ Collected transactions from users;
    $TEE.Run(WaitForBlock(), \mathcal{C}, x)$

RunPlayer():

    if $PLAYER\_QUEUE[playerID]$ is not empty **then**
        $\mathcal{C}_{new} \leftarrow PickChain(playerID, \mathcal{C})$ // Defined in Fig 6
        if $\mathcal{C}_{new} \neq \mathcal{C}$ **then**
            $\mathcal{C} \leftarrow \mathcal{C}_{new}$; $x \leftarrow$ Collected transactions from users
            $TEE.Run(WaitForBlock, \mathcal{C}, x)$ // Wait on TEE for the next block
        end if
    else
        if $TEE.Poll() \neq Incomplete \wedge TEE.Poll() \neq \perp$ **then**
            // It seems the player is a leader
            $(B, WaitCert) \leftarrow TEE.Poll()$; $B.\pi.WaitCert \leftarrow WaitCert$
            Add B to $\mathcal{C}$; $Broadcast(\mathcal{C})$
            // Again, repeat for the next leader election
            $x \leftarrow$ Collected transactions; $TEE.Run(WaitForBlock, \mathcal{C}, x)$
        end if
    end if

Fig. 5. Ideal functionality of ET consensus protocol

(defined in Fig. 6) to replace (if applicable) its own local chain. If $PickChain()$ updates the local chain, our player stops competing for the last election and calls $TEE.Run(WaitForBlock, \mathcal{C}, \cdots)$ to start a new competition.

PickChain(integer i denoting the player index, current chain $\mathcal{C}$):

  for each $\mathcal{C}^*$ in $PLAYER\_QUEUE[i]$ **do**
    // Check if the chain is valid and longer than the current chain
    // In case of a tie, keep the current chain
    if $(Length(\mathcal{C}^*) > Length(\mathcal{C})) \wedge IsChainValid(\mathcal{C}^*)$ **then** $\mathcal{C} \leftarrow \mathcal{C}^*$ **end if**
  end for
  return $\mathcal{C}$

IsChainValid(chain $\mathcal{C}^* = \{B_1, B_2, \ldots B_\ell\}$):

  if B_1 is not the genesis block **then** return $false$ **end if**
  for each block B_i in $\mathcal{C}^*$ except B_1 **do**
    $\mathcal{C}_{i-1} \leftarrow (B_1, \cdots, B_{i-1})$
    // Verify that the current block is pointing to the previous block
    if ($B_i.s \neq \mathcal{H}(B_{i-1})$) **then** return $false$
    // Verify that the block is not created ahead of its previous block
    else if $(B_i.\pi.timestamp < B_i.\pi.WaitTime + B_{i-1}.\pi.timestamp)$
    then return $false$
    // Verify the $WaitCert$ and content for the block
    else if $!ValidBlock(B_i, \mathcal{C}_{i-1}) \vee !\textbf{IsCertValid}_{TEE}(B_i.\pi.WaitCert,$
                                 $B_i.\pi.WaitTime \| WaitForBlock \| (\mathcal{C}_{i-1}, B_i.x))$
    then return $false$
    else continue
    end if
  end for
  // Verify that the last block is not created ahead of time
  if ($B_\ell.\pi.timestamp \geq$ current-round) **then** return $false$ **end if**
  // If z-test is running, verify that the chain satisfies z-test property
  if ($z_{\epsilon',\lambda}(\mathcal{C}, B_\ell.\pi.playerID) = 0$) **then** return $false$ **end if**
  return $true$

Fig. 6. Chain selection mechanism for ET consensus (the part in red is only applicable when z-test is used as defined in Definition 4.)

Given an existing chain $\mathcal{C}$, the leader election mechanism works very much like a lottery algorithm: a player wins an election if their $WaitTime$ (picked from a pre-defined probability distribution P) is smallest among all players. The TEE runs $WaitForBlock(\mathcal{C})$ (defined in Fig. 7) for a player to generate $WaitTime$.

Collision Resolution: It is possible that two players get the same $WaitTime$. In that case, both the players broadcast their chains in the same round, each chain with a newly added block – it is considered a collision.

Each player handles collision locally in the following way (refer to Fig. 6 for the pseudocode representation): If two chains $C1$ and $C2$ are of same length, and the last blocks in $C1$ and $C2$ were generated at rounds t_1 and t_2 respectively. Among t_1 and t_2, whichever is smaller the corresponding chain is chosen. However, if $t_1 = t_2$, the collision is not resolved; the player can choose any one of the chains as the current chain and keeps mining for that chain. If C_1 and C_2 are of different lengths, the longer chain is chosen by the player.

Note that, since we have a synchronized round based model and the players have access to a reliable broadcast mechanism, it might seem unlikely to have $t_1 \neq t_2$. However, a compromised player might choose not to broadcast his chain, or selectively send the chain to some players.

WaitForBlock(chain C, transactions x)

    if (TEE.GetCounterValue() $\geq Length(C)$) **then** return $\bot$
    else TEE.CounterSet($Length(C)$) **end if**
    $waitTime \leftarrow$ draw an element from P; $sleep(waitTime)$
    $B \leftarrow CreateBlock(waitTime, C, x)$; **return** B

CreateBlock(time delay t, chain C, transactions x):

    create an empty block B; $B.x \leftarrow x$ // Add transactions
    $B.s \leftarrow \mathcal{H}(C.head)$ // Point to the last block of the existing chain
    $B.\pi.timestamp \leftarrow$ current-round; $B.\pi.WaitTime \leftarrow t$
    $B.\pi.playerID \leftarrow$ current player ID; **return** B

Fig. 7. Function to be run under Trusted Execution Environment (TEE)

Probability Distribution for WaitTime. In our protocol, the TEE generates the $WaitTime$ by sampling from a probability distribution. In our case, we use a geometric distribution where the probability of success in each round is p.[3] The parameters of the probability distribution are defined by the protocol, and are globally known. Each $WaitTime$ is independent of all previous ones and all other players. We denote the probability distribution with P.

Due to the memorylessness of geometric distribution adversarial parties gain no information about the sampled wait times until the wait time actually expires and TEE releases the block. The following lemma captures this fact.

Lemma 1. *The event that any party generates a block in a given round happens with probability at most p over the random coins of that party's TEE. This event is independent of all other random coins in the protocol as well as adversarial choices.*

Proof (Proof Sketch for Lemma 1).

The probability of block generation by an honest party can only be influenced if a new block arrives. However, because the adversary has no knowledge about

---

[3] Here we are considering the version of geometric distribution where trial number $WaitTime$ is the first successful trial.

the current wait times of honest or adversarial parties, drawing a new wait time is exactly same as drawing a new element from the probability distribution with replacement, and hence, is independent of the current wait times or any past wait times.

The memorylessness property of geometric distribution ensures that the probability of generating a block by an honest party is p in a given round, independent of if the party has queried a new wait time in that round or not. An adversarial party can draw a new wait time in two ways:

1. if the party decides to discard the current wait time and draw a new wait time,
2. or, after the completion of the current wait time.

In the first case, the probability for the adversarial party to generate a block in a given round still remains p since the wait time is stored inside the TEE and the party does not see it. In the second case, the probability is trivially p. Note here, we assume that the adversarial party always generates a block, when the TEE time expires.   □

With the above lemma in place the security proof for ET consensus with trusted timer is very similar to that of bitcoin [29] and provides exactly the same security properties; we skip the detailed proof here and refer to [29]; in Appendix 6.4 we summarize the security properties achieved by the protocol for completeness.

4   ET Consensus with Z-Test

We already know that operations within a TEE may be subject to attacks [32, 34, 36, 49]. In PoET, PoL, and ET consensus with TEEs, we are mainly concerned about two forms of attack: accelerating the trusted timer and impersonating (or stealing the secret keys from) a TEE. In both cases, an attacker can create an invalid leadership claim and break the security of the protocol.

To address this issue, PoET implements a "z-test" (or more accurately, it implements a "1 sample z-test") that limits the number of blocks any validator can win in some (large) consecutive set of blocks. The "z-test" is based on the observation that while any validator can win any block (the fairness principle), the probability that a particular validator wins a disproportionately large number of blocks is extremely low.

4.1   Our ET Consensus Protocol with z-Test

While the PoET z-test is an excellent innovation, we cannot prove the security of any ET consensus protocols using that z-test. We implement a slightly different z-test—PoET rate-limits what percentage of blocks any given participant can win on the entire chain, while we rate-limit each participant's block wins over a sliding window of time (or, in our protocol, a sliding window of rounds). An adversary can decide not create blocks for a long time, then create enough in a short window to violate consensus while bypassing the z-test by PoET; however, our z-test would catch such attacks. Given the distribution of block creation, we can figure out the expectation of (and appropriate other statistics around) how many blocks a player wins over a particular time period. Deviating too far from this results in future blocks being declared invalid.[4]

For a consecutive set of rounds S, we denote number of adversarial blocks in a chain $\mathcal{C}$ by $ADV_{\mathcal{C}}(S)$. In other words, $ADV_{\mathcal{C}}(S) = |\{B \in \mathcal{C} : \text{round}(B) \in S \text{ and } \text{id}(B) \text{ is corrupted. }\}|$. For a player $i \in [1, n]$, $Z_{\mathcal{C}}(i, S)$ denotes the number of blocks in chain $\mathcal{C}$ produced by player i, created in rounds in S, i.e. $Z_{\mathcal{C}}(i, S) = |\{B \in \mathcal{C} : \text{round}(B) \in S \text{ and } \text{id}(B) = i\}|$. Hence, for a chain $\mathcal{C}$ and set of rounds S, we have $ADV_{\mathcal{C}}(S) = \sum_{\substack{i \in [1,n] \\ i \text{ is corrupted}}} Z_{\mathcal{C}}(i, S)$.

Definition 4. *Let $\mathcal{C}$ be a chain. For $\epsilon' \in (0, 1)$ and $\lambda > 0$ the function $z_{\epsilon', \lambda} : \mathcal{C} \times [1, ..., n] \to \{0, 1\}$ be defined in the following way:*

$$z_{\epsilon', \lambda}(\mathcal{C}, i) = \left\{ \begin{array}{cc} 0 & \begin{array}{c} \textit{if } \exists \textit{ set of consecutive rounds } S \textit{ s.t.} \\ |S| \geq \lambda \textit{ and } Z_{\mathcal{C}}(i, S) > (1 + \epsilon')p|S| \end{array} \\ 1 & \textit{otherwise} \end{array} \right\} \tag{1}$$

$z_{\epsilon', \lambda}(\mathcal{C}, i) = 0$ *if a party i has contributed more than the allowed number of blocks in chain $\mathcal{C}$.*

We set our z-test parameters so that honest parties will only be affected with negligible probability, so our z-test has no negative impact on honest blockchain operation. Our new z-test can effectively stop an adversary from concentrating a high number of blocks in a very small amount of time and allows us to state concrete facts about the security of our protocol with the z-test.

4.2   Modification in the Protocol with Z-Test

In this section, we do not assume any integrity of the TEE. Hence, adversarial parties can generate arbitrarily many valid blocks per round. However, honest parties apply the 'z-test' before accepting a chain, which checks that no single player is producing substantially more than their fair share of the blocks.

Although we do not assume any security of any TEE (or even the existence of a TEE), the probability any honest party generates a block in any given round still remains p. This holds because adversarial parties cannot influence the wait time distributions of honest parties. We capture this in the following lemma. We skip the proof here because it is very similar to the proof of Lemma 1.

Lemma 2. *The event that any honest party generates a block in a given round happens with probability p, over the random coins of that party's TEE. This event is independent of all other random coins in the protocol as well as adversarial choices.*

---

[4] We also note that this change helps us to address the attacks in [19].

5   Security of ET Consensus with Z-Test

Even though z-test is a powerful assumption, the adversary can still essentially allocate their blocks however they want over the given time periods. In addition, the adversary can also create many different small forks or chains like a "nothing at stake" attacker [14]. It is important to note that the z-test bounds the behaviour of the adversary on *each* chain, not globally. Therefore, we use a slightly modified honest majority assumption (where we require slightly more honest parties) compared to bitcoin, and prove that honest parties are "stronger" than the adversary on each *valid* chain.

To prove the desired security properties for ET_{ztest}, we assume cryptographic security of the hash function and the signature scheme, and an honest majority assumption (formally stated below).

Definition 5 (Honest Majority Assumption). *Suppose n is the total number of parties, and out of them t parties are corrupted. Then we require that* $t < (1 - \delta)(n - t)$, *where* $\max\left(\frac{2f+\epsilon+\epsilon'-f^2-f\epsilon}{1+\epsilon'}, \frac{1+\epsilon+2\epsilon'-2\epsilon'f-2\epsilon f}{2(1+\epsilon')(1-f)}\right) < \delta \leq 1$, $\epsilon \in (0,1)$ *and* $\epsilon' > 0$.

We shall use the following boolean random variables for the proofs:

- $HON_i^{\geq 1}$ is defined to be 1 if *at least* one honest party creates a block at round i and 0 otherwise.
- HON_i^1 is defined to be 1 if exactly one *single* honest party creates a block at round i and 0 otherwise.
- $ADV_{i,j}$ is defined to be 1 if the jth dishonest party creates a block at round i and 0 otherwise[5]. We also define, $ADV_i := \sum_j ADV_{i,j}$.
- $HON_{i,j}$ is defined to be 1 if jth honest player successfully generated a block at round i and 0 otherwise. We denote $HON_{.,i}(S) = \sum_{r \in S} HON_{r,i}$.

Below, we mention an inequality that we will use often.

$$f < p(n - t) < \frac{f}{1 - f} \tag{2}$$

Note, the first inequality is a straight forward application of Bernoulli's inequality which says for real $x > -1$ and integer $r \geq 0$ we have, $(1+x)^r > 1+rx$. The second inequality is another application of Bernoulli's inequality after applying the following inequality $(1 - p)^{-(n-t)} > (1 + p)^{n-t}$.

---

[5] The adversary actually has a choice to try to mine in a specific round or not. However, without loss of generality we can consider an adversary who always tries to do so, as the adversary is always free to discard a successfully mined block. This assumption helps us in defining random variables $ADV_{i,j}$ in terms of pure probabilistic events.

5.1 Typical Execution

We slightly modify the definition of typical execution from the bitcoin backbone work [28] and use here. More specifically, we do not impose any condition on adversarial success, because without integrity of the trusted execution environment the adversary is free to generate as many valid blocks as it wants (although, if they generate too many, they will be rejected by honest parties using the z-test property).

Definition 6 (Typical Execution). *An execution of r_{end} rounds, is $(\epsilon, \epsilon', \lambda)$-typical, for some $\epsilon \in (0,1), \epsilon' > 0$, if for any set S of at least λ consecutive rounds the following hold:*

(a) $(1-\epsilon)\mathbb{E}[HON^{\geq 1}(S)] < HON^{\geq 1}(S) < (1+\epsilon)\mathbb{E}[HON^{\geq 1}(S)]$
   and $(1-\epsilon)\mathbb{E}[HON^1(S)] < HON^1(S)$
(b) For all honest players i, $HON_{.,i}(S) < (1+\epsilon')\mathbb{E}[HON_{.,i}(S)]$

Theorem 1. *An execution of r_{end} rounds is $(\epsilon, \epsilon', \lambda)$-typical with probability at least $1 - r_{end}(e^{-\Omega(\epsilon^2 \lambda f)} + (n-t)e^{-\Omega(\epsilon'^2 \lambda p)})$.*

Proof (Sketch). Note, there are $(n-t)$ honest parties and for every honest party i, we have $\mathbb{E}[HON_{.,i}(S)] = p|S|$. The theorem follows with a Chernoff bound. $\square$

Now, let us look at some more properties of a typical execution under z-test. Later in this section, we are going to use those properties to analyze the chain growth and chain quality properties.

Lemma 3. *For any set S of at least λ consecutive rounds, the following properties hold in a typical execution where C is a chain adopted by an honest party.*

(a) $(1-\epsilon)f|S| < HON^{\geq 1}(S) < (1+\epsilon)f|S|$
(b) $ADV_C(S) < \frac{(1+\epsilon')t}{(n-t)(1-f)(1-\epsilon)}HON^{\geq 1}(S)$
(c) $2ADV_C(S) < HON^1(S)$
(d) $ADV_C(S) < (1-f-\epsilon)f|S|$

Proof. Recall, $\mathbb{E}[HON^{\geq 1}(S)] = f|S|$. Hence, part (a) readily follows from definition of typical execution (Definition 6). The chain C got adopted by an honest party, hence it passed the 'z-test' for all parties. As $|S| \geq \lambda$, for all players $i \in [1,n]$ we have $Z_C(i,S) < (1+\epsilon')p|S|$. Hence,

$$ADV_C(S) = \sum_{\substack{i \in [1,n] \\ i \text{ is corrupted}}} Z_C(i,S) < (1+\epsilon')pt|S| < \frac{(1+\epsilon')tf}{(n-t)(1-f)}|S| \quad (3)$$

The last inequality above uses inequality (2). Now we can prove part (b) by applying $HON^{\geq 1}(S)$ lower bound from part (a). For part (c), from the definition of typical execution we have,

$$HON^1(S) > (1-\epsilon)\mathbb{E}[HON^1(S)]$$
$$= (1-\epsilon)(n-t)p(1-p)^{n-t-1}|S|$$
$$> (1-\epsilon)(n-t)p(1-p)^{n-t}|S|$$

$$> (1 - \epsilon)(n - t)p(1 - p(n - t))|S| \qquad \text{By Bernoulli's inequality}$$

$$> (1 - \epsilon)(n - t)p(1 - \frac{f}{1 - f})|S| \qquad \text{By Inequality 2}$$

$$= \frac{(1 - \epsilon)(1 - 2f)}{(1 + \epsilon')(1 - f)} \frac{(n - t)}{t}(1 + \epsilon')pt|S|$$

$$> \frac{(1 - \epsilon)(1 - 2f)}{(1 + \epsilon')(1 - f)} \frac{(n - t)}{t} ADV_C(S) \qquad \text{By Inequality 3}$$

$$> \frac{(1 - \epsilon)(1 - 2f)}{(1 + \epsilon')(1 - f)(1 - \delta)} ADV_C(S) \qquad \text{Definition 5}$$

From the honest majority assumption or Definition 5 we also have

$$\frac{1 + \epsilon + 2\epsilon' - 2\epsilon'f - 2\epsilon f}{2(1 + \epsilon')(1 - f)} < \delta < 1,$$

which in turn implies $\frac{(1-\epsilon)(1-2f)}{(1+\epsilon')(1-f)(1-\delta)} > 2$. This completes the proof of part (c). For part (d), from Inequality (3) we have

$$ADV_C(S) < (1 + \epsilon')pt|S|$$

$$< (1 + \epsilon')(1 - \delta)p(n - t)|S| \qquad \text{By Definition 5}$$

$$< (1 + \epsilon')(1 - \delta)\frac{f}{1 - f}|S| \qquad \text{By Inequality (2)}$$

$$= \frac{(1 + \epsilon')(1 - \delta)}{(1 - f)(1 - f - \epsilon)}(1 - f - \epsilon)f|S|$$

From honest majority assumption we also have $\frac{2f + \epsilon + \epsilon' - f^2 - f\epsilon}{1 + \epsilon'} < \delta < 1$, which in turn implies $\frac{(1+\epsilon')(1-\delta)}{(1-f)(1-f-\epsilon)} < 1$. This completes the proof of part (d). □

5.2 Chain Growth Properties

Now, we want to prove the chain growth property for ET consensus with z-test. However, the property crucially depends upon the fact that in a typical execution, honestly generated blocks never get rejected because of the 'z-test'. We note that this property is easy to achieve with what should be fairly typical parameter settings: namely, with $\epsilon \leq \epsilon'$.

Lemma 4. *In a typical execution, let C_1 and C_2 be two chains which were adopted by some honest parties. Suppose B_1 and B_2 are the k-th blocks of chains C_1 and C_2 respectively. If $id(B_1)$ is an honest user and $round(B_1)$ is a uniquely successful round, then either $B_1 = B_2$ or $id(B_2)$ is corrupted.*

Proof. For contradiction, we assume $B_1 \neq B_2$ and $id(B_2)$ is honest. Security of the signature scheme implies the blocks B_1 and B_2 are actually created by $id(B_1)$ and $id(B_2)$. As, $round(B_1)$ is uniquely successful round and both $id(B_1)$

and $\mathrm{id}(B_2)$ are honest, we have $\mathrm{round}(B_1) \neq \mathrm{round}(B_2)$. Suppose, $\mathrm{round}(B_1) < \mathrm{round}(B_2)$; as both of the players are honest $\mathrm{id}(B_2)$ must have received the chain ending in B_1 with length k on or before $\mathrm{round}(B_2)$. This implies position of the block B_2 must be greater than k, which is a contradiction. The cryptographic security of the hash function ensures an honest party creates a block at position k and that adversarial players cannot insert that block at a different position. A similar argument holds for the case $\mathrm{round}(B_1) < \mathrm{round}(B_2)$. □

Lemma 5 (Chain Growth Lemma). *In a typical execution, suppose an honest party has adopted a chain of length ℓ at round r. Then, by round $h > r$, every honest party has adopted a chain of length at least $\ell + \sum_{i=r}^{h-1} HON_i^{\geq 1}$.*

Proof. We prove the above theorem using induction on $h \geq r + 1$.

Induction base: The protocol has moved only one round after round r, hence $h = r + 1$. If at round r, an honest party has a chain of length ℓ, every honest party will adopt a chain of length at least ℓ by round $r + 1$. Additionally, if $HON_r^{\geq 1} = 0$, the statement follows directly. If $HON_r^{\geq 1} = 1$, the successful honest party will broadcast a chain of length $\ell + 1 = \ell + HON_r^{\geq 1}$, and all honest parties will adopt a chain of at least that length by round $h = r + 1$.

Inductive step: Let us assume that every honest party has adopted a chain of length at least $\ell' = \ell + \sum_{i=r}^{h-2} HON_i^{\geq 1}$ by round $h - 1$.

Now, two things could have happened on round $h - 1$:

1. $HON_{h-1}^{\geq 1} = 0$, in which case $\sum_{i=r}^{h-1} HON_i^{\geq 1} = \sum_{i=r}^{h-2} HON_i^{\geq 1}$. Hence, the statement follows.
2. $HON_{h-1}^{\geq 1} = 1$, in that case a successful honest party will broadcast a chain of length at least $\ell' + 1$ in round $h - 1$. By round s, all honest parties will adopt a chain of length at least $\ell' + 1 = \ell + \sum_{i=r}^{h-2} HON_i^{\geq 1} + 1 = \ell + \sum_{i=r}^{h-1} HON_i^{\geq 1}$.

□

Lemma 6 (Chain Growth Upper Bound). *Suppose $\mathcal{C}$ is a chain adopted by an honest party during a typical execution. For any $k \geq \max(2\lambda f, 4)$, let $B_m, B_{m+1}, \cdots, B_{m+k-1}$ be k consecutive blocks of the chain $\mathcal{C}$. Then, we have*

$$||[\mathrm{round}(B_m), \mathrm{round}(B_{m+k-1})]|| \geq \frac{k}{2f}.$$

Proof. Suppose $S' = [\mathrm{round}(B_m), \mathrm{round}(B_{m+k-1})]$. For contradiction let us assume $|S'| < \frac{k}{2f}$. Consider the set S of consecutive rounds such that $S \supseteq S'$ and $|S| = \lceil \frac{k}{2f} \rceil$. Security of the signature scheme along with the fact chain $\mathcal{C}$ has been adopted by an honest party ensures $HON^{\geq 1}(S') + ADV_{\mathcal{C}}(S') \geq k$. As

$S' \subseteq S$, this in turn implies $HON^{\geq 1}(S) + ADV_{\mathcal{C}}(S) \geq k$. As, $|S| \geq \lambda$, we can apply Lemma 3 and it implies the following.

$$
\begin{aligned}
HON^{\geq 1}&(S) + ADV_{\mathcal{C}}(S) \\
&< (1+\epsilon)f|S| + (1 - f - \epsilon)f|S| \\
&< (2 - f)f|S| \\
&< (2 - f)f(\frac{k}{2f} + 1) \qquad\qquad\qquad \text{Since } |S| = \lceil \frac{k}{2f} \rceil < \frac{k}{2f} + 1 \\
&\leq k - \frac{kf}{2} + 2f - f^2 < k + f(1 - k/4) < k. \qquad\qquad \text{Since } k \geq 4
\end{aligned}
$$

This shows we have a contradiction.   □

Lemma 6 provides us an upper limit on the rate of chain growth. It says that at least $\frac{k}{2f}$ rounds are required for a valid chain to grow by k blocks. Additionally, note that, for $f > 0.5$ the number of rounds to generate k blocks becomes less than k, which is not possible because multiple blocks in the same round will only increase forks, not the chain length. That necessarily means any $f > 0.5$ will not improve the chain growth, instead only increase the fork rate. That is why we should always consider $f \leq 0.5$.

A corollary to chain growth lemma(Lemma 5), Lemma 3 and Lemma 6 is the following theorem.

Theorem 2 (chain-growth). *In a typical execution, the chain growth property holds with parameters $\tau = (1 - \epsilon)f$, $\sigma = 2f$ and $r_g > \lambda$.*

The above theorem provides an upper bound as well as a lower bound on the total number of blocks added to a chain $\mathcal{C}$ given a sequence of rounds S with a length $s > r_g$. For s rounds, the number of blocks x added to the chain $\mathcal{C}$ is upper bounded by σs and lower bounded by τs.

5.3   Common Prefix Property

Here we prove that honest parties eventually agree on a common chain in our ET consensus with z-test protocol. The main difference from bitcoin backbone analysis [28] is the following: In bitcoin, the total number of blocks an adversary can produce is bounded (with some probability, of course). However, in our ET consensus with z-test protocol, the z-test only allows us to bound the number of blocks *per chain*. So an adversary could create a theoretically infinite number of chains and generate blocks on all of them. It turns out, though, that this per-chain restriction is actually pretty strong. Below we present the formal proof.

Lemma 7 (Common Prefix Lemma). *In a typical execution, for two chains $\mathcal{C}_1$ and $\mathcal{C}_2$ with $len(\mathcal{C}_2) \geq len(\mathcal{C}_1)$, if $\mathcal{C}_1$ is adopted by an honest party at round r, and $\mathcal{C}_2$ is either adopted by an honest party or broadcasted by an honest party at round r, then $\mathcal{C}_1^{\lceil k} \preceq \mathcal{C}_2$ and $\mathcal{C}_2^{\lceil k} \preceq \mathcal{C}_1$, for all $k \geq \max(2\lambda f, 4)$.*

Proof. Let us assume, for contradiction, there exists a $k > 2\lambda f$ such that $C_1^{\lceil k} \npreceq C_2$ or $C_2^{\lceil k} \npreceq C_1$. Suppose, B^* be the last block on the common prefix of C_1 and C_2 such that $\mathrm{id}(B^*)$ is honest. Let us denote $\mathrm{round}(B^*) = r^*$. Note, B^* can be genesis block, in which case $r^* = 0$.

Now, we define $S = \{i : r^* < i < r\}$. Suppose, $B_m, B_{m+1}, \cdots, B_{m+k'-1}$ are k' consecutive blocks of the chain C_1, where B_m is the next block after $B*$ and $B_{m+k'-1}$ is the last block of C_1. Clearly, $k' \geq k \geq \max(2\lambda f, 4)$ and we can apply Lemma 6. This implies, $|[\mathrm{round}(B_m), \mathrm{round}(B_{m+k'-1})]| \geq \frac{k'}{2f} \geq \lambda$. We also know, $S \supseteq [\mathrm{round}(B_m), \mathrm{round}(B_{m+k'-1})]$. Hence, $|S| \geq \lambda$ (i.e., the execution during S is a typical execution with overwhelming probability) and Lemma 3 applies for the set of rounds S.

For a uniquely successful round $u \in S$, let j_u be the position at which the uniquely successful honest party created the block. J be the set of positions at which honest parties created the blocks on uniquely successful rounds. $J = \{j_u : u \in S, HON_u^1 = 1\}$. Suppose the maximum value of the set J is $\max(J)$. Then, $\mathrm{len}(C_1) \geq \max(J)$, since C_1 is adopted by an honest party at round r, by which the honest party has already received a chain of length $\max(J)$.

Since, $\mathrm{len}(C_2) \geq \mathrm{len}(C_1)$, j^{th} block exists in both the chains C_1 and C_2 for all $j \in J$. We denote such blocks by $B_{1,j}$ and $B_{2,j}$ respectively. Now, we want to claim for all $j \in J$ at least one of the players between $\mathrm{id}(B_{1,j})$ and $\mathrm{id}(B_{1,j})$ is corrupted. By Lemma 4, if both $\mathrm{id}(B_{1,j})$ and $\mathrm{id}(B_{1,j})$ are honest then we must have $B_{1,j} = B_{2,j}$. Cryptographic strength (collision resistance) of the hash function implies $B_j = B_{1,j} = B_{2,j}$ belongs to the common prefix of chains C_1 and C_2. However, we also know $\mathrm{round}(B_j) > \mathrm{round}(B^*)$ and B^* is the last block in the common prefix such that $\mathrm{id}(B^*)$ is honest. This implies a contradiction.

Now, we have established the fact that for all $j \in J$ at least one of the players between $\mathrm{id}(B_{1,j})$ and $\mathrm{id}(B_{2,j})$ is corrupted. Hence, total number of blocks B such that $\mathrm{id}(B)$ is corrupted, $B \in C_1 \cup C_2$ and $\mathrm{round}(B) \in S$ must be more than or equal to size of set J. Hence,

$$ADV_{C_1}(S) + ADV_{C_2}(S) \geq |\{B : B \in C_1 \cup C_2 \text{ and } \mathrm{round}(B) \in S\}|$$
$$\geq |J| = HON^1(S).$$

However, for a typical execution with $|S| \geq \lambda$, by Lemma 3 we have

$$ADV_{C_1}(S), ADV_{C_2}(S) < \frac{HON^1(S)}{2}.$$

Hence, contradiction. Therefore, we can say that for all $k > 2\lambda f$, it holds that $C_1^{\lceil k} \preceq C_2$ and $C_2^{\lceil k} \preceq C_1$. $\qquad\square$

Intuitively, if $C_1^{\lceil k} \npreceq C_2$ or $C_2^{\lceil k} \npreceq C_1$, the number of adversarial blocks for both the chains combined is more than the total number of honest blocks, for the parts of the chains where they don't have a common honest block. And that is not possible for a typical execution, because the number of adversarial blocks for a chain C during a sequence of rounds S is limited by $ADV_C(S) < \frac{HON^1(S)}{2}$.

Common Prefix Lemma shows that the honest parties eventually agree on a common chain. Once a transaction is included in a block B, the transaction becomes irreversible once honest parties have mined enough number of blocks extending after B. The common prefix lemma directly implies the following security theorem about the common prefix property.

Theorem 3 (Common Prefix). *In a typical execution the common prefix property holds with parameter $\ell_{cf} \geq \max(2\lambda f, 4)$.*

5.4   Chain Quality Property

Now we want to prove the property that at least a constant fraction of blocks are added by honest parties in a chain C that is adopted by an honest party. That eventually ensures, because of common prefix property, that the common chain agreed on by the honest parties has at least a constant fraction of honest blocks.

Theorem 4 (Chain Quality). *In a typical execution, the chain quality property holds with parameters $\ell_q \geq \max(2\lambda f, 4)$ and $\mu = 1 - \frac{(1+\epsilon')t}{(n-t)(1-f)(1-\epsilon)}$ for any chain adopted by any honest party.*

Proof. Let us consider a chain C, which has been adopted by an honest party P at round r, such that $\text{len}(C) > \ell_q$. Suppose C consists of sequence of blocks $(B_1, B_2, \ldots, B_{\text{len}(C)})$ and $(B_u, B_{u+1}, \ldots, B_{u+\ell_q-1})$ is an arbitrary ℓ_q length subsequence of C, such that $\ell_q \geq \max(2\lambda f, 4)$.

Let $(B_{u'}, B_{u'+1} \ldots, B_{u'+L-1})$ be the shortest subsequence of C containing $(B_u, B_{u+1}, \ldots, B_{u+\ell_q-1})$ (i.e. $u' \leq u$ and $L \geq \ell_q$) such that:

1. $\text{id}(B_{u'})$ is honest
2. there exists an honest party which adopted the chain $(B_1, B_2, \ldots, B_{u'+L-1})$

Observe that B_1 is genesis block and $\text{id}(B_1)$ is honest by definition. We know that an honest party P adopted the chain C and $\text{len}(C) > \ell_q$. Hence, the whole chain C trivially satisfies the above properties, except it might not the shortest one. This shows existence of the shortest subsequence $B_{u'}, B_{u'+1} \ldots, B_{u'+L-1}$. Suppose, $r_1 = \text{round}(B_{u'})$ and the earliest round at which the chain $(B_1, B_2, \ldots, B_{u'+L-1})$ got adopted by an honest party is r_2. Let S be the sequence of rounds defined as $S = \{r : r_1 \leq r < r_2\}$. Observe that

$$S \supseteq [\text{round}(B_{u'}), \text{round}(B_{u'+L-1})] \supseteq [\text{round}(B_u), \text{round}(B_{u+\ell_q-1})].$$

Hence, by Lemma 6, we have $|S| \geq \ell_q/2f \geq \lambda$ and the properties of typical execution are applicable (Lemma 3) for the set of rounds S.

Let x be the number of honest blocks in the ℓ_q length sequence. In other words $x = |\{B \in (B_u, B_{u+1}, \ldots, B_{u+\ell_q-1}) | \text{id}(B) \text{ is honest}\}|$. For contradiction, we assume the chain quality property does not hold for this ℓ_q length sequence of blocks $(B_u, B_{u+1}, \ldots, B_{u+\ell_q-1})$. Hence, $x < \mu\ell_q \leq \mu L$.

As the chain $(B_1, B_2, \ldots, B_{u'+L-1})$ got adopted by an honest party in round r_2; for all $i \in [u', u' + L - 1]$ we have $\texttt{round}(B_i) \in S$. As $[u, u + \ell_q - 1] \subseteq [u', u' + L - 1]$, from our contradiction assumption we have

$$ADV_{\mathcal{C}}(S) \geq |\{B \in (B_u, B_{u+1}, \ldots, B_{u+\ell_q-1}) | \texttt{id}(B) \text{ is corrupted}\}|$$
$$= L - x > (1 - \mu)L \tag{4}$$

Now, Lemma 5 implies $u' + L - 1 \geq u' + HON^{\geq 1}(S)$ or equivalently $L > HON^{\geq 1}(S)$. Hence inequality (4) can be rewritten as $ADV_{\mathcal{C}}(S) > (1 - \mu)HON^{\geq 1}(S)$. As we have seen before, $|S| \geq \lambda$. Hence, by Lemma 3

$$(1 - \mu)HON^{\geq 1}(S) = \frac{(1 + \epsilon')t}{(n - t)(1 - f)(1 - \epsilon)}HON^{\geq 1}(S) > ADV_{\mathcal{C}}(S)$$

Therefore we have our desired contradiction $ADV_{\mathcal{C}}(S) > ADV_{\mathcal{C}}(S)$. $\qquad\square$

The chain quality property guarantees that there will be at least $\mu\ell_q$ honest blocks given a chain of length ℓ_q. For example, when 20% of the miners are dishonest, $\epsilon' = \epsilon = 0.2$, and $f = 0.2$, we have $\mu = 0.53$—which means at least 53% blocks in the chain are honest. We refer to Table 2 for more examples.

6   Discussion and Practical Application

6.1   Parameter Choices

We want to set the z-test parameter ϵ' in such a way that an honest block is excluded from a chain only with negligible probability. We therefore recommend setting $\epsilon = \epsilon'$. In Table 2 we show some examples with possible values of ϵ, f, δ and how the parameters $\tau, \sigma, \ell_{cf}, \mu$ corresponding to the security properties(namely, chain growth, common prefix and chain quality) vary. Table 2 shows that we can vary $(f + \epsilon)$ up to 1, when $\delta = 1$ (which means all the protocol parties are honest). For $\epsilon = 0.2$ and $f = 0.2$, δ can be as low as 0.75, which means the protocol can tolerate up to 20% dishonest protocol parties. For small values of ϵ and f, ET consensus with z-test can tolerate up to 33% dishonest parties.

6.2   Implications of z-Test Security

In addition to lending evidence to support that the actual PoET protocol (and other similar protocols like proof of luck) is resilient to the compromise of some TEEs, we show a pretty surprising fact: basic proof of work consensus with a z-test *but no actual proofs of work, just "promises" from users* still remains secure with an honest majority assumption! Table 3 shows that our ET protocol without TEEs is not terribly worse (in terms of security) than ET consensus with trusted timer (and, similarly, bitcoin in the bitcoin backbone protocol).

While these numbers are not incredibly tight, the δ factors indicate that our proofs hold even when the number of adversarial parties is a (relatively large)

Table 2. How the security property parameters $(\tau, \sigma, r_g, \ell_{cf}, \ell_q, \mu)$ of ET consensus with z-test corresponding to chain growth, common prefix and chain quality properties vary based on the protocol parameters $\delta, \epsilon, f, \lambda$. The first column presents the values of ϵ and f defined in the honest majority assumption, the second column the minimum δ (accurate up to two decimal places) to satisfy the honest majority assumption; the third, fourth, fifth, sixth, seventh, and eighth columns are τ, σ, r_g, ℓ_{cf}, ℓ_q and μ respectively as described in Sect. 5. For all the cases, we use $\epsilon' = \epsilon$, and $\lambda \gg 4$. Note that f in our case is actually derived from p, however, to be comparable with similar works [7, 28, 29] we use f in the table.

Protocol parameters	δ	τ	σ	r_g	ℓ_{cf}	ℓ_q	μ
$\epsilon = 0.05, f = 0.05$	0.58	0.0475	0.1	λ	0.1λ	0.1λ	0.51
$\epsilon = 0.1, f = 0.1$	0.64	0.09	0.2	λ	0.2λ	0.2λ	0.51
$\epsilon = 0.2, f = 0.2$	0.75	0.16	0.4	λ	0.4λ	0.4λ	0.53
$\epsilon = 0.3, f = 0.3$	0.85	0.21	0.6	λ	0.6λ	0.6λ	0.60
$\epsilon = 0.4, f = 0.3$	0.88	0.18	0.6	λ	0.6λ	0.6λ	0.6
$\epsilon = 0.4, f = 0.4$	0.93	0.24	0.8	λ	0.8λ	0.8λ	0.72
$\epsilon = 0.5, f = 0.4$	0.95	0.2	0.8	λ	0.8λ	0.8λ	0.65
$\epsilon = 0.6, f = 0.4$	0.96	0.16	0.8	λ	0.8λ	0.8λ	0.73
$\epsilon = 0.5, f = 0.5$	1	0.25	1	λ	λ	λ	1

Table 3. Relationship between f and minimum δ in ET consensus with trusted timer, ET consensus with z-test. The f and the corresponding minimum δ values are exactly same for Bitcoin consensus and ET with trusted timer, and therefore, we do not include a separate column for Bitcoin in the table.

f	ET with trusted timer $\delta_{\min}$	ET with z-test $\delta_{\min}$
0.05	0.3	0.58
0.1	0.6	0.64

constant fraction (up to 33%) of the total number of players. This indicates that current TEE-based consensus systems like PoET that are used "in the wild" are, at least in theory, secure, although we would need to change the z-test in PoET in order for our proofs to apply.

Although the security proofs of ET consensus with z-test hold without any TEE assumptions, as long as the honest majority assumption holds, we recommend using the protocol in combination with TEE (e.g., Intel SGX) to ensure only a small number of malicious participants.

6.3   Performance Improvement

Even though, in our protocol description, we make ET_{ztest} wait on the TEE to generate a block, the security analysis does not depend on that. And therefore, a player can just query the $WaitTime$ and $WaitCert$ from the TEE, and still, all the security properties will hold. This can be very useful in practice, because if each round is small enough querying the TEE every round can be really inefficient.

6.4 Applications of Our Results

In [28], the authors show that the bitcoin backbone protocol almost immediately implies a Byzantine fault tolerant consensus protocol and a public ledger. The same results apply to our protocols, so we omit the full proofs and descriptions here. An inquisitive reader can refer to Sects. 5 and 6 of [28].

Acknowledgment. We thank the anonymous reviewers for their helpful comments. We thank Dan Middleton for the useful discussions.

Appendix: Security of ET Consensus with Trusted Timer

Assuming that the hash function and the signature scheme are cryptographically secure through our $Cert\,()$ functionality, and assuming integrity of the TEE, we can prove that the security properties of our ET consensus protocol with trusted timer are exactly same as that of Bitcoin. This fact is a direct implication of Lemma 1, and the security proofs are extremely similar to that of Bitcoin. Here we skip the proofs and present the key security properties.

All of the security guarantees hold if there are enough honest parties in the system, where the exact amount that is "enough" depends on other parameters of the system. Below, we formally state the honest majority assumption.

Definition 7 (Honest Majority Assumption). *Suppose n is the total number of parties, and out of them t parties are corrupted. If δ is the advantage of honest parties, then we require that $t < (1 - \delta)(n - t)$, where $3f + 3\epsilon < \delta \leq 1$, where ϵ is a positive fraction (used in various concentration bounds) and f is the probability that at least one honest party creates a block at a given round.*

For a security parameter λ, total number of parties $n \in poly(\lambda)$, and with the above honest majority assumption the following security theorems can be derived about our ET consensus protocol with trusted timer.

Theorem 5 (chain-growth). *The chain growth property holds with parameters $\tau = (1 - \epsilon)f$, $\sigma = 2f$ and $r_g > \lambda$ with overwhelming probability.*

Theorem 6 (Common Prefix). *The common prefix property holds with parameter $\ell_{cf} \geq \max(2\lambda f, 4)$ with overwhelming probability.*

Theorem 7 (Chain Quality). *With overwhelming probability the chain quality property holds with parameters $\ell_q \geq \max(2\lambda f, 4)$ and $\mu = 1 - (1 + \frac{\delta}{2})\frac{t}{n-t} - \frac{\epsilon}{1-\epsilon} > 1 - (1 + \frac{\delta}{2})\frac{t}{n-t} - \frac{\delta}{2}$ for any chain adopted by any honest party.*

References

1. Bitcoin energy consumption index. https://digiconomist.net/bitcoin-energy-consumption
2. Introduction to hyperledger sawtooth. https://sawtooth.hyperledger.org/docs/core/releases/latest/introduction.html
3. Poet 1.0 specification. https://sawtooth.hyperledger.org/docs/core/releases/1.0/architecture/poet.html
4. Trusted time and monotonic counters with intel software guard extensions platform services. https://software.intel.com/sites/default/files/managed/1b/a2/Intel-SGX-Platform-Services.pdf
5. Andreina, S., Bohli, J.-M., Karame, G.O., Li, W., Marson, G.A.: Pots - a secure proof of tee-stake for permissionless blockchains. Cryptology ePrint Archive, Report 2018/1135 (2018). https://eprint.iacr.org/2018/1135
6. Androulaki, E., et al.: Hyperledger fabric: a distributed operating system for permissioned blockchains. In: Proceedings of the Thirteenth EuroSys Conference, p. 30. ACM (2018)
7. Badertscher, C., Maurer, U., Tschudi, D., Zikas, V.: Bitcoin as a transaction ledger: a composable treatment. In: Katz, J., Shacham, H. (eds.) CRYPTO 2017. LNCS, vol. 10401, pp. 324–356. Springer, Cham (2017). https://doi.org/10.1007/978-3-319-63688-7_11
8. Barak, B., et al.: On the (im)possibility of obfuscating programs. In: Kilian, J. (ed.) CRYPTO 2001. LNCS, vol. 2139, pp. 1–18. Springer, Heidelberg (2001). https://doi.org/10.1007/3-540-44647-8_1
9. Benet, J., Greco, N.: Filecoin: a decentralized storage network. Protocol Labs (2018)
10. Bentov, I., Gabizon, A., Mizrahi, A.: Cryptocurrencies without proof of work. In: Clark, J., Meiklejohn, S., Ryan, P.Y.A., Wallach, D., Brenner, M., Rohloff, K. (eds.) FC 2016. LNCS, vol. 9604, pp. 142–157. Springer, Heidelberg (2016). https://doi.org/10.1007/978-3-662-53357-4_10
11. Bessani, A., Sousa, J., Alchieri, E.E.: State machine replication for the masses with BFT-SMART. In: 2014 44th Annual IEEE/IFIP International Conference on Dependable Systems and Networks, pp. 355–362. IEEE (2014)
12. Boneh, D., Bonneau, J., Bünz, B., Fisch, B.: Verifiable delay functions. In: Shacham, H., Boldyreva, A. (eds.) CRYPTO 2018. LNCS, vol. 10991, pp. 757–788. Springer, Cham (2018). https://doi.org/10.1007/978-3-319-96884-1_25
13. Bowman, M., Das, D., Mandal, A., Montgomery, H.: On elapsed time consensus protocols. https://eprint.iacr.org/2021/086.pdf
14. Brown-Cohen, J., Narayanan, A., Psomas, C.-A., Weinberg, S.M.: Formal barriers to longest-chain proof-of-stake protocols. CoRR, abs/1809.06528 (2018)
15. Buterin, V., Griffith, V.: Casper the friendly finality gadget. CoRR, abs/1710.09437 (2017)
16. Cachin, C.: Architecture of the hyperledger blockchain fabric. In: Workshop on Distributed Cryptocurrencies and Consensus Ledgers, vol. 310 (2016)
17. Cachin, C., Vukolić, M.: Blockchains consensus protocols in the wild. arXiv preprint arXiv:1707.01873 (2017)
18. Castro, M., Liskov, B., et al.: Practical byzantine fault tolerance. In: OSDI, vol. 99, pp. 173–186 (1999)

19. Chen, L., Xu, L., Shah, N., Gao, Z., Lu, Y., Shi, W.: On security analysis of proof-of-elapsed-time (PoET). In: Spirakis, P., Tsigas, P. (eds.) SSS 2017. LNCS, vol. 10616, pp. 282–297. Springer, Cham (2017). https://doi.org/10.1007/978-3-319-69084-1_19

20. Cohen, B., Pietrzak, K.: The chia network blockchain (2019)

21. Corso, A.: Performance analysis of proof-of-elapsed-time (poet) consensus in the sawtooth blockchain framework (2019)

22. Daian, P., Pass, R., Shi, E.: Snow white: provably secure proofs of stake. Technical report, Cryptology ePrint Archive, Report 2016/919, 2016 (2016)

23. Dang, H., Dinh, T.T.A., Loghin, D., Chang, E.-C., Lin, Q., Ooi, B.C.: Towards scaling blockchain systems via sharding. In: Proceedings of the 2019 International Conference on Management of Data, pp. 123–140 (2019)

24. David, B., Gaži, P., Kiayias, A., Russell, A.: Ouroboros Praos: an adaptively-secure, semi-synchronous proof-of-stake blockchain. In: Nielsen, J.B., Rijmen, V. (eds.) EUROCRYPT 2018. LNCS, vol. 10821, pp. 66–98. Springer, Cham (2018). https://doi.org/10.1007/978-3-319-78375-8_3

25. Dolev, D., Reischuk, R.: Bounds on information exchange for Byzantine agreement. J. ACM **32**(1), 191–204 (1985)

26. Dziembowski, S., Faust, S., Kolmogorov, V., Pietrzak, K.: Proofs of space. In: Gennaro, R., Robshaw, M. (eds.) CRYPTO 2015. LNCS, vol. 9216, pp. 585–605. Springer, Heidelberg (2015). https://doi.org/10.1007/978-3-662-48000-7_29

27. Eyal, I., Gencer, A.E., Sirer, E.G., Van Renesse, R.: Bitcoin-ng: a scalable blockchain protocol. In: NSDI, pp. 45–59 (2016)

28. Garay, J., Kiayias, A., Leonardos, N.: The bitcoin backbone protocol: analysis and applications. In: Oswald, E., Fischlin, M. (eds.) EUROCRYPT 2015. LNCS, vol. 9057, pp. 281–310. Springer, Heidelberg (2015). https://doi.org/10.1007/978-3-662-46803-6_10

29. Garay, J., Kiayias, A., Leonardos, N.: The bitcoin backbone protocol with chains of variable difficulty. In: Katz, J., Shacham, H. (eds.) CRYPTO 2017. LNCS, vol. 10401, pp. 291–323. Springer, Cham (2017). https://doi.org/10.1007/978-3-319-63688-7_10

30. Gervais, A., Karame, G.O., Wüst, K., Glykantzis, V., Ritzdorf, H., Capkun, S.: On the security and performance of proof of work blockchains. In: Proceedings of the 2016 ACM SIGSAC Conference on Computer and Communications Security, pp. 3–16. ACM (2016)

31. Kiayias, A., Russell, A., David, B., Oliynykov, R.: Ouroboros: a provably secure proof-of-stake blockchain protocol. In: Katz, J., Shacham, H. (eds.) CRYPTO 2017. LNCS, vol. 10401, pp. 357–388. Springer, Cham (2017). https://doi.org/10.1007/978-3-319-63688-7_12

32. Kocher, P., et al.: Spectre attacks: exploiting speculative execution. In: 40th IEEE Symposium on Security and Privacy (S&P 2019) (2019)

33. Kogias, E.K., Jovanovic, P., Gailly, N., Khoffi, I., Gasser, L., Ford, B.: Enhancing bitcoin security and performance with strong consistency via collective signing. In: 25th USENIX Security Symposium (USENIX Security 2016), pp. 279–296 (2016)

34. Koruyeh, E.M., Khasawneh, K.N., Song, C., Abu-Ghazaleh, N.: Spectre returns! Speculation attacks using the return stack buffer. In: 12th USENIX Workshop on Offensive Technologies (WOOT 2018) (2018)

35. Kwon, J.: Tendermint: consensus without mining. Draft v. 0.6, fall (2014)

36. Lipp, M., et al.: Meltdown: reading kernel memory from user space. In: 27th USENIX Security Symposium (USENIX Security 2018), pp. 973–990 (2018)

37. Liu, J., Li, W., Karame, G.O., Asokan, N.: Scalable byzantine consensus via hardware-assisted secret sharing. IEEE Trans. Comput. **68**(1), 139–151 (2019)
38. Madison, J.: Federalist no. 51. The Federalist Papers (1788)
39. Mazieres, D.: The stellar consensus protocol: a federated model for internet-level consensus. Stellar Development Foundation (2015)
40. Milutinovic, M., He, W., Wu, H., Kanwal, M.: Proof of luck: an efficient blockchain consensus protocol. In: Proceedings of the 1st Workshop on System Software for Trusted Execution, p. 2. ACM (2016)
41. Nakamoto, S.: Bitcoin: a peer-to-peer electronic cash system. http://bitcoin.org/bitcoin.pdf
42. Nayak, K., Kumar, S., Miller, A., Shi, E.: Stubborn mining: generalizing selfish mining and combining with an eclipse attack. In: 2016 IEEE European Symposium on Security and Privacy (EuroS&P), pp. 305–320. IEEE (2016)
43. Pass, R., Shi, E.: Fruitchains: a fair blockchain. In: Proceedings of the ACM Symposium on Principles of Distributed Computing, pp. 315–324. ACM (2017)
44. Pass, R., Shi, E.: The sleepy model of consensus. In: Takagi, T., Peyrin, T. (eds.) ASIACRYPT 2017. LNCS, vol. 10625, pp. 380–409. Springer, Cham (2017). https://doi.org/10.1007/978-3-319-70697-9_14
45. Pass, R., Shi, E.: Thunderella: blockchains with optimistic instant confirmation. In: Nielsen, J.B., Rijmen, V. (eds.) EUROCRYPT 2018. LNCS, vol. 10821, pp. 3–33. Springer, Cham (2018). https://doi.org/10.1007/978-3-319-78375-8_1
46. Santos Veronese, G., Correia, M., Neves Bessani, A., Lung, L.C., Verissimo, P.: Efficient Byzantine fault-tolerance. IEEE Trans. Comput. **62**, 16–30 (2013)
47. Shi, Z., Zhou, H., Hu, Y., Jayachander, S., de Laat, C., Zhao, Z.: Operating permissioned blockchain in clouds: a performance study of hyperledger sawtooth. In: 2019 18th International Symposium on Parallel and Distributed Computing (ISPDC), pp. 50–57. IEEE (2019)
48. Tamer Özsu, M., Valduriez, P.: Correction to: principles of distributed database systems. In: Principles of Distributed Database Systems, pp. C1–C2. Springer, Cham (2020). https://doi.org/10.1007/978-3-030-26253-2_13
49. Van Bulck, J., et al.: Foreshadow: extracting the keys to the intel SGX kingdom with transient out-of-order execution. In: 25th USENIX Security Symposium (USENIX Security 2016), pp. 991–1008 (2018)
50. Vukolić, M.: The quest for scalable blockchain fabric: proof-of-work vs. BFT replication. In: Camenisch, J., Kesdoğan, D. (eds.) iNetSec 2015. LNCS, vol. 9591, pp. 112–125. Springer, Cham (2016). https://doi.org/10.1007/978-3-319-39028-4_9
51. Yin, M., Malkhi, D., Reiter, M.K., Gueta, G.G., Abraham, I.: HotStuff: BFT consensus with linearity and responsiveness. In: Proceedings of the 2019 ACM Symposium on Principles of Distributed Computing, pp. 347–356. ACM (2019)

Time-Release Cryptography from Minimal Circuit Assumptions

Samuel Jaques[1]([⊠]), Hart Montgomery[2], Razvan Rosie[3], and Arnab Roy[2]

[1] Oxford University, Oxford, UK
sam@samueljaques.com
[2] Fujitsu Research of America, Sunnyvale, CA, USA
hmontgomery@fujitsu.com
[3] University of Luxembourg, Esch-sur-Alzette, Luxembourg
razvan.rosie@uni.lu

Abstract. *Time-release* cryptography requires problems that take a long time to solve and take just as long even with significant computational resources. While time-release cryptography originated with the seminal paper of Rivest, Shamir and Wagner ('96), it has gained special visibility recently due to new time-release primitives, like *verifiable delay functions* (VDFs) and *sequential proofs of work*, and their novel blockchain applications. In spite of this recent progress, security definitions remain inconsistent and fragile, and foundational treatment of these primitives is scarce. Relationships between the various time-release primitives are elusive, with few connections to standard cryptographic assumptions.

We systematically address these drawbacks. We define formal notions of *sequential functions*, the building blocks of time-release cryptography. The new definitions are robust against change of machine models, making them more amenable to complexity theoretic treatment. We demonstrate the equivalence of various types of sequential functions under standard cryptographic assumptions. The time-release primitives in the literature (such as those defined by Bitansky *et al.* (ITCS '16)) imply that these primitives exist, as well as the converse.

However, showing that a given construction is a sequential function is a hard circuit lower bound problem. To our knowledge, no results show that standard cryptographic assumptions imply any sequentiality. For example, repeated squaring over RSA groups is assumed to be sequential, but nothing connects this conjecture to standard hardness assumptions. To circumvent this, we construct a function that we prove is sequential if there *exists* any sequential function, without needing any specific knowledge of this hypothetical function. Our techniques use universal circuits and fully homomorphic encryption and generalize some of the elegant techniques of the recent work on lattice NIZKs (Canetti *et al.*, STOC '19).

Using our reductions and sequential function constructions, we build VDFs and sequential proofs of work from fully homomorphic encryption, incremental verifiable computation, and the existence of a sequential function. Though our constructions are theoretical in nature and not competitive with existing techniques, they are built from much weaker assumptions than known constructions.

© Springer Nature Switzerland AG 2021
A. Adhikari et al. (Eds.): INDOCRYPT 2021, LNCS 13143, pp. 584–606, 2021.
https://doi.org/10.1007/978-3-030-92518-5_26

1 Introduction

[1]Many security assumptions assume a certain problem cannot be solved within some computational budget, such as 2^{80} operations, but give no restriction on whether these computations are done in parallel or serially. In contrast, time-release cryptography adds an extra flavour of assumption: a problem can be solved in less than a specified amount of *time*, even with enormous parallel computing resources.

The field of sequential (or "time-release") crypto dates back to 1996, when Rivest, Shamir, and Wagner first proposed time-lock puzzles [44]. A time-lock puzzle is a problem for which it is easy to generate a problem instance but which requires a moderate amount of *sequential* computation to solve. The authors of [44] proposed that repeated squaring on a group of unknown order is an inherently sequential function, and so far this has been the core idea behind almost all non-random oracle primitives in time-release cryptography. Boneh and Naor [12] followed up by building timed commitment schemes, Garay *et al.* [23] considered resource-fairness in multi-party computation, but time-release cryptography was a relatively quiet field until the advent of blockchain [36].

Much of the most recent work has focused on *verifiable delay functions*. A verifiable delay function is a function that requires T sequential steps of computation and has a unique output on every input that can be verified efficiently in time "almost" independent of T. This means any "honest" user with a relatively small amount of computing power should be able to compute the function in almost the same time as an "adversarial" user with substantial parallel computing resources.

The genesis of this work was a construction by Lenstra and Wesolowski called Sloth [31]. Approximately two years later, Boneh *et al.* wrote the seminal VDF paper [10] which formally defined and introduced the notion of a VDF. More efficient constructions from Weselowski [50] and Pietrzak [41] followed this, as well as more analysis of these constructions [11].

Other interesting VDF constructions include *tight* VDFs in [21], giving a greater theoretical understanding to the problem. VDFs have been built from elliptic curve isogenies [20,46]. The imminent use of VDFs in blockchains has even prompted work on more efficient parallel field operations [37,38].

The complexity requirements of VDFs have also attracted attention. In their paper on continuous VDFs, Ephraim *et al.* [22] connect the existence of a VDF to the computation of Nash equilibria. Mahmoody *et al.* show that VDFs satisfying perfect uniqueness and tight VDFs are impossible to construct in a black-box way solely from ideal hash functions [34]. Rotem *et al.* [45] show that what they call "generic group delay functions" which model the known VDF constructions which require hidden-order groups, meaning that we are unlikely to be able to build VDFs from group-based assumptions without groups of unknown order.

Recently there has been substantial interest in sequential primitives. There have been a number of constructions on time-lock puzzles [9], including a new notion of *homomorphic* time-lock puzzles that allow for greater efficiency [13,35]. Mahmoody

---

[1] This is a condensed version of our full result; the full version with all supporting details is at https://eprint.iacr.org/2020/755.

et al. [33] defined a primitive called a *publicly verifiable sequential proof of work*, which is similar to a VDF except the verifying solution may not be unique. More recently, Cohen and Pietrzak [18] showed a simpler construction[2].

Verifiable delay functions have a number of exciting applications, including randomness beacons [17,42], resource-efficient blockchains [29,30,39], and proofs of replication [4]. In fact, the Ethereum Foundation and a number of other blockchain entities are rapidly pushing towards building practical VDFs in order to better scale Ethereum [16]. Potentially billions of dollars [1] will rely on a secure VDF construction in the near future, so it is important that we have a secure construction. We encourage interested readers to refer to [10] for a full treatment of the applications of VDFs and time-release cryptography.

1.1 Models of Computation and Time

The existing models of computation in time-release cryptography works [10,44,50] are based on parallel random access machines. Boneh et al. [10] define a notion of (t, ϵ)-sequentiality for functions: the function can be honestly computed in time t, while no adversary will have a non-negligible chance of computing it within time $(1 - \epsilon)t$. Of course if the adversary has a vastly superior machine compared to an honest evaluator, it can even accelerate the honest computation. So such a possibility is implicit in the notion, although not explicitly encoded in the definition.

However, this notion is not robust to changes in machine models, which makes a complexity-theoretic treatment difficult. For example, if we analyze a function in the circuit model, which is common in cryptography, it is natural to take the depth as the run time and the width as the amount of parallelism. However, the adversary may execute this in a random access machine which may shave off a $\log(\lambda)$ factor in evaluation time.

We therefore ask: is there a notion of sequential functions that is independent of the specific, perhaps distinct, models adopted by the honest and adversarial evaluators, as long as these models are reasonable in some sense? If so, can we relate these notions to each other, to standard time-release primitives, and to standard cryptographic notions?

1.2 Assumptions of Existing Constructions

If we examine all of the above constructions of time-release cryptography, then we notice that there are some common threads. In particular, all of the constructions we have mentioned (except for [9], which we will mention in more detail later) explicitly rely on one (or both) of the following assumptions: that repeatedly computing a random oracle on its own output is an inherently sequential operation, and that repeated squaring in a group of unknown order is an inherently sequential operation. Each of these assumptions has some unfortunate drawbacks.

The Random Oracle Assumption. The random oracle sequentiality assumption in the above papers is typically a more precise statement of the following form: given a random oracle $H : \mathcal{X} \to \mathcal{X}$, if it takes h time to compute H on a single input $x \in \mathcal{X}$, then

---

[2] The [18] result also improved the [33] result in a number of ways that are important for our results.

it takes $\Omega(hk)$ time to compute $H^k(x)$, where $H^k(x) = H(...H(x))$ for k computations of H. While there may be more complicated bounds involved, this is the general structure of typical random oracle assumptions.

However, this is a very strong assumption on random oracle models. The random oracle model [6] assumes that an adversary has *black-box* access to a random oracle: in other words, they can query the oracle on inputs of their choice, and receive back the corresponding outputs. For some cryptographic protocols, such as digital signatures, the protocols reasonably fit the scheme. In the case of time-release cryptography, this black-box assumption no longer holds. An adversary generally must have the circuit description of a random oracle in order to compute any sequential functions, and we must assume that *given a circuit description of H* an adversary cannot find another circuit that computes H^k much faster than k evaluations of H. This is a strong requirement for concrete hash functions, and while it seems to hold for popular choices of hash functions that are used as random oracles such as SHA256, it remains to be seen if researchers will be able to parallelize "chained" computations of random oracle instantiations such as SHA256, particularly once there are large financial incentives to do so.

Even more clearly defying the random oracle assumption, random oracle VDF constructions not only require access to the circuit of the random oracle, but the proofs of correctness are built around the circuit itself [10]. In fact, with only black-box access to H, tight VDFs are impossible [21].

Groups of Unknown Order. The more prominent sequentiality assumption made in VDFs and other sequential crypto primitives is that repeated squaring in a group of unkown order is inherently sequential (e.g. [41,50]. More precisely, many constructions assume that with a description of a group $\mathbb{G}$ that does not include the order, and a generator $g \in \mathbb{G}$, then it takes $\Omega(T)$ time to compute g^{2^T}. This assumption can be generalized to include arbitrary powers other than squaring, which some constructions use.

This assumption is already known to be false: Bernstein and Sorenson [7] showed that modular exponentation of 2^T can be parallelized with $T^{1+o(1)}$ processors to a depth of $O(T/\lg \lg T)$. While this algorithm is not a strong practical concern, it highlights that these assumptions are tenuous. There are no known reductions relating the hardness of computing modular exponentiation of 2^T with any traditionally hard problems over groups of unknown order, such as factoring, even for exponentially-sized T.

Finally, we would be neglectful if we did not mention that efficient quantum computers can determine the order of groups in polynomial time [47]. Recently [45] showed that delay functions on groups require an unknown order, meaning that unless we find a non-generic way to use groups of known order, we will need to completely scrap this assumption if quantum computing becomes viable.

Ideal Assumptions. Naturally, we want to ask: can we do better? If so, how? Traditonal complexity theorists have studied parallel complexity for quite some time [5], but devoted less attention to parallel *average-case* complexity, which would be applicable to cryptographic protocols[3]. [9] define average-case non-parallelizing languages and show that they imply one-way functions, but we would like a reverse implication. Ideally we could build some sequential function F such that violating the sequentiality of F allowed for some traditional cryptographic assumption to be broken. But this style of reduction seems difficult, since we currently have no way of relating sequentiality assumptions to traditional cryptographic assumptions.

On the other hand, could we build time-release cryptography from two assumptions: a very broad assumption stating that *some* sequential function of a certain type existed, and a traditional cryptographic assumption? Assuming only the existence of some non-parallelizing language, and a specific randomized encoding, [9] construct a concrete time-lock puzzle. This is fairly close to ideal, since the existence of sequential functions is necessary for things like VDFs in the first place. Can we do this for VDFs?

Related Work. There has been some progress on building sequential cryptographic primitives from better assumptions. In [9], Bitansky *et al.* show how to construct time-locked puzzles from randomized encodings [3] assuming the existence of what they call a t-non-parallelizing language. Informally, a t-non-parallelizing language is decidable in time t, but hard for circuits of depth substantially smaller than t. Notably, the authors of [9] only need to assume *worst-case* hardness of the non-parallelizing language, avoiding average case assumptions of sequentiality.

Bitansky *et al.* show two main constructions of TLPs from randomized encodings. The first, an (essentially) optimal construction from *succinct* randomized encodings, has the drawback that the only known way to construct such randomized encodings uses indistinguishability obfuscation (iO) [8,24]. The second construction is of *weak* TLPs (similar to the primitive given in the random oracle construction of [33]) from randomized encodings that are implied by one-way functions.

The [9] construction is, to our knowledge, the only known construction of time-release cryptographic primitives that does not rely on a concrete sequentiality assumption. As such, we will refer to it frequently in the paper. However, the only "optimal" construction relies on iO, which is a strong assumption.

1.3   Our Contributions

We develop new notions of sequential functions and show that we can build time-release cryptography from general circuit assumptions and fully homomorphic encryption. We substantially advance the line of work started in [9] by showing several new constructions of time-release primitives, as well as some implications between them all.

Sequential Function Notions. Informally, we allow distinct models for a challenger (the honest user) and the adversary, which we call $\mathcal{M}_C$ and $\mathcal{M}_A$, respectively. A *sequential* computation in both models takes time proportional to some function of a security parameter λ and a time parameter k. $\mathcal{M}_A$ is allowed to be more powerful (up to some factors) than $\mathcal{M}_C$ with respect to λ but should be no more powerful with respect to k.

---

[3] There has been some work done on average-case parallel complexity with respect to memory hardness [2].

In this paradigm, we will consider (t_C, t_A)-sequentiality to model the gap between an honest user and an adversary rather than the notion of (t, ϵ) sequentiality as in [10]. Our modeling here reflects the fact that an adversary may have faster hardware or a better model of computation than the challenger, which is not reflected in previous definitions. We develop several variants of the notion in terms of adaptivity and iterativity and show the equivalence of the existence of these notions with the assumption of fully homomorphic encryption.

Sequential Function Constructions. Our core construction is an iterative sequential function (ISF) from minimal circuit assumptions. In particular, we show how to build an ISF from the following ingredients:

- **The existence** of an iterative sequential function (ISF).
- A fully homomorphic encryption (FHE) scheme.

We emphasize that we do not actually need to know a construction of an ISF, we just need the knowledge that one exists within some set of parameters. We need an FHE scheme that allows us to compute potentially a superpolynomially large number of operations, so we will unfortunately need to assume circular-secure LWE [43] because we will need to bootstrap [25]. Concretely, our scheme uses the GSW FHE scheme in [26].

Circuit Framework. We define a circuit-based framework and assumptions for time-release cryptography. In Sect. 5, we show that our minimal circuit assumptions both imply and are implied by the the t-non-parallelizing language assumption of [9] up to some small loss factors. We specifically use the circuit model and we focus on "search" problems instead of decision problems because these apply more directly to recent time-release cryptographic primitives. To our knowledge, there has not been a model around sequential computation for VDFs and other "modern" sequential primitives that is as fine-grained as this one, so we think that this framework may be useful for future work in the space of time-release cryptography.

Applications. [10] showed that an iterated sequential function (ISF), together with incremental verifiable computation (IVC), can produce a VDF. This implies that if there exists an ISF, an FHE, and IVC, then our construction can create a VDF.

By definition, a VDF, proof of sequential work, or a time-lock puzzle are all sequential functions. Thus the existence of any of these primitives implies that ISFs exist, which in turn implies that VDFs exist. Our results provide some connection between these time-release cryptography assumptions, illustrated in Fig. 1.

1.4 Paper Outline

Section 2 covers some preliminary material. Section 3 introduces our new definitions for various flavours of sequential functions, and also proves their equivalence if FHE exists. We discuss our main assumption about the existence of a sequential function. In Sect. 4, we construct our ISF, proving it is sequential from our existential circuit assumption and FHE. Section 5 relates our sequential function ideas to non-parallelizing languages, the notion of sequentiality defined in [9].

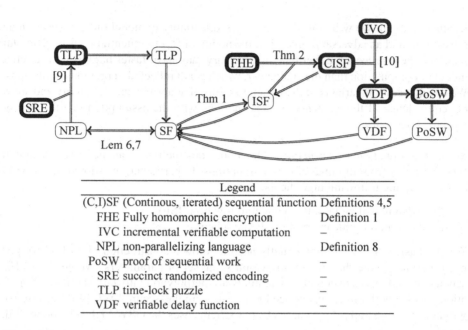

Legend	
(C,I)SF (Continous, iterated) sequential function	Definitions 4,5
FHE Fully homomorphic encryption	Definition 1
IVC incremental verifiable computation	–
NPL non-parallelizing language	Definition 8
PoSW proof of sequential work	–
SRE succinct randomized encoding	–
TLP time-lock puzzle	–
VDF verifiable delay function	–

Fig. 1. Relation between time-release cryptography assumptions. Thin borders indicate existential assumptions (e.g., there exists an ISF) and thick borders indicate constructive assumptions (e.g., the construction in Sect. 4 is an ISF). Unlabelled arrows are consequences that follow directly from definitions.

2   Preliminaries

In this section we provide background material and definitions for our constructions and reductions. Experienced cryptographers should be familiar with the content, although the notation might be unfamiliar in some cases.

2.1   Fully Homomorphic Encryption

We now briefly go over definitions and notation for fully homomorphic encryption (FHE) [25]. We base our presentation off of [14] because we use FHE in a similar manner as they do.

Definition 1. *Fully Homomorphic Encryption: A fully homomorphic encryption (FHE) scheme FHE* $=$ $(\mathsf{Gen}, \mathsf{Enc}, \mathsf{Dec}, \mathsf{Eval})$ *consists of four PPT algorithms such that* $(\mathsf{Gen}, \mathsf{Enc}, \mathsf{Dec})$ *is a public key encryption scheme and*

- $\mathsf{Eval}\,(\mathsf{pk}, f, \mathsf{ct}_1, ..., \mathsf{ct}_n) \to \mathsf{ct}'$ *takes as input the public key* pk, *a function* f *(represented by a Boolean circuit), and a vector of ciphertexts* $(\mathsf{ct}_1, ..., \mathsf{ct}_n)$. *Eval outputs another ciphertext* ct' *which has size that is polynomial in* λ *(and, without loss of generality, linear in the output length of* f*).*

– *For any* $(\mathsf{pk}, \mathsf{sk}) \leftarrow \mathsf{Gen}\left(1^\lambda\right)$, *any vector of messages* $(m_1, ..., m_n)$ *and any circuit* $\mathcal{C} : \{0, 1\}^n \rightarrow \{0, 1\}$ *it holds with probability* 1 *that*

$$\mathsf{Dec}\left(\mathsf{sk}, \mathsf{Eval}\left(\mathsf{pk}, \mathcal{C}, \mathsf{Enc}\left(\mathsf{pk}, m_1\right), ..., \mathsf{Enc}\left(\mathsf{pk}, m_n\right)\right)\right) = \mathcal{C}\left(m_1, ..., m_n\right)$$

Definition 2. *Circular Secure Encryption: A public key encryption scheme PKE is said to be* circular secure *if the following distribution for* $m = 0^{|\mathsf{sk}|}$ *and* $m = \mathsf{sk}$ *is computationally indistinguishable:*

$$\left\{(\mathsf{pk}, \mathsf{sk}) \leftarrow \mathsf{Gen}\left(1^\lambda\right) : (\mathsf{pk}, \mathsf{Enc}\left(\mathsf{pk}, m\right))\right\}$$

2.2 Universal Circuits

Our construction needs a universal circuit [19,32,49] for homomorphic computation of encrypted circuits. We define this below. Our work will focus on the circuit model with boolean gates of fan-in 2.

Definition 3. *Universal Circuit: A circuit* $\mathcal{UC}_{d,g}^{n,m}$ *is called a universal circuit if it contains* n *true input variables,* m *true output variables, and* g *distinguished universal gates such that for any circuit* C *of size* $g_c \leq g$ *and depth* $d_c \leq d$, *there is an efficiently computable configuration for* $\mathcal{UC}$ *such that the ith distinguished universal gate of* $\mathcal{UC}$ *computes the same function as the ith gate of* C *for* $1 \leq i \leq g_c$.

Let $\tilde{C}$ *denote the bitwise representation of some circuit* C *with* $g_c \leq g$ *gates,* n *true input variables, and* m *true output variables. We define the following convention:*

$$\mathcal{UC}_{d,g}^{n,m}\left(\tilde{C}, x_1, ..., x_n\right) = C\left(x_1, ..., x_n\right) = m_1, ..., m_n$$

3 Sequential Functions

In this section we define sequential functions and related primitives and prove equivalence results between different notions of sequential functions. We also relate our new definitions to previous work, such as [10] and [9]. We start by introducing our models of computation, as these will motivate many of our new definitions.

3.1 Models of Computation

We assume two models of computations $\mathcal{M}_C$ and $\mathcal{M}_A$, respectively, for the challenger and the adversary. Each has resources parameterized by the security parameter λ.

Typically, $\mathcal{M}_C$ will have $poly(\lambda)$ parallelism, whereas $\mathcal{M}_A$ may have $2^{o(\lambda)}$ parallelism. The precise subexponential resources of $\mathcal{M}_A$ must be polynomial in the delay T, but not enough to break the security of the FHE scheme we will use[4]. Rather than clutter our notation, we will refer to the parallelism of $\mathcal{M}_A$ as $2^{o(\lambda)}$.

---

[4] In fact, we need the FHE to be secure against "efficient" sub-exponential adversaries. In practical terms, this makes no difference, since any adversary against our model could be used to attack FHE in a different context.

These two models allow us to define (t_C, t_A)-sequential functions. Informally, $\mathcal{M}_C$ can compute such a function in time t_C, and t_A is the fastest time that an algorithm in $\mathcal{M}_A$ can compute the same function.

User Model. For $\mathcal{M}_C$, we want to capture general computations and have universal simulation. That is, there is a universal algorithm U in $\mathcal{M}_C$ such that U can simulate all algorithms F in $\mathcal{M}_C$, given a description of F as input. Running U should take time at most $O(poly(\lambda))$ more than F. Such models include uniform boolean circuits, uniform arithmetic circuits, Turing machines, and parallel random access machines with polynomial parallelism.

Our constructions and reductions will use both universal circuits and FHE. Since we will need to keep track of the circuit overhead of these primitives in order to properly describe our constructions and reductions, we will actually require four different computational models:

1. The model $\mathcal{M}_C$ which can compute a (t_C, t_A)-sequential function. There must be a universal circuit which can simulate $\mathcal{M}_C$.
2. The model $\mathcal{M}_{UC}$ in which a universal circuit can run. $\mathcal{M}_{UC}$ must be homomorphically computable by the FHE.
3. The model $\mathcal{M}_{FHE}$ in which the fully homomorphic encryption is performed and the universal circuit homomorphically evaluated.
4. The adversarial model $\mathcal{M}_A$.

We choose $\mathcal{M}_C$ to be a boolean circuit model with gates of fan-in two, with unit cost and unit depth for all 16 possible gates. Assuming a (t_C, t_A)-sequential function exists is a stronger assumption if $\mathcal{M}_C$ is less powerful. Unfortunately, even if a stronger model is a more realistic model of an actual user, we must choose a weaker model $\mathcal{M}_C$ so that a universal circuit exists that can efficiently evaluate circuits in this model.

We choose $\mathcal{M}_{UC}$ to be a boolean circuit model, since this accommodates a universal circuit, but we restrict the gate set so it can be easily evaluated homomorphically.

We also model $\mathcal{M}_{FHE}$ as a boolean circuit of bounded fan-in, simply for ease of analysis. Since this is the model that actually computes the construction, it should be similar to $\mathcal{M}_A$. If not, we risk losing logarithmic factors in the sequentiality.

We assume throughout that the security of the FHE scheme is sub-exponential in both T and λ. For example, if $T = \Theta(\lambda^{\log \lambda})$, then $O(T^{\log T}) = O(\lambda^{\log^3 \lambda})$ is subexponential in both λ and T, even though T is subexponential in λ as well.

Adversarial Parallelism. If the adversary were allowed an exponential number of gates, then they could compute any circuit in depth logarithmic in the input size by hardcoding the truth table of the function being computed. To avoid such pitfalls, we prevent the model $\mathcal{M}_A$ from having exponential parallelism. Previous works [10] also only allow subexponential parallelism to the adversary.

We still allow an adversary to reduce circuit depth from d to d', with an increase in circuit size of $\Omega(2^{d-d'})$ [28]. This means with $poly(k, \lambda)$ size, they can reduce the depth of a circuit by an *additive* factor of $O(\log k + \log \lambda)$. This allows us to choose a slightly smaller $t'_A(\lambda)$ such that $kt_A(\lambda) - O(\log k + \log \lambda) \geq kt'_A(\lambda)$ for al $k \leq 2^{o(\lambda)}$ and retain the linear scaling.

The key observation for our model is that we are more flexible in allowing an adversary to compute a sequential function *once* very quickly – up to $poly(\lambda)$ faster than $\mathcal{M}_C$ – but we still have the restriction that computing such a function k times in sequence takes time proportional to k times the original computation.

Choice of Models. While $\mathcal{M}_A$ has more resources than $\mathcal{M}_C$, we assume they are fundamentally the same type of computational model. A specific function might be a tight sequential function when both $\mathcal{M}_A$ and $\mathcal{M}_C$ are boolean circuit models, but may become loose if $\mathcal{M}_A$ is a more powerful PRAM model.

For our construction, we assume a (t_C, t_A)-sequential function in a boolean circuit model, in order to evaluate the function with a universal circuit. This means that if a more powerful model like PRAM is more appropriate to the real hardware for both $\mathcal{M}_C$ and $\mathcal{M}_A$, the adversary can use that power while the honest users must still use the universal circuit. This could create a gap between the tightness of the sequential function we assume to exist, and the provable tightness of our construction.

To exploit this gap an adversary must recompile the FHE and universal circuit for faster evaluation with their PRAM, and still produce the same output as the honest user. This seems implausible, but our methods cannot rule it out. However, we assume that since all possible models can simulate each other up to poly-logarithmic factors, which bounds the tightness loss.

3.2 Definitions of Sequential Functions

In this work, instead of considering (t, ϵ)-sequentiality as in [10], we will consider (t_C, t_A)-sequentiality. If $\mathcal{M}_C = \mathcal{M}_A$ (except for the allowed parallelisms), then these definitions are trivially equivalent with $t = t_C$ and $\epsilon = 1 - \frac{t_A}{t_C}$.

We view sequential functions in practice to have three phases, captured in the (Setup, Gen, Eval) tuple in Definition 4. The infrequent Setup phase generates public parameters from the required cryptographic strength. Then the instance generation function Gen produces a seed value. Finally, the evaluation function Eval runs on the seed for a desired duration and outputs a value. We require that honest participants can efficiently perform these phases, but for security we disallow adversaries to output the same value too soon.

The syntax and security of sequential functions have freedom along two dimensions. The first is which of the three phases require the duration parameter. The most inflexible situation ("selective") is when the duration needs to be decided at the setup phase. This restricts all runtime instances to the same duration parameter. Isogeny-based VDFs are in this category [20,46]. We can relax this restriction to make the setup independent of the delay parameter, but the instance generation phase must select its own ("adaptive"). The least restrictive case is when even the instance generation is duration independent ("dynamic"). Here the evaluation can select its desired duration.

The second dimension is iterativity, where the evaluation function has a repetitive structure composed of rounds. A repetitive structure is not only more convenient, but also enables some primitive constructions, such as VDFs by using IVC and SNARKs [10,21] and continuous VDFs [22]. We can have all possible conjuctions of adaptivity and iterativity.

In an iterative sequential function where only Eval requires the duration parameter, Eval is allowed to select a different round function for each duration parameter. We can relax this further and allow the round function to be independent of the duration parameter ("continous"). This allows us to extend the duration at any point by computing more iterations of the round function. This captures the idea of a self-composable VDF from [21]. We take the name from continuous VDFs [22], though a continuous VDF requires the proofs to also be produced iteratively.

Some of the implications among these primitives follow from the definitions. We show some non-trivial implications in this section. Remarkably, the existence of all these notions are equivalent assuming FHE and restricting evaluation to polynomial space in the security parameter.

Definition 4 (Sequential Functions). *A selective sequential function (SSF)* $F =$ (Setup, Gen, Eval) *is defined as the following tuple of algorithms:*

Setup(1^λ $\boxed{,k}$) $\rightarrow$ pp: *On input the security parameter* 1^λ $\boxed{, \text{and } k \in 2^{o(\lambda)}}$, *the setup algorithm returns the public parameters* pp. *By convention, the public parameters encode an input domain* X *and an output domain* Y.

Gen(pp $\boxed{,k}$)) $\rightarrow x$: *On input the public parameters* pp $\boxed{, \text{and } k \in 2^{o(\lambda)}}$, *the instance generation algorithm samples a random input* $x \leftarrow X$.

Eval(pp, x, k) $\rightarrow y$: *On input the public parameters* pp, *an input* $x \in X$, *and* $k \in 2^{o(\lambda)}$, *the evaluation algorithm returns an output* $y \in Y$.

*An SSF is an **Adaptive Sequential Function (ASF)** if* Setup *is independent of* k. *An ASF is a **Dynamic Sequential Function (DSF)** if* Gen *is independent of* k.

An SF F *satisfies* $(t_C(\lambda), t_A(\lambda))$-*sequentiality for machine models* $(\mathcal{M}_C, \mathcal{M}_A)$ *if the following hold:*

1. *There exists an algorithm in the computational model* $\mathcal{M}_C$ *such that for all* k *and for all* x *that can be output by* Gen, *it computes* Eval *in at most time* $k \cdot t_C(\lambda)$.
2. *For all* $\lambda \in \mathbb{N}$ *and for all tuples of PPT machines* $(\mathcal{A}_0, \mathcal{A}_1, \mathcal{A}_2)$, *such that* $\mathcal{A}_2$ *runs in time strictly less than* $k \cdot t_A(\lambda)$ *in the computational model* $\mathcal{M}_A$, *there exists a negligible function* $negl$ *such that:*
   (a) If F *is a selective sequential function:*

$$\Pr\left[y = y' \middle| \begin{array}{l} (k, \tau_0) \leftarrow \mathcal{A}_0(1^\lambda), \ \text{pp} \leftarrow \text{Setup}(1^\lambda, k), \\ \tau_1 \leftarrow \mathcal{A}_1(\text{pp}, k, \tau_0), \ x \leftarrow \text{Gen}(\text{pp}, k), \\ y' \leftarrow \mathcal{A}_2(\text{pp}, x, k, \tau), \ y \leftarrow \text{Eval}(\text{pp}, x, k) \end{array} \right] = negl(\lambda)$$

   (b) If F *is an adaptive sequential function:*

$$\Pr\left[y = y' \middle| \begin{array}{c} \text{pp} \leftarrow \text{Setup}(1^\lambda), \ (k, \tau) \leftarrow \mathcal{A}_1(\text{pp}), \\ x \leftarrow \text{Gen}(\text{pp}, k), \\ y' \leftarrow \mathcal{A}_2(\text{pp}, x, k, \tau), \ y \leftarrow \text{Eval}(\text{pp}, x, k) \end{array} \right] = negl(\lambda)$$

   (c) If F *is a dynamic sequential function:*

$$\Pr\left[y = y' \middle| \begin{array}{c} \text{pp} \leftarrow \text{Setup}(1^\lambda), \ (k, \tau) \leftarrow \mathcal{A}_1(\text{pp}), \\ x \leftarrow \text{Gen}(\text{pp}) \\ y' \leftarrow \mathcal{A}_2(\text{pp}, x, k, \tau), \ y \leftarrow \text{Eval}(\text{pp}, x, k) \end{array} \right] = negl(\lambda)$$

We now consider the relationship between these definitions. By definition, we have DSF $\implies$ ASF $\implies$ SSF as properties, but FHE allows us to show the reverse implications in terms of existence.

Lemma 1. *If a selective sequential function and FHE exist, then a dynamic sequential function exists.*

Proof. Given an SSF SF, we construct another sequential function SF_1 by moving the setup step from SF to the gen step:

SF_1.Setup($1^\lambda, k$) $\to$ pp: Output pp $= \epsilon$.

SF_1.Gen(pp, k) $\to$ x: Sample pp$'$ $\leftarrow$ SF.Setup($1^\lambda, k$) and x' $\leftarrow$ SF.Gen(pp$', k$).
   Output $x = ($pp$', x')$.

SF_1.Eval(pp, x, k) $\to$ y: Output SF.Eval(pp$', x', k$).

This is also an SSF. To show this, let $(\mathcal{A}_0^{SF_1}, \mathcal{A}_1^{SF_1}, \mathcal{A}_2^{SF_1})$ be an SSF adversary against SF_1. We construct an SSF adversary $(\mathcal{A}_0^{SF}, \mathcal{A}_1^{SF}, \mathcal{A}_2^{SF})$ against SF:

$\mathcal{A}_0^{SF}(1^\lambda) \to (k, \tau_0)$: Sample and output $(k, \tau_0) \leftarrow \mathcal{A}_0^{SF_1}(1^\lambda)$.

$\mathcal{A}_1^{SF}($pp, $k, \tau_0) \to \tau$: Sample and output $\tau \leftarrow \mathcal{A}_1^{SF_1}(\epsilon, k, \tau_0)$.

$\mathcal{A}_2^{SF}($pp, $x, k, \tau) \to y$: Sample and output $y \leftarrow \mathcal{A}_2^{SF_1}(\epsilon, (pp, x), k, \tau)$.

The advantages of $(\mathcal{A}_0^{SF_1}, \mathcal{A}_1^{SF_1}, \mathcal{A}_2^{SF_1})$ and $(\mathcal{A}_0^{SF}, \mathcal{A}_1^{SF}, \mathcal{A}_2^{SF})$ are the same.

We now construct a hybrid sequential function SF_2 using the FHE scheme:

SF_2.Setup($1^\lambda, k$) $\to$ pp: Output pp $= \epsilon$.

SF_2.Gen(pp, k) $\to$ x: Sample pk $\leftarrow$ FHE.Gen(1^λ). Let l be the $poly(\lambda)$ size output
   bound of SF_1.Gen(pp, $\cdot$). Sample $x' \leftarrow SF_1$.Gen(pp, k) and pad it to l bits. Sample
   ct $\leftarrow$ FHE.Enc(pk, x'). Output $x = ($pk, ct$)$.

SF_2.Eval(pp, x, k) $\to$ y: Let P_E be the algorithm SF_1.Eval(pp, $\cdot, k$).
   Output FHE.Eval(pk, P_E, ct).

An SSF adversary against SF_2 can be used to construct an SSF adversary against SF_1 by instantiating its own instance of FHE before passing the challenges on, though it loses a poly-logarithmic overhead to compute the FHE. Thus, SF_2 is also an SSF.

Finally, we construct SF_3 as follows:

SF_3.Setup(1^λ) $\to$ pp: Output pp $= \epsilon$.

SF_3.Gen(pp) $\to$ x: Sample pk $\leftarrow$ FHE.Gen(1^λ). Let l be the $poly(\lambda)$ size output
   bound of SF_1.Gen(pp, $\cdot$). Sample ct $\leftarrow$ FHE.Enc(pk, 0^l). Output $x = ($pk, ct$)$.

SF_3.Eval(pp, x, k) $\to$ y: Let P_E be the algorithm SF_1.Eval($\cdot, \cdot, k$).
   Output FHE.Eval(pk, P_E, ct).

SF_3 can be syntactically structured as an SSF by simply ignoring any input k in the Setup and Gen functions. The semantic security of FHE implies that the outputs of SF_3 and SF_2 are indistinguishable, and hence since SF_2 is SSF-sequential, so is SF_3.

Now we show that SF_3 is a DSF. To do this we build an SSF adversary (SSF.$\mathcal{A}_0^{SF_3}$, SSF.$\mathcal{A}_1^{SF_3}$, SSF.$\mathcal{A}_2^{SF_3}$) from a DSF adversary (DSF.$\mathcal{A}_1^{SF_3}$, DSF.$\mathcal{A}_2^{SF_3}$). The only difference between these types of adversary is that SSF adversaries are restricted to choose k before the setup phase, so we construct the SSF adversary as:

SSF.$\mathcal{A}_0^{SF_3}(1^\lambda) \rightarrow (k, \tau_0)$: Sample and output $(k, \tau_0) \leftarrow$ DSF.$\mathcal{A}_1^{SF_3}(\epsilon)$.

SSF.$\mathcal{A}_1^{SF_3}(\mathsf{pp}, k, \tau_0) \rightarrow \tau$: Output $\tau = \tau_0$.

SSF.$\mathcal{A}_2^{SF_3}(\mathsf{pp}, x, k, \tau) \rightarrow y$: Sample and output $y \leftarrow$ DSF.$\mathcal{A}_2^{SF_3}(\epsilon, x, k, \tau)$.

If (DSF.$\mathcal{A}_1^{SF_3}$, DSF.$\mathcal{A}_2^{SF_3}$) is a successful DSF adversary, then (SSF.$\mathcal{A}_0^{SF_3}$, SSF.$\mathcal{A}_1^{SF_3}$, SSF.$\mathcal{A}_2^{SF_3}$) is a successful SSF adversary because we simply changed the order of steps that depend only on fixed inputs.

Following all the reductions, the SSF-sequentiality of SF implies that SF_3 is DSF-sequential.

Iterative Sequential Functions. We next define iterative sequential functions.

Definition 5. *An Iterative Sequential Function (ISF) is a Sequential Function such that the* Eval *function is iterative: there exists a function* Round *such that* Eval(pp, x, k) = $(\mathsf{Round}(\mathsf{pp}, \cdot, k))^{(k)}(x)$. *We have Selective, Adaptive and Dynamic Iterative Sequential Functions defined in the same way as Sequential Functions. In addition, we say that a DISF is a Continuous ISF (CISF) if* Round *is also independent of* k.

By definition, we have CISF $\implies$ DISF $\implies$ AISF $\implies$ SISF, The proof of the converse follows that of Lemma 1.

Lemma 2. *If a selective iterative sequential function and FHE exist, then a continuous iterative sequential function exists.*

Proof. We construct the same series of hybrids ISF_1, ISF_2, and ISF_3 as in the proof of Lemma 1, except that ISF_2 and ISF_3 homomorphically evaluate the round function iteratively. This means that ISF_3.Round(pp, x, k) will output FHE.Eval(pk, P_E, ct) for $P_E = SF_1$.Round(pp, $\cdot, k$).

We then construct ISF_4, where we set $P_E' = SF_1$.Round(pp, $\cdot, \cdot$), with a round function of FHE.Eval(pk, P_E', ct, ct$_k$) for ct$_k$ = FHE.Enc(k). This is identical, except the round number k is now encrypted, so it is also a sequential function.

This allows us to switch ct$_k$ with ct$_0$, an encryption of 0, for ISF_5. An adversary breaking ISF_5 but not ISF_4 distinguishes between an encryption of 0 and of k, and thus breaks semantic security of FHE. Thus ISF_5 is secure as a sequential function, and since the round function is now independent of k, it is a CISF.

An iterative sequential function of any type (selective, adaptive, or dynamic) implies the existence of a non-iterative sequential function of the same type. For the converse:

Theorem 1. *DSF $\implies$ DISF, provided DSF.*Eval *runs in poly-space in* λ. *Similarly, ASF $\implies$ AISF and SSF $\implies$ SISF with the same poly-space restrictions.*

Proof. Let C_Ω be an algorithm in model $\mathcal{M}_C$ that takes a configuration description M (in the model $\mathcal{M}_C$) of length $poly(\lambda)$ and outputs the configuration resulting after the simulation of t_C steps, which also has length $poly(\lambda)$. C_Ω will only introduce a $poly(\lambda)$ overhead in time. We define the DISF as follows:

- Setup $(1^\lambda) \to$ pp:
  - Let $[E]$ denote the description of DSF.Eval(), and $s(\lambda)$ define the upper limit of its space requirement.
  - Sample $pp_0 \leftarrow$ DSF.Setup(1^λ)
  - Output pp $= (pp_0, [E], s(\lambda))$.
- Gen (pp):
  - Sample $x \leftarrow$ DSF.Gen(pp_0).
  - Output $M_0 = ([E], x, 0)$ padded to make it $s(\lambda)$-bits.
- Round (pp, M, k):
  - Given input M, if $M = ([E], x, 0)$ for some x, set $\hat{M} = ([E], x, k)$, otherwise set $\hat{M} = M$.
  - Output $C_\Omega(\hat{M})$, padded to make it $s(\lambda)$-bits.

In the first round, C_Ω acts on $([E], x, k)$ and produces the t_C step advance of the evaluation of DSF.Eval(x, k). In subsequent rounds it just advances in steps of t_C over the previous configuration, as expected.

The proof can be simply adapted for the other two implications ASF $\implies$ AISF and SSF $\implies$ SISF with the same poly-space restrictions.

Overall Picture. Figure 2 shows the overall relationship between all of the sequential functions we have defined. The existence of any type implies the existence of any of the others, though perhaps with a $poly(\lambda)$ loss of tightness.

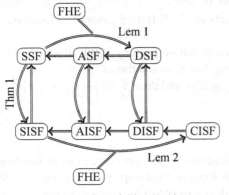

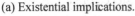

(a) Existential implications.

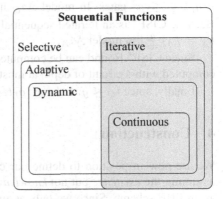

(b) Set containments.

Fig. 2. Relations between sequential function definitions. $\{S, A, D\}$SF are $\{$sequential, adaptive, dynamic$\}$ sequential functions (Definition 4). $\{S, A, D, C\}$ISF are $\{$sequential, adaptive, dynamic, continuous$\}$ iterated sequential functions (Definition 5). Unlabelled arrows represent implications that follow directly from definitions

3.3 Main Assumption

We do not know of any primitives that are provably sequential in a rigorous sense. Like other works, we will make an assumption that some sort of sequential function exists. Our goal is that this assumption should be as weak as possible, and that we only need the *existence* of such a function–not necessarily the *knowledge* of one. This core assumption is that continous ISFs exist:

Definition 6 (Circuit Assumption $\mathsf{CKT}_{t_C,t_A,d,g,n}$). *There exists a CISF, denoted CISF*, with (t_C,t_A)-sequentiality such that $f^* = CISF^*$.Round has a circuit of at most g gates, at most d depth, and at most n inputs and n outputs.*

We assume that CISF* is a boolean circuit with fan-in 2, although all circuit models are interchangeable up to polynomial loss. Though we assume the strongest type of ISF, Lemma 2 shows that the types of ISF are also interchangeable up to polynomial loss.

Our circuit assumption may not hold for all parameters, e.g., all iterated sequential functions may require many more gates g than their depth d. The bounds below allow us to choose values of d, g, and n that are likely to capture a CISF, if it exists.

Lemma 3. *The assumption $\mathsf{CKT}_{t_C,t_A,d,g,n}$ implies $\mathsf{CKT}_{t'_C,t'_A,d',g',n}$, where $d' = g$, $g' = g^2$, $t'_C = d' - o(d')$ and $\frac{d'}{t'_A} \leq 2\frac{t_C}{t_A}$.*

Proof. Let CISF* $= (\mathsf{Setup}, \mathsf{Gen}, \mathsf{Eval}, \mathsf{Round})$ be a continous iterated sequential function implied by the circuit assumption. Let CISF$'$ be identical to CISF*, except CISF$'$.Round consists of repeating CISF*.Round for $\lfloor g/t_C \rfloor$ iterations, which will have $g\lfloor g/t_C \rfloor \leq g^2$ gates. In model $\mathcal{M}_C$ it runs in time $t'_C := t_C \cdot \lfloor \frac{g}{t_C} \rfloor = g - o(g)$. Because CISF* is an iterated sequential function, CISF$'$.Round cannot run faster than $t'_A := t_A \lfloor \frac{g}{t_C} \rfloor$ in model $\mathcal{M}_A$.

Since CISF*.Round can be computed in a circuit of depth t_C, CISF$'$.Round can be computed with a circuit of depth at most $t_C \lfloor g/t_C \rfloor \leq g$, and thus $d' := g$.

Finally, since $t_C \leq g$ we have $\lfloor g/t_C \rfloor \geq g/2t_C$, and thus $\frac{d'}{t'_A} = \frac{g}{t_A \lfloor g/t_C \rfloor} \leq 2\frac{t_C}{t_A}$. $\qquad \blacksquare$

4 Construction

We are now in position to define our construction of an iterated sequential function assuming the *existence* but not *knowledge* of some iterated sequential function as well as an FHE scheme. Since we only assume the existence of an ISF, we do not need to have one as an input to our scheme.

The starting point of our construction is not any of the recent VDF constructions; rather, it is the beautiful line of work on building NIZKs from lattice assumptions [14,15,40]. The core technique of these papers (that we will also use) is the idea of computing a universal circuit (Definition 3) [48] homomorphically over encrypted data. Suppose we are given an encryption of a circuit description $\tilde{C}$ and an encryption of a program input $\mathbf{x}$, which we will refer to as $\mathsf{Enc}\left(\tilde{c}\right)$ and $\mathsf{Enc}(\mathbf{x})$, respectively. If Eval denotes the FHE evaluation function under the appropriate public key, then we can compute

$$\text{Eval}\left(\mathcal{UC}_{g,d}^{n,m}\left(\cdot\right), \text{Enc}\left(\tilde{\mathcal{C}}\right), \text{Enc}\left(\mathbf{x}\right)\right) = \text{Enc}\left(\mathcal{C}\left(\mathbf{x}\right)\right).$$

In words, we homomorphically compute the universal circuit on an encrypted description of a circuit $\mathcal{C}$ and an encrypted input to the circuit $\mathbf{x}$, and get a valid encryption of $\mathcal{C}\left(\mathbf{x}\right)$. Due to FHE security, the encrypted circuit description $\tilde{\mathcal{C}}$ is indistinguishable from random–so someone computing the universal circuit in this way (without the secret key) cannot determine whether they are computing $\mathcal{C}$ or any other circuit that meets the requirements of the parameters n, m, g, and d.

The authors of [14,40] use this to show correlation intractability, which allows them to use a lattice-based hash function in the place of random oracles for NIZKs. Here, we use this to argue that an adversary cannot distinguish whether they are evaluating a sequential function.

We assume that a (t_C, t_A)-iterated sequential function f exists, and can be evaluated homomorphically as an input to the universal circuit. Wrapping f in this way produces a function that is still sequential, since evaluating this circuit gives the output of f encrypted, and we know the output of f cannot be found faster than the bound t_A. Since the FHE and universal circuit add only a polynomial parallelization overhead, honest users can use the homomorphic wrapper of f as a sequential function, albeit with some loss in tightness, as the overheads increase t_C.

So far this requires us to encode f as a circuit. If we knew exactly what function f is, then we could use f directly, but we may not know such a function. However, thanks to FHE, during the setup phase we can encrypt *any* circuit (even an all-zeros string), and no adversary can distinguish this from an encryption of f. Hence, by the semantic security of the FHE, they will not be able to evalute this circuit homomorphically any faster than they could evaluate f, even though the setup does not know anything about f except some bound on the circuit size.

Since we only rely on the *existence* of some f, this means that as long as any sequential function (or VDF) exists, then this construction is a sequential function.

Unfortunately, our constructions based on this intuition are not remotely practical: honest parties will need a huge amount of computational parallelism to compute our core sequential function. Instead, we view our constructions as a theoretical advancement that will hopefully spur further improvements in this area, and that maybe one day some constructions in this vein will be practical.

4.1 Formal Definition

Our ISF is a continuous ISF (CISF) in the sense of Sect. 3, as the subroutines Setup, Gen and Round are all independent of k. We use a universal circuit $\mathcal{UC}_{d,g}^{n,n}$ (Definition 3), and we assume the existence of a fully homomorphic encryption scheme FHE = (Gen, Enc, Dec, Eval) (Definition 1).

Definition 7 (CISF$_{FHE}$ construction). *The continous iterated sequential function CISF$_{FHE}$ is defined as follows:*

- Setup $\left(1^\lambda\right) \to$ pp:

- *Select g, k, and d to be in $O(poly(\lambda))$, such that $n \in \Omega(\lambda)$ and $g = d^2$ (see Lemma 3). These parameterize the number of gates, the input size, and depth, respectively, of a universal circuit.*
- *Let b denote the largest number of bits required to represent the circuit portion of the input to $\mathcal{UC}_{d,g}^{n,n} (\cdot)$.*
- *Sample $(\mathsf{pk}, \mathsf{sk}) \leftarrow FHE.\mathsf{Gen}\left(1^\lambda\right)$ and $\mathsf{ct}_{ckt} \leftarrow \langle FHE.\mathsf{Enc}\left(\mathsf{pk}, 0\right)\rangle_{i=1}^{b}$.*
- *Output the tuple $\mathsf{pp} = (\mathsf{pk}, \mathsf{ct}_{ckt})$.*
- Gen (pp):
  - *Sample and output $\mathbf{x} \leftarrow \langle FHE.\mathsf{Enc}\left(\mathsf{pk}, 0\right)\rangle_{i=1}^{n}$.*
- Round $(\mathsf{pp}, \mathbf{x})$:
  - *Output $FHE.\mathsf{Eval}\left(\mathsf{pk}, \mathcal{UC}_{d,g}^{n,n}, \mathsf{ct}_{ckt}, \mathbf{x}\right)$.*
- Eval $(\mathsf{pp}, \mathbf{x}, k)$:
  - *Output $\left(\mathsf{Round}\left(\mathsf{pk}, \mathcal{UC}_{d,g}^{n,n}, \mathsf{ct}_{ckt}, \cdot\right)\right)^{(k)} (\mathbf{x})$.*

FHE.Eval may be probabilistic, but we can instead use any pseudorandom bits for its random input to make it deterministic to fit the definition of Round. This will not impact the proof of Theorem 2.

4.2 Sequentiality

Here we show that CISF_{FHE} is a continous ISF as long as there exists a continuous ISF. Since we must assume FHE for this construction, then Lemma 2 and Theorem 1 show that the existence of any type of sequential function implies that CISF_{FHE} is a continuous ISF.

Our construction adds two constant overheads to the scheme: κ_{UC}, the overhead to compute a circuit with a universal circuit, and κ_{FHE}, the overhead to compute a circuit homomorphically with an FHE scheme. These constants are a function only of the security parameter λ[5]. Here we show that evaluating a sequential function with either a universal circuit or an FHE scheme is also sequential.

Recall Definition 6, which defines $\mathsf{CKT}_{t_C, t_A, d, g, n}$ as the assumption that there exists some (t_C, t_A) continous ISF, simulatable by $\mathcal{UC}_{d,g}^{n,n}$.

Lemma 4 (UC Sequentiality). *Assuming $\mathsf{CKT}_{t'_C, t'_A, d, g, n}$, there exists a continous ISF, $\mathrm{CISF}_n = (\mathsf{Setup}, \mathsf{Gen}, \mathsf{Eval})$ with round function f, such that $(\mathsf{Setup}, \mathsf{Gen}, \mathcal{UC}_{g, g^2}^{n,n}(f, \cdot))$ is a (t_C, t_A) continous ISF, with $t_C = \kappa_{UC} g$ and $t_A = t'_A \lfloor \frac{g}{t_C} \rfloor$.*

Proof. Lemma 3 strengthens the circuit assumption to $\mathsf{CKT}_{t''_C, t''_A, g, g^2, n}$ with $t''_C = g$ and $t''_A = t'_A \lfloor \frac{g}{t_C} \rfloor$, implying the existence of CISF_n. Cook and Hoover's universal circuit [19, Theorem 1] shows that κ_{UC} can be made constant.

Lemma 5 (FHE Sequentiality). *If $CISF = (\mathsf{Setup}, \mathsf{Gen}, \mathsf{Eval})$ is an iterated (t'_C, t'_A)-sequential function such that $CISF.\mathsf{Eval}$ has circuit $\mathcal{C}$, then $CISF' = (\mathsf{Setup}', \mathsf{Gen}', \mathsf{Eval}')$ is an iterated (t_C, t_A)-sequential function, with $t_C = (\kappa_{FHE} + o(1))t'_C$ and $t_A = t'_A$, where*

---

[5] Details in full version.

- $\mathsf{Setup}'(1^\lambda) \to (\mathsf{pp}_1 := CISF.\mathsf{Setup}(1^\lambda), \mathsf{pp}_2 := FHE.\mathsf{Gen}(1^\lambda))$
- $\mathsf{Gen}'((\mathsf{pp}_1, \mathsf{pp}_2)) \to FHE.\mathsf{Enc}(\mathsf{pp}_2, CISF.\mathsf{Gen}(\mathsf{pp}_1))$
- $\mathsf{Eval}'((\mathsf{pp}_1, \mathsf{pp}_2), k, \mathbf{x}) = (FHE.\mathsf{Eval}(\mathsf{pp}, \mathcal{C}, \cdot))^{(k)}(\mathbf{x})$

Proof. If we decrypt the output of Eval', then it acts as a circuit to compute the iterated sequential function CISF, and this cannot run faster than t_A. The overhead for these computations is κ_{FHE}, and decrypting the output adds the $o(1)$ term.

Finally, we prove that our scheme is sequential even if the encrypted public parameters do not encode a sequential function.

Theorem 2 (Sequentiality). *Let $CISF_{FHE}$ be instantiated with parameters d, $g = d^2$, and n. Assuming $\mathsf{CKT}_{t'_C, t'_A, d, d, n}$ and CPA-2 security of FHE, $CISF_{FHE}$ is a (t_C, t_A)-iterated sequential function, where $t_C = (\kappa_{FHE}\kappa_{UC} + o(1))d$ and $t_A = (\frac{t'_A}{t_C} - o(1))d$.*

Proof. The circuit assumption and Lemma 4 imply that there exists CISF = (Setup, Gen, Eval), a CISF, with a round function f that $\mathcal{UC}^{n,n}_{d,d^2}$ can simulate.

We now play an adaptive security game with an oracle for an FHE scheme with public key pk. First we run Gen and get a random message m, and we send this to the FHE oracle to get an input $\mathbf{x}$. Then for the challenge, we send $m_0 = \{0\}^b$ and m_1 as the circuit for f. We receive a ciphertext ct_c for $c \in \{0, 1\}$, and we set $\mathsf{pp}_c = (\mathsf{pk}, \mathsf{ct}_c)$ to be the public parameters of our construction.

Suppose that $(\mathcal{A}_1, \mathcal{A}_2)$ breaks the sequentiality of $CISF_{FHE}$. We set $(k, \tau) \leftarrow \mathcal{A}_1(\mathsf{pp}_c)$ and then set $y_A \leftarrow \mathcal{A}_2(\mathsf{pp}_c, \mathbf{x}, k, \tau)$, which runs in some time T_A. We also honestly compute $y \leftarrow CISF_{FHE}(\mathsf{pp}_c, k, \mathbf{x})$.

By our assumption that $\mathcal{A}_2$ breaks the iterated sequentiality of $CISF_{FHE}$, if $c = 0$ then $y = y_A$ and $T_A < kt_A$. However, if $c = 1$, then both statements cannot be true: since the ciphertext encodes the circuit for a CISF, then the construction is a sequential function by Lemma 5, so $\mathcal{A}_2$ cannot produce the correct answer y in time $T_A < kt_A$. Thus, we can compare y to y_A, and T_A to kt_A, and deduce the original value of c, breaking the semantic security of FHE. Honestly computing $CISF_{FHE}$ requires only $k \cdot poly(\lambda) \leq 2^{o(\lambda)}$ resources, so this is a computationally feasible attack.

5 Non-Parallelizing Languages

Bitansky *et al.* defined a primitive called a *non-parallelizing language* in their work on time-locked puzzles [9]. We modify their definition slightly to use our $(\mathcal{M}_C, \mathcal{M}_A)$ approach and then show equivalences between our definition of adaptive sequential function and the definition of a non-parallelizing language. Informally, an adaptive sequential function is akin to the "search problem" variant of a non-parallel language.

Definition 8. *An average-case non-parallelizing language ensemble with gap ϵ is a set of languages $\{\mathcal{L}_{\lambda, t}\}_{\lambda, t \in \mathbb{N}}$, where $\mathcal{L}_{\lambda, t} \subseteq \{0, 1\}^\lambda$, that satisfies:*

Completeness: *For all $\lambda \in \mathbb{N}$ and $t \leq 2^{o(\lambda)}$, there exists a decision algorithm $\mathcal{L}$ in model $\mathcal{M}_C$ such that for all λ and t and all inputs $x \in \{0, 1\}^\lambda$, $\mathcal{L}(t, x)$ runs in time t and outputs 1 if and only if $x \in \mathcal{L}_{\lambda, t}$.*

Average-case non-parallelizing: *There exists an efficient sampler* Gen *such that for every family of circuits* $\mathcal{A} = \{\mathcal{A}_\lambda\}_{\lambda \in \mathbb{N}}$ *in model* $\mathcal{M}_A$ *with parallelism at most* $2^{o(\lambda)}$, *there exists a negligible function* negl *such that for all* λ *and* t, *if the run-time of* $\mathcal{A}_\lambda < (1 - \epsilon)t$, *then*

$$\Pr\left[\mathcal{A}_\lambda(x) = \mathcal{L}(t, x) \mid x \leftarrow \mathsf{Gen}(1^\lambda, t)\right] \le negl(\lambda).$$

Lemma 6. *The existence of a* (t_C, t_A) *ASF implies an average case non-parallelizing language of gap* $\epsilon = 1 - \frac{t_A}{t_C} + o(1)$.

Proof. Our proof is a relatively basic application of the Goldreich-Levin Theeorem [27]. A critical fact necessary for the proof to work is that queries in the Goldreich-Levin algorithm (as stated in theorem) are nonadaptive and thus can be computed in parallel.

Let ASF = (Setup, Gen, Eval) be an ASF and let pp = Setup(1^λ). We let $T = kt_C(\lambda)$ and l be the bit-length of the outputs of Gen(pp, k). We create a language $\mathcal{L}_{\lambda,T} \subseteq \{0,1\}^{l+l}$ as the set of all strings (pp, $\mathbf{x}$, r) such that $\langle \mathsf{Eval}(\mathsf{pp}, k, \mathbf{x}), r \rangle \equiv 1$ mod 2. The behaviour of Eval may be undefined if $\mathbf{x}$ is not the output of Gen; we include such strings in $\mathcal{L}_{\lambda,T}$ if Eval runs in T and produces a well-formed output with odd parity with r.

Finding the parity with Eval satisfies the completeness property, since Eval runs in time $kt_C(\lambda) = T$. If Eval fails to run in that time or does not produce a well-formed output, the string is not in the language by definition and we can correctly output 0.

We let ASF.Gen be the efficient sampler for the languages. If $\mathcal{L}_{\lambda,T}$ are not average-case non-parallelizing, then there is a parallel circuit $\mathcal{A}$ that decides $\mathcal{L}_{\lambda,T}$ with probability greater than $\frac{1}{2} + p$ in time less than $(1 - \epsilon)T$ on the outputs of Gen. The Goldreich-Levin algorithm will then find the output of Eval by running $\mathcal{A}$ for $O(p^{-2}\lambda^{1+o(1)})$ inputs [27]; however, this is less than $2^{o(\lambda)}$, and these can be run in parallel, since the output of the algorithm is just the bitwise majority of the outputs of $\mathcal{A}$. Thus, the total time will be less than $(1 - \epsilon)T + O(\log(p) + \log(\lambda))$. If we let $\epsilon = 1 - \frac{t_A}{t_C} + \delta$, then this equals

$$kt_C(\lambda) - \delta kt_C(\lambda) + O(\log(p) + \log(\lambda)).$$

If δ is large enough this contradicts the sequentiality of ASF, and a large enough δ is still $o(1)$ in terms of λ.

Lemma 7. *If there exists an average-case non-parallelizing languages of gap* ϵ, *then there is a* $(1, 1 - \epsilon)$ *ASF.*

Proof. Suppose we have a language $\mathcal{L}_{\lambda,t}$ which is average-case non-parallelizing of gap ϵ. It comes with an algorithm $\mathcal{L}$ with decides the language. We set Setup(1^λ) $\rightarrow \lambda$. The definition of non-parallelizing implies a sampler $\mathcal{L}$.Gen, and we define the Gen function for the ASF as λ repetitions of $\mathcal{L}$.Gen, outputting $\mathbf{x} = (\mathbf{x}_1, \ldots, \mathbf{x}_\lambda)$. We then define

$$\mathsf{Eval}(\mathsf{pp}, k, \mathbf{x}) \rightarrow \mathcal{L}(k, \mathbf{x}_1) \| \mathcal{L}(k, \mathbf{x}_2) \| \ldots \| \mathcal{L}(k, \mathbf{x}_\lambda).$$

Since $\mathcal{L}$ can be run in time k for any t, Eval runs in time $k \cdot 1$.

If $(\mathcal{A}_1, \mathcal{A}_2)$ breaks sequentiality of this ASF, then $\mathcal{A}_1$ can be run once to produce k, since Setup produces only the public information λ. Then $\mathcal{A}_2$ produces the output of Eval in time less than $kt_A := k(1 - \epsilon)$, and the output of Eval decides the language $\mathcal{L}_{\lambda,k}$ with non-negligible probablity, contradicting the average-case non-parallelization of $\mathcal{L}_{\lambda,t}$.

Lemma 8. *If there exist a worst-case non-parallelizing language of gap ϵ, then there is a $(\kappa_{FHE}, 1 - \epsilon)$ ASF, where κ_{FHE} is the sequential overhead of FHE.*

Proof. Suppose we have a languages $\mathcal{L}_{\lambda,t}$ which is *worst*-case non-parallelizing of gap ϵ. As before, it comes with an algorithm $\mathcal{L}$ with decides the language. We sample pk $\leftarrow$ FHE.Gen (1^λ) and set Setup$(1^\lambda) \rightarrow$ (pk, λ). Let S be the sampler implied by the definition of $\mathcal{L}_{\lambda,t}$, and set Gen to be

$$\mathsf{FHE.Enc}\,(\mathbf{x}_1 \leftarrow S \| \mathbf{x}_2 \leftarrow S \| \dots \| \mathbf{x}_\lambda \leftarrow S)$$

Finally, we set

$$\mathsf{Eval}\,(\mathsf{pp}, k, \mathbf{x}) \rightarrow \mathsf{FHE.Eval}\,(\mathcal{L}\,(k, \cdot)\,, \mathbf{x}_1) \| \dots \| \mathsf{FHE.Eval}\,(\mathcal{L}_\lambda\,(k, \cdot)\,, \mathbf{x}_\lambda)$$

This has the exact same structure as in lemma 7 except for the fact that the input string is encrypted and we are evaluating everything homomorphically. Thus, our argument would follow immediately for average-case non-parallelizing languates.

However, the FHE scheme hides the input of Eval (effectively the output from Gen). So, by the security of the FHE scheme, an adversary cannot tell whether this is a random input or a specially tailored one. Using a simple hybrid argument, we can switch out the input $\mathbf{x}$ for arbitrary (i.e. worst-case) value, which completes the proof.

The [26] FHE encryption scheme can have sequential overhead of $O\left(\log^{1+\epsilon} \lambda\right)$ for any $\epsilon > 0^6$, which means we can instantiate the implied construction from the above lemma with relatively good parameters.

Acknowledgements. Samuel Jaques was supported by the University of Oxford Clarendon fund.

References

1. https://coinmarketcap.com/currencies/ethereum/
2. Alwen, J., Serbinenko, V.: High parallel complexity graphs and memory-hard functions. In: Servedio, R.A., Rubinfeld, R., (Eds.), 47th ACM STOC, pp. 595–603. ACM Press, June 2015
3. Applebaum, B., Ishai, Y., Kushilevitz, E.: Cryptography in NC⁰. In 45th FOCS, pp. 166–175. IEEE Computer Society Press, October 2004
4. Armknecht, F., Barman, L., Bohli, J.-M., Karame, G.O.: Mirror: enabling proofs of data replication and retrievability in the cloud. In: Holz, T., Savage, S. (eds.) USENIX Security 2016, pp. 1051–1068. USENIX Association, August 2016
5. Arora, S., Barak, B.: Computational Complexity: A Modern Approach. Cambridge University Press, Cambridge (2009)

---

[6] For details, please see the full version.

6. Bellare, M., Rogaway, P.: Random oracles are practical: a paradigm for designing efficient protocols. In: Denning, D.E., Pyle, R., Ganesan, R., Sandhu, R.S., Ashby, V., (Eds.) ACM CCS 93, pp. 62–73. ACM Press, November 1993

7. Bernstein, D.J., Sorenson, J.P.: Modular exponentiation via the explicit Chinese remainder theorem. Math. Comput. **76**(257), 443–454 (2007)

8. Bitansky, N., Garg, S., Lin, H., Pass, R., Telang, S.: Succinct randomized encodings and their applications. In: Servedio, R.A., Rubinfeld, R., (Eds.), 47th ACM STOC, pp. 439–448. ACM Press, June 2015

9. Bitansky, N., Goldwasser, S., Jain, A., Paneth, O., Vaikuntanathan, V., Waters, B.: Time-lock puzzles from randomized encodings. In: Sudan, M. (ed.) ITCS 2016, pp. 345–356. ACM, January 2016

10. Boneh, D., Bonneau, J., Bünz, B., Fisch, B.: Verifiable delay functions. In: Shacham, H., Boldyreva, A. (eds.) CRYPTO 2018. LNCS, vol. 10991, pp. 757–788. Springer, Cham (2018). https://doi.org/10.1007/978-3-319-96884-1_25

11. Boneh, D., Bünz, B., Fisch, B.: A survey of two verifiable delay functions. Cryptology ePrint Arch., Rep. 2018/712 (2018). https://eprint.iacr.org/2018/712

12. Boneh, D., Naor, M.: Timed commitments. In: Bellare, M. (ed.) CRYPTO 2000. LNCS, vol. 1880, pp. 236–254. Springer, Heidelberg (2000). https://doi.org/10.1007/3-540-44598-6_15

13. Brakerski, Z., Döttling, N., Garg, S., Malavolta, G.: Leveraging linear decryption: rate-1 fully-homomorphic encryption and time-lock puzzles. In: Hofheinz, D., Rosen, A. (eds.) TCC 2019. LNCS, vol. 11892, pp. 407–437. Springer, Cham (2019). https://doi.org/10.1007/978-3-030-36033-7_16

14. Canetti, R., et al.: Fiat-Shamir: from practice to theory. In: Charikar, M., Cohen, E. (Eds.) 51st ACM STOC, pp. 1082–1090. ACM Press, June 2019

15. Canetti, R., Chen, Y., Reyzin, L., Rothblum, R.D.: Fiat-Shamir and correlation intractability from strong KDM-secure encryption. In: Nielsen, J.B., Rijmen, V. (eds.) EUROCRYPT 2018. LNCS, vol. 10820, pp. 91–122. Springer, Cham (2018). https://doi.org/10.1007/978-3-319-78381-9_4

16. Chen, M., et al.: Diogenes: lightweight scalable RSA modulus generation with a dishonest majority. Cryptology ePrint Arch., Rep. 2020/374 (2020). https://eprint.iacr.org/2020/374

17. Clark, J., Hengartner, U.: On the use of financial data as a random beacon. EVT/WOTE, 89 (2010)

18. Cohen, B., Pietrzak, K.: Simple proofs of sequential work. In: Nielsen, J.B., Rijmen, V. (eds.) EUROCRYPT 2018. LNCS, vol. 10821, pp. 451–467. Springer, Cham (2018). https://doi.org/10.1007/978-3-319-78375-8_15

19. Cook, S.A., Hoover, H.J.: A depth-universal circuit. SIAM J. Comput. **14**(4), 833–839 (1985)

20. De Feo, L., Masson, S., Petit, C., Sanso, A.: Verifiable delay functions from Supersingular isogenies and pairings. In: Galbraith, S.D., Moriai, S. (eds.) ASIACRYPT 2019. LNCS, vol. 11921, pp. 248–277. Springer, Cham (2019). https://doi.org/10.1007/978-3-030-34578-5_10

21. Döttling, N., Garg, S., Malavolta, G., Vasudevan, P.N.: Tight verifiable delay functions. In: Galdi, C., Kolesnikov, V. (eds.) SCN 2020. LNCS, vol. 12238, pp. 65–84. Springer, Cham (2020). https://doi.org/10.1007/978-3-030-57990-6_4

22. Ephraim, N., Freitag, C., Komargodski, I., Pass, R.: Continuous verifiable delay functions. In: Canteaut, A., Ishai, Y. (eds.) EUROCRYPT 2020. LNCS, vol. 12107, pp. 125–154. Springer, Cham (2020). https://doi.org/10.1007/978-3-030-45727-3_5

23. Garay, J., MacKenzie, P., Prabhakaran, M., Yang, K.: Resource fairness and composability of cryptographic protocols. In: Halevi, S., Rabin, T. (eds.) TCC 2006. LNCS, vol. 3876, pp. 404–428. Springer, Heidelberg (2006). https://doi.org/10.1007/11681878_21

24. Garg, S., Gentry, C., Halevi, S., Raykova, M., Sahai, A., Waters, B.: Candidate indistinguishability obfuscation and functional encryption for all circuits. In: 54th FOCS, pp. 40–49. IEEE Computer Society Press, October 2013

25. Gentry, C.: Fully homomorphic encryption using ideal lattices. In: Mitzenmacher, M. (Ed.) 41st ACM STOC, pp. 169–178. ACM Press, May/June 2009

26. Gentry, C., Sahai, A., Waters, B.: Homomorphic encryption from learning with errors: conceptually-simpler, asymptotically-faster, attribute-based. In: Canetti, R., Garay, J.A. (eds.) CRYPTO 2013. LNCS, vol. 8042, pp. 75–92. Springer, Heidelberg (2013). https://doi.org/10.1007/978-3-642-40041-4_5

27. Goldreich, O., Levin, L.A.: A hard-core predicate for all one-way functions. In: 21st ACM STOC, pp. 25–32. ACM Press, May 1989

28. Golovnev, A., Kulikov, A.S., Williams, R.R.: Circuit depth reductions (2018)

29. Kiayias, A., Russell, A., David, B., Oliynykov, R.: Ouroboros: a provably secure proof-of-stake blockchain protocol. In: Katz, J., Shacham, H. (eds.) CRYPTO 2017. LNCS, vol. 10401, pp. 357–388. Springer, Cham (2017). https://doi.org/10.1007/978-3-319-63688-7_12

30. Protocol Labs. Filecoin: a decentralized storage network (2017). https://filecoin.io/filecoin.pdf

31. Lenstra, A.K., Wesolowski, B.: Trustworthy public randomness with sloth, unicorn, and trx. Int. J. Appl. Crypt. **3**(4), 330–343 (2017)

32. Lipmaa, H., Mohassel, P., Sadeghian, S.: Valiant's universal circuit: improvements, implementation, and applications. Cryptology ePrint Arch., Rep. 2016/017 (2016). https://eprint.iacr.org/2016/017

33. Mahmoody, M., Moran, T., Vadhan, S.P.: Publicly verifiable proofs of sequential work. In: Kleinberg, R.D. (Ed.) ITCS 2013, pp. 373–388. ACM, January 2013

34. Mahmoody, M., Smith, C., Wu, D.J.: Can verifiable delay functions be based on random oracles? In: ICALP 2020, LIPIcs, pp. 83:1–83:17. Schloss Dagstuhl (2020)

35. Malavolta, G., Thyagarajan, S.A.K.: Homomorphic time-lock puzzles and applications. In: Boldyreva, A., Micciancio, D. (eds.) CRYPTO 2019. LNCS, vol. 11692, pp. 620–649. Springer, Cham (2019). https://doi.org/10.1007/978-3-030-26948-7_22

36. Nakamoto, S.: Bitcoin: a peer-to-peer electronic cash system. Technical report, Manubot (2019)

37. Öztürk, E.: Modular multiplication algorithm suitable for low-latency circuit implementations. Cryptology ePrint Arch., Rep. 2019/826 (2019). https://eprint.iacr.org/2019/826

38. Öztürk, E.: Design and implementation of a low-latency modular multiplication algorithm. IEEE Trans. Circuits Syst. I Regul. Pap. **67**, 1902–1911 (2020)

39. Park, S., Kwon, A., Fuchsbauer, G., Gaži, P., Alwen, J., Pietrzak, K.: SpaceMint: a cryptocurrency based on proofs of space. In: Meiklejohn, S., Sako, K. (eds.) FC 2018. LNCS, vol. 10957, pp. 480–499. Springer, Heidelberg (2018). https://doi.org/10.1007/978-3-662-58387-6_26

40. Peikert, C., Shiehian, S.: Noninteractive zero knowledge for NP from (plain) learning with errors. In: Boldyreva, A., Micciancio, D. (eds.) CRYPTO 2019. LNCS, vol. 11692, pp. 89–114. Springer, Cham (2019). https://doi.org/10.1007/978-3-030-26948-7_4

41. Pietrzak, K.: Simple verifiable delay functions. In: Blum, A., (Ed.) ITCS 2019, vol. 124, pp. 60:1–60:15. LIPIcs, January 2019

42. Rabin, M.O.: Transaction protection by beacons. J. Comput. Syst. Sci. **27**(2), 256–267 (1983)

43. Regev, O.: On lattices, learning with errors, random linear codes, and cryptography. In: Gabow, H.N., Fagin, R. (Eds.) 37th ACM STOC, pp. 84–93. ACM Press, May 2005

44. Rivest, R.L., Shamir, A., Wagner, D.A.: Time-lock puzzles and timed-release crypto (1996)

45. Rotem, L., Segev, G., Shahaf, I.: Generic-group delay functions require hidden-order groups. In: Canteaut, A., Ishai, Y. (eds.) EUROCRYPT 2020. LNCS, vol. 12107, pp. 155–180. Springer, Cham (2020). https://doi.org/10.1007/978-3-030-45727-3_6

46. Shani, B.: A note on isogeny-based hybrid verifiable delay functions. Cryptology ePrint Arch., Rep. 2019/205 (2019). https://eprint.iacr.org/2019/205

47. Shor, P.W.: Polynomial-time algorithms for prime factorization and discrete logarithms on a quantum computer. SIAM Rev. **41**(2), 303–332 (1999)
48. Valiant, L.G.: Universal circuits (preliminary report). In: Proceedings of the Eighth Annual ACM Symposium on Theory of Computing, pp. 196–203 (1976)
49. Wegener, I.: The complexity of Boolean Functions. BG Teubner (1987)
50. Wesolowski, B.: Efficient verifiable delay functions. In: Ishai, Y., Rijmen, V. (eds.) EURO-CRYPT 2019. LNCS, vol. 11478, pp. 379–407. Springer, Cham (2019). https://doi.org/10.1007/978-3-030-17659-4_13

Succinct Publicly-Certifiable Proofs
Or, Can a Blockchain Verify a Designated-Verifier Proof?

Matteo Campanelli and Hamidreza Khoshakhlagh[✉]

Aarhus University, Aarhus, Denmark
{matteo,hamidreza}@cs.au.dk

Abstract. We study zero-knowledge arguments where proofs are: of knowledge, short, publicly-verifiable and produced without interaction. While zkSNARKs satisfy these requirements, we build such proofs in a constrained theoretical setting: in the standard-model—i.e., without a random oracle—and without assuming public-verifiable SNARKs (or even NIZKs, for some of our constructions) or primitives currently known to imply them.

We model and construct a new primitive, SPuC (Succinct Publicly-Certifiable System), where: a party can prove knowledge of a witness w by publishing a proof π_0; the latter can then be certified non-interactively by a committee sharing a secret; any party in the system can now verify the proof through its certificates; the total communication complexity should be sublinear in $|w|$. We construct SPuCs *generally* from (leveled) FHE, homomorphic signatures and linear-only encryption, all instantiatable from lattices and thus plausibly quantum-resistant. We also construct them in the two-party case replacing FHE with the simpler primitive of homomorphic secret-sharing.

Our model has practical applications in blockchains and in other protocols where there exist committees sharing a secret and it is necessary for parties to prove knowledge of a solution to some puzzle. Our constructions can be seen as a way to compile a designated-verifier SNARK into a proof system with a flavor of public-verifiability with similar efficiency features of the starting dvSNARK (e.g., proving time).

We show that one can construct a version of SPuCs with robust proactive security from similar assumptions. In a proactively secure model the committee reshares its secret from time to time. Such a model is robust if the committee members can prove they performed this resharing step correctly. Along the way to our goal we define and build Proactive Universal Thresholdizers, a proactive version of the Universal Thresholdizer defined in Boneh et al. [Crypto 2018].

1 Introduction

We consider the setting where, at any given moment in time, users can post a puzzle on a blockchain. Later some other user may come along and show to everybody that they know a solution to the puzzle without necessarily leaking it (i.e., in zero-knowledge). This scenario has numerous applications to problems

© Springer Nature Switzerland AG 2021
A. Adhikari et al. (Eds.): INDOCRYPT 2021, LNCS 13143, pp. 607–631, 2021.
https://doi.org/10.1007/978-3-030-92518-5_27

in secure decentralized computing that have received much attention lately—these include but are not limited to: showing that the parties are following some internal protocol [29], storing and retrieving secrets with functionalities close to extractable witness encryption [31], zero-knowledge contingent payments [17] and showing knowledge of secret inputs to general smart-contracts [16].

For a solution to the problem above to be useful, we do not only require that all the users can verify the proof to a puzzle, but we also need to pose efficiency requirements. A *scalable* solution should involve minimal interaction among parties—ideally the *puzzle-solver* should post its proof and then disappear—and low bandwidth—short proofs.

In principle, a perfect candidate for this setting are publicly-verifiable succinct non-interactive arguments of knowledge (or pv-SNARKs) [4] with zero-knowledge properties. In this work, however, we shall seek solutions that do not require publicly-verifiable SNARKs. *Our choice is motivated by exploring different (and, plausibly, weaker) assumptions while obtaining post-quantum secure constructions.* In our solutions we do not only avoid using pv-SNARKs, but also any *publicly-verifiable proof for non-deterministic computations* (that is, NIZKs for NP \ P). We discuss the rationale of this choice in Sect. 1.2.

Committees Certifying Proofs without Interaction. We consider a model which is almost as non-interactive as that of pv-SNARKs, but in which we add one more hop. At the high-level our model works as follows. At each moment in time there exists a committee holding a secret (the secret being shared among the committee members)[1]. This secret permits them to publicly "certify" a proof publicly posted by anybody claiming they know a solution to a puzzle. Certifying a proof happens in a threshold fashion: a prover holding a witness w, outputs a succinct proof π_0; the parties in the committee can then process it broadcasting a "partial certificate", which any node in the network can check whether to consider it valid; if at least d (out of the total N) committee members broadcasted a valid certificate, these can be combined through a deterministic algorithm to obtain the bit b determining acceptance/rejection of π_0. The protocol is required to stay secure as long as the adversary corrupts less than a certain fraction of committee members.

Naturally, a general MPC-based solution is always applicable in this scenario. Our challenge, however, is to keep the efficiency requirements of low interaction/bandwidth sketched above. Specifically we need to guarantee that: *(i)* parties require no interaction among each other for proving, certification or verification[2]; *(ii)* all messages—the proof π_0 as well as the partial certificates—are short (sublinear in the witness size).

YOSO-style Proactive Committees. The requirements sketched above are sufficient for the setting where a certifying committee is *static* (this is our vanilla SPuC model in Sect. 2). We also study a version of our protocol where the com-

---

[1] Such a committee is not an uncommon architectural choice. See, e.g. [3,27].

[2] Naturally we require certifying parties to wait for proof π_0 to be posted publicly.

mittee changes over time and can proactively reshare its shares. The challenge for us is to make these protocols *robust* and *YOSO-style*, staying within our weak-assumptions framework as much as possible. Requiring robustness means that the resharing parties can prove whether they reshared correctly. YOSO (You Only Speak Once) [27] requires more elaboration: when performing the resharing (as well as in other parts of the protocol) parties should not interact among each other, instead they speak only once and then can potentially disappear. For us, the YOSO-style requirement means that, after the parties have been assigned their roles as members of the certifying committees[3] they need to speak only once. Their message will consist of the certificate for the (potentially many) proofs π_0-s publicly posted during their time holding the role.

1.1 Contributions and Overview

A Model for SPuCs. We provide a formal model for Succinct Publicly Certifiable proofs (SPuCs), which we describe in Sect. 2. Our security notions all refer to an adversary controlling up to $d - 1$ of the N committee members. We require properties analogous to those for proof systems: *unbounded zero-knowledge*—an adversary cannot learn anything even after (adaptively) querying many proofs and certificates on them—and *strong knowledge-soundness*—given an adversary providing a verifying proof and certificates for a statement stmt one can extract a valid witness from them. The last notion can be paraphrased as: no adversary can forge a certified proof π_0 and (up to $d - 1$) valid certificates for stmt and π_0 without knowing a witness for stmt. While these definitions intuitively are extensions of the corresponding notions for designated-verifier NIZKs, we find them to be non-trivial and require some care (for example, in modeling appropriate oracles for the zero-knowledge simulator). Finally we require our proofs and certificates to be of total size sublinear in the witness size.

A General Construction for SPuCs. We provide a general construction for SPuCs from designated-verifier SNARKs and a primitive called Universal Thresholdizers (UT) introduced in [8]. Informally a UT generalizes threshold primitives such as threshold encryption or signatures. The setup of a UT takes as input a secret x and produces some public parameters and N secret keys which, in our setting, will be given to the members of the certifying committee. These allow the secret-holders to non-interactively and jointly compute any circuit C on the secret without knowing the secret. Each of these "local computations" from the secret holders can be verified as being valid. If at least d of them are valid they can be recombined to reconstruct $C(x)$.

---

[3] This happens through some nomination mechanism that we just posit and do not model explicitly in this paper. For example, one could use the nominating committee techniques in [3]. After being nominated the committee members can potentially remain anonymous to the rest of the network. This can be done for example through ephemeral public-keys and anonymous public-key encryption [3].

Our second ingredient are designated-verifier (dv) SNARKs. In a dvSNARK a proof π for a statement stmt can be verified only by a party holding a verification-key vk through Verify(vk, stmt, π). To preserve soundness of the system it is important that the designated-verifier key remains secret from a malicious prover.

We show that thresholdizers from [8] can be used to construct SPuCs by injecting $x = $ vk as a secret in the UT and compute functions of the type $C_{\mathsf{stmt},\pi}(\cdot) = $ Verify($\cdot$, stmt, π) through it. Although this construction is arguably simple, showing we can apply UT to obtain our desired argument-like system has some non-trivial aspects to it. First, despite the generality of the threshold-like setting in the UT definition, its security definition is incompatible with that in the SPuC setting: the latter involves additional oracles—e.g. a proof oracle for true statements in the zero-knowledge experiment—and additional experiments extractability. Second, we do not require the "full universality" of these thresholdizers, but only that their supported computations include dvSNARK verification. This may be a low-complexity computation, involving for example a decryption and a zero-test on a low-degree polynomial [6]. This is significantly less complex than the proven relation $\mathcal{R}$. Finally, to obtain zero-knowledge in SPuCs we observe that the dvSNARK used in the construction does not need to satisfy the usual notion of zero-knowledge for designated-verifier NIZKs; a weaker notion suffices. We introduce and model this notion, dubbed "key-less zero-knowledge", which we believe to be of independent interest. We show that some existing dvSNARKs already satisfy this notion, namely all those obtained through the popular compiler from Non-Interactive Linear Proofs (NILPs) [32] described in [6]. We also observe that it is possible to obtain dvSNARKs satisfying this notion by compiling a (non zero-knowledge) pvSNARKs with a public-key encryption scheme.

Quantum-Resistant Instantiations from Homomorphic Primitives and Linear-Only Encryption. By "opening the boxes" of UT and dvSNARKs we show we can instantiate our SPuC construction requiring the existence of: (leveled) Fully Homomorphic Encryption (FHE) [25][4], Homomorphic Signatures (HS) with context-hiding[5] properties [30] and linear-only encryption [6,11] (we require the existence of *all* these primitives). Given an encryption of x, FHE allows computing an encryption of $f(x)$ using only public parameters; *leveled* FHE ensures correctness only for functions of a bounded depth d specified at setup time. HS allows to perform the same on signatures. Linear-only encryption [6,11] is a form of linearly-homomorphic encryption with guaranteed limited malleability.

We elaborate more on the relation between publicly-verifiable NIZKs and these abstract primitives in Sect. 1.2. Our construction for SPuCs is quantum-

---

[4] More precisely, we require leveled Threshold FHE, which is shown to be implied by leveled FHE with the mild requirement of moderate decryption "noise bound"[8].

[5] Context-hiding states that a signature $\sigma_{f,x}$, authenticating $f(x)$ and obtained homomorphically from a signature on x, reveals nothing about x.

resistant: all the above primitives can be instantiated from lattices. This is of particular relevance since there are no results on publicly-verifiable zero-knowledge arguments with short proofs in the standard model. The only other construction of pvNIZKs from lattices does not have succinct proofs [35]; the constructions in [11,12,24] are for designated-verifiers.

One relatively minor challenge for us here is making sure that UT can be built through the abstract primitives above. The construction for UT in [8] is based on NIZKs, which we want to avoid. Although [8] informally mentions that one could replace NIZKs with context-hiding homomorphic signatures, there is no formal construction in the paper[6].

We also show yet one more construction of UT for the two-party case replacing FHE with the simpler notion of (two-party) homomorphic secret sharing (HSS), which can be also built from lattices [15]. An HSS scheme allows to share a secret x and to let the share-holders compute shares of $C(x)$ for any circuit C.

A Practical Perspective. If applied to an efficient dvSNARK—potentially one more efficient than pvSNARKs—then one could leverage our constructions to obtain a public-verifiability-flavored proof system preserving some of the efficiency features of the starting dvSNARK (e.g. proving time and to some extent succinctness). We believe our constructions can be practical: their overhead for certifying dvSNARK proofs is arguably low since we apply homomorphic cryptography to very small circuits (those for dvSNARK verification) and so is the communication overhead for each certificate (whose number, however, scales with the chosen threshold). Nonetheless it seems unclear what scheme could *currently* be used for such instantiation. To the best of our knowledge, despite recent advances [33] it is still an open problem to obtain dvSNARKs without random oracles that could beat pvSNARKs in practice (especially for prover's time).

Proactive SPuCs from Proactive UT (pUT). We consider the setting where the committee is not fixed but it can proactively reshare its secret at every round without interaction. We construct a proactive variant of SPuCs through a proactive variant of UT (pUT) which we introduce in this paper. The construction of pSPuC from pUT is analog to that SPuC from UT, i.e. applying a thresholdizer for a designated-verifier SNARK. Our model for proactive SPuCs is straightforward once defining SPuCs and pUT. We present it in full details in the full version of this paper.

A Construction of pUT from Special UT (sUT). To convert a UT into its proactive version we need to enable the committee members to reshare (or "hand over") their secret keys. Some prior techniques for doing this allow each party to prove they are resharing correctly but they use NIZKs [3,31]. For our alternative approach, we observe that what needs to be handed over to the next committee

---

[6] A formal construction from homomorphic signatures is present in [9] but it relies on the specifics of the underlying homomorphic encryption scheme.

are reshares of some trapdoor computed inside the UT setup. We cannot directly perform secret shares of it at handover time because there is no party holding it (whoever computed it is now disappeared or it was not a single entity but a protocol execution).

The solution to the problem above comes from UT itself. UT can be used to verifiably compute functions on some secret obliviously (without knowing the secret). Can we then extend UT to perform oblivious computation, not only an injected secret x, but on its own trapdoor (a secret computed during the execution of UT.Setup(x))? With this tool in our hands we could then let the committee members obliviously compute some resharing function Reshare.

We show we can extend UT to support general (controlled) evaluations of its own trapdoor obtaining a new primitive we call sUT. A sUT is like a UT but it allows evaluations on two secrets: some secret x specified (through algorithm sUT.PartEval) at setup time and its own trapdoor (through an analog of the partial evaluation algorithm, called sUT.TrapEval). We are able to construct sUT using almost the same assumptions as for UT: we still require homomorphic signatures and FHE, but we need to also assume circular security of the latter (namely, we should be able to securely encrypt its own decryption key in it).

We then show how to construct pUT by applying the algorithm TrapEval of sUT on a function that generates a new secret and provides its share. Other techniques of our construction for pUT are inspired by the YOSO-style ones in [3] where the committee members of the new epoch can access their share by opening a ciphertext encrypted with an ephemeral public key (of which they only know the decryption key).

Both pUT and sUT are of independent interest and can be applied in contexts of "cryptography-as-a-service" as those described in [3] (Fig. 1).

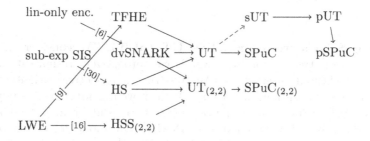

Fig. 1. Dependency diagram of assumptions and constructions. Suffix "(2, 2)" denotes two-parties. The dashed line refers to non blackbox constructions and additionally requires circular (KDM) security for the TFHE scheme. Plausible constructions for linear-only encryption can be instantiated from LWE [11].

1.2 Further Theoretical Motivation and Assumptions

Our goal is to build SPuCs through assumptions that are weaker than publicly-verifiable zero-knowledge SNARKs and NIZKs. Also, our goal is to stay in the standard model (without random oracles). In the next paragraphs we discuss some of the motivation behind this and how our constructions relate to these goals. Our hope is that this work can provide a new lens on constructions relying on publicly-verifiable proof systems.

Through this work, we want to make the following observation:

> In the standard model, we can obtain robust systems for succinct zero-knowledge proofs, without interaction among the prover and verifier even if publicly-verifiable NIZKs or SNARKs do not exist. It is possible to extend these results to the case of proactive resharing without relying on publicly-verifiable SNARKs.

Why not Using Publicly-Verifiable SNARKs? We know that succinct arguments in general require non-falsifiable assumptions (in case of black-box reductions) [28]. Constructions of publicly-verifiable SNARKs usually go around this by: the sometimes problematic Fiat-Shamir in the random-oracle model; knowledge-of-exponent-like assumptions or idealized settings such as the generic or algebraic group models (e.g., [1,22,32]). Since our constructions use results implying designated-verifier SNARKs, we cannot get around the result in [28] and will have underlying non-falsifiable assumption (those required for linear-only encryption [6,11]). Nonetheless we remark that our results still hold without a random oracle and in the following paragraphs we argue that there is still an advantage in moving from pvSNARKs to dvSNARKs as an assumption.

Advantages of Assuming dvSNARKs Instead of pvSNARKs. We observe it is plausible that dvSNARKs may require strictly weaker assumptions than pvS-NARKs. In fact, we know that publicly-verifiable SNARKs are not a stronger primitive than designated-verifier SNARKs since we can always construct the latter from pvSNARK by encrypting the proof under the verifier's public key. We still do not know whether there is a theoretical separation between these two notions though.

Even if dvSNARKs were not strictly weaker than pvSNARKs as a primitive in the standard model, we might still obtain them from *different* (and, potentially, more plausible) assumptions. For example, consider the pvSNARK constructions in [23] and the dvSNARK constructions in [11,12,24]. Although all non-falsifiable, the mathematical objects they refer to are quite different (respectively, groups with bilinear pairings and lattices). We point that there also exist other constructions in the standard model such as the publicly verifiable arguments in [36], but they are based on the indistinguishability obfuscation, which is yet not standard.

Finally, SPuCs and their constructions relying on dvSNARKs, can be motivated by post-quantum security. We observe that, to the best of our knowledge, *there are no known constructions for pvSNARKs in the standard-model that are resistant to quantum attacks.* In fact, only recently the community learned about the possibility of post-quantum non-interactive zero-knowledge (with non-succinct proofs) [35].

On not Requiring Publicly-Verifiable NIZKs in General. Our constructions for SPuCs not only do not require publicly-verifiable SNARKs, but they do not require publicly-verifiable NIZKs in general either. None of the assumptions we rely on—linear-only encryption, leveled FHE (or two-party HSS) and (context-hiding) homomorphic signatures—are known to imply pvNIZKs[7]. We observe that homomorphic signatures with the context-hiding property can be seen as a variant of non-interactive zero-knowledge (with short proofs) for *deterministic* computations on authenticated data. However, they do not allow to prove anything on general non-deterministic computations since witnesses can possibly be unauthenticated. The reason our work can afford this is that we use a trusted setup that "bootstraps" the system creating secret keys for authentication (homomorphic signatures) and threshold homomorphic decryption and signing the initial set of shares. After this step no party is assumed to have access to these secrets. We remark that it is possible to replace the trusted setup with an MPC execution. This, at the same time, shows a limitation of our work: for this MPC to run efficiently one would probably require publicly-verifiable NIZKs (interactive approaches should also be possible though). We leave alternative approaches to the latter as future work.

On Assuming Homomorphic Cryptography for Small Computations. We remark that although we often express our assumptions as *general* "Fully" Homomorphic Encryption and (context-hiding) Homomorphic Signature in general, our requirements are actually weaker. We only need homomorphic properties on computations as decryption, PRFs and the final low-degree test of some designated-verifier SNARKs [6]. These are all computable in the class NC^1 [2].

1.3   Other Related Work

The work in [5] also discusses how to compose (unleveled) FHE and "proofs" of the verification algorithms to obtain succinct arguments of knowledge (in their Sect. 9). The differences between their work and ours is that we use a primitive that checks only deterministic computation (we use homomorphic signatures; they use NIZK arguments of knowledge) and that their construction cannot achieve public-verifiability from designated-verifiability. On the other hand, to obtain the latter, we work in a slightly different security model and we add one "hop" in the protocol.

---

[7] Unleveled FHE—where homomorphic operations work correctly for any polynomial-size function $f(x)$ without any depth bound—does imply *designated-verifier* NIZKs [20]. The recent work in [18] shows, however, that circular (KDM-secure) unleveled FHE even implies pvNIZKs. For our proactive extensions, we assume KDM-secure *leveled* FHE for NC^1 which is known to imply (circular-secure) unleveled FHE through bootstrapping [25]. We observe, however, that while the assumptions in our proactive constructions are sufficient to imply pvNIZKs, they do not require the standard FHE bootstrapping, significantly improving the efficiency of homomorphic operations. Finally, circular-secure leveled FHE is not known to imply pvSNARKs.

The work in [26] investigates approaches to minimizing proof size. Their work requires a slightly different primitive called fully homomorphic hybrid encryption, and differently from us, requires it to support any computation (whereas we require that only for the circuit of the verifier in a designated-verifier SNARK).

Notation and Basic Background. For any positive integer n, $[n]$ denotes the set $\{1, \ldots, n\}$. We denote vectors in boldface. We use the notation $O_\lambda(f(n))$ to denote $O(p(\lambda)f(n))$ where p is some polynomial in the security parameter. We consider all adversaries to be stateful.

2   A Definition of SPuC

In this section we define our primitive SPuC-s.

Definition 1. *Let $P = [\mathsf{N}]$ be a set of parties. A SPuC Π with a (d, N)-threshold access structure and relation family $(\mathsf{RSet}_\lambda)_{\lambda \in \mathbb{N}}$ with completeness error $c = c(\lambda)$ and soundness error $\epsilon = \epsilon(\lambda)$ is a tuple of PPT algorithms* (Setup, Prv, PartCert, PartCertVfy, Vfy) *such that*

- Setup$(1^\lambda, \mathcal{R}, \mathsf{d}, \mathsf{N}) \to (\mathsf{pp}, \{\mathsf{sk}_1, \ldots, \mathsf{sk}_\mathsf{N}\})$: On input the description of $\mathcal{R}$ and threshold parameters d, N, the setup algorithm outputs public parameters pp and a set of verification state shares $\mathsf{sk}_1, \ldots, \mathsf{sk}_\mathsf{N}$.
- Prv$(\mathsf{pp}, \mathsf{stmt}, \mathsf{w}) \to \pi_0$: On input pp, a statement stmt and a witness w, the prover algorithm outputs a proof π_0.
- PartCert$(\mathsf{sk}_i, \mathsf{stmt}, \pi_0) \to \pi^{(i)}$: On input a verification state share sk_i, a statement stmt and a proof π_0, the partial public prover algorithm outputs a partial proof $\pi^{(i)}$ related to the partial certifier i.
- PartCertVfy$(\mathsf{pp}, \mathsf{stmt}, \pi_0, \pi^{(i)}) \to \{0, 1\}$: On input pp, a statement stmt, a proof π_0 and a partial proof $\pi^{(i)}$, the partial verifier outputs a bit $b \in \{0, 1\}$.
- Vfy$(\mathsf{pp}, \mathsf{stmt}, \pi_0, B) \to \{0, 1\}$: On input pp, a statement stmt, a proof π_0 and a set $B = \{\pi^{(i)}\}_{i \in I_S}$ for some $S \subseteq [\mathsf{N}]$ with index set I_S, the verifier algorithm outputs a bit $b \in \{0, 1\}$.

Remark 1. Although we do not make it explicit in the syntax, the public parameters can be split in two: prover-related (used in Prv) and verifier-related (used verification algorithms) parameters. The former of size potentially growing with $|\mathcal{R}|$, while the latter of independent size and concretely much smaller.

We require the following properties.

Correctness. For all $\lambda \in \mathbb{N}$, $\mathcal{R} \in \mathsf{RSet}_\lambda$, $(\mathsf{stmt}, \mathsf{w}) \in \mathcal{R}$, any set S with cardinality no smaller than d, we have that the following probability is at least $1 - c(\lambda)$

$$\Pr\left[\begin{array}{c} (\mathsf{pp}, \{\mathsf{sk}_1, \ldots, \mathsf{sk}_\mathsf{N}\}) \leftarrow \mathsf{Setup}(\mathcal{R}, \mathsf{d}, \mathsf{N}) \\ \pi_0 \leftarrow \mathsf{Prv}(\mathsf{pp}, \mathsf{stmt}, \mathsf{w}) \ : \ \mathsf{Vfy}(\mathsf{pp}, \mathsf{stmt}, \pi_0, \{\pi^{(i)}\}_{i \in I_S}) = 1 \\ \pi^{(i)} \leftarrow \mathsf{PartCert}(\mathsf{sk}_i, \mathsf{stmt}, \pi_0) \end{array}\right]$$

Moreover, for any statement stmt^*, proof π_0^* and for any set of partial proofs $B = \{\pi^{*(i)}\}_{i \in I_S}$ such that $\mathsf{Vfy}(\mathsf{pp}, \mathsf{stmt}^*, \pi_0^*, B) = 1$, it should hold for all $i \in I_S$,

$$\Pr[\mathsf{PartCertVfy}(\mathsf{pp}, \mathsf{stmt}^*, \pi_0^*, \pi^{*(i)}) = 1] \geq 1 - c(\lambda)$$

where $(\mathsf{pp}, \{\mathsf{sk}_1, \ldots, \mathsf{sk}_N\}) \leftarrow \mathsf{Setup}(\mathcal{R}, \mathsf{d}, \mathsf{N})$.

Succinctness. The running time of Verify is $O_\lambda(\mathsf{d}(|\mathsf{stmt}| + \log(|\mathsf{w}|)))$ and the size of each proof and certificate is $O_\lambda(\log(|\mathsf{w}|))$.

Robustness. We require that for all $\lambda \in \mathbb{N}$, $\mathcal{R} \in \mathsf{RSet}_\lambda$, it holds that for any PPT adversary $\mathcal{A}$, the following experiment called $\mathsf{Expt}_{\mathcal{A},\mathsf{robust}}(1^\lambda)$ outputs 1 with negligible probability.

1. The challenger runs $(\mathsf{pp}, \{\mathsf{sk}_1, \ldots, \mathsf{sk}_N\}) \leftarrow \mathsf{Setup}(\mathcal{R}, \mathsf{d}, \mathsf{N})$ and then sends $(\mathsf{pp}, \{\mathsf{sk}_1, \ldots, \mathsf{sk}_N\})$ to $\mathcal{A}$.
2. $\mathcal{A}$ outputs a statement stmt^*, a proof π_0^* and a partial proof $\pi^{*(i)}$.
3. The challenger returns 1 if $\mathsf{PartCertVfy}(\mathsf{pp}, \mathsf{stmt}^*, \pi_0^*, \pi^{*(i)}) = 1$ and $\pi^{*(i)} \neq \mathsf{PartCert}(\mathsf{sk}_i, \mathsf{stmt}^*, \pi_0^*)$.

Knowledge Soundness. We require that if an adversary is able to convince the verifier, then we can extract a valid witness from it. Intuition about the experiment: the adversary chooses a corruption set and gets the secret keys for that set. It is then given oracle access to partial proofs from all the other parties.

Definition 2 (Knowledge Soundness). *For all $\lambda \in \mathbb{N}$, $\mathcal{R} \in \mathsf{RSet}_\lambda$ and for all (non-uniform) efficient stateful adversaries $\mathcal{A}$ there exists a (non-uniform) efficient extractor $\mathcal{E}$ such that $\Pr[\mathsf{KSND}_{\mathcal{A},\mathcal{E}}(1^\lambda) = 1] \leq \mathsf{negl}(\lambda)$*

$\underline{\mathsf{KSND}_{\mathcal{A},\mathcal{E}}(1^\lambda)}$

$(\mathsf{pp}, \mathbf{sk} = (\mathsf{sk}_1, \ldots, \mathsf{sk}_N)) \leftarrow \mathsf{Setup}(1^\lambda, \mathcal{R}, \mathsf{d}, \mathsf{N})$

$C \leftarrow \mathcal{A}(\mathsf{pp})$ where $|C| = \mathsf{d} - 1$

$(h, \mathsf{stmt}, \pi_0, \pi_{i_1}, \ldots, \pi_{i_{d-1}}) \leftarrow \mathcal{A}^{\mathcal{O}_{\mathrm{prf}}}(\mathsf{pp}, (\mathsf{sk}_j)_{j \in C})$ where $h \in [\mathsf{N}] \setminus C$

$\pi_h \leftarrow \mathsf{PartCert}(\mathsf{sk}_h, \mathsf{stmt}, \pi_0)$

$\mathsf{w} \leftarrow \mathcal{E}^{\mathcal{O}_{\mathrm{prf}}}(\mathsf{pp})$

Output 1 iff $\mathcal{R}(\mathsf{stmt}, \mathsf{w}) \neq 1 \wedge \mathsf{Verify}(\mathsf{pp}, \pi_0, (\pi_h, \pi_{i_1}, \ldots, \pi_{i_{d-1}})) = 1$

The oracle $\mathcal{O}_{\mathrm{prf}}$ above works as follows: given a pair (stmt', π_0') the adversary is given all the responses $\mathsf{PartCert}(\mathsf{sk}_i, \mathsf{stmt}', \pi_0')$ for $i \in [\mathsf{N}]$.

NB: Above, the extractor does not need to take as input π_h since it can always obtain it from the (deterministic) proof oracle it has access to by emulating the adversary's behavior. This approach to modeling the extractor has the advantage of not requiring an explicit trapdoor (we remark that constructions of this type are possible [6]), thus allowing for a somewhat stronger notion. We follow

$$ZK_{\mathcal{A}}^{world\in\{hon,sim\}}(1^\lambda)$$

if world = hon then

    $(pp, \mathbf{sk} = (sk_1, \ldots, sk_N)) \leftarrow Setup(1^\lambda, \mathcal{R}, d, N)$

else

    $(pp, \mathbf{sk} = (sk_1, \ldots, sk_N)) \leftarrow S_1(\mathcal{R}, d, N)$

$C \leftarrow \mathcal{A}(pp)$ where $|C| = d - 1$

guess $\leftarrow \mathcal{A}^{\mathcal{O}_{zk}^{world}}(pp, (sk_j)_{j\in C})$

Output 1 iff guess = world

$\mathcal{O}_{zk}^{hon}(tag, inp)$

if tag = part-proofs then

    Parse inp as $(stmt, \pi_0)$

    $(\pi_i)_{i\in[N]} \leftarrow (PartCert(sk_i, stmt, \pi_0))_{i\in[N]}$

    return $(\pi_1, \ldots, \pi_N)$

if tag = valid-x then

    Parse inp as $(stmt, w)$

    if $(stmt, w) \notin \mathcal{R}$ then return $\bot$

    return $Prv(pp, stmt, w)$

$\mathcal{O}_{zk}^{sim}(tag, inp)$

if tag = part-proofs then

    Parse inp as $(stmt, \pi_0)$

    $(\pi_i)_{i\in[N]} \leftarrow (S_{prt}(\mathbf{sk}, stmt, \pi_0))_{i\in[N]}$

    return $(\pi_1, \ldots, \pi_N)$

if tag = valid-x then

    Parse inp as $(stmt, w)$

    if $(stmt, w) \notin \mathcal{R}$ then return $\bot$

    return $S_{prf}(\mathbf{sk}, stmt)$

Fig. 2. ZK experiment. Oracles take as input tag $\in \{part\text{-}proofs, valid\text{-}x\}$ and some stmt whose structure depends on the tag.

a similar line of modeling when defining strong knowledge-soundness for dvS-NARKs (Definition 4).

Zero-Knowledge. In the zero-knowledge experiment we let the adversary to corrupt a certain subset of parties and then access to two types of oracles:

- one in which it supplies a statement stmt (not necessarily in the language) and some π_0 and gets the partial certificates from all the secret key holders;
- one analog to the oracle for standard zero-knowledge where, given a pair statement–witness satisfying the relation, it receives a proof together with certificates for it.

Definition 3 (Zero-Knowledge). *We say SPuC with a* (d, N)-*threshold access structure is zero-knowledge if there exists a stateful efficient simulator tuple* $S = (S_1, S_{prt}, S_{prf})$ *such that for all* $\lambda \in \mathbb{N}$, *all* $\mathcal{R} \in RSet_\lambda$ *and all PPT adversary* $\mathcal{A}$, *we have that*

$$| \Pr[ZK_{\mathcal{A}}^{hon}(1^\lambda) = 1] - \Pr[ZK_{\mathcal{A}}^{sim}(1^\lambda) = 1]| \leq negl(\lambda)$$

where the experiments are defined in Fig. 2.

3   Construction of SPuC

In this section we describe constructions of (non-proactive) SPuC and discuss its instantiations. The goal of Subsect. 3.1 is to serve as a warm-up to some of the challenges of constructing SPuC-s and informally describes a limited construction. We provide preliminaries for our general SPuC construction—universal thresholdizers, UT, and designated-verifier SNARKs—in Subsect. 3.2. We then proceed to describe two instantiations of UT, both based on lattices. In Subsect. 3.5 we present a general construction (no limitations on threshold and number of parties) from Threshold FHE and context-hiding homomorphic signatures (HS). We present a simpler, more efficient construction for the two-party case based on homomorphic-secret sharing (HSS) in Subsect. 3.6.

3.1   Warm-Up: A Straw-Man Construction

The following construction—based only on the existence of (zero-knowledge) designated-verifier SNARKs—exemplifies some of the properties we desire in a succinct publicly-certifiable scheme. Although arguably simpler than our other constructions we find it to have stronger limitations, discussed below. Thus we keep its presentation informal.

Assuming the existence of a designated-verifier SNARK scheme (see next section), we can construct a SPuC with N certifiers and threshold d as follows.

- At setup time we generate N different setups $(ek_i, vk_i) \leftarrow dvKeyGen(1^\lambda, \mathcal{R})$, publish the N evaluation keys and a secret verification key vk_i to each of the committee members.
- The algorithm Prv would then produce N designated-verifier proofs π_i^{dv}, each with a different evaluation key ek_i for $i \in [N]$.
- Each certifier i in the committee (algorithm PartCert) would return a bit stating acceptance or rejection of the respective π_i^{dv} using vk_i and signed with a key of the respective committee member.
- Given a set B of acceptance/rejection bits of size at least d, a verifier would then accept if all the bits in B are 1 and otherwise reject.

For simplicity we have not presented algorithm PartCertVfy which can be achieved with techniques similar to ours. The construction just described satisfies knowledge soundness and zero-knowledge. its main limitations are a high concrete and asymptotic efficiency and that it is not immediate how to extend it efficiently to a proactively secure construction. For efficiency, notice that we require N designated-verifier setups, which is very expensive (especially if we want to replace the setup stage with an MPC execution). It is also expensive in practice to require that a prover would run N times the proving algorithm. The construction does not technically satisfy succinctness for the same reason: the output of Prv depends on the number of shares. Even if this were acceptable asymptotically (e.g., considering N a constant) this incurs high concrete costs. In addition and in contrast to our constructions, it forces the runner of the algorithm Prv to store N evaluation keys (each of size at least linear in the size of the relation $\mathcal{R}$). This dependency on N is less problematic if this parameter is small. Extending this construction to the proactive case would seem to require regenerating the verification keys (the adversary could learn d of them through different epochs and so they cannot remain the same). It is unclear how to perform this new setup without an interactive MPC or a trusted authority.

3.2 Building Block Primitives: UT and dvSNARKs

We now describe the building blocks for our general construction.

UT. Universal thresholdizers (UTs) are a primitive that can be used to thresholdize a system. A UT scheme with a (d, N)-threshold access structure consists of four algorithms (Setup, Eval, Verify, Combine). The setup algorithm Setup takes in a secret value x and divides it into a set of shares $s_1, \ldots, s_N$, which are given to N users. Each user, on input a circuit C, calls Eval and uses their shares s_i to compute an evaluation share y_i of $C(x)$. The verification algorithm Verify can be used to check whether y_i was computed correctly. Finally, for a set $B = \{y_i\}$ for which $|B| \geq d$, the algorithm Combine can be used to combine these evaluation shares and produce $y = C(x)$.

For a UT scheme to be secure, it should hold that the shares $s_1, \ldots, s_N$, together with the evaluation shares y_i can be simulated only given access to the circuit C and its output on the secret value x (i.e., $C(x)$). In addition, the robustness property states that no PPT adversary should be able to produce an incorrectly computed evaluation share y_i for a circuit C if the verification algorithm Verify accepts it.

Theorem 1 (Implicit in [8]). *If there exists leveled Threshold FHE and compact context-hiding homomorphic signatures (HS) then there exists UT. It is possible to construct leveled Threshold FHE from LWE.*

dvSNARKs. A dvSNARK has a key-generation algorithm dvKeyGen which returns an evaluation key ek and a verification key vk for an NP relation $\mathcal{R}$. The prover $\mathcal{P}_{\mathsf{SNARK}}$ takes in ek, a statement stmt and a witness w, and outputs a proof π, which can be verified through algorithm $\mathcal{V}_{\mathsf{SNARK}}$ taking as input (stmt, π), and the (secret) vk. Key properties of a dvSNARKs are: *Succinctness* (its proofs are short), *Knowledge-soundness* (we can extract a valid witness from a verifying proof), *Zero-knowledge* (a proof does not reveal anything more than the truth of the statement). There are constructions of dvSNARKs from linear-only encryptions [6,11] (which can be plausibly instantiated from LWE).

3.3 A General Construction for SPuC

Our construction is in Fig. 3.

Theorem 2. *(informal) If there exists UT and zero-knowledge dvSNARKs then there exists a secure SPuC.*

$\mathsf{Setup}(1^\lambda, \mathcal{R}, \mathsf{d}, \mathsf{N})$

$\mathsf{dvKeyGen}(1^\lambda, \mathcal{R}) \to (\mathsf{ek}, \mathsf{vk})$

$(\mathsf{pp}_{\mathsf{UT}}, \mathsf{sk}_{\mathsf{UT},1}, \dots, \mathsf{sk}_{\mathsf{UT},\mathsf{N}}) \leftarrow \mathsf{UT.Setup}(\mathsf{d}, \mathsf{N}, \mathsf{vk})$

$\mathbf{return}\ (\mathsf{pp} = (\mathsf{ek}, \mathsf{pp}_{\mathsf{UT}}), \{\mathsf{sk}_i = \mathsf{sk}_{\mathsf{UT},i}\}_{i \in [\mathsf{N}]})$

$\mathsf{Prv}(\mathsf{pp} = (\mathsf{ek}, \mathsf{pp}_{\mathsf{UT}}), \mathsf{stmt}, \mathsf{w})$ $\qquad$ $\mathsf{Vfy}(\mathsf{pp}, \mathsf{stmt}, \pi_0, (\pi^{(i)})_{i \in I_S})$

$\mathbf{return}\ \pi_0 \leftarrow \mathsf{dvProve}(\mathsf{ek}, \mathsf{stmt}, \mathsf{w})$ $\quad$ $\mathbf{return}\ \mathsf{UT.Combine}(\mathsf{pp}_{\mathsf{UT}}, (\pi^{(i)})_{i \in I_S})$

$\mathsf{PartCert}(\mathsf{sk}_i, \mathsf{stmt}, \pi_0)$ $\qquad\qquad$ $\mathsf{PartCertVfy}(\mathsf{pp}, \mathsf{stmt}, \pi_0, \pi^{(i)})$

$\pi^{(i)} \leftarrow \mathsf{UT.PartEval}(\mathsf{sk}_{\mathsf{UT},i}, C_{\mathsf{stmt}, \pi_0})$ $\quad$ $\mathbf{return}\ \mathsf{UT.Verify}(\mathsf{pp}_{\mathsf{UT}}, C_{\mathsf{stmt}, \pi_0}, \pi^{(i)})$

s.t. $C_{\mathsf{stmt}, \pi_0}(\cdot) := \mathsf{dvVerify}(\cdot, \mathsf{stmt}, \pi_0)$ $\quad$ s.t. $C_{\mathsf{stmt}, \pi_0}(\cdot) := \mathsf{dvVerify}(\cdot, \mathsf{stmt}, \pi_0)$

Fig. 3. Construction of SPuC from UT

Remark 2 (Weakening Zero-Knowledge Requirements for dvSNARKs). The result above (as well as its corollaries) only require a weaker notion than standard zero-knowledge for dvNIZKs: *key-less* zero-knowledge, which we introduce (Definition 5). The notion states that a proof leaks nothing to any adversary without the verification key. This is less stringent than the standard zero-knowledge requirement where we require a proof to leak nothing even to an adversary *holding a verification-key*. We show this weaker notion is sufficient to obtain (full) zero-knowledge in our model as formalized in Definition 3. We provide further discussion in the full version where we also argue how it may allow for simpler and more efficient designated-verifier SNARKs to be plugged into our construction.

3.4 Proof of Security

Completeness and robustness follow straightforwardly from the equivalent properties of UT [8]. We prove knowledge soundness and zero-knowledge. We first recall two formal definitions for dvSNARKs that we will use in the proof. The definition of strong knowledge-soundness is an adaptation of that in [19].

Definition 4 (Strong Knowledge-Soundness). *For all* $\lambda \in \mathbb{N}$ *and for all (non-uniform) efficient adversaries* $\mathcal{A}_{dv}$ *there exists a (non-uniform) efficient extractor* $\mathcal{E}_{dv}$ *such that*

$$\Pr\left[\begin{array}{c} (\mathsf{ek}, \mathsf{vk}) \leftarrow \mathsf{dvKeyGen}(1^\lambda, \mathcal{R}) \\ (\mathsf{stmt}, \pi) \leftarrow \mathcal{A}_{dv}^{\mathcal{O}_{dv}(\mathsf{vk}, \cdot)}(\mathsf{ek}) \\ \mathsf{w} \leftarrow \mathcal{E}_{dv}^{\mathcal{O}_{dv}(\mathsf{vk}, \cdot)}(\mathsf{ek}) \end{array} : \begin{array}{c} \mathcal{R}(\mathsf{stmt}, \mathsf{w}) \neq 1 \wedge \\ \mathcal{V}_{\mathsf{SNARK}}(\mathsf{vk}, \mathsf{stmt}, \pi) = 1 \end{array}\right] \leq \mathsf{negl}(\lambda)$$

where $\mathcal{O}_{dv}(\mathsf{vk}, \cdot) := \mathcal{V}_{\mathsf{SNARK}}(\mathsf{vk}, \cdot)$

Definition 5 ((Unbounded) Key-Less Zero-Knowledge). *We say dvS-NARK* $\Pi_{\mathsf{SNARK}} = (\mathsf{dvKeyGen}, \mathcal{P}_{\mathsf{SNARK}}, \mathcal{V}_{\mathsf{SNARK}})$ *is key-less zero-knowledge if there exists a stateful efficient simulator S such that for all* $\lambda \in \mathbb{N}$ *and all PPT adversary* $\mathcal{A}$, *we have that* $|\Pr[\mathsf{kIZK}_{\mathcal{A}}^{\mathsf{hon}}(1^{\lambda}) = 1] - \Pr[\mathsf{kIZK}_{\mathcal{A}}^{\mathsf{sim}}(1^{\lambda}) = 1]| \leq \mathsf{negl}(\lambda)$

$\mathsf{kIZK}_{\mathcal{A}}^{\mathsf{world} \in \{\mathsf{hon}, \mathsf{sim}\}}(1^{\lambda})$

$(\mathsf{ek}, \mathsf{vk}) \leftarrow \mathsf{dvKeyGen}(1^{\lambda}, \mathcal{R}); \mathsf{guess} \leftarrow \mathcal{A}^{\mathcal{O}_{\mathsf{kl\text{-}zk}}^{\mathsf{world}}}(\mathsf{ek}); \mathsf{Output}\ 1\ \text{iff guess} = \mathsf{world}$

---

where $\mathcal{O}_{\mathsf{kl\text{-}zk}}^{\mathsf{hon}}(\mathsf{stmt}, \mathsf{w})$ (resp. $\mathcal{O}_{\mathsf{kl\text{-}zk}}^{\mathsf{sim}}(\mathsf{stmt}, \mathsf{w})$) return $\mathcal{P}_{\mathsf{SNARK}}(\mathsf{ek}, \mathsf{stmt}, \mathsf{w})$ (resp. $S(\mathsf{ek}, \mathsf{stmt})$) if $(\mathsf{stmt}, \mathsf{w}) \in \mathcal{R}$. Both oracles return $\perp$ if $(\mathsf{stmt}, \mathsf{w}) \notin \mathcal{R}$.

In our proofs below we also use UT security, which is a special case of sUT security with no trapdoor evaluation oracle, described formally in Definition 7.

Lemma 1 (Knowledge Soundness). *The construction in Fig. 3 is knowledge sound (Definition 2) if UT is Universal Thresholdizer and DV is a designated-verifier SNARK with strong knowledge-soundness (Definition 4).*

Proof. Consider an adversary $\bar{\mathcal{A}}$ in the knowledge soundness experiment of Definition 2 for some $\lambda, \mathsf{N} \in \mathbb{N}$. Let us construct an adversary $\mathcal{A}_{\mathsf{dv}}$ for the strong knowledge-soundness experiment as in Fig. 4. We construct an extractor $\bar{\mathcal{E}}$ that internally runs the knowledge soundness extractor $\mathcal{E}_{\mathsf{dv}}$, corresponding to $\mathcal{A}_{\mathsf{dv}}$. We claim that the extractor outputs a witness with high probability if $\bar{\mathcal{A}}$ produces a valid proof with high probability. First observe that (x, π_0), output of $\mathcal{A}_{\mathsf{dv}}$, must verify successfully with probability negligibly close to that of $\bar{\mathcal{A}}$. This follows from the definition of $S = (S_1^{\mathsf{UT}}, S_2^{\mathsf{UT}})$, security of UT as well as its verification and evaluation correctness: the output of $\mathcal{O}'$ in $\mathcal{A}_{\mathsf{dv}}$ must be computationally indistinguishable from $\mathsf{dvVerify}(\mathsf{vk}, \cdot)$ (the oracle $\mathcal{O}_{\mathsf{dv}}$ in Strong Knowledge-Soundness definition) otherwise we would be able to distinguish between the simulated π_i-s and the honestly computed ones in UT security. By definition of $\mathcal{A}_{\mathsf{dv}}$ the output of $\bar{\mathcal{E}}$ must be a valid witness with probability close to that of $\mathcal{E}_{\mathsf{dv}}$. To show why, we observe that the oracle $\mathcal{O}''$ in the extractor $\bar{\mathcal{E}}$ must have, by construction, an output indistinguishable from that of $\mathsf{dvVerify}(\mathsf{vk}, \cdot)$; we can conclude this by invoking verification and evaluation correctness. □

Lemma 2 (Zero-Knowledge). *The construction in Fig. 3 is zero-knowledge (Definition 3) if UT is Universal Thresholdizer and DV is a designated-verifier SNARK with key-less zero-knowledge (Definition 5).*

Proof. Our goal is to build $S = (S_1, S_{\mathsf{prt}}, S_{\mathsf{prf}})$ where S_1 is the simulator for the setup. We shall do that by invoking the security definition of UT[8] and the definition of key-less zero-knowledge (Definition 5). From these theorems it follows the

---

[8] For the definition of UT security, we refer to the sUT security in Fig. 6. Note that UT security is a special case where there is no trapdoor evaluation oracle.

$\mathcal{A}_{\mathrm{dv}}^{\mathcal{O}_{\mathrm{dv}}}(\mathsf{ek})$

Let $S = (S_1^{\mathrm{UT}}, S_2^{\mathrm{UT}})$ be the simulator from the UT security;

$(\mathsf{pp}, s_1, \ldots, s_N, st) \leftarrow S_1^{\mathrm{UT}}(1^\lambda); \quad C \leftarrow \bar{\mathcal{A}}(\mathsf{pp})$

Define oracle $\mathcal{O}'(\mathsf{stmt}', \pi_0')$ as :

$\quad b \leftarrow \mathcal{O}_{\mathrm{dv}}(\mathsf{stmt}', \pi_0')$

$\quad (\pi_i)_{i \in [N]} \leftarrow S_2^{\mathrm{UT}}(\mathsf{pp}, C_{\mathsf{stmt}', \pi_0'}, b, st)$

$\quad\quad$ where $C_{\mathsf{stmt}', \pi_0'}$ is the verification circuit (as in construction)

$\quad$ **return** $(\pi_i)_{i \in [N]}$

$(h, \mathsf{stmt}, \pi_0, \pi_{i_1}, \ldots, \pi_{i_{d-1}}) \leftarrow \bar{\mathcal{A}}^{\mathcal{O}_{\mathrm{prf}}}(\mathsf{pp}, (s_i)_{i \in C})$

return (stmt, π_0)

$\bar{\mathcal{E}}^{\mathcal{O}_{\mathrm{prf}}}(\mathsf{pp})$

Define oracle $\mathcal{O}''(\mathsf{stmt}'', \pi_0'')$ as :

$\quad (\pi_i)_{i \in [N]} \leftarrow \mathcal{O}_{\mathrm{prf}}(\mathsf{stmt}'', \pi_0'')$

$\quad$ Find set of d proofs π^* s.t. $\mathsf{SPuC.PartCertVfy}(\mathsf{pp}, \mathsf{stmt}, \pi_0'', \pi_j^*) = 1 \; \forall j \in [\mathsf{d}]$

$\quad$ If $\exists \pi^*$ output $\mathsf{SPuC.Vfy}(\mathsf{pp}, \mathsf{stmt}, \pi_0'', \pi^*)$; o.w. output 0

$\mathsf{w} \leftarrow \mathcal{E}_{\mathrm{dv}}^{\mathcal{O}''}(\mathsf{ek})$

return w

Fig. 4. Construction of $\mathcal{A}_{\mathrm{dv}}$ in the proof of Lemma 1

existence of simulators respectively $S^{\mathrm{UT}} = (S_1^{\mathrm{UT}}, S_2^{\mathrm{UT}})$ and S^{klzk}. We then define S_1 so that: it first runs $(\mathsf{ek}, \mathsf{vk}) \leftarrow \mathsf{dvKeyGen}(\mathcal{R})$; then $(\mathsf{pp}_{\mathrm{UT}}, \mathsf{sk}) \leftarrow S_1^{\mathrm{UT}}(1^\lambda, N)$; then it outputs a public key $(\mathsf{ek}, \mathsf{pp}_{\mathrm{UT}})$ and a simulation trapdoor $(\mathsf{sk}, \mathsf{vk})$. We shall then define S as $S := (S_1, S_{\mathrm{prt}} = S_2^{\mathrm{UT}}, S_{\mathrm{prf}} = S^{\mathrm{klzk}})$.

Claim 1. The output of S_1 is indistinguishable from that of the honest setup. This follows directly from the definition of S_1^{UT} and from UT security.

Hybrid Experiments. Let $q(\lambda) = \mathsf{poly}(\lambda)$ be an upper bound on the number of oracle queries of the adversary in the experiment in Definition 3. For each $i \in \{0, 1, \ldots, q(\lambda)\}$ we define a hybrid zero-knowledge experiment $\mathcal{H}_i$ as in figure. For all oracle queries $j \in [q(\lambda)]$ the oracle $\mathcal{O}_{\mathrm{zk}}^i$ acts as follows: for query $j \leq i$ the adversary receives honest generated queries (from $\mathcal{O}_{\mathrm{zk}}^{\mathrm{hon}}$); for query $j > i$ receives simulated queries ($\mathcal{O}_{\mathrm{zk}}^{\mathrm{sim}}$). Notice that hybrid $\mathcal{H}_0$ corresponds to $\mathsf{ZK}^{\mathrm{hon}}$ and hybrid $\mathcal{H}_{q(\lambda)}$ to $\mathsf{ZK}^{\mathrm{sim}}$. It is now sufficient to prove the following claim.

Claim 2. for all $i \in [q(\lambda)]$ $\mathcal{H}_{i-1} \approx \mathcal{H}_i$. Notice that the oracles in Fig. 2 are such that for any $\mathsf{tag} \in \{\mathsf{part\text{-}proofs}, \mathsf{valid\text{-}x}\}$ $\mathcal{O}_{\mathrm{zk}}^{\mathrm{hon}}(\mathsf{tag}, \mathsf{inp}) \approx \mathcal{O}_{\mathrm{zk}}^{\mathrm{sim}}(\mathsf{tag}, \mathsf{inp})$. This is because of the security of the UT and the (key-less) zero-knowledge property of the dvSNARK. If two consecutive hybrids were distinguishable then it would be possible to distinguish either of the two oracles with non-negligible probability since the $i - 1$ queries can be efficiently implemented.

$\mathcal{H}^i_\mathcal{A}(1^\lambda, N)$

$(\mathsf{pp_{UT}}, \mathsf{sk} = (sk_1, \ldots, sk_N)) \leftarrow S_1^{\mathsf{UT}}(1^\lambda, \mathcal{R}, N);\ C \leftarrow \mathcal{A}(\mathsf{pp})$ where $|C| = \mathsf{d} - 1$

Output guess $\leftarrow \mathcal{A}^{\mathcal{O}^i_{\mathsf{zk}}}(\mathsf{pp_{UT}}, (s_j)_{j \in C})$ where $h \in [N] \setminus C$

□

3.5   A General Construction of UT from TFHE and HS ([8])

As informally described in [8], we can construct UT from TFHE and context-hiding HS. TFHE can itself be built from FHE with moderate "noise bound" (roughly, a measure of the noise at the decryption stage), which we can obtain for our purposes from LWE [8]. In the full version we formally build for the first time UT from homomorphic signatures ([8] only contains formal description and proofs for a pvNIZK-based construction).

Intuition on Construction. We exploit Threshold FHE, where one can encrypt a message x (TFHE.Enc), publicly obtain a ciphertext of an evaluation $C(x)$ for a circuit C, members of a committee can provide partial decryptions of a ciphertext through (a share of) a secret key, which can then be publicly combined to obtain a plaintext. When we run UT.Setup(x) we encrypt the secret x through the TFHE and provide a share of the TFHE secret key to each of the committee members. The evaluation and combination algorithm of UT invoke respectively the partial decryption and combination algorithm of TFHE. To provide robustness we use homomorphic signatures: we let each committee member sign the output of the partial decryption. They can carry this out homomorphically (using HS.Eval), as they are given a signature of their secret key share at setup time (through HS.Sign).

Corollary 1. *(informal) If there exists leveled Threshold FHE for* NC^1, *compact context-hiding Homomorphic Signatures and zero-knowledge dvSNARKs then there exists a secure SPuC.*

Efficiency. We can instantiate our construction with dvSNARKs obtained through Square-Span Programs [21] compiled with the results in [6] and homomorphic signatures from [30]. The output of Prove consists of a constant number of ciphertexts each encrypting a field element. Its total size would then be $O_\lambda(1)$.

The size of each certificate is $O_\lambda(\log(|\mathsf{stmt}|))$ which we can derive as follows. First observe that the signatures in [30] after evaluation remain of a size lower than some bound on the depth of the homomorphic computation. Looking inside the TFHE-based UT construction from [8] (formalized in the full version) and the compiler in [6], we see that the homomorphic computation consists of a partial TFHE decryption on top of a procedure f_{dv}. On input a signed secret of size $O_\lambda(|stmt|)$ procedure f_{dv} decrypts the aforementioned ciphertexts and performs a zero-test on a low-degree multivariate polynomial with $O(n)$ variables. Hence a bound on the depth of f_{dv} is $O_\lambda(\log(|stmt|))$. The partial decryption on top of it adds a factor $poly(\lambda)$.

3.6   A Construction of UT from HSS and HS for the (2, 2) Setting

In Fig. 5 we describe a novel construction for (two-party) UT based on Homomorphic Secret-Sharing [13]. It works similarly to the construction from TFHE. We recall that HS denotes the homomorphic signature scheme and we denote by using HS.Eval and by HS.Sign respectively the algorithms for homomorphic evaluation of signatures and for initially signing a message. We can instantiate HSS[9] from LWE through the construction in [15]. While the (2, 2)-case for UT is subsumed by the general construction from Sect. 3.5, our HSS-based construction requires simpler and more efficient primitives (see discussion of efficiency of TFHE vs HSS in [15]). Moreover, although our main focus is quantum-resistant constructions, HSS allows for a wider type of instantiations, for example from DDH as in [13][10] (not known to imply (leveled) FHE).

Corollary 2. *(informal) If there exists two-party-HSS for* NC^1, *context-hiding HS and zero-knowledge dvSNARKs then there exists a two-party SPuC.*

Remark 3 (On UT and Robust HSS). We observe that the notion of UT is very close to *robust* homomorphic secret-sharing scheme (see, e.g., Sect. 2 in [14]). We, however, present it in the language of UT because it allows to use for the same framework as that of our Sect. 3.5 and for continuity with [8].

4   Proactive UT and Proactive SPuC

We define a new primitive pUT, proactive version of UT where the committee members can change constantly. The protocol is divided in epochs with a handover stage at the end of each. During each epoch t, the members of committee $(\mathcal{C}_t)$ can carry out oblivious evaluations as in UT and later hand over their shares to the next committee $\mathcal{C}_{t+1}$. We require these steps to be non-interactive and robust (roughly, the resharing phase should be publicly verifiable).

After being nominated (a nomination stage is out of the scope of this paper and we merely posit it) the committee member i for the next epoch holds an

---

[9] A (2-party) HSS consists of algorithms: Share to secret share a message, Eval to homomorphically produce a partial evaluation of a function f on the message x given a share, Combine to publicly recombine the evaluation shares into $f(x)$.

[10] This instantiation is still plausibly weaker than publicly-verifiable NIZKs; the recent breakthrough in [34] requires a *sub-exponential* version of DDH to build pvNIZKs.

$\mathsf{UT}_{(2,2)}.\mathsf{Setup}(1^\lambda, \mathsf{d} = 2, \mathsf{N} = 2, x)$

$(\mathsf{sk}_{\mathsf{hs}}, \mathsf{pk}_{\mathsf{hs}}) \leftarrow \mathsf{HS.Setup}(1^\lambda)$

$\mathbf{sk} \leftarrow \mathsf{UT}_{(2,2)}\text{-}\mathsf{AuxSetup}(x, \mathsf{sk}_{\mathsf{hs}})$

return $(\mathsf{pp} := \mathsf{pk}_{\mathsf{hs}}, \mathbf{sk})$

$\mathsf{UT}_{(2,2)}\text{-}\mathsf{AuxSetup}(x, \mathsf{sk}_{\mathsf{hs}})$

$(\mathsf{share}_1, \mathsf{share}_2) \leftarrow \mathsf{HSS.Share}(1^\lambda, x)$

for $i = 1, 2$:

   $\mathsf{sk}'_i[\mathsf{hs}] \leftarrow \mathsf{HS.Sign}(\mathsf{sk}_{\mathsf{hs}}, \text{``}i\text{''}, \mathsf{share}_i)$

   $\mathsf{sk}'_i := (\mathsf{share}_i, \mathsf{sk}'_i[\mathsf{hs}])$

   return $(\mathsf{sk}'_1, \mathsf{sk}'_2)$

$\mathsf{UT}_{(2,2)}.\mathsf{PartEval}(\mathsf{pp} := \mathsf{pk}_{\mathsf{hs}}, \mathsf{sk}_i, i, C)$

$y_i \leftarrow \mathsf{HSS.Eval}_i(\mathsf{share}_i, C)$

$\sigma_i \leftarrow \mathsf{HS.Eval}(\mathsf{pk}_{\mathsf{hs}}, \text{``}i\text{''}, C_{\mathsf{HSSEval}}, \mathsf{sk}_i[\mathsf{hs}])$

  where $C_{\mathsf{HSSEval}} := \mathsf{HSS.Eval}_i(\cdot, C)$

return (y_i, σ_i)

$\mathsf{UT}_{(2,2)}.\mathsf{Combine}(\mathsf{pp} := \mathsf{pk}_{\mathsf{hs}}, y_1, y_2)$

return $\mathsf{HSS.Combine}(y_1, y_2)$.

$\mathsf{UT}_{(2,2)}.\mathsf{VfyEval}(\mathsf{pp} := \mathsf{pk}_{\mathsf{hs}}, \pi_i = (y_i, \sigma_i), i, C)$

return $\mathsf{HS.Verify}(\mathsf{pk}_{\mathsf{hs}}, \text{``}i\text{''}, y_i, \sigma_i, C_{\mathsf{HSSEval}})$

  where $C_{\mathsf{HSSEval}} := \mathsf{HSS.Eval}_i(\cdot, C)$

Fig. 5. 2-party UT Construction, $\mathsf{UT}_{(2,2)}$, from HSS and HS.

ephemeral secret key esk_i. Its share of the secret will be encrypted with a corresponding ephemeral public key epk_i. For this purpose a pUT is coupled with a public-key encryption scheme PK.

Here we present an overview of the model and the construction. Further details can be found in the full version.

4.1 Proactive UT: Model Description

A pUT extends the syntax of UT with algorithms for resharing, reconstruction and related verification: – $\mathsf{pUT.Reshare}(\mathsf{pp}, \mathsf{sk}_i^t, i, \mathbf{epk}^{t+1}) \rightarrow (y_i^{\mathsf{resh}}, \sigma_i^{\mathsf{resh}})$: using a partial secret key sk_i^t this algorithm performs a (partial) handover of secret i to the committee in epoch $t + 1$. – $\mathsf{pUT.VfyReshare}(\mathsf{pp}, \mathbf{epk}^t, (y_i^{\mathsf{resh}}, \sigma_i^{\mathsf{resh}}), i) \rightarrow \{0, 1\}$: The algorithm verifies if party i carried out a resharing step correctly. – $\mathsf{pUT.Reconstruct}(\mathsf{pp}, \mathsf{esk}_j, (y_i^{\mathsf{resh}})_{i\in[\mathsf{d}]}) \rightarrow \mathsf{sk}_j^{t+1}$: Having d shares (y_i^{resh}), the algorithm reconstruct a secret share sk_j^{t+1} through esk_j.

4.2 Building Block: Special UT (sUT)

We construct pUT from another novel primitive, sUT. If a pUT extends UT with resharing features, a sUT extends it with a special type of oblivious evaluation. Recall that in UT committee members can obliviously compute functions on a secret x, provided as *input* to the UT setup. In sUT, on the other hand, we also allow to compute functions on secrets of the sUT itself (a trapdoor generated at setup time). This very powerful type of evaluation will be useful in pUT to

$\mathsf{Expt}_{\mathcal{A},\mathsf{sUT}}^{\mathsf{world} \in \{\mathsf{real},\mathsf{ideal}\}} \left(1^\lambda, \mathsf{d}, \mathsf{N}\right):$

1. $x \leftarrow \mathcal{A}(1^\lambda, \mathsf{d}, \mathsf{N})$
2. if world = real then $(\mathsf{pp}, \mathsf{s}_1, \ldots, \mathsf{s}_\mathsf{N}, \mathsf{trapd}) \leftarrow \mathsf{sUT}.\mathsf{Setup}\left(1^\lambda, \mathsf{d}, \mathsf{N}, x\right)$
3. else if world = ideal then $(\mathsf{pp}, \mathsf{s}_1, \ldots, \mathsf{s}_\mathsf{N}, \mathsf{trapd}) \leftarrow \mathcal{S}_S\left(1^\lambda, \mathsf{d}, \mathsf{N}\right).$
4. $\mathcal{A}$ outputs a corruption set $\mathcal{C}$ of size $\mathsf{d} - 1$
5. The challenger provides the shares $\{\mathsf{s}_i\}_{i \in \mathcal{C}}$ to $\mathcal{A}$.
6. $\mathcal{A}$ can ask for a polynomial number of adaptive queries to the oracle $\mathcal{O}_{\mathsf{sUT}}^{\mathsf{world}}$ (defined below).
7. Adversary outputs a guess guess
8. Return 1 iff guess = world

The oracle $\mathcal{O}_{\mathsf{sUT}}^{\mathsf{world}}$ can receive in input either a tuple $(\mathsf{trapdquery}, z)$ or a tuple (xquery, C). The first asks for a query evaluation on the trapdoor; the other for the secret x. For the case $(\mathsf{trapdquery}, z)$, the oracle samples a circuit from sampler D as $C \leftarrow_{\$} D(\mathsf{trapd}, z)$, returns circuit C and partial evaluation $\{y_i \leftarrow \mathsf{sUT}.\mathsf{TrapdEval}(\mathsf{pp}, \mathsf{s}_i, C)\}_{i \in [\mathsf{N}]}$. For the case (xquery, C) the oracle responds with:

- if world = real then return $\{y_i \leftarrow \mathsf{sUT}.\mathsf{Eval}(\mathsf{pp}, \mathsf{s}_{i,T}, C)\}_{i \in [\mathsf{N}]}$
- if world = ideal then return $\{y_i\}_{i \in [\mathsf{N}]} \leftarrow \mathcal{S}_E(\mathsf{trapd}, C, C(x))$

Fig. 6. Security experiment for sUT

reshare the trapdoor itself. Naturally we need to somehow constrain the type of evaluations allowed to the adversary. In order to do this we allow two types of evaluation queries: one unconstrained (on the secret x) and one (on the sUT trapdoor) with respect to a circuit sampler.

Definition 6 (Circuit Sampler). *A circuit sampler D is a PPT that on input a string z returns a circuit $C \leftarrow D(z)$ of size polynomial in $|z|$.*

Definition 7. *(sUT Security) A sUT scheme satisfies security with respect to circuit sampler D if there exists a PPT algorithm $\mathcal{S} = (\mathcal{S}_S, \mathcal{S}_E)$ such that for all λ, for any PPT adversary $\mathcal{A}$, the following experiments $\mathsf{Exp}_{\mathcal{A},\mathsf{sUT}}^{\mathsf{real}}\left(1^\lambda, \mathsf{d}, \mathsf{N}\right) \approx \mathsf{Exp}_{\mathcal{A},\mathsf{sUT}}^{\mathsf{ideal}}\left(1^\lambda, \mathsf{d}, \mathsf{N}\right)$ (see Fig. 6).*

A Construction for sUT. We extend the construction from [8] to prove evaluations on the sUT trapdoor. The TrapdEval function works exactly as PartEval but on a different ciphertext (which encrypts the trapdoor). The construction is using almost the same assumptions as for UT, namely homomorphic signatures and FHE, but we need to also assume circular security of the latter as we should be able to securely encrypt its own decryption key. A construction of sUT is in Fig. 7. We prove its security in the full version.

$\mathsf{sUT.Setup}(1^\lambda, \mathsf{d}, \mathsf{N}, x)$ $\mathsf{AuxSetup}(s)$

$(\mathsf{sk}_\mathsf{hs}, \mathsf{pk}_\mathsf{hs}) \leftarrow \mathsf{HS.Setup}(1^\lambda)$

$(\mathsf{sk}_\mathsf{fhe}, \mathsf{pk}_\mathsf{fhe}) \leftarrow \mathsf{TFHE.KeyGenAux}(1^\lambda, \mathsf{d}, \mathsf{N})$

$\mathsf{ct}_x \leftarrow \mathsf{TFHE.Enc}(\mathsf{pk}_\mathsf{fhe}, x)$

$\rho \leftarrow_\$ \mathsf{rnd}$

$\mathsf{trapd} := (\mathsf{sk}_\mathsf{fhe}, \mathsf{sk}_\mathsf{hs}, \rho)$

$\mathbf{sk} \leftarrow \mathsf{AuxSetup}(\mathsf{trapd})$

$\mathsf{ct}_\mathsf{tpd} \leftarrow \mathsf{TFHE.Enc}(\mathsf{pk}_\mathsf{fhe}, \mathsf{trapd})$

$\mathbf{return}\ (\mathsf{pp} := (\mathsf{pk}_\mathsf{fhe}, \mathsf{pk}_\mathsf{hs}, \mathsf{ct}_x, \mathsf{ct}_\mathsf{tpd}), \mathbf{sk}, \mathsf{trapd})$

$\mathsf{AuxSetup}(s)$

Parse s as $s = (\mathsf{sk}_\mathsf{fhe}, \mathsf{sk}_\mathsf{hs}, \rho)$

Parse ρ as $\rho = (\rho[SS], \rho_1[\mathsf{hs}], \dots, \rho_\mathsf{N}[\mathsf{hs}])$

$\mathsf{sk}'_1[\mathsf{fhe}], \dots, \mathsf{sk}'_\mathsf{N}[\mathsf{fhe}] \leftarrow \mathsf{SS}(\mathsf{d}, \mathsf{N}, \mathsf{sk}_\mathsf{fhe}, \rho[SS])$

$\mathbf{for}\ i = 1, \dots, \mathsf{N}$

     $\mathsf{sk}'_i[\mathsf{hs}] \leftarrow \mathsf{HS.Sign}(\mathsf{sk}_\mathsf{hs}, \text{``}i\text{''}, \mathsf{sk}'_i[\mathsf{fhe}]; \rho_i[\mathsf{hs}])$

     $\mathsf{sk}'_i := (\mathsf{sk}'_i[\mathsf{fhe}], \mathsf{sk}'_i[\mathsf{hs}])$

$\mathbf{return}\ \mathsf{sk}'_1, \dots \mathsf{sk}'_\mathsf{N}$

$\mathsf{sUT.PartEval}(\mathsf{pp} := (\mathsf{pk}_\mathsf{fhe}, \mathsf{pk}_\mathsf{hs}, \mathsf{ct}_x, \mathsf{ct}_\mathsf{tpd}), \mathsf{sk}_i, i, C)$

$\mathsf{ct}' \leftarrow \mathsf{TFHE.Eval}(\mathsf{pk}_\mathsf{fhe}, \mathsf{ct}_x, C)$

$y_i \leftarrow \mathsf{TFHE.PartDec}(\mathsf{sk}_i[\mathsf{fhe}], \mathsf{ct}')$

$\sigma_i \leftarrow \mathsf{HS.Eval}(\mathsf{pk}_\mathsf{hs}, \text{``}i\text{''}, C_\mathsf{Dec}, \mathsf{sk}_i[\mathsf{hs}])$

     where $C_\mathsf{Dec} := \mathsf{TFHE.PartDec}(\cdot, \mathsf{ct}')$

$\mathbf{return}\ (y_i, \sigma_i)$

$\mathsf{sUT.TrapdEval}(\mathsf{pp} := (\mathsf{pk}_\mathsf{fhe}, \mathsf{pk}_\mathsf{hs}, \mathsf{ct}_x, \mathsf{ct}_\mathsf{tpd}), \mathsf{sk}_i, i, C)$

$\mathsf{ct}' \leftarrow \mathsf{TFHE.Eval}(\mathsf{pk}_\mathsf{fhe}, \mathsf{ct}_\mathsf{tpd}, C)$

$y_i \leftarrow \mathsf{TFHE.PartDec}(\mathsf{sk}_i[\mathsf{fhe}], \mathsf{ct}')$

$\sigma_i \leftarrow \mathsf{HS.Eval}(\mathsf{pk}_\mathsf{hs}, \text{``}i\text{''}, C_\mathsf{Dec}, \mathsf{sk}_i[\mathsf{hs}])$

     where $C_\mathsf{Dec} := \mathsf{TFHE.PartDec}(\cdot, \mathsf{ct}')$

$\mathbf{return}\ (y_i, \sigma_i)$

$\mathsf{sUT.VfyEval}(\mathsf{pp} := (\mathsf{pk}_\mathsf{fhe}, \mathsf{pk}_\mathsf{hs}), \pi_i = (y_i, \sigma_i), i, C)$

$\mathsf{ct}' \leftarrow \mathsf{TFHE.Eval}(\mathsf{pk}_\mathsf{fhe}, \mathsf{ct}_x, C)$

$\mathbf{return}\ \mathsf{HS.Verify}(\mathsf{pk}_\mathsf{hs}, \text{``}i\text{''}, y_i, \sigma_i, C_\mathsf{Dec})$

     where $C_\mathsf{Dec} := \mathsf{TFHE.PartDec}(\cdot, \mathsf{ct}')$

$\mathsf{sUT.VfyTrapdEval}(\mathsf{pp} := (\mathsf{pk}_\mathsf{fhe}, \mathsf{pk}_\mathsf{hs}), \pi_i = (y_i, \sigma_i), i, C)$

$\mathsf{ct}' \leftarrow \mathsf{TFHE.Eval}(\mathsf{pk}_\mathsf{fhe}, \mathsf{ct}_\mathsf{tpd}, C)$

$\mathbf{return}\ \mathsf{HS.Verify}(\mathsf{pk}_\mathsf{hs}, \text{``}i\text{''}, y_i, \sigma_i, C_\mathsf{Dec})$

     where $C_\mathsf{Dec} := \mathsf{TFHE.PartDec}(\cdot, \mathsf{ct}')$

$\mathsf{sUT.Combine}(\mathsf{pp} := (\mathsf{pk}_\mathsf{fhe}, \mathsf{pk}_\mathsf{hs}), y_1, \dots, y_\mathsf{d})$

$\mathbf{return}\ \mathsf{TFHE.Dec}(\mathsf{pk}_\mathsf{fhe}, \{y_1, \dots, y_\mathsf{d}\}).$

Fig. 7. Our sUT Construction.

4.3 Construction of pUT

We give a construction based on a homomorphic signature HS, a threshold fully homomorphic encryption scheme TFHE, and PRFs PRF. Our construction is in fact based on the sUT construction by applying the algorithm TrapEval of pUT on a "resharing" function $\mathcal{F}^\mathsf{resh}_{t, \mathbf{epk}^{t+1}}$, tied to our sUT construction (see also Fig. 8)

$\mathsf{pUT.Setup}(1^\lambda, \mathsf{d}, \mathsf{N}, \mathbf{epk}^0, x) \to (\mathsf{pp}, \mathbf{ct})$

   $(\mathsf{pp}, \mathbf{sk}, \mathsf{trapd}) \leftarrow \mathsf{sUT.Setup}(1^\lambda, \mathsf{d}, \mathsf{N}, x)$

   Parse trapd as $(\mathsf{sk}_{\mathsf{fhe}}, \mathsf{sk}_{\mathsf{hs}}, \rho)$

   $\mathbf{ct} \leftarrow \mathcal{F}^{\mathrm{resh}}_{0, \mathbf{epk}^0}(\mathsf{sk}_{\mathsf{fhe}}, \mathsf{sk}_{\mathsf{hs}}, \rho)$

   return $(\mathsf{pp}, \mathbf{ct})$

$\mathsf{pUT.Reshare}(\mathsf{sk}^t_i, i, \mathbf{epk}^{t+1}) \to (y^{\mathrm{resh}}_i, \sigma^{\mathrm{resh}}_i)$

   return $\mathsf{sUT.TrapdEval}(\mathsf{pp}, \mathsf{sk}^t_i, \mathcal{F}^{\mathrm{resh}}_{t, \mathbf{epk}^{t+1}})$

$\mathsf{pUT.VfyReshare}(\mathsf{pp}, \mathbf{epk}^t, (y^{\mathrm{resh}}_i, \sigma^{\mathrm{resh}}_i), i)$

   return $\mathsf{sUT.VfyEval}(\mathsf{pp}, (y^{\mathrm{resh}}_i, \sigma^{\mathrm{resh}}_i), i, \mathcal{F}^{\mathrm{resh}}_{t, \mathbf{epk}^{t+1}})$

$\mathsf{pUT.Reconstruct}(\mathsf{pp}, esk^t_j, (y^{\mathrm{resh}}_i)_{i \in [\mathsf{d}]})$

   $\mathsf{ct}_j \leftarrow \mathsf{sUT.Combine}(\mathsf{pp}, (y^{\mathrm{resh}}_i)_{i \in [\mathsf{d}]}))$

   return $\mathsf{sk}^{t+1}_j := \mathsf{Dec}_{esk^t_j}(\mathsf{ct}_j)$

$\mathsf{pUT.Eval} := \mathsf{sUT.Eval}$

$\mathsf{pUT.VfyEval} := \mathsf{sUT.VfyEval}$

$\mathsf{pUT.Combine} := \mathsf{sUT.Combine}$

$\mathcal{F}^{\mathrm{resh}}_{t, \mathbf{epk}^{t+1}}(s)$

   Parse s as $s = (\mathsf{sk}_{\mathsf{fhe}}, \mathsf{sk}_{\mathsf{hs}}, \rho)$

   $(\rho^{t+1}_{\mathsf{SS}}, \rho^{t+1}_{\mathsf{hs},1}, \dots, \rho^{t+1}_{\mathsf{hs},\mathsf{N}}, \rho^{t+1}_{\mathsf{ct},1}, \dots, \rho^{t+1}_{\mathsf{ct},\mathsf{N}}) = \mathsf{PRF}_\rho(t+1)$

   $(\mathsf{sk}'_i[\mathsf{fhe}])_{i \in [\mathsf{N}]} \leftarrow \mathsf{SS.Share}(\mathsf{d}, \mathsf{N}, \mathsf{sk}_{\mathsf{fhe}}, \rho^{t+1}_{\mathsf{SS}})$

   for $i = 1, \dots, \mathsf{N}$

      $\mathsf{sk}'_i[\mathsf{hs}] \leftarrow \mathsf{HS.Sign}(\mathsf{sk}_{\mathsf{hs}}, \text{``}(i,t)\text{''}, \mathsf{sk}'_i[\mathsf{fhe}], \rho^{t+1}_{\mathsf{hs},i})$

      $\mathsf{sk}'_i := (\mathsf{sk}'_i[\mathsf{fhe}], \mathsf{sk}'_i[\mathsf{hs}])$

      $\mathsf{ct}_i \leftarrow \mathsf{Enc}_{epk^{t+1}_i}(\mathsf{sk}'_i; \rho^{t+1}_{\mathsf{ct},i})$

   return $\mathsf{ct}_1, \dots \mathsf{ct}_\mathsf{N}$

Fig. 8. pUT Construction and the auxiliary resharing functionality

that generates a new secret and then creates, signs and encrypts its shares for the next epoch. Other techniques of our construction for pUT are inspired by the YOSO-style ones in [3] where the committee members of the new epoch can access their share by opening a ciphertext encrypted with an ephemeral public key (of which they only know the decryption key). The main intuition is that a committee member can carry out homomorphic computation on the encrypted secrets and then certify through homomorphic signatures their partial decryption. The result can publicly be combined to obtain the function output. The construction of pUT is in Fig. 8.

Theorem 3. *(Informal) We can construct sUT for a "family of resharing functions" from compact context-hiding homomorphic signatures and leveled TFHE with KDM security [7, 10]. We can construct pUT from the same assumptions.*

4.4 From pUT to pSPuC

Proactive SPuCs extend the SPuC model in the same way as pUT extends UT. A pSPuC includes algorithms (Reshare, VfyReshare, Reconstruct) to allow the committee members to hand over their secrets for certification. Once defined (and constructed) pUTs, a construction for pSPuCs is straightforward: it is the same as the one for SPuCs, but we replace UT with pUT. We provide further details in the full version of this paper.

Acknowledgements. We thank the anonymous reviewers, as well as Jesper Buus Nielsen, Mahak Pancholi and Antonio Faonio for useful discussions around this work. Matteo Campanelli was supported by the Carlsberg Foundation under the Semper Ardens Research Project CF18-112 (BCM). Hamidreza Khoshakhlagh was funded by the Concordium Foundation under Concordium Blockchain Research Center, Aarhus.

References

1. Ames, S., Hazay, C., Ishai, Y., Venkitasubramaniam, M.: Ligero: lightweight sublinear arguments without a trusted setup, pp. 2087–2104 (2017)
2. Applebaum, B.: Cryptography in Constant Parallel Time. Springer Science & Business Media, Heidelberg (2013)
3. Benhamouda, F., et al.: Can a public blockchain keep a secret? In: Pass, R., Pietrzak, K. (eds.) TCC 2020. LNCS, vol. 12550, pp. 260–290. Springer, Cham (2020). https://doi.org/10.1007/978-3-030-64375-1_10
4. Bitansky, N., et al.: The hunting of the snark. J. Cryptol. **30**(4), 989–1066 (2017)
5. Bitansky, N., Canetti, R., Chiesa, A., Tromer, E.: From extractable collision resistance to succinct non-interactive arguments of knowledge, and back again, pp. 326–349 (2012)
6. Bitansky, N., Chiesa, A., Ishai, Y., Ostrovsky, R., Paneth, O.: Succinct non-interactive arguments via linear interactive proofs, pp. 315–333 (2013)
7. Black, J., Rogaway, P., Shrimpton, T.: Encryption-scheme security in the presence of key-dependent messages. In: Nyberg, K., Heys, H. (eds.) SAC 2002. LNCS, vol. 2595, pp. 62–75. Springer, Heidelberg (2003). https://doi.org/10.1007/3-540-36492-7_6

8. Boneh, D., et al.: Threshold cryptosystems from threshold fully homomorphic encryption, pp. 565–596 (2018)
9. Boneh, D., Gennaro, R., Goldfeder, S., Kim, S.: A lattice-based universal thresholdizer for cryptographic systems. IACR Cryptol. ePrint Arch. **2017**, 251 (2017)
10. Boneh, D., Halevi, S., Hamburg, M., Ostrovsky, R.: Circular-secure encryption from decision Diffie-Hellman, pp. 108–125 (2008)
11. Boneh, D., Ishai, Y., Sahai, A., Wu, D.J.: Lattice-based SNARGs and their application to more efficient obfuscation, pp. 247–277 (2017)
12. Boneh, D., Ishai, Y., Sahai, A., Wu, D.J.: Quasi-optimal SNARGs via linear multiprover interactive proofs, pp. 222–255 (2018)
13. Boyle, E., Gilboa, N., Ishai, Y.: Breaking the circuit size barrier for secure computation under DDH, pp. 509–539 (2016)
14. Boyle, E., Gilboa, N., Ishai, Y., Lin, H., Tessaro, S.: Foundations of homomorphic secret sharing, pp. 21:1–21:21 (2018)
15. Boyle, E., Kohl, L., Scholl, P.: Homomorphic secret sharing from lattices without FHE, pp. 3–33 (2019)
16. Bünz, B., Agrawal, S., Zamani, M., Boneh, D.: Zether: towards privacy in a smart contract world, pp. 423–443 (2020)
17. Campanelli, M., Gennaro, R., Goldfeder, S., Nizzardo, L.: Zero-knowledge contingent payments revisited: attacks and payments for services, pp. 229–243 (2017)
18. Canetti, R., et al.: Fiat-shamir: from practice to theory, pp. 1082–1090 (2019)
19. Chaidos, P., Couteau, G.: Efficient designated-verifier non-interactive zeroknowledge proofs of knowledge, pp. 193–221 (2018)
20. Damgård, I., Fazio, N., Nicolosi, A.: Non-interactive zero-knowledge from homomorphic encryption, pp. 41–59 (2006)
21. Danezis, G., Fournet, C., Groth, J., Kohlweiss, M.: Square span programs with applications to succinct NIZK arguments, pp. 532–550 (2014)
22. Fuchsbauer, G., Kiltz, E., Loss, J.: The algebraic group model and its applications, pp. 33–62 (2018)
23. Gennaro, R., Gentry, C., Parno, B., Raykova, M.: Quadratic span programs and succinct NIZKs without PCPs, pp. 626–645 (2013)
24. Gennaro, R., Minelli, M., Nitulescu, A., Orrù, M.: Lattice-based zk-SNARKs from square span programs, pp. 556–573 (2018)
25. Gentry, C.: Fully homomorphic encryption using ideal lattices, pp. 169–178 (2009)
26. Gentry, C., Groth, J., Ishai, Y., Peikert, C., Sahai, A., Smith, A.D.: Using fully homomorphic hybrid encryption to minimize non-interative zero-knowledge proofs. J. Cryptol. **28**(4), 820–843 (2015)
27. Gentry, C., et al.: YOSO: you only speak once. In: Malkin, T., Peikert, C. (eds.) CRYPTO 2021. LNCS, vol. 12826, pp. 64–93. Springer, Cham (2021). https://doi.org/10.1007/978-3-030-84245-1_3
28. Gentry, C., Wichs, D.: Separating succinct non-interactive arguments from all falsifiable assumptions, pp. 99–108 (2011)
29. Goldreich, O., Micali, S., Wigderson, A.: How to play any mental game or a completeness theorem for protocols with honest majority, pp. 218–229 (1987)
30. Gorbunov, S., Vaikuntanathan, V., Wichs, D.: Leveled fully homomorphic signatures from standard lattices, pp. 469–477 (2015)
31. Goyal, V., Kothapalli, A., Masserova, E., Parno, B., Song, Y.: Storing and retrieving secrets on a blockchain. IACR Cryptol. ePrint Arch. **2020**, 504 (2020)
32. Groth, J.: On the size of pairing-based non-interactive arguments, pp. 305–326 (2016)

33. Ishai, Y., Su, H., Wu, D.J.: Shorter and faster post-quantum designated-verifier zksnarks from lattices. Cryptology ePrint Archive, Report 2021/977 (2021). https://ia.cr/2021/977

34. Jain, A., Jin, Z.: Non-interactive zero knowledge from sub-exponential DDH. In: Canteaut, A., Standaert, F.X. (eds.) EUROCRYPT 2021. LNCS, vol. 12696, pp. 3–32. Springer, Cham (2021). https://doi.org/10.1007/978-3-030-77870-5_1

35. Peikert, C., Shiehian, S.: Noninteractive zero knowledge for NP from (plain) learning with errors. In: Boldyreva, A., Micciancio, D. (eds.) CRYPTO 2019. LNCS, vol. 11692, pp. 89–114. Springer, Cham (2019). https://doi.org/10.1007/978-3-030-26948-7_4

36. Sahai, A., Waters, B.: How to use indistinguishability obfuscation: deniable encryption, and more, pp. 475–484 (2014)

Author Index

Printed in the United States
by Baker & Taylor Publisher Services